UNIVERSITY CASEBOOK SERIES®

COPYRIGHT

UNFAIR COMPETITION, AND RELATED TOPICS BEARING ON THE PROTECTION OF WORKS OF AUTHORSHIP

ELEVENTH EDITION

by

RALPH S. BROWN
Late Simon E. Baldwin Professor of Law
Yale University

ROBERT C. DENICOLA
Margaret Larson Professor of Intellectual Property
University of Nebraska

FOUNDATION PRESS

University Casebook Series is a trademark registered in the U.S. Patent and Trademark Office.

© 1958, 1960, 1974, 1978, 1985, 1990, 1995, 1998, 2002 FOUNDATION PRESS
© 2005 THOMSON REUTERS/FOUNDATION PRESS
© 2009 By THOMSON REUTERS/FOUNDATION PRESS
© 2013 by LEG, Inc. d/b/a West Academic Publishing
  610 Opperman Drive
  St. Paul, MN 55123
  1-800-313-9378

West, West Academic Publishing, and West Academic are trademarks of West Publishing Corporation, used under license.

Printed in the United States of America

ISBN: 978–1–60930–239–9

Mat #41350426

To Christine

PREFACE

The First Edition of this casebook was the product of a collaboration between Professor Benjamin Kaplan of Harvard and Professor Ralph Brown of Yale—two giant figures in twentieth-century intellectual property law. Their book was the first casebook published on copyright law. Professor Kaplan's elevation to the bench precluded his direct participation in later editions, but the casebook continued to benefit from his generous counsel. Ralph Brown remained the principal force behind six subsequent editions. I had the pleasure of working with Ralph on four of those editions.[a]

Like its predecessors, this Eleventh Edition is distinctive in giving substantial attention to topics related to copyright, especially unfair competition. Copyright and its many cousins—unfair competition, publicity rights, moral rights, and corners of contract—continue to expand. The frequent amendments to the Copyright Act demand discussion, and the growth of unfair competition appears relentless. As a consequence, this casebook has steadily increased in length. Although the book is still manageable in size, probably no course will cover every page. To help with organization, virtually all the materials on federal copyright law appear in Part I. Most of that can be covered even in a two-credit course.

Copyright law is undergoing major transformations as new technologies spawn new challenges. The technology of photocopying still eludes control even as it is supplanted by digital dissemination. The "broadcast" media continue to change shape with new forms of transmission and new means of reception. Copyright law had barely digested computer programs when it was forced to confront the enormous capacity of the Internet to disseminate works of authorship. In the face of emerging technologies, can either Congress or the courts effectively secure to authors the exclusive right to their writings without undermining the ultimate purpose of the constitutional grant?

In spite of all these matters, the emphasis here remains on fundamentals. In their Preface to the First Edition, Professors Kaplan and Brown recalled Justice Story's now famous observation that copyrights, in company with patents, "approach, nearer than any other class of cases belonging to forensic discussions, to what may be called the metaphysics of the law, where the distinctions are, or at least may be, very subtle and refined, and, sometimes, almost evanescent."[b] Who is an "author"? What is a "writing"? What are the exclusive rights of authors in their writings and what, on the other hand, is "fair use"? The courts continue to instruct us almost daily on all these questions. It is impossible to predict what may come next, except to mark the obvious and portentous acceleration of the technologies that disseminate works of authorship. Meanwhile, there is a wealth of issues, some old and some new, to tantalize and entertain both students and teachers.

---

[a] Ralph Brown's contributions to the law of intellectual property are recounted in R. Denicola, Freedom to Copy, 108 Yale L.J. 1661 (1999), part of a Symposium in Ralph's honor published by the *Yale Law Journal*. Ralph's admiration for his original co-author is evident in his review of Benjamin Kaplan's most famous work, *An Unhurried View of Copyright* (Columbia Univ. Press 1967). R. Brown, Book Review, 80 Harv.L.Rev. 1621 (1967).

[b] Folsom v. Marsh, 9 Fed.Cas. 342, 344 (C.C.D.Mass.1841) (No. 4901).

SUMMARY OF CONTENTS

TABLE OF CONTENTS

TABLE OF CASES

The principal cases are in bold type.

COPYRIGHT

UNFAIR COMPETITION,
AND RELATED TOPICS
BEARING ON THE
PROTECTION OF WORKS OF
AUTHORSHIP

The Congress shall have the Power ... To Promote the Progress of Science and useful Arts, by securing for limited Times to Authors and Inventors the exclusive Right to their respective Writings and Discoveries.

Constitution of the United States, Article I, Section 8

PART 1

COPYRIGHT

CHAPTER 1

THE BOUNDARIES OF COPYRIGHT

1. A FIRST LOOK AT COPYRIGHT

Sony Corp. of America v. Universal City Studios, Inc.

Supreme Court of the United States, 1984.
464 U.S. 417, 104 S.Ct. 774.

■ JUSTICE STEVENS delivered the opinion of the Court.

Petitioners manufacture and sell home video tape recorders. Respondents own the copyrights on some of the television programs that are broadcast on the public airwaves. Some members of the general public use video tape recorders sold by petitioners to record some of these broadcasts, as well as a large number of other broadcasts. The question presented is whether the sale of petitioners' copying equipment to the general public violates any of the rights conferred upon respondents by the Copyright Act. *Issue*

Respondents commenced this copyright infringement action against petitioners in the United States District Court for the Central District of California in 1976. Respondents alleged that some individuals had used Betamax video tape recorders (VTR's) to record some of respondents' copyrighted works which had been exhibited on commercially sponsored television and contended that these individuals had thereby infringed respondents' copyrights. Respondents further maintained that petitioners were liable for the copyright infringement allegedly committed by Betamax consumers because of petitioners' marketing of the Betamax VTR's. Respondents sought no relief against any Betamax consumer. Instead, they sought money damages and an equitable accounting of profits from petitioners, as well as an injunction against the manufacture and marketing of Betamax VTR's. *Universal didn't seek damages from customers — sought $ & injunction*

After a lengthy trial, the District Court denied respondents all the relief they sought and entered judgment for petitioners. 480 F.Supp. 429 (1979). The United States Court of Appeals for the Ninth Circuit reversed the District Court's judgment on respondent's copyright claim, holding petitioners liable for contributory infringement and ordering the District Court to fashion appropriate relief. 659 F.2d 963 (1981). We granted certiorari, 457 U.S. 1116 (1982); since we had not completed our study of the case last Term, we ordered reargument, 463 U.S. 1226 (1983). We now reverse. * * * *DCH for π Sony. ACH reversed & held them liable for contributory infringement 9th Cir*

The lengthy trial of the case in the District Court concerned the private, home use of VTR's for recording programs broadcast on the public airwaves without charge to the viewer. No issue concerning the transfer of tapes to other persons, the use of home-recorded tapes for public performances, or the copying of programs transmitted on pay or cable television systems was raised. See 480 F.Supp. 429, 432–433, 442 (1979). * * *

5 to 4 decision

3

II

Article I, Sec. 8 of the Constitution provides that:

"The Congress shall have Power . . . to Promote the Progress of Science and useful Arts, by securing for limited Times to Authors and Inventors the exclusive Right to their respective Writings and Discoveries."

The monopoly privileges that Congress may authorize are neither unlimited nor primarily designed to provide a special private benefit. Rather, the limited grant is a means by which an important public purpose may be achieved. It is intended to motivate the creative activity of authors and inventors by the provision of a special reward, and to allow the public access to the products of their genius after the limited period of exclusive control has expired.

"The copyright law, like the patent statute, makes reward to the owner a secondary consideration. In Fox Film Corp. v. Doyal, 286 U.S. 123, 127, Chief Justice Hughes spoke as follows respecting the copyright monopoly granted by Congress, 'The sole interest of the United States and the primary object in conferring the monopoly lie in the general benefits derived by the public from the labors of authors.' It is said that reward to the author or artist serves to induce release to the public of the products of his creative genius." United States v. Paramount Pictures, 334 U.S. 131, 158.

As the text of the Constitution makes plain, it is Congress that has been assigned the task of defining the scope of the limited monopoly that should be granted to authors or to inventors in order to give the public appropriate access to their work product. Because this task involves a difficult balance between the interests of authors and inventors in the control and exploitation of their writings and discoveries on the one hand, and society's competing interest in the free flow of ideas, information, and commerce on the other hand, our patent and copyright statutes have been amended repeatedly.[10]

From its beginning, the law of copyright has developed in response to significant changes in technology. Indeed, it was the invention of a new form of copying equipment—the printing press—that gave rise to the original need for copyright protection.[12] Repeatedly, as new developments have occurred in this country, it has been the Congress that has fashioned the

---

[10] In its Report accompanying the comprehensive revision of the Copyright Act in 1909, the Judiciary Committee of the House of Representatives explained this balance:

"The enactment of copyright legislation by Congress under the terms of the Constitution is not based upon any natural right that the author has in his writings, . . . but upon the ground that the welfare of the public will be served and progress of science and useful arts will be promoted by securing to authors for limited periods the exclusive rights to their writings.

"In enacting a copyright law Congress must consider . . . two questions: First, how much will the legislation stimulate the producer and so benefit the public, and, second, how much will the monopoly granted be detrimental to the public? The granting of such exclusive rights, under the proper terms and conditions, confers a benefit upon the public that outweighs the evils of the temporary monopoly." H.R.Rep. No. 2222, 60th Cong., 2d Sess. 7 (1909).

[12] "Copyright protection became necessary with the invention of the printing press and had its early beginnings in the British censorship laws. The fortunes of the law of copyright have always been closely connected with freedom of expression, on the one hand, and with technological improvements in means of dissemination, on the other. Successive ages have drawn different balances among the interest of the writer in the control and exploitation of his intellectual property, the related interest of the publisher, and the competing interest of society in the untrammeled dissemination of ideas." Foreword to B. Kaplan, An Unhurried View of Copyright vii–viii (1967).

new rules that new technology made necessary. Thus, long before the enactment of the Copyright Act of 1909, 35 Stat. 1075, it was settled that the
protection given to copyrights is wholly statutory. Wheaton v. Peters, 33
U.S. (8 Peters) 591, 661–662 (1834). The remedies for infringement "are
only those prescribed by Congress." Thompson v. Hubbard, 131 U.S. 123,
151 (1889). * * *

In a case like this, in which Congress has not plainly marked our
course, we must be circumspect in construing the scope of rights created by
a legislative enactment which never contemplated such a calculus of interests. In doing so, we are guided by Justice Stewart's exposition of the correct approach to ambiguities in the law of copyright:

> "The limited scope of the copyright holder's statutory monopoly,
> like the limited copyright duration required by the Constitution, re-
> flects a balance of competing claims upon the public interest: Creative
> work is to be encouraged and rewarded, but private motivation must
> ultimately serve the cause of promoting broad public availability of lit-
> erature, music, and the other arts. The immediate effect of our copy-
> right law is to secure a fair return for an 'author's' creative labor. But
> the ultimate aim is, by this incentive, to stimulate artistic creativity
> for the general public good. 'The sole interest of the United States and
> the primary object in conferring the monopoly,' this Court has said, 'lie
> in the general benefits derived by the public from the labors of au-
> thors.' Fox Film Corp. v. Doyal, 286 U.S. 123, 127. See Kendall v.
> Winsor, 21 How. 322, 327–328; Grant v. Raymond, 6 Pet. 218, 241–
> 242. When technological change has rendered its literal terms ambigu-
> ous, the Copyright Act must be construed in light of this basic pur-
> pose." Twentieth Century Music Corp. v. Aiken, 422 U.S. 151, 156
> (footnotes omitted).

Copyright protection "subsists . . . in original works of authorship fixed
in any tangible medium of expression." 17 U.S.C. § 102(a). This protection
has never accorded the copyright owner complete control over all possible
uses of his work. Rather, the Copyright Act grants the copyright holder "exclusive" rights to use and to authorize the use of his work in five qualified
ways, including reproduction of the copyrighted work in copies. Id., § 106.
All reproductions of the work, however, are not within the exclusive domain
of the copyright owner; some are in the public domain. Any individual may
reproduce a copyrighted work for a "fair use;" the copyright owner does not
possess the exclusive right to such a use. Compare id., § 106 with id., § 107.

"Anyone who violates any of the exclusive rights of the copyright owner," that is, anyone who trespasses into his exclusive domain by using or
authorizing the use of the copyrighted work in one of the five ways set forth
in the statute, "is an infringer of the copyright." Id., § 501(a). Conversely,
anyone who is authorized by the copyright owner to use the copyrighted
work in a way specified in the statute or who makes a fair use of the work
is not an infringer of the copyright with respect to such use.

The Copyright Act provides the owner of a copyright with a potent ar-
senal of remedies against an infringer of his work, including an injunction
to restrain the infringer from violating his rights, the impoundment and
destruction of all reproductions of his work made in violation of his rights,
a recovery of his actual damages and any additional profits realized by the
infringer or a recovery of statutory damages, and attorneys fees. Id.,
§§ 502–505.

The two respondents in this case do not seek relief against the Betamax users who have allegedly infringed their copyrights. Moreover, this is not a class action on behalf of all copyright owners who license their works for television broadcast, and respondents have no right to invoke whatever rights other copyright holders may have to bring infringement actions based on Betamax copying of their works. As was made clear by their own evidence, the copying of the respondents' programs represents a small portion of the total use of VTR's. It is, however, the taping of respondents own copyrighted programs that provides them with standing to charge Sony with contributory infringement. To prevail, they have the burden of proving that users of the Betamax have infringed their copyrights and that Sony should be held responsible for that infringement.

[The Court next considered the issue of contributory infringement and concluded that Sony could be liable only if the Betamax had no substantial noninfringing uses. That portion of the Court's opinion is considered at p. 399 infra.]

IV

The question is thus whether the Betamax is capable of commercially significant noninfringing uses. In order to resolve that question, we need not explore *all* the different potential uses of the machine and determine whether or not they would constitute infringement. Rather, we need only consider whether on the basis of the facts as found by the District Court a significant number of them would be noninfringing. Moreover, in order to resolve this case we need not give precise content to the question of how much use is commercially significant. For one potential use of the Betamax plainly satisfies this standard, however it is understood: private, noncommercial time-shifting in the home. It does so both (A) because respondents have no right to prevent other copyright holders from authorizing it for their programs, and (B) because the District Court's factual findings reveal that even the unauthorized home time-shifting of respondents' programs is legitimate fair use.

A.   *Authorized Time–Shifting*

Each of the respondents owns a large inventory of valuable copyrights, but in the total spectrum of television programming their combined market share is small. The exact percentage is not specified, but it is well below 10%. If they were to prevail, the outcome of this litigation would have a significant impact on both the producers and the viewers of the remaining 90% of the programming in the Nation. No doubt, many other producers share respondents' concern about the possible consequences of unrestricted copying. Nevertheless the findings of the District Court make it clear that time-shifting may enlarge the total viewing audience and that many producers are willing to allow private time-shifting to continue, at least for an experimental time period. * * *

If there are millions of owners of VTR's who make copies of televised sports events, religious broadcasts, and educational programs such as *Mister Rogers' Neighborhood,* and if the proprietors of those programs welcome the practice, the business of supplying the equipment that makes such copying feasible should not be stifled simply because the equipment is used by some individuals to make unauthorized reproductions of respondents' works. The respondents do not represent a class composed of all copyright holders. Yet a finding of contributory infringement would inevitably frustrate the interests of broadcasters in reaching the portion of their audience that is available only through time-shifting. * * *

B.   *Unauthorized Time–Shifting*

Even unauthorized uses of a copyrighted work are not necessarily infringing. An unlicensed use of the copyright is not an infringement unless it conflicts with one of the specific exclusive rights conferred by the copyright statute. Twentieth Century Music Corp. v. Aiken, 422 U.S. 151, 154–155. Moreover, the definition of exclusive rights in § 106 of the present Act is prefaced by the words "subject to sections 107 through 118." Those sections describe a variety of uses of copyrighted material that "are not infringements of copyright notwithstanding the provisions of § 106." The most pertinent in this case is § 107, the legislative endorsement of the doctrine of "fair use."

[The Court concluded that "home time-shifting" is a fair use under § 107 and thus does not infringe the copyright owner's exclusive rights. "[T]ime-shifting merely enables a viewer to see such a work which he had been invited to witness in its entirety free of charge * * *." The portion of the Court's opinion dealing with fair use is reprinted at p. 341 infra.]

V

"The direction of Art. I is that *Congress* shall have the power to promote the progress of science and the useful arts. When, as here, the Constitution is permissive, the sign of how far Congress has chosen to go can come only from Congress." Deepsouth Packing Co. v. Laitram Corp., 406 U.S. 518, 530 (1972).

One may search the Copyright Act in vain for any sign that the elected representatives of the millions of people who watch television every day have made it unlawful to copy a program for later viewing at home, or have enacted a flat prohibition against the sale of machines that make such copying possible.

It may well be that Congress will take a fresh look at this new technology, just as it so often has examined other innovations in the past. But it is not our job to apply laws that have not yet been written. Applying the copyright statute, as it now reads, to the facts as they have been developed in this case, the judgment of the Court of Appeals must be reversed.

It is so ordered.

[Justice Blackmun's dissent, in which Justices Marshall, Powell and Rehnquist joined, is reprinted in part at p. 344 infra.]

NOTES AND QUESTIONS

(1) Sections 102 and 106 are the bedrock provisions of the Copyright Act. Section 102 describes the subject matter of copyright. According to the 1976 House Report, the list of works in that section is "illustrative and not limitative."[a]

---

[a]   H.R.Rep. No. 94–1476, 94th Cong., 2d Sess. 53 (1976). (This authoritative Report, cited here simply as the House Report (H.R.Rep.), will be quoted frequently in these materials.) A statement of policy by the Copyright Office views the legislative history as indicating "that Congress intended the statute to be flexible as to the scope of established categories, but also that Congress also intended to retain control of the designation of entirely new categories of authorship." 77 Fed.Reg. 37607 (June 22, 2012).

[Editors' footnotes throughout this casebook are lettered. Footnotes from judicial opinions and other materials, when reprinted, retain their original numbering. Footnotes are omitted without indication.]

Some of the works listed in § 102 are defined in § 101; the general category of "original works of authorship" is not. The subject matter of copyright is further amplified in §§ 103–105.

Section 106 enumerates the exclusive rights granted to the owner of a copyright. These rights are subject to the complicated set of limitations and qualifications in §§ 107–122. Almost all of these sections will be taken up in the course of these materials.

§106 is exclusive rights granted to the owner

Given the basic structure of the Copyright Act—broadly defined rights followed by a series of specific limitations—is Part V of the Court's opinion in *Sony* a sensible approach to the statute? The Court of Appeals had taken a different view of the structure of the Copyright Act:

> The statutory framework is unambiguous; the grant of exclusive rights is only limited by the statutory exceptions. * * * The issue is not whether Congress exhibited an intent to protect a copyright holder from certain reproduction of his works. It had already expressed its intent to do so by extending the "bundle of rights" set forth in § 106 to copyright owners, *subject to specific sections,* to-wit: §§ 107–118. Consequently, our concern must be whether Congress has exhibited the intent to limit the rights of copyright owners in ways not specified in §§ 107–118. (659 F.2d 963, 966)

J. Litman, Lawful Personal Use, 85 Tex.L.Rev. 1871 (2007), argues against an interpretive approach that assumes all uses are unlawful unless specifically exempted by the copyright act.

(2) Looking ahead, what facts would be relevant in deciding whether the time-shifting in *Sony* should be permitted as a "fair use"?

• commercial
• private or public
• all or part
• copiable (stream vs. download)

(3) What interests justify the recognition of exclusive rights in "works of authorship"? The incentive rationale offered by the Court in *Sony* is a traditional response. Since works of authorship are intangible, without copyright protection it would be difficult for creators to capture the economic value of their creations. (Would the creator's head start in the market provide sufficient reward?) In a case to be considered later, the Supreme Court said:

> The economic philosophy behind the clause empowering Congress to grant patents and copyrights is the conviction that encouragement of individual effort by personal gain is the best way to advance public welfare through the talents of authors and inventors in "Science and useful Arts." Sacrificial days devoted to such creative activities deserve rewards commensurate with the services rendered.

Mazer v. Stein, p. 124 infra. Does the last sentence appeal to interests beyond incentive? A former United States Register of Copyrights has said that "the fundamental claim of copyright is one of justice." D. Ladd, The Harm of the Concept of Harm in Copyright, 30 J.Copyr.Soc'y 421, 425 (1983), but M. Hamilton, Copyright at the Supreme Court: A Jurisprudence of Deference, 47 J.Copyr.Soc'y 317 (2000), finds steadfast rejection of a natural rights theory in the Supreme Court's copyright decisions.[b]

---

[b]   C. Dallon, The Problem with Congress and Copyright Law: Forgetting the Past and Ignoring the Public Interest, 44 Santa Clara L.Rev. 365 (2004), carefully details the long history supporting a public interest as opposed to a natural right theory of copyright. S. Ghosh, Deprivatizing Copyright, 54 Case W.Res.L.Rev. 1 (2004), justifies a public interest model by arguing that copyright law represents a privatization of the government's role in promoting

What costs are incurred by recognizing exclusive rights in works of authorship? Legal restrictions on dissemination and use seem particularly wasteful since, unlike tangible goods, works of authorship can be enjoyed by an unlimited number of users without depriving anyone else of the work. Exclusive rights not only interfere with the public's enjoyment of the work, but also with the creation of new works derived from the original. But all this assumes that the original work has been created in the first place, which returns us to the incentive rationale. Copyright is in part a balance between the benefits derived from encouraging the creation of works and the costs of restricting access. (Could the need for incentive be met without restricting dissemination and use? Would a system of direct government subsidies be preferable to copyright?) Note too that some industries, fashion and consumer product design, for example, have a long history of innovation despite the absence of copyright protection. Since the United States has become a major exporter of works of authorship, our copyright law also reflects an interest in generating revenue from foreign sales.

indivisible

The economic and moral arguments underlying the recognition of exclusive rights in works of authorship are discussed in R. Brown, Eligibility for Copyright Protection: A Search for Principled Standards, 70 Minn.L.Rev. 579 (1985). For an expansive treatment of similar themes, see W. Gordon, An Inquiry into the Merits of Copyright: The Challenges of Consistency, Consent, and Encouragement Theory, 41 Stan.L.Rev. 1343 (1989).[c]

The incentive rationale for copyright is challenged in R. Breyer, The Uneasy Case for Copyright: A Study of Copyright in Books, Photocopies, and Computer Programs, 84 Harv.L.Rev. 281 (1970). See generally W. Landes and R. Posner, An Economic Analysis of Copyright Law, 18 J.Leg.Stud. 325 (1989).[d]

---

culture; S. Stadler, Forging a Truly Utilitarian Copyright, 91 Iowa L. Rev. 609 (2006), uses copyright in fine art to argue that if the public interest is truly paramount, some authors should get less protection, and some none at all. However, A. Ng, The Social Contract and Authorship: Allocating Entitlements in the Copyright System, 19 Fordham Intell.Prop., Media & Ent.L.J. 413 (2009), catalogs the benefits of a natural rights perspective on copyright.

[c]   S. Sterk, Rhetoric and Reality in Copyright Law, 94 Mich.L.Rev. 1197 (1996), attributes the contours of modern copyright law to the political power of the copyright industries. M. Pollack, What Is Congress Supposed to Promote? Defining Progress in Art. I, Sec. 8, Cl. 8 of the U.S. Constitution, 80 Neb.L.Rev. 754 (2001), concludes that the constitutional goal of "progress" means "dissemination." Reliance on property analogies to explain copyright is questioned in S. Sterk, Intellectualizing Property: The Tenuous Connections Between Land and Copyright, 83 Wash. U. L.Q. 417 (2005), and T. Bell, Copyright as Intellectual (Property) Privilege, 58 Syracuse L.Rev. 523 (2008), but D. Fagundes, Property Rhetoric and the Public Domain, 94 Minn.L.Rev. 652 (2010), points out that since property law includes the concept of public entitlements, a property perspective can push back against overly broad assertions of rights.

[d]   Recall, too, Samuel Johnson's famous remark: "No man but a blockhead ever wrote, except for money." 3 Boswell, *Life of Johnson* 19 (1934 ed.). But R. Tushnet, Economics of Desire: Fair Use and Marketplace Assumptions, 51 Will. & Mary L.Rev. 513 (2009), reminds us that the desire to create often springs from non-economic motives, and D. Long, Dissonant Harmonization: Limitations on "Cash N' Carry" Creativity, 70 Alb.L.Rev. 1163 (2007), urges more study on the kinds of rights that actually encourage authorship. D. Oliar and C. Sprigman, There's No Free Laugh (Anymore), 94 Va.L.Rev. 1787 (2008), uses stand-up comedy to illustrate that social norms can sometimes serve as an alternative to copyright protection.

COPYRIGHT AND THE PUBLIC DOMAIN

Prior to January 1, 1978, the effective date of the 1976 Copyright Act, many works of authorship were protected, if at all, under state rather than federal law. As we will see, the 1976 Act dramatically reduced (but did not quite eliminate) the role of state copyright law. See § 301. State protection of artistic and intellectual works had come to be called "common law copyright." Much of it did in fact spring from the process of judicial decision-making that we know as the common law, but the states sometimes enacted copyright statutes too. So it is not quite correct to refer to state copyright as "common law copyright," but it remains a familiar usage.

Sometimes, however, a work may fall beyond the protection of both state and federal copyright law. It is then in the public domain, meaning approximately that anyone may copy or use it. But note that the constitutional clause quoted in *Sony* also authorizes rights for inventors in their discoveries. Inventors may obtain patents, and what is claimed in a patent is not free for public use. The states do not have patent statutes and there are no "common law" patents, but state trade secret law also creates rights in intellectual property. Finally, in Part Two of these materials we will see other legal doctrines that can have the effect of creating exclusive rights in intellectual property and that thus limit the public domain.

These materials will be concerned largely with obtaining and maintaining exclusive rights. Relegation to the public domain may sometimes appear to be an inferior sort of thing that happens to deserving authors when for some reason they lose control of their creations. Viewed in another way, the public domain is the accumulated wisdom of the ages. Justice Brandeis' dissent in International News Service v. Associated Press, p. 596 infra, reminds us that "The general rule of law is, that the noblest of human productions—knowledge, truths ascertained, conceptions, and ideas—become, after voluntary communication to others, free as the air to common use."

Thomas Jefferson was even more eloquent:

If nature has made any one thing less susceptible than all others of exclusive property, it is the action of the thinking power called an idea, which an individual may exclusively possess as long as he keeps it to himself; but the moment it is divulged, it forces itself into the possession of every one, and the receiver cannot dispossess himself of it. Its peculiar character, too, is that no one possesses the less, because every other possess the whole of it. He who receives an idea from me, receives instructions himself without lessening mine; as he who lights his taper at mine, receives light without darkening me. That ideas should freely spread from one to another over the globe, for the moral and mutual instruction of man, and improvement of his condition, seems to have been peculiarly and benevolently designed by nature, when she made them, like fire, expansible over all space, without lessening their density in any point, and like the air in which we breathe, move and have our physical being, incapable of confinement or exclusive appropriation.[e]

---

[e]   13 Writings of Thomas Jefferson 333–34 (Lipscomb ed., 1904) (letter to I. McPherson, Aug. 13, 1813). The function of the public domain in preserving access to the raw material of future authorship is emphasized in J. Litman, The Public Domain, 39 Emory L.J. 965 (1990). For a similar argument drawn from the concept of "progress" as embodied in the Patent and

A NOTE ON REFERENCE WORKS

The leading treatises on copyright law are M. and D. Nimmer, Nimmer on Copyright (Matthew Bender) and P. Goldstein, Goldstein on Copyright (Wolters Kluwer). Other texts include H. Abrams, The Law of Copyright (Thomson West); W. Patry, Patry on Copyright (Thomson West). The Copyright Law Reporter (CCH) provides a convenient collection of legislative, judicial, and administrative materials. The United States Patent Quarterly (BNA) reports copyright cases, along with cases on patents, trademarks, and unfair competition. Current developments can be followed in the weekly Patent, Trademark & Copyright Journal (BNA).[f]

2. COPYRIGHT DISTINCT FROM PROPERTY RIGHTS IN OBJECTS

Pushman v. New York Graphic Society, Inc.

Court of Appeals of New York, 1942.
287 N.Y. 302, 39 N.E.2d 249.

■ DESMOND, JUDGE. Plaintiff, who is an artist, brought this suit in 1940 for an injunction to enjoin the defendants from making reproductions of a painting executed by plaintiff and which he had sold outright to the University of Illinois in 1930, for $3,600. This painting was not copyrighted under the copyright laws of the United States. Special Term denied the injunction and dismissed the complaint on the merits, writing an opinion and decision, 25 N.Y.S.2d 32, in which it is said that the only question in the case is as to whether an artist after giving an absolute and unconditional bill of sale of his painting, still retains such a common law copyright in it as to be able to prevent commercial reproduction. Appellate Division, First Department, one of the justices dissenting, affirmed without opinion. 262 A.D. 729, 28 N.Y.S.2d 711.

Plaintiff, Pushman, has an international reputation as an artist, for his execution of still life subjects in color. He has been painting for fifty years; his original works command substantial prices and many of them are held by museums and collectors. In 1930 he completed the painting, entitled "When Autumn is Here," which is the subject of this action. He turned the painting over for sale to Grand Central Art Galleries which seems to be a mutual organization of artists for sale of their works, as agent for them. All the evidence is that the plaintiff did not state that he was seeking to reserve reproduction rights in his painting and that he made no such reservation at any time up to and including the sale to the University. There is evidence here of a general practice of this gallery whereby whenever it sold a painting to a purchaser who was in the reproduction business, which of course would not include the University, the Gallery negotiated a separate written agreement between the artist and the purchaser covering reproduction rights. Pushman never expressly au-

---

Copyright Clause, see M. Chon, Postmodern "Progress": Reconsidering the Copyright and Patent Power, 34 DePaul L.Rev. 97 (1993).

[f]   A. Bartow, The Hegemony of the Copyright Treatise, 73 U.Cin.L.Rev. 581 (2004), criticizes what she sees as excessive judicial deference to the *Nimmer* copyright treatise.

did not authorize, did not forbid

thorized the Gallery to sell the rights to reproduce this painting, nor did he forbid it. Shortly after this painting was sent to the Gallery for sale, the manager of the Gallery took it and a number of others to the University of Illinois where he exhibited them publicly for sale. The University chose seven of these paintings, including the one by plaintiff here in suit. The University would not pay plaintiff's asking price of $5,000 and so the Gallery sold it to the University for $3,600. All this took place in 1930. The painting remained at the University until 1940 when the University sold to the defendant, New York Graphic Society, Inc., the right to make reproductions. The trial proofs had been made by defendants and the reproductions were about to be put on the market when plaintiff learned of the project and brought this suit. * * *

We are, of course, concerned here with the so-called common law copyright, not statutory copyright. This common law copyright is sometimes called the right of first publication. There is no question but that it is a different and independent right from the usual right of ownership of an article of personal property. Stephens v. Cady, 14 How. 528, 530. The Stephens case quotes Lord Mansfield as saying it is "a property in notion, and has no corporeal tangible substance." There is no doubt that in New York State the

NY law

separate common law copyright or control of the right to reproduce belongs to the artist or author until disposed of by him and will be protected by the courts. Oertel v. Wood, 40 How.Prac. 10; Howitt v. Street & Smith Publications, Inc., 276 N.Y. 345, 350, 12 N.E.2d 435. Such is the holding of the case of Werckmeister v. Springer Lithographing Co., C.C., 63 F. 808, at page 811, which says that the painting itself may be transferred without a transfer of the common law rights of publishing or restricting publication, and that the ownership of the painting itself does not necessarily carry with it the common law copyright. The same thing is held in Caliga v. Inter–Ocean Newspaper Co., 7 Cir., 157 F. 186, 188, affirmed 215 U.S. 182. Palmer v. DeWitt, 47 N.Y. 532, 7 Am.Rep. 480, is not direct authority either way on the case before us.

We are not helped here by the cases which say that an artist's separate common law copyright does not necessarily pass with the sale of the painting. The question is whether it did pass with the sale of this painting. We

Rule ★

think it follows from the authorities above cited that it did so pass and that an artist must, if he wishes to retain or protect the reproduction right, make some reservation of that right when he sells the painting. The Parton case [Parton v. Prang, 18 F.Cas. 1273 (C.C.D.Mass.1872) (No. 10,784)] has always been considered as so holding. There are seemingly contrary expressions in some cases, such as the dictum in Stephens v. Cady, 14 How. at page 531, that the right to reproduce "will not pass with the manuscript unless included by express words in the transfer." Appellant cites also other authorities which say that the sale of a work of art does not carry with it the right of reproduction "unless such was the evident intent of the parties." But this begs the question. What was the intent of the parties? The whole tenor of the Prang case, as we read it, is that an ordinary, straight

intent to convey whole prop.

out bill of sale shows an intention to convey the artist's whole property in his picture. Here there is no substantial proof of a contrary intent.

We are not entering into a separate discussion as to whether by this sale *and* the public exhibition the artist is to be held to have "published" the work so that his common law right is lost. Special Term so held. See Keene v. Kimball, 16 Gray, Mass., 545, 77 Am.Dec. 426; Baker v. Taylor, Fed.Cas. No. 782. Nor need we examine into the equities, as did Special

Term. Our conclusion is that under the cases and the texts, this unconditional sale carried with it the transfer of the common law copyright and right to reproduce. Plaintiff took no steps to withhold or control that right. "The courts cannot read words of limitation into a transfer which the parties do not choose to use." *Dam v. Kirk La Shelle Co.*, 2 Cir., 175 F. 902, 904, 20 Ann.Cas. 1173.

Holding for Δ — sale carries transfer of CL copyright & right to reproduce

The judgment of the Appellate Division should be affirmed, with costs.

■ LEHMAN, C.J., and LOUGHRAN, FINCH, RIPPEY, LEWIS, and CONWAY, JJ., concur.

Judgment affirmed.

Chamberlain v. Feldman

300 N.Y. 135, 89 N.E.2d 863 (1949).

Judge Desmond, again writing for a unanimous court, reached a different conclusion on these facts. "In 1876, Samuel L. Clemens, under his pen name of 'Mark Twain', wrote a story entitled 'A Murder, A Mystery and A Marriage', and in the same year offered the manuscript to William Dean Howells, editor of the Atlantic Monthly, for publication. There followed, during the same year, some correspondence between Twain and Howells, in which was discussed an unusual project which the author had in mind: he proposed that a number of other famous writers of the period (such as Bret Harte and Howells himself) be enlisted, each to write his own final chapter for the work, so that for the mystery set up in the first few chapters, each author would compose a solution, in addition to, or in competition with Twain's own denouement. In other words, as planned by Twain, there was to be a common plot for the story, with a number of different endings. For one reason or another, including the reluctance of famous writers to dance to a rival's music, Twain's pet scheme came to nothing. Twenty years later, an entry in Twain's diary dated March 18, 1897, records a rather vague hope of the author to 'make a skeleton novelette plot and write all the stories myself' or use it as the basis for a prize story competition. Whether that entry referred to 'A Murder, A Mystery and A Marriage' we do not know, but there is undisputed proof, credited by both courts below, that when Mark Twain died in 1910, the manuscript of 'A Murder, A Mystery and A Marriage' was not found among his effects and had never been published anywhere, by anyone.

"In 1945, defendant Feldman bought the original manuscript (holographic *[handwritten]* and signed) at an auction sale, in New York City, of the rare books and manuscripts that had been in the possession, during his life, of Dr. James Brentano Clemens (no kin of Mark Twain) and had passed by inheritance to Dr. Clemens' wife. How Dr. Clemens came to have the writing is unknown. Mr. Feldman sought permission from plaintiffs, who are the present owners of all literary property formerly belonging to Mark Twain and not otherwise disposed of, to publish the work, but permission was refused. Defendant Feldman went ahead with the publication, however, and this suit was brought to enjoin him from reproducing or publishing the story, in any way. The complaint prays also for a direction to defendant to cancel a purported statutory copyright entered by defendant in the office of the Federal Register of Copyrights. It is not claimed that this statutory copyrighting, or attempt at such, was with the permission of plaintiffs, or any of them."

Twain's unpublished book was published. even though owner said not to

injunction

TCH

ACH

The trial court found that Mark Twain had transferred the manuscript without reserving the common law copyright, but the Appellate Division "found no basis for presuming or inferring such a grant by Twain." The Court of Appeals agreed with the Appellate Division.

Rule

"With the facts in that posture, little problem remains. The common-law copyright, or right of first publication, is a right different from that of ownership of the physical paper; the first of those rights does not necessarily pass with the second; and 'the separate common law copyright or control of the right to reproduce belongs to the artist or author until disposed of by him and will be protected by the courts' (see Pushman v. New York Graphic Soc., 287 N.Y. 302, 307, 39 N.E.2d 249, 250, supra, and cases cited thereat; see similarly, as to statutory copyright, U.S. Code, tit. 17, § 27, 17 U.S.C.A. § 27). Since it has here been found to be the fact that, however the manu-

Reason script left the possession of the author, he never intended that it be published, it follows that defendant could not have bought the publication rights. Feldman did not have publication rights.

"A recent commentary on this case, 62 Harv.L.Rev. 1406–1407, suggests that it may be contrary to sound policy to keep meritorious literary achievement out of the public domain for so long a time as is here involved. Without expressing any views of our own as to the advisability of permitting literary flowers so to blush unseen, we state our agreement with the last sentence of that Law Review article, in which it is pointed out that any such change of public policy must be the doing of the Legislature."

SCH The judgment of the Appellate Division perpetually restraining the defendant from publishing or reproducing the story was affirmed.

NOTES AND QUESTIONS

(1) Twain's story finally appeared in *The Atlantic Monthly* in July, 2001, 125 years after its original submission, after the magazine purchased the publication rights. For a possible explanation of the timing, see § 303 on the duration of copyright in unpublished works.

Can *Chamberlain* be distinguished from *Pushman?* See also Forward v. Thorogood, 985 F.2d 604 (1st Cir.1993), involving a band that had given the organizer of a 1976 recording session the resulting demo tapes "for his own enjoyment." The court said that the transfer of the tapes did not carry with it the common law copyright in the unpublished recordings.

(2) The presumption invoked in *Pushman* that an unrestricted transfer of a work of fine art also conveys the common law right of reproduction was altered by statute in New York in 1966. See N.Y. Arts & Cult.Aff.L. § 14.01. Several other states have similar statutes. See, e.g., Cal.Civ.C. § 982(c); Or.Rev.Stat. § 359.355. All reserve reproduction rights to the artist unless expressly transferred in writing. (These statutes, however, have no effect as to transfers after Jan. 1, 1978, the effective date of the 1976 Copyright Act. See Ronald Litoff, Ltd. v. American Express Co., 621 F.Supp. 981 (S.D.N.Y.1985), holding that a claim for unauthorized reproduction brought under the New York statute is preempted by § 301(a) of the Copyright Act.)

before 1978— production rights stay w/ artist by default

Suppose Pushman had created and sold his painting in 2013. Who would own the reproduction rights? See § 202 and § 204(a).

(3) Notice the reference at the conclusion of the *Pushman* case to the possibility that the artist might have lost his common law copyright through "publication." We will hear more of "publication" in the sections that follow.

RIGHTS IN LETTERS

Another vivid example of the separation of the copyright from the material object occurs with letters. In his famous Digest of the Law of Copyright (1878), Sir James Stephens summarized the law of letters in the familiar way as follows: "A person who writes and sends a letter to another retains his copyright in such letter, except in so far as the particular circumstances of the case may give a right to publish such letter to the person addressed, or to his representatives, but the property in the material on which the letter is written passes to the person to whom it is sent, so as to entitle him to destroy or transfer it." S. Warren and L. Brandeis relate the sender's right to prevent publication of the letter—and, indeed, all rights to prevent publication of "thoughts, sentiments, and emotions, expressed through the medium of writings or of the arts"—to "the more general right of the individual to be let alone." The Right to Privacy, 4 Harv.L.Rev. 193, 205 (1890).

[handwritten margin note: don't print that; leave me alone —Brandeis]

The proposition that the recipient of a letter owns the physical paper seems traceable at least in part to the idea that if the rule were otherwise an unreasonable burden would be cast on the receiver to hold the letter for the benefit of the sender. See Baker v. Libbie, 210 Mass. 599, 97 N.E. 109 (1912) (executor of the will of Mary Baker G. Eddy, founder of the Christian Science religion, failed in an effort to restrain an auction of letters that had been written by Mrs. Eddy to a relative).

NOTES AND QUESTIONS

(1) What circumstances might entitle the recipient of a letter to publish it without the sender's permission? Cf. Diamond v. Am–Law Pub. Corp., 745 F.2d 142 (2d Cir.1984), upholding a defense of "fair use" raised by *The American Lawyer* magazine in connection with its publication of a letter criticizing a story that the magazine had written about the sender. The letter said in part, "You are authorized to publish this letter but only in its entirety"; the magazine published only excerpts, omitting a portion attacking the magazine and its editor.

Letters sent by reclusive author J.D. Salinger to neighbors and friends (including his New Hampshire neighbor Learned Hand) were at the center of another dispute. The letters had been donated by the recipients to various libraries. The defendant Hamilton, in preparing a biography of Salinger, gained access to the letters, but only after signing library forms restricting reproduction. Quoted and paraphrased portions of the letters appeared in the biography. Should Salinger's copyright interest prevail? The Second Circuit's analysis of Hamilton's "fair use" defense is considered at p. 338 infra. See also Lish v. Harper's Magazine Foundation, 807 F.Supp. 1090 (S.D.N.Y.1992), rejecting *Harper's* claims of fair use and free speech in connection with its publication of a letter written by a well-known editor to the students in his creative writing class.

(2) How can the receiver's property right in the physical paper be accommodated to the sender's right of publication? Should the burden be on the sender to retain a copy? How much of this remains relevant in an age of texts and emails? J. Harrison, Privacy, Copyright, and Letters, 3 Elon L.Rev. 161 (2012), maintains that privacy rather than copyright is the more appropriate concept for thinking about communications like letters, emails, and text messages.

3. SEPARATING STATUTORY COPYRIGHT, COMMON LAW COPYRIGHT, AND THE PUBLIC DOMAIN

The materials in this section probe the boundaries between statutory copyright, common law copyright, and the public domain. The 1976 Act dramatically altered the old landscape, in which the concept of "publication" had been the dominant feature. The emphasis now is on fixation, so that an eligible work proceeds directly into federal copyright when it is "fixed in any tangible medium of expression." § 102. At the end of the preceding section we looked at the rules that have grown up around rights in letters. Consider instead what property rights the parties to an oral conversation have in the content of what they say or hear.

Estate of Hemingway v. Random House

Court of Appeals of New York, 1968.
23 N.Y.2d 341, 296 N.Y.S.2d 771, 244 N.E.2d 250.

■ CHIEF JUDGE FULD. On this appeal—involving an action brought by the estate of the late Ernest Hemingway and his widow against the publisher and author of a book, entitled "Papa Hemingway"—we are called upon to decide, primarily, whether conversations of a gifted and highly regarded writer may become the subject of common-law copyright, even though the speaker himself has not reduced his words to writing.

Issue

Hemingway died in 1961. During the last 13 years of his life, a close friendship existed between him and A.E. Hotchner, a younger and far less well-known writer. Hotchner, who met Hemingway in the course of writing articles about him, became a favored drinking and traveling companion of the famous author, a frequent visitor to his home and the adapter of some of his works for motion pictures and television. During these years, Hemingway's conversation with Hotchner, in which others sometimes took part, was filled with anecdote, reminiscence, literary opinion and revealing comment about actual persons on whom some of Hemingway's fictional characters were based. Hotchner made careful notes of these conversations soon after they occurred, occasionally recording them on a portable tape recorder.

During Hemingway's lifetime, Hotchner wrote and published several articles about his friend in which he quoted some of this talk at length. Hemingway, far from objecting to this practice, approved of it. Indeed, the record reveals that other writers also quoted Hemingway's conversation without any objection from him, even when he was displeased with the articles themselves.

After Hemingway's death, Hotchner wrote "Papa Hemingway," drawing upon his notes and his recollections, and in 1966 it was published by the defendant Random House. Subtitled "a personal memoir", it is a serious and revealing biographical portrait of the world-renowned writer. Woven through the narrative, and giving the book much of its interest and character, are lengthy quotations from Hemingway's talk, as noted or remembered by Hotchner. Included also are two chapters on Hemingway's final illness and suicide in which Hotchner, writing of his friend with obvious feeling and sympathy, refers to events, and even to medical information, to which he was privy as an intimate of the family. Hemingway's widow, Mary, is mentioned frequently in the book, and is sometimes quoted, but only incidentally.

The complaint, which seeks an injunction and damages, alleges four causes of action. The first three, in which the Estate of Hemingway and his widow join as plaintiffs, are, briefly stated, (1) that "Papa Hemingway" consists, in the main, of literary matter composed by Hemingway in which he had a common-law copyright; (2) that publication would constitute an unauthorized appropriation of Hemingway's work and would compete unfairly with his other literary creations; and (3) that Hotchner wrongfully used material which was imparted to him in the course of a confidential and fiduciary relationship with Hemingway. In the fourth cause of action, Mary Hemingway asserts that the book invades the right to privacy to which she herself is entitled under section 51 of the Civil Rights Law, Consol.Laws, c. 6.

The plaintiffs moved for a preliminary injunction. The motion was denied (49 Misc.2d 726, 268 N.Y.S.2d 531, affd. 25 A.D.2d 719, 269 N.Y.S.2d 366), and the book was thereafter published. After its publication, the defendants sought and were granted summary judgment dismissing all four causes of action. The Appellate Division unanimously affirmed the resulting orders and granted the plaintiffs leave to appeal to this court.

Turning to the first cause of action, we agree with the disposition made below but on a ground more narrow than that articulated by the court at Special Term. It is the position of the plaintiffs (under this count) that Hemingway was entitled to a common-law copyright on the theory that his directly quoted comment, anecdote and opinion were his "literary creations", his "literary property", and that the defendant Hotchner's note-taking only performed the mechanics of recordation. And, in a somewhat different vein, the plaintiffs argue that "[w]hat for Hemingway was oral one day would be or could become his written manuscript the next day", that his speech, constituting not just a statement of his ideas but the very form in which he conceived and expressed them, was as much the subject of common-law copyright as what he might himself have committed to paper.

Common-law copyright is the term applied to an author's proprietary interest in his literary or artistic creations before they have been made generally available to the public. It enables the author to exercise control over the first publication of his work or to prevent publication entirely—hence, its other name, the "right of first publication". (Chamberlain v. Feldman, 300 N.Y. 135, 139, 89 N.E.2d 863, 864.) No cases deal directly with the question whether it extends to conversational speech and we begin, therefore, with a brief review of some relevant concepts in this area of law.

It must be acknowledged—as the defendants point out—that nearly a century ago our court stated that common-law copyright extended to " '[e]very new and innocent product of mental labor which has been *embodied in writing, or some other material form*' ". (Palmer v. De Witt, 47 N.Y. 532, 537; emphasis supplied.) And, more recently, it has been said that "an author has no property right in his ideas unless * * * given embodiment in a tangible form." (O'Brien v. RKO Radio Pictures, D.C., 68 F.Supp. 13, 14.)

However, as a noted scholar in the field has observed, "the underlying rationale for common law copyright (i.e., the recognition that a property status should attach to the fruits of intellectual labor) is applicable regardless of whether such labor assumes tangible form" (Nimmer, Copyright, § 11.1, p. 40). The principle that it is not the tangible embodiment of the author's work but the creation of the work itself which is protected finds recognition in a number of ways in copyright law.

One example, with some relevance to the problem before us, is the treatment which the law has accorded to personal letters—a kind of half-conversation in written form. * * *

Letters, however—like plays and public addresses, written or not—have distinct, identifiable boundaries and they are, in most cases, only occasional products. Whatever difficulties attend the formulation of suitable rules for the enforcement of rights in such works (see, e.g., Note, Personal Letters: In Need of a Law of Their Own, 44 Iowa L.Rev. 705), they are relatively manageable. However, conversational speech, the distinctive behavior of man, is quite another matter, and subjecting any part of it to the restraints of common-law copyright presents unique problems.

One such problem—and it was stressed by the court at Special Term (Schweitzer, J.)[2]—is that of avoiding undue restraints on the freedoms of speech and press and, in particular, on the writers of history and of biographical works of the genre of Boswell's "Life of Johnson". The safeguarding of essential freedoms in this area is, though, not without its complications. The indispensable right of the press to report on what people have *done,* or on what has *happened* to them or on what they have *said in public* (see Time, Inc. v. Hill, 385 U.S. 374; Curtis Pub. Co. v. Butts, 388 U.S. 130; Associated Press v. Walker, 388 U.S. 130) does not necessarily imply an unbounded freedom to publish whatever they may have *said in private conversation,* any more than it implies a freedom to copy and publish what people may have put down in *private writings.*

Copyright, both common-law and statutory, rests on the assumption that there are forms of expression, limited in kind, to be sure, which should not be divulged to the public without the consent of their author. The purpose, far from being restrictive, is to encourage and protect intellectual labor. (See Note, Copyright: Right to Common Law Copyright in Conversation of a Decedent, 67 Col.L.Rev. 366, 367, commenting on the decision denying the plaintiffs before us a preliminary injunction, 49 Misc.2d 726, 268 N.Y.S.2d 531.) The essential thrust of the First Amendment is to prohibit improper restraints on the *voluntary* public expression of ideas; it shields the man who wants to speak or publish when others wish him to be quiet. There is necessarily, and within suitably defined areas, a concomitant freedom *not* to speak publicly, one which serves the same ultimate end as freedom of speech in its affirmative aspect.

The rules of common-law copyright assure this freedom in the case of written material. However, speech is now easily captured by electronic devices and, consequently, we should be wary about excluding all possibility of protecting a speaker's right to decide when his words, uttered in private dialogue, may or may not be published at large. Conceivably, there may be

---

[2]   Another problem—also remarked by the court—is the difficulty of measuring the relative self-sufficiency of any one party's contributions to a conversation, although it may be, in the case of some kinds of dialogue or interview, that the difficulty would not be greater than in deciding other questions of degree, such as plagiarism. (See, e.g., Nichols v. Universal Pictures Corp., C.C., 45 F.2d 119.)

limited and special situations in which an interlocutor brings forth oral statements from another party which both understand to be the unique intellectual product of the principal speaker, a product which would qualify for common-law copyright if such statements were in writing. Concerning such problems, we express no opinion; we do no more than raise the questions, leaving them open for future consideration in cases which may present them more sharply than this one does.

On the appeal before us, the plaintiffs' claim to common-law copyright may be disposed of more simply and on a more narrow ground.

The defendant Hotchner asserts—without contradiction in the papers before us—that Hemingway never suggested to him or to anyone else that he regarded his conversational remarks to be "literary creations" or that he was of a mind to restrict Hotchner's use of the notes and recordings which Hemingway knew him to be accumulating. On the contrary, as we have already observed, it had become a continuing practice, during Hemingway's lifetime, for Hotchner to write articles about Hemingway, consisting largely of quotations from the latter's conversation—and of all of this Hemingway approved. In these circumstances, authority to publish must be implied, thus negativing the reservation of any common-law copyright.

Assuming, without deciding, that in a proper case a common-law copyright in certain limited kinds of spoken dialogue might be recognized, it would, at the very least, be required that the speaker indicate that he intended to mark off the utterance in question from the ordinary stream of speech, that he meant to adopt it as a unique statement and that he wished to exercise control over its publication. In the conventional common-law copyright situation, this indication is afforded by the creation of the manuscript itself. It would have to be evidenced in some other way if protection were ever to be accorded to some forms of conversational dialogue.

Such an indication is, of course, possible in the case of speech. It might, for example, be found in prefatory words or inferred from the circumstances in which the dialogue takes place.[3] Another way of formulating such a rule might to be to say that, although, in the case of most intellectual products, the courts are reluctant to find that an author has "published," so as to lose his common-law copyright (see Nimmer, Copyright, § 58.2, pp. 226–228), in the case of conversational speech—because of its unique nature—there should be a presumption that the speaker has not reserved any common-law rights unless the contrary strongly appears. However, we need not carry such speculation further in the present case since the requisite conditions are plainly absent here.

For present purposes, it is enough to observe that Hemingway's words and conduct, far from making any such reservation, left no doubt of his willingness to permit Hotchner to draw freely on their conversation in writing about him and to publish such material. What we have said disposes of the plaintiffs' claim both to exclusive and to joint copyright and we need not consider this aspect of the case any further. It follows, therefore, that the courts below were eminently correct in dismissing the first cause of action.

---

[3] This was the situation in Jenkins v. News Syndicate Co., 128 Misc. 284, 219 N.Y.S. 196. The plaintiff alleged that she had had a conference with a newspaper editor in which she described in detail the proposed content of some articles she was requested to write. Later, she decided not to write them and the newspaper thereupon published an "interview" with her, precisely quoting much of her conversation with the editor. The court held that she had stated a cause of action for damages on the theory of common-law copyright.

[The court also held that plaintiffs were not entitled to relief on their claims for unfair competition, breach of a confidential relationship, and invasion of privacy.]

In brief, then, it is our conclusion that, since no triable issues have been raised, the courts below very properly dismissed the complaint.

The orders appealed from should be affirmed, with costs.

■ JUDGES BURKE, SCILEPPI, BERGAN, KEATING, BREITEL, and JASEN concur.

Orders affirmed.

ACH affirmed
all COA dismissed

NOTES AND QUESTIONS

(1) How could a speaker desiring common law protection "indicate that he intended to mark off the utterance in question from the ordinary stream of speech"? Would the requirement be equally applicable to more formal "talk" such as an extemporaneous lecture? *Should* state law protect such works, or should some form of fixation be required? A claim of common law copyright in an interview was rejected in Falwell v. Penthouse Int'l, Ltd., 521 F.Supp. 1204 (W.D.Va.1981).

CA statute

A California statute (Cal.Civ.C. § 980(a)(1)) states that the "author of any original work of authorship that is not fixed in any tangible medium of expression has an exclusive ownership in the representation or expression thereof * * *." It also states that such "ownership" may be transferred. § 982(a). Would such a statute alter the outcome or reasoning in *Hemingway*?

Suppose that a private company hires undergraduate students enrolled in popular courses to take class notes that the company then makes available on its web site for a fee. Does the professor have a copyright claim that could prevent the practice? See Leibowitz, At Yale's Demand, a Web Site Drops Lecture Notes From the University's Classes, Chronicle of Higher Ed., March 17, 2000, p. A49. California now extends statutory protection to unfixed "academic presentations." Cal.Educ.C. § 66450.

Fed. copyright protection
only for works fixed in
tangible medium
State law can protect
unfixed

(2) Federal copyright protection is available only to works "fixed in any tangible medium of expression." § 102. Section 301(b) expressly allows state law copyright in works that remain unfixed. The 1976 House Report offers some examples: "choreography that has never been filmed or notated, an extemporaneous speech, 'original works of authorship' communicated solely through conversations or live broadcasts, and a dramatic sketch or musical composition improvised or developed from memory and without being recorded or written down." H.R.Rep. p. 131.

A lecture or speech that has been written down on paper or saved on a computer hard drive prior to its delivery is "fixed", thus triggering federal copyright protection (see § 302(a) and the § 101 definition of "created") and preempting state copyright (see § 301). Suppose the speaker has merely prepared notes. Is that a fixation? Of what? The entire speech? The portion the speaker could reconstruct using the notes? Only the portion actually written down? See the definition of "fixed" in § 101. And what if a completely extemporaneous speech is recorded by the speaker at the time it is delivered? Note the special provision in the statutory definition of "fixed" for live transmissions that are being simultaneously recorded.[g] Doesn't that imply that there is no claim under the 1976 Act against someone who copies material from a live lecture that is being simultaneously recorded but *not* transmitted? At the conclusion of such a recorded performance, however, the work would be "fixed" and thus protected against subsequent copiers.

(3) Suppose A's conversation is recreated by B in a copyrighted book. C then copies those portions of the book that purport accurately to represent A's words. In an action by B, is C liable for copyright infringement? Has C taken an "original" work of *B's* authorship? If A's words were part of a conversation with B, could the conversation as a whole be considered a "joint work" of A and B? See § 201(a) and the definition of "joint work" in § 101. See also Urantia Foundation v. Maaherra, 114 F.3d 955 (9th Cir.1997) (questions put by humans to "celestial beings" contributed to the structure and arrangement of the "revelations," providing sufficient human authorship for copyright). Compare Quinto v. Legal Times of Washington, Inc., 506 F.Supp. 554 (D.D.C.1981) (arrangement and selection of quotations is copyrightable) with Suid v. Newsweek Magazine, 503 F.Supp. 146 (D.D.C.1980) (no infringement where the selection and arrangement of the quotations were not copied).

(4) A number of states have enacted statutes that make it a crime to record a live musical performance for commercial sale without the consent of the "owner"—a practice sometimes described as "bootlegging". See, e.g., Fla.S.A. § 540.11(2)(a)(3); S.C. Code § 16–11–915. In 1994, Congress extended federal protection to live musical performances. 17 U.S.C. § 1101. Although § 1101 incorporates the civil remedies applicable to copyright infringement, it does not create a "copyright" in live performances; the performances are not "fixed" and thus are ineligible for copyright protection under the 1976 Act. Section 1101 does not preempt continued protection of live performances under state law. § 1101(d). The court in Kiss Catalog, Ltd. v. Passport Int'l Prods., 405 F.Supp.2d 1169 (C.D.Cal.2005), held that § 1101 was a valid exercise of congressional power under the Commerce Clause. "That the Statute might provide 'copyright-like' or 'copyright-related' protection to matters clearly not covered by the Copyright Clause is not important. One need only find an alternative source of constitutional authority."

Congress also imposed substantial criminal penalties for bootlegging. See 18 U.S.C. § 2319A (reprinted in the Statutory Supplement). The criminal statute was upheld in the face of a constitutional challenge in United States v. Moghadam, 175 F.3d 1269 (11th Cir.1999), cert. denied, 529 U.S. 1036 (2000). Although the legislative history suggests that Congress was acting pursuant to its power under the Patent and Copyright Clause, the court declined to decide whether copyright could "encompass live performances that are merely capable of being reduced to tangible form, but have not been." Holding "that the Copyright Clause does not envision that Congress is positively forbidden from extending copyright-like protection under other constitutional clauses, such as the Commerce Clause, to works of authorship that may not meet the fixation requirement inherent in the term 'Writings,'" the court upheld the statute on the basis of the congressional power over interstate commerce. Carefully limit-

---

[g]   The exception for simultaneously recorded transmissions was applied in Pacific and Southern Co. v. Duncan, 744 F.2d 1490 (11th Cir.1984), to uphold federal copyright in television news broadcasts despite the fact that the station typically erased the tapes after seven days.

ing its decision to the criminal statute and "express[ing] no opinion on Section 1101's constitutionality," the Second Circuit in United States v. Martignon, 492 F.3d 140 (2d Cir.2007), held that the criminal statute did not create property rights in expression since it gave only the government the right to exclude others from the protected performances. Thus, it is not a copyright law and there is "no need to examine whether it violates limits of the Copyright Clause * * *."[h]

A NOTE ON FIXATION

Why does federal copyright law insist on fixation in a tangible form? The requirement is obviously a convenient way to avoid the difficulties posed by ephemeral works, but it may also have a constitutional dimension. Recall the reference in Article I, Sec. 8 to "Authors" and their "Writings." The latter has been interpreted by the Supreme Court "to include any *physical rendering* of the fruits of creative intellectual or aesthetic labor." Goldstein v. California, p. 614 infra (emphasis added). If "Writings" entail tangibility, unfixed works are beyond the reach of Congress, at least with respect to its authority under the copyright clause. Thus, works must be fixed in a tangible form in order to qualify for federal copyright. The Copyright Act calls these tangible forms—the material objects in which works are fixed—"copies" and "phonorecords." Both are defined in § 101. "Phonorecords" are material objects in which sounds (other than sounds that are part of an audiovisual work) are fixed. A compact disc containing musical works, for example, is a "phonorecord." "Copies" are everything else in which works of authorship can be embodied. A book is a "copy," as is a painting or a movie DVD. Some of this is summed up in the House Report:

> "[C]opies" and "phonorecords" together will comprise all of the material objects in which copyrightable works are capable of being fixed. The definitions of these terms in section 101, together with their usage in section 102 and throughout the bill, reflect a fundamental distinction between the "original work" which is the product of "authorship" and the multitude of material objects in which it can be embodied. Thus, in the sense of the bill, a "book" is not a work of authorship, but is a particular kind of "copy." Instead, the author may write a "literary work," which in turn can be embodied in a wide range of "copies" and "phonorecords," including books, periodicals, computer punch cards, microfilm, tape recordings, and so forth. It is possible to have an "original work of authorship" without having a "copy" or "phonorecord" embodying it, and it is also possible to have a "copy" or "phonorecord" embodying something that does not qualify as an "original work of authorship." The two essential elements—original work and tangible object—must merge through fixation in order to produce subject matter copyrightable under the statute. (H.R.Rep. p. 53.)

The distinction between phonorecords and copies was intended to do more than harass the uninitiated. Rights and duties under the 1976 Act

    h   An argument that Congress can legislate under the commerce clause without regard to the limits of the copyright clause is made in T. Nachbar, Intellectual Property and Constitutional Norms, 104 Colum.L.Rev. 272 (2004); C. Dallon, The Anti–Bootlegging Provisions: Congressional Power and Constitutional Limitations, 13 Vand.J.Ent. & Tech.L. 255 (2011), also concludes that the Commerce Clause provides a sound constitutional basis for both the civil and criminal anti-bootlegging provisions; J. Fromer, The Intellectual Property Clause's External Limitations, 61 Duke L.J. 1329 (2012), offers a general framework for evaluating the constitutionality of attempts to use other federal powers to promote "science and useful arts."

sometimes turn on the kind of material object in which the work is embodied.

As Note (2) following the *Hemingway* case illustrates, the seemingly clear-cut event of fixation still has its ambiguities. Consider the controversy that erupted when a fireworks company warned in an announcement for an upcoming fireworks display that the show was protected under federal copyright law and reproduction in video recordings or photographs was prohibited. The American Society of Media Photographers objected, arguing that a fireworks display is not fixed in a tangible medium of expression. 3 ABA Sect. of Intell.Prop.L. Bull. (No.2) 1 (Oct. 1998). Would it matter if the fireworks display is conducted according to a written script detailing the nature, timing, and location of each explosion? The Seventh Circuit in Kelley v. Chicago Park Dist., 635 F.3d 290 (7th Cir.), cert. denied, 132 S.Ct. 380 (2011), held that "a garden is simply too changeable to satisfy the primary purpose of fixation; its appearance is too inherently variable to supply a baseline for determining questions of copyright creation and infringement." L. Heymann, How to Write a Life: Some Thoughts on Fixation and the Copyright/Privacy Divide, 51 Will. & Mary L.Rev. 825 (2009), examines the cultural as well as the legal significance of fixation.

fireworks [handwritten]

"PUBLICATION" BEFORE AND AFTER THE 1976 ACT

Section 302(a) of the 1976 Act provides that "copyright in a work created on or after January 1, 1978, subsists from its creation * * *." "A work is 'created' when it is fixed in a copy or phonorecord for the first time." § 101. Since state copyright protection for works within the subject matter of the federal statute is preempted by § 301, *fixation* is the dividing-line between state common law copyright and federal statutory protection.

publication → fixation [handwritten]

Before the 1976 Copyright Act took effect on January 1, 1978, the reach of common law copyright was much more extensive. The dividing-line between common law and federal copyright was ordinarily defined by the act of *publication*. Unpublished works belonged to state law. Once a work was published, it was protected, if at all, by the federal copyright statutes that were passed beginning in 1790 under the authority of the constitutional clause.

The line between unpublished and published works was first drawn by history. A celebrated eighteenth-century English case raised questions about the nature of literary property—did it exist at all at common law? Did it exist after publication? Did the first statutory copyright created by the Statute of Anne in 1710 (reprinted in the Statutory Supplement) displace common law rights? In Donaldson v. Becket,[i] the House of Lords, while affirming the existence of a common law copyright of unlimited duration, held that a *published* work could be protected only for the term of years provided by the statute (and, less clearly, that during that term the only remedies were those provided in the statute). The English statute and cases clearly influenced the shape and development of copyright law in this

---

[i] 2 Bro.P.C. 129, 1 Eng.Rep. 837, 4 Burr. 2408 (H.L.1774). Consult B. Kaplan, An Unhurried View of Copyright (1967), Chap. 1. R. Curtin, The "Capricious Privilege": Rethinking the Origins of Copyright under the Tudor Regime, 59 J.Copyr. Soc'y 391 (2012), examining an exclusive printing privilege granted by Henry VIII two centuries before the Statute of Anne, finds that like modern copyright, it was motivated by a desire to increase public knowledge.

country. When similar issues came before the Supreme Court in Wheaton v. Peters, 33 U.S. 591 (1834), p. 32 infra, a similar result was reached within the framework of the Constitution and the supremacy clause.[j] Thus, once a work had been published, its author was entitled only to the protection offered by the federal copyright statute. If the statutory formalities (chiefly the requirement of a copyright notice) had not been met, the work fell into the public domain.

For English and American legislators of the eighteenth and early nineteenth century, the subject matter of copyright was, almost entirely, books. Books were something printed and published; before that they were manuscripts, which remained under common law protection. Indeed, the Statute of Anne spoke only of books; the first American copyright statute in 1790 (reprinted in the Statutory Supplement), appropriately for a new-found land, covered maps and charts as well as books.

1802-historical, print
1831- musical comps.
1865- photos
1870- fine arts

Meanwhile, beyond the paradigm of the book and its manuscript, the range of works that sought and got federal copyright protection was expanding: in 1802, to "any historical or other print"; in 1831, to musical compositions; in 1865, to photographs; and in 1870, to paintings, drawings and other productions "intended as works of fine arts." All these, while unpublished, had common law protection.

The thorough-going revision of federal copyright law in 1909 made a brave try at delimiting the spheres of common law and federal copyright. (The 1909 Act is reproduced in the Statutory Supplement.) Section 2 was a flat affirmation that

> Nothing in this title shall be construed to annul or limit the right of the author or proprietor of an unpublished work, at common law or in equity, to prevent the copying, publication, or use of such unpublished work without his consent, and to obtain damages therefor.

Yet at the same time, § 12 of the 1909 Act created a route to federal copyright for certain works "of which copies are not reproduced for sale," that is, for certain unpublished works. Simple deposit requirements provided statutory protection for unpublished dramatic works, lectures, musical compositions, motion pictures, photographs, and other artistic works. Section 12, however, was not viewed as preemptive of common law rights. Rather, it was construed as affording an option. But if an author registered an unpublished work under § 12, it came to be agreed that this choice amounted to a displacement of common law rights.

Despite the alternative offered to some unpublished works by § 12, the primary means of acquiring federal copyright under the 1909 Act was through the mechanism provided in § 10: "Any person entitled thereto by this title may secure copyright for his work by publication thereof with the notice of copyright required by this title."

Since it was "publication" that divested the author of common law rights and, if accompanied by the appropriate formalities, initiated protection under the 1909 Act, courts were regularly called upon to determine what sorts of activities amounted to "publication." Some situations seemed easy enough. If the author of a literary work sold or otherwise distributed

---

[j]   These historic cases are re-examined in H. Abrams, The Historic Foundation of American Copyright Law: Exploding the Myth of Common Law Copyright, 29 Wayne L.Rev. 1119 (1983). The changing American perspectives on the Statute of Anne are chronicled in O. Bracha, The Statute of Anne: An American Mythology, 47 Houston L.Rev. 877 (2010).

copies to the general public, publication had occurred. Other works presented greater difficulties. With respect to works of art like paintings and sculpture, for example, would common law protection be jeopardized if the artist publicly exhibited the work but did not distribute reproductions? The answer was never quite clear.

In the case of dramatic and musical works, the issue of public performance created particular concern. The influential decision of the Supreme Court in Ferris v. Frohman, 223 U.S. 424 (1912), held that the public performance of a dramatic work was not a publication. A play could be exploited forever on the stage with perpetual common law copyright protection.

The position that public performance was not a publication that divested common law rights extended equally and easily to musical compositions. But the defense of common law rights in musical compositions had a harder time resisting the argument that widespread dissemination of the music on phonograph records constituted publication. The issues here were shaped—or rather distorted—by another famous Supreme Court decision.

In White–Smith Music Publishing Co. v. Apollo Co., 209 U.S. 1 (1908), the Court rejected an attempt to enjoin the infringement of federal copyright in two songs, "Little Cotton Dolly" and "Kentucky Babe," published in the form of sheet music. The acts of alleged infringement were the manufacture and sale by the defendant of perforated music rolls which, used in connection with player pianos, produced plaintiff's melodies in sound.

The Supreme Court concluded that the copyrights had not been infringed since the piano rolls could not be considered "copies" of the musical works within the meaning of the copyright act. "What is meant by a copy? * * * The [definition] which most commends itself to our judgment * * * defines a copy of a musical composition to be 'a written or printed record of it in intelligible notation.'" Piano rolls were not "copies" since "even those skilled in the making of these rolls are unable to read them as musical compositions."

The specific holding in *White–Smith* that copyright owners could not control the mechanical reproduction of their songs in piano rolls (or more significantly, in phonograph records) was soon modified by § 1(e) of the 1909 Act. That section established a compulsory licensing scheme that remains to this day (see § 115 and p. 550 infra), but the 1909 Act accomplished this without specifically overruling the Supreme Court's narrow interpretation of "copy."

Although *White–Smith* dealt only with the question of what constituted an infringing "copy" of a copyrighted work, many saw in it wider implications. If phonograph records and other "unintelligible" embodiments were not copies of the work for purposes of infringement, perhaps they were also not copies for purposes of determining whether their distribution by the copyright owner was a publication of the work. Although the case law did not consistently support such a view, many practitioners took the position that the sale and distribution of phonograph records was not a publication of the underlying musical composition, leaving common law protection intact.[k]

---

[k] The Second Circuit in Rosette v. Rainbo Record Mfg. Corp., 546 F.2d 461 (2d Cir.1976), adhered to the proposition that the distribution of phonorecords was not a publication of the musical work under the 1909 Act, but the Ninth Circuit disagreed in La Cienega Music Co. v. ZZ Top, 53 F.3d 950 (9th Cir.), cert. denied, 516 U.S. 927 (1995). A 1997 amendment added

The combined thrust of *White-Smith* and *Ferris* had considerable impact on the burgeoning broadcast industry. Broadcasts were performances, and so under *Ferris* neither divested common law rights in the works they embodied nor provided entrée to the federal statutory protection available for published works. And even when the broadcasts were recorded on videotape, *White-Smith's* emphasis on intelligibility impeded access to federal copyright.[l]

By the middle of the twentieth century, almost everyone agreed that the 1909 Copyright Act was outmoded, cumbersome, and at times, virtually unworkable. Although there was talk of revision, the 1909 Act survived for another quarter-century while a multitude of industries and interest groups struggled to construct the compromises ultimately embodied in the Copyright Act of 1976.[m]

Those who first encounter copyright law long after the passage of the 1976 Act may be tempted to dismiss all this as ancient history. The 1976 Act installs fixation in "copies" or "phonorecords" as the threshold of federal protection, and the definitions of these terms in § 101 sweep away the arcane distinctions that emanated from *White-Smith*. But the past cannot be discarded so easily. For the millions of works created under the prior law, their status on January 1, 1978, the effective date of the 1976 Act, is crucial. Protection of works then under federal copyright was continued, indeed expanded, by the 1976 Act, and existing unpublished works then under common law protection were automatically brought within the scope of federal copyright. §§ 303, 304. But the 1976 Act did not provide protection for works that had already entered the public domain.[n] As to this, the old rules about publication remain decisive.

The old law of publication also remains important in another way. Although no longer marking the boundary between common law and federal copyright, publication retains significance under the 1976 Act. For some works, the duration of copyright is measured from the year of first publication. § 302(c). The rights of foreign authors under § 104 can turn on whether publication has occurred. Remedies under the Act can also depend upon whether the work has been published. See § 412. Reproduction rights of libraries, § 108, and the availability of the public broadcasting compulsory license, § 118, turn on publication, as do other rights. Publication also triggers the obligation to deposit copies of the work with the Copyright Office, § 407, and, prior to 1989, it determined whether a notice of copyright was necessary to insure continued protection for the work. §§ 401, 402. For all these purposes the 1976 Act created its own definition of publication in § 101. This statutory law of publication is in part a codification of what had gone before, and the prior law continues to influence interpretation of the 1976 Act.[o]

---

§ 303(b) to the 1976 Act, which overrules *La Cienega Music* and confirms the prior understanding under the 1909 Act.

[l]   The Copyright Office did not accept videotapes for registration until 1961.

[m]   See generally R. Brown, Unification: A Cheerful Requiem for Common–Law Copyright, 24 UCLA L.Rev. 1070 (1977). The contentious negotiations among the interest groups who in effect drafted the 1976 Act are detailed in J. Litman, Copyright, Compromise, and Legislative History, 72 Cornell L.Rev. 857 (1987).

[n]   17 U.S.C.A. Trans. and Supp. Provisions § 103.

[o]   D. Gerhardt, Copyright Publication: An Empirical Study, 87 Notre Dame L.Rev. 135 (2011), examines the case law on publication in all of its various contexts; T. Cotter, Toward a Functional Definition of Publication in Copyright Law, 92 Minn.L.Rev. 1724 (2008), considers

Estate of Martin Luther King, Jr., Inc. v. CBS, Inc.

United States Court of Appeals, Eleventh Circuit, 1999.
194 F.3d 1211.

■ Before ANDERSON, CHIEF JUDGE, RONEY, SENIOR CIRCUIT JUDGE, and COOK, SENIOR DISTRICT JUDGE.

■ ANDERSON, CHIEF JUDGE:

The Estate of Martin Luther King, Jr., Inc. brought this copyright infringement action against CBS, Inc. after CBS produced a video documentary that used, without authorization, portions of civil rights leader Dr. Martin Luther King's famous "I Have a Dream" speech at the March on Washington on August 28, 1963. The district court granted summary judgment to CBS on the ground that Dr. King had engaged in a general publication of the speech, placing it into the public domain. See Estate of Martin Luther King, Jr., Inc. v. CBS, Inc., 13 F.Supp.2d 1347 (N.D.Ga.1998). We now reverse.*

[handwritten: DC H for Δ]

I.   FACTS

The facts underlying this case form part of our national heritage and are well-known to many Americans. On the afternoon of August 28, 1963, the Southern Christian Leadership Conference ("SCLC") held the March on Washington ("March") to promote the growing civil rights movement. The events of the day were seen and heard by some 200,000 people gathered at the March, and were broadcast live via radio and television to a nationwide audience of millions of viewers. The highlight of the March was a rousing speech that Dr. Martin Luther King, Jr., the SCLC's founder and president, gave in front of the Lincoln Memorial ("Speech"). The Speech contained the famous utterance, "I have a dream . . . ," which became symbolic of the civil rights movement. The SCLC had sought out wide press coverage of the March and the Speech, and these efforts were successful; the Speech was reported in daily newspapers across the country, was broadcast live on radio and television, and was extensively covered on television and radio subsequent to the live broadcast.

On September 30, 1963, approximately one month after the delivery of the Speech, Dr. King took steps to secure federal copyright protection for the Speech under the Copyright Act of 1909, and a certificate of registration of his claim to copyright was issued by the Copyright Office on October 2, 1963. Almost immediately thereafter, Dr. King filed suit in the Southern District of New York to enjoin the unauthorized sale of recordings of the Speech and won a preliminary injunction on December 13, 1963. See King v. Mister Maestro, Inc., 224 F.Supp. 101 (S.D.N.Y.1963).

[handwritten: King secures fed © protection]

For the next twenty years, Dr. King and the Estate enjoyed copyright protection in the Speech and licensed it for a variety of uses, and renewed the copyright when necessary. In 1994, CBS entered into a contract with the Arts & Entertainment Network to produce a historical documentary series entitled "The 20th Century with Mike Wallace." One segment was

---

the nature and consequences of publication and suggests that works might be considered published for some purposes but not others.

* Chief Judge Anderson and Judge Cook comprise the majority holding that there has been no publication of the speech that destroyed Dr. King's common law copyright protection. Chief Judge Anderson's reasoning is set out in this opinion; Judge Cook's related but somewhat different reasoning is set out in his separate opinion.

devoted to "Martin Luther King, Jr. and The March on Washington." That episode contained material filmed by CBS during the March and extensive footage of the Speech (amounting to about 60% of its total content). CBS, however, did not seek the Estate's permission to use the Speech in this manner and refused to pay royalties to the Estate. The instant litigation ensued.

On summary judgment, the district court framed the issue as "whether the public delivery of Dr. King's speech . . . constituted a general publication of the speech so as to place it in the public domain." 13 F.Supp.2d at 1351. After discussing the relevant case law, the district court held that Dr. King's "performance coupled with such wide and unlimited reproduction and dissemination as occurred concomitant to Dr. King's speech during the March on Washington can be seen only as a general publication which thrust the speech into the public domain." Id. at 1354. Thus, the district court granted CBS's motion for summary judgment. The Estate now appeals to this Court.

II.   DISCUSSION

* * *

Because of the dates of the critical events, the determinative issues in this case are properly analyzed under the Copyright Act of 1909 ("1909 Act"), rather than the Copyright Act of 1976 ("1976 Act") that is currently in effect. See Brown v. Tabb, 714 F.2d 1088, 1091 (11th Cir.1983) ("[T]he determination whether a work entered the public domain prior to the effective date of the 1976 Act must be made according to the copyright law as it existed before that date."). The question is whether Dr. King's attempt to obtain statutory copyright protection on September 30, 1963 was effective, or whether it was a nullity because the Speech had already been forfeited to the public domain via a general publication.

Under the regime created by the 1909 Act, an author received state common law protection automatically at the time of creation of a work. See 1 Melville B. Nimmer & David Nimmer, Nimmer on Copyright § 4.01[B] (1998) [hereinafter *Nimmer*]. This state common law protection persisted until the moment of a general publication. See Silverman v. CBS Inc., 632 F.Supp. 1344, 1353 (S.D.N.Y.1986). When a general publication occurred, the author either forfeited his work to the public domain, see, e.g., White v. Kimmell, 193 F.2d 744 (9th Cir.1952), or, if he had therebefore complied with federal statutory requirements, converted his common law copyright into a federal statutory copyright. See *Mister Maestro*, 224 F.Supp. at 105 ("The [statutory] copyright may be obtained before publication of such works but as soon as publication occurs there must be compliance with the requirements as to published works."); see generally 1 *Nimmer* § 4.01[B].

In order to soften the hardship of the rule that publication destroys common law rights, courts developed a distinction between a "general publication" and a "limited publication." *Brown*, 714 F.2d at 1091 (citing American Vitagraph, Inc. v. Levy, 659 F.2d 1023, 1026–27 (9th Cir.1981)). Only a general publication divested a common law copyright. See id. A general publication occurred "when a work was made available to members of the public at large without regard to their identity or what they intended to do with the work." Id. (citing Burke v. National Broadcasting Co., 598 F.2d 688, 691 (1st Cir.1979)). Conversely, a non-divesting limited publication was one that communicated the contents of a work to a select group and for a limited purpose, and without the right of diffusion, reproduction, distribution or sale. See id. (citing *White*, 193 F.2d at 746–47). The issue before us is whether Dr. King's delivery of the Speech was a general publication.

[handwritten: Issue — was delivery of Speech a gen. pub.?]

Numerous cases stand for the proposition that the performance of a work is not a general publication. See, e.g., Ferris v. Frohman, 223 U.S. 424 (1912) ("The public representation of a dramatic composition, not printed and published, does not deprive the owner of his common-law right .... [T]he public performance of the play is not an abandonment of it to the public use."); Nutt v. National Inst. Incorporated for the Improvement of Memory, 31 F.2d 236, 238 (2d Cir.1929) ("The author of a literary composition, as a lecture, may profit from public delivery, but that does not constitute the kind of publication which deprives him of the protection of the copyright statute .... "); *Mister Maestro*, 224 F.Supp. at 106 ("The copyright statute itself plainly shows that 'oral delivery' of an address is not a dedication to the public."); * * * cf. American Tobacco Co. v. Werckmeister, 207 U.S. 284, 299 (1907) (no general publication where there is merely "the exhibition of a work of art at a public exhibition") * * *.

It appears from the case law that a general publication occurs only in two situations. First, a general publication occurs if tangible copies of the work are distributed to the general public in such a manner as allows the public to exercise dominion and control over the work. * * * Second, a general publication may occur if the work is exhibited or displayed in such a manner as to permit unrestricted copying by the general public. See *American Tobacco*, 207 U.S. at 300 ("We do not mean to say that the public exhibition of a painting or statue, where all might see and freely copy it, might not amount to [divestive] publication .... "); * * * Letter Edged in Black Press, Inc. v. Public Bldg. Comm'n of Chicago, 320 F.Supp. 1303, 1311 (N.D.Ill.1970) (invoking this exception where "there were no restrictions on copying [of a publicly displayed sculpture] and no guards preventing copying" and "every citizen was free to copy the maquette for his own pleasure and camera permits were available to members of the public"). * * *

[handwritten: general publication in 2 ways: 1. tangible copies of work distributed to gen public allowing dominion control over work; 2. displayed in way to permit unrestricted copying by public]

The case law indicates that distribution to the news media, as opposed to the general public, for the purpose of enabling the reporting of a contemporary newsworthy event, is only a limited publication. For example, in Public Affairs Assoc., Inc. v. Rickover, 284 F.2d 262 (D.C.Cir.1960), vacated on other grounds, 369 U.S. 111 (1962), the court said that general publication occurs only when there is "a studied effort not only to secure publicity for the contents of the addresses through the channels of information, but to *go beyond customary sources of press or broadcasting* in distributing the addresses to any interested individual." Id. at 270 (emphasis added). Although the *Rickover* court ultimately held that a general publication had occurred, it contrasted the "limited use of the addresses by the press for fair comment," i.e., limited publication, with "the unlimited distribution to anyone who was interested," i.e., general publication. Id. at 271. See also *Mister Maestro*, 224 F.Supp. at 107 (taking the position that solicitation of news coverage and distribution to the media amounts to only a limited publication); * * *

With the above principles in mind, in the summary judgment posture of this case and on the current state of this record, we are unable to conclude that CBS has demonstrated beyond any genuine issue of material fact that Dr. King, simply through his oral delivery of the Speech, engaged in a general publication making the Speech "available to members of the public at large without regard to their identity or what they intended to do

[handwritten: Reasons]

with the work." *Brown*, 714 F.2d at 1091. A performance, no matter how broad the audience, is not a publication; to hold otherwise would be to upset a long line of precedent. This conclusion is not altered by the fact that the Speech was broadcast live to a broad radio and television audience and was the subject of extensive contemporaneous news coverage. We follow the above cited case law indicating that release to the news media for contemporary coverage of a newsworthy event is only a limited publication.[4] * * *

Because there exist genuine issues of material fact as to whether a general publication occurred, we must reverse the district court's grant of summary judgment for CBS. It would be inappropriate for us to address CBS's other arguments, e.g., fair use and the First Amendment, because the district court did not address them, and because the relevant facts may not yet be fully developed. Of course, we express no opinion on the eventual merits of this litigation. The judgment of the district court is reversed and remanded for further proceedings not inconsistent with this opinion.

Reversed and Remanded.

■ COOK, SENIOR DISTRICT JUDGE, concurring in part and dissenting in part:
         * * *

The district court held that a general publication had occurred on the basis of the combined presence of three factors; namely, (1) the performance of the speech by Dr. King during the March on Washington, (2) its contemporaneous wide dissemination by the press, through the broadcasting and print media, which resulted from the concerted efforts of the March organizers to gain media attention, and (3) the lack of restrictions, explicit, implicit, or in practice, on the copying or reproduction of the speech by the

---

[4] We emphasize the summary judgment posture of this case, which necessitates that we disregard evidence that may be important or even dispositive at trial. In other words, in this summary judgment posture, we consider only the evidence with respect to which there is no genuine issue of material fact. This evidence includes only the fact of the oral delivery of the Speech to a large audience and the fact that the sponsors of the event including Dr. King sought and successfully obtained live broadcasts on radio and television and extensive contemporary coverage in the news media. In this regard, we do not consider at this stage of the litigation two potentially important pieces of evidence brought to our attention by CBS. First, an advance text of the Speech was apparently available in a press tent on the day of the speech. According to an eyewitness affidavit submitted by CBS, members of the public at large—not merely the press—were permitted access to the press tent and were given copies of the advance text. However, the Estate has proffered affidavits which contradict the statements of the CBS witness, and suggest that access was controlled by the SCLC within reasonable means. Moreover, the Estate argues that much of the content of the Speech was generated extemporaneously by Dr. King and was not contained in this advance text—an argument that we do not consider but that can be explored by the district court. Finding genuine issues of material fact with respect to the availability of the advance text to the general public, the district court disregarded CBS's allegations in this regard. 13 F.Supp.2d at 1353 n. 5. We agree, and do likewise.

Second, CBS has produced a September 1963 issue of the SCLC's newsletter in which the text of the Speech was reprinted in its entirety, with no copyright notice. The newsletter was widely circulated to the general public. Indeed, at oral argument, the Estate conceded that this reprinting of the Speech and wide distribution of the newsletter would constitute a general publication, if it were authorized by Dr. King. However, the Estate has raised the issue that Dr. King did not authorize this reprinting and distribution of the Speech. Finding genuine issues of fact in this regard, the district court disregarded this evidence. We agree, and do likewise. Finally, we note that the opinion in *Mister Maestro*, 224 F.Supp. at 104, suggests that there may have been evidence of subsequent rebroadcasts of the Speech in movie houses and sales of phonograph records. We do not consider any such evidence because CBS has not argued in this appeal that such evidence is relevant at this stage. Moreover, the opinion in *Mister Maestro* suggests that there may be genuine issues of material fact (e.g., authorization) with respect to such evidence.

press or public. See Estate of Martin Luther King, Jr., Inc. v. CBS, Inc., 13 F.Supp.2d 1347, 1353 (N.D.Ga.1998) * * *. While agreeing with Chief Judge Anderson that the speech was not placed into the public domain on the basis of these factors, I do not reach this conclusion because of the limited publication rule. Rather, I rely upon the more fundamental principle that, in the context of performed works, none of these factors may be properly considered as having contributed to a general or limited publication in the absence of an authorized dissemination of a tangible copy of the work without copyright notice. * * *

■ RONEY, SENIOR CIRCUIT JUDGE, dissenting:

I respectfully dissent on the ground that the district court correctly held there was a general publication. I would affirm on the basis of the district court opinion. * * *

NOTES AND QUESTIONS ON PUBLICATION

(1) Was the distribution of Dr. King's speech, in any real sense, "limited"? Does the result nevertheless seem equitable? What was the rationale for the rule that a "general" publication divested common law rights in works of authorship? For another illustration of the limited publication doctrine, see Academy of Motion Picture Arts & Sciences v. Creative House Promotions, Inc., 944 F.2d 1446 (9th Cir.1991), in which the court found that the restricted distribution of the Oscar statuette was a limited publication and thus protection had not been lost for lack of a copyright notice.

(2) In connection with publication under the 1909 Act, consider the following quotation from American Vitagraph v. Levy, 659 F.2d 1023 (9th Cir.1981): "[P]ublication may be more readily found if the issue is whether the copyright statute has been complied with than if forfeiture of common law rights is involved." This notion that the distribution necessary to cause the loss of common law rights (divestive publication) was greater than that required to bring a work within the protection of the 1909 Act through publication with copyright notice (investive publication) may help explain much of the case law on publication. Although protection under the 1976 Act commences upon fixation, prior to the 1989 amendments (see p. 34 infra) compliance with the copyright notice provisions upon publication of the work was a prerequisite to continued copyright protection. Which of the former concepts of publication corresponds more closely to its role in this statutory scheme?

(3) The rule that public performance is not publication is continued under the 1976 Act. (See the § 101 definition of "publication.") As for public display of a work, the House Report offers this comment:

> It should be noted that, under the definition of "publication" in section 101, there would no longer be any basis for holding, as a few court decisions have done in the past, that the public display of a work of art under some conditions (e.g., without restriction against its reproduction) would constitute publication of the work. (H.R.Rep. p. 144.)

(4) Suppose an author posts her work on a public website. Is that a "publication"? Getaped.com, Inc. v. Cangemi, 188 F.Supp.2d 398 (S.D.N.Y.2002), held that since the *sine qua non* of publication is the ability of the public to acquire tangible copies of the work, a work has been published when the copyright owner makes it accessible to the public on the Internet.

(5) Assume that Dr. King had delivered his speech just after the passage of the 1976 Act. Would the speech have been protected by federal copyright at the time of his address? Would the events of the day have threatened the continuation of that protection? A similar case arose at the 1988 Democratic National Convention. Jesse Jackson gave a speech to the convention carried live by the major television networks. Copies of the speech had been provided to the press prior to its delivery; Jackson's national campaign office distributed additional copies in the weeks that followed. None apparently bore a notice of copyright. When the defendant began marketing a videotape of the convention address, Jackson brought an infringement action. Although § 401 at the time made copyright notice mandatory on published copies, the court granted a preliminary injunction, finding that the omission of notice was probably excused under one or more of the exceptions to the notice requirement in § 405(a), which are taken up in the next section. Jackson v. MPI Home Video, 694 F.Supp. 483 (N.D.Ill.1988).

Would there be any risk of forfeiture if Dr. King's speech and its distribution to the press occurred today? See § 401.

4. THE STATUTORY FORMALITIES

FORMALITIES AND COPYRIGHT

Procedural formalities have played a central role in American copyright law. They have often tripped up an incautious author or publisher. This is in part a legacy of the famous case of Wheaton v. Peters, 33 U.S. (8 Pet.) 591 (1834). The contestants were Wheaton, the reporter of decisions for the Supreme Court from 1816 to 1827, and his successor, Peters, who published a series of Condensed Reports that included his predecessor's headnotes and commentary.[p] (The Court in this case declared that no reporter could have copyright in the opinions themselves.) The defense was that Wheaton and his publishers had not met all the statutory requirements for obtaining a federal copyright. This apparent flaw in his copyrights led Wheaton (represented by Daniel Webster) to assert the persistence of common law copyright after publication, to which the federal copyright statute was only complementary and remedial. He thus recreated in this country the controversy over the nature of literary property that had come to a climax in England in Donaldson v. Becket, p. 23 supra, where the House of Lords had ruled that the Statute of Anne supplanted common law rights after publication. The Supreme Court took a parallel view with respect to our statute. It superseded the author's common law rights in published works, which the Court doubted had ever existed anyway. Rights in published works were therefore subject to the statutory formalities:

"This right, as has been shown, does not exist at common law—it originated, if at all, under the acts of Congress. No one can deny that when the legislature are about to vest an exclusive right in an author or an inventor, they have the power to prescribe the conditions on which such right shall be enjoyed; and that no one can avail himself of such right who does not substantially comply with the requisitions of the law. * * *

---

[p] An informative history of the early Supreme Court reporters and the controversy between Wheaton and Peters is offered in C. Joyce, The Rise of the Supreme Court Reporter: An Institutional Perspective on the Marshall Court Ascendancy, 83 Mich.L.Rev. 1291 (1985).

"The Act of Congress under which Mr. Wheaton, one of the complainants, in his capacity of reporter, was required to deliver eighty copies of each volume of his reports to the department of state, and which were, probably, faithfully delivered, does not exonerate him from the deposite of a copy under the act of 1790. The eighty volumes were delivered for a different purpose; and cannot excuse the deposite of the one volume as specially required."

So, despite the fact that as the reporter for the Supreme Court Wheaton apparently delivered eighty copies to the Department of State, he was not excused from depositing in the same office "the one volume as specially required" by the copyright statute. The case was remanded to ascertain the facts. For every volume of the reports that did not comply with the statutory formalities, the complaint as to it was to be dismissed.q

The statutory formalities were modified from time to time, and indeed, the 1909 Act was supposed to represent a considerable relaxation. It made acquisition of copyright on publication seemingly easy—all that was necessary was a notice of copyright on the published copies. But the statutory scheme was still cumbersome. At least a half-dozen sections of the 1909 Act held implications for the notice requirement, and it continued to trap the unwary.r A few examples will suffice.

In Group Publishers, Inc. v. Winchell, 86 F.Supp. 573 (S.D.N.Y.1949), copyright was lost because an assignee substituted its own name in the copyright notice before recording the assignment with the Copyright Office: "Strict compliance with the statutory requirements is essential to the perfection of the copyright itself and failure fully to conform to the form of notice prescribed by the act results in abandonment of the right and a dedication of one's work to the public." One case dismissed an infringement action because the plaintiff's notice appeared on the back cover rather than on the "title page or the page immediately following" as required by § 20 of the 1909 Act. J.A. Richards, Inc. v. New York Post, 23 F.Supp. 619 (S.D.N.Y.1938). Another case withheld protection from a series of cartoons because the notice did not contain the name of the copyright owner, despite the appearance of his name in the title legend of the cartoons. Moger v. WHDH, Inc., 194 F.Supp. 605 (D.Mass.1961). Some judges, however, worked hard to avoid declaring a forfeiture against a deserving claimant who had failed to clear all the statutory hurdles. Thus, phrases such as "substantial compliance" and "adequate" notice sometimes appeared in the case law.

During the lengthy revision process that culminated in the 1976 Act, some urged that the requirement of a copyright notice be eliminated.s The structure of the 1976 Act offered some support for this view, since it was now fixation rather than publication that marked the beginning of federal protection. The case for elimination also drew upon international copyright

---

q Future Supreme Court Justice Oliver Wendell Holmes was defeated by the statutory formalities when he sought as executor of his father's estate to enjoin an infringement of *The Autocrat of the Breakfast Table*, published by the senior Holmes in twelve successive issues of the *Atlantic Monthly*. Since the issues of the magazine were not copyrighted, a later attempt to secure copyright on the complete work was held ineffective. Holmes v. Hurst, 174 U.S. 82 (1899).

r As with publication, the old rules retain significance. The notice requirements of the 1909 Act determine whether a work published prior to 1978 is in the public domain.

s See generally V. Doyal *et al.*, Notice of Copyright, Copyr. Law Revision Study No. 7 (1957), in 1 Studies on Copyr. 229 (1963); W. Blaisdell, Commercial Use of the Copyright Notice, Copyr. Law Revision Study No. 8 (1959), id. at 275.

law. Most of the nations of the world had no copyright notice requirements and their systems were predominantly free of other formalities. This was one of the differences that had long prevented our adherence to the Berne Convention, the primary multinational copyright treaty. (See p. 810 infra.) The drafters of the 1976 Act attempted an elaborate compromise. The philosophy of the Act as initially adopted is described in the legislative history:

> A requirement that the public be given formal notice of every work in which copyright is claimed was a part of the first U.S. copyright statute enacted in 1790, and since 1802 our copyright laws have always provided that the published copies of copyrighted works must bear a specified notice as a condition of protection. Under the present law the copyright notice serves four principal functions:

> *[handwritten: notice functions]*

> (1) It has the effect of placing in the public domain a substantial body of published material that no one is interested in copyrighting;

> (2) It informs the public as to whether a particular work is copyrighted;

> (3) It identifies the copyright owner; and

> (4) It shows the date of publication.

> Ranged against these values of a notice requirement are its burdens and unfairness to copyright owners. One of the strongest arguments for revision of the present statute has been the need to avoid the arbitrary and unjust forfeitures now resulting from unintentional or relatively unimportant omissions or errors in the copyright notice. It has been contended that the disadvantages of the notice requirement outweigh its values and that it should therefore be eliminated or substantially liberalized.

> The fundamental principle underlying the notice provisions of the bill is that the copyright notice has real values which should be preserved, and that this should be done by inducing use of notice without causing outright forfeiture for errors or omissions. Subject to certain safeguards for innocent infringers, protection would not be lost by the complete omission of copyright notice from large numbers of copies or from a whole edition, if registration for the work is made before or within 5 years after publication. Errors in the name or date in the notice could be corrected without forfeiture of copyright. (H.R.Rep. p. 143.)

[handwritten: notice became optional]

This compromise survived for barely a decade. With the coming into effect on March 1, 1989 of the Berne Convention Implementation Act, P.L. 100–569, 102 Stat. 2853, notice of copyright became optional, ending the notice requirement that had endured in various forms for only a year short of two centuries.

NOTES AND QUESTIONS ON COPYRIGHT NOTICE

(1) The principal copyright notice provisions are § 401 and § 402. As enacted in 1976, both sections required notice of copyright on all published works. The amendments effective in 1989 replaced "shall" with "may", thus ending mandatory copyright notice. Habit, together with the small remedial advantage offered in § 401(d) and § 402(d), will doubtless insure its continued presence on most works. (An exception may be works of fine art, where the appearance of a copyright notice has sometimes been decried as a defacement or mutilation.) Are there also practical benefits to the continued use of a copyright notice?

The legislative history of the Berne Implementation Act indicates an apparent intent to eliminate the requirement of notice only for works first published after March 1, 1989. "The proposed legislation abolishes mandatory notice of copyright for works first published after the law comes into effect." H.R.Rep. No. 100–609, 100th Cong., 2d Sess. 45 (1988). But consider the introductory language in § 405—doesn't it imply that an omission of notice from copies distributed after the effective date of the amendment will not invalidate the copyright regardless of when the work was first published? The Copyright Office in Circular 1, Copyright Basics (2012), "does not take a position on whether copies of works first published with notice before March 1, 1989, which are distributed on or after March 1, 1989, must bear the copyright notice." In Encore Shoe Corp. v. Bennett Industries, Inc., 18 U.S.P.Q.2d 1874 (D.Mass.1991), the court said in dictum that if a satisfactory copyright notice had appeared on pre–1989 publications, an omission of notice on post-amendment publications did not threaten the copyright.

The form and placement of notice sufficient to provide the remedial advantages offered in § 401(d) (and, for pre–1989 distributions, to preserve the validity of the copyright) are prescribed in § 401(b) and (c). As indicated in § 401(c), Copyright Office regulations offer specific examples of satisfactory affixation.[t] See 37 C.F.R. § 201.20. Hopefully, the copyright notice following the title page of this casebook is a further example of compliance. (Is it necessary to include the dates of earlier editions? See § 401(b)(2).)

Consider the form of notice specified in § 401(b). What is the purpose of including "the year of first publication"? How often will that date be useful in determining when copyright expires? See § 302.

Will the notice necessarily identify the owner of the copyright? Recall that copyrights can be transferred. The name appearing in the copyright notice on existing copies will not magically change to reflect a subsequent assignment.

(2) Examine the label on a compact disc. Why is there typically no § 401 notice of copyright for the musical works recorded on the disc? What is the function of the notice that *does* appear? See §§ 401 and 402, together with the § 101 definitions of "copies," "phonorecords," and "sound recordings."

(3) A copyright notice reminds users that the work is protected by copyright law, but the notice can also be misleading. Consider a work that incorporates substantial material from the public domain. The copyright notice will not reflect the fact that only a portion of the work is protected, and indeed may create the opposite impression. Only when the public domain material consists of works of the United States Government (which are excluded from copyright under § 105) is the public likely to be protected by a more informative notice.

---

[t]   The general prescription in § 401(c) that notice be affixed so as to "give reasonable notice of the claim of copyright" was found satisfied in Forry, Inc. v. Neundorfer, Inc., 837 F.2d 259 (6th Cir.1988), by a notice that appeared on the underside of a microchip attached to a circuit board. The court noted that the copyrighted computer program could not be duplicated unless the chip was first removed from the board.

See § 403.[u] (Should this casebook have a § 403 notice in view of its extensive use of federal judicial opinions? What would such a notice say?)

———

As we have seen, for publications before Jan. 1, 1978, the effective date of the 1976 Act, the notice requirements of the 1909 Act determine whether the work has entered the public domain. For publications occurring after March 1, 1989, copyright notice is no longer required. For publications between Jan. 1, 1978 and March 1, 1989, an omission or error in the notice can cause a forfeiture of copyright, but as the following case illustrates, the omission or error might be excused or cured under the complicated set of provisions in §§ 404–06.

Hasbro Bradley, Inc. v. Sparkle Toys, Inc.

United States Court of Appeals, Second Circuit, 1985.
780 F.2d 189.

Before FRIENDLY, MANSFIELD and WINTER, CIRCUIT JUDGES.

■ FRIENDLY, CIRCUIT JUDGE:

The companies involved in this copyright case in the District Court for the Southern District of New York are Takara Co., Ltd. ("Takara"), a Japanese company that designed the toys here in question; plaintiff Hasbro Bradley, Inc. ("Hasbro"), a large American toy manufacturer and seller that acquired Takara's rights to United States copyrights for the toys; and defendant Sparkle Toys, Inc. ("Sparkle"), a smaller American toy manufacturer and seller that copied the toys in Asia from models manufactured by Takara which did not carry the copyright notice required by § 401 of the Copyright Act of 1976 (the "Act"), 17 U.S.C. § 101 et seq., and by Article III(1) of the Revised Universal Copyright Convention (U.C.C.), 25 U.S.T. 1341 (1971), to which the United States and Japan are parties. The appeal, by Sparkle, is from an order of Judge Broderick entered April 29, 1985, granting Hasbro a preliminary injunction prohibiting Sparkle from "distributing, selling, marketing, promoting, advertising, imitating or exploiting, in this country, its toys, formerly denoted 'Trans Robot,' which are in violation of plaintiff's registered copyrights in the sculptural embodiments of its 'Topspin' and 'Twin Twist' toys."

"Topspin" and "Twin Twist" (the "toys") are part of Hasbro's "The Transformers" series of changeable robotic action figures. The sculptural expressions of the toys are original designs of Takara, which manufactures "The Transformers" for Hasbro. Takara authored the designs in the summer of 1983 and by the end of November had completed molds for manufacturing the toys. These molds did not contain a copyright notice. Takara avers that the omission was due to the facts that Japanese law does not recognize copyright in toy products and that Takara was unaware that American law does recognize copyright in such works but requires notice,

DCH for π injunction

———

[u] In Matthew Bender & Co. v. West Pub. Co., 240 F.3d 116 (2d Cir.2001), the Second Circuit rejected the trial court's attempt to justify an award of attorney's fees against West Publishing Company based on West's failure to include in the copyright notice on its judicial reporters a statement delineating the aspects of the reports in which it claimed copyright. The Second Circuit held that the sole consequence of failing to provide the more elaborate notice specified by § 403 for works that incorporate U.S. Government material is that the alleged infringer is no longer prohibited by § 401(d) from asserting an innocent infringement defense in mitigation of damages. J. Mazzone, Copyfraud, 81 N.Y.U.L.Rev. 1026 (2006), proposes legislative and judicial penalties to deter false claims of copyright in public domain works.

even on copies of the work distributed outside the United States, for copyright protection to be claimed inside the United States. Production of the unmarked toys began in December 1983 and ended in February 1984. Between January and March, approximately 213,000 of the unmarked toys were sold; thereafter, sales were minor and were made only to remove inventory. Whether the unmarked toys were sold only in Asia or some of them were sold as well in the United States is in dispute. * * *

As previously stated, there is also no dispute that before the assignment of Takara's copyrights to Hasbro approximately 213,000 of the toys were sold, mostly in Japan, without copyright notice. This omission of notice from toys sold by Takara or with its authority outside the United States violated § 401(a) of the Act, which requires:

> Whenever a work protected under this title is published in the United States *or elsewhere* by authority of the copyright owner, a notice of copyright as provided by this section shall be placed on all publicly distributed copies from which the work can be visually perceived, either directly or with the aid of a machine or device.

(Emphasis added.) * * *

It is not contended that the omission of notice from the toys could have been excused under either subsections (1) or (3) of § 405(a); rather, reliance is placed on subsection (2). In effect, § 405(a)(2) allows a person who publishes a copyrightable work without notice to hold a kind of incipient copyright in the work for five years thereafter: if the omission is cured in that time through registration and the exercise of "a reasonable effort . . . to add notice to all copies . . . that are distributed to the public in the United States after the omission has been discovered," the copyright is perfected and valid retroactively for the entire period after cure; if the omission is not cured in that time, the incipient copyright never achieves enforceability. The *quid pro quo* in the Act for persons who have been misled by the omission of copyright notice before the cure is the more liberal provision of § 405(b), as compared with § 21 of the 1909 Act, regarding innocent infringers, of which more hereafter. * * *

The issue thus becomes whether Hasbro has cured Takara's omission of notice under § 405(a)(2). There is no question that Hasbro, as Takara's assignee, is permitted to effect cure through its own efforts. The "copyright claimant" entitled under the Act to register a copyright in the United States may be either the author of the work or his assignee, and any registration is of the work *per se* and redounds to the benefit of the assignor as well as the assignee. 3 *Nimmer,* supra, § 10.02[C][2], at 10–33. Not disputing this, Sparkle argues that Hasbro cannot effect cure under § 405(a)(2) because Takara's omission of notice was deliberate.

On its face, § 405(a)(2) is not restricted to unintentional omissions. Its language permits cure if registration is made "within five years after *the publication without notice*"—not, as Sparkle would read it, "the [unintentional] publication without notice." The difference between the broad language of § 405(a) and the more limited language of § 21 of the 1909 Act * * * shows that Congress no longer wished to deal only with omissions of notice due to accident or mistake. Moreover, the legislative history of the 1976 Act affords ample demonstration that Congress intended to bring deliberate omissions within the ambit of § 405(a)(2). The House Report comments with respect to § 405(a) that "[u]nder the proposed law a work published without any copyright notice will still be subject to statutory protection for at least 5 years, whether the omission was partial or total, *unintentional or deliberate.*" *House Report*, supra, at 147 (emphasis added), reprinted in 1976 U.S. Code Cong. & Ad. News at 5763. * * *

Against this, Sparkle relies on Judge Sand's opinion in Beacon Looms, Inc. v. S. Lichtenberg & Co., 552 F.Supp. 1305 (S.D.N.Y.1982), and on Professor Nimmer's approval of the reasoning of that opinion, see 2 *Nimmer,* supra, § 7.13[B][3].

The result in *Beacon Looms* depended almost entirely on the language in § 405(a)(2) that reasonable efforts to affix notice need begin only "after the omission has been discovered." Judge Sand reasoned that since "one cannot 'discover' an omission that has been deliberate," 552 F.Supp. at 1310, to permit the cure of deliberate omissions would do violence to the unambiguous "plain meaning" of the statute. * * *

With due respect, we cannot agree with *Beacon Looms.* The operative language of the statute in this context comes at the beginning of § 405(a), covers all three methods of cure, and is not restricted in any way. The language relied on by Judge Sand, which comes at the end of § 405(a)(2), is relevant only with respect to unmarked copies that have been publicly distributed in the United States. More important, the premise of the argument—namely, that a deliberate omission cannot be "discovered"—is unsound. As discussed above, an assignee or licensee may effect cure under § 405(a)(2) on behalf of itself and its assignor or licensor. In such a situation—the very one presented in this case—no violence is done to the statutory language by saying that the omission, though deliberate on the part of the assignor or licensor, was "discovered" by the person later attempting to cure it. Similarly, a deliberate omission at a lower level of a corporate hierarchy might well be "discovered," in realistic terms, by someone at a higher level. Instances like these at least indicate that the "discovered" language does not reveal a plain intent to exclude all deliberate omissions. * * *

* * * We therefore conclude that the omission of notice from the toys, even if deliberate on Takara's part, was subject to cure under § 405(a)(2), and we pass on to the question whether Hasbro in fact effectuated cure.

Apart from Sparkle's contention that Hasbro committed fraud on the Copyright Office [the court's discussion of this issue is omitted], there is no dispute that Hasbro validly registered its copyrights in the Takara designs within five years of publication of the unmarked toys, thus satisfying one of the two requirements for cure under § 405(a)(2). Sparkle admits also that Hasbro has affixed notice to all of the toys since sold under its authority in the United States and elsewhere. It argues, however, that Hasbro did not make "a reasonable effort" to affix notice to toys from the unmarked batch initially produced by Takara and thus failed to satisfy the second requirement of § 405(a)(2). * * *

We are content, however, to leave undecided the question whether Hasbro would be obligated under § 405(a)(2) to make a reasonable effort to affix notice even with respect to unmarked toys distributed in the United States by persons other than itself or Takara. At this juncture, Sparkle has yet to produce credible evidence that any of the unmarked toys have been publicly distributed in the United States *at all,* let alone evidence of who distributed them. Whether any unmarked toys were introduced into the United States and, if so, who introduced them and what efforts to mark them would be reasonable are questions that can be resolved at trial when Hasbro seeks a permanent injunction. * * *

Turning finally to Sparkle's claim that it should have been recognized as an innocent infringer under § 405(b), we think the record did not contain sufficient information for the district judge to have decided this issue, and he properly declined to do so. However, it should be promptly dealt with, either on an application by Hasbro for a permanent injunction or on one by Sparkle for a declaration of its rights.

Affirmed.

ACH for π injunction

NOTES AND QUESTIONS ON OMISSION OF NOTICE

(1) The "reasonable effort" to add notice after the omission has been discovered[v] that is required for cure under § 405(a)(2) does not extend to copies already distributed to the public. It does extend, however, to copies in the hands of distributors and retailers, in addition to those still in the possession of the copyright owner. See Lifshitz v. Walter Drake & Sons, Inc., 806 F.2d 1426 (9th Cir.1986) (lack of effort to remedy the omission of notice on copies held by an independent distributor prevented cure); Shapiro & Son Bedspread Corp. v. Royal Mills Associates, 764 F.2d 69 (2d Cir.1985) (reversing a summary judgment against the copyright owner since the rapid turnover of retailers' inventory made efforts to add notice useless).

(2) According to § 405(a)(1), if notice was omitted from only a "relatively small number of copies," copyright protection is not endangered. Is "relatively small number" to be taken in an absolute sense ("a few") or in a relative sense ("a small proportion of the total")? Is an omission of notice from four hundred copies too many? From four hundred out of a total of forty thousand? Compare Original Appalachian Artworks, Inc. v. Toy Loft, Inc., 684 F.2d 821 (11th Cir.1982) (1 per cent (400 out of 40,000) is a "relatively small number") with Donald Frederick Evans & Associates, Inc. v. Continental Homes, Inc., 785 F.2d 897 (11th Cir.1986) (2,500 (2.4 per cent of the total) "is a significant number in the absolute sense").

(3) Section 405(a)(3) states that an omission of notice by a third party will not invalidate the copyright if the owner had in writing conditioned the authorization to publish on use of the notice. Does this imply that omissions in violation of oral or implied conditions *are* divestive? If so, the rule is more restrictive than prior law. See Judge Learned Hand's resolution of a dispute between Superman and Captain Marvel in National Comics Pub. v. Fawcett Pub., 191 F.2d 594 (2d Cir.1951), supplemented, 198 F.2d 927 (2d Cir.1952).

(4) The notice requirement has been especially troublesome for authors who contribute to a "collective work," another term defined in § 101. The 1909 Act in § 19 required notice in the name of the "copyright proprietor." This created difficulties in light of the judicial tendency under the 1909 Act to view copyright as an indivisible bundle of rights. Since a partial assignment was impossible, anything less than a complete transfer of copyright created a mere license. Licensees were not "proprietors," and thus a notice in their name technically did

---

[v] When is an omission of copyright notice "discovered"? Compare Hardwick Airmasters, Inc. v. Lennox Indus., Inc., 78 F.3d 1332 (8th Cir.1996) (claimant discovers the omission when he learns that his rights have been infringed, even if unaware of the legal significance of the omission) with Charles Garnier, Paris v. Andin Int'l, Inc., 36 F.3d 1214 (1st Cir.1994) (focusing on when the claimant learned of the legal consequences of the omission). The latter case also held that the § 405(a)(2) requirement to add notice on subsequently distributed copies applies even as to copies distributed after March 1, 1989, when mandatory notice was otherwise abolished.

not comply with the 1909 Act. The 1976 Act in § 404 specifically authorizes copyright notice in the name of the publisher of a collective work regardless of copyright ownership in the individual contributions. Even if the author of an article gives a journal or magazine a mere license to publish, notice in the name of the publisher is thus sufficient to secure the remedial advantage of § 401(d), and in the case of a pre–1989 publication, to preserve the validity of the author's copyright.[w] With respect to pre–1989 publications, a contributor who has not transferred the copyright is subject to the rather slight risk that an infringer who deals with the person named in the notice may invoke the good faith defense in § 406(a). What sort of showing is necessary under § 406(a) to establish good faith reliance on a license from the person named in the notice? Does good faith require some measure of reasonableness in an objective sense, or will a pure heart suffice? See Quinto v. Legal Times of Washington, Inc., 506 F.Supp. 554 (D.D.C.1981), involving a contribution to a law school newspaper.

(5) The 1976 Act in § 201(d)(2) rejects the concept of indivisibility. The rights comprising copyright may now be separately owned. What consequences does this have for the copyright notice as specified in § 401 and § 402? Both refer to "the name of the owner of copyright." Note the definitions of "copyright owner" and "transfer of copyright ownership" in § 101. Does all this imply that assignees or exclusive licensees of specific rights should use their own names in the notice? Professor Nimmer thinks not. See Nimmer on Copyright § 10.02[C]. An incorrect name will not in any case threaten the validity of the copyright, even on pre–1989 publications. See § 406(a).

(6) If, as in *Hasbro*, even deliberate omissions of notice on pre–1989 publications could be cured under § 405(a)(2), the usefulness of the notice requirement was substantially reduced. Users relying on the absence of notice receive a measure of protection in § 405(b), but even these "innocent" infringers can be forced to disgorge profits and discontinue use. The House Report could offer only this advice: "Persons who undertake major enterprises * * * should check the Copyright Office registration records before starting even where copies have been published without notice." H.R.Rep. p. 148.

With its tolerance of defective notice and its liberal opportunities for cure, the 1976 Act effectively emasculated the requirement of copyright notice. It was thus a short step to the 1989 amendments that formally eliminated the notice requirement.

(7) As *Hasbro* indicates, the notice requirement under § 401 of the 1976 Act is applicable to works published both "in the United States or elsewhere." Prior to the elimination of the notice requirement in 1989, publication abroad without a notice of copyright could thus inject the work into the public domain, at least with respect to protection here.[x] As part of the 1994 legislation implementing

---

[w] Why are advertisements excepted from the rule in § 404(a) permitting copyright notice in the name of the collective work publisher? See Canfield v. Ponchatoula Times, 759 F.2d 493 (5th Cir.1985).

[x] The status of works published abroad without notice of copyright prior to the effective date of the 1976 Act is less certain. Compare Twin Books Corp. v. Walt Disney Co., 83 F.3d 1162 (9th Cir.1996) (adhering to Heim v. Universal Pictures Co., 154 F.2d 480 (2d Cir.1946), and holding that under the 1909 Act copyright in *Bambi, A Life in the Woods* was not lost due to its 1923 publication without notice in Germany) with 37 C.F.R. § 202.2(a)(3) (works first published abroad before Jan. 1, 1978, must have an adequate copyright notice). *Twin Books* was followed in Societe Civile Succession Guino v. Renoir, 549 F.3d 1182 (9th Cir.2008), which held that a 1917 publication without notice in France of sculptures by Pierre–Auguste Renoir did not cause the works to enter the public domain in the United States. The restoration of

the Uruguay Round Trade Agreement that created the World Trade Organization, Congress in § 104A of the Copyright Act automatically restored copyright, as of Jan. 1, 1996, in foreign works that had fallen into the public domain in the United States because of non-compliance with statutory formalities such as notice or renewal of copyright. A restored copyright lasts for the remainder of the copyright term that the work would have enjoyed if it had not entered the public domain. To be eligible for restoration, the foreign work must not be in the public domain in its source country, it must not have been published in the United States within 30 days of its first publication abroad, and the author must be a national or domiciliary of a country other than the United States that belongs to the World Trade Organization or the Berne Convention or is covered by a Presidential proclamation. (Thus, copyright restoration does *not* apply to works by U.S. authors that entered the public domain because of non-compliance with required formalities.)

[handwritten margin note: copyright restoration not for US citizens]

Section 104A provides a measure of protection to users who have been exploiting a work in which copyright is restored in reliance on its former public domain status. After the owner of a restored copyright files the required notice, such a "reliance party" must stop reproducing the work, but can continue to sell off existing stock for twelve months. They can also continue to exploit existing derivative works upon payment of "reasonable compensation." The exception for existing derivative works was at issue in Dam Things from Denmark v. Russ Berrie & Co., 290 F.3d 548 (3d Cir.2002). The plaintiff's copyright in its troll dolls, originally lost due to improper notice, had been restored under § 104A; it sought an injunction against a defendant who was selling dolls copied from photographs of the plaintiff's products. The defendant argued that it was entitled to a mandatory license as a reliance party who had created derivative works prior to the restoration of copyright. The case was remanded to determine whether the defendant's dolls embodied sufficient additional creativity to qualify as derivative works.

The restoration of copyrights in foreign works under § 104A was upheld by the Supreme Court against claims that it exceeded congressional power under the Copyright Clause and violated the First Amendment in Golan v. Holder, 132 S.Ct. 873 (2012). "Neither the Copyright and Patent Clause nor the First Amendment, we hold, makes the public domain, in any and all cases, a territory that works may never exit." As to any limitation under the Copyright Clause, Judge Ginsburg's opinion stated, "Nothing in the text of the Copyright Clause confines the 'Progress of Science' exclusively to 'incentives for creation.' * * * Evidence from the founding, moreover, suggest that inducing *dissemination*—as opposed to creation—was viewed as an appropriate means to promote science. See Nachbar, Constructing Copyright's Mythology, 6 Green Bag 2d 327, 44 (2002) * * *. Congress rationally could have concluded that adherence to Berne 'promotes the diffusion of knowledge,' Brief for Petitioners 4." The First Amendment was also no bar to restoration. "Section [104A] leaves undisturbed the 'idea/expression' distinction and the 'fair use' defense. Moreover, Congress adopted measures to ease the transition from a national scheme to an international copyright regime: It deferred the date from which enforcement runs, and it cushioned the impact of restoration on 'reliance parties' who exploited foreign works denied protection before [§ 104A] took effect. * * * And

[handwritten margin note: Golan]

---

copyright provisions in § 104A, applicable to certain public domain works, were thus irrelevant; instead, the court held that the sculptures were protected under § 303(a) as works "created before January 1, 1978, but not theretofore in the public domain or copyrighted.

nothing in the historical record, congressional practice, or our own jurisprudence warrants exceptional First Amendment solicitude for copyrighted works that were once in the public domain."

DEPOSIT

Section 407(a) of the Copyright Act requires the copyright owner to deposit in the Copyright Office "two complete copies of the best edition" of the work within three months after publication. (Note the singularly unhelpful definition of "best edition" in § 101. See 37 C.F.R. § 202.19.) Copyright Office regulations exempt some works and require only one copy of others. The deposits enrich the collections of the Library of Congress. (The Library, located in Washington just beyond the U.S. Supreme Court Building, is an architectural wonder too often overlooked.) A failure to make the required deposit has no immediate legal consequences; it may elicit, however, a demand from the Acquisitions Division of the Copyright Office. Refusal to comply with a demand for deposit leaves the copyright owner subject to the penalties prescribed in § 407(d). Note that forfeiture of copyright is *not* among them.[y]

REGISTRATION

A system of copyright registration has long been a feature of American copyright law. The Copyright Office once offered these justifications for the registration system:

a.   *Value to copyright owners*

Registration provides, for authors and other copyright owners, a permanent and official record of their copyright claims. It furnishes them with proof of the existence of their works at a particular time and the facts supporting their copyright claims. Particularly important to them is the certificate of registration, which constitutes prima facie evidence of the stated facts and is generally accepted in trade circles as proof of copyright.

b.   *Value to users*

Registration serves other purposes, perhaps even more important, for persons who wish to use copyright materials. It provides accessible official records from which they can obtain information regarding the existence and basis of a copyright claim, the extent of the claim (e.g., in a new version of a preexisting work), its duration, and its initial ownership. In conjunction with the records of assignments and other transfers of ownership, it enables users to trace title to the copyright.[z]

---

[y]   The constitutionality of the deposit requirement was sustained against fifth and first amendment challenges in Ladd v. Law & Technology Press, 762 F.2d 809 (9th Cir.1985), cert. denied, 475 U.S. 1045 (1986). At that time, § 407 required deposit only upon publication with notice of copyright; the deposit thus could be seen as a kind of fee imposed on those who voluntarily sought the protection of the Act. Under the 1989 amendments, deposit is triggered by the mere fact of publication. Does this alter the constitutional arguments?

[z]   Report of the Register of Copyrights on the General Revision of the U.S. Copyright Law, House Comm. on the Judiciary, 87th Cong., 1st Sess. 72 (Comm. Print 1961), in 2 Studies on Copyr. 1199, 1272 (1963).

Registration is governed by §§ 408–410. Both published and unpublished works may be registered. Since registration is intended in part to inaugurate an official record of the copyright so that ownership can be determined, the registration provisions should be viewed together with § 205 on recordation of transfers. Copyright Office registration records can be accessed through Westlaw, LexisNexis, and at the Copyright Office web site at www. copyright.gov.

Despite the benefits ascribed to registration, the Copyright Act eschews the most obvious means of insuring a comprehensive public record. Section 408(a) is explicit that "registration is not a condition of copyright protection."[aa] Since registration is not compulsory, Congress determined that it "should therefore be induced in some practical way." H.R.Rep. p. 158. This effort is carried forward in §§ 410–412.

Section 410(c) offers an inducement to registration by providing that a certificate of registration obtained within five years of first publication is prima facie evidence of the validity of the copyright and of the facts stated in the certificate, thus shifting to an alleged infringer the burden of contesting ownership and copyrightability. (Why the five-year limitation? Are more tardy registrations less likely to be reliable?) Commencement of an infringement action is itself barred "until preregistration[bb] or registration of the copyright claim has been made," or "registration has been refused" by the Copyright Office. § 411(a).[cc] The limitation on the recovery of statutory damages and attorney's fees in § 412 for infringements of unregistered works provides a particularly compelling incentive to register. The speculative nature of actual damages and profits often precludes their recovery in copyright litigation—preserving the ability to recover statutory damages under § 504(c) and attorney's fees under § 505 is thus of particular importance.[dd] Finally, the practical effect of registration in enhancing the marketability of a work is itself a significant inducement to register.

Registration of copyright is a straight-forward process. It must be done using a registration form available at the Copyright Office web site— www.copyright.gov. The form can be submitted electronically or completed online, printed, and submitted by mail. The Register of Copyrights is authorized under § 708(b) to periodically adjust the fee for registration and

---

[aa] But recall § 405(a)(2), which requires registration within five years in order to cure an omission of notice on pre–1989 publications.

[bb] In order to increase protection for categories of works that are frequently infringed prior to publication, Congress in 2005 amended § 408 to allow for preregistration of certain unpublished works that are being prepared for commercial distribution. Copyright Office rules permit preregistration of motion pictures, sound recordings, musical works, literary works, computer programs, and advertising photographs. Preregistration is done electronically at the Copyright Office web site. Section 411 was amended to allow the commencement of an infringement action based on preregistration, and 412 permits the recovery of attorney's fees and statutory damages as long as preregistration occurred before commencement of the infringement and is followed by a timely registration.

[cc] After reviewing a split among the circuits, the Ninth Circuit in Cosmetic Ideas, Inc. v. IAC/Interactivecorp., 606 F.3d 612 (9th Cir.), cert. denied, 131 S.Ct. 686 (2010), held that the requirement in § 411(a) making registration a prerequisite to instituting an infringement action was satisfied by receipt of the registration application at the Copyright Office. According to the court, requiring the applicant to wait until the Copyright Office acts on the application would create needless delay since under § 411(a) the applicant is entitled to proceed with the action even if registration is refused. Is there a policy argument for requiring a plaintiff to wait until the Copyright Office has acted?

[dd] The severity of the remedial consequences of delayed registration are criticized in J. Tehranian, The Emperor Has No Copyright: Registration, Cultural Hierarchy, and the Myth of American Copyright Militancy, 24 Berk.Tech.L.J. 1399 (2009).

the Copyright Office has proposed a new registration fee of $45 to $100 depending on the method of submission. The form and fee must be accompanied by the deposit specified in § 408(b). In general, deposit of one copy of unpublished and two copies of published works is required. For some published works, the regulations provide that deposit of a single copy will suffice. For others, "identifying material" such as a photograph is sufficient. See 37 C.F.R. §§ 202.20, 202.21. A modern Michelangelo, for example, is not required to ship a copy of his *David* to the Copyright Office. Unpublished works and works published only in electronic form can be deposited electronically as part of an online registration; otherwise, hard copies must be sent to the Copyright Office. Deposits submitted as part of the registration process also satisfy the mandatory deposit requirement of § 407. See generally J. Hawes and B. Dietz, Copyright Registration Practice (Thomson West).

The Copyright Office determines whether "the material deposited constitutes copyrightable subject matter and that the other legal and formal requirements of this title have been met." § 410(a). The scope of the examination is limited. The Copyright Office will of course take note of obvious discrepancies between the application and the deposited copies, but it does not undertake to verify the information supplied by the applicant; in particular, it does not attempt to verify the applicant's claim to be the author of the work.

The Copyright Office operates under a "rule of doubt"—a work will be registered as long as there is at least a reasonable doubt as to whether the work is copyrightable. Only a small percentage of the applications for registration are ultimately rejected.[ee] The registration process can take several months, but "special handling" to reduce processing time is available in certain circumstances for a substantial fee.

The volume of registrations is impressive. The Copyright Office receives more than a half-million registration applications every year. Unpublished works account for about one-third of the total.

[ee] An administrative appeal from an initial adverse decision on registration can be taken to the Copyright Office Review Board. Section 701(e) subjects decisions of the Copyright Office to judicial review under the Administrative Procedure Act (5 U.S.C.A. § 551 et seq.). In reflecting on the appropriate scope of judicial review, consider the comments of Judge Silberman, concurring in Atari Games Corp. v. Oman, 888 F.2d 878 (D.C.Cir.1989): "We must bear in mind that when we review the Register's determination to accept or reject an application for registration, we do not make a final decision on the copyrightability of the item. In fact, as the majority opinion recognizes, the Copyright Office's imprimatur is worth only a rebuttable presumption as to copyrightability in an infringement action. * * * Every time the Register denies registration for too little creativity it cannot be expected to issue an opinion that compares with the learned offerings of my colleagues. I think that is why the courts have generally thought abuse of discretion to be the appropriate standard to review the Office's denial of a registration. Since the applicant can gain full judicial review of copyrightability in an infringement action, the costs of forcing too fine an analysis and too extensive an explanation of a denial of registration are not worth the benefits—particularly when reviewing a question which has unavoidably subjective aspects such as how much creativity is sufficient to force the Copyright Office to register a proffered work." See also Darden v. Peters, 488 F.3d 277 (4th Cir.2007), cert. denied, 552 U.S. 1230 (2008) (reviewing a denial of registration under an abuse of discretion standard). The various alternatives for review available to an applicant who has been denied registration are examined in T. Field, Judicial Review of Copyright Examination, 44 Idea 479 (2004).

CHAPTER 2

THE SUBJECT MATTER OF COPYRIGHT

1. ORIGINAL WORKS OF AUTHORSHIP

Burrow–Giles Lithographic Co. v. Sarony

Supreme Court of the United States, 1884.
111 U.S. 53, 4 S.Ct. 279.

■ MILLER, J. This is a writ of error to the Circuit Court for the Southern District of New York. Plaintiff [in error] is a lithographer, and defendant a photographer, with large business in those lines in the city of New York. The suit was commenced by an action at law in which Sarony was plaintiff and the lithographic company was defendant, the plaintiff charging the defendant with violating his copyright in regard to a photograph, the title of which is "Oscar Wilde, No. 18." A jury being waived, the court made a finding of facts on which a judgment in favor of the plaintiff was rendered for the sum of $600 for the plates and 85,000 copies sold and exposed to sale, and $10 for copies found in his possession, as penalties under section 4965 of the Revised Statutes. * * *

[handwritten: TCH for Sarony]

The constitutional question is not free from difficulty. The eighth section of the first article of the Constitution is the great repository of the powers of Congress, and by the eighth clause of that section Congress is authorized "to promote the progress of science and useful arts, by securing, for limited times to authors and inventors, the exclusive right to their respective writings and discoveries." The argument here is that a photograph is not a writing nor the production of an author. * * *

[handwritten: Issue]

It is insisted in argument, that a photograph being a reproduction on paper of the exact features of some natural object or of some person, is not a writing of which the producer is the author.

Section 4952 of the Revised Statutes places photographs in the same class as things which may be copyrighted with "books, maps, charts, dramatic or musical compositions, engravings, cuts, prints, paintings, drawings, statues, statuary, and models or designs intended to be perfected as works of the fine arts." * * *

The first Congress of the United States, sitting immediately after the formation of the Constitution, enacted that the "author or authors of any map, chart, book, or books, being a citizen or resident of the United States, shall have the sole right and liberty of printing, reprinting, publishing, and vending the same for the period of fourteen years from the recording of the title thereof in the clerk's office, as afterwards directed." 1 Stat. p. 124, § 1.

Oscar Wilde—the Sarony photograph

This statute not only makes maps and charts subjects of copyright, but mentions them before books in the order of designation. The second section of an act to amend this act, approved April 29, 1802, 2 Stat. 171, enacts that from the first day of January thereafter he who shall invent and design, engrave, etch or work, or from his own works shall cause to be designed and engraved, etched or worked, any historical or other print or prints shall have the same exclusive right for the term of 14 years from recording the title thereof as prescribed by law.

By the first section of the act of February 3, 1831, 4 Stat. 436, entitled "An act to amend the several acts respecting copyright," musical compositions and cuts, in connection with prints and engravings, are added, and the period of protection is extended to 28 years. The caption or title of this act uses the word "copyright" for the first time in the legislation of Congress.

The construction placed upon the Constitution by the first act of 1790, and the act of 1802, by the men who were contemporary with its formation, many of whom were members of the convention which framed it, is of itself entitled to very great weight, and when it is remembered that the rights thus established have not been disputed during a period of nearly a century, it is almost conclusive.

Unless, therefore, photographs can be distinguished in the classification on this point from the maps, charts, designs, engravings, etchings, cuts, and other prints, it is difficult to see why Congress cannot make them the subject of copyright as well as the others.

These statutes certainly answer the objection that books only, or writing in the limited sense of a book and its author, are within the constitutional provision. Both these words are susceptible of a more enlarged definition than this. An author in that sense is "he to whom anything owes its origin; originator; maker; one who completes a work of science or literature." Worcester. So, also, no one would now claim that the word "writing" in this clause of the Constitution, though the only word used as to subjects in regard to which authors are to be secured, is limited to the actual script of the author, and excludes books and all other printed matter. By writings in that clause is meant the literary productions of those authors, and Congress very properly has declared these to include all forms of writing, printing, engraving, etching, etc., by which the ideas in the mind of the author are given visible expression. The only reason why photographs were not included in the extended list in the act of 1802 is probably that they did not exist, as photography as an art was then unknown, and the scientific principle on which it rests, and the chemicals and machinery by which it is operated, have all been discovered long since that statute was enacted.

Nor is it to be supposed that the framers of the Constitution did not understand the nature of copyright and the objects to which it was commonly applied, for copyright, as the exclusive right of a man to the production of his own genius or intellect, existed in England at that time, and the contest in the English courts, finally decided by a very close vote in the House of Lords, whether the statute of 8 Anne, c. 19, which authorized copyright for a limited time, was a restraint to that extent on the common law or not, was then recent. * * *

We entertain no doubt that the Constitution is broad enough to cover an act authorizing copyright of photographs, so far as they are representatives of original intellectual conceptions of the author.

But it is said that an engraving, a painting, a print, does embody the intellectual conception of its author, in which there is novelty, invention, originality, and therefore comes within the purpose of the Constitution in securing its exclusive use or sale to its author, while the photograph is the mere mechanical reproduction of the physical features or outlines of some object, animate or inanimate, and involves no originality of thought or any novelty in the intellectual operation connected with its visible reproduction in shape of a picture. That while the effect of light on the prepared plate may have been a discovery in the production of these pictures, and patents could properly be obtained for the combination of the chemicals, for their application to the paper or other surface, for all the machinery by which the light reflected from the object was thrown on the prepared plate, and for all the improvements in this machinery, and in the materials, the remainder of the process is merely mechanical, with no place for novelty, invention, or originality. It is simply the manual operation, by the use of these instruments and preparations, of transferring to the plate the visible representation of some existing object, the accuracy of this representation being its highest merit.

This may be true in regard to the ordinary production of a photograph, and, further, that in such case a copyright is no protection. On the question as thus stated we decide nothing.

In regard, however, to the kindred subject of patents for invention, they cannot by law be issued to the inventor until the novelty, the utility, and the actual discovery or invention by the claimant have been established by proof before the Commissioner of Patents; and when he has secured such a patent, and undertakes to obtain redress for a violation of his right in a court of law, the question of invention, of novelty, of originality, is always open to examination. Our copyright system has no such provision for previous examination by a proper tribunal as to the originality of the book, map, or other matter offered for copyright. A deposit of two copies of the article or work with the Librarian of Congress, with the name of the author and its title page, is all that is necessary to secure a copyright. It is, therefore, much more important that when the supposed author sues for a violation of his copyright, the existence of those facts of originality, of intellectual production, of thought, and conception on the part of the author should be proved, than in the case of a patent right. In the case before us we think this has been done.

The third finding of facts says, in regard to the photograph in question, that it is a "useful, new, harmonious, characteristic, and graceful picture, and that plaintiff made the same . . . entirely from his own original mental conception, to which he gave visible form by posing the said Oscar Wilde in front of the camera, selecting and arranging the costume, draperies, and other various accessories in said photograph, arranging the subject so as to present graceful outlines, arranging and disposing the light and shade, suggesting and evoking the desired expression, and from such disposition, arrangement, or representation, made entirely by plaintiff, he produced the picture in suit."

These findings, we think, show this photograph to be an original work of art, the product of plaintiff's intellectual invention, of which plaintiff is the author, and of a class of inventions for which the Constitution intended that Congress should secure to him the exclusive right to use, publish and sell, as it has done by section 4952 of the Revised Statutes. * * *

The judgment of the Circuit Court is accordingly affirmed.[a]   *SCH affirms for π*

NOTES AND QUESTIONS

(1) The subject matter of copyright as described in § 102(a) consists of "original works of authorship." What does this encompass? Recall that the constitutional grant of authority to Congress speaks of "Authors" and their "Writings." The 1909 Act in § 4 had addressed "all the writings of an author." This phrase raised the issue of whether the scope of the 1909 Act was meant to be coextensive with the constitutional grant, in effect making decisions on protectable subject matter an issue of constitutional interpretation. To avoid this result, courts interpreted § 4 more narrowly than the constitutional clause. In explaining the change in phraseology in the 1976 Act, the House Report offers these comments: "In using the phrase 'original works of authorship,' rather than 'all the writings of an author' now in section 4 of the statute, the committee's purpose is to avoid exhausting the constitutional power of Congress to legislate in this field, and to eliminate the uncertainties arising from the latter phrase." H.R.Rep. p. 51. However, "original works of authorship" must ultimately take its meaning from the more general concepts of "Authors" and "Writings." But what, in turn, do those terms mean? Note the definitions offered by Justice Miller in *Sarony*. Recall also the Supreme Court's description of "Writings" in Goldstein v. California, quoted at p. 22 supra.

(2) Is Sarony's photograph a "work of authorship"? Are *all* photographs "works of authorship"? Are you comfortable with how the Supreme Court resolved the former question?

What about "the ordinary production of a photograph," the question that the Court reserves? French law took a narrow view of what photographs qualify for copyright, protecting only those of an "artistic or documentary character." (The limitation was eventually dropped.) So did British law until the 1956 statute declared that copyright would subsist in photographs "irrespective of artistic quality." After a detailed review of the history of copyright in photography, Judge Pauley in SHL Imaging, Inc. v. Artisan House, Inc., 117 F.Supp.2d 301 (S.D.N.Y.2000), acknowledged that there was no uniform test to determine copyrightability in photographs but noted that "[t]he technical aspects of photography imbue the medium with almost limitless creative potential." The court held that the plaintiff's photographs of mirrored picture frames intended for advertising were copyrightable in view of the plaintiff's choice of lighting and the selection of camera angle, lens, and filter.[b]

---

[a] In the Trade–Mark Cases, 100 U.S. 82 (1879), the question was whether federal power to enact trademark registration laws could be supported under the Patent and Copyright Clause. Congress had not attempted to invoke the commerce power, and the trademark statute of 1870, 16 Stat. 198, was part of a revision of the copyright and patent laws. Justice Miller, writing for a unanimous Court, said that a trademark could not be considered the discovery of an inventor nor the writing of an author. "While the word *writings* may be liberally construed, as it has been, to include original designs for engravings, prints, & c., it is only such as are *original,* and are founded in the creative powers of the mind. The writings which are to be protected are the fruits of intellectual labor, embodied in the form of books, prints, engravings, and the like. The trade-mark may be, and generally is, the adoption of something already in existence as the distinctive symbol of the party using it."

[b] The history of photography and the assertion of "authorship" in *Sarony* are examined in C. Farley, The Lingering Effects of Copyright's Response to the Invention of Photography, 65 U.Pitt.L.Rev. 385 (2004); E. Subotnik, Originality Proxies: Toward a Theory of Copyright and Creativity, 76 Brooklyn L.Rev. 1487 (2011), concludes that a heightened standard of originality is inappropriate for works like photographs. E. Judge and D. Gervais, Of Silos and

Bleistein v. Donaldson Lithographing Co.

Supreme Court of the United States, 1903.
188 U.S. 239, 23 S.Ct. 298.

■ MR. JUSTICE HOLMES delivered the opinion of the court:

This case comes here from the United States Circuit Court of Appeals for the Sixth Circuit by writ of error. * * * It is an action brought by the plaintiffs in error to recover the penalties prescribed for infringements of copyrights. * * * The alleged infringements consisted in the copying in reduced form of three chromolithographs prepared by employees of the plaintiffs for advertisements of a circus owned by one Wallace. Each of the three contained a portrait of Wallace in the corner and lettering bearing some slight relation to the scheme of decoration, indicating the subject of the design and the fact that the reality was to be seen at the circus. One of the designs was of an ordinary ballet, one of a number of men and women, described as the Stirk family, performing on bicycles, and one of groups of men and women whitened to represent statues. The Circuit Court directed a verdict for the defendant on the ground that the chromolithographs were not within the protection of the copyright law, and this ruling was sustained by the Circuit Court of Appeals. Courier Lithographing Co. v. Donaldson Lithographing Co., 104 F. 993.

There was evidence warranting the inference that the designs belonged to the plaintiffs, they having been produced by persons employed and paid by the plaintiffs in their establishment to make those very things. Gill v. United States, 160 U.S. 426, 435; Colliery Engineer Co. v. United Correspondence Schools Co., 94 F. 152; Carte v. Evans, 27 F. 861. It fairly might be found also that the copyrights were taken out in the proper names. * * *

We shall do no more than mention the suggestion that painting and engraving unless for a mechanical end are not among the useful arts, the progress of which Congress is empowered by the Constitution to promote. The Constitution does not limit the useful to that which satisfies immediate bodily needs. Burrow–Giles Lithographing Co. v. Sarony, 111 U.S. 53. It is obvious also that the plaintiff's case is not affected by the fact, if it be one, that the pictures represent actual groups—visible things. They seem from the testimony to have been composed from hints or description, not from sight of a performance. But even if they had been drawn from the life, that fact would not deprive them of protection. The opposite proposition would mean that a portrait by Velasquez or Whistler was common property because others might try their hand on the same face. Others are free to copy the original. They are not free to copy the copy. Blunt v. Patten, 400 Fed.Cas. No. 1,580. See Kelly v. Morris, L.R. 1 Eq. 697; Morris v. Wright, L.R. 5 Ch. 279. The copy is the personal reaction of an individual upon nature. Personality always contains something unique. It expresses its singularity even in handwriting, and a very modest grade of art has in it something irreducible, which is one man's alone. That something he may copyright unless there is a restriction in the words of the act.

If there is a restriction it is not to be found in the limited pretensions of these particular works. The least pretentious picture has more originality in it than directories and the like, which may be copyrighted. Drone,

Constellations: Comparing Notions of Originality in Copyright Law, 27 Cardozo Arts & Ent.L.J. 375 (2009), examines international conceptions of originality in copyright law.

Copyright, 153. See Henderson v. Tompkins, 60 F. 758, 765. The amount of training required for humbler efforts than those before us is well indicated by Ruskin. "If any young person, after being taught what is, in polite circles, called 'drawing,' will try to copy the commonest piece of real *work,*—suppose a lithograph on the title page of a new opera air, or a woodcut in the cheapest illustrated newspaper of the day—they will find themselves entirely beaten." Elements of Drawing, first ed. 3. There is no reason to doubt that these prints in their *ensemble* and in all their details, in their design and particular combinations of figures, lines and colors, are the original work of the plaintiffs' designer. If it be necessary, there is express testimony to that effect. It would be pressing the defendant's right to the verge, if not beyond, to leave the question of originality to the jury upon the evidence in this case, as was done in Hegeman v. Springer, 110 F. 374.

* * * Certainly works are not the less connected with the fine arts because their pictorial quality attracts the crowd and therefore gives them a real use—if use means to increase trade and to help to make money. A picture is none the less a picture and none the less a subject of copyright that it is used for an advertisement. And if pictures may be used to advertise soap, or the theatre, or monthly magazines, as they are, they may be used to advertise a circus. Of course, the ballet is as legitimate a subject for illustration as any other. A rule cannot be laid down that would excommunicate the paintings of Degas. * * *

It would be a dangerous undertaking for persons trained only to the law to constitute themselves final judges of the worth of pictorial illustrations, outside of the narrowest and most obvious limits. At the one extreme some works of genius would be sure to miss appreciation. Their very novelty would make them repulsive until the public had learned the new language in which their author spoke. It may be more than doubted, for instance, whether the etchings of Goya or the paintings of Manet would have been sure of protection when seen for the first time. At the other end, copyright would be denied to pictures which appealed to a public less educated than the judge. Yet if they command the interest of any public, they have a commercial value—it would be bold to say that they have not an aesthetic and educational value—and the taste of any public is not to be treated with contempt. It is an ultimate fact for the moment, whatever may be our hopes for a change. That these pictures had their worth and their success is sufficiently shown by the desire to reproduce them without regard to the plaintiffs' rights. See Henderson v. Tompkins, 60 F. 758, 765. We are of opinion that there was evidence that the plaintiffs have rights entitled to the protection of the law.

The judgment of the Circuit Court of Appeals is reversed; the judgment of the Circuit Court is also reversed and the cause remanded to that court with directions to set aside the verdict and grant a new trial.

The Stirk Family

■ MR. JUSTICE HARLAN, dissenting:

Judges Lurton, Day and Severens, of the Circuit Court of Appeals, *Say not copyright because they were ads* concurred in affirming the judgment of the District Court. Their views were thus expressed in an opinion delivered by Judge Lurton: "What we hold is this: That if a chromo, lithograph, or other print, engraving, or picture has no other use than that of a mere advertisement, and no value aside from this function, it would not be promotive of the useful arts, within the meaning of the constitutional provision, to protect the 'author' in the exclusive use thereof, and the copyright statute should not be construed as including such a publication, if any other construction is admissible. If a mere label simply designating or describing an article to which it is attached, and which has no value separated from the article, does not come within the constitutional clause upon the subject of copyright, it must follow that a pictorial illustration designed and useful only as an advertisement, and having no intrinsic value other than its function as an advertisement, must be equally without the obvious meaning of the Constitution. It must have some connection with the fine arts to give it intrinsic value, and that it shall have is the meaning which we attach to the act of June 18, 1874 (18 Stat. at L. 78, chap. 301, U.S.Comp.Stat.1901, p. 3411), amending the provisions of the copyright law. We are unable to discover anything useful or meritorious in the design copyrighted by the plaintiffs in error other than as an advertisement of acts to be done or exhibited to the public in Wallace's show. No evidence, aside from the deductions which are to be drawn from the prints themselves, was offered to show that these designs had any original artistic qualities. The jury could not reasonably have found merit or value aside from the purely business object of advertising a show, and the instruction to find for the defendant was not error. Many other points have been urged as justifying the result reached in the court below. We find it unnecessary to express an opinion upon them, in view of the conclusion already announced. The judgment must be affirmed." Courier Lithographing Co. v. Donaldson Lithographing Co., 104 F. 993, 996.

I entirely concur in these views, and therefore dissent from the opinion and judgment of this court. The clause of the Constitution giving Congress power to promote the progress of science and useful arts, by securing for limited terms to authors and inventors the exclusive right to their respective works and discoveries, does not, as I think, embrace a mere advertisement of a circus.

■ MR. JUSTICE McKENNA authorizes me to say that he also dissents.

NOTES AND QUESTIONS

(1) Justice Holmes' famous opinion barely responds to the dissenting view that the posters were disqualified from copyright because they were advertisements. Yet, "there can be no question that Judge Lurton [in the opinion for the Court of Appeals] * * * correctly and fairly stated what was then generally thought to be the law with reference to advertising matter being the subject of copyright." Sanborn, J., in Ansehl v. Puritan Pharmaceutical Co., 61 F.2d 131, 134 (8th Cir.), cert. denied, 287 U.S. 666 (1932). *Ansehl* reviews the decisions that *Bleistein* effectively overruled and describes the subsequent acceptance of advertising material as a subject of copyright. *Should* materials such as magazine advertisements and television commercials be considered works of authorship eligible for copyright protection? What of labels and other packaging materials? See p. 588 infra. The justification for extending the incentive of copyright to advertising is questioned in L. Ramsey, Intellectual Property Rights in Advertising, 12 Mich.Telecomm. & Tech.L.Rev. 189 (2006).

(2) Would Justice Holmes agree with the approach pursued by Justice Miller in upholding the copyrightability of Sarony's photograph of Oscar Wilde? Can judgments of aesthetic merit be avoided in determining eligibility for copyright?[c] Should the standard of copyrightability differ for the various kinds of works listed in § 102?

At the beginning of the revision process leading to the 1976 Act, a 1961 Report of the Register of Copyrights recommended that under the new statute a copyrightable work "must represent an appreciable amount of creative authorship." House Comm. on the Judiciary, 87th Cong., 1st Sess., Copyright Law Revision 9 (1961). This standard was eventually abandoned. The House Report, commenting on the phrase "original works of authorship" in § 102, says that it is "intended to incorporate without change the standard of originality established by the courts under the present copyright statute. This standard does not include requirements of novelty, ingenuity, or esthetic merit, and there is no intention to enlarge the standard of copyright to require them." H.R.Rep. p. 51. The legislative history of the 1976 Act as it relates to the "creativity" requirement is reviewed in R. VerSteeg, Sparks in the Tinderbox: *Feist*, "Creativity," and the Legislative History of the 1976 Copyright Act, 56 U.Pitt.L.Rev. 549 (1995).[d]

Congress has determined that works falling within the eight illustrative categories in § 102 can be "works of authorship." But there remains the problem of deciding whether a work fits within one of those categories. Is a single sentence a "literary work"? Is a drawing that consists of a few lines a "graphic work"? Does the amount of "creativity" matter?

(3) John Muller & Co. v. New York Arrows Soccer Team, 802 F.2d 989 (8th Cir.1986), concerned an attempt to obtain copyright registration for the insignia of a soccer team. The insignia looked something like this:

---

[c] C. Farley, Judging Art, 79 Tulane L.Rev. 805 (2005), urges courts to acknowledge aesthetic issues in deciding what is "art", and D. Zimmerman, It's an Original!(?): In Pursuit of Copyright's Elusive Essence, 28 Colum.J.L. & Arts 187 (2005), wonders whether it would be so terrible if we demanded quality in return for copyright protection. M. Madison, Beyond Creativity: Copyright as Knowledge Law, 12 Vand.J.Ent. & Tech.L. 817 (2010), concludes that the basis for copyright should shift from creativity to the production and dissemination of knowledge.

[d] A. Durham, Copyright and Information Theory: Toward an Alternative Model of "Authorship," 2004 B.Y.U.L.Rev. 69, uses information theory to interpret "authorship" as selection and freedom from constraint, but J. Harrison, Rationalizing the Allocative/Distributive Relationship in Copyright, 32 Hofstra L.Rev. 853 (2004), argues that a higher standard of authorship would lower the costs of copyright by focusing on those efforts most likely to advance the public interest; G. Parchomovsky and A. Stein, Originality, 95 Va.L.Rev. 1505 (2009), suggests calibrating the scope of an author's rights to the quantum of originality in the work.

[F2708]

A "work of authorship"? The Eighth Circuit upheld a denial of registration. A similar result was reached in another case involving a fabric design consisting of "two inch stripes, with small grid squares superimposed." The Register's finding that the work did not meet the "minimal amount of creative authorship" necessary for copyright was affirmed. Jon Woods Fashions, Inc. v. Curran, 8 U.S.P.Q.2d 1870 (S.D.N.Y.1988). Compare Prince Group, Inc. v. MTS Products, 967 F.Supp. 121 (S.D.N.Y.1997), agreeing with the Copyright Office that the plaintiff's polka dot fabric design was copyrightable; the dots were not perfect circles nor uniformly colored and were arranged in imperfect diagonal lines.

(4) In Toro Co. v. R & R Products Co., 787 F.2d 1208 (8th Cir.1986), the court held that numbers that were arbitrarily assigned to designate machine parts lacked sufficient authorship for copyright. A manufacturer claiming infringement of the numbers used to identify its screw fasteners had the opposite problem in Southco, Inc. v. Kanebridge Corp., 390 F.3d 276 (3d Cir.2004), cert. denied, 546 U.S. 813 (2005); far from being arbitrary, its numbers were completely determined by a numbering system linked to the characteristics of the item. In an *en banc* decision the Third Circuit said that the numbers lacked creativity; the numbering system itself was also unprotectable as an idea. Two judges dissented on the latter issue, arguing that the plaintiff's numbering rules could qualify as protected expression. Numbers used as part of a classification scheme for dental procedures did get copyright protection in American Dental Ass'n v. Delta Dental Plans Ass'n, 126 F.3d 977 (7th Cir.1997); the court held that the numbers reflected creative decisions about how to classify the particular procedures. That approach was questioned by the Sixth Circuit in ATC Distrib. Group, Inc. v. Whatever It Takes Transmissions & Parts, Inc., 402 F.3d 700 (6th Cir.2005). The court said that the plaintiff's transmission parts catalog was not copyrightable since the classification scheme was an unprotectable idea and the parts numbers themselves did not express any of the creative ideas inherent in the classification system.

(5) According to a Copyright Office regulation, the following are not subject to copyright: "Words and short phrases such as names, titles, and slogans; familiar symbols or designs; mere variations of typographic ornamentation, lettering or coloring; mere listing of ingredients or contents." 37 C.F.R. § 202.1(a). What is the justification for these exclusions? In Magic Marketing, Inc. v. Mailing Services, Inc., 634 F.Supp. 769 (W.D.Pa.1986), the regulation was invoked to reject a claim of infringement relating to phrases such as "Priority Message: Contents Require Immediate Attention" and "Gift Check Enclosed" printed on envelopes. The regulation was also cited in Publications Int'l, Ltd. v. Meredith Corp., 88 F.3d 473 (7th Cir.1996), which rejected a plaintiff's claim of copyright in recipes for delicacies such as Swiss 'n Cheddar Cheeseball appearing in *Discover Dannon—50 Fabulous Recipes with Yogurt*; the listings of ingredients and instructions were mere facts with no creative expression. But in Applied Innovations, Inc. v. Regents of Univ. of Minnesota, 876 F.2d 626 (8th Cir.1989), the Eighth Circuit held the regulation inapplicable to "short, simple, declarative sentences" such as "No one seems to understand me" and "I am a good mixer" used in a personality test.

Is the requirement of sufficient "authorship" best understood as a qualitative or a quantitative standard?

(6) Literary merit is apparently not a significant consideration in crafting the first message sent on a new medium of communication. The first telephone call, made in 1876 by Alexander Graham Bell to his laboratory assistant Thomas Watson in an adjoining room, was "Mr. Watson, come here—I want to see you." The first email message, sent in 1971 from one computer to another sitting right beside it by engineer Ray Tomlinson (who also introduced the "@" character in email addresses) was "QWERTYUIOP"—the top row of letters on a standard keyboard. The first text message, sent by British engineer Neil Papworth in 1992, was "Merry Christmas." The first tweet, sent in 2006 by Twitter co-founder Jack Dorsey, was apparently an automated message reading "just setting up my twttr." Are *any* of these first messages copyrightable? What about the last email, text, or tweet that *you* sent?

(7) An increasing number of judicial opinions draw an explicit distinction between the requirements of "originality" and "work of authorship."[e] Does § 102(a) encourage such usage? (Compare the terminology in the first and second sentences.) Other decisions subsume both requirements under a more expansive concept of "originality." See, e.g., Feist Publications, Inc. v. Rural Telephone Service Co., p. 75 infra: "Original, as the term is used in copyright, means only that the work was independently created by the author (as opposed to copied from other works), and that it possesses at least some minimal degree of creativity." The Supreme Court went on to say, "To be sure, the requisite level of creativity is extremely low; even a slight amount will suffice. The vast majority of works make the grade quite easily, as they possess some creative spark, 'no matter how crude, humble or obvious' it may be."

(8) Consider also works that owe their existence to the application of computer technology. Computer-generated graphics and music are now common in the broadcast and film industries. More mundane illustrations are a mailing list created through the electronic manipulation of a database and a computer-generated list of random numbers useful to statisticians. An unusual example was presented to the Copyright Office for registration in 1993. A computer was programmed to "think" like author Jacqueline Susann by inputting thousands of "rules" based on a detailed analysis of two of her steamier novels. (There was apparently an agreement of some sort with the author's estate). The computer

---

[e]   See, e.g., Baltimore Orioles, Inc. v. Major League Baseball Players Ass'n, 805 F.2d 663, 668 n. 6 (7th Cir.1986), cert. denied, 480 U.S. 941 (1987). "Although the requirements of independent creation and intellectual labor both flow from the constitutional prerequisite of authorship and the statutory reference to original works of authorship, courts often engender confusion by referring to both concepts by the term 'originality.' For the sake of clarity, we shall use 'originality' to mean independent authorship and 'creativity' to denote intellectual labor."

then asked a series of questions, the programmer answered, and the machine produced a novel entitled *Just This Once*. The originator of the software says he wrote about one-quarter of the prose, the computer wrote a quarter, and half was a "collaboration of man and machine." A reviewer, comparing the book to a work in the same genre by author Jackie Collins, said that "if you like this stuff, you'd be much better off with the one written by the computer." See 46 Pat., Tm. & Copyr.J. (BNA) 397 (1993). Are such computer-generated works copyrightable? Who is the author?

The question of computer-generated works was among those considered early in the digital era by the National Commission on New Technological Uses of Copyrighted Works (CONTU) that was established by Congress in 1974 to examine the copyright issues presented by computer technology. The 1978 CONTU Report concluded that "the author is the one who employs the computer," and that such works present "no special problem." As for copyrightability, the Report said, "The eligibility of any work for protection by copyright depends not upon the device or devices used in its creation, but rather upon the presence of at least minimal human creative effort at the time the work is produced." CONTU Rep. p. 45.

Is there sufficient creative authorship on the part of a user who enters several words into a poetry writing program and awaits the result? Is there a case for authorship of the resulting poem in the creator of the software? A case for joint authorship with the user of the software? These and other possibilities are considered in P. Samuelson, Allocating Ownership Rights in Computer–Generated Works, 47 U.Pitt.L.Rev. 1185 (1986), which reluctantly acquiesces in the CONTU position. R. Clifford, Intellectual Property in the Era of the Creative Computer Program: Will the True Creator Please Stand Up?, 71 Tul.L.Rev. 1675 (1997), argues that the output of an autonomously creative computer program isn't (and shouldn't be) copyrightable. E. Lee, Digital Originality, 14 Vand.J.Ent. & Tech.L. 919 (2012), applies the originality requirement to the output of new technologies like 3-D printers.

A number of zoos raise money through the sale of paintings done by elephants and other animals. In 2005, a London auction house sold three "abstract" paintings by Congo, a chimpanzee who died in 1964, for more than $25,000. Picasso is said to have had a Congo painting hanging in his studio. N.Y. Times, June 22, 2005, p. E2. Are such works protected by copyright? The Copyright Office apparently requires at least some measure of human authorship for registration. Compendium II: Copyright Office Practices 503.03(a).

(9) Is the determination of copyrightability an issue for the jury in an infringement action? In denying a motion for summary judgment in Lotus Development Corp. v. Borland Int'l, Inc., 788 F.Supp. 78 (D.Mass.1992), Judge Keeton offered the following comments on the copyrightability of elements of the user interface of the Lotus 1–2–3 spreadsheet program that were allegedly copied by defendant Borland in its Quattro spreadsheet program:

"The legal test for determining copyrightability * * * is a standard requiring an evaluative mixed law-fact determination, as distinguished from a bright-line rule calling for a finding about disputed historical facts such as who did what, where, and when. Moreover, this standard is far more heavily loaded with public policy implications than most other standards more commonly used in law, of which the negligence standard is an example. Juries applying the copyrightability standard would not be required or even permitted to explain their reasoning. They would be free as a practical matter to reach decisions inconsistent with the balance struck by Congress, as interpreted by the courts. * * *

"For all these reasons, I reach the tentative conclusion * * * that at least in the circumstances of this case (and probably more generally, though I need not so determine here), the issue or issues of copyrightability, including any fact questions bearing upon them, must be determined by the court, not the jury."[f]

Other courts have reached a different conclusion. In North Coast Industries v. Jason Maxwell, Inc., p. 74 infra, the court said that whether the plaintiff's design was sufficiently different from earlier works to be copyrightable must be left to the trier of fact. The Second Circuit in Matthew Bender & Co. v. West Pub. Co., 158 F.3d 674 (2d Cir.1998), cert. denied, 526 U.S. 1154 (1999), said, "Because we treat the question of whether particular elements of a work demonstrate sufficient originality and creativity to warrant copyright protection as a question for the factfinder—here the judge—we will not reverse the district court's findings unless clearly erroneous."

Alfred Bell & Co., Limited v. Catalda Fine Arts, Inc.

United States Court of Appeals, Second Circuit, 1951.
191 F.2d 99.

■ Before CHASE, CLARK and FRANK, CIRCUIT JUDGES.

The facts are reported in the opinions of the district judge. See 74 F.Supp. 973, and 86 F.Supp. 399.

[The facts as stated by Judge Smith in the District Court were these:

"The plaintiff, a British print producer and dealer, member of the Fine Arts Trade Guild, copyrighted in the United States eight mezzotint engravings of old masters produced at its order by three mezzotint engravers.

"The defendants, a color lithographer, a dealer in lithographs and the dealer's president, produced and sold color lithographs of the eight mezzotints. * * *

" * * * The mezzotint method lends itself to a fairly realistic reproduction of oil paintings. It is a tedious process requiring skill and patience and is, therefore, rather expensive compared with modern color photographic processes.

"The artists employed to produce these mezzotint engravings in suit attempted faithfully to reproduce paintings in the mezzotint medium so that the basic idea, arrangement, and color scheme of each painting are those of the original artist. The mezzotint engraving process is performed by first rocking a copper plate, that is, drawing across the plate under pressure a hand tool having many fine and closely spaced teeth. The tool is drawn across the plate many times in various directions so that the plate is roughened by the process. The outlines of the engraving are then placed upon the plate either by tracing with carbon paper from a photograph of the original work which it is desired to reproduce in this medium or by a

---

[f] See also Judge Easterbrook's comment in Pivot Point Int'l, Inc. v. Charlene Prods., Inc., 932 F.Supp. 220 (N.D.Ill.1996), that whether plaintiff's mannequin heads were copyrightable "is a question of law, which the court will decide."; Yankee Candle Co. v. Bridgewater Candle Co., 259 F.3d 25 (1st Cir.2001) ("The extent to which [plaintiff's works] contain protected expression is a matter of law, determined by the court.").

tracing taken from such a photograph on gelatine sheets transferred to the copper plate by rubbing carbon black or some similar substance in the lines of the tracing on the gelatine sheet and transferring of them by pressing the sheet upon the copper plate. With the image on the roughened plate the engraver then scrapes with a hand tool the picture upon the plate, obtaining light and shade effects by the depth of the scraping of the roughened plate or ground. When the plate is completed, trial prints are taken from it and it may be altered to make the final result to the satisfaction of the engraver. When it is completed and a satisfactory proof drawn from the plate, a thin steel coating is applied to it to preserve it during the printing of the final article, of which several hundred may be drawn from such a steel-faced plate before noticeable wearing of the plate. The final product is a print in color called in the trade a proof. The color is applied to the plate by hand before each print or proof is drawn from the plate. The color may be applied to the plate by the artist, but usually is done by one or more printers who follow a sample print or color guide in applying the colored ink in the depressions made by the engraver on the plate. It is possible by this process to make quite a satisfactory reproduction of the original painting in whatever size desired (the size of the photograph governing the size of the engraving), preserving the softness of line which is characteristic of the oil painting. It is not, however, possible to make a photographic copy of the painting by this method exact in all its details. The work of the engraver upon the plate requires the individual conception, judgment and execution by the engraver on the depth and shape of the depressions in the plate to be made by the scraping process in order to produce in this other medium the engraver's concept of the effect of the oil painting. No two engravers can produce identical interpretations of the same oil painting. * * *

"Concededly the defendants used proofs taken from the plaintiff's plates and sold by the plaintiff, carrying notice of plaintiff's copyright, as the subjects of their colored photoengravings."]

■ FRANK, CIRCUIT JUDGE:

1. Congressional power to authorize both patents and copyrights is contained in Article 1, § 8 of the Constitution. In passing on the validity of patents, the Supreme Court recurrently insists that this constitutional provision governs. On this basis, pointing to the Supreme Court's consequent requirement that, to be valid, a patent must disclose a high degree of uniqueness, ingenuity and inventiveness, the defendants assert that the same requirement constitutionally governs copyrights. As several sections of the Copyright Act—e.g., those authorizing copyrights of "reproductions of works of art," maps, and compilations—plainly dispense with any such high standard, defendants are, in effect, attacking the constitutionality of those sections. But the very language of the Constitution differentiates (a) "authors" and their "writings" from (b) "inventors" and their "discoveries." Those who penned the Constitution, of course, knew the difference. The pre-revolutionary English statutes had made the distinction. In 1783, the Continental Congress had passed a resolution recommending that the several states enact legislation to "secure" to authors the "copyright" of their books. Twelve of the thirteen states (in 1783–1786) enacted such statutes. Those of Connecticut and North Carolina covered books, pamphlets, maps, and charts.

Moreover, in 1790, in the year after the adoption of the Constitution, the first Congress enacted two statutes, separately dealing with patents and copyrights. The patent statute, enacted April 10, 1790, 1 Stat. 109, provided that patents should issue only if the Secretary of State, Secretary of War and the Attorney General, or any two of them "shall deem the invention or discovery sufficiently useful and important"; the applicant for a patent was obliged to file a specification "so particular" as "to distinguish the invention or discovery from other things before known and used * * *"; the patent was to constitute *prima facie* evidence that the patentee was "the first and true inventor or * * * discoverer * * * of the thing so specified." The Copyright Act, enacted May 31, 1790, 1 Stat. 124, covered "maps, charts, and books". A printed copy of the title of any map, chart or book was to be recorded in the Clerk's office of the District Court, and a copy of the map, chart or book was to be delivered to the Secretary of State within six months after publication. Twelve years later, Congress in 1802, 2 Stat. 171, added, to matters that might be copyrighted, engravings, etchings and prints.

Thus legislators peculiarly familiar with the purpose of the Constitutional grant, by statute, imposed far less exacting standards in the case of copyrights. They authorized the copyrighting of a mere map which, patently, calls for no considerable uniqueness. They exacted far more from an inventor. And, while they demanded that an official should be satisfied as to the character of an invention before a patent issued, they made no such demand in respect of a copyright. In 1884, in Burrow–Giles Lithographic Co. v. Sarony, 111 U.S. 53, 57, the Supreme Court, adverting to these facts said: "The construction placed upon the Constitution by the first act of 1790 and the act of 1802, by the men who were contemporary with its formation, many of whom were members of the convention which framed it, is of itself entitled to very great weight, and when it is remembered that the rights thus established have not been disputed during a period of nearly a century, it is almost conclusive." Accordingly, the Constitution, as so interpreted, recognizes that the standards for patents and copyrights are basically different.

The defendants' contention apparently results from the ambiguity of the word "original." It may mean startling, novel or unusual, a marked departure from the past. Obviously this is not what is meant when one speaks of "the original package," or the "original bill," or (in connection with the "best evidence" rule) an "original" document; none of those things is highly unusual in creativeness. "Original" in reference to a copyrighted work means that the particular work "owes its origin" to the "author."[8] No large measure of novelty is necessary. Said the Supreme Court in Baker v. Selden, 101 U.S. 99, 102–103: "The copyright of the book, if not pirated from other works, would be valid without regard to the novelty, or want of novelty, of its subject-matter. The novelty of the art or thing described or explained has nothing to do with the validity of the copyright. * * *."

In Bleistein v. Donaldson Lithographing Co., 188 U.S. 239, 250, 252, the Supreme Court cited with approval Henderson v. Tompkins, C.C., 60 F. 758, where it was said, 60 F. at page 764: "There is a *very broad distinction between what is implied in the word 'author,' found in the constitution, and the word 'inventor.' The latter carries an implication which excludes the results of only ordinary skill, while nothing of this is necessarily involved in the former.* Indeed, the statutes themselves make broad distinctions on this point. So much as relates to copyrights * * * is expressed, so far as this particular is concerned, by the mere words, 'author, inventor, designer or proprietor,' with such aid as may be derived from the words 'written, composed

---

8   Burrow–Giles Lithographic Co. v. Sarony, 111 U.S. 53, 57–58.

or made,' * * *. But *a multitude of books rest safely under copyright, which show only ordinary skill and diligence in their preparation.* Compilations are noticeable examples of this fact. With reference to this subject, the courts have not undertaken to assume the functions of critics, or to measure carefully the degree of originality, or literary skill or training involved."

It is clear, then, that nothing in the Constitution commands that copyrighted matter be strikingly unique or novel. Accordingly, we were not ignoring the Constitution when we stated that a "copy of something in the public domain" will support a copyright if it is a "distinguishable variation";[10] or when we rejected the contention that "like a patent, a copyrighted work must be not only original, but new", adding, "That is not * * * the law as is obvious in the case of maps or compendia, where later works will necessarily be anticipated."[11] All that is needed to satisfy both the Constitution and the statute is that the "author" contributed something more than a "merely trivial" variation, something recognizably "his own."[12] Originality in this context "means little more than a prohibition of actual copying."[13] No matter how poor artistically the "author's" addition, it is enough if it be his own. Bleistein v. Donaldson Lithographing Co., 188 U.S. 239, 250.

On that account, we have often distinguished between the limited protection accorded a copyright owner and the extensive protection granted a patent owner. So we have held that "independent reproduction of a copyrighted * * * work is not infringement",[14] whereas it is *vis a vis* a patent. Correlative with the greater immunity of a patentee is the doctrine of anticipation which does not apply to copyrights: The alleged inventor is chargeable with full knowledge of all the prior art, although in fact he may be utterly ignorant of it. The "author" is entitled to a copyright if he independently contrived a work completely identical with what went before; similarly, although he obtains a valid copyright, he has no right to prevent another from publishing a work identical with his, if not copied from his. A patentee, unlike a copyrightee, must not merely produce something "original"; he must also be "the first inventor or discoverer."[15] "Hence it is possible to have a plurality of valid copyrights directed to closely identical or even identical works. Moreover, none of them, if independently arrived at without copying, will constitute an infringement of the copyright of the others."[16] * * *

2.   We consider untenable defendants' suggestion that plaintiff's mezzotints could not validly be copyrighted because they are reproductions of works in the public domain. Not only does the Act include "Reproductions of a work of art",[19] but—while prohibiting a copyright of "the original

---

[10] Gerlach–Barklow Co. v. Morris & Bendien, 2 Cir., 23 F.2d 159, 161.

[11] Sheldon v. Metro–Goldwyn Pictures Corp., 2 Cir., 81 F.2d 49, 53. See also Ricker v. General Electric Co., 2 Cir., 162 F.2d 141, 142.

[12] Chamberlin v. Uris Sales Corp., 2 Cir., 150 F.2d 512; cf. Gross v. Seligman, 2 Cir., 212 F. 930.

[13] Hoague–Sprague Corp. v. Frank C. Meyer, Inc., D.C.N.Y., 31 F.2d 583, 586. See also as to photographs Judge Learned Hand in Jewelers Circular Publishing Co. v. Keystone Pub. Co., D.C.N.Y., 274 F. 932, 934. * * *

[14] Arnstein v. Edward B. Marks Music Corp., 2 Cir., 82 F.2d 275; Ricker v. General Electric Co., 2 Cir., 162 F.2d 141, 142.

[15] See Amdur, Copyright Law and Practice (1936) 70.

[16] Id. * * *

[19] 17 U.S.C.A. § 5.

text of any work * * * in the public domain"[20]—it explicitly provides for the copyrighting of "translations, or other versions of works in the public domain".[21] The mezzotints were such "versions." They "originated" with those who made them, and—on the trial judge's findings well supported by the evidence—amply met the standards imposed by the Constitution and the statute. There is evidence that they were not intended to, and did not, imitate the paintings they reproduced. But even if their substantial departures from the paintings were inadvertent, the copyrights would be valid. A copyist's bad eyesight or defective musculature, or a shock caused by a clap of thunder, may yield sufficiently distinguishable variations. Having hit upon such a variation unintentionally, the "author" may adopt it as his and copyright it.[25]

Accordingly, defendants' arguments about the public domain become irrelevant. They could be relevant only in their bearing on the issue of infringement, i.e., whether the defendants copied the mezzotints. But on the findings, again well grounded in the evidence, we see no possible doubt that defendants, who did deliberately copy the mezzotints, are infringers. For a copyright confers the exclusive right to copy the copyrighted work—a right not to have others copy it. Nor were the copyrights lost because of the reproduction of the mezzotints in catalogues. * * *

NOTES AND QUESTIONS

(1) In the terminology of the 1976 Act, the plaintiff's mezzotints are "derivative works." See § 101. Section 103(a) brings derivative works within the subject matter of copyright. Note the fundamental limitation on the scope of protection for derivative works in § 103(b). What do the copyrights in plaintiff's mezzotints protect? What difficulties does this create in determining infringement?

(2) The defendant in Pickett v. Prince, 207 F.3d 402 (7th Cir.2000), was the singer sometimes known as Prince, who since 1992 had referred to himself by a symbol resembling an Egyptian hieroglyph. The plaintiff, without obtaining Prince's permission, made a guitar in the shape of the symbol. Soon afterwards, Prince began to appear in public playing a similar guitar. Plaintiff sued for copyright infringement and Prince counterclaimed for infringement of his copyrighted symbol. Judge Posner concluded that the plaintiff's guitar was a derivative work based on Prince's symbol; since the plaintiff did not have permission to incorporate Prince's copyrighted symbol into the derivative work, plaintiff was prevented from claiming copyright in the guitar by the rule in § 103(a) that precludes protection for parts of a derivative work in which copyrighted material has been unlawfully used. See also Palladium Music, Inc. v. EatSleepMusic, Inc., 398 F.3d 1193 (10th Cir.2005), holding the copyrights in the plaintiff's sound recordings invalid because it did not have permission to use the underlying musical works.

---

[20]   17 U.S.C.A. § 8 (formerly § 7).

[21]   17 U.S.C.A. § 7 (formerly § 6). * * *

[25]   Consider inadvertent errors in a translation. Compare cases holding that a patentable invention may stem from an accidental discovery. See, e.g., Radiator Specialty Co. v. Buhot, 3 Cir., 39 F.2d 373, 376; Nichols v. Minnesota Mining & Mfg. Co., 4 Cir., 109 F.2d 162, 165; New Wrinkle v. Fritz, D.C.W.D.N.Y., 45 F.Supp. 108, 117; Byerley v. Sun Co., 3 Cir., 184 F. 455, 456–457. Many great scientific discoveries have resulted from accidents, e.g., the galvanic circuit and the x-ray.

NOTE ON STANDARDS FOR COPYRIGHTS AND PATENTS

Judge Frank in Alfred Bell v. Catalda ably expressed the conventional understanding that Congress has the power to cast one balance sheet for copyrights and another for patents, and that both history and policy explain most of the differences. Does it assist the case for differing treatment of copyright and patent to read Art. I, § 8, cl. 8, as though it contained two separable grants? Thus:

> The Congress shall have power:

> To promote the progress of science, by securing for limited times to authors the exclusive right to their writings.

> To promote the progress of useful arts, by securing for limited times to inventors the exclusive right to their discoveries.

This reading acquired a casual endorsement by the Supreme Court in Graham v. John Deere Co., 383 U.S. 1, 5 (1966). Within this structure, how should one define "science" and "useful arts"? What did "science" and "useful art" mean in 1787? (The term "useful art" appeared in the patent statute until 1952.) But this dual reading does nothing to describe the gap between the modest requirement of original authorship for copyright and the demanding statutory standards for patent.

Graham v. Deere

The patent statute comprises Title 35 of the U.S. Code. Section 101 describes the subject matter eligible for a patent:

§ 101 Patentable subject matter

> Whoever invents or discovers any new and useful process, machine, manufacture, or composition of matter, or any new and useful improvement thereof, may obtain a patent therefor, subject to the conditions and requirements of this title.

Section 103 adds a further requirement. Its negative form exemplifies the observation that it is easier to say what is not patentable than what is:

§ 103

> A patent for a claimed invention may not be obtained * * * if the differences between the claimed invention and the prior art are such that the claimed invention as a whole would have been obvious before the effective filing date of the claimed invention to a person having ordinary skill in the art to which the claimed invention pertains. Patentablity shall not be negated by the manner in which the invention was made.

The "non-obvious" requirement in § 103 came before the Supreme Court in Graham v. John Deere Co., 383 U.S. 1 (1966). Justice Clark began by observing that,

Non-obvious

> After a lapse of 15 years, the Court again focuses its attention on the patentability of inventions under the standard of Art. 1, § 8, cl. 8 of the Constitution and under the conditions prescribed by the laws of the United States. Since our last expression on patent validity, Great A. & P. Tea Co. v. Supermarket Equipment Corp., 340 U.S. 147 (1950), the Congress has for the first time expressly added a third statutory dimension to the two requirements of novelty and utility that had been the sole statutory test since the Patent Act of 1793. This is the test of obviousness * * *.

The Supreme Court offered this guidance to the lower courts and the Patent and Trademark Office:

Under § 103, the scope and content of the prior art are to be determined; differences between the prior art and the claims at issue are to be ascertained; and the level of ordinary skill in the pertinent art resolved. Against this background, the obviousness or nonobviousness of the subject matter is determined. Such secondary considerations as commercial success, long felt but unsolved needs, failure of others, etc., might be utilized to give light to the circumstances surrounding the origin of the subject matter sought to be patented. As indicia of obviousness or nonobviousness, these inquiries may have relevancy.

The Supreme Court again emphasized the non-obvious requirement in KSR International Co. v. Teleflex, 550 U.S. 398 (2007), holding that when the claimed invention consists of a combination of elements found in the prior art, a finding of obviousness does not require proof of an explicit prior teaching, suggestion, or motivation to combine the existing elements.

The test of utility had a rare exposition by the Supreme Court in Brenner v. Manson, 383 U.S. 519 (1966). One view of the utility requirement has been to say that the market will determine whether an invention is useful. There was accordingly little need to frame and apply a legal restriction, except for the limiting cases characterized long ago by Justice Story as "injurious to the morals, the health, or the good order of society." Bedford v. Hunt, 3 Fed.Cas. 37 (C.C.D.Mass.1817) (No. 1,217). But the Court of Customs and Patent Appeals had decided in 1950 that a new compound for which there was no known use was not patentable, Application of Bremner, 182 F.2d 216 (C.C.P.A.1950), and the Supreme Court in *Brenner* pushed a step beyond this position by directing the Patent and Trademark Office to refuse a patent for the *process* of producing a compound of no practical utility. Consult E. Kitch, Graham v. John Deere Co.: New Standards for Patents, 1966 Sup.Ct.Rev. 293 (1967).

Finally, we should note that concern with "originality" is more acute in patent than in copyright. The Patent Act generally precludes a patent if "the claimed invention was patented, described in a printed publication, or in public use, on sale, or otherwise available to the public before the effective filing date of the claimed invention." 35 U.S.C. § 102(a)(1). For copyright, as Judge Frank reminds us in *Alfred Bell,* independent creation is sufficient. J. Fromer, A Psychology of Intellectual Property, 104 Nw.U.L.Rev. 1441 (2010), relates the dissimilar standards for copyright and patent to the different natures of artistic and scientific creativity, with implications for the appropriate subject matter of each regime.

The concept of an inventor's "discoveries" is, at bottom, a constitutional question, like the essentials of an author's "writings." Within the Constitution's bounds, the statutes can and do limit the categories of discoveries and writings that Congress deems eligible for patent or copyright protection. For patents, as for copyrights, there are problems of what is "statutory subject matter" within the deceptively simple language of § 101. See, e.g., Diamond v. Chakrabarty, 447 U.S. 303 (1980), finding a genetically engineered bacterium to be patentable. Some of these problems—the patentability of computer programs notably—are relevant for us and will be taken up later.

The leading treatises on patent law are M. Adelman, Patent Law Perspectives (Matthew Bender); D. Chisum, Chisum on Patents (Matthew Bender); and Moy's Walker on Patents (Thomson West).

ORIGINALITY IN WORKS DERIVED FROM PREEXISTING SOURCES

Italian Book Co. v. Rossi

United States District Court, Southern District of New York, 1928.
27 F.2d 1014.

■ THACHER, DISTRICT JUDGE. When Paolo Citorello, a Sicilian sailor, sang and played his guitar on a long ocean voyage, Sicilian folk songs he had heard and forgotten came back to his memory. He did not know how to read music, and such parts of the words and music as he could remember he sang and played by ear. What he could not remember he improvised. In this way he learned a song which he claimed as his own composition. At the end of the voyage he sang and played it to the representative of a company manufacturing phonograph records. The score was arranged for him by another, and upon his application a copyright was obtained, which he assigned to the plaintiff. The defendants have copied the copyrighted song, claiming that it is an old Sicilian folk song, the words of which were published as early as 1871.

How much of Citorello's composition was subconscious repetition of this old song, as he had heard it sung, and how much of it was original with him, no one can say. No doubt he had heard some variation of the old song and was trying to remember it, but the product differed in words and music from any version of it that has been proved, although the theme was the same and the music quite similar. To the extent of such differences he was the author of the new arrangement of the words and music of an old song. That these differences were of some importance may be inferred from the plaintiff's commercial success in selling it and the defendants' desire to appropriate it. There must have been something which Citorello added which brought the old song back into popularity with his own people in this country, and sufficient, I think, to support his claim of copyright. Gerlach–Barklow Co. v. Morris & Bendien, 23 F.2d 159 (C.C.A.2d.). Of course, the defendants could make their own improvisation of the old song, or could copy it without change. They were free to copy the original, but not to copy Citorello's variation. I am satisfied that they did not go back to the original, but simply appropriated the Citorello song, making colorable changes in a clumsy effort to conceal their infringement.

Decree for plaintiff in usual form.

NOTES AND QUESTIONS

(1) Wihtol v. Wells, 231 F.2d 550 (7th Cir.1956), was about a hymn, with words and music copyrighted by Wihtol, who testified that he recalled the tune from his childhood in Latvia. When challenged by Wells, a defendant who had copied portions of the song, Wihtol's copyright was upheld. The Seventh Circuit said that the tune was old, "But it was original work on plaintiff's part when, some thirty years later, he devised a calculated melody score thus putting it in shape

for all to read." (See also, involving the same hymn, Wihtol v. Crow, 309 F.2d 777 (8th Cir.1962), one of the first "photocopying" cases, brought against a choirmaster who had run off 48 copies for his high school choir.)

In Tempo Music, Inc. v. Famous Music Corp., 838 F.Supp. 162 (S.D.N.Y.1993), the court said that a one note variation in Duke Ellington's jazz standard *Satin Doll,* which may have arisen from a typographical error, was not a copyrightable derivative work, but the court refused to hold as a matter of law that a harmony created to accompany the original tune could not be sufficiently creative to support a claim to copyright. See also Woods v. Bourne Co., 60 F.3d 978 (2d Cir.1995), excluding from copyright "stylized version[s]" and "cocktail pianist variations" of existing songs.

(2) The creator of an arrangement or adaptation of an old melody may in reality get substantial control over the underlying work, as illustrated by the *Rossi* case. This may be viewed as the reward for rescuing a song from oblivion; it may also be a racket, when performers are led to believe that they must pay to use collections of works that are old or of unknown authorship. Should disclaimers of copyright in public domain material be required as a condition of protection for the new material? How could a composer disclose and disclaim the public domain elements used to create a derivative work? P. Heald, Reviving the Rhetoric of the Public Interest: Choir Directors, Copy Machines, and New Arrangements of Public Domain Music, 46 Duke L.J. 241 (1996), concludes that many claims of copyright in new variations of musical works fail even the loosest interpretation of the creativity requirement, but still generate royalties because users are frequently unable to make comparisons with the original works.

(3) The various recordings of a popular song made possible by the compulsory license in § 115 (see p. 550 infra) often differ from the original composition. Can the licensee claim copyright in the new version as a derivative work? See § 115(a)(2).

(4) Suppose a folk song is known only through one or more versions under copyright. Is it permissible to reconstruct the public domain original from the copyrighted adaptations? Similar questions also arise in connection with other derivative works. Recall Justice Holmes' statement in *Bleistein,* p. 50 supra: "Others are free to copy the original. They are not free to copy the copy." Is this always true? Whether the "original" is a scene or a face, as in *Bleistein,* or an earlier work in the public domain, portions of the original work become embodied in the copyrighted derivative work. Must a second author seek out the original, or is there a privilege to extract it, if possible, from the first author's "copy"? It has been suggested that "[i]t might have been better * * * had Holmes resisted the temptation to turn a phrase," because it has sometimes led courts to forget that "[i]f a portion of the work has been copied from other sources and thus lacks originality, that portion is not a work of authorship. Since this renders unprotectable that component of the work, absent a copyright on the source, others are free to use it as they will, without returning to the original."[g]

---

[g] R. Denicola, Copyright in Collections of Facts: A Theory for the Protection of Nonfiction Literary Works, 81 Colum.L.Rev. 516, 523 (1981).

L. Batlin & Son, Inc. v. Snyder

536 F.2d 486 (2d Cir.), cert. denied, 429 U.S. 857 (1976).

[handwritten: Requirement of creativity in]

"Uncle Sam mechanical banks have been on the American scene at least since June 8, 1886, when Design Patent No. 16,728, issued on a toy savings bank of its type. The basic delightful design has long since been in the public domain. The banks are well documented in collectors' books and known to the average person interested in Americana. A description of the bank is that Uncle Sam, dressed in his usual stove pipe hat, blue full dress coat, starred vest and red and white striped trousers, and leaning on his umbrella, stands on a four-or five-inch wide base, on which sits his carpet-bag. A coin may be placed in Uncle Sam's extended hand. When a lever is pressed, the arm lowers, and the coin falls into the bag, while Uncle Sam's whiskers move up and down. The base has an embossed American eagle on it with the words 'Uncle Sam' on streamers above it, as well as the word 'Bank' on each side. Such a bank is listed in a number of collectors' books, the most recent of which may be F.H. Griffith, Mechanical Banks (1972 ed.) where it was listed as No. 280, and is said to be not particularly rare."

Snyder took an antique Uncle Sam bank to Hong Kong and had a reduced plastic version of it designed and manufactured there, in which he claimed copyright. Batlin bought cast iron Uncle Sam banks from Taiwan, and he ordered plastic models from Hong Kong that may well have come from the same mold as Snyder's. Both were refused entry by U.S. Customs because of Snyder's copyright.

Batlin brought an action for a declaration that Snyder's copyright was invalid. He won a preliminary injunction restraining enforcement of the copyright in the District Court, but it was set aside by a panel of the Court of Appeals. The preliminary injunction restraining enforcement of Snyder's copyright was reinstated on reconsideration en banc. *[handwritten: TCH for π ACH for D then injunction reinstated]*

Judge Oakes, for a 6–3 majority, accepted the findings of Judge Metzner, 394 F.Supp. 1389, 1394 (S.D.N.Y.1975), that the differences between the public domain prototype and Snyder's plastic replica lay only in the direction of making it simpler and cheaper. He also agreed that the copyright test of originality has a "low threshold," and that Mazer v. Stein, p. 124 infra, "established that mass-produced commercial objects with a minimal element of artistic craftsmanship may satisfy the statutory requirement of [a work of art]." But, with respect to a reproduction of a work of art, he endorsed Nimmer's view that "the mere reproduction of a work of art in a different medium should not constitute the required originality." Referring to Sunset House Distributing Corp. v. Doran, 304 F.2d 251 (9th Cir.1962), where a copyright was upheld in a figure of Santa Claus, Judge Oakes said, "We do not follow the *Doran* case. We do follow the school of cases in this circuit and elsewhere supporting the proposition that to support a copyright there must be at least some substantial variation, not merely a trivial variation such as might occur in the translation to a different medium." *[handwritten: difference was making it simpler & cheaper]*

Both the court's opinion and the dissent by Judge Meskill dwell on Alva Studios, Inc. v. Winninger, 177 F.Supp. 265 (S.D.N.Y.1959), where the work in which copyright was upheld was a reduced scale reproduction, for museum sales, of Rodin's "Hand of God." Judge Oakes distinguished *Alva Studios* by emphasizing the inaccessibility of the original and that "a significant public benefit accrues from its precise, artistic reproduction." *[handwritten: making painting smaller is OK because its inaccessible & significant benefit to public to reproduce]*

Bridgeman Art Library, Ltd. v. Corel Corp.

36 F.Supp.2d 191 (S.D.N.Y.1999).

"On November 13, 1998, this Court granted defendant's motion for summary judgment dismissing plaintiff's copyright infringement claim on the alternative grounds that the allegedly infringed works—color transparencies of paintings which themselves are in the public domain—were not original and therefore not permissible subjects of valid copyright and, in any case, were not infringed.[1] It applied United Kingdom law in determining whether plaintiff's transparencies were copyrightable. The Court noted, however, that it would have reached the same result under United States law."

Plaintiff Bridgeman was an English company that had acquired rights to market high quality photographic reproductions of public domain paintings from the museums that owned the works. Bridgeman distributed the reproductions in the form of color transparencies and digital files on CD–ROMs. It accused defendant Corel of marketing a CD–ROM containing copies of the reproductions. In an earlier decision, Judge Kaplan had concluded that since most of the reproductions were produced and first published in the United Kingdom, their copyrightability should be governed by U.K. law, and he held that under U.K. law the works were not entitled to protection. On a motion for reconsideration, Judge Kaplan first reviewed his conclusion on the choice of law. Since the Berne Convention is not self-executing under U.S. law, the 1976 Copyright Act is the exclusive source of protection for foreign works in the United States. Statutory protection for foreign works under § 104(b) is limited to "works specified by sections 102 and 103," which in turn limit protection to "original works of authorship." Reversing his earlier conclusion, Judge Kaplan held that the copyrightability of the reproductions was thus governed by U.S. law.

"In Burrow–Giles Lithographic Co v. Sarony, the Supreme Court held that photographs are 'writings' within the meaning of the Copyright Clause and that the particular portrait at issue in that case was sufficiently original—by virtue of its pose, arrangement of accessories in the photograph, and lighting and the expression the photographer evoked—to be subject to copyright. The Court, however, declined to decide whether 'the ordinary production of a photograph' invariably satisfies the originality requirement. While Judge Learned Hand later suggested that the 1909 Copyright Act protected photographs independent of their originality,[29] his view ultimately was rejected by the Supreme Court.[30] Nevertheless, there is broad scope for copyright in photographs because 'a very modest expression of personality will constitute sufficient originality.'[31]

"As the Nimmers have written, there 'appear to be at least two situations in which a photograph should be denied copyright for lack of originality,' one of which is directly relevant here: 'where a photograph of a photograph or other printed matter is made that amounts to nothing more than slavish copying.'[32] The authors thus conclude that a slavish photographic copy of a painting would lack originality, although they suggest the possi-

---

[1]   The Bridgeman Art Library, Ltd. v. Corel Corp., 25 F.Supp.2d 421 (S.D.N.Y.1998).

[29]   Jewelers' Circular Pub. Co. v. Keystone Pub. Co., 274 F. 932, 934 (S.D.N.Y.1921), aff'd, 281 F. 83 (2d Cir.), cert. denied, 259 U.S. 581 (1922).

[30]   Feist Pub., Inc. v. Rural Tel. Serv. Co., 499 U.S. 340, 350–53 (1991).

[31]   Nimmer Section 2.08[E][1], at 2–130.

[32]   Id. Section 2.08[E][2], at 2–131.

bility that protection in such a case might be claimed as a 'reproduction of a work of art.'[33] But they immediately go on to point out that this suggestion is at odds with the Second Circuit's *in banc* decision in L. Batlin & Son, Inc. v. Snyder. * * *

"There is little doubt that many photographs, probably the overwhelming majority, reflect at least the modest amount of originality required for copyright protection. 'Elements of originality . . . may include posing the subjects, lighting, angle, selection of film and camera, evoking the desired expression, and almost any other variant involved.'[39] But 'slavish copying,' although doubtless requiring technical skill and effort, does not qualify.[40] As the Supreme Court indicated in *Feist*, 'sweat of the brow' alone is not the 'creative spark' which is the *sine qua non* of originality.[41] It therefore is not entirely surprising that an attorney for the Museum of Modern Art, an entity with interests comparable to plaintiff's and its clients, not long ago presented a paper acknowledging that a photograph of a two-dimensional public domain work of art 'might not have enough originality to be eligible for its own copyright.'[42]

"In this case, plaintiff by its own admission has labored to create 'slavish copies' of public domain works of art. While it may be assumed that this required both skill and effort, there was no spark of originality—indeed, the point of the exercise was to reproduce the underlying works with absolute fidelity. Copyright is not available in these circumstances. * * *

"Plaintiff's motion for reargument and reconsideration of this Court's order granting summary judgment dismissing the complaint is granted. Nevertheless, on reargument and reconsideration, defendant Corel Corporation's motion for summary judgment dismissing the complaint is granted."

Gracen v. Bradford Exchange

698 F.2d 300 (7th Cir.1983).

Bradford makes "collectors' plates." It had a license from MGM to make a set of plates illustrated with characters from the well-known film *The Wizard of Oz*, notably portraying Judy Garland as Dorothy. In a competition for paintings (based on photographs from the movie) that would "evoke all the warm feeling the people have for the film and its actors," Jorie Gracen, a clerical employee of Bradford and an amateur painter, won. But there was a falling-out over terms, and Bradford commissioned Auckland, an artist, to redo the portrait of Garland/Dorothy. Gracen obtained a

---

[33] Id.

[39] Rogers v. Koons, 960 F.2d 301, 307 (2d Cir.), cert. denied, 506 U.S. 934 (1992); accord, Leibovitz v. Paramount Pictures Corp., 137 F.3d 109, 116 (2d Cir.1998).

[40] In Hearn v. Meyer, 664 F.Supp. 832 (S.D.N.Y.1987), Judge Leisure held on the authority of *Batlin* that "slavish copies" of public domain reproductions of public domain original works of art were not copyrightable despite the great skill and effort involved in the copying process, and minor but unintentional variations between the copies and the works copied.

[41] 499 U.S. 340.

[42] Beverly Wolff, Copyright, in ALI-ABA Course of Study, Legal Problems of Museum Administration, 1989 ALI-ABA 27, at *48 (available on Westlaw). See also Lynne A. Greenburg, The Art of Appropriation: Puppies, Piracy, and Post–Modernism, 11 Cardozo Arts & Ent.L.J. 1, 20–21 (1992) (photographic copies of original art photographs taken by the famous photographer, Edward Weston, which were made to "deconstruct the myth of the masterpiece" not copyrightable).

copyright and joined MGM as a defendant when she sued Bradford and Auckland for infringing her painting. This led to a counterclaim that Gracen had no authority to copy and display the MGM image of Dorothy, and in the trial court Gracen wound up on the wrong end of a $1500 summary judgment.

Judge Posner for the Court of Appeals found that the counterclaim raised questions of implied authority and of a possible oral license to Gracen that made summary judgment inappropriate. He then moved to the validity of her copyright:

"Miss Gracen reminds us that judges can make fools of themselves pronouncing on aesthetic matters. But artistic originality is not the same thing as the legal concept of originality in the Copyright Act. Artistic originality indeed might inhere in a detail, a nuance, a shading too small to be apprehended by a judge. * * * A portrait is not unoriginal for being a good likeness.

"But especially as applied to derivative works, the concept of originality in copyright law has as one would expect a legal rather than aesthetic function—to prevent overlapping claims."

Judge Posner then discussed the problems of proof that would arise as Auckland tried to establish that he copied from the MGM photographs and not from Gracen's derivative painting. As for originality, "the purpose of the term in copyright law is not to guide aesthetic judgments but to assure a sufficiently gross difference between the underlying and the derivative work to avoid entangling subsequent artists depicting the underlying work in copyright problems.

"We are speaking, however, only of the requirement of originality in derivative works. If a painter paints from life, no court is going to hold that his painting is not copyrightable because it is an exact photographic likeness. * * *

" * * * If Miss Gracen had painted Judy Garland from life, her painting would be copyrightable even if we thought it *kitsch;* but a derivative work must be substantially different from the underlying work to be copyrightable. This is the test of L. Batlin & Son, Inc. v. Snyder, 536 F.2d at 491, a decision of the Second Circuit—the nation's premier copyright court—sitting en banc. * * *

"We agree with the district court that under the test of *Batlin* Miss Gracen's painting, whatever its artistic merit, is not an original derivative work within the meaning of the Copyright Act."

The Gracen Painting

A Photograph From *The Wizard of Oz*

NOTES AND QUESTIONS ON ORIGINALITY IN DERIVATIVE WORKS

(1) What is the rationale for a requirement of substantial variation? Is Judge Posner's argument in *Gracen* convincing? Commenting on the language in *Gracen* that "a derivative work must be substantially different from the underlying work," the Seventh Circuit later cautioned that "the originality requirement for derivative works is no more demanding than the originality requirement for other works" and "the key inquiry is whether there is sufficient nontrivial expressive variation in the derivative work to make it distinguishable from the underlying work in some meaningful way." Schrock v. Learning Curve Int'l, Inc., 586 F.3d 513 (7th Cir.2009). The Ninth Circuit, invoking *Gracen*,

Non trivial expressive variation

argued that the requirement of an adequate distinction between the derivative and underlying works was mandated by the affirmation in § 103(b) that copyright in a derivative works does not affect the scope of copyright in the preexisting material; granting plaintiff a copyright on its inflatable costumes based on copyrighted characters "would have the practical effect of providing [plaintiff] with a de facto monopoly on all inflatable costumes depicting the copyrighted characters." Entertainment Research Group, Inc. v. Genesis Creative Group, Inc., 122 F.3d 1211 (9th Cir.1997), cert. denied, 523 U.S. 1021 (1998). Did Jorie Gracen's painting evince less "originality" than the mezzotints described in *Alfred Bell?*

D. Olson, Copyright Originality, 48 Mo.L.Rev. 29, 55 (1983), declares that the "implications" of the *Batlin* decision "are awesome." How so? Consider the suggestion made in P. Page, The Works: Distinguishing Derivative Creations Under Copyright, 5 Cardozo Art. & Ent.L.J. 415 (1986), that "[w]hat the author adds to the work of his predecessors should be judged as though it were placed on a blank canvas or other naked medium." Is that possible? See also R. VerSteeg, Rethinking Originality, 34 Wm. & Mary L.Rev. 801 (1993), an ambitious attempt to define the requisite creativity necessary for "authorship."

(2) The decision in *Bridgeman* creates problems for museums seeking to raise money through the marketing of reproductions. That's just as it should be according to K. Butler, Keeping the World Safe from Naked–Chicks–In–Art Refrigerator Magnets: The Plot to Control Art Images in the Public Domain Through Copyrights in Photographic and Digital Reproductions, 21 Hastings Comm/Ent L.J. 55 (1998), who argues that by physically limiting the copying of works in their collections and then claiming copyright in their own licensed reproductions, museums are subverting the public domain.

Bridgeman was cited with approval by the Tenth Circuit in Meshwerks, Inc. v. Toyota Motor Sales U.S.A., Inc., 528 F.3d 1258 (10th Cir.2008), cert. denied, 555 U.S. 1138 (2009). Plaintiff sued for infringement of its "digital models" of Toyota cars. The models were made by mapping data points on the cars onto a computer grid and then using modeling software to connect the points to form a "wire frame" computer depiction of the vehicles. Employees of the plaintiff then manually "fine-tuned" the lines of the frame to complete the model. Finding that the digital wire-frame models "depict only those unadorned vehicles, having stripped away all lighting, angle, perspective, and 'other ingredients' associated with an original expression," the court concluded that the models were insufficiently original to warrant copyright protection.

(3) The majority in *Batlin* accepted the copyrightability of a precise, small-scale reproduction of Rodin's "Hand of God." Can you frame an acceptable rationale for that result—or for rejecting it?

(4) Consider these two palm tree designs used by a plaintiff on beach towels with sufficient success to inspire imitation. The original design on the left, marketed in the 1960s, had entered the public domain. In 1976 the plaintiff created the "new" design on the right in which it now asserts a copyright against a competitor selling an exact copy. What result? See Sherry Manufacturing Co. v. Towel King of Florida, Inc., 753 F.2d 1565 (11th Cir.1985).

SHERRY'S ORIGINAL DESIGN   SHERRY'S NEW DESIGN

(5) The Dutch painter Piet Mondrian was renowned for his use of bounded geometric shapes in a uniquely characteristic style. French fashion designer Yves St. Laurent was the first to adapt Mondrian's designs to women's clothing in the 1960s. A clothing designer for North Coast Industries, undeniably influenced by Mondrian and St. Laurent, created "Style 7114." When a competitor began selling clothing with a similar design, North Coast sued for infringement. The district court gave summary judgment to the defendant, finding that the variations between the St. Laurent design and plaintiff's Style 7114 were too trivial to support a copyright.

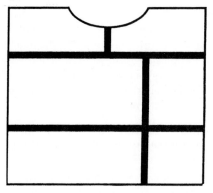
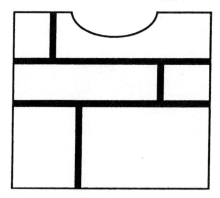

Yves St. Laurent's rendition of a Mondrian painting   Style 7114

The Ninth Circuit disagreed in North Coast Industries v. Jason Maxwell, Inc., 972 F.2d 1031 (9th Cir.1992), holding that the plaintiff was entitled to a trial on the issue of copyrightability. "If we were to accept the view that, as a matter of law the differences in the placement of geometric shapes should be regarded as trivial, we would be forced to conclude that Mondrian's creativity with geometric shapes ended with his first painting, and that he went on to paint the same painting a thousand times. This is not the judgment of art history, and it cannot be the correct judgment of a court as a matter of law." Is this consistent with the distinction between a legal and aesthetic conception of originality in derivative works drawn by Judge Posner in *Gracen?*

(6) Modern computer technology permits the creation of "colorized" versions of classic black and white motion pictures. Is the colorized version a copyrightable derivative work? The Copyright Office announced in 1987 that it would accept *will register color remakes* such works for registration.[h] The specter of a colorized *Citizen Kane,* however, *of black & white movies* stirs emotions, and the "right" to make such works has been hotly debated. That question raises the issue of "moral rights," a topic to be considered later. See p. 738 infra.

COMPILATIONS

Feist Publications, Inc. v. Rural Telephone Service Co.

Supreme Court of the United States, 1991.
499 U.S. 340, 111 S.Ct. 1282.

■ JUSTICE O'CONNOR delivered the opinion of the Court.

This case requires us to clarify the extent of copyright protection available to telephone directory white pages.

I

Rural Telephone Service Company is a certified public utility that provides telephone service to several communities in northwest Kansas. It is subject to a state regulation that requires all telephone companies operating in Kansas to issue annually an updated telephone directory. Accordingly, as a condition of its monopoly franchise, Rural publishes a typical telephone directory, consisting of white pages and yellow pages. The white pages list in alphabetical order the names of Rural's subscribers, together with their towns and telephone numbers. The yellow pages list Rural's business subscribers alphabetically by category and feature classified advertisements of various sizes. Rural distributes its directory free of charge to its subscribers, but earns revenue by selling yellow pages advertisements.

Feist Publications, Inc., is a publishing company that specializes in area-wide telephone directories. Unlike a typical directory, which covers only a particular calling area, Feist's area-wide directories cover a much larger geographical range, reducing the need to call directory assistance or consult multiple directories. The Feist directory that is the subject of this litigation covers 11 different telephone service areas in 15 counties and contains 46,878 white pages listings—compared to Rural's approximately *white & yellow* 7,700 listings. Like Rural's directory, Feist's is distributed free of charge and includes both white pages and yellow pages. Feist and Rural compete vigorously for yellow pages advertising.

---

[h] In Maljack Prod., Inc. v. UAV Corp., 964 F.Supp. 1416 (C.D.Cal.1997), aff'd on other grounds, 160 F.3d 1223 (9th Cir.1998), cert. denied, 526 U.S. 1158 (1999), the court agreed with the Copyright Office that the "panning and scanning" done to a movie to fit the images onto a television screen also resulted in a copyrightable derivative work.

* * * To obtain white pages listings for its area-wide directory, Feist approached each of the 11 telephone companies operating in northwest Kansas and offered to pay for the right to use its white pages listings.

Of the 11 telephone companies, only Rural refused to license its listings to Feist. Rural's refusal created a problem for Feist, as omitting these listings would have left a gaping hole in its area-wide directory, rendering it less attractive to potential yellow pages advertisers. * * *

Unable to license Rural's white pages listings, Feist used them without Rural's consent. Feist began by removing several thousand listings that fell outside the geographic range of its area-wide directory, then hired personnel to investigate the 4,935 that remained. These employees verified the data reported by Rural and sought to obtain additional information. As a result, a typical Feist listing includes the individual's street address; most of Rural's listings do not. Notwithstanding these additions, however, 1,309 of the 46,878 listings in Feist's 1983 directory were identical to listings in Rural's 1982–1983 white pages. Four of these were fictitious listings that Rural had inserted into its directory to detect copying.

Rural sued for copyright infringement in the District Court for the District of Kansas taking the position that Feist, in compiling its own directory, could not use the information contained in Rural's white pages. * * * The District Court granted summary judgment to Rural, explaining that "[c]ourts have consistently held that telephone directories are copyrightable" and citing a string of lower court decisions. 663 F.Supp. 214, 218 (1987). In an unpublished opinion, the Court of Appeals for the Tenth Circuit affirmed "for substantially the reasons given by the district court." * * *

II

A

This case concerns the interaction of two well-established propositions. The first is that facts are not copyrightable; the other, that compilations of facts generally are. Each of these propositions possesses an impeccable pedigree. That there can be no valid copyright in facts is universally understood. The most fundamental axiom of copyright law is that "[n]o author may copyright his ideas or the facts he narrates." Harper & Row, Publishers, Inc. v. Nation Enterprises, 471 U.S. 539, 556. Rural wisely concedes this point, noting in its brief that "[f]acts and discoveries, of course, are not themselves subject to copyright protection." At the same time, however, it is beyond dispute that compilations of facts are within the subject matter of copyright. Compilations were expressly mentioned in the Copyright Act of 1909, and again in the Copyright Act of 1976.

There is an undeniable tension between these two propositions. Many compilations consist of nothing but raw data—i.e., wholly factual information not accompanied by any original written expression. On what basis may one claim a copyright in such a work? Common sense tells us that 100 uncopyrightable facts do not magically change their status when gathered together in one place. Yet copyright law seems to contemplate that compilations that consist exclusively of facts are potentially within its scope.

The key to resolving the tension lies in understanding why facts are not copyrightable. The *sine qua non* of copyright is originality. To qualify for copyright protection, a work must be original to the author. See *Harper & Row,* supra, at 547–549. Original, as the term is used in copyright, means only that the work was independently created by the author (as opposed to copied from other works), and that it possesses at least some minimal degree of creativity. 1 M. Nimmer & D. Nimmer, Copyright §§ 2.01[A], [B] (1990) (hereinafter Nimmer). To be sure, the requisite level of creativity is extremely low; even a slight amount will suffice. The vast majority of works make the grade quite easily, as they possess some creative spark, "no matter how crude, humble or obvious" it might be. Id., § 1.08[C][1]. Originality does not signify novelty; a work may be original even though it closely resembles other works so long as the similarity is fortuitous, not the result of copying. To illustrate, assume that·two poets, each ignorant of the other, compose identical poems. Neither work is novel, yet both are original and, hence, copyrightable. See Sheldon v. Metro–Goldwyn Pictures Corp., 81 F.2d 49, 54 (2d Cir.1936).

Originality is a constitutional requirement. The source of Congress' power to enact copyright laws is Article I, § 8, cl. 8, of the Constitution, which authorizes Congress to "secur[e] for limited Times to Authors . . . the exclusive Right to their respective Writings." In two decisions from the late 19th Century—The Trade–Mark Cases, 100 U.S. (10 Otto) 82 (1879); and Burrow–Giles Lithographic Co. v. Sarony, 111 U.S. 53 (1884)—this Court defined the crucial terms "authors" and "writings." In so doing, the Court made it unmistakably clear that these terms presuppose a degree of originality.

In *The Trade–Mark Cases,* the Court addressed the constitutional scope of "writings." For a particular work to be classified "under the head of writings of authors," the Court determined, "originality is required." 100 U.S., at 94. The Court explained that originality requires independent creation plus a modicum of creativity: "[W]hile the word *writings* may be liberally construed, as it has been, to include original designs for engraving, prints, & c., it is only such as are *original,* and are founded in the creative powers of the mind. The writings which are to be protected are *the fruits of intellectual labor,* embodied in the form of books, prints, engravings, and the like." Ibid. (emphasis in original).

In *Burrow–Giles,* the Court distilled the same requirement from the Constitution's use of the word "authors." The Court defined "author," in a constitutional sense, to mean "he to whom anything owes its origin; originator; maker." 111 U.S., at 58 (internal quotations omitted). As in *The Trade–Mark Cases,* the Court emphasized the creative component of originality. It described copyright as being limited to "original intellectual conceptions of the author," ibid., and stressed the importance of requiring an author who accuses another of infringement to prove "the existence of those facts of originality, of intellectual production, of thought, and conception." Id., at 59–60.

The originality requirement articulated in *The Trade–Mark Cases* and *Burrow–Giles* remains the touchstone of copyright protection today. * * *

It is this bedrock principle of copyright that mandates the law's seemingly disparate treatment of facts and factual compilations. "No one may claim originality as to facts." [Nimmer] § 2.11[A], p. 2–157. This is because facts do not owe their origin to an act of authorship. The distinction is one between creation and discovery: the first person to find and report a particular fact has not created the fact; he or she has merely discovered its existence. To borrow from *Burrow–Giles,* one who discovers a fact is not its "maker" or "originator." 111 U.S., at 58. "The discoverer merely finds and records." Nimmer § 2.03[E]. Census takers, for example, do not "create" the population figures that emerge from their efforts; in a sense, they copy these figures from the world around them. Denicola, Copyright in Collections of Facts: A Theory for the Protection of Nonfiction Literary Works, 81 Colum.L.Rev. 516, 525 (1981) (hereinafter Denicola). * * *

Factual compilations, on the other hand, may possess the requisite originality. The compilation author typically chooses which facts to include, in what order to place them, and how to arrange the collected data so that they may be used effectively by readers. These choices as to selection and arrangement, so long as they are made independently by the compiler and entail a minimal degree of creativity, are sufficiently original that Congress may protect such compilations through the copyright laws. Nimmer §§ 2.11[D], 3.03; Denicola 523, n. 38. * * *

This protection is subject to an important limitation. The mere fact that a work is copyrighted does not mean that every element of the work may be protected. Originality remains the *sine qua non* of copyright; accordingly, copyright protection may extend only to those components of a work that are original to the author. * * * In *Harper & Row,* for example, we explained that President Ford could not prevent others from copying bare historical facts from his autobiography, see 471 U.S., at 556–557, but that he could prevent others from copying his "subjective descriptions and portraits of public figures." Id., at 563. Where the compilation author adds no written expression but rather lets the facts speak for themselves, the expressive element is more elusive. The only conceivable expression is the manner in which the compiler has selected and arranged the facts. * * *

This inevitably means that the copyright in a factual compilation is thin. Notwithstanding a valid copyright, a subsequent compiler remains free to use the facts contained in another's publication to aid in preparing a competing work, so long as the competing work does not feature the same selection and arrangement. * * *

It may seem unfair that much of the fruit of the compiler's labor may be used by others without compensation. As Justice Brennan has correctly observed, however, this is not "some unforeseen byproduct of a statutory scheme." *Harper & Row,* 471 U.S., at 589 (dissenting opinion). It is, rather, "the essence of copyright," ibid., and a constitutional requirement. The primary objective of copyright is not to reward the labor of authors, but "[t]o promote the Progress of Science and useful Arts." Art. I, § 8, cl. 8. Accord Twentieth Century Music Corp. v. Aiken, 422 U.S. 151, 156 (1975). To this end, copyright assures authors the right to their original expression, but encourages others to build freely upon the ideas and information conveyed by a work. *Harper & Row,* supra, at 556–557. This principle, known as the idea/expression or fact/expression dichotomy, applies to all works of authorship. As applied to a factual compilation, assuming the absence of original written expression, only the compiler's selection and arrangement may be protected; the raw facts may be copied at will. This result is neither unfair nor unfortunate. It is the means by which copyright advances the progress of science and art.

* * *

This, then, resolves the doctrinal tension: Copyright treats facts and factual compilations in a wholly consistent manner. Facts, whether alone or as part of a compilation, are not original and therefore may not be copyrighted. A factual compilation is eligible for copyright if it features an original selection or arrangement of facts, but the copyright is limited to the

facts are not original

particular selection or arrangement. In no event may copyright extend to the facts themselves.

B

[The Court explained that a misreading of the 1909 statute "caused some lower courts temporarily to lose sight of [the originality] requirement." The 1909 statute only implicitly called for original authorship, and its catalog of registrable works included without qualification "directories, gazetteers, and other compilations." § 5(a). This led some courts, including Jeweler's Circular Pub. Co. v. Keystone Pub. Co., 281 Fed. 83 (2d Cir.1922), "to infer erroneously that directories and the like were copyrightable *per se*."]

Making matters worse, these courts developed a new theory to justify the protection of factual compilations. Known alternatively as "sweat of the brow" or "industrious collection," the underlying notion was that copyright was a reward for the hard work that went into compiling facts. The classic formulation of the doctrine appeared in *Jeweler's Circular Publishing Co.*, 281 Fed., at 88:

> "The right to copyright a book upon which one has expended labor in its preparation does not depend upon whether the materials which he has collected consist or not of matters which are publici juris, or whether such materials show literary skill *or originality,* either in thought or in language, or anything more than industrious collection. The man who goes through the streets of a town and puts down the names of each of the inhabitants, with their occupations and their street number, acquires material of which he is the author" (emphasis added).

The "sweat of the brow" doctrine had numerous flaws, the most glaring being that it extended copyright protection in a compilation beyond selection and arrangement—the compiler's original contributions—to the facts themselves. Under the doctrine, the only defense to infringement was independent creation. A subsequent compiler was "not entitled to take one word of information previously published," but rather had to "independently wor[k] out the matter for himself, so as to arrive at the same result from the same common sources of information." Id., at 88–89 (internal quotations omitted). "Sweat of the brow" courts thereby eschewed the most fundamental axiom of copyright law—that no one may copyright facts or ideas. * * *

* * * [T]hey handed out proprietary interests in facts and declared that authors are absolutely precluded from saving time and effort by relying upon the facts contained in prior works. In truth, "[i]t is just such wasted effort that the proscription against the copyright of ideas and facts . . . [is] designed to prevent." Rosemont Enterprises, Inc. v. Random House, Inc., 366 F.2d 303, 310 (2d Cir.1966), cert. denied, 385 U.S. 1009 (1967). "Protection for the fruits of such research . . . may in certain circumstances be available under a theory of unfair competition. But to accord copyright protection on this basis alone distorts basic copyright principles in that it creates a monopoly in public domain materials without the necessary justification of protecting and encouraging the creation of 'writings' by 'authors.' " Nimmer § 3.04, p. 3–23 (footnote omitted).

C

* * *

Congress [in the 1976 Act] took another step to minimize confusion by deleting the specific mention of "directories . . . and other compilations" in § 5 of the 1909 Act. As mentioned, this section had led some courts to conclude that directories were copyrightable *per se* and that every element of a directory was protected. In its place, Congress enacted two new provisions. First, to make clear that compilations were not copyrightable *per se,* Congress provided a definition of the term "compilation." Second, to make clear that the copyright in a compilation did not extend to the facts themselves, Congress enacted 17 U.S.C. § 103.

def of compilation

The definition of "compilation" is found in § 101 of the 1976 Act. It defines a "compilation" in the copyright sense as "a work formed by the collection and assembly of preexisting materials or of data *that* are selected, coordinated, or arranged *in such a way that* the resulting work as a whole constitutes an original work of authorship" (emphasis added).

The purpose of the statutory definition is to emphasize that collections of facts are not copyrightable *per se*. It conveys this message through its tripartite structure, as emphasized above by the italics. The statute identifies three distinct elements and requires each to be met for a work to qualify as a copyrightable compilation: (1) the collection and assembly of preexisting material, facts, or data; (2) the selection, coordination, or arrangement of those materials; and (3) the creation, by virtue of the particular selection, coordination, or arrangement, of an "original" work of authorship. * * *

required elements to a compilation

At first glance, the first requirement does not seem to tell us much. It merely describes what one normally thinks of as a compilation—a collection of pre-existing material, facts, or data. What makes it significant is that it is not the *sole* requirement. It is not enough for copyright purposes that an author collects and assembles facts. To satisfy the statutory definition, the work must get over two additional hurdles. In this way, the plain language indicates that not every collection of facts receives copyright protection. Otherwise, there would be a period after "data."

The third requirement is also illuminating. It emphasizes that a compilation, like any other work, is copyrightable only if it satisfies the originality requirement ("an *original* work of authorship"). Although § 102 states plainly that the originality requirement applies to all works, the point was emphasized with regard to compilations to ensure that courts would not repeat the mistake of the "sweat of the brow" courts by concluding that fact-based works are treated differently and measured by some other standard. As Congress explained it, the goal was to "make plain that the criteria of copyrightable subject matter stated in section 102 apply with full force to works . . . containing preexisting material." H.R.Rep. [No. 94–1476], at 57; S.Rep. [No. 94–473], at 55.

The key to the statutory definition is the second requirement. It instructs courts that, in determining whether a fact-based work is an original work of authorship, they should focus on the manner in which the collected facts have been selected, coordinated, and arranged. This is a straightforward application of the originality requirement. Facts are never original, so the compilation author can claim originality, if at all, only in the way the facts are presented. To that end, the statute dictates that the principal focus should be on whether the selection, coordination, and arrangement are sufficiently original to merit protection.

Not every selection, coordination, or arrangement will pass muster. This is plain from the statute. It states that, to merit protection, the facts must be selected, coordinated, or arranged "in such a way" as to render the work as a whole original. This implies that some "ways" will trigger copyright, but that others will not. * * * Otherwise, the phrase "in such a way" is meaningless and Congress should have defined "compilation" simply as "a work formed by the collection and assembly of preexisting materials or data that are selected, coordinated, or arranged." That Congress did not do so is dispositive. In accordance with "the established principle that a court should give effect, if possible, to every clause and word of a statute," Moskal v. United States, 498 U.S. 103, 109–110 (1990) (internal quotations omitted), we conclude that the statute envisions that there will be some fact-based works in which the selection, coordination, and arrangement are not sufficiently original to trigger copyright protection.

"in such a way"

As discussed earlier, however, the originality requirement is not particularly stringent. A compiler may settle upon a selection or arrangement that others have used; novelty is not required. Originality requires only that the author make the selection or arrangement independently (i.e., without copying that selection or arrangement from another work), and that it display some minimal level of creativity. Presumably, the vast majority of compilations will pass this test, but not all will. There remains a narrow category of works in which the creative spark is utterly lacking or so trivial as to be virtually nonexistent. See generally Bleistein v. Donaldson Lithographing Co., 188 U.S. 239, 251 (1903) (referring to "the narrowest and most obvious limits"). Such works are incapable of sustaining a valid copyright. Nimmer § 2.01[B].

Even if a work qualifies as a copyrightable compilation, it receives only limited protection. This is the point of § 103 of the Act. * * *

As § 103 makes clear, copyright is not a tool by which a compilation author may keep others from using the facts or data he or she has collected. "The most important point here is one that is commonly misunderstood today: copyright . . . has no effect one way or the other on the copyright or public domain status of the preexisting material." H.R.Rep., at 57; S.Rep., at 55. The 1909 Act did not require, as "sweat of the brow" courts mistakenly assumed, that each subsequent compiler must start from scratch and is precluded from relying on research undertaken by another. See, e.g., *Jeweler's Circular Publishing Co.*, 281 Fed., at 88–89. Rather, the facts contained in existing works may be freely copied because copyright protects only the elements that owe their origin to the compiler—the selection, coordination, and arrangement of facts. * * *

The 1976 revisions have proven largely successful in steering courts in the right direction. A good example is Miller v. Universal City Studios, Inc., 650 F.2d, at 1369–1370: "A copyright in a directory . . . is properly viewed as resting on the originality of the selection and arrangement of the factual material, rather than on the industriousness of the efforts to develop the information. Copyright protection does not extend to the facts themselves, and the mere use of information contained in a directory without a substantial copying of the format does not constitute infringement" (citation omitted). Additionally, the Second Circuit, which almost 70 years ago issued the classic formulation of the "sweat of the brow" doctrine in *Jeweler's Circular Publishing Co.*, has now fully repudiated the reasoning of that decision. See, e.g., Financial Information, Inc. v. Moody's Investors Service, Inc., 808 F.2d 204, 207 (2d Cir.1986), cert. denied, 484 U.S. 820 (1987); Financial Information, Inc. v. Moody's Investors Service, Inc., 751 F.2d 501, 510 (2d Cir.1984) (Newman, J., concurring); Hoehling v. Universal City Studios, Inc., 618 F.2d 972, 979 (2d Cir.1980). Even those scholars who believe that "industrious collection" should be rewarded seem to recognize that this is beyond the scope of existing copyright law. Denicola 516 ("the very vocabulary of copyright is ill suited to analyzing property rights in works of nonfiction"); id., at 520–521, 525; Ginsburg [Creation and Commercial Value: Copyright Protection of Works of Information, 90 Colum.L.Rev. 1865 (1990)] 1876, 1870.

III

There is no doubt that Feist took from the white pages of Rural's directory a substantial amount of factual information. At a minimum, Feist copied the names, towns, and telephone numbers of 1,309 of Rural's subscribers. Not all copying, however, is copyright infringement. To establish infringement, two elements must be proven: (1) ownership of a valid copyright, and (2) copying of constituent elements of the work that are original. See *Harper & Row,* 471 U.S., at 548. The first element is not at issue here; Feist appears to concede that Rural's directory, considered as a whole, is subject to a valid copyright because it contains some foreword text, as well as original material in its yellow pages advertisements.

The question is whether Rural has proved the second element. In other words, did Feist, by taking 1,309 names, towns, and telephone numbers from Rural's white pages, copy anything that was "original" to Rural? Certainly, the raw data does not satisfy the originality requirement. Rural may have been the first to discover and report the names, towns, and telephone numbers of its subscribers, but this data does not " 'ow[e] its origin' " to Rural. *Burrow–Giles,* 111 U.S., at 58. * * *

Rural essentially concedes the point by referring to the names, towns, and telephone numbers as "preexisting material." Section 103(b) states explicitly that the copyright in a compilation does not extend to "the preexisting material employed in the work."

The question that remains is whether Rural selected, coordinated, or arranged these uncopyrightable facts in an original way. As mentioned, originality is not a stringent standard; it does not require that facts be presented in an innovative or surprising way. It is equally true, however, that the selection and arrangement of facts cannot be so mechanical or routine as to require no creativity whatsoever. The standard of originality is low, but it does exist. * * *

The selection, coordination, and arrangement of Rural's white pages do not satisfy the minimum constitutional standards for copyright protection. As mentioned at the outset, Rural's white pages are entirely typical. Persons desiring telephone service in Rural's service area fill out an application and Rural issues them a telephone number. In preparing its white pages, Rural simply takes the data provided by its subscribers and lists it alphabetically by surname. The end product is a garden-variety white pages directory, devoid of even the slightest trace of creativity.

Rural's selection of listings could not be more obvious: it publishes the most basic information—name, town, and telephone number—about each person who applies to it for telephone service. This is "selection" of a sort, but it lacks the modicum of creativity necessary to transform mere selection into copyrightable expression. Rural expended sufficient effort to make the white pages directory useful, but insufficient creativity to make it original.

We note in passing that the selection featured in Rural's white pages may also fail the originality requirement for another reason. Feist points out that Rural did not truly "select" to publish the names and telephone numbers of its subscribers; rather, it was required to do so by the Kansas Corporation Commission as part of its monopoly franchise. See 737 F.Supp., at 612. Accordingly, one could plausibly conclude that this selection was dictated by state law, not by Rural.

Nor can Rural claim originality in its coordination and arrangement of facts. The white pages do nothing more than list Rural's subscribers in alphabetical order. This arrangement may, technically speaking, owe its origin to Rural; no one disputes that Rural undertook the task of alphabetizing the names itself. But there is nothing remotely creative about arranging names alphabetically in a white pages directory. It is an age-old practice, firmly rooted in tradition and so commonplace that it has come to be expected as a matter of course. * * * It is not only unoriginal, it is practically inevitable. This time-honored tradition does not possess the minimal creative spark required by the Copyright Act and the Constitution.

We conclude that the names, towns, and telephone numbers copied by Feist were not original to Rural and therefore were not protected by the copyright in Rural's combined white and yellow pages directory. As a constitutional matter, copyright protects only those constituent elements of a work that possess more than a *de minimis* quantum of creativity. Rural's white pages, limited to basic subscriber information and arranged alphabetically, fall short of the mark. As a statutory matter, 17 U.S.C. § 101 does not afford protection from copying to a collection of facts that are selected, coordinated, and arranged in a way that utterly lacks originality. Given that some works must fail, we cannot imagine a more likely candidate. Indeed, were we to hold that Rural's white pages pass muster, it is hard to believe that any collection of facts could fail.

Because Rural's white pages lack the requisite originality, Feist's use of the listings cannot constitute infringement. This decision should not be construed as demeaning Rural's efforts in compiling its directory, but rather as making clear that copyright rewards originality, not effort. As this Court noted more than a century ago, " 'great praise may be due to the plaintiffs for their industry and enterprise in publishing this paper, yet the law does not contemplate their being rewarded in this way.' " Baker v. Selden, 101 U.S., at 105.

The judgment of the Court of Appeals is

Reversed.

■ JUSTICE BLACKMUN concurs in the judgment.

BellSouth Advertising & Pub. Corp. v. Donnelley Information Pub., Inc.

999 F.2d 1436 (11th Cir.1993), cert. denied, 510 U.S. 1101 (1994).

"[W]e are called upon to apply *Feist Publications* * * *, which addressed copyright protection for a 'white pages' telephone directory, to resolve the infringement claims presented to us concerning a directory of a different color. * * * The pivotal issue in this case is whether that which was copied by the alleged infringer was protected by the registered claim of compilation copyright. * * *

"BellSouth Advertising & Publishing Corporation ('BAPCO') is a wholly owned subsidiary of BellSouth Corporation ('BellSouth') created for the purpose of preparing, publishing and distributing telephone directories. Using telephone listing information supplied by Southern Bell Telephone and Telegraph Company ('Southern Bell'), another wholly owned subsidiary of BellSouth, BAPCO publishes a classified, 'yellow pages,' advertising directory for the Greater Miami area. The BAPCO directory is organized into an alphabetical list of business classifications. Each business-rate telephone service subscriber is listed in alphabetical order under one appropriate heading without charge. A subscriber may purchase cross listings under different business classifications or advertisements to appear along with its business listing.

"After BAPCO published its 1984 directory for the Greater Miami area, Donnelley Information Publishing, Inc. and Reuben H. Donnelley Corp. (collectively 'Donnelley') began promoting and selling classified advertisements to be placed in a competitive classified directory for the Greater Miami area. To generate a list of business telephone subscribers to be solicited for placement in its directory, Donnelley gave copies of BAPCO's directory to Appalachian Computer Services, Inc. ('ACS'), a data entry company. Donnelley first marked each listing in the BAPCO directory with one alphanumeric code indicating the size and type of advertisement purchased by the subscriber and a similar code indicating the type of business represented by the BAPCO heading under which the listing appeared. For each listing appearing in the BAPCO directory, ACS created a computer data base containing the name, address, and telephone number of the subscriber, as well as the codes corresponding to business type and unit of advertising. From this data base, Donnelley printed sales lead sheets, listing this information for each subscriber, to be used to contact business telephone subscribers to sell advertisements and listings in the Donnelley directory. Relying on this information copied from the BAPCO directory, Donnelley ultimately prepared its own competitive directory for the Greater Miami area."

The district court had granted summary judgment in favor of BAPCO, and the judgment was affirmed by a panel of the Eleventh Circuit, 933 F.2d 952 (11th Cir.1991). However, the panel decision had been vacated and a rehearing *en banc* ordered at 977 F.2d 1435 (11th Cir.1992).

"[T]he district court found that BAPCO engaged in feats of coordination and arrangement to generate its yellow pages directory. The court explains that BAPCO arranged its directory in an alphabetized list of business types, with individual businesses listed in alphabetical order under the applicable headings. The Copyright Act protects 'original works of authorship.' 17 U.S.C. § 102(a). BAPCO's arrangement and coordination is 'entirely typical' for a business directory. *Feist*, 499 U.S. at 362." (In a footnote, Judge Birch said, "While the listings in BAPCO's yellow pages required somewhat more organization and arrangement than the white pages directory considered in *Feist*, BAPCO's claim of 'originality' must be resolved by comparison to other business telephone directories. * * * ")

"The district court also identified acts of coordination and arrangement in the particular system of headings used in the BAPCO directory. * * *

" * * * BAPCO failed to present evidence that, even if copied, its heading structure constitutes original expression warranting copyright protection. Initially, many of the selected headings, for example 'Attorneys' or 'Banks,' represent such an obvious label for the entities appearing under these headings as to lack the requisite originality for copyright protection. BAPCO can claim no copyright in the idea of dividing churches by denomination or attorneys by area of specialty. Further, any expressive act in including a category such as 'Banks' or in dividing 'Attorneys' into categories such as 'Bankruptcy' or 'Criminal Law' would lose copyright protection because it would merge with the idea of listing such entities as a class of businesses in a business directory. The evidence submitted by Donnelley also establishes that many of BAPCO's headings result from certain standard industry practices, such as the recommendations of the National Yellow Pages Sales Association, with regard to the selection and phrasing of headings in business directories. Finally, as established by the testimony of BAPCO's representatives, the ultimate appearance of a particular subscriber under a certain heading is determined by the subscriber's willingness to purchase those listings in the BAPCO directory. While BAPCO may select the headings that are offered to the subscriber, it is the subscriber who selects from those alternatives the headings under which the subscriber will appear in the copyrighted directory. The headings that actually appear in the directory thus, do not owe their origin to BAPCO and BAPCO has claimed no copyright in the larger universe of headings that are offered to subscribers. Thus, the elements of selection, coordination and arrangement identified by the district court, and purportedly copied by Donnelley, as a matter of law, do not display the originality required to merit copyright protection. * * *.

"We reverse the judgment of the district court granting summary judgment to BAPCO on its claim of copyright infringement and enter judgment in favor of Donnelley on this claim."

Judge Hatchett in dissent remained unconvinced. "The majority's holding establishes a rule of law that transforms the multi-billion dollar classified publishing industry from a business requiring the production of a useful directory based on multiple layers of creative decision-making, into a business requiring no more than a successful race to a data processing agency to copy another publisher's copyrighted work-product. * * *

"The clearest example of BAPCO's original selection is its choice of the classified headings that would be included in the 1984 Yellow Pages. * * * BAPCO selected the approximate 7,000 classified heading in the 1984 Yellow Pages from the 4,700 primary headings and approximately 34,000 related headings in the BAPCO headings book. BAPCO presented the undisputed testimony of Gerald Brown that the BAPCO headings book is not standardized to coincide with the menu of classified headings used in National Yellow Page Sales Association (NYPSA) publications. Moreover, even if BAPCO's selection of classified headings is similar to other NYPSA publications, it would still be copyrightable under *Feist* so long as BAPCO selected independently. See *Feist*, 499 U.S. at 362 (holding that 'originality does not signify novelty; a work may be original even though it closely resembles other works so long as the similarity is fortuitous, not the result of copying')." (In a footnote Judge Hatchett argued, "In reasoning that BAPCO's selection of headings lack originality because many resemble NYPSA headings, the majority completely ignores the *Feist* Court's holding that an independent selection of data need not be 'novel' in order to be deemed original.")

"The originality of BAPCO's arrangement of business listings under a particular classified heading is also clear under the standard definition of 'arrangement' in the copyright laws. * * * Because most business subscribers offer multiple product lines, goods, and services, Johnson testified that BAPCO sales representatives were responsible for itemizing the products or services of a business subscriber, determining the degree of importance or profitability to the business, and recommending an appropriate classified heading for listing the business in the 1984 Yellow Pages." Judge Hatchett also noted that BAPCO's "Heading Committee" had final responsibility for deciding whether a classified heading selected by a customer was appropriate. "Accordingly, the evidence is clear that BAPCO's arrangement was in no sense mechanical. On the contrary, the 1984 Yellow Pages reflects several layers of BAPCO choices on grouping 106,398 business listings under approximately 7,000 classified headings, which BAPCO selected from a heading book containing 4,700 primary entries and 34,000 related headings."

Key Pub., Inc. v. Chinatown Today Pub. Enterprises

945 F.2d 509 (2d Cir.1991).

"This appeal concerns the scope of copyright protection provided a classified telephone directory published by appellee Key Publications, Inc. ('Key'). Appellants Galore Enterprises, Inc. and Ma Kam Yee ('Galore' and 'Ma'), appeal from Judge Ward's holding that their publication, the 1990 Chinese American–Life Guide ('Galore Directory'), infringed Key's copyright in the 1989–90 Chinese Business Guide & Directory ('1989–90 Key Directory'). We hold that the 1989–90 Key Directory is subject to copyright protection, but that the Galore Directory does not infringe Key's copyright. We therefore reverse. * * *

"This appeal specifically concerns the yellow pages listings contained in the 1989–90 Key Directory. Key's president, Lynn Wang, is responsible for assembling the Key directories. Beginning in 1983, Ms. Wang collected business cards from doctors and lawyers associated with the Chinese–American community, banks that did business in the Chinese–American community, and other establishments she thought ought to be included in the yellow pages section of the Directory. Additionally, a 'modest percentage,' in the words of the district court, of the listings in the 1984 Key Directory were copied from another compilation, the 1981 Chinese American Restaurant Directory ('Restaurant Directory'). Some of the copied listings were presumably included in later directories, including the 1989–90 Key Directory. The information collected in the 1989–90 Key Directory was sorted by type of business; each listing is placed in one of over 260 different categories; and each of the approximately 9000 listings consists of an English and a Chinese name, an address, and a telephone number. * * * The yellow pages of the Galore Directory contain approximately 2000 listings divided among twenty-eight different categories. Like the 1989–90 Key Directory, business establishments of interest to the New York Chinese–American community are listed in the Galore Directory. About seventy-five percent, or 1500, of the businesses listed in the Galore Directory are also listed in the 1989–90 Key Directory. * * *

[handwritten: 751. similarity]

"[O]nly if the selection, coordination, or arrangement of listings in the directory is sufficiently original or creative will the directory be entitled to a copyright. Selection implies the exercise of judgment in choosing which facts from a given body of data to include in a compilation. * * * In assembling the directory, Ms. Wang had to select from a multitude of businesses in New York and elsewhere those of greatest interest to her audience—the New York City Chinese–American community. * * * Ms. Wang testified that she excluded from the directory those businesses she did not think would remain open for very long, such as certain insurance brokers, take-out restaurants, and traditional Chinese medical practitioners. This testimony alone indicates thought and creativity in the selection of businesses included in the 1989–90 Key Directory. * * *

[handwritten: Key's originality]

"In addition, the arrangement of the Key Directory is original within the meaning of the copyright laws. Arrangement 'refers to the ordering or grouping of data into lists or categories that go beyond the mere mechanical grouping of data as such, for example, the alphabetical, chronological, or sequential listings of data.' Copyright Office, Guidelines for Registration of Fact–Based Compilations 1 (Rev. Oct. 11, 1989), * * *. The 1989–90 Key Directory contains over 9000 listings divided among approximately 260 different categories. The format of the Key Directory is common to most classified directories, and particular categories have, of course, been used in other classified directories, e.g., 'ACCOUNTANTS,' 'BRIDAL SHOPS,' and 'SHOE STORES.' Nevertheless, some of the categories are of particular interest to the Chinese–American community and not common to yellow pages, e.g., 'BEAN CURD & BEAN SPROUT SHOPS.' And there is no evidence that the arrangement and designation of categories was copied from, or is substantially similar to, another directory. The lack of novelty is, as noted, not a bar to copyright protection."

[handwritten: def of arrangement]

Although Key's copyright was upheld, the court concluded that the Galore Directory was not an infringement. "What must be shown is substantial similarity between those elements, and only those elements, that provide copyrightability to the allegedly infringed compilation. * * * With regard to the arrangement of listings in the Galore Directory, it can hardly be described as even remotely similar to the arrangement utilized by the 1989–90 Key Directory. The Galore Directory contains only twenty-eight different categories, set out in APPENDIX A. The 1989–90 Key Directory contains over 260 different categories, set out in APPENDIX B. Not only is the magnitude of the difference in the number of categories enormous, but only three of the twenty-eight categories in the Galore Directory duplicate categories in the 1989–90 Key Directory. A facial examination thus readily reveals great dissimilarity. * * *

"Of course, as noted supra, infringement may also be found if there is a substantial similarity in the selection of businesses listed in the two publications. The district court found that seventy-five percent of the 2000 listings, 1500 listings, included in the Galore Directory duplicated listings contained in the 1989–90 Key Directory. The district court also found that the 1500 duplicate listings resulted from deliberate copying by Galore and Ma.

"However, the 1989–90 Key Directory contains over 9000 listings. Thus, just seventeen percent (1500/9000) of the listings in the 1989–90 Key Directory were also printed in the Galore Directory. Moreover, the listings copied do not come primarily from any particular portion of the 1989–90 Key Directory; no category of the 1989–90 Key Directory containing more than a few entries is duplicated in total in the Galore Directory. For exam-

[handwritten: few entries are duplicated for key]

ple, of the 124 accountants listed in the 1989–90 Key Directory, only forty-two are also listed in the Galore Directory. Finally, at least twenty-five percent of the listings in the Galore Directory are not in the 1989–90 Key Directory.

"We conclude that, as a matter of law, the Galore Directory does not infringe the 1989–90 Key Directory."

NOTES AND QUESTIONS

(1) Does the *BellSouth* case move beyond *Feist* in limiting protection for compilations of facts? Is it inconsistent with *Key Publications*?

Examples of compilations that have survived the *Feist* analysis include a "pitching form" in Kregos v. Associated Press, 937 F.2d 700 (2d Cir.1991), that combined nine statistics relating to the past performances of the opposing pitchers in upcoming baseball games. Judge Newman noted that "there are at least scores of available statistics about pitching performances available to be calculated from the underlying data and therefore thousands of combinations of data that a selector can chose to include in a pitching form." But the plaintiff lost a subsequent appeal on the issue of infringement; plaintiff's copyright was "limited to the particular selections he made," and defendant AP's pitching form had 10 statistics, only six of which were the same as the plaintiff's. 3 F.3d 656 (2d Cir.1993), cert. denied, 510 U.S. 1112 (1994). In Lipton v. Nature Co., 71 F.3d 464 (2d Cir.1995), the plaintiff's selection and "aesthetic" arrangement of so-called "terms of venery" (a pride of lions, a murder of crows, a parliament of owls), culled from fifteenth century manuscripts and published under the title *An Exaltation of Larks* was found sufficiently original to support an infringement claim against a defendant who sold posters bearing a strikingly similar compilation.

(2) Consider the following pre-*Feist* case. Would the outcome remain the same if the case was litigated today? Plaintiffs published *Sport Americana Baseball Card Price Guide.* "The Guide lists some 18,000 different baseball cards and in each case furnishes the going market price. * * * The Guide also gives the prices for each card according to its condition: mint, very good/excellent and fair/good. In addition, the cards are placed into two groups; premium or star cards, and common cards. There are approximately 5,000 of the former, and they are considered particularly valuable because of the player featured on the card, e.g., a hall of famer, a rookie of the year, or because of the team on which he plays, or because of some characteristic of the card itself, such as an imperfection or the scarcity of the card. Common cards consist of the remaining cards listed in the series covered." Three months after publication of the *Guide,* the defendants began to publish *Card Price Update,* a monthly listing of baseball card prices. "CPU was published in a newspaper form, indicated the trends in prices by a plus or minus and listed separately only premium cards; however, its listing contained substantially the same 5,000 cards that the Guide had listed as premium cards. * * * [M]any of the prices and pictures in CPU are the same as those in the Guide, and a number of inadvertent errors in the Guide, including misspellings, inconsistent use of abbreviations and obvious omissions, are repeated in CPU." The court concluded that the *Guide* was copyrightable, and that the defendants had infringed. Eckes v. Card Prices Update, 736 F.2d 859 (2d Cir.1984).

(3) As the *Eckes* case illustrates, the presence of common errors can be compelling evidence of copying. See, e.g., Lakedale Tel. Co. v. Fronteer Directory Co., 230 U.S.P.Q. 694 (D.Minn.1986). The "errors" in a copyrighted work are not always inadvertent. See Rockford Map Pub., Inc. v. Directory Service Co., 768 F.2d 145 (7th Cir.1985), cert. denied, 474 U.S. 1061 (1986), in which bogus middle initials of landowners on a plat map, spelling out the name of the copyright owner, also appeared on the defendant's map. (Do publishers of casebooks employ similar stratagems?) Proof of copying through common errors, however, does not necessarily establish infringement. See Cooling Systems and Flexibles, Inc. v. Stuart Radiator, Inc., 777 F.2d 485 (9th Cir.1985) (copied errors were part of uncopyrightable factual material).

[handwritten margin note: common errors in copyrighten material can be evidence of copying]

[handwritten margin note: Paper towns]

(4) One way to avoid the limitations on the scope of copyright protection for compilations is to convince the court that the compiled items are themselves copyrightable. In CDN Inc. v. Kapes, 197 F.3d 1256 (9th Cir.1999), the plaintiff was the publisher of a weekly newsletter containing prices for collectible coins. It complained about a defendant who had used the prices as a baseline for a price list available on the Internet. Plaintiff did not allege copying of its selection or arrangement, arguing instead that "the prices themselves are sufficiently original as compilations to sustain a copyright." The Ninth Circuit agreed. "CDN's process to arrive at wholesale prices begins with examining the major coin publications to find relevant retail price information. CDN then reviews this data to retain only that information it considers to be the most accurate and important. Prices for each grade of coin are determined with attention to whether the coin is graded by a professional service (and which one). CDN also reviews the online networks for the bid and ask prices posted by dealers. * * * CDN also considers the impact of public auctions and private sales, and analyzes the effect of the economy and foreign policies on the price of coins. As the district court found, CDN does not republish data from another source or apply a set formula or rule to generate prices. The prices CDN creates are compilations of data that represent its best estimate of the value of the coins."

The Ninth Circuit's opinion relied on a similar result reached by the Second Circuit in CCC Information Services, Inc. v. Maclean Hunter Market Reports, Inc., 44 F.3d 61 (2d Cir.1994), cert. denied, 516 U.S. 817 (1995), which held used car valuations copyrightable: "[The] valuations were neither reports of historical prices nor mechanical derivations of historical prices or other data. Rather, they represent predictions by the Red Book editors of future prices estimated to cover specified geographic regions. According to Maclean's evidence, these predictions were based not only on a multitude of data sources, but also on professional judgment and expertise." Does the statement of a coin's value or a used car's price represent a work of authorship?

[handwritten margin note: used car valuations are copyrightable]

The Second Circuit distinguished its decision on car valuations in N.Y. Mercantile Exchange, Inc. v. IntercontinentalExchange, Inc., 497 F.3d 109 (2d Cir.2007), cert. denied, 552 U.S. 1259 (2008), when a commodity exchange claimed protection for the daily settlement prices of commodity futures contracts. First, since the *CCC Information* case found that the compilation as a whole was protectable, the court said the holding that the individual car prices were copyrightable was dicta. Second, the used car prices represented predictions of value created by the editors, while the settlement prices here were arguably facts based on actual trades. In any event, even if the settlement prices were copyrightable, the merger doctrine (see p. 109) operated to bar protection since all possible expressions of the settlement prices must take the same form.

Judge Katzmann also concluded that unlike the editors in *CCC Information*, the plaintiff here did not need the incentive of copyright; establishing settlement prices was necessary to its business and was also required by law. J. Hughes, Created Facts and the Flawed Ontology of Copyright Law, 83 Notre Dame L.Rev. 43 (2007), concludes that the law should protect "created facts" like the car valuations in *CCC Information* if copyright's incentive is necessary to the creation of the "facts," but D. Burk, Method and Madness in Copyright Law, 2007 Utah L.Rev. 587, argues that cases like *CCC Information* in effect protect the underlying processes that produce the protected output. A. Durham, Speaking of the World: Fact, Opinion, and the Originality Standard of Copyright, 33 Ariz.St.L.J. 791 (2001), criticizes cases that find protectable originality in "facts," however derived.

The decisions in *CDN* and *CCC Information* were invoked in Health Grades v. Robert Wood Johnson Univ. Hospital, Inc., 634 F.Supp.2d 1226 (D.Colo.2009), to justify the denial of a motion to dismiss a copyright infringement claim brought against a hospital that had copied information about its "star ratings" and awards from plaintiff Health Grades' website. The complaint alleged that the healthcare ratings were the product of Health Grades' collection of data from various sources, which it then analyzed using its own proprietary methodologies. "Health Grades has sufficiently alleged that the ratings and awards copied by RWJ are original compilations of fact subject to copyright protection, rather than 'discovered' facts outside the protection of copyright." A similar result was reached in National Football Scouting, Inc. v. Rang, 2012 WL 6444226 (W.D.Wash.2012), finding grades given to college football players by NFL scouts copyrightable. The varying judicial responses to claims of protection for "ratings" are analyzed in J. Grimmelmann, Three Theories of Copyright in Ratings, 14 Vand.J.Ent. & Tech.L. 851 (2010).

(5) Commentary on *Feist* has been profuse. See, e.g., R. Dreyfuss, A *Wiseguy's* Approach to Information Products: Muscling Copyright and Patent Into a Unitary Theory of Intellectual Property, 1992 Sup.Ct.Rev. 195, worrying about the preservation of incentives to compile and arguing for greater flexibility in defining rights and remedies in preference to an all or nothing approach; D. Shipley, Thin But Not Anorexic: Copyright Protection for Compilations and Other Fact Works, 15 J.Intell.Prop. 91 (2007), thinks that case-by-case applications of *Feist* are working well to preserve a proper balance between access and protection.

(6) A notable feature of the *Feist* opinion is its repetitive invocation of the Constitution (at least 13 times) as the source of the requirement of original authorship. This constitutional emphasis is decried in P. Heald, The Vices of Originality, 1991 Sup.Ct.Rev. 143 (1992), but applauded for its steadying influence in H. Abrams, Originality and Creativity in Copyright Law, 55 L. & Contemp.Prob. (No. 2) 3 (1992). It is a recurring theme among the commentators that the Supreme Court did little to clarify the concept of "authorship"—the apparently modest requirement of some minimal creativity.

———

PROBLEM: West publishes judicial opinions in the familiar series of books known as the National Reporter System. After receiving an opinion from a court, West checks the accuracy of the citations and adds headnotes and a synopsis. West then separates state and federal opinions. State opinions are then divided by geographic region and assigned to the appropriate regional reporter. Federal decisions are separated according to the level of the issuing court. District court decisions are further divided by separating bankruptcy decisions and federal rules decisions from other district court decisions.

After the decisions are designated for a particular reporter series, they are assigned to the current volume of the series and arranged within the volume. Decisions in the *Federal Reporter*, for example, are arranged by circuit, although typically there are more than one group of each circuit's opinions in a single volume. The volumes and pages are numbered sequentially.

Mead Data Central operated LEXIS, the computer-assisted legal research service. Mead Data announced its intention to add "star pagination" to the decisions in its database. This feature would consist of "page breaks" inserted into the text of opinions in LEXIS. The "page breaks" are brackets containing the page numbers from the West report of the case, inserted into the text of the LEXIS opinion at the point where one West page ends and the next begins. The feature would permit LEXIS users to cite to the specific page of the West reporter on which a relevant quotation or point of law appears without actually consulting the West reporter volume. West responded to Mead Data's announcement with a complaint alleging infringement of the copyright in its compilation of cases and moved for a preliminary injunction. Does West have a copyright in its arrangement of judicial opinions? If so, does the star pagination feature infringe that copyright?

In West Publishing Co. v. Mead Data Central, Inc., 799 F.2d 1219 (8th Cir.1986), cert. denied, 479 U.S. 1070 (1987), the Eighth Circuit held that the "labor, talent, and judgment" used to arrange the cases was sufficient for copyright. Star pagination was an infringement since it could allow LEXIS users to page through the cases in the order in which they appeared in the West reporter. After the decision on the preliminary injunction, the case proceeded to trial, but the suit was settled when the parties agreed to a license. The decision and settlement are criticized in L. Patterson and C. Joyce, Monopolizing the Law: The Scope of Copyright Protection for Law Reports and Statutory Codes, 36 UCLA. L.Rev. 719 (1989).

More recently, the Second Circuit in Matthew Bender & Co. v. West Pub. Co., 158 F.3d 693 (2d Cir.1998), cert. denied, 526 U.S. 1154 (1999), held in a 2–1 decision that star pagination to West reporters appearing in the defendant's CD–ROM collection of judicial opinions was not an infringement. The court found it unnecessary to decide whether West's arrangement of cases was copyrightable, since star pagination did not infringe any copyright that West might have in its arrangement. According to the court, the arrangement of cases was already revealed through the defendant's use of parallel citations to the West reports at the beginning of every case, which even West agreed was a permissible fair use. The addition of star pagination merely revealed the location of the internal page breaks in the West reports, which the court said were not copyrightable. Alternatively, the court held that the CD–ROMs did not reproduce West's arrangement—the cases were not physically fixed on the discs in the sequence found in the West reporters, and "[a]t least absent some invitation, incentive, or facilitation not in the record here, a copyrighted arrangement is not infringed by a CD–ROM disc if a machine can perceive the arrangement only after another person uses the machine to re-arrange the material into the copyrightholder's arrangement." In a separate 2–1 decision, the Second Circuit affirmed a declaratory judgment that West's addition of parallel citations, attorney information, and procedural history to the opinions was not copyrightable. (The defendant had not copied West's syllabi, headnotes, or key numbers.) Matthew Bender & Co. v. West Pub. Co., 158 F.3d 674 (2d Cir.1998), cert. denied, 526 U.S. 1154 (1999).[i]

NOTES ON DATABASES

(1) A computer database is in essence an automated compilation—a collection of information capable of being manipulated and retrieved by an appropriate search program. WESTLAW and LEXIS are computer databases. So is the computerized listing of names and numbers used by telephone companies. The House Report states that the term "literary work * * * includes computer data bases." H.R.Rep. p. 54.

The issue of copyright in computer databases was among those examined by the National Commission on New Technological Uses of Copyrighted Works. The CONTU Report in 1978 concluded that computer databases are eligible for protection as "compilations" under the Copyright Act. It is often difficult, however, to think in terms of an arrangement of information in a computer database. The format in which the information is stored depends primarily on the nature of the particular storage media, and the form in which the information is retrieved is often controlled by the user. The CONTU Report concludes that an "unauthorized taking of substantial segments of a copyrighted data base should be considered infringing." CONTU Rep. p. 42. Is this consistent with the Supreme Court's subsequent decision in *Feist*?

(2) Are compilations sufficiently distinctive to justify a separate statutory regime more precisely attuned than copyright to the nature and value of such works? In 1996, the European Union adopted a Directive on Legal Protection of Databases that requires member nations to grant protection against unauthorized "extraction" and "reutilization" of a "substantial part" of a database, irrespective of the work's eligibility for copyright. Protection for foreign databases is available within the EU only on the basis of reciprocal protection for EU databases in the foreign country.[j] There have also been proposals for an international system of sui generis database protection, but the push for an international treaty has been stalled by a coalition of scientific and educational organizations and developing nations.[k]

Sui generis

---

[i]   Would anything prevent another copier from simply duplicating and selling the first copier's CD–ROM? Soon after its victory over West, Matthew Bender was forced to defend its own compilation of judicial decisions against another legal publisher that copied from Matthew Bender to produce a rival product. Matthew Bender relied on state law, alleging that the defendant committed fraud in accessing the database and also violated a shrinkwrap license. Matthew Bender & Co. v. Jurisline.Com LLC, 91 F.Supp.2d 677 (S.D.N.Y.2000). The case was settled.

[j]   In 2005, the European Commission published DG Internal Market and Services Working Paper, First Evaluation of Directive 96/9/EC on the Legal Protection of Databases (Dec. 12, 2005). After stating that "[t]he economic impact of the 'sui generis' right on database production is unproven," the report noted that "[t]he ratio of European/US database production, which was nearly 1:2 in 1996, has become 1:3 in 2004." "[T]here has been a considerable growth in database production in the US, whereas, in the EU, the introduction of 'sui generis' protection appears to have had the opposite effect. With respect to 'non-original' databases, the assumption that more and more layers of IP protection means more innovation and growth appears not to hold up."

[k]   C. McManis, Database Protection in the Digital Information Age, 7 Roger Williams U.L.Rev. 7 (2001), counsels against broad database protection propelled by a desire for reciprocal protection abroad; J. Gibson, Re–Reifying Data, 80 Notre Dame L.Rev. 163 (2004), concludes that any expansion of database protection should be accompanied by a deposit requirement to assure whatever public access the legal entitlement allows.

Attempts to enact sui generis database protection in the United States began in 1996. In light of *Feist*'s emphasis on the constitutional basis of originality, does Congress have the power to protect unoriginal compilations? Could it rely on its authority under the commerce clause? A 1997 Copyright Office report on database protection prepared at the request of the Senate Judiciary Committee declined to offer a recommendation on sui generis legislation; it did, however, address the constitutional issue: "To the extent that the legislation promotes different policies from copyright, and does so in a different manner, it is similar to trademark law, and therefore seems likely to survive a constitutional challenge." The report also raised first amendment concerns, although it concluded that a legislative pronouncement confirming that individual facts remain in the public domain might be sufficient.[1] Meanwhile, the push for sui generis database protection continues amid concern by researchers and librarians that increased protection would undermine access to information essential to research. Producers continue to complain that because of the reciprocity requirement in the European Union Database Directive, American database developers will remain at a disadvantage until the U.S. adopts its own protection scheme. Some of the proposals are reviewed in J. Reichman and P. Uhlir, Database Protection at the Crossroads: Recent Developments and Their Impact on Science and Technology, 14 Berk.Tech.L.J. 793 (1999), which advocates a cautious approach limiting protection to unfair uses that harm the market for the database. J. Lipton, Balancing Private Rights and Public Policies: Reconceptalizing Property in Databases, 18 Berk.Tech.L.J. 773 (2003), suggests sui generis protection tempered by compulsory licenses and government supervision.[m]

(3) Looking ahead, could *state* law prohibit the reproduction of factual information contained in a compilation? A number of cases indicate that § 301 of the Copyright Act preempts such state protection. See, e.g., Financial Information, Inc. v. Moody's Investors Service, Inc., 808 F.2d 204 (2d Cir.1986), cert. denied, 484 U.S. 820 (1987).

---

[1] The constitutional constraints on the protection of databases are examined in P. Heald, The Extraction/Duplication Dichotomy: Constitutional Line–Drawing in the Database Debate, 62 Ohio St.L.J. 933 (2001), and M. Pollack, The Right to Know?: Delimiting Database Protection at the Juncture of the Commerce Clause, the Intellectual Property Clause, and the First Amendment, 17 Cardozo Arts & Ent.L.J. 47 (1999). J. Hughes, How Extra–Copyright Protection of Databases Can be Constitutional, 28 U. Dayton L.Rev. 159 (2003), speculates on how to craft a database bill that will pass constitutional muster.

[m] The House Energy and Commerce Committee, reporting unfavorably on a database bill in 2004, offered this analysis: "[Since *Feist*], the proponents of the legislation have produced no compelling evidence that there is any danger to the continued prosperity of the database industry. In fact, a 2003 report by Dr. Martha E. Williams entitled, *The State of Databases Today*, showed an increase in the total number of databases as well as an increase in the private sector's share of the database market. * * * [T]here has been a steady shift in database production, away from government and academic production and toward private sector production. In 1990, government databases made up 17% of the database market, academic databases made up 12%, and private sector databases made up 68%. By 2002, the private sector had grown to constitute 90% of the total database market." H.R.Rep. No. 108–437, 108th Cong., 2d Sess. 2–3 (2004).

MAPS

United States v. Hamilton

United States Court of Appeals, Ninth Circuit, 1978.
583 F.2d 448.

■ Before KILKENNY, SNEED, and KENNEDY, CIRCUIT JUDGES.

■ KENNEDY, CIRCUIT JUDGE:

The defendant in this criminal case admitted making and selling precise reproductions of a map bearing a copyright. The sole issue on appeal is whether the map that the defendant copied was of such originality that its copyright was valid. That inquiry requires us to decide a question of copyright law not addressed by previous decisions in this circuit.

The defendant, Edward S. Hamilton, was charged with two counts of knowing and willful infringement of a copyright in violation of 17 U.S.C. § 104.[1] [Section 104 of the 1909 Act imposed criminal penalties for willful infringement.]

The district court, sitting without a jury, found the defendant guilty and imposed a $700 fine. We find, as did the district court, that the copyright is valid; and the conviction is affirmed.

The maps involved in this case show the boundaries, roads, terrain, features, and improved areas of Ada County, Idaho. KDB Enterprises, a company which specializes in making maps of the Pacific Northwest and which holds about ninety copyrights for various maps, produced a map of Ada County, Idaho in 1970 and obtained copyright for it. KDB then produced a second map of Ada County in 1973 and received a certificate of copyright covering the new matter included on that map. The defendant here was charged with infringing the 1973 copyright by reproducing this second map, and all that is before us is the validity of the copyright for the map of later date.

Hamilton's principal contention, both here and in the trial court, has been that KDB's 1973 map lacks the quality of originality requisite for obtaining a copyright because it was merely a synthesis of information already depicted on maps in the public domain. The 1973 map did show terrain features which had been physically located by a KDB employee and which did not appear on any preexisting map. But a contribution which is more than merely trivial is required in order to satisfy the originality requirement of the Constitution and the copyright statutes, Alfred Bell & Co. v. Catalda Fine Arts, Inc., 191 F.2d 99, 102–03 (2d Cir.1951), and the defendant claims KDB's terrain investigations were so minimal that the 1973 map is not an original work. On the record before us it is a close question whether the extent of the geographic investigation done by KDB was so substantial that, considered alone, it can support the map copyright. We therefore find it necessary to decide whether the map maker's selection, arrangement, and presentation of terrain features which were already either in the public domain or subject to separate copyright (that KDB had a right to use) may be considered as part of the efforts and skill which constitute a cartographer's authorship.

---

[1] The alleged copyright infringement took place prior to the January 1, 1978 effective date of the 1976 General Revision of Copyright Law. 17 U.S.C. § 101 et seq. (1976).

The Third Circuit has held that a map which represents a new combination of information already in the public domain lacks any element worthy of copyright protection. *Amsterdam v. Triangle Publications*, 93 F.Supp. 79 (E.D.Pa.1950), aff'd on opinion below, 189 F.2d 104 (3d Cir.1951). The *Amsterdam* court stated that a map may not be put under copyright unless "the publisher of the map in question obtains originally some of that information by the sweat of his own brow." 93 F.Supp. at 82. Thus, under the *Amsterdam* rule, as applied to this case, only those portions of the map recorded as a result of direct observation of terrain features would support the copyright. * * *

Amsterdam and perhaps the copyright cases from this circuit cited above suggest that we should insist upon a standard of originality that is more demanding in cases respecting maps than with other works subject to copyright. If this approach reflects a concern that cartographers might be excluded entirely from using valuable maps in the public domain because a private party has a previous copyright on a map which utilizes the public domain information, the fear, of course, is a false one; for the fact that one person studies other works so as to produce from those elements a new work with sufficient originality to obtain a copyright does not prevent a different author from making independent use of his own skills and efforts to do precisely the same thing. In this respect, the danger of removing a whole subject area from the public realm of experimentation and design does not exist, as it does under the patent laws, which permit the owner of a valid patent to exclude others from infringement even if they created the object or device solely by efforts of their own.

Amsterdam appears to rest on the judgment that the only facet of cartography that can result in an original product, the only feature of the art worth protecting, results from direct observation. However, we are unable to find a persuasive reason for adopting this premise, and we therefore decline to rule that maps present considerations that are distinct from all other copyright cases. Expression in cartography is not so different from other artistic forms seeking to touch upon external realities that unique rules are needed to judge whether the authorship is original. Recording by direct observation is only one measure of a cartographer's skill and talent, and originality should not be made synonymous with a requirement that features of a copyrighted map be observed and recorded directly before they will be entitled to copyright protection. For this reason, we think the *Amsterdam* rule is theoretically unsound. We are aware that under the conventional standards for determining originality a cartographer occasionally may have some difficulty proving that his map is an original compilation rather than a mere imitation. But this problem of proof does not justify failing to protect the many cartographers whose claims of original work can be established. Not protecting the product of creative compilation or synthesis would discourage progress in the field of cartography much more than the difficulty in a few cases of proving originality under the conventional standards. * * *

* * * Trivial elements of compilation and arrangement, of course, are not copyrightable since they fall below the threshold of originality. For example, it is well-settled that copyright of a map does not give the author an exclusive right to the coloring, symbols, and key used in delineating boundaries of and locations within the territory depicted. *Perris v. Hexamer*, 99 U.S. (9 Otto) 674, 675–76 (1878); *Christianson v. West Publishing Co.*, 149 F.2d 202, 203–04 (9th Cir.1945).

That maps have sufficient originality to support a copyright has been recognized since the first copyright statute, enacted in 1790, provided coverage for "maps, charts, and books." 1 Stat. 124 (1790). The early cases recognized that "[t]he elements of the copyright [in a map] consist in the selection, arrangement, and presentation of the component parts." General Drafting Co. v. Andrews, 37 F.2d 54, 55 (2d Cir.1930). See Emerson v. Davies, 8 Fed.Cas. 615, 619 (Cir.Ct.D.Mass.1845) (Story, J.). We rule that elements of compilation which amount to more than a matter of trivial selection may, either alone or when taken into consideration with direct observation, support a finding that a map is sufficiently original to merit copyright protection. Beginning with the Supreme Court's decision in Burrow–Giles Lithographic Co. v. Sarony, 111 U.S. 53 (1884), the courts have carefully delineated selection of subject, posture, background, lighting, and perhaps even perspective alone as protectible elements of a photographer's work. See, e.g., Time, Inc. v. Bernard Geis Associates, 293 F.Supp. 130, 141–43 (S.D.N.Y.1968). Similar attention to rewarding the cartographer's art requires us to recognize that the elements of authorship embodied in a map consist not only of the depiction of a previously undiscovered landmark or the correction or improvement of scale or placement, but also in selection, design, and synthesis.[5]

The record below establishes that there are elements both of synthesis from public sources and independent observation in the efforts used to create the 1973 map, and we find that, taken together, they support the validity of the 1973 copyright.

KDB used an Idaho Department of Highways map as the principal base in preparing the 1973 map. It relied upon the 1970 KDB map for some data added to the base. Substantial portions of the roads, landmarks, and features depicted on the 1973 KDB map also appear on maps published by United States Geological Survey, United States Forest Service, and the Bureau of Land Management. We think that the compilation that produced the 1973 map was a result of substantial creative efforts, and we weigh it heavily in support of the finding that the 1973 map was an original work.

In addition to the compilation and synthesis from the other maps, which were put in evidence, the court also found that "a significant portion" of the information on the 1973 KDB map, including rifle ranges, landing strips, motorcycle and jeep trails, landmarks, and names of subdivisions came from other sources. It is clear from the record that at least some of this information was derived from personal observations of a KDB employee who checked the motorcycle trails and other landmarks by ground and aerial observations. The parties differ as to whether the sources of the added information were in the public domain or were from direct observations of the KDB employees, but in our view of the matter that is irrelevant since synthesis can be an element of originality. The new information, when taken into account with the compilation and synthesis from the maps that were introduced in evidence, makes the 1973 map an original one that is subject to copyright. We conclude that the 1973 KDB map was an original

---

[5] We emphasize that compilations or new arrangements of material which represent merely trivial additions to or omissions from a preexisting map will not support a copyright absent some additional original work. For example, copying the outline of the United States and the boundaries of each state cannot be said to involve any element of original choice or arrangement. Christianson v. West Publishing Co., 149 F.2d 202 (9th Cir.1945). Similarly, the selection of principal cities of North America partly from memory and partly from census reports is "far from constituting such originality as to form a basis for copyright." Andrews v. Guenther Publishing Co., 60 F.2d 555, 557 (S.D.N.Y.1932).

product of significant efforts expended by those skilled in the cartographer's art. The copyright was valid. This being the only issue raised by Hamilton on appeal, his conviction must be affirmed.

Mason v. Montgomery Data, Inc.

967 F.2d 135 (5th Cir.1992).

Mason claimed copyright in a series of maps showing the ownership of real estate in Montgomery County, Texas. The information depicted on Mason's maps came from several sources, including tax and survey records, title abstracts, and existing city and county maps. He claimed infringement when title companies began to make unauthorized copies. The defendants did not dispute that Mason independently created his maps; the issue was whether the maps possessed the "minimal degree of creativity" required under *Feist*.

"Mason's maps pass muster under *Feist* because Mason's selection, coordination, and arrangement of the information that he depicted are sufficiently creative to qualify his maps as original 'compilations' of facts. * * * In his deposition and affidavit, Mason explained the choices that he independently made to select information from numerous and sometimes conflicting sources, and to depict that information on his maps.

"Mason's maps also possess sufficient creativity to merit copyright protection as pictorial and graphic works of authorship. Historically, most courts have treated maps solely as compilations of facts. * * * The Copyright Act, however, categorizes maps not as factual compilations but as 'pictorial, graphic, and sculptural works'—a category that includes photographs and architectural plans. * * *

"Because Mason's maps possess sufficient creativity in both the selection, coordination, and arrangement of the facts that they depict, and as in the pictorial, graphic nature of the way that they do so, we find no error in the district court's determination that Mason's maps are original."

NOTES AND QUESTIONS

(1) Both KDB's and Mason's maps were derivative works. What leeway to copy might this give the defendants? See § 103. Cf. C.S. Hammond & Co. v. International College Globe, Inc., 210 F.Supp. 206 (S.D.N.Y.1962) (defendant used plaintiff's globe and other sources; no infringement found). On the "thin" protection available to maps under the *Feist* rationale, see the Second Circuit's decision in Streetwise Maps, Inc. v. VanDam, Inc., 159 F.3d 739 (2d Cir.1998), limiting protection to the plaintiff's original selection and arrangement of expressive elements, including colors. *Mason* and the issue of copyright protection for maps in the post-*Feist* era are reviewed in D. Karjala, Copyright in Electronic Maps, 35 Jurimetrics J. 395 (1995), sensing a return to "sweat of the brow" protection.

(2) The defendants in *Mason* also challenged the copyrightability of the maps under the "merger" doctrine, which holds, roughly, that when there is only one way to express an idea, copying will be permitted in order to avoid giving the first author a monopoly over the idea itself. See p. 109 infra. The court rejected the defense, holding that protection for Mason's maps "will not grant Mason a monopoly over the idea [of an effective pictorial expression of land ownership], because other mapmakers can express the same idea differently." The court distinguished its earlier decision in Kern River Gas Transmission Co. v. Coastal Corp., 899 F.2d 1458 (5th Cir.), cert. denied, 498 U.S. 952 (1990), in which the court applied the merger doctrine to deny copyright to a map depicting the proposed location of a gas pipeline.

2. THE LIMITS OF STATUTORY SUBJECT MATTER

Baker v. Selden

Supreme Court of the United States, 1880.
101 U.S. 99.

■ MR. JUSTICE BRADLEY delivered the opinion of the court.

Charles Selden, the testator of the complainant in this case, in the year 1859 took the requisite steps for obtaining the copyright of a book, entitled "Selden's Condensed Ledger, or Bookkeeping Simplified," the object of which was to exhibit and explain a peculiar system of book-keeping. In 1860 and 1861, he took the copyright of several other books, containing additions to and improvements upon the said system. The bill of complaint was filed against the defendant, Baker, for an alleged infringement of these copyrights. The latter, in his answer, denied that Selden was the author or designer of the books, and denied the infringement charged, and contends on the argument that the matter alleged to be infringed is not a lawful subject of copyright.

The parties went into proofs, and the various books of the complainant, as well as those sold and used by the defendant, were exhibited before the examiner, and witnesses were examined on both sides. A decree was rendered for the complainant, and the defendant appealed.

The book or series of books of which the complainant claims the copyright consists of an introductory essay explaining the system of book-keeping referred to, to which are annexed certain forms or blanks, consisting of ruled lines, and headings, illustrating the system and showing how it is to be used and carried out in practice. This system effects the same results as book-keeping by double entry; but, by a peculiar arrangement of columns and headings, presents the entire operation, of a day, a week, or a month, on a single page, or on two pages facing each other, in an account-book. The defendant uses a similar plan so far as results are concerned; but makes a different arrangement of the columns, and uses different headings. If the complainant's testator had the exclusive right to the use of the system explained in his book, it would be difficult to contend that the defendant does not infringe it, notwithstanding the difference in his form of arrangement; but if it be assumed that the system is open to public use, it seems to be equally difficult to contend that the books made and sold by the defendant are a violation of the copyright of the complainant's book considered merely as a book explanatory of the system. Where the truths of a science or the methods of an art are the common property of the whole world, any author has the right to express the one, or explain and use the other, in his own way. As an author, Selden explained the system in a particular way. It may be conceded that Baker makes and uses account-books arranged on substantially the same system; but the proof fails to show that he has violated the copyright of Selden's book, regarding the latter merely as an explanatory work; or that he has infringed Selden's right in any way, unless the latter became entitled to an exclusive right in the system.

The evidence of the complainant is principally directed to the object of showing that Baker uses the same system as that which is explained and illustrated in Selden's books. It becomes important, therefore, to determine whether, in obtaining the copyright of his books, he secured the exclusive right to the use of the system or method of book-keeping which the said books are intended to illustrate and explain. It is contended that he has secured such exclusive right, because no one can use the system without using substantially the same ruled lines and headings which he has appended to his books in illustration of it. In other words, it is contended that the ruled lines and headings, given to illustrate the system, are a part of the book, and, as such, are secured by the copyright; and that no one can make or use similar ruled lines and headings, or ruled lines and headings made and arranged on substantially the same system, without violating the copyright. And this is really the question to be decided in this case. Stated in another form, the question is, whether the exclusive property in a system of book-keeping can be claimed, under the law of copyright, by means of a book in which that system is explained? The complainant's bill, and the case made under it, are based on the hypothesis that it can be.

It cannot be pretended, and indeed it is not seriously urged, that the ruled lines of the complainant's account-book can be claimed under any special class of objects, other than books, named in the law of copyright existing in 1859. The law then in force was that of 1831, and specified only books, maps, charts, musical compositions, prints, and engravings. An account-book, consisting of ruled lines and blank columns, cannot be called by any of these names unless by that of a book.

There is no doubt that a work on the subject of book-keeping, though only explanatory of well-known systems, may be the subject of a copyright; but, then, it is claimed only as a book. Such a book may be explanatory either of old systems, or of an entirely new system; and, considered as a book, as the work of an author, conveying information on the subject of book-keeping, and containing detailed explanations of the art, it may be a very valuable acquisition to the practical knowledge of the community. But there is a clear distinction between the book, as such, and the art which it is intended to illustrate. The mere statement of the proposition is so evident, that it requires hardly any argument to support it. The same distinction may be predicated of every other art as well as that of book-keeping. A treatise on the composition and use of medicines, be they old or new; on the construction and use of ploughs, or watches, or churns; or on the mixture and application of colors for painting or dyeing; or on the mode of drawing lines to produce the effect of perspective,—would be the subject of copyright; but no one would contend that the copyright of the treatise would give the exclusive right to the art or manufacture described therein. The copyright of the book, if not pirated from other works, would be valid without regard to the novelty, or want of novelty, of its subject-matter. The novelty of the art or thing described or explained has nothing to do with the validity of the copyright. To give to the author of the book an exclusive property in the art described therein, when no examination of its novelty has ever been officially made, would be a surprise and a fraud upon the public. That is the province of letters-patent, not of copyright. The claim to an invention or discovery of an art or manufacture must be subjected to the examination of the Patent Office before an exclusive right therein can be obtained; and it can only be secured by a patent from the government.

The difference between the two things, letters-patent and copyright, may be illustrated by reference to the subjects just enumerated. Take the case of medicines. Certain mixtures are found to be of great value in the healing art. If the discoverer writes and publishes a book on the subject (as regular physicians generally do), he gains no exclusive right to the manufacture and sale of the medicine; he gives that to the public. If he desires to acquire such exclusive right, he must obtain a patent for the mixture as a new art, manufacture, or composition of matter. He may copyright his book, if he pleases; but that only secures to him the exclusive right of printing and publishing his book. So of all other inventions or discoveries.

The copyright of a book on perspective, no matter how many drawings and illustrations it may contain, gives no exclusive right to the modes of drawing described, though they may never have been known or used before. By publishing the book, without getting a patent for the art, the latter is given to the public. The fact that the art described in the book by illustrations of lines and figures which are reproduced in practice in the application of the art, makes no difference. Those illustrations are the mere language employed by the author to convey his ideas more clearly. Had he used words of description instead of diagrams (which merely stand in the place of words), there could not be the slightest doubt that others, applying the art to practical use, might lawfully draw the lines and diagrams which were in the author's mind, and which he thus described by words in his book.

The copyright of a work on mathematical science cannot give to the author an exclusive right to the methods of operation which he propounds, or to the diagrams which he employs to explain them, so as to prevent an engineer from using them whenever occasion requires. The very object of publishing a book on science or the useful arts is to communicate to the world the useful knowledge which it contains. But this object would be frustrated if the knowledge could not be used without incurring the guilt of piracy of the book. And where the art it teaches cannot be used without employing the methods and diagrams used to illustrate the book, or such as are similar to them, such methods and diagrams are to be considered as necessary incidents to the art, and given therewith to the public; not given for the purpose of publication in other works explanatory of the art, but for the purpose of practical application.

Of course, these observations are not intended to apply to ornamental designs, or pictorial illustrations addressed to the taste. Of these it may be said, that their form is their essence, and their object, the production of pleasure in their contemplation. This is their final end. They are as much the product of genius and the result of composition, as are the lines of the poet or the historian's periods. On the other hand, the teachings of science and the rules and methods of useful art have their final end in application and use; and this application and use are what the public derive from the publication of a book which teaches them. But as embodied and taught in a literary composition or book, their essence consists only in their statement. This alone is what is secured by the copyright. The use by another of the same methods of statement, whether in words or illustrations, in a book published for teaching the art, would undoubtedly be an infringement of the copyright.

ONE OF SELDEN'S BOOKKEEPING FORMS

[F2709]

Recurring to the case before us, we observe that Charles Selden, by his books, explained and described a peculiar system of book-keeping, and illustrated his method by means of ruled lines and blank columns, with proper headings on a page, or on successive pages. Now, whilst no one has a right to print or publish his book, or any material part thereof, as a book intended to convey instruction in the art, any person may practice and use the art itself which he has described and illustrated therein. The use of the art is a totally different thing from a publication of the book explaining it. The copyright of a book on book-keeping cannot secure the exclusive right to make, sell, and use account-books prepared upon the plan set forth in such book. Whether the art might or might not have been patented, is a question which is not before us. It was not patented, and is open and free to the use of the public. And, of course, in using the art, the ruled lines and headings of accounts must necessarily be used as incident to it.

The plausibility of the claim put forward by the complainant in this case arises from a confusion of ideas produced by the peculiar nature of the art described in the books which have been made the subject of copyright. In describing the art, the illustrations and diagrams employed happen to correspond more closely than usual with the actual work performed by the operator who uses the art. Those illustrations and diagrams consist of ruled lines and headings of accounts; and it is similar ruled lines and headings of accounts which, in the application of the art, the book-keeper makes with his pen, or the stationer with his press; whilst in most other cases the diagrams and illustrations can only be represented in concrete forms of wood, metal, stone, or some other physical embodiment. But the principle is the same in all. The description of the art in a book, though entitled to the benefit of copyright, lays no foundation for an exclusive claim to the art itself. The object of the one is explanation; the object of the other is use. The former may be secured by copyright. The latter can only be secured, if it can be secured at all, by letters-patent. * * *

The conclusion to which we have come is, that blank account-books are not the subject of copyright; and that the mere copyright of Selden's book did not confer upon him the exclusive right to make and use account-books, ruled and arranged as designated by him and described and illustrated in said book.

The decree of the Circuit Court must be reversed, and the cause remanded with instructions to dismiss the complainant's bill; and it is

So ordered.

Fc reversed for Δ

NOTES AND QUESTIONS

(1) Is the "art" vs. "description of the art" distinction raised in Baker v. Selden merely an alternative form of the "idea" vs. "expression of the idea" distinction put forward in other cases and codified in § 102(b)?

(2) Does the Supreme Court assume that the plaintiff's "art" can be practiced only by means of substantially similar forms? Is this consistent with the Court's description of the defendant's account books? If similar forms are necessary to the system, is the Court's distinction between copying for use and copying for explanation appropriate? Can the distinction be maintained in view of the Court's holding, as stated at the conclusion of its opinion, "that blank account-books are not the subject of copyright"?

NOTES ON THE DENIAL OF COPYRIGHT IN "BLANK FORMS"

deny copyright to forms that don't convey info

(1) The Copyright Office has a regulation, 37 C.F.R. § 202(1)(c), denying copyright to "[b]lank forms, such as time cards, graph paper, account books, diaries, bank checks, scorecards, address books, report forms, order forms and the like, which are designed for recording information and do not in themselves convey information." Is this proposition required by Baker v. Selden? Or is it merely an application of the general criteria of "authorship"? Is the Copyright Office justified in requiring some level of expository content as a condition of copyright?

The Copyright Office in 1979 announced a rulemaking inquiry "regarding blank forms," but concluded the study in 1980 with a detailed statement in 45 Fed.Reg. 63297 that reviewed the case law and affirmed the blank form regulation as firmly based on both Baker v. Selden and the general requirement of "original, creative expression." See Bibbero Systems, Inc. v. Colwell Systems, Inc., 893 F.2d 1104 (9th Cir.1990), denying copyright in a medical claim form despite the inclusion of instructions, checklists, and assignment of claims provisions, but noting that "cases interpreting the blank forms rule do not yield a consistent line of reasoning"; Utopia Provider Sys., Inc. v. Pro–Med Clinical Sys., LLC, 596 F.3d 1313 (11th Cir.2010) (templates used by emergency room doctors were not copyrightable because the selection and arrangement of the requested information were not sufficiently original.)

(2) Taylor Instrument Cos. v. Fawley–Brost Co., 139 F.2d 98 (7th Cir.1943), cert. denied, 321 U.S. 785 (1944), was a suit for infringement of copyrighted charts used in connection with plaintiff's recording thermometers. Defendant's charts were copied from plaintiff's and in some instances bore symbols indicating that they fit the plaintiff's instruments. The court found plaintiff's charts uncopyrightable. In Brown Instrument Co. v. Warner, 161 F.2d 910 (D.C.Cir.), cert. denied, 332 U.S. 801 (1947), where the Copyright Office was upheld in refusing registration for a similar recording chart, the court said that *Taylor Instrument* was correctly decided and "moreover, that the case is controlled by Baker v. Selden." Judge Edgerton wrote:

> Articles intended for practical use in cooperation with a machine are not copyrightable. White–Smith Music Pub. Co. v. Apollo Co., 209 U.S. 1. Both law and policy forbid monopolizing a machine except within the comparatively narrow limits of the patent system. In several patents on recording machines, the necessary printed chart is rightly claimed as one of the operative elements. Since the machines which cooperate with the charts in suit are useless without them, to copyright the charts would in effect continue appellant's monopoly of its machines beyond the time authorized by the patent law.

Continental Casualty Co. v. Beardsley

United States Court of Appeals, Second Circuit, 1958.
253 F.2d 702.
Certiorari denied, 358 U.S. 816.

■ Before HINCKS and LUMBARD, CIRCUIT JUDGES, and DIMOCK, DISTRICT JUDGE.

■ HINCKS, CIRCUIT JUDGE. These are cross-appeals arising out of a suit brought by Continental Casualty Company (Continental) which sought a declaratory judgment that defendants' copyrights were invalid together with an injunction, an accounting, and counsel fees. Continental also demanded damages for unfair competition and violation of the antitrust laws. The defendant, Beardsley, counterclaimed alleging infringement by Continental of his valid copyrights and that Continental was liable for unfair competition. The District Court held that the material in question was not properly copyrightable; that, even if it were, the copyright had been lost; and, further, that there was no infringement. The District Court granted the declaratory relief sought by Continental and an injunction. It rejected the unfair competition claims of both parties and Continental's antitrust claim and its request for an accounting and counsel fees. Each party has appealed from every adverse ruling below. In addition, Beardsley contends that in any event the injunction is too broad.

Copyrightability

This controversy had its inception in the late 1930's. Defendant Beardsley was an insurance broker (also a member of the bar) who allegedly developed a blanket bond to cover replacement of lost securities which would operate *in futuro.* In September 1939, he published his "plan" in a six-page pamphlet. The entire pamphlet carried a copyright notice and Continental admits that the introductory three pages of narrative are validly copyrighted. As to these three pages, however, there is no claim of infringement. Continental contended below, and the court agreed, that the remaining three pages of forms to carry out the "plan" were not copyrightable. The forms included a proposed bond, an affidavit of loss and indemnity agreement, and drafts of an instruction letter and board resolutions. Beardsley had also devised various insurance instruments, some but not all of which he had copyrighted.

We find nothing which, as a matter of law, prevents the copyrighting of forms and insurance instruments such as those now before us. * * *

Notwithstanding this general authority in support of the copyrightability of forms, Continental relies upon Baker v. Selden, 101 U.S. 99. * * *

In Baker v. Selden, supra, the subject-matter was such that the explanation of the system could be treated as separable from account books prepared and arranged for the practice of the system. But not so here. For inseparably included in Beardsley's bonds and affidavits, which constitute the means for the practice of his Plan, is language explanatory of the Plan. Consequently, the holding of Baker v. Selden is not applicable here. See also Taylor Instrument Companies v. Fawley–Brost Co., 7 Cir., 139 F.2d 98, certiorari denied 321 U.S. 785, chart for recording temperatures; Aldrich v. Remington–Rand, D.C.N.D.Texas, 52 F.Supp. 732, sheets for keeping tax records; Page v. Wisden, 20 L.T.R. (n.s.) 435, cricket scoring sheet. And since the Constitution and Copyright Act read directly upon all the forms here involved, we hold them to be copyrightable.

This resolution of the question of copyrightability raises several very serious questions as to the scope of the protection granted which we now come to consider.

Infringement

We agree completely with the conclusion of the trial court that Beardsley did not succeed in proving infringement. * * *

There have been several cases dealing with the copyrighting of insurance and similar forms. Significantly, they uniformly are decided by holdings of non-infringement and leave undecided the copyrightability point.[3] These cases have set a stiff standard for proof of infringement.

In Dorsey v. Old Surety Life Ins. Co., 10 Cir., 98 F.2d 872, 874, the court found non-infringement declaring, "To constitute infringement in such cases a showing of appropriation in the exact form or substantially so of the copyrighted material should be required."

---

[3] We have had to decide the copyright question here because one portion of the judgment appealed from enjoined Beardsley from claiming a copyright on any of his forms.

In Crume v. Pacific Mut. Life Ins. Co., 7 Cir., 140 F.2d 182, certiorari denied 322 U.S. 755, the court found non-infringement of plaintiff's pamphlet describing a method for reorganizing insurance companies. As in all of these cases, the court was keenly aware that to prohibit similarity of language would have the effect of giving the copyright owner a monopoly on his idea—which the cases uniformly deny to copyright owners. Thus, the court stated, 140 F.2d at pages 184–185:

" * * * In the instant situation there is no room for the skill of the mechanic or artisan in utilizing the plan or the method disclosed. Its use, to which the public is entitled, can be effected solely by the employment of words descriptive thereof. In our view, where the use can be effected only in such manner, there can be no infringement even though the plan or method be copied. We realize that such a view leaves little, if any, protection to the copyright owners; in fact, it comes near to invalidating the copyright. This situation, however, results from the fact that the practical use of the art explained by the copyright and lodged in the public domain can be attained solely by the employment of language which gives expression to that which is disclosed." Further, "We also observe that such comparison [of the documents] adds strength to the view heretofore expressed that defendant's rightful use of the art disclosed could only be accomplished by the employment of words which describe plaintiff's method. To hold that an idea, plan, method or art described in a copyright is open to the public but that it can be used only by the employment of different words and phrases which mean the same thing, borders on the preposterous. It is to exalt the accomplishment of a result by indirect means which could not be done directly. It places a premium upon evasion and makes this the test of infringement. Notwithstanding some authorities which support a theory permitting such a result, we think it is wrong and disapprove it." * * *

These cases indicate that in the fields of insurance and commerce the use of specific language in forms and documents may be so essential to accomplish a desired result and so integrated with the use of a legal or commercial conception that the proper standard of infringement is one which will protect as far as possible the copyrighted language and yet allow free use of the thought beneath the language. The evidence here shows that Continental in so far as it has used the language of Beardsley's forms has done so only as incidental to its use of the underlying idea. Chautauqua School of Nursing v. National School of Nursing, 2 Cir., 238 F. 151. In so doing it has not infringed.

[Judge Hincks concluded that Beardsley's copyright had in any event been forfeited by general publication of the forms without a notice of copyright. Beardsley's claim for unfair competition was also rejected since Continental had done nothing to suggest that its plan had anything to do with Beardsley.]

Modified and affirmed.

Morrissey v. Procter & Gamble Company

United States Court of Appeals, First Circuit, 1967.
379 F.2d 675.

■ Before ALDRICH, CHIEF JUDGE, MCENTEE and COFFIN, CIRCUIT JUDGES.

■ ALDRICH, CHIEF JUDGE. This is an appeal from a summary judgment for the defendant. The plaintiff, Morrissey, is the copyright owner of a set of rules for a sales promotional contest of the "sweepstakes" type involving the social security numbers of the participants. Plaintiff alleges that the defendant, Procter & Gamble Company, infringed, by copying, almost precisely, Rule 1. In its motion for summary judgment, based upon affidavits and depositions, defendant denies that plaintiff's Rule 1 is copyrightable material, and denies access. The district court held for the defendant on both grounds.

Taking the second ground first, the defendant offered affidavits or depositions of all of its allegedly pertinent employees, all of whom denied having seen plaintiff's rules. Although the plaintiff, by deposition, flatly testified that prior to the time the defendant conducted its contest he had mailed to the defendant his copyrighted rules with an offer to sell, the court ruled that the defendant had "proved" nonaccess, and stated that it was "satisfied that no material issue as to access * * * lurks * * * [in the record.]"

The court did not explain whether it considered defendant's showing to have constituted proof overcoming the presumption of receipt arising from plaintiff's testimony of mailing, or whether it felt there was an unsatisfied burden on the plaintiff to show that the particularly responsible employees of the defendant had received his communication. Either view would have been error. A notice to the defendant at its principal office, as this one assertedly was, is proper notice. There is at least an inference that the letter reached its proper destination. Even if we assume that if, at the trial of the case, it should be found that the particular employees of the defendant responsible for the contest were in fact without knowledge of plaintiff's rules, defendant would be free of a charge of copying, cf. Pinci v. Twentieth Century–Fox Film Corp., S.D.N.Y., 1951, 95 F.Supp. 884; Dezendorf v. Twentieth Century–Fox Film Corp., S.D.Cal., 1940, 32 F.Supp. 359, aff'd, 9 Cir., 118 F.2d 561, on a motion for summary judgment a plaintiff should not have to go to the point of showing that every employee of a corporate defendant received his notification. Nor can it be said that no issue of fact as to access "lurks" merely because it seems to the court that plaintiff's own proof has been satisfactorily contradicted. Nothing is clearer than this on a motion for summary judgment; if a party has made an evidentiary showing warranting a favorable inference, contradiction cannot eliminate it. Summary judgment may not be granted where there is the "slightest doubt as to the facts." Peckham v. Ronrico Corp., 1 Cir., 1948, 171 F.2d 653, 657; Arnstein v. Porter, 2 Cir., 1946, 154 F.2d 464, 468. Defendant's argument misreads Dressler v. MV Sandpiper, 2 Cir., 1964, 331 F.2d 130. The presumption arising from mailing remained in the case.[1] * * *

The second aspect of the case raises a more difficult question. Before discussing it we recite plaintiff's Rule 1, and defendant's Rule 1, the italicizing in the latter being ours to note the defendant's variations or changes.

"1. Entrants should print name, address and social security number on a boxtop, or a plain paper. Entries must be accompanied by * * * boxtop or by plain paper on which the name * * * is copied from any source. Official rules are explained on * * * packages or leaflets obtained from dealer. If you do not have a social security number you may use the name and number of any member of your immediate family living with you. Only the per-

---

[1]   The court did not discuss, nor need we, the additional fact that the almost exact following of plaintiff's wording and format in an area in which there is at least some room for maneuverability, might be found of itself to contradict defendants' denial of access. Cf. Arnstein v. Porter, supra.

son named on the entry will be deemed an entrant and may qualify for prize.

"Use the correct social security number belonging to the person named on entry * * * wrong number will be disqualified." (Plaintiff's Rule)

"1. Entrants should print name, address and *Social Security* number on a Tide boxtop, or *on* [a] plain paper. Entries must be accompanied by Tide boxtop *(any size)* or by plain paper on which the name 'Tide' is copied from any source. Official rules are *available* on Tide Sweepstakes packages, or *on* leaflets *at* Tide dealers, *or you can send a stamped, self-addressed envelope to*: Tide 'Shopping Fling' Sweepstakes, P.O. Box 4459, Chicago 77, Illinois.

"If you do not have a *Social Security* number, you may use the name and number of any member of your immediate family living with you. Only the person named on the entry will be deemed an entrant and may qualify for a prize.

"Use the correct Social Security number, belonging to the person named on *the* entry—wrong numbers will be disqualified." (Defendant's Rule)

The district court, following an earlier decision, Gaye v. Gillis, D.Mass., 1958, 167 F.Supp. 416, took the position that since the substance of the contest was not copyrightable, which is unquestionably correct, Baker v. Selden, 1879, 101 U.S. 99; Affiliated Enterprises v. Gruber, 1 Cir., 1936, 86 F.2d 958; Chamberlin v. Uris Sales Corp., 2 Cir., 1945, 150 F.2d 512, and the substance was relatively simple, it must follow that plaintiff's rule sprung directly from the substance and "contains no original creative authorship." 262 F.Supp. at 738. This does not follow. Copyright attaches to form of expression, and defendant's own proof, introduced to deluge the court on the issue of access, itself established that there was more than one way of expressing even this simple substance. Nor, in view of the almost precise similarity of the two rules, could defendant successfully invoke the principle of a stringent standard for showing infringement which some courts apply when the subject matter involved admits of little variation in form of expression. E.g., Dorsey v. Old Surety Life Ins. Co., 10 Cir., 1938, 98 F.2d 872, 874 ("a showing of appropriation in the exact form or substantially so."); Continental Casualty Co. v. Beardsley, 2 Cir., 1958, 253 F.2d 702, 705, cert. denied, 358 U.S. 816 ("a stiff standard for proof of infringement.").

Nonetheless, we must hold for the defendant. When the uncopyrightable subject matter is very narrow, so that "the topic necessarily requires," Sampson & Murdock Co. v. Seaver–Radford Co., 1 Cir., 1905, 140 F. 539, 541; cf. Kaplan, An Unhurried View of Copyright, 64–65 (1967), if not only one form of expression, at best only a limited number, to permit copyrighting would mean that a party or parties, by copyrighting a mere handful of forms, could exhaust all possibilities of future use of the substance. In such circumstances it does not seem accurate to say that any particular form of expression comes from the subject matter. However, it is necessary to say that the subject matter would be appropriated by permitting the copyrighting of its expression. We cannot recognize copyright as a game of chess in which the public can be checkmated. Cf. Baker v. Selden, supra.

Upon examination the matters embraced in Rule 1 are so straightforward and simple that we find this limiting principle to be applicable. Furthermore, its operation need not await an attempt to copyright all possible forms. It cannot be only the last form of expression which is to be condemned, as completing defendant's exclusion from the substance. Rather, in these circumstances, we hold that copyright does not extend to the subject matter at all, and plaintiff cannot complain even if his particular expression was deliberately adopted.

Affirmed.

Herbert Rosenthal Jewelry Corp. v. Kalpakian
446 F.2d 738 (9th Cir.1971).

Plaintiff charged defendants with infringing its copyright in a pin in the shape of a bee formed of gold and encrusted with jewels. After discussing the distinction between idea and expression, the court affirmed a judgment for the defendants: "We think the production of jeweled bee pins is a larger private preserve than Congress intended to be set aside in the public market without a patent. A jeweled bee pin is therefore an 'idea' that defendants were free to copy. * * * The difficulty, as we have noted, is that on this record the 'idea' and its 'expression' appear to be indistinguishable. There is no greater similarity between the pins of plaintiff and defendants than is inevitable from the use of jewel-encrusted bee forms in both.

"When the 'idea' and its 'expression' are thus inseparable, copying the 'expression' will not be barred, since protecting the 'expression' in such circumstances would confer a monopoly of the 'idea' upon the copyright owner free of the conditions and limitations imposed by the patent law." The court cited *Baker* and *Morrissey,* with a "see also" to *Continental Casualty.*

Can the court be correct on the facts? Judge Friendly for the Second Circuit had earlier upheld an injunction apparently directed against copying the same pin, with no mention of *Baker.* See Herbert Rosenthal Jewelry Corp. v. Grossbardt, 436 F.2d 315 (2d Cir.1970).

NOTES AND QUESTIONS

(1) Courts have sometimes found legal forms uncopyrightable on the ground that they lack originality; an unspoken assumption may be that judges feel on surer ground here than with works of art. See Donald v. Zack Meyer's T.V. Sales & Service, 426 F.2d 1027 (5th Cir.1970), cert. denied, 400 U.S. 992 (1971), in which a "common legal form" was held uncopyrightable. "The plaintiff did no original legal research which resulted in a significant addition to the standard conditional sales contract or chattel mortgage forms; he merely made trivial word changes by combining various forms and servilely imitating the already stereotyped language found therein." The same plaintiff lost again in Donald v. Uarco Business Forms, 344 F.Supp. 338 (W.D.Ark.1972), aff'd, 478 F.2d 764 (8th Cir.1973). Accord, M.M. Business Forms Corp. v. Uarco, Inc., 472 F.2d 1137 (6th Cir.1973). These outcomes have been sharply criticized. See D. Olson, The Legal Protection of Printed Systems, 81 W.Va.L.Rev. 45 (1979). Other cases have been more generous, especially with elaborate "forms." In Edwin K. Williams & Co. v. Edwin K. Williams & Co.–East, 542 F.2d 1053 (9th Cir.1976), cert. denied, 433 U.S. 908 (1977), the court found that a book of accounting forms, with several pages of instructions, "constituted an integrated work entitled to copyright protection." See also Baldwin Cooke Co. v. Keith Clark, Inc., 383 F.Supp. 650 (N.D.Ill.), aff'd, 505 F.2d 1250 (7th Cir.1974), extending copy-

right protection to an "Executive Planner"—a combination calendar, diary, information, and appointment book. The court found the Planner copyrightable as a compilation, distinguishing *Morrissey* and *M.M. Business Forms,* supra, because "[n]one of the works involved in those cases approach the sophistication and complexity of format and arrangement involved here."

Exex. planner
= (c)

(2) Consider, as to forms, game rules[n], and other instances where exposition and the matter expounded are closely entwined, which approach is preferable: copyright, but with a high standard for infringement, as in *Continental Casualty,* or no copyright, as in *Morrissey?*

(3) *Baker* and *Morrissey* have become parents to the doctrine of "merger." A subsequent case, describing the concept as "a close cousin to the idea/expression dichotomy," said that under the doctrine of merger "copyright protection will be denied to even some *expressions* of ideas if the idea behind the expression is such that it can be expressed only in a very limited number of ways. The doctrine is designed to prevent an author from monopolizing an idea merely by copyrighting a few expressions of it." Toro Co. v. R & R Products Co., 787 F.2d 1208, 1212 (8th Cir.1986). The court there declined to invoke the doctrine in connection with a parts numbering system. The doctrine was also held inapplicable to the expression of questions on the SAT test. Educational Testing Services v. Katzman, 793 F.2d 533 (3d Cir.1986). A combination of the merger doctrine and the "blank form" rule, however, was successfully invoked in Matthew Bender & Co. v. Kluwer Law Book Pub., Inc., 672 F.Supp. 107 (S.D.N.Y.1987), to deny copyright to charts in a legal textbook presenting information on damage awards. A professor's model of electron behavior was an unprotectable idea; protection for the equations and figures used to express the model was held to be precluded by the merger doctrine in Seng-Tiong Ho v. Taflove, 648 F.3d 489 (7th Cir.2011). See Professor Nimmer's criticism of the merger doctrine in Nimmer on Copyright § 2.18.

doctrine of merger

When a photographer who had taken a series of photos of Skyy's blue vodka bottle brought an infringement action against the company after it used another photographer's substantially similar photographs in a marketing campaign, the Ninth Circuit said that the "litigation is fundamentally about how many ways one can create an advertising photograph * * * of a blue vodka bottle. We conclude that there are not many." Because of the merger of idea and expression, only "virtually identical copying" would be actionable. Ets–Hokin v. Skyy Spirits, Inc., 323 F.3d 763 (9th Cir.2003).

The Eleventh Circuit in BUC International Corp. v. International Yacht Council Ltd., 489 F.3d 1129 (11th Cir.2007), emphasized that application of the merger doctrine requires a sensitive determination of what constitutes the underlying idea. Defendant MLS Solutions, accused of infringing the selection and arrangement of section headings in BUC's compilation of yacht listings, argued that protection was precluded by the merger doctrine. "The first relevant inquiry in deciding how to apply the merger doctrine calls for a determination of precisely what the idea and its expression are. Generally speaking, BUC's idea was how to present brokers with information about a boat. BUC expressed this idea by selecting certain features of a boat that it thought would be important to brokers, and arranging them according to what [BUC] thought was the most

---

[n]   A narrow view of the copyrightability of games, based on the exclusion of "system" in § 102(b), is proposed in B. Boyden, Games and Other Uncopyrightable Systems, 18 Geo. Mason L.Rev. 439 (2011).

important information first. While MLS Solutions would have us define the idea more narrowly, i.e., dividing a vessel listing by rooms or other features of a boat, we think that definition skews the analysis in favor of finding merger. Articulating the idea and expression is not merely an exercise in semantics; it is a policy decision that must be carefully drawn. By defining the idea around the contours of the chosen expression, MLS Solutions attempts to cast the idea and the expression as one. This type of analysis would swallow up the idea-expression dichotomy, and the merger doctrine would become the rule instead of the exception. A more balanced conception of the idea here yields the conclusion that BUC's idea was to present yacht brokers with information about boats." Since there were many ways to select and organize information in a yacht listing, the defendant's merger argument was rejected.

Appeals to the doctrine of merger arise regularly in cases involving computer programs. A broad application of the doctrine is rejected in the following case on copyrightability. The merger doctrine also appears in the materials on infringement of copyright in computer programs, p. 244 infra.

COPYRIGHT IN COMPUTER PROGRAMS

Apple Computer, Inc. v. Franklin Computer Corp.

United States Court of Appeals, Third Circuit, 1983.
714 F.2d 1240.
Certiorari dismissed, 464 U.S. 1033 (1984).

■ Before HUNTER, HIGGINBOTHAM and SLOVITER, CIRCUIT JUDGES.

■ SLOVITER, CIRCUIT JUDGE.

I.

INTRODUCTION

Apple Computer, Inc. appeals from the district court's denial of a motion to preliminarily enjoin Franklin Computer Corp. from infringing the copyrights Apple holds on fourteen computer programs. * * *

II.

FACTS AND PROCEDURAL HISTORY

Apple, one of the computer industry leaders, manufactures and markets personal computers (microcomputers), related peripheral equipment such as disk drives (peripherals), and computer programs (software). It presently manufactures Apple II computers and distributes over 150 programs. Apple has sold over 400,000 Apple II computers, employs approximately 3,000 people, and had annual sales of $335,000,000 for fiscal year 1981. One of the byproducts of Apple's success is the independent development by third parties of numerous computer programs which are designed to run on the Apple II computer.

Franklin, the defendant below, manufactures and sells the ACE 100 personal computer and at the time of the hearing employed about 75 people and had sold fewer than 1,000 computers. The ACE 100 was designed to be "Apple compatible," so that peripheral equipment and software developed for use with the Apple II computer could be used in conjunction with the

ACE 100. Franklin's copying of Apple's operating system computer programs in an effort to achieve such compatibility precipitated this suit. * * *

There are three levels of computer language in which computer programs may be written. High level language, such as the commonly used BASIC or FORTRAN, uses English words and symbols, and is relatively easy to learn and understand (e.g., "GO TO 40" tells the computer to skip intervening steps and go to the step at line 40). A somewhat lower level language is assembly language, which consists of alphanumeric labels (e.g., "ADC" means "add with carry"). Statements in high level language, and apparently also statements in assembly language, are referred to as written in "source code." The third, or lowest level computer language, is machine language, a binary language using two symbols, 0 and 1, to indicate an open or closed switch (e.g., "01101001" means, to the Apple, add two numbers and save the result). Statements in machine language are referred to as written in "object code." * * *

A computer program can be stored or fixed on a variety of memory devices, two of which are of particular relevance for this case. The ROM (Read Only Memory) is an internal permanent memory device consisting of a semi-conductor "chip" which is incorporated into the circuitry of the computer. A program in object code is embedded on a ROM before it is incorporated in the computer. Information stored on a ROM can only be read, not erased or rewritten.[3] * * *

Computer programs can be categorized by function as either application programs or operating system programs. Application programs usually perform a specific task for the computer user, such as word processing, checkbook balancing, or playing a game. In contrast, operating system programs generally manage the internal functions of the computer or facilitate use of application programs. The parties agree that the fourteen computer programs at issue in this suit are operating system programs.[4]

Apple filed suit in the United States District Court for the Eastern District of Pennsylvania pursuant to 28 U.S.C. § 1338 on May 12, 1982, alleging that Franklin was liable for copyright infringement of the fourteen computer programs, patent infringement, unfair competition, and misappropriation. Franklin's answer in respect to the copyright counts included the affirmative defense that the programs contained no copyrightable subject matter. * * *

---

[3] In contrast to the permanent memory devices a RAM (Random Access Memory) is a chip on which volatile internal memory is stored which is erased when the computer's power is turned off.

[4] [Three of the] fourteen programs at issue, briefly described, are:

(1) *Autostart ROM* is sold as part of the Apple Computer and is embedded on a ROM chip. The program has also been published in source code as part of a copyrighted book, the Apple II manual. When the computer's power is turned on, Autostart ROM performs internal routines that turn on the circuits in the computer and make its physical parts (e.g. input/output devices, screen, and memory) ready for use.

(2) *Applesoft* is Apple's version of the Beginner's All-purpose Symbolic Instruction Code (BASIC) language. The program is stored in ROM and is sold as part of the computer. Applesoft translates instructions written in the higher-level BASIC language into the lower-level machine code that the computer understands. * * *

(5) *DOS 3.3,* the disk operating system program, provides the instructions necessary to control the operation between the disk system (disk drive) and the computer itself. It controls the reading and writing functions of the disks and includes other routines which put all the data transfers in sequence. * * *

Δ: no copyrightable ss

After expedited discovery, Apple moved for a preliminary injunction to restrain Franklin from using, copying, selling, or infringing Apple's copyrights. The district court held a three day evidentiary hearing limited to the copyright infringement claims. Apple produced evidence at the hearing in the form of affidavits and testimony that programs sold by Franklin in conjunction with its ACE 100 computer were virtually identical with those covered by the fourteen Apple copyrights. The variations that did exist were minor, consisting merely of such things as deletion of reference to Apple or its copyright notice. * * *

Δ agreed they copied

Said not feasible to write its own programs

Franklin did not dispute that it copied the Apple programs. Its witness admitted copying each of the works in suit from the Apple programs. Its factual defense was directed to its contention that it was not feasible for Franklin to write its own operating system programs. David McWherter, now Franklin's vice-president of engineering, testified he spent 30–40 hours in November 1981 making a study to determine if it was feasible for Franklin to write its own Autostart ROM program and concluded it was not because "there were just too many entry points in relationship to the number of instructions in the program." Entry points at specific locations in the program can be used by programmers to mesh their application programs with the operating system program. McWherter concluded that use of the identical signals was necessary in order to ensure 100% compatibility with application programs created to run on the Apple computer. * * * Apple introduced evidence that Franklin could have rewritten programs, including the Autostart ROM program, and that there are in existence operating programs written by third parties which are compatible with Apple II.

Franklin's principal defense at the preliminary injunction hearing and before us is primarily a legal one, directed to its contention that the Apple operating system programs are not capable of copyright protection.

The district court denied the motion for preliminary injunction by order and opinion dated July 30, 1982. Apple moved for reconsideration in light of this court's decision in Williams Electronics, Inc. v. Artic International, Inc., 685 F.2d 870 (3d Cir.1982), which was decided August 2, 1982, three days after the district court decision. The district court denied the motion for reconsideration. We have jurisdiction of Apple's appeal pursuant to 28 U.S.C. § 1292(a)(1).

III.

THE DISTRICT COURT OPINION

* * *

We read the district court opinion as presenting the following legal issues: (1) whether copyright can exist in a computer program expressed in object code, (2) whether copyright can exist in a computer program embedded on a ROM, (3) whether copyright can exist in an operating system program, and (4) whether independent irreparable harm must be shown for a preliminary injunction in copyright infringement actions.

Issues

IV.

DISCUSSION

A.

Copyrightability of a Computer Program Expressed in Object Code

Certain statements by the district court suggest that programs expressed in object code, as distinguished from source code, may not be the proper subject of copyright. We find no basis in the statute for any such concern. Furthermore, our decision in Williams Electronics, Inc. v. Artic International, Inc., supra, laid to rest many of the doubts expressed by the district court.

In 1976, after considerable study, Congress enacted a new copyright law to replace that which had governed since 1909. Act of October 19, 1976, Pub.L. No. 94–553, 90 Stat. 2541 (codified at 17 U.S.C. §§ 101 et seq.). Under the law, two primary requirements must be satisfied in order for a work to constitute copyrightable subject matter—it must be an "original wor[k] of authorship" and must be "fixed in [a] tangible medium of expression." * * *

Although section 102(a) does not expressly list computer programs as works of authorship, the legislative history suggests that programs were considered copyrightable as literary works. See H.R.Rep. No. 1476, 94th Cong., 2d Sess. 54, reprinted in 1976 U.S.Code Cong. & Ad. News 5659, 5667 (" 'literary works' . . . includes . . . computer programs"). Because a Commission on New Technological Uses ("CONTU") had been created by Congress to study, inter alia, computer uses of copyrighted works, Pub.L. No. 93–573, § 201, 88 Stat. 1873 (1974), Congress enacted a status quo provision, section 117, in the 1976 Act concerning such computer uses pending the CONTU report and recommendations.[6]

The CONTU Final Report recommended that the copyright law be amended, inter alia, "to make it explicit that computer programs, to the extent that they embody an author's original creation, are proper subject matter of copyright." National Commission on New Technological Uses of Copyrighted Works, Final Report 1 (1979) [hereinafter CONTU Report]. CONTU recommended two changes relevant here: that section 117, the status quo provision, be repealed and replaced with a section limiting exclusive rights in computer programs so as "to ensure that rightful possessors of copies of computer programs may use or adapt these copies for their use," id.; and that a definition of computer program be added to section 101. Id. at 12. Congress adopted both changes. Act of Dec. 12, 1980, Pub.L. No. 96–517, § 10, 94 Stat. 3015, 3028. The revisions embodied CONTU's recommendations to clarify the law of copyright of computer software. H.R.Rep. No. 1307, 96th Cong., 2d Sess. 23, reprinted in 1980 U.S.Code Cong. & Ad. News 6460, 6482.

The 1980 amendments added a definition of a computer program:

> A "computer program" is a set of statements or instructions to be used directly or indirectly in a computer in order to bring about a certain result.

17 U.S.C. § 101. The amendments also substituted a new section 117 which provides that "it is not an infringement for the owner of a copy of a computer program to make or authorize the making of another copy or adaptation of that computer program" when necessary to "the utilization of the computer program" or "for archival purposes only." 17 U.S.C. § 117. The parties agree that this section is not implicated in the instant lawsuit. The language of the provision, however, by carving out an exception to the normal proscriptions against copying, clearly indicates that programs are copyrightable and are otherwise afforded copyright protection.

---

[6] Section 117 applied only to the scope of protection to be accorded copyrighted works when used in conjunction with a computer and not to the copyrightability of programs. H.R.Rep. No. 1476, at 116, reprinted in 1976 U.S.Code Cong. & Ad. News at 5731.

* * *

Programs are copyrightable [handwritten margin note]

The district court here questioned whether copyright was to be limited to works "designed to be 'read' by a human reader [as distinguished from] read by an expert with a microscope and patience", 545 F.Supp. at 821. The suggestion that copyrightability depends on a communicative function to individuals stems from the early decision of White–Smith Music Publishing Co. v. Apollo Co., 209 U.S. 1 (1908), which held a piano roll was not a copy of the musical composition because it was not in a form others, except perhaps for a very expert few, could perceive. See 1 Nimmer on Copyright § 2.03[B][1] (1983). However, it is clear from the language of the 1976 Act and its legislative history that it was intended to obliterate distinctions engendered by *White–Smith.* H.R.Rep. No. 1476, supra, at 52, reprinted in 1976 U.S.Code Cong. & Ad. News at 5665.

§ 102(a) [handwritten margin note]

Under the statute, copyright extends to works in any tangible means of expression *"from which they can be perceived,* reproduced, or otherwise communicated, either directly or *with the aid of machine or device."* 17 U.S.C. § 102(a) (emphasis added). Further, the definition of "computer program" adopted by Congress in the 1980 amendments is "sets of statements or instructions to be used *directly or indirectly* in a computer in order to bring about a certain result." 17 U.S.C. § 101 (emphasis added). As source code instructions must be translated into object code before the computer can act upon them, only instructions expressed in object code can be used "directly" by the computer. See Midway Manufacturing Co. v. Strohon, 564 F.Supp. 741 at 750–751 (N.D.Ill.1983). This definition was adopted following the CONTU Report in which the majority clearly took the position that object codes are proper subjects of copyright. See CONTU Report at 21.
* * *

Literary work : § 101 [handwritten margin note]

The district court also expressed uncertainty as to whether a computer program in object code could be classified as a "literary work." However, the category of "literary work", one of the seven copyrightable categories, is not confined to literature in the nature of Hemingway's *For Whom the Bell Tolls.* The definition of "literary works" in section 101 includes expression not only in words but also "numbers, or other . . . numerical symbols or indicia", thereby expanding the common usage of "literary works." Cf. Harcourt, Brace & World, Inc. v. Graphic Controls Corp., 329 F.Supp. 517, 523–24 (S.D.N.Y.1971) (the symbols designating questions or response spaces on exam answer sheets held to be copyrightable "writings" under 1909 Act); Reiss v. National Quotation Bureau, Inc., 276 F. 717 (S.D.N.Y.1921) (code book of coined words designed for cable use copyrightable). Thus a computer program, whether in object code or source code, is a "literary work" and is protected from unauthorized copying, whether from its object or source code version. Accord Midway Mfg. Co. v. Strohon, 564 F.Supp. at 750–751; see also GCA Corp. v. Chance, [217 U.S.P.Q. 718, 719–20 (N.D.Cal.1982).]

Program is a lit. work [handwritten margin note]

B.

Copyrightability of a Computer Program Embedded on a ROM

Just as the district court's suggestion of a distinction between source code and object code was rejected by our opinion in *Williams* issued three days after the district court opinion, so also was its suggestion that embodiment of a computer program on a ROM, as distinguished from in a traditional writing, detracts from its copyrightability. In *Williams* we rejected the argument that "a computer program is not infringed when the program is loaded into electronic memory devices (ROMs) and used to control the activity of machines." 685 F.2d at 876. Defendant there had argued that there can be no copyright protection for the ROMs because they are utilitarian objects or machine parts. We held that the statutory requirement of "fixation", the manner in which the issue arises, is satisfied through the embodiment of the expression in the ROM devices. * * *

C.

Copyrightability of Computer Operating System Programs

We turn to the heart of Franklin's position on appeal which is that computer operating system programs, as distinguished from application programs, are not the proper subject of copyright "regardless of the language or medium in which they are fixed." Brief of Appellee at 15 (emphasis deleted). Apple suggests that this issue too is foreclosed by our *Williams* decision because some portion of the program at issue there was in effect an operating system program. Franklin is correct that this was not an issue raised by the parties in *Williams* and it was not considered by the court. Thus we consider it as a matter of first impression.

Franklin contends that operating system programs are *per se* excluded from copyright protection under the express terms of section 102(b) of the Copyright Act, and under the precedent and underlying principles of Baker v. Selden, 101 U.S. 99 (1879). These separate grounds have substantial analytic overlap. * * *

Franklin reads Baker v. Selden as "stand[ing] for several fundamental principles, each presenting . . . an insuperable obstacle to the copyrightability of Apple's operating systems." It states:

> First, *Baker* teaches that use of a system itself does not infringe a copyright on the description of the system. Second, *Baker* enunciates the rule that copyright does not extend to purely utilitarian works. Finally, *Baker* emphasizes that the copyright laws may not be used to obtain and hold a monopoly over an idea. In so doing, *Baker* highlights the principal difference between the copyright and patent laws—a difference that is highly pertinent in this case.

Brief of Appellee at 22.

Section 102(b) of the Copyright Act, the other ground on which Franklin relies, appeared first in the 1976 version, long after the decision in Baker v. Selden. * * * It is apparent that section 102(b) codifies a substantial part of the holding and dictum of Baker v. Selden. See 1 Nimmer on Copyright § 2.18[D], at 2–207.

We turn to consider the two principal points of Franklin's argument.

1. *"Process", "System" or "Method of Operation"*

Franklin argues that an operating system program is either a "process", "system", or "method of operation" and hence uncopyrightable. Franklin correctly notes that underlying section 102(b) and many of the statements for which Baker v. Selden is cited is the distinction which must be made between property subject to the patent law, which protects discoveries, and that subject to copyright law, which protects the writings describing such discoveries. However, Franklin's argument misapplies that distinction in this case. Apple does not seek to copyright the method which instructs the computer to perform its operating functions but only the instructions themselves. The method would be protected, if at all, by the patent law, an issue as yet unresolved. See Diamond v. Diehr, 450 U.S. 175 (1981).

Franklin's attack on operating system programs as "methods" or "processes" seems inconsistent with its concession that application programs are an appropriate subject of copyright. Both types of programs instruct the computer to do something. Therefore, it should make no difference for purposes of section 102(b) whether these instructions tell the computer to help prepare an income tax return (the task of an application program) or to translate a high level language program from source code into its binary language object code form (the task of an operating system program such as "Applesoft", see note 4 supra). Since it is only the instructions which are protected, a "process" is no more involved because the instructions in an operating system program may be used to activate the operation of the computer than it would be if instructions were written in ordinary English in a manual which described the necessary steps to activate an intricate complicated machine. There is, therefore, no reason to afford any less copyright protection to the instructions in an operating system program than to the instructions in an application program. * * *

Franklin also argues that the operating systems cannot be copyrighted because they are "purely utilitarian works" and that Apple is seeking to block the use of the art embodied in its operating systems. This argument stems from the following dictum in Baker v. Selden:

> The very object of publishing a book on science or the useful arts is to communicate to the world the useful knowledge which it contains. But this object would be frustrated if the knowledge could not be used without incurring the guilt of piracy of the book. And where the art it teaches cannot be used without employing the methods and diagrams used to illustrate the book, or such as are similar to them, such methods and diagrams are to be considered as necessary incidents to the art, and given therewith to the public; not given for the purpose of publication in other works explanatory of the art, but for the purpose of practical application.

101 U.S. at 103. We cannot accept the expansive reading given to this language by some courts, see, e.g., Taylor Instrument Companies v. Fawley–Brost Co., 139 F.2d 98 (7th Cir.1943), cert. denied, 321 U.S. 785 (1944). In this respect we agree with the views expressed by Professor Nimmer in his treatise. See 1 Nimmer on Copyright § 2.18[C].

Although a literal construction of this language could support Franklin's reading that precludes copyrightability if the copyright work is put to a utilitarian use, that interpretation has been rejected by a later Supreme Court decision. In Mazer v. Stein, 347 U.S. 201, 218 (1954), the Court stated: "We find nothing in the copyright statute to support the argument that the intended use or use in industry of an article eligible for copyright bars or invalidates its registration. We do not read such a limitation into the copyright law." Id. at 218. The CONTU majority also rejected the expansive view some courts have given Baker v. Selden, and stated, "That the words of a program are used ultimately in the implementation of a process should in no way affect their copyrightability." Id. at 21. It referred to "copyright practice past and present, which recognizes copyright protection for a work of authorship regardless of the uses to which it may be put." Id. The Commission continued: "The copyright status of the written rules for a game *or a system for the operation of a machine* is unaffected by the fact that those rules direct the actions of those who play the game or *carry out the process*." Id. (emphasis added). * * *

Perhaps the most convincing item leading us to reject Franklin's argument is that the statutory definition of a computer program as a set of instructions to be used in a computer in order to bring about a certain result, 17 U.S.C. § 101, makes no distinction between application programs and operating programs. * * *

2. *Idea/Expression Dichotomy*

Franklin's other challenge to copyright of operating system programs relies on the line which is drawn between ideas and their expression. Baker v. Selden remains a benchmark in the law of copyright for the reading given it in Mazer v. Stein, supra, where the Court stated, "Unlike a patent, a copyright gives no exclusive right to the art disclosed; protection is given only to the expression of the idea—not the idea itself." 347 U.S. at 217 (footnote omitted). * * *

* * * We believe that in the context before us, a program for an operating system, the line must be a pragmatic one, which also keeps in consideration "the preservation of the balance between competition and protection reflected in the patent and copyright laws". Herbert Rosenthal Jewelry Corp. v. Kalpakian, 446 F.2d 738, 742 (9th Cir.1971). As we stated in Franklin Mint Corp. v. National Wildlife Art Exchange, Inc., 575 F.2d 62, 64 (3d Cir.), cert. denied, 439 U.S. 880 (1978), "Unlike a patent, a copyright protects originality rather than novelty or invention." In that opinion, we quoted approvingly the following passage from Dymow v. Bolton, 11 F.2d 690, 691 (2d Cir.1926):

> Just as a patent affords protection only to the means of reducing an inventive idea to practice, so the copyright law protects the means of expressing an idea; and it is as near the whole truth as generalization can usually reach that, *if the same idea can be expressed in a plurality of totally different manners, a plurality of copyrights may result,* and no infringement will exist.

(emphasis added).

We adopt the suggestion in the above language and thus focus on whether the idea is capable of various modes of expression. If other programs can be written or created which perform the same function as an Apple's operating system program, then that program is an expression of the idea and hence copyrightable. In essence, this inquiry is no different than that made to determine whether the expression and idea have merged, which has been stated to occur where there are no or few other ways of expressing a particular idea. See, e.g., Morrissey v. Procter & Gamble Co., 379 F.2d 675, 678–79 (1st Cir.1967); Freedman v. Grolier Enterprises, Inc., 179 U.S.P.Q. 476, 478 (S.D.N.Y.1973) ("[c]opyright protection will not be given to a form of expression necessarily dictated by the underlying subject matter"); CONTU Report at 20.

The district court made no findings as to whether some or all of Apple's operating programs represent the only means of expression of the idea underlying them. Although there seems to be a concession by Franklin that at least some of the programs can be rewritten, we do not believe that the record on that issue is so clear that it can be decided at the appellate level. Therefore, if the issue is pressed on remand, the necessary finding can be made at that time.

Franklin claims that whether or not the programs can be rewritten, there are a limited "number of ways to arrange operating systems to enable a computer to run the vast body of Apple-compatible software", Brief of Appellee at 20. This claim has no pertinence to either the idea/expression dichotomy or merger. The idea which may merge with the expression, thus making the copyright unavailable, is the idea which is the subject of the expression. The idea of one of the operating system programs is, for example, how to translate source code into object code. If other methods of expressing that idea are not foreclosed as a practical matter, then there is no merger. Franklin may wish to achieve total compatibility with independently developed application programs written for the Apple II, but that is a commercial and competitive objective which does not enter into the somewhat metaphysical issue of whether particular ideas and expressions have merged. * * *

V.

For the reasons set forth in this opinion, we will reverse the denial of the preliminary injunction and remand to the district court for further proceedings in accordance herewith.

Rev'd/Remand

NOTES AND QUESTIONS ON COPYRIGHT IN COMPUTER PROGRAMS

(1) The *Apple* decision drew mixed reviews. See, e.g., P. Samuelson, CONTU Revisited: The Case Against Copyright Protection for Computer Programs in Machine Readable Form, 1984 Duke L.J. 663 (1984). T. Hardy, The Copyrightability of New Works of Authorship: "XML Schemas" as an Example, 38 Hous.L.Rev. 855 (2001), argues that the copyrightability of a new "thing" should depend on whether protection would increase the quantity or quality of such works. International treaty obligations now require the United States to treat both source and object code as "literary works." See Trade-Related Aspects of Intellectual Property (TRIPS), art. 10.

Did the court give adequate attention to the public interest in compatibility? D. Karjala, Copyright Protection of Operating Software, Copyright Misuse, and Antitrust, 9 Cornell J.L. & Pub.Pol. 161 (2000), concludes that strong copyright protection for operating systems, coupled with network effects that increase a program's value in proportion to the number of users, will inexorably produce a single dominant firm—with Microsoft as an example.

(2) Registration of copyright in computer software does not necessarily require disclosure of the entire program; only the first and last twenty-five pages of the program, in source code, are required. Even less will suffice if the program contains trade secrets. See 37 C.F.R. § 202.20(c)(2)(vii). Is there a policy favoring public access to works claiming the benefits of federal copyright? When "publication" was the crucial event for federal protection, the answer seemed to be yes. Now copyright subsists from creation, although registration is still a prerequisite to enforcement.°

Only 1st & last 25 pages

(3) In the early years of the computer age, trade secret law was the most common means of preventing the unauthorized copying of software. Trade secret law is well-suited to the protection of programs developed for internal use by a single company. For programs sold or licensed to others, the requisite secrecy might still be maintained through the use of confidentiality agreements. Com-

---

° A Copyright Office regulation designed to maintain secrecy for registrations of "secure tests" was upheld in National Conference of Bar Examiners v. Multistate Legal Studies, Inc., 692 F.2d 478 (7th Cir.1982), cert. denied, 464 U.S. 814 (1983). The court said, "In sum, the statutory scheme of the Copyright Act demonstrates that the deposit provisions are not for the purpose of disclosure." What *is* the purpose?

puware Corp. v. Serena Software International, Inc., 77 F.Supp.2d 816 (E.D.Mich.1999), held that the deposit of computer software for copyright registration did not as a matter of law vitiate the secrecy necessary for trade secret protection, citing regulations prohibiting duplication of the deposited materials that are available for inspection at the Copyright Office.

(4) The 1980 amendments to the Copyright Act sponsored by CONTU added the definition of "computer program" in § 101 and the exemptions for utilization and backup copies in § 117. The amendments are interpreted in P. Maggs, Computer Programs as the Object of Intellectual Property in the United States of America, 30 Am.J.Comp.L. 251 (1982 Supp.).

Section 117 is not without its ambiguities. Are its exemptions, for example, applicable to licensees as well as purchasers of computer programs? In MAI Systems Corp. v. Peak Computer, Inc., 991 F.2d 511 (9th Cir.1993), cert. dism'd, 510 U.S. 1033 (1994), the Ninth Circuit said no. The Federal Circuit disagreed in DSC Communications Corp. v. Pulse Communications, Inc., 170 F.3d 1354 (Fed.Cir.), cert. denied, 528 U.S. 923 (1999), holding that a licensee could be an "owner of a copy of a computer program" for purposes of § 117. Ownership of a copy turned on facts such as whether the right to possession of the copy was perpetual, whether it was obtained through a one-time payment, and whether the right to use the copy was encumbered by restrictions inconsistent with ownership such as limitations on the right to transfer the copy or to use it with hardware not authorized by the copyright owner. The Second Circuit took a similarly broad view of "owner" in Krause v. Titleserv, Inc., 402 F.3d 119 (2d Cir.), cert. denied, 546 U.S. 1002 (2005). However, the Ninth Circuit in Vernor v. Autodesk, Inc., 621 F.3d 1102 (9th Cir. 2010), cert. denied, 132 S.Ct. 105 (2011), reaffirmed its holding in *MAI Systems* that narrowly interpreted who is an "owner" for purposes of invoking the § 117 "essential step in the utilization of the computer program" defense to copying. "It may seem intuitive that every lawful user of a copyrighted software program whether they own their copies or are merely licensed to use them, should be entitled to an 'essential step defense' that provides that they do not infringe simply by using a computer program that they lawfully acquired. However, the Copyright Act confers this defense only on owners of software copies. See 17 U.S.C. § 117. In contrast, a licensee's right to use the software, including the right to copy the software into RAM, is conferred by the terms of its license agreement."

The Ninth Circuit in *MAI Systems* also concluded that a computer service company that caused a copy of the plaintiff's operating system software to be created in RAM memory when it turned on a licensee's computer during a diagnostic procedure was an infringer. That result was legislatively overruled in 1998 by the addition of § 117(c), which permits the owner of a computer to make or authorize another to make a copy of a program that is lawfully contained in the computer for purposes of computer maintenance or repair. Section 117(c) is analyzed in Storage Tech. Corp. v. Custom Hardware Eng'g & Consulting, Inc., 421 F.3d 1307 (Fed.Cir.2005).[p]

---

[p]   L. Gibbons, Entrepreneurial Copyright Fair Use: Let the Independent Contractor Stand in the Shoes of the User, 57 Ark.L.Rev. 539 (2004), goes further, arguing that the rights of software owners should always be exercisable through independent contractors; S. McJohn, Fair Use of Copyrighted Software, 28 Rutgers L.J. 593 (1997), argues that "copying" a computer program by turning on a computer in the course of maintenance or repair is in any event a fair use.

§ 117(a)(1)

Section 117(a)(1) recognizes the right of an owner of a copy of a computer program to make a copy as part of "an essential step in the utilization of the computer program." Would the exemption apply, for example, to loading the program into a computer for the purpose of analyzing rather than "running" the program? The Fifth Circuit in Vault Corp. v. Quaid Software Ltd., 847 F.2d 255 (5th Cir.1988), held that the exemption applied. And what is the scope of the "adaptation" right recognized in § 117(a)(1)? Why would the modification of a computer program by a user be an infringement in any event? See Aymes v. Bonelli, 47 F.3d 23 (2d Cir.1995) (§ 117 adaptation right was successfully invoked to avoid infringement of the copyright owner's exclusive right to prepare derivative works). In *Krause*, supra, the court held that the § 117 adaptation right covered the addition of features to better serve the needs of the user. The adaptation right is considered in R. Nimmer and P. Krauthaus, Copyright and Software Technology Infringement: Defining Third Party Development Rights, 62 Ind.L.J. 13 (1986); L. Mtima, So Dark the Con(tu) of Man: The Quest for a Software Derivative Work Right in § 117, 70 U.Pitt.L.Rev. 1 (2008), attempts to reconcile the adaptation right in § 117 with the copyright owner's exclusive derivative right in § 106.

Consider also § 117(a)(2) and the right to make "archival" copies. Does this exemption apply when the purchased copy is not subject to the mechanical or electronic failures that can destroy software embodied in disks or hard drives? See Atari, Inc. v. JS & A Group, Inc., 597 F.Supp. 5 (N.D.Ill.1983) (exemption was not applicable to the program for the PAC–MAN video game embodied in ROM chips). However, the court in *Vault,* supra, in an expansive reading of § 117(a)(2), said that the owner of a program is entitled to make an archival copy in order to guard against *any* risk of destruction. The § 117 exemptions are analyzed in R. Kreiss, Section 117 of the Copyright Act, 1991 B.Y.U.L.Rev. 1497.

(5) Many software companies use "shrink-wrap" or "click-on" licenses with their mass-marketed programs. The licenses usually say that by tearing open the package or by clicking on "agree," the consumer has consented to the terms of the agreement. The licenses often purport to retain title to the product in the seller, with the buyer being characterized as a "licensee." They typically contain provisions limiting rental, modification, disassembly, and copying. Are such "licenses" enforceable under basic contract principles of offer and acceptance? Are they "unconscionable" or in violation of recognized public policy as evidenced by the rights of users recognized under § 117?

Clickwrap cases

Pro Cd ↗

Shrink-wrap licenses survived a major challenge in ProCD, Inc. v. Zeidenberg, 86 F.3d 1447 (7th Cir.1996), when the Seventh Circuit overturned a district court decision that had found the license accompanying the plaintiff's CD–ROM telephone directory unenforceable as a matter of contract law and preempted under § 301 of the Copyright Act. Plaintiff's product, compiled from over 3,000 telephone directories, was sold in a box that indicated the sale was subject to restrictions contained in the enclosed license agreement. The license, which was printed in the manual and encoded on the CD–ROM, permitted only noncommercial use and provided for a refund if the buyer found the terms unacceptable. Defendant nevertheless put the directory on the Internet, available to users for a fee. The district court found the license unenforceable because the terms were not available to the buyer prior to purchase. Judge Easterbrook, citing purchases of insurance, airline tickets, and other transactions in which payment precedes the communication of detailed terms, held that "[n]otice on the outside, terms on the inside, and a right to return the software for a refund if the terms are unacceptable," followed by buyer's use of the product, were sufficient to establish an enforceable contract. (Judge Easterbrook's argument that enforcing the contractual restriction against commercial use facilitates price discrimination between consumer and commercial purchasers to the ultimate benefit of consumers is questioned in W. Gordon, Intellectual Property as Price Discrimination: Implications for Contract, 73 Chi.-Kent L.Rev. 1367 (1998), which notes that the § 106 exclusive rights already facilitate price discrimination by copyright owners.) Judge Easterbrook also disagreed with the district court's conclusion that the contractual restriction on use of the uncopyrightable contents of the telephone directory was preempted by federal copyright law. M. Lemley, Intellectual Property and Shrinkwrap Licenses, 68 S.Cal.L.Rev. 1239 (1995), strongly supports the approach taken by the district court. Louisiana has a statute validating certain restrictions imposed on purchasers of software through shrink-wrap licenses. See La.Rev.Stat. §§ 51:1961–66. Is the statute preempted by federal copyright law? The Fifth Circuit in *Vault,* supra, held that to the extent the statute conflicts with the rights granted to users under § 117, it is preempted.

PATENT PROTECTION FOR COMPUTER PROGRAMS

Although the Copyright Office began accepting computer programs for registration in 1964, the Patent and Trademark Office was more reluctant to enter the field. The PTO did not believe that computer programs were patentable subject matter, and it did not have the resources to search the prior art in this mushrooming industry. Inventors tried to describe computer applications as processes, or to claim a computer following a particular program as a novel machine. They found support in the Court of Customs and Patent Appeals, which first directed the PTO to issue a patent essentially for a computer program in Application of Prater, 415 F.2d 1393 (C.C.P.A.1969). The C.C.P.A. continued its push for software patents in Application of Benson, 441 F.2d 682 (C.C.P.A.1971). When *Benson* reached the Supreme Court as Gottschalk v. Benson, 409 U.S. 63 (1972), Justice Douglas reversed, arguing that a "method of programming a general purpose digital computer to convert signals from binary coded decimal form into pure binary form" described a process so broad that "the patent would wholly pre-empt the mathematical formula and in practical effect would be a patent on the algorithm itself." Before such patents should issue, "considered action by the Congress is needed."

The Court of Customs and Patent Appeals continued to press for patentability, doing battle with both the Patent and Trademark Office and the Supreme Court. In the next computer-related case to reach the Supreme Court, Dann v. Johnston, 425 U.S. 219 (1976), the claimed invention was disposed of as obvious. Next, in Parker v. Flook, 437 U.S. 584 (1978), Justice Stevens for the Court said that the only novel element in the invention was an equation or algorithm for computing "alarm limits" in chemical processes; this was unpatentable. But three justices dissented. The Court of Customs and Patent Appeals persisted. Finally, two more Justices were won over, and in the following case a software-related patent survived, 5–4.

Diamond v. Diehr

450 U.S. 175 (1981).

The patent at issue involved a process for curing rubber. During the curing process sensors inside a mold continually take temperature readings and send them to a computer. When the rubber is cured to the desired specifications, the program sends a message that causes the mold to open. Justice Rehnquist, writing for the majority, said:

"[W]e think that a physical and chemical process for molding precision synthetic rubber products falls within the § 101 categories of possibly patentable subject matter. * * *

"Our conclusion regarding respondents' claims is not altered by the fact that in several steps of the process a mathematical equation and a programmed digital computer are used. This Court has undoubtedly recognized limits to § 101 and every discovery is not embraced within the statutory terms. Excluded from such patent protection are laws of nature, physical phenomena and abstract ideas. * * *

"Our recent holdings in Gottschalk v. Benson, supra, and Parker v. Flook, supra, both of which are computer-related, stand for nothing more than these long-established principles. * * *

"In contrast, the respondents here do not seek to patent a mathematical formula. Instead, they seek patent protection for a process of curing synthetic rubber. Their process admittedly employs a well-known mathematical equation [i.e., the Arrhenius equation, a standard calculation named for its inventor], but they do not seek to pre-empt the use of that equation. Rather, they seek only to foreclose from others the use of that equation in conjunction with all of the other steps in their claimed process. * * * Obviously, one does not need a 'computer' to cure natural or synthetic rubber, but if the computer use incorporated in the process patent significantly lessens the possibility of 'overcuring' or 'undercuring,' the process as a whole does not thereby become unpatentable subject matter. * * *

"In this case, it may later be determined that the respondents' process is not deserving of patent protection because it fails to satisfy the statutory conditions of novelty under § 102 or nonobviousness under § 103. A rejection on either of these grounds does not affect the determination that respondents' claims recited subject matter which was eligible for patent protection under § 101. * * *

" * * * We recognize, of course, that when a claim recites a mathematical formula (or scientific principle or phenomenon of nature), an inquiry must be made into whether the claim is seeking patent protection for that formula in the abstract. * * * [I]nsignificant postsolution activity will not transform an unpatentable principle into a patentable process. * * * On the other hand, when a claim containing a mathematical formula implements or applies that formula in a structure or process which, when considered as a whole, is performing a function which the patent laws were designed to protect (e.g., transforming or reducing an article to a different state or thing), then the claim satisfies the requirements of § 101."

Justice Stevens' dissent, joined by Brennan, Marshall, and Blackmun, maintained that since the only new element of the process was an unpatentable algorithm, the process as a whole was unpatentable. The Court's decision in Parker v. Flook, he said, was controlling; the postsolution activity that distinguished respondents' process from the *Flook* alarm limit was not itself novel, so *Flook,* he argued, dictated that the entire process was unpatentable.

NOTES AND QUESTIONS

(1) Spurred by the obvious importance of computer technology in our modern economy, lower court cases after *Diehr* have continued to expand the availability of patent protection for software. The Court of Appeals for the Federal Circuit (successor to the Court of Customs and Patent Appeals) became adept at finding sufficient integration of a computer program with a claimed process or machine to avoid the bar against patenting abstract ideas. In re Alappat, 33 F.3d 1526 (Fed.Cir.1994), held that a claim directed to a machine that used a mathematical program to create a smooth waveform on an oscilloscope was patentable subject matter. "This is not a disembodied mathematical concept which may be characterized as an 'abstract idea,' but rather a specific machine to produce a useful, concrete, and tangible result. * * * Alappat admits that claim 15 would read on a general purpose computer programmed to carry out the claimed invention, but argues that this alone does not justify holding claim 15 unpatentable as directed to nonstatutory subject matter. We agree. We have held that such programming creates a new machine, because a general purpose computer in effect becomes a special purpose computer once it is programmed to perform particular functions pursuant to instructions from program software." In State Street Bank and Trust Co. v. Signature Financial Group, Inc., 149 F.3d 1368 (Fed.Cir.1998), cert. denied, 525 U.S. 1093 (1999), the Federal Circuit upheld the patentability of a computer-implemented investment accounting system. "Today we hold that the transformation of data, representing discrete dollar amounts, by a machine through a series of mathematical calculations into a final share price, constitutes a practical application of a mathematical algorithm, formula, or calculation, because it produces 'a useful, concrete and tangible result' * * *." The Federal Circuit later abandoned the "useful, concrete and tangible result" formulation in In re Bilski, 545 F.3d 943 (Fed.Cir.2008), holding in a business method case that the test for determining whether a claim went to an abstract idea or to patentable subject matter was whether "(1) it is tied to a particular machine or apparatus, or (2) it transforms a particular article into a different state or thing." When *Bilski* reached the Supreme Court as Bilski v. Kappos, 130 S.Ct. 3218 (2010), the Court held "that the machine-or-transformation test is a useful and important clue, an investigative tool, for determining whether some claimed inventions are processes under § 101. The machine-or-transformation test is not the sole test for deciding whether an invention is a patent-eligible 'process.'"

A panel of the Federal Circuit took advantage of the Supreme Court's broadened inquiry in *Bilski* to uphold the patentability of a computerized investment trading platform in CLS Bank Int'l v. Alice Corp. PTY. Ltd., 685 F.3d 1341 (Fed.Cir.2012). "Today, computers play a role in every part of our daily life. They are found in everything from toasters to transponders. The computer, with all of its hardware and software variations, may be one of the greatest inventions of all time, and there can be no question that advances in computer technology have fostered and will continue to foster innovation in all areas of science and technology. Many patents drawn to inventions implemented in computer hardware or software, however, are argued not to pass the machine-or-transformation test. Thus, courts must sometimes look beyond the machine-or-transformation test to distinguish eligible from ineligible computer-related claims." However, after a rehearing en banc, the Federal Circuit held that the claims were not directed to eligible subject matter under § 101. 2013 WL 1920941 (Fed.Cir.2013). Besides the *per curiam* opinion for the court, the ten judges produced five concurring and dissenting opinions, as well as some "Additional Reflections" by the Chief Judge. There was little consensus on how to interpret the judicially-created "abstract ideas" limitation on eligible subject matter. Describing the court as "irreconcilably fractured", Judge Moore in dissent hoped for further guidance from the Supreme Court.

(2) Remember that eligible subject matter must also satisfy the statutory requirements of novelty, utility, and non-obviousness. By some estimates the PTO now issues 40,000 software-related patents every year. J. Bessen, A Generation of Software Patents, 18 B.U.J.Sci. & Tech.L. 241 (2012). A former Director of the PTO has said that patents on software are "every bit as well deserved" as patents on air flight, the electric bulb, and innovations that enabled the industrial revolution. 85 Pat., Tm. & Copyr.J (BNA) 126 (2012).

(3) Is the patchwork of copyright, trade secret, and patent law adequate for the protection of software? Is it more than adequate? Does it overprotect, for example, in the long duration of copyright or patent? Are computer programs of such importance, and are their characteristics sufficiently distinctive, that a specially-tailored body of law should be adopted for their protection? A major effort to resurrect the sui generis alternative for software protection is made in P. Samuelson, R. Davis, M. Kapor, and J. Reichman, A Manifesto Concerning the Legal Protection of Computer Programs, 94 Colum.L.Rev. 2308 (1994). A. Miller, Copyright Protection for Computer Programs, Databases, and Computer–Generated Works: Is Anything New Since CONTU?, 106 Harv.L.Rev. 977 (1993), defends the assimilation of software into copyright as originally advocated in the CONTU Report, but J. Lipton, IP's Problem Child: Shifting the Paradigms for Software Protection, 58 Hastings L.J. 205 (2006), urges the elimination of copyright for software.

COPYRIGHT IN COMMERCIAL DESIGN

Mazer v. Stein

Supreme Court of the United States, 1954.
347 U.S. 201, 74 S.Ct. 460.

■ MR. JUSTICE REED delivered the opinion of the Court.

This case involves the validity of copyrights obtained by respondents for statuettes of male and female dancing figures made of semi-vitreous china. The controversy centers around the fact that although copyrighted as "works of art," the statuettes were intended for use and used as bases for table lamps, with electric wiring, sockets and lamp shades attached.

Respondents are partners in the manufacture and sale of electric lamps. One of the respondents created original works of sculpture in the form of human figures by traditional clay-model technique. From this model, a production mold for casting copies was made. The resulting statuettes, without any lamp components added, were submitted by the respondents to the Copyright Office for registration as "works of art" or reproductions thereof under § 5(g) or § 5(h) of the copyright law, and certificates of registration issued. Sales (publication in accordance with the statute) as fully equipped lamps preceded the applications for copyright registration of the statuettes. 17 U.S.C. (Supp. V, 1952) §§ 10, 11, 13, 209; Rules and Regulations, 37 CFR, 1949, §§ 202.8 and 202.9. Thereafter, the statuettes were sold in quantity throughout the country both as lamp bases and as statuettes. The sales in lamp form accounted for all but an insignificant portion of respondents' sales.

Sold as lamps & statues

Petitioners are partners and, like respondents, make and sell lamps. Without authorization, they copied the statuettes, embodied them in lamps and sold them.

The instant case is one in a series of reported suits brought by respondents against various alleged infringers of the copyrights, all presenting the same or a similar question. Because of conflicting decisions, we granted certiorari. * * *

Petitioners, charged by the present complaint with infringement of respondents' copyrights of reproductions of their works of art, seek here a reversal of the Court of Appeals decree upholding the copyrights. Petitioners in their petition for certiorari present a single question:

ACH for π

"Can statuettes be protected in the United States by copyright when the copyright applicant intended primarily to use the statuettes in the form of lamp bases to be made and sold in quantity and carried the intentions into effect?

issue

"Stripped down to its essentials, the question presented is: Can a lamp manufacturer copyright his lamp bases?"

The first paragraph accurately summarizes the issue. The last gives it a quirk that unjustifiably, we think, broadens the controversy. The case requires an answer, not as to a manufacturer's right to register a lamp base but as to an artist's right to copyright a work of art intended to be reproduced for lamp bases. As petitioners say in their brief, their contention "questions the validity of the copyright based upon the actions of respondents." Petitioners question the validity of a copyright of a work of art for "mass" production. "Reproduction of a work of art" does not mean to them unlimited reproduction. Their position is that a copyright does not cover industrial reproduction of the protected article. Thus their reply brief states: "When an artist becomes a manufacturer or a designer for a manufacturer he is subject to the limitations of design patents and deserves no more consideration than any other manufacturer or designer." It is not the right to copyright an article that could have utility under § 5(g) and (h), * * * that petitioners oppose. Their brief accepts the copyrightability of the great carved golden salt cellar of Cellini but adds: "If, however, Cellini designed and manufactured this item in quantity so that the general public could have salt cellars, then an entirely different conclusion would be reached. In such case, the salt cellar becomes an article of manufacture having utility in addition to its ornamental value and would therefore have to be protected by design patent." It is publication as a lamp and registration as a statue to gain a monopoly in manufacture that they assert is such a misuse of copyright as to make the registration invalid.

No unfair competition question is presented. The constitutional power of Congress to confer copyright protection on works of art or their reproductions is not questioned.[5] Petitioners assume, as Congress has in its enact-

---

[5]   We do not reach for constitutional questions not raised by the parties. * * *

ments and as do we, that the constitutional clause empowering legislation "To promote the Progress of Science and useful Arts, by securing for limited Times to Authors and Inventors the exclusive Right to their respective Writings and Discoveries", Art. I, § 8, cl. 8, includes within the term "Authors" the creator of a picture or a statue. The Court's consideration will be limited to the question presented by the petition for the writ of certiorari. In recent years the question as to utilitarian use of copyrighted articles has been much discussed.

Const grant

In answering that issue, a review of the development of copyright coverage will make clear the purpose of the Congress in its copyright legislation. In 1790 the First Congress conferred a copyright on "authors of any map, chart, book or books already printed." Later, designing, engraving and etching were included; in 1831 musical compositions; dramatic compositions in 1856; and photographs and negatives thereof in 1865.

1870

The Act of 1870 defined copyrightable subject matter as: ". . . any book, map, chart, dramatic or musical composition, engraving, cut, print, or photograph or negative thereof, or of a painting, drawing, chromo, *statue, statuary, and of models or designs intended to be perfected as works of the fine arts.*" (Emphasis supplied.) The italicized part added three-dimensional work of art to what had been protected previously. In 1909 Congress again enlarged the scope of the copyright statute. The new Act provided in § 4: "That the works for which copyright may be secured under this Act shall include all the writings of an author." Some writers interpret this section as being coextensive with the constitutional grant, but the House Report, while inconclusive, indicates that it was "declaratory of existing law" only. Section 5 relating to classes of writings in 1909 read as shown in the margin with subsequent additions not material to this decision.[19] Significant for our purposes was the deletion of the fine-arts clause of the 1870 Act. Verbal distinctions between purely aesthetic articles and useful works of art ended insofar as the statutory copyright language is concerned.

1909

The practice of the Copyright Office, under the 1870 and 1874 Acts and before the 1909 Act, was to allow registration "as works of the fine arts" of articles of the same character as those of respondents now under challenge. Seven examples appear in the Government's brief *amicus curiae.*[22] In 1910, interpreting the 1909 Act, the pertinent Copyright Regulations read as shown in the margin.[23] Because, as explained by the Government, this regulation "made no reference to articles which might fairly be considered works of art although they might also serve a useful purpose," it was reworded in 1917 as shown below.[24] The *amicus* brief gives sixty ex-

---

[19] [The Court's footnote sets out § 5 of the Act of 1909.]

[22] E.g., "A female figure bearing an urn in front partly supported by drapery around the head. The figure nude from the waist up and below this the form concealed by conventionalized skirt draperies which flow down and forward forming a tray at the base. Sides and back of skirt in fluted form. The whole being designed as a candlestick with match tray. The figure standing and bent forward from hips and waist."

[23] "Works of art.—This term includes all works belonging fairly to the so-called fine arts. (Paintings, drawings, and sculpture.)

"Productions of the industrial arts utilitarian in purpose and character are not subject to copyright registration, even if artistically made or ornamented." Rules and Regulations for the Registration of Claims to Copyright, Bulletin No. 15 (1910), 8.

[The rest of this 1910 regulation, which the Court's footnote omits, was as follows: "No copyright exists in toys, games, dolls, advertising novelties, instruments or tools of any kind, glassware, embroideries, garments, laces, woven fabrics, or any similar articles."]

[24] "Works of art and models or designs for works of art.—This term includes all works belonging fairly to the so-called fine arts. (Paintings, drawings, and sculpture.)

amples selected at five-year intervals, 1912–1952, said to be typical of registrations of works of art possessing utilitarian aspects.[25] The current pertinent regulation, published in 37 CFR, 1949, § 202.8, reads thus: "Works of art (Class G)—(a)—In General. This class includes works of artistic craftsmanship, in so far as their form but not their mechanical or utilitarian aspects are concerned, such as artistic jewelry, enamels, glassware, and tapestries, as well as all works belonging to the fine arts, such as paintings, drawings and sculpture. . . . " So we have a contemporaneous and long-continued construction of the statutes by the agency charged to administer them that would allow the registration of such a statuette as is in question here.

This Court once essayed to fix the limits of the fine arts.[27] That effort need not be appraised in relation to this copyright issue. It is clear Congress intended the scope of the copyright statute to include more than the traditional fine arts. Herbert Putnam, Esq., then Librarian of Congress and active in the movement to amend the copyright laws, told the joint meeting of the House and Senate Committees:

> "The term 'works of art' is deliberately intended as a broader specification than 'works of the fine arts' in the present statute with the idea that there is subject-matter (for instance, of applied design, not yet within the province of design patents), which may properly be entitled to protection under the copyright law."[28]

The successive acts, the legislative history of the 1909 Act and the practice of the Copyright Office unite to show that "works of art" and "reproductions of works of art" are terms that were intended by Congress to include the authority to copyright these statuettes. Individual perception of the beautiful is too varied a power to permit a narrow or rigid concept of art. As a standard we can hardly do better than the words of the present Regulation, § 202.8, supra, naming the things that appertain to the arts. They must be original, that is, the author's tangible expression of his ideas. Compare Burrow–Giles Lithographic Co. v. Sarony, 111 U.S. 53, 59–60. Such expression, whether meticulously delineating the model or mental image or conveying the meaning by modernistic form or color, is copyrightable. What cases there are confirm this coverage of the statute.[30]

"The protection of productions of the industrial arts, utilitarian in purpose and character, even if artistically made or ornamented depends upon action under the patent law; but registration in the Copyright Office has been made to protect artistic drawings notwithstanding they may afterwards be utilized for articles of manufacture." 37 CFR, 1939, § 201.4(7).

[25]   E.g., "Lighting fixture design. By F.E. Guitini. [Bowl-shaped bracket embellished with figure of half-nude woman standing in bunch of flowers.] Copyright December 28, 1912. Registration number G 42645. Copyright claimant: Kathodion Bronze Works, New York."

[27]   United States v. Perry, 146 U.S. 71.

[28]   Arguments before the Committees on Patents of the Senate and House of Representatives, conjointly, on S. 6330 and H.R. 19853, To Amend and Consolidate the Arts Respecting Copyright, 59th Cong., 1st Sess., June 6–9, 1906, p. 11. * * *

[30]   Burrow–Giles Lithographic Co. v. Sarony, 111 U.S. 53; Bleistein v. Donaldson Lithographing Co., 188 U.S. 239, 250; Louis De Jonge & Co. v. Breuker & Kessler Co., C.C., 182 F. 150, 152; F.W. Woolworth Co. v. Contemporary Arts, 1 Cir., 193 F.2d 162, 164; see same case, 344 U.S. 228; Yuengling v. Schile, C.C., 12 F. 97, 100; Schumacher v. Schwencke, C.C., 25 F. 466; Pellegrini v. Allegrini, D.C., 2 F.2d 610.

THE PRINCIPAL STATUETTE IN MAZER v. STEIN.

The conclusion that the statues here in issue may be copyrighted goes far to solve the question whether their intended reproduction as lamp stands bars or invalidates their registration. This depends solely on statutory interpretation. Congress may after publication protect by copyright any writing of an author. Its statute creates the copyright. It did not exist at common law even though he had a property right in his unpublished work.

But petitioners assert that congressional enactment of the design patent laws should be interpreted as denying protection to artistic articles embodied or reproduced in manufactured articles. They say: "Fundamentally and historically, the Copyright Office is the repository of what each claimant considers to be a cultural treasure, whereas the Patent Office is the repository of what each applicant considers to be evidence of the advance in industrial and technological fields." Their argument is that design patents require the critical examination given patents to protect the public against monopoly. Attention is called to Gorham Mfg. Co. v. White, 14 Wall. 511, interpreting the design patent law of 1842, 5 Stat. 544, granting a patent to anyone who by "their own industry, genius, efforts, and expense, may have invented or produced any new and original design for a manufacture. . . . " A pattern for flat silver was there upheld. The intermediate and present law differs little. "Whoever invents any new, original and ornamental design for an article of manufacture may obtain a patent therefor, . . . " subject generally to the provisions concerning patents for invention. § 171, 66 Stat. 805, 35 U.S.C.A. § 171. As petitioner sees the effect of the design patent law: "If an industrial designer can not satisfy the novelty requirements of the design patent laws, then his design as used on articles of manufacture can be copied by anyone." Petitioner has furnished the Court a booklet of numerous design patents for statuettes, bases for table lamps and similar articles for manufacture, quite indistinguishable in type from the copyrighted statuettes here in issue.[35] Petitioner urges that overlapping of patent and copyright legislation so as to give an author or inventor a choice between patents and copyrights should not be permitted. We assume petitioner takes the position that protection for a statuette for industrial use can only be obtained by patent, if any protection can be given.

As we have held the statuettes here involved copyrightable, we need not decide the question of their patentability. Though other courts have passed upon the issue as to whether allowance by the election of the author or patentee of one bars a grant of the other, we do not. We do hold that the patentability of the statuettes, fitted as lamps or unfitted, does not bar copyright as works of art. Neither the Copyright Statute nor any other says that because a thing is patentable it may not be copyrighted. We should not so hold.

Unlike a patent, a copyright gives no exclusive right to the art disclosed; protection is given only to the expression of the idea—not the idea itself. Thus, in Baker v. Selden, 101 U.S. 99, the Court held that a copyrighted book on a peculiar system of bookkeeping was not infringed by a similar book using a similar plan which achieved similar results where the alleged infringer made a different arrangement of the columns and used different headings. The distinction is illustrated in Fred Fisher, Inc. v. Dillingham, D.C., 298 F. 145, 151, when the court speaks of two men, each a perfectionist, independently making maps of the same territory. Though the maps are identical each may obtain the exclusive right to make copies of his own particular map, and yet neither will infringe the other's copyright. Likewise a copyrighted directory is not infringed by a similar directory which is the product of independent work. The copyright protects originality rather than novelty or invention—conferring only "the sole right of multiplying copies."[41] Absent copying there can be no infringement of copyright. Thus, respondents may not exclude others from using statuettes of

---

[35] E.g., Design Patent 170.445 Base for table lamps, a fanciful statuette of a girl standing in front of a high rock in bathing costume.

[41] Jeweler's Circular Pub. Co. v. Keystone Publishing, 2 Cir., 281 F. 83, 94, 26 A.L.R. 571.

human figures in table lamps; they may only prevent use of copies of their statuettes as such or as incorporated in some other article. Regulation § 202.8, supra, makes clear that artistic articles are protected in "form but not their mechanical or utilitarian aspects." See Stein v. Rosenthal, D.C., 103 F.Supp. 227, 231. The dichotomy of protection for the aesthetic is not beauty and utility but art for the copyright and the invention of original and ornamental design for design patents. We find nothing in the copyright statute to support the argument that the intended use or use in industry of an article eligible for copyright bars or invalidates its registration. We do not read such a limitation into the copyright law.

Nor do we think the subsequent registration of a work of art published as an element in a manufactured article, is a misuse of the copyright. This is not different from the registration of a statuette and its later embodiment in an industrial article.

"The copyright law, like the patent statutes, makes reward to the owner a secondary consideration." United States v. Paramount Pictures, 334 U.S. 131, 158. However, it is "intended definitely to grant valuable enforceable rights to authors, publishers, etc., without burdensome requirements; 'to afford greater encouragement to the production of literary [or artistic] works of lasting benefit to the world.'" Washingtonian Pub. Co. v. Pearson, 306 U.S. 30, 36.

The economic philosophy behind the clause empowering Congress to grant patents and copyrights is the conviction that encouragement of individual effort by personal gain is the best way to advance public welfare through the talents of authors and inventors in "Science and useful Arts." Sacrificial days devoted to such creative activities deserve rewards commensurate with the services rendered.

Affirmed.

■ Opinion of MR. JUSTICE DOUGLAS, in which MR. JUSTICE BLACK concurs.

An important constitutional question underlies this case—a question which was stirred on oral argument but not treated in the briefs. It is whether these statuettes of dancing figures may be copyrighted. Congress has provided that "works of art," "models or designs for works of art," and "reproductions of a work of art" may be copyrighted, 17 U.S.C. § 5; and the Court holds that these statuettes are included in the words "works of art." But may statuettes be granted the monopoly of the copyright?

Article I, § 8 of the Constitution grants Congress the power "To promote the Progress of Science and useful Arts, by securing for limited Times to Authors . . . the exclusive Right to their respective Writings . . . . " The power is thus circumscribed: it allows a monopoly to be granted only to "authors" for their "writings." Is a sculptor an "author" and is his statue a "writing" within the meaning of the Constitution? We have never decided the question. * * *

The interests involved in the category of "works of art," as used in the copyright law, are considerable. The Copyright Office has supplied us with a long list of such articles which have been copyrighted—statuettes, book ends, clocks, lamps, door knockers, candlesticks, inkstands, chandeliers, piggy banks, sundials, salt and pepper shakers, fish bowls, casseroles, and ash trays. Perhaps these are all "writings" in the constitutional sense. But to me, at least, they are not obviously so. It is time that we came to the problem full face. I would accordingly put the case down for reargument.

NOTES AND QUESTIONS

(1) What is the holding of *Mazer?* That all utilitarian objects are copyrightable as "sculptural works"? That an otherwise copyrightable "work of art" will not forfeit protection if it is reproduced as part of a useful article?

(2) *Should* a light bulb protruding from the head of Rodin's *The Thinker* render the work uncopyrightable?

————

DESIGN PATENT

One argument urged on the Supreme Court in Mazer v. Stein was that protection for the design of a useful article is the exclusive province of federal design patent law. Since 1842, design patent protection has been available for the appearance of an "article of manufacture." 5 Stat. 544 (1842). The current Patent Act at 35 U.S.C.A. § 171 provides:

§ 171.   Patents for designs

Whoever invents any new, original and ornamental design for an article of manufacture may obtain a patent therefor, subject to the conditions and requirements of this title.

The provisions of this title relating to patents for inventions shall apply to patents for designs, except as otherwise provided.

The second sentence of § 171 subjects design patents to the demanding standards applied to other patents, including the "non-obvious" requirement in § 103. The next case grapples with the consequences.

In re Nalbandian

United States Court of Customs and Patent Appeals, 1981.
661 F.2d 1214.

■ Before MARKEY, CHIEF JUDGE, and RICH, BALDWIN, MILLER and NIES, JUDGES.

■ NIES, JUDGE.

This appeal is from the decision of the Patent and Trademark Office (PTO) Board of Appeals (board) affirming the rejection under 35 U.S.C. § 103 by the examiner of appellant's application, serial No. 792,482, filed April 29, 1977, for "Combined Tweezer and Spotlight." We affirm.

denied design patent

The claimed ornamental design is for an implement referred to as an illuminable tweezer. The primary reference on which the examiner and the board relied is U.S. Patent Des. 175,259, issued to Johnson et al. (Johnson) on August 2, 1955, also for an illuminable tweezer. The respective designs are reproduced below:

Appellant's

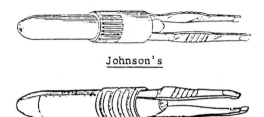

Johnson's

* * *

The sole issue on appeal is whether appellant's design would have been obvious within the meaning of 35 U.S.C. § 103. In the words of the statute, are

> . . . the differences between the subject matter sought to be patented and the prior art . . . such that the subject matter as a whole would have been obvious at the time the invention was made to a person having ordinary skill in the art to which said subject matter pertains[?]

In In re Laverne, 356 F.2d 1003 (1966), this court specifically rejected the interpretation generally given to the statutory language "one of ordinary skill in the art" as referring to a designer. The court concluded that this interpretation would not effectuate the intent of Congress to promote progress in designs since it would result in the denial of patent protection for the work of competent designers. Accordingly, it was held that the obviousness of designs over the prior art must be tested by the eyes of the "ordinary intelligent man," who was also referred to as the "ordinary observer."

Since the *Laverne* decision, the Second, Third, Tenth and District of Columbia circuits have specifically considered the "ordinary observer" test set forth therein and rejected it. These circuits continue to interpret "one of ordinary skill" as requiring obviousness to be tested from the viewpoint of the "ordinary designer." Since board decisions may be reviewed by the District of Columbia Circuit as well as this court, the PTO has been faced with two standards in design cases.

We believe it is appropriate to close this schism. Accordingly, with this case we hold that the test of *Laverne* will no longer be followed. In design cases we will consider the fictitious person identified in § 103 as "one of ordinary skill in the art" to be the designer of ordinary capability who designs articles of the type presented in the application. This approach is consistent with Graham v. John Deere Co., 383 U.S. 1 (1966), which requires that the level of ordinary skill *in the pertinent art be determined.* * * *

Rejection of the "ordinary observer" test under 35 U.S.C. § 103 does not preclude its application in other contexts. The "ordinary observer" test was applied in determining whether a claim to a design had been infringed as long ago as Gorham Co. v. White, 81 U.S. (14 Wall.) 511 (1871). Further, the "ordinary observer" test has been applied when determining anticipation under § 102 by courts which apply the "ordinary designer" test under § 103.

Applying the "ordinary designer" test of § 103 to the case at bar, the question is whether the changes made by appellant in the Johnson design

for an illuminated tweezer would have been obvious to an ordinary designer of such implements. As noted, the claimed design is substantially identical in overall configuration to the design shown in Johnson for the same
type of article. The differences in the finger grips of a slightly different
shape and the straight, rather than slightly curved pincers, are de minimis.
We also agree that it is well within the skill of an ordinary designer in the
art to make the modification of the fluting and that it would have been obvious to do so. Such changes do not achieve a patentably distinct design. In
re Lamb, 286 F.2d 610 (1961). We agree, therefore, that the PTO has shown
a prima facie case of obviousness. * * *

Affirmed.

■ RICH, JUDGE, concurring.

A majority of my colleagues choose to swing the court into alignment
with the three circuits which have affirmatively rejected the reasoning of
our fifteen-year old *In re Laverne* opinion which, until now, this court has
always unanimously accepted without question.

Laverne thus being dead, I deem it appropriate, as the father of the so-
called "ordinary observer" test (as applied to 35 U.S.C. § 103), to say a few
kind words over the corpse.

From the passages quoted from my opinion by the majority, it will be
seen that what was written in 1966 was a response to the examiner's reliance on what would be produced by "the expected skill of a competent designer," perhaps an imaginary person of somewhat greater skill than the
imaginary "ordinary designer" now enthroned by the majority. I was interested in retaining within the ambit of the patent system the made-for-hire
products of "competent designers" so businessmen or corporations would
find it economically advantageous to employ them, thus carrying out the
objective of 35 U.S.C. § 171, to promote the ornamental design of articles of
manufacture.

The majority is not now talking of "competent designers" but of "ordinary designers" from which it follows that there may be extraordinary designers who will produce unobvious designs which ordinary designers will
not routinely produce. It is probably true, as the majority says, that all this
is just semantics and courts will, with phraseology of their own choosing,
continue to find designs patentable or unpatentable according to their judicial "hunches."

The real problem, however, is not whether the § 103 fictitious "person"
is an ordinary observer or an ordinary designer but with the necessity under Title 35 of finding unobviousness in a design. The problem long ante-
dates 1952 and its Patent Act and existed from the beginning, the pre–1952
test being the presence of "invention" in a design. The problem was well
known to the drafters of the 1952 Act (of which I was one) and it was also
known that many prior legislative efforts had been made to solve it.[1] When

---

[1]   Records I made in the mid 50's show that, beginning in 1914, some 45 bills were introduced in the House and Senate directed to some improved form of protection for designs. Many
of these bills were, of course, duplicates, substantially the same bill being introduced in each
house or reintroduced in successive years. Those interested in the history can examine Barbara A. Ringer's 70–page *Bibliography on Design Protection* published for Copyright Office use
June 1, 1955, and an enlarged 160–page version or "supplement" compiled by W. Strauss,
Varmer, Caruthers, and Berger on June 1, 1959, bearing the same title. Fabulous amounts of
time and effort have been poured into solving the design protection problem with, to date, no
legislative solution. See also Kelsey M. Mott's two-installment article The Standard of Orna-
mentality in the United States Design Patent Law, 48 ABA J. 548, 643 (June, July 1962).

work on revision of the patent statutes began in 1950, a deliberate decision was made not to attempt any solution of the "controversial design problem" but simply to retain the substance of the existing design patent statute and attack the design problem at a later date, after the new Title 35 had been enacted.

Thus it was that the patentability of designs came to be subject to the new § 103 which was written with an eye to the kinds of inventions encompassed by § 101 with no thought at all of how it might affect designs. Therefore, the design protection problem was in no way made better; perhaps it was made worse. * * *

The point of this review is to call attention to the resulting presently pending legislation, H.R. 20, 97th Congress, 1st Session, introduced January 5, 1981, by Mr. Railsback, a bill "To amend the copyright law, title 17 of the United States Code, to provide for protection of ornamental designs of useful articles." The present case and its companion, In re Spreter, 661 F.2d 1220 (Cust. & Pat.App.), concurrently decided, are but the latest examples of the need for a law tailored to the problems of designers, of their employers and clients in the business world, and of the government agencies now concerned. The now-pending legislation is substantially the same bill introduced in 1957, after the refining process of *24 years of legislative consideration. It is time to pass it* and get the impossible issue of obviousness in design patentability cases off the backs of the courts and the Patent and Trademark Office, giving some sense of certainty to the business world of what designs can be protected and how. * * *

NOTES ON DESIGN PATENTS

(1) Design patents have issued for the ornamental designs of objects ranging from hosiery reinforcements to cement mixer trucks.[q] Some cases reflect persistent attempts to capture the *function* of an article indirectly by means of a design patent claim, but courts resist this backdoor approach when they detect it. See, e.g., Best Lock Corp. v. Ilco Unican Corp., 94 F.3d 1563 (Fed.Cir.1996) (design patent on the shape of key blanks was declared invalid; the shape was dictated by function because of the necessary compatibility with the corresponding lock). In Richardson v. Stanley Works, Inc., 597 F.3d 1288 (Fed.Cir.2010), an action for infringement of a design patent on a multi-function carpentry tool, the Federal Circuit held that the trial court was correct in factoring out functional aspects of the patented design. "If the patented design is primarily functional rather than ornamental, the patent is invalid. * * * However, when the design also contains ornamental aspects, it is entitled to a design patent whose scope is limited to those aspects alone and does not extent to any functional elements of the claimed article."

(2) The overlap between the subject matters of design patent and copyright raises the possibility of dual protection. Early cases put the creator to an election. The Supreme Court in *Mazer* noted the prior case law, but found it unnecessary to consider the election doctrine since the plaintiff had not sought a design patent.

---

[q] See Glen Raven Knitting Mills, Inc. v. Sanson Hosiery Mills, Inc., 189 F.2d 845 (4th Cir.1951); In re Koehring, 37 F.2d 421 (C.C.P.A.1930). The appearance of a stadium grandstand, In re Hadden, 20 F.2d 275 (D.C.Cir.1927), and even the design produced by jets of water in a fountain, In re Hruby, 373 F.2d 997 (C.C.P.A.1967), have been found to fall within the statutory subject matter. For a more modern illustration, see Apple, Inc. v. Samsung Electronics Co., 678 F.3d 1314 (Fed.Cir.2012) (design patents on Apple's iPhone and iPad).

In 1974, the Court of Customs and Patent Appeals repudiated the election doctrine. It reversed a Patent and Trademark Office decision rejecting a design patent application for a previously copyrighted watch bearing a caricature of Spiro Agnew (Spiro who?). In re Yardley, 493 F.2d 1389 (C.C.P.A.1974). The Copyright Office, however, continued to refuse copyright registration to patented designs until 1995, when it too finally abandoned the election doctrine. See 60 Fed.Reg. 15605 (1995).

(3) Does the "non-obvious" standard for ornamental designs under patent law require the kind of artistic judgments generally eschewed by copyright law? T. Lindgren, The Sanctity of Design Patent: Illusion or Reality?, 10 Okla. City U.L.Rev. 195 (1985), reports that about 70% of the design patents challenged in federal courts between 1964 and 1983 were held *invalid*. Although the sample produced by cases attacking validity is undoubtedly biased toward questionable patents, the statistics nevertheless appear to vindicate the prevailing mistrust of design patent protection. The tide eventually turned as the Federal Circuit increasingly exercised its exclusive appellate jurisdiction over patents to uphold validity. See, e.g., Avia Group Int'l, Inc. v. L.A. Gear California, Inc., 853 F.2d 1557 (Fed.Cir.1988).

In contrast to the relative ease with which a copyright registration can be secured, obtaining a design patent is, as with other patents, a difficult business. The applicant (or realistically, the applicant's attorney, who must be licensed to practice before the Patent and Trademark Office) must file an elaborate application detailing the claim. The PTO then conducts a search to determine novelty and nonobviousness. This may take considerable time—in some cases several years. Costs (including filing fees, issuance fees, and attorney's fees) mount quickly, particularly if protection is sought for a number of new designs.

The design patent, if issued, has a term of fourteen years. 35 U.S.C.A. § 173. The degree of similarity that will constitute infringement of a patented design is measured with reference to the reaction of an "ordinary observer," Gorham Manufacturing Co. v. White, 81 U.S. 511 (1871), who is familiar with the prior art, Egyptian Goddess, Inc. v. Swisa, Inc., 543 F.3d 665 (Fed.Cir.2008), cert. denied, 129 S.Ct. 1917 (2009).

On design patents, see generally D. Chisum, Chisum on Patents, Chap. 23.

USEFUL ARTICLES AFTER *MAZER*

Soon after Mazer v. Stein, the regulations of the Copyright Office were amended to reflect the Supreme Court's holding. Registration of copyright in a "work of art" would not be affected by "the use of the work, the number of copies reproduced, or the fact that it appears on a textile material or textile product." 37 C.F.R. § 202.10(b) (1957) (current version at 37 C.F.R. § 202.10(a)). As this language suggests, textile designers were a major beneficiary of the new rule.

Before *Mazer,* manufacturers seeking protection for textile designs had hard going. See Cheney Brothers v. Doris Silk Corp., p. 647 infra; Verney Corp. v. Rose Fabric Converters Corp., 87 F.Supp. 802 (S.D.N.Y.1949). Design patents were presumably available, but the delays and expense associated with the application process and the requirements of novelty and nonobviousness made them an unattractive alternative. Copyright was far better suited to the protection of such evanescent creations, and after *Mazer* they were securely within its scope. See Peter Pan Fabrics, Inc. v. Martin Weiner Corp., p. 208 infra. Indeed, graphic designs on utilitarian articles ranging from shoe soles to dinnerware were now within the subject matter of copyright. See SCOA Industries, Inc. v. Famolare, Inc., 192 U.S.P.Q. 216 (S.D.N.Y.1976); Syracuse China Corp. v. Stanley Roberts, Inc., 180 F.Supp. 527 (S.D.N.Y.1960).

Copyright claims embracing three-dimensional aspects of utilitarian objects presented greater difficulties. As the Copyright Office regulation quoted by the Supreme Court in *Mazer* indicates, jewelry had already found a place within the statutory scheme, but perhaps jewelry is not really a utilitarian object. Cf. § 101 (definition of "useful article").[r] A dancing figure used as a lamp base was now within the subject matter of copyright, but what of the design of a dress, the contours of an automobile, or the shape of a silver tea service?

The Copyright Office, determined to preclude protection for all manner of industrial design, promulgated a regulation limiting copyright in utilitarian articles. The regulation inspired the formulation ultimately adopted in the 1976 Copyright Act. The Act includes a narrow codification of *Mazer* in § 113(a); the distinctions between works of applied art and industrial design pursued in the former regulation now appear in the § 101 definitions of "useful article" and "pictorial, graphic, and sculptural works." The regulation and its statutory offspring are analyzed in the following case.

Kieselstein–Cord v. Accessories By Pearl, Inc.

United States Court of Appeals, Second Circuit, 1980.
632 F.2d 989.

■ Before OAKES and VAN GRAAFEILAND, CIRCUIT JUDGES, and WEINSTEIN, DISTRICT JUDGE.

■ OAKES, CIRCUIT JUDGE:

This case is on a razor's edge of copyright law. It involves belt buckles, utilitarian objects which as such are not copyrightable. But these are not ordinary buckles; they are sculptured designs cast in precious metals—decorative in nature and used as jewelry is, principally for ornamentation. We say "on a razor's edge" because the case requires us to draw a fine line under applicable copyright law and regulations. Drawing the line in favor of the appellant designer, we uphold the copyrights granted to him by the Copyright Office and reverse the district court's grant of summary judgment, 489 F.Supp. 732, in favor of the appellee, the copier of appellant's designs.

Appellant Barry Kieselstein–Cord designs, manufactures exclusively by handcraftsmanship, and sells fashion accessories. To produce the two buckles in issue here, the "Winchester" and the "Vaquero," he worked from original renderings which he had conceived and sketched. * * *

* * * Sales of both buckles were made primarily in high fashion stores and jewelry stores, bringing recognition to appellant as a "designer." This recognition included a 1979 Coty American Fashion Critics' Award for his

---

[r]   See Donald Bruce & Co. v. B.H. Multi Com Corp., 964 F.Supp. 265 (N.D.Ill.1997), holding that a ring is not a "useful article" under the § 101 definition since it "is purely ornamental, its sole purpose is to portray its appearance."

work in jewelry design as well as election in 1978 to the Council of Fashion Designers of America. Both the Winchester and the Vaquero buckles, donated by appellant after this lawsuit was commenced, have been accepted by the Metropolitan Museum of Art for its permanent collection.

As the court below found, appellee's buckles "appear to be line-for-line copies but are made of common metal rather than" precious metal. Appellee admitted to copying the Vaquero and selling its imitations, and to selling copies of the Winchester. Indeed some of the order blanks of appellee's customers specifically referred to "Barry K Copy," "BK copy," and even "Barry Kieselstein Knock-off." Thus the only legal questions for the court below were whether the articles may be protected under the copyright statutes and, if so, whether the copyrights were adequate under the laws. * * *

* * * The thrust of appellee's argument, as well as of the court's decision below, is that appellant's buckles are not copyrightable because they are "useful articles" with no "pictorial, graphic, or sculptural features that can be identified separately from, and are capable of existing independently of, the utilitarian aspects" of the buckles. The 1976 copyright statute does not provide for the copyrighting of useful articles except to the extent that their designs incorporate artistic features that can be identified separately from the functional elements of the articles. See 17 U.S.C. §§ 101, 102. With respect to this question, the law adopts the language of the longstanding Copyright Office regulations, 37 C.F.R. § 202.10(c) (1977)[3] (revoked Jan. 5, 1978, 43 Fed.Reg. 965, 966 (1978)). The regulations in turn were adopted in the mid–1950's, under the 1909 Act, in an effort to implement the Supreme Court's decision in Mazer v. Stein, 347 U.S. 201 (1954). See H.R.Rep. No. 1476, 94th Cong., 2d Sess. 54–55 (1976), reprinted in [1976] U.S.Code Cong. & Admin. News, pp. 5659, 5668 [hereinafter cited as *House Report*]. The Court in *Mazer,* it will be recalled, upheld the validity of copyrights obtained for statuettes of male and female dancing figures despite the fact that they were intended for use and used as bases for table lamps, with electric wiring, sockets, and lampshades attached. *Mazer* itself followed a "contemporaneous and long-continued construction" by the Copyright Office of the 1870 and 1874 Acts as well as of the 1909 Act, under which the case was decided. 347 U.S. at 211–13. As Professor Nimmer points out, however,

---

[3]   37 C.F.R. § 202.10, reprinted in 4 Nimmer on Copyright, App. 11, at 11–13 to 11–14 (1980), provided as follows:

Works of Art (Class G)

(a) General[.] This class includes published or unpublished works of artistic craftsmanship, insofar as their form but not their mechanical or utilitarian aspects are concerned, such as artistic jewelry, enamels, glassware, and tapestries, as well as works belonging to the fine arts, such as paintings, drawings and sculpture. [Revoked Jan. 1, 1978, 43 Fed.Reg. 965, 966 (1978).]

(b) In order to be acceptable as a work of art, the work must embody some creative authorship in its delineation or form. The registrability of a work of art is not affected by the intention of the author as to the use of the work, the number of copies reproduced, or the fact that it appears on a textile material or textile product. The potential availability of protection under the design patent law will not affect the registrability of a work of art, but a copyright claim in a patented design or in the drawings or photographs in a patent application will not be registered after the patent has been issued. [Current version at 37 C.F.R. § 202.10(b) (1979).]

(c) If the sole intrinsic function of an article is its utility, the fact that the article is unique and attractively shaped will not qualify it as a work of art. However, if the shape of a utilitarian article incorporates features, such as artistic sculpture, carving, or pictorial representation, which can be identified separately and are capable of existing independently as a work of art, such features will be eligible for registration. [Revoked Jan. 1, 1978, 43 Fed.Reg. 965, 966 (1978).]

the Copyright Office's regulations in the mid–1950's that purported to "implement" this decision actually limited the Court's apparent open-ended extension of copyright protection to all aesthetically pleasing useful articles. See 1 Nimmer, supra, § 2.08[B], at 2–88 to 2–89. * * *

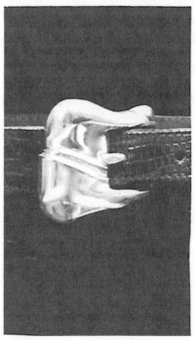 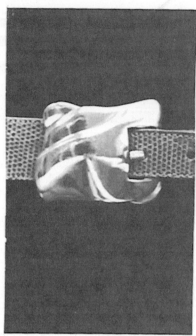

Winchester   Vaquero

We are left nevertheless with the problem of determining when a pictorial, graphic, or sculptural feature "can be identified separately from, and [is] capable of existing independently of, the utilitarian aspects of the article," 17 U.S.C. § 101. This problem is particularly difficult because, according to the legislative history explored by the court below, such separability may occur either "physically or conceptually," *House Report* at 55, [1976] U.S.Code Cong. & Admin. News at 5668. As the late Judge Harold Leventhal observed in his concurrence in Esquire, Inc. v. Ringer, 591 F.2d 796, 807 (D.C.Cir.1978), cert. denied, 440 U.S. 908 (1979), legislative policy supports the Copyright Office's "effort to distinguish between the instances where the aesthetic element is conceptually severable and the instances where the aesthetic element is inextricably interwoven with the utilitarian aspect of the article." Examples of conceptual separateness as an artistic notion may be found in many museums today and even in the great outdoors. Professor Nimmer cites Christo's "Running Fence" as an example of today's "conceptual art": it "did not contain sculptural features that were physically separable from the utilitarian aspects of the fence, but the whole point of the work was that the artistic aspects of the work were conceptually separable." 1 Nimmer, supra, § 2.08[B] at 2–94. * * *

We see in appellant's belt buckles conceptually separable sculptural elements, as apparently have the buckles' wearers who have used them as ornamentation for parts of the body other than the waist. The primary ornamental aspect of the Vaquero and Winchester buckles is conceptually separable from their subsidiary utilitarian function. This conclusion is not at variance with the expressed congressional intent to distinguish copyrightable applied art and uncopyrightable industrial design, *House Report* at 55, [1976] U.S.Code Cong. & Admin.News at 5668. Pieces of applied art, these buckles may be considered jewelry, the form of which is subject to copyright protection, * * *.

We reverse the grant of summary judgment to the appellee and remand the case for consideration of whether appellant has satisfied the copyright notice requirements.

■ WEINSTEIN, DISTRICT JUDGE (dissenting):

The trial judge was correct on both the law and the facts for the reasons given in his excellent opinion holding that plaintiff was not entitled to copyright protection. Kieselstein–Cord v. Accessories By Pearl, Inc., 489 F.Supp. 732 (S.D.N.Y.1980). The works sued on are, while admirable aesthetically pleasing examples of modern design, indubitably belt buckles and nothing else; their innovations of form are inseparable from the important function they serve—helping to keep the tops of trousers at waist level.

The conclusion that affirmance is required is reached reluctantly. The result does deny protection to designers who use modern three-dimensional abstract works artfully incorporated into a functional object as an inseparable aspect of the article while granting it to those who attach their independent representational art, or even their trite gimmickry, to a useful object for purposes of enhancement. Moreover, this result enables the commercial pirates of the marketplace to appropriate for their own profit, without any cost to themselves, the works of talented designers who enrich our lives with their intuition and skill. The crass are rewarded, the artist who creates beauty is not. All of us are offended by the flagrant copying of another's work. This is regrettable, but it is not for this court to twist the law in order to achieve a result Congress has denied. * * *

Interpretation and application of the copyright statute is facilitated by House Report No. 94–1476, U.S.Code Cong. & Admin.News 1976, p. 5658, by the Committee on the Judiciary. It explicitly indicated that the rule of *Mazer* was incorporated.

In accordance with the Supreme Court's decision in Mazer v. Stein, 347 U.S. 201 (1954), works of "applied art" encompass all original pictorial, graphic, and sculptural works that are intended to be or have been embodied in useful articles, regardless of factors such as mass production, commercial exploitation, and the potential availability of design patent protection . . .

The Committee has added language to the definition of "pictorial, graphic, and sculptural works" in an effort to make clearer the distinction between works of applied art protectable under the bill and industrial designs not subject to copyright protection. * * *

* * *

In adopting this amendatory language [the separability test in § 101], the Committee is seeking to draw as clear a line as possible between copyrightable works of applied art and uncopyrighted works of industrial design. A two-dimensional painting, drawing, or graphic work is still capable of being identified as such when it is printed on or applied to utilitarian articles such as textile fabrics, wallpaper, containers, and the like. The same is true when a statue or carving is used to embellish an industrial product or, as in the *Mazer* case, is incorporated into a product without losing its ability to exist independently as a work of art. On the other hand, *although the shape of an industrial product may be aesthetically satisfying and valuable, the Committee's intention is not to offer it copyright protection under the bill.* Unless the shape of an automobile, airplane, ladies' dress, food processor, television set, or any other industrial product contains some element that, physically or conceptually, can be identified as separable from the utilitarian aspects of that article, the design would not be copyrighted under the bill. The test of separability and independence from "the utilitarian aspects of the article" does not depend upon the nature of the design— that is, even if the appearance of an article is determined by aesthetic (as opposed to functional) considerations, only elements, if any, which can be identified separately from the useful article as such are copyrightable. *And, even if the three-dimensional design contains some such element (for example, a carving on the back of a chair or a floral relief design on silver flatware), copyright protection would extend only to that element, and would not cover the overall configuration of the utilitarian article as such.*

1976 U.S.Code Cong. & Admin.News, pp. 5667–5668. (Emphasis supplied.)

Congress considered and declined to enact legislation that would have extended copyright protection to "[t]he 'design of a useful article' . . . including its two-dimensional or three-dimensional features of shape and surface, which make up the appearance of the article." H.R. 2223, Title II, § 201(b)(2), 94th Cong., 1st Sess. (January 28, 1975). * * *

The distinctions between copyrightable "pictorial, graphic and sculptural works" and noncopyrightable industrial "designs" reflect serious concerns about the promotion of competition, the widespread availability of quality products and the advancement of technology through copying and modification. * * *

Important policies are obviously at stake. Should we encourage the artist and increase the compensation to the creative? Or should we allow cheap reproductions which will permit our less affluent to afford beautiful artifacts? Appellant sold the original for $600.00 and up. Defendant's version went for one-fiftieth of that sum.

Thus far Congress and the Supreme Court have answered in favor of commerce and the masses rather than the artists, designers and the well-to-do. Any change must be left to those higher authorities. The choices are legislative not judicial.

———————

Esquire, Inc. v. Ringer
591 F.2d 796 (D.C.Cir.1978), cert. denied, 440 U.S. 908 (1979).

"This case," Judge Bazelon said, "presents the question whether the overall shape of certain outdoor lighting fixtures is eligible for copyright as a 'work of art.' The Register of Copyrights determined that the overall shape or configuration of such articles is not copyrightable. The district court disagreed, and issued a writ of mandamus directing the Register to enter the claim to copyright. Esquire, Inc. v. Ringer, 414 F.Supp. 939 (D.D.C.1976). For the reasons expressed below, we reverse."

Esquire had filed applications for copyright registration in connection with the designs of several outdoor lights. The Copyright Office, relying on § 202.10(c) of its former regulations (quoted in footnote 3 in *Kieselstein-*

Cord), found the designs uncopyrightable. "The Register interprets § 202.10(c) to bar copyright registration of the overall shape or configuration of a utilitarian article, no matter how aesthetically pleasing that shape or configuration may be." The court found the Register's interpretation "reasonable and well-supported." "In the Register's view, registration of the overall shape or configuration of utilitarian articles would lead to widespread copyright protection for industrial design. The Register reasons that aesthetic considerations enter into the design of most useful articles. Thus, if overall shape or configuration can qualify as a 'work of art,' 'the whole realm of consumer products—garments, toasters, refrigerators, furniture, bathtubs, automobiles, etc.—and industrial products designed to have aesthetic appeal—subway cars, computers, photocopying machines, typewriters, adding machines, etc.—must also qualify as works of art.'" That, the court believed, was beyond the intent of Congress, based in part on the legislative history of the 1976 Act, not yet then in effect.

Judge Bazelon expressed some sympathy for the district court's conclusion that the Register's interpretation of § 202.10(c) "amounted to impermissible discrimination" against modern abstract sculpture in favor of "the realistic or the ornate." He concluded, however, that the nondiscrimination principle espoused in *Bleistein,* p. 50 supra, should not be allowed to "undermine other plainly legitimate goals of copyright law—in this case the congressional directive that copyright protection should not be afforded to industrial designs."

NOTES AND QUESTIONS ON SEPARABILITY

(1) In *Esquire*, the Copyright Office maintained that the "overall shape or configuration of a utilitarian article" is not copyrightable. The Court of Appeals apparently agreed. Is that a sensible rule? Is it consistent with *Kieselstein–Cord?* The automatic exclusion of overall shape is difficult to reconcile with a number of decisions recognizing copyright in the shapes of a variety of useful articles.[s] Would the *Esquire* rationale preclude copyright in the overall shape of a Mickey Mouse telephone if the electronics were hidden in Mickey's tummy? Suppose that Esquire's outdoor lighting fixtures had consisted of giant dancing figures clutching halogen flood lights in uplifted hands. Would the Register or the court have reached a different conclusion?

---

[s] E.g., Animal Fair, Inc. v. AMFESCO Indus., Inc., 620 F.Supp. 175 (D.Minn.1985), aff'd, 794 F.2d 678 (8th Cir.1986) (bear paw design of slippers); R. Dakin & Co. v. A & L Novelty Co., 444 F.Supp. 1080 (E.D.N.Y.1978) (animal-shaped pajama bags). Consider also Ted Arnold Ltd. v. Silvercraft, 259 F.Supp. 733 (S.D.N.Y.1966), involving a copyright registration issued for a "simulation of an antique telephone" used to house a pencil sharpener. The court found the work copyrightable, arguing that the telephone casing could be physically separated from the utilitarian pencil sharpener. Judge MacMahon also responded to the argument that the work had been created specifically for a utilitarian use. "There was still room here for considerable artistic expression. * * * Customers are paying fifteen dollars for it, not because it sharpens pencils uncommonly well, but because it is also a decorative conversation piece."

ONE OF THE ESQUIRE LIGHTING FIXTURES

(2) The House Report's reference to "conceptually * * * separable" elements was dismissed by Judge Bazelon in *Esquire* as an "isolated reference." *Kieselstein–Cord* obviously disagrees. Should *physical* separability be required?

(3) The separability standard embodied in the § 101 definition of "pictorial, graphic, and sculptural works" applies only to the design of a "useful article." This term too is defined in § 101. What does the definition comprehend? An automobile presumably is a useful article; a portrait is not. What of a model airplane? A sheet of wrapping paper depicting a Christmas scene? A bust of Beethoven, useful in holding down papers or holding up books? See Poe v. Missing Persons, 745 F.2d 1238 (9th Cir.1984), where the issue was whether "Aquatint No. 5" was a "swimsuit" or a "work of art which portrayed an article of clothing." The "work" as depicted in the court's opinion resembles a partially transparent bikini. A "useful article"?

Brandir International, Inc. v. Cascade Pacific Lumber Co.

United States Court of Appeals, Second Circuit, 1987.
834 F.2d 1142.

■ Before OAKES and WINTER, CIRCUIT JUDGES, and ZAMPANO, DISTRICT JUDGE.

■ OAKES, CIRCUIT JUDGE:

In passing the Copyright Act of 1976 Congress attempted to distinguish between protectable "works of applied art" and "industrial designs not subject to copyright protection." See H.R.Rep. No. 1476, 94th Cong., 2d Sess. 54, reprinted in 1976 U.S.Code Cong. & Admin.News 5659, 5667 (hereinafter H.R.Rep. No. 1476). The courts, however, have had difficulty framing tests by which the fine line establishing what is and what is not copyrightable can be drawn. Once again we are called upon to draw such a line, this time in a case involving the "RIBBON Rack," a bicycle rack made of bent tubing that is said to have originated from a wire sculpture. (A photograph of the rack is contained in the appendix to this opinion.) We are also called upon to determine whether there is any trademark protection available to the manufacturer of the bicycle rack, appellant Brandir International, Inc. The Register of Copyright, named as a third-party defendant under the statute, 17 U.S.C. § 411, but electing not to appear, denied copyrightability. In the subsequent suit brought in the United States District Court for the Southern District of New York, Charles S. Haight, Jr., Judge, the district court granted summary judgment on both the copyright and trademark claims to defendant Cascade Pacific Lumber Co., d/b/a Columbia Cascade Co., manufacturer of a similar bicycle rack. We affirm as to the copyright claim, but reverse and remand as to the trademark claim.

Against the history of copyright protection well set out in the majority opinion in Carol Barnhart Inc. v. Economy Cover Corp., 773 F.2d 411, 415–18 (2d Cir.1985), and in Denicola, Applied Art and Industrial Design: A Suggested Approach to Copyright in Useful Articles, 67 Minn.L.Rev. 707, 709–17 (1983), Congress adopted the Copyright Act of 1976. The "works of art" classification of the Copyright Act of 1909 was omitted and replaced by reference to "pictorial, graphic, and sculptural works," 17 U.S.C. § 102(a)(5). According to the House Report, the new category was intended to supply "as clear a line as possible between copyrightable works of applied art and uncopyrighted works of industrial design." H.R.Rep. No. 1476, at 55, U.S.Code Cong. & Admin.News 1976, p. 5668. * * *

In Carol Barnhart Inc. v. Economy Cover Corp., 773 F.2d 411 (2d Cir.1985), a divided panel of this circuit affirmed a district court grant of summary judgment of noncopyrightability of four life-sized, anatomically correct human torso forms. *Carol Barnhart* distinguished *Kieselstein–Cord,* but it surely did not overrule it. The distinction made was that the ornamented surfaces of the *Kieselstein–Cord* belt buckles "were not in any respect required by their utilitarian functions," but the features claimed to be aesthetic or artistic in the *Carol Barnhart* forms were "inextricably intertwined with the utilitarian feature, the display of clothes." 773 F.2d at 419. But cf. Animal Fair, Inc. v. Amfesco Indus., Inc., 620 F.Supp. 175, 186–88 (D.Minn.1985) (holding bear-paw design conceptually separable from the utilitarian features of a slipper), aff'd mem., 794 F.2d 678 (8th Cir.1986). As Judge Newman's dissent made clear, the *Carol Barnhart* majority did not dispute "that 'conceptual separability' is distinct from 'physical separability' and, when present, entitles the creator of a useful article to a copyright on its design." 773 F.2d at 420.

[handwritten margin note: Barnhart]

[handwritten margin note: Conceptual vs. physic,]

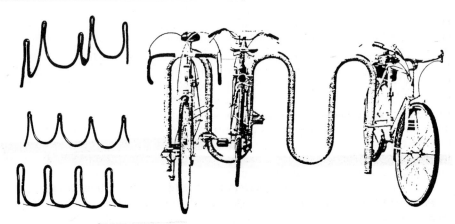

LEVINE'S WIRE SCULPTURES AND THE RIBBON
BICYCLE RACK

"Conceptual separability" is thus alive and well, at least in this circuit. The problem, however, is determining exactly what it is and how it is to be applied. Judge Newman's illuminating discussion in dissent in *Carol Barnhart*, see 773 F.2d at 419–24, proposed a test that aesthetic features are conceptually separable if "the article . . . stimulate[s] in the mind of the beholder a concept that is separate from the concept evoked by its utilitarian function." Id. at 422. This approach has received favorable endorsement by at least one commentator, W. Patry, Latman's The Copyright Law 43–45 (6th ed. 1986), who calls Judge Newman's test the "temporal displacement" test. It is to be distinguished from other possible ways in which conceptual separability can be tested, including whether the primary use is as a utilitarian article as opposed to an artistic work, whether the aesthetic aspects of the work can be said to be "primary," and whether the article is marketable as art, none of which is very satisfactory. But Judge Newman's test was rejected outright by the majority as "a standard so ethereal as to amount to a 'nontest' that would be extremely difficult, if not impossible, to administer or apply." 773 F.2d at 419 n. 5.

Perhaps the differences between the majority and the dissent in *Carol Barnhart* might have been resolved had they had before them the Denicola article on Applied Art and Industrial Design: A Suggested Approach to Copyright in Useful Articles, supra. There, Professor Denicola points out that although the Copyright Act of 1976 was an effort " 'to draw as clear a line as possible,' " in truth "there is no line, but merely a spectrum of forms and shapes responsive in varying degrees to utilitarian concerns." 67 Minn.L.Rev. at 741. Denicola argues that "the statutory directive requires a distinction between works of industrial design and works whose origins lie outside the design process, despite the utilitarian environment in which they appear." He views the statutory limitation of copyrightability as "an attempt to identify elements whose form and appearance reflect the unconstrained perspective of the artist," such features not being the product of industrial design. Id. at 742. "Copyrightability, therefore, should turn on the relationship between the proffered work and the process of industrial design." Id. at 741. He suggests that "the dominant characteristic of industrial design is the influence of nonaesthetic, utilitarian concerns" and hence concludes that copyrightability "ultimately should depend on the extent to which the work reflects artistic expression uninhibited by functional considerations." Id. To state the Denicola test in the language of conceptual separability, if design elements reflect a merger of aesthetic and functional considerations, the artistic aspects of a work cannot be said to be conceptually separable from the utilitarian elements. Conversely, where design elements can be identified as reflecting the designer's artistic judgment exercised independently of functional influences, conceptual separability exists.

We believe that Professor Denicola's approach provides the best test for conceptual separability and, accordingly, adopt it here for several reasons. First, the approach is consistent with the holdings of our previous cases. In *Kieselstein–Cord,* for example, the artistic aspects of the belt buckles reflected purely aesthetic choices, independent of the buckles' function, while in *Carol Barnhart* the distinctive features of the torsos—the accurate anatomical design and the sculpted shirts and collars—showed clearly the influence of functional concerns. Though the torsos bore artistic features, it was evident that the designer incorporated those features to further the usefulness of the torsos as mannequins. Second, the test's emphasis on the influence of utilitarian concerns in the design process may help, as Denicola notes, to "alleviate the de facto discrimination against nonrepresentational art that has regrettably accompanied much of the current analysis." Id. at 745.[3] Finally, and perhaps most importantly, we think Denicola's test will not be too difficult to administer in practice. The work itself will continue to give "mute testimony" of its origins. In addition, the parties will be required to present evidence relating to the design process and the nature of the work, with the trier of fact making the determination whether the aesthetic design elements are significantly influenced by functional considerations.

Turning now to the facts of this case, we note first that Brandir contends, and its chief owner David Levine testified, that the original design of the RIBBON Rack stemmed from wire sculptures that Levine had created, each formed from one continuous undulating piece of wire. These sculptures were, he said, created and displayed in his home as a means of personal expression, but apparently were never sold or displayed elsewhere. He also created a wire sculpture in the shape of a bicycle and states that he did not give any thought to the utilitarian application of any of his sculptures until he accidentally juxtaposed the bicycle sculpture with one of the self-standing wire sculptures. It was not until November 1978 that Levine seriously began pursuing the utilitarian application of his sculptures, when a friend, G. Duff Bailey, a bicycle buff and author of numerous articles about urban cycling, was at Levine's home and informed him that the sculptures would make excellent bicycle racks, permitting bicycles to be parked under the overloops as well as on top of the underloops. Following this meeting, Levine met several times with Bailey and others, completing the designs for the RIBBON Rack by the use of a vacuum cleaner hose, and submitting his drawings to a fabricator complete with dimensions. The Brandir RIBBON Rack began being nationally advertised and promoted for sale in September 1979. * * *

---

[3] We are reminded not only by Judge Gesell in the district court in *Esquire,* 414 F.Supp. 939, 941 (D.D.C.1976), but by Holmes in Bleistein v. Donaldson Lithographing Co., 188 U.S. 239, 251–52 (1903), by Mazer v. Stein, 347 U.S. at 214, and by numerous other opinions, that we judges should not let our own view of styles of art interfere with the decisionmaking process in this area. Denicola suggests that the shape of a Mickey Mouse telephone is copyrightable because its form is independent of function, and "[a] telephone shape owing more to Arp, Brancusi, or Moore than Disney may be equally divorced from utilitarian influence." 67 Minn.L.Rev. at 746. This is true, of course, of the artist Christo's "Running Fence," approved (following Professor Nimmer) as an example of conceptual separability in *Kieselstein–Cord,* 632 F.2d at 993.

Applying Professor Denicola's test to the RIBBON Rack, we find that the rack is not copyrightable. It seems clear that the form of the rack is influenced in significant measure by utilitarian concerns and thus any aesthetic elements cannot be said to be conceptually separable from the utilitarian elements. This is true even though the sculptures which inspired the RIBBON Rack may well have been—the issue of originality aside—copyrightable. * * *

Had Brandir merely adopted one of the existing sculptures as a bicycle rack, neither the application to a utilitarian end nor commercialization of that use would have caused the object to forfeit its copyrighted status. Comparison of the RIBBON Rack with the earlier sculptures, however, reveals that while the rack may have been derived in part from one o[r] more "works of art," it is in its final form essentially a product of industrial design. In creating the RIBBON Rack, the designer has clearly adapted the original aesthetic elements to accommodate and further a utilitarian purpose. These altered design features of the RIBBON Rack, including the spacesaving, open design achieved by widening the upper loops to permit parking under as well as over the rack's curves, the straightened vertical elements that allow in-and above-ground installation of the rack, the ability to fit all types of bicycles and mopeds, and the heavy-gauged tubular construction of rustproof galvanized steel, are all features that combine to make for a safe, secure, and maintenance-free system of parking bicycles and mopeds. Its undulating shape is said in *Progressive Architecture,* January 1982, to permit double the storage of conventional bicycle racks. Moreover, the rack is manufactured from 2 and 3/8 Binch standard steam pipe that is bent into form, the six-inch radius of the bends evidently resulting from bending the pipe according to a standard formula that yields bends having a radius equal to three times the nominal internal diameter of the pipe. * * *

It is unnecessary to determine whether to the art world the RIBBON Rack properly would be considered an example of minimalist sculpture. The result under the copyright statute is not changed. Using the test we have adopted, it is not enough that, to paraphrase Judge Newman, the rack may stimulate in the mind of the reasonable observer a concept separate from the bicycle rack concept. While the RIBBON Rack may be worthy of admiration for its aesthetic qualities alone, it remains nonetheless the product of industrial design. Form and function are inextricably intertwined in the rack, its ultimate design being as much the result of utilitarian pressures as aesthetic choices. Indeed, the visually pleasing proportions and symmetricality of the rack represent design changes made in response to functional concerns. Judging from the awards the rack has received, it would seem in fact that Brandir has achieved with the RIBBON Rack the highest goal of modern industrial design, that is, the harmonious fusion of function and aesthetics. Thus there remains no artistic element of the RIBBON Rack that can be identified as separate and "capable of existing independently, of, the utilitarian aspects of the article." Accordingly, we must affirm on the copyright claim.

[The court ordered a remand for further consideration of the trademark infringement claim. See p. 142 infra.]

■ WINTER, CIRCUIT JUDGE, concurring in part and dissenting in part:

Although I concur in the reversal of the district court's grant of summary judgment on the trademark and unfair competition claims, I respectfully dissent from the majority's discussion and disposition of the copyright claim.

My colleagues, applying an adaptation of Professor Denicola's test, hold that the aesthetic elements of the design of a useful article are not conceptually separable from its utilitarian aspects if "[f]orm and function are inextricably intertwined" in the article, and "its ultimate design [is] as much the result of utilitarian pressures as aesthetic choices." Applying that test to the instant matter, they observe that the dispositive fact is that "in creating the Ribbon Rack, [Levine] has clearly adapted the *original* aesthetic elements to accommodate and further a utilitarian purpose." (emphasis added). The grounds of my disagreement are that: (1) my colleagues' adaptation of Professor Denicola's test diminishes the statutory concept of "conceptual separability" to the vanishing point; and (2) their focus on the process or sequence followed by the particular designer makes copyright protection depend upon largely fortuitous circumstances concerning the creation of the design in issue. * * *

My colleagues also allow too much to turn upon the process or sequence of design followed by the designer of the Ribbon Rack. They thus suggest that copyright protection would have been accorded "had Brandir merely adopted . . . as a bicycle rack" an enlarged version of one of David Levine's original sculptures rather than one that had wider upper loops and straightened vertical elements. I cannot agree that copyright protection for the Ribbon Rack turns on whether Levine serendipitously chose the final design of the Ribbon Rack during his initial sculptural musings or whether the original design had to be slightly modified to accommodate bicycles. Copyright protection, which is intended to generate incentives for designers by according property rights in their creations, should not turn on purely fortuitous events. For that reason, the Copyright Act expressly states that the legal test is how the final article is perceived, not how it was developed through various stages. * * *

MORE NOTES AND QUESTIONS ON SEPARABILITY

(1) In Hart v. Dan Chase Taxidermy Supply Co., 86 F.3d 320 (2d Cir.1996), the Second Circuit distinguished the human torso forms in the *Barnhart* case discussed in *Brandir* and agreed with the Fourth Circuit's conclusion in Superior Form Builders, Inc. v. Dan Chase Taxidermy Supply Co., 74 F.3d 488 (4th Cir.), cert. denied, 519 U.S. 809 (1996), that animal taxidermy mannequins are not useful articles and thus not subject to the separability limitation; the function of animal mannequins is to portray their own form (see the definition of "useful article" in § 101), while the purpose of the torsos in *Barnhart* was to display clothing. The Fourth Circuit's decision in *Superior Form Builders* alternatively concluded that even if taxidermy mannequins are useful articles, they would be copyrightable under the *Brandir* test for separability.

The Seventh Circuit in Pivot Point International, Inc. v. Charlene Products, Inc., 372 F.3d 913 (7th Cir.2004), identified six different tests for determining separability and then adopted the analysis in *Brandir* to uphold copyright in a mannequin head used for hair styling.

(2) The *Brandir* test was adopted with a qualification in National Theme Productions, Inc. v. Jerry B. Beck, Inc., 696 F.Supp. 1348 (S.D.Cal.1988). Plaintiff claimed copyright in a series of masquerade costumes; Judge Thompson said the costumes had an intrinsic utilitarian function and were therefore useful articles. He concurred with *Brandir* "to the extent it requires one to look to an artist or designer's creative process, and the decisions going into that process, in creating a useful article," but questioned the Second Circuit's emphasis on the sequence and chronology of creative decisions. The costumes were copyrightable since they embodied "aesthetic judgments exercised independently of functional considerations."

In Whimsicality, Inc. v. Rubie's Costume Co. 891 F.2d 452 (2d Cir.1989), the Second Circuit held that an application for copyright registration describing costumes as "soft sculpture" constituted a misrepresentation to the Copyright Office that invalidated the registration. But on remand, the district court accepted an affidavit from a Copyright Office examiner that "soft sculpture" was a term routinely allowed by the Copyright Office and that the costumes had been registered as containing separable artistic elements. 836 F.Supp. 112 (E.D.N.Y.1993). Cf. Masquerade Novelty, Inc. v. Unique Industries, Inc., 912 F.2d 663 (3d Cir.1990) (plaintiff's animal nose masks are not useful articles and thus copyrightable). A Copyright Office Policy Decision declares that while masks can generally be registered, costumes are useful articles and will not be registered unless they contain separable pictorial, graphic, or sculptural features. 56 Fed.Reg. 56530 (1991). The Fifth Circuit in Galiano v. Harrah's Operating Co., 416 F.3d 411 (5th Cir.2005), held that uniforms worn by casino workers were useful articles and not copyrightable under the separability standard; plush animal-themed Halloween costumes, on the other hand, might contain conceptually separable features entitled to copyright and thus a claim for infringement should not have been dismissed. Chosun Int'l, Inc. v. Chrisha Creations, Ltd., 413 F.3d 324 (2d Cir.2005).

(3) Ralph Brown, commenting on his co-author's suggestions as described in *Brandir,* has said, "I have no quarrel with Denicola's aspirations for the criteria which should guide the Copyright Office and then the courts in making their judgments. I do have qualms about the practicality of the criteria. How are we to verify the impulses that guided a designer's hand? * * * It seems to leave too much room for self-serving declarations of aesthetic aims, even if such declarations could be deflated by cross-examination or simple skepticism." R. Brown, Design Protection: An Overview, 34 UCLA L.Rev. 1341, 1350–53 (1987).

(4) Could the plaintiff in *Brandir* have successfully claimed that the defendant infringed the copyright in the original wire sculptures? Would § 113(b), discussed in the following note, preclude such a claim?

(5) Consider this ploy. An automobile manufacturer, intent on circumventing the limitations on copyright in useful articles, obtains a copyright registration for a photograph or clay model of next year's design. (Note that neither work is a "useful article.") The manufacturer then argues that unauthorized production of the car portrayed in the work would infringe the copyright in the photo or model. If this stratagem works, the separability test becomes irrelevant. It has long been the position of the Copyright Office that although others may not reproduce the photograph or model, the law is and should be that "copyright in a pictorial, graphic, or sculptural work, portraying a useful article as such, does not extend to the manufacture of the useful article itself." Report of the Register of Copyrights, General Revision of the U.S. Copyright Law, House Comm. on the Judiciary, 87th Cong., 1st Sess. 15 (1961). In the Register's Supplementary Report of 1965, p. 48, two lines of relevant cases are identified. One line includes Jack Adelman, Inc. v. Sonners & Gordon, Inc., 112 F.Supp. 187

(S.D.N.Y.1934), which held that copyright in a drawing of a dress "secured no exclusive monopoly of the dress shown in the drawing." It also includes Kashins v. Lightmakers, 155 F.Supp. 202 (S.D.N.Y.1956), holding that the plaintiff's copyrighted catalog containing photographs of its lamps was not infringed by the defendant's manufacture of similar lamps or the subsequent publication of a catalog containing photographs of the imitations.[t] The other line of cases identified in the Supplementary Report consists of two decisions holding that copyright in two-dimensional cartoon characters is infringed by three-dimensional dolls (see p. 215 infra), plus Jones Brothers Co. v. Underkoffler, 16 F.Supp. 729 (M.D.Pa.1936). The latter ruled that copyright in a drawing of a cemetery monument was infringed by construction of the depicted monument. Can these two lines of cases be distinguished? Do the latter cases involve depictions of "useful articles" not themselves copyrightable? The Supplementary Report surprisingly concluded that it had not been possible "to find any statutory formulation that would express the distinction satisfactorily." The principle concern was "to make clear that there is no intention to change the present law." The result is the extraordinary cop-out in § 113(b).

[handwritten margin note: drawn cartoon characters are infringed by 3d dolls]

(6) At this point, if not long before, one might well ask if the distinctions pursued in the 1976 Act are worth the effort. Would dire consequences follow if the whole of industrial design was brought within the subject matter of copyright? Would some alternative form of protection be preferable?

For a searching comparative view of design protection, see two articles by J. Reichman, Design Protection in Domestic and Foreign Copyright Law: From the Berne Revision of 1948 to the Copyright Act of 1976, 1983 Duke L.J. 1143, and Design Protection After the Copyright Act of 1976, 31 J.Copyr.Soc'y 267 (1984).

PROPOSED DESIGN PROTECTION LEGISLATION

Several of the preceding decisions take note of proposals for separate design protection legislation. The limitations of both design patent and copyright have prompted a persistent search for alternatives. One such proposal was included as Title II, Protection of Ornamental Designs of Useful Articles, in the 1976 Copyright Revision Bill. It met the fate of its predecessors.[u]

Title II would have provided a maximum of ten years protection for "an original ornamental design of a useful article." The House Judiciary Committee deleted Title II in 1976, and the Senate conferees concurred. The House Report explained:

---

[t] A more recent illustration is Russell v. Trimfit, Inc., 428 F.Supp. 91 (E.D.Pa.1977), aff'd, 568 F.2d 770 (3d Cir.1978). Plaintiff registered drawings of socks with separate compartments for each toe. Her infringement action against a manufacturer of the socks was summarily dismissed. The court noted that there was no allegation that defendant had reproduced plaintiff's drawings; it had only manufactured the article they depicted. Similarly, copyright in a drawing of a shoe did not prevent a competing shoe maker from manufacturing the shoe in competition with the copyright owner. Eliya, Inc. v. Kohl's Dept. Stores, 82 U.S.P.Q.2d 1088 (S.D.N.Y.2006).

[u] Counting unsuccessful design protection bills is apparently a popular pastime. See, e.g., footnote 1 in *Nalbandian,* supra, and footnote 12 in *Esquire,* 591 F.2d at 800 n.12 (counting 70 bills).

Title II of S. 22 as passed by the Senate would create a new limited form of copyright protection for "original" designs which are clearly a part of a useful article, regardless of whether such designs could stand by themselves, separate from the article itself. Thus designs of useful articles which do not meet the design patent standard of "novelty" would for the first time be protected.

S. 22 is a copyright revision bill. The Committee chose to delete Title II in part because the new form of design protection provided by Title II could not truly be considered copyright protection and therefore appropriately within the scope of copyright revision. * * *

Finally, the Committee will have to examine further the assertion of the Department of Justice, which testified in opposition to the Title, that Title II would create a new monopoly which has not been justified by a showing that its benefits will outweigh the disadvantage of removing such designs from free public use. (H.R.Rep. p. 50.)

Proponents of design protection were left with only an invitation to try again.

Design legislation proponents argue that increased protection for designs is necessary to stimulate innovation and to protect American jobs against competition from foreign knock-offs; opponents counter that design protection would stifle competition and injure consumers. The proponents had been kept at bay by an opposing coalition of consumer groups, manufacturers of after-market repair parts, and insurance companies fearful of monopoly pricing on automobile replacement parts. The first breach in the defense came in 1998 when the Digital Millennium Copyright Act added Chapter 13 to Title 17.

Chapter 13 creates an elaborate system of protection for "an original design of a useful article which makes the article attractive or distinctive in appearance to the purchasing or using public * * *." § 1301(a). However, the definition of "useful article" is currently limited to "a vessel hull or deck, including a plug or mold * * *." § 1301(b). Protection lasts for ten years (§ 1305(a)), commencing from the date of registration or public exhibition or sale. § 1304. There are provisions for notice (a "D" in a circle) and registration, and protection is lost if an application for registration is not filed within two years after the design is made public. § 1310. A protected design is infringed by making, importing, or selling any useful article the design of which has been copied from the protected design without the owner's consent. § 1308–09. There are provisions for awarding injunctions, damages, and profits. § 1322–23. Protection under Chapter 13 terminates if a design patent is issued. § 1329.

The statute's generalized form invites expansion beyond vessel hulls and decks. Do we need a general design protection law to spur investment in product design? In an article in *Time* detailing the renaissance in American design, the president of the Industrial Designers Society says, "This is the new Golden Age of design" and offers this explanation: "When industries are competing at equal price and functionality, design is the only differential that matters." Gibney and Luscombe, The Redesigning of America, Time, March 20, 2000, p. 66. In 1988, a small electronics company redesigned its principal product, a compact antenna, to look like a piece of modern sculpture. According to the company's founder, orders increased 400 to 500 percent "purely because of the design." N.Y. Times, Feb. 12, 1989, p. F3. Does this argue for—or against—increased design protection?

NOTES ON DESIGN LEGISLATION, TYPEFACE, AND MASK WORKS

(1) Can you describe what a general design protection law would cover that now falls outside the subject matters of copyright and design patent?

(2) Title II of the 1976 revision bill would have done little for fashion designers; § 202(e) excluded three-dimensional aspects of apparel. (What groups might support such an exclusion?) In the world of fashion, copying of designs has long been stigmatized as "piracy," especially by the originators of high-priced lines who have seen their creations quickly duplicated for mass markets. The search for protection has a history—mostly of frustration—reaching back almost a century. We have already seen that apart from the protection of fabric designs, copyright is of little use in the fashion industry. Design patents are available, but the standard of inventiveness and the protracted application process generally eliminates them as a practical alternative.[v] As to the possibility of relief under common law unfair competition, see p. 647 infra.[w]

Bills have been introduced since 2006 to extend the design protection regime in Chapter 13 to fashion design, defined as "the appearance as a whole of an article of apparel, including its ornamentation" that provides "a unique, distinguishable, non-trivial and non-utilitarian variation over prior designs." "Apparel" includes clothing, gloves, footwear, handbags, belts, and eyeglass frames. Protection would last for three years, and the standard for infringement is heightened by requiring that the defendant's copy is "so similar in appearance as to be likely to be mistaken for the protected design." See 82 Pat., Tm. & Copyr.J. (BNA) 385 (2011). Digital technologies are said to have made the piracy problem more acute, as images of new designs from fashion shows are transmitted instantly around the world and automated design and manufacturing systems begin producing knockoffs within days. Wilson, Before Models Can Turn Around, Knockoffs Fly, N.Y. Times, Sept. 4, 2007, p. A1. Advocating passage of fashion protection, the director of the Council of Fashion Designers of America said, "America is the world fashion leader and yet it is basically the only industrialized country that does not provide protection for fashion design." Klein, In Copycats vs. Copyright, the Knock–Off Wins, Wash. Post, Aug. 22, 2010, p. G1. Does that make a strong case for protection? C. Hemphill and J. Suk, The Law, Culture, and Economics of Fashion, 61 Stan.L.Rev. 1147 (2009), advocates limited fashion protection that would prevent close copying. However, an article by K. Raustiala and C. Sprigman, The Piracy Paradox: Innovation and Intellectual Property in Fashion Design, 92 Va.L.Rev. 1687 (2006), examining how the fashion industry has thrived despite (and indeed perhaps because of) the absence of protection, concludes that copying hastens market saturation and thus continually drives the fashion cycle toward new looks.

(3) Technological changes introduced in the printing industry in the 1960s led to pressure for copyright or other protection for typeface designs. The House Report defines "typeface" as "a set of letters, numbers, or other symbolic characters, whose forms are related by repeating design elements consistently ap-

---

[v]   For an example of design patent protection for "fashion," see Crocs, Inc. v. Int'l Trade Comm., 598 F.3d 1294 (Fed.Cir.2010), involving a design patent on Crocs footwear.

[w]   Some of the rich history of fashion piracy is recounted in Agins, Fashion Knockoffs Hit Stores Before Originals as Designers Seethe, Wall St.J., Aug. 8, 1994, p. A1. As might be expected, French law is apparently more sympathetic to the fashion designer. See Spindler, A Ruling by French Court Finds Copyright in a Design, N.Y. Times, May 19, 1994, p. D4, reporting on a successful suit by Yves Saint Laurent against Ralph Lauren for copying a black tuxedo dress.

plied in a notational system and are intended to be embodied in articles whose intrinsic utilitarian function is for use in composing text or other cognizable combinations of characters." H.R.Rep. p. 55. The switch from metal fonts to photocomposition, which employed film strips rather than brass matrices, made the copying of typeface designs relatively inexpensive. Design patents were available, subject to the usual requirements, but the switch from metal to printed film fonts seemed to strengthen the claim to copyright. The Copyright Office had refused to accept typeface designs for registration as a "work of art" under the 1909 Act. See Eltra Corp. v. Ringer, 579 F.2d 294 (4th Cir.1978). Typeface manufacturers pressed their case during the revision process. For a time it appeared that Title II might afford a measure of relief. With the demise of Title II, the question of copyright became decisive.

The implications of extending copyright to typeface designs were unclear. Opponents feared that manufacturers would use their exclusive rights to enforce tying arrangements between their typeface designs and typesetting equipment. There was also general unease over potential liability for printed material composed with infringing type. See the Register's Second Supplementary Report on the General Revision 201–02 (Draft 1975). The House Report announced an intention to exclude typeface design from copyright, at least for the present:

> The Committee has considered, but chosen to defer, the possibility of protecting the design of typefaces. * * * The Committee does not regard the design of typeface, as thus defined, to be a copyrightable "pictorial, graphic, or sculptural work" within the meaning of this bill and the application of the dividing line in section 101. (H.R.Rep. p. 55.)

In the 1980s, technological change again created pressure for copyright in typeface—this time in the programs and digital data used by computers to generate fonts. The Copyright Office initially required registrants of computer programs that generate digitized typeface to disclaim copyright in the digitized representations themselves. 53 Fed.Reg. 38110 (1988). It eventually dropped the disclaimer and instead amended its regulation on Materials Not Subject to Copyright, adding "(e) Typeface as typeface" to the list of exclusions. 37 C.F.R. § 202.1(e). J. Lipton, To © or Not To ©? Copyright and Innovation in the Digital Typeface Industry, 43 U.C. Davis L.Rev. 143 (2009), uses the typeface industry to analyze claims for extending copyright to currently unprotected products. E. Rosenblatt, A Theory of IP's Negative Space, 34 Colum.J.L. & Arts 317 (2011), pursues the factors that may justify withholding exclusive rights from certain forms of creative works.

(4) Modern electronic technology relies on tiny components called semiconductor chips. They consist of layers of metallic and insulating materials on which patterns are etched or deposited. They are expensive to design, but cheap to reproduce. The patterns or "mask works" that are embodied in semiconductor chips are the subject of Chapter 9 of Title 17, added by the Semiconductor Chip Protection Act of 1984. The amendment establishes sui generis protection tailored to the unique characteristics of "mask works."

The requirement of originality in mask works is strengthened by the exclusion of "staple, commonplace, or familiar" designs. § 902(b). The "owner" has the exclusive right to reproduce the mask work and to import or distribute chips in which the work is embodied, although a measure of protection is afforded to "innocent" infringers. §§ 905, 907. There is a registration system,

[handwritten margin note: implications of extending to typeface design]

§ 908, and protection terminates if registration is not made within two years of first commercial use. There is also a notice provision, § 909, (this one with an "M" in a circle), but notice is not a condition of protection. Protection lasts for 10 years, commencing on registration or use. § 904. There are complex provisions protecting foreign mask works, designed to encourage protection of U.S. mask works abroad. §§ 902 and 914.

[handwritten margin note: protection of mask work is terminated if not registered w/in 2 years]

[handwritten margin note: Ⓜ]

[handwritten margin note: 10 year protection]

A major innovation appears in § 906 of the Act. That section permits reproduction of a protected mask work for purposes of analysis and evaluation; more significantly, it permits others to incorporate the results of such efforts into their own "original" mask work. It is an attempt to encourage the creation of improved derivative works through reverse engineering. In Brooktree Corp. v. Advanced Micro Devices, Inc., 977 F.2d 1555 (Fed.Cir.1992), after holding that the traditional test of "substantial similarity" applies to determine the infringement of mask works, the court examined the defendant's "paper trail" of study and analysis to distinguish legitimate reverse engineering from actionable piracy. The court concluded that the "paper trail" indicated only that the defendant made an unsuccessful attempt to analyze the plaintiff's chip before resorting to copying. The Ninth Circuit in Altera Corp. v. Clear Logic, Inc., 424 F.3d 1079 (9th Cir.2005), upheld a jury verdict that the defendant's mask work was substantially similar to the plaintiff's and was not the result of legitimate reverse engineering permitted under § 906.

[handwritten margin note: reverse engineering is ok to let others incorporate the results into their own work]

[handwritten margin note: • Reproduction of a protected mask work]

"Equivalent" rights under state law in mask works are preempted, § 912, but the Semiconductor Chip Protection Act does not affect rights or remedies available under federal copyright or patent law. (Would the configurations and patterns embodied in semiconductor chips be protectable as "pictorial, graphic, and sculptural works" under the definition in § 101?)

[handwritten margin note: Equivalent rights are preempt,]

The Semiconductor Chip Protection Act spawned substantial commentary, including a treatise, R. Stern, Semiconductor Chip Protection (Wolters Kluwer), and a Symposium: The Semiconductor Chip Protection Act of 1984 and Its Lessons, 70 Minn.L.Rev. 263 (1985). See also C. McManis, International Protection for Semiconductor Chip Designs, 22 Geo.Wash.J. Int'l L. & Econ. 331 (1988).

(5) Should the Semiconductor Chip Protection Act be viewed as a model for sui generis protection for other works? What subject matter would be appropriate for specialized treatment? Ornamental designs of useful articles? Computer programs? Compilations? What are the costs and benefits of the sui generis approach? An analogy to copyright in computer software is invoked in C. Holman, Copyright for Engineered DNA: An Idea Whose Time Has Come?, 113 W.Va.L.Rev. 699 (2011), to argue for copyright in engineered genetic sequences.

ARCHITECTURE

Robert R. Jones Associates, Inc. v. Nino Homes

United States Court of Appeals, Sixth Circuit, 1988.
858 F.2d 274.

■ Before MARTIN, JONES and MILBURN, CIRCUIT JUDGES.

■ BOYCE F. MARTIN, JR., CIRCUIT JUDGE.

Nino Homes and Michele Lochirco appeal the judgment entered by the district court in favor of Robert R. Jones Associates, Inc. The district court held that Nino Homes and Lochirco had violated the Copyright Act of 1976, 17 U.S.C. § 101 et seq., by copying Jones Associates' registered architectural drawings and by using those unauthorized copies to construct several houses, and the district court awarded Jones Associates actual damages, attorneys' fees, and prejudgment interest, 686 F.Supp. 160. This appeal presents a rather unusual question: whether the damages recoverable because of the infringement of copyrighted architectural drawings include, not only the losses attributable to the infringer's unauthorized reproduction of the copyrighted article, but also the losses suffered as a result of the infringer's subsequent use of the infringing copies. We affirm the finding of unlawful copying and subsequent use, but we reverse as to attorneys' fees and prejudgment interest.

Robert R. Jones Associates, Inc. designs, builds, and sells custom-made houses. Nino Homes also constructs and sells new houses. Michele Lochirco is the principal shareholder and president of Nino Homes, and he is also the company's chief executive and operating officer.

In 1980, Jones Associates hired an architect to prepare a complete set of architectural drawings, including floor plans and elevations, for a house which was eventually called the "Aspen". These plans were based on design concepts generated by Robert R. Jones, the sole shareholder of Jones Associates. After receiving the completed plans from the architect, Jones Associates constructed two model houses in accordance with the Aspen plans, one in the Grosse Pines subdivision in Rochester, Michigan, the other in the Maplewood North subdivision in West Bloomfield, Michigan. In order to promote sales of its houses in those two subdivisions, Jones Associates distributed to potential buyers brochures which contained abridged floor plans of the Aspen.

In June 1983, one of those potential customers informed Robert Jones that a competing developer was constructing houses that were very similar to the Aspen. Jones subsequently investigated this tip, and, while driving through Nino Homes' Clinton River Valley subdivision, a development less than three miles from Jones Associates' Grosse Pines subdivision, he recognized one of the houses as being nearly identical to his design. Jones then checked the building permit at the construction site, and from the information contained on the permit, Jones was able to locate the building plans filed by Nino Homes with the Rochester Hills Township. After examining these plans, Jones concluded that his Aspen plans had been copied, so he promptly registered the complete architectural drawings and the abridged floor plans. Immediately thereafter, Jones sent a letter to Nino Homes demanding that construction of the allegedly identical house cease. When Nino Homes denied that its house, which it called the "Riverside", was a copy of the Aspen, Jones Associates commenced this action.

During the trial which followed, Jones Associates offered evidence that Nino Homes had unlawfully copied its Aspen plans. The record shows that Nino Homes had hired an architectural firm called Diebele–Ginter to design a house. Before construction of the house initially designed by Diebele–Ginter had begun, however, Lochirco apparently gave Clifford Ginter, one of the two partners in the architectural firm, a photocopy of the Aspen abridged floor plans contained in the promotional brochure. According to the testimony of Richard J. Diebele, Ginter's partner, Lochirco instructed Ginter to copy these plans for use by Nino Homes. The photocopy allegedly given by Lochirco to Ginter, who died before the case went to trial, was subsequently discovered in Diebele–Ginter's files and introduced into evidence by Jones Associates.

On the basis of this evidence, and other documents which showed that the Riverside design was virtually identical to the Aspen design, the district court concluded that Nino Homes and Diebele–Ginter had infringed upon Jones Associates' copyright. The court then found that, had Nino Homes not sold seven houses which were built according to the infringing copies, Jones Associates would have sold seven additional houses. Therefore, the court awarded actual damages in the amount of $298,870: $212,550 for presumed profits not earned by Jones Associates because of Nino Homes' infringement, and $86,320 for the profits earned by Nino Homes from the sale of the houses built pursuant to the infringing plans. * * *

Nino Homes contends that the district court used an improper standard to compute the damages it awarded to Jones Associates. The court held that Jones Associates was entitled to recover the profits it would have earned on the sale of additional houses had Nino Homes not used infringing copies of the Aspen plans to build houses which it sold. Nino Homes maintains that this "lost profits" standard is not the appropriate measure of damages in an action for copyright infringement where the protected work is architectural plans. Rather, Nino Homes argues, the proper standard is the fair market value of the architectural plans at the time of the infringement. We disagree. * * *

Architectural plans, however, "are subject to certain qualifications peculiar to this form of work." 1 Nimmer § 2.08[D][2][a] at 2–105. The copyright statute "does not afford, to the owner of a copyright in a work that portrays a useful article as such, any greater or lesser rights with respect to the making, distribution, or display of the useful article so portrayed than those afforded to such works under the law . . . in effect on December 31, 1977." 17 U.S.C. § 113(b). A "useful article" is one which has "an intrinsic utilitarian function." Id. at § 1.01. Because any building or house undoubtedly falls within this definition, architectural plans necessarily depict a useful article and are subject to this restriction. Therefore, the owner of a copyright in architectural plans has statutory copyright protection in the building depicted in those plans only to the extent that such protection was recognized by the law prior to January 1, 1978. The limitations of this protection were initially set by the Supreme Court in Baker v. Selden, 101 U.S. (11 Otto) 99 (1879).

* * * In essence, the plaintiff in *Baker* could prevent the unauthorized reproduction of the actual book, but, unless he had a patent, the plaintiff could not prevent others from using the accounting forms, the useful article embodied in the book.

The doctrine enunciated in Baker v. Selden is particularly problematic where architectural plans are the copyrighted items because the principal value of such creative works lies in their use in constructing a building. If *Baker* is applied strictly, and the Copyright Act is interpreted as merely prohibiting others from selling copyrighted plans and not from using the plans to construct other buildings, then the statute may not afford the kind of protection necessary to give architects adequate incentive to create new architectural designs. Conversely, giving the owner of a copyright in architectural plans the right to prevent others from constructing buildings substantially similar to the one depicted in the copyrighted plans, without requiring the architect to show that the design is novel as opposed to merely original, would give architects unwarranted monopoly powers with the result that the costs of houses and other buildings would rise unnecessarily. Other courts have also struggled to balance these competing concerns—to remain faithful to *Baker,* yet afford architects the protection Congress clearly intended to provide them. * * *

In Imperial Homes Corp. v. Lamont, 458 F.2d 895 (5th Cir.1972), a builder advertised its houses by distributing brochures which contained a copy of the floor plan from the complete set of copyrighted architectural drawings. After visiting one of the builder's houses and obtaining one of the brochures, a potential customer proceeded to develop a set of drawings for a house which was to be substantially similar to the builder's design. The builder brought an action for copyright infringement and sought to enjoin the customer from using the allegedly infringing plans.

The court in *Imperial Homes* recognized that the *Baker* decision warned against extending a copyright into a patent. The court reasoned that "no copyrighted architectural plans . . . may clothe their author with the exclusive right to reproduce the dwelling pictured." Id. at 899. The court, though, then stated that nothing in Baker v. Selden "prevents such a copyright from vesting the law's grant of an exclusive right to make copies of the copyrighted plans so as to instruct a would-be builder on how to proceed to construct the dwelling pictured." Id. Therefore, although the court expressly did "not hold that the [defendants] were in anywise restricted by the existence of Imperial's copyright from reproducing a substantially identical residential dwelling," the court held that, "if copyrighted architectural drawings of the originator of such plans are imitated or transcribed in whole or in part, infringement occurs." Id. * * *

Another federal district court recently addressed a similar issue. In Demetriades v. Kaufmann [680 F.Supp. 658 (S.D.N.Y.1988)], a real estate developer brought a copyright infringement action to enjoin another developer from completing construction of a house which the defendant conceded was being built pursuant to plans which were merely tracings of the plaintiff's copyrighted plans. The court recognized that, under Baker v. Selden, although the plaintiff may have a valid copyright in the architectural plans that served as the basis for its uniquely designed house, that copyright "protection simply does not extend to the design or the house itself absent a design patent." Demetriades v. Kaufmann, 680 F.Supp. at 665. The court held, however, "that the unauthorized reproduction of copyrighted architectural plans constitutes infringement." Id. Accordingly, although the court refused to enjoin construction of the defendant's substantially similar house, the court enjoined the defendants from further, unauthorized copying of plaintiff's architectural plans, and, of greater significance in the matter before us, the court "further enjoined [the defendants] from relying on any infringing copies of those plans." Id. at 666.[4]

The rule which emerges from these cases is that one may construct a house which is identical to a house depicted in copyrighted architectural

---

[4]   In Muller v. Triborough Bridge Authority, 43 F.Supp. 298 (S.D.N.Y.1942), the court held that the copyright in a plan for the construction of an approach to a highway bridge did not give the copyright owner the power to prevent someone else from using the copyrighted plan to build the actual structure. The court in *Demetriades,* though, felt its decision was consistent with *Muller,* presumably because it was unclear in *Muller* whether the defendants had made infringing copies or had merely used the copyrighted original to construct the approach. See Demetriades v. Kaufmann, 680 F.Supp. at 664.

plans, but one may not directly copy those plans and then use the infringing copy to construct the house. As a logical extension of this rule, we hold that, where someone makes infringing copies of another's copyrighted architectural plans, the damages recoverable by the copyright owner include the losses suffered as a result of the infringer's subsequent use of the infringing copies. Accordingly, the measure of damages in this case is the profits Jones Associates would have made on houses it would have sold but for Nino Homes' unauthorized duplication of the Aspen plans and Nino Homes' use of its infringing copies to build its Riverside houses. Therefore, the district court's decision to award Jones Associates $212,550 for profits it would have earned but for Nino Homes' sale of seven houses built pursuant to the infringing plans is correct.

An identical house can be built but not directly from the copied plans

damages
- *profits would have made*

In a copyright infringement action, the copyright owner is also entitled to recover "any profits of the infringer that are attributable to the infringement *and are not taken into account in computing the actual damages.*" 17 U.S.C. § 504(b) (emphasis added). Here, however, where the infringer's profit per house is less than the copyright owner's profit margin, and where all of the infringer's sales were counted as sales lost by the copyright owner, all of the infringer's profits attributable to the infringement were already taken into account in the actual damages awarded to the copyright owner. Therefore, the district court's decision to add Nino Homes' profits of $86,320 to the award of Jones Associates' lost profits constitutes the kind of double recovery clearly precluded by the statute. Accordingly, that aspect of the district court's decision is reversed.

[The court went on to conclude that the award of attorney's fees was improper under § 412(2) because the infringement occurred before registration; the relevant date was when the plans were copied, not when construction occurred. The court also vacated the award of prejudgment interest, noting that the Copyright Act, unlike the Patent Act, contains no express authorization for prejudgment interest.]

NOTES ON COPYRIGHT IN ARCHITECTURAL PLANS

(1) *Jones Associates* restates the general rule that unauthorized construction is not itself an infringement of the copyright in architectural plans. A few courts, however, have indicated a willingness to enjoin construction as a remedy for infringement when the copyrighted plans have also been copied. See Herman Frankel Organization v. Wolfe, 184 U.S.P.Q. 819 (E.D.Mich.1974); see also Nucor Corp. v. Tennessee Forging Steel Service, Inc., 476 F.2d 386 (8th Cir.1973).

Construction

Would the rule that construction alone does not infringe the copyright in plans apply if some aspect of the structure depicted in the plans (a gargoyle, perhaps, or a design in wrought iron) is itself eligible for copyright? In Jones Brothers Co. v. Underkoffler, 16 F.Supp. 729 (M.D.Pa.1936), it was held that copyright in the drawing of a cemetery monument was infringed by construction of the depicted monument. Can that case be distinguished from the construction in *Jones Associates?*

(2) The scope of protection for architectural plans was explored by Judge Leval writing for the Second Circuit in Attia v. Society of New York Hospital, 201 F.3d 50 (2d Cir.1999), cert. denied, 531 U.S. 843 (2000). Plaintiff had prepared preliminary drawings for a proposed hospital expansion; he complained that the architects who won the design contract infringed his drawings by incorpo-

rating features from the drawings into their own design drawings for the project.

"The problem of distinguishing an idea from its expression is particularly acute when the 'work of authorship' is of a functional nature, as is a plan for the accomplishment of an architectural or engineering project. As a generalization, to the extent that such plans include generalized notions of where to place functional elements, how to route the flow of traffic, and what methods of construction and principles of engineering to rely on, these are 'ideas' that may be taken and utilized by a successor without violating the copyright of the original 'author' or designer. * * * [W]e do not mean to suggest that, in the domain of copyrighted architectural depictions, only final construction drawings can contain protected expression. And we express no view whether, in other circumstances, an architect's sketches of visual elements (for example, Frank Lloyd Wright's preliminary sketches of the facade of the Guggenheim Museum) might include the type of expressive content entitled to copyright protection. Plaintiff's drawings in this case, however, at least to the extent copied, consisted only of generalized ideas and concepts * * *."

Judge Leval later distinguished the decision in *Attia* when a land surveyor sued for infringement of a site plan for an assisted living facility. The detailed specifications for preparation of the site amounted to more than the kinds of generalized ideas held unprotectable in *Attia*. Sparaco v. Lawler, Matusky, Skelly, Engineers LLP, 303 F.3d 460 (2d Cir.2002), cert. denied, 538 U.S. 945 (2003).

(3) The rules relating to common law copyright in architectural plans remain relevant because the 1976 Act offers no protection to works that had already entered the public domain through a general publication without copyright notice. Common law protection for architectural plans was a fragile thing. Local building ordinances often require the filing of plans in a public office. One line of cases took the view that these filings amounted to a general publication; others cases disagreed. Construction also could threaten common law protection because a number of decisions saw construction as a publication of the underlying plans. Again, other cases disagreed, sometimes distinguishing design aspects easily observable in the structure from details shown only in the underlying plans. Much of the case law is reviewed in Edgar H. Wood Associates v. Skene, 347 Mass. 351, 197 N.E.2d 886 (1964).

Issues of publication and notice also retain significance under the 1976 Act for architectural plans distributed prior to the elimination of the notice requirement in 1989. In John G. Danielson, Inc. v. Winchester–Conant Properties, Inc., 322 F.3d 26 (1st Cir.2003), a defendant who had copied plans for a condominium development argued that the copyright had been forfeited in 1987 by publication of the plans without a copyright notice. The court disagreed. Display of the plans before neighborhood groups and public officials were not "publications" under the definition in § 101, nor was their inclusion in a cable television broadcast of a public meeting. Copies filed with public officials or distributed to contractors and consultants constituted only "limited" publications that did not require a copyright notice. Inclusion of the plans in a videotape of a public meeting that was available for borrowing at the public library was also not a problem, since that had not been done "by authority of the copyright owner" as required under § 401.

NOTES ON COPYRIGHT IN ARCHITECTURAL WORKS

(1) The Berne Convention specifically lists "works * * * of architecture" among the subject matter to be protected by member nations. When the United States joined the Berne Convention in 1989, a reference to "architectural plans" was added to the § 101 definition of "pictorial, graphic, and sculptural works" in an attempt to meet our treaty obligations. The House Report accompanying the 1976 Act had already made clear that "[a]n architect's plans and drawings would, of course, be protected by copyright." H.R.Rep. p. 55. However, protection for architectural *works* (as distinguished from architectural *plans*) remained severely limited by the separability requirement applicable to copyright in useful articles: "[W]here the only elements of shape in an architectural design are conceptually inseparable from the utilitarian aspects of the structure, copyright protection for the design would not be available." Id. A 1989 report by the Copyright Office concluded that Berne demanded greater protection for architectural works. Congress responded in 1990 with the Architectural Works Copyright Protection Act.

The 1990 amendments added "architectural works" to the list of protectable subject matter in § 102(a), with an accompanying definition in § 101. Protection extends to "the design of a building" (whether embodied in an actual building or in plans or drawings), subject to the limitations in § 120(a), which allow others to take and display photographs of the completed building,[x] and § 120(b), which allows the owner of the building to alter or destroy it. The legislation also added § 301(b)(4), which protects state and local preservation, zoning, and building codes from preemption. The scope and effect of the architectural works amendment are described in the legislative history:

> [T]he term ["building"] encompassed habitable structures such as houses and office buildings. It also covers structures that are used, but not inhabited, by human beings, such as churches, pergolas, gazebos, and garden pavilions. * * *

> This provision amends section 102, title 17, United States Code, to create a new category of protected subject matter "architectural works." By creating a new category of protectible subject matter in new section 102(a)(8), and, therefore, by deliberately not encompassing architectural works as pictorial, graphic, or sculptural works in existing section 102(a)(5), the copyrightability of architectural works shall not be evaluated under the separability test applicable to pictorial, graphic, or sculptural works embodied in useful articles. * * *

> The Committee does not suggest, though, that in evaluating the copyrightability or scope of protection for architectural works, the Copyright Office or the courts should ignore functionality. A two-step analysis is envisioned. First, an architectural work should be examined to determine whether there are original design elements present, including overall shape and interior architecture. If such design elements are present, a second step is reached to examine whether the design elements are functionally required. If the design elements are not functionally required, the

---

[x] Section 120(a) was applied in *Leicester v. Warner Bros.*, 232 F.3d 1212 (9th Cir.2000), to insulate the defendant movie studio from liability for casting a Los Angeles building with accompanying towers and gates as the Gotham City Bank in its *Batman Forever* movie.

*If not reg →
protectable regardless
of separabilty*

work is protectible without regard to physical or conceptual separability. As a consequence, contrary to the Committee's report accompanying the 1976 Copyright Act with respect to industrial products, the aesthetically pleasing overall shape of an architectural work would be protected under this bill. H.R.Rep. No. 101–735, 101st Cong.2d Sess. 20–21 (1990).

Separate registrations are required by the Copyright Office for claims in architectural plans as "pictorial, graphic and sculptural works" and for claims in the underlying "architectural works." 37 C.F.R. § 202.11(c)(4).

(2) Trek Leasing, Inc. v. United States, 66 Fed.Cl. 8 (2005), involved a suit against the United States for constructing a post office building that allegedly infringed a post office constructed by the plaintiff. The court, noting that the definition of "architectural work" in § 101 excludes "individual standard features," held that the hallmarks of a popular architectural style are not protectable, nor are features specified in the U.S. Postal Service standards. After filtering out the unprotectable elements of the copyrighted work, the new post office was not substantially similar. (Judge Birch in Intervest Const., Inc. v. Canterbury Estate Homes, Inc., 554 F.3d 914 (11th Cir.2008), analogized the protection of architectural works to the "thin" protection afforded to compilations.) The owner of a copyright in an architectural work depicting a high-rise building was unsuccessful in an infringement action against the builders of the Trump Palace in Florida. Although the Trump building used alternating concave and convex sections and partially exposed elevator towers that were present in the plaintiff's design, the Eleventh Circuit held that the defendants' expression of those features was sufficiently different to justify summary judgment. Oravec v. Sunny Isles Luxury Ventures, L.C., 527 F.3d 1218 (11th Cir.2008). Another plaintiff had greater success with an architectural work claim in Shine v. Childs, 382 F.Supp.2d 602 (S.D.N.Y.2005). Plaintiff, an architecture student at Yale, produced a model for a skyscraper as part of a design course; it was evaluated by a panel of experts that included the defendant, who later unveiled a similar design proposal for the World Trade Center site. Invoking the "total concept and feel" standard, the court concluded that ordinary observers might disagree on whether the designs were substantially similar; defendant's motion for summary judgment was denied. D. Shipley, The Architectural Works Copyright Protection Act at Twenty: Has Full Protection Made a Difference?, 18 J.Intell.Prop.L. 1 (2010), finds that the extension of copyright to architectural works has had little impact during its first twenty years.

(3) Might other forms of protection serve the architect? Design patents are available. See In re Hadden, 20 F.2d 275 (D.C.Cir.1927) ("Modern Athletic Stadia"). But patent and copyright aside, are there circumstances in which a defendant should be prohibited from duplicating the design of a building in which a competitor conducts business? Compare Fotomat Corp. v. Cochran, 437 F.Supp. 1231 (D.Kan.1977), with Fotomat Corp. v. Photo Drive–Thru, Inc., 425 F.Supp. 693 (D.N.J.1977). The design of a hole on a golf course was protected on a trademark theory when a defendant built a replica of the hole on another course. Pebble Beach Co. v. Tour 18 I Ltd., 155 F.3d 526 (5th Cir.1998). (What sort of confusion, if any, might such copying create?) The Rock and Roll Hall of Fame, however, was unsuccessful when it asserted trademark rights in the design of its building, created by celebrated architect I. M. Pei, against a defendant who was selling posters that depicted the unique structure. Rock and Roll Hall of Fame and Museum, Inc. v. Gentile Prod., 134 F.3d 749 (6th Cir.1998).

CHOREOGRAPHY AND PANTOMIME

The movement of dancers can be described, although imprecisely, in words. By the use of Labanotation—a system of hieroglyphics that can be related to the musical score—a considerable degree of descriptive precision can be attained. Dance can also be recorded on film or videotape, or portrayed through computer graphics. That dance can be captured and reduced to a written or electronic record, however, does not dispose of the question of copyrightability.

Case law prior to the 1976 Act was scanty. In Fuller v. Bemis, 50 Fed. 926 (S.D.N.Y.1892), the plaintiff copyrighted a word description of her "Serpentine Dance," which according to the petition had won her "great profit and credit." The infringement complained of was "the production by defendant of this 'dramatic composition' upon the public stage, with merely colorable alterations." The court stated that "[i]t is essential to [a dramatic] composition that it should tell some story," and spoke of plaintiff's dance as "portraying no character, depicting no emotion." A preliminary injunction was denied. Copyright Office regulations under the 1909 Act permitted registration under the category of "[d]ramatic or dramatico-musical compositions" for "[c]horeographic works of a dramatic character," but excluded "descriptions of dance steps and other physical gestures, including ballroom and social dances or choreographic works which do not tell a story, develop a character or emotion, or otherwise convey a dramatic concept or idea."

Pantomimes could more easily be seen as a species of dramatic work, and therefore copyrightable. An early case extended protection to a "railroad scene" in a play (it was the business of the villain tying the heroine to the tracks), even though it was mostly in pantomime. Daly v. Palmer, 6 Fed.Cas. 1132 (C.C.S.D.N.Y.1868) (No. 3552). But copyright protection for dramatic compositions could not reach more abstract movement.

In the 1976 Act, Cinderella goes to the ball. "Pantomimes and choreographic works" are now one of the eight categories of works listed in § 102. The Act does not define these terms—the drafters believed them to "have fairly settled meanings." H.R.Rep. p. 53. The House Report does say, however, that " 'choreographic works' do not include social dance steps and simple routines." Why not? Is this merely an application of the independent creation and creative authorship requirements?

'76
Pantomime of choreograph added

NOTES AND QUESTIONS ON CHOREOGRAPHY

The Jan. 23, 1989 issue of *Sports Illustrated* reports on a claim by a San Antonio dermatologist and an Austin writer to copyright in a football formation. The formation, which the "authors" called the I–Bone, had been described by them in a 1984 article that appeared in a magazine for coaches. The claimants had also created a playbook for the I–Bone. During the 1988 football season the authors claimed that they saw the University of Colorado using the formation in a game against Oklahoma. (Colorado lost, 17–14.) The two authors threatened legal action unless the university acknowledged them as the creators of the formation. The Colorado coaching staff, which called its formation the Power–Bone, claimed independent creation. Assume instead that the coaching staff had used the I–Bone playbook. Can the plays be seen as a form of copyrightable choreography? Would drawing the plays on a blackboard infringe the copyright? Would running the plays during a game infringe? Can copyright be obtained in aerobic exercise routines, or in the competitive routines of a gymnast or figure skater, or in the movements produced by a diver, or by a basketball player participating in a slam dunk contest? According to a Copyright Office Statement of Policy, "a selection, coordination, or arrangement of functional physical movements such as sports movements, exercises, and other ordinary motor activities alone do not represent the type of authorship intended to be protected under copyright law as a choreographic work." 77 Fed.Reg. 37605 (June 22, 2012).

Horgan v. Macmillan

789 F.2d 157 (2d Cir.1986).

In 1954, renowned choreographer George Balanchine created his own version of the ballet "The Nutcracker." The ballet has become a classic. In 1981, Balanchine registered the work with the Copyright Office, depositing a videotape of a New York City Ballet Company dress rehearsal. The work has been licensed to numerous other ballet companies.

In 1985, the executrix of Balanchine's estate learned that the defendant was planning to publish a book about the New York City Ballet's performance of the work. Interspersed with the book's narration is a series of 60 color photographs of scenes from the Ballet Company's production. The estate sought an injunction, arguing that the book was both an infringing reproduction of the ballet and an unauthorized derivative work. Defendant Macmillan claimed that little if any of Balanchine's original choreography was shown in the photographs and noted that the plaintiff made no claim to copyright in the costumes or sets. The trial court found for Macmillan: "The still photographs in the Nutcracker book, numerous though they are, catch dancers in various attitudes at specific instances of time; they do not, nor do they intend to, take or use the underlying choreography. The staged performance could not be recreated from them."

The Second Circuit remanded, holding that the trial judge had applied the wrong standard. Judge Feinberg said that "the standard for determining copyright infringement is not whether the original could be recreated from the allegedly infringing copy, but whether the latter is 'substantially similar' to the former." He also said that the district judge "took a far too limited view of the extent to which choreographic material may be conveyed in the medium of still photography." Among other issues to be determined on remand was "the degree to which the choreography would be distinguishable in the photographs without the costumes and sets."

NOTE

The number of copyright registrations for choreography and pantomimes is small. The fixation of choreographic works in tangible form is largely irrelevant to the day to day business of creating, teaching, and performing dance. Most dance remains unfixed, and the role of federal copyright is thus a modest one.[y] As an unfixed work, dance remains eligible for protection under common

---

[y]   The relative indifference to copyright on the part of choreographers is illustrated in Macauley, In Dance, Borrowing is a Tradition, N.Y. Times, Nov. 21, 2011, p. C1.

law copyright, but there are few cases. See Dane v. M. & H. Co., 136 U.S.P.Q. 426 (N.Y.Sup.Ct.1963).

———————

WORKS OF THE UNITED STATES GOVERNMENT

Schnapper v. Foley

United States Court of Appeals, District of Columbia Circuit, 1981.
667 F.2d 102.
Certiorari denied, 455 U.S. 948 (1982).

■ Before ROBINSON, CHIEF JUDGE, McGOWAN, SENIOR CIRCUIT JUDGE, and PARKER, UNITED STATES DISTRICT JUDGE for the District of Columbia Circuit.

■ McGOWAN, SENIOR CIRCUIT JUDGE:

[The Administrative Office of the United States Courts commissioned Pittsburgh public broadcasting station WQED to produce a series of television films dramatizing famous cases arising in the early years of the Republic. The series, entitled "Equal Justice Under Law," was transmitted by the Public Broadcasting Service to its affiliates across the country.

[Plaintiff Schnapper and his Public Affairs Press alleged that the production contract required WQED to copyright the films and to assign the copyrights to the Government. (The Government denied that any such assignments had taken place.) Plaintiff asserted that the copyrights restricted public access to the films because permission for commercial broadcast had been refused. He also complained that the copyrights prevented him from publishing the text of the films. The complaint sought "both injunctive and declaratory relief not only to void the copyright subsisting in 'Equal Justice Under Law' but also to prevent the defendants from committing in the future acts that appellants contend are unlawful."

[The District Court dismissed the complaint. The Court of Appeals, *DCH dismissed* proceeding on the assumption that the copyrights had been assigned to the *ACH affirmed* Government, affirmed the dismissal.]

The most plausible point of departure for considering appellants' claims on the merits lies in their assertion that the copyright laws, both old and new, do not permit the registration of works commissioned by the Government, or the subsequent assignment of copyrights subsisting therein to the Government. As the series was copyrighted in 1976 under the old Copyright Act, and appellants seek a broad injunction of future applicability under the new Act, we will decide the fate of appellants' claims with respect to both the old and new Copyright Acts.

The status of works produced pursuant to a Government commission does not present any difficult problems under the new Copyright Act. Section 105 of the new Act, 17 U.S.C. § 105 (Supp. I 1977) states in its entirety:

> Copyright protection under this title is not available for any work of the United States Government, but the United States Government is not precluded from receiving and holding copyrights transferred to it by assignment, bequest, or otherwise.

The statute defines a "work of the United States" as one "prepared by . . . *def of work of the US* an employee of the United States Government as part of that person's offi-

new copyright act allows copyright for federally commissioned works

cial duties." 17 U.S.C. § 101 (Supp. I 1977). It is readily observable, therefore, that the language of the new Copyright Act does not prohibit copyright protection for federally commissioned works.

Whatever doubt there may be left after reading the statute is wholly dispelled by the legislative history, which states plainly that these commissioned works may be eligible for copyright protection:

> The bill deliberately avoids making any sort of outright, unqualified prohibition against copyright in works prepared under Government contract or grant. There may well be cases where it would be in the public interest to deny copyright . . . . However, there are almost certainly many other cases where the denial of copyright protection would be unfair or would hamper the production and publication of important works.

H.R.Rep. No. 1476, 94th Cong., 2d Sess. 59 (1976), U.S.Code Cong. & Admin.News 1976, pp. 5659, 5672. That report also states that the government agency may withhold copyright protection from the author if it would be in the public interest to do so or if the commission is merely an alternative to producing the work in-house. Id.; see also 1 Nimmer on Copyright § 5.06[B][2] n. 19.2. In this case, however, the government did not choose to withhold copyright protection from WQED.

Although section 105 explicitly allows the Government to obtain a copyright by assignment, appellants argue that section 105 does not comprehend an assignment of a federally commissioned work. They assert that this commission and assignment constitute an effort to avoid the proscription of copyright subsisting in works produced by the Government, and is therefore prohibited by the new law. In support of this analysis they cite the following passage of Professor Nimmer's treatise:

> Could the U.S. Government thus claim a copyright in a work by this indirect method which it would be precluded from claiming if the work were in the first instance made in a for hire relationship? It seems unlikely that the courts would permit such a subterfuge.

1 Nimmer on Copyright § 5.06[B][3].

Without laying down a broad rule, we are reluctant to cabin the discretion of government agencies to arrange ownership and publication rights with private contractors absent some reasonable showing of a congressional desire to do so. The legislative history noted above indicates a desire to vest the government with some flexibility in making these arrangements. The House Report provides no strong indicia of congressional intent that would lead this court to void the alleged assignment provision. It states, "The effect of section 105 is intended to place all works of the United States Government . . . in the public domain." H.R.Rep. No. 1476, 94th Cong., 2d Sess. 59 (1976), U.S.Code Cong. & Admin.News 1976, p. 5672. Works of the United States were defined by section 101 to comprise works created by Government employees carrying out their official duties. Section 105, therefore, is not necessarily subverted by assigning to the Government the copyright in a commissioned work that is neither produced by current or former employees nor related to the official duties of any Government employee, as here. Had the Government employees been detailed as consultants or employees of WQED, we might more readily find the purported assignment to be a "subterfuge," but without any such allegation we simply lack the statutory warrant to void the assignment.

The 1909 Act similarly provides no basis on which to deny copyright protection to a work commissioned by the Government or to void an alleged assignment of that work to the Government. * * *

We have come to the conclusion that neither the old nor the new copyright law proscribes, the registration of works commissioned by the Government for copyright, and that Congress possessed the power to enact these laws. In addition, when there is no allegation that the Government and the contractor have attempted to subvert the copyright laws through an assignment subsequent to registration of a commissioned work, we find that the copyright laws, in their present as well as former incarnation, will permit such an assignment. * * *

Appellants contend that the application of the copyright laws to works commissioned by the Government is, if authorized by Congress, violative of the First Amendment. * * *

Appellants' surviving First Amendment claims number but two: (1) that they have a constitutional right to reprint the screenplays for commercial gain, and (2) that the defendants acted unconstitutionally in failing to disclose the extent of government involvement in the series. Neither is meritorious. * * *

[The court here quoted Judge Fuld's comment in Estate of Hemingway v. Random House, p. 16 supra, that there is a "freedom *not* to speak publicly."] * * *

Chief Judge Fuld's statements explain why this court should not compel WQED to issue a license even if offered a royalty or other payment. The First Amendment interests to which he adverted are not based upon a desire for pecuniary gain, but upon the author's freedom to speak or remain silent as an end in itself. * * * We therefore conclude that the liberty of WQED to grant or deny a license to appellants, either gratuitously or for compensation, does not offend either the First Amendment or its underlying values.

For similar reasons, we are not inclined to grant appellants' request that we require public broadcasters to, in the words of the complaint, "disclose[ ] the existence or extent of government control of the content of the films," Complaint ¶ 15, on First Amendment grounds. The First Amendment cannot be used to force the unwilling author to speak when he would rather remain silent, as we have just explained supra.

Underlying the appellants' First Amendment assault on the copyright obtained for "Equal Justice Under Law" is their professed concern that the Government may one day attempt to use the copyright law as an instrument of censorship. They seem to argue that if the Pentagon Papers [see New York Times Co. v. United States, 403 U.S. 713 (1971)] could have been copyrighted, their publication could have been enjoined. * * *

We are aware that there is at least a theoretical possibility that some copyright laws may be used by some nations as instruments of censorship. Fears had been expressed, for example, that the Soviet Union would, through use of a compulsory-assignment provision in its domestic copyright laws, attempt to prevent foreign publication of dissident works whose copyright it had assumed. See Newcity, The Universal Copyright Convention as an Instrument of Repression: The Soviet Experiment, in Copyright Law Symposium No. 24 (1980). The congressional response to this perceived threat was 17 U.S.C. § 201(e) (Supp. I 1977), protecting authors from involuntary transfers. * * *

We are unaware, however, of any effort on the part of the United States Government to throttle free expression through use of the copyright laws, and we are not inclined to hypothesize such an effort nor to hand down a decision invalidating an act of Congress on that hypothetical basis. It is important in this regard to recall that there is no tenable allegation in this case that any person interested in viewing "Equal Justice Under Law" has been denied the opportunity to do so, or that copies of the films and their scripts are other than freely available for public inspection.

We are confident that should the day come when the Government denies someone access to a work produced at its direction on the basis of a copyright, and if the doctrine of fair use and the distinction between an idea and its expression fail to vindicate adequately that person's interests—although we have no reason to believe that they would—the courts of the United States would on the basis of facts, not hypotheses, consider afresh the First Amendment interests implicated thereby. We are sure that they will comprehend the difference between that case and this one. * * *

The judgment of the District Court from which this appeal was taken is affirmed.

It is so ordered.

NOTES ON WORKS OF THE U.S. GOVERNMENT

(1) Section 105, in conjunction with the definition of a "work of the United States Government" in § 101, prohibits both the United States and its employees from copyrighting works created in the course of official business. The House Report notes that the exclusion pertains to unpublished as well as published works.

Not every work produced by a government employee is a "work of the United States Government." The House Report tells us that an "official or employee would not be prevented from securing copyright in a work written at that person's own volition and outside his or her duties, even though the subject matter involves the Government work or professional field of the official or employee." H.R.Rep. p. 58. See Public Affairs Associates, Inc. v. Rickover, 268 F.Supp. 444 (D.D.C.1967), holding that speeches delivered to the Harvard Club and the American Public Power Association by nuclear power advocate Admiral Hyman Rickover were his "private property which he was entitled to copyright."

(2) "Equal Justice Under Law" was not produced by an "officer or employee of the United States Government." It was the work of private parties acting pursuant to a government contract. *Schnapper* holds that such works may be copyrighted by their creators. This aspect of the court's decision is supported by the House Report's discussion of § 105:

> * * * As the bill is written, the Government agency concerned could determine in each case whether to allow an independent contractor or grantee to secure copyright in works prepared in whole or in part with the use of Government funds. The argument that has been made against allowing copyright in this situation is that the public should not be required to pay a "double subsidy," and that it is inconsistent to prohibit copyright in works by Government employees while permitting private copyrights in a growing body of works created by persons who are paid with Government funds. Those arguing in favor of potential copyright protection have

stressed the importance of copyright as an incentive to creation and dissemination in this situation and the basically different policy considerations applicable to works written by Government employees and those applicable to works prepared by private organizations with the use of Federal funds. * * *

* * * Where, under the particular circumstances, Congress or the agency involved finds that the need to have a work freely available outweighs the need of the private author to secure copyright, the problem can be dealt with by specific legislation, agency regulations, or contractual restrictions. (H.R.Rep. p. 59.)

(3) Section 105 states that the federal government is not prohibited from holding copyrights "transferred to it by assignment, bequest, or otherwise." *Schnapper* says this language comprehends assignments of copyrights in works that were created at the instigation of the Government. Are you convinced by the court's analysis? Professor Nimmer was not. See Nimmer on Copyright § 5.13[C]. However, *Schnapper* was followed in United States v. Washington Mint, LLC, 115 F.Supp.2d 1089 (D.Minn.2000), upholding the Government's claim of copyright in the design of the Sacagawea dollar coin. Although coins are usually designed by employees of the U.S. Mint, this design had been done by a private artist as part of a design competition involving both Mint employees and invited artists. The outside artists had been required to assign their rights in the designs to the Government in order to participate in the competition. The court granted a preliminary injunction against sales of replica coins by the defendant.

(4) Section 105 does not preclude *state* or *local* governmental entities from claiming copyright in the output of *their* officers and employees. See National Conference of Bar Examiners v. Multistate Legal Studies, Inc., 495 F.Supp. 34 (N.D.Ill.1980), aff'd, 692 F.2d 478 (7th Cir.1982), cert. denied, 464 U.S. 814 (1983) (state bar examinations held copyrightable). A long-standing judicial exception, however, precludes copyright in state judicial opinions and statutes. See Banks v. Manchester, 128 U.S. 244 (1888); State of Georgia v. Harrison Co., 548 F.Supp. 110 (N.D.Ga.1982), vacated, 559 F.Supp. 37 (N.D.Ga.1983). (*Federal* judicial opinions and statutes are in the public domain by virtue of § 105.) The exception does not extend to synopses or headnotes appended by private publishers. Callaghan v. Myers, 128 U.S. 617 (1888). (Recall also West's claim of copyright in its selection and arrangement of opinions, p. 90 supra.) One court, after an extensive review of the case law, concluded that privately drafted codes that are subsequently incorporated into state law might be ineligible for copyright. Building Officials & Code Administrators Int'l, Inc. v. Code Tech., Inc., 628 F.2d 730 (1st Cir.1980). However, the Second Circuit rejected an argument under *Building Officials* that a state's adoption of a legal standard that incorporated a copyrighted compilation of used cars values resulted in the compilation's loss of copyright. CCC Information Services, Inc. v. Maclean Hunter Market Reports, Inc., 44 F.3d 61 (2d Cir.1994), cert. denied, 516 U.S. 817 (1995).[z] In an en banc decision on the copyrightability of privately drafted

---

[z]   The Ninth Circuit followed *CCC Information Services* in Practice Management Information Corp. v. American Medical Ass'n, 121 F.3d 516 (9th Cir.1997), opinion amended, 133 F.3d 1140 (9th Cir.), cert. denied, 524 U.S. 952 (1998) (AMA's medical procedure coding system did not lose its copyright upon adoption by a federal agency for use on Medicare forms).

codes, the Fifth Circuit ordered the dismissal of an infringement claim brought against Peter Veeck (son of legendary baseball team owner Bill Veeck). *Veeck v. Southern Building Code Congress Int'l, Inc.*, 293 F.3d 791 (5th Cir.2002) (en banc), cert. denied, 539 U.S. 969 (2003). A private building code had been adopted by two local towns, and Veeck had posted the code on his web site. "Our short answer is that as *law*, the model codes enter the public domain and are not subject to the copyright holder's exclusive prerogatives." The majority distinguished cases like *CCC Information Services* that concern statutory references to extrinsic standards. "The copyrighted works do not 'become law' merely because a statute refers to them."[aa]

(5) One consequence of § 105 should not be overlooked. In the words of the House Report, it "means that, as far as the copyright law is concerned, the Government could not restrain the employee or official from disseminating the work if he or she chooses to do so." H.R.Rep. p. 59.[bb] The plaintiff in *Schnapper* apparently argued that allowing assignments to the Government of copyright in works produced under Government commission could become "an instrument of censorship." Professor Kaplan has reminded us that the development of copyright law owes much to the English Crown's fear of the newly-invented printing press. See B. Kaplan, An Unhurried View of Copyright 2–6 (1967). The plaintiff's reference in *Schnapper* to the *Pentagon Papers* case was not entirely unfounded. During the Vietnam War, the United States, in an unsuccessful attempt to stop publication in the *New York Times* of portions of a 47–volume government report on the U.S. role in Southeast Asia, had argued to the Supreme Court in New York Times Co. v. U.S., 403 U.S. 713 (1971), that the documents leaked to the *Times* were the "literary property" of the United States. See The Pentagon Papers as Published by the New York Times 689 (Quadrangle Books 1971).

In County of Suffolk v. First American Real Estate Solutions, 261 F.3d 179 (2d Cir.2001), a county brought an infringement claim against a commercial publisher who was marketing copies of the county's real estate maps. Rejecting an analogy to state statutes and judicial opinions, the court held that the maps were eligible for copyright; it also held that New York's Freedom of Information Law, which requires state agencies to "make available for public inspection and copying all records," did not abrogate the county's copyright. Accord, Seago v. Horry County, 378 S.C. 414, 663 S.E.2d 38 (2008). However, a Florida appellate court reached the opposite conclusion when a county official tried to extract a royalty for commercial use of the county's real estate maps; the court said that the Florida Constitution and the state public records statutes preclude a claim of copyright absent authorization from the state legislature. Microdecisions, Inc. v. Skinner, 889 So.2d 871 (Fla.App.2004), cert. denied, 546 U.S. 1033 (2005).

[aa] S. Ghosh, Legal Code and the Need for a Broader Functionality Doctrine in Copyright, 50 J.Copyr. Soc'y 71 (2003), applauds the result in *Veeck*, but argues that the decision should rest on a broad view of the merger doctrine that would preserve access, not only to ideas, but also to "functional" expression.

On the application of copyright (and fair use) to litigation documents prepared by private attorneys, see D. Isaacs, Highest Form of Flattery? Application of the Fair Use Defense Against Copyright Claims for Unauthorized Appropriation of Litigation Documents, 71 Mo.L.Rev. 391 (2006). See also T. Field, From Custom to Law in Copyright, 49 Idea 125 (2008), describing the few contested cases.

[bb] Section 105 did not prevent the Government from seeking to regain physical possession of a document removed without permission by a former employee in Pfeiffer v. Central Intelligence Agency, 60 F.3d 861 (D.C.Cir.1995).

COPYRIGHT AND MORALITY

May copyright be held and enforced in obscene publications? A 1958 opinion of the U.S. Attorney General cautiously concluded that the Register was not without power to withhold registration, but found that the law "imposes no duty upon him to deny registration of such claims." 41 Op. Att'y Gen. No. 73, 121 U.S.P.Q. 329 (1958).

The Copyright Office apparently makes no attempt to curb registration for obscenity. (How could it, in light of the Supreme Court's emphasis on "community standards"? See Miller v. California, 413 U.S. 15 (1973).) Despite some older cases to the contrary, recent judicial decisions have also rejected obscenity defenses in infringement actions. See Mitchell Brothers Film Group v. Cinema Adult Theater, 604 F.2d 852 (5th Cir.1979), cert. denied, 445 U.S. 917 (1980); Jartech, Inc. v. Clancy, 666 F.2d 403 (9th Cir.), cert. denied, 459 U.S. 826 (1982). However, while not deciding whether obscenity is a defense to infringement, the court in Devils Films, Inc. v. Nectar Video, 29 F.Supp.2d 174 (S.D.N.Y.1998), concluded that it should not assist the plaintiff in marketing its obscene tapes by granting a request to seize unlicensed copies.

What of material published with intent to deceive or defraud? In Belcher v. Tarbox, 486 F.2d 1087 (9th Cir.1973), the court said it was no defense to an infringement action that the plaintiff's horse race handicapping system might be fraudulent: "There is nothing in the Copyright Act to suggest that the courts are to pass upon the truth or falsity, the soundness or unsoundness, of the views embodied in a copyrighted work." The Ninth Circuit in Dream Games, Inc. v. PC Onsite, 561 F.3d 983 (9th Cir.2009), relied on both the obscenity and fraudulent content cases to conclude that a copyright owner's illegal use of a gambling video game did not deprive the work of copyright protection.

Finally, it might be noted that morality survives in § 2(a) of the federal Trademark Act, 15 U.S.C.A. § 1052(a), which forbids the registration of a trademark that "comprises immoral, deceptive, or scandalous matter." The mark "Bubby Trap" for brassieres was denied registration, but "Badass" for musical instruments was not.[cc]

[cc] See In re Runsdorf, 171 U.S.P.Q. 443 (Trademark Trial & App.Bd.1971); In re Leo Quan Inc., 200 U.S.P.Q. 370 (Trademark Trial & App.Bd.1978). See generally J. McCarthy, Trademarks and Unfair Competition § 19.77.

CHAPTER 3

SCOPE OF PROTECTION: INFRINGEMENT

1. IDEAS AND EXPRESSION IN WORKS OF FICTION

Nichols v. Universal Pictures Corp.

United States Circuit Court of Appeals, Second Circuit, 1930.
45 F.2d 119.
Certiorari denied, 282 U.S. 902 (1931).

■ Before L. HAND, SWAN, and AUGUSTUS N. HAND, CIRCUIT JUDGES.

■ L. HAND, CIRCUIT JUDGE. The plaintiff is the author of a play, "Abie's Irish Rose," which it may be assumed was properly copyrighted under section five, subdivision (d), of the Copyright Act, 17 U.S.C.A. § 5(d). The defendant produced publicly a motion picture play, "The Cohens and The Kellys," which the plaintiff alleges was taken from it. As we think the defendant's play too unlike the plaintiff's to be an infringement, we may assume, arguendo, that in some details the defendant used the plaintiff's play as will subsequently appear, though we do not so decide. It therefore becomes necessary to give an outline of the two plays.

"Abie's Irish Rose" presents a Jewish family living in prosperous circumstances in New York. The father, a widower, is in business as a merchant, in which his son and only child helps him. The boy has philandered with young women, who to his father's great disgust have always been Gentiles, for he is obsessed with a passion that his daughter-in-law shall be an orthodox Jewess. When the play opens the son, who has been courting a young Irish Catholic girl, has already married her secretly before a Protestant minister, and is concerned to soften the blow for his father, by securing a favorable impression of his bride, while concealing her faith and race. To accomplish this he introduces her to his father at his home as a Jewess, and lets it appear that he is interested in her, though he conceals the marriage. The girl somewhat reluctantly falls in with the plan; the father takes the bait, becomes infatuated with the girl, concludes that they must marry, and assumes that of course they will, if he so decides. He calls in a rabbi, and prepares for the wedding according to the Jewish rite.

Meanwhile the girl's father, also a widower, who lives in California, and is as intense in his own religious antagonism as the Jew, has been called to New York, supposing that his daughter is to marry an Irishman and a Catholic. Accompanied by a priest, he arrives at the house at the moment when the marriage is being celebrated, but too late to prevent it, and the two fathers, each infuriated by the proposed union of his child to a heretic, fall into unseemly and grotesque antics. The priest and the rabbi become friendly, exchange trite sentiments about religion, and agree that the match is good. Apparently out of abundant caution, the priest celebrates the marriage for a third time, while the girl's father is inveigled away. The second act closes with each father, still outraged, seeking to find some way by which the union, thus trebly insured, may be dissolved.

The last act takes place about a year later, the young couple having meanwhile been abjured by each father, and left to their own resources. They have had twins, a boy and a girl, but their fathers know no more than that a child has been born. At Christmas each, led by his craving to see his grandchild, goes separately to the young folks' home, where they encounter each other, each laden with gifts, one for a boy, the other for a girl. After some slapstick comedy, depending upon the insistence of each that he is right about the sex of the grandchild, they become reconciled when they learn the truth, and that each child is to bear the given name of a grand-parent. The curtain falls as the fathers are exchanging amenities, and the Jew giving evidence of an abatement in the strictness of his orthodoxy.

"The Cohens and The Kellys" presents two families, Jewish and Irish, living side by side in the poorer quarters of New York in a state of perpetu-al enmity. The wives in both cases are still living, and share in the mutual animosity, as do two small sons, and even the respective dogs. The Jews have a daughter, the Irish a son; the Jewish father is in the clothing busi-ness; the Irishman is a policeman. The children are in love with each other, and secretly marry, apparently after the play opens. The Jew, being in great financial straits, learns from a lawyer that he has fallen heir to a large fortune from a great-aunt, and moves into a great house, fitted luxu-riously. Here he and his family live in vulgar ostentation, and here the Irish boy seeks out his Jewish bride, and is chased away by the angry fa-ther. The Jew then abuses the Irishman over the telephone, and both be-come hysterically excited. The extremity of his feelings makes the Jew sick, so that he must go to Florida for a rest, just before which the daughter dis-closes her marriage to her mother.

On his return the Jew finds that his daughter has borne a child; at first he suspects the lawyer, but eventually learns the truth and is over-come with anger at such a low alliance. Meanwhile, the Irish family who have been forbidden to see the grandchild, go to the Jew's house, and after a violent scene between the two fathers in which the Jew disowns his daughter, who decides to go back with her husband, the Irishman takes her back with her baby to his own poor lodgings. The lawyer, who had hoped to marry the Jew's daughter, seeing his plan foiled, tells the Jew that his for-tune really belongs to the Irishman, who was also related to the dead wom-an, but offers to conceal his knowledge, if the Jew will share the loot. This the Jew repudiates, and, leaving the astonished lawyer, walks through the rain to his enemy's house to surrender the property. He arrives in great dejection, tells the truth, and abjectly turns to leave. A reconciliation en-sues, the Irishman agreeing to share with him equally. The Jew shows some interest in his grandchild, though this is at most a minor motive in the reconciliation, and the curtain falls while the two are in their cups, the Jew insisting that in the firm name for the business, which they are to car-ry on jointly, his name shall stand first.

It is of course essential to any protection of literary property, whether at common-law or under the statute, that the right cannot be limited liter-ally to the text, else a plagiarist would escape by immaterial variations. That has never been the law, but, as soon as literal appropriation ceases to be the test, the whole matter is necessarily at large, so that, as was recent-ly well said by a distinguished judge, the decisions cannot help much in a new case. Fendler v. Morosco, 253 N.Y. 281, 292, 171 N.E. 56. When plays are concerned, the plagiarist may excise a separate scene [Daly v. Webster, 56 F. 483 (C.C.A.2); Chappell v. Fields, 210 F. 864 (C.C.A.2); Chatterton v. Cave, L.R. 3 App.Cas. 483]; or he may appropriate part of the dialogue (Warne v. Seebohm, L.R. 39 Ch.D. 73). Then the question is whether the part so taken is "substantial," and therefore not a "fair use" of the copyrighted work; it is the same question as arises in the case of any other copyrighted work. Marks v. Feist, 290 F. 959 (C.C.A.2); Emerson v. Davies, Fed.Cas. No. 4436, 3 Story, 768, 795–797. But when the plagiarist does not take out a block in situ, but an abstract of the whole, decision is more troublesome. Upon any work, and especially upon a play, a great number of patterns of increasing generality will fit equally well, as more and more of the incident is left out. The last may perhaps be no more than the most general statement of what the play is about, and at times might consist only of its title; but there is a point in this series of abstractions where they are no longer protected, since otherwise the playwright could prevent the use of his "ideas," to which, apart from their expression, his property is never extended. Holmes v. Hurst, 174 U.S. 82, 86; Guthrie v. Curlett, 36 F.2d 694 (C.C.A.2). Nobody has ever been able to fix that boundary, and nobody ever can. In some cases the question has been treated as though it were analogous to lifting a portion out of the copyrighted work (Rees v. Melville, MacGillivray's Copyright Cases [1911–1916], 168); but the analogy is not a good one, because though the skeleton is a part of the body, it pervades and supports the whole. In such cases we are rather concerned with the line between expression and what is expressed. As respects plays, the controversy chiefly centers upon the characters and sequence of incident, these being the substance.

We did not in Dymow v. Bolton, 11 F.2d 690, hold that a plagiarist was never liable for stealing a plot; that would have been flatly against our rulings in Dam v. Kirk La Shelle Co., 175 F. 902 and Stodart v. Mutual Film Co., 249 F. 513, affirming my decision in (D.C.) 249 F. 507; neither of which we meant to overrule. We found the plot of the second play was too different to infringe, because the most detailed pattern, common to both, eliminated so much from each that its content went into the public domain; and for this reason we said, "this mere subsection of a plot was not susceptible of copyright." But we do not doubt that two plays may correspond in plot closely enough for infringement. How far that correspondence must go is another matter. Nor need we hold that the same may not be true as to the characters, quite independently of the "plot" proper, though, as far as we know, such a case has never arisen. If Twelfth Night were copyrighted, it is quite possible that a second comer might so closely imitate Sir Toby Belch or Malvolio as to infringe, but it would not be enough that for one of his characters he cast a riotous knight who kept wassail to the discomfort of the household, or a vain and foppish steward who became amorous of his mistress. These would be no more than Shakespeare's "ideas" in the play, as little capable of monopoly as Einstein's Doctrine of Relativity, or Darwin's theory of the Origin of Species. It follows that the less developed the characters, the less they can be copyrighted; that is the penalty an author must bear for marking them too indistinctly.

In the two plays at bar we think both as to incident and character, the defendant took no more—assuming that it took anything at all—than the law allowed. The stories are quite different. One is of a religious zealot who insists upon his child's marrying no one outside his faith; opposed by another who is in this respect just like him, and is his foil. Their difference in race is merely an obbligato to the main theme, religion. They sink their differences through grandparental pride and affection. In the other, zealotry is wholly absent; religion does not even appear. It is true that the parents are hostile to each other in part because they differ in race; but the marriage of their son to a Jew does not apparently offend the Irish family at all, and it exacerbates the existing animosity of the Jew, principally because he has become rich, when he learns it. They are reconciled through the honesty of the Jew and the generosity of the Irishman; the grandchild has nothing whatever to do with it. The only matter common to the two is a quarrel between a Jewish and an Irish father, the marriage of their children, the birth of grandchildren and a reconciliation.

If the defendant took so much from the plaintiff, it may well have been because her amazing success seemed to prove that this was a subject of enduring popularity. Even so, granting that the plaintiff's play was wholly original, and assuming that novelty is not essential to a copyright, there is no monopoly in such a background. Though the plaintiff discovered the vein, she could not keep it to herself; so defined, the theme was too generalized an abstraction from what she wrote. It was only a part of her "ideas."

Nor does she fare better as to her characters. It is indeed scarcely credible that she should not have been aware of those stock figures, the low comedy Jew and Irishman. The defendant has not taken from her more than their prototypes have contained for many decades. If so, obviously so to generalize her copyright, would allow her to cover what was not original with her. But we need not hold this as matter of fact, much as we might be justified. Even though we take it that she devised her figures out of her brain de novo, still the defendant was within its rights.

There are but four characters common to both plays, the lovers and the fathers. The lovers are so faintly indicated as to be no more than stage properties. They are loving and fertile; that is really all that can be said of them, and anyone else is quite within his rights if he puts loving and fertile lovers in a play of his own, wherever he gets the cue. The plaintiff's Jew is quite unlike the defendant's. His obsession is his religion, on which depends such racial animosity as he has. He is affectionate, warm and patriarchal. None of these fit the defendant's Jew, who shows affection for his daughter only once, and who has none but the most superficial interest in his grandchild. He is tricky, ostentatious and vulgar, only by misfortune redeemed into honesty. Both are grotesque, extravagant and quarrelsome; both are fond of display; but these common qualities make up only a small part of their simple pictures, no more than any one might lift if he chose. The Irish fathers are even more unlike; the plaintiff's a mere symbol for religious fanaticism and patriarchal pride, scarcely a character at all. Neither quality appears in the defendant's, for while he goes to get his grandchild, it is rather out of a truculent determination not to be forbidden, than from pride in his progeny. For the rest he is only a grotesque hobbledehoy, used for low comedy of the most conventional sort, which any one might borrow, if he chanced not to know the exemplar.

The defendant argues that the case is controlled by my decision in Fisher v. Dillingham (D.C.) 298 F. 145. Neither my brothers nor I wish to throw doubt upon the doctrine of that case, but it is not applicable here. We assume that the plaintiff's play is altogether original, even to an extent that in fact it is hard to believe. We assume further that, so far as it has been anticipated by earlier plays of which she knew nothing, that fact is immaterial. Still, as we have already said, her copyright did not cover everything that might be drawn from her play; its content went to some extent into the public domain. We have to decide how much, and while we are as aware as any one that the line, wherever it is drawn, will seem arbitrary, that is no excuse for not drawing it; it is a question such as courts must answer in nearly all cases. Whatever may be the difficulties a priori, we have no question on which side of the line this case falls. A comedy based upon conflicts between Irish and Jews, into which the marriage of their children enters, is no more susceptible of copyright than the outline of Romeo and Juliet.

The plaintiff has prepared an elaborate analysis of the two plays, showing a "quadrangle" of the common characters, in which each is represented by the emotions which he discovers. She presents the resulting parallelism as proof of infringement, but the adjectives employed are so general as to be quite useless. Take for example the attribute of "love" ascribed to both Jews. The plaintiff has depicted her father as deeply attached to his son, who is his hope and joy; not so, the defendant, whose father's conduct is throughout not actuated by any affection for his daughter, and who is merely once overcome for the moment by her distress when he has violently dismissed her lover. "Anger" covers emotions aroused by quite different occasions in each case; so do "anxiety," "despondency" and "disgust." It is unnecessary to go through the catalogue for emotions are too much colored by their causes to be a test when used so broadly. This is not the proper approach to a solution; it must be more ingenuous, more like that of a spectator, who would rely upon the complex of his impressions of each character.

We cannot approve the length of the record, which was due chiefly to the use of expert witnesses. Argument is argument whether in the box or at the bar, and its proper place is the last. The testimony of an expert upon such issues, especially his cross-examination, greatly extends the trial and contributes nothing which cannot be better heard after the evidence is all submitted. It ought not to be allowed at all; and while its admission is not a ground for reversal, it cumbers the case and tends to confusion, for the more the court is led into the intricacies of dramatic craftsmanship, the less likely it is to stand upon the firmer, if more naïve, ground of its considered impressions upon its own perusal. We hope that in this class of cases such evidence may in the future be entirely excluded, and the case confined to the actual issues; that is, whether the copyrighted work was original, and whether the defendant copied it, so far as the supposed infringement is identical. * * *

Decree affirmed.

Reyher v. Children's Television Workshop

533 F.2d 87 (2d Cir.), cert. denied, 429 U.S. 980 (1976).

Plaintiff's book for children, "My Mother is the Most Beautiful Woman in the World," retold the folktale of a lost Russian child who could describe his mother only in the words of the title. The search for the mother was hampered because objectively she was quite homely. Defendant's Sesame Street television playlet and two-page magazine recreation, called "The Most Beautiful Woman in the World," located the same story in Africa.

"The difficult task in an infringement action is to distill the nonprotected idea from protected expression. * * * While the line between idea and expression may not be susceptible to overly helpful generalization, it has been emphasized repeatedly that the essence of infringement lies in taking not a general theme but its particular expression through similarities of treatment, details, scenes, events, and characterizations."

Judge Meskill said the question was "whether defendants in the instant case utilized the idea in Reyher's book or instead descended so far into the concrete as to invade her expression." Finding the works "not similar in mood, details or characterization," the court affirmed a dismissal of the infringement claim.

Sheldon v. Metro–Goldwyn Pictures Corp.

United States Circuit Court of Appeals, Second Circuit, 1936.
81 F.2d 49.
Certiorari denied 298 U.S. 669.

■ Before L. HAND, SWAN, and CHASE, CIRCUIT JUDGES.

■ L. HAND, CIRCUIT JUDGE. The suit is to enjoin the performance of the picture play, "Letty Lynton," as an infringement of the plaintiffs' copyrighted play, "Dishonored Lady." The plaintiffs' title is conceded, so too the validity of the copyright; the only issue is infringement. The defendants say that they did not use the play in any way to produce the picture; the plaintiffs discredit this denial because of the negotiations between the parties for the purchase of rights in the play, and because the similarities between the two are too specific and detailed to have resulted from chance. The judge thought that, so far as the defendants had used the play, they had taken only what the law allowed, that is, those general themes, motives, or ideas in which there could be no copyright. Therefore he dismissed the bill.

An understanding of the issue involves some description of what was in the public demesne, as well as of the play and the picture. In 1857 a Scotch girl, named Madeleine Smith, living in Glasgow, was brought to trial upon an indictment in three counts; two for attempts to poison her lover, a third for poisoning him. The jury acquitted her on the first count, and brought in a verdict of "Not Proven" on the second and third. The circumstances of the prosecution aroused much interest at the time not only in Scotland but in England; so much indeed that it became a cause célèbre, and that as late as 1927 the whole proceedings were published in book form. An outline of the story so published, which became the original of the play here in suit, is as follows: The Smiths were a respectable middle-class family, able to send their daughter to a "young ladies' boarding school"; they supposed her protected not only from any waywardness of her own, but from the wiles of seducers. In both they were mistaken, for when at the age of twenty-one she met a young Jerseyman of French blood, Emile L'Angelier, ten years older, and already the hero of many amorous adventures, she quickly succumbed and poured out her feelings in letters of the utmost ardor and indiscretion, and at times of a candor beyond the standards then, and even yet, permissible for well-nurtured young women. They wrote each other as though already married, he assuming to dictate her conduct and even her feelings; both expected to marry, she on any terms, he with the approval of her family. Nevertheless she soon tired of him and engaged herself to a man some twenty years older who was a better match, but for whom she had no more than a friendly complaisance. L'Angelier was not, however, to be fobbed off so easily; he threatened to expose her to her father by showing her letters. She at first tried to dissuade him by appeals to their tender memories, but finding this useless and thinking herself otherwise undone, she affected a return of her former passion and invited him to visit her again. Whether he did, was the turning point of the trial; the evidence, though it really left the issue in no doubt, was too indirect to satisfy the jury, perhaps in part because of her advocate's argument that to kill him only insured the discovery of her letters. It was shown that she had several times bought or tried to buy poison,—prussic acid and arsenic,—and that twice before his death L'Angelier became violently ill, the second time on the day after her purchase. He died of arsenical poison, which the prosecution charged that she had given him in a cup of chocolate. At her trial, Madeleine being incompetent as a witness, her advocate proved an alibi by the testimony of her younger sister that early on the night of the murder as laid in the indictment, she had gone to bed with Madeleine, who had slept with her throughout the night. As to one of the attempts her betrothed swore that she had been with him at the theatre.

This was the story which the plaintiffs used to build their play. As will appear they took from it but the merest skeleton, the acquittal of a wanton young woman, who to extricate herself from an amour that stood in the way of a respectable marriage, poisoned her lover. The incidents, the characters, the mis en scène, the sequence of events, were all changed; nobody disputes that the plaintiffs were entitled to their copyright. All that they took from the story they might probably have taken, had it even been copyrighted. Their heroine is named Madeleine Cary; she lives in New York, brought up in affluence, if not in luxury; she is intelligent, voluptuous, ardent and corrupt; but, though she has had a succession of amours, she is capable of genuine affection. Her lover and victim is an Argentinian, named Moreno, who makes his living as a dancer in night-clubs. Madeleine has met him once in Europe before the play opens, has danced with him, has excited his concupiscence; he presses presents upon her. The play opens in his rooms, he and his dancing partner who is also his mistress, are together; Madeleine on the telephone recalls herself to him and says she wishes to visit him, though it is already past midnight. He disposes of his mistress by a device which does not deceive her and receives Madeleine; at once he falls to wooing her, luring her among other devices by singing a Gaucho song. He finds her facile and the curtain falls in season.

The second act is in her home, and introduces her father, a bibulous dotard, who has shot his wife's lover in the long past; Laurence Brennan, a self-made man in the fifties, untutored, self-reliant and reliable, who has had with Madeleine a relation, half paternal, half amorous since she grew up; and Denis Farnborough, a young British labor peer, a mannekin to delight the heart of well ordered young women. Madeleine loves him; he loves Madeleine; she will give him no chance to declare himself, remembering her mottled past and his supposedly immaculate standards. She confides to Brennan, who makes clear to her the imbecility of her self-denial; she accepts this enlightenment and engages herself to her high-minded paragon after confessing vaguely her evil life and being assured that to post-war generations all such lapses are peccadillo.

In the next act Moreno, who has got wind of the engagement, comes to her house. Disposing of Farnborough, who chances to be there, she admits Moreno, acknowledges that she is to marry Farnborough, and asks him to accept the situation as the normal outcome of their intrigue. He refuses to be cast off, high words pass, he threatens to expose their relations, she raves at him, until finally he knocks her down and commands her to go to his apartment that morning as before. After he leaves full of swagger, her eye lights on a bottle of strychnine which her father uses as a drug; her fingers slowly close upon it; the audience understands that she will kill Moreno. Farnborough is at the telephone; this apparently stiffens her resolve, showing her the heights she may reach by its execution.

JUDGE LEARNED HAND

His opinions for more than half a century illuminated the law of copyright and unfair competition. What George Wharton Pepper said of the *Sheldon* opinion can be many times justly repeated about Judge Hand's writing: "The entire opinion exhibits craftsmanship at its best and is entitled to be ranked as a model of judicial style." 60 Harv.L.Rev. 333, 341 (1947).

The scene then shifts again to Moreno's apartment; his mistress must again be put out, most unwillingly for she is aware of the situation; Madeleine comes in; she pretends once more to feel warmly, she must wheedle him for he is out of sorts after the quarrel. Meanwhile she prepares to poison him by putting the strychnine in coffee, which she asks him to make ready. But in the course of these preparations during which he sings her again his Gaucho song, what with their proximity, and this and that, her animal ardors are once more aroused and drag her, unwillingly and protesting, from her purpose. The play must therefore wait for an hour or more until, relieved of her passion, she appears from his bedroom and while breakfasting puts the strychnine in his coffee. He soon discovers what has happened and tries to telephone for help. He does succeed in getting a few words through, but she tears away the wire and fills his dying ears with her hatred and disgust. She then carefully wipes away all traces of her fingerprints and manages to get away while the door is being pounded in by those who have come at his call.

The next act is again at her home on the following evening. Things are going well with her and Farnborough and her father, when a district attorney comes in, a familiar of the household, now in stern mood; Moreno's mistress and a waiter have incriminated Madeleine, and a cross has been found in Moreno's pocket, which he superstitiously took off her neck the night before. The district attorney cross-questions her, during which Farnborough several times fatuously intervenes; she is driven from point to point almost to an avowal when as a desperate plunge she says she spent the night with Brennan. Brennan is brought to the house and, catching the situation after a moment's delay, bears her out. This puts off the district attorney until seeing strychnine brought to relieve the father, his suspicions spring up again and he arrests Madeleine. The rest of the play is of no consequence here, except that it appears in the last scene that at the trial where she is acquitted, her father on the witness stand accounts for the absence of the bottle of strychnine which had been used to poison Moreno.

At about the time that this play was being written an English woman named Lowndes wrote a book called Letty Lynton, also founded on the story of Madeleine Smith. Letty Lynton lives in England; she is eighteen years old, beautiful, well-reared and intelligent, but wayward. She has had a more or less equivocal love affair with a young Scot, named McLean, who worked in her father's chemical factory, but has discarded him, apparently before their love-making had gone very far. Then she chances upon a young Swede—half English—named Ekebon, and their acquaintance quickly becomes a standardized amour, kept secret from her parents, especially her mother, who is an uncompromising moralist, and somewhat estranged from Letty anyway. She and her lover use an old barn as their place of assignation; it had been fitted up as a play house for Letty when she was a child. Like Madeleine Smith she had written her lover a series of indiscreet letters which he has kept, for though he is on pleasure bent Ekebon has a frugal mind, and means to marry his sweetheart and set himself up for life. They are betrothed and he keeps pressing her to declare it to her parents, which she means never to do. While he is away in Sweden, Letty meets an unmarried peer considerably older than she, poor but intelligent and charming; he falls in love with her and she accepts him, more because it is a good match than for any other reason, though she likes him well enough, and will make him suppose that she loves him.

Thereupon Ekebon reappears, learns of Letty's new betrothal, and threatens to disclose his own to her father, backing up his story with her letters. She must at once disown her peer and resume her engagement with him. His motive, like L'Angelier's, is ambition rather than love, though conquest is a flattery and Letty a charming morsel. His threats naturally throw Letty into dismay; she has come to loathe him and at any cost must get free, but she has no one to turn to. In her plight she thinks of her old suitor, McLean, and goes to the factory only to find him gone. He has taught her how to get access to poisons in his office and has told of their effect on human beings. At first she thinks of jumping out the window, and when she winces at that, of poisoning herself; that would be easier. So she selects arsenic which is less painful and goes away with it; it is only when she gets home that she thinks of poisoning Ekebon. Her mind is soon made up, however, and she makes an appointment with him at the barn; she has told her father, she writes, and Ekebon is to see him on Monday, but meanwhile on Sunday they will meet secretly once more. She has prepared to go on a week-end party and conceals her car near the barn. He comes; she welcomes him with a pretence of her former ardors, and tries to get back her letters. Unsuccessful in this she persuades him to drink a cup of chocolate into which she puts the arsenic. After carefully washing the pans and cups, she leaves with him, dropping him from her car near his home; he being still unaffected. On her way to her party she pretends to have broken down and by asking the help of a passing cyclist establishes an alibi. Ekebon dies at his home attended by his mistress; the letters are discovered and Letty is brought before the coroner's inquest and acquitted chiefly through the alibi, for things look very bad for her until the cyclist appears.

The defendants, who are engaged in producing speaking films on a very large scale in Hollywood, California, had seen the play and wished to get the rights. They found, however, an obstacle in an association of motion picture producers presided over by Mr. Will Hays, who thought the play obscene; not being able to overcome his objections, they returned the copy of the manuscript which they had had. That was in the spring of 1930, but in the autumn they induced the plaintiffs to get up a scenario, which they hoped might pass moral muster. Although this did not suit them after the plaintiffs prepared it, they must still have thought in the spring of 1931 that they could satisfy Mr. Hays, for they then procured an offer from the plaintiffs to sell their rights for $30,000. These negotiations also proved abortive because the play continued to be objectionable, and eventually they cried off on the bargain. Mrs. Lowndes' novel was suggested to Thalberg, one of the vice-presidents of the Metro–Goldwyn Company, in July, 1931, and again in the following November, and he bought the rights to it in December. At once he assigned the preparation of a play to Stromberg, who had read the novel in January, and thought it would make a suitable play for an actress named, Crawford, just then not employed. Stromberg chose Meehan, Tuchock and Brown to help him, the first two with the scenario, the third with the dramatic production. All these four were examined by deposition; all denied that they had used the play in any way whatever; all agreed that they had based the picture on the story of Madeleine Smith and on the novel, "Letty Lynton." All had seen the play, and Tuchock had read the manuscript, as had Thalberg, but Stromberg, Meehan and Brown swore that they had not; Stromberg's denial being however worthless, for he had originally sworn the contrary in an affidavit. They all say that work began late in November or early in December, 1931, and the picture was finished by the end of March. To meet these denials, the plaintiffs appeal to the substantial identity between passages in the picture and those parts of the play which are original with them.

The picture opens in Montevideo where Letty Lynton is recovering from her fondness for Emile Renaul. She is rich, luxurious and fatherless, her father having been killed by his mistress's husband; her mother is seared, hard, selfish, unmotherly; and Letty has left home to escape her, wandering about in search of excitement. Apparently for the good part of a year she has been carrying on a love affair with Renaul; twice before she has tried to shake loose, has gone once to Rio where she lit another flame, but each time she has weakened and been drawn back. Though not fully declared as an amour, there can be no real question as to the character of her attachment. She at length determines really to break loose, but once again her senses are too much for her and it is indicated, if not declared, that she spends the night with Renaul. Though he is left a vague figure on-ly indistinctly associated with South America somewhere or other, the part was cast for an actor with a marked foreign accent, and it is plain that he was meant to be understood, in origin anyway, as South American, like Moreno in the play. He is violent, possessive and sensual; his power over Letty lies in his strong animal attractions. However, she escapes in the morning while he is asleep, whether from his bed or not is perhaps uncer-tain; and with a wax figure in the form of a loyal maid—Letty in the novel had one—boards a steamer for New York. On board she meets Darrow, a young American, the son of a rich rubber manufacturer, who is coming back from a trip to Africa. They fall in love upon the faintest provocation and become betrothed before the ship docks, three weeks after she left Montevi-deo. At the pier she finds Renaul who has flown up to reclaim her. She must in some way keep her two suitors apart, and she manages to dismiss Darrow and then to escape Renaul by asking him to pay her customs du-ties, which he does. Arrived home her mother gives her a cold welcome and refuses to concern herself with the girl's betrothal. Renaul is announced; he has read of the betrothal in the papers and is furious. He tries again to stir her sensuality by the familiar gambit, but this time he fails; she slaps his face and declares that she hates him. He commands her to come to his apartment that evening; she begs him to part with her and let her have her life; he insists on renewing their affair. She threatens to call the police; he rejoins that if so her letters will be published, and then he leaves. Desper-ate, she chances on a bottle of strychnine, which we are to suppose is an accoutrement of every affluent household, and seizes it; the implication is of intended suicide, not murder. Then she calls Darrow, tells him that she will not leave with him that night for his parents' place in the Adirondacks as they had planned; she renews to him the pledge of her love, without him she cannot live, an intimation to the audience of her purpose to kill herself.

That evening she goes to Renaul's apartment in a hotel armed with her strychnine bottle, for use on the spot; she finds him cooling champagne, but in bad temper. His caresses which he bestows plentifully enough, again stir her disgust not her passions, but he does not believe it and assumes that she will spend the night with him. Finding that he will not return the letters, she believes herself lost and empties the strychnine into a wine glass. Again he embraces her; she vilifies him; he knocks her down; she vili-fies him again. Ignorant of the poison he grasps her glass, and she, perceiv-ing it, lets him drink. He woos her again, this time with more apparent success, for she is terrified; he sings a Gaucho song to her, the same one that has been heard at Montevideo. The poison begins to work and, at length supposing that she has meant to murder him, he reaches for the telephone; she forestalls him, but she does not tear out the wire. As he slowly dies, she stands over him and vituperates him. A waiter enters; she steps behind a curtain; he leaves thinking Renaul drunk; she comes out, wipes off all traces of her fingerprints and goes out, leaving however her rubbers which Renaul had taken from her when she entered.

Next she and Darrow are found at his parents' in the Adirondacks; while there a detective appears, arrests Letty and takes her to New York; she is charged with the murder of Renaul; Darrow goes back to New York with her. The finish is at the district attorney's office; Letty and Darrow, Letty's mother, the wax serving maid are all there. The letters appear incriminating to an elderly rather benevolent district attorney; also the customs slip and the rubbers. Letty begins to break down; she admits that she went to Renaul's room, not to kill him but to get him to release her. Darrow sees that that story will not pass, and volunteers that she came to his room at a hotel and spent the night with him. Letty confirms this and mother, till then silent, backs up their story; she had traced them to the hotel and saw the lights go out, having ineffectually tried to dissuade them. The maid still further confirms them and the district attorney, not sorry to be discomfited, though unbelieving, discharges Letty.

We are to remember that it makes no difference how far the play was anticipated by works in the public demesne which the plaintiffs did not use. The defendants appear not to recognize this, for they have filled the record with earlier instances of the same dramatic incidents and devices, as though, like a patent, a copyrighted work must be not only original, but new. That is not however the law as is obvious in the case of maps or compendia, where later works will necessarily be anticipated. At times, in discussing how much of the substance of a play the copyright protects, courts have indeed used language which seems to give countenance to the notion that, if a plot were old, it could not be copyrighted. London v. Biograph Co. (C.C.A.) 231 F. 696; Eichel v. Marcin (D.C.) 241 F. 404. But we understand by this no more than that in its broader outline a plot is never copyrightable, for it is plain beyond peradventure that anticipation as such cannot invalidate a copyright. Borrowed the work must indeed not be, for a plagiarist is not himself pro tanto an "author"; but if by some magic a man who had never known it were to compose anew Keats's Ode on a Grecian Urn, he would be an "author," and, if he copyrighted it, others might not copy that poem, though they might of course copy Keats's. Bleistein v. Donaldson Lithographing Co., 188 U.S. 239, 249; Gerlach–Barklow Co. v. Morris & Bendien, Inc., 23 F.2d 159, 161 (C.C.A.2); Weil, Copyright Law, p. 234. But though a copyright is for this reason less vulnerable than a patent, the owner's protection is more limited, for just as he is no less an "author" because others have preceded him, so another who follows him, is not a tort-feasor unless he pirates his work. Jewelers' Circular Publishing Co. v. Keystone Co., 281 F. 83, 92 (C.C.A.2); General Drafting Co. v. Andrews, 37 F.2d 54, 56 (C.C.A.2); Williams v. Smythe (C.C.) 110 F. 961; American, etc., Directory Co. v. Gehring Pub. Co. (D.C.) 4 F.2d 415; New Jersey, etc., Co. v. Barton Business Service (D.C.) 57 F.2d 353. If the copyrighted work is therefore original, the public demesne is important only on the issue of infringement; that is, so far as it may break the force of the inference to be drawn from likenesses between the work and the putative piracy. If the defendant has had access to other material which would have served him as well, his disclaimer becomes more plausible.

In the case at bar there are then two questions: First, whether the defendants actually used the play; second, if so, whether theirs was a "fair use." The judge did not make any finding upon the first question, as we said at the outset, because he thought the defendants were in any case justified; in this following our decision in Nichols v. Universal Pictures Corporation, 45 F.2d 119. The plaintiffs challenge that opinion because we said that "copying" might at times be a "fair use"; but it is convenient to define such a use by saying that others may "copy" the "theme," or "ideas," or the like, of a work, though not its "expression." At any rate so long as it is clear what is meant, no harm is done. In the case at bar the distinction is not so important as usual, because so much of the play was borrowed from the story of Madeleine Smith, and the plaintiffs' originality is necessarily limited to the variants they introduced. Nevertheless, it is still true that their whole contribution may not be protected; for the defendants were entitled to use, not only all that had gone before, but even the plaintiffs' contribution itself, if they drew from it only the more general patterns; that is, if they kept clear of its "expression." We must therefore state in detail those similarities which seem to us to pass the limits of "fair use." Finally, in concluding as we do that the defendants used the play pro tanto, we need not charge their witnesses with perjury. With so many sources before them they might quite honestly forget what they took; nobody knows the origin of his inventions; memory and fancy merge even in adults. Yet unconscious plagiarism is actionable quite as much as deliberate. Buck v. Jewell–La Salle Realty Co., 283 U.S. 191, 198; Harold Lloyd Corporation v. Witwer, 65 F.2d 1, 16 (C.C.A.9); Fred Fisher, Inc. v. Dillingham (D.C.) 298 F. 145.

The defendants took for their mis en scène the same city and the same social class; and they chose a South American villain. The heroines had indeed to be wanton, but Letty Lynton "tracked" Madeleine Cary more closely than that. She is overcome by passion in the first part of the picture and yields after announcing that she hates Renaul and has made up her mind to leave him. This is the same weakness as in the murder scene of the play, though transposed. Each heroine's waywardness is suggested as an inherited disposition; each has had an errant parent involved in scandal; one killed, the other becoming an outcast. Each is redeemed by a higher love. Madeleine Cary must not be misread; it is true that her lust overcomes her at the critical moment, but it does not extinguish her love for Farnborough; her body, not her soul, consents to her lapse. Moreover, her later avowal, which she knew would finally lose her her lover, is meant to show the basic rectitude of her nature. Though it does not need Darrow to cure Letty of her wanton ways, she too is redeemed by a nobler love. Neither Madeleine Smith, nor the Letty of the novel, were at all like that; they wished to shake off a clandestine intrigue to set themselves up in the world; their love as distinct from their lust, was pallid. So much for the similarity in character.

Coming to the parallelism of incident, the threat scene is carried out with almost exactly the same sequence of event and actuation; it has no prototype in either story or novel. Neither Ekebon nor L'Angelier went to his fatal interview to break up the new betrothal; he was beguiled by the pretence of a renewed affection. Moreno and Renaul each goes to his sweetheart's home to detach her from her new love; when he is there, she appeals to his better side, unsuccessfully; she abuses him, he returns the abuse and commands her to come to his rooms, she pretends to agree, expecting to finish with him one way or another. True, the assault is deferred in the picture from this scene to the next, but it is the same dramatic trick. Again, the poison in each case is found at home, and the girl talks with her betrothed just after the villain has left and again pledges him her faith. Surely the sequence of these details is pro tanto the very web of the authors' dramatic expression; and copying them is not "fair use."

The death scene follows the play even more closely; the girl goes to the villain's room as he directs; from the outset he is plainly to be poisoned while they are together. (The defendants deny that this is apparent in the picture, but we cannot agree. It would have been an impossible dénoument on the screen for the heroine, just plighted to the hero, to kill herself in desperation, because the villain has successfully enmeshed her in their mutual past; yet the poison is surely to be used on some one.) Moreno and Renaul each tries to arouse the girl by the memory of their former love, using among other aphrodisiacs the Gaucho song; each dies while she is there, incidentally of strychnine not arsenic. In extremis each makes for the telephone and is thwarted by the girl; as he dies, she pours upon him her rage and loathing. When he is dead, she follows the same ritual to eradicate all traces of her presence, but forgets telltale bits of property. Again these details in the same sequence embody more than the "ideas" of the play; they are its very raiment.

Finally in both play and picture in place of a trial, as in the story and the novel, there is substituted an examination by a district attorney; and this examination is again in parallel almost step by step. A parent is present; so is the lover; the girl yields progressively as the evidence accumulates; in the picture, the customs slip, the rubbers and the letters; in the play, the cross and the witnesses, brought in to confront her. She is at the breaking point when she is saved by substantially the same most unexpected alibi; a man declares that she has spent the night with him. That alibi there introduced is the turning point in each drama and alone prevents its ending in accordance with the classic canon of tragedy; i.e., fate as an inevitable consequence of past conduct, itself not evil enough to quench pity. It is the essence of the authors' expression, the very voice with which they speak.

We have often decided that a play may be pirated without using the dialogue. Daly v. Palmer, Fed.Cas. No. 3,552, 6 Blatch. 256; Daly v. Webster, 56 F. 483, 486, 487; Dam v. Kirk La Shelle Co., 175 F. 902, 907; Chappell & Co. v. Fields, 210 F. 864. Dymow v. Bolton, 11 F.2d 690; and Nichols v. Universal Pictures Corporation, supra, 45 F.2d 119, do not suggest otherwise. Were it not so, there could be no piracy of a pantomime, where there cannot be any dialogue; yet nobody would deny to pantomime the name of drama. Speech is only a small part of a dramatist's means of expression; he draws on all the arts and compounds his play from words and gestures and scenery and costume and from the very looks of the actors themselves. Again and again a play may lapse into pantomime at its most poignant and significant moments; a nod, a movement of the hand, a pause, may tell the audience more than words could tell. To be sure, not all this is always copyrighted, though there is no reason why it may not be, for those decisions do not forbid which hold that mere scenic tricks will not be protected. Serrana v. Jefferson (C.C.) 33 F. 347; Barnes v. Miner (C.C.) 122 F. 480; Bloom et al. v. Nixon (C.C.) 125 F. 977. The play is the sequence of the confluents of all these means, bound together in an inseparable unity; it may often be most effectively pirated by leaving out the speech, for which a substitute can be found, which keeps the whole dramatic meaning. That as it appears to us is exactly what the defendants have done here; the dramatic significance of the scenes we have recited is the same, almost to the letter. True, much of the picture owes nothing to the play; some of it is plainly drawn from the novel; but that is entirely immaterial; it is enough that substantial parts were lifted; no plagiarist can excuse the wrong by showing how much of his work he did not pirate. We cannot avoid the conviction that, if the picture was not an infringement of the play, there can be none short of taking the dialogue.

The decree will be reversed and an injunction will go against the picture together with a decree for damages and an accounting. The plaintiffs will be awarded an attorney's fee in this court and in the court below, both to be fixed by the District Court upon the final decree.

Holding for π

NOTES AND QUESTIONS ON IDEAS AND EXPRESSION

(1) In what respects do the similarities between "Abie's Irish Rose" and "The Cohens and The Kellys" differ from those shared by "Dishonored Lady" and "Letty Lynton"? Recall that § 102(b) prohibits protection for ideas. Can you describe the copyrightable "expression" appropriated by the latter work? Is Judge Hand's use of the term "fair use" in *Sheldon* consistent with its meaning in § 107 of the 1976 Act?

(2) Section 106(1) gives a copyright owner the exclusive right "to reproduce the copyrighted work." Judge Hand, in describing the defendants' infringement in *Sheldon*, states that "it is enough that substantial parts were lifted." The standard for infringement of a copyright owner's reproduction right is often said to be "substantial similarity." See Nimmer on Copyright § 13.03. When are similarities "substantial"? Cases to follow offer various formulations. For now, consider the comments of Judge Woolsey in the court below, responding to the plaintiff's contention that the impression of the play and picture on the "average playgoer" was the appropriate criterion: "In a situation such as I have here, however, I must, as the trier of the facts, have a more Olympian viewpoint than the average playgoer. I must look at the two opposing productions, the Play and the Picture, not only comparatively, but, as it were, genealogically," taking into account "the common origin of the plot of both the Play and Picture in a mid-nineteenth century trial." What is the rationale for such an approach?

Should harm to the copyright owner be relevant in determining whether the similarity between two works is "substantial"? An affirmative argument is made in L. Lape, The Metaphysics of the Law: Bringing Substantial Similarity Down to Earth, 98 Dick.L.Rev. 181 (1994).

(3) K. Umbreit, A Consideration of Copyright, 87 U.Pa.L.Rev. 932 (1939), attacked the idea/expression distinction as not fairly descriptive of the cases and related the trend he saw toward broader protection of works to the decay of "classicism" and its preoccupation with form rather than content. Half a century later this thesis, which had influenced B. Kaplan, An Unhurried View of Copyright 24 (1967), flowered in the sudden attention devoted by literary scholars to copyright and the nature of authorship. See, e.g., The Construction of Authorship: Textual Appropriation in Law and Literature (M. Woodmansee and P. Jaszi ed.) (1993), a collection of essays first published in 10 Cardozo Arts & Ent.L.J. No. 2 (1992). The editors declare, "Taken as a whole these studies of writing practices from the Renaissance to the present suggest that the modern regime of authorship, far from being timeless and universal, is a relatively recent formation—the result of a quite radical reconceptualization of the creative process that culminated less than 200 years ago in the heroic self-presentation of Romantic poets. * * * Prior to this apotheosis of authorship words and texts circulated more freely * * * not because surveillance was lax, but because more corporate and collaborative norms of writing prevailed." O. Bracha, The Ideology of Authorship Revisited: Authors, Markets, and Liberal Values in Early American Copyright, 118 Yale L.J. 186 (2008), traces our modern (and inconsistent) conception of authorship to the social and economic struggles of the 19th century.

(4) Several commentators have questioned the utility of the idea/expression dichotomy as a criterion for judging infringement. See, e.g., A. Cohen, Copyright Law and the Myth of Objectivity: The Idea–Expression Dichotomy and the Inevitability of Artistic Value Judgments, 66 Ind.L.Rev. 175 (1990) (lacking a "philosophical or objective basis" for distinguishing ideas from expression, assessments of the artistic value of the appropriated material predominate); L. Kurtz, Speaking to the Ghost: Idea and Expression in Copyright, 47 U.Miami L.Rev. 1221 (1993) (protection should not unduly interfere with the ability of later authors to create).

(5) Suppose, unlike in *Nichols* or *Sheldon*, a defendant reproduces some of the actual language from a copyrighted work. How should the issue of substantial similarity be approached in a case that involves literal copying? What factors, in addition to the amount taken, might influence the outcome?[a]

SOME REPRESENTATIVE LITERARY INFRINGEMENT CASES

The following cases illustrate the techniques of comparing allegedly infringed and infringing works, a matter that requires such lengthy descriptions as to preclude useful summaries. The cases selected involve works of some past or present popularity.

Lewys v. O'Neill, 49 F.2d 603 (S.D.N.Y.1931) (Eugene O'Neill's "Strange Interlude"); Kustoff v. Chaplin, 120 F.2d 551 (9th Cir.1941) ("Modern Times"); McConnor v. Kaufman, 49 F.Supp. 738 (S.D.N.Y.), aff'd, 139 F.2d 116 (2d Cir.1943) ("The Man Who Came to Dinner"); MacDonald v. Du Maurier, 75 F.Supp. 655 (S.D.N.Y.1948) (see also, on motion for judgment on the pleadings, 144 F.2d 696 (2d Cir.1944)) ("Rebecca"); Musto v. Meyer, 434 F.Supp. 32 (S.D.N.Y.1977), aff'd, 598 F.2d 609 (2d Cir.1979) (Sherlock Holmes and the "Seven Per Cent Solution"); Alexander v. Haley, 460 F.Supp. 40 (S.D.N.Y.1978) ("Roots") (This plaintiff lost, but another got a substantial settlement. See 'Roots' Plagiarism Case is Settled, N.Y. Times, Dec. 15, 1978, p. 1.); Litchfield v. Spielberg, 736 F.2d 1352 (9th Cir.1984), cert. denied, 470 U.S. 1052 (1985) ("E.T.—The Extraterrestrial"); Zambito v. Paramount Pictures Corp., 613 F.Supp. 1107 (E.D.N.Y.) aff'd, 788 F.2d 2 (2d Cir.1985) ("Raiders of the Lost Ark"); Denker v. Uhry, 820 F.Supp. 722 (S.D.N.Y.1992), aff'd, 996 F.2d 301 (2d Cir.1993) ("Driving Miss Daisy"); Williams v. Crichton, 84 F.3d 581 (2d Cir.1996) ("Jurassic Park"); Chase–Riboud v. Dreamworks, Inc., 987 F.Supp. 1222

---

[a] In Andreas v. Volkswagen, Inc., 336 F.3d 789 (8th Cir.2003), the court upheld a $965,000 jury verdict against an automobile company that copied nine words from an artist's drawing and short text for use in a television commercial. (Most of the award consisted of a portion of the company's profits on car sales during the period that the commercial aired.) What, if anything, might justify liability for such a small taking?

(C.D.Cal.1997) ("Amistad"); Allen v. Scholastic Inc., 739 F.Supp.2d 642 (S.D.N.Y.2011) ("Harry Potter and the Goblet of Fire").

See also Brown v. Perdue, 76 U.S.P.Q.2d 1012 (S.D.N.Y.2005), aff'd, 177 Fed.Appx. 121 (2d Cir.), cert. denied, 549 U.S. 1047 (2006) (summary judgment to the author of *The Da Vinci Code*, holding that the novel did not infringe two earlier works). A British court also rejected an infringement claim brought against *The Da Vinci Code* by the authors of a different work. The decision in the High Court contained its own secret code consisting of italicized letters scattered throughout the opinion. The code was cracked using the Fibonacci Sequence, a famous numerical sequence mentioned in *The Da Vinci Code*. Lyall and Marks, Broken: The Code in the "Da Vinci Code" Ruling, N.Y. Times, April 28, 2006, p. A8. The High Court decision was upheld by the Court of Appeal.

Interesting opinions arising out of television include Bradbury v. CBS, 287 F.2d 478 (9th Cir.), cert. dism'd, 368 U.S. 801 (1961) ("Fahrenheit 451"); Davis v. E.I. DuPont de Nemours & Co., 240 F.Supp. 612 (S.D.N.Y.1965) ("Ethan Frome"); Bevan v. CBS, 329 F.Supp. 601 (S.D.N.Y.1971) ("Hogan's Heroes"). See Goodson–Todman Enterprises, Ltd. v. Kellogg Co., 513 F.2d 913 (9th Cir.1975) ("To Tell the Truth"); Twentieth Century–Fox Film Corp. v. MCA, Inc., 715 F.2d 1327 (9th Cir.1983) ("Star Wars" and "Battlestar Galactica"); Funky Films, Inc. v. Time Warner Ent. Co., 462 F.3d 1072 (9th Cir.2006) (HBO's "Six Feet Under").

2. MUSIC

This Section deals with the infringement of one musical composition by another. On infringement by public performance, see p. 273 infra; on infringement by unlicensed recording, see p. 550 infra.

Three Boys Music Corp. v. Bolton

United States Court of Appeals, Ninth Circuit, 2000.
212 F.3d 477.
Certiorari denied, 531 U.S. 1126 (2001).

■ Before FLETCHER, D. W. NELSON, and BRUNETTI, CIRCUIT JUDGES.

■ D. W. NELSON, CIRCUIT JUDGE:

In 1994, a jury found that Michael Bolton's 1991 pop hit, "Love Is a Wonderful Thing," infringed on the copyright of a 1964 Isley Brothers' song of the same name. The district court denied Bolton's motion for a new trial and affirmed the jury's award of $5.4 million. * * *

The Isley Brothers, one of this country's most well-known rhythm and blues groups, have been inducted into the Rock and Roll Hall of Fame. They helped define the soul sound of the 1960s with songs such as "Shout," "Twist and Shout," and "This Old Heart of Mine," and they mastered the funky beats of the 1970s with songs such as "Who's That Lady," "Fight the Power," and "It's Your Thing." In 1964, the Isley Brothers wrote and recorded "Love is a Wonderful Thing" for United Artists. The Isley Brothers received a copyright for "Love is a Wonderful Thing" from the Register of Copyrights on February 6, 1964. The following year, they switched to the famous Motown label and had three top–100 hits including "This Old Heart of Mine."

Hoping to benefit from the Isley Brothers' Motown success, United Artists released "Love is a Wonderful Thing" in 1966. The song was not released on an album, only on a 45–record as a single. Several industry publications predicted that "Love is a Wonderful Thing" would be a hit—"Cash Box" on August 27, 1966, "Gavin Report" on August 26, 1966, and "Billboard" on September 10, 1966. On September 17, 1966, Billboard listed "Love is a Wonderful Thing" at number 110 in a chart titled "Bubbling Under the Hot 100." The song was never listed on any other Top 100 charts. In 1991, the Isley Brothers' "Love is a Wonderful Thing" was released on compact disc. See Isley Brothers, *The Isley Brothers—The Complete UA Sessions,* (EMI 1991).

Michael Bolton is a singer/songwriter who gained popularity in the late 1980s and early 1990s by reviving the soul sound of the 1960s. Bolton has orchestrated this soul-music revival in part by covering old songs such as Percy Sledge's "When a Man Love a Woman" and Otis Redding's "(Sittin' on the) Dock of the Bay." Bolton also has written his own hit songs. In early 1990, Bolton and Goldmark wrote a song called "Love Is a Wonderful Thing." Bolton released it as a single in April 1991, and as part of Bolton's album, "Time, Love and Tenderness." Bolton's "Love Is a Wonderful Thing" finished 1991 at number 49 on Billboard's year-end pop chart.

On February 24, 1992, Three Boys Music Corporation filed a copyright infringement action for damages against the appellants under 17 U.S.C. §§ 101 et seq. (1988). The parties agreed to a trifurcated trial. On April 25, 1994, in the first phase, the jury determined that the appellants had infringed the Isley Brothers' copyright. At the end of second phase five days later, the jury decided that Bolton's "Love Is a Wonderful Thing" accounted for 28 percent of the profits from "Time, Love and Tenderness." The jury also found that 66 percent of the profits from commercial uses of the song could be attributed to the inclusion of infringing elements. On May 9, 1994, the district court entered judgment in favor of the Isley Brothers based on the first two phases. * * *

On December 5, 1996, the district court adopted the findings of the Special Master's Amended Report about the allocation of damages (third phrase). In the final judgment entered against the appellants, the district court ordered Sony Music to pay $4,218,838; Bolton to pay $932,924; Goldmark to pay $220,785; and their music publishing companies to pay $75,900. They timely appealed.

Proof of copyright infringement is often highly circumstantial, particularly in cases involving music. A copyright plaintiff must prove (1) ownership of the copyright; and (2) infringement—that the defendant copied protected elements of the plaintiff's work. See Smith v. Jackson, 84 F.3d 1213, 1218 (9th Cir.1996) (citation omitted). Absent direct evidence of copying, proof of infringement involves fact-based showings that the defendant had "access" to the plaintiff's work and that the two works are "substantially similar." Id. * * *

As a general matter, the standard for reviewing jury verdicts is whether they are supported by "substantial evidence"—that is, such relevant evidence as reasonable minds might accept as adequate to support a conclusion. * * *

A.   *Access*

Proof of access requires "an opportunity to view or to copy plaintiff's work." Sid and Marty Krofft Television Productions, Inc. v. McDonald's

Corp., 562 F.2d 1157, 1172 (9th Cir.1977). This is often described as providing a "reasonable opportunity" or "reasonable possibility" of viewing the plaintiff's work. 4 Melville B. Nimmer & David Nimmer, Nimmer on Copyright, § 13.02[A], at 13–19 (1999); Jason v. Florida, 526 F.Supp. 774, 775 (C.D.Cal.1981), aff'd, 698 F.2d 966 (9th Cir.1982). We have defined reasonable access as "more than a 'bare possibility.' " * * *

Circumstantial evidence of reasonable access is proven in one of two ways: (1) a particular chain of events is established between the plaintiff's work and the defendant's access to that work (such as through dealings with a publisher or record company), or (2) the plaintiff's work has been widely disseminated. * * *

Proof of widespread dissemination is sometimes accompanied by a theory that copyright infringement of a popular song was subconscious. Subconscious copying has been accepted since Learned Hand embraced it in a 1924 music infringement case: "Everything registers somewhere in our memories, and no one can tell what may evoke it . . . . Once it appears that another has in fact used the copyright as the source of this production, he has invaded the author's rights. It is no excuse that in so doing his memory has played him a trick." Fred Fisher, Inc. v. Dillingham, 298 F. 145, 147–48 (S.D.N.Y.1924). In *Fred Fisher*, Judge Hand found that the similarities between the songs "amount[ed] to identity" and that the infringement had occurred "probably unconsciously, what he had certainly often heard only a short time before." Id. at 147.

In modern cases, however, the theory of subconscious copying has been applied to songs that are more remote in time. ABKCO Music, Inc. v. Harrisongs, Ltd., 722 F.2d 988 (2d Cir.1983) is the most prominent example. In *ABKCO,* the Second Circuit affirmed a jury's verdict that former Beatle George Harrison, in writing the song "My Sweet Lord," subconsciously copied The Chiffons' "He's So Fine," which was released six years earlier. See id. at 997, 999. Harrison admitted hearing "He's So Fine" in 1963, when it was number one on the Billboard charts in the United States for five weeks and one of the top 30 hits in England for seven weeks. See id. at 998. * * *

The Isley Brothers' access argument was based on a theory of widespread dissemination and subconscious copying. They presented evidence supporting four principal ways that Bolton and Goldmark could have had access to the Isley Brothers' "Love is a Wonderful Thing":

(1) Bolton grew up listening to groups such as the Isley Brothers and singing their songs. In 1966, Bolton and Goldmark were 13 and 15, respectively, growing up in Connecticut. Bolton testified that he had been listening to rhythm and blues music by black singers since he was 10 or 11, "appreciated a lot of Black singers," and as a youth was the lead singer in a band that performed "covers" of popular songs by black singers. Bolton also testified that his brother had a "pretty good record collection."

(2) Three disk jockeys testified that the Isley Brothers' song was widely disseminated on radio and television stations where Bolton and Goldmark grew up. * * *

(3) Bolton confessed to being a huge fan of the Isley Brothers and a collector of their music. Ronald Isley testified that when Bolton saw Isley at the Lou Rawls United Negro College Fund Benefit concert in 1988, Bolton said, "I know this guy. I go back with him. I have all his stuff." Angela

Winbush, Isley's wife, testified about that meeting that Bolton said, "This man needs no introduction. I know everything he's done."

(4) Bolton wondered if he and Goldmark were copying a song by another famous soul singer. Bolton produced a work tape attempting to show that he and Goldmark independently created their version of "Love Is a Wonderful Thing." On that tape of their recording session, Bolton asked Goldmark if the song they were composing was Marvin Gaye's "Some Kind of Wonderful." * * *

The appellants contend that the Isley Brothers' theory of access amounts to a "twenty-five-years-after-the-fact-subconscious copying claim." Indeed, this is a more attenuated case of reasonable access and subconscious copying than *ABKCO*. * * * Nor did the Isley Brothers ever claim that Bolton's and Goldmark's song is so "strikingly similar" to the Isley Brothers' that proof of access is presumed and need not be proven. * * *

Although we might not reach the same conclusion as the jury regarding access, we find that the jury's conclusion about access is supported by substantial evidence. * * *

B.   *Substantial Similarity*

* * * It is well settled that a jury may find a combination of unprotectible elements to be protectible * * * because " 'the over-all impact and effect indicate substantial appropriation.' " [*Krofft,* 562 F.2d at 1169] (quoting Malkin v. Dubinsky, 146 F.Supp. 111, 114 (S.D.N.Y.1956)).

1.   *Evidence of Substantial Similarity*

Bolton and Goldmark argue that there was insufficient evidence of substantial similarity because the Isley Brothers' expert musicologist, Dr. Gerald Eskelin, failed to show that there was copying of a *combination* of unprotectible elements. On the contrary, Eskelin testified that the two songs shared a combination of five unprotectible elements: (1) the title hook phrase (including the lyric, rhythm, and pitch); (2) the shifted cadence; (3) the instrumental figures; (4) the verse/chorus relationship; and (5) the fade ending. Although the appellants presented testimony from their own expert musicologist, Anthony Ricigliano, he conceded that there were similarities between the two songs and that he had not found the combination of unprotectible elements in the Isley Brothers' song "anywhere in the prior art." The jury heard testimony from both of these experts and "found infringement based on a unique compilation of those elements." We refuse to interfere with the jury's credibility determination, nor do we find that the jury's finding of substantial similarity was clearly erroneous.

2.   *Independent Creation*

Bolton and Goldmark also contend that their witnesses rebutted the Isley Brothers' prima facie case of copyright infringement with evidence of independent creation. By establishing reasonable access and substantial similarity, a copyright plaintiff creates a presumption of copying. The burden shifts to the defendant to rebut that presumption through proof of independent creation. See Granite Music Corp. v. United Artists Corp., 532 F.2d 718, 721 (9th Cir.1976).

The appellants' case of independent creation hinges on three factors: the work tape demonstrating how Bolton and Goldmark created their song, Bolton and Goldmark's history of songwriting, and testimony that their arranger, Walter Afanasieff, contributed two of five unprotectible elements that they allegedly copied. The jury, however, heard the testimony of Bolton, Goldmark, Afanasieff, and Ricigliano about independent creation. The *Bolton may have subconsciously thought he was copying* work tape revealed evidence that Bolton may have subconsciously copied a song that he believed to be written by Marvin Gaye. Bolton and Goldmark's history of songwriting presents no direct evidence about this case. And Afanasieff's contributions to Bolton and Goldmark's song were described by the appellants' own expert as "very common." Once again, we refuse to disturb the jury's determination about independent creation. The substantial evidence of copying based on access and substantial similarity was such *affirm DCH for π* that a reasonable juror could reject this defense. * * *

AFFIRMED.

NOTES AND QUESTIONS ON "COPYING"

(1) A web site maintained by the USC School of Law at mcir.usc.edu contains audio files of the songs involved in many famous musical infringement cases, including the two works at issue in *Bolton*.

(2) In the Fred Fisher v. Dillingham case discussed in *Bolton*, Judge Learned Hand held that composer Jerome Kern had infringed the plaintiff's song "Dardanella," a popular hit of the early 1920s. Although there was no similarity in the melodies of the works, the accompaniment in Kern's song included eight notes, written in two measures and repeated again and again, that were identical to eight notes in the accompaniment in "Dardanella." The defendant had introduced evidence of a similar series of notes in works that predated "Dardanella"; Judge Hand held that the earlier works did not invalidate the plaintiff's copyright since there was no evidence that they had played any role in the creation of "Dardanella." According to A. Shafter, Musical Copyright (2d ed. 1939), before the "Dardanella" case it was common practice to establish a public domain equivalent to the plaintiff's composition for the purpose of destroying the validity of the copyright. Fred Fisher v. Dillingham, by restating the rule that only originality and not novelty is necessary for copyright, effectively eliminated from consideration obscure works to which the plaintiff likely had no access. However, Judge Hand also restated the rule that a defendant remains free to use the public domain, so the existence of similar works remains relevant if the defendant can show that he copied from those works and not from the plaintiff's song.

(3) On the necessity of proving access by the defendant to the copyrighted work, consider Selle v. Gibb, 741 F.2d 896 (7th Cir.1984). A jury verdict for the plaintiff was set aside because no inference of access was plausible. Gibb, one of the Bee Gees, had composed "How Deep Is Your Love" at an isolated recording session; plaintiff's song, although registered, was unpublished, unrecorded, and unperformed, except on two or three occasions by his own band in Chicago. Copies of the music had been sent to several music publishing companies. The Seventh Circuit recognized that when "the plaintiff does not have direct evidence of access, then an inference of access may still be established circumstantially by proof of similarity which is so striking that the possibilities of independent creation, coincidence and prior common source are, as a practical matter, precluded."[b] Judge Cudahy went on to conclude, however, "that no matter

---

[b]   The two songs *were* remarkably similar. "The similarities between the Bee Gees' hit from *Saturday Night Fever* and the unpublished *Let It End* are amusing; it seems to defy chance that two composers could have hit upon the same ugly tune." Walsh, Has Somebody Stolen Their Song?, Time, Oct. 19, 1987, p. 86.

how great the similarity between the two works, it is not their similarity *per se* which establishes access; rather, their similarity tends to prove access in light of the nature of the works, the particular musical genre involved and other circumstantial evidence of access. In other words, striking similarity is just one piece of circumstantial evidence tending to show access and must not be considered in isolation; it must be considered together with other types of circumstantial evidence relating to access. As a threshold matter, therefore, it would appear that there must be at least some other evidence which would establish a reasonable possibility that the complaining work was *available* to the alleged infringer."

The concept of "striking similarity" also loomed large in another claim against the composer of a popular hit. In Gaste v. Kaiserman, 863 F.2d 1061 (2d Cir.1988), the plaintiff alleged that his song, "Pour Toi," written in 1956 as part of the score for a French movie, had been infringed in 1973 by the defendant Kaiserman (better known as Morris Albert) in composing the internationally successful "Feelings." The principal theory of access to the plaintiff's virtually unknown song was strained: one of the plaintiff's employees testified that in the 1950s he had sent copies of the sheet music to the owner of the defendant's Brazilian publisher. Plaintiff's musical expert, after pointing out general similarities between the two songs, identified "a unique musical 'fingerprint' "—he called it an "evaded resolution"—occurring at the same place in both works. He said that he had never seen this particular method of modulation. The trial judge instructed the jury that if works are "strikingly similar," then "access does not have to be proven." The Second Circuit, in an opinion by Judge Newman, upheld a verdict for the plaintiff. Responding to the defendant's reliance on Selle v. Gibb, supra, Judge Newman said, "Appellants contend that undue reliance on striking similarity to show access precludes protection for the author who independently creates a similar work. However, the jury is only *permitted* to infer access from striking similarity; it need not do so. Though striking similarity alone can raise an inference of copying, that inference must be reasonable in light of all the evidence."

In an opinion by Judge Posner, the Seventh Circuit later withdrew from *Selle v. Gibb*'s apparent insistence on independent proof of access even in cases of striking similarity. "[W]e do not read our decision in *Selle* to hold or imply, in conflict with the *Gaste* decision, that no matter how closely the works resemble each other, the plaintiff must produce some (other) evidence of access. * * * Access (and copying) may be inferred when two works are so similar to each other and not to anything in the public domain that it is likely that the creator of the second work copied the first, but the inference can be rebutted by disproving access or otherwise showing independent creation * * *." Ty, Inc. v. GMA Accessories, Inc., 132 F.3d 1167 (7th Cir.1997).

(4) A newspaper article on the trial of an infringement suit lodged by a reggae musician named Patrick Alley against Mick Jagger and his "Just Another Night" sets a colorful scene. "In the course of the seven-day trial, presided over by Judge Gerard L. Goettel, a Juilliard faculty member played piano; a top Jamaican studio musician, Sly Dunbar, played drums, and Mr. Jagger sang snatches of 'Jumpin' Jack Flash,' 'Brown Sugar,' and 'Miss You' from the witness stand." In addition to taped performances of the two works, Jagger, arguing independent creation, played working tapes to show the genesis of his song, and "lawyers for both sides sang a few lines." The jury did not find infringement. (The article also notes an out-of-court payment by Ray Parker Jr. in settlement of a claim relating to alleged similarities between his song "Ghostbusters" and "I Want a New Drug" by Huey Lewis and the News.) Pareles, U.S. Jury Says Jagger Did Not Steal Hit Song, N.Y. Times, April 27, 1988, p. C.22. Rapper Vanilla Ice may be best remembered for lifting part of the 1981 song "Under Pressure" by David Bowie and Queen for his No. 1 hit "Ice Ice Baby." A settlement was reached after Bowie and Queen threatened a lawsuit. Morse, Setting the New Market in Sampling, Boston Globe, March 3, 2002, p. L1.

In Bridgeport Music, Inc. v. UMG Recordings, Inc., 585 F.3d 267 (6th Cir.2009), "fragmented literal similarity" sufficient to constitute infringement was found when the hip-hop group Public Announcement copied the phrase "Bow wow wow, yippie yo, yippie yea" and the repetitive use of the word "dog" along with the sound of rhythmic panting from George Clinton's song *Atomic Dog* for use in *D.O.G. in Me*.

Two articles by M. Carroll, Whose Music Is It Anyway?, 72 U.Cinn.L.Rev. 1405 (2004), and The Struggle for Music Copyright, 57 Fla.L.Rev. 907 (2005), recount the history of proprietary claims in music and its implications for contemporary disputes; K. Greene, Copyright, Culture and Black Music: A Legacy of Unequal Protection, 21 Hastings Comm/Ent L.J. 339 (1999), argues that copyright's emphasis on fixation of specific forms of expression disfavors African–American innovators in genres like jazz, blues, and rap; Y Liebesman, Downstream Copyright Infringers, 60 U.Kan.L.Rev. 1 (2011), wonders whether someone who legally downloads a song that infringes an earlier work would themselves be liable for copyright infringement.

(5) Are our modern ideas about authorship and infringement too idealistic? In a review of a production of John Gay's *The Beggar's Opera* (1728), music critic Richard Morrison, recounting how classical music has thrived on recycled melodies, points out how much poorer our musical heritage would be if current notions of copyright infringement had applied. He argues that Bach, for example, took melodies for a number of his works from hymns in the Lutheran hymnbook (which in many cases the Lutherans themselves had lifted from minstrel songs and ballads). When a friend remarked to Brahms that the finale of his *First Symphony* sounded a lot like the *Ode to Joy* from Beethoven's Ninth, Brahms responded that "any fool can hear that." Of the sixty-nine songs in the original version of *The Beggar's Opera* (described by Morrison as "the *magnum opus* of plagiarism"), apparently none had an original melody. Gay even took a tune from his popular contemporary George Frideric Handel, who could hardly complain since Handel himself was perhaps the biggest borrower of all. Handel, however, vastly improved whatever he took. "Handel took other men's pebbles and polished them into diamonds," according to composer William Boyce. Should that excuse the borrowing? The Times, April 7, 1993, p. 29.[c]

---

[c]   Literature offers its own illustrations. T.S. Eliot once remarked, "Immature poets imitate; mature poets steal." *Philip Massinger*, in The Sacred Wood: Essays on Poetry and Criticism (1920). Giants like Chaucer, Virgil, and Milton were all voracious appropriators. See A. Lindey, Plagiarism and Originality 65–77 (1952). According to one analysis, Shakespeare— described by Lindey as evincing "a marked propensity for avoiding unnecessary invention"— copied 1,771 lines and paraphrased another 2,373 in producing the 6,033 lines in *Henry VI, Pts. I, II, and III*. Id. at 73–75. O. Arewa, The Freedom to Copy: Copyright, Creation, and Context, 41 U.C. Davis L.Rev. 477 (2007), argues that modern copyright law undervalues the importance of copying in the creative process.

Arnstein v. Porter

United States Circuit Court of Appeals, Second Circuit, 1946.
154 F.2d 464.

Appeal from the District Court of the United States for the Southern District of New York.

Action by Ira B. Arnstein against Cole Porter for infringement of copyrights, infringement of right to uncopyrighted musical compositions and wrongful use of the titles of others. From a judgment dismissing action on defendant's motion for summary judgment, the plaintiff appeals.

Modified in part; otherwise reversed and remanded.

Plaintiff, a citizen and resident of New York, brought this suit, charging infringement by defendant, a citizen and resident of New York, of plaintiff's copyrights to several musical compositions, infringement of his rights to other uncopyrighted musical compositions, and wrongful use of the titles of others. Plaintiff, when filing his complaint, demanded a jury trial. Plaintiff took the deposition of defendant, and defendant, the deposition of plaintiff. Defendant then moved for an order striking out plaintiff's jury demand, and for summary judgment. Attached to defendant's motion papers were the depositions, phonograph records of piano renditions of the plaintiff's compositions and defendant's alleged infringing compositions, and the court records of five previous copyright infringement suits brought by plaintiff in the court below against other persons, in which judgments had been entered, after trials, against plaintiff. Defendant also moved for dismissal of the action on the ground of "vexatiousness."

Plaintiff alleged that defendant's "Begin the Beguine" is a plagiarism from plaintiff's "The Lord Is My Shepherd" and "A Mother's Prayer." Plaintiff testified, on deposition, that "The Lord Is My Shepherd" had been published and about 2,000 copies sold, that "A Mother's Prayer" had been published, over a million copies having been sold. In his depositions, he gave no direct evidence that defendant saw or heard these compositions. He also alleged that defendant's "My Heart Belongs to Daddy" had been plagiarized from plaintiff's "A Mother's Prayer."

Plaintiff also alleged that defendant's "I Love You" is a plagiarism from plaintiff's composition "La Priere," stating in his deposition that the latter composition had been sold. He gave no direct proof that plaintiff knew of this composition.

He also alleged that defendant's song "Night and Day" is a plagiarism of plaintiff's song "I Love You Madly," which he testified had not been published but had once been publicly performed over the radio, copies having been sent to divers radio stations but none to defendant; a copy of this song, plaintiff testified, had been stolen from his room. He also alleged that "I Love You Madly" ["Night and Day"?] was in part plagiarized from "La Priere." He further alleged that defendant's "You'd Be So Nice To Come Home To" is plagiarized from plaintiff's "Sadness Overwhelms My Soul." He testified that this song had never been published or publicly performed but that copies had been sent to a movie producer and to several publishers. He also alleged that defendant's "Don't Fence Me In" is a plagiarism of plaintiff's song "A Modern Messiah" which has not been published or publicly performed; in his deposition he said that about a hundred copies had been sent to divers radio stations and band leaders but that he sent no copy to defendant. Plaintiff said that defendant "had stooges right along to follow me, watch me, and live in the same apartment with me," and that plaintiff's room had been ransacked on several occasions. Asked how he knew that defendant had anything to do with any of these "burglaries," plaintiff said, "I don't know that he had to do with it, but I only know that he could have." He also said " * * * many of my compositions had been published. No one had to break in to steal them. They were sung publicly."

Defendant in his deposition categorically denied that he had ever seen or heard any of plaintiff's compositions or had had any acquaintance with any person said to have stolen any of them.

The prayer of plaintiff's original complaint asked "at least one million dollars out of the millions the defendant has earned and is earning out of all the plagiarism." In his amended complaint the prayer is "for judgment against the defendant in the sum of $1,000,000 as damages sustained by the plagiarism of all the compositions named in the complaint." Plaintiff, not a lawyer, appeared pro se below and on this appeal.

■ Before L. HAND, CLARK, and FRANK, CIRCUIT JUDGES.

■ FRANK, CIRCUIT JUDGE:

1.   Plaintiff with his complaint filed a jury demand which defendant moved to strike out. Defendant urges that the relief prayed in the complaint renders a jury trial inappropriate. We do not agree. Plaintiff did not ask for an injunction but solely for damages. Such a suit is an action at "law." That it is founded solely on a statute does not deprive either party of a right to a trial by jury; an action for treble damages under the Sherman Act is likewise purely statutory, but it is triable at "law" and by a jury as of right.

2.   The principal question on this appeal is whether the lower court, under Rule 56, properly deprived plaintiff of a trial of his copyright infringement action. The answer depends on whether "there is the slightest doubt as to the facts." Doehler Metal Furniture Co. v. United States, 2 Cir., 149 F.2d 130, 135 * * *. In applying that standard here, it is important to avoid confusing two separate elements essential to a plaintiff's case in such a suit: (a) that defendant copied from plaintiff's copyrighted work and (b) that the copying (assuming it to be proved) went so far as to constitute improper appropriation.

As to the first—copying—the evidence may consist (a) of defendant's admission that he copied or (b) of circumstantial evidence—usually evidence of access—from which the trier of the facts may reasonably infer copying. Of course, if there are no similarities, no amount of evidence of access will suffice to prove copying. If there is evidence of access and similarities exist, then the trier of the facts must determine whether the similarities are sufficient to prove copying. On this issue, analysis ("dissection") is relevant, and the testimony of experts may be received to aid the trier of the facts. If evidence of access is absent, the similarities must be so striking as to preclude the possibility that plaintiff and defendant independently arrived at the same result.

If copying is established, then only does there arise the second issue, that of illicit copying (unlawful appropriation). On that issue (as noted more in detail below) the test is the response of the ordinary lay hearer; accordingly, on that issue, "dissection" and expert testimony are irrelevant.

In some cases, the similarities between the plaintiff's and defendant's work are so extensive and striking as, without more, both to justify an inference of copying and to prove improper appropriation. But such double-purpose evidence is not required; that is, if copying is otherwise shown, proof of improper appropriation need not consist of similarities which, standing alone, would support an inference of copying.

Each of these two issues—copying and improper appropriation—is an issue of fact. If there is a trial, the conclusions on those issues of the trier of the facts—of the judge if he sat without a jury, or of the jury if there was a jury trial—bind this court on appeal, provided the evidence supports those findings, regardless of whether we would ourselves have reached the same conclusions. But a case could occur in which the similarities were so striking that we would reverse a finding of no access, despite weak evidence of access (or no evidence thereof other than the similarities); and similarly as to a finding of no illicit appropriation.

3.   We turn first to the issue of copying. After listening to the compositions as played in the phonograph recordings submitted by defendant, we find similarities; but we hold that unquestionably, standing alone, they do not compel the conclusion, or permit the inference, that defendant copied. The similarities, however, are sufficient so that, if there is enough evidence of access to permit the case to go to the jury, the jury may properly infer that the similarities did not result from coincidence.

Summary judgment was, then, proper if indubitably defendant did not have access to plaintiff's compositions. Plainly that presents an issue of fact. On that issue, the district judge, who heard no oral testimony, had before him the depositions of plaintiff and defendant. The judge characterized plaintiff's story as "fantastic"; and, in the light of the references in his opinion to defendant's deposition, the judge obviously accepted defendant's denial of access and copying. Although part of plaintiff's testimony on deposition (as to "stooges" and the like) does seem "fantastic," yet plaintiff's credibility, even as to those improbabilities, should be left to the jury. If evidence is "of a kind that greatly taxes the credulity of the judge, he can say so, or, if he totally disbelieves it, he may announce that fact, leaving the jury free to believe it or not." * * * We should not overlook the shrewd proverbial admonition that sometimes truth is stranger than fiction.

But even if we were to disregard the improbable aspects of plaintiff's story, there remain parts by no means "fantastic." On the record now before us, more than a million copies of one of his compositions were sold; copies of others were sold in smaller quantities or distributed to radio stations or band leaders or publishers, or the pieces were publicly performed. If, after hearing both parties testify, the jury disbelieves defendant's denials, it can, from such facts, reasonably infer access. It follows that, as credibility is unavoidably involved, a genuine issue of material fact presents itself. * * *

We do not believe that, in a case in which the decision must turn on the reliability of witnesses, the Supreme Court, by authorizing summary judgments, intended to permit a "trial by affidavits," if either party objects. That procedure which, so the historians tell us, began to be outmoded at common law in the 16th century, would, if now revived, often favor unduly the party with the more ingenious and better paid lawyer. Grave injustice might easily result. * * *

4.   Assuming that adequate proof is made of copying, that is not enough; for there can be "permissible copying," copying which is not illicit. Whether (if he copied) defendant unlawfully appropriated presents, too, an issue of fact. The proper criterion on that issue is not an analytic or other

comparison of the respective musical compositions as they appear on paper or in the judgment of trained musicians.[19] The plaintiff's legally protected interest is not, as such, his reputation as a musician but his interest in the potential financial returns from his compositions which derive from the lay public's approbation of his efforts. The question, therefore, is whether defendant took from plaintiff's works so much of what is pleasing to the ears of lay listeners, who comprise the audience for whom such popular music is composed, that defendant wrongfully appropriated something which belongs to the plaintiff.

Surely, then, we have an issue of fact which a jury is peculiarly fitted to determine.[22] Indeed, even if there were to be a trial before a judge, it would be desirable (although not necessary) for him to summon an advisory jury on this question.

We should not be taken as saying that a plagiarism case can never arise in which absence of similarities is so patent that a summary judgment for defendant would be correct. Thus suppose that Ravel's "Bolero" or Shostakovitch's "Fifth Symphony" were alleged to infringe "When Irish Eyes Are Smiling."[23] But this is not such a case. For, after listening to the playing of the respective compositions, we are, at this time, unable to conclude that the likenesses are so trifling that, on the issue of misappropriation, a trial judge could legitimately direct a verdict for defendant.

At the trial, plaintiff may play, or cause to be played, the pieces in such manner that they may seem to a jury to be inexcusably alike, in terms of the way in which lay listeners of such music would be likely to react. The plaintiff may call witnesses whose testimony may aid the jury in reaching its conclusion as to the responses of such audiences. Expert testimony of musicians may also be received, but it will in no way be controlling on the issue of illicit copying, and should be utilized only to assist in determining the reactions of lay auditors. The impression made on the refined ears of musical experts or their views as to the musical excellence of plaintiff's or defendant's works are utterly immaterial on the issue of misappropriation; for the views of such persons are caviar to the general—and plaintiff's and defendant's compositions are not caviar. * * *

[After disposing of some minor points, Judge Frank considered defendant's motion for dismissal of the action as vexatious, pointing to five similar actions that Arnstein had brought against other defendants.]

* * * [W]e regard it as entirely improper to give any weight to other actions lost by plaintiff. * * * Absent the factors which make up res judicata (not present here), each case must stand on its own bottom, subject, of course, to the doctrine of stare decisis. Succumbing to the temptation to consider other defeats suffered by a party may lead a court astray; see, e.g., Southern Pacific Co. v. Bogert, 250 U.S. 483, 489, note 1. When a particular suit is vexatious, sometimes at its conclusion the court can give some redress to the victorious party. Perhaps the Legislature can and should meet this problem more effectively. But we surely must not do so, as defendant here would have us do, by prejudging the merits of the case before us.

---

[19] Where plaintiff relies on similarities to prove copying (as distinguished from improper appropriation) paper comparisons and the opinions of experts may aid the court.

[22] It would, accordingly, be proper to exclude tone-deaf persons from the jury, cf. Chatterton v. Cave, 3 A.C. 483, 499–501, 502–504 [H.L.1878].

[23] In such a case, the complete absence of similarity would negate both copying and improper appropriation.

Modified in part; otherwise reversed and remanded. * * *

■ CLARK, CIRCUIT JUDGE (dissenting). While the procedure followed below seems to me generally simple and appropriate, the defendant did make one fatal tactical error. In an endeavor to assist us, he caused to be prepared records of all the musical pieces here involved, and presented these transcriptions through the medium of the affidavit of his pianist. Though he himself did not stress these records and properly met plaintiff's claims as to the written music with his own analysis, yet the tinny tintinnabulations of the music thus canned resounded through the United States Courthouse to the exclusion of all else, including the real issues in the case. Of course, sound is important in a case of this kind, but it is not so important as to falsify what the eye reports and the mind teaches. Otherwise plagiarism would be suggested by the mere drumming of repetitious sound from our usual popular music, as it issues from a piano, orchestra, or hurdy-gurdy—particularly when ears may be dulled by long usage, possibly artistic repugnance or boredom, or mere distance which causes all sounds to merge. And the judicial eardrum may be peculiarly insensitive after long years of listening to the "beat, beat, beat" (I find myself plagiarizing from defendant and thus in danger of my brothers' doom) of sound upon it, though perhaps no more so than the ordinary citizen juror—even if tone deafness is made a disqualification for jury service, as advocated.

Pointing to the adscititious fortuity inherent in the stated standard is, it seems to me, the fact that after repeated hearings of the records, I could not find therein what my brothers found. The only thing definitely mentioned seemed to be the repetitive use of the note e^2 in certain places by both plaintiff and defendant, surely too simple and ordinary a device of composition to be significant. In our former musical plagiarism cases we have, naturally, relied on what seemed the total sound effect; but we have also analyzed the music enough to make sure of an intelligible and intellectual decision. Thus in Arnstein v. Edward B. Marks Music Corp., 2 Cir., 82 F.2d 275, 277, Judge L. Hand made quite an extended comparison of the songs, concluding, inter alia: " * * * the seven notes available do not admit of so many agreeable permutations that we need be amazed at the reappearance of old themes, even though the identity extend through a sequence of twelve notes." See also the discussion in Marks v. Leo Feist, Inc., 2 Cir., 290 F. 959, and Darrell v. Joe Morris Music Co., 2 Cir., 113 F.2d 80, where the use of six similar bars and of an eight-note sequence frequently repeated were respectively held not to constitute infringement, and Wilkie v. Santly Bros., 2 Cir., 91 F.2d 978, affirming, D.C.S.D.N.Y., 13 F.Supp. 136, certiorari denied Santly Bros. v. Wilkie, 302 U.S. 735, where use of eight bars with other similarities amounting to over three-quarters of the significant parts was held infringement.[1]

---

[1]   In accord is Shafter, Musical Copyright, 2d Ed.1939, c. 6, particularly p. 205, where the author speaks of "the 'comparative method,' worked out by Judge Learned Hand with great success," and "his successful method of analysis," citing Hein v. Harris, C.C.S.D.N.Y., 175 F. 875, affirmed 2 Cir., 183 F. 107, and Haas v. Leo Feist, Inc., D.C.S.D.N.Y., 234 F. 105; and p. 194, where he approves of Judge Yankwich's course in attaching an exhibit of analysis to his opinion in Hirsch v. Paramount Pictures, Inc., D.C.S.D.Cal., 17 F.Supp. 816—"this sensible procedure," "a splendid model for future copyright decisions." I find nowhere any suggestion of two steps in adjudication of this issue, one of finding copying which may be approached with musical intelligence and assistance of experts, and another that of illicit copying which must be approached with complete ignorance; nor do I see how rationally there can be any such difference, even if a jury—the now chosen instrument of musical detection—could be expected to separate those issues and the evidence accordingly. If there is actual copying, it is actionable, and there are no degrees; what we are dealing with is the claim of similarities suf-

It is true that in Arnstein v. Broadcast Music, Inc., 2 Cir., 137 F.2d 410, 412, we considered "dissection" or "technical analysis" not the proper approach to support a finding of plagiarism, and said that it must be "more ingenuous, more like that of a spectator, who would rely upon the complex of his impressions." But in its context that seems to me clearly sound and in accord with what I have in mind. Thus one may look to the total impression to repulse the charge of plagiarism where a minute "dissection" might dredge up some points of similarity. Hence one cannot use a purely theoretical disquisition to supply a tonal resemblance which does not otherwise exist. Certainly, however, that does not suggest or compel the converse— that one must keep his brain in torpor for fear that otherwise it would make clear differences which do exist. Music is a matter of the intellect as well as the emotions; that is why eminent musical scholars insist upon the employment of the intellectual faculties for a just appreciation of music. * * *d

NOTES AND QUESTIONS

(1) Suppose that a plaintiff can establish that the defendant derived her song by playing plaintiff's song backward. A. Shafter, Musical Copyright 213 (2d ed. 1939), argues that this would be an infringement. Do you agree? Would Judge Frank or Judge Clark?

(2) Despite Arnstein v. Porter, summary judgments are often granted to defendants in infringement cases. In Walker v. Time Life Films, Inc., 784 F.2d 44 (2d Cir.), cert. denied, 476 U.S. 1159 (1986), for example, Judge Feinberg for the Second Circuit said that "a district court may determine noninfringement as a matter of law on a motion for summary judgment either when the similarity concerns only noncopyrightable elements of plaintiff's work, or when no reasonable trier of fact could find the works substantially similar." The court affirmed a summary judgment in favor of the producers of the movie "Fort Apache: The Bronx" in the face of an infringement claim by the author of "Fort Apache," an anecdotal account of life in a South Bronx precinct of the New York Police Department. The Ninth Circuit, although noting that "as a general rule, summary judgment is not highly favored on the substantial similarity issue in copyright cases," Berkic v. Crichton, 761 F.2d 1289 (9th Cir.), cert. denied, 474 U.S. 826 (1985), has said that "there is no special standard" for summary judgment on substantial similarity. Frybarger v. International Business Machines Corp., 812 F.2d 525 (9th Cir.1987). D. Wanat, Copyright Law: Infringement of Musical Works and the Appropriateness of Summary Judgment under the FRCP, Rule 56(c), 39 U. Memphis L.Rev. 1037 (2009), looks at summary judgments in musical infringement cases.

(3) In Hoehling v. Universal City Studios, Inc., p. 235 infra, the Second Circuit, quoting Arnstein, said that a plaintiff "must demonstrate that defendants 'copied' his work and that they 'improperly appropriated' his 'expression.' " The court added that "[o]rdinarily, wrongful appropriation is shown by proving a 'substantial similarity' of copyrightable expression." In the "Fort Apache" case, supra, the court said that Arnstein and Hoehling required the plaintiff to "show that his book was 'copied,' by proving access and substantial similarity between

---

ficient to justify the inference of copying. This is a single deduction to be made intelligently, not two with the dominating one to be made blindly.

ᵈ   A subsequent jury verdict for Cole Porter was affirmed at 158 F.2d 795 (2d Cir.1946), cert. denied, 330 U.S. 851 (1947).

the works, and also show that his expression was 'improperly appropriated,' by proving that the similarities relate to copyrightable material." In a later case, the Second Circuit noted that "the presence of a 'substantial similarity' requirement in both prongs of the analysis—actual copying and improper appropriation—creates the potential for unnecessary confusion." Laureyssens v. Idea Group, Inc., 964 F.2d 131 (2d Cir.1992). The court then proceeded to restate the required elements:

> A plaintiff must first show that his or her work was actually copied. Copying may be established either by direct evidence of copying or by indirect evidence, including access to the copyrighted work, similarities that are probative of copying between the works, and expert testimony. If actual copying is established, a plaintiff must then show that the copying amounts to an improper appropriation by demonstrating that substantial similarity to protected material exists between the two works.

EXPERT TESTIMONY IN INFRINGEMENT CASES

The use of expert witnesses in musical infringement cases has been commonplace since the earliest American cases. See Reed v. Carusi, 20 Fed.Cas. 431 (C.C.D.Md.1845) (No. 11,642), where the defendant brought in experts to point out the dissimilarities between his ballad and the plaintiff's. However, a jury verdict went for the plaintiff.

The majority in *Arnstein* is hostile to expert testimony on the issue of "improper appropriation." Judge Clark in dissent fears that the majority invites drowning the judgment of the trier of fact in an unanalyzed welter of seemingly similar sounds. But any expert testimony and close analysis offered on the issue of "copying" also will likely influence the determination of "improper appropriation."[e] And the majority does allow expert testimony even on "improper appropriation," limited to proving the probable reaction of "lay listeners of such music."[f] In Baxter v. MCA, Inc., 812 F.2d 421 (9th Cir.), cert. denied, 484 U.S. 954 (1987), the Ninth Circuit, in a case in which the alleged infringing work was the musical theme from the motion picture "E.T.: The Extra–Terrestrial," took the similar position that " '[a]nalytic dissection' and expert testimony are not called for; the gauge of substantial similarity is the response of the ordinary lay hearer," citing *Arnstein*.

In Rottlund Co. v. Pinnacle Corp., 452 F.3d 726 (8th Cir.2006), a jury verdict against the owner of copyrighted architectural works and plans who claimed infringement by competing home builders was overturned because the trial court had admitted expert testimony on whether there was substantial similarity of expression. However, in another architecture case, the First Circuit, noting that "the need for expert testimony may be greater in cases involving complex subject matters where an ordinary observer may find it difficult to properly evaluate the similarity of two works without the aid of expert testimony," left it to the trial judge to determine whether ex-

---

[e]   For an example of (conflicting) expert testimony on the "copying" issue, see Repp v. Webber, 132 F.3d 882 (2d Cir.1997), cert. denied, 525 U.S. 815 (1998), involving Andrew Lloyd Webber and the "Phantom Song" from *The Phantom of the Opera.*

[f]   In Kohus v. Mariol, 328 F.3d 848 (6th Cir.2003), a case involving the alleged infringement of a technical drawing, the Sixth Circuit said that expert testimony would be admissible to educate the trier of fact on the perspective of the trained engineers for whom the drawing was intended.

pert testimony would be helpful on the issue of substantial similarity. T–Peg, Inc. v. Vermont Timber Works, Inc., 459 F.3d 97 (1st Cir.2006).

Why eschew the potential insights afforded by a detailed or expert comparison of the alleged infringed and infringing works in favor of the visceral reaction of an "ordinary lay hearer"? Does the choice reflect a decision about the underlying purpose of copyright law? Should the standard focus on the reaction of an ordinary person—or on the reaction of an ordinary member of the audience to whom the work is directed? Which standard is adopted in Arnstein v. Porter? See Dawson v. Hinshaw Music Inc., 905 F.2d 731 (4th Cir.), cert. denied, 498 U.S. 981 (1990), adopting an "intended audience" interpretation of the ordinary observer test for works directed at consumers with specialized knowledge or expertise.[g]

3. SUBSTANTIAL SIMILARITY IN VISUAL WORKS

Steinberg v. Columbia Pictures Industries, Inc.

United States District Court, Southern District of New York, 1987.
663 F.Supp. 706.

■ STANTON, DISTRICT JUDGE.

In these actions for copyright infringement, plaintiff Saul Steinberg is suing the producers, promoters, distributors and advertisers of the movie "Moscow on the Hudson" ("Moscow"). Steinberg is an artist whose fame derives in part from cartoons and illustrations he has drawn for *The New Yorker* magazine. Defendant Columbia Pictures Industries, Inc. (Columbia) is in the business of producing, promoting and distributing motion pictures, including "Moscow." * * *

Plaintiff alleges that defendants' promotional poster for "Moscow" infringes his copyright on an illustration that he drew for *The New Yorker* and that appeared on the cover of the March 29, 1976 issue of the magazine, in violation of 17 U.S.C. §§ 101–810. Defendants deny this allegation and assert the affirmative defenses of fair use as a parody, estoppel and laches.

Defendants have moved, and plaintiff has cross-moved, for summary judgment. For the reasons set forth below, this court rejects defendants' asserted defenses and grants summary judgment on the issue of copying to plaintiff. * * *　*SJ for π*

The essential facts are not disputed by the parties despite their disagreements on nonessential matters. On March 29, 1976, *The New Yorker* published as a cover illustration the work at issue in this suit, widely known as a parochial New Yorker's view of the world. The magazine

registered this illustration with the United States Copyright Office and subsequently assigned the copyright to Steinberg. Approximately three months later, plaintiff and *The New Yorker* entered into an agreement to print and sell a certain number of posters of the cover illustration.

---

g　J. Lund, An Empirical Examination of the Lay Listener Test in Music Composition Copyright Infringement, 11 Va. Sports & Ent.L.J. 137 (2011), finds that the impressions of lay listeners in music composition cases are often improperly influenced by similarities or dissimilarities in the performance elements of the sound recordings of the compositions that are played to the jury.

THE
NEW YORKER

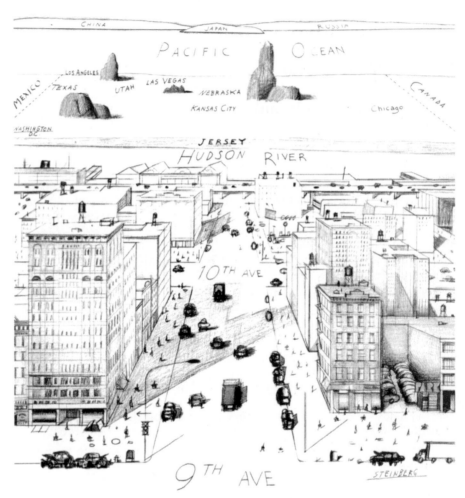

© Saul Steinberg. Reproduced by permission.

Reproduced by permission of Columbia Pictures.

It is undisputed that unauthorized duplications of the poster were made and distributed by unknown persons, although the parties disagree on the extent to which plaintiff attempted to prevent the distribution of those counterfeits. Plaintiff has also conceded that numerous posters have been created and published depicting other localities in the same manner that he depicted New York in his illustration. These facts, however, are irrelevant to the merits of this case, which concerns only the relationship between plaintiff's and defendants' illustrations.

Defendants' illustration was created to advertise the movie "Moscow on the Hudson," which recounts the adventures of a Muscovite who defects in New York. In designing this illustration, Columbia's executive art director, Kevin Nolan, has admitted that he specifically referred to Steinberg's poster, and indeed, that he purchased it and hung it, among others, in his office. Furthermore, Nolan explicitly directed the outside artist whom he retained to execute his design, Craig Nelson, to use Steinberg's poster to achieve a more recognizably New York look. Indeed, Nelson acknowledged having used the facade of one particular edifice, at Nolan's suggestion that it would render his drawing more "New York-ish." Curtis Affidavit ¶ 28(c). While the two buildings are not identical, they are so similar that it is impossible, especially in view of the artist's testimony, not to find that defendants' impermissibly copied plaintiff's.[1]

To decide the issue of infringement, it is necessary to consider the posters themselves. Steinberg's illustration presents a bird's eye view across a portion of the western edge of Manhattan, past the Hudson River and a telescoped version of the rest of the United States and the Pacific Ocean, to a red strip of horizon, beneath which are three flat land masses labeled China, Japan and Russia. The name of the magazine, in *The New Yorker's* usual typeface, occupies the top fifth of the poster, beneath a thin band of blue wash representing a stylized sky.

The parts of the poster beyond New York are minimalized, to symbolize a New Yorker's myopic view of the centrality of his city to the world. The entire United States west of the Hudson River, for example, is reduced to a brown strip labeled "Jersey," together with a light green trapezoid with a few rudimentary rock outcroppings and the names of only seven cities and two states scattered across it. The few blocks of Manhattan, by contrast, are depicted and colored in detail. The four square blocks of the city, which occupy the whole lower half of the poster, include numerous buildings, pedestrians and cars, as well as parking lots and lamp posts, with water towers atop a few of the buildings. The whimsical, sketchy style and spiky lettering are recognizable as Steinberg's.

The "Moscow" illustration depicts the three main characters of the film on the lower third of their poster, superimposed on a bird's eye view of New York City, and continues eastward across Manhattan and the Atlantic Ocean, past a rudimentary evocation of Europe, to a clump of recognizably Russian-styled buildings on the horizon, labeled "Moscow." The movie credits appear over the lower portion of the characters. The central part of the poster depicts approximately four New York city blocks, with fairly detailed buildings, pedestrians and vehicles, a parking lot, and some water towers and lamp posts. Columbia's artist added a few New York landmarks at apparently random places in his illustration, apparently to render the locale more easily recognizable. Beyond the blue strip labeled "Atlantic Ocean," Europe is represented by London, Paris and Rome, each anchored by a single landmark (although the landmark used for Rome is the Leaning Tower of Pisa).

---

[1]   Nolan claimed also to have been inspired by some of the posters that were inspired by Steinberg's; such secondary inspiration, however, is irrelevant to whether or not the "Moscow" poster infringes plaintiff's copyright by having impermissibly copied it.

The horizon behind Moscow is delineated by a red crayoned strip, above which are the title of the movie and a brief textual introduction to the plot. The poster is crowned by a thin strip of blue wash, apparently a stylization of the sky. This poster is executed in a blend of styles: the three characters, whose likenesses were copied from a photograph, have realistic faces and somewhat sketchy clothing, and the city blocks are drawn in a fairly detailed but sketchy style. The lettering on the drawing is spiky, in block-printed handwritten capital letters substantially identical to plaintiff's, while the printed texts at the top and bottom of the poster are in the typeface commonly associated with *The New Yorker* magazine.[2]

To succeed in a copyright infringement action, a plaintiff must prove ownership of the copyright and copying by the defendant. Reyher v. Children's Television Workshop, 533 F.2d 87, 90 (2d Cir.1976); Durham Industries, [Inc. v. Tomy Corp., 630 F.2d 905, 911 (2d Cir.1980)]; Novelty Textile Mills, Inc. v. Joan Fabrics Corp., 558 F.2d 1090, 1092 (2d Cir.1977). There is no substantial dispute concerning plaintiff's ownership of a valid copyright in his illustration. Therefore, in order to prevail on liability, plaintiff need establish only the second element of the cause of action.

[handwritten margin note: π had ownership of valid copyright; π nudd to prove ∆ copied]

"Because of the inherent difficulty in obtaining direct evidence of copying, it is usually proved by circumstantial evidence of access to the copyrighted work and substantial similarities as to protectible material in the two works." *Reyher,* 533 F.2d at 90, citing Arnstein v. Porter, 154 F.2d 464, 468 (2d Cir.1946). See also *Novelty Textile Mills,* 558 F.2d at 1092. "Of course, if there are no similarities, no amount of evidence of access will suffice to prove copying." Arnstein v. Porter, 154 F.2d at 468. See also *Novelty Textile Mills,* 558 F.2d at 1092 n. 2. * * *

The definition of "substantial similarity" in this circuit is "whether an average lay observer would recognize the alleged copy as having been appropriated from the copyrighted work." Ideal Toy Corp. v. Fab–Lu Ltd., 360 F.2d 1021, 1022 (2d Cir.1966); Silverman v. CBS, Inc., [632 F.Supp. 1344, 1351–52 (S.D.N.Y.1986)]. A plaintiff need no longer meet the severe "ordinary observer" test established by Judge Learned Hand in Peter Pan Fabrics, Inc. v. Martin Weiner Corp., 274 F.2d 487 (2d Cir.1960). Uneeda Doll Co., Inc. v. Regent Baby Products Corp., 355 F.Supp. 438, 450 (E.D.N.Y.1972). Under Judge Hand's formulation, there would be substantial similarity only where "the ordinary observer, unless he set out to detect the disparities, would be disposed to overlook them, and regard their aesthetic appeal as the same." 274 F.2d at 489. * * *

In determining whether there is substantial similarity between two works, it is crucial to distinguish between an idea and its expression. * * *

There is no dispute that defendants cannot be held liable for using the *idea* of a map of the world from an egocentrically myopic perspective. No rigid principle has been developed, however, to ascertain when one has gone beyond the idea to the expression, and "[d]ecisions must therefore inevitably be ad hoc." Peter Pan Fabrics, Inc. v. Martin Weiner Corp., 274 F.2d 487, 489 (2d Cir.1960) (L. Hand, J.). As Judge Frankel once observed, "Good eyes and common sense may be as useful as deep study of reported and unreported cases, which themselves are tied to highly particularized facts." Couleur International Ltd. v. Opulent Fabrics, Inc., 330 F.Supp. 152, 153 (S.D.N.Y.1971).

---

2   The typeface is not a subject of copyright, but the similarity reinforces the impression that defendants copied plaintiff's illustration.

Even at first glance, one can see the striking stylistic relationship between the posters, and since style is one ingredient of "expression," this relationship is significant. Defendants' illustration was executed in the
sketchy, whimsical style that has become one of Steinberg's hallmarks.
Both illustrations represent a bird's eye view across the edge of Manhattan
and a river bordering New York City to the world beyond. Both depict approximately four city blocks in detail and become increasingly minimalist
as the design recedes into the background. Both use the device of a narrow
band of blue wash across the top of the poster to represent the sky, and
both delineate the horizon with a band of primary red.[3]

The strongest similarity is evident in the rendering of the New York
City blocks. Both artists chose a vantage point that looks directly down a
wide two-way cross street that intersects two avenues before reaching a
river. Despite defendants' protestations, this is not an inevitable way of
depicting blocks in a city with a grid-like street system, particularly since
most New York City cross streets are one-way. Since even a photograph
may be copyrighted because "no photograph, however simple, can be unaffected by the personal influence of the author," Time Inc. v. Bernard Geis
Assoc., 293 F.Supp. 130, 141 (S.D.N.Y.1968), quoting *Bleistein,* supra, one
can hardly gainsay the right of an artist to protect his choice of perspective
and layout in a drawing, especially in conjunction with the overall concept
and individual details. Indeed, the fact that defendants changed the names
of the streets while retaining the same graphic depiction weakens their
case: had they intended their illustration realistically to depict the streets
labeled on the poster, their four city blocks would not so closely resemble
plaintiff's four city blocks. Moreover, their argument that they intended the
jumble of streets and landmarks and buildings to symbolize their Muscovite protagonist's confusion in a new city does not detract from the strong
similarity between their poster and Steinberg's.

While not all of the details are identical, many of them could be mistaken for one another; for example, the depiction of the water towers, and
the cars, and the red sign above a parking lot, and even many of the individual buildings. The shapes, windows, and configurations of various edi-
fices are substantially similar. The ornaments, facades and details of
Steinberg's buildings appear in defendants', although occasionally at other
locations. In this context, it is significant that Steinberg did not depict any
buildings actually erected in New York; rather, he was inspired by the general appearance of the structures on the West Side of Manhattan to create
his own New York-ish structures. Thus, the similarity between the buildings depicted in the "Moscow" and Steinberg posters cannot be explained by
an assertion that the artists happened to choose the same buildings to
draw. The close similarity can be explained only by the defendants' artist
having copied the plaintiff's work. Similarly, the locations and size, the errors and anomalies of Steinberg's shadows and streetlight, are meticulously
imitated.

In addition, the Columbia artist's use of the childlike, spiky block print
that has become one of Steinberg's hallmarks to letter the names of the

---

[3]   Defendants claim that since this use of thin bands of primary colors is a traditional
Japanese technique, their adoption of it cannot infringe Steinberg's copyright. This argument
ignores the principle that while "[o]thers are free to copy the original . . . [t]hey are not free to
copy the copy." Bleistein v. Donaldson Lithographing Co., 188 U.S. 239, 250 (1903) (Holmes,
J.). Cf. Dave Grossman Designs, Inc. v. Bortin, 347 F.Supp. 1150, 1156–57 (N.D.Ill.1972) (an
artist may use the same subject and style as another "so long as the second artist does not
substantially copy [the first artist's] specific expression of his idea.")

streets in the "Moscow" poster can be explained only as copying. There is no inherent justification for using this style of lettering to label New York City streets as it is associated with New York only through Steinberg's poster.

While defendants' poster shows the city of Moscow on the horizon in far greater detail than anything is depicted in the background of plaintiff's illustration, this fact alone cannot alter the conclusion. "Substantial similarity" does not require identity, and "duplication or near identity is not necessary to establish infringement." [Sid & Marty Krofft Television Productions, Inc. v. McDonald's Corp., 562 F.2d 1157, 1167 (9th Cir.1977)]. Neither the depiction of Moscow, nor the eastward perspective, nor the presence of randomly scattered New York City landmarks in defendants' poster suffices to eliminate the substantial similarity between the posters. As Judge Learned Hand wrote, "no plagiarist can excuse the wrong by showing how much of his work he did not pirate." Sheldon v. Metro–Goldwyn Pictures Corp., 81 F.2d 49, 56 (2d Cir.), cert. denied, 298 U.S. 669 (1936). * * *

I also reject defendants' argument that any similarities between the works are unprotectible *scenes a faire,* or "incidents, characters or settings which, as a practical matter, are indispensable or standard in the treatment of a given topic." [Walker v. Time Life Films, Inc., 615 F.Supp. 430, 434 (S.D.N.Y.1985), aff'd, 784 F.2d 44 (2d Cir.), cert. denied, 476 U.S. 1159 (1986)]. See also *Reyher,* 533 F.2d at 92. It is undeniable that a drawing of New York City blocks could be expected to include buildings, pedestrians, vehicles, lampposts and water towers. Plaintiff, however, does not complain of defendants' mere use of these elements in their poster; rather, his complaint is that defendants copied his *expression* of those elements of a street scene. * * *

[The court next rejected defendants' "parody" defense under the fair use doctrine, finding that the movie poster was not intended to parody the Steinberg illustration. Judge Stanton then turned to the defendants' defenses of estoppel and laches.]

Defendants base their assertions of these equitable defenses on the following factual claims: (1) plaintiff's alleged "deliberate inaction" for eight years in the face of numerous counterfeits of his poster and adaptations of his idea to various other localities; * * *

The record, however, does not support defendants' claims. First, Steinberg specifically requested that *The New Yorker* magazine attempt to identify the sources of the counterfeit posters and prevent their continued distribution. As for the so-called adaptations of Steinberg's idea, there is no evidence that they infringed his copyright or that anyone ever believed that they did. As plaintiff freely and necessarily admits, the law does not protect an idea, but only the specific expression of that idea. The examples that defendants use to support their defense can at most be considered derivative of Steinberg's idea; none is a close copy of the poster itself, as defendants' is.

[Plaintiff's motion for summary judgment was granted.]

NOTES AND QUESTIONS ON INFRINGEMENT OF VISUAL WORKS

(1) What happened to the two-step approach espoused in Arnstein v. Porter? Judicial conflation of the "copying" and "improper appropriation" elements remains common, prompted in part by the relevance of "substantial similarity" to both elements of the plaintiff's case. See, e.g., the court's infringement analysis in Three Boys Music Corp. v. Bolton, p. 187 supra.

Did Columbia Pictures copy the "idea" of Steinberg's illustration? Did Columbia Pictures copy Steinberg's "expression" of that idea? (Do you find the two posters, which were not reproduced in the court's opinion, less similar than Judge Stanton's description suggests?) Is the court correct in treating Steinberg's "style" and "choice of perspective" as part of his copyrightable expression? Compare Kerr v. New Yorker Magazine, 63 F.Supp.2d 320 (S.D.N.Y.1999), in which an illustrator alleged that the July 10, 1995 cover of the *New Yorker* magazine—"Manhattan Mohawk"—was copied from his 1989 drawing, "New York Hairline." "Both pictures depict a male figure with a 'Mohawk' haircut (completely bald except for one strip of hair down the center of the head) in the shape of the Manhattan skyline. * * * There can be no dispute that defendants cannot be held liable for using the idea of the New York City skyline on someone's head. See Steinberg v. Columbia Pictures Ind., Inc., 663 F.Supp. 706, 711 (S.D.N.Y.1987). Here, the similarities between the pictures are the 'idea' of skyline as a haircut, and the other uncopyrightable elements which the 'expression' of this 'idea' might reasonably be expected to include: eyes, nose, mouth, a figure in profile, and certain N.Y. buildings. * * * This is not a case like *Steinberg*, 663 F.Supp. 706, where the defendant copied the plaintiff's style, as well as copying the actual imaginary buildings which plaintiff depicted."

(2) Judge Stanton's opinion in *Steinberg* declines to adopt the test for substantial similarity formulated by Learned Hand in Peter Pan Fabrics, Inc. v. Martin Weiner Corp., 274 F.2d 487 (2d Cir.1960). That case involved infringement in the textile industry, a crowded and litigious field that has afforded numerous opportunities for judicial pronouncements on substantial similarity. Judge Hand, upholding a preliminary injunction in favor of the owner of a design called "Byzantium," wrote:

"The test for infringement of a copyright is of necessity vague. In the case of verbal 'works' it is well settled that although the 'proprietor's' monopoly extends beyond an exact reproduction of the words, there can be no copyright in the 'ideas' disclosed but only in their 'expression.' Obviously, no principle can be stated as to when an imitator has gone beyond copying the 'idea,' and has borrowed its 'expression.' Decisions must therefore inevitably be *ad hoc*. In the case of designs, which are addressed to the aesthetic sensibilities of an observer, the test is, if possible, even more intangible. No one disputes that the copyright extends beyond a photographic reproduction of the design, but one cannot say how far an imitator must depart from an undeviating reproduction to escape infringement. In deciding that question one should consider the uses for which the design is intended, especially the scrutiny that observers will give to it as used. In the case at bar we must try to estimate how far its overall appearance will determine its aesthetic appeal when the cloth is made into a garment. Both designs have the same general color, and the arches, scrolls, rows of symbols, etc. on one resemble those on the other though they are not identical. Moreover, the patterns in which these figures are distributed to make up the design as a whole are not identical. However, the ordinary observer, unless he set out to detect the disparities, would be disposed to overlook them, and regard their aesthetic appeal as the same. That is enough; and indeed, it is all that can be said, unless protection against infringement is to be denied because of variants irrelevant to the purpose for which the design is intended."

How does Judge Hand's formulation differ from the one recited in *Steinberg,* which asks whether an observer "would recognize the alleged copy as having been appropriated from the copyrighted work"? In Ideal Toy Corp. v. Fab–Lu Ltd., 360 F.2d 1021 (2d Cir.1966), the doll infringement case from which the latter standard is taken, the test is followed by a citation to Hand's opinion in *Peter Pan Fabrics.* Judge Lumbard, in another textile design case, thought the two formulations interchangeable. See Dolori Fabrics, Inc. v. Limited, Inc., 662 F.Supp. 1347 (S.D.N.Y.1987). Judge Newman injected a note of caution in Beaudin v. Ben and Jerry's Homemade, Inc., 95 F.3d 1 (2d Cir.1996), holding that the ice cream maker's cow hats did not infringe plaintiff's black and white fabric design for cow jeans; when the quantum of originality is slight, only very close copying will infringe.

Another test for substantial similarity asks, again from the perspective of an ordinary observer, whether the defendant has captured "the total concept and feel" of the plaintiff's work. That phrase originated in Roth Greeting Cards v. United Card Co., 429 F.2d 1106 (9th Cir.1970), an interesting case about the copyrightability and infringement of greeting cards. The standard has gained increasing usage, spurred especially by its recitation in Sid & Marty Krofft Television Productions, Inc. v. McDonald's Corp., another Ninth Circuit decision that appears at p. 219 infra. "Total concept and feel" now seems to be the principal test for substantial similarity of expression in the Ninth Circuit; it also has made appearances in other circuits.[h] Is the test a useful guide to decision? Does it stretch too broadly in defining infringement? None of the cases seem to pay any attention to the inclusion of "concept" in the catalog of subject matter excluded from copyright protection in § 102(b).

The Second Circuit offered this analysis of the "total concept and feel" standard: "Essentially, the total-concept-and-feel locution functions as a reminder that, while the infringement analysis must *begin* by dissecting the copyrighted work into its component parts in order to clarify precisely what is not original, infringement analysis is not *simply* a matter of ascertaining similarity between components viewed in isolation. For the defendant may infringe on the plaintiff's work not only through literal copying of a portion of it, but also by parroting properties that are apparent only when the numerous aesthetic decisions embodied in the plaintiff's work of art—the excerpting, modifying, and arranging of public domain compositions, if any, together with the development and representation of wholly new motifs and the use of texture and color, etc.—are considered in relation to one another." However, the court went on to endorse Professor Nimmer's view that " 'total concept and feel' should not be viewed as a *sine qua non* for infringement—similarity that is otherwise actionable cannot be rendered defensible simply because of a different 'concept and feel'." Tufenkian Import/Export Ventures, Inc. v. Einstein Moomjy, Inc., 338 F.3d 127 (2d Cir.2003).

(3) Video games now rival textile designs as a fertile ground for litigation. See, e.g., Tetris Holding, LLC v. Xio Interactive, Inc., 863 F.Supp.2d 394 (D.N.J.2012) (although the defendant was free to use the idea of *Tetris*—fitting different shaped pieces together to form complete lines—the particular style, design, shape and movement of the *Tetris* pieces was protectable expression);

---

[h] See, e.g., Lyons Partnership, L.P. v. Morris Costumes, Inc., 243 F.3d 789 (4th Cir.2001); Knitwaves, Inc. v. Lollytogs, Ltd., 71 F.3d 996 (2d Cir.1995); Hartman v. Hallmark Cards, Inc., 833 F.2d 117 (8th Cir.1987); Atari, Inc. v. North American Philips Consumer Electronics Corp., 672 F.2d 607 (7th Cir.), cert. denied, 459 U.S. 880 (1982).

Data East USA, Inc. v. Epyx, Inc., 862 F.2d 204 (9th Cir.1988). Video games, dolls, and toys can raise questions about when it is proper to find infringing substantial similarity in situations where there is an extensive public domain and a demand for naturalistic depictions. One approach is to be cautious about copyrightability. See, e.g., Kuddle Toy, Inc. v. Pussycat–Toy Co., 183 U.S.P.Q. 642 (E.D.N.Y.1974) (insufficient originality in various versions of the classic teddy bear); Florabelle Flowers v. Joseph Markovits, Inc., 296 F.Supp. 304 (S.D.N.Y.1968) (insufficient originality in plastic flowers). Another is to emphasize the limits of the plaintiff's copyright protection. See, e.g., Incredible Tech., Inc. v. Virtual Tech., Inc., 400 F.3d 1007 (7th Cir.2005) (narrow protection for a video golf game); Data East USA, Inc., supra (similarities in video games follow from the idea of a martial arts game); Eden Toys, Inc. v. Marshall Field & Co., 675 F.2d 498 (2d Cir.1982) (no infringement because all snowmen dolls necessarily look alike).

(4) Can an ordinary observer test for substantial similarity deal adequately with the dichotomy between ideas and expression? Consider McCulloch v. Albert E. Price, Inc., 823 F.2d 316 (9th Cir.1987). Plaintiff marketed a red dinner plate bearing a white floral design with the words "You Are Special Today" in white letters; defendant entered the market with a plate bearing the same phrase, although it was white with red letters and apparently had a different floral design. The court said that the question of infringement turned on "whether the 'ordinary reasonable person' would find the 'total concept and feel' of the works showed substantial similarity." Defendant argued that the uncopyrightable text should be discounted in evaluating substantial similarity; plaintiff responded that "proper analysis of this issue requires that all of the elements of the work, including the uncopyrightable text, be considered as a whole in determining copyright infringement." The court agreed with the plaintiff and affirmed a finding of infringement. Is this a sound result? See also Roulo v. Russ Berrie & Co., p. 653 infra, eschewing dissection and upholding a jury verdict that the defendant's greeting cards infringed the unique combination of otherwise common elements that characterized plaintiff's "sensitive verse" cards. Compare Concrete Machinery Co. v. Classic Lawn Ornaments, Inc., 843 F.2d 600 (1st Cir.1988), involving a menagerie of lawn statuary. Instructing the lower court on the standard for a preliminary injunction, the First Circuit said that "on rehearing, the court should 'dissect' the works to identify those aspects which [plaintiff] likely will be able to show are protected expression and were copied by [defendant]. Then, focusing on those aspects which are protected expression, the court should determine whether [plaintiff] is likely to prove, under the ordinary observer test, that [defendant's] works are substantially similar to its own."

The Ninth Circuit refined its approach to substantial similarity in Aliotti v. R. Dakin & Co., 831 F.2d 898 (9th Cir.1987), a case about stuffed toy dinosaurs. Although adhering to the ordinary observer test, the court announced a qualification: "Although even unprotectable material should be considered when determining if there is substantial similarity of expression, see *McCulloch,* 823 F.2d at 320–21, no substantial similarity may be found under the intrinsic test where analytic dissection demonstrates that all similarities in expression arise from the use of common ideas." Because the similarities between the toys resulted either from the physiognomy of dinosaurs or the nature of stuffed animals, there was no infringement. The Ninth Circuit echoed that limitation in Satava v. Lowry, 323 F.3d 805 (9th Cir.), cert. denied, 540 U.S. 983

(2003), when it reversed a preliminary injunction won by a sculptor against a copier of his glass-in-glass jellyfish sculptures. Citing *Aliotti*, the court said that "no copyright protection may be afforded to the idea of producing a glass-in-glass jellyfish sculpture or to the elements of expression that naturally follow from the idea of such a sculpture." The court then offered a broader synthesis, stating "that a *combination* of unprotectable elements may qualify for copyright protection." However, "[o]ur case law suggests, and we now hold today, that a combination of unprotectable elements is eligible for copyright protection only if those elements are numerous enough and their selection and arrangement original enough that their combination constitutes an original work of authorship." Here, there was insufficient authorship. "The selection of the clear glass, oblong shroud, bright colors, proportion, vertical orientation, and stereotyped jellyfish form, considered together, lacks the quantum of originality needed to merit copyright protection."

Should the nature of the substantial similarity analysis reflect the type of works at issue? *McCulloch,* supra, defending its "totalities" approach to the "You Are Special Today" plate, said that "factual" works would require a different approach. See, e.g., Cooling Systems and Flexibles, Inc. v. Stuart Radiator, Inc., 777 F.2d 485 (9th Cir.1985), rejecting "total concept and feel" in favor of a comparison of "the very small amount of protectible expression" in plaintiff's radiator catalog. S. Balganesh, The Normativity of Copying in Copyright Law, 62 Duke L.J. 203 (2012), emphasizes the central role of substantial similarity in modulating the scope of copyright to achieve an appropriate level of protection; R. Tushnet, Worth a Thousand Words: The Images of Copyright, 125 Harv.L.Rev. 683 (2012), concludes that copyright rhetoric designed for textual works does not yield a stable framework for analyzing copyright in images.

(5) The issue of "substantial similarity" arose in a different context when Judge Newman considered a claim brought by the owner of a copyrighted poster that had appeared without permission in the background of a scene in the defendants' television series. "In cases involving visual works, like the pending one, the quantitative component of substantial similarity also concerns the observability of the copied work—the length of time the copied work is observable in the allegedly infringing work and such factors as focus, lighting, camera angles, and prominence." The court concluded that a four or five second segment in which most of the work was visible (although not in perfect focus), reinforced by briefer segments in which smaller portions could be seen, was sufficient to establish actionable copying; it also reversed a summary judgment of fair use. Ringgold v. Black Entertainment Television, Inc., 126 F.3d 70 (2d Cir.1997).

Distinguishing the facts in *Ringgold*, the Second Circuit in Sandoval v. New Line Cinema Corp., 147 F.3d 215 (2d Cir.1998), found that the plaintiff had failed to establish substantial similarity in connection with the defendant's use of ten of the plaintiff's photographs in a movie. Although the photos were visible for more than 35 seconds, they were never in focus and appeared primarily in the distant background. Motion picture and television studios typically employ "clearance" specialists to license copyrighted works that appear in their productions.

"Popover"
(Figure 1)

"Obee"
(Figure 2)

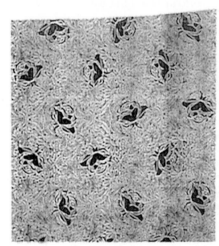

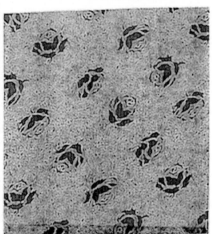

Folio's "Pattern 1365"
(Figure 3)

Lida's "Baroque Rose 7480"
(Figure 4)

(6) Assuming access and a valid copyright, is plaintiff's toy ostrich "Popover" (see Figure 1) infringed by defendant's "Obee" (Figure 2)? See Gund, Inc. v. Russ Berrie & Co., 701 F.Supp. 1013 (S.D.N.Y.1988).

Is plaintiff Folio's fabric design "Pattern 1365" (Figure 3) infringed by defendant Lida's "Baroque Rose 7480" (Figure 4)? Does it matter that the plaintiff took the background for its design from a work in the public domain? See Folio Impressions, Inc. v. Byer California, 937 F.2d 759 (2d Cir.1991).

(7) Computer technology has raised new problems for the owners of copyrights in visual works, especially photographs. Photographs can be scanned and converted into digital data capable of being manipulated in a computer. The digital data can be altered to produce a new scene that never existed, and parts of different works can be combined into a single image. *National Geographic*, for example, created a public controversy in 1982 when it "moved" two Egyptian pyramids closer together to fit a photograph onto its cover. Similarly, digital video can be altered frame by frame. The technology offers significant savings to producers—a handful of marching soldiers can be digitally cloned to create an infantry regiment or a photograph of Big Ben can be manipulated into the background of a movie or television scene shot in California. Is it an infringement to take a cloud or a tree from a copyrighted photograph and use it as background in a new picture? Does unauthorized digital alteration by a licensee who has permission to reproduce the work infringe the copyright owner's exclusive right to prepare derivative works?

The plaintiff in Tiffany Design, Inc. v. Reno–Tahoe Specialty, Inc., 55 F.Supp.2d 1113 (D.Nev.1999), had created a cityscape of Las Vegas through computer manipulation of aerial photographs in which it held copyrights. A defendant scanned the plaintiff's cityscape into a computer and incorporated several of the buildings into its own image of Las Vegas. The court granted summary judgment to the plaintiff on its claim that scanning the image into the defendant's computer was itself a violation of the § 106(1) reproduction right. In light of the defendant's argument that it had radically modified the images of the buildings, the court denied the plaintiff's motion for summary judgment on its claim that the defendant's final picture was an infringing derivative work under § 106(2); the issue of substantial similarity raised a question of fact to be determined at trial.

(8) Three-dimensional printing is on its way, along with the inevitable copyright issues. Users who make home copies of copyrighted sculptural works, three-dimensional versions of copyrighted characters, or copies of useful articles that include copyrightable elements will no doubt be pursued by copyright owners, as will third-parties who supply unauthorized plans and data sets used to make the reproductions.

A NOTE ON COPYING THE COPY

(1) Recall Justice Holmes' remark in *Bleistein:* "Others are free to copy the original. They are not free to copy the copy." Consider the variation on the original subject—copy—second copy sequence that arises when an artist depicts something from nature, sells the copyright in that work, and then returns to the same subject. Two cases invite comparison:

(1) "One Rochlitz, an artist, posed a model in the nude, and therefrom produced a photograph, which he named the 'Grace of Youth.' A copyright was obtained therefor; all the artist's rights being sold and assigned to complainants. Two years later the same artist placed the same model in the identical pose, with the single exception that the young woman now wears a smile and holds a cherry stem between her teeth. He took a photograph of this pose, which he called 'Cherry Ripe'; this second photograph is published by defendants * * *." On this statement of facts, taken from Gross v. Seligman, 212 Fed. 930 (2d Cir.1914), is the second photograph an infringement? It was held that it was. But had Rochlitz copied the copy, or copied the original?

(2) Gilbert, "a nationally recognized wildlife artist," created a painting in 1972 entitled "Cardinals on Apple Blossom." Copyright was assigned to the Na-

tional Wildlife Art Exchange, which sold prints of the painting. During 1975 and 1976, Gilbert created another painting called "The Cardinal" as part of a series for the Franklin Mint. "In painting 'The Cardinal,' Gilbert used some of the same source material he had utilized for 'Cardinals on Apple Blossom,' including preliminary sketches from his collection, photographs, slides, and a working drawing. In addition, however, he used other slides of foliage taken after completion of the earlier painting and sketches specifically developed for 'The Cardinal,' as well as a series of cardinal photographs. He did not use the stuffed bird specimens which had served as models for 'Cardinals on Apple Blossom.' " National sued for copyright infringement. In Franklin Mint Corp. v. National Wildlife Art Exchange, 575 F.2d 62 (3d Cir.), cert. denied, 439 U.S. 880 (1978), the Third Circuit agreed with the trial court that there was no infringement. After noting "that there are indeed obvious similarities," partly because "in ornithological art * * * minute attention to detail of plumage and other physical characteristics is required and the stance of the birds must be anatomically correct," the court said that "there are also readily apparent dissimilarities"—which it detailed. "[W]hile the ideas are similar, the expressions are not. A pattern of differences is sufficient to establish a diversity of expression rather than only an echo."

Are these cases distinguishable on the facts, or is there a difference in approach, in that a watercolorist is treated differently from a photographer. If the latter, which subsequent artist should be held to a greater variety of treatment? Judge Weis' elegant opinion in *Franklin Mint* raises other points, including "the tendency of some painters to return to certain basic themes time and time again." Cf. Schiller & Schmidt, Inc. v. Nordisco Corp., 969 F.2d 410 (7th Cir.1992) (when the author of the two works is the same, similarities are less probative of copying).

Can similar issues arise in other art forms? An article in the *New York Times,* Bishop, A Victory for the Creative Process, Nov. 11, 1988, p. B.5, reports on an infringement suit brought by Fantasy Records, owner of the copyrights in songs composed by John Fogerty for Creedence Clearwater Revival from 1967 to 1972. Fantasy claimed that Fogerty had infringed himself by copying his 1970 hit "Run Through the Jungle" when he wrote "Old Man Down the Road" for his 1985 album "Centerfield." Fogerty's attorney argued that "[w]hat similarities there were between the two songs were the result of Mr. Fogerty having written both of them. Both of them came out of the same musical vocabulary." The jury found that the songs were not substantially similar. (The litigation ultimately produced an opinion by the Supreme Court on the standards governing the award of attorney's fees under the Copyright Act. See Fogerty v. Fantasy, Inc., p. 577 infra.)

(2) Consider a different variation on Justice Holmes' sequence, namely, the "recreation" of a copyrighted photograph by a different photographer. In Alt v. Morello, 227 U.S.P.Q. 49 (S.D.N.Y.1985), the plaintiff, a young photographer, "created a photograph depicting a Cross pen and pencil positioned at an angle on a dark grid against a dark background, with the tips of the pen and pencil in a yellow toned circle lit from below." The defendant, an established advertising photographer who had seen the plaintiff's work, created a photograph that the court found "virtually the same," although the pen and pencil were of a different brand, the angle between them was slightly different, and the circle was a different shade of yellow. (The defendant's photograph was published in a source book widely used by advertising directors, leading many to assume that it was the plaintiff who had copied.) The court found infringement; statutory damages were set at $20,000.[i] See Kisch v. Ammirati & Puris Inc., 657 F.Supp. 380 (S.D.N.Y.1987), where the plaintiff's work was a black and white photograph of a seated woman holding a concertina, taken in a small corner of a nightclub with a mural in the background. The defendant created an advertisement for lime juice by taking a color photograph of musician John Lurie seated in front of the same mural, holding a saxophone. A table and a bottle of lime juice were included in the defendant's photo, but the lighting and camera angles were similar. The defendant, conceding access, moved for summary judgment. What result?

Leigh v. Warner Bros., Inc., 212 F.3d 1210 (11th Cir.2000), involved a plaintiff commissioned to take a photograph for the cover of the novel *Midnight in the Garden of Good and Evil, A Savannah Story*, by John Berendt. Plaintiff chose to photograph a sculpture in a Savannah cemetery known as *The Bird Girl*. In making a movie based on the novel, Warner Brothers, with permission from the sculptor's heir, made a replica and placed it in a different location in the same cemetery; images of the scene appeared in the film and photographs were used in promotional materials. Although "plaintiff may have been the first to think of the statue as evocative of the novel's mood and as an appropriate symbol of the book's themes," he had no rights in the appearance of either the statue or the cemetery; his copyright was limited to his "selection of lighting, shading, timing, angle, and film." The court found that the film sequences featuring *The Bird Girl* were not substantially similar to the protected elements of the plaintiff's photograph and affirmed a summary judgment. However, the similarities between the plaintiff's photograph and the photos that the defendant used to promote the film were sufficient to preclude summary judgment on the claim that those photos were infringements.

4. COPYRIGHT IN CHARACTERS

King Features Syndicate v. Fleischer
United States Circuit Court of Appeals, Second Circuit, 1924.
299 Fed. 533.

■ Before ROGERS, HOUGH, AND MANTON, CIRCUIT JUDGES.

■ MANTON, CIRCUIT JUDGE. Appellant, the owner of the copyright of a book of cartoons known as "Barney Google and Spark Plug," sues the appellees, who are manufacturers of toys, and who manufacture a toy horse which they have fashioned after, labeled, and sold as "Spark Plug" and "Sparky." The appellant has been and is engaged, among other things, in selling, publishing, and syndicating to the publishers of newspapers, cartoons and com-

---

[i] See also Woods v. Universal City Studios, Inc., 920 F.Supp.2d 62 (S.D.N.Y.1996), holding that the plaintiff's pencil drawing was infringed by a recreation of the scene in the defendant's motion picture *12 Monkeys*. In Harney v. Sony Television, Inc., 704 F.3d 173 (1st Cir.2013), a photographer who had taken a photograph of a criminal with a daughter in a pink coat riding piggy-back on his shoulders sued a movie studio that recreated the photo using actors who starred in a television movie about the criminal. The original photo had played a role in the police investigation. According to the court, "subject matter that the photographer did not create could be viewed as 'facts' that, like ideas, are not entitled to copyright protection." The photographer's copyright did not extend to the piggy-back pose or pink coat; only creative aspects such as the light tones and framing of the scene were protectable, and as to those there was no substantial similarity.

ic strips, which are in turn published under a license from appellant. These newspapers have a wide and large reading public, and the cartoons and comic strips have great value to the publishers. The appellant's employee prepared cartoons—that is, sketches and drawings—in series of representations of a male character known as "Barney Google," which depicts a character in a variety of ludicrous situations coupled with descriptive reading matter or dialogue. From July, 1922, these cartoons appeared almost daily, and included a characteristic representation of a new grotesque and comic race horse called "Spark Plug," sometimes referred to as "Sparky." Both figures, the man and the horse, are found to be the creation of the appellant's employee. * * *

The appellees' infringement consisted of the reproduction of a substantial portion of the copyright, and also in publishing it as an advertisement in the trade paper entitled "Plaything" and in the newspaper called "Billboard." The principal act of infringement, however, is the manufacturing and sale of a grotesque figure or toy, an exact reproduction of the horse "Spark Plug," or "Sparky," as copyrighted by the appellant. * * *

The question presented to us is whether manufacturing and duplicating the horse as a figure doll is a copy of the copyrighted idea of the appellant's. * * *

We do not think it avoids the infringement of the copyright to take the substance or idea, and produce it through a different medium, and picturing in shape and details in sufficient limitation to make it a true copy of the character thought of by the appellant's employee. Doing this is omitting the work of the artisan, but appropriating the genius of the artist. Falk v. Howell & Co. (C.C.) 37 F. 202. * * *

* * * The Copyright Act protects the conception of humor which a cartoonist may produce, as well as the conception of genius which an artist or sculptor may use. Hill v. Whalen (D.C.) 220 F. 359.

In the *Hill* Case, the complainant was the licensee of cartoon characters known as "Mutt and Jeff." The defendants produced a dramatic performance calling it "In Cartoonland." The characters were costumed exactly like the figures of "Mutt and Jeff," the cartoons, and their actions and speech were in harmony with the spirit of the cartoons. The court enjoined the defendants, upon the ground that representations of "Mutt and Jeff" dramatically was calculated to injuriously affect the copyright of the cartoons. A reproduction in materials of the copyrighted cartoon character, it would seem, is equally a violation of the copyright of the cartoon. Empire Amusement Co. v. Wilton (C.C.) 134 F. 132. * * *

Here the book was copyrightable, and embodied the pictorial illustration of the horse "Sparky." The artist's concept of humor was embodied in the copyrightable form, was addressed to the contemplation of the observer and the reader; its essence was the concept of humor which that form embodied. We think it cannot be copied, by manufacturing a toy or doll as the appellees did, without taking the copyrightable form of that concept, and without at the same time taking the commercial value—the fruits of the cartoonist's genius which consisted in his capacity to entertain and amuse.

Decree reversed.

Detective Comics, Inc. v. Bruns Publications, Inc.

United States Circuit Court of Appeals, Second Circuit, 1940.
111 F.2d 432.

■ Before L. HAND, AUGUSTUS N. HAND, and CHASE, CIRCUIT JUDGES.

■ AUGUSTUS N. HAND, CIRCUIT JUDGE. The complainant is the owner of eleven copyrights for a like number of monthly issues of a periodical known as "Action Comics". Judge Woolsey found that these copyrights were infringed by a magazine of the defendant Bruns Publications Inc., (hereinafter called Bruns) and known as "Wonderman" [28 F.Supp. 399]. He found infringement both by Bruns and by the defendants Kable News Company and Interborough News Co., who were the distributing agents of Bruns. The defendants all had access to complainant's periodicals, which had a wide sale.

We have compared the alleged infringing magazine of Bruns with the issues of "Action Comics" and are satisfied that the finding that Bruns copied the pictures in the complainant's periodical is amply substantiated. *△ copied* Each publication portrays a man of miraculous strength and speed called "Superman" in "Action Comics" and "Wonderman" in the magazine of *Superman ⇒ Wonderman* Bruns. The attributes and antics of "Superman" and "Wonderman" are closely similar. Each at times conceals his strength beneath ordinary clothing but after removing his cloak stands revealed in full panoply in a skintight acrobatic costume. The only real difference between them is that "Superman" wears a blue uniform and "Wonderman" a red one. Each is termed the champion of the oppressed. Each is shown running toward a full moon "off into the night", and each is shown crushing a gun in his powerful hands. "Superman" is pictured as stopping a bullet with his person and "Wonderman" as arresting and throwing back shells. Each is depicted as shot at by three men, yet as wholly impervious to the missiles that strike him. "Superman" is shown as leaping over a twenty story building, and "Wonderman" as leaping from building to building. "Superman" and "Wonderman" are each endowed with sufficient strength to rip open a steel door. Each is described as being the strongest man in the world and each as battling against "evil and injustice."

Defendants attempt to avoid the copyright by the old argument that various attributes of "Superman" find prototypes or analogues among the heroes of literature and mythology. But if the author of "Superman" has portrayed a comic Hercules, yet if his production involves more than the presentation of a general type he may copyright it and say of it: "A poor thing but mine own". Perhaps the periodicals of the complainant are foolish rather than comic, but they embody an original arrangement of incidents and a pictorial and literary form which preclude the contention that Bruns was not copying the antics of "Superman" portrayed in "Action Comics". We think it plain that the defendants have used more than general types and ideas and have appropriated the pictorial and literary details embodied in the complainant's copyrights.

We have repeatedly held that irrespective of the sources from which the author of a work may derive the material which he uses, a picture or writing which is his own production cannot be copied. The prior art is only relevant as bearing on the question whether an alleged infringer has copied the author or has taken his material directly from the prior art. Sheldon v. Metro–Goldwyn Pictures Corporation, 2 Cir., 81 F.2d 49, 53.

So far as the pictorial representations and verbal descriptions of "Superman" are not a mere delineation of a benevolent Hercules, but embody an arrangement of incidents and literary expressions original with the author, they are proper subjects of copyright and susceptible of infringement because of the monopoly afforded by the act. Since the complainant is not entitled to a monopoly of the mere character of a "Superman" who is a blessing to mankind (Nichols v. Universal Pictures Corp., 2 Cir., 45 F.2d 119), we think the language of clause 4(c) of the decree somewhat too sweeping. It should be modified so as to read as follows: "(c) From printing, publishing, offering for sale or selling, or in any way distributing any cartoon or cartoons, or any periodical or book portraying any of the feats of strength or powers performed by 'Superman' or closely imitating his costume or appearance in any feat whatever."[j] * * *

The decree modified as provided in this opinion is affirmed, but without costs or any allowance for counsel fees upon this appeal.

NOTES AND QUESTIONS ON CARTOON CHARACTERS

(1) Is the language of the decree, as modified, consistent with the rest of the opinion? What change, if any, was accomplished by the modification? Do the visual similarities between "Superman" and "Wonderman" as described by the court seem sufficient in themselves to constitute infringement under the rationale of the "Spark Plug" case? Was there an appropriation of other protected "expression"?

(2) In a later "Superman" case, the adversary was "Captain Marvel." National Comics Pub., Inc. v. Fawcett Pub., Inc., 191 F.2d 594 (2d Cir.1951). Judge L. Hand, in an opinion chiefly about problems of copyright notice, said that in the *Detective Comics* case "we limited the copyright to the specific exploits of 'Superman' as each picture portrayed them." In a per curiam response to a Petition to Clarify Opinion," 198 F.2d 927 (1952), the court further explained:

> [W]e did not find which of the strips, which the plaintiff put in suit "Fawcett" had infringed: i.e., copied so closely as to be actionable under Detective Comics v. Bruns Publications, 2 Cir., 111 F.2d 432. That will demand a comparison of each strip put in suit by the plaintiff with "Fawcett's" strip, which the plaintiff asserts does so closely copy that particular strip. Each such comparison really involves the decision of a separate claim; there is no escape from it. The plaintiff may put in suit as many strips as it pleases, but it must prove infringement of each, or it will lose as to that strip.

Is the requirement of a "strip-by-strip" analysis consistent with the decision in *Detective Comics*?

(3) In Atari v. North American Philips Consumer Electronics Corp., 672 F.2d 607 (7th Cir.), cert. denied, 459 U.S. 880 (1982), Judge Wood directed the entry of a preliminary injunction against an infringement of the audiovisual display of the plaintiff's PAC–MAN video game, based on the defendant's "substantial

---

[j]　The paragraph before modification read as follows: "(c) From printing, publishing, offering for sale or selling, or in any way distributing any cartoon or cartoons, or any periodical, book, magazine or other publication containing any cartoon or cartoons, portraying the figure of or embodiment of plaintiff's cartoon character Superman as set forth in plaintiff's copyrighted works (plaintiff's exhibits 12 to 22 inclusive in evidence herein) or any figure which is a copy or imitation thereof." Record on Appeal, p. 180.

appropriation of the PAC–MAN characters * * *. The expression of the central figure as a 'gobbler' and the pursuit figures as 'ghost monsters' distinguishes PAC–MAN from conceptually similar video games. * * * Those characters are wholly fanciful creations, without reference to the real world."

(4) The right to control the exploitation of a character beyond its original medium as recognized in the "Spark Plug" case can be extraordinarily valuable. Marvel Comics, purchased in 2009 by Disney for over $4 billion, earns the vast majority of its income from film and merchandising licenses for its comic book characters like Spider-Man, Iron Man, Captain America, and X-Men. Although now over 80 years old, Mickey Mouse and his Disney companions, together with Winnie the Pooh and friends (also controlled by Disney), still gross billions of dollars annually.

Sid & Marty Krofft Television Productions, Inc. v. McDonald's Corp.

United States Court of Appeals, Ninth Circuit, 1977.
562 F.2d 1157.

■ Before CARTER, GOODWIN, and SNEED, CIRCUIT JUDGES.

■ JAMES M. CARTER, CIRCUIT JUDGE:

This is a copyright infringement action. Plaintiffs Sid and Marty Krofft Television Productions, Inc., and Sid and Marty Krofft Productions, Inc. were awarded $50,000.00 in their action against defendants McDonald's Corporation and Needham, Harper & Steers, Inc. Defendants were found to have infringed plaintiffs' "H.R. Pufnstuf" children's television show by the production of their "McDonaldland" television commercials. * * *

Facts

In 1968, Sid and Marty Krofft were approached by the NBC television network to create a children's television program for exhibition on Saturday morning. The Kroffts spent the next year creating the H.R. Pufnstuf television show, which was introduced on NBC in September 1969. The series included several fanciful costumed characters, as well as a boy named Jimmy, who lived in a fantasyland called "Living Island," which was inhabited by moving trees and talking books. The television series became extremely popular and generated a line of H.R. Pufnstuf products and endorsements.

In early 1970, Marty Krofft, the President of both Krofft Television and Krofft Productions and producer of the show, was contacted by an executive from Needham, Harper & Steers, Inc., an advertising agency. He was told that Needham was attempting to get the advertising account of McDonald's hamburger restaurant chain and wanted to base a proposed campaign to McDonald's on the H.R. Pufnstuf characters. The executive wanted to know whether the Kroffts would be interested in working with Needham on a project of this type.

Needham and the Kroffts were in contact by telephone six or seven more times. By a letter dated August 31, 1970, Needham stated it was going forward with the idea of a McDonaldland advertising campaign based on the H.R. Pufnstuf series. It acknowledged the need to pay the Kroffts a fee for preparing artistic designs and engineering plans. Shortly thereafter, Marty Krofft telephoned Needham only to be told that the advertising campaign had been cancelled.

In fact, Needham had already been awarded McDonald's advertising account and was proceeding with the McDonaldland project. Former employees of the Kroffts were hired to design and construct the costumes and sets for McDonaldland. Needham also hired the same voice expert who supplied all of the voices for the Pufnstuf characters to supply some of the voices for the McDonaldland characters. In January 1971, the first of the McDonaldland commercials was broadcast on network television. They continue to be broadcast.

Prior to the advent of the McDonaldland advertising campaign, plaintiffs had licensed the use of the H.R. Pufnstuf characters and elements to the manufacturers of toys, games, lunch boxes, and comic books. In addition, the H.R. Pufnstuf characters were featured in Kellogg's cereal commercials and used by the Ice Capades. After the McDonaldland campaign, which included the distribution of toys and games, plaintiffs were unable to obtain new licensing arrangements or extend existing ones.[3] In the case of the Ice Capades, the H.R. Pufnstuf characters were actually replaced by the McDonaldland characters. * * *

[A jury, after a three-week trial, returned a verdict in favor of the plaintiffs.]

Proof of Infringement

It has often been said that in order to establish copyright infringement a plaintiff must prove ownership of the copyright and "copying" by the defendant. See, e.g., Reyher v. Children's Television Workshop, 533 F.2d 87, 90 (2 Cir.1976); Universal Athletic Sales Co. v. Salkeld, 511 F.2d 904, 907 (3 Cir.1975); 2 M. Nimmer on Copyright § 141 at 610–11 (1976) (hereinafter "Nimmer"). "Copying," in turn, is said to be shown by circumstantial evidence of access to the copyrighted work and substantial similarity between the copyrighted work and defendant's work. Reyher v. Children's Television Workshop, supra, 533 F.2d at 90; 2 Nimmer § 141.2 at 613. But an analysis of the cases suggests that these statements frequently serve merely as boilerplate to copyright opinions.

Under such statements, infringement would be established upon proof of ownership, access, and substantial similarity. Application of this rule, however, would produce some untenable results. For example, a copyright could be obtained over a cheaply manufactured plaster statue of a nude. Since ownership of a copyright is established, subsequent manufacturers of statues of nudes would face the grave risk of being found to be infringers if their statues were substantially similar and access were shown. The burden of proof on the plaintiff would be minimal, since most statues of nudes would in all probability be substantially similar to the cheaply manufactured plaster one.

Clearly the scope of copyright protection does not go this far. A limiting principle is needed. This is provided by the classic distinction between an "idea" and the "expression" of that idea. It is an axiom of copyright law that the protection granted to a copyrighted work extends only to the particular expression of the idea and never to the idea itself. Mazer v. Stein, 347 U.S. 201, 217–18 (1954); Baker v. Selden, 101 U.S. 99, 102–03 (1879). This principle attempts to reconcile two competing social interests: reward-

---

[3]   The evidence reveals that certain persons with whom plaintiffs dealt for licensing believed that the H.R. Pufnstuf characters were being licensed to McDonald's for use in their McDonaldland campaign. Accordingly, they did not pursue licensing arrangements for the characters themselves.

ing an individual's creativity and effort while at the same time permitting the nation to enjoy the benefits and progress from use of the same subject matter.

The real task in a copyright infringement action, then, is to determine whether there has been copying of the expression of an idea rather than just the idea itself. "[N]o one infringes, unless he descends so far into what is concrete [in a work] as to invade . . . [its] expression." National Comics Publications v. Fawcett Publications, 191 F.2d 594, 600 (2 Cir.1951). Only this expression may be protected and only it may be infringed.

[margin handwriting: infringement is copying of the idea or the expression; infringe when invading expression]

The difficulty comes in attempting to distill the unprotected idea from the protected expression. No court or commentator in making this search has been able to improve upon Judge Learned Hand's famous "abstractions test" articulated in Nichols v. Universal Pictures Corporation, * * *. See also Chafee, Reflections on the Law of Copyright, 45 Colum.L.Rev. 503 (1945) * * *.

The test for infringement therefore has been given a new dimension. There must be ownership of the copyright and access to the copyrighted work. But there also must be substantial similarity not only of the general ideas but of the expressions of those ideas as well. Thus two steps in the analytic process are implied by the requirement of substantial similarity.

The determination of whether there is substantial similarity in ideas may often be a simple one. Returning to the example of the nude statue, the idea there embodied is a simple one—a plaster recreation of a nude human figure. A statue of a horse or a painting of a nude would not embody this idea and therefore could not infringe. The test for similarity of ideas is still a factual one, to be decided by the trier of fact. See International Luggage Registry v. Avery Products Corp., 541 F.2d 830, 831 (9 Cir.1976); Williams v. Kaag Manufacturers, Inc., 338 F.2d 949, 951 (9 Cir.1964).

[margin handwriting: Substantial similarity decided by trier of fact]

We shall call this the "extrinsic test." It is extrinsic because it depends not on the responses of the trier of fact, but on specific criteria which can be listed and analyzed. Such criteria include the type of artwork involved, the materials used, the subject matter, and the setting for the subject. Since it is an extrinsic test, analytic dissection and expert testimony are appropriate. Moreover, this question may often be decided as a matter of law.

[margin handwriting: extrinsic test; criteria]

The determination of when there is substantial similarity between the forms of expression is necessarily more subtle and complex. As Judge Hand candidly observed, "Obviously, no principle can be stated as to when an imitator has gone beyond copying the 'idea,' and has borrowed its 'expression.' Decisions must therefore inevitably be ad hoc." Peter Pan Fabrics, Inc. v. Martin Weiner Corp., 274 F.2d 487, 489 (2 Cir.1960). If there is substantial similarity in ideas, then the trier of fact must decide whether there is substantial similarity in the expressions of the ideas so as to constitute infringement.

The test to be applied in determining whether there is substantial similarity in expressions shall be labeled an intrinsic one—depending on the response of the ordinary reasonable person. See International Luggage Registry v. Avery Products Corp., supra, 541 F.2d at 831; Harold Lloyd Corp. v. Witwer, 65 F.2d 1, 18–19 (9 Cir.1933). See generally Nimmer § 143.5. It is intrinsic because it does not depend on the type of external criteria and analysis which marks the extrinsic test. As this court stated in Twentieth Century–Fox Film Corp. v. Stonesifer, 140 F.2d 579, 582 (9 Cir.1944):

[margin handwriting: intrinsic test depends on response of ordinary reasonable person]

"The two works involved in this appeal should be considered and tested, not hypercritically or with meticulous scrutiny, but by the observations and impressions of the average reasonable reader and spectator."

Because this is an intrinsic test, analytic dissection and expert testimony are not appropriate.

This same type of bifurcated test was announced in Arnstein v. Porter, [p. 194 supra]. * * *

We believe that the court in *Arnstein* was alluding to the idea-expression dichotomy which we make explicit today. When the court in *Arnstein* refers to "copying" which is not itself an infringement, it must be suggesting copying merely of the work's idea, which is not protected by the copyright. To constitute an infringement, the copying must reach the point of "unlawful appropriation," or the copying of the protected expression itself. We analyze this distinction in terms both of the elements involved—idea and expression—and of the tests to be used—extrinsic and intrinsic—in an effort to clarify the issues involved.

The Tests Applied

In the context of this case, the distinction between these tests is important. Defendants do not dispute the fact that they copied the idea of plaintiffs' Pufnstuf television series—basically a fantasyland filled with diverse and fanciful characters in action. They argue, however, that the expressions of this idea are too dissimilar for there to be an infringement. They come to this conclusion by dissecting the constituent parts of the Pufnstuf series—characters, setting, and plot—and pointing out the dissimilarities between these parts and those of the McDonaldland commercials.

This approach ignores the idea-expression dichotomy alluded to in *Arnstein* and analyzed today. Defendants attempt to apply an extrinsic test by the listing of dissimilarities in determining whether the expression they used was substantially similar to the expression used by plaintiffs. That extrinsic test is inappropriate; an intrinsic test must here be used. * * *

The present case demands an even more intrinsic determination because both plaintiffs' and defendants' works are directed to an audience of children. This raises the particular factual issue of the impact of the respective works upon the minds and imaginations of young people. * * *

Defendants would have this court ignore that intrinsic quality which they recognized to embark on an extrinsic analysis of the two works. For example, in discussing the principal characters—Pufnstuf and Mayor McCheese—defendants point out:

" 'Pufnstuf' wears what can only be described as a yellow and green dragon suit with a blue cummerband from which hangs a medal which says 'mayor'. 'McCheese' wears a version of pink formal dress—'tails'—with knicker trousers. He has a typical diplomat's sash on which is written 'mayor', the 'M' consisting of the McDonald's trademark of an 'M' made of golden arches."

So not only do defendants remove the characters from the setting, but dissect further to analyze the clothing, colors, features, and mannerisms of each character. We do not believe that the ordinary reasonable person, let alone a child, viewing these works will even notice that Pufnstuf is wearing a cummerbund while Mayor McCheese is wearing a diplomat's sash. * * *

We have viewed representative samples of both the H.R. Pufnstuf show and McDonaldland commercials. It is clear to us that defendants' works are substantially similar to plaintiffs'.[9] They have captured the "total concept and feel" of the Pufnstuf show. Roth Greeting Cards v. United Card Co., 429 F.2d 1106, 1110 (9 Cir.1970). We would so conclude even if we were sitting as the triers of fact. There is no doubt that the findings of the jury in this case are not clearly erroneous. * * *

Δ's work sub. similar

Access

In addition to substantial similarity, a plaintiff must show access in order to prove infringement. * * *

In this case, representatives of Needham actually visited the Kroffts' headquarters in Los Angeles to discuss the engineering and design work necessary to produce the McDonaldland commercials. They did this after they had been awarded the contract by McDonald's and apparently with no intention to work with the Kroffts. We believe that this degree of access justifies a lower standard of proof to show substantial similarity. Since the subjective test applies, it is impossible to quantify this standard. But there is no question it is met here. * * *

Conclusion

The judgment of the district court finding infringement is affirmed. The McDonald commercials are based on the same ideas as the H.R. Pufnstuf series. The expression of that idea is sufficiently similar so that a jury applying an intrinsic test could find infringement. This is especially true here since there was strong evidence of access. * * *

[On remand, the trial court awarded over $1 million in statutory damages. 221 U.S.P.Q. 114 (C.D.Cal.1983).]

Shaw v. Lindheim

919 F.2d 1353 (9th Cir.1990).

Shaw, a well-known television writer and producer, developed a pilot script for a television series entitled "The Equalizer" under a contract with Lindheim, a programming executive at NBC. NBC declined to produce the show, and Lindheim subsequently took a position at Universal Television. Lindheim later wrote a series treatment, also called "The Equalizer," that became the pilot for a CBS series of that name. Shaw claimed that both the pilot and series infringed the copyright in his original script. The district court, holding as a matter of law that there was no substantial similarity of expression, granted summary judgment to the defendants. The summary

DCH for Δ no sub. sim

---

[9] Even a dissection of the two works reveals their similarities. The "Living Island" locale of Pufnstuf and "McDonaldland" are both imaginary worlds inhabited by anthromorphic plants and animals and other fanciful creatures. The dominant topographical features of the locales are the same: trees, caves, a pond, a road, and a castle. Both works feature a forest with talking trees that have human faces and characteristics.

The characters are also similar. Both lands are governed by mayors who have disproportionately large round heads dominated by long wide mouths. They are assisted by "Keystone cop" characters. Both lands feature strikingly similar crazy scientists and a multi-armed evil creature.

It seems clear that such similarities go beyond merely that of the idea into the area of expression. The use of the basic idea of the works does not inevitably result in such similarities. Certainly a jury applying an intrinsic test could find such similarities of expression substantial.

judgment was reversed on appeal in an opinion by Judge Alarcon that reinterpreted the Ninth Circuit's infringement analysis in *Krofft*.

"*Krofft* defined the extrinsic test as a 'test for similarity of ideas' under which 'analytic dissection and expert testimony are appropriate.' 562 F.2d at 1164. The intrinsic test, according to *Krofft,* should measure 'substantial similarity in expressions . . . depending on the response of the ordinary reasonable person . . . . [I]t does not depend on the type of external criteria and analysis which marks the extrinsic test.' Id. In decisions under the intrinsic test, 'analytic dissection and expert testimony are not appropriate.' Id.

"Relying on this language, panels applying *Krofft* to literary works have included a lengthy list of concrete elements under the extrinsic test. Whereas *Krofft* listed 'the type of artwork involved, the materials used, the subject matter, and the setting for the subject' as criteria for consideration under the extrinsic test, id., a series of opinions beginning with the district court opinion in Jason v. Fonda, 526 F.Supp. 774 (C.D.Cal.1981), aff'd and incorporated by reference, 698 F.2d 966 (9th Cir.1982), have listed 'plot, themes, dialogue, mood, setting, pace, and sequence' as extrinsic test criteria. 526 F.Supp. at 777; see also * * * [Narell v. Freeman, 872 F.2d 907, 912 (9th Cir.1989)] (adding 'characters' to the list and transforming 'sequence' into 'sequence of events').

"Now that it includes virtually every element that may be considered concrete in a literary work, the extrinsic test as applied to books, scripts, plays, and motion pictures can no longer be seen as a test for mere similarity of ideas. Because the criteria incorporated into the extrinsic test encompass all objective manifestations of creativity, the two tests are more sensibly described as objective and subjective analyses of *expression,* having strayed from *Krofft's* division between expression and ideas. * * * Indeed, a judicial determination under the intrinsic test is now virtually devoid of analysis, for the intrinsic test has become a mere subjective judgment as to whether two literary works are or are not similar. * * *

"We must determine in this matter whether a party that demonstrates a triable issue of fact under the extrinsic test has made a sufficient showing of substantial similarity to defeat a summary judgment motion. As noted above, the extrinsic test focuses on 'specific similarities between the plot, theme, dialogue, mood, setting, pace, characters, and sequence of events . . . . "The actual concrete elements that make up the total sequence of events and the relationships between the major characters." ' *Narell,* 872 F.2d at 912 (quoting [Berkic v. Crichton, 761 F.2d 1289, 1294 (9th Cir.), cert. denied, 474 U.S. 826 (1985)]). These are the measurable, objective elements that constitute a literary work's expression. Because these elements are embodied in the extrinsic test, we hold that it is improper for a court to find, as the district court did, that there is no substantial similarity as a matter of law after a writer has satisfied the extrinsic test. To conclude otherwise would allow a court to base a grant of summary judgment on a purely subjective determination of similarity. * * *

" * * * Once a court has established that a triable question of objective similarity of expression exists, by analysis of each element of the extrinsic test, its inquiry should proceed no further. What remains is a subjective assessment of the 'concept and feel' of two works of literature—a task no more suitable for a judge than for a jury."

Judge Alarcon, acknowledging that titles are not themselves eligible for copyright (see p. 685 infra), held that the defendants' admitted copying

Titles aren't copyrightable [handwritten margin note]

of Shaw's title was nevertheless relevant in determining whether there was substantial similarity of protected expression. The court found similarities in the theme and plot of the works and concluded the comparison with an analysis of the respective characters.

"As the district court noted, both the dialogue and the characters in the respective works share some striking similarities. A particularly glaring example of similar personal traits is revealed by a comparison of the principal characters in both works. As the district court found, both scripts have 'similar lead characters . . . . Both leads are well dressed, wealthy and have expensive tastes. The most striking similarity is their self-assuredness, and unshakeable faith in the satisfactory outcome of any difficult situation.' Although James Bond may have the Equalizers' demeanor and the Ghostbusters may have their penchant for unpopular assignments, the totality of the similarities between the two characters goes beyond the necessities of the 'Equalizer' theme and belies any claim of literary accident. We find that defendants' copying of the Equalizer character and other characters extends to elements of protected expression. Because the similarities between the principals in each script and among the other common characters point to copying of more than a general theme or plot idea, they support the district court's finding that Shaw raised a triable issue of fact regarding substantial similarity under the extrinsic test. * * *

"We conclude that Shaw has satisfied the extrinsic test for literary works and thus has presented a triable issue of fact regarding substantial similarity of protected expression."

NOTES AND QUESTIONS

(1) Is the two-step, "extrinsic"/"intrinsic" approach announced in *Krofft* the same as the "copying"/"improper appropriation" approach pursued in Arnstein v. Porter?[k] Or is the two-step process simply a way to keep cases where there is clearly no infringement away from the jury? The Ninth Circuit's mode of analysis in *Krofft* is criticized in A. Cohen, Masking Copyright Decisionmaking: The Meaninglessness of Substantial Similarity, 20 U.C. Davis L.Rev. 719 (1987).

(2) The "extrinsic"/"intrinsic" formulation was further elaborated by the Ninth Circuit in Swirsky v. Carey, 376 F.3d 841 (9th Cir.2004), which reversed a summary judgment awarded to defendant singer/composer Mariah Carey. The trial court had held that the plaintiffs failed to establish that their song and Carey's "Thank God I Found You" were substantially similar under the "extrinsic" test. Judge Canby, writing for the Court of Appeals, explained the "extrinsic" test this way:

"The extrinsic test considers whether two works share a similarity of ideas and expression as measured by external, objective criteria. * * * The extrinsic test requires 'analytic dissection of a work and expert testimony.' [Three Boys Music v. Bolton], 212 F.3d at 485. 'Analytic dissection' requires breaking the works 'down into their constituent elements and comparing those elements for proof of copying as measured by "substantial similarity." ' Rice v. Fox Broad. Co., 148 F.Supp.2d 1029, 1051 (C.D.Cal.2001), reversed on other grounds, 330 F.3d 1170 (9th Cir.2003). Because the requirement is one of substantial simi-

---

[k] In footnote 7 of his opinion in *Krofft*, Judge Carter wrote: " * * * We do not resurrect the *Arnstein* approach today. Rather, we formulate an extrinsic-intrinsic test for infringement based on the idea-expression dichotomy. We believe that the *Arnstein* court was doing nearly the same thing. But the fact that it may not have been does not subtract from our analysis."

larity to *protected* elements of the copyrighted work, it is essential to distinguish between the protected and unprotected material in a plaintiff's work."

Judge Canby acknowledged the difficulty of applying the "extrinsic" test to works like music or art that lack "distinct elements of idea and expression." Nevertheless, "[t]he extrinsic test does serve the purpose of permitting summary judgment in clear cases of non-infringement, and it informs the factfinder of some of the complexities of the medium in issue while guiding attention toward protected elements and away from unprotected elements of a composition."

Walt Disney Productions v. Air Pirates

581 F.2d 751 (9th Cir.1978), cert. denied, 439 U.S. 1132 (1979).

"This case involves the admitted copying of plaintiff Walt Disney Productions' ('Disney') cartoon characters in defendants' adult 'counter-culture' comic books. The present defendants are three individuals and two business entities operated by them. The complaint alleges that they infringed Disney copyrights, a Disney trademark and engaged in unfair competition, trade disparagement and interference with Disney's business. Disney sought injunctive relief, destruction of infringing materials, damages, costs and attorney's fees. * * *

"The individual defendants have participated in preparing and publishing two magazines of cartoons entitled 'Air Pirates Funnies.' The characters in defendants' magazines bear a marked similarity to those of plaintiff. The names given to defendants' characters are the same names used in plaintiff's copyrighted work. However, the themes of defendants' publications differ markedly from those of Disney. While Disney sought only to foster 'an image of innocent delightfulness,' defendants supposedly sought to convey an allegorical message of significance. Put politely by one commentator, the 'Air Pirates' was 'an "underground" comic book which had placed several well-known Disney cartoon characters in incongruous settings where they engaged in activities clearly antithetical to the accepted Mickey Mouse world of scrubbed faces, bright smiles and happy endings.' It centered around 'a rather bawdy depiction of the Disney characters as active members of a free thinking, promiscuous, drug ingesting counterculture.' Note, Parody, Copyrights and the First Amendment, 10 U.S.F.L.Rev. 564, 571, 582 (1976)."

The defendants argued that "characters are never copyrightable and therefore cannot in any way constitute a copyrightable component part. That argument flies in the face of a series of cases dating back to 1914 that have held comic strip characters protectable under the old Copyright Act." * * *

"It is true that this Court's opinion in Warner Brothers Pictures v. Columbia Broadcasting System, 216 F.2d 945 (9th Cir.1954), certiorari denied, 348 U.S. 971, lends some support to the position that characters ordinarily are not copyrightable. There the mystery writer Dashiell Hammett and his publisher entered into a 1930 contract with Warner Brothers giving the movie production company copyright and various other rights to a 'certain story * * * entitled Maltese Falcon' involving the fictional detective Sam Spade. In 1946, Hammett and other defendants used the Maltese Falcon characters in other writings, causing Warner Brothers to sue for copyright infringement and 'unfair use and competition.' After pointing out the sophisticated nature of the plaintiff, we construed the contracts between the parties and held:

> 'We are of the opinion that since the use of characters and character names are nowhere specifically mentioned in the agreements [including the assignment of copyright instrument], but that other items, including the title, "The Maltese Falcon", and their use are specifically mentioned as being granted [to Warner Brothers], that the character rights with the names cannot be held to be within the grants, and that under the doctrine of *ejusdem generis,* general language cannot be held to include them.' (Footnote omitted.)

"After so holding, Judge Stephens' opinion considered 'whether it was ever intended by the copyright statute that characters with their names should be under its protection.' In that context he concluded that such a restriction on Hammett's future use of a character was unreasonable, at least when the characters were merely vehicles for the story and did not 'really constitute' the story being told. Judge Stephens' reasons for that conclusion provide an important indication of the applicability of that conclusion to comic book characters as opposed to literary characters. In reasoning that characters 'are always limited and always fall into limited patterns,' Judge Stephens recognized that it is difficult to delineate distinctively a literary character. Cf. Nichols v. Universal Pictures Corp., 45 F.2d 119 (2d Cir.1930), certiorari denied, 282 U.S. 902. When the author can add a visual image, however, the difficulty is reduced. See generally 1 Nimmer on Copyright § 30. Put another way, while many literary characters may embody little more than an unprotected idea (see Sid & Marty Krofft Television v. McDonald's Corp., 562 F.2d 1157 (9th Cir.1977)), a comic book character, which has physical as well as conceptual qualities, is more likely to contain some unique elements of expression. Because comic book characters therefore are distinguishable from literary characters, the *Warner Brothers* language does not preclude protection of Disney's characters."

The court rejected a defense of parody as fair use. "By copying the images in their entirety, the defendants took more than was necessary to place firmly in the reader's mind the parodied work and those specific attributes that are to be satirized." It also rejected a first amendment defense. Disney's summary judgment on its copyright claim was affirmed, but summary judgment on trademark and unfair competition counts was reversed in the absence of an uncontested showing that purchasers were likely to be confused as to the source of the defendants' comics, which the court thought unlikely.

NOTES AND QUESTIONS ON LITERARY CHARACTERS

(1) Warner Brothers v. CBS—the "Sam Spade" case discussed in *Air Pirates*—had erected a virtually insurmountable obstacle to copyright in literary characters. (Note the peculiar alignment of interests in that case, with Dashiell ~~The Thin Man~~ Hammett, the author, arguing that his character was *not* copyrightable.) Compare Judge Hand's dictum on literary characters in *Nichols,* p. 171 supra.

The Ninth Circuit returned to literary characters, and to the "Sam Spade" case, in Olson v. NBC, Inc., 855 F.2d 1446 (9th Cir.1988). The court affirmed a judgment in favor of defendant NBC against allegations that its television series "The A–Team" infringed the characters in the plaintiff's screenplay. The court said that the standard in the "Sam Spade" case was "arguably dicta," but found that the plaintiff could not prevail even under a more lenient test of copyrightability. Referring to Judge Hand's formulation in *Nichols,* the court said that the plaintiff's characters were neither Malvolio nor Sir Toby Belch (nor Mickey Mouse or Superman, distinguishing the graphic character cases). The Ninth Circuit's subsequent decision in Shaw v. Lindheim confirmed its acceptance of literary characters as copyrightable subject matter.

(2) Protection for literary characters was recognized in Filmvideo Releasing Corp. v. Hastings, 509 F.Supp. 60 (S.D.N.Y.), aff'd on other grounds, 668 F.2d 91 (2d Cir.1981). Judge Werker enjoined the performance of twenty-three motion pictures based on Clarence Mulford's "Hopalong Cassidy" books. (The films, made under license from the author, had entered the public domain because the copyrights had not been renewed; the books, however, were still under copyright.) "In my opinion, these characters [Hopalong, Windy, Johnny, and Lucky] and others were sufficiently delineated, developed and well known to the public to be copyrightable. The use of these characters for the purposes intended by Filmvideo therefore would constitute infringement * * * irrespective and independent of the similarity of the story line."

The character of "Tarzan" was held copyrightable in a district court decision dealing with the termination of a license, but in affirming, the Second Circuit thought it unnecessary to express a view on "the venerable question as to whether and in what circumstances an author's creation of a fictional character can be protected by copyright." Burroughs v. Metro–Goldwyn–Mayer, 519 F.Supp. 388 (S.D.N.Y.1981), aff'd, 683 F.2d 610 (2d Cir.1982). The Second Circuit did eventually confirm the copyrightability of literary characters when the issue again reached the court in Silverman v. CBS Inc., 870 F.2d 40 (2d Cir.), cert. denied, 492 U.S. 907 (1989). The plaintiff sought a declaration that the characters from the "Amos 'n Andy" radio programs broadcast between 1928 and 1948 were now in the public domain; he wanted to use the characters in a musical comedy. Judge Newman said that the characters "were sufficiently delineated in the pre–1948 radio programs to have been placed in the public domain when the scripts entered the public domain." (Is a finding of sufficient delineation necessary to this aspect of the holding?) He also said, however, that plaintiff could not use "any further delineation of the characters contained in the post–1948 radio scripts and the television scripts and programs" if CBS could establish valid copyrights in those programs.

(3) Sherlock Holmes was first introduced to readers by Arthur Conan Doyle in *A Study in Scarlet*, published in 1887. Doyle's final Holmes story, *The Adventure of Shoscombe Old Place*, was published in the United States in 1927. Is it possible that some or even all uses of the Sherlock Holmes character might still constitute copyright infringement? For some of the complicated history of rights in the world's most famous detective, see Schuessler, Suit Says Sherlock Belongs to the Ages, N.Y. Times, March 7, 2013, p. C1. In Warner Bros. Entertainment, Inc. v. X One X Productions, 644 F.3d 584 (8th Cir.2011), the court held that the defendant could use depictions of characters from *The Wizard of Oz* and *Gone with the Wind* taken from motion picture publicity materials that had been published without copyright notice, but it could not combine or manipulate the images in ways that captured expressive aspects of the characters from the subsequent copyrighted films.

(4) In the Silverman v. CBS case described in Note (2), Judge Newman also held that CBS had abandoned any trademark rights in the "Amos 'n Andy" name. (See p. 707 infra.) Names cannot be copyrighted. See 37 C.F.R. § 202.1(a) (quoted at p. 55 supra). Can the use of an identical name for a character in a subsequent work nevertheless contribute to a finding of substantial similarity? Will it not conjure up the attributes of the named character as delineated in the original work? Is that "copying"?

An argument against copyright protection for literary characters is mounted in F. Nevins, Copyright + Character = Catastrophe, 39 J.Copyr. Soc'y 303 (1992). D. Karjala, Harry Potter, Tanya Grotter, and the Copyright Derivative Work, 38 Ariz.St.L.J. 17 (2006), concludes that the creators of fictional characters have too much control over subsequent variations, especially when the use extends to other cultures.

Warner Brothers, Inc. v. American Broadcasting Companies, Inc.

United States Court of Appeals, Second Circuit, 1983.
720 F.2d 231.

■ Before MANSFIELD, MESKILL, and NEWMAN, CIRCUIT JUDGES.

■ NEWMAN, CIRCUIT JUDGE:

The primary issue raised by this appeal is whether as a matter of law the fictional character Ralph Hinkley, the principal figure in a television series, "The Greatest American Hero," is not sufficiently similar to the fictional character Superman, the hero of comic books, television, and more recently films, so that claims of copyright infringement and unfair competition may be dismissed without consideration by a jury. * * *

I.

Many of the significant facts are set out in our prior opinion affirming the denial of plaintiffs' motion for a preliminary injunction. Warner Bros. Inc. v. American Broadcasting Companies, Inc., 654 F.2d 204 (2d Cir.1981). Plaintiffs own the copyrights in various works embodying the character Superman and have thereby acquired copyright protection for the character itself. See Detective Comics, Inc. v. Bruns Publications, Inc., 111 F.2d 432 (2d Cir.1940). Since the creation of Superman in 1938, plaintiffs have exploited their rights with great success, portraying Superman in several media and licensing the character for a variety of merchandising purposes. Through plaintiffs' efforts, Superman has attained an extremely high degree of exposure and recognition.

In 1978, building on previous Superman works, plaintiff Warner Bros., Inc. released a motion picture entitled "Superman, The Movie" (*Superman I*) and more recently two sequels. * * *

The substantial commercial success of *Superman I* and the attendant publicity prompted many requests for licenses permitting use of the Superman character in connection with the merchandising of toys, greeting cards, apparel, and other products. It also led ABC to seek a license for production of a television series about "Superboy" based on the early adventures of Superman. Plaintiffs, who were planning to make their own sequels and derivative works, refused ABC permission to proceed with its proposed project.

Unable to obtain this license, ABC assigned to Cannell, the principal of the third-party defendant production company, the task of creating a "pilot" program for a TV series involving a superhero. Cannell produced a program, and subsequently a weekly series, entitled "The Greatest American Hero" (*Hero*), which he described as being about "what happens when you [the average person] become Superman." *Hero's* protagonist, Ralph Hinkley, was given attributes intended to identify him as an "ordinary guy." Hinkley is portrayed as a young high school teacher attempting to cope with a recent divorce, a dispute over the custody of his son, and the strain that his domestic problems place upon his work and his relationship with his girlfriend. Although Hinkley is attractive, his physical appearance is not imposing: he is of medium height with a slight build and curly, somewhat unkempt, blond hair. * * *

* * * Hinkley as a superhero is not an unqualified success. He uses his superpowers awkwardly and fearfully. When flying, Hinkley shouts with fright and makes crash-landings, sometimes crumpling in a heap or skidding nearly out of control to a stop. Though protected from bullets by his costume, Hinkley cringes and cowers when shot at by villains. * * *

The *Hero* series contains several visual effects and lines that inevitably call Superman to mind, sometimes by way of brief imitation, sometimes by mention of Superman or another character from the Superman works, and sometimes by humorous parodying or ironic twisting of well-known Superman phrases. Hinkley's suit invests him with most of Superman's powers, and the suit, like Superman's, is a tight-fitting leotard with a chest insignia and a cape. Their outfits differ in that Superman wears a blue leotard with red briefs, boots, and cape, while Hinkley's costume is a red leotard with a tunic top, no boots, and a black cape. In one scene, as Hinkley is running at super speed, smoke emerges from his footsteps, and the sound of a locomotive is heard. A similar scene occurs in *Superman I,* though even without seeing the movie it would be difficult not to be reminded by the *Hero* scene of Superman, who is regularly described as "more powerful than a locomotive." When Hinkley first views himself in a mirror holding his costume in front of him, he says, "It's a bird . . . it's a plane . . . it's Ralph Hinkley." The youngster, Jerry, watching Hinkley's unsuccessful first effort to fly, tells him, "Superman wouldn't do it that way." In a scene with his girlfriend, who is aware of the powers that come with the magic costume, Hinkley says, "Look at it this way . . . you're already one step up on Lois Lane. She never found out who Clark Kent really was." * * *

Prior to the start of the trial the District Judge, apparently harboring doubts as to the need for a trial, conducted an extended pretrial conference, lasting two weeks, to afford an opportunity to review the evidence to be offered by the plaintiffs. In the course of the pretrial conference, Chief Judge Motley ruled that the responses to an audience survey commissioned by the plaintiffs were inadmissible, "because they were too general to be of any benefit to the jury with respect to . . . the copyright claim."[4] The District Judge also excluded all expert testimony on the copyright claim, including testimony, sought to be introduced by plaintiffs, offered to show the inabil-

---

[4]   The survey asked the following three questions:

(1) Was there anything about the character Ralph Hinkley that reminded you of any other character you had seen before?

(2) Did any scenes from that TV movie [*Hero*] remind you of scenes from any other TV programs or movies in theatres or on TV?

(3) Aside from the actors, do you think that the people who wrote or made this movie were responsible for any other TV programs or movies in theatres or on TV?

ity of young children to perceive the differences between Hinkley and Superman. * * *

* * * On December 16, 1981, the District Judge concluded that no reasonable jury could find that the parties' works were substantially similar and granted summary judgment to defendants on the entire copyright claim. * * *

II.

The basic issues concerning the copyright infringement claim are whether the *Hero* and *Superman* works are substantially similar so as to support an inference of copying and whether the lack of substantial similarity is so clear as to fall outside the range of reasonably disputed fact questions requiring resolution by a jury. The similarity to be assessed must concern the expression of ideas, not the ideas themselves, Reyher v. Children's Television Workshop, 533 F.2d 87, 90–91 (2d Cir.), cert. denied, 429 U.S. 980 (1976); Nichols v. Universal Pictures Corp., 45 F.2d 119, 121 (2d Cir.1930), cert. denied, 282 U.S. 902 (1931), a distinction easier to assert than to apply, see Peter Pan Fabrics, Inc. v. Martin Weiner Corp., 274 F.2d 487, 489 (2d Cir.1960) (decisions "inevitably . . . ad hoc"). Though the issue of substantial similarity is frequently a fact issue for jury resolution, see Twentieth Century–Fox Film Corp. v. MCA, Inc., 715 F.2d 1327 (9th Cir.1983); Hoehling v. Universal City Studios, Inc., 618 F.2d 972, 977 (2d Cir.), cert. denied, 449 U.S. 841 (1980), we have recognized that a court may determine non-infringement as a matter of law on a motion for summary judgment, either because the similarity between two works concerns only "*non*-copyrightable elements of the plaintiff's work," id., or because no reasonable jury, properly instructed, could find that the two works are substantially similar, Durham Industries, Inc. v. Tomy Corp., 630 F.2d 905, 918 (2d Cir.1980). See Twentieth Century–Fox Film Corp. v. MCA, Inc., supra, at 1330 & n. 6; 3 Nimmer on Copyright § 12.10 (1983) (hereafter "Nimmer"). Before assessing the District Court's determination that summary judgment was appropriate in this case, we consider the principles that guide decision in this area. * * *

When, as in this case, the claim concerns infringement of a character, rather than a story, the idea-expression distinction has proved to be especially elusive. In *Nichols,* Hand applied his "abstractions" test in determining that neither the plot nor the characters of "Abie's Irish Rose" were infringed by a similar play called "The Cohens and the Kellys." He noted that no case then decided had found infringement of a character described only by written word, although he recognized the possibility that a literary character could be sufficiently delineated to support a claim of infringement by a second comer, 45 F.2d at 121. Copyrightability of a literary character has on occasion been recognized, Burroughs v. Metro–Goldwyn–Mayer, Inc., 519 F.Supp. 388, 391 (S.D.N.Y.1981) (Tarzan), aff'd with issue expressly left open, 683 F.2d 610, 621 (2d Cir.1982). However, there has been no doubt that copyright protection is available for characters portrayed in cartoons, even before *Nichols,* e.g., King Features Syndicate v. Fleischer, 299 Fed. 533 (2d Cir.1924) (Barney Google's horse, Spark Plug); * * *

In determining whether a character in a second work infringes a cartoon character, courts have generally considered not only the visual resemblance but also the totality of the characters' attributes and traits. * * * A pertinent consideration, formulated in a case concerning greeting cards in which characters were one element of the art work, Roth Greeting Cards v.

United Card Co., 429 F.2d 1106, 1110 (9th Cir.1970), is the extent to which the allegedly infringing character captures the "total concept and feel" of the copyrighted character. * * *

* * * A story has a linear dimension: it begins, continues, and ends. If a defendant copies substantial portions of a plaintiff's sequence of events, he does not escape infringement by adding original episodes somewhere along the line. A graphic or three-dimensional work is created to be perceived as an entirety. Significant dissimilarities between two works of this sort inevitably lessen the similarity that would otherwise exist between the total perceptions of the two works. The graphic rendering of a character has aspects of both the linear, literary mode and the multi-dimensional total perception. What the character thinks, feels, says, and does and the descriptions conveyed by the author through the comments of other characters in the work episodically fill out a viewer's understanding of the character. At the same time, the visual perception of the character tends to create a dominant impression against which the similarity of a defendant's character may be readily compared, and significant differences readily noted.

Ultimately, care must be taken to draw the elusive distinction between a substantially similar character that infringes a copyrighted character despite slight differences in appearance, behavior, or traits, and a somewhat similar though non-infringing character whose appearance, behavior, or traits, and especially their combination, significantly differ from those of a copyrighted character, even though the second character is reminiscent of the first one. Stirring one's memory of a copyrighted character is not the same as appearing to be substantially similar to that character, and only the latter is infringement. See Ideal Toy Corp. v. Kenner Products Division of General Mills Fun Group, Inc., 443 F.Supp. 291, 305 (S.D.N.Y.1977). * * *

Applying these principles to this case, we conclude that Chief Judge Motley correctly entered summary judgment for the defendants on the claim of copyright infringement. Plaintiffs make no claim that the *Hero* pilot, subsequent episodes, or "promos" infringed the story of any Superman works. Their contention is that the *Hero* character, Ralph Hinkley, is substantially similar to Superman and that the *Hero* works impermissibly copied what plaintiffs call the "indicia" of Superman, a concept broad enough to include Superman's costume, his abilities, the well-known lines associated with him—in short, anything occurring in the *Hero* works that might remind a viewer of Superman.

The total perception of the Hinkley character is not substantially similar to that of Superman. On the contrary, it is profoundly different. Superman looks and acts like a brave, proud hero, who has dedicated his life to combating the forces of evil. Hinkley looks and acts like a timid, reluctant hero, who accepts his missions grudgingly and prefers to get on with his normal life. Superman performs his superhuman feats with skill, verve, and dash, clearly the master of his own destiny. Hinkley is perplexed by the superhuman powers his costume confers and uses them in a bumbling, comical fashion. In the genre of superheros, Hinkley follows Superman as, in the genre of detectives, Inspector Clouseau follows Sherlock Holmes.

However, we do not accept defendants' mode of analysis whereby every skill the two characters share is dismissed as an idea rather than a protected form of expression. That approach risks elimination of any copyright protection for a character, unless the allegedly infringing character looks and behaves exactly like the original. A character is an aggregation of the particular talents and traits his creator selected for him. That each one may be an idea does not diminish the expressive aspect of the combination. But just as similarity cannot be rejected by isolating as an idea each characteristic the characters have in common, it cannot be found when the total perception of all the ideas as expressed in each character is fundamentally different. * * *

* * * Appellants were prepared to offer expert testimony to show that some children would not perceive the negatives when the announcer says that Hinkley "may be unable to leap tall buildings in a single bound," "may be slower than a speeding bullet," and "may be less powerful than a locomotive." We do not doubt that some viewers may miss the point, but their misunderstanding does not establish infringement. Perhaps if *Hero* were a children's series, aired on Saturday mornings among the cartoon programs, we would have greater concern for the risk that lines intended to contrast Hinkley with Superman might be mistakenly understood to suggest that *Hero* was a Superman program. Cf. Ideal Toy Corp. v. Fab–Lu, Ltd., 261 F.Supp. 238, 241–42 (S.D.N.Y.1966) (children's perception of television commercial for dolls). But when a work is presented to a general audience of evening television viewers, the possible misperception of some young viewers cannot prevent that audience from seeing a program that will readily be recognized by the "average lay observer," Ideal Toy Corp. v. Fab–Lu Ltd., 360 F.2d 1021, 1022 (2d Cir.1966), as poking fun at, rather than copying, a copyrighted work.

Our conclusion is not altered by plaintiffs' proffered evidence of a survey of persons who viewed the *Hero* pilot. The survey reported, among other things, that of the 45% of those interviewed who said Hinkley reminded them of some other character, 74% (33% of the entire sample) said they were reminded of Superman. We appreciate the problem plaintiffs confronted in designing the survey. If they asked too pointed a question, e.g., "Do you think Hinkley is substantially similar to Superman?", they would have been faulted for using a leading question. On the other hand, their open-ended questions caused Chief Judge Motley to rule the entire survey inadmissible because the responses were "too general." 530 F.Supp. at 1197 n. 3. That dilemma simply illustrates the problems that arise when surveys are sought to be used as an aid in determining issues of copyright infringement. See Ideal Toy Corp. v. Kenner Products Division of General Mills Fun Group, Inc., supra, 443 F.Supp. at 304 (cautioning against "the dangerous precedent of allowing trial by the court to be replaced by trial by public opinion poll"). The "substantial similarity" that supports an inference of copying sufficient to establish infringement of a copyright is not a concept familiar to the public at large. It is a term to be used in a courtroom to strike a delicate balance between the protection to which authors are entitled under an act of Congress and the freedom that exists for all others to create their works outside the area protected against infringement. We need not and do not decide whether survey evidence of the sort tendered in this case would be admissible to aid a jury in resolving a claim of substantial similarity that lies within the range of reasonable factual dispute. However, when a trial judge has correctly ruled that two works are not substantially similar as a matter of law, that conclusion is not to be altered by the availability of survey evidence indicating that some people applying some standard of their own were reminded by one work of the other. Courts have an important responsibility in copyright cases to monitor the outer limits within which juries may determine reasonably disputed issues of fact. If a case lies beyond those limits, the contrary view of a properly drawn sample of the population, or even of a particular jury, cannot be permitted to enlarge (or diminish) the scope of statutory protection enjoyed by a copyright proprietor. * * *

[Judge Motley's summary judgment had also disposed of the plaintiff's trademark and unfair competition counts. The Court of Appeals affirmed in a crisp discussion declaring that "as with claims of copyright infringement, courts retain an important authority to monitor the outer limits of substantial similarity within which a jury is permitted to make the factual determination whether there is a likelihood of confusion as to source." A statutory claim of trademark "dilution" met a similar fate: "Even if Superman's trademarks are not as indestructible as the character that spawned them, no reasonable jury could find that the *Hero* series or 'promos' blurred or tarnished those marks."]

The judgment of the District Court is affirmed.

NOTES AND QUESTIONS

(1) If Arnstein v. Porter's opposition to summary judgment is now discredited, does *Warner Brothers* stretch too far in the opposite direction?

(2) Does *Warner Brothers* introduce still another approach to adjudicating infringement? Is it significant that Judge Newman's opinion makes no reference to the two-step techniques of *Arnstein* or *Krofft?*

(3) Superman, although born a cartoon character, became in maturity a star of television and motion pictures. Consider other characters created expressly for such media—Kramer of *Seinfeld,* for example, or Darth Vader of *Star Wars.* Are they more akin, for purposes of copyrightability and infringement, to cartoon characters or to literary characters?[1] Is it relevant that the visual dimension of movie and television characters often consists chiefly of the physical appearance of a particular actor? On copyright issues relating to digitally-created screen characters, see L. Kurtz, Digital Actors and Copyright—From *The Polar Express* to *Simone*, 21 Santa Clara Computer & High Tech.L.J. 783 (2005).

(4) Any appraisal of the total scope of protection available for characters must await exposure in Part Two of this casebook to the law of unfair competition. Both the copyright and unfair competition dimensions are comprehensively reviewed in L. Kurtz, The Independent Legal Lives of Fictional Characters, 1986 Wis.L.Rev. 429 (1986).

---

[1]   See Anderson v. Stallone, 11 U.S.P.Q.2d 1161 (C.D.Cal.1989), distinguishing the literary character cases and holding that "Rocky" as delineated in the movie series is a protectable character. In Metro–Goldwyn–Mayer, Inc. v. American Honda Motor Co., 900 F.Supp. 1287 (C.D.Cal.1995), the court granted the plaintiff motion picture studio a preliminary injunction protecting the "James Bond" character as expressed in sixteen movies against defendant Honda's television commercial in which a villain jumps from a helicopter onto the roof of a car occupied by a Bond-like character and female companion who release the car's detachable roof to make their escape.

5. NONFICTION WORKS

Hoehling v. Universal City Studios, Inc.

United States Court of Appeals, Second Circuit, 1980.
618 F.2d 972.
Certiorari denied 449 U.S. 841.

■ Before KAUFMAN, CHIEF JUDGE, TIMBERS, CIRCUIT JUDGE, and WERKER, DISTRICT JUDGE.

■ IRVING R. KAUFMAN, CHIEF JUDGE: * * *

This litigation arises from three separate accounts of the triumphant introduction, last voyage, and tragic destruction of the Hindenburg, the colossal dirigible constructed in Germany during Hitler's reign. The zeppelin, the last and most sophisticated in a fleet of luxury airships, which punctually floated its wealthy passengers from the Third Reich to the United States, exploded into flames and disintegrated in 35 seconds as it hovered above the Lakehurst, New Jersey Naval Air Station at 7:25 p.m. on May 6, 1937. * * *

Appellant A.A. Hoehling published *Who Destroyed the Hindenburg?*, a full-length book based on his exhaustive research in 1962. Mr. Hoehling studied the investigative reports, consulted previously published articles and books, and conducted interviews with survivors of the crash as well as others who possessed information about the Hindenburg. His book is presented as a factual account, written in an objective, reportorial style.

The first half recounts the final crossing of the Hindenburg, from Sunday, May 2, when it left Frankfurt, to Thursday, May 6, when it exploded at Lakehurst. Hoehling describes the airship, its role as an instrument of propaganda in Nazi Germany, its passengers and crew, the danger of hydrogen, and the ominous threats received by German officials, warning that the Hindenburg would be destroyed. The second portion, headed *The Quest,* sets forth the progress of the official investigations, followed by an account of Hoehling's own research. In the final chapter, spanning eleven pages, Hoehling suggests that all proffered explanations of the explosion, save deliberate destruction, are unconvincing. He concludes that the most likely saboteur is one Eric Spehl, a "rigger" on the Hindenburg crew who was killed at Lakehurst.

According to Hoehling, Spehl had motive, expertise, and opportunity to plant an explosive device, constructed of dry-cell batteries and a flashbulb, in "Gas Cell 4," the location of the initial explosion. An amateur photographer with access to flashbulbs, Spehl could have destroyed the Hindenburg to please his ladyfriend, a suspected communist dedicated to exploding the myth of Nazi invincibility.

Ten years later appellee Michael MacDonald Mooney published his book, *The Hindenburg*. Mooney's endeavor might be characterized as more literary than historical in its attempt to weave a number of symbolic themes through the actual events surrounding the tragedy. His dominant theme contrasts the natural beauty of the month of May, when the disaster occurred, with the cold, deliberate progress of "technology." The May theme is expressed not simply by the season, but also by the character of Spehl, portrayed as a sensitive artisan with needle and thread. The Hindenburg, in contrast, is the symbol of technology, as are its German creators and the Reich itself. The destruction is depicted as the ultimate triumph of nature over technology, as Spehl plants the bomb that ignites the hydrogen. Developing this theme from the outset, Mooney begins with an extended review of man's efforts to defy nature through flight, focusing on the evolution of the zeppelin. This story culminates in the construction of the Hindenburg, and the Nazis' claims of its indestructibility. Mooney then traces the fateful voyage, advising the reader almost immediately of Spehl's scheme. The book concludes with the airship's explosion.

Mooney acknowledges, in this case, that he consulted Hoehling's book, and that he relied on it for some details. * * *

After Mooney prepared an outline of his anticipated book, his publisher succeeded in negotiations to sell the motion picture rights to appellee Universal City Studios. * * *

The Gidding screenplay follows what is known in the motion picture industry as a "Grand Hotel" formula, developing a number of fictional characters and subplots involving them. This formula has become standard fare in so-called "disaster" movies, which have enjoyed a certain popularity in recent years. In the film, which was released in late 1975, a rigger named "Boerth," who has an anti-Nazi ladyfriend, plans to destroy the airship in an effort to embarrass the Reich. Nazi officials, vaguely aware of sabotage threats, station a Luftwaffe intelligence officer on the zeppelin, loosely resembling a Colonel Erdmann who was aboard the Hindenburg. This character is portrayed as a likable fellow who soon discovers that Boerth is the saboteur. Boerth, however, convinces him that the Hindenburg should be destroyed and the two join forces, planning the explosion for several hours after the landing at Lakehurst, when no people would be on board. In Gidding's version, the airship is delayed by a storm, frantic efforts to defuse the bomb fail, and the Hindenburg is destroyed. * * *

Upon learning of Universal's plans to release the film, Hoehling instituted this action against Universal for copyright infringement and common law unfair competition in the district court for the District of Columbia in October 1975. Judge Smith declined to issue an order restraining release of the film in December, and it was distributed throughout the nation.

* * * After the completion of discovery, both Mooney and Universal moved for summary judgment, Fed.R.Civ.P. 56, which was granted on August 1, 1979.

It is undisputed that Hoehling has a valid copyright in his book. To prove infringement, however, he must demonstrate that defendants "copied" his work and that they "improperly appropriated" his "expression." See Arnstein v. Porter, 154 F.2d 464, 468 (2d Cir.1946). Ordinarily, wrongful appropriation is shown by proving a "substantial similarity" of *copyrightable* expression. See Nichols v. Universal Pictures Corp., 45 F.2d 119, 121 (2d Cir.1930), cert. denied, 282 U.S. 902 (1931). Because substantial similarity is customarily an extremely close question of fact, see *Arnstein,* supra, 154 F.2d at 468, summary judgment has traditionally been frowned upon in copyright litigation, id. at 474. Nevertheless, while *Arnstein's* influence in other areas of the law has been diminished, see SEC v. Research Automation Corp., 585 F.2d 31 (2d Cir.1978); 6 Moore's Federal Practice ¶ 56.17[14] (2d ed. 1976), a series of copyright cases in the Southern District of New York have granted defendants summary judgment when all alleged similarity related to *non*-copyrightable elements of the plaintiff's work, see, e.g., Alexander v. Haley, 460 F.Supp. 40 (S.D.N.Y.1978); Musto v. Meyer, 434 F.Supp. 32 (S.D.N.Y.1977); Gardner v.

Nizer, 391 F.Supp. 940 (S.D.N.Y.1975); Fuld v. National Broadcasting Co., 390 F.Supp. 877 (S.D.N.Y.1975). These cases signal an important development in the law of copyright, permitting courts to put "a swift end to meritless litigation" and to avoid lengthy and costly trials. Quinn v. Syracuse Model Neighborhood Corp., 613 F.2d 438, 445 (2d Cir.1980); accord, Donnelly v. Guion, 467 F.2d 290, 293 (2d Cir.1972); American Manufacturers Mutual Insurance Co. v. American Broadcasting–Paramount Theatres, Inc., 388 F.2d 272, 278 (2d Cir.1967). Drawing on these cases, Judge Metzner assumed both copying and substantial similarity, but concluded that all similarities pertained to various categories of non-copyrightable material. Accordingly, he granted appellees' motion for summary judgment. We affirm the judgment of the district court.

Hoehling's principal claim is that both Mooney and Universal copied the essential plot of his book—i.e., Eric Spehl, influenced by his girlfriend, sabotaged the Hindenburg by placing a crude bomb in Gas Cell 4. * * *

* * * [Mooney and Universal] argue that Hoehling's plot is an "idea," and ideas are not copyrightable as a matter of law. See Sheldon v. Metro–Goldwyn Pictures Corp., 81 F.2d 49, 54 (2d Cir.), cert. denied, 298 U.S. 669 (1936).

Hoehling, however, correctly rejoins that while ideas themselves are not subject to copyright, his "expression" of *his* idea is copyrightable. Id. at 54. He relies on Learned Hand's opinion in *Sheldon,* supra, at 50, holding that *Letty Lynton* infringed *Dishonored Lady* by copying its story of a woman who poisons her lover, and Augustus Hand's analysis in Detective Comics, Inc. v. Bruns Publications, Inc., 111 F.2d 432 (2d Cir.1940), concluding that the exploits of "Wonderman" infringed the copyright held by the creators of "Superman," the original indestructible man. Moreover, Hoehling asserts that, in both these cases, the line between "ideas" and "expression" is drawn, in the first instance, by the fact finder.

Sheldon and *Detective Comics,* however, dealt with works of fiction, where the distinction between an idea and its expression is especially elusive. But, where, as here, the idea at issue is an interpretation of an historical event, our cases hold that such interpretations are not copyrightable as a matter of law. In Rosemont Enterprises, Inc. v. Random House, Inc., 366 F.2d 303 (2d Cir.1966), cert. denied, 385 U.S. 1009 (1967), we held that the defendant's biography of Howard Hughes did not infringe an earlier biography of the reclusive alleged billionaire. Although the plots of the two works were necessarily similar, there could be no infringement because of the "public benefit in encouraging the development of historical and biographical works and their public distribution." Id. at 307; accord, Oxford Book Co. v. College Entrance Book Co., 98 F.2d 688 (2d Cir.1938). To avoid a chilling effect on authors who contemplate tackling an historical issue or event, broad latitude must be granted to subsequent authors who make use of historical subject matter, including theories or plots. Learned Hand counseled in Myers v. Mail & Express Co., 36 C.O.Bull. 478, 479 (S.D.N.Y.1919), "[t]here cannot be any such thing as copyright in the order of presentation of the facts, nor, indeed, in their selection."

In the instant case, the hypothesis that Eric Spehl destroyed the Hindenburg is based entirely on the interpretation of historical facts, including Spehl's life, his girlfriend's anti-Nazi connections, the explosion's origin in Gas Cell 4, Spehl's duty station, discovery of a dry-cell battery among the wreckage, and rumors about Spehl's involvement dating from a 1938 Gestapo investigation. Such an historical interpretation, whether or not it originated with Mr. Hoehling, is not protected by his copyright and can be freely used by subsequent authors.

The same reasoning governs Hoehling's claim that a number of specific facts, ascertained through his personal research, were copied by appellees.[6] The cases in this circuit, however, make clear that factual information is in the public domain. See, e.g., *Rosemont Enterprises, Inc.,* supra, 366 F.2d at 309; *Oxford Book Co.,* supra, 98 F.2d at 691. Each appellee had the right to "avail himself of the facts contained" in Hoehling's book and to "use such information, whether correct or incorrect, in his own literary work." Greenbie v. Noble, 151 F.Supp. 45, 67 (S.D.N.Y.1957). Accordingly, there is little consolation in relying on cases in other circuits holding that the fruits of original research are copyrightable. See, e.g., Toksvig v. Bruce Publications Corp., 181 F.2d 664, 667 (7th Cir.1950); Miller v. Universal City Studios, Inc., 460 F.Supp. 984 (S.D.Fla.1978). Indeed, this circuit has clearly repudiated *Toksvig* and its progeny. In *Rosemont Enterprises, Inc.,* supra, 366 F.2d at 310, we refused to "subscribe to the view that an author is absolutely precluded from saving time and effort by referring to and relying upon prior published material . . . . It is just such wasted effort that the proscription against the copyright of ideas and facts . . . are designed to prevent." Accord, 1 Nimmer on Copyright § 2.11 (1979).

The remainder of Hoehling's claimed similarities relate to random duplications of phrases and sequences of events. For example, all three works contain a scene in a German beer hall, in which the airship's crew engages in revelry prior to the voyage. Other claimed similarities concern common German greetings of the period, such as "Heil Hitler," or songs, such as the German National anthem. These elements, however, are merely *scenes a faire,* that is "incidents, characters or settings which are as a practical matter indispensable, or at least standard, in the treatment of a given topic." [Alexander v. Haley, 460 F.Supp. 40, 45 (S.D.N.Y.1978)]; accord, Bevan v. Columbia Broadcasting System, Inc., 329 F.Supp. 601, 607 (S.D.N.Y.1971). Because it is virtually impossible to write about a particular historical era or fictional theme without employing certain "stock" or standard literary devices, we have held that *scenes a faire* are not copyrightable as a matter of law. See Reyher v. Children's Television Workshop, 533 F.2d 87, 91 (2d Cir.), cert. denied, 429 U.S. 980 (1976).

All of Hoehling's allegations of copying, therefore, encompass material that is non-copyrightable as a matter of law, rendering summary judgment entirely appropriate. We are aware, however, that in distinguishing between themes, facts, and *scenes a faire* on the one hand, and copyrightable expression on the other, courts may lose sight of the forest for the trees. By factoring out similarities based on non-copyrightable elements, a court runs the risk of overlooking wholesale usurpation of a prior author's expression.

---

[6]   In detailed comparisons of his book with Mooney's work and Universal's motion picture, Hoehling isolates 266 and 75 alleged instances of copying, respectively. Judge Metzner correctly pointed out that many of these allegations are patently frivolous. The vast majority of the remainder deals with alleged copying of historical facts. It would serve no purpose to review Hoehling's specific allegations in detail in this opinion. The following ten examples, however, are illustrative: (1) Eric Spehl's age and birthplace; (2) Crew members had smuggled monkeys on board the Graf Zeppelin; (3) Germany's ambassador to the United States dismissed threats of sabotage; (4) A warning letter had been received from a Mrs. Rauch; (5) The Hindenburg's captain was constructing a new home in Zeppelinheim; (6) Eric Spehl was a photographer; (7) The airship flew over Boston; (8) The Hindenburg was "tail heavy" before landing; (9) A member of the ground crew had etched his name in the zeppelin's hull; and (10) The navigator set the Hindenburg's course by reference to various North Atlantic islands.

A verbatim reproduction of another work, of course, even in the realm of nonfiction, is actionable as copyright infringement. See Wainwright Securities, Inc. v. Wall Street Transcript Corp., 558 F.2d 91 (2d Cir.1977), cert. denied, 434 U.S. 1014 (1978). Thus, in granting or reviewing a grant of summary judgment for defendants, courts should assure themselves that the works before them are not virtually identical. In this case, it is clear that all three authors relate the story of the Hindenburg differently.

In works devoted to historical subjects, it is our view that a second author may make significant use of prior work, so long as he does not bodily appropriate the expression of another. *Rosemont Enterprises, Inc.,* supra, 366 F.2d at 310. This principle is justified by the fundamental policy undergirding the copyright laws—the encouragement of contributions to recorded knowledge. The "financial reward guaranteed to the copyright holder is but an incident of this general objective, rather than an end in itself." Berlin v. E.C. Publications, Inc., 329 F.2d 541, 543–44 (2d Cir.), cert. denied, 379 U.S. 822 (1964). Knowledge is expanded as well by granting new authors of historical works a relatively free hand to build upon the work of their predecessors.[7] * * *

The judgment of the district court is affirmed.

Nash v. CBS, Inc.

899 F.2d 1537 (7th Cir.1990).

"John Dillinger, Public Enemy No. 1, died on July 22, 1934, at the Biograph Theater in Chicago. He emerged from the air conditioned movie palace into a sweltering evening accompanied by two women, one wearing a red dress. The 'lady in red', Anna Sage, had agreed to betray his presence for $10,000. Agents of the FBI were waiting. Alerted by Polly Hamilton, the other woman, Dillinger wheeled to fire, but it was too late. A hail of bullets cut him down, his .45 automatic unused."

Nash, an author with a fascination for crimes and criminals, believed that it was not Dillinger who died that night at the Biograph. In his book *The Dillinger Dossier,* published in 1983, Nash concludes that Dillinger had learned of the trap and dispatched a small-time hoodlum who looked like him to take his place. Nash describes numerous discrepancies between Dillinger's physical appearance and the dead man, and notes that Dillinger's father had the corpse encased in concrete before burial. The FBI, Nash believed, mortified that it got the wrong man, went along with the cover-up, planting Dillinger's fingerprints in the morgue. After interviewing numerous people connected with Dillinger and the FBI, Nash claimed to have tracked Dillinger to the west coast, where he says Dillinger married and survived at least until 1979.

"Someone in Hollywood must have read *The Dillinger Dossier,* however, because in 1984 CBS broadcast an episode of its *Simon and Simon* series entitled *The Dillinger Print.*" The central premise of the episode is that Dillinger is alive and living in San Diego. There are references to the physical discrepancies between Dillinger and the corpse, and one of the characters plants a fake Dillinger fingerprint on a gun used in a bank robbery.

---

[7]   We note that publication of Mooney's book and release of the motion picture revived long dormant interest in the Hindenburg. As a result, Hoehling's book, which had been out of print for some time, was actually re-released after the film was featured in theaters across the country.

Nash filed suit for copyright infringement. CBS, conceding access and the copying of factual material, moved for summary judgment. The trial court granted the motion, holding that the television episode did not appropriate any copyrightable material. Judge Easterbrook, writing for the Seventh Circuit, agreed.

" * * * Intellectual (and artistic) progress is possible only if each author builds on the work of others. No one invents even a tiny fraction of the ideas that make up our cultural heritage. Once a work has been written and published, any rule requiring people to compensate the author slows progress in literature and art, making useful expressions 'too expensive', forcing authors to re-invent the wheel, and so on. Every work uses scraps of thought from thousands of predecessors, far too many to compensate even if the legal system were frictionless, which it isn't. Because any new work depends on others even if unconsciously, broad protection of intellectual property also creates a distinct possibility that the cost of litigation—old authors trying to get a 'piece of the action' from current successes—will prevent or penalize the production of new works, even though the claims be rebuffed. Authors as a group therefore might prefer limited protection for their writings—they gain in the ability to use others' works more than they lose in potential royalties. See William M. Landes & Richard A. Posner, An Economic Analysis of Copyright Law, 18 J.Legal Studies 325, 332–33, 349–59 (1989).

"Yet to deny authors all reward for the value their labors contribute to the works of others *also* will lead to inefficiently little writing, just as surely as excessively broad rights will do. The prospect of reward is an important stimulus for thinking and writing, especially for persons such as Nash who are full-time authors. Before the first work is published, broad protection of intellectual property seems best; after it is published, narrow protection seems best. At each instant some new works are in progress, and every author is simultaneously a creator in part and a borrower in part. In these roles, the same person has different objectives. Yet only one rule can be in force. This single rule must achieve as much as possible of these inconsistent demands. Neither Congress nor the courts has the information that would allow it to determine which is best. Both institutions must muddle through, using not a fixed rule but a sense of the consequences of moving dramatically in either direction.

"If Nash had written a novel that another had translated into a screenplay, this would be a difficult case. Although *The Dillinger Print* is substantially original, it does not matter that almost all of the second author's expression is new. '[N]o plagiarist can excuse the wrong by showing how much of his work he did not pirate.' Sheldon v. Metro–Goldwyn Pictures Corp., 81 F.2d 49, 56 (2d Cir.1936) (L. Hand, J.). The TV drama took from Nash's works the idea that Dillinger survived and retired to the west coast, and employed many of the ingredients that Nash used to demonstrate that the man in the Cook County morgue was not Dillinger. CBS even used one of Nash's books as a prop: 'Twentieth Century Desperadoes' in *The Dillinger Print* is a ringer for Nash's *Bloodletters and Badmen*. To see that *The Dillinger Print* is in a sense a 'derivative work', we need only imagine how we would react if Nash had written a short story based on the premise that Dillinger was really a woman masquerading as a man, and CBS had used a switch in sex roles as the centerpiece of a drama. In such an event we would need to decide, as Hand did in *Sheldon,* whether the portions CBS took over were qualitatively so important that the original author's market would be diminished excessively by a rule allowing similar appropriations in the regular course.

"Nash does not portray *The Dillinger Dossier* and its companion works as fiction, however, which makes all the difference. The inventor of Sherlock Holmes controls that character's fate while the copyright lasts; the first person to conclude that Dillinger survived does not get dibs on history. If Dillinger survived, that fact is available to all. Nash's rights lie in his expression: in his words, in his arrangement of facts (his deployment of narration interspersed with interviews, for example), but not in the naked 'truth'. *The Dillinger Print* does not use any words from *The Dillinger Dossier* or Nash's other books; it does not take over any of Nash's presentation but instead employs a setting of its own invention with new exposition and development. Physical differences between Dillinger and the corpse, planted fingerprints, photographs of Dillinger and other gangsters in the 1930s, these and all the rest are facts as Nash depicts them. (Nash did not take the photographs and has no rights in them; *The Dillinger Print* used the photos but not Nash's arrangement of them.)" Judge Easterbrook then turned to the Second Circuit's decision in *Hoehling*.

"*Hoehling* suggested that '[t]o avoid a chilling effect on authors who contemplate tackling an historical issue or event, broad latitude must be granted to subsequent authors who make use of historical subject matter, including theories or plots'. 618 F.2d at 978. As our opinion in [Toksvig v. Bruce Pub. Co., 181 F.2d 664 (7th Cir.1950)] shows, we are not willing to say that 'anything goes' as long as the first work is about history. *Toksvig* held that the author of a biography of Hans Christian Andersen infringed the copyright of the author of an earlier biography by using portions of Andersen's letters as well as some of the themes and structure. *Hoehling* rejected *Toksvig,* see 618 F.2d at 979, concluding that '[k]nowledge is expanded . . . by granting new authors of historical works a relatively free hand to build upon the work of their predecessors.' Id. at 980 (footnote omitted). With respect for our colleagues of the east, we think this goes to the extreme of looking at incentives only *ex post*. The authors in *Hoehling* and *Toksvig* spent years tracking down leads. If all of their work, right down to their words, may be used without compensation, there will be too few original investigations, and facts will not be available on which to build.

"In *Toksvig* the first author, who knew Danish, spent three years learning about Andersen's life; the second author, who knew no Danish, wrote her biography in less than a year by copying out of the first book scenes and letters that the original author discovered or translated. Reducing the return on such effort, by allowing unhindered use, would make the initial legwork less attractive and so less frequent. Copyright law does not protect hard work (divorced from expression), and hard work is not an essential ingredient of copyrightable expression * * *; to the extent *Toksvig* confuses work or ideas with expression, it has been justly criticized. * * * We need not revisit *Toksvig* on its own facts to know that it is a mistake to hitch up at *either* pole of the continuum between granting the first author a right to forbid all similar treatments of history and granting the second author a right to use anything he pleases of the first's work."

Concluding that CBS had used Nash's "analysis of history but none of his expression," the court affirmed the summary judgment.

NOTES AND QUESTIONS ON COPYRIGHT IN RESEARCH

(1) Both *Hoehling* and *Nash* refer to Toksvig v. Bruce Pub. Co., 181 F.2d 664 (7th Cir.1950). Plaintiff Toksvig spent three years working with original Danish sources in writing a biography of author Hans Christian Andersen. The defendant (who, as Judge Easterbrook notes in *Nash,* could not read Danish), wrote a novel based on Andersen's life, apparently quoting twenty-four passages from the plaintiff's translations of letters written by Andersen. Not content to rest the defendant's liability solely on that appropriation, the court noted that the defendant had also "obtained much value from the use in her work of many of the original concepts and ideas of plaintiff as to Andersen and his relationship with other persons * * *."

If the defendant had refrained from lifting specific language, *should* she be permitted to utilize the factual material in the biography as the basis for a novel? A second biography?

(2) The decision in Miller v. Universal City Studios, Inc., 460 F.Supp. 984 (S.D.Fla.1978), invoked along with *Toksvig* by the plaintiff in *Hoehling*, was later reversed by the Fifth Circuit, 650 F.2d 1365 (5th Cir.1981). The litigation had its origins in a bizarre Georgia kidnaping in 1971. The victim, rescued from the underground coffin in which she had been imprisoned for five days, collaborated with the plaintiff reporter on a book detailing her ordeal. The reporter spent more than 2,500 hours on the book. Universal City Studios (after unsuccessfully attempting to purchase movie rights to the book) produced a television film portraying the crime. An internal memorandum indicated that the account depicted in the film had been constructed in large measure from the information in the plaintiff's book. The issue on appeal was the propriety of a jury instruction that read in part: "Moreover, if an author, in writing a book concerning factual matters, engages in research on those matters, his research is copyrightable"; the jury found infringement. Rejecting *Toksvig* in favor of *Hoehling,* the Fifth Circuit ordered a new trial: "The valuable distinction in copyright law between facts and the expression of facts cannot be maintained if research is held to be copyrightable."[m]

The Supreme Court, in a "fair use" case to be considered later, remarked on *Hoehling* and the problems posed by nonfiction works: "Especially in the realm of factual narrative, the law is currently unsettled regarding the ways in which uncopyrightable elements combine with the author's original contributions to form protected expression. Compare Wainwright Securities Inc. v. Wall Street Transcript Corp., [p. 322 infra] (protection accorded author's analysis, structuring of material and marshalling of facts), with [*Hoehling*] (limiting pro-

---

[m]   In Castle Rock Ent., Inc. v. Carol Pub. Group, 150 F.3d 132 (2d Cir.1998), the Second Circuit affirmed a summary judgment against a defendant who published a quiz book entitled *The Seinfeld Aptitude Test* devoted to testing readers' recollection of events from the *Seinfeld* television series. The court rejected the defendant's argument that it had copied only unprotected "facts" about the show. "Unlike the facts in a phone book * * * each 'fact' tested by *The SAT* is in reality fictitious expression created by *Seinfeld*'s authors." Relying on *Castle Rock,* the court in Warner Bros. Enter. Inc. v. RDR Books, 575 F.Supp.2d 513 (S.D.N.Y.2008), held against a Harry Potter fanatic who had written a *Harry Potter Lexicon* consisting of an alphabetical compilation of descriptions and commentary on the names, places, spells, and characters in the J.K. Rowling books. The case is analyzed in A. Schwabach, The Harry Potter Lexicon and the World of Fandom: Fan Fiction, Outsider Works, and Copyright, 70 U.Pitt.L.Rev. 387 (2009).

tection to ordering and choice of words).” Harper & Row, Publishers v. Nation Enterprises, p. 323 infra.[n]

On the *scenes a faire* doctrine described by Judge Kaufman in *Hoehling,* see L. Kurtz, Copyright: The Scenes A Faire Doctrine, 41 Fla.L.Rev. 79 (1989).

(3) The Ninth Circuit in Landsberg v. Scrabble Crossword Game Players, Inc., 736 F.2d 485 (9th Cir.), cert. denied, 469 U.S. 1037 (1984), relied on both *Hoehling* and *Miller* in a valiant effort to explicate the principles applicable to nonfiction works. The plaintiff complained that Selchow & Righter, producer of the *Scrabble* crossword game, had infringed the copyright in his manuscript entitled “Championship Scrabble Strategy.” The defendant had produced a similar handbook after negotiating for rights to the plaintiff’s manuscript (in bad faith, according to the district court). The district court found infringement, but the Ninth Circuit disagreed:

“One consequence of the policy in favor of free use of ideas is that the degree of substantial similarity required to show infringement varies according to the type of work and the ideas expressed in it [citing *Krofft,* p. 219 supra]. Some ideas can be expressed in myriad ways, while others allow only a narrow range of expression. Fictional works generally fall into the first category.” The standard for “substantial similarity” for fictional works therefore may be relatively low.

“Factual works are different. Subsequent authors wishing to express the ideas contained in a factual work often can choose from only a narrow range of expression. For example, Landsberg’s work states that ‘[t]he poor player simply attempts to make as many points as possible each turn.’ The idea contained in that statement cannot be expressed in a wide variety of ways. Just about any subsequent expression of that idea is likely to appear to be a substantially similar paraphrase of the words with which Landsberg expressed the idea. Therefore, similarity of expression may have to amount to verbatim reproduction or very close paraphrasing before a factual work will be deemed infringed. * * *

“We have reviewed Landsberg’s work, S & R’s work, and Exhibit 45, a comparative table of similarities between the two works. While we find similarities between the two works, we think there is no more than the similarity that must unavoidably be produced by anyone who wishes to use and restate the unprotectable ideas contained in Landsberg’s work.

“S & R’s work does not duplicate the selection, coordination, and arrangement of the ideas in Landsberg’s work, so we need not decide whether a work that rephrased in the same order as the original a substantial part of the ideas in another work might be held to infringe that work as a compilation, see 17 U.S.C.A. §§ 101, 103, even though none of the rephrasings of the individual ideas would constitute infringement when viewed in isolation.”

The case was remanded to the district court to determine whether the plaintiff might have a claim for breach of an “implied-in-fact” contract to pay

---

[n]   Cases claiming infringement of textbooks may be less interesting than the history or biography cases, but they too can require extensive comparisons. See McGraw–Hill, Inc. v. Worth Pub. Inc., 335 F.Supp. 415 (S.D.N.Y.1971); Meredith Corp. v. Harper & Row, Inc., 378 F.Supp. 686 (S.D.N.Y.), aff’d per curiam, 500 F.2d 1221 (2d Cir.1974) (preliminary injunction; on final judgment, see 413 F.Supp. 385 (S.D.N.Y.1975)); Morrison v. Solomons, 494 F.Supp. 218 (S.D.N.Y.1980) (similarities successfully explained during the defendant’s *twenty-two days* on the witness stand).

him for his ideas. That question brought the parties back before the Ninth Circuit two years later. See p. 243 infra.

(4) The commitment to preserve unrestricted access to facts is evident in an odd series of cases denying protection to fictional material that has been represented as fact. See, e.g., Mosley v. Follett, 209 U.S.P.Q. 1109 (S.D.N.Y.1980); Oliver v. Saint Germain Foundation, 41 F.Supp. 296 (S.D.Cal.1941). The facts of the *Oliver* case are particularly odd, even for California. The defendant was permitted to appropriate material from a copyrighted work because it had been represented by the plaintiff as the revelations of a deceased entity from another world. Would the interest in access to factual information be compromised if account were taken of the reasonable expectations of the copier? But see Arica Institute, Inc. v. Palmer, 970 F.2d 1067 (2d Cir.1992) (estoppel bars any claim of authorship in material represented as fact, even if a reasonable reader might not believe the representation).

6. COMPUTER PROGRAMS

Computer Associates International, Inc. v. Altai, Inc.

United States Court of Appeals, Second Circuit, 1992.
982 F.2d 693.

■ Before ALTIMARI, MAHONEY and WALKER, CIRCUIT JUDGES.

■ WALKER, CIRCUIT JUDGE.

* * *

Among other things, this case deals with the challenging question of whether and to what extent the "non-literal" aspects of a computer program, that is, those aspects that are not reduced to written code, are protected by copyright. While a few other courts have already grappled with this issue, this case is one of first impression in this circuit. As we shall discuss, we find the results reached by other courts to be less than satisfactory. Drawing upon long-standing doctrines of copyright law, we take an approach that we think better addresses the practical difficulties embedded in these types of cases. In so doing, we have kept in mind the necessary balance between creative incentive and industrial competition. * * *

BACKGROUND

We assume familiarity with the facts set forth in the district court's comprehensive and scholarly opinion. See Computer Assocs. Int'l, Inc. v. Altai, Inc., 775 F.Supp. 544, 549–55 (E.D.N.Y.1991). Thus, we summarize only those facts necessary to resolve this appeal.

I.   COMPUTER PROGRAM DESIGN

Certain elementary facts concerning the nature of computer programs are vital to the following discussion. The Copyright Act defines a computer program as "a set of statements or instructions to be used directly or indirectly in a computer in order to bring about a certain result." 17 U.S.C. § 101. In writing these directions, the programmer works "from the general to the specific." Whelan Assoc., Inc. v. Jaslow Dental Lab., Inc., 797 F.2d 1222, 1229 (3d Cir.1986), cert. denied, 479 U.S. 1031 (1987). See generally Steven R. Englund, Note, Idea, Process, or Protected Expression?: Determining the Scope of Copyright Protection of the Structure of Computer Programs, 88 Mich.L.Rev. 866, 867–73 (1990) (hereinafter "Englund"); Peter S. Menell, An Analysis of the Scope of Copyright Protection for Application Programs, 41 Stan.L.Rev. 1045, 1051–57 (1989) (hereinafter "Menell"); Mark T. Kretschmer, Note, Copyright Protection For Software Architecture: Just Say No!, 1988 Colum.Bus.L.Rev. 823, 824–27 (1988) (hereinafter "Kretschmer"); Peter G. Spivack, Comment, Does Form Follow Function? The Idea/Expression Dichotomy In Copyright Protection of Computer Software, 35 U.C.L.A.L.Rev. 723, 729–31 (1988) (hereinafter "Spivack").

The first step in this procedure is to identify a program's ultimate function or purpose. An example of such an ultimate purpose might be the creation and maintenance of a business ledger. Once this goal has been achieved, a programmer breaks down or "decomposes" the program's ultimate function into "simpler constituent problems or 'subtasks,'" Englund, at 870, which are also known as subroutines or modules. See Spivack, at 729. In the context of a business ledger program, a module or subroutine might be responsible for the task of updating a list of outstanding accounts receivable. Sometimes, depending upon the complexity of its task, a subroutine may be broken down further into sub-subroutines.

Having sufficiently decomposed the program's ultimate function into its component elements, a programmer will then arrange the subroutines or modules into what are known as organizational or flow charts. Flow charts map the interactions between modules that achieve the program's end goal. See Kretschmer, at 826. * * *

"The functions of the modules in a program together with each module's relationships to other modules constitute the 'structure' of the program." Englund, at 871. Additionally, the term structure may include the category of modules referred to as "macros." A macro is a single instruction that initiates a sequence of operations or module interactions within the program. * * *

In fashioning the structure, a programmer will normally attempt to maximize the program's speed, efficiency, as well as simplicity for user operation, while taking into consideration certain externalities such as the memory constraints of the computer upon which the program will be run. See id.; Kretschmer, at 826; Menell, at 1052. "This stage of program design often requires the most time and investment." Kretschmer, at 826.

Once each necessary module has been identified, designed, and its relationship to the other modules has been laid out conceptually, the resulting program structure must be embodied in a written language that the computer can read. This process is called "coding," and requires two steps. *Coding steps* *(1)* *Whelan,* 797 F.2d at 1230. First, the programmer must transpose the program's structural blueprint into a source code. This step has been described as "comparable to the novelist fleshing out the broad outline of his plot by crafting from words and sentences the paragraphs that convey the ideas." Kretschmer, at 826. The source code may be written in any one of several computer languages, such as COBAL, FORTRAN, BASIC, EDL, etc., depending upon the type of computer for which the program is intended. *Whelan,* 797 F.2d at 1230. Once the source code has been completed, the *(2)* second step is to translate or "compile" it into object code. Object code is the binary language comprised of zeros and ones through which the computer directly receives its instructions. Id., at 1230–31; Englund, at 868 & n. 13. * * *

II.   FACTS

* * *

The subject of this litigation originates with one of CA's marketed programs entitled CA–SCHEDULER. CA–SCHEDULER is a job scheduling program designed for IBM mainframe computers. Its primary functions are straightforward: to create a schedule specifying when the computer should run various tasks, and then to control the computer as it executes the schedule. CA–SCHEDULER contains a sub-program entitled ADAPTER, also developed by CA. ADAPTER is not an independently marketed product of CA; it is a wholly integrated component of CA–SCHEDULER and has no capacity for independent use.

adapter is part of
Scheduler, not separate

Nevertheless, ADAPTER plays an extremely important role. It is an "operating system compatibility component," which means, roughly speaking, it serves as a translator. An "operating system" is itself a program that manages the resources of the computer, allocating those resources to other programs as needed. The IBM System 370 family of computers, for which CA–SCHEDULER was created, is, depending upon the computer's size, designed to contain one of three operating systems: DOS/VSE, MVS, or CMS. As the district court noted, the general rule is that "a program written for one operating system, e.g., DOS/VSE, will not, without modification, run under another operating system such as MVS." Computer Assocs., 775 F.Supp. at 550. ADAPTER's function is to translate the language of a given program into the particular language that the computer's own operating system can understand.

* * *

Starting in 1982, Altai began marketing its own job scheduling program entitled ZEKE. The original version of ZEKE was designed for use in conjunction with a VSE operating system. By late 1983, in response to customer demand, Altai decided to rewrite ZEKE so that it could be run in conjunction with an MVS operating system.

At that time, James P. Williams ("Williams"), then an employee of Altai and now its President, approached Claude F. Arney, III ("Arney"), a computer programmer who worked for CA. Williams and Arney were longstanding friends, and had in fact been co-workers at CA for some time before Williams left CA to work for Altai's predecessor. Williams wanted to recruit Arney to assist Altai in designing an MVS version of ZEKE.

At the time he first spoke with Arney, Williams was aware of both the CA–SCHEDULER and ADAPTER programs. However, Williams was not involved in their development and had never seen the codes of either program. When he asked Arney to come work for Altai, Williams did not know that ADAPTER was a component of CA–SCHEDULER.

Arney, on the other hand, was intimately familiar with various aspects of ADAPTER. While working for CA, he helped improve the VSE version of ADAPTER, and was permitted to take home a copy of ADAPTER's source code. This apparently developed into an irresistible habit, for when Arney left CA to work for Altai in January, 1984, he took with him copies of the source code for both the VSE and MVS versions of ADAPTER. He did this in knowing violation of the CA employee agreements that he had signed.

Once at Altai, Arney and Williams discussed design possibilities for adapting ZEKE to run on MVS operating systems. Williams, who had created the VSE version of ZEKE, thought that approximately 30% of his original program would have to be modified in order to accommodate MVS. Arney persuaded Williams that the best way to make the needed modifications was to introduce a "common system interface" component into ZEKE. He did not tell Williams that his idea stemmed from his familiarity with ADAPTER. They decided to name this new component-program OSCAR.

Arney went to work creating OSCAR at Altai's offices using the ADAPTER source code. The district court accepted Williams' testimony that no one at Altai, with the exception of Arney, affirmatively knew that Arney had the ADAPTER code, or that he was using it to create OSCAR/VSE. * * * When the dust finally settled, Arney had copied approximately 30% of OSCAR's code from CA's ADAPTER program.

The first generation of OSCAR programs was known as OSCAR 3.4. From 1985 to August 1988, Altai used OSCAR 3.4 in its ZEKE product, as well as in programs entitled ZACK and ZEBB. In late July 1988, CA first learned that Altai may have appropriated parts of ADAPTER. After confirming its suspicions, CA secured copyrights on its 2.1 and 7.0 versions of CA–SCHEDULER. CA then brought this copyright and trade secret misappropriation action against Altai.

Apparently, it was upon receipt of the summons and complaint that Altai first learned that Arney had copied much of the OSCAR code from ADAPTER. After Arney confirmed to Williams that CA's accusations of copying were true, Williams immediately set out to survey the damage. Without ever looking at the ADAPTER code himself, Williams learned from Arney exactly which sections of code Arney had taken from ADAPTER.

Upon advice of counsel, Williams initiated OSCAR's rewrite. The project's goal was to save as much of OSCAR 3.4 as legitimately could be used, and to excise those portions which had been copied from ADAPTER. Arney was entirely excluded from the process, and his copy of the ADAPTER code was locked away. Williams put eight other programmers on the project, none of whom had been involved in any way in the development of OSCAR 3.4. Williams provided the programmers with a description of the ZEKE operating system services so that they could rewrite the appropriate code. The rewrite project took about six months to complete and was finished in mid-November 1989. The resulting program was entitled OSCAR 3.5.

From that point on, Altai shipped only OSCAR 3.5 to its new customers. Altai also shipped OSCAR 3.5 as a "free upgrade" to all customers that had previously purchased OSCAR 3.4. While Altai and Williams acted responsibly to correct Arney's literal copying of the ADAPTER program, copyright infringement had occurred.

* * *

DISCUSSION

While both parties originally appealed from different aspects of the district court's judgment, Altai has now abandoned its appellate claims. In particular, Altai has conceded liability for the copying of ADAPTER into OSCAR 3.4 and raises no challenge to the award of $364,444 in damages on that score. Thus, we address only CA's appeal from the district court's rulings that: (1) Altai was not liable for copyright infringement in developing OSCAR 3.5; and (2) in developing both OSCAR 3.4 and 3.5, Altai was not liable for misappropriating CA's trade secrets. * * *

I.   COPYRIGHT INFRINGEMENT

* * * For the purpose of analysis, the district court assumed that Altai had access to the ADAPTER code when creating OSCAR 3.5. See *Computer Assocs.,* 775 F.Supp. at 558. Thus, in determining whether Altai had unlawfully copied protected aspects of CA's ADAPTER, the district court narrowed its focus of inquiry to ascertaining whether Altai's OSCAR 3.5 was substantially similar to ADAPTER. Because we approve Judge Pratt's conclusions regarding substantial similarity, our analysis will proceed along the same assumption.

As a general matter, and to varying degrees, copyright protection extends beyond a literary work's strictly textual form to its non-literal components. As we have said, "[i]t is of course essential to any protection of literary property . . . that the right cannot be limited literally to the text, else a plagiarist would escape by immaterial variations." Nichols v. Universal Pictures Co., 45 F.2d 119, 121 (2d Cir.1930) (L. Hand, J.), cert. denied, 282 U.S. 902 (1931). Thus, where "the fundamental essence or structure of one work is duplicated in another," 3 Nimmer, § 13.03[A][1], at 13–24, courts have found copyright infringement. * * *

A.   Copyright Protection for the Non-literal Elements of Computer Programs

It is now well settled that the literal elements of computer programs, i.e., their source and object codes, are the subject of copyright protection. See *Whelan,* 797 F.2d at 1233 (source and object code); * * * Here, as noted earlier, Altai admits having copied approximately 30% of the OSCAR 3.4 program from CA's ADAPTER source code, and does not challenge the district court's related finding of infringement.

In this case, the hotly contested issues surround OSCAR 3.5. As recounted above, OSCAR 3.5 is the product of Altai's carefully orchestrated rewrite of OSCAR 3.4. After the purge, none of the ADAPTER source code remained in the 3.5 version; thus, Altai made sure that the literal elements of its revamped OSCAR program were no longer substantially similar to the literal elements of CA's ADAPTER. * * *

CA argues that, despite Altai's rewrite of the OSCAR code, the resulting program remained substantially similar to the *structure* of its ADAPTER program. As discussed above, a program's structure includes its non-literal components such as general flow charts as well as the more specific organization of inter-modular relationships, parameter lists, and macros. In addition to these aspects, CA contends that OSCAR 3.5 is also substantially similar to ADAPTER with respect to the list of services that both ADAPTER and OSCAR obtain from their respective operating systems. We must decide whether and to what extent these elements of computer programs are protected by copyright law.

The statutory terrain in this area has been well explored. See Lotus Dev. Corp. v. Paperback Software Int'l, 740 F.Supp. 37, 47–51 (D.Mass.1990); see also *Whelan,* 797 F.2d at 1240–42; Englund, at 885–90; Spivack, at 731–37. The Copyright Act affords protection to "original works of authorship fixed in any tangible medium of expression." 17 U.S.C. § 102(a). This broad category of protected "works" includes "literary works," id. at § 102(a)(1), which are defined by the Act as "works, other than audiovisual works, expressed in words, numbers, or other verbal or numerical symbols or indicia, regardless of the nature of the material objects, such as books, periodicals, manuscripts, phonorecords, film, tapes, disks, or cards, in which they are embodied." 17 U.S.C. § 101. While computer programs are not specifically listed as part of the above statutory definition, the legislative history leaves no doubt that Congress intended them to be considered literary works. See H.R.Rep. No. 1476, 94th Cong., 2d Sess. 54, reprinted in 1976 U.S.C.C.A.N. 5659, 5667 (hereinafter "House Report"); *Whelan,* 797 F.2d at 1234; Apple Computer, 714 F.2d at 1247.

The syllogism that follows from the foregoing premises is a powerful one: if the non-literal structures of literary works are protected by copyright; and if computer programs are literary works, as we are told by the legislature; then the non-literal structures of computer programs are protected by copyright. See *Whelan,* 797 F.2d at 1234 ("By analogy to other literary works, it would thus appear that the copyrights of computer programs can be infringed even absent copying of the literal elements of the program."). We have no reservation in joining the company of those courts that have already ascribed to this logic. * * * However, that conclusion does not end our analysis. We must determine the scope of copyright protection that extends to a computer program's non-literal structure.

As a caveat, we note that our decision here does not control infringement actions regarding categorically distinct works, such as certain types of screen displays. These items represent products of computer programs, rather than the programs themselves, and fall under the copyright rubric of audiovisual works. If a computer audiovisual display is copyrighted separately as an audiovisual work, apart from the literary work that generates it (i.e., the program), the display may be protectable regardless of the underlying program's copyright status. * * *

(1) Idea vs. Expression Dichotomy

    * * *

The doctrinal starting point in analyses of utilitarian works, is the seminal case of Baker v. Selden, 101 U.S. 99 (1879). * * *

To the extent that an accounting text and a computer program are both "a set of statements or instructions . . . to bring about a certain result," 17 U.S.C. § 101, they are roughly analogous. In the former case, the processes are ultimately conducted by human agency; in the latter, by electronic means. In either case, as already stated, the processes themselves are not protectable. But the holding in *Baker* goes farther. The Court concluded that those aspects of a work, which "must necessarily be used as incident to" the idea, system or process that the work describes, are also not copyrightable. 101 U.S. at 104. Selden's ledger sheets, therefore, enjoyed no copyright protection because they were "necessary incidents to" the system of accounting that he described. Id. at 103. From this reasoning, we conclude that those elements of a computer program that are necessarily incidental to its function are similarly unprotectable.

While Baker v. Selden provides a sound analytical foundation, it offers scant guidance on how to separate idea or process from expression, and moreover, on how to further distinguish protectable expression from that expression which "must necessarily be used as incident to" the work's underlying concept. In the context of computer programs, the Third Circuit's noted decision in *Whelan* has, thus far, been the most thoughtful attempt to accomplish these ends.

The court in *Whelan* faced substantially the same problem as is presented by this case. There, the defendant was accused of making off with the non-literal structure of the plaintiff's copyrighted dental lab management program, and employing it to create its own competitive version. In assessing whether there had been an infringement, the court had to determine which aspects of the programs involved were ideas, and which were expression. In separating the two, the court settled upon the following conceptual approach: "[T]he line between idea and expression may be drawn with reference to the end sought to be achieved by the work in question. In other words, *the purpose or function of a utilitarian work would be the work's idea, and everything that is not necessary to that purpose or function would be part of the expression of the idea . . . .* Where there are various means of achieving the desired purpose, then the particular means chosen is not necessary to the purpose; hence, there is expression, not idea." 797 F.2d at 1236 (citations omitted). The "idea" of the program at issue in *Whelan* was identified by the court as simply "the efficient management of a dental laboratory." Id. at n. 28.

So far, in the courts, the *Whelan* rule has received a mixed reception. * * *

Whelan has fared even more poorly in the academic community, where its standard for distinguishing idea from expression has been widely criticized for being conceptually overbroad. * * * The leading commentator in the field has stated that, "[t]he crucial flaw in [*Whelan's*] reasoning is that it assumes that only one 'idea,' in copyright law terms, underlies any computer program, and that once a separable idea can be identified, everything else must be expression." 3 Nimmer § 13.03(F), at 13–62.34. This criticism focuses not upon the program's ultimate purpose but upon the reality of its structural design. As we have already noted, a computer program's ultimate function or purpose is the composite result of interacting subroutines. Since each subroutine is itself a program, and thus, may be said to have its own "idea," *Whelan's* general formulation that a program's overall purpose equates with the program's idea is descriptively inadequate.

Accordingly, we think that Judge Pratt wisely declined to follow *Whelan*. See *Computer Assocs.,* 775 F.Supp. at 558–60. * * *

(2) Substantial Similarity Test for Computer Program Structure: Abstraction—Filtration—Comparison

We think that *Whelan's* approach to separating idea from expression in computer programs relies too heavily on metaphysical distinctions and does not place enough emphasis on practical considerations. * * *

As discussed herein, we think that district courts would be well-advised to undertake a three-step procedure, based on the abstractions test utilized by the district court, in order to determine whether the non-literal elements of two or more computer programs are substantially similar. This approach breaks no new ground; rather, it draws on such familiar copyright doctrines as merger, *scenes a faire,* and public domain. In taking this approach, however, we are cognizant that computer technology is a dynamic field which can quickly outpace judicial decisionmaking. Thus, in cases where the technology in question does not allow for a literal application of the procedure we outline below, our opinion should not be read to foreclose the district courts of our circuit from utilizing a modified version.

In ascertaining substantial similarity under this approach, a court would first break down the allegedly infringed program into its constituent structural parts. Then, by examining each of these parts for such things as incorporated ideas, expression that is necessarily incidental to those ideas, and elements that are taken from the public domain, a court would then be able to sift out all non-protectable material. Left with a kernel, or possible kernels, of creative expression after following this process of elimination, the court's last step would be to compare this material with the structure of an allegedly infringing program. The result of this comparison will determine whether the protectable elements of the programs at issue are substantially similar so as to warrant a finding of infringement. It will be helpful to elaborate a bit further.

Step One: Abstraction

As the district court appreciated, see *Computer Assocs.,* 775 F.Supp. at 560, the theoretic framework for analyzing substantial similarity expounded by Learned Hand in the *Nichols* case is helpful in the present context. In *Nichols,* we enunciated what has now become known as the "abstractions" test for separating idea from expression * * *.

As applied to computer programs, the abstractions test will comprise the first step in the examination for substantial similarity. Initially, in a manner that resembles reverse engineering on a theoretical plane, a court should dissect the allegedly copied program's structure and isolate each level of abstraction contained within it. This process begins with the code and ends with an articulation of the program's ultimate function. Along the way, it is necessary essentially to retrace and map each of the designer's steps—in the opposite order in which they were taken during the program's creation. See Background: Computer Program Design, supra.

As an anatomical guide to this procedure, the following description is helpful: "At the lowest level of abstraction, a computer program may be thought of in its entirety as a set of individual instructions organized into a hierarchy of modules. At a higher level of abstraction, the instructions in the lowest-level modules may be replaced conceptually by the functions of those modules. At progressively higher levels of abstraction, the functions of higher-level modules conceptually replace the implementations of those modules in terms of lower-level modules and instructions, until finally, one is left with nothing but the ultimate function of the program . . . . A program has structure at every level of abstraction at which it is viewed. At low levels of abstraction, a program's structure may be quite complex; at the highest level it is trivial." Englund, at 897–98. Cf. Spivack, at 774.

Step Two: Filtration

Once the program's abstraction levels have been discovered, the substantial similarity inquiry moves from the conceptual to the concrete. Professor Nimmer suggests, and we endorse, a "successive filtering method" for separating protectable expression from non-protectable material. See generally 3 Nimmer § 13.03[F]. This process entails examining the structural components at each level of abstraction to determine whether their particular inclusion at that level was "idea" or was dictated by considerations of efficiency, so as to be necessarily incidental to that idea; required by factors external to the program itself; or taken from the public domain and hence is nonprotectable expression. See also Kretschmer, at 844–45 (arguing that program features dictated by market externalities or efficiency concerns are unprotectable). The structure of any given program may reflect some, all, or none of these considerations. Each case requires its own fact specific investigation.

Strictly speaking, this filtration serves "the purpose of defining the scope of plaintiff's copyright." Brown Bag Software v. Symantec Corp., 960 F.2d 1465, 1475 (9th Cir.) (endorsing "analytic dissection" of computer programs in order to isolate protectable expression), cert. denied, 506 U.S. 869 (1992). By applying well developed doctrines of copyright law, it may ultimately leave behind a "core of protectable material." 3 Nimmer § 13.03[F][5], at 13–72. Further explication of this second step may be helpful.

(a) Elements Dictated by Efficiency

The portion of Baker v. Selden, discussed earlier, which denies copyright protection to expression necessarily incidental to the idea being expressed, appears to be the cornerstone for what has developed into the doctrine of merger. * * *

CONTU recognized the applicability of the merger doctrine to computer programs. In its report to Congress it stated that: "[C]opyrighted language may be copied without infringing when there is but a limited number of ways to express a given idea . . . . In the computer context, this means that when specific instructions, even though previously copyrighted, are the only and essential means of accomplishing a given task, their later use by another will not amount to infringement." CONTU Report at 20. While this statement directly concerns only the application of merger to program code, that is, the textual aspect of the program, it reasonably suggests that the doctrine fits comfortably within the general context of computer programs.

Furthermore, when one considers the fact that programmers generally strive to create programs "that meet the user's needs in the most efficient manner," Menell, at 1052, the applicability of the merger doctrine to computer programs becomes compelling. In the context of computer program design, the concept of efficiency is akin to deriving the most concise logical proof or formulating the most succinct mathematical computation. Thus, the more efficient a set of modules are, the more closely they approximate the idea or process embodied in that particular aspect of the program's structure.

While, hypothetically, there might be a myriad of ways in which a programmer may effectuate certain functions within a program,—i.e., express the idea embodied in a given subroutine—efficiency concerns may so narrow the practical range of choice as to make only one or two forms of expression workable options. See 3 Nimmer § 13.03[F][2], at 13–63; see also *Whelan,* 797 F.2d at 1243 n. 43 ("It is true that for certain tasks there are only a very limited number of file structures available, and in such cases the structures might not be copyrightable . . . . "). Of course, not all program structure is informed by efficiency concerns. See Menell, at 1052 (besides efficiency, simplicity related to user accommodation has become a programming priority). It follows that in order to determine whether the merger doctrine precludes copyright protection to an aspect of a program's structure that is so oriented, a court must inquire "whether the use of *this particular set* of modules is necessary efficiently to implement that part of the program's process" being implemented. Englund, at 902. If the answer is yes, then the expression represented by the programmer's choice of a specific module or group of modules has merged with their underlying idea and is unprotected. Id. at 902–03. * * *

(b) Elements Dictated By External Factors

We have stated that where "it is virtually impossible to write about a particular historical era or fictional theme without employing certain 'stock' or standard literary devices," such expression is not copyrightable.

Hoehling v. Universal City Studios, Inc., 618 F.2d 972, 979 (2d Cir.), cert. denied, 449 U.S. 841 (1980). * * * This is known as the *scenes a faire* doctrine, and like "merger," it has its analogous application to computer programs. Cf. [Data East USA, Inc. v. Epyx, Inc., 862 F.2d 204, 208 (9th Cir.1988)] (applying *scenes a faire* to a home computer video game).

Professor Nimmer points out that "in many instances it is virtually impossible to write a program to perform particular functions in a specific computing environment without employing standard techniques." 3 Nimmer § 13.03[F][3], at 13–65. This is a result of the fact that a programmer's freedom of design choice is often circumscribed by extrinsic considerations such as (1) the mechanical specifications of the computer on which a particular program is intended to run; (2) compatibility requirements of other programs with which a program is designed to operate in conjunction; (3) computer manufacturers' design standards; (4) demands of the industry being serviced; and (5) widely accepted programming practices within the computer industry. Id. at 13–65–71.

Courts have already considered some of these factors in denying copyright protection to various elements of computer programs. * * *

Building upon this existing case law, we conclude that a court must also examine the structural content of an allegedly infringed program for elements that might have been dictated by external factors.

(c) Elements Taken From the Public Domain

Closely related to the non-protectability of *scenes a faire,* is material found in the public domain. Such material is free for the taking and cannot be appropriated by a single author even though it is included in a copyrighted work. See E.F. Johnson Co. v. Uniden Corp. of America, 623 F.Supp. 1485, 1499 (D.Minn.1985); see also *Sheldon,* 81 F.2d at 54. We see no reason to make an exception to this rule for elements of a computer program that have entered the public domain by virtue of freely accessible program exchanges and the like. See 3 Nimmer § 13.03[F][4]; see also *Brown Bag Software,* 960 F.2d at 1473 (affirming the district court's finding that " '[p]laintiffs may not claim copyright protection of an . . . expression that is, if not standard, then commonplace in the computer software industry.' "). Thus, a court must also filter out this material from the allegedly infringed program before it makes the final inquiry in its substantial similarity analysis.

Step Three: Comparison

The third and final step of the test for substantial similarity that we believe appropriate for non-literal program components entails a comparison. Once a court has sifted out all elements of the allegedly infringed program which are "ideas" or are dictated by efficiency or external factors, or taken from the public domain, there may remain a core of protectable expression. In terms of a work's copyright value, this is the golden nugget. See *Brown Bag Software,* 960 F.2d at 1475. At this point, the court's substantial similarity inquiry focuses on whether the defendant copied any aspect of this protected expression, as well as an assessment of the copied portion's relative importance with respect to the plaintiff's overall program. * * *

(3) Policy Considerations

We are satisfied that the three step approach we have just outlined not only comports with, but advances the constitutional policies underlying the

Copyright Act. Since any method that tries to distinguish idea from expression ultimately impacts on the scope of copyright protection afforded to a particular type of work, "the line [it draws] must be a pragmatic one, which also keeps in consideration 'the preservation of the balance between competition and protection . . . . ' " [Apple Computer, Inc. v. Franklin Computer Corp., 714 F.2d 1240, 1253 (3d Cir.1983), cert. dismissed, 464 U.S. 1033 (1984)].

CA and some *amici* argue against the type of approach that we have set forth on the grounds that it will be a disincentive for future computer program research and development. At bottom, they claim that if programmers are not guaranteed broad copyright protection for their work, they will not invest the extensive time, energy and funds required to design and improve program structures. While they have a point, their argument cannot carry the day. The interest of the copyright law is not in simply conferring a monopoly on industrious persons, but in advancing the public welfare through rewarding artistic creativity, in a manner that permits the free use and development of non-protectable ideas and processes. * * *

Furthermore, we are unpersuaded that the test we approve today will lead to the dire consequences for the computer program industry that plaintiff and some *amici* predict. To the contrary, serious students of the industry have been highly critical of the sweeping scope of copyright protection engendered by the *Whelan* rule, in that it "enables first comers to 'lock up' basic programming techniques as implemented in programs to perform particular tasks." Menell, at 1087; see also Spivack, at 765 (*Whelan* "results in an inhibition of creation by virtue of the copyright owner's quasi-monopoly power"). * * *

B. The District Court Decision

We turn now to our review of the district court's decision in this particular case. At the outset, we must address CA's claim that the district court erred by relying too heavily on the court appointed expert's "personal opinions on the factual and legal issues before the court." * * *

The well-established general rule in this circuit has been to limit the use of expert opinion in determining whether works at issue are substantially similar [citing Arnstein v. Porter, 154 F.2d 464 (2d Cir.1946)]. * * *

Historically, *Arnstein*'s ordinary observer standard had its roots in "an attempt to apply the 'reasonable person' doctrine as found in other areas of the law to copyright." 3 Nimmer § 13.03[E][2], at 13–62.10–11. That approach may well have served its purpose when the material under scrutiny was limited to art forms readily comprehensible and generally familiar to the average lay person. However, in considering the extension of the rule to the present case, we are reminded of Holmes' admonition that, "[t]he life of the law has not been logic: it has been experience." O.W. Holmes, Jr., *The Common Law* 1 (1881).

Thus, in deciding the limits to which expert opinion may be employed in ascertaining the substantial similarity of computer programs, we cannot disregard the highly complicated and technical subject matter at the heart of these claims. Rather, we recognize the reality that computer programs are likely to be somewhat impenetrable by lay observers—whether they be judges or juries—and, thus, seem to fall outside the category of works contemplated by those who engineered the *Arnstein* test. * * *

In making its finding on substantial similarity with respect to computer programs, we believe that the trier of fact need not be limited by the strictures of its own lay perspective. * * * Rather, we leave it to the discretion of the district court to decide to what extent, if any, expert opinion, regarding the highly technical nature of computer programs, is warranted in a given case.

In so holding, we do not intend to disturb the traditional role of lay observers in judging substantial similarity in copyright cases that involve the aesthetic arts, such as music, visual works or literature. * * *

II.   TRADE SECRET PREEMPTION

[The court, after a rehearing, concluded that Computer Associates' trade secret claims against Altai were not preempted under § 301 of the Copyright Act.]

CONCLUSION

In adopting the above three step analysis for substantial similarity between the non-literal elements of computer programs, we seek to insure two things: (1) that programmers may receive appropriate copyright protection for innovative utilitarian works containing expression; and (2) that non-protectable technical expression remains in the public domain for others to use freely as building blocks in their own work. At first blush, it may seem counter-intuitive that someone who has benefitted to some degree from illicitly obtained material can emerge from an infringement suit relatively unscathed. However, so long as the appropriated material consists of non-protectable expression, "[t]his result is neither unfair nor unfortunate. It is the means by which copyright advances the progress of science and art." [Feist Publications, Inc. v. Rural Tel. Serv. Co., 499 U.S. 340, 350 (1991)].

Furthermore, we underscore that so long as trade secret law is employed in a manner that does not encroach upon the exclusive domain of the Copyright Act, it is an appropriate means by which to secure compensation for software espionage.

Accordingly, we affirm the judgment of the district court in part; vacate in part; and remand for further proceedings. The parties shall bear their own costs of appeal, including the petition for rehearing.

■ [JUDGE ALTIMARI dissented from the court's preemption analysis.]

NOTES ON INFRINGEMENT OF COMPUTER PROGRAMS

(1) In a subsequent decision, the Second Circuit refused to enjoin Computer Associates from pursuing the same infringement claim against Altai under French copyright law. Computer Associates Int'l, Inc. v. Altai, Inc., 126 F.3d 365 (2d Cir.1997), cert. denied, 523 U.S. 1106 (1998).

Does Judge Walker's analogy to the scope of protection accorded other kinds of literary works provide a convincing justification for extending protection to the "non-literal" elements of computer programs? A case for protection limited to literal copying is made in P. Goldstein, Infringement of Copyright in Computer Programs, 47 U.Pitt.L.Rev. 1119 (1986). D. Karjala, A Coherent Theory for the Copyright Protection of Computer Software and Recent Judicial Interpretations, 66 U.Cinn.L.Rev. 53 (1997), advocates narrow protection limited to aspects of computer programs that are subject to fast and cheap duplication, thus barring only literal copying or close derivatives.[o]

(2) Is *Computer Associates* correct in rejecting the analysis in Whelan Associates v. Jaslow Dental Laboratories, which viewed a computer program's overall "purpose or function" as the unprotected "idea" and any structural aspects not essential to the performance of that purpose or function as protectable "expression"? Did *Whelan* carry software protection into the forbidden realm of "idea, procedure, process, system, [or] method of operation"?

The "basic three-part analysis" in *Computer Associates* was adopted by the Tenth Circuit in Gates Rubber Co. v. Bando Chemical Indus., Ltd., 9 F.3d 823 (10th Cir.1993), which rejected the lower court's reliance on *Whelan*. "Filtration should eliminate from comparison the unprotectable elements of ideas, processes, facts, public domain information, merger material, *scenes a faire* material, and other unprotectable elements suggested by the particular facts of the program under examination." Although emphasizing that the copying of unprotectable elements cannot serve as the basis for liability, the court said that a comparison of the works as a whole may be useful in determining the fact of copying. The Eleventh Circuit in Bateman v. Mnemonics, Inc., 79 F.3d 1532 (11th Cir.1996), said that although the technique pursued in *Computer Associates* was formulated for non-literal copying, a similar analysis can be appropriate in cases of literal copying. Judge Baer in Harbor Software, Inc. v. Applied Systems, Inc., 925 F.Supp. 1042 (S.D.N.Y.1996), held that the abstraction and filtration necessary to determine the scope of copyright in a computer program is a matter for the court; the jury's role is limited to comparing protectable elements.

If *Computer Associates* is right in its conclusion that the protection granted in *Whelan* is excessive, does the filtration method move too far in the opposite direction? Is it possible that the sifting required by *Computer Associates* may be so fine as to ignore expressive selections and arrangements of unprotectable programming elements? In a subsequent non-literal copying case, the Second Circuit argued that the comparison of programs at successively higher levels of abstraction facilitates protection for original combinations and interrelationships of individually unprotected design elements. Softel, Inc. v. Dragon Medical and Scientific Communications, Inc., 118 F.3d 955 (2d Cir.1997), cert. denied, 523 U.S. 1020 (1998).

(3) Is *Computer Associates* correct in abandoning the ordinary observer test for substantial similarity in the case of computer programs? Is it relevant that the legislative history of the Semiconductor Chip Protection Act (p. 152 supra) says that expert testimony should be admissible on the issue of substantial similarity of mask works? See S.Rep. No. 98–425, 98th Cong., 2d Sess. 18 (1984).

(4) The legitimacy of "reverse engineering" of computer programs was the central issue in Sega Enterprises Ltd. v. Accolade, Inc., 977 F.2d 1510 (9th Cir.1992). Sega marketed video games played through its "Genesis" console. Accolade, desiring to develop games that would be compatible with the Genesis console, copied Sega's software in the course of "disassembling" the object code embedded in the Sega game cartridges and console chip in order to reconstruct

---

[o]   The clearest form of software infringement—complete duplication in the form of pirated copies—is a major problem for software producers. The Business Software Alliance, an industry trade group, claims on its web site that in 2011, 42 per cent of the computer software around the world was pirated, with an asserted value of $63 billion.

the source code. Accolade then produced games that were compatible with Genesis, but the games did not contain any of Sega's programming. The court concluded that although Accolade's "intermediate copying" would ordinarily constitute infringement, "where disassembly is the only way to gain access to the ideas and functional elements embodied in a copyrighted computer program and where there is a legitimate reason for seeking such access, disassembly is a fair use of the copyrighted work, as a matter of law." The court's discussion of the fair use factors in § 107 emphasized the public benefit in having more "independently designed video game programs offered for use with the Genesis console." This benefit overrode the presumption that copying for commercial purposes is not a fair use, especially since the direct objective of the copying was analysis rather than resale. See also Atari Games Corp. v. Nintendo Inc., 975 F.2d 832 (Fed.Cir.1992), in which the Federal Circuit had jurisdiction (because a patent was involved) over another intermediate copying case, with Ninth Circuit law controlling. Atari was struggling to break the electronic "lock" that controlled entry into the Nintendo game console. The court said that Atari could have made fair use of the Nintendo program to derive unprotected ideas and processes; it also indicated that Atari could incorporate into its games aspects of the Nintendo program necessary to unlock the Nintendo console. Atari's copying, however, had gone further (and it had also gotten a copy of Nintendo's source code by perpetrating a fraud on the Copyright Office). The court affirmed a preliminary injunction.

The defendant in Sony Computer Ent., Inc. v. Connectix Corp., 203 F.3d 596 (9th Cir.), cert. denied, 531 U.S. 871 (2000), successfully invoked *Sega* to overcome a claim that it had infringed the copyright in the software contained in Sony's PlayStation game console. Connectix sold a program called Virtual Game Station that allowed games designed for the PlayStation to be played on personal computers. Connectix's product did not contain any of Sony's copyrighted software. However, Sony's software had been repeatedly copied during the development of the defendant's product. The district court concluded that this "intermediate copying" was not a fair use and enjoined the sale of the Virtual Game Station. The Ninth Circuit reversed. Although the defendant's product might cause Sony to lose some PlayStation sales, Connectix's wholly new product "is a legitimate competitor" to the PlayStation console and thus the economic loss to Sony did not preclude a finding of fair use.ᴾ

Reverse engineering of computer programs is now constrained by § 1201 of the Copyright Act, added in 1998 as part of the Digital Millennium Copyright Act. That section establishes a general prohibition against circumventing technological measures that control access to a copyrighted work. Although § 1201(f) contains an exception if the circumvention is for the purpose of reverse engineering a computer program, the exception is limited to analysis necessary to achieve interoperability of computer programs.

(5) Consider again the question raised at p. 124 supra—should the protection of computer programs be achieved through some form of sui generis legislation analogous to that protecting semiconductor chips?

ᴾ   For a comparative analysis, see C. McManis, Intellectual Property Protection and Reverse Engineering of Computer Programs in the U.S. and the European Community, 8 High Tech.L.J. 25 (1993).

Lotus Development Corp. v. Borland International, Inc.

United States Court of Appeals, First Circuit, 1995.
49 F.3d 807.
Affirmed per curiam, 516 U.S. 233 (1996).

■ Before TORRUELLA, CHIEF JUDGE, BOUDIN and STAHL, CIRCUIT JUDGES.

■ STAHL, CIRCUIT JUDGE:

This appeal requires us to decide whether a computer menu command hierarchy is copyrightable subject matter. In particular, we must decide whether, as the district court held, plaintiff-appellee Lotus Development Corporation's copyright in Lotus 1–2–3, a computer spreadsheet program, was infringed by defendant-appellant Borland International, Inc., when Borland copied the Lotus 1–2–3 menu command hierarchy into its Quattro and Quattro Pro computer spreadsheet programs. See Lotus Dev. Corp. v. Borland Int'l, Inc., 788 F.Supp. 78 (D.Mass.1992) (*"Borland I"*); Lotus Dev. Corp. v. Borland Int'l, Inc., 799 F.Supp. 203 (D.Mass.1992) (*"Borland II"*); Lotus Dev. Corp. v. Borland Int'l, Inc., 831 F.Supp. 202 (D.Mass.1993) (*"Borland III"*); Lotus Dev. Corp. v. Borland Int'l, Inc., 831 F.Supp. 223 (D.Mass.1993) (*"Borland IV"*).

I.

Background

Lotus 1–2–3 is a spreadsheet program that enables users to perform accounting functions electronically on a computer. Users manipulate and control the program via a series of menu commands, such as "Copy," "Print," and "Quit." Users choose commands either by highlighting them on the screen or by typing their first letter. In all, Lotus 1–2–3 has 469 commands arranged into more than 50 menus and submenus.

Lotus 1–2–3, like many computer programs, allows users to write what are called "macros." By writing a macro, a user can designate a series of command choices with a single macro keystroke. Then, to execute that series of commands in multiple parts of the spreadsheet, rather than typing the whole series each time, the user only needs to type the single pre-programmed macro keystroke, causing the program to recall and perform the designated series of commands automatically. Thus, Lotus 1–2–3 macros shorten the time needed to set up and operate the program.

Borland released its first Quattro program to the public in 1987, after Borland's engineers had labored over its development for nearly three years. Borland's objective was to develop a spreadsheet program far superior to existing programs, including Lotus 1–2–3. In Borland's words, "[f]rom the time of its initial release . . . Quattro included enormous innovations over competing spreadsheet products."

The district court found, and Borland does not now contest, that Borland included in its Quattro and Quattro Pro version 1.0 programs "a *virtually identical* copy of the entire 1–2–3 menu tree." *Borland III*, 831 F.Supp. at 212 (emphasis in original). In so doing, Borland did not copy any of Lotus's underlying computer code; it copied only the words and structure of Lotus's menu command hierarchy. Borland included the Lotus menu command hierarchy in its programs to make them compatible with Lotus 1–2–3 so that spreadsheet users who were already familiar with Lotus 1–2–3 would be able to switch to the Borland programs without having to learn new commands or rewrite their Lotus macros.

In its Quattro and Quattro Pro version 1.0 programs, Borland achieved compatibility with Lotus 1–2–3 by offering its users an alternate user interface, the "Lotus Emulation Interface." By activating the Emulation Interface, Borland users would see the Lotus menu commands on their screens and could interact with Quattro or Quattro Pro as if using Lotus 1–2–3, albeit with a slightly different looking screen and with many Borland options not available on Lotus 1–2–3. In effect, Borland allowed users to choose how they wanted to communicate with Borland's spreadsheet programs: either by using menu commands designed by Borland, or by using the commands and command structure used in Lotus 1–2–3 augmented by Borland-added commands.

Lotus filed this action against Borland in the District of Massachusetts on July 2, 1990, four days after a district court held that the Lotus 1–2–3 "menu structure, taken as a whole—including the choice of command terms [and] the structure and order of those terms," was protected expression covered by Lotus's copyrights. Lotus Dev. Corp. v. Paperback Software Int'l, 740 F.Supp. 37, 68, 70 (D.Mass.1990) ("*Paperback*").[1] * * *

[Both parties filed motions for summary judgment.] Because so many variations were possible, the district court concluded that the Lotus developers' choice and arrangement of command terms, reflected in the Lotus menu command hierarchy, constituted copyrightable expression. [Granting summary judgment, the district court held that Borland had infringed Lotus's copyright in its menu commands and structure, but concluded that a trial was necessary to determine the extent of the infringement.]

Immediately following the district court's summary judgment decision, Borland removed the Lotus Emulation Interface from its products. Thereafter, Borland's spreadsheet programs no longer displayed the Lotus 1–2–3 menus to Borland users, and as a result Borland users could no longer communicate with Borland's programs as if they were using a more sophisticated version of Lotus 1–2–3. Nonetheless, Borland's programs continued to be partially compatible with Lotus 1–2–3, for Borland retained what it called the "Key Reader" in its Quattro Pro programs. Once turned on, the Key Reader allowed Borland's programs to understand and perform some Lotus 1–2–3 macros. * * * Accordingly, people who wrote or purchased macros to shorten the time needed to perform an operation in Lotus 1–2–3 could still use those macros in Borland's programs. The district court permitted Lotus to file a supplemental complaint alleging that the Key Reader infringed its copyright.

[In two separate trials, the district court held that both the Emulation Interface and the Key Reader contained "a virtually identical copy" of the Lotus menu tree and entered a permanent injunction against Borland, from which Borland appealed.]

II.

Discussion

On appeal, Borland does not dispute that it factually copied the words and arrangement of the Lotus menu command hierarchy. Rather, Borland argues that it "lawfully copied the unprotectable menus of Lotus 1–2–3." Borland contends that the Lotus menu command hierarchy is not copy-

---

[1]   Judge Keeton presided over both the *Paperback* litigation and this case.

rightable because it is a system, method of operation, process, or procedure foreclosed from protection by 17 U.S.C. § 102(b). Borland also raises a number of affirmative defenses.

A. Copyright Infringement Generally

To establish copyright infringement, a plaintiff must prove "(1) ownership of a valid copyright, and (2) copying of constituent elements of the work that are original." Feist Publications, Inc. v. Rural Tel. Serv. Co., 499 U.S. 340, 361 (1991); * * *

In this appeal, we are faced only with whether the Lotus menu command hierarchy is copyrightable subject matter in the first instance, for Borland concedes that Lotus has a valid copyright in Lotus 1–2–3 as a whole and admits to factually copying the Lotus menu command hierarchy. * * *

B. Matter of First Impression

Whether a computer menu command hierarchy constitutes copyrightable subject matter is a matter of first impression in this court. While some other courts appear to have touched on it briefly in dicta, see, e.g., Autoskill, Inc. v. National Educ. Support Sys., Inc., 994 F.2d 1476, 1495 n. 23 (10th Cir.), cert. denied, 510 U.S. 916 (1993), we know of no cases that deal with the copyrightability of a menu command hierarchy standing on its own (i.e., without other elements of the user interface, such as screen displays, in issue). Thus we are navigating in uncharted waters.

Borland vigorously argues, however, that the Supreme Court charted our course more than 100 years ago when it decided Baker v. Selden, 101 U.S. 99 (1879). * * * Borland argues:

> The facts of Baker v. Selden, and even the arguments advanced by the parties in that case, are identical to those in this case. The only difference is that the "user interface" of Selden's system was implemented by pen and paper rather than by computer.

To demonstrate that Baker v. Selden and this appeal both involve accounting systems, Borland even supplied this court with a video that, with special effects, shows Selden's paper forms "melting" into a computer screen and transforming into Lotus 1–2–3.

We do not think that Baker v. Selden is nearly as analogous to this appeal as Borland claims. Of course, Lotus 1–2–3 is a computer spreadsheet, and as such its grid of horizontal rows and vertical columns certainly resembles an accounting ledger or any other paper spreadsheet. Those grids, however, are not at issue in this appeal for, unlike Selden, Lotus does not claim to have a monopoly over its accounting system. Rather, this appeal involves Lotus's monopoly over the commands it uses to operate the computer. Accordingly, this appeal is not, as Borland contends, "identical" to Baker v. Selden.

C. Altai

Before we analyze whether the Lotus menu command hierarchy is a system, method of operation, process, or procedure, we first consider the applicability of the test the Second Circuit set forth in Computer Assoc. Int'l, Inc. v. Altai, Inc., 982 F.2d 693 (2d Cir.1992). The Second Circuit designed its *Altai* test to deal with the fact that computer programs, copyrighted as "literary works," can be infringed by what is known as "nonliteral" copying, which is copying that is paraphrased or loosely paraphrased *non-literal copying is* rather than word for word. See id. at 701 (citing nonliteral-copying cases); *paraphrase, not word for word* * * *

In the instant appeal, we are not confronted with alleged nonliteral copying of computer code. Rather, we are faced with Borland's deliberate, literal copying of the Lotus menu command hierarchy. Thus, we must determine not whether nonliteral copying occurred in some amorphous sense, but rather whether the literal copying of the Lotus menu command hierarchy constitutes copyright infringement.

While the *Altai* test may provide a useful framework for assessing the alleged nonliteral copying of computer code, we find it to be of little help in assessing whether the literal copying of a menu command hierarchy constitutes copyright infringement. In fact, we think that the *Altai* test in this context may actually be misleading because, in instructing courts to abstract the various levels, it seems to encourage them to find a base level that includes copyrightable subject matter that, if literally copied, would make the copier liable for copyright infringement. While that base (or literal) level would not be at issue in a nonliteral-copying case like *Altai,* it is precisely what is at issue in this appeal. We think that abstracting menu command hierarchies down to their individual word and menu levels and then filtering idea from expression at that stage, as both the *Altai* and the district court tests require, obscures the more fundamental question of whether a menu command hierarchy can be copyrighted at all. The initial inquiry should not be whether individual components of a menu command hierarchy are expressive, but rather whether the menu command hierarchy as a whole can be copyrighted. * * *

D.   *The Lotus Menu Command Hierarchy: A "Method of Operation"*

Borland argues that the Lotus menu command hierarchy is uncopyrightable because it is a system, method of operation, process, or procedure foreclosed from copyright protection by 17 U.S.C. § 102(b). * * *

We think that "method of operation," as that term is used in § 102(b), refers to the means by which a person operates something, whether it be a car, a food processor, or a computer. Thus a text describing how to operate something would not extend copyright protection to the method of operation itself; other people would be free to employ that method and to describe it in their own words. Similarly, if a new method of operation is used rather than described, other people would still be free to employ or describe that method.

We hold that the Lotus menu command hierarchy is an uncopyrightable "method of operation." The Lotus menu command hierarchy provides the means by which users control and operate Lotus 1–2–3. If users wish to copy material, for example, they use the "Copy" command. If users wish to print material, they use the "Print" command. Users must use the command terms to tell the computer what to do. Without the menu command hierarchy, users would not be able to access and control, or indeed make use of, Lotus 1–2–3's functional capabilities.

The Lotus menu command hierarchy does not merely explain and present Lotus 1–2–3's functional capabilities to the user; it also serves as the method by which the program is operated and controlled. The Lotus menu command hierarchy is different from the Lotus long prompts [brief explanations of the highlighted menu commands], for the long prompts are not necessary to the operation of the program; users could operate Lotus 1–2–3 even if there were no long prompts.[9] The Lotus menu command hierarchy is also different from the Lotus screen displays, for users need not "use" any expressive aspects of the screen displays in order to operate Lotus 1–2–3; because the way the screens look has little bearing on how users control the program, the screen displays are not part of Lotus 1–2–3's "method of operation"[10] The Lotus menu command hierarchy is also different from the underlying computer code, because while code is necessary for the program to work, its precise formulation is not. In other words, to offer the same capabilities as Lotus 1–2–3, Borland did not have to copy Lotus's underlying code (and indeed it did not); to allow users to operate its programs in substantially the same way, however, Borland had to copy the Lotus menu command hierarchy. Thus the Lotus 1–2–3 code is not an uncopyrightable "method of operation."

The district court held that the Lotus menu command hierarchy, with its specific choice and arrangement of command terms, constituted an "expression" of the "idea" of operating a computer program with commands arranged hierarchically into menus and submenus. *Borland II,* 799 F.Supp. at 216. Under the district court's reasoning, Lotus's decision to employ hierarchically arranged command terms to operate its program could not foreclose its competitors from also employing hierarchically arranged command terms to operate their programs, but it did foreclose them from employing the specific command terms and arrangement that Lotus had used. In effect, the district court limited Lotus 1–2–3's "method of operation" to an abstraction.

Accepting the district court's finding that the Lotus developers made some expressive choices in choosing and arranging the Lotus command terms, we nonetheless hold that that expression is not copyrightable because it is part of Lotus 1–2–3's "method of operation." We do not think that "methods of operation" are limited to abstractions; rather, they are the means by which a user operates something. If specific words are essential to operating something, then they are part of a "method of operation" and, as such, are unprotectable. This is so whether they must be highlighted, typed in, or even spoken, as computer programs no doubt will soon be controlled by spoken words.

The fact that Lotus developers could have designed the Lotus menu command hierarchy differently is immaterial to the question of whether it is a "method of operation." In other words, our initial inquiry is not whether the Lotus menu command hierarchy incorporates any expression. Rather, our initial inquiry is whether the Lotus menu command hierarchy is a "method of operation." Concluding, as we do, that users operate Lotus 1–2–3 by using the Lotus menu command hierarchy, and that the entire Lotus menu command hierarchy is essential to operating Lotus 1–2–3, we do not inquire further whether that method of operation could have been designed differently. The "expressive" choices of what to name the command terms

---

[9]   As the Lotus long prompts are not before us on appeal, we take no position on their copyrightability, although we do note that a strong argument could be made that the brief explanations they provide "merge" with the underlying idea of explaining such functions. See Morrissey v. Procter & Gamble Co., 379 F.2d 675, 678–79 (1st Cir.1967) (when the possible ways to express an idea are limited, the expression "merges" with the idea and is therefore uncopyrightable; when merger occurs, identical copying is permitted).

[10]   As they are not before us on appeal, we take no position on whether the Lotus 1–2–3 screen displays constitute original expression capable of being copyrighted.

and how to arrange them do not magically change the uncopyrightable menu command hierarchy into copyrightable subject matter. * * *

In many ways, the Lotus menu command hierarchy is like the buttons used to control, say, a video cassette recorder ("VCR"). A VCR is a machine that enables one to watch and record video tapes. Users operate VCRs by pressing a series of buttons that are typically labelled "Record, Play, Reverse, Fast Forward, Pause, Stop/Eject." That the buttons are arranged and labeled does not make them a "literary work," nor does it make them an "expression" of the abstract "method of operating" a VCR via a set of labeled buttons. Instead, the buttons are themselves the "method of operating" the VCR.

When a Lotus 1–2–3 user chooses a command, either by highlighting it on the screen or by typing its first letter, he or she effectively pushes a button. Highlighting the "Print" command on the screen, or typing the letter "P," is analogous to pressing a VCR button labeled "Play."

Just as one could not operate a buttonless VCR, it would be impossible to operate Lotus 1–2–3 without employing its menu command hierarchy. Thus the Lotus command terms are not equivalent to the labels on the VCR's buttons, but are instead equivalent to the buttons themselves. Unlike the labels on a VCR's buttons, which merely make operating a VCR easier by indicating the buttons' functions, the Lotus menu commands are essential to operating Lotus 1–2–3. Without the menu commands, there would be no way to "push" the Lotus buttons, as one could push unlabeled VCR buttons. While Lotus could probably have designed a user interface for which the command terms were mere labels, it did not do so here. Lotus 1–2–3 depends for its operation on use of the precise command terms that make up the Lotus menu command hierarchy. * * *

That the Lotus menu command hierarchy is a "method of operation" becomes clearer when one considers program compatibility. Under Lotus's theory, if a user uses several different programs, he or she must learn how to perform the same operation in a different way for each program used. For example, if the user wanted the computer to print material, then the user would have to learn not just one method of operating the computer such that it prints, but many different methods. We find this absurd. The fact that there may be many different ways to operate a computer program, or even many different ways to operate a computer program using a set of hierarchically arranged command terms, does not make the actual method of operation chosen copyrightable; it still functions as a method for operating the computer and as such is uncopyrightable.

Consider also that users employ the Lotus menu command hierarchy in writing macros. Under the district court's holding, if the user wrote a macro to shorten the time needed to perform a certain operation in Lotus 1–2–3, the user would be unable to use that macro to shorten the time needed to perform that same operation in another program. Rather, the user would have to rewrite his or her macro using that other program's menu command hierarchy. This is despite the fact that the macro is clearly the user's own work product. We think that forcing the user to cause the computer to perform the same operation in a different way ignores Congress's direction in § 102(b) that "methods of operation" are not copyrightable. * * *

We also note that in most contexts, there is no need to "build" upon other people's expression, for the ideas conveyed by that expression can be conveyed by someone else without copying the first author's expression. In the context of methods of operation, however, "building" requires the use of the precise method of operation already employed; otherwise, "building" would require dismantling, too. Original developers are not the only people entitled to build on the methods of operation they create; anyone can. Thus, Borland may build on the method of operation that Lotus designed and may use the Lotus menu command hierarchy in doing so. * * *

III.

Conclusion

Because we hold that the Lotus menu command hierarchy is uncopyrightable subject matter, we further hold that Borland did not infringe Lotus's copyright by copying it. Accordingly, we need not consider any of Borland's affirmative defenses. The judgment of the district court is

Reversed.

■ BOUDIN, CIRCUIT JUDGE, concurring.

* * * Most of the law of copyright and the "tools" of analysis have developed in the context of literary works such as novels, plays, and films. In this milieu, the principal problem—simply stated, if difficult to resolve—is to stimulate creative expression without unduly limiting access by others to the broader themes and concepts deployed by the author. The middle of the spectrum presents close cases; but a "mistake" in providing too much protection involves a small cost: subsequent authors treating the same themes must take a few more steps away from the original expression.

The problem presented by computer programs is fundamentally different in one respect. The computer program is a *means* for causing something to happen; it has a mechanical utility, an instrumental role, in accomplishing the world's work. Granting protection, in other words, can have some of the consequences of *patent* protection in limiting other people's ability to perform a task in the most efficient manner. Utility does not bar copyright (dictionaries may be copyrighted), but it alters the calculus.

Of course, the argument *for* protection is undiminished, perhaps even enhanced, by utility: if we want more of an intellectual product, a temporary monopoly for the creator provides incentives for others to create other, different items in this class. But the "cost" side of the equation may be different where one places a very high value on public access to a useful innovation that may be the most efficient means of performing a given task. Thus, the argument for extending protection may be the same; but the stakes on the other side are much higher.

It is no accident that patent protection has preconditions that copyright protection does not—notably, the requirements of novelty and non-obviousness—and that patents are granted for a shorter period than copyrights. * * *

Requests for the protection of computer menus present the concern with fencing off access to the commons in an acute form. A new menu may be a creative work, but over time its importance may come to reside more in the investment that has been made by users in learning the menu and in building their own mini-programs—macros—in reliance upon the menu. Better typewriter keyboard layouts may exist, but the familiar QWERTY keyboard dominates the market because that is what everyone has learned to use. See P. David, CLIO and the Economics of QWERTY, 75

Am.Econ.Rev. 332 (1985). The QWERTY keyboard is nothing other than a menu of letters. * * *

Thus, for me the question is not whether Borland should prevail but on what basis. Various avenues might be traveled, but the main choices are between holding that the menu is not protectable by copyright and devising a new doctrine that Borland's use is privileged. No solution is perfect and no intermediate appellate court can make the final choice.

To call the menu a "method of operation" is, in the common use of those words, a defensible position. * * *

A different approach would be to say that Borland's use is privileged because, in the context already described, it is not seeking to appropriate the advances made by Lotus' menu; rather, having provided an arguably more attractive menu of its own, Borland is merely trying to give former Lotus users an option to exploit their own prior investment in learning or in macros. The difference is that such a privileged use approach would not automatically protect Borland if it had simply copied the Lotus menu (using different codes), contributed nothing of its own, and resold Lotus under the Borland label. * * *

But a privileged use doctrine would certainly involve problems of its own. It might more closely tailor the limits on copyright protection to the reasons for limiting that protection; but it would entail a host of administrative problems that would cause cost and delay, and would also reduce the ability of the industry to predict outcomes. Indeed, to the extent that Lotus' menu is an important standard in the industry, it might be argued that any use ought to be deemed privileged.

In sum, the majority's result persuades me and its formulation is as good, if not better, than any other that occurs to me now as within the reach of courts. Some solutions (e.g., a very short copyright period for menus) are not options at all for courts but might be for Congress. In all events, the choices are important ones of policy, not linguistics, and they should be made with the underlying considerations in view.

NOTE

The Supreme Court granted Lotus's petition for certiorari. Lotus argued that the First Circuit had misread § 102(b) to automatically bar copyright protection for any aspect of a computer program that embodies a "method of operation," regardless of the extent of its expressive elements. With Justice Stevens not participating, the decision was affirmed per curiam by an equally divided Court. 516 U.S. 233 (1996).

Apple Computer, Inc. v. Microsoft Corp.
35 F.3d 1435 (9th Cir.1994), cert. denied, 513 U.S. 1184 (1995).

Apple, maker of the MacIntosh computer, sued Microsoft, developer of the Windows operating systems, alleging that Microsoft had gone beyond the scope of its license from Apple in creating Windows 2.03 and 3.0 and in licensing NewWave to Hewlett–Packard. Microsoft in defense challenged the copyrightability of dozens of the elements of the MacIntosh user interface. Apple attempted to sweep aside the defense by arguing that the individual elements were all protected by its claim of copyright in MacIntosh's overall "desktop" graphical interface. In a series of rulings the district court interpreted Microsoft's license to cover most of the similarities, and then dissected the works to conclude that most of the remaining similarities did not relate to protectable elements. "Some visual displays are or become so closely tied to the functional purpose of the article that they become standard. * * * Such standards in a graphical user interface would enlarge the market for computers by making it easier to learn how to use them." 799 F.Supp. 1006 (N.D.Cal.1992). The district court concluded that any infringement of Apple's user interface as a whole would require virtual identity; it later granted Microsoft's motion for summary judgment under the virtual identity standard. 821 F.Supp. 616 (N.D.Cal.1993).

The Court of Appeals affirmed the summary judgment and remanded for further consideration of Microsoft's request for attorney's fees. Referring to Microsoft's license from Apple, Judge Rymer said that the district court "correctly decided first to identify which visual displays in Windows 2.03, 3.0 and NewWave are licensed and which are not."

"The district court then properly proceeded to distinguish ideas from expression, and to 'dissect' unlicensed elements in order to determine whether the remaining similarities lack originality, flow naturally from basic ideas, or are one of the few ways in which a particular idea can be expressed given the constraints of the computer environment. Dissection is not inappropriate even though GUIs [graphical user interfaces] are thought of as the 'look and feel' of a computer, because copyright protection extends only to protectable elements of expression.

"Having found that the similarities in Windows 2.03 and 3.0 consist only of unprotectable or licensed elements, and that the similarities between protectable elements in Apple's works and NewWave are de minimis, the district court did not err by concluding that, to the extent there is creative expression left in how the works are put together, as a whole they can receive only limited protection. When the range of protectable and unauthorized expression is narrow, the appropriate standard for illicit copying is virtual identity."

Reviewing the arguments made by Apple on appeal, the court remarked that "all of these contentions boil down to the same thing: Apple wants an overall comparison of its works to the accused works for substantial similarity rather than virtual identity." However, the court held that "considering the license and the limited number of ways that the basic ideas of the Apple GUI can be expressed differently, we conclude that only 'thin' protection, against virtually identical copying, is appropriate."

NOTES AND QUESTIONS

(1) Is *Lotus* correct in rejecting District Judge Keeton's "abstraction" approach that tried to separate the unprotected idea of operating a spreadsheet program through commands hierarchically arranged into menus from the expression of that idea through the choice of specific command terms and arrangements?

Under *Lotus*, would the graphical user interface of the MacIntosh computer that was before the Ninth Circuit in *Apple Computer* be classified as a "method of operation" and hence excluded from copyright? What about a computer's operating system program—is it too a "method of operation" according to the analysis in *Lotus*? Are you convinced by the court's policy argument in favor of compatibility? Recall the different response to similar arguments in Apple Computer v. Franklin Computer, p. 110 supra.

In Mitel, Inc. v. Iqtel, Inc., 124 F.3d 1366 (10th Cir.1997), the Tenth Circuit rejected *Lotus Development*'s interpretation of the rule in § 102(b) precluding copyright in a "method of operation." The plaintiff was seeking protection for a set of over sixty four-digit numeric command codes used with a piece of telecommunications equipment known as a call controller. The defendant produced a competing controller and programmed it to respond to the plaintiff's codes. Referring to the district court's determination that the plaintiff's codes were an unprotected method of operation, Judge Tacha said, "The First Circuit reached a similar conclusion in *Lotus* * * *. The *Lotus* court concluded that the question whether a work is excluded from protection under section 102(b) logically precedes consideration of whether the individual components of the work are 'expressive.' * * * Section 102(b) does not extinguish the protection accorded a particular expression of an idea merely because that expression is embodied in a method of operation at a higher level of abstraction. Rather, sections 102(a) & (b) interact to secure ideas for public domain and to set apart an author's particular expression for further scrutiny to ensure that copyright protection will 'promote the . . . useful Arts.' U.S. Const. art. I, § 8, cl. 8. Our abstraction-filtration-comparison approach is directed to achieving this balance." The trial court's denial of a preliminary injunction was nonetheless affirmed since the court found that the plaintiff's arbitrary assignment of numbers to particular functions lacked the creativity necessary for copyright.

L. Weinreb, Copyright for Functional Expression, 111 Harv.L.Rev. 1149 (1998), viewing copyright law as a series of descriptive conventions rather than purposive rules, defends the outcome in *Lotus* as consistent with the dichotomy between literary works and machines. G. Lunney, *Lotus v. Borland*: Copyright and Computer Programs, 70 Tulane L.Rev. 2397 (1996), also applauds the result (but not the rationale) of *Lotus*.

(2) When Google developed its Android platform for smartphones, it used the Java programming language. Oracle claimed that Google had infringed 37 of its Java application programming interfaces (API)—essentially groups of pre-written programs designed to carry out specific routines. Google replicated the names, organization, and functions of the APIs, but with 97 percent different programming code, in order to allow Java applications to run on its devices. After a detailed review of the case law on copyright in computer programs, Judge Alsup in Oracle America, Inc. v. Google Inc., 872 F.Supp.2d 974 (N.D.Cal.2012), dismissed Oracle's claims for copyright infringement. The specific routines or methods were unprotectable ideas. Anyone was free to carry out the same functions with their own programming code. The organization of the routines was a command structure for a system of operation and thus uncopyrightable under § 102(b). The three percent of the plaintiff's code that had been copied related to the names and specifications of the programs and its use was necessary to achieve interoperability.

(3) Screen displays are often a dominant feature of the interface between a computer program and the user. Early cases were divided on whether copyright in a computer program extends to the screen displays that the program generates. Compare Broderbund Software, Inc. v. Unison World, Inc., 648 F.Supp. 1127 (N.D.Cal.1986), with Digital Communications Associates, Inc. v. Softklone Distributing Corp., 659 F.Supp. 449 (N.D.Ga.1987). Since 1988, the Copyright

Office has taken the position that "all copyrightable expression owned by the same claimant and embodied in a computer program, or first published as a unit with a computer program, including computer screen displays, is considered a single work and should be registered on a single application form." 53 Fed.Reg. 21817 (1988).

When judging infringement of certain screen displays, notably video games, the courts have generally invoked the standards used for other audiovisuals works. Is a different analysis appropriate for screen displays that form part of a functional interface with the user of a computer program? Compare Atari, Inc. v. North American Philips Consumer Electronics Corp., 672 F.2d 607 (7th Cir.), cert. denied, 459 U.S. 880 (1982), with Manufacturers Tech., Inc. v. Cams, Inc., 706 F.Supp. 984 (D.Conn.1989). In MiTek Holdings, Inc. v. Arce Engineering Co., 89 F.3d 1548 (11th Cir.1996), the court followed the Ninth Circuit's approach in *Apple Computer* and required "bodily appropriation of expression" or "virtual identicality" to establish infringement of copyright in a compilation of elements in a user interface. What justifies this heightened standard for infringement? A limited range of available expression? An interest in standardization?

(4) Does the public interest in standardization and compatibility justify analytic dissection that eliminates from copyright aspects of a computer interface that reflect attempts to respond to consumer preferences and expectations? Does the interest in standardized displays and command structures and compatible data formats justify application of the merger doctrine? (Recall Franklin Computer's unsuccessful merger argument in Apple Computer, Inc. v. Franklin Computer Corp., p. 110 supra.) The Fifth Circuit in Engineering Dynamics, Inc. v. Structural Software, Inc., 26 F.3d 1335 (5th Cir.1994), endorsed the abstraction-filtration-comparison method for determining copyright in a user interface consisting primarily of input and output formats, but ordered a remand "to determine whether the existence of industry standards precludes copyright protection."

7. SOUND RECORDINGS

This Section deals with the infringement of sound recordings by unauthorized duplication. Infringement by unauthorized public performance is considered at p. 273 infra; on the imitation of sound recordings, see p. 669 infra.

As the market for records became larger and more lucrative in the 1950s and 60s, so did the opportunities for sellers of unauthorized copies, commonly referred to as "pirates." Congress responded to the pleas of the record companies in 1971 with amendments to the 1909 Copyright Act creating a new, although limited, copyright in sound recordings "fixed, published and copyrighted" on or after February 15, 1972.[q] The Sound Recording Amendments of 1971 were eventually superseded by § 114 of the 1976 Act.

----

[q]   Pub.L. No. 92–140, 85 Stat. 391. On the protection of older sound recordings, see § 301(c) and p. 668 infra.

"Sound recordings" are defined in § 101; they are fixed in "phonorecords." (Note that sound tracks of motion pictures and other audiovisual works are excluded from the definition—those works are protected as components of the audiovisual work.) Sound recordings typically consist of a recorded performance and should be distinguished from the underlying musical, literary, or dramatic work being performed. Like other copyrightable works, sound recordings must satisfy the requirements of originality and authorship. What are the possible sources of creative authorship in a sound recording? There is also a special form of copyright notice in § 402 for sound recordings—the letter P in a circle.

Rights in sound recordings, framed with an eye toward the record pirate, are carefully circumscribed in § 114(b). The exclusive rights of reproduction and the preparation of derivative works are limited to physical duplication of the sound recording and exclude mere imitation.[r]

The ease with which CDs can be duplicated fostered a brisk market in pirated discs. Large CD burners can churn out copies of popular recordings in vast numbers. By some estimates, pirated copies account for over one-third of global CD sales. The trade became so stable that some sellers of counterfeit CDs even accept returns. Referring to her usual seller of pirated CDs, one New York customer said, "Everybody buys from him. The quality is very good. He's reputable and he's honest." Zittel, The Pirates of Pop Music Fill Streets with $5 CDs, N.Y. Times, Sept. 9, 1999, p. E1. (In addition to civil liability for copyright infringement, there are substantial criminal penalties for record piracy. See § 506 and 18 U.S.C.A. §§ 2318–19.) Despite the continuing problem with traditional record piracy, the attention of the record companies is now focused on what the industry views as an even greater threat—unauthorized distribution of sound recordings over the Internet. That issue is taken up in the next chapter.

DIGITAL SAMPLING

The limits of the reproduction right in sound recordings are being tested by the phenomenon of digital sampling. The digital recording of music makes it possible to extract bits of sound and to manipulate the samples in endless ways. As an early example, consider the handiwork of one New York sound engineer who "plugged into his sampler the sound of Madonna screaming 'hey!' on her song 'Like a Virgin,' raised it an octave and dropped the new sound into a few parts of a coming song by Jamie Bernstein. He took a horn blast from a James Brown song and turned it into a lush, mellow tone for a Japanese singer's love ballad. 'I didn't feel at all like I was ripping James Brown off,' he says." Miller, High–Tech Alteration of Sights and Sounds Divides Art World, Wall St.J., Sept. 1, 1987, p. 1.

What rights, if any, does sampling violate? Is it an infringement of the copyright in a sound recording to remove a sample of sound and put it into a new recording? How should one approach issues of substantial similarity and fair use? If the sample lasts, say, a few seconds, is it even a copyrightable entity? And at what point are rights in the underlying musical composition infringed? Few cases have been litigated, perhaps because record com-

---

[r]   Protection of sound recordings under § 114 is not limited to record piracy. See Agee v. Paramount Communications, Inc., 59 F.3d 317 (2d Cir.1995) (unauthorized reproduction of a sound recording on the sound track of a television program infringed the owner's reproduction right under § 114).

panies sample other companies' recordings as often as their own recordings are sampled. The court in one early case, relying more on the Ten Commandments than on any principle of copyright law, enjoined the sale of an album by rapper Biz Markie containing samples taken from Gilbert O'Sullivan's *Alone Again (Naturally)*, citing plaintiff's ownership of both the music and sound recording copyrights. Grand Upright Music Ltd. v. Warner Bros. Records, Inc., 780 F.Supp. 182 (S.D.N.Y.1991). Another court denied a sampler's motion for summary judgment because it had not established as a matter of law that the sampled portions of the copyrighted song were insubstantial; since the plaintiff owned only the song and not the sound recording, however, the defendant did get summary judgment on the sound recording infringement claim. Jarvis v. A & M Records, 827 F.Supp. 282 (D.N.J.1993). A plaintiff who owned the copyright in an underlying musical work sampled by Beastie Boys lost on a motion for summary judgment in Newton v. Diamond, 388 F.3d 1189 (9th Cir.2004), cert. denied, 545 U.S. 1114 (2005). The defendants had sampled a three-note sequence and one background note lasting six seconds from the plaintiff's recording of his flute composition. The defendants had a license from the owner of the sound recording, but plaintiff claimed infringement of his musical composition. The court concluded that the three-note sequence, considered without of any of the distinctive audio elements from the licensed sound recording, was de minimis; the defendants' work thus was not substantially similar to the copyrighted musical work.

Record companies have grown more cautious about using unlicensed samples and now routinely pay for a license, but some artists such as The Eagles, Led Zeppelin, and the Beatles rarely authorize any sampling of their work. See Jones, Haven't I Heard that "Whoop" (or "Hoop") Somewhere Before?, N.Y. Times, Dec. 22, 1996, Sec. 2, p. 44. That caution may be redoubled in light of the following decision by the Sixth Circuit.

Bridgeport Music, Inc. v. Dimension Films
410 F.3d 792 (6th Cir. 2005).

The plaintiff owned the copyright in a sound recording of "Get Off Your Ass and Jam" by George Clinton, Jr. and the Funkadelics. The defendant used a two-second sample of a guitar solo playing an "arpeggiated chord"— three notes of a chord played in succession rather than struck together. The sample was lowered in pitch and "looped" into a seven-second segment that appeared at five separate places in a recording used on the sound track of the defendant's movie. The district court, applying a standard of substantial similarity, found that no reasonable juror would recognize the sample as having been appropriated from the copyrighted sound recording; it granted summary judgment to the defendant. The Sixth Circuit reversed.

Judge Guy began by noting that § 114(b) limits the exclusive reproduction right in a sound recording to duplications that recapture the actual sounds. "This means that the world at large is free to imitate or simulate the creative work fixed in the recording so long as an actual copy of the sound recording itself is not made. That leads us directly to the issue in this case. If you cannot pirate the whole sound recording, can you 'lift' or 'sample' something less than the whole. Our answer to that question is in the negative."

"Section 114(b) provides that '[t]he exclusive right of the owner of cop- *[§114(b)]* yright in a sound recording under clause (2) of section 106 is limited to the right to prepare a derivative work in which the actual sounds fixed in the sound recording are rearranged, remixed, or otherwise altered in sequence or quality.'" In a footnote, the court said, "'The import of this language is that it does not matter how much a digital sampler alters the actual sounds or whether the ordinary lay observer can or cannot recognize the song or the artist's performance of it. Since the exclusive right encompasses rearranging, remixing, or otherwise altering the actual sounds, the statute by its own terms precludes the use of a substantial similarity test,'" quoting S. Latham, Newton v. Diamond: Measuring the Legitimacy of Unauthorized Compositional Sampling—A Clue Illuminated and Obscured, 26 Hastings Comm/Ent L.J. 119, 125 (2003). "In other words, a sound recording owner has the exclusive right to 'sample' his own recording. We find much to recommend this interpretation."

"To begin with, there is ease of enforcement. Get a license or do not *[get license or don't sample]* sample. We do not see this as stifling creativity in any significant way. It must be remembered that if an artist wants to incorporate a 'riff' from another work in his or her recording, he is free to duplicate the sound of that 'riff' in the studio. Second, the market will control the license price and keep it within bounds. The sound recording copyright holder cannot exact a *[license price controlled by market]* license fee greater than what it would cost the person seeking the license to just duplicate the sample in the course of making the new recording. Third, sampling is never accidental. It is not like the case of a composer who has a *[sampling not incidental]* melody in his head, perhaps not even realizing that the reason he hears this melody is that it is the work of another which he had heard before. When you sample a sound recording you know you are taking another's work product. * * *

"Finally, and unfortunately, there is no Rosetta stone for the interpretation of the copyright statute. We have taken a 'literal reading' approach. The legislative history is of little help because digital sampling wasn't being done in 1971. If this is not what Congress intended or is not what they would intend now, it is easy enough for the record industry, as they have done in the past, to go back to Congress for a clarification or change in the law."

NOTES AND QUESTIONS

(1) Is *Bridgeport Music* correct in interpreting the language in § 114(b) limiting a sound recording owner's protection against derivative works to uses that take actual sounds as meaning that *any* taking of actual sounds is an infringement? Do the court's policy arguments provide a convincing justification for that interpretation? *Bridgeport Music*'s per se rule against sampling was rejected by the district court in Saregama India Ltd. v. Mosley, 687 F.Supp.2d 1325 (S.D.Fla. 2009), aff'd on other grounds, 635 F.3d 1284 (11th Cir. 2011). According to Judge Seitz, "The *Bridgeport* court appears to interpret [§ 114(b)] to mean that protection in a copyrighted sound recording extends to *every* sound fixed in the work such that a sample of *any* sound automatically constitutes infringement. However, a more plausible reading of this provision is that pro- *[plausible reading of 114(b)]* tection in a sound recording 'do[es] not extend' to sound recordings which, although *similar-sounding*, do not capture *any* sounds from the copyrighted sound recording." The court granted summary judgment to a defendant who had taken a one-second sample from the plaintiff's work because no reasonable jury could find the works substantially similar. J. Cromer Young, Harry Potter and the Three Second Crime: Are We Vanishing the De Minimis Defense from Copyright Law?, 36 N.Mex.L.Rev. 261 (2006), is critical of *Bridgeport* and other intrusions on a de minimis defense, but T. Reilly, Debunking the Top Three Myths of Digital Sampling, 31 Colum.J.L. & Arts 355 (2008), stoutly defends *Bridgeport* and urges the music industry to adopt a comprehensive licensing regime. A proposal for compulsory licensing of samples is offered in W. Henslee, Marybeth Peters Is Almost Right: An Alternative to Her Proposals to Reform the Compulsory License Scheme for Music, 48 Washburn L.J. 107 (2008).

Mashups, created by combining material from two or more sound recordings, typically involve more extensive and more easily recognizable takings. May they nevertheless be a fair use? O. Arewa, From J.C. Bach to Hip Hop: Musical Borrowing, Copyright and Cultural Context, 84 N.Car.L.Rev. 547 (2006), argues the copyright law fails to accommodate the artistic requirements of genres like hip hop; T. Evans, Sampling, Looping, and Mashing . . . Oh My!: How Hip Hop Music is Scratching More Than the Surface of Copyright Law, 21 Ford.Intell.Prop., Media & Ent.L.J. 843 (2011), criticizes *Bridgeport* and urges recognition of a kind of reverse engineering privilege to make innovative use of sound recordings; H. Anderson, "Criminal Minded?": Mixtape DJs, the Piracy Paradox, and Lessons for the Recording Industry, 76 Tenn.L.Rev. 111 (2008), concludes that the recording industry has misjudged the economic impact of "mixtape" DJs who remix existing recordings.

(2) E. Ulmer, The Rome Convention for the Protection of Performers, Producers of Phonograms, and Broadcasting Organizations, 10 Bull.Copyr. Soc'y 90, 165, 219 (1962), is a full description of a 1961 treaty aimed at establishing an international regime of protection for performers and record producers, including rights against unauthorized fixation, reproduction, and broadcast (but available only to performers and producers from contracting states). The United States declined to join the Rome Convention. In 1971, a conference in Geneva proposed a simple ban on the unauthorized duplication of sound recordings. The 1971 Sound Recording Amendment to the 1909 Copyright Act met the requirements of this Convention for the Protection of Producers of Phonograms Against Unauthorized Duplication of Their Phonograms, and it entered into force with respect to the United States in 1974.

In foreign systems, performers' rights are often described as "neighboring rights"—*droit voisins*. "Neighboring rights derive their name from the fact that their origins are to be found in the neighborhood of copyright. However, neighboring rights not only differ from copyright in the extent of protection afforded them, but also with regard to the subjects to which they relate: the subjects of copyright are literary and artistic works; the subjects of neighboring rights are performances, phonograms and broadcasts." Ulmer, supra, at 165. In the United States, protection for performers and producers of works such as sound recordings and televisions broadcasts is accomplished through copyright, thus entitling foreign performers and producers to similar protection in the U.S. under the national treatment requirement of the Berne Convention. When foreign countries declare a right to be outside of copyright—a neighboring right—they are free to treat the right as they wish, with no obligation to foreign nationals under Berne.

(3) At a 1996 conference in Geneva sponsored by the World Intellectual Property Organization (WIPO), representatives adopted a treaty intended to secure protection for sound recordings in the emerging digital environment. The Performances and Phonograms Treaty (reprinted in the Statutory Supplement) recognizes on behalf of performers and producers an exclusive right to reproduce and distribute their recordings and includes an obligation of national treatment for the citizens of other contracting states. Performers are also given the exclusive right to authorize the broadcast or fixation of their unfixed performances. With an eye toward the electronic delivery of sound recordings, Articles 10 and 14 of the treaty recognize on behalf of performers and producers the exclusive right to authorize the distribution of their recordings to the public "by wire or wireless means, in such a way that members of the public may access them from a place and at a time individually chosen by them." The treaty also requires adequate legal protection against the circumvention of technological security measures used to prevent violations of the owner's rights and against the removal or alteration of "rights management information"—information that identifies the work and specifies the terms and conditions of use. About ninety countries have ratified the treaty. The United States implemented the Performances and Phonograms Treaty through the Digital Millennium Copyright Act in 1998. We will hear more about the DMCA in the next chapter.

8. PERFORMANCE RIGHTS

An exclusive right of public performance (now § 106(4)) was first granted to the owners of copyrights in musical works by an act of 1897 (29 Stat. 481). It seems to have had little practical importance,[s] even though it was not restricted to performances that were "for profit"—a limitation on the performance right that was introduced in the 1909 Copyright Act. In 1914, the American Society of Composers, Authors and Publishers (ASCAP) was formed by Victor Herbert, John Philip Sousa, and other famous figures in the music industry to monitor and license the public performance of music. In a series of cases during the first half of the twentieth century, ASCAP and other copyright owners managed to expand the boundaries of the public performance for profit right under the 1909 Act. They were uniformly successful, for example, in obtaining recognition that performances carrying even an indirect economic advantage were still "for profit." See, e.g., Herbert v. Shanley Co., 242 U.S. 591 (1917). The "for profit" requirement was ultimately eliminated in § 106(4) of the 1976 Act, but the issue survives in the form of an exemption for certain non-profit performances in § 110(4). "Public" and "performance" were also generously interpreted under the 1909 Act until the Supreme Court took a sharp turn beginning with the *Fortnightly* case.

Fortnightly Corp. v. United Artists Television, Inc.

Supreme Court of the United States, 1968.
392 U.S. 390, 88 S.Ct. 2084.

■ MR. JUSTICE STEWART delivered the opinion of the Court.

The petitioner, Fortnightly Corporation, owns and operates community antenna television (CATV) systems in Clarksburg and Fairmont, West Virginia. There were no local television broadcasting stations in that immedi-

---

[s] "There is no record of a single cent being collected under that law." ASCAP, The Story of ASCAP 12 (1948).

ate area until 1957. Now there are two, but, because of hilly terrain, most residents of the area cannot receive the broadcasts of any additional stations by ordinary rooftop antennas. Some of the residents have joined in erecting larger cooperative antennas in order to receive more distant stations, but a majority of the householders in both communities have solved the problem by becoming customers of the petitioner's CATV service. * * *

During 1960, when this proceeding began, the petitioner's systems provided customers with signals of five television broadcasting stations, three located in Pittsburgh, Pennsylvania; one in Steubenville, Ohio; and one in Wheeling, West Virginia. The distance between those cities and Clarksburg and Fairmont ranges from 52 to 82 miles. The systems carried all the programming of each of the five stations * * *.

[Respondent United Artist Television licensed the television stations to broadcast motion pictures on which it held the copyrights, and these broadcasts were carried by petitioner to its customers. The licenses did not authorize CATV carriage. Respondent prevailed on infringement claims in the courts below.] * * *

At the outset it is clear that the petitioner's systems did not "perform" the respondent's copyrighted works in any conventional sense of that term, or in any manner envisaged by the Congress that enacted the law in 1909. But our inquiry cannot be limited to ordinary meaning and legislative history, for this is a statute that was drafted long before the development of the electronic phenomena with which we deal here. In 1909 radio itself was in its infancy, and television had not been invented. We must read the statutory language of 60 years ago in the light of drastic technological change. * * *

The television broadcaster in one sense does less than the exhibitor of a motion picture or stage play; he supplies his audience not with visible images but only with electronic signals. The viewer conversely does more than a member of a theater audience; he provides the equipment to convert electronic signals into audible sound and visible images. Despite these deviations from the conventional situation contemplated by the framers of the Copyright Act, broadcasters have been judicially treated as exhibitors, and viewers as members of a theater audience. Broadcasters perform. Viewers do not perform. Thus, while both broadcaster and viewer play crucial roles in the total television process, a line is drawn between them. One is treated as active performer; the other, as passive beneficiary.

When CATV is considered in this framework, we conclude that it falls on the viewer's side of the line. Essentially, a CATV system no more than enhances the viewer's capacity to receive the broadcaster's signals; it provides a well-located antenna with an efficient connection to the viewer's television set. * * * We have been invited by the Solicitor General in an *amicus curiae* brief to render a compromise decision in this case that would, it is said, accommodate various competing considerations of copyright, communications, and antitrust policy. We decline the invitation. That job is for Congress. We take the Copyright Act of 1909 as we find it. With due regard to changing technology, we hold that the petitioner did not under that law "perform" the respondent's copyrighted works.

The judgment of the Court of Appeals is reversed.

■ MR. JUSTICE DOUGLAS and MR. JUSTICE MARSHALL took no part in the consideration or decision of this case.■ MR. JUSTICE HARLAN took no part in the decision of this case.

■ MR. JUSTICE FORTAS dissented.

Teleprompter Corp. v. Columbia Broadcasting System, Inc.
415 U.S. 394 (1974).

This was a carefully presented test case. CBS charged infringement of representative programs by five CATV installations belonging to the defendant. Noting that *Fortnightly* was based on simpler technology that did nothing more than bring in telecasts otherwise blocked by mountainous terrain, CBS pointed out that CATV systems now import signals from distant markets and originate programming on non-broadcast channels, which makes them more akin to and competitive with regular broadcasters. The Court of Appeals held that "when a CATV system imports distant signals it is no longer within the ambit of the *Fortnightly* doctrine." 476 F.2d 338 (2d Cir.1973).

The Supreme Court, with Justice Stewart again writing, rejected the attempt to distinguish distant signals and found no significant difference from *Fortnightly*. "By importing signals that could not normally be received with current technology in the community it serves, a CATV system does not, for copyright purposes, alter the function it performs for its subscribers. * * * The reception and rechanneling of these signals for simultaneous viewing is essentially a viewer function, irrespective of the distance between the broadcasting station and the ultimate viewer."

Twentieth Century Music Corp. v. Aiken
United States Supreme Court, 1975.
422 U.S. 151, 95 S.Ct. 2040.

■ MR. JUSTICE STEWART delivered the opinion of the Court.

The question presented by this case is whether the reception of a radio broadcast of a copyrighted musical composition can constitute copyright infringement, when the copyright owner has licensed the broadcaster to perform the composition publicly for profit.

The respondent George Aiken owns and operates a small fast-service food shop in downtown Pittsburgh, Pa., known as "George Aiken's Chicken." Some customers carry out the food they purchase, while others remain and eat at counters or booths. Usually the "carry-out" customers are in the restaurant for less than five minutes, and those who eat there seldom remain longer than 10 or 15 minutes.

A radio with outlets to four speakers in the ceiling receives broadcasts of music and other normal radio programing at the restaurant. Aiken usually turns on the radio each morning at the start of business. Music, news, entertainment, and commercial advertising broadcast by radio stations are thus heard by Aiken, his employees, and his customers during the hours that the establishment is open for business.

[Petitioners' copyrighted songs were heard in Aiken's shop. The broadcaster had an ASCAP license, but Aiken did not. Aiken lost in the District Court, but won in the Court of Appeals, 500 F.2d 127 (3d Cir.1974), which relied on *Fortnightly* and *Teleprompter*.] * * *

The precise statutory issue in the present case is whether Aiken infringed upon the petitioners' exclusive right, under the Copyright Act of

1909, 17 U.S.C.A. § 1(e), "[t]o perform the copyrighted work publicly for profit." We may assume that the radio reception of the musical compositions in Aiken's restaurant occurred "publicly for profit." See Herbert v. Shanley, 242 U.S. 591. The dispositive question, therefore, is whether this radio reception constituted a "performance" of the copyrighted works. * * *

* * *[A]s the Court of Appeals in this case perceived, this Court has in two recent decisions explicitly disavowed the view that the reception of an electronic broadcast can constitute a performance, when the broadcaster himself is licensed to perform the copyrighted material that he broadcasts. * * *

To hold in this case that the respondent Aiken "performed" the petitioners' copyrighted works would thus require us to overrule two very recent decisions of this Court. But such a holding would more than offend the principles of *stare decisis;* it would result in a regime of copyright law that would be both wholly unenforceable and highly inequitable.

The practical unenforceability of a ruling that all of those in Aiken's position are copyright infringers is self-evident. One has only to consider the countless business establishments in this country with radio or television sets on their premises—bars beauty shops, cafeterias, car washes, dentists' offices, and drive-ins—to realize the total futility of any evenhanded effort on the part of copyright holders to license even a substantial percentage of them.[12]

And a ruling that a radio listener "performs" every broadcast that he receives would be highly inequitable for two distinct reasons. First, a person in Aiken's position would have no sure way of protecting himself from liability for copyright infringement except by keeping his radio set turned off. For even if he secured a license from ASCAP, he would have no way of either foreseeing or controlling the broadcast of compositions whose copyright was held by someone else. Secondly, to hold that all in Aiken's position "performed" these musical compositions would be to authorize the sale of an untold number of licenses for what is basically a single public rendition of a copyrighted work. The exaction of such multiple tribute would go far beyond what is required for the economic protection of copyright owners,[14] * * *.

For the reasons stated in this opinion, the judgment of the Court of Appeals is affirmed.

It is so ordered.

■ MR. JUSTICE BLACKMUN, concurring in the result.

---

[12] The Court of Appeals observed that ASCAP now has license agreements with some 5,150 business establishments in the whole country, 500 F.2d, at 129, noting that these include "firms which employ on premises sources for music such as tape recorders and live entertainment." Id., at n. 4. As a matter of so-called "policy" or "practice," we are told, ASCAP has not even tried to exact licensing agreements from commercial establishments whose radios have only a single speaker.

[14] The petitioners have not demonstrated that they cannot receive from a broadcaster adequate royalties based upon the total size of the broadcaster's audience. On the contrary, the respondent points out that generally copyright holders can and do receive royalties in proportion to advertising revenues of licensed broadcasters, and a broadcaster's advertising revenues reflect the total number of its listeners, including those who listen to the broadcasts in public business establishments.

* * * Respondent Aiken hardly was an innocent "listener," as the Court seems to characterize him throughout its opinion * * *.

* * * Aiken installed four loudspeakers in his small shop. This, obviously, was not done for his personal use and contentment so that he might hear the broadcast, in any corner he might be, above the noise of commercial transactions. It was done for the entertainment and edification of his customers. It was part of what Mr. Aiken offered his trade, and it added, in his estimation, to the atmosphere and attraction of his establishment. Viewed in this light, respondent is something more than a mere listener and is not so simply to be categorized. * * *

■ MR. CHIEF JUSTICE BURGER, with whom MR. JUSTICE DOUGLAS joins, dissenting.

* * * My primary purpose in writing is not merely to express disagreement with the Court but to underscore what has repeatedly been stated by others as to the need for legislative action. * * *

NOTES AND QUESTIONS ON PUBLIC PERFORMANCE

(1) The preceding opinions from the Supreme Court called upon Congress to act, and Congress responded in the 1976 Copyright Act. The response on cable television will be surveyed in a later chapter. The exclusive right of public performance appears now in § 106(4) (supported by definitions of "perform," "publicly," and "transmit" in § 101), but it is elaborately qualified in § 110.

[handwritten: Altered stat definitions]

Consider first the statutory definitions—do they overrule the Supreme Court's interpretation of public performance under the 1909 Act? They were clearly so intended:

> Under the definitions of "perform," "display," "publicly," and "transmit" in section 101, the concepts of public performance and public display cover not only the initial rendition or showing, but also any further act by which that rendition or showing is transmitted or communicated to the public. Thus, for example: a singer is performing when he or she sings a song; a broadcasting network is performing when it transmits his or her performance (whether simultaneously or from records); a local broadcaster is performing when it transmits the network broadcast; a cable television system is performing when it retransmits the broadcast to its subscribers; and any individual is performing whenever he or she plays a phonorecord embodying the performance or communicates the performance by turning on a receiving set. (H.R.Rep. p. 63.)

[handwritten: broadcast is when a performance is transmitted]

The performance right encompasses only *public* performances—singing in the shower will not infringe, at least absent unusual circumstances. The § 101 definition of "publicly" was construed in Columbia Pictures Indus., Inc. v. Redd Horne, Inc., 749 F.2d 154 (3d Cir.1984), which held that "in-store rentals" of movie cassettes constituted public performance; the tapes were played in viewing rooms (complete with popcorn) that accommodated two to four people. "Simply because the cassettes can be viewed in private does not mitigate the essential fact that Maxwell's is unquestionably open to the public." In *Redd Horne,* store employees ran the cassettes from a central location. The customers in Columbia Pictures Indus., Inc. v. Aveco, Inc., 800 F.2d 59 (3d Cir.1986), took the cassettes into the viewing rooms. The court held that it was still a public performance.[t]

In National Football League v. PrimeTime 24 Joint Venture, 211 F.3d 10 (2d Cir.2000), cert. denied, 532 U.S. 941 (2001), the NFL complained about a satellite carrier that was uplinking transmissions of NFL football games in the United States and providing the broadcasts to its subscribers in Canada. The defendant argued that any public performance occurred when the transmissions were downlinked to the Canadian customers and thus could not trigger liability under U.S. law. The Second Circuit disagreed, holding that "each step" in the process by which the works are delivered to the public constitutes a public performance or display, and thus the uplink in the United States was itself an infringement. (The NFL and other professional sports leagues now have a bigger problem—unauthorized streaming of live game broadcasts over the Internet; the pirated feeds compete with both authorized broadcasts and the leagues' own subscription Internet packages.)

(2) Both *Redd Horne* and *PrimeTime 24* were distinguished in Cartoon Network LP v. CSC Holdings, Inc., 536 F.3d 121 (2d Cir.2008), cert. denied, 129 S.Ct. 2890 (2009), when copyright owners objected to a new service proposed by Cablevision called Remote Storage DVR. The service allowed customers who did not have a DVR to record programs on Cablevision's own central servers and play back the shows using their standard cable box. When a customer wanted to record a program, it was saved on a portion of Cablevision's hard drive allocated to that customer. Playback was accomplished by transmitting the unique copy to the customer; the transmission could be decoded only by that subscriber's cable box. As for the copying itself, the court concluded that the "copies produced by the RS–DVR system are 'made' by the RS–DVR customer" and thus Cablevision was not directly liable for the reproduction. The copyright owners also argued that the transmission of the recorded programs back to the customers was a public performance. Since the RS–DVR system transmitted a unique copy to only the requesting subscriber, the court said that the performance was not "to the public," despite the plaintiffs' argument that Cablevision was transmitting copies of the same program to numerous users.

WNET, Thirteen v. Aereo, Inc.

712 F.3d 676 (2d Cir.2013) .

"Aereo, Inc. ('Aereo') enables its subscribers to watch broadcast television programs over the internet for a monthly fee. Two groups of plaintiffs, holders of copyrights in programs broadcast on network television, filed copyright infringement actions against Aereo in the United States District Court for the Southern District of New York. They moved for a preliminary injunction barring Aereo from transmitting programs to its subscribers while the programs are still airing, claiming that those transmissions infringe their exclusive right to publicly perform their works. The district court (Nathan, J.) denied the motion, concluding that the plaintiffs were

---

[t]   Major motion pictures studios, operating through the Motion Picture Licensing Corporation, offer licenses to non-profit organizations, businesses, and governmental institutions for public performances of movies. See the MPLC web site at www.mplc.com. S. Stadler, Performance Values, 83 Notre Dame L.Rev. 697 (2008), argues for substantial reductions in the performance right that would force owners to rely more on revenue from the distribution of copies.

unlikely to prevail on the merits in light of our prior decision in Cartoon Network LP, LLLP v. CSC Holdings, Inc., 536 F.3d 121 (2d Cir.2008) ('*Cablevision*'). We agree and affirm the order of the district court denying the motion for a preliminary injunction. * * *

" * * * Aereo's primary means of transmitting a program to a user is via an internet browser, which users can access on their computers. Aereo users can also watch programs on mobile devices such as tablets or smart phones using mobile applications. * * * " When a user selects a program, Aereo assigns a specific tiny antenna to that user; the captured broadcast is then recorded on a portion of Aereo's hard drive reserved for that subscriber. The program is streamed to the user using that specific copy.

"The Act also states: 'To perform or display a work "publicly" means * * * (2) to transmit or otherwise communicate a performance or display of the work to a place specified by clause (1) or to the public, by means of any device or process, whether the members of the public capable of receiving the performance or display receive it in the same place or in separate places and at the same time or at separate times.'

"Plaintiffs claim that Aereo's transmissions of broadcast television programs while the programs are airing on broadcast television fall within the plain language of the Transmit Clause and are analogous to the re-transmissions of network programing made by cable systems, which the drafters of the 1976 Copyright Act viewed as public performances. They therefore believe that Aereo is publicly performing their copyrighted works without a license. * * *

"The *Cablevision* court began by discussing the language and legislative history of the Transmit Clause. 536 F.3d at 134–35. * * * As the language makes plain, in determining whether a transmission is to the public it is important 'to discern who is "capable of receiving" the performance being transmitted.' Id. (quoting 17 U.S.C. § 101). *Cablevision* then decided that 'capable of receiving the performance' refers not to the performance of the underlying work being transmitted but rather to the transmission itself, since the 'transmission of a performance is itself a performance.' Id. The Court therefore concluded that 'the transmit clause directs us to examine who precisely is "capable of receiving" *a particular transmission of a performance.*' 536 F.3d at 135 (emphasis added). * * *

"We discuss *Cablevision's* interpretation of the Transmit Clause in such detail because that decision establishes four guideposts that determine the outcome of this appeal. First and most important, the Transmit Clause directs courts to consider the potential audience of the individual transmission. See id. at 135. If that transmission is 'capable of being received by the public' the transmission is a public performance; if the potential audience of the transmission is only one subscriber, the transmission is not a public performance, except as discussed below. Second and following from the first, private transmissions--that is those not capable of being received by the public--should not be aggregated. It is therefore irrelevant to the Transmit Clause analysis whether the public is capable of receiving the same underlying work or original performance of the work by means of many transmissions. See id. at 135–37. Third, there is an exception to this no-aggregation rule when private transmissions are generated from the same copy of the work. In such cases, these private transmissions *should* be aggregated, and if these aggregated transmissions from a single copy enable the public to view that copy, the transmissions are public performances. See id. at 137–38. * * *

" * * * Plaintiffs argue that discrete transmissions should be aggregated to determine whether they are public performances. * * * Plaintiffs first argue that because Aereo's discrete transmissions enable members of the public to receive 'the same performance (i.e., Aereo's retransmission of a program)' they are transmissions made 'to the public.' * * * But this is nothing more than the *Cablevision* plaintiffs' interpretation of the Transmit Clause, as it equates Aereo's transmissions with the original broadcast made by the over-the-air network rather than treating Aereo's transmissions as independent performances. See 536 F.3d at 136. This approach was explicitly rejected by the *Cablevision* court."

The court concluded that Aereo's transmissions were not public performances and affirmed the denial of the preliminary injunction. Judge Chin dissented, calling Aereo's technology platform "a sham." "Even assuming Aereo's system limits the potential audience for each transmission, and even assuming each of its subscribers receives a unique recorded copy, Aereo still is transmitting the programming 'to the public.' "

(The television networks had greater success against a different company using similar technology to stream broadcast programming in Fox Television Stations, Inc. v. BarryDriller Content Sys., 2012 WL 6784498 (C.D.Cal.2012). Rejecting *Cartoon Networks*, the court held that even the transmission of unique copies made for specific users could be a public performance since the § 101 definition did not require that the transmission to the public be made from the same copy of the work. However, given the possibility of differing views among the circuits, the district court limited the preliminary injunction to the geographic area of the Ninth Circuit.)

NOTES AND QUESTIONS ON THE EXEMPTIONS IN § 110

(1) Certain public performances are exempt under § 110. Note first that most of the exemptions apply only to specific types of works, although the classroom exemption in § 110(1) refers simply to "a work," as does § 110(5)(A). Would a school play performed in a high school auditorium be exempt under the classroom exemption in § 110(1)? The House Report at p. 82 says that it would not. Why not?

(2) The exemption in § 110(2) governing performances and displays in the course of educational transmissions was rewritten in 2002 by the Technology, Education, and Copyright Harmonization (TEACH) Act, Pub.L.No. 107–273, in order to accommodate digital transmissions. The former exemption was expanded beyond nondramatic literary and musical works to include "reasonable and limited portions of any other work." To the extent technologically feasible, reception of the transmission must be limited to students officially enrolled in the course. Section 110(2) specifically authorizes digital transmissions, including asynchronous access by students, but the school must apply technological measures that "reasonably prevent" retention and further dissemination. Provisions added at the conclusion of § 110 protect an educational institution from liability for transient or temporary copies created during an authorized digital transmission; amendments to § 112(f) permit schools to make copies of works for use in authorized transmissions, but with a prohibition against converting analog works to digital formats if a useable digital version is available.

(3) Could the § 110(3) exemption for performances in the course of worship services be challenged as an impermissible preference to religion? (What does the phrase "of a religious nature" in § 110(3) modify? Apparently it was intended to limit only the category of "dramatico-musical work." See H.R.Rep. p. 84.)

(4) The exemption in § 110(4) for certain non-profit performances replaces the general "for profit" limitation on the performance right under the 1909 Act. When is a performance "without any purpose of direct or indirect commercial advantage"? According to the House Report, "This provision expressly adopts the principle established by the court decisions construing the 'for profit' limitation: that public performances given or sponsored in connection with any commercial or profit-making enterprises are subject to the exclusive rights of the copyright owner even though the public is not charged for seeing or hearing the performance." H.R.Rep. p. 85.[u]

Would a performance by a school orchestra conducted by a music teacher who receives an annual salary be excluded from § 110(4) as involving "payment of any fee or other compensation for the performance"? The House Report indicates that it would not. Id. Would the half-time performance of a high school or college band at a football game be exempt under § 110(4)? Does it matter if there is radio or television coverage of the half-time festivities?

Why, in the event of an admission charge, is the copyright owner allowed to prohibit use of the work? The House Report states that "otherwise, owners could be compelled to make involuntary donations to the fund-raising activities of causes to which they are opposed." H.R.Rep. p. 86. But how will the copyright owner know of the intended use? Apparently users are not required to provide advance notice; the Copyright Office regulations leave the initiative with the copyright owner. 37 C.F.R. § 201.13.

(5) Section 110(5) responds to the *Aiken* problem. As originally enacted, § 110(5) consisted only of what is now § 110(5)(A), exempting "the public reception of a transmission on a single receiving apparatus of a kind commonly used in private homes." If a tavern owner installs a television, the resulting public performances are exempt. (What of a large high-definition television—is it "a single receiving apparatus of a kind commonly used in private homes"?[v]) Suppose a tavern owner records installments of "reality" shows and then provides a saturnalia of viewing on the weekend. That is probably an infringement. Why? Or, on a standard stereo, a restaurant owner plays CDs of copyrighted music. Is

---

[u]   ASCAP suffered a public relations nightmare when it attempted to sign up the nation's camp grounds to public performance licenses. News accounts, reporting that ASCAP was going after groups like the Girl Scouts, were full of stories about scouts afraid to sing *Puff the Magic Dragon* around the campfire. Would that be exempt under § 110(4)? Insisting that it had only meant to license performances by professional musicians at large resort camps, ASCAP returned the fees to 16 Girl Scout camps that had paid for licenses. Bumiller, ASCAP Asks Royalties from Girl Scouts, and Regrets It, N.Y. Times, Dec. 17, 1996, p. B1.

In re Cellco Partnership, 663 F.Supp.2d 363 (S.D.N.Y.2009), held that a ringtone playing on a cellphone does not usually constitute a public performance, and even if the audience is sufficiently large to qualify as "public," the performance would comfortably fit within the exemption for nonprofit public performances in § 110(4).

[v]   Churches across the country hurriedly canceled plans for Super Bowl parties when attorneys for the National Football League insisted that the viewing parties would be legal only if the churches limited themselves to a single home-size television of 55–inches or less and did not charge admission. Senator Arlen Specter then introduced a bill that would allow churches to show live broadcasts of professional football games on any kind of equipment as long as they did not charge for the performance. 75 Pat., Tm. & Copyr.J. (BNA) 359 (2008). The National Football League quickly responded with a letter indicating that it would no longer object to live showings of the Super Bowl on church premises, regardless of the screen size. Balt. Sun, Feb. 22, 2008, p. 16Z.

that within the safety of § 110(5)? And what of George Aiken and his "radio with outlets to four speakers in the ceiling"? The House Report at p. 87 said that it considered the *Aiken* case "to represent the outer limit of the exemption," but the exemption for the public reception of non-dramatic musical works was subsequently expanded by § 110(5)(B).

(6) The Fairness in Music Licensing Act, Pub.L. No. 105–298, added § 110(5)(B) in 1998. Note first that § 110(5)(B) applies only to the performance of a nondramatic musical work, whether embodied in a radio or television transmission.[w] The subsection offers a blanket exemption for reception by establishments that have less than 2,000 gross square feet of space (or less than 3,750 square feet in the case of food and drinking establishments). Implementing definitions of "establishment," "food or drinking establishment," and "gross square feet of space" were added in § 101. For businesses that exceed the square-footage limitations, the reception is still exempt if the business uses no more than six speakers (not more than four in any one room) or four televisions (not more than one per room). A study prepared for ASCAP indicated that 70 per cent of eating and drinking establishments and 45 per cent of retail businesses are exempt under § 110(5)(B). 60 Pat., Tm. & Copyr.J. (BNA) 282 (2000).

At the instigation of the European Union, the World Trade Organization ruled in 2000 that the exemptions to the public performance right for musical works in § 110(5)(B) are incompatible with U.S. obligations under the WTO's TRIPS agreement. The U.S. maintained that the economic impact of the exemptions was de minimis and fell within art. 13 of TRIPS, which permits exceptions to exclusive rights "which do not conflict with a normal exploitation of the work and do not unreasonably prejudice the legitimate interests of the right holder." However, the WTO concluded that § 110(5)(B) violated our obligation under art. 11 of the Berne Convention to protect the public performance right and hence was a violation of our obligation under art. 9.1 of TRIPS to comply with Berne. A claim that the original exemption in § 110(5)(A) also violated TRIPS was rejected, although that conclusion was based in part on the assumption that performances of nondramatic musical works are no longer exempt under § 110(5)(A) in light of their specific treatment in § 110(5)(B). 60 Pat., Tm. & Copyr.J. (BNA) 282 (2000). A WTO arbitration panel set damages at $1.1 million annually, which the EU could enforce through trade sanctions. Pat., Tm. & Copyr.L. Daily (BNA) (Oct. 16, 2001). The dispute was temporarily settled in 2003 when the U.S. agreed to pay damages to EU performing rights societies, but the agreement includes an understanding that the U.S. will eventually amend § 110(5)(B) to comply with the WTO ruling. Pat., Tm. & Copyr.L. Daily (BNA) (June 25, 2003). M. Landau, Fitting United States Copyright Law Into the International Scheme: Foreign and Domestic Challenges to Recent Legislation, 23 Ga.St.U.L.Rev. 847 (2007), reviews the current status of the dispute.

(7) The § 110(10) exemption for fraternal and veterans' organizations was added in 1982. Why should they be exempt? Note the limited inclusion of college fraternities and sororities.

(8) Hotel and apartment house retransmissions are exempt under § 111(a)(1). For what uses would a hotel now need a performing rights license? A hotel

Handwritten margin note: WTO 110(5)(B) violated art. 11 of BC to protect public perf ∴ = violation of TRIPS

---

w   Performances of audiovisual works like game broadcasts in sports bars are generally licensed through the cable or satellite company that provides the video; they charge the bars a higher fee to cover licensing payments to copyright owners.

renting videodiscs that guests took to their rooms (which were equipped with players and large-screen televisions) did not need a license; the guest rooms were not "public." Columbia Pictures Indus., Inc. v. Professional Real Estate Investors, 866 F.2d 278 (9th Cir.1989). But in On Command Video Corp. v. Columbia Pictures Indus., 777 F.Supp. 787 (N.D.Cal.1991), the court held that electronic delivery of videotaped movies from a central location to individual hotel rooms involved a transmission to the public and was not exempt. And another hotel needed a license when it used a satellite dish to bring in ESPN and HBO. ESPN, Inc. v. Edinburg Community Hotel, Inc., 735 F.Supp. 1334 (S.D.Tex.1986). Why? See § 111(b).

PUBLIC PERFORMANCE OF SOUND RECORDINGS

(1) Early attempts at common law to control the public performance of sound recordings (as distinguished from the musical works embodied in the recordings) produced famous cases and irreconcilable results.[x] Proposals to create an exclusive public performance right in sound recordings, which would be especially valuable against broadcasters, were rebuffed during the revision process leading to the 1976 Act. Proponents got only a directive to the Register of Copyrights to report with recommendations on a performance right for sound recordings. The Report of the Register of Copyrights on Performance Rights in Sound Recordings was duly submitted in 1978; it strongly supported an exclusive right of public performance for sound recordings. "Broadcasters and other commercial users of recordings have performed them without permission or payment for generations. Users today look upon any requirement that they pay royalties as an unfair imposition in the nature of a 'tax.' However, any economic burden on the users of recordings for public performance is heavily outweighed, not only by the commercial benefits accruing directly from the use of copyrighted sound recordings, but also by the direct and indirect damage done to performers whenever recordings are used as a substitute for live performances." The Report also responded to the broadcasters' traditional argument that the benefits accruing to performers and record companies from the free airplay of their recordings is adequate compensation for the performance. "This is the strongest argument put forward by broadcasters and other users. There is no question that broadcasting and jukebox performances give some recordings the kind of exposure that benefits their producers and individual performers through increased sales and popularity. * * * The opportunity for benefit through increased sales, no matter how significant it may be temporarily for some 'hit records,' can hardly justify the outright denial of any performing rights to any sound recordings."

The Record Industry Association of America and various organizations representing performing artists have continued their battle for a general public performance right for sound recordings. Since satellite, cable, and Internet music providers must now pay royalties as a result of the digital performance right in sound recordings (see Note (2) infra), the record companies think they may be able to convince Congress as a matter of equity to make radio stations pay as well. The radio stations, taking advantage of their free access to the airwaves, have run advertisements railing against a "tax" that could "bankrupt local radio stations" in order to pay "[g]iant rec-

---

[x] Compare Waring v. WDAS Broadcasting Station, Inc., 327 Pa. 433, 194 A. 631 (1937), with RCA Manuf. Co. v. Whiteman, 114 F.2d 86 (2d Cir.), cert. denied, 311 U.S. 712 (1940).

ord companies, most of which are in foreign countries." The record companies and performers note that a performance right could bring in $100 to $150 million in royalties from foreign countries, which now refuse to pay American sound recording owners for foreign radio performances based on the lack of reciprocity for performances of foreign recordings in the U.S. Plambeck, Dispute Heats Up Over Proposed New Fees for Playing Songs on the Radio, N.Y. Times, March 8, 2010, p. B3. The National Association of Broadcasters continues to emphasize the promotional value of the free airplay they provide, quoting both performers ("You can text, Twitter and website your ass off and it's not going to have one-tenth the impact radio has"—country music singer Kix Brooks) and record company executives ("[R]adio remains the best way to get new music into listener's lives"—Sony BMG Executive Vice President Butch Waugh). NAB Statement, States News Service, March 15, 2011. One compromise pushed by the radio stations includes a federal law to force cellphone manufacturers to make their devices capable of receiving radio broadcasts. The cellphone industry is not amused. 80 Pat., Tm. & Copyr.J. (BNA) 839 (2010).

G. Myers and G. Howard, The Future of Music: Reconfiguring Public Performance Rights, 17 J.Intell.Prop.L. 207 (2010), advocates full performance rights for sound recordings, as does W. Henslee, What's Wrong with U.S.? Why the United States Should Have a Public Performance Right for Sound Recordings, 13 Vand.J.Ent. & Tech.L. 739 (2011). M. LaFrance, From Whether to How: The Challenge of Implementing a Full Public Performance Right in Sound Recordings, 2 Harv.J. Sports & Ent.L. 221 (2011), examines the practical difficulties in effectuating a full-blown performance right. Clear Channel, the nation's largest radio broadcaster, recently entered a groundbreaking contract with a country music record label that represents performers like Taylor Swift and Tim McGraw. The deal requires royalties for radio performances in exchange for reduced royalties for online performances. Sisario, Radio Royalty Deal Offers Hope for Industrywide Pact, N.Y. Times, June 11, 2012, p. B2. For now at least, the U.S. remains virtually alone in refusing to recognize a general public performance right in sound recordings.

(2) In 1995 Congress passed the Digital Performance Right in Sound Recordings Act, Pub.L. No. 104–39. The Act creates a new—but sharply limited—public performance right for sound recordings. The amendments made by the Act begin with a deceptively simple addition to the list of exclusive rights—§ 106(6) now recognizes, for sound recordings, an exclusive right "to perform the copyrighted work publicly by means of a digital audio transmission," supported by a definition of "digital transmission" in § 101. However, the digital performance right for sound recordings is subject to the dizzying series of limitations imposed in §§ 114(d)–(j).

Note first that the performance right in sound recordings is limited to digital transmissions; it does not apply to analog transmissions of sound recordings such as traditional AM or FM broadcasts, or to public performances that do not involve a transmission, such as playing CDs as background music at a restaurant. Since the right covers only sound recordings, it does not apply to transmissions of audiovisual works (see § 114(j)(5)).

Even some digital transmissions of sound recordings are exempt under § 114(d)(1), primarily a "nonsubscription broadcast transmission." Thus, radio stations can continue to broadcast sound recordings without liability even if they switch to digital technology. Other types of digital transmissions—"subscription transmissions"—do fall within the scope of the digital performance right but may be eligible for a compulsory license at fees set by voluntary negotiations or by the Copyright Royalty Board. "Subscription transmissions" are controlled transmissions to recipients who pay to receive them. Satellite radio and digital cable music channels are the chief examples. They are eligible for the compulsory license if, among other conditions, they are not "interactive," basically meaning that they do not permit a recipient to hear a particular sound recording on request. There are also restrictions on publishing advance programming schedules and playing too many selections from a given recording or performer in a specified time period. All this is geared to preventing subscription services from cutting too heavily into sales of pre-recorded music. Half of the compulsory licensing fees are reserved for performers (45 per cent to the featured artists on the sound recording and 2 1/2 per cent each to funds for non-featured vocalists and musicians); the other half of the fee goes to the record company that owns the copyright in the sound recording. Subscription transmissions that do not qualify for the compulsory license—primarily interactive transmissions—must be licensed by the copyright owner. The distribution of proceeds from such licenses is determined by the terms of the performers' contracts with the record company.

Eligible for compulsory license if not interactive & do not permit a recipient to hear song req.

1/2 of compulsory lic. fees → perf.

1/2 → Record company

IF DNQ (interactive) → must be lic. by the © owner

(3) Uncertainty about the status of webcasting—streaming sound recordings over the Internet—led to a 1998 amendment to § 114 that included even nonsubscription webcasting within the digital performance right. The programming capabilities of webcasting (single artist channels, for example) and the ability of listeners to influence the selection of recordings were viewed as a the threat to music sales. The amendment also extended the compulsory license to cover noninteractive webcasts. The Copyright Office has determined that AM/FM broadcasters who simultaneously stream their programming over the Internet are subject to the webcasting rules. 65 Fed.Reg. 77292. That determination was upheld in Bonneville Int'l Corp. v. Peters, 347 F.3d 485 (3d Cir.2003).

In 2002, the Librarian of Congress set the compulsory license rate for webcasts at .07 cents per performance per listener. The record companies complained that the rate was too low, but webcasters, who had been pushing for a rate based on a percentage of revenue, said the flat rate would force many small webcasters, including college stations, off the Internet. The Librarian's decision was ultimately upheld in Beethoven.com LLC v. Librarian of Congress, 394 F.3d 939 (D.C.Cir.2005). Small webcasters sought relief from Congress, which responded with the Small Webcaster Settlement Act of 2002, Pub.L.No. 107–321. The amendments authorized the recording industry to enter into agreements with small webcasters on alternative rates for the compulsory license. Controversy over webcasting rates has continued with each new rate-setting determination. The Copyright Royalty Board set new rates in 2007 that imposed a $500 per channel fee and higher per performance rates for stations that exceed a monthly performance threshold. Webcasters, who still support a percentage of revenue approach, objected again, pointing out that large webcasters often have hundreds of separate channels and small webcasters would be increasingly burdened by the escalating per performance rates. The compulsory rates were largely upheld when webcasters appealed the determination to the D.C. Circuit. Intercollegiate Broadcast Sys., Inc. v. Copyright Royalty Bd., 571 F.3d 69 (D.C.Cir.2009). However, the court vacated and remanded the annual $500 per channel fee. Congress had already stepped in again with the Webcaster Settlement Act of 2008, Pub.L.No. 110–435, giving webcasters an opportunity to negotiate alternative rates. Agreements were

2002: .07 / lic.

reached that cap the per channel fees and allow small webcasters to pay a percentage of revenue. 77 Pat., Tm. & Copyr.J. (BNA) 446 (2009). Meanwhile, Congress reacted yet again with the Webcaster Settlement Act of 2009, P.L. No. 111–36, which extended the authority of the record industry to negotiate rates with the webcasters that effectively replace the rates set by the CRB. Various groups of webcasters have now reached agreements that run through 2015. For commercial webcasters who are not a party to an agreement, the CRB has established rates for the 2011–2015 period that rise to .23 cents per performance per listener by 2015. Large commercial webcasters like Pandora continue to argue that their rates should be based on a percentage of revenue using the standards in § 801(b) that are applicable to other digital performers like satellite and cable music providers, rather than the "willing buyer and a willing seller" standard currently used for internet providers under § 114(f)(2)(B). 85 Pat., Tm. & Copyr.J. (BNA) 168 (2012). (Satellite providers like SiriusXM paid a compulsory royalty rate of 9 percent of gross revenue in 2013, rising to 11 percent by 2017.)

Webcasters and the record companies are also arguing over the degree of listener influence necessary to make a webcast "interactive" and ineligible for the compulsory license. The Second Circuit in Arista Records, LLC v. Launch Media, Inc., 578 F.3d 148 (2d Cir.2009), cert. denied, 130 S.Ct. 1290 (2010), became the first appellate court to decide when a webcasting service is "interactive." LAUNCHcast enabled its users to create "stations" that would play songs within a particular genre or songs similar to those of a particular artist. Section 114(j)(7) defines an "interactive service" as one "that enables a member of the public to receive a transmission of a program specially created for the recipient, or on request, a transmission of a particular sound recording." A LAUNCHcast user could not request a particular song on demand; as for the reception of a "specially created" program, the court held that the individualized "stations" did not ensure a degree of predictability that would make the service a substitute for purchasing the music. LAUNCHcast was thus not "interactive" for purposes of the § 114 compulsory license.

(4) SoundExchange, the agency that collects royalties for non-exempt digital performances of sound recordings, now pays out over $400 million a year. Sisario, Royalties from Digital Radio Start to Carry Weight, N.Y. Times, June 18, 2012, p. B4. Distributions are likely to increase as satellite radio adds to its subscriber base. The biggest headache is tracking down less well-known performers who are owed a share of the pool.

PERFORMING RIGHTS ORGANIZATIONS

ASCAP

The organization and operation of ASCAP are described in the following excerpts from a paper by Herman Finkelstein, a long-time general counsel of ASCAP.[y]

----

[y] Public Performance Rights in Music and Performance Rights Societies, originally in Seven Copyright Problems Analyzed 69 (1952), revised and separately published in 1956 and 1961 by the author; excerpts reproduced by permission from the 1961 publication. The operation of ASCAP is also described in I. Koenigsberg, Performing Rights in Music and Performing Rights Organizations, Revisited, 50 J.Copyr.Soc'y 355 (2003). For additional information, see the ASCAP web site at www.ascap.com.

"The performing right which will be discussed here is limited to musical compositions—particularly the non-dramatic, or so-called 'small' rights in such works.[z] In addition to the American Society of Composers, Authors and Publishers, which has been in existence since 1914, there are other licensing organizations such as Broadcast Music, Inc. (BMI) which is owned by and operated for the radio broadcast industry; and a third organization known as SESAC, Inc., originally called the Society of European Stage Authors and Composers. This organization is privately owned. * * *

"The American Society of Composers, Authors and Publishers unlike any of the other licensing organizations mentioned is made up entirely of composers, authors and publishers. It is a nonprofit organization. After payment of expenses, all of its receipts are divided equally between writers on the one hand and their publishers on the other. * * *

"The members, as I have said, grant only the non-dramatic rights. * * * Members license their works directly for the legitimate stage. Dramatic performances on television or radio are also reserved to and handled by the members independently of the Society.

"Users of music have the option of dealing individually with the members of the Society, or collectively with the Society. As a practical matter, of course, a radio station, or other large scale users of copyrighted musical works would find it wholly impractical to deal with individual copyright owners.

"The need for bulk licensing of performing rights is nowhere more evident than in the radio and television field where program directors require the greatest latitude in building their shows while protecting the station, its sponsors and artists from claims of infringement. The networks and most local stations have license agreements with ASCAP, BMI and SESAC, Inc. Network programs are cleared at the source by the Society, that is, if a network broadcasts a program using music in the Society's repertory, the network's license covers all the interconnected stations picking up that program. On purely local programs, the individual stations have their own agreement. * * *

"Although radio and television together constitute the most extensive users of copyrighted musical compositions in the Society's repertory, a great variety of users obtain licenses to perform the vast repertory of compositions made available by the Society. These include restaurants, taverns, dance halls, hotels, department stores and such wired music concerns as Muzak, Seeburg and others. Of late, factories and similar industrial establishments have become important users of music. * * *

"The royalties collected by the Society are divided equally between the publishers and the writers. The publishers have their system of distribution and the writers have theirs. There are these overriding principles applicable both to writer and publisher-director: consideration must be given to the number of works that a member contributes, their nature, character,

---

[z] Rights to perform songs in a dramatic setting are sometimes called "grand rights" and have their own problems of definition, licensing, and protection. See M. Krasilovsky, S. Shemel, J. Gross, and J. Feinstein, This Business of Music (2007). On the often severe restrictions imposed on dramatic performances of well-known songs by the copyright successors to deceased composers and lyricists, see O'Toole, Ego, Paranoia and Power in the Land of Musical Rights, N.Y. Times, May 30, 1993, Sec. 2, p. 1. O. Arewa, Copyright on Catfish Row: Musical Borrowing, *Porgy and Bess,* and Unfair Use, 37 Rutgers L.J. 277 (2006), bemoans the (excessive) control that copyright gives to heirs and suggests a separation of control and compensation rights.

prestige, the length of time they have been a part of the catalogue of the Society, and their vogue and popularity; and primary consideration must be given to the performances of the members' works."

Reg by Sherman Act

The present structure of ASCAP is to a large extent regulated by a consent decree under the Sherman Act. The initial decree in 1941 resulted from a consent judgment that terminated a civil complaint filed against ASCAP by the Department of Justice. That early decree prohibited ASCAP from acquiring or asserting exclusive licensing rights in its members' music. The decree also prohibited discrimination among licensees similarly situated. ASCAP was required to offer per-program licenses to broadcasters under which fees are based only on programs that use the licensed music as an alternative to blanket licenses based on total revenues. The decree enjoined ASCAP from refusing to offer per-song licenses to users other than broadcasters.

The consent decree of 1941 was amended in 1950 to require ASCAP to distribute revenues to members primarily on the basis of objective surveys and to ease the requirements for membership and withdrawal. The 1950 amendment also provided for the court to determine a reasonable royalty if the applicant and ASCAP were unable to agree. (Section 513 of the 1976 Act, added in 1998, now allows small users to bring a rate determination proceeding within their home circuit rather than in the Southern District of New York.) A further consent order dealing primarily with revenue distribution was approved in 1960.[aa] In 2001, at the request of ASCAP and the Department of Justice, the court approved a new amended judgment that replaced the prior decrees. See CCH 2001–2 Trade Cases ¶ 73,474 (S.D.N.Y.2001). The new order eases some of the former membership and distribution rules and streamlines rate determination proceedings, but members still have the unrestricted right to license their own works. It also continues ASCAP's obligation to offer a license to any user on a non-discriminatory basis and to offer per program licenses that afford a genuine choice to broadcasters. There are also new provisions designed for on-line performances.

ASCAP licensing rates vary with the type and size of the establishment and the nature of the performance (live, recorded music, broadcast reception, etc.). Rates for corporations depend on the number of employees, and colleges pay based on the number of students.

BMI

Corp. w/stock
• K w/s pub q wrtr

The broadcasters in 1941 created an organization that has become a formidable rival to ASCAP. Broadcast Music, Inc., usually known as BMI, is not a performing rights society with a membership of writers and publishers like ASCAP. It is a corporation, and its stock is owned by broadcasters. It deals with writers and publishers entirely on a contractual basis. Performances are measured through station logs and sampling, and are paid for entirely on a current basis, without the income-leveling formulas used by ASCAP. This has the result of providing larger initial payments for some young composers than are available from ASCAP.

[aa]   The ASCAP consent decrees are in CCH 1940–43 Trade Cases ¶ 56,104; 1950-51 id. ¶ 62,595; 1960 id. ¶ 69,612.

BMI also operates under the terms of an antitrust consent decree (see CCH 1940–43 Trade Cases ¶ 56,096), but the restrictions of the decree are not comparable to the extensive control over ASCAP. A 1966 revision of the consent decree provides that publishers and writers must be free to give their own non-exclusive licenses, and the duration of BMI contracts is limited to five years. (CCH 1966 Trade Cases ¶ 71,941.) A 1994 modification of the 1966 decree (CCH 1996–1 Trade Cases ¶ 71,378) created a mechanism for judicial resolution of licensing fee disputes. A writer must decide whether to sign up with BMI or with ASCAP. Many music publishers, operating through corporations, have both an ASCAP firm and a BMI firm.[bb]

BMI claims contracts with about 500,000 songwriters, composers and music publishers, compared to about 435,000 ASCAP members, although the BMI song catalog, at 7.5 million compositions, is smaller than ASCAP's 8.5 million. The gross income of BMI and ASCAP is about the same; together they take in more than $1.75 billion a year.[cc] With royalties from CD sales dropping due to Internet file-sharing, performance royalties now account for the majority of most songwriters' compensation.[dd]

Private Antitrust Actions Against ASCAP and BMI: The "Blanket License"

In K–91, Inc. v. Gershwin Pub. Corp., 372 F.2d 1 (9th Cir.1967), cert. denied, 389 U.S. 1045 (1968), a radio station resisted an infringement action by claiming that ASCAP and its members were violating the antitrust laws. Judge Barnes wrote:

"We agree with the trial court that the activities of ASCAP do not constitute a combination in restraint of trade or a monopoly within the meaning of the Sherman Act. ASCAP is certainly a combination, but not every combination is a combination in restraint of trade or a monopoly. ASCAP cannot be accused of fixing prices because every applicant to ASCAP has a right under the consent decree to invoke the authority of the United States District Court for the Southern District of New York to fix a reasonable fee whenever the applicant believes that the price proposed by ASCAP is unreasonable, and ASCAP has the burden of proving the price reasonable. In other words, so long as ASCAP complies with the decree, it is not the price fixing authority. We cannot agree with the contention that the danger of unreasonable activity that might arise from ASCAP's activities makes everything that it does a violation of the antitrust laws, when those of its potential activities that might have this effect are prohibited by the decree. No contention is here made that ASCAP's actual activities do not comply

---

[bb] For additional information, see the BMI web site at www.bmi.com. A day on the road with a BMI licensing executive is described in Bowe, The Copyright Enforcers, N.Y. Times, Aug. 8, 2010, Sec. MM, p. 38.

[cc] With over 8 million performances, *You've Got that Lovin' Feeling*, written in 1964 by Phil Spector, Barry Mann, and Cynthia Weil, was the most performed song in the BMI catalog during the twentieth century, beating out *Never My Love, Yesterday,* and *Stand By Me.* According to ASCAP, *Happy Birthday to You* was its most performed song of the century, followed by *Tea for Two, Moon River*, and *Over the Rainbow.*

[dd] The one-stop shopping for music performance rights (really three stops, with ASCAP, BMI, and SESAC) may be breaking down. Sony/ATV withdrew its digital performance rights from the licensing collectives and directly negotiated higher music performance royalties with online music provider Pandora. Other large music owners may follow a similar approach to the digital performance market. Atkinson, Sony's Music Mojo, N.Y. Post, Jan. 17, 2013, p. 33.

with the decree. In short, we think that as a potential combination in restraint of trade, ASCAP has been 'disinfected' by the decree."

Undismayed by these barriers, CBS in 1969 sued ASCAP and BMI, alleging that the customary "blanket" and "program" licenses violated the antitrust laws. CBS proposed that it be permitted to negotiate a "per use" license that would measure payments chiefly by the actual use of the repertory. CBS lost in the district court, 400 F.Supp. 737 (S.D.N.Y.1975), but the Second Circuit reversed. 562 F.2d 130 (2d Cir.1977). Distinguishing (or rejecting) K–91 v. Gershwin, the appellate court held that blanket licensing was price-fixing. When the Supreme Court reviewed that conclusion on appeal in Broadcast Music, Inc. v. CBS, Inc., 441 U.S. 1 (1979), it decided that the blanket license was not a *per se* violation of the Sherman Act. For one thing, it found that the convenience and flexibility of the blanket license made it a product distinct from the aggregation of songs. The Supreme Court then concluded:

" * * * [T]he blanket license cannot be wholly equated with a simple horizontal arrangement among competitors. ASCAP does set the price for its blanket license, but that license is quite different from anything any individual owner could issue. The individual composers and authors have neither agreed not to sell individually in any other market nor use the blanket license to mask price fixing in such other markets. Moreover, the substantial restraints placed on ASCAP and its members by the consent decree must not be ignored. The District Court found that there was no legal, practical, or conspiratorial impediment to CBS obtaining individual licenses; CBS, in short, had a real choice.

"With this background in mind, which plainly enough indicates that over the years, and in the face of available alternatives, the blanket license has provided an acceptable mechanism for at least a large part of the market for the performing rights to copyrighted musical compositions, we cannot agree that it should automatically be declared illegal in all of its many manifestations. Rather, when attacked, it should be subjected to a more discriminating examination under the rule of reason. It may not ultimately survive that attack, but that is not the issue before us today."

On remand, the Second Circuit found close examination unnecessary. CBS had the burden of proving that the blanket license had restrained competition, and the burden had not been met. CBS v. ASCAP, 620 F.2d 930 (2d Cir.1980), cert. denied, 450 U.S. 970 (1981).

It was then the turn of the *local* television stations to take on ASCAP, BMI, and the blanket license. All of the local stations depend heavily on syndicated programs. Complaining of the illegality and unfairness of blanket licenses, the local stations urged that the performing rights societies should be required to license performance rights through the syndicators ("source licensing"), who now buy only synchronization rights—the right to record the music on the program.

The district court found that the local stations had no viable alternative to blanket licenses (unlike CBS, which supposedly could manage direct licensing from composers if it wanted to), so there was a violation of § 1 of the Sherman Act. The Court of Appeals disagreed. Buffalo Broadcasting Co. v. ASCAP, 546 F.Supp. 274 (S.D.N.Y.1982), rev'd, 744 F.2d 917 (2d Cir.1984), cert. denied, 469 U.S. 1211 (1985). It found that the impracticability of alternatives had not been established. As for the inability of the local broadcasters to induce syndicators to obtain performance licenses, that was not established either. There is competition in the syndication market, and that market might not be "unresponsive to aggregate demand from stations willing to pay a reasonable price for source licensing of music performing rights."

Cable television operators also challenged the blanket license, but their antitrust claim against BMI was rejected in National Cable Television Ass'n, Inc. v. Broadcast Music, Inc., 772 F.Supp. 614 (D.D.C.1991).

9. DISTRIBUTION, DISPLAY, AND DERIVATIVE RIGHTS

THE DISTRIBUTION RIGHT

Among the exclusive rights reserved to the owner of a copyright is the right "to distribute copies" of the work to the public. § 106(3). The right is described succinctly in the House Report: "Under this provision the copyright owner would have the right to control the first public distribution of an authorized copy or phonorecord of his work, whether by sale, gift, loan, or some rental or lease arrangement. Likewise, any unauthorized public distribution of copies or phonorecords that were unlawfully made would be an infringement." H.R.Rep. p. 62. An independent distribution right thus enables a copyright owner to secure relief against vendors (even ones with no knowledge of the infringement) as well as against the producers of infringing material.

"Distribution" is not defined in § 101. Does it require an actual transfer of a copy, or will offering to transfer a copy or making a copy available for transfer suffice? In Hotaling v. Church of Jesus Christ of Latter–Day Saints, 118 F.3d 199 (4th Cir.1997), the plaintiff had copyrighted a collection of genealogical research materials; defendant purchased a copy for its main library and made several microfiche copies that it sent to branch libraries. The three-year statute of limitations prevented a suit for unauthorized reproduction, but the plaintiff contended that the defendant had also infringed by "distributing" the copies within the limitations period. The court reversed a summary judgment in favor of the library, holding that "[w]hen a public library adds a work to its collection, lists the work in its index or catalog system, and makes the work available to the borrowing public, it has completed all the steps necessary for distribution to the public" in violation of § 106(3). The court seemed worried that otherwise the plaintiff would be prejudiced by the library's failure to keep records of public use. However, in several "file-sharing" cases brought by record companies against defendants who had made copies of sound recordings available for transfer over file-sharing networks, the courts held that "distribution" requires evidence of an actual transfer. See, e.g., Atlantic Recording Corp. v. Howell, 554 F.Supp.2d 976 (D.Ariz.2008); London–Sire Records, Inc. v. Doe 1, 542 F.Supp.2d 153 (D.Mass.2008).

As the House Report indicates, the distribution right also extends to the distribution of authorized copies. In that context, however, the copyright owner's exclusive right is limited by § 109, which incorporates what is commonly, although somewhat inaccurately, known as the "first sale" doctrine.

[handwritten margin notes: Distribution defined. © v. of genealogical research matls & made several copies]

UMG Recordings, Inc. v. Augusto

United States Court of Appeals, Ninth Circuit, 2011.
628 F.3d 1175.

■ Before CANBY, CALLAHAN, and IKUTA, CIRCUIT JUDGES.

■ CANBY, CIRCUIT JUDGE:

UMG Recordings appeals the district court's grant of summary judgment in favor of defendant Troy Augusto on UMG's claim of copyright infringement in violation of § 501 of the Copyright Act, which entitles copyright owners to institute an action for infringement of the exclusive right to distribute copies of the copyrighted work. See 17 U.S.C. §§ 501(a), (b), 106(3) (2006). The copies in issue comprise eight specially-produced compact discs, each embodying a copyrighted sound recording. UMG, the copyright owner, used the discs solely for marketing purposes, sending them unsolicited to individuals such as music critics and radio disc jockeys. Although Augusto was not one of those individuals, he managed to obtain the discs from various sources. He later sold them at auction, an act which UMG contends infringed its exclusive right to distribute the discs.

Augusto asserts that UMG's initial distribution of the discs effected a transfer of ownership of the discs to the recipients, rendering the discs subject to the "first sale" doctrine, which permits one who has acquired ownership of a copy to dispose of that copy without the permission of the copyright owner. See id. § 109(a). UMG argues that the statements on the discs and the circumstances of their distribution granted only a license to each recipient, not a transfer of ownership (or "sale") of the copy. Absent a sale, UMG remained the owner of the discs and, accordingly, the defense of the first sale doctrine would be out of Augusto's reach. We conclude that the mailing indeed did effect a sale of the discs to the recipients for purposes of the first sale doctrine, and we affirm the order of the district court. * * *

Like many music companies, UMG ships specially-produced promotional CDs to a large group of individuals ("recipients"), such as music critics and radio programmers, that it has selected. There is no prior agreement or request by the recipients to receive the CDs. UMG does not seek or receive payment for the CDs, the content and design of which often differs from that of their commercial counterparts. UMG ships the promotional CDs by means of the United States Postal Service and United Parcel Service. Relatively few of the recipients refuse delivery of the CDs or return them to UMG, and UMG destroys those that are returned.

Most of the promotional CDs in issue in this case bore a statement (the ...notional statement") similar to the following:

> ...his CD is the property of the record company and is licensed to the ...ended recipient for personal use only. Acceptance of this CD shall ...titute an agreement to comply with the terms of the license. Re-...r transfer of possession is not allowed and may be punishable ...federal and state laws.

> ...CDs bore a more succinct statement, such as "Promotional Use ...ale."

> ...s not among the select group of individuals slated to re-...onal CDs. He nevertheless managed to acquire numerous ...which he sold through online auctions at eBay.com. Au-...ertised the CDs as "rare . . . industry editions" and ...Promo CDs."

After several unsuccessful attempts at halting the auctions through eBay's dispute resolution program, UMG filed a complaint against Augusto in the United States District Court for the Central District of California, alleging that Augusto had infringed UMG's copyrights in eight promotional CDs for which it retained the "exclusive right to distribute." The district court granted summary judgment in favor of Augusto, and UMG appealed. We have jurisdiction of the appeal pursuant to 28 U.S.C. § 1291. * * *

Although UMG, as the owner of the copyright, has exclusive rights in the promotional CDs, "[e]xemptions, compulsory licenses, and defenses found in the Copyright Act narrow [those] rights." Wall Data Inc. v. Los Angeles Cnty. Sheriff's Dept., 447 F.3d 769, 777 (9th Cir.2006) (citing 17 U.S.C. §§ 107–22). Augusto invokes the "first sale" doctrine embodied in § 109(a) of the Act. 17 U.S.C. § 109(a). He argues that the circumstances attending UMG's distribution of the discs effected a "sale" (transfer of ownership) of the discs to the original recipients and that, under the "first sale" doctrine, the recipients and subsequent owners of those particular copies were permitted to sell or otherwise dispose of those copies without authorization by the copyright holder. * * *

UMG, on the other hand, contends that the promotional statement effected a license with the recipients and, because the recipients were not owners but licensees of the CDs, neither they nor Augusto were entitled to sell or otherwise transfer the CDs. See Quality King Distribs., Inc. v. L'anza Research Int'l, Inc., 523 U.S. 135 (1998) ("[B]ecause the protection afforded by § 109(a) is available only to the 'owner' of a lawfully made copy . . . , the first sale doctrine would not provide a defense to . . . any nonowner such as a bailee, a licensee, a consignee, or one whose possession of the copy was unlawful."); Am. Int'l Pictures, Inc. v. Foreman, 576 F.2d 661, 664 (5th Cir.1978) ("[U]nless title to the copy passes through a first sale by the copyright holder, subsequent sales do not confer good title.").

The first sale doctrine provides that "the owner of a particular copy or phonorecord lawfully made under [the Act], or any person authorized by such owner, is entitled, without the authority of the copyright owner, to sell or otherwise dispose of the possession of that copy or phonorecord." 17 U.S.C. § 109(a). Notwithstanding its distinctive name, the doctrine applies not only when a copy is first sold, but when a copy is given away or title is otherwise transferred without the accouterments of a sale. See 4 Patry on Copyright § 13:15; see also United States v. Atherton, 561 F.2d 747, 750 (9th Cir.1977) ("The 'sale' embodied in the first sale concept is a term of art."). "[O]nce the copyright owner places a copyrighted item in the stream of commerce . . . , he has exhausted his exclusive statutory right to control its distribution." Quality King, 523 U.S. at 152. The seminal illustration of the principle is found in Bobbs–Merrill Co. v. Straus, 210 U.S. 339 (1908), where a copyright owner unsuccessfully attempted to restrain the resale of a copyrighted book by including in it the following notice: "The price of this book at retail is $1 net. No dealer is licensed to sell it at a less price, and a sale at less price will be treated as an infringement of the copyright." Id. The Court noted that the statutory grant to a copyright owner of the "sole right of vending" the work did not continue after the first sale of a given copy. Id. at 349–50. "The purchaser of a book, once sold by authority of the owner of the copyright, may sell it again, although he could not publish a new edition of it." Id. at 350. The attempt to limit resale below a certain price was therefore held invalid. Id. at 351.

The rule of *Bobbs-Merrill* remains in full force, enshrined as it is in § 109(a) of the Act: a copyright owner who transfers title in a particular copy to a purchaser or donee cannot prevent resale of that particular copy. We have recognized, however, that not every transfer of possession of a copy transfers title. Particularly with regard to computer software, we have recognized that copyright owners may create licensing arrangements so that users acquire only a license to use the particular copy of software and do not acquire title that permits further transfer or sale of that copy without the permission of the copyright owner. Our most recent example of that rule is Vernor v. Autodesk, Inc., 621 F.3d 1102 (9th Cir.2010). Others are Wall Data Inc. v. Los Angeles Cnty. Sheriff's Dept., 447 F.3d 769 (9th Cir.2006); Triad Sys. Corp. v. Se. Express Co., 64 F.3d 1330 (9th Cir.1995); MAI Sys. Corp. v. Peak Computer, Inc., 991 F.2d 511 (9th Cir.1993). All of these cases dealt with the question whether arrangements with consumers amounted to sales of copies, or succeeded in awarding only licenses. They recognized that the mere labeling of an arrangement as a license rather than a sale, although it was a factor to be considered, was not by itself dispositive of the issue. See, e.g., *Vernor,* 621 F.3d at 1109 (construing United States v. Wise, 550 F.2d 1180, 1190–92 (9th Cir.1977)).

The same question is presented here. Did UMG succeed in creating a license in recipients of its promotional CDs, or did it convey title despite the restrictive labeling on the CDs? We conclude that, under all the circumstances of the CDs' distribution, the recipients were entitled to use or dispose of them in any manner they saw fit, and UMG did not enter a license agreement for the CDs with the recipients. Accordingly, UMG transferred title to the particular copies of its promotional CDs and cannot maintain an infringement action against Augusto for his subsequent sale of those copies.

Our conclusion that the recipients acquired ownership of the CDs is based largely on the nature of UMG's distribution. First, the promotional CDs are dispatched to the recipients without any prior arrangement as to those particular copies. The CDs are not numbered, and no attempt is made to keep track of where particular copies are or what use is made of them. As explained in greater detail below, although UMG places written restrictions in the labels of the CDs, it has not established that the restrictions on the CDs create a license agreement. * * *

There are additional reasons for concluding that UMG's distribution of the CDs did not involve a consensual licensing operation. Some of the statements on the CDs and UMG's purported method of securing agreement to licenses militate against a conclusion that any licenses were created. The sparest promotional statement, "Promotional Use Only–Not for Sale," does not even purport to create a license. But even the more detailed statement is flawed in the manner in which it purports to secure agreement from the recipient. The more detailed statement provides:

> This CD is the property of the record company and is licensed to the intended recipient for personal use only. Acceptance of this CD shall constitute an agreement to comply with the terms of the license. Resale or transfer of possession is not allowed and may be punishable under federal and state laws.

It is one thing to say, as the statement does, that "acceptance" of the CD constitutes an agreement to a license and its restrictions, but it is quite another to maintain that "acceptance" may be assumed when the recipient makes no response at all. This record reflects no responses. Even when the evidence is viewed in the light most favorable to UMG, it does not show that any recipients agreed to enter into a license agreement with UMG when they received the CDs.

Because the record here is devoid of any indication that the recipients agreed to a license, there is no evidence to support a conclusion that licenses were established under the terms of the promotional statement. Accordingly, we conclude that UMG's transfer of possession to the recipients, without meaningful control or even knowledge of the status of the CDs after shipment, accomplished a transfer of title.

No indication that they accepted

The district court based its decision in favor of Augusto in part on somewhat different grounds from those we have adopted. The district court first held that the licensing language in the detailed promotional statement did not create a license because it lacked any provision for UMG to regain possession of the CDs. In this ruling, the district court relied upon our decision in United States v. Wise, 550 F.2d 1180 (9th Cir.1977). In *Wise,* we dealt with several contracts, each denominated as a license, by which motion picture studios conveyed films to various recipients.

The issue was whether any of these licenses actually constituted a sale for purposes of the first sale doctrine. We held all but one of the conveyances to be licenses, pointing out that they were designated as licenses, reserved title in the studio, and provided for return or destruction of the prints after use. See id . at 1191–92. We held one purported license to be a sale, however, because in addition to the payment of a "cost" price (which did not alone establish a sale), there was no provision for return of the print to the studio; permanent possession was granted to the recipient. See id.

Wise

whether any of licenses constituted a sale

• Return provision = one indication

Return of possession is not invariably required in a license, however. We have since read *Wise* and our software licensing cases

to prescribe three considerations that we may use to determine whether a software user is a licensee, rather than an owner of a copy. First, we consider whether the copyright owner specifies that a user is granted a license. Second, we consider whether the copyright owner significantly restricts the user's ability to transfer the software. Finally, we consider whether the copyright owner imposes notable use restrictions.

considerations whether software user is licensee or owner

Vernor, 621 F.3d at 1110–11 (footnote omitted).

This formulation, however, applies in terms to software users, and software users who order and pay to acquire copies are in a very different position from that held by the recipients of UMG's promotional CDs. As we have already explained, UMG has virtually no control over the unordered CDs it issues because of its means of distribution, and it has no assurance that any recipient has assented or will assent to the creation of any license or accept its limitations. UMG also does not require the ultimate return of the promotional CDs to its possession. Although the failure to require return of the CDs may not, by itself, conclusively establish a sale under our precedent, it is one more indication that UMG had no control over the promotional CDs once it dispatched them. UMG thus did not retain "sufficient incidents of ownership" over the promotional copies "to be sensibly considered the owner of the cop[ies]." Krause v. Titleserv, Inc., 402 F.3d 119, 124 (2d Cir.2005). * * *

UMG has no control
• no assurance
• Return not req

UMG's distribution of the promotional CDs under the circumstances effected a sale (transfer of title) of the CDs to the recipients. Further sale of those copies was therefore permissible without UMG's authorization. The judgment of the district court dismissing UMG's copyright infringement action against Augusto is therefore

AFFIRMED.

NOTES AND QUESTIONS ON THE "FIRST SALE" DOCTRINE

(1) Note that § 109(a) limits only the copyright owner's distribution right—the owner of a copy is not privileged to intrude on other exclusive rights such as reproduction or public performance.

(2) A copyright owner who merely leases or lends copies of the work retains exclusive distribution rights, § 109(d), but distinctions between sales and leases are not always easily drawn. Vernor v. Autodesk, Inc., 621 F.3d 1102 (9th Cir.2010), cert. denied, 132 S.Ct. 105 (2011), quoted by Judge Canby in *UMG Recordings,* involved computer design software used by architects and engineers. Autodesk sold its software to customers pursuant to a software license agreement under which Autodesk retained title to the copies and granted customers a nonexclusive and nontransferable license to use the software. The license prohibited customers from transferring the software without permission and restricted activities such as modification and reverse engineering. Vernor bought copies of the software from an Autodesk customer and resold them on eBay. Vernor then brought a declaratory judgment action to establish that the resales did not infringe Autodesk's copyright. The court concluded that Autodesk's customers were licensees and thus not entitled under the first sale doctrine to transfer title to Vernor. The sales by both the customer and Vernor thus infringed Autodesk's exclusive right to distribute copies under § 106(3).

J. Rothchild, The Incredible Shrinking First–Sale Rule: Are Software Resale Limits Lawful?, 57 Rutgers L.Rev. 1 (2004), argues that courts should not permit software sellers to avoid the first sale doctrine by characterizing transfers as "licenses." L. Gibbons, Stop Mucking Up Copyright Law: A Proposal for a Federal Common Law of Contract, 35 Rutgers L.J. 959 (2004), urges courts to adopt uniform federal interpretations of contracts that control rights in copyrighted works.

(3) The popularity first of VCRs and then DVD players generated a lively market in pre-recorded movies. Purchases by video rental companies account for a substantial portion of the market. The "first sale" doctrine prevented the motion picture studios from gaining direct control over the once-lucrative rental business. When a studio sells a DVD, both private and commercial purchasers are free to rent or resell it as they choose, just as a library that has acquired ownership of a book is free to lend it without accounting to the copyright owner.

Could motion picture studios gain control over the rental market through contractual limitations attached to DVD sales? Would rentals in violation of such contractual restrictions constitute an infringement of the distribution right? If there has been a "first sale," albeit with restrictions, they would not. The House Report confirms this point: "This does not mean that conditions on future disposition of copies or phonorecords, imposed by a contract between their buyer and seller, would be unenforceable between the parties as a breach of contract, but it does mean that they could not be enforced by an action for infringement of copyright." H.R.Rep. p. 79. The remedy in contract is itself problematic, however, in light of the general disinclination to enforce agreements restraining trade or alienation. There is also considerable difficulty in binding remote vendees to a contract; restrictive legends generally will not suffice. The movie studies did eventually capture a share of the home rental market by offering discounts to rental chains in exchange for a contractual share of rental revenues.

Since a "first sale" does not impair the performance right, a purchaser who subsequently rents or lends the copy for a public performance may be liable as a contributory infringer. See Kalem Co. v. Harper Brothers, 222 U.S. 55 (1911).

(4) There are numerous web sites on which customers can arrange swaps of used CDs, DVDs, and video games. Are the trades protected under the first sale doctrine? Must the traders delete any digital copies of the works that they may have made? What about sales on eBay of used iPods already loaded with thousands of songs downloaded from iTunes or copied from the seller's CD collection? A company called ReDigi offered a service that allowed users to upload music purchased from iTunes to the company's server for resale. The seller's copy was then deleted. In Capitol Records, LLC v. ReDigi, Inc., 2013 WL 1286134 (S.D.N.Y.2013), the court held that the service infringed the reproduction right by making new copies. "It is beside the point that the original phonorecord no longer exists." There was also a violation of the distribution right, despite the first sale doctrine, since the user was not transferring possession of the "particular copy or phonorecord" that they owned. A. Perzanowski and J. Schultz, Digital Exhaustion, 58 UCLA L.Rev. 889 (2011), argues for the development of judicial rules that preserve the benefits of the first sale doctrine in the digital marketplace.

(5) Like the movie studios, the record industry also worried about the rental market; the ease of home duplication magnified the threat posed by commercial rentals. In 1984, citing record rental advertisements bragging, "Never, ever buy another record"[ee], the industry secured an amendment to the Copyright Act adding § 109(b)(1)(A). The Record Rental Amendment of 1984 excludes the commercial rental of phonorecords from the protection afforded by the first sale doctrine.[ff] Why was Congress moved to intervene in record but not video rentals? (As part of the World Trade Organization's TRIPS agreement (see p. 814 infra), member countries agree to recognize rights against the commercial rental of phonorecords, computer programs (see Note (6) infra), and "cinematographic works," but the obligation with respect to the latter works accrues only if rentals are "materially impairing" the exclusive right of reproduction.)

(6) Encouraged by the success of the record industry, software producers sought similar relief against the growing practice of commercial software rental. The ease of duplication here too presented a major threat to copyright owners. Armed with advertisements from rental firms boasting that customers could "save a bundle" by renting popular software "at a fraction of the cost," 40 Pat., Tm. & Copyr.J. (BNA) 290 (1990), the software industry won an amendment to § 109(b) prohibiting the commercial rental of computer programs.[gg]

[ee] See H.R.Rep. No. 98–987, 98th Cong., 2d Sess. (1984).

[ff] The court in Brilliance Audio, Inc. v. Haights Cross Communications, Inc., 474 F.3d 365 (6th Cir. 2007), used both the reference in § 109(b)(1)(A) to "musical works embodied therein" and the legislative history's focus on the music industry to conclude that the prohibition against commercial rentals of sound recordings does not apply to the commercial rental of audio books.

[gg] The prohibition against commercial software rental was successfully invoked in Central Point Software, Inc. v. Global Software & Accessories, Inc., 880 F.Supp. 957

There is an exception for video games and for programs embodied in machines or products that preclude routine copying. There is also an exception for software lending by nonprofit libraries. (The copyright warning required under § 109(b)(2)(A) on copies of software lent by libraries is prescribed in 37 C.F.R. § 201.24.)

(7) Several nations, notably Great Britain, Germany, and the Scandinavian countries, have implemented schemes to compensate authors for library lending—a recognition of a public lending right. (A 1992 European Union Directive, recodified in 2006, requiring all EU countries to adopt compensation schemes for public lending has apparently not been widely implemented. See 69 Pat., Tm. & Copyr.J. (BNA) 550 (2005).) Should a similar right be recognized here? Where would the money come from? From overburdened library budgets? From library patrons? In a panel discussion on the public lending right, an editor of this casebook is quoted as arguing, "If you want people to read more, you don't make it more expensive." 34 Pat., Tm. & Copyr.J. (BNA) 41 (1987).

(8) The copyright owner's exclusive right of public display, § 106(5), is the first statutory recognition of an exclusive right to show the copyrighted work to the public. It too is subject to a "first sale" defense, § 109(c), which allows the owner of a lawful copy "to display that copy publicly, either directly or by the projection of no more than one image at a time, to viewers present at the place where the copy is located." The exemption does not permit the transmission of an image beyond the place where the work is physically located; even when the object and the viewers are in the same place, simultaneous projection of images on multiple television or computer screens would seem to violate the "one image at a time" restriction in § 109(c). "The committee's intention is to preserve the traditional privilege of the owner of a copy to display it directly, but to place reasonable restrictions on the ability to display it indirectly in such a way that the copyright owner's market for reproduction and distribution of copies would be affected." H.R.Rep. p. 80. Note too that some of the limitations in § 110 on a copyright owner's exclusive right of public performance also apply to the public display right.

(9) When National Basketball Association player Rasheed Wallace was playing for the Portland Trail Blazers in 1998, he told a Portland tattoo artist that he wanted an Egyptian-themed family scene with a king and queen and three children and an image of the sun. The tattoo artist researched the idea and came up with a design that he placed on Wallace's arm. Wallace paid $450. Six years later the artist learned that Nike had created an advertisement featuring Wallace that centered on the tattoo. He filed a federal lawsuit for copyright infringement against Wallace and Nike. Green, Ink is Dry on Tattoo But Not on Lawsuit, The Oregonian, Feb. 15, 2005, p. A1. Assuming that the artist owns the copyright in the design, is the public display right infringed when Wallace plays basketball in front of a packed arena? When he plays in a televised game? Does Nike's advertisement infringe any of the artist's exclusive rights? How far would an implied license defense extend? The suit was ultimately settled. A character in the Warner Brothers film *The Hangover Part II* wakes up with a facial tattoo recognizable as the same one sported since 2003 by boxer Mike Tyson, who also appears in the film. The tattoo artist who created the work for Tyson sued Warner Brothers for copyright infringement. Warner Brothers as-

---

(E.D.N.Y.1995), to stop a "deferred billing plan" that allowed customers to return software after five days and pay only a "restocking fee."

serted a fair use right to parody both Tyson and the tattoo, but it quickly settled. Cohen, "Hangover 2" Settles Suit from Artist Over Tattoo, N.Y. Times, June 22, 2011, p. B9.

INFRINGING IMPORTATION

Section 602(a) of the 1976 Copyright Act states, "Importation into the United States, without the authority of the owner of copyright under this title, of copies or phonorecords of a work that have been acquired outside the United States is an infringement of the exclusive right to distribute copies or phonorecords under section 106, actionable under section 501."[hh] Note that the restriction on importation is not limited to infringing copies. "Section 602 * * * deals with two separate situations: importation of 'piratical' articles (that is, copies or phonorecords made without any authorization of the copyright owner), and unauthorized importation of copies or phonorecords that were lawfully made." H.R.Rep. p. 169. By recording the copyright registration and paying the required fee, a copyright owner can enlist the aid of U.S. Customs and Border Protection in preventing entry of pirated copies. 19 C.F.R. § 133.31 et seq.

The chief interpretive difficulty in § 602(a) comes from its reference to the exclusive right to distribute copies or phonorecords under § 106; does this incorporate into § 602 the first sale limitations on the distribution right in § 109?

Kirtsaeng v. John Wiley & Sons, Inc.

Supreme Court of the United States, 2013.
___ U.S. ___, 133 S.Ct. 1351.

■ JUSTICE BREYER delivered the opinion of the Court.

Section 106 of the Copyright Act grants "the owner of copyright under this title" certain "exclusive rights," including the right "to distribute copies . . . of the copyrighted work to the public by sale or other transfer of ownership." 17 U.S.C. § 106(3). These rights are qualified, however, by the application of various limitations set forth in the next several sections of the Act, §§ 107 through 122. Those sections, typically entitled "Limitations on exclusive rights," include, for example, the principle of "fair use" (§ 107), permission for limited library archival reproduction, (§ 108), and the doctrine at issue here, the "first sale" doctrine (§ 109).

§106(3)

exceptions 107–122

Section 109(a) sets forth the "first sale" doctrine as follows:

§109–first sale doctrine

"Notwithstanding the provisions of section 106(3) [the section that grants the owner exclusive distribution rights], the owner of a particular copy or phonorecord *lawfully made under this title* . . . is entitled,

---

[hh] Section 602(a) includes limited exceptions covering importation for governmental, private, or scholarly use, including the right under § 602(a)(3)(B) to import no more than one copy of a work at a time for the private use of the importer. The latter exception attracted increased attention in light of the ease with which works can be purchased from abroad over the Internet. Holders of American publishing rights in works like the *Harry Potter* series were alarmed at the number of readers purchasing copies through foreign online bookstores like the British subsidiary of Amazon.com, especially when the foreign version was published in advance of the U.S. publication. See Carvajal, Young Wizard is Best Seller and Copyright Challenge, N.Y. Times, Apr. 1, 1999, p. E1.

without the authority of the copyright owner, to sell or otherwise dispose of the possession of that copy or phonorecord." (Emphasis added.)

Thus, even though § 106(3) forbids distribution of a copy of, say, the copyrighted novel Herzog without the copyright owner's permission, § 109(a) adds that, once a copy of Herzog has been lawfully sold (or its ownership otherwise lawfully transferred), the buyer of *that copy* and subsequent owners are free to dispose of it as they wish. In copyright jargon, the "first sale" has "exhausted" the copyright owner's § 106(3) exclusive distribution right.

> *[handwritten margin note: once the copyrighted thing has been sold/transferred the owner of the copy & all that follow can dispose of it as they want to]*

What, however, if the copy of Herzog was printed abroad and then initially sold with the copyright owner's permission? Does the "first sale" doctrine still apply? Is the buyer, like the buyer of a domestically manufactured copy, free to bring the copy into the United States and dispose of it as he or she wishes?

To put the matter technically, an "importation" provision, § 602(a)(1), says that

> "[i]mportation into the United States, without the authority of the owner of copyright under this title, of copies . . . of a work that have been acquired outside the United States is an infringement of the exclusive right to distribute copies . . . *under section 106* . . . ." 17 U.S.C. § 602(a)(1) (2006 ed., Supp. V) (emphasis added).

Thus § 602(a)(1) makes clear that importing a copy without permission violates the owner's exclusive distribution right. But in doing so, § 602(a)(1) refers explicitly to the *§ 106(3)* exclusive distribution right. As we have just said, § 106 is by its terms "[s]ubject to" the various doctrines and principles contained in §§ 107 through 122, including § 109(a)'s "first sale" limitation. Do those same modifications apply—in particular, does the "first sale" modification apply—when considering whether § 602(a)(1) prohibits importing a copy?

> *[handwritten margin note: 602(a)(1) - importing w/o permission violates owners exclusive rights]*

In Quality King Distributors, Inc. v. L'anza Research Int'l, Inc., 523 U.S. 135, 145 (1998), we held that § 602(a)(1)'s reference to § 106(3)'s exclusive distribution right incorporates the later subsections' limitations, including, in particular, the "first sale" doctrine of § 109. Thus, it might seem that, § 602(a)(1) notwithstanding, one who buys a copy abroad can freely import that copy into the United States and dispose of it, just as he could had he bought the copy in the United States.

But *Quality King* considered an instance in which the copy, though purchased abroad, was initially manufactured in the United States (and then sent abroad and sold). This case is like *Quality King* but for one important fact. The copies at issue here were manufactured abroad. That fact is important because § 109(a) says that the "first sale" doctrine applies to "a particular copy or phonorecord *lawfully made under this title*." And we must decide here whether the five words, "lawfully made under this title," make a critical legal difference.

Putting section numbers to the side, we ask whether the "first sale" doctrine applies to protect a buyer or other lawful owner of a copy (of a copyrighted work) lawfully manufactured abroad. Can that buyer bring that copy into the United States (and sell it or give it away) without obtaining permission to do so from the copyright owner? Can, for example, someone who purchases, say at a used bookstore, a book printed abroad subsequently resell it without the copyright owner's permission?

In our view, the answers to these questions are, yes. We hold that the "first sale" doctrine applies to copies of a copyrighted work lawfully made abroad.

Holding

first sale applies to copies of copyrighted work made abroad

I

A

Respondent, John Wiley & Sons, Inc., publishes academic textbooks. Wiley obtains from its authors various foreign and domestic copyright assignments, licenses and permissions—to the point that we can, for present purposes, refer to Wiley as the relevant American copyright owner. See 654 F.3d 210, 213, n. 6 (C.A.2 2011). Wiley often assigns to its wholly owned foreign subsidiary, John Wiley & Sons (Asia) Pte Ltd., rights to publish, print, and sell Wiley's English language textbooks abroad. App. to Pet. for Cert. 47a–48a. Each copy of a Wiley Asia foreign edition will likely contain language making clear that the copy is to be sold only in a particular country or geographical region outside the United States. 654 F.3d, at 213. * * *

Wiley is American copyright owner

assign right to publish to its foreign subsid.

Petitioner, Supap Kirtsaeng, a citizen of Thailand, moved to the United States in 1997 to study mathematics at Cornell University. Ibid. He paid for his education with the help of a Thai Government scholarship which required him to teach in Thailand for 10 years on his return. Brief for Petitioner 7. Kirtsaeng successfully completed his undergraduate courses at Cornell, successfully completed a Ph. D. program in mathematics at the University of Southern California, and then, as promised, returned to Thailand to teach. Ibid. While he was studying in the United States, Kirtsaeng asked his friends and family in Thailand to buy copies of foreign edition English-language textbooks at Thai book shops, where they sold at low prices, and mail them to him in the United States. Id., at 7–8. Kirtsaeng would then sell them, reimburse his family and friends, and keep the profit. App. to Pet. for Cert. 48a–49a.

Bought books in Thailand + then re

B

In 2008 Wiley brought this federal lawsuit against Kirtsaeng for copyright infringement. 654 F.3d, at 213. Wiley claimed that Kirtsaeng's unauthorized importation of its books and his later resale of those books amounted to an infringement of Wiley's § 106(3) exclusive right to distribute as well as § 602's related import prohibition. 17 U.S.C. §§ 106(3) (2006 ed.), 602(a) (2006 ed., Supp. V). See also § 501 (2006 ed.) (authorizing infringement action). App. 204–211. Kirtsaeng replied that the books he had acquired were "'lawfully made'" and that he had acquired them legitimately. Record in No. 1:08–CV–7834–DCP (SDNY), Doc. 14, p. 3. Thus, in his view, § 109(a)'s "first sale" doctrine permitted him to resell or otherwise dispose of the books without the copyright owner's further permission. Id., at 2–3.

π complaint

infringement of dist.

Δ argues

The District Court held that Kirtsaeng could not assert the "first sale" defense because, in its view, that doctrine does not apply to "foreign-manufactured goods" (even if made abroad with the copyright owner's permission). App. to Pet. for Cert. 72a. The jury then found that Kirtsaeng had willfully infringed Wiley's American copyrights by selling and importing without authorization copies of eight of Wiley's copyrighted titles. And it assessed statutory damages of $600,000 ($75,000 per work). 654 F.3d, at 215.

DC said no first sale b/c doesn't apply to foreign manu goods

On appeal, a split panel of the Second Circuit agreed with the District Court. Id., at 222. * * *

2CH affirmed DCH

II

Issue

We must decide whether the words "lawfully made under this title" restrict the scope of § 109(a)'s "first sale" doctrine geographically. The Second Circuit, the Ninth Circuit, Wiley, and the Solicitor General (as *amicus*) all read those words as imposing a form of *geographical* limitation. The Second Circuit held that they limit the "first sale" doctrine to particular copies "made in territories *in which the Copyright Act is law*," which (the Circuit says) are copies "manufactured domestically," not "outside of the United States." 654 F.3d, at 221–222 (emphasis added). * * *

Δ argues

Δ: non.geo

Kirtsaeng, however, reads the words "lawfully made under this title" as imposing a *non*-geographical limitation. He says that they mean made "in accordance with" or "in compliance with" the Copyright Act. Brief for Petitioner 26. In that case, § 109(a)'s "first sale" doctrine would apply to copyrighted works as long as their manufacture met the requirements of American copyright law. In particular, the doctrine would apply where, as here, copies are manufactured abroad with the permission of the copyright owner. See § 106 (referring to the owner's right to authorize).

A non-geo reading is better

In our view, § 109(a)'s language, its context, and the common-law history of the "first sale" doctrine, taken together, favor a *non*-geographical interpretation. We also doubt that Congress would have intended to create the practical copyright-related harms with which a geographical interpretation would threaten ordinary scholarly, artistic, commercial, and consumer activities. See Part II–D, infra. We consequently conclude that Kirtsaeng's nongeographical reading is the better reading of the Act.

A

The language of § 109(a) read literally favors Kirtsaeng's nongeographical interpretation, namely, that "lawfully made under this title" means made "in accordance with" or "in compliance with" the Copyright Act. * * *

To read the clause geographically, Wiley, like the Second Circuit and the Solicitor General, must first emphasize the word "under." Indeed, Wiley reads "under this title" to mean "in conformance with the Copyright Act *where the Copyright Act is applicable*." Brief for Respondent 15. Wiley must then take a second step, arguing that the Act " is applicable" only in the United States. Ibid. * * *

* * * Where, precisely, is the Copyright Act "applicable"? The Act does not instantly *protect* an American copyright holder from unauthorized piracy taking place abroad. But that fact does not mean the Act is *inapplicable* to copies made abroad. As a matter of ordinary English, one can say that a statute imposing, say, a tariff upon "any rhododendron grown in Nepal" applies to *all* Nepalese rhododendrons. And, similarly, one can say that the American Copyright Act is *applicable* to *all* pirated copies, including those printed overseas. Indeed, the Act itself makes clear that (in the Solicitor General's language) foreign-printed pirated copies are "subject to" the Act. § 602(a)(2) (2006 ed., Supp. V) (referring to importation of copies "the making of which either constituted an infringement of copyright, or which would have constituted an infringement of copyright if this title had been applicable"); Brief for United States 5. See also post, at 6 (suggesting that "made under" may be read as "subject to").

The appropriateness of this linguistic usage is underscored by the fact that § 104 of the Act itself says that works *"subject to protection under this title"* include unpublished works "without regard to the nationality or domicile of the author," and works "first published" in any one of the nearly 180 nations that have signed a copyright treaty with the United States. §§ 104(a), (b) (2006 ed.) (emphasis added); § 101 (2006 ed., Supp. V) (defining "treaty party"); U.S. Copyright Office, Circular No. 38A, International Copyright Relations of the United States (2010). Thus, ordinary English permits us to say that the Act "applies" to an Irish manuscript lying in its author's Dublin desk drawer as well as to an original recording of a ballet performance first made in Japan and now on display in a Kyoto art gallery. * * *

D

Associations of libraries, used-book dealers, technology companies, consumer-goods retailers, and museums point to various ways in which a geographical interpretation would fail to further basic constitutional copyright objectives, in particular "promot[ing] the Progress of Science and useful Arts." U.S. Const., Art. I, § 8, cl. 8.

The American Library Association tells us that library collections contain at least 200 million books published abroad (presumably, many were first published in one of the nearly 180 copyright-treaty nations and enjoy American copyright protection under 17 U.S.C. § 104, see supra, at 10); that many others were first published in the United States but printed abroad because of lower costs; and that a geographical interpretation will likely require the libraries to obtain permission (or at least create significant uncertainty) before circulating or otherwise distributing these books. Brief for American Library Association et al. as Amici Curiae 4, 15–20. * * *

Used-book dealers tell us that, from the time when Benjamin Franklin and Thomas Jefferson built commercial and personal libraries of foreign books, American readers have bought used books published and printed abroad. Brief for Powell's Books Inc. et al. as Amici Curiae 7 (citing M. Stern, Antiquarian Bookselling in the United States (1985)). The dealers say that they have "operat[ed] . . . for centuries" under the assumption that the "first sale" doctrine applies. Brief for Powell's Books 7. But under a geographical interpretation a contemporary tourist who buys, say, at Shakespeare and Co. (in Paris), a dozen copies of a foreign book for American friends might find that she had violated the copyright law. The used-book dealers cannot easily predict what the foreign copyright holder may think about a reader's effort to sell a used copy of a novel. And they believe that a geographical interpretation will injure a large portion of the used-book business.

Technology companies tell us that "automobiles, microwaves, calculators, mobile phones, tablets, and personal computers" contain copyrightable software programs or packaging. Brief for Public Knowledge et al. as Amici Curiae 10. See also Brief for Association of Service and Computer Dealers International, Inc., et al. as Amici Curiae 2. Many of these items are made abroad with the American copyright holder's permission and then sold and imported (with that permission) to the United States. Brief for Retail Litigation Center, Inc., et al. as Amici Curiae 4. A geographical interpretation would prevent the resale of, say, a car, without the permission of the holder of each copyright on each piece of copyrighted automobile software. Yet there is no reason to believe that foreign auto manufacturers regularly obtain this kind of permission from their software component suppliers, and Wiley did not indicate to the contrary when asked. See Tr. of Oral Arg. 29–30. Without that permission a foreign car owner could not sell his or her used car.

Retailers tell us that over \$2.3 trillion worth of foreign goods were imported in 2011. Brief for Retail Litigation Center 8. American retailers buy many of these goods after a first sale abroad. Id., at 12. And, many of these items bear, carry, or contain copyrighted "packaging, logos, labels, and product inserts and instructions for [the use of] everyday packaged goods from floor cleaners and health and beauty products to breakfast cereals." Id., at 10–11. The retailers add that American sales of more traditional copyrighted works, "such as books, recorded music, motion pictures, and magazines" likely amount to over \$220 billion. Id., at 9. See also id., at 10 (electronic game industry is \$16 billion). A geographical interpretation would subject many, if not all, of them to the disruptive impact of the threat of infringement suits. Id., at 12.

Art museum directors ask us to consider their efforts to display foreign-produced works by, say, Cy Twombly, Rene Magritte, Henri Matisse, Pablo Picasso, and others. See supra, at 10 (describing how § 104 often makes such works "subject to" American copyright protection). A geographical interpretation, they say, would require the museums to obtain permission from the copyright owners before they could display the work, see supra, at 15—even if the copyright owner has already sold or donated the work to a foreign museum. Brief for Association of Art Museum Directors et al. as *Amici Curiae* 10–11. What are the museums to do, they ask, if the artist retained the copyright, if the artist cannot be found, or if a group of heirs is arguing about who owns which copyright? Id., at 14. * * *

Finally, the fact that harm has proved limited so far may simply reflect the reluctance of copyright holders so far to assert geographically based resale rights. They may decide differently if the law is clarified in their favor. Regardless, a copyright law that can work in practice only if unenforced is not a sound copyright law. It is a law that would create uncertainty, would bring about selective enforcement, and, if widely unenforced, would breed disrespect for copyright law itself.

Thus, we believe that the practical problems that petitioner and his *amici* have described are too serious, too extensive, and too likely to come about for us to dismiss them as insignificant—particularly in light of the ever-growing importance of foreign trade to America. * * *

III

Wiley and the dissent make several additional important arguments in favor of the geographical interpretation. *First,* they say that our *Quality King* decision strongly supports its geographical interpretation. In that case we asked whether the Act's "importation provision," now § 602(a)(1) (then § 602(a)), barred importation (without permission) of a copyrighted item (labels affixed to hair care products) where an American copyright owner authorized the first sale and export of hair care products with copyrighted labels made in the United States, and where a buyer sought to import them back into the United States without the copyright owner's permission. 523 U.S., at 138–139.

We held that the importation provision did *not* prohibit sending the products back into the United States (without the copyright owner's permission). * * *

We also explained why we rejected the claim that our interpretation would make § 602(a)(1) pointless. Those advancing that claim had pointed out that the 1976 Copyright Act amendments retained a prior anti-piracy provision, prohibiting the importation of *pirated* copies. *Quality King,* supra, at 146. Thus, they said, § 602(a)(1) must prohibit the importation of lawfully made copies, for to allow the importation of those lawfully made copies *after a first sale,* as *Quality King'* s holding would do, would leave § 602(a)(1) without much to prohibit. It would become superfluous, without any real work to do.

We do not believe that this argument is a strong one. Under *Quality King*'s interpretation, § 602(a)(1) would still forbid importing (without permission, and subject to the exceptions in § 602(a)(3)) copies lawfully made abroad, for example, where (1) a foreign publisher operating as the licensee of an American publisher prints copies of a book overseas but, prior to any authorized sale, seeks to send them to the United States; (2) a foreign printer or other manufacturer (if not the "owner" for purposes of § 109(a), e.g., before an authorized sale) sought to send copyrighted goods to the United States; (3) "a book publisher transports copies to a wholesaler" and the wholesaler (not yet the owner) sends them to the United States, see Copyright Law Revision, pt. 4, at 211 (giving this example); or (4) a foreign film distributor, having leased films for distribution, or any other licensee, consignee, or bailee sought to send them to the United States. * * *

In *Quality King* we rejected the "superfluous" argument for similar reasons. But, when rejecting it, we said that, where an author gives exclusive American distribution rights to an American publisher and exclusive British distribution rights to a British publisher, "presumably *only those [copies] made by the publisher of the United States edition would be 'lawfully made under this title'* within the meaning of § 109(a)." 523 U.S., at 148 (emphasis added). Wiley now argues that this phrase in the *Quality King* opinion means that books published abroad (under license) must fall outside the words "lawfully made under this title" and that we have consequently already given those words the geographical interpretation that it favors. *[Quality King opinion]* *[Wiley argues]*

We cannot, however, give the *Quality King* statement the legal weight for which Wiley argues. The language "lawfully made under this title" was not at issue in *Quality King*; the point before us now was not then fully argued; we did not canvas the considerations we have here set forth; we there said nothing to suggest that the example assumes a "first sale"; and we there hedged our statement with the word "presumably." Most importantly, the statement is pure dictum. It is dictum contained in a rebuttal to a counterargument. And it is *unnecessary* dictum even in that respect. Is the Court having once written dicta calling a tomato a vegetable bound to deny that it is a fruit forever after? * * *

Third, Wiley and the dissent claim that a nongeographical interpretation will make it difficult, perhaps impossible, for publishers (and other copyright holders) to divide foreign and domestic markets. We concede that is so. A publisher may find it more difficult to charge different prices for the same book in different geographic markets. But we do not see how these facts help Wiley, for we can find no basic principle of copyright law that suggests that publishers are especially entitled to such rights. * * *

* * * Whether copyright owners should, or should not, have more than ordinary commercial power to divide international markets is a matter for Congress to decide. We do no more here than try to determine what decision Congress has taken. * * *

IV

For these reasons we conclude that the considerations supporting Kirtsaeng's nongeographical interpretation of the words "lawfully made under this title" are the more persuasive. The judgment of the Court of Appeals is reversed, and the case is remanded for further proceedings consistent with this opinion.

It is so ordered.

■ JUSTICE KAGAN, with whom JUSTICE ALITO joins, concurring.

I concur fully in the Court's opinion. Neither the text nor the history of 17 U.S.C. § 109(a) supports removing first-sale protection from every copy of a protected work manufactured abroad. See ante, at 8–16, 28–31. I recognize, however, that the combination of today's decision and Quality King Distributors, Inc. v. L'anza Research Int'l, Inc., 523 U.S. 135 (1998), constricts the scope of § 602(a)(1)'s ban on unauthorized importation. I write to suggest that any problems associated with that limitation come not from our reading of § 109(a) here, but from *Quality King* 's holding that § 109(a) limits § 602(a)(1). * * *

At bottom, John Wiley (together with the dissent) asks us to misconstrue § 109(a) in order to restore § 602(a)(1) to its purportedly rightful function of enabling copyright holders to segment international markets. I think John Wiley may have a point about what § 602(a)(1) was designed to do; that gives me pause about *Quality King's* holding that the first-sale doctrine limits the importation ban's scope. But the Court today correctly declines the invitation to save § 602(a)(1) from *Quality King* by destroying the first-sale protection that § 109(a) gives to every owner of a copy manufactured abroad. That would swap one (possible) mistake for a much worse one, and make our reading of the statute only less reflective of Congressional intent. If Congress thinks copyright owners need greater power to restrict importation and thus divide markets, a ready solution is at hand— not the one John Wiley offers in this case, but the one the Court rejected in *Quality King.*

■ JUSTICE GINSBURG, with whom JUSTICE KENNEDY joins, and with whom JUSTICE SCALIA joins except as to Parts III and V–B–1, dissenting.

    * * *

I

* * * As the District Court and the Court of Appeals concluded, see 654 F.3d 210, 221–222 (C.A.2 2011); App. to Pet. for Cert. 70a–73a, application of the *Quality King* analysis to the facts of this case would preclude any invocation of § 109(a). Petitioner Supap Kirtsaeng imported and then sold at a profit over 600 copies of copyrighted textbooks printed outside the United States by the Asian subsidiary of respondent John Wiley & Sons, Inc. (Wiley). App. 29–34. See also ante, at 3–5 (opinion of the Court). In the words the Court used in *Quality King,* these copies "were 'lawfully made' not under the United States Copyright Act, but instead, under the law of some other country." 523 U.S., at 147. Section 109(a) therefore does not apply, and Kirtsaeng's unauthorized importation constitutes copyright infringement under § 602(a)(1).

The Court does not deny that under the language I have quoted from *Quality King,* Wiley would prevail. Ante, at 27. Nevertheless, the Court dismisses this language, to which all Members of the *Quality King* Court subscribed, as ill-considered dictum. Ante, at 27–28. I agree that the discussion was dictum in the sense that it was not essential to the Court's judgment. See *Quality King,* 523 U.S., at 154 (Ginsburg, J., concurring) ("[W]e do not today resolve cases in which the allegedly infringing imports were manufactured abroad."). But I disagree with the Court's conclusion that this dictum was ill considered. Instead, for the reasons explained below, I would hold, consistently with *Quality King* 's dictum, that § 602(a)(1) authorizes a copyright owner to bar the importation of a copy manufactured abroad for sale abroad.

would adopt QK dictum

II

The text of the Copyright Act demonstrates that Congress intended to provide copyright owners with a potent remedy against the importation of foreign-made copies of their copyrighted works. As the Court recognizes, *ante,* at 3, this case turns on the meaning of the phrase "lawfully made under this title" in § 109(a). In my view, that phrase is most sensibly read as referring to instances in which a copy's creation is governed by, and conducted in compliance with, Title 17 of the U.S.Code. * * *

Not only does the Court adopt an unnatural construction of the § 109(a) phrase "lawfully made under this title." Concomitantly, the Court reduces § 602(a)(1) to insignificance. As the Court appears to acknowledge, see *ante,* at 26, the only independent effect § 602(a)(1) has under today's decision is to prohibit unauthorized importations carried out by persons who merely have possession of, but do not own, the imported copies. See 17 U.S.C. § 109(a) (§ 109(a) applies to any *"owner* of a particular copy or phonorecord lawfully made under this title" (emphasis added)). If this is enough to avoid rendering § 602(a)(1) entirely "superfluous," *ante,* at 26, it hardly suffices to give the owner's importation right the scope Congress intended it to have. Congress used broad language in § 602(a)(1); it did so to achieve a broad objective. * * * The Court's decision also overwhelms 17 U.S.C. § 602(a)(3)'s exceptions to § 602(a)(1)'s importation prohibition. 2 P. Goldstein, Copyright § 7.6.1.2(a), p. 7:141 (3d ed.2012) (hereinafter Goldstein). Those exceptions permit the importation of copies without the copyright owner's authorization for certain governmental, personal, scholarly, educational, and religious purposes. 17 U.S.C. § 602(a)(3). Copies imported under these exceptions "will often be lawfully made gray market goods purchased through normal market channels abroad." 2 Goldstein § 7.6.1.2(a), at 7:141. But if, as the Court holds, such copies can in any event be imported by virtue of § 109(a), § 602(a)(3)'s work has already been done. For example, had Congress conceived of § 109(a)'s sweep as the Court does, what earthly reason would there be to provide, as Congress did in § 602(a)(3)(C), that a library may import "no more than five copies" of a non-audiovisual work for its "lending or archival purposes"? * * *

Exceptions provide sufficient protch

III

* * *

The current text of § 602(a)(1) was finally enacted into law in 1976. See Copyright Act of 1976, § 602(a), 90 Stat. 2589–2590. The House and Senate Committee Reports on the 1976 Act demonstrate that Congress understood, as did the Copyright Office, just what that text meant. Both Reports state:

"Section 602 [deals] with two separate situations: importation of 'piratical' articles (that is, copies or phonorecords made without any authorization of the copyright owner), and unauthorized importation of copies or phonorecords that were lawfully made. *The general approach of sec-*

tion 602 is to make unauthorized importation an act of infringement in both cases, but to permit the Bureau of Customs to prohibit importation only of 'piratical' articles." S.Rep. No. 94–473, p. 151 (1975) (emphasis added). See also H.R.Rep. No. 94–1476, p. 169 (1976) (same).

In sum, the legislative history of the Copyright Act of 1976 is hardly "inconclusive." *Ante,* at 28. To the contrary, it confirms what the plain text of the Act conveys: Congress intended § 602(a)(1) to provide copyright owners with a remedy against the unauthorized importation of foreign-made copies of their works, even if those copies were made and sold abroad with the copyright owner's authorization. * * *

NOTES AND QUESTIONS

(1) How might the foreign marketing practices of copyright owners change in response to the decision in *Kirtsaeng*? Higher prices for foreign versions? Greater reliance on digital sales? Does the legislative history quoted in Justice Ginsburg's dissent indicate that Congress did indeed intend that copyright owners could maintain separate markets for their works sold abroad?

(2) If Congress is moved to intervene in the importation issue, would it be better to state that the first sale doctrine does not apply to copies manufactured abroad, or instead to state that the first sale doctrine is simply inapplicable in actions for unauthorized importation under § 602(a)?

THE RIGHT TO PREPARE DERIVATIVE WORKS

(1) The owner of a copyright enjoys the exclusive right "to prepare derivative works based upon the copyrighted work." § 106(2). The House Report offers this explanation: "The exclusive right to prepare derivative works, specified separately in clause (2) of section 106, overlaps the exclusive right of reproduction to some extent. It is broader than that right, however, in the sense that reproduction requires fixation in copies or phonorecords, whereas the preparation of a derivative work, such as a ballet, pantomime, or improvised performance, may be an infringement even though nothing is ever fixed in tangible form." After referring to the definition of a "derivative work" in § 101, the Report continues: "Thus, to constitute a violation of section 106(2), the infringing work must incorporate a portion of the copyrighted work in some form; for example, a detailed commentary on a work or a programmatic musical composition inspired by a novel would not normally constitute infringement under this clause." H.R.Rep. p. 62.

Fixation aside, what, if anything, does the § 106(2) derivative right add to the protection already afforded to a copyright owner by the reproduction right in § 106(1)? In Litchfield v. Spielberg, 736 F.2d 1352 (9th Cir.1984), cert. denied, 470 U.S. 1052 (1985), plaintiff Litchfield claimed that Steven Spielberg's motion picture "E.T.—The Extra Terrestrial" infringed her copyrighted musical "Lokey from Maldemar." Responding to her argument that *E.T.* was a derivative work based on *Lokey,* Judge Wright said: "Litchfield apparently believes that she does not have to show substantial similarity to show that *E.T.* is a derivative work." The court did not agree. "To prove infringement, one must show substantial similarity. * * * Litchfield's arguments that section 106(2) radically altered the protection afforded by the law of copyright are frivolous." See also Vault Corp. v. Quaid Software Ltd., 847 F.2d 255 (5th Cir.1988), using the absence of substantial similarity to reject a claim that the defendant's "unlocking" program infringed the plaintiff's derivative rights in its anti-copying software.

The exclusive right to prepare derivative works may be useful to a copyright owner who objects to changes in the work made by a licensee of the reproduction right. The plaintiff in Kennedy v. National Juvenile Detention Ass'n, 187 F.3d 690 (7th Cir.1999), cert. denied, 528 U.S. 1159 (2000), relied on this argument when the organization he worked for as a consultant made revisions to a report that he had submitted. His argument was rejected, however, on the grounds that his consulting agreement gave the defendant a license "to reproduce, publish, and to use such material in whole or in part," which the court interpreted to include a right to create derivative works.

D. Bambauer, Faulty Math: The Economics of Legalizing the Grey Album, 59 Ala.L.Rev. 345 (2008), concludes that from an economic perspective, a separate derivative right is difficult to justify, and C. Sprigman, Copyright and the Rule of Reason, 7 J.Telecomm. & High Tech.L. 317 (2009), argues that the incentive rationale should at least require proof of harm to the copyright owner in the case of unauthorized derivative works. L. Heymann, The Trademark/Copyright Divide, 60 SMU L.Rev. 55 (2007), notes that some complaints about derivative uses are actually attempts to avoid unwelcome associations with the original and hence are more trademark than copyright.

(2) Can the derivative right ensnare a defendant who has not reproduced even a portion of the copyrighted work? See National Bank of Commerce v. Shaklee Corp., 503 F.Supp. 533 (W.D.Tex.1980), finding copyright infringement in a defendant's insertion of advertising material into purchased copies of the plaintiff's book that the defendant distributed to its customers as a promotion. Is this result consistent with the "rebinding" cases that protect defendants who recondition copyrighted books, including turning paperbacks into hardcover? See, e.g., Lantern Press, Inc. v. American Pub. Co., 419 F.Supp. 1267 (E.D.N.Y.1976). In Paramount Pictures Corp. v. Video Broadcasting Systems, Inc., 724 F.Supp. 808 (D.Kan.1989), the court said that a video rental store's insertion of advertisements at the beginning of movie cassettes was not an infringement of the motion picture studios' right to create derivative works since the defendant had not "recast, transformed, or adapted" the films, quoting from the statutory definition of a "derivative work."

Lee v. A.R.T. Company

United States Court of Appeals, Seventh Circuit, 1997.
125 F.3d 580.

■ Before BAUER, EASTERBROOK, and DIANE P. WOOD, CIRCUIT JUDGES.

■ EASTERBROOK, CIRCUIT JUDGE.

Annie Lee creates works of art, which she sells through her firm Annie Lee & Friends. Deck the Walls, a chain of outlets for modestly priced art, is among the buyers of her works, which have been registered with the Register of Copyrights. One Deck the Walls store sold some of Lee's notecards and small lithographs to A.R.T. Company, which mounted the works on ceramic tiles (covering the art with transparent epoxy resin in the process) and resold the tiles. Lee contends that these tiles are derivative works, which under 17 U.S.C. § 106(2) may not be prepared without the permission of the copyright proprietor. She seeks both monetary and injunctive relief. Her position has the support of two cases holding that A.R.T.'s business violates the copyright laws. Munoz v. Albuquerque A.R.T. Co., 38 F.3d 1218 (9th Cir.1994), affirming without published opinion, 829 F.Supp. 309 (D.Alaska 1993); Mirage Editions, Inc. v. Albuquerque A.R.T. Co., 856 F.2d 1341 (9th Cir.1988). *Mirage Editions,* the only full appellate discussion, dealt with pages cut from books and mounted on tiles; the court of appeals' brief order in *Munoz* concludes that the reasoning of *Mirage Editions* is equally applicable to works of art that were sold loose. Our district court disagreed with these decisions and entered summary judgment for the defendant. 925 F.Supp. 576 (N.D.Ill.1996).

Now one might suppose that this is an open and shut case under the doctrine of first sale, codified at 17 U.S.C. § 109(a). A.R.T. bought the work legitimately, mounted it on a tile, and resold what it had purchased. Because the artist could capture the value of her art's contribution to the finished product as part of the price for the original transaction, the economic rationale for protecting an adaptation as "derivative" is absent. See William M. Landes & Richard A. Posner, An Economic Analysis of Copyright Law, 17 J. Legal Studies 325, 353–57 (1989). An alteration that includes (or consumes) a complete copy of the original lacks economic significance. One work changes hands multiple times, exactly what § 109(a) permits, so it may lack legal significance too. But § 106(2) creates a separate exclusive right, to "prepare derivative works", and Lee believes that affixing the art to the tile is "preparation," so that A.R.T. would have violated § 106(2) even if it had dumped the finished tiles into the Marianas Trench. For the sake of argument we assume that this is so and ask whether card-on-a-tile is a "derivative work" in the first place.

"Derivative work" is a defined term:

> A "derivative work" is a work based upon one or more preexisting works, such as a translation, musical arrangement, dramatization, fictionalization, motion picture version, sound recording, art reproduction, abridgment, condensation, or any other form in which a work may be recast, transformed, or adapted. A work consisting of editorial revisions, annotations, elaborations, or other modifications which, as a whole, represent an original work of authorship, is a "derivative work".

17 U.S.C. § 101. The district court concluded that A.R.T.'s mounting of Lee's works on tile is not an "original work of authorship" because it is no different in form or function from displaying a painting in a frame or placing a medallion in a velvet case. No one believes that a museum violates § 106(2) every time it changes the frame of a painting that is still under copyright, although the choice of frame or glazing affects the impression the art conveys, and many artists specify frames (or pedestals for sculptures) in detail. *Munoz* and *Mirage Editions* acknowledge that framing and other traditional means of mounting and displaying art do not infringe authors' exclusive right to make derivative works. Nonetheless, the Ninth Circuit held, what A.R.T. does creates a derivative work because the epoxy resin bonds the art to the tile. Our district judge thought this a distinction without a difference, and we agree. If changing the way in which a work of art will be displayed creates a derivative work, and if Lee is right about what "prepared" means, then the derivative work is "prepared" when the art is mounted; what happens later is not relevant, because the violation of the § 106(2) right has already occurred. If the framing process does not cre-

ate a derivative work, then mounting art on a tile, which serves as a flush frame, does not create a derivative work. * * *

Lee wages a vigorous attack on the district court's conclusion that A.R.T.'s mounting process cannot create a derivative work because the change to the work "as a whole" is not sufficiently original to support a copyright. Cases such as Gracen v. Bradford Exchange, Inc., 698 F.2d 300 (7th Cir.1983), show that neither A.R.T. nor Lee herself could have obtained a copyright in the card-on-a-tile, thereby not only extending the period of protection for the images but also eliminating competition in one medium of display. After the Ninth Circuit held that its mounting process created derivative works, A.R.T. tried to obtain a copyright in one of its products; the Register of Copyrights sensibly informed A.R.T. that the card-on-a-tile could not be copyrighted independently of the note card itself. But Lee says that this is irrelevant—that a change in a work's appearance may infringe the exclusive right under § 106(2) even if the alteration is too trivial to support an independent copyright. Pointing to the word "original" in the second sentence of the statutory definition, the district judge held that "originality" is essential to a derivative work. This understanding has the support of both cases and respected commentators. E.g., L. Batlin & Son, Inc. v. Snyder, 536 F.2d 486 (2d Cir.1976); Melville B. Nimmer & David Nimmer, 1 Nimmer on Copyrights § 3.03 (1997). Pointing to the fact that the first sentence in the statutory definition omits any reference to originality, Lee insists that a work may be derivative despite the mechanical nature of the transformation. This view, too, has the support of both cases and respected commentators. E.g., Lone Ranger Television, Inc. v. Program Radio Corp., 740 F.2d 718, 722 (9th Cir.1984); Paul Goldstein, Copyright: Principles, Law and Practice § 5.3.1 (2d ed. 1996) (suggesting that a transformation is covered by § 106(2) whenever it creates a "new work for a different market").

Fortunately, it is not necessary for us to choose sides. Assume for the moment that the first sentence recognizes a set of non-original derivative works. To prevail, then, Lee must show that A.R.T. altered her works in one of the ways mentioned in the first sentence. The tile is not an "art reproduction"; A.R.T. purchased and mounted Lee's original works. That leaves the residual clause: "any other form in which a work may be recast, transformed, or adapted." None of these words fits what A.R.T. did. Lee's works were not "recast" or "adapted". "Transformed" comes closer and gives the Ninth Circuit some purchase for its view that the permanence of the bond between art and base matters. Yet the copyrighted note cards and lithographs were not "transformed" in the slightest. The art was bonded to a slab of ceramic, but it was not changed in the process. It still depicts exactly what it depicted when it left Lee's studio. See William F. Patry, Copyright Law and Practice 823–24 (1994) (disapproving *Mirage Editions* on this ground).[1] If mounting works a "transformation," then changing a painting's frame or a photograph's mat equally produces a derivative work. Indeed, if Lee is right about the meaning of the definition's first sentence, then any alteration of a work, however slight, requires the author's permission. We asked at oral argument what would happen if a purchaser jotted a note on one of the note cards, or used it as a coaster for a drink, or cut it in half, or if a collector applied his seal (as is common in Japan); Lee's counsel

---

[1] Scholarly disapproval of *Mirage Editions* has been widespread. Goldstein § 5.3 at 5:81–82; Nimmer & Nimmer § 3.03; Wendy J. Gordon, On Owning Information: Intellectual Property and the Restitutionary Impulse, 78 Va.L.Rev. 149, 255 n. 401 (1992).

replied that such changes prepare derivative works, but that as a practical matter artists would not file suit. A definition of derivative work that makes criminals out of art collectors and tourists is jarring despite Lee's gracious offer not to commence civil litigation.

If Lee (and the Ninth Circuit) are right about what counts as a derivative work, then the United States has established through the back door an extraordinarily broad version of authors' moral rights, under which artists may block any modification of their works of which they disapprove. No European version of *droit moral* goes this far. Until recently it was accepted wisdom that the United States did not enforce any claim of moral rights; even bowdlerization of a work was permitted unless the modifications produced a new work so different that it infringed the exclusive right under § 106(2). Compare WGN Continental Broadcasting Co. v. United Video, Inc., 693 F.2d 622 (7th Cir.1982), with Gilliam v. American Broadcasting Companies, Inc., 538 F.2d 14, 24 (2d Cir.1976). The Visual Artists Rights Act of 1990, Pub.L. 101–650, 104 Stat. 5089, 5123–33, moves federal law in the direction of moral rights, but the cornerstone of the new statute, 17 U.S.C. § 106A, does not assist Lee. Section 106A(a)(3)(A) gives an artist the right to "prevent any intentional distortion, mutilation, or other modification of that work which would be prejudicial to his or her honor or reputation". At oral argument Lee's lawyer disclaimed any contention that the sale of her works on tile has damaged her honor or reputation. What is more, § 106A applies only to a "work of visual art", a new term defined in § 101 to mean either a unique work or part of a limited edition (200 copies or fewer) that has been "signed and consecutively numbered by the author". Lee's note cards and lithographs are not works of visual art under this definition, so she could not invoke § 106A even if A.R.T.'s use of her works to produce kitsch had damaged her reputation. It would not be sound to use § 106(2) to provide artists with exclusive rights deliberately omitted from the Visual Artists Rights Act. We therefore decline to follow *Munoz* and *Mirage Editions*.

no infringement

Affirmed.

NOTES AND QUESTIONS

(1) What rationales support recognition of a right in the copyright owner to prevent alterations to purchased copies of the work? A. Cohen, When Does a Work Infringe the Derivative Works Right of a Copyright Owner?, 17 Cardozo Arts & Ent.L.J. 623 (1999), suggests that consumptive uses such as the defendant's ceramic tiles in *Lee* should be considered infringing only if the use is not a reasonably expected one for which the copyright owner was presumptively compensated through the original sale.

(2) Does the *Mirage Editions* case described in *Lee* restrict the *use* of a copyrighted work? "The right to control the use of a work, although granted to inventors, has never been part of copyright except as performance may be considered 'use.' Indeed, the absence of a 'use right' helps justify the relatively casual approach to granting copyright as opposed to the more searching tests for patentability." R. Brown, Eligibility for Copyright Protection: A Search for Principled Standards, 70 Minn.L.Rev. 579, 588–89 (1985).

(3) The Portland Maine Public Library hit upon an unusual scheme for books that it would otherwise discard—it invited local artists to alter them as they pleased. The resulting works were returned to the library for circulation. Some of the artists reworked the text, for example, by changing the male and female gender pronouns in *Men Who Hate Women and the Women Who Love Them*. One artist put wheels and a lease on a dog training manual; another turned Walt Whitman's *Leaves of Grass* into a potted patch of turf in which the waving blades of grass are lines cut from the book. Sutherland, Wear This Book (But Bring It Back Friday), N.Y. Times, April 23, 2006, Sec. 2, p. 30. Could such uses infringe the derivative right?

(4) Should infringement of the derivative right turn on whether the defendant has contributed original authorship—the issue reserved by the court in *Lee*? Recall that the concept of a derivative work as defined in § 101 is used to determine both infringement of the derivative right in pre-existing works under § 106(2) and the copyrightability of the new work under § 103.

The defendant in Peker v. Masters Collection, 96 F.Supp.2d 216 (E.D.N.Y.2000), purchased poster prints of plaintiff's oil paintings for around $5 and then, after adding paint to the posters in a process that replicated the original oil painting, sold the replica paintings for several hundred dollars. Denying plaintiff's claim for infringement of its exclusive right to prepare derivative works, the court said that the replicas did not possess sufficient originality to be independently copyrightable, and hence were not "derivative works." However, the court did hold the defendant liable for violating the plaintiff's reproduction right; the replicas reproduced plaintiff's original paintings and the fact that the defendant had purchased copies of the posters provided no defense to its "transmogrification" of the posters into the original works.

(5) The Directors Guild of America and several motion picture studios became involved in a dispute with companies marketing technologies that produce sanitized versions of Hollywood movies. One company purchased movie DVDs and inserted codes at various points corresponding to designated levels of violence, nudity, sex, and profanity. When the coded DVD is played on one of the company's specially-designed DVD players, the user can choose among different levels of filtering and the player will automatically skip the offending images or dialogue. The directors were unhappy about what they saw as a distortion of their work—a *Saving Private Ryan* with less violence, or *Titanic* without the scene in which Leonardo DiCaprio sketches a nude Kate Winslet. Does either the company or a consumer who uses the technology infringe the studios' derivative rights? (Is it any different from simply fast-forwarding past the scenes?) In 2005, Congress added § 110(11), which protects the purveyors and users of DVD filtering technology as long as no fixed copy of the edited version is created.

Judge Matsch in Clean Flicks, LLC v. Soderbergh, 433 F.Supp.2d 1236 (D.Colo.2006), noted that the amendment in § 110(11) does not apply to companies like Clean Flicks that sell edited copies of movies. The studios claimed that the practice violated their reproduction, derivative, and distribution rights; the companies argued it was a fair use, emphasizing that they purchased a new DVD of the movie every time they edited and then recorded an altered version for sale to a customer. The court said that the fair use defense was not applicable because the companies were exploiting the movies in a market that the copyright owners had chosen not to enter. Judge Matsch held that there was no violation of the derivative right since the companies had added nothing new to the films and hence the new versions were not sufficiently transformative to qualify as derivative works under the statute. However, the court held that the companies were liable for infringing the reproduction right when they recorded the edited version onto a blank DVD, and they were also infringing the distribution right. A. Durham, Consumer Modification of Copyrighted Works, 81 Ind.L.J. 851 (2006), pushes for recognition of a general right in consumers to make their own modifications to works for private use.

Lewis Galoob Toys, Inc. v. Nintendo of America, Inc.

United States Court of Appeals, Ninth Circuit, 1992.
964 F.2d 965.
Certiorari denied, 507 U.S. 985 (1993).

■ Before FARRIS and RYMER, CIRCUIT JUDGES, and KENYON, DISTRICT JUDGE.

■ FARRIS, CIRCUIT JUDGE:

DCH

Nintendo of America appeals the district court's judgment following a bench trial (1) declaring that Lewis Galoob Toys' Game Genie does not violate any Nintendo copyrights and dissolving a temporary injunction and (2) denying Nintendo's request for a permanent injunction enjoining Galoob from marketing the Game Genie. Lewis Galoob Toys, Inc. v. Nintendo of America, Inc., 780 F.Supp. 1283 (N.D.Cal.1991). We have appellate jurisdiction pursuant to 15 U.S.C. § 1121 and 28 U.S.C. §§ 1291 and 1292(a)(1). We affirm.

FACTS

The Nintendo Entertainment System is a home video game system marketed by Nintendo. To use the system, the player inserts a cartridge containing a video game that Nintendo produces or licenses others to produce. By pressing buttons and manipulating a control pad, the player controls one of the game's characters and progresses through the game. The games are protected as audiovisual works under 17 U.S.C. § 102(a)(6).

games protected by AV
Works under 102(6)(6)

The Game Genie is a device manufactured by Galoob that allows the player to alter up to three features of a Nintendo game. For example, the Game Genie can increase the number of lives of the player's character, increase the speed at which the character moves, and allow the character to float above obstacles. The player controls the changes made by the Game Genie by entering codes provided by the Game Genie Programming Manual and Code Book. The player also can experiment with variations of these codes.

* * * The Game Genie is inserted between a game cartridge and the Nintendo Entertainment System. The Game Genie does not alter the data that is stored in the game cartridge. Its effects are temporary.

DISCUSSION

1. *Derivative work*

The Copyright Act of 1976 confers upon copyright holders the exclusive right to prepare and authorize others to prepare derivative works based on their copyrighted works. See 17 U.S.C. § 106(2). Nintendo argues that the district court erred in concluding that the audiovisual displays created by the Game Genie are not derivative works. * * *

A derivative work must incorporate a protected work in some concrete or permanent "form." The Copyright Act defines a derivative work as follows:

> A "derivative work" is a work based upon one or more preexisting works, such as a translation, musical arrangement, dramatization, fictionalization, motion picture version, sound recording, art reproduction, abridgment, condensation, *or any other form in which a work may be recast, transformed, or adapted.* A work consisting of editorial revisions, annotations, elaborations, or other modifications which, as a whole, represent an original work of authorship, is a "derivative work."

[handwritten: def derivative work]

17 U.S.C. § 101 (emphasis added). The examples of derivative works provided by the Act all physically incorporate the underlying work or works. The Act's legislative history similarly indicates that "the infringing work must incorporate a portion of the copyrighted work in some form." 1976 U.S.Code Cong. & Admin.News 5659, 5675. See also Mirage Editions, Inc. v. Albuquerque A.R.T. Co., 856 F.2d 1341, 1343–44 (9th Cir.1988) (discussing same), cert. denied, 489 U.S. 1018 (1989). * * *

The district court's finding that no independent work is created, see *Galoob,* 780 F.Supp. at 1291, is supported by the record. The Game Genie merely enhances the audiovisual displays (or underlying data bytes) that originate in Nintendo game cartridges. The altered displays do not incorporate a portion of a copyrighted work in some concrete or permanent *form.* Nintendo argues that the Game Genie's displays are as fixed in the hardware and software used to create them as Nintendo's original displays. Nintendo's argument ignores the fact that the Game Genie cannot produce an audiovisual display; the underlying display must be produced by a Nintendo Entertainment System and game cartridge. Even if we were to rely on the Copyright Act's definition of "fixed," we would similarly conclude that the resulting display is not "embodied," see 17 U.S.C. § 101, in the Game Genie. It cannot be a derivative work.

[handwritten: △ enhances the AV displays]

Mirage Editions is illustrative. Albuquerque A.R.T. transferred artworks from a commemorative book to individual ceramic tiles. See *Mirage Editions,* 856 F.2d at 1342. We held that "[b]y borrowing and mounting the preexisting, copyrighted individual art images without the consent of the copyright proprietors . . . [Albuquerque A.R.T.] has prepared a derivative work and infringed the subject copyrights." Id. at 1343. The ceramic tiles *physically* incorporated the copyrighted works in a form that could be sold. Perhaps more importantly, sales of the tiles supplanted purchasers' demand for the underlying works. Our holding in *Mirage Editions* would have been much different if Albuquerque A.R.T. had distributed lenses that merely enabled users to view several artworks simultaneously. * * *

[handwritten: mirage holding]

Nintendo relies heavily on Midway Mfg. Co. v. Artic Int'l, Inc., 704 F.2d 1009 (7th Cir.), cert. denied, 464 U.S. 823 (1983). *Midway* can be distinguished. The defendant in *Midway,* Artic International, marketed a computer chip that could be inserted in Galaxian video games to speed up the rate of play. The Seventh Circuit held that the speeded-up version of Galaxian was a derivative work. Id. at 1013–14. Artic's chip substantially copied and *replaced* the chip that was originally distributed by Midway. Purchasers of Artic's chip also benefited economically by offering the altered game for use by the general public. The Game Genie does not physically incorporate a portion of a copyrighted work, nor does it supplant demand for a component of that work. The court in *Midway* acknowledged that the Copyright Act's definition of "derivative work" "must be stretched to accommodate speeded-up video games." Id. at 1014. Stretching that definition further would chill innovation and fail to protect "society's competing interest in the free flow of ideas, information, and commerce." Sony Corp. of America v. Universal Studios, Inc., 464 U.S. 417 (1984).

In holding that the audiovisual displays created by the Game Genie are not derivative works, we recognize that technology often advances by improvement rather than replacement. * * * Some time ago, for example, computer companies began marketing spell-checkers that operate within existing word processors by signalling the writer when a word is misspelled. These applications, as well as countless others, could not be produced and marketed if courts were to conclude that the word processor and spell-checker combination is a derivative work based on the word processor alone. The Game Genie is useless by itself, it can only enhance, and cannot duplicate or recaste, a Nintendo game's output. It does not contain or produce a Nintendo game's output in some concrete or permanent form, nor does it supplant demand for Nintendo game cartridges. Such innovations rarely will constitute infringing derivative works under the Copyright Act. * * *

2. *Fair use*

* * * The district court concluded that, even if the audiovisual displays created by the Game Genie are derivative works, Galoob is not liable under 17 U.S.C. § 107 because the displays are a fair use of Nintendo's copyrighted displays. * * *

Much of the parties' dispute regarding the fair use defense concerns the proper focus of the court's inquiry: (1) Galoob or (2) consumers who purchase and use the Game Genie. Nintendo's complaint does not allege direct infringement, nor did it try the case on that theory. The complaint, for example, alleges only that "Galoob's marketing advertising [sic], promoting and selling of Game Genie has and will *contribute to* the creation of infringing derivatives of Nintendo's copyrighted . . . games." (emphasis added). Contributory infringement is a form of third party liability. See Melville B. Nimmer & David Nimmer, 3 Nimmer on Copyright § 12.04[A][2], at 12–68 (1991). The district court properly focused on whether consumers who purchase and use the Game Genie would be infringing Nintendo's copyrights by creating (what are now assumed to be) derivative works.

[The court agreed that the use was fair, relying on the conclusion of the lower court that use of the Game Genie by consumers was a noncommercial use that did not threaten Nintendo's actual or potential market; there was no reasonable likelihood that Nintendo would sell similarly altered versions of its games.]

NOTES AND QUESTIONS

(1) Did Judge Farris adequately distinguish the Seventh Circuit's decision in *Midway*? That case offered this justification for its decision to treat the speeded-up game as an infringing derivative work: "A speeded-up video game is a substantially different product from the original game. As noted, it is more exciting to play and it requires some creative effort to produce. For that reason the owner of the copyright on the game should be entitled to monopolize it on the same theory that he is entitled to monopolize the derivative works specifically listed in § 101."

[handwritten margin note: sped-up game is infringement]

In emphasizing that the Game Genie neither incorporated nor produced an altered version of Nintendo's game in a permanent form, did the court in *Galoob* ignore the absence in § 106(2) of any requirement that the infringing derivative work be embodied in a copy or phonorecord? Is the result nonetheless preferable to *Midway*?

Galoob was distinguished by the Ninth Circuit in Micro Star v. FormGen Inc., 154 F.3d 1107 (9th Cir.1998). FormGen owned the copyright in *Duke Nukem 3D*, a "very cool" computer game according to Judge Kozinski. The game contained a variety of different levels, each with a different combination of scenery, aliens, and challenges. The game also came with a utility program that enabled players to create their own levels, along with a license that prohibited sale but not free distribution of the new levels. Micro Star downloaded 300 user-created levels that had been placed on the Internet and marketed the collection on a CD–ROM. The files did not contain any of the copyrighted artwork from the game—they merely directed the game to use images stored in the game's own permanent art library. FormGen claimed infringement of its derivative right; Micro Star argued that the files were not derivative works since they did not contain any infringing material. Judge Kozinski said that the files "described" the resulting audiovisual displays, and the new levels were essentially unauthorized "sequels" that infringed FormGen's copyright in the story embodied in its game.

(2) Cases such as *Midway* and *Galoob* are of special interest to software producers. Do users who modify copyrighted programs infringe the derivative right? Cf. § 117. See P. Samuelson, Modifying Copyrighted Software: Adjusting Copyright Doctrine to Accommodate a Technology, 28 Jurimetrics J. 179 (1988), arguing that the answer should be no. Are software companies that sell add-ons or enhancement programs designed to improve the performance of existing software liable as direct or contributory infringers even if their products contain none of the copyright owner's protected code? Who should profit from the added value of the enhanced software?

+ Nominative determinism
+ Looking glass self

CHAPTER 4

SCOPE OF PROTECTION: THE LIMITS OF LIABILITY

1. FAIR USE

"The judicial doctrine of fair use, one of the most important and well-
established limitations on the exclusive right of copyright owners, would be
given express statutory recognition for the first time in section 107. * * *

"The statement of the fair use doctrine in section 107 offers some guidance to users in determining when the principles of the doctrine apply.
However, the endless variety of situations and combinations of circumstances that can rise in particular cases precludes the formulation of exact
rules in the statute. The bill endorses the purpose and general scope of the
judicial doctrine of fair use, but there is no disposition to freeze the doctrine
in the statute, especially during a period of rapid technological change. Beyond a very broad statutory explanation of what fair use is and some of the
criteria applicable to it, the courts must be free to adapt the doctrine to
particular situations on a case-by-case basis. Section 107 is intended to restate the present judicial doctrine of fair use, not to change, narrow, or enlarge it in any way." H.R.Rep. pp. 65–66.

———

Two cases involving Boston worthies first gave the fair use doctrine
definition and a name. The term "fair use" apparently appeared for the first
time in Lawrence v. Dana, 15 Fed.Cas. 26 (C.C.D.Mass.1869) (No. 8,136), in
which author-attorney Richard Henry Dana, Jr., was found to have infringed the work of an earlier editor in his preparation of a new edition of
Wheaton's *Elements of International Law.* But Justice Story some twenty-
eight years earlier in Folsom v. Marsh had already spoken of the "nice balance" that determines the question of infringement.

Folsom v. Marsh
9 Fed.Cas. 342, No. 4901 (C.C.D.Mass.1841).

Justice Story was confronted with what he described as "one of those
intricate and embarrassing questions, arising in the administration of civil
justice, in which it is not, from the peculiar nature and character of the
controversy, easy to arrive at any satisfactory conclusion, or to lay down
any general principles applicable to all cases. Patents and copyrights," he
observed, "approach, nearer than any other class of cases belonging to forensic discussions, to what may be called the metaphysics of the law, where
the distinctions are, or at least may be, very subtle and refined, and, sometimes, almost evanescent." The Rev. Charles W. Upham, in his *Life of
Washington in the Form of an Autobiography,* derived 353 of its 866 pages
from letters and other documents that had first appeared in Jared Sparks'
monumental *Writings of President Washington,* a work of nearly 7,000 pages in twelve volumes, which had been published by the plaintiffs. Justice
Story decided that the plaintiffs held the copyright in all but a few of Washington's letters. He further decided that the defendants could not justify

319

their work as an "abridgment" (considered lawful at the time of this decision); so the defendants infringed unless their contention was accepted that they had a privilege to select and use the plaintiffs' materials in a new work of their own. "The question, then, is, whether this is a justifiable use of the original materials, such as the law recognizes as no infringement of the copyright of the plaintiffs. * * * It is certainly not necessary, to constitute an invasion of copyright, that the whole of a work should be copied, or even a large portion of it, in form or in substance. If so much is taken, that the value of the original is sensibly diminished, or the labors of the original author are substantially to an injurious extent appropriated by another, that is sufficient, in point of law, to constitute a piracy pro tanto. * * * In short, we must often, in deciding questions of this sort, look to the nature and objects of the selections made, the quantity and value of the materials used, and the degree in which the use may prejudice the sale, or diminish the profits, or supersede the objects, of the original work." With the hope that "some means may be found, to produce an amicable settlement of this unhappy controversy," Justice Story enjoined the defendants from further distribution of Upham's book.

Time Inc. v. Bernard Geis Associates

United States District Court, Southern District of New York, 1968.
293 F.Supp. 130.

■ WYATT, DISTRICT JUDGE.

This is a motion by plaintiff for summary judgment "interlocutory in character" on the issue of liability alone, as authorized by Rule 56(c) of the Federal Rules of Civil Procedure. * * *

When President Kennedy was killed in Dallas on November 22, 1963, Abraham Zapruder, a Dallas dress manufacturer, was by sheer happenstance at the scene taking home movie pictures with his camera. His film— an historic document and undoubtedly the most important photographic evidence concerning the fatal shots—was bought a few days later by Life; parts of the film were printed in several issues of the magazine. As to these issues and their contents (including, of course, the Zapruder pictures) and as to the film itself, Life has complied with all provisions of the Copyright Act (17 U.S.C. § 1 and following; the Act).

Defendant Thompson has written a book, "Six Seconds in Dallas" (the Book), which is a study of the assassination. It is a serious, thoughtful and impressive analysis of the evidence. The Book contains a number of what are called "sketches" but which are in fact copies of parts of the Zapruder film. Defendant Bernard Geis Associates (Associates), a partnership, published the Book on November 18, 1967 and defendant Random House, Inc. has been distributing the Book to the public. Defendant Bernard Geis is the only general partner of Associates.

This action was commenced on December 1, 1967. The complaint in a single count charges that certain frames of the Zapruder film were "stolen surreptitiously" from Life by Thompson and that copies of these frames appear in the Book as published. The complaint avers that the conduct of defendants is an infringement of statutory copyrights, an unfair trade practice, and unfair competition. * * *

President Johnson on November 29, 1963 appointed a Commission with Chief Justice Warren as Chairman (the Commission) to investigate the killing of President Kennedy. This Commission on September 24, 1964 submitted its lengthy report (the Warren Report) and all the evidence before it.

The Commission made extensive use of the Zapruder film, and placed great reliance on it, as evidenced in the Report (for example, pp. 97, 98–115). Six of the Zapruder frames are shown in the body of the Report (at pp. 100–103, 108, 114) and some 160 Zapruder frames are included (in volume XVIII) in the Exhibits of the Commission printed and submitted with the Report. * * *

There gradually developed a substantial volume of criticism of the Report, centered on its findings (Report, pp. 18, 22) that all the shots were fired from one place and that the person firing those shots acted alone.

Thompson was among those particularly interested in the Report; he became convinced that the Report was incomplete and he doubted its principal conclusion. * * *

[Thompson became a consultant to Life and without authorization photographed frames from the Zapruder film. Life repeatedly denied Thompson permission to use the photographs in his book, stating that it was corporate policy "not to allow anyone the use of any part of this film in the United States," that the film was "an invaluable asset of the corporation," and that "its use will be limited to our publications and enterprises." Thompson and the other defendants then hired an artist who made charcoal sketches from the photos for use in "Six Seconds in Dallas."]

There is thus an infringement by defendants unless the use of the copyrighted material in the Book is a "fair use" outside the limits of copyright protection. * * *

There is an initial reluctance to find any fair use by defendants because of the conduct of Thompson in making his copies and because of the deliberate appropriation in the Book, in defiance of the copyright owner. Fair use presupposes "good faith and fair dealing". Schulman, Fair Use and the Revision of the Copyright Act, 53 Iowa L.Rev. 832 (1968). On the other hand it was not the nighttime activities of Thompson which enabled defendants to reproduce copies of Zapruder frames in the Book. They could have secured such frames from the National Archives, or they could have used the reproductions in the Warren Report or in the issues of Life itself. Moreover, while hope by a defendant for commercial gain is not a significant factor in this Circuit, there is a strong point for defendants in their offer to surrender to Life all profits of Associates from the Book as royalty payment for a license to use the copyrighted Zapruder frames. It is also a fair inference from the facts that defendants acted with the advice of counsel.

In determining the issue of fair use, the balance seems to be in favor of defendants.

There is a public interest in having the fullest information available on the murder of President Kennedy. Thompson did serious work on the subject and has a theory entitled to public consideration. While doubtless the theory could be explained with sketches of the type used at page 87 of the Book and in The Saturday Evening Post, the explanation actually made in the Book with copies is easier to understand. The Book is not bought because it contained the Zapruder pictures; the Book is bought because of the theory of Thompson and its explanation, supported by Zapruder pictures.

There seems little, if any, injury to plaintiff, the copyright owner. There is no competition between plaintiff and defendants. Plaintiff does not sell the Zapruder pictures as such and no market for the copyrighted work appears to be affected. Defendants do not publish a magazine. There are projects for use by plaintiff of the film in the future as a motion picture or in books, but the effect of the use of certain frames in the Book on such projects is speculative. It seems more reasonable to speculate that the Book would, if anything, enhance the value of the copyrighted work; it is difficult to see any decrease in its value. * * *

The motion of plaintiff is denied.

The Clerk is directed to enter judgment in favor of defendants.

So ordered.

Iowa State University Research Foundation, Inc. v. American Broadcasting Co.

621 F.2d 57 (2d Cir.1980).

Plaintiff held the copyright in a film biography of Dan Gable, a student at Iowa State University who won a gold medal in wrestling at the 1972 Munich Olympics. ABC, without authorization, used a two and a half minute segment from the film during its Olympic coverage. When sued for infringement, ABC raised a fair use defense. The court affirmed a judgment in favor of the plaintiff.

"The doctrine of fair use, originally created and articulated in case law, permits courts to avoid rigid application of the copyright statute when, on occasion, it would stifle the very creativity which that law is designed to foster. * * *

"The network relies most heavily on the first factor—the purpose and character of its use. It claims it was engaged in the laudable pursuit of disseminating the life history of an important public figure involved in an event of intense public interest. * * *

"This argument proves too much. * * * The public interest in the free flow of information is assured by the law's refusal to recognize a valid copyright in facts. * * * The fair use doctrine is not a license for corporate theft, empowering a court to ignore a copyright whenever it determines the underlying work contains material of possible public importance. Indeed, we do not suppose that appellants would embrace their own defense theory if another litigant sought to apply it to the ABC evening news."

On the issue of market effect, the court concluded that "ABC did foreclose a significant potential market to [plaintiff]—sale of its film for use on television in connection with the Olympics. In fact, because of its exclusive right to televise the games, ABC monopolized that market. When ABC telecast *Champion* without purchasing the film, it usurped an extremely significant market."

Wainwright Securities, Inc. v. Wall Street Transcript Corp.

558 F.2d 91 (2d Cir.1977), cert. denied, 434 U.S. 1014 (1978).

This case rejected a fair use defense raised by the publisher of a weekly financial newspaper that promised its readers "a fast-reading, pinpointed account of heavy-weight reports from the top institutional research firms." The plaintiff, unhappy with the defendant's practice of publishing abstracts of its copyrighted research reports, sought a preliminary injunction.

"It is, of course, axiomatic that 'news events' may not be copyrighted. * * * What is protected is the manner of expression, the author's analysis or interpretation of events [query], the way he structures his material and marshals facts, his choice of words, and the emphasis he gives to particular developments." The court noted that the defendant had contributed no independent research or analysis.

"The copying by the Transcript is easily distinguishable from the reporting of the Wainwright research reports by other publications. The Wall Street Journal articles referred to by appellants, for example, were published a year apart. There apparently was no attempt to provide readers regularly with summaries of the Wainwright reports and there is no indication that the Wall Street Journal launched an advertising campaign portraying itself as a publisher of the same financial analyses available to large investors, but at a lower price. By contrast, the appellants' use of the Wainwright reports was blatantly self-serving, with the obvious intent, if not the effect, of fulfilling the demand for the original work. * * * This was not legitimate coverage of a news event; instead it was, and there is no other way to describe it, chiseling for personal profit." The court affirmed a preliminary injunction.

Harper & Row, Publishers, Inc. v. Nation Enterprises

Supreme Court of the United States, 1985.
471 U.S. 539, 105 S.Ct. 2218.

■ JUSTICE O'CONNOR delivered the opinion of the Court.

This case requires us to consider to what extent the "fair use" provision of the Copyright Revision Act of 1976, 17 U.S.C. § 107 (hereinafter the Copyright Act), sanctions the unauthorized use of quotations from a public figure's unpublished manuscript. In March 1979, an undisclosed source provided The Nation magazine with the unpublished manuscript of "A Time to Heal: The Autobiography of Gerald R. Ford." Working directly from the purloined manuscript, an editor of The Nation produced a short piece entitled "The Ford Memoirs—Behind the Nixon Pardon." The piece was timed to "scoop" an article scheduled shortly to appear in Time Magazine. Time had agreed to purchase the exclusive right to print prepublication excerpts from the copyright holders, Harper & Row, Publishers, Inc. (hereinafter Harper & Row) and Reader's Digest Association, Inc. (hereinafter Reader's Digest). As a result of The Nation article, Time canceled its agreement. Petitioners brought a successful copyright action against The Nation. On appeal, the Second Circuit reversed the lower court's finding of infringement, holding that The Nation's act was sanctioned as a "fair use" of the copyrighted material. We granted certiorari, 467 U.S. 1214 (1984), and we now reverse.

I

In February 1977, shortly after leaving the White House, former President Gerald R. Ford contracted with petitioners Harper & Row and Reader's Digest, to publish his as yet unwritten memoirs. The memoirs were to contain "significant hitherto unpublished material" concerning the Watergate crisis, Mr. Ford's pardon of former President Nixon and "Mr. Ford's reflections on this period of history, and the morality and personalities involved." App. to Pet. for Cert. C–14–C–15. In addition to the right to publish the Ford memoirs in book form, the agreement gave petitioners the exclusive right to license prepublication excerpts, known in the trade as "first serial rights." Two years later, as the memoirs were nearing completion, petitioners negotiated a prepublication licensing agreement with Time, a weekly news magazine. Time agreed to pay $25,000, $12,500 in advance and an additional $12,500 at publication, in exchange for the right to excerpt 7,500 words from Mr. Ford's account of the Nixon pardon. The issue featuring the excerpts was timed to appear approximately one week before shipment of the full length book version to bookstores. Exclusivity was an important consideration; Harper & Row instituted procedures designed to maintain the confidentiality of the manuscript, and Time retained the right to renegotiate the second payment should the material appear in print prior to its release of the excerpts.

Two to three weeks before the Time article's scheduled release, an unidentified person secretly brought a copy of the Ford manuscript to Victor Navasky, editor of The Nation, a political commentary magazine. Mr. Navasky knew that his possession of the manuscript was not authorized and that the manuscript must be returned quickly to his "source" to avoid discovery. 557 F.Supp. 1067, 1069 (S.D.N.Y.1983). He hastily put together what he believed was "a real hot news story" composed of quotes, paraphrases, and facts drawn exclusively from the manuscript. Ibid. Mr. Navasky attempted no independent commentary, research or criticism, in part because of the need for speed if he was to "make news" by "publish[ing] in advance of publication of the Ford book." App. 416–417. The 2,250 word article, reprinted in the Appendix to this opinion, appeared on April 3, 1979. As a result of The Nation's article, Time canceled its piece and refused to pay the remaining $12,500. * * *

II

We agree with the Court of Appeals that copyright is intended to increase and not to impede the harvest of knowledge. But we believe the Second Circuit gave insufficient deference to the scheme established by the Copyright Act for fostering the original works that provide the seed and substance of this harvest. The rights conferred by copyright are designed to assure contributors to the store of knowledge a fair return for their labors. Twentieth Century Music Corp. v. Aiken, 422 U.S. 151 (1975). * * *

Creation of a nonfiction work, even a compilation of pure fact, entails originality. See, e.g., Schroeder v. William Morrow & Co., 566 F.2d 3 (C.A.7 1977) (copyright in gardening directory); cf. Burrow–Giles Lithographic Co. v. Sarony, 111 U.S. 53, 58 (1884) (originator of a photograph may claim copyright in his work). The copyright holders of "A Time to Heal" complied with the relevant statutory notice and registration procedures. See §§ 106, 401, 408; App. to Pet. for Cert. C–20. Thus there is no dispute that the unpublished manuscript of "A Time to Heal," as a whole, was protected by § 106 from unauthorized reproduction. Nor do respondents dispute that verbatim copying of excerpts of the manuscript's original form of expression would constitute infringement unless excused as fair use. See 1 M. Nimmer, Nimmer on Copyright § 2.11[B], p. 2–159 (1984) (hereinafter Nimmer). Yet copyright does not prevent subsequent users from copying from a prior author's work those constituent elements that are not original—for example, quotations borrowed under the rubric of fair use from other copyrighted works, facts, or materials in the public domain—as long as such use does not unfairly appropriate the author's original contributions. Ibid.; A. Latman, Fair Use of Copyrighted Works (1958), reprinted as Study No. 14 in Copyright Law Revision Studies Nos. 14–16, Prepared for the Senate Committee on the Judiciary, 86th Cong., 2d Sess., 7 (1960) (hereinafter Latman). Perhaps the controversy between the lower courts in this case over copyrightability is more aptly styled a dispute over whether The Nation's appropriation of unoriginal and uncopyrightable elements encroached on the originality embodied in the work as a whole. Especially in the realm of factual narrative, the law is currently unsettled regarding the ways in which uncopyrightable elements combine with the author's original contributions to form protected expression. Compare Wainwright Securities Inc. v. Wall Street Transcript Corp., 558 F.2d 91 (C.A.2 1977) (protection accorded author's analysis, structuring of material and marshaling of facts), with Hoehling v. Universal City Studios, Inc., 618 F.2d 972 (C.A.2 1980) (limiting protection to ordering and choice of words). See, e.g., 1 Nimmer § 2.11[D], at 2–164–2–165.

We need not reach these issues, however, as The Nation has admitted to lifting verbatim quotes of the author's original language totaling between 300 and 400 words and constituting some 13% of The Nation article. In using generous verbatim excerpts of Mr. Ford's unpublished manuscript to lend authenticity to its account of the forthcoming memoirs, The Nation effectively arrogated to itself the right of first publication, an important marketable subsidiary right. For the reasons set forth below, we find that this use of the copyrighted manuscript, even stripped to the verbatim quotes conceded by The Nation to be copyrightable expression, was not a fair use within the meaning of the Copyright Act.

Holding

III

A

Fair use was traditionally defined as "a privilege in others than the owner of the copyright to use the copyrighted material in a reasonable manner without his consent." H. Ball, Law of Copyright and Literary Property 260 (1944) (hereinafter Ball). The statutory formulation of the defense of fair use in the Copyright Act of 1976 reflects the intent of Congress to codify the common-law doctrine. 3 Nimmer § 13.05. Section 107 requires a case-by-case determination whether a particular use is fair, and the statute notes four nonexclusive factors to be considered. This approach was "intended to restate the [pre-existing] judicial doctrine of fair use, not to change, narrow, or enlarge it in any way." H.R.Rep. No. 94–1476, p. 66 (1976) (hereinafter House Report). * * *

traditional dcf fair use

§ 107 case by case determ & has 4 non-exclusive factors to consider

Perhaps because the fair use doctrine was predicated on the author's implied consent to "reasonable and customary" use when he released his work for public consumption, fair use traditionally was not recognized as a defense to charges of copying from an author's as yet unpublished works. Under common-law copyright, "the property of the author . . . in his intellectual creation [was] absolute until he voluntarily part[ed] with the same." American Tobacco Co. v. Werckmeister, 207 U.S. 284, 299 (1907); 2 Nimmer § 8.23, at 8–273. This absolute rule, however, was tempered in practice by the equitable nature of the fair use doctrine. In a given case, factors such as implied consent through *de facto* publication on performance or dissemination of a work may tip the balance of equities in favor of prepublication use. See Copyright Law Revision—Part 2: Discussion and Comments on Report of the Registrar of Copyrights on General Revision of the U.S. Copyright Law, 88th Cong., 1st Sess., at 27 (H.R.Comm. Print, 1963) (discussion suggesting works disseminated to the public in a form not constituting a technical "publication" should nevertheless be subject to fair use); 3 Nimmer § 13.05, at 13–62, n. 2. But it has never been seriously disputed that "the fact that the plaintiff's work is unpublished . . . is a factor tending to negate the defense of fair use." Ibid. Publication of an author's expression before he has authorized its dissemination seriously infringes the author's right to decide when and whether it will be made public, a factor not present in fair use of published works. Respondents contend, however, that Congress, in including first publication among the rights enumerated in § 106, which are expressly subject to fair use under § 107, intended that fair use would apply *in pari materia* to published and unpublished works. The Copyright Revision Act does not support this proposition.

*** [The 1976 Act] recognized for the first time a distinct statutory right of first publication, which had previously been an element of the common-law protections afforded unpublished works. The Report of the House Committee on the Judiciary confirms that "Clause (3) of section 106, establishes the exclusive right of publications. . . . Under this provision the copyright owner would have the right to control the first public distribution of an authorized copy . . . of his work." Id., at 62.

Though the right of first publication, like the other rights enumerated in § 106, is expressly made subject to the fair use provision of § 107, fair use analysis must always be tailored to the individual case. Id., at 65; 3 Nimmer § 13.05[A]. The nature of the interest at stake is highly relevant to whether a given use is fair. From the beginning, those entrusted with the task of revision recognized the "overbalancing reasons to preserve the common law protection of undisseminated works until the author or his successor chooses to disclose them." Copyright Law Revision, Report of the Register of Copyrights on the General Revision of the U.S. Copyright Law, 87th Cong., 1st Sess., 41 (Comm.Print 1961). The right of first publication implicates a threshold decision by the author whether and in what form to release his work. First publication is inherently different from other § 106 rights in that only one person can be the first publisher; as the contract with Time illustrates, the commercial value of the right lies primarily in exclusivity. Because the potential damage to the author from judicially enforced "sharing" of the first publication right with unauthorized users of his manuscript is substantial, the balance of equities in evaluating such a claim of fair use inevitably shifts. ***

*** We conclude that the unpublished nature of a work is "[a] key, though not necessarily determinative, factor" tending to negate a defense of fair use. Senate Report, at 64. See 3 Nimmer § 13.05, at 13–62, n. 2; W. Patry, The Fair Use Privilege in Copyright Law 125 (1985) (hereinafter Patry).

We also find unpersuasive respondents' argument that fair use may be made of a soon-to-be-published manuscript on the ground that the author has demonstrated he has no interest in nonpublication. This argument assumes that the unpublished nature of copyrighted material is only relevant to letters or other confidential writings not intended for dissemination. It is true that common-law copyright was often enlisted in the service of personal privacy. See Brandeis & Warren, The Right to Privacy, 4 Harv.L.Rev. 193, 198–199 (1890). In its commercial guise, however, an author's right to choose when he will publish is no less deserving of protection. The period encompassing the work's initiation, its preparation, and its grooming for public dissemination is a crucial one for any literary endeavor. The Copyright Act, which accords the copyright owner the "right to control the first public distribution" of his work, House Report, at 62, echos the common law's concern that the author or copyright owner retain control throughout this critical stage. See generally Comment, The Stage of Publication as a "Fair Use" Factor: Harper & Row, Publishers v. Nation Enterprises, 58 St. John's L.Rev. 597 (1984). The obvious benefit to author and public alike of assuring authors the leisure to develop their ideas free from fear of expropriation outweighs any short term "news value" to be gained from premature publication of the author's expression. * * *

B

Respondents, however, contend that First Amendment values require a different rule under the circumstances of this case. The thrust of the decision below is that "[t]he scope of [fair use] is undoubtedly wider when the information conveyed relates to matters of high public concern." Consumers Union of the United States, Inc. v. General Signal Corp., 724 F.2d 1044, 1050 (C.A.2 1983) (construing Harper & Row, Publishers, Inc. v. Nation Enterprises, 723 F.2d 195 (1983) (case below), as allowing advertiser to quote Consumer Reports), cert. denied, 469 U.S. 823 (1984). Respondents advance the substantial public import of the subject matter of the Ford memoirs as grounds for excusing a use that would ordinarily not pass muster as a fair use—the piracy of verbatim quotations for the purpose of "scooping" the authorized first serialization. Respondents explain their copying of Mr. Ford's expression as essential to reporting the news story it claims the book itself represents. In respondents' view, not only the facts contained in Mr. Ford's memoirs, but "the precise manner in which [he] expressed himself [were] as newsworthy as what he had to say." Brief for Respondents 38–39. Respondents argue that the public's interest in learning this news as fast as possible outweighs the right of the author to control its first publication.

The Second Circuit noted, correctly, that copyright's idea/expression dichotomy "strike[s] a definitional balance between the First Amendment and the Copyright Act by permitting free communication of facts while still protecting an author's expression." 723 F.2d, at 203. No author may copyright his ideas or the facts he narrates. 17 U.S.C. § 102(b). See, e.g., New York Times Co. v. United States, 403 U.S. 713, 726, n.* (1971) (BRENNAN, J., concurring) (Copyright laws are not restrictions on freedom of speech as copyright protects only form of expression and not the ideas expressed); 1 Nimmer § 1.1[B][2]. As this Court long ago observed: "[T]he news element—the information respecting current events contained in the literary production—is not the creation of the writer, but is a report of matters that ordinarily are *publici juris;* it is the history of the day." International News Service v. Associated Press, 248 U.S. 215, 234 (1918). But copyright assures those who write and publish factual narratives such as "A Time to Heal" that they may at least enjoy the right to market the original expression contained therein as just compensation for their investment. Cf. Zacchini v. Scripps–Howard Broadcasting Co., 433 U.S. 562, 575 (1977).

Respondents' theory, however, would expand fair use to effectively destroy any expectation of copyright protection in the work of a public figure. Absent such protection, there would be little incentive to create or profit in financing such memoirs, and the public would be denied an important source of significant historical information. The promise of copyright would be an empty one if it could be avoided merely by dubbing the infringement a fair use "news report" of the book. See Wainwright Securities, Inc. v. Wall Street Transcript Corp., 558 F.2d 91 (C.A.2 1977), cert. denied, 434 U.S. 1014 (1978).

Nor do respondents assert any actual necessity for circumventing the copyright scheme with respect to the types of works and users at issue here. Where an author and publisher have invested extensive resources in creating an original work and are poised to release it to the public, no legitimate aim is served by preempting the right of first publication. The fact that the words the author has chosen to clothe his narrative may of themselves be "newsworthy" is not an independent justification for unauthorized copying of the author's expression prior to publication. * * *

In our haste to disseminate news, it should not be forgotten that the Framers intended copyright itself to be the engine of free expression. By establishing a marketable right to the use of one's expression, copyright supplies the economic incentive to create and disseminate ideas. This Court stated in Mazer v. Stein:

> "The economic philosophy behind the clause empowering Congress to grant patents and copyrights is the conviction that encouragement of individual effort by personal gain is the best way to advance public welfare through the talents of authors and inventors in 'Science and useful Arts.'" 347 U.S. 201, 219 (1954).

And again in Twentieth Century Music Corp. v. Aiken:

> "The immediate effect of our copyright law is to secure a fair return for an 'author's' creative labor. But the ultimate aim is, by this incentive, to stimulate [the creation of useful works] for the general public good." 422 U.S., at 156.

It is fundamentally at odds with the scheme of copyright to accord lesser rights in those works that are of greatest importance to the public. Such a notion ignores the major premise of copyright and injures author and public alike. "[T]o propose that fair use be imposed whenever the 'social value [of dissemination] . . . outweighs any detriment to the artist,' would be to propose depriving copyright owners of their right in the property precisely when they encounter those users who could afford to pay for it." Gordon, Fair Use as Market Failure: A Structural and Economic Analysis of the *Betamax* Case and its Predecessors, 82 Colum.L.Rev. 1600, 1615 (1982). And as one commentator has noted: "If every volume that was in the public interest could be pirated away by a competing publisher, . . . the public [soon] would have nothing worth reading." Sobel, Copyright and the First Amendment: A Gathering Storm?, 19 ASCAP Copyright Law Symposium 43, 78 (1971). * * *

In view of the First Amendment protections already embodied in the Copyright Act's distinction between copyrightable expression and uncopyrightable facts and ideas, and the latitude for scholarship and comment traditionally afforded by fair use, we see no warrant for expanding the doctrine of fair use to create what amounts to a public figure exception to copyright. Whether verbatim copying from a public figure's manuscript in a given case is or is not fair must be judged according to the traditional equities of fair use.

IV

* * * The four factors identified by Congress as especially relevant in determining whether the use was fair are: (1) the purpose and character of the use; (2) the nature of the copyrighted work; (3) the substantiality of the portion used in relation to the copyrighted work as a whole; (4) the effect on the potential market for or value of the copyrighted work. We address each one separately.

Purpose of the Use. The Second Circuit correctly identified news reporting as the general purpose of The Nation's use. News reporting is one of the examples enumerated in § 107 to "give some idea of the sort of activities the courts might regard as fair use under the circumstances." Senate Report, at 61. This listing was not intended to be exhaustive, see id.; § 101 (definition of "including" and "such as"), or to single out any particular use as presumptively a "fair" use. The drafters resisted pressures from special interest groups to create presumptive categories of fair use, but structured the provision as an affirmative defense requiring a case by case analysis. See H.R.Rep. No. 83, 90th Cong., 1st Sess., 37 (1967); Patry 477, n. 4. "[W]hether a use referred to in the first sentence of section 107 is a fair use in a particular case will depend upon the application of the determinative factors, including those mentioned in the second sentence." Senate Report, at 62. The fact that an article arguably is "news" and therefore a productive use is simply one factor in a fair use analysis. * * *

The fact that a publication was commercial as opposed to nonprofit is a separate factor that tends to weigh against a finding of fair use. "[E]very commercial use of copyrighted material is presumptively an unfair exploitation of the monopoly privilege that belongs to the owner of the copyright." Sony Corp. v. Universal City Studios, Inc., 464 U.S., at 451. In arguing that the purpose of news reporting is not purely commercial, The Nation misses the point entirely. The crux of the profit/nonprofit distinction is not whether the sole motive of the use is monetary gain but whether the user stands to profit from exploitation of the copyrighted material without paying the customary price. See Roy Export Co. Establishment v. Columbia Broadcasting System, Inc., 503 F.Supp., at 1144; 3 Nimmer § 13.05[A][1], at 13–71, n. 25.3. * * *

Nature of the Copyrighted Work. Second, the Act directs attention to the nature of the copyrighted work. "A Time to Heal" may be characterized as an unpublished historical narrative or autobiography. The law generally recognizes a greater need to disseminate factual works than works of fiction or fantasy. * * * Some of the briefer quotes from the memoirs are arguably necessary adequately to convey the facts; for example, Mr. Ford's characterization of the White House tapes as the "smoking gun" is perhaps so integral to the idea expressed as to be inseparable from it. Cf. 1 Nimmer § 1.10[C]. But The Nation did not stop at isolated phrases and instead excerpted subjective descriptions and portraits of public figures whose power lies in the author's individualized expression. Such use, focusing on the most expressive elements of the work, exceeds that necessary to disseminate the facts.

The fact that a work is unpublished is a critical element of its "nature." 3 Nimmer § 13.05[A]; Comment, 58 St. John's L.Rev., at 613. Our prior discussion establishes that the scope of fair use is narrower with respect to unpublished works. While even substantial quotations might qualify as fair use in a review of a published work or a news account of a speech that had been delivered to the public or disseminated to the press, see House Report, at 65, the author's right to control the first public appearance of his expression weighs against such use of the work before its release. The right of first publication encompasses not only the choice whether to publish at all, but also the choices when, where, and in what form first to publish a work. * * *

Amount and Substantiality of the Portion Used. Next, the Act directs us to examine the amount and substantiality of the portion used in relation to the copyrighted work as a whole. In absolute terms, the words actually quoted were an insubstantial portion of "A Time to Heal." The District Court, however, found that "[T]he Nation took what was essentially the heart of the book." 557 F.Supp., at 1072. We believe the Court of Appeals erred in overruling the District Judge's evaluation of the qualitative nature of the taking. See, e.g., Roy Export Co. Establishment v. Columbia Broadcasting System, Inc., 503 F.Supp., at 1145 (taking of 55 seconds out of one hour and twenty-nine minute film deemed qualitatively substantial). A Time editor described the chapters on the pardon as "the most interesting and moving parts of the entire manuscript." Reply Brief for Petitioners 16, n. 8. The portions actually quoted were selected by Mr. Navasky as among the most powerful passages in those chapters. He testified that he used verbatim excerpts because simply reciting the information could not adequately convey the "absolute certainty with which [Ford] expressed himself," App. 303; or show that "this comes from President Ford," id., at 305; or carry the "definitive quality" of the original, id., at 306. In short, he quoted these passages precisely because they qualitatively embodied Ford's distinctive expression.

As the statutory language indicates, a taking may not be excused merely because it is insubstantial with respect to the *infringing* work. As Judge Learned Hand cogently remarked, "no plagiarist can excuse the wrong by showing how much of his work he did not pirate." Sheldon v. Metro–Goldwyn Pictures Corp., 81 F.2d 49, 56 (CA2), cert. denied, 298 U.S. 669 (1936). Conversely, the fact that a substantial portion of the infringing work was copied verbatim is evidence of the qualitative value of the copied material, both to the originator and to the plagiarist who seeks to profit from marketing someone else's copyrighted expression.

Stripped to the verbatim quotes,[8] the direct takings from the unpublished manuscript constituted at least 13% of the infringing article. See Meeropol v. Nizer, 560 F.2d 1061, 1071 (C.A.2 1977) (copyrighted letters constituted less than 1% of infringing work but were prominently featured). The Nation article is structured around the quoted excerpts which serve as its dramatic focal points. See Appendix, infra. In view of the expressive value of the excerpts and their key role in the infringing work, we cannot agree with the Second Circuit that the "magazine took a meager, indeed an infinitesimal amount of Ford's original language." 723 F.2d, at 209.

---

[8]   See Appendix, infra, at 570. The Court of Appeals found that only "approximately 300 words" were copyrightable but did not specify which words. The court's discussion, however, indicates it excluded from consideration those portions of The Nation's piece that, although copied verbatim from Ford's manuscript, were quotes attributed by Ford to third persons and quotations from Government documents. At oral argument, counsel for The Nation did not dispute that verbatim quotes and very close paraphrase could constitute infringement. Tr. of Oral Arg. 24–25. Thus the Appendix identifies as potentially infringing only verbatim quotes or very close paraphrase and excludes from consideration Government documents and words attributed to third persons. The Appendix is not intended to endorse any particular rule of copyrightability but is intended merely as an aid to facilitate our discussion.

Effect on the Market. Finally, the Act focuses on "the effect of the use upon the potential market for or value of the copyrighted work." This last factor is undoubtedly the single most important element of fair use.[9] See 3 Nimmer § 13.05[A], at 13–76, and cases cited therein. "Fair use, when properly applied, is limited to copying by others which does not materially impair the marketability of the work which is copied." 1 Nimmer § 1.10[D], at 1–87. The trial court found not merely a potential but an actual effect on the market. Time's cancellation of its projected serialization and its refusal to pay the $12,500 were the direct effect of the infringement. The Court of Appeals rejected this fact finding as clearly erroneous, noting that the record did not establish a causal relation between Time's nonperformance and respondents' unauthorized publication of Mr. Ford's *expression* as opposed to the facts taken from the memoirs. We disagree. Rarely will a case of copyright infringement present such clear-cut evidence of actual damage. Petitioners assured Time that there would be no other authorized publication of *any* portion of the unpublished manuscript prior to April 23, 1979. *Any* publication of material from chapters 1 and 3 would permit Time to renegotiate its final payment. Time cited The Nation's article, which contained verbatim quotes from the unpublished manuscript, as a reason for its nonperformance. * * *

More important, to negate fair use one need only show that if the challenged use "should become widespread, it would adversely affect the *potential* market for the copyrighted work." Sony Corp. v. Universal City Studios, Inc., 464 U.S., at 451 (emphasis added); id., at 484, and n. 36 (collecting cases) (dissenting opinion). This inquiry must take account not only of harm to the original but also of harm to the market for derivative works. See Iowa State University Research Foundation, Inc. v. American Broadcasting Cos., 621 F.2d 57 (C.A.2 1980); Meeropol v. Nizer, supra, at 1070; Roy Export v. Columbia Broadcasting System, Inc., 503 F.Supp., at 1146. "If the defendant's work adversely affects the value of any of the rights in the copyrighted work (in this case the adaptation [and serialization] right) the use is not fair." 3 Nimmer § 13.05[B], at 13–77—13–78 (footnote omitted).

It is undisputed that the factual material in the balance of The Nation's article, besides the verbatim quotes at issue here, was drawn exclusively from the chapters on the pardon. The excerpts were employed as featured episodes in a story about the Nixon pardon—precisely the use petitioners had licensed to Time. The borrowing of these verbatim quotes from the unpublished manuscript lent The Nation's piece a special air of authenticity—as Navasky expressed it, the reader would know it was Ford speaking and not The Nation. App. 300c. Thus it directly competed for a share of the market for prepublication excerpts. The Senate Report states:

> "With certain special exceptions . . . a use that supplants any part of the normal market for a copyrighted work would ordinarily be considered an infringement." Senate Report, at 65.

---

[9] Economists who have addressed the issue believe the fair use exception should come into play only in those situations in which the market fails or the price the copyright holder would ask is near zero. See, e.g., T. Brennan, Harper & Row v. The Nation, Copyrightability and Fair Use, Dept. of Justice Economic Policy Office Discussion Paper, 13–17 (1984); Gordon, Fair Use as Market Failure: A Structural and Economic Analysis of the *Betamax* Case and its Predecessors, 82 Colum.L.Rev. 1600, 1615 (1982). As the facts here demonstrate, there is a fully functioning market that encourages the creation and dissemination of memoirs of public figures. In the economists' view, permitting "fair use" to displace normal copyright channels disrupts the copyright market without a commensurate public benefit.

Placed in a broader perspective, a fair use doctrine that permits extensive prepublication quotations from an unreleased manuscript without the copyright owner's consent poses substantial potential for damage to the marketability of first serialization rights in general. "Isolated instances of minor infringements, when multiplied many times, become in the aggregate a major inroad on copyright that must be prevented." Ibid.

V

* * *

The Nation conceded that its verbatim copying of some 300 words of direct quotation from the Ford manuscript would constitute an infringement unless excused as a fair use. Because we find that The Nation's use of these verbatim excerpts from the unpublished manuscript was not a fair use, the judgment of the Court of Appeals is reversed and remanded for further proceedings consistent with this opinion.

It is so ordered.

APPENDIX TO OPINION OF THE COURT

The portions of The Nation article which were copied verbatim from "A Time to Heal," excepting quotes from Government documents and quotes attributed by Ford to third persons, are identified in boldface in the text. See n. 8, ante, at 565. The corresponding passages in the Ford manuscript are footnoted.

[The Appendix to the Supreme Court's opinion contains the complete text of The Nation article, with parallel references to the Ford manuscript. Only a portion is reproduced below.]

THE FORD MEMOIRS BEHIND THE NIXON PARDON

In his memoirs, *A Time To Heal,* which Harper & Row will publish in late May or early June, former President Gerald R. Ford says that the idea of giving a blanket pardon to Richard M. Nixon was raised before Nixon resigned from the Presidency by Gen. Alexander Haig, who was then the White House chief of staff.

Ford also writes that, but for a misunderstanding, he might have selected Ronald Reagan as his 1976 running mate, that Washington lawyer Edward Bennett Williams, a Democrat, was his choice for head of the Central Intelligence Agency, that Nixon was the one who first proposed Rockefeller for Vice President, and that he regretted his **"cowardice"**[1] in allowing Rockefeller to remove himself from Vice Presidential contention. Ford also describes his often prickly relations with Henry Kissinger.

The Nation obtained the 655–page typescript before publication. Advance excerpts from the book will appear in *Time* in mid-April and in *The Reader's Digest* thereafter. Although the initial print order has not been decided, the figure is tentatively set at 50,000; it could change, depending upon the public reaction to the serialization.

Ford's account of the Nixon pardon contains significant new detail on the negotiations and considerations that surrounded it. According to Ford's version, the subject was first broached to him by General Haig on August 1, 1974, a week before Nixon resigned. General Haig revealed that the newly

---

[1] I was angry at myself for showing cowardice in not saying to the ultra-conservatives, "It's going to be Ford and Rockefeller, whatever the consequences." p. 496.

transcribed White House tapes were the equivalent of the **"smoking gun"**[2] and that Ford should prepare himself to become President.

Ford was deeply hurt by Haig's revelation: **"Over the past several months Nixon had repeatedly assured me that he was not involved in Watergate, that the evidence would prove his innocence, that the matter would fade from view."**[3] Ford had believed him, but he let Haig explain the President's alternatives.

He could **"ride it out"**[4] or he could resign, Haig said. He then listed the different ways Nixon might resign and concluded by pointing out that **Nixon could agree to leave in return for an agreement that the new President, Ford, would pardon him.**[5] Although Ford said it would be improper for him to make any recommendation, he basically agreed with Haig's assessment and adds, **"Because of his references to the pardon authority, I did ask Haig about the extent of a President's pardon power."**[6]

"It's my understanding from a White House lawyer," Haig replied, "that a President does have authority to grant a pardon even before criminal action has been taken against an individual."

But because Ford had neglected to tell Haig he thought the idea of a resignation conditioned on a pardon was improper, his press aide, Bob Hartmann, suggested that Haig might well have returned to the White House and told President Nixon that he had mentioned the idea and Ford seemed comfortable with it. "Silence implies assent."

Ford then consulted with White House special counsel James St. Clair, who had no advice one way or the other on the matter more than pointing out that he was not the lawyer who had given Haig the opinion on the pardon. Ford also discussed the matter with Jack Marsh, who felt that the mention of a pardon in this context was a "time bomb," and with Bryce Harlow, who had served six Presidents and who agreed that **the mere mention of a pardon "could cause a lot of trouble."**[7]

As a result of these various conversations, Vice President Ford called Haig and read him a written statement: "I want you to understand that I have no intention of recommending what the President should do about resigning or not resigning and that nothing we talked about yesterday afternoon should be given any consideration in whatever decision the President may wish to make."

Despite what Haig had told him about the "smoking gun" tapes, Ford told a Jackson, Mich., luncheon audience later in the day that **the Presi-**

---

[2]   [I]t contained the so-called smoking gun. p. 3.

[3]   [O]ver the past several months Nixon had repeatedly assured me that he was not involved in Watergate, that the evidence would prove his innocence, that the matter would fade from view. p. 7.

[4]   The first [option] was that he could try to "ride it out" by letting impeachment take its natural course through the House and the Senate trial, fighting against conviction all the way. p. 4.

[5]   Finally, Haig said that according to some on Nixon's White House staff, Nixon could agree to leave in return for an agreement that the new President—Gerald Ford—would pardon him. p. 5.

[6]   Because of his references to pardon authority, I did ask Haig about the extent of a President's pardon power. pp. 5–6.

[7]   Only after I had finished did [Bryce Harlow] let me know in no uncertain terms that he agreed with Bob and Jack, that the mere mention of the pardon option could cause a lot of trouble in the days ahead. p. 18.

dent was not guilty of an impeachable offense. "Had I said otherwise at that moment," he writes, "the whole house of cards might have collapsed."[8]

In justifying the pardon, Ford goes out of his way to assure the reader that "compassion for Nixon as an individual hadn't prompted my decision at all."[9] Rather, he did it because he had "to get the monkey off my back one way or the other."[10] * * *

Ultimately, Ford sums up the philosophy underlying his decision as one he picked up as a student at Yale Law School many years before. "I learned that public policy often took precedence over a rule of law. Although I respected the tenet that no man should be above the law, public policy demanded that I put Nixon—and Watergate—behind us as quickly as possible."[17]

Later, when Ford learned that Nixon's phlebitis had acted up and his health was seriously impaired, he debated whether to pay the ailing former President a visit. "If I made the trip it would remind everybody of Watergate and the pardon. If I didn't, people would say I lacked compassion."[18] Ford went:

He was stretched out flat on his back. There were tubes in his nose and mouth, and wires led from his arms, chest and legs to machines with orange lights that blinked on and off. His face was ashen, and I thought I had never seen anyone closer to death.[19] * * *

■ JUSTICE BRENNAN, with whom JUSTICE WHITE and JUSTICE MARSHALL join, dissenting.

The Court holds that The Nation's quotation of 300 words from the unpublished 200,000–word manuscript of President Gerald R. Ford infringed the copyright in that manuscript, even though the quotations related to a historical event of undoubted significance—the resignation and pardon of President Richard M. Nixon. Although the Court pursues the laudable goal of protecting "the economic incentive to create and disseminate ideas," ante, at 558, this zealous defense of the copyright owner's prerogative will, I fear, stifle the broad dissemination of ideas and information copyright is intended to nurture. Protection of the copyright owner's economic interest is achieved in this case through an exceedingly narrow definition of the scope of fair use. The progress of arts and sciences and the robust public debate essential to an enlightened citizenry are ill served by this constricted reading of the fair use doctrine. See 17 U.S.C. § 107. I therefore respectfully dissent.

---

[8] During the luncheon I repeated my assertion that the President was not guilty of an impeachable offense. Had I said otherwise at that moment, the whole house of cards might have collapsed. p. 21.

[9] But compassion for Nixon as an individual hadn't prompted my decision at all. p. 266.

[10] I had to get the monkey off my back one way or another. p. 236.

[17] Years before, at Yale Law School, I'd learned that public policy often took precedence over a rule of law. Although I respected the tenet that no man should be above the law, public policy demanded that I put Nixon—and Watergate—behind us as quickly as possible. p. 256.

[18] My staff debated whether or not I ought to visit Nixon at the Long Beach hospital, only half an hour away. If I made the trip, it would remind everyone of Watergate and the pardon. If I didn't, people would say I lacked compassion. I ended their debate as soon as I found out it had begun. Of course I would go. p. 298.

[19] He was stretched out flat on his back. There were tubes in his nose and mouth, and wires led from his arms, chest and legs to machines with orange lights that blinked on and off. His face was ashen, and I thought I had never seen anyone closer to death. p. 299.

I

A

This case presents two issues. First, did The Nation's use of material from the Ford manuscript in forms other than direct quotation from that manuscript infringe Harper & Row's copyright. Second, did the quotation of approximately 300 words from the manuscript infringe the copyright because this quotation did not constitute "fair use" within the meaning of § 107 of the Copyright Act. 17 U.S.C. § 107. The Court finds no need to resolve the threshold copyrightability issue. The use of 300 words of quotation was, the Court finds, beyond the scope of fair use and thus a copyright infringement. Because I disagree with the Court's fair use holding, it is necessary for me to decide the threshold copyrightability question.

B

* * * Not surprisingly, the test for infringement has defied precise formulation. In general, though, the inquiry proceeds along two axes: *how closely* has the second author tracked the first author's particular language and structure of presentation; and *how much* of the first author's language and structure has the second author appropriated. * * *

The Language. Much of the information The Nation conveyed was not in the form of paraphrase at all, but took the form of synopsis of lengthy discussions in the Ford manuscript. In the course of this summary presentation, The Nation did use occasional sentences that closely resembled language in the original Ford manuscript. But these linguistic similarities are insufficient to constitute an infringement for three reasons. First, some leeway must be given to subsequent authors seeking to convey facts because those "wishing to express the ideas contained in a factual work often can choose from only a narrow range of expression." Landsberg v. Scrabble Crossword Game Players, Inc., 736 F.2d 485, 488 (C.A.9 1984). Second, much of what The Nation paraphrased was material in which Harper & Row could claim no copyright.[10] Third, The Nation paraphrased nothing approximating the totality of a single paragraph, much less a chapter or the work as a whole. At most The Nation paraphrased disparate isolated sentences from the original. A finding of infringement based on paraphrase generally requires far more close and substantial a tracking of the original language than occurred in this case. See, e.g., Wainwright Securities v. Wall Street Transcript Corp., 558 F.2d 91 (C.A.2 1977).

The Structure of Presentation. The article does not mimic Mr. Ford's structure. The information The Nation presents is drawn from scattered sections of the Ford work and does not appear in the sequence in which Mr. Ford presented it. Some of The Nation's discussion of the pardon does roughly track the order in which the Ford manuscript presents information about the pardon. With respect to this similarity, however, Mr. Ford has done no more than present the facts chronologically and cannot claim infringement when a subsequent author similarly presents the facts of histo-

---

[10] Often the paraphrasing was of statements others had made to Mr. Ford. E.g., ante, at 571 ("He could 'ride it out' or he could resign, Haig said"). See generally ante, at 570–579. No copyright can be asserted in the verbatim representation of such statements of others. 17 U.S.C. § 102. See Suid v. Newsweek Magazine, 503 F.Supp., at 148; Rokeach v. Avco Embassy Pictures Corp., 197 USPQ, at 161. Other paraphrased material came from Government documents in which no copyright interest can be claimed. For example, the article quotes from a memorandum prepared by Henry S. Ruth, Jr., in his official capacity as assistant to Watergate Special Prosecutor Leon Jaworski. See ante, at 573. This document is a work of the United States Government. See 17 U.S.C. § 105.

ry in a chronological manner. Also, it is difficult to suggest that a 2000–word article could bodily appropriate the structure of a 200,000–word book. Most of what Mr. Ford created, and most of the history he recounted, was simply not represented in The Nation's article.

When The Nation was not quoting Mr. Ford, therefore, its efforts to convey the historical information in the Ford manuscript did not so closely and substantially track Mr. Ford's language and structure as to constitute an appropriation of literary form.

II

The Nation is thus liable in copyright only if the quotation of 300 words infringed any of Harper & Row's exclusive rights under § 106 of the Act. Section 106 explicitly makes the grant of exclusive rights "[s]ubject to section 107 through 118." 17 U.S.C. § 106. * * *

With respect to a work of history, particularly the memoirs of a public official, the statutorily prescribed analysis cannot properly be conducted without constant attention to copyright's crucial distinction between protected literary form and unprotected information or ideas. The question must always be: Was the subsequent author's use of *literary form* a fair use within the meaning of § 107, in light of the purpose for the use, the nature of the copyrighted work, the amount of literary form used, and the effect of this use of literary form on the value of or market for the original? * * *

The urge to compensate for subsequent use of information and ideas is perhaps understandable. An inequity seems to lurk in the idea that much of the fruit of the historian's labor may be used without compensation. This, however, is not some unforeseen by-product of a statutory scheme intended primarily to ensure a return for works of the imagination. Congress made the affirmative choice that the copyright laws should apply in this way: "Copyright does not preclude others from using the ideas or information revealed by the author's work. It pertains to the literary . . . form in which the author expressed intellectual concepts." H.R.Rep. No. 94–1476, at 56–57. This distinction is at the essence of copyright. The copyright laws serve as the "engine of free expression," ante, at 558, only when the statutory monopoly does not choke off multifarious indirect uses and consequent broad dissemination of information and ideas. To ensure the progress of arts and sciences and the integrity of First Amendment values, ideas and information must not be freighted with claims of proprietary right.

In my judgment, the Court's fair use analysis has fallen to the temptation to find copyright violation based on a minimal use of literary form in order to provide compensation for the appropriation of information from a work of history. The failure to distinguish between information and literary form permeates every aspect of the Court's fair use analysis and leads the Court to the wrong result in this case. Application of the statutorily prescribed analysis with attention to the distinction between information and literary form leads to a straightforward finding of fair use within the meaning of § 107.

[Justice Brennan then proceeded to consider the four fair use factors. With regard to purpose, he said that The Nation's use was news reporting furthering the public interest in the dissemination of information; he also rejected the majority's reliance on the commercial nature of the use: "Many uses § 107 lists as paradigmatic examples of fair use, including criticism, comment, and *news reporting*, are generally conducted for profit in this country, a fact of which Congress was obviously aware when it enacted § 107."

[The nature of the work, Justice Brennan believed, also supported a finding of fair use. The scope of fair use for factual and historical works is broad, and a "categorical presumption against prepublication fair use" was unwarranted.

[On the amount and substantiality of the use, he emphasized that appropriations of information and ideas are irrelevant to the issue of substantiality, and that the borrowing of copyrightable material must be judged in light of the purpose of the use.

[Finally, with respect to market effect, Justice Brennan thought that the majority had failed to distinguish between the appropriation of information and the appropriation of literary form; only injury resulting from the latter was relevant to the fair use analysis. "Wholly apart from these quoted words, The Nation published significant information and ideas from the Ford manuscript. If it was this publication of information, and not the publication of the few quotations, that caused Time to abrogate its serialization agreement, then whatever the negative effect on the serialization market, that effect was the product of wholly legitimate activity."]

NOTES AND QUESTIONS

(1) Would the Supreme Court have reached a different conclusion if *The Nation* had published its article *after* publication of the Ford memoirs? Arguing in opposition to "the near presumption against fair use" of unpublished works, K. Crews, Fair Use of Unpublished Works: Burdens of Proof and the Integrity of Copyright, 31 Ariz.St.L.J. 1 (1999), suggests that copyright owners should have the burden of proving that the use will interfere with genuine publication plans or privacy interests. K. O'Neill, Against Dicta: A Legal Method for Rescuing Fair Use for the Right of First Publication, 89 Calif.L.Rev. 369 (2001), reviews the practices adopted by publishers in the wake of the case law on unpublished works.

Is it possible, as urged in Justice Brennan's dissent, to separate the economic consequences of *The Nation*'s appropriation of expression from its appropriation of facts? If the defendant could establish that *Time* would have canceled its prepublication agreement even if the article in *The Nation* had included no quotations, would the use then be fair?[a]

Eight years after the decision in *Harper & Row,* the courts of England reached a somewhat different conclusion on remarkably parallel facts. *The Downing Street Years,* the memoirs of former British Prime Minister Margaret Thatcher, were soon to be published by HarperCollins; *The Sunday Times* had purchased serialization rights, with excerpts scheduled to appear just before publication of the book. The British newspaper *Daily Mirror* obtained a stolen copy of the manuscript and initiated a series of articles on the book, including excerpts, with particular emphasis on Lady Thatcher's disapproving remarks about her successor, John Major. (The *Daily Mirror* articles appeared during a

---

[a] *Time* had prepublication rights scooped again in 1995 when *Newsweek* somehow got a pre-release copy of Colin Powell's memoir, *My American Journey. Newsweek*'s article, which beat publication of *Time*'s excerpts and the book by a week, carefully avoided direct quotation, instead adopting the form of an analysis of the book's contents by senior *Newsweek* correspondents. Carmody, Time Questions Newsweek on Powell Memoirs Scoop, N.Y. Times, Sept. 6, 1995, p. D6.

Conservative Party conference at which Thatcher made a public display of support for Major.) HarperCollins and *The Sunday Times* sought an injunction against publication of additional excerpts, arguing copyright infringement and breach of confidence. The injunction was denied by the High Court in a decision affirmed by the Court of Appeal. The judges thought that the "extreme step" of enjoining publication was not warranted in light of the plaintiffs' ability to pursue a subsequent damage action against the defendant. But the judges also relied on the "public interest" in access to Thatcher's comments about Prime Minister Major, particularly in light of the image of unity portrayed at the Conservative Party conference. The Sunday Times, Oct. 10, 1993, Sec. 3, p. 6. If Harper & Row had realized that a copy of the Ford manuscript had been given to *The Nation* in time to seek an injunction, would a restraint on publication have been upheld by the Supreme Court?

(2) *Harper & Row* was invoked in Salinger v. Random House, Inc., 811 F.2d 90 (2d Cir.), cert. denied, 484 U.S. 890 (1987), which presented the issue of whether a biographer of author J.D. Salinger had made fair use of his subject's unpublished letters. The letters had been donated to libraries by their recipients; they were made available to biographer Hamilton under agreements forbidding reproduction or publication. The biography quoted some 200 words, but Judge Newman also found numerous passages that "closely paraphrase" portions of the letters. (He gives as an example a quotation from Salinger describing 1940 presidential candidate Wendell Wilkie: "He looks to me like a guy who makes his wife keep a scrapbook for him"; the biography states that Salinger "had fingered [Wilkie] as the sort of fellow who makes his wife keep an album of his press clippings.") The Second Circuit rejected the claim of fair use, placing "special emphasis on the unpublished nature of Salinger's letters." Judge Leval in the district court, 650 F.Supp. 413 (S.D.N.Y.1986), had expressed sympathy with the biographer's argument that departure from Salinger's own words "distorts, sacrificing both accuracy and vividness of description." Judge Newman, remanding for a preliminary injunction, responded: "But the biographer has no inherent right to copy the 'accuracy' or the 'vividness' of the letter writer's expression. Indeed, 'vividness of description' is precisely an attribute of the author's expression that he is entitled to protect." Judge Newman emphasized that biographer Hamilton remained free to fashion a work that reported the facts contained in the letters.

Craft v. Kobler, 667 F.Supp. 120 (S.D.N.Y.1987), which involved a biographer's quotation and paraphrase of 3,500 words from the published writings of composer Igor Stravinsky, afforded Judge Leval the opportunity for a rejoinder: "I agree with the defendants that the fair use doctrine gives latitude to the biographer of an author to quote limited excerpts of published copyrighted work to illustrate the descriptive skill, wit, power, vividness, and originality of the author's writing." *Salinger,* he said, "refers only to takings from *unpublished* copyrighted materials." Judge Leval concluded, however, that the defendant's "appropriations of copyrighted materials are too extensive and important, and their justification too slight to support an overall claim of fair use." Distribution of the book was enjoined.

Judge Leval had another round with the Second Circuit over fair use of unpublished works in New Era Pub. Int'l, ApS v. Henry Holt and Co., 873 F.2d 576 (2d Cir.1989), cert. denied, 493 U.S. 1094 (1990). The work in question, *Bare–Faced Messiah,* was a hostile exposé of the life of the late L. Ron Hubbard, the founder of Scientology. The plaintiff held Hubbard's copyrights, including unpublished diaries and letters, from which the defendant copied many excerpts. Judge Leval found 44 of them infringing. 695 F.Supp. 1493 (S.D.N.Y.1988). However, he declined to convert a temporary restraining order into an injunction, and left the plaintiff to monetary relief. He said that much of the author's use of Hubbard's expression was necessary to support critical judgments about Hubbard's life and character. The public interest in the material, even though it was unpublished, raised first amendment concerns that weighed against the customary remedy of an injunction. Judge Miner for the Second Circuit repudiated almost every step of Judge Leval's analysis, reaffirming the strong protection that *Salinger* and *Harper & Row* give to unpublished material. The court saw no copyright ground for withholding the injunction and reasserted the prevailing view that the fair use doctrine adequately protects free speech interests (see p. 367 infra). However, the appellate court affirmed the denial of an injunction on the basis of laches since New Era had not commenced its action until the first printing of 12,000 copies had been shipped. Chief Judge Oakes concurred in the laches argument only; as to the propriety of an injunction absent laches, he wrote, "I totally disagree." The pointed debate continued in the denial of a rehearing en banc, this time in opinions by Judges Miner and Newman. 884 F.2d 659 (2d Cir.1989).[b]

A Hubbard biographer was again before the Second Circuit in New Era Pub. Int'l, ApS v. Carol Pub. Group, 904 F.2d 152 (2d Cir.), cert. denied, 498 U.S. 921 (1990), which upheld the defendant's fair use defense in connection with quotations from Hubbard's *published* works; the quotations were used to convey Hubbard's "hypocrisy and pomposity, qualities that may best (or only) be revealed through direct quotation." See also Wright v. Warner Books, Inc., 953 F.2d 731 (2d Cir.1991) ("sparing use" of unpublished writings in a biography of author Richard Wright held to be fair use).

(3) Authors complained to Congress that in reaction to cases like Salinger v. Random House and New Era Pub. v. Henry Holt, their publishers were forbidding them from quoting unpublished sources. See 42 Pat., Tm. & Copyr.J. (BNA) 147 (1991). Congress responded in 1992 with an amendment adding the final sentence to § 107 that emphasizes the continued applicability of the traditional fair use factors to unpublished works. Pub.L. 102–492 (1992). Supporters in the Senate described the amendment as "designed to undo the harm caused by the overly restrictive standards adopted in *Salinger* and *New Era,* and to clearly and indisputably reject the view that the unpublished nature of the work triggers a virtual per se ruling against a finding of fair use." 44 Pat., Tm. & Copyr.J. (BNA) 633 (1992). The history of the amendment is recounted in D. Wanat, Fair Use and the 1992 Amendment to Section 107 of the 1976 Copyright Act, 1 Vill. Sports & Ent.L.J. 47 (1994).

(4) A defense of news reporting as fair use succeeded in Nunez v. Caribbean Int'l News Corp., 235 F.3d 18 (1st Cir.2000), when a newspaper reproduced a photograph of a naked Miss Universe Puerto Rico taken by the plaintiff photographer and distributed as part of a modeling portfolio. The existence of the photograph had stirred debate about whether the model should retain her crown. The court concluded that it would be difficult for the newspaper to explain the

---

[b]   The disputes within the Second Circuit spilled over into extra-judicial pronouncements. See P. Leval, Toward a Fair Use Standard, 103 Harv.L.Rev. 1105 (1990); R. Miner, Exploiting Stolen Text: Fair Use or Fair Play?, 37 J.Copyr.Soc'y 1 (1989); J. Newman, Not the End of History: The Second Circuit Struggles with Fair Use, id. at 12; J. Oakes, Copyrights and Copyremedies: Unfair Use and Injunctions, 18 Hofstra L.Rev. 983 (1990).

controversy without reproducing the photograph. "Unauthorized reproduction of professional photographs by newspapers will generally violate the Copyright Act of 1976; in this context, however, where the photograph itself is particularly newsworthy, the newspaper acquired it in good faith, and the photograph has already been disseminated, a fair use exists under 17 U.S.C. § 107." *Nunez* was distinguished and a fair use defense rejected in Monge v. Maya Magazines, Inc., 688 F.3d 1164 (9th Cir.2012), when a celebrity gossip magazine published photos of the plaintiffs' clandestine wedding. The photographs had not previously been published and unlike *Nunez*, the photos here were not themselves the news story. There was a sharp dissent.

(5) The Second Circuit in NXIVM Corp. v. Ross Institute, 364 F.3d 471 (2d Cir.), cert. denied, 543 U.S. 1000 (2004), refused to read *Harper & Row* as standing for the proposition that a defendant's possession of the copyrighted work must be authorized in order to succeed with a fair use defense; although the defendant's bad faith in acquiring a copy of the plaintiff's work through a breach of confidence was relevant in applying the first statutory factor, the presence of bad faith was not dispositive. The court affirmed the denial of a preliminary injunction sought against a defendant who posted quotations and criticism of the plaintiff's confidential seminar manual on a web site.

R. Kasunic, Is That All There Is? Reflections on the Nature of the Second Fair Use Factor, 31 Colum.J.L. & Arts 529 (2008), argues that "the nature of the copyrighted work factor" should include an analysis of the incentives that drove the creation of the work; see also C. Bohannan, Copyright Harm, Foreseeability, and Fair Use, 85 Wash.U.L.Rev. 969 (2007), concluding that the fair use defense should be denied only when the use is likely to affect the owner's ex ante decision to create or distribute the work.[c]

Commenting on the "amount" factor in § 107, Judge Posner in Chicago Board of Ed. v. Substance, Inc., 354 F.3d 624 (7th Cir.2003), cert. denied, 543 U.S. 816 (2004), said, "[T]he fair use copier must copy no more than is reasonably necessary (not strictly necessary—room must be allowed for judgment, and judges must not police criticism with a heavy hand) to enable him to pursue an aim that the law recognizes as proper, in this case the aim of criticizing the copyrighted work effectively." The court held that a teacher who criticized standardized tests used by the school board went too far in publishing the entire content of six of the secure tests.

In Worldwide Church of God v. Philadelphia Church of God, Inc., 227 F.3d 1110 (9th Cir.2000), cert. denied, 532 U.S. 958 (2001), the plaintiff church held the copyright in a religious tract written by its General Pastor, Hebert Armstrong; it had discontinued distribution of the work after Armstrong's death, citing changed views on doctrinal issues. Two of the plaintiff's former ministers formed the defendant church and distributed copies of the work to church members. A fair use claim was rejected. Arguing that the fourth fair use factor refers not only to market effect but also to the "value of the copyrighted work," the court said that the defendant's distribution of the work could divert both

---

[c]   An empirical analysis of fair use cases in B. Beebe, An Empirical Study of U.S. Copyright Fair Use Opinions, 1978–2005, 156 U.Pa.L.Rev. 549 (2008), concludes that courts rely primarily on the first and fourth fair use factors and permit more fair use than the leading cases might suggest. L. Heymann, A Tale of (At Least) Two Authors: Focusing Copyright Law on Process Over Product, 34 J.Corp.L. 1009 (2009), thinks fair use should turn not only on the nature of the defendant's use but also on the strength of the plaintiff's interest in enforcing the copyright.

members and contributions from the plaintiff. S. Jamar, Religious Use of Copyrighted Works After *Smith*, *RFRA*, and *Eldred*, 32 Cardozo L.Rev. 1879 (2011), urges greater accommodation under copyright law for the use of religious works.

(6) An imposing demonstration of the ambiguity and incoherence of the "factors" approach to fair use is mounted in W. Fisher, Reconstructing the Fair Use Doctrine, 101 Harv.L.Rev. 1659 (1988); M. Madison, A Pattern–Oriented Approach to Fair Use, 45 Will. & Mary L.Rev. 1525 (2004), argues for a reinterpretation of fair use organized around favored social practices rather than the statutory factors in § 107. N. Snow, Judges Playing Jury: Constitutional Conflicts in Deciding Fair Use on Summary Judgment, 44 U.C. Davis L.Rev. 483 (2010), argues that courts are wrong in treating fair use as an issue of law; he also argues that the burden should be on the copyright owner rather than the user. N. Snow, Proving Fair Use: Burden of Proof as Burden of Speech, 31 Cardozo L.Rev. 1781 (2010).

(7) Book publishers sometimes insert notices like this: "No part of this book may be reproduced in any form without the permission of the publisher." What is the legal effect of such a notice? Is fair use premised on consent? Are such notices likely to have extralegal effects?

Sony Corp. of America v. Universal City Studios, Inc.

Supreme Court of the United States, 1984.
464 U.S. 417, 104 S.Ct. 774.

[Other portions of the Supreme Court's opinion appear at p. 3 supra and p. 399 infra.]

■ JUSTICE STEVENS. * * *

B. *Unauthorized Time–Shifting*

Even unauthorized uses of a copyrighted work are not necessarily infringing. An unlicensed use of the copyright is not an infringement unless it conflicts with one of the specific exclusive rights conferred by the copyright statute. Twentieth Century Music Corp. v. Aiken, 422 U.S. 151. Moreover, the definition of exclusive rights in § 106 of the present Act is prefaced by the words "subject to sections 107 through 118." Those sections describe a variety of uses of copyrighted material that "are not infringements of copyright notwithstanding the provisions of § 106." The most pertinent in this case is § 107, the legislative endorsement of the doctrine of "fair use."

That section identifies various factors that enable a court to apply an "equitable rule of reason" analysis to particular claims of infringement. Although not conclusive, the first factor requires that "the commercial or nonprofit character of an activity" be weighed in any fair use decision. If the Betamax were used to make copies for a commercial or profit-making purpose, such use would presumptively be unfair. The contrary presumption is appropriate here, however, because the District Court's findings plainly establish that time-shifting for private home use must be characterized as a noncommercial, nonprofit activity. Moreover, when one considers the nature of a televised copyrighted audiovisual work, see 17 U.S.C. § 107(2), and that time-shifting merely enables a viewer to see such a work which he had been invited to witness in its entirety free of charge, the fact that the entire work is reproduced, see id., at § 107(3), does not have its ordinary effect of militating against a finding of fair use.

This is not, however, the end of the inquiry because Congress has also directed us to consider "the effect of the use upon the potential market for or value of the copyrighted work." Id., at § 107(4). The purpose of copyright is to create incentives for creative effort. Even copying for noncommercial purposes may impair the copyright holder's ability to obtain the rewards that Congress intended him to have. But a use that has no demonstrable effect upon the potential market for, or the value of, the copyrighted work need not be prohibited in order to protect the author's incentive to create. The prohibition of such noncommercial uses would merely inhibit access to ideas without any countervailing benefit.

Thus, although every commercial use of copyrighted material is presumptively an unfair exploitation of the monopoly privilege that belongs to the owner of the copyright, noncommercial uses are a different matter. A challenge to a noncommercial use of a copyrighted work requires proof either that the particular use is harmful, or that if it should become widespread, it would adversely affect the potential market for the copyrighted work. Actual present harm need not be shown; such a requirement would leave the copyright holder with no defense against predictable damage. Nor is it necessary to show with certainty that future harm will result. What is necessary is a showing by a preponderance of the evidence that *some* meaningful likelihood of future harm exists. If the intended use is for commercial gain, that likelihood may be presumed. But if it is for a noncommercial purpose, the likelihood must be demonstrated.

In this case, respondents failed to carry their burden with regard to home time-shifting. The District Court described respondents' evidence as follows:

> "Plaintiffs' experts admitted at several points in the trial that the time-shifting without librarying would result in 'not a great deal of harm.' Plaintiffs' greatest concern about time-shifting is with 'a point of important philosophy that transcends even commercial judgment.' They fear that with any Betamax usage, 'invisible boundaries' are passed: 'the copyright owner has lost control over his program.'" 480 F.Supp., at 467.

Later in its opinion, the District Court observed:

> "Most of plaintiffs' predictions of harm hinge on speculation about audience viewing patterns and ratings, a measurement system which Sidney Sheinberg, MCA's president, calls a 'black art' because of the significant level of imprecision involved in the calculations." Id., at 469.

There was no need for the District Court to say much about past harm. "Plaintiffs have admitted that no actual harm to their copyrights has occurred to date." Id., at 451.

On the question of potential future harm from time-shifting, the District Court offered a more detailed analysis of the evidence. It rejected respondents' "fear that persons 'watching' the original telecast of a program [would] not be measured in the live audience and the ratings and revenues will [dec]rease," by observing that current measurement technology allows the [Bet]amax audience to be reflected. Id., at 466. It rejected respondents' pre[dict]ion "that live television or movie audiences will decrease as more people [wat]ch Betamax tapes as an alternative," with the observation that "[t]here is no factual basis for [the underlying] assumption." Ibid. It rejected respondents' "fear that time-shifting will reduce audiences for telecast reruns," and concluded instead that "given current market practices, this should aid plaintiffs rather than harm them." Ibid. And it declared that respondents' suggestion "that theater or film rental exhibition of a program will suffer because of time-shift recording of that program" "lacks merit." 480 F.Supp., at 467.

After completing that review, the District Court restated its overall conclusion several times, in several different ways. "Harm from time-shifting is speculative and, at best, minimal." Ibid. "The audience benefits from the time-shifting capability have already been discussed. It is not implausible that benefits could also accrue to plaintiffs, broadcasters, and advertisers, as the Betamax makes it possible for more persons to view their broadcasts." Ibid. "No likelihood of harm was shown at trial, and plaintiffs admitted that there had been no actual harm to date." Id., at 468–469. "Testimony at trial suggested that Betamax may require adjustments in marketing strategy, but it did not establish even a likelihood of harm." Id., at 469. "Television production by plaintiffs today is more profitable than it has ever been, and, in five weeks of trial, there was no concrete evidence to suggest that the Betamax will change the studios' financial picture." Ibid.

The District Court's conclusions are buttressed by the fact that to the extent time-shifting expands public access to freely broadcast television programs, it yields societal benefits. Earlier this year, in Community Television of Southern California v. Gottfried, 459 U.S. 498, 508, n. 12 (1983), we acknowledged the public interest in making television broadcasting more available. Concededly, that interest is not unlimited. But it supports an interpretation of the concept of "fair use" that requires the copyright holder to demonstrate some likelihood of harm before he may condemn a private act of time-shifting as a violation of federal law.

When these factors are all weighed in the "equitable rule of reason" balance, we must conclude that this record amply supports the District Court's conclusion that home time-shifting is fair use. In light of the findings of the District Court regarding the state of the empirical data, it is clear that the Court of Appeals erred in holding that the statute as presently written bars such conduct.[40] * * *

---

[40] The Court of Appeals chose not to engage in any "equitable rule of reason" analysis in this case. Instead, it assumed that the category of "fair use" is rigidly circumscribed by a requirement that every such use must be "productive." It therefore concluded that copying a television program merely to enable the viewer to receive information or entertainment that he would otherwise miss because of a personal scheduling conflict could never be fair use. That understanding of "fair use" was erroneous.

Congress has plainly instructed us that fair use analysis calls for a sensitive balancing of interests. The distinction between "productive" and "unproductive" uses may be helpful in calibrating the balance, but it cannot be wholly determinative. Although copying to promote a scholarly endeavor certainly has a stronger claim to fair use than copying to avoid interrupting a poker game, the question is not simply two-dimensional. For one thing, it is not true that all copyrights are fungible. Some copyrights govern material with broad potential secondary markets. Such material may well have a broader claim to protection because of the greater potential for commercial harm. Copying a news broadcast may have a stronger claim to fair use than copying a motion picture. And, of course, not all uses are fungible. Copying for commercial gain has a much weaker claim to fair use than copying for personal enrichment. But the notion of social "productivity" cannot be a complete answer to this analysis. A teacher who copies to prepare lecture notes is clearly productive. But so is a teacher who copies for the sake of broadening his personal understanding of his specialty. Or a legislator who copies for the sake of broadening her understanding of what her constituents are watching; or a constituent who copies a news program to help make a decision on how to vote.

■ JUSTICE BLACKMUN, with whom JUSTICE MARSHALL, JUSTICE POWELL, and JUSTICE REHNQUIST join, dissenting. * * *

There are situations, nevertheless, in which strict enforcement of this monopoly would inhibit the very "Progress of Science and useful Arts" that copyright is intended to promote. An obvious example is the researcher or scholar whose own work depends on the ability to refer to and to quote the work of prior scholars. * * * The scholar's work, in other words, produces external benefits from which everyone profits. In such a case, the fair use doctrine acts as a form of subsidy—albeit at the first author's expense—to permit the second author to make limited use of the first author's work for the public good. See Latman [Fair Use of Copyrighted Works, Copyr. Law Revision Study No. 14, 31 (1958)]; Gordon, Fair Use as Market Failure: A Structural Analysis of the *Betamax* Case and its Predecessors, 82 Colum.L.Rev. 1600, 1630 (1982).

A similar subsidy may be appropriate in a range of areas other than pure scholarship. The situations in which fair use is most commonly recognized are listed in § 107 itself; fair use may be found when a work is used "for purposes such as criticism, comment, news reporting, teaching, . . . scholarship, or research." The House and Senate Reports expand on this list somewhat, and other examples may be found in the case law. Each of these uses, however, reflects a common theme: each is a *productive* use, resulting in some added benefit to the public beyond that produced by the first author's work. The fair use doctrine, in other words, permits works to be used for "socially laudable purposes." See Copyright Office, Briefing Papers on Current Issues, reprinted in 1975 House Hearings 2051, 2055. I am aware of no case in which the reproduction of a copyrighted work for the sole benefit of the user has been held to be fair use. * * *

The making of a videotape recording for home viewing is an ordinary rather than a productive use of the Studios' copyrighted works. The District Court found that "Betamax owners use the copy for the same purpose as the original. They add nothing of their own." 480 F.Supp., at 453. Although applying the fair use doctrine to home VTR recording, as Sony argues, may increase public access to material broadcast free over the public airwaves, I think Sony's argument misconceives the nature of copyright. Copyright gives the author a right to limit or even to cut off access to his work. * * *

I recognize, nevertheless, that there are situations where permitting even an unproductive use would have no effect on the author's incentive to create, that is, where the use would not affect the value of, or the market for, the author's work. Photocopying an old newspaper clipping to send to a friend may be an example; pinning a quotation on one's bulletin board may be another. In each of these cases, the effect on the author is truly *de minimis*. Thus, even though these uses provide no benefit to the public at large, no purpose is served by preserving the author's monopoly, and the use may be regarded as fair. * * *

Making a copy of a copyrighted work for the convenience of a blind person is expressly identified by the House Committee Report as an example of fair use, with no suggestion that anything more than a purpose to entertain or to inform need motivate the copying. In a hospital setting, using a VTR to enable a patient to see programs he would otherwise miss has no productive purpose other than contributing to the psychological well-being of the patient. Virtually any time-shifting that increases viewer access to television programming may result in a comparable benefit. The statutory language does not identify any dichotomy between productive and nonproductive time-shifting, but does require consideration of the economic consequences of copying.

I therefore conclude that, at least when the proposed use is an unproductive one, a copyright owner need prove only a *potential* for harm to the market for or the value of the copyrighted work. * * *

The Studios have identified a number of ways in which VTR recording could damage their copyrights. VTR recording could reduce their ability to market their works in movie theaters and through the rental or sale of prerecorded videotapes or videodiscs; it also could reduce their rerun audience, and consequently the license fees available to them for repeated showings. Moreover, advertisers may be willing to pay for only "live" viewing audiences, if they believe VTR viewers will delete commercials or if rating services are unable to measure VTR use; if this is the case, VTR recording could reduce the license fees the Studios are able to charge even for first-run showings. Library-building may raise the potential for each of the types of harm identified by the Studios, and time-shifting may raise the potential for substantial harm as well. * * *

It is thus apparent from the record and from the findings of the District Court that time-shifting does have a substantial adverse effect upon the "potential market for" the Studios' copyrighted works. Accordingly, even under the formulation of the fair use doctrine advanced by Sony, time-shifting cannot be deemed a fair use. * * *

NOTES AND QUESTIONS

(1) The plaintiffs sought a rehearing in the Supreme Court, arguing that the issues should not be resolved "on the basis of facts that have demonstrably changed so radically in the five years since the district court made the findings on which this Court so heavily relies." They contended that technological innovations had increased the likelihood that commercials would be deleted from recordings or skipped during playback, thus reducing the licensing value of their works. Their petition was denied at 465 U.S. 1112 (1984).[d] When the papers of Justice Marshall were opened to the public by the Library of Congress shortly after his death, they revealed that Justice Stevens' majority opinion in *Sony* was originally written as the dissent; Justice Blackmun had been assigned to write a majority opinion affirming the defendants' liability, but it became the dissent when Justice O'Connor was persuaded to join in Justice Stevens' opinion. J. Band and A. McLaughlin, The Marshall Papers: A Peek Behind the Scenes at the Making of *Sony v. Universal*, 17 Colum.J.L. & Arts 427 (1993).

---

[d]   The negative impact of television recording on the audience for commercials may be overstated. The Nielson rating company now includes commercials watched during DVR playback in its television program ratings, and nearly half of the viewers watching a recorded show still watch the commercials. Carter, TV Finds that Mortal Foe, DVR, Is a Friend After All, N.Y. Times, Nov. 2, 2009, p. B1. Viewers even get significant information from ads that they see while fast-forwarding. Story, Engaging at Any Speed?, N.Y. Times, July 3, 2007, p. C1. The calculus may change, however, with the arrival of a new DVR from Dish Network that customers can set to record every prime-time show on the four major networks, storing them for eight days. During playback, the DVR can be set to automatically skip over commercials. An attempt by the networks to get a preliminary injunction was rebuffed in Fox Broadcasting Co. v. Dish Network, LLC, 2012 WL 5938563 (C.D.Cal.2012). Relying on Cartoon Network LP v. CSC Holdings, p. 413 infra, Judge Gee held that the copying was done by the users rather than by Dish, thus precluding liability against Dish for direct infringement. As to contributory liability, the court held that the users' copying was protected under *Sony*. (The court did find that quality assurance copies made by Dish to insure that the commercial skipping feature was properly encoding the programming was not a fair use, but the network had failed to show that those copies resulted in the irreparable harm necessary for a preliminary injunction.)

The Ninth Circuit in *Sony* had concluded that reproduction of a work in order to use it for its intrinsic purpose is not fair use—a proposition the court attempted to support by an analysis of the fair use factors: the copying did not further a traditionally accepted purpose of fair use; the nature of the works as entertainment counted against fair use; entire works had been reproduced; and the cumulative effect of mass reproduction serving the same purpose as the originals diminished the plaintiffs' market. Was the Supreme Court correct in rejecting this analysis? Should copying for personal use *ever* be an infringement? S. Stadler, Copyright as Trade Regulation, 155 U.Pa.L.Rev. 899 (2007), broadly advocates conceptualizing infringement as a prohibition on unfair competition and thus limited to unauthorized distributions in a relevant market; G. Lunney, Copyright, Private Copying, and Discrete Public Goods, 12 Tulane J.Tech. & Intell.Prop. 1 (2009), offers an economic analysis that questions the rationale for prohibiting copying for private use. Formulation of a fair use variant specifically calibrated to technological uses is suggested in E. Lee, Technological Fair Use, 83 S.Cal.L.Rev. 797 (2010).

The motion picture industry badly misjudged the impact of home video technology. For many years the studios made more money from sales of movie cassettes and DVDs than they got from box-office receipts, although the DVD market is now shrinking due to video-on-demand and online streaming. F. Pasquale, Breaking the Vicious Circularity: *Sony*'s Contribution to the Fair Use Doctrine, 55 Case W.Res.L.Rev. 777 (2005), praises *Sony* for adopting an analysis that permits consideration of the positive economic effects of the use on the copyrighted work.

(2) An influential perspective on fair use is offered in W. Gordon, Fair Use as Market Failure: A Structural and Economic Analysis of the *Betamax* Case and its Predecessors, 82 Colum.L.Rev. 1600 (1982), which takes the view that "fair use is ordinarily granted when the market cannot be relied upon to allow socially desirable access to, and use of, copyrighted works," because of, for example, high transaction costs or the presence of externalities. In Excuse and Justification in the Law of Fair Use: Transaction Costs Have Always Been *Part* of the Story, 50 J.Copyr.Soc'y 149 (2003), Professor Gordon adds that fair use may also be justified when market norms are an inappropriate criteria because of significant nonmonetizable interests. Compare M. Sag, Beyond Abstraction: The Law and Economics of Copyright Scope and Doctrinal Efficiency, 81 Tul.L.Rev. 187 (2006), concluding that a market failure model of fair use is superior to any balancing of costs and benefits, with G. Lunney, Fair Use and Market Failure: *Sony* Revisited, 82 B.U.L.Rev. 975 (2002), rejecting a market failure rationale for *Sony*, positing instead a broad conception of the public interest. S. McJohn, Fair Use and Privatization in Copyright, 35 San Diego L.Rev. 61 (1998), argues that a model limited to overcoming transaction costs is too narrow—fair use should also insure that mechanical applications of the exclusive rights do not result in de facto protection of noncopyrightable elements.

(3) The Board of Educational Services in Erie County, New York, was created under state law to provide educational services to local schools. It maintained a library of 4,500 videotapes, most of them obtained through off-the-air recording. A catalog of its holdings was distributed to teachers, and upon request, a copy of the desired videotape would be furnished. In a suit brought by copyright owners, a fair use defense was unsuccessful. Why? Encyclopedia Britannica Ed. Corp. v. Crooks, 542 F.Supp. 1156 (W.D.N.Y.1982) (see also 558 F.Supp. 1247 (W.D.N.Y.1983)).

Representatives of various educational organizations, copyright owners, and creative guilds and unions, at the urging of the House Judiciary Committee, negotiated guidelines on the application of fair use to off-the-air recording by non-profit educational institutions. Since the guidelines were not completed until 1981, they cannot be considered part of the legislative history of the 1976 Act. They do, however, appear in the Congressional Record with the endorsement of the Chair of the House Subcommittee with jurisdiction over intellectual property. The guidelines require that recordings be made only at the request of individual teachers. The tapes must be erased within 45 days. They may be used for instructional purposes (twice only) during the first 10 school days of the retention period, after which use is limited to "teacher evaluation." 127 Cong.Rec. 24048–49 (Oct. 14, 1981).

(4) A fair use defense raised by a defendant who had copied the plaintiff's videotape of the 1992 Los Angeles riots from an authorized network news broadcast and then transmitted the copy to other news organizations was rejected in Los Angeles News Service v. Reuters Television Int'l, Ltd., 149 F.3d 987 (9th Cir.1998), cert. denied, 525 U.S. 1141 (1999); the use was commercial and not transformative and would diminish the market for news footage.[e] A fair use defense was also unsuccessful in Pacific and Southern Co., Inc. v. Duncan, 744 F.2d 1490 (11th Cir.1984), cert. denied, 471 U.S. 1004 (1985), involving a commercial "news clipping" service that sold videotapes of television news broadcasts to the subjects of the news reports.

(5) Suppose a consumer rents a favorite movie and makes a copy for personal use. Fair use? For many years the movie industry incorporated anti-copying technology into pre-recorded videocassettes. It finally gained legislative support for its anti-copying effort in 1998 when § 1201(k) was added to the 1976 Act as part of the Digital Millennium Copyright Act. Under that subsection, analog VCRs manufactured, imported, or sold in the U.S. must incorporate copy-control technology that will prevent duplication of encoded tapes or transmissions. As usual, technology moved faster than law, and videocassettes and VCRs were soon obsolete. As for anti-copying measures on DVDs, see p. 460 infra.

The movie studios aggressively pursue commercial copiers—chiefly street vendors and flea markets selling pirated discs to consumers. The Motion Picture Association of America has its own investigatory staff to search out commercial pirates, backed by the substantial criminal penalties for piracy in 18 U.S.C.A. § 2319. Many major films are available on the street even before they come out in theaters as a result of copies "borrowed" from editing facilities or

---

[e]   The same plaintiff overcame a fair use defense to unauthorized performance when the Ninth Circuit ruled against a local television station that obtained a copy of the plaintiff's news tape from another station and without permission broadcast thirty seconds of the tape during several news programs; the court thought that allowing such use would undermine the investment made by independent news organizations like the plaintiff. Los Angeles News Service v. KCAL–TV Channel 9, 108 F.3d 1119 (9th Cir.), cert. denied, 522 U.S. 823 (1997). In yet another Ninth Circuit decision involving the same tape, however, a fair use defense prevailed. The plaintiff sued Court TV in connection with its use of a few seconds of the tape as part of an introductory "teaser" for its news coverage of the trial of two participants in the riots and also as part of an introductory montage for one of its regular news shows. Although the uses were commercial and only the montage was transformative, the court upheld a summary judgment in favor of Court TV. The portion used, although the most valuable and pertinent, was small and did not harm plaintiff's market either for news coverage of the riot or news reporting in general. Los Angeles News Service v. CBS Broadcasting, Inc., 305 F.3d 924, amended, 313 F.3d 1093 (9th Cir.2002).

advance screenings; pirated copies of almost all major films are available within a day or two of their theatrical release. Some of the copies come from camcorders smuggled into movie theaters by customers. Several states enacted laws that make it a crime to operate a recording device in a movie theater. According to a Los Angeles City Attorney, "If you carry a [camcorder] into a movie theater, you have to ask yourself, 'Do I feel lucky?'." Garrison, Chief, Sheriff, Vow Crackdown on Movie Pirates, L.A. Times, Dec. 5, 2003, p. B3. Congress joined the fray in 2005 with a law that makes recording a motion picture in a movie theater a federal crime. 18 U.S.C. § 2319B. It also expanded liability for criminal copyright infringement under § 506 to include unauthorized Internet distribution of motion pictures that have not yet been marketed in copies for sale to the general public.

(6) The issue of home copying looms even larger in the music industry. Does *Sony* compel the conclusion that off-the-air copying of musical works is a fair use? (Is such copying likely to be only for purposes of time-shifting?) Is it fair use to make a copy of a newly-purchased CD to keep in your car? A copy for a friend to keep in *her* car? What about copying music files from a CD onto your iPod? The web site of the Recording Industry Association of America once had this to say about purchased CDs: "If you choose to take your own CDs and make copies for yourself on your computer or portable music player, that's great. It's your music and we want you to enjoy it at home, at work, in the car and on the jogging trail." www.riaa.com (visited June 1, 2007). Similarly, counsel for the record companies said during oral argument before the Supreme Court in Metro–Goldwyn–Mayer Studios v. Grokster (see p. 440 infra), "The record companies, my clients, have said, for some time now, and it's been on their Website for some time now, that it's perfectly lawful to take a CD that you've purchased, upload it onto your computer, put it into your iPod." 2005 WL 832356 (Or. Arg., March 29, 2005, p. 14). However, in an administrative submission in connection with the Copyright Office's anticircumvention rulemaking (see p. 459 infra), the RIAA said this: "Nor does the fact that permission to make a copy in particular circumstances is often or even 'routinely' given * * * necessarily establish that the copying is a fair use when the copyright owner withholds that authorization. In this regard, the statement attributed to counsel for copyright holders in the *Grokster* case * * * is simply about authorization, not about fair use." Joint Reply Comments of Ass'n of Amer. Pub., et al., at 22 (Feb. 2, 2006). The submission went on to say, "Similarly, creating a back-up copy of a music CD is not a non-infringing use * * *." The RIAA web site now opines that "there's no legal 'right' to copy the copyrighted music on a CD onto a CD–R." However, it concedes that burning a copy of the CD or transferring a copy onto a computer hard drive or portable music player "won't usually raise concerns" as long as the copy is made from an authorized CD that you own and is for "personal use"—giving the copy away or lending it to others for copying is expressly excluded. (visited January 3, 2013).[f] A. Perzanowski and J. Schultz,

---

[f] Both Google and Amazon introduced "cloud" music services that allow users to upload their music to the companies' web servers and then access the songs on their cellphones, tablets, and computers. The companies claimed that they did not need licenses from the record companies since the users upload the songs themselves, just as if they put the songs on their iPod or backed up their computer. Miller, Google to Unveil Service to Let Users Stream Their Music, N.Y. Times, May 10, 2011, p. B5. Are the services on firm legal ground? Apple launched a similar system, but unlike Google and Amazon, it had negotiated licenses with the record companies. The licenses permit Apple to offer a more efficient system that scans users' music files and then matches their songs to a master collection of music already stored on Apple's

Copyright Exhaustion and the Personal Use Dilemma, 96 Minn.L.Rev. 2067 (2012), argues broadly that consumers who buy copies should always be able to copy them for personal use.

Although the RIAA has been somewhat ambivalent about consumers copying purchased music for their personal use, copying for friends is a different matter. The RIAA and the Motion Picture Association of America both see "schoolyard" piracy—giving physical copies to friends—as a grave threat. They face an uphill battle. Although eighty per cent of teens surveyed thought it was illegal to download music from unauthorized file-sharing networks, sixty-nine percent said it was legal to copy a CD borrowed from a friend who purchased the original. According to one teen, "I think you're allowed to make, like, two or three copies of a CD you bought and give them to friends. It's only once you make five copies, or copy a CD of stolen music, that it's illegal." Duhigg, The Entertainment Poll, L.A. Times, Aug. 9, 2006, p. 1.

(7) The music industry first faced the issue of digital copying in the 1980s with the development of digital audio tape, or DAT, capable of recording music on tape in a digital format. The record companies worried that consumers would use DAT recorders to make perfect copies of compact discs and digital broadcasts. The record industry thought that it had secured significant relief in 1992 when representatives of the electronics industry, songwriters, and the record companies agreed on a new anti-copying technology and a system of royalties on "digital audio recording devices" and digital recording media. The agreement was enacted into law as the Audio Home Recording Act, Pub.L. 102–563, 106 Stat. 4237 (1992). The Act is codified in Chapter 10 of Title 17. Section 1002 prohibits the importation, manufacture, or distribution of a "digital audio recording device" unless the device is equipped with a "serial copy management system"—an electronic system that prevents "serial copying," defined in § 1001 essentially as the digital copying of a *copy* of a digital recording. (The system does not prevent users from making an unlimited number of copies of an *original* digital recording.) There is also a prohibition in § 1002 against importing, manufacturing, or distributing devices designed to circumvent the serial copy management system. Importers and manufacturers who distribute digital audio recording devices are required to pay a royalty based on the price of the unit. There is also a royalty imposed on the distribution of digital audio recording media such as blank DAT tapes. § 1003. Two-thirds of the money is distributed to the record companies and performers; the remaining one-third goes to the music publishers and composers. § 1006.

Although used by professionals, the DAT recorders that spawned the 1992 amendment were a flop with consumers, primarily because the record companies generally refused to release pre-recorded music in the DAT format. A comprehensive analysis of the Act in L. Kurlantzick and J. Pennino, The Audio Home Recording Act of 1992 and the Formation of Copyright Policy, 45 J.Copyr.Soc'y 497 (1998), concludes that the music industry never made a persuasive case to justify the royalty scheme.

As part of the compromise that made the Audio Home Recording Act possible, § 1008 bars claims of contributory copyright infringement against the manufacturer of a "digital audio recording device" or an analog recording device; it also bars claims of direct infringement against consumers who make

---

servers, eliminating the need to upload files. Helft, Apple Unveils a "Cloud" Storage Service for Music, Photos and Files, N.Y. Times, June 7, 2011, p. B1.

noncommercial use of such devices to produce digital or analog copies of musical recordings.

(8) The shortcomings of the Audio Home Recording Act became apparent in Recording Industry Ass'n of America v. Diamond Multimedia Systems, Inc., 180 F.3d 1072 (9th Cir.1999), when the record companies failed to secure a preliminary injunction against the distribution of the Rio, an early portable digital music player that could copy MP3 music files from a computer hard drive. The plaintiffs argued that the Rio violated the Audio Home Recording Act because it did not incorporate the Serial Copy Management System and no royalties had been paid on sales of the Rio. (The SCMS would not have prevented the copying of MP3 files into the Rio in any event, since MP3 files do not contain the coding necessary to trigger the system.)

The issue was whether the Rio was a "digital audio recording device" covered by Chapter 10. A "digital audio recording device" is defined in § 1001 as a device designed "for the primary purpose of * * * making a digital audio copied recording for private use." A "digital audio copied recording" is a digital reproduction of a "digital musical recording." A "digital musical recording" in turn is "a material object (i) in which are fixed, in a digital format, only sounds, and material, statements, or instructions incidental to those fixed sounds * * *." The Ninth Circuit held that this narrow definition didn't cover music files fixed on a computer hard drive; the Rio thus was not a "digital audio recording device" since it did not copy "digital musical recordings." Neither presumably is an iPod.

The Ninth Circuit's opinion in *Diamond Multimedia* emphasizes that personal computers are not "digital audio recording devices" subject to the rules in Chapter 10 since computers are not designed primarily for the purpose of making digital audio copies. One consequence of the narrow scope of the Audio Home Recording Act is that the devices most commonly used by consumers to make copies of music—computers—are beyond the scope of Chapter 10. However, another consequence is that the immunity from suit granted in § 1008 to consumers for noncommercial copying by means of a "digital audio recording device" or an "analog recording device" does not cover copying accomplished by means of a computer. Thus, when a consumer transfers a music file obtained from a purchased CD or music download from her computer to her iPod, the copying is not immune under § 1008, although it may still of course be a fair use.[g]

A & M Records, Inc. v. Napster, Inc.
239 F.3d 1004 (9th Cir.2001).

Record companies and music publishers brought a copyright infringement action against Napster, the first popular file-sharing network. The suit alleged that Napster was a contributory and vicarious infringer because it facilitated the infringement of copyrighted musical works and sound recordings by Napster users. Judge Beezer, noting that "[s]econdary liability for copyright infringement does not exist in the absence of direct infringement by a third party," turned first to the question of whether us-

---

[g]   M. Carpenter, Space Age Love Song: The Mix Tape in a Digital Universe, 11 Nev.L.J. 44 (2010), laments the inability of the Audio Home Recording Act or fair use to insulate the creation of mixed tape compilations made for family and friends.

ers of the Napster system were engaged in fair use. "We agree that plaintiffs have shown that Napster users infringe at least two of the copyright holders' exclusive rights: the rights of reproduction, § 106(1); and distribution, § 106(3). Napster users who upload file names to the search index for others to copy violate plaintiffs' distribution rights. Napster users who download files containing copyrighted music violate plaintiffs' reproduction rights."

"Napster contends that its users do not directly infringe plaintiffs' copyrights because the users are engaged in fair use of the material. * * *

"1. Purpose and Character of the Use * * *

"The district court first concluded that downloading MP3 files does not transform the copyrighted work. *Napster*, 114 F.Supp.2d at 912. This conclusion is supportable. Courts have been reluctant to find fair use when an original work is merely retransmitted in a different medium. * * *

"This 'purpose and character' element also requires the district court to determine whether the allegedly infringing use is commercial or noncommercial. See [Campbell v. Acuff–Rose Music, Inc., 510 U.S. 569, 584–85.] A commercial use weighs against a finding of fair use but is not conclusive on the issue. Id. The district court determined that Napster users engage in commercial use of the copyrighted materials largely because (1) 'a host user sending a file cannot be said to engage in a personal use when distributing that file to an anonymous requester' and (2) 'Napster users get for free something they would ordinarily have to buy.' *Napster*, 114 F.Supp.2d at 912. The district court's findings are not clearly erroneous. * * * In the record before us, commercial use is demonstrated by a showing that repeated and exploitative unauthorized copies of copyrighted works were made to save the expense of purchasing authorized copies."

As to "the nature of the copyrighted work," Judge Beezer said that the songs and sound recordings were creative works, which counted against a finding of fair use. On the amount factor, the court said that copying an entire work also weighed against a finding of fair use.

"4. Effect of Use on Market * * *

"Addressing this factor, the district court concluded that Napster harms the market in 'at least' two ways: it reduces audio CD sales among college students and it 'raises barriers to plaintiffs' entry into the market for the digital downloading of music.' *Napster*, 114 F.Supp.2d at 913. * * *

"As for defendant's experts, plaintiffs objected to the report of Dr. Peter S. Fader, in which the expert concluded that Napster is *beneficial* to the music industry because MP3 music file-sharing stimulates more audio CD sales than it displaces. * * * The court decided the generality of the report rendered it 'of dubious reliability and value.' The court did not exclude the report, however, but chose 'not to rely on Fader's findings in determining the issues of fair use and irreparable harm.'

"The district court cited both the Jay and Fine Reports in support of its finding that Napster use harms the market for plaintiffs' copyrighted musical compositions and sound recordings by reducing CD sales among college students. The district court cited the Teece Report to show the harm Napster use caused in raising barriers to plaintiffs' entry into the market for digital downloading of music. * * *

"Napster further argues that the district court erred in rejecting its evidence that the users' downloading of 'samples' increases or tends to increase audio CD sales. The district court, however, correctly noted that 'any potential enhancement of plaintiffs' sales . . . would not tip the fair use analysis conclusively in favor of defendant.' Id. at 914. We agree that increased sales of copyrighted material attributable to unauthorized use should not deprive the copyright holder of the right to license the material. See *Campbell*, 510 U.S. at 591 n. 21 ('Even favorable evidence, without more, is no guarantee of fairness. Judge Leval gives the example of the film producer's appropriation of a composer's previously unknown song that turns the song into a commercial success; the boon to the song does not make the film's simple copying fair.'); see also [L.A. Times v. Free Republic, 54 U.S.P.Q.2d 1453, 1471–72 (C.D.Cal.2000)]. Nor does positive impact in one market, here the audio CD market, deprive the copyright holder of the right to develop identified alternative markets, here the digital download market. See id. at 1469–71. * * *

"Napster also maintains that space-shifting is a fair use. Space-shifting occurs when a Napster user downloads MP3 music files in order to listen to music he already owns on audio CD. See id. at 915–16. Napster asserts that we have already held that space-shifting of musical compositions and sound recordings is a fair use. See Recording Indus. Ass'n of Am. v. Diamond Multimedia Sys., Inc., 180 F.3d 1072, 1079 (9th Cir.1999) ('Rio [a portable MP3 player] merely makes copies in order to render portable, or "space-shift," those files that already reside on a user's hard drive . . . . Such copying is a paradigmatic noncommercial personal use.'). See also generally *Sony*, 464 U.S. at 423 (holding that 'time-shifting,' where a video tape recorder owner records a television show for later viewing, is a fair use).

"We conclude that the district court did not err when it refused to apply the 'shifting' analyses of *Sony* and *Diamond*. Both *Diamond* and *Sony* are inapposite because the methods of shifting in these cases did not also simultaneously involve distribution of the copyrighted material to the general public; the time or space-shifting of copyrighted material exposed the material only to the original user. * * *

"We find no error in the district court's determination that plaintiffs will likely succeed in establishing that Napster users do not have a fair use defense."

The court also rejected Napster's argument that the actions of its users were protected by § 1008 of the Audio Home Recording Act.

"The statute states in part:

> *No action may be brought under this title alleging infringement of copyright* based on the manufacture, importation, or distribution of a digital audio recording device, a digital audio recording medium, an analog recording device, or an analog recording medium, or *based on the noncommercial use by a consumer of such a device or medium* for making digital musical recordings or analog musical recordings.

17 U.S.C. § 1008 (emphases added). Napster contends that MP3 file exchange is the type of 'noncommercial use' protected from infringement actions by the statute. Napster asserts it cannot be secondarily liable for users' nonactionable exchange of copyrighted musical recordings. * * *

"We agree with the district court that the Audio Home Recording Act does not cover the downloading of MP3 files to computer hard drives. First, '[u]nder the plain meaning of the Act's definition of digital audio recording devices, computers (and their hard drives) are not digital audio recording devices because their "primary purpose" is not to make digital audio copied recordings.' Recording Indus. Ass'n of Am. v. Diamond Multimedia Sys., Inc., 180 F.3d 1072, 1078 (9th Cir.1999). Second, notwithstanding Napster's claim that computers are 'digital audio recording devices,' computers do not make 'digital music recordings' as defined by the Audio Home Recording Act. Id. at 1077 (citing S. Rep. 102–294) ('There are simply no grounds in either the plain language of the definition or in the legislative history for interpreting the term "digital musical recording" to include songs fixed on computer hard drives.').''

NOTES

(1) The Ninth Circuit went on to uphold a preliminary injunction against Napster on grounds of both contributory and vicarious copyright infringement. That issue is taken up later in this chapter.

(2) Judge Easterbrook agreed with *Napster* and held in BMG Music v. Gonzalez, 430 F.3d 888 (7th Cir.2005), cert. denied, 547 U.S. 1130 (2006), that downloading copyrighted music from a file-sharing network is not a fair use. See also the full-blown analysis and rejection of a fair use defense to file-sharing in Sony BMG Music Ent. v. Tenenbaum, 672 F.Supp.2d 217 (D.Mass.2009).

PARODY

Elsmere Music, Inc. v. National Broadcasting Co.
482 F.Supp. 741 (S.D.N.Y.), aff'd, 623 F.2d 252 (2d Cir.1980).

"In the dark days of 1977, when the City of New York teetered on the brink of bankruptcy and its name had become synonymous with sin, there came forth upon the land a message of hope. On the television screens of America there appeared the image of a top-hatted Broadway showgirl, backed by an advancing phalanx of dancers, chanting:

'I–I–I–I–I–I Love New Y-o-o-o-o-o-o-rk!'

Repeated again and again (to musical accompaniment), with increasing intensity throughout the commercial, this slogan was to become the theme for an extensive series of advertisements that were to bring the nation assurances from the stars of Broadway, ranging from Dracula to the Cowardly Lion, that all was well, and that they too *loved* New York. * * *

"The success of this campaign did not go unnoticed in the entertainment world. On May 20, 1978, the popular weekly variety program 'Saturday Night Live' ('SNL') performed a comedy sketch over defendant National Broadcasting Company's network. In this sketch the cast of SNL, portraying the mayor and the members of the Chamber of Commerce of the biblical city of Sodom, are seen discussing Sodom's poor public image with out of towners, and the effect this was having on the tourist trade. In an attempt to recast the City's image in a more positive light, a new advertising campaign emphasizing the less sensational aspects of Sodom nightlife is unveiled. As the highlight of this campaign the song 'I Love Sodom' is sung *a cappella* by a chorus line of three SNL regulars to the tune of 'I Love New York,' with the words 'I Love Sodom' repeated three times."

[handwritten margin note: SNL comedy sketch]

borrowing was fair use

Judge Goettel held that the borrowing was a fair use. In a per curiam affirmance consisting chiefly of a footnote, the Second Circuit took a broad view of the precedents:

"The District Court concluded, among other things, that the parody did not make more extensive use of appellant's song than was necessary to 'conjure up' the original. 482 F.Supp. at 747. While we agree with this conclusion, we note that the concept of 'conjuring up' an original came into the copyright law not as a limitation on how much of an original may be used, but as a recognition that a parody frequently needs to be more than a fleeting evocation of an original in order to make its humorous point. Columbia Pictures Corp. v. National Broadcasting Co., 137 F.Supp. 348, 354 (S.D.Cal.1955). A parody is entitled at least to 'conjure up' the original. Even more extensive use would still be fair use, provided the parody builds upon the original, using the original as a known element of modern culture and contributing something new for humorous effect or commentary."

Campbell v. Acuff–Rose Music, Inc.

Supreme Court of the United States, 1994.
510 U.S. 569, 114 S.Ct. 1164.

■ JUSTICE SOUTER delivered the opinion of the Court.

Issue

We are called upon to decide whether 2 Live Crew's commercial parody of Roy Orbison's song, "Oh, Pretty Woman," may be a fair use within the meaning of the Copyright Act of 1976, 17 U.S.C. § 107 (1988 ed. and Supp. IV). Although the District Court granted summary judgment for 2 Live Crew, the Court of Appeals reversed, holding the defense of fair use barred by the song's commercial character and excessive borrowing. Because we hold that a parody's commercial character is only one element to be weighed in a fair use enquiry, and that insufficient consideration was given to the nature of parody in weighing the degree of copying, we reverse and remand.

I

In 1964, Roy Orbison and William Dees wrote a rock ballad called "Oh, Pretty Woman" and assigned their rights in it to respondent Acuff–Rose Music, Inc. See Appendix A. Acuff–Rose registered the song for copyright protection.

Petitioners Luther R. Campbell, Christopher Wongwon, Mark Ross, and David Hobbs, are collectively known as 2 Live Crew, a popular rap music group. In 1989, Campbell wrote a song entitled "Pretty Woman" which he later described in an affidavit as intended, "through comical lyrics, to satirize the original work . . . . " On July 5, 1989, 2 Live Crew's manager informed Acuff–Rose that 2 Live Crew had written a parody of "Oh, Pretty Woman," that they would afford all credit for ownership and authorship of the original song to Acuff–Rose, Dees, and Orbison, and that they were willing to pay a fee for the use they wished to make of it. Enclosed with the letter were a copy of the lyrics and a recording of 2 Live Crew's song. See Appendix B. Acuff–Rose's agent refused permission, stating that "I am aware of the success enjoyed by 'The 2 Live Crews', but I must inform you that we cannot permit the use of a parody of 'Oh, Pretty Woman'." Nonetheless, in June or July 1989, 2 Live Crew released records, cassette tapes, and compact discs of "Pretty Woman" in a collection of songs entitled "As Clean As They Wanna Be." The albums and compact discs identify the authors of "Pretty Woman" as Orbison and Dees and its publisher as Acuff–Rose. * * *

II

It is uncontested here that 2 Live Crew's song would be an infringement of Acuff–Rose's rights in "Oh, Pretty Woman," under the Copyright Act of 1976, 17 U.S.C. § 106, but for a finding of fair use through parody.[4]
* * *

In Folsom v. Marsh, 9 F. Cas. 342 (No. 4,901) (CCD Mass.1841), Justice Story distilled the essence of law and methodology from the earlier cases: "look to the nature and objects of the selections made, the quantity and value of the materials used, and the degree in which the use may prejudice the sale, or diminish the profits, or supersede the objects, of the original work." Id. at 348. Thus expressed, fair use remained exclusively judge-made doctrine until the passage of the 1976 Copyright Act * * *.

C. 1.

The task is not to be simplified with bright-line rules, for the statute, like the doctrine it recognizes, calls for case-by-case analysis. [Harper & Row, Publishers, Inc. v. Nation Enterprises, 471 U.S. 539, 560 (1985); Sony Corp. of America v. Universal City Studios, Inc., 464 U.S. 417, 448 and n. 31 (1984); H.R.Rep. No. 94–1476, pp. 65–66 (1976); S.Rep. No. 94–473, p. 62 (1975).] The text employs the terms "including" and "such as" in the preamble paragraph to indicate the "illustrative and not limitative" function of the examples given, § 101; see *Harper & Row,* supra, 471 U.S., at 561, which thus provide only general guidance about the sorts of copying that courts and Congress most commonly had found to be fair uses. Nor may the four statutory factors be treated in isolation, one from another. All are to be explored, and the results weighed together, in light of the purposes of copyright. See Leval [Toward a Fair Use Standard, 103 Harv.L.Rev. 1105, 1110–11 (1990).][10] * * *

A

The first factor in a fair use enquiry is "the purpose and character of the use, including whether such use is of a commercial nature or is for non-profit educational purposes." § 107(1). This factor draws on Justice Story's formulation, "the nature and objects of the selections made." Folsom v. Marsh, supra, at 348. The enquiry here may be guided by the examples given in the preamble to § 107, looking to whether the use is for criticism, or comment, or news reporting, and the like, see § 107. The central purpose of this investigation is to see, in Justice Story's words, whether the new work merely "supersede[s] the objects" of the original creation, Folsom v. Marsh, supra, at 348; accord, *Harper & Row,* supra, at 562 ("supplanting" the original), or instead adds something new, with a further purpose or dif-

use

---

[4] * * * 2 Live Crew concedes that it is not entitled to a compulsory license under § 115 because its arrangement changes "the basic melody or fundamental character" of the original. § 115(a)(2).

[10] Because the fair use enquiry often requires close questions of judgment as to the extent of permissible borrowing in cases involving parodies (or other critical works), courts may also wish to bear in mind that the goals of the copyright law, "to stimulate the creation and publication of edifying matter," Leval 1134, are not always best served by automatically granting injunctive relief when parodists are found to have gone beyond the bounds of fair use. See 17 U.S.C. § 502(a) (court "*may* . . . grant . . . injunctions on such terms as it may deem reasonable to prevent or restrain infringement") (emphasis added); Leval 1132 (while in the "vast majority of cases, [an injunctive] remedy is justified because most infringements are simply piracy," such cases are "worlds apart from many of those raising reasonable contentions of fair use" where "there may be a strong public interest in the publication of the secondary work [and] the copyright owner's interest may be adequately protected by an award of damages for whatever infringement is found"); Abend v. MCA, Inc., 863 F.2d 1465, 1479 (C.A.9 1988) (finding "special circumstances" that would cause "great injustice" to defendants and "public injury" were injunction to issue), aff'd sub nom. Stewart v. Abend, 495 U.S. 207 (1990).

ferent character, altering the first with new expression, meaning, or message; it asks, in other words, whether and to what extent the new work is "transformative." Leval 1111. Although such transformative use is not absolutely necessary for a finding of fair use, *Sony,* supra, at 455, n. 40,[11] the goal of copyright, to promote science and the arts, is generally furthered by the creation of transformative works. Such works thus lie at the heart of the fair use doctrine's guarantee of breathing space within the confines of copyright, see, e.g., *Sony,* supra, at 478–480 (BLACKMUN, J., dissenting), and the more transformative the new work, the less will be the significance of other factors, like commercialism, that may weigh against a finding of fair use.

This Court has only once before even considered whether parody may be fair use, and that time issued no opinion because of the Court's equal division. Benny v. Loew's Inc., 239 F.2d 532 (C.A.9 1956), aff'd sub nom. Columbia Broadcasting System, Inc. v. Loew's Inc., 356 U.S. 43 (1958). Suffice it to say now that parody has an obvious claim to transformative value, as Acuff–Rose itself does not deny. Like less ostensibly humorous forms of criticism, it can provide social benefit, by shedding light on an earlier work, and, in the process, creating a new one. We thus line up with the courts that have held that parody, like other comment or criticism, may claim fair use under § 107. * * *

The germ of parody lies in the definition of the Greek *parodeia,* quoted in Judge Nelson's Court of Appeals dissent, as "a song sung alongside another." 972 F.2d, at 1440, quoting 7 Encyclopedia Britannica 768 (15th ed. 1975). Modern dictionaries accordingly describe a parody as a "literary or artistic work that imitates the characteristic style of an author or a work for comic effect or ridicule,"[12] or as a "composition in prose or verse in which the characteristic turns of thought and phrase in an author or class of authors are imitated in such a way as to make them appear ridiculous."[13] For the purposes of copyright law, the nub of the definitions, and the heart of any parodist's claim to quote from existing material, is the use of some elements of a prior author's composition to create a new one that, at least in part, comments on that author's works. See, e.g., Fisher v. Dees [794 F.2d 432, 437 (C.A.9 1986)]; MCA, Inc. v. Wilson, 677 F.2d 180, 185 (C.A.2 1981). If, on the contrary, the commentary has no critical bearing on the substance or style of the original composition, which the alleged infringer merely uses to get attention or to avoid the drudgery in working up something fresh, the claim to fairness in borrowing from another's work diminishes accordingly (if it does not vanish), and other factors, like the extent of its commerciality, loom larger.[14] Parody needs to mimic an original to make

---

[11]   The obvious statutory exception to this focus on transformative uses is the straight reproduction of multiple copies for classroom distribution.

[12]   The American Heritage Dictionary 1317 (3d ed. 1992).

[13]   11 The Oxford English Dictionary 247 (2d ed. 1989).

[14]   A parody that more loosely targets an original than the parody presented here may still be sufficiently aimed at an original work to come within our analysis of parody. If a parody whose wide dissemination in the market runs the risk of serving as a substitute for the original or licensed derivatives (see infra, discussing factor four), it is more incumbent on one claiming fair use to establish the extent of transformation and the parody's critical relationship to the original. By contrast, when there is little or no risk of market substitution, whether because of the large extent of transformation of the earlier work, the new work's minimal distribution in the market, the small extent to which it borrows from an original, or other factors, taking parodic aim at an original is a less critical factor in the analysis, and looser forms of parody may be found to be fair use, as may satire with lesser justification for the borrowing than would otherwise be required.

its point, and so has some claim to use the creation of its victim's (or collective victims') imagination, whereas satire can stand on its own two feet and so requires justification for the very act of borrowing.[15] See Ibid.; Bisceglia, Parody and Copyright Protection: Turning the Balancing Act Into a Juggling Act, in ASCAP, Copyright Law Symposium, No. 34, p. 25 (1987).

[handwritten: parody v. satire]

The fact that parody can claim legitimacy for some appropriation does not, of course, tell either parodist or judge much about where to draw the line. Like a book review quoting the copyrighted material criticized, parody may or may not be fair use, and petitioner's suggestion that any parodic use is presumptively fair has no more justification in law or fact than the equally hopeful claim that any use for news reporting should be presumed fair, see *Harper & Row,* 471 U.S., at 561. The Act has no hint of an evidentiary preference for parodists over their victims, and no workable presumption for parody could take account of the fact that parody often shades into satire when society is lampooned through its creative artifacts, or that a work may contain both parodic and nonparodic elements. Accordingly, parody, like any other use, has to work its way through the relevant factors, and be judged case by case, in light of the ends of the copyright law.

Here, the District Court held, and the Court of Appeals assumed, that 2 Live Crew's "Pretty Woman" contains parody, commenting on and criticizing the original work, whatever it may have to say about society at large. As the District Court remarked, the words of 2 Live Crew's song copy the original's first line, but then "quickly degenerat[e] into a play on words, substituting predictable lyrics with shocking ones ... [that] derisively demonstrat[e] how bland and banal the Orbison song seems to them." 754 F.Supp., at 1155 (footnote omitted). Judge Nelson, dissenting below, came to the same conclusion, that the 2 Live Crew song "was clearly intended to ridicule the white-bread original" and "reminds us that sexual congress with nameless streetwalkers is not necessarily the stuff of romance and is not necessarily without its consequences. The singers (there are several) have the same thing on their minds as did the lonely man with the nasal voice, but here there is no hint of wine and roses." 972 F.2d, at 1442. Although the majority below had difficulty discerning any criticism of the original in 2 Live Crew's song, it assumed for purposes of its opinion that there was some. Id., at 1435–1436, and n. 8.

We have less difficulty in finding that critical element in 2 Live Crew's song than the Court of Appeals did, although having found it we will not take the further step of evaluating its quality. The threshold question when fair use is raised in defense of parody is whether a parodic character may reasonably be perceived.[16] Whether, going beyond that, parody is in good taste or bad does not and should not matter to fair use. * * *

[handwritten: ☆ good or bad taste. don't matter for fair use]

The Court of Appeals, however, immediately cut short the enquiry into 2 Live Crew's fair use claim by confining its treatment of the first factor essentially to one relevant fact, the commercial nature of the use. The court then inflated the significance of this fact by applying a presumption osten-

---

[15]   Satire has been defined as a work "in which prevalent follies or vices are assailed with ridicule," 14 The Oxford English Dictionary 500 (2d ed. 1989), or are "attacked through irony, derision, or wit," The American Heritage Dictionary 1604 (3d ed. 1992).

[16]   The only further judgment, indeed, that a court may pass on a work goes to an assessment of whether the parodic element is slight or great, and the copying small or extensive in relation to the parodic element, for a work with slight parodic element and extensive copying will be more likely to merely "supersede the objects" of the original. See infra, discussing factors three and four.

upp. ct. error

sibly culled from *Sony,* that "every commercial use of copyrighted material is presumptively . . . unfair . . . . " *Sony,* 464 U.S., at 451. In giving virtually dispositive weight to the commercial nature of the parody, the Court of Appeals erred.

The language of the statute makes clear that the commercial or non-profit educational purpose of a work is only one element of the first factor enquiry into its purpose and character. * * * If, indeed, commerciality carried presumptive force against a finding of fairness, the presumption would swallow nearly all of the illustrative uses listed in the preamble paragraph of § 107, including news reporting, comment, criticism, teaching, scholarship, and research, since these activities "are generally conducted for profit in this country." *Harper & Row,* supra, at 592 (Brennan, J., dissenting). Congress could not have intended such a rule, which certainly is not inferable from the common-law cases, arising as they did from the world of letters in which Samuel Johnson could pronounce that "[n]o man but a blockhead ever wrote, except for money." 3 Boswell's Life of Johnson 19 (G. Hill ed. 1934). * * *

B

The second statutory factor, "the nature of the copyrighted work," § 107(2), draws on Justice Story's expression, the "value of the materials used." Folsom v. Marsh, 9 F.Cas., at 348. This factor calls for recognition that some works are closer to the core of intended copyright protection than others, with the consequence that fair use is more difficult to establish when the former works are copied. * * * We agree with both the District Court and the Court of Appeals that the Orbison original's creative expression for public dissemination falls within the core of the copyright's protective purposes. 754 F.Supp., at 1155–1156; 972 F.2d, at 1437. This fact, however, is not much help in this case, or ever likely to help much in separating the fair use sheep from the infringing goats in a parody case, since parodies almost invariably copy publicly known, expressive works.

C

The third factor asks whether "the amount and substantiality of the portion used in relation to the copyrighted work as a whole," § 107(3) (or, in Justice Story's words, "the quantity and value of the materials used," Folsom v. Marsh, supra, at 348) are reasonable in relation to the purpose of the copying. Here, attention turns to the persuasiveness of a parodist's justification for the particular copying done, and the enquiry will harken back to the first of the statutory factors, for, as in prior cases, we recognize that the extent of permissible copying varies with the purpose and character of the use. * * *

The District Court considered the song's parodic purpose in finding that 2 Live Crew had not helped themselves overmuch. 754 F.Supp., at 1156–1157. The Court of Appeals disagreed, stating that "[w]hile it may not be inappropriate to find that no more was taken than necessary, the copying was qualitatively substantial . . . . We conclude that taking the heart of the original and making it the heart of a new work was to purloin a substantial portion of the essence of the original." 972 F.2d, at 1438.

The Court of Appeals is of course correct that this factor calls for thought not only about the quantity of the materials used, but about their quality and importance, too. In *Harper & Row,* for example, the Nation had taken only some 300 words out of President Ford's memoirs, but we signalled the significance of the quotations in finding them to amount to "the heart of the book," the part most likely to be newsworthy and important in licensing serialization. 471 U.S., at 564–566, 568 (internal quotation marks omitted). We also agree with the Court of Appeals that whether "a substantial portion of the infringing work was copied verbatim" from the copyrighted work is a relevant question, see id., at 565, for it may reveal a dearth of transformative character or purpose under the first factor, or a greater likelihood of market harm under the fourth; a work composed primarily of an original, particularly its heart, with little added or changed, is more likely to be a merely superseding use, fulfilling demand for the original.

Where we part company with the court below is in applying these guides to parody, and in particular to parody in the song before us. Parody presents a difficult case. Parody's humor, or in any event its comment, necessarily springs from recognizable allusion to its object through distorted imitation. Its art lies in the tension between a known original and its parodic twin. When parody takes aim at a particular original work, the parody must be able to "conjure up" at least enough of that original to make the object of its critical wit recognizable. See, e.g., [Elsmere Music, Inc. v. National Broadcasting Co., 482 F.Supp. 741 (S.D.N.Y.), aff'd, 623 F.2d 252, 253 n. 1 (C.A.2 1980)]; Fisher v. Dees, 794 F.2d, at 438–439. What makes for this recognition is quotation of the original's most distinctive or memorable features, which the parodist can be sure the audience will know. Once enough has been taken to assure identification, how much more is reasonable will depend, say, on the extent to which the song's overriding purpose and character is to parody the original or, in contrast, the likelihood that the parody may serve as a market substitute for the original. But using some characteristic features cannot be avoided.

We think the Court of Appeals was insufficiently appreciative of parody's need for the recognizable sight or sound when it ruled 2 Live Crew's use unreasonable as a matter of law. It is true, of course, that 2 Live Crew copied the characteristic opening bass riff (or musical phrase) of the original, and true that the words of the first line copy the Orbison lyrics. But if quotation of the opening riff and the first line may be said to go to the "heart" of the original, the heart is also what most readily conjures up the song for parody, and it is the heart at which parody takes aim. Copying does not become excessive in relation to parodic purpose merely because the portion taken was the original's heart. If 2 Live Crew had copied a significantly less memorable part of the original, it is difficult to see how its parodic character would have come through. See Fisher v. Dees, 794 F.2d, at 439.

This is not, of course, to say that anyone who calls himself a parodist can skim the cream and get away scot free. In parody, as in news reporting, see *Harper & Row,* supra, context is everything, and the question of fairness asks what else the parodist did besides go to the heart of the original. It is significant that 2 Live Crew not only copied the first line of the original, but thereafter departed markedly from the Orbison lyrics for its own ends. 2 Live Crew not only copied the bass riff and repeated it, but also produced otherwise distinctive sounds, interposing "scraper" noise, overlaying the music with solos in different keys, and altering the drum beat. See 754 F.Supp., at 1155. This is not a case, then, where "a substantial portion" of the parody itself is composed of a "verbatim" copying of the original. It is not, that is, a case where the parody is so insubstantial, as compared to the copying, that the third factor must be resolved as a matter of law against the parodists.

Suffice it to say here that, as to the lyrics, we think the Court of Appeals correctly suggested that "no more was taken than necessary," 972 F.2d, at 1438, but just for that reason, we fail to see how the copying can be excessive in relation to its parodic purpose, even if the portion taken is the original's "heart." As to the music, we express no opinion whether repetition of the bass riff is excessive copying, and we remand to permit evaluation of the amount taken, in light of the song's parodic purpose and character, its transformative elements, and considerations of the potential for market substitution sketched more fully below.

D

The fourth fair use factor is "the effect of the use upon the potential market for or value of the copyrighted work." § 107(4). It requires courts to consider not only the extent of market harm caused by the particular actions of the alleged infringer, but also "whether unrestricted and widespread conduct of the sort engaged in by the defendant . . . would result in a substantially adverse impact on the potential market" for the original. Nimmer § 13.05[A][4], p. 13–102.61 (footnote omitted); accord *Harper & Row,* 471 U.S., at 569; Senate Report, p. 65; Folsom v. Marsh, 9 F.Cas., at 349. The enquiry "must take account not only of harm to the original but also of harm to the market for derivative works." *Harper & Row,* supra, 471 U.S. at 568. * * *

* * * In assessing the likelihood of significant market harm, the Court of Appeals quoted from language in *Sony* that " '[i]f the intended use is for commercial gain, that likelihood may be presumed. But if it is for a noncommercial purpose, the likelihood must be demonstrated.' " 972 F.2d, at 1438, quoting *Sony,* 464 U.S., at 451. * * *

No "presumption" or inference of market harm that might find support in *Sony* is applicable to a case involving something beyond mere duplication for commercial purposes. *Sony*'s discussion of a presumption contrasts a context of verbatim copying of the original in its entirety for commercial purposes, with the noncommercial context of *Sony* itself (home copying of television programming). In the former circumstances, what *Sony* said simply makes common sense: when a commercial use amounts to mere duplication of the entirety of an original, it clearly "supersede[s] the objects," Folsom v. Marsh, 9 F.Cas., at 348, of the original and serves as a market replacement for it, making it likely that cognizable market harm to the original will occur. *Sony,* 464 U.S., at 451. But when, on the contrary, the second use is transformative, market substitution is at least less certain, and market harm may not be so readily inferred. Indeed, as to parody pure and simple, it is more likely that the new work will not affect the market for the original in a way cognizable under this factor, that is, by acting as a substitute for it ("supersed[ing] [its] objects"). * * *

We do not, of course, suggest that a parody may not harm the market at all, but when a lethal parody, like a scathing theater review, kills demand for the original, it does not produce a harm cognizable under the Copyright Act. Because "parody may quite legitimately aim at garroting the original, destroying it commercially as well as artistically," B. Kaplan, An Unhurried View of Copyright 69 (1967), the role of the courts is to distinguish between "[b]iting criticism [that merely] suppresses demand [and] copyright infringement[, which] usurps it." Fisher v. Dees, 794 F.2d, at 438.

This distinction between potentially remediable displacement and unremediable disparagement is reflected in the rule that there is no protectable derivative market for criticism. The market for potential derivative uses includes only those that creators of original works would in general develop or license others to develop. Yet the unlikelihood that creators of imaginative works will license critical reviews or lampoons of their own productions removes such uses from the very notion of a potential licensing market. "People ask . . . for criticism, but they only want praise." S. Maugham, Of Human Bondage 241 (Penguin ed. 1992). Thus, to the extent that the opinion below may be read to have considered harm to the market for parodies of "Oh, Pretty Woman," see 972 F.2d, at 1439, the court erred. * * *[22]

In explaining why the law recognizes no derivative market for critical works, including parody, we have, of course, been speaking of the later work as if it had nothing but a critical aspect (i.e., "parody pure and simple," * * *). But the later work may have a more complex character, with effects not only in the arena of criticism but also in protectable markets for derivative works, too. In that sort of case, the law looks beyond the criticism to the other elements of the work, as it does here. 2 Live Crew's song comprises not only parody but also rap music, and the derivative market for rap music is a proper focus of enquiry, see *Harper & Row,* 471 U.S., at 568; Nimmer § 13.05[B]. Evidence of substantial harm to it would weigh against a finding of fair use, because the licensing of derivatives is an important economic incentive to the creation of originals. See 17 U.S.C. § 106(2) (copyright owner has rights to derivative works). Of course, the only harm to derivatives that need concern us, as discussed above, is the harm of market substitution. The fact that a parody may impair the market for derivative uses by the very effectiveness of its critical commentary is no more relevant under copyright than the like threat to the original market.[24]

Although 2 Live Crew submitted uncontroverted affidavits on the question of market harm to the original, neither they, nor Acuff–Rose, introduced evidence or affidavits addressing the likely effect of 2 Live Crew's parodic rap song on the market for a nonparody, rap version of "Oh, Pretty Woman." And while Acuff–Rose would have us find evidence of a rap market in the very facts that 2 Live Crew recorded a rap parody of "Oh, Pretty Woman" and another rap group sought a license to record a rap derivative, there was no evidence that a potential rap market was harmed in any way by 2 Live Crew's parody, rap version. The fact that 2 Live Crew's parody sold as part of a collection of rap songs says very little about the parody's effect on a market for a rap version of the original, either of the music alone or of the music with its lyrics. The District Court essentially passed on this issue, observing that Acuff–Rose is free to record "whatever version of the original it desires," 754 F.Supp., at 1158; the Court of Appeals went the other way by erroneous presumption. Contrary to each treatment, it is impossible to deal with the fourth factor except by recognizing that a silent record on an important factor bearing on fair use disentitled the proponent of the defense, 2 Live Crew, to summary judgment. The evidentiary hole will doubtless be plugged on remand.

---

[22] We express no opinion as to the derivative markets for works using elements of an original as vehicles for satire or amusement, making no comment on the original or criticism of it.

[24] In some cases it may be difficult to determine whence the harm flows. In such cases, the other fair use factors may provide some indicia of the likely source of the harm. A work whose overriding purpose and character is parodic and whose borrowing is slight in relation to its parody will be far less likely to cause cognizable harm than a work with little parodic content and much copying.

III

It was error for the Court of Appeals to conclude that the commercial nature of 2 Live Crew's parody of "Oh, Pretty Woman" rendered it presumptively unfair. No such evidentiary presumption is available to address either the first factor, the character and purpose of the use, or the fourth, market harm, in determining whether a transformative use, such as parody, is a fair one. The court also erred in holding that 2 Live Crew had necessarily copied excessively from the Orbison original, considering the parodic purpose of the use. We therefore reverse the judgment of the Court of Appeals and remand for further proceedings consistent with this opinion.

It is so ordered.

APPENDIX A

"Oh, Pretty Woman" by Roy Orbison and William Dees

Pretty Woman, walking down the street,

Pretty Woman, the kind I like to meet,

Pretty Woman, I don't believe you, you're not the truth,

No one could look as good as you

Mercy

Pretty Woman, won't you pardon me,

Pretty Woman, I couldn't help but see,

Pretty Woman, that you look lovely as can be

Are you lonely just like me?

Pretty Woman, stop a while,

Pretty Woman, talk a while,

Pretty Woman give your smile to me

Pretty Woman, yeah, yeah, yeah

Pretty Woman, look my way,

Pretty Woman, say you'll stay with me

'Cause I need you, I'll treat you right

Come to me baby, Be mine tonight

Pretty Woman, don't walk on by,

Pretty Woman, don't make me cry,

Pretty Woman, don't walk away,

Hey, O.K.

If that's the way it must be, O.K.

I guess I'll go on home, it's late

There'll be tomorrow night, but wait!

What do I see

Is she walking back to me?

Yeah, she's walking back to me!

Oh, Pretty Woman.

APPENDIX B
"Pretty Woman" as Recorded by 2 Live Crew

Pretty Woman walkin' down the street

Pretty woman girl you look so sweet

Pretty woman you bring me down to that knee

Pretty woman you make me wanna beg please

Oh, pretty woman

Big hairy woman you need to shave that stuff

Big hairy woman you know I bet it's tough

Big hairy woman all that hair it ain't legit

'Cause you look like 'Cousin It'

Big hairy woman

Bald headed woman girl your hair won't grow

Bald headed woman you got a teeny weeny afro

Bald headed woman you know your hair could look nice

Bald headed woman first you got to roll it with rice

Bald headed woman here, let me get this hunk of biz for ya

Ya know what I'm saying you look better than rice a roni

Oh bald headed woman

Big hairy woman come on in

And don't forget your bald headed friend

Hey pretty woman let the boys

Jump in

Two timin' woman girl you know you ain't right

Two timin' woman you's out with my boy last night

Two timin' woman that takes a load off my mind

Two timin' woman now I know the baby ain't mine

Oh, two timin' woman

Oh pretty woman

■ JUSTICE KENNEDY, concurring.

I agree that remand is appropriate and join the opinion of the Court, with these further observations about the fair use analysis of parody. * * *

* * * It is not enough that the parody use the original in a humorous fashion, however creative that humor may be. The parody must target the original, and not just its general style, the genre of art to which it belongs, or society as a whole (although if it targets the original, it may target those features as well). See Rogers v. Koons, 960 F.2d 301, 310 (C.A.2 1992) ("[T]hough the satire need not be only of the copied work and may . . . also be a parody of modern society, the copied work must be, at least in part, an object of the parody"); Fisher v. Dees, 794 F.2d 432, 436 (C.A.9 1986) ("[A] humorous or satiric work deserves protection under the fair-use doctrine only if the copied work is at least partly the target of the work in question"). This prerequisite confines fair use protection to works whose very subject is the original composition and so necessitates some borrowing from

it. See MCA, Inc. v. Wilson, 677 F.2d 180, 185 (C.A.2 1981) ("[I]f the copyrighted song is not at least in part an object of the parody, there is no need to conjure it up") * * *.

The fair use factors thus reinforce the importance of keeping the definition of parody within proper limits. More than arguable parodic content should be required to deem a would-be parody a fair use. Fair use is an affirmative defense, so doubts about whether a given use is fair should not be resolved in favor of the self-proclaimed parodist. We should not make it easy for musicians to exploit existing works and then later claim that their rendition was a valuable commentary on the original. * * *

The Court decides it is "fair to say that 2 Live Crew's song reasonably could be perceived as commenting on the original or criticizing it, to some degree." * * * While I am not so assured that 2 Live Crew's song is a legitimate parody, the Court's treatment of the remaining factors leaves room for the District Court to determine on remand that the song is not a fair use. As future courts apply our fair use analysis, they must take care to ensure that not just any commercial takeoff is rationalized *post hoc* as a parody.

With these observations, I join the opinion of the Court.

NOTES AND QUESTIONS ON PARODY

(1) Is 2 Live Crew's claim of fair use helped—or hurt—by the fact that they were refused a license to use *Oh, Pretty Woman?* In footnote 18 of its opinion the Supreme Court said, "[W]e reject Acuff–Rose's argument that 2 Live Crew's request for permission to use the original should be weighed against a finding of fair use. Even if good faith were central to fair use, 2 Live Crew's actions do not necessarily suggest that they believed their version was not fair use; the offer may simply have been made in a good faith effort to avoid this litigation. If the use is otherwise fair, then no permission need be sought or granted. Thus, being denied permission to use a work does not weigh against a finding of fair use." J. Gibson, Risk Aversion and Rights Accretion in Intellectual Property Law, 116 Yale L.J. 882 (2007), makes the point that risk-averse users often seek licenses when none are needed; the existence of those licenses may then help copyright owners justify a legal entitlement covering the licensed market; J. Rothman, The Questionable Use of Custom in Intellectual Property, 93 Va.L.Rev. 1899 (2007), decries decisions that rely on industry clearance practices and other litigation avoidance measures in defining the scope of copyright exemptions like fair use.

(2) In assessing the strength of the defendants' fair use defense, the Court distinguishes "parody" from "satire." In those terms, how would you characterize the Saturday Night Live sketch at issue in *Elsmere*? See also Rogers v. Koons, 960 F.2d 301 (2d Cir.), cert. denied, 506 U.S. 934 (1992), which rejected a "parody" claim by flamboyant artist Jeff Koons, who closely copied plaintiff's postcard depicting a row of puppies (and got $367,000 for three duplicate originals); although the defendant's work may be "a satirical critique of our materialistic society," the court said that a parody defense requires that "the copied work be, at least in part, an object of the parody." Koons had better luck in a subsequent appearance before the Second Circuit. In Blanch v. Koons, 467 F.3d 244 (2d Cir.2006), the court upheld a summary judgment in his favor in a suit brought by a photographer; a portion of a fashion photograph taken by the plaintiff had been copied by Koons in a collage painting. Citing *Campbell,* the court said that

the portion taken was reasonable in relation to Koons' purpose to evoke a certain style of mass communication.

Campbell's emphasis on the extent of a defendant's parodic commentary on the original was pursued in Leibovitz v. Paramount Pictures Corp., 137 F.3d 109 (2d Cir.1998). Plaintiff owned the copyright in a photograph of a nude and pregnant Demi Moore that had appeared on the cover of *Vanity Fair*; defendant photographed a pregnant model in a similar pose and after superimposing the head of actor Leslie Nielsen, used the photo to advertise a new movie. Judge Newman, finding fair use, said the defendant's advertisement could be perceived as commenting on the pretentiousness of the original photograph and its interpretation of feminine beauty.

After holding that whether a work is a parody for purposes of fair use is a question of law, the Ninth Circuit in Mattel, Inc. v. Walking Mountain Productions, 353 F.3d 792 (9th Cir.2003), concluded that photographs depicting plaintiff's Barbie doll in danger from various household appliances (e.g., "Barbie Enchiladas," showing four Barbie dolls wrapped in tortillas in a casserole dish inside an oven) were parodies commenting on Barbie's influence on gender roles—and a fair use. B. Keller and R. Tushnet, Even More Parodic Than the Real Thing: Parody Lawsuits Revisited, 94 Trademark Rep. 979 (2004), questions the wisdom of a distinction between parody and satire; R. Kasunic, The Problem of Meaning in Non–Discursive Expression, 57 J.Copyr. Soc'y 399 (2010), discusses the difficulty of applying fair use to visual works.

(3) What if the second artist disclaims any intention to comment on the original work or its genre? In Cariou v. Prince, 2013 WL 1760521 (2d Cir.2013), the defendant, an appropriation artist, had incorporated photographs of Rastafarians in Jamaica into a series of paintings. The photos, taken from the plaintiff's book, were variously enlarged, cropped, tinted, and partially painted over. The defendant testified that he had no interest in the original meanings of the photographs. "What is critical is how the work in question appears to the reasonable observer, not simply what an artist might say about a particular piece or body of work. Prince's work could be transformative even without commenting on Cariou's work or culture * * *." The court found that most of the uses were fair, but remanded on five works that made less substantial changes. H. Holland, Social Semiotics in the Fair Use Analysis, 24 Harv.J.L. & Tech. 335 (2011), agrees that for purposes of fair use, the "transformativeness" of a work should include new meanings and functions of the work attributable to the audience, independent of the creator's intent; L. Heymann, Everything is Transformative: Fair Use and Reader Response, 31 Colum.J.L. & Arts 445 (2008), similarly concludes that the degree of "transformation" should be judged from a user perspective; N. Schaumann, An Artist's Privilege, 15 Cardozo Arts & Ent.L.J. 249 (1997), argues more broadly that "artists should be free to copy whatever they like," at least absent a competitive threat to the original.

(4) Yoko Ono and the children of John Lennon failed in their pursuit of a preliminary injunction against the use of a fifteen-second clip from Lennon's "Imagine" in a film critical of the theory of evolution. The producers used the clip, including the lyrics, "Nothing to kill or die for/And no religion too," following an interview with a scientist who predicted that religion would eventually be displaced by science. Tracking the analysis in Blanch v. Koons, Judge Stein ruled that the use was transformative, even though the song had not been altered. "Defendants use is nonetheless transformative because they put the song to a different purpose, selected an excerpt containing the ideas they wished to critique, paired the music and lyrics with images that contrast with the song's utopian expression, and placed the excerpt in the context of a debate regarding the role of religion in public life." Also, there was no evidence that permitting this transformative use "will usurp the market for licensing the song for traditional uses." Lennon v. Premise Media Corp., 556 F.Supp.2d 310 (S.D.N.Y.2008). (The case was settled after the film's producers agreed to cut the song from the DVD version.) This view of "transformativeness" was echoed by Judge Traxler, affirming a finding of fair use by an online plagiarism detection service that stored class papers submitted for analysis by high school students: "[T]he use of a copyrighted work need not alter or augment the work to be transformative in nature. Rather, it can be transformative in function or purpose without altering or actually adding to the original work." A.V. ex rel. Vanderhye v. iParadigms, LLC, 562 F.3d 630 (4th Cir.2009).

The Supreme Court's decision in Campbell v. Acuff–Rose and Yoko Ono's defeat in Lennon v. Premise Media are both criticized in W. Henslee, You Can't Always Get What You Want, But If You Try Sometimes You Can Steal It and Call It Fair Use, 58 Cath.U.L.Rev. 663 (2009). An empirical study in M. Sag, Predicting Fair Use, 73 Ohio St.L.Rev. 47 (2012), finds that transformativeness is a robust predictor of fair use outcomes; L. Lape, Transforming Fair Use: The Productive Use Factor in Fair Use Doctrine, 58 Alb.L.Rev. 677 (1995), worries that emphasis on transformative use will displace a more general analysis of the social utility of the defendant's use.

(5) In connection with the fourth fair use factor, Justice Souter in *Campbell* says that "there is no protectable derivative market for criticism"; only harm to the market for the original or for derivative uses that creators would likely develop or license counts against a fair use claim. On remand, what kinds of evidence would be relevant in measuring the potential harm to the derivative market for a non-parody rap version of the plaintiff's song?[h]

(6) A number of commentators have expressed concern about the potential chilling effect of the vague standards applicable to works like parodies. What could be done to decrease uncertainty? Would some sort of compulsory license be feasible? See S. Burr, Artistic Parody: A Theoretical Construct, 14 Cardozo Arts & Ent.L.J. 65 (1996); Ex ante determinations of fair use? See J. Mazzone, Administering Fair Use, 51 Will. & Mary L.Rev. 395 (2009); Statutory safe harbors? See G. Parchomovsky and K. Goldman, Fair Use Harbors, 93 Va.L.Rev. 1483 (2007). C. Newman, Transformation in Property and Copyright, 56 Vill.L.Rev. 251 (2011), would remove some of the uncertainty of fair use through a more stringent understanding of substantial similarity.

(7) If, as Justice Souter believes, a parody is unlikely to affect the market for the original, why do copyright owners litigate these cases? To be able to sell licenses to parody? To protect the esteem of the plaintiff or the work? Is it relevant that many of the parodies in recent cases are arguably in poor taste?

---

[h]   After the remand by the Supreme Court, the case was settled when the parties agreed to a license. Nashville Banner, June 5, 1996, p. B2.

A NOTE ON COPYRIGHT AND THE FIRST AMENDMENT

A series of law review articles in the 1970s asked if there was an inherent conflict between freedom of speech and proprietary rights in forms of expression.[i] The traditional judicial response has been no. The Ninth Circuit, for example, has said that the idea-expression dichotomy adequately accommodates the competing interests: "The 'marketplace of ideas' is not limited by copyright because copyright is limited to protection of expression." Sid & Marty Krofft Television Productions, Inc. v. McDonald's Corp., 562 F.2d 1157, 1170 (9th Cir.1977). But are there situations in which the first amendment demands access, not merely to ideas, but also to copyrighted expression? The fair use doctrine will often insure the necessary access. The Second Circuit in *Wainwright Securities,* p. 322 supra, noted that "Conflicts between interests protected by the first amendment and the copyright laws thus far have been resolved by application of the fair use doctrine." See, e.g., Los Angeles News Service v. Tullo, 973 F.2d 791 (9th Cir.1992) ("First Amendment considerations are relevant in determining whether the purpose of copying a work and the nature of the work copied militate in favor of finding a given use of a particular work to be a 'fair use' * * *."). Recall too the Supreme Court's endorsement of this view in *Harper & Row*: "In view of the First Amendment protections already embodied in the Copyright Act's distinction between copyrightable expression and uncopyrightable facts and ideas, and the latitude for scholarship and comment traditionally afforded by fair use, we see no warrant for expanding the doctrine of fair use to create what amounts to a public figure exception to copyright."

Is the fair use doctrine indeed sufficient to mediate copyright and free speech interests? If Time, Inc. had suffered substantial economic injury as a result of Thompson's use of the Zapruder frames in his book on the Kennedy assassination, for example, would the defendants still have prevailed on their fair use defense? Would it be constitutional to hold the defendants liable for the use?[j] In *Wainwright Securities* the Second Circuit indicated that in some cases (although not that one) courts might be required to recognize, apart from fair use, a first amendment limitation on copyright protection. The Ninth Circuit in *Sid & Marty Krofft* made a similar concession, although it thought such instances "rare," and limited to "graphic expressions of newsworthy events." (Is it true, as the court stated in a footnote, that "[b]ecause there are available alternatives in the form of expressing any verbal ideas, first amendment considerations should not limit copyright protection in this area"? 562 F.2d at 1171 n. 17.)

A. Garfield, The First Amendment as a Check on Copyright Rights, 23 Hastings Comm/Ent L.J. 587 (2001), worries that free speech concerns are not adequately considered in fair use and idea/expression analysis. The emphasis on "transformative" copying in fair use analysis obscures the free speech implications of other copying according to R. Tushnet, Copy This Essay: How Fair Use Doctrine Harms Free Speech and How Copying Serves It, 114 Yale L.J. 535 (2004); L. Lockridge, The Myth of Copyright's

---

[i] See R. Denicola, Copyright and Free Speech: Constitutional Limitations on the Protection of Expression, 67 Calif.L.Rev. 283 (1979); P. Goldstein, Copyright and the First Amendment, 70 Colum.L.Rev. 983 (1970); and M. Nimmer, Does Copyright Abridge the First Amendment Guarantees of Free Speech and Press?, 17 U.C.L.A.L.Rev. 1180 (1970).

[j] J. Bauer, Copyright and the First Amendment: Comrades, Combatants, or Uneasy Allies?, 67 Wash. & Lee L.Rev. 831 (2010), thinks that, fair use aside, Thompson had a first amendment right to use the Zapruder film.

Fair Use Doctrine as a Protector of Free Speech, 24 Santa Clara Computer & High Tech.L.J. 31 (2007), similarly concludes that the emphasis on non-commercial and transformative use limits the ability of fair use to safeguard free speech.

Does the Supreme Court's rejection of the defendant's free speech argument in *Harper & Row* foreclose the possibility of a discrete first amendment defense to copyright infringement? The Supreme Court in Eldred v. Ashcroft, 537 U.S. 186 (2003), p. 481 infra, had this to say about copyright and the first amendment: "The Copyright Clause and First Amendment were adopted close in time. This proximity indicates that, in the Framer's view, copyright's limited monopolies are compatible with free speech principles. * * * We recognize that the D.C. Circuit spoke too broadly when it declared copyrights 'categorically immune from challenges under the First Amendment.' 239 F.3d at 375. But when, as in this case, Congress has not altered the traditional contours of copyright protection, further First Amendment scrutiny is unnecessary." R. Ku, F(r)ee Expression? Reconciling Copyright and the First Amendment, 57 Case W.Res.L.Rev. 863 (2007), uses copyright as understood by the framers as the baseline for determining when changes to copyright law require first amendment scrutiny; L. Bloom, Copyright Under Siege: The First Amendment Front, 9 Computer L.Rev & Tech.J. 41 (2004), defends the traditional reconciliation of copyright and free speech endorsed by the Supreme Court.

An attempt to rekindle judicial interest in the first amendment implications of copyright is made in A. Garfield, The Case for First Amendment Limits on Copyright Law, 35 Hofstra L.Rev. 1169 (2007); M. Madison, Complexity and Copyright in Contradiction, 18 Cardozo Arts & Ent.L.J. 125 (2000), moves beyond a traditional first amendment analysis, arguing for a richer interplay between copyright and freedom of speech; J. Rothman, Liberating Copyright: Thinking Beyond Free Speech, 95 Cornell L.Rev. 463 (2010), concludes that constitutional constraints on copyright premised on liberty and due process are more promising than first amendment arguments.

PHOTOCOPYING AND ELECTRONIC REPRODUCTION

Does the reader of a book infringe the copyright if she copies by hand passages for her own use? According to common understanding, she does not. May she not then use a photocopier to speed the process? But we quickly come to limiting cases: what if a large corporation makes hundreds of photocopies of technical articles for use by employees engaged in a profit-making enterprise?

American Geophysical Union v. Texaco Inc.

United States Court of Appeals, Second Circuit, 1994.
60 F.3d 913.
Certiorari dismissed, 516 U.S. 1005 (1995).

■ Before NEWMAN, WINTER and JACOBS, CIRCUIT JUDGES.

■ NEWMAN, CHIEF JUDGE.

This interlocutory appeal presents the issue of whether, under the particular circumstances of this case, the fair use defense to copyright infringement applies to the photocopying of articles in a scientific journal.

This issue arises on the appeal of defendant Texaco Inc. from the July 23, 1992, order of the United States District Court for the Southern District of New York (Pierre N. Leval, Judge) holding, after a limited-issue bench trial, that the photocopying of eight articles from the *Journal of Catalysis* for use by one of Texaco's researchers was not fair use. See American Geophysical Union v. Texaco Inc., 802 F.Supp. 1 (S.D.N.Y.1992). Though not for precisely the same reasons, we agree with the District Court's conclusion *not fair use* that this particular copying was not fair use and therefore affirm.

Background

The District Court Proceedings. Plaintiffs American Geophysical Union and 82 other publishers of scientific and technical journals (the "publishers") brought a class action claiming that Texaco's unauthorized photocopying of articles from their journals constituted copyright infringement. Among other defenses, Texaco claimed that its copying was fair use under section 107 of the Copyright Act, 17 U.S.C. § 107 (1988). Since it appeared likely that the litigation could be resolved once the fair use defense was adjudicated, the parties agreed that an initial trial should be limited to whether Texaco's copying was fair use, and further agreed that this issue would be submitted for decision on a written record.

Although Texaco employs 400 to 500 research scientists, of whom all or most presumably photocopy scientific journal articles to support their Texaco research, the parties stipulated—in order to spare the enormous expense of exploring the photocopying practices of each of them—that one scientist would be chosen at random as the representative of the entire group. The scientist chosen was Dr. Donald H. Chickering, II, a scientist at Texaco's research center in Beacon, New York. For consideration at trial, the publishers selected from Chickering's files photocopies of eight particular articles from the *Journal of Catalysis*. * * *

Essential Facts. Employing between 400 and 500 researchers nationwide, Texaco conducts considerable scientific research seeking to develop new products and technology primarily to improve its commercial performance in the petroleum industry. As part of its substantial expenditures in support of research activities at its Beacon facility, Texaco subscribes to many scientific and technical journals and maintains a sizable library with these materials. Among the periodicals that Texaco receives at its Beacon research facility is the *Journal of Catalysis* ("*Catalysis*"), a monthly publication produced by Academic Press, Inc., a major publisher of scholarly journals and one of the plaintiffs in this litigation. Texaco had initially purchased one subscription to *Catalysis* for its Beacon facility, and increased its total subscriptions to two in 1983. Since 1988, Texaco has maintained three subscriptions to *Catalysis*. * * *

The copies of the eight articles from *Catalysis* found in Chickering's files that the parties have made the exclusive focus of the fair use trial were photocopied in their entirety by Chickering or by other Texaco employees at Chickering's request. Chickering apparently believed that the material and data found within these articles would facilitate his current or future professional research. The evidence developed at trial indicated that Chickering did not generally use the *Catalysis* articles in his research immediately upon copying, but placed the photocopied articles in his files to have them available for later reference as needed. Chickering became aware of six of the photocopied articles when the original issues of *Catalysis* containing the articles were circulated to him. He learned of the other two articles upon seeing a reference to them in another published article.

As it turned out, Chickering did not have occasion to make use of five of the articles that were copied.

Discussion

I. The Nature of the Dispute

The parties and many of the *amici curiae* have approached this case as if it concerns the broad issue of whether photocopying of scientific articles is fair use, or at least the only slightly more limited issue of whether photocopying of such articles is fair use when undertaken by a research scientist engaged in his own research. Such broad issues are not before us. Rather, we consider whether Texaco's photocopying by 400 or 500 scientists, as represented by Chickering's example, is a fair use. This includes the question whether such institutional, systematic copying increases the number of copies available to scientists while avoiding the necessity of paying for license fees or for additional subscriptions. We do not deal with the question of copying by an individual, for personal use in research or otherwise (not for resale), recognizing that under the fair use doctrine or the *de minimis* doctrine, such a practice by an individual might well not constitute an infringement. In other words, our opinion does not decide the case that would arise if Chickering were a professor or an independent scientist engaged in copying and creating files for independent research, as opposed to being employed by an institution in the pursuit of his research on the institution's behalf. * * *

A. Fair Use and Photocopying

* * * [I]f the issue were open, we would seriously question whether the fair use analysis that has developed with respect to works of authorship alleged to use portions of copyrighted material is precisely applicable to copies produced by mechanical means. * * *

* * * However, we learn from the Supreme Court's consideration of copying achieved by use of a videotape recorder that mechanical copying is to be assessed for fair use purposes under the traditional mode of analysis, including the four statutory factors of section 107. See [Sony Corp. of America v. Universal City Studios, Inc., 464 U.S. 417, 447–56 (1984).] We therefore are obliged to apply that analysis to the photocopying that occurred in this case.

B. The Precise Copyrights at Issue

We must first identify precisely the copyrighted works alleged to be infringed, since certain arguments made on appeal seem to focus on different works. The publishers typically hold two separate sets of copyrights in their journal publications. As a consequence of the publishers' requirement that authors transfer their copyrights when their articles are accepted for publication, the publishers usually possess the copyrights that subsist in each individual article appearing within their journals. Moreover, to the extent that the compilation of a journal issue involves an original work of authorship, the publishers possess a distinct copyright in each journal issue as a collective work, see 17 U.S.C. § 103; see also 17 U.S.C. § 101 (defining "compilation" and "collective work"). See generally Feist Publications, Inc. v. Rural Telephone Service Co., 499 U.S. 340, 356–61 (1991) (discussing extent of copyright protection in compilations and collective works).

From the outset, this lawsuit concerned alleged infringement of the copyrights in individual journal articles, copyrights assigned by the authors to the publishers. More specifically, by virtue of the parties' stipulation, this case now concerns the copyrights in the eight articles from *Catalysis* found in Chickering's files, copyrights now owned by Academic Press. There are no allegations that raise questions concerning Academic Press's potential copyrights in whole issues or annual volumes of *Catalysis* as collective works.

C.   Burdens of Proof and Standard of Review

Fair use serves as an affirmative defense to a claim of copyright infringement, and thus the party claiming that its secondary use of the original copyrighted work constitutes a fair use typically carries the burden of proof as to all issues in the dispute. See [Campbell v. Acuff–Rose Music, Inc., 510 U.S. 569, 590 (1994)]. Moreover, since fair use is a "mixed question of law and fact," [Harper & Row Pub., Inc. v. Nation Enterprises, 471 U.S. 539, 560 (1985)], we review the District Court's conclusions on this issue *de novo,* though we accept its subsidiary findings of fact unless clearly erroneous, see [Twin Peaks Prod., Inc. v. Publications Int'l, Ltd., 996 F.2d 1366, 1374 (2d Cir.1993)].

II.   The Enumerated Fair Use Factors of Section 107

* * *

A.   First Factor: Purpose and Character of Use

* * * In Chickering's own words, the copies of the articles were made for "my personal convenience," since it is "far more convenient to have access in my office to a photocopy of an article than to have to go to the library each time I wanted to refer to it." Affidavit of Donald Chickering at 11 (submitted as direct trial testimony) [hereinafter Chickering testimony]. Significantly, Chickering did not even have occasion to use five of the photocopied articles at all, further revealing that the photocopies of the eight *Catalysis* articles were primarily made just for "future retrieval and reference." Id.

It is true that photocopying these articles also served other purposes. The most favorable for Texaco is the purpose of enabling Chickering, if the need should arise, to go into the lab with pieces of paper that (a) were not as bulky as the entire issue or a bound volume of a year's issues, and (b) presented no risk of damaging the original by exposure to chemicals. And these purposes might suffice to tilt the first fair use factor in favor of Texaco if these purposes were dominant. * * *

The photocopying of these eight *Catalysis* articles may be characterized as "archival"—i.e., done for the primary purpose of providing numerous Texaco scientists (for whom Chickering served as an example) each with his or her own personal copy of each article without Texaco's having to purchase another original journal. The photocopying "merely 'supersede[s] the objects' of the original creation," *Campbell,* 510 U.S. at 579 (quoting Folsom v. Marsh, 9 F.Cas. 342, 348 (No. 4,901) (C.C.D.Mass.1841)), and tilts the first fair use factor against Texaco. We do not mean to suggest that no instance of archival copying would be fair use, but the first factor tilts against Texaco in this case because the making of copies to be placed on the shelf in Chickering's office is part of a systematic process of encouraging employee researchers to copy articles so as to multiply available copies while avoiding payment.

Texaco criticizes three aspects of the District Court's analysis of the first factor. Relying largely on the Supreme Court's discussion of fair use in *Sony,* the District Court suggested that a secondary user will "win" this first factor by showing a "transformative (or productive) nonsuperseding use of the original, or [a] noncommercial use, generally for a socially beneficial or widely accepted purpose." 802 F.Supp. at 12. The District Court then concluded that Texaco's copying is "neither transformative nor noncommercial," id. at 13: not transformative because Texaco "simply makes mechanical photocopies of the entirety of relevant articles" and the "primary aspect" of Texaco's photocopying is to multiply copies, see id. at 13–15; and not noncommercial because, though it facilitates research, this research is conducted solely for commercial gain, see id. at 15–16. * * *

1.   *Commercial use.* We generally agree with Texaco's contention that the District Court placed undue emphasis on the fact that Texaco is a for-profit corporation conducting research primarily for commercial gain. Since many, if not most, secondary users seek at least some measure of commercial gain from their use, unduly emphasizing the commercial motivation of a copier will lead to an overly restrictive view of fair use. See *Campbell,* 510 U.S. at 584 * * *. Though the Supreme Court had stated in *Sony* that every commercial use was "presumptively" unfair, see 464 U.S. at 451, that Court and lower courts have come to explain that the commercial nature of a secondary use simply " 'tends to weigh against a finding of fair use.' " *Campbell,* 510 U.S. at 585 (quoting *Harper & Row,* 471 U.S. at 562) * * *.

We do not mean to suggest that the District Court overlooked these principles; in fact, the Court discussed them insightfully, see 802 F.Supp. at 12–13. Rather, our concern here is that the Court let the for-profit nature of Texaco's activity weigh against Texaco without differentiating between a direct commercial use and the more indirect relation to commercial activity that occurred here. Texaco was not gaining direct or immediate commercial advantage from the photocopying at issue in this case—i.e., Texaco's profits, revenues, and overall commercial performance were not tied to its making copies of eight *Catalysis* articles for Chickering. Cf. Basic Books, Inc. v. Kinko's Graphics Corp., 758 F.Supp. 1522 (S.D.N.Y.1991) (revenues of reprographic business stemmed directly from selling unauthorized photocopies of copyrighted books). Rather, Texaco's photocopying served, at most, to facilitate Chickering's research, which in turn might have led to the development of new products and technology that could have improved Texaco's commercial performance. Texaco's photocopying is more appropriately labeled an "intermediate use." See [Sega Enterprises Ltd. v. Accolade, Inc., 977 F.2d 1510, 1522–23 (9th Cir.1992)] (labeling secondary use "intermediate" and finding first factor in favor of for-profit company, even though ultimate purpose of copying was to develop competing commercial product, because immediate purpose of copying computer code was to study idea contained within computer program). * * *

As noted before, in this particular case the link between Texaco's commercial gain and its copying is somewhat attenuated: the copying, at most, merely facilitated Chickering's research that might have led to the production of commercially valuable products. Thus, it would not be accurate to conclude that Texaco's copying of eight particular *Catalysis* articles amounted to "commercial exploitation," especially since the immediate goal of Texaco's copying was to facilitate Chickering's research in the sciences, an objective that might well serve a broader public purpose. See *Twin Peaks,* 996 F.2d at 1375; *Sega Enterprises,* 977 F.2d at 1522. Still, we need not ignore the for-profit nature of Texaco's enterprise, especially since we can confidently conclude that Texaco reaps at least some indirect economic advantage from its photocopying. As the publishers emphasize, Texaco's photocopying for Chickering could be regarded simply as another "factor of production" utilized in Texaco's efforts to develop profitable products. Conceptualized in this way, it is not obvious why it is fair for Texaco to avoid having to pay at least some price to copyright holders for the right to photocopy the original articles.

2. *Transformative Use.* * * *

Texaco suggests that its conversion of the individual *Catalysis* articles through photocopying into a form more easily used in a laboratory might constitute a transformative use. However, Texaco's photocopying merely transforms *the material object* embodying the intangible article that is the copyrighted original work. * * *

Even though Texaco's photocopying is not technically a transformative use of the copyrighted material, we should not overlook the significant independent value that can stem from conversion of original journal articles into a format different from their normal appearance. See generally *Sony,* 464 U.S. at 454, 455 n. 40 (acknowledging possible benefits from copying that might otherwise seem to serve "no productive purpose"); [L. Weinreb, Fair's Fair: A Comment on the Fair Use Doctrine, 103 Harv.L.Rev. 1137, 1143 & n. 29 (1990)] (discussing potential value from nontransformative copying). As previously explained, Texaco's photocopying converts the individual *Catalysis* articles into a useful format. Before modern photocopying, Chickering probably would have converted the original article into a more serviceable form by taking notes, whether cursory or extended;[10] today he can do so with a photocopying machine. Nevertheless, whatever independent value derives from the more usable format of the photocopy does not mean that every instance of photocopying wins on the first factor. In this case, the predominant archival purpose of the copying tips the first factor against the copier, despite the benefit of a more usable format.

notetaking-like use is fair use

3. *Reasonable and Customary Practice.* Texaco contends that Chickering's photocopying constitutes a use that has historically been considered "reasonable and customary." We agree with the District Court that whatever validity this argument might have had before the advent of the photocopying licensing arrangements discussed below in our consideration of the fourth fair use factor, the argument today is insubstantial. As the District Court observed, "To the extent the copying practice was 'reasonable' in 1973 [when *Williams & Wilkins* was decided], it has ceased to be 'reasonable' as the reasons that justified it before [photocopying licensing] have ceased to exist." 802 F.Supp. at 25. * * *

B.   Second Factor: Nature of Copyrighted Work

     * * *

Though a significant measure of creativity was undoubtedly used in the creation of the eight articles copied from *Catalysis,* even a glance at their content immediately reveals the predominantly factual nature of the-

---

[10] In stating that a handwritten copy would have been made, we do not mean to imply that such copying would necessarily have been a fair use. Despite the 1973 dictum in [Williams & Wilkins Co. v. United States, 487 F.2d 1345 (Ct.Cl.1973), aff'd by equally divided Court, 420 U.S. 376 (1975)] asserting that "it is almost unanimously accepted that a scholar can make a handwritten copy of an entire copyrighted article for his own use . . . ," 487 F.2d at 1350, the current edition of the Nimmer treatise reports that "[t]here is no reported case on the question of whether a single handwritten copy of all or substantially all of a book or other protected work made for the copier's own private use is an infringement or fair use." 3 Nimmer on Copyright § 1305[E][4][a], at 13–229

se works. Moreover, though we have previously recognized the importance of strong copyright protection to provide sufficient incentives for the creation of scientific works, see [Weissmann v. Freeman, 868 F.2d 1313, 1325 (2d Cir.1989)], nearly every category of copyrightable works could plausibly assert that broad copyright protection was essential to the continued vitality of that category of works.

Ultimately, then, the manifestly factual character of the eight articles precludes us from considering the articles as "within the core of the copyright's protective purposes," *Campbell*, 510 U.S. at 586; see also *Harper & Row*, 471 U.S. at 563 ("The law generally recognizes a greater need to disseminate factual works than works of fiction or fantasy."). Thus, in agreement with the District Court, we conclude that the second factor favors Texaco.

C.   Third Factor: Amount and Substantiality of Portion Used

The third statutory fair use factor is "the amount and substantiality of the portion used in relation to the copyrighted work as a whole." 17 U.S.C. § 107(3). The District Court concluded that this factor clearly favors the publishers because Texaco copied the eight articles from *Catalysis* in their entirety. * * *

Texaco's suggestion that we consider that it copied only a small percentage of the total compendium of works encompassed within *Catalysis* is superficially intriguing, especially since *Catalysis* is traditionally marketed only as a periodical by issue or volume. However, as the District Court recognized, each of the eight articles in *Catalysis* was separately authored and constitutes a discrete "original work[ ] of authorship," 17 U.S.C. § 102. As we emphasized at the outset, each article enjoys independent copyright protection, which the authors transferred to Academic Press, and what the publishers claim has been infringed is the copyright that subsists in each individual article—not the distinct copyright that may subsist in each journal issue or volume by virtue of the publishers' original compilation of these articles. The only other appellate court to consider the propriety of photocopying articles from journals also recognized that each article constituted an entire work in the fair use analysis. See *Williams & Wilkins*, 487 F.2d at 1353. * * *

Finally, though we are sensitive to Texaco's claim that the third factor serves merely as a proxy for determining whether a secondary use significantly interferes with demand for the original—a concern echoed by some commentators, see William W. Fisher III, Reconstructing the Fair Use Doctrine, 101 Harv.L.Rev. 1661, 1678 (1988) [hereinafter Fisher, *Reconstructing Fair Use*]—we think this factor serves a further end that advances the fair use analysis. Specifically, by focussing on the amount and substantiality of the original work used by the secondary user, we gain insight into the purpose and character of the use as we consider whether the quantity of the material used was "reasonable in relation to the purpose of the copying." See *Campbell*, 510 U.S. at 586. In this case, the fact that Texaco photocopied the eight *Catalysis* articles in their entirety weakens its assertion that the overriding purpose and character of its use was to enable the immediate use of the article in the laboratory and strengthens our view that the predominant purpose and character of the use was to establish a personal library of pertinent articles for Chickering. Cf. id. at 586–87 (intimating that extent of copying can provide insight into primary purpose of copying).

D.   Fourth Factor: Effect Upon Potential Market or Value

　　　* * *

In analyzing the fourth factor, it is important (1) to bear in mind the precise copyrighted works, namely the eight journal articles, and (2) to recognize the distinctive nature and history of "the potential market for or value of" these particular works. Specifically, though there is a traditional market for, and hence a clearly defined value of, *journal issues and volumes,* in the form of per-issue purchases and journal subscriptions, there is neither a traditional market for, nor a clearly defined value of, *individual journal articles.* As a result, analysis of the fourth factor cannot proceed as simply as would have been the case if Texaco had copied a work that carries a stated or negotiated selling price in the market.

Like most authors, writers of journal articles do not directly seek to capture the potential financial rewards that stem from their copyrights by personally marketing copies of their writings. Rather, like other creators of literary works, the author of a journal article "commonly sells his rights to publishers who offer royalties in exchange for their services in producing and marketing the author's work." *Harper & Row,* 471 U.S. at 547. In the distinctive realm of academic and scientific articles, however, the only form of royalty paid by a publisher is often just the reward of being published, publication being a key to professional advancement and prestige for the author, see *Weissmann,* 868 F.2d at 1324 (noting that "in an academic setting, profit is ill-measured in dollars. Instead, what is valuable is recognition because it so often influences professional advancement and academic tenure."). The publishers in turn incur the costs and labor of producing and marketing authors' articles, driven by the prospect of capturing the economic value stemming from the copyrights in the original works, which the authors have transferred to them. Ultimately, the monopoly privileges conferred by copyright protection and the potential financial rewards therefrom are not directly serving to motivate authors to write individual articles; rather, they serve to motivate publishers to produce journals, which provide the conventional and often exclusive means for disseminating these individual articles. It is the prospect of such dissemination that contributes to the motivation of these authors. * * *

　　1.   *Sales of Additional Journal Subscriptions, Back Issues, and Back Volumes.* Since we are concerned with the claim of fair use in copying the eight individual articles from *Catalysis,* the analysis under the fourth factor must focus on the effect of Texaco's photocopying upon the potential market for or value of these individual articles. Yet, in their respective discussions of the fourth statutory factor, the parties initially focus on the impact of Texaco's photocopying of individual journal articles upon the market for *Catalysis* journals through sales of *Catalysis* subscriptions, back issues, or back volumes.

As a general matter, examining the effect on the marketability of the composite work containing a particular individual copyrighted work serves as a useful means to gauge the impact of a secondary use "upon the potential market for or value of" that individual work, since the effect on the marketability of the composite work will frequently be directly relevant to the effect on the market for or value of that individual work. Quite significantly, though, in the unique world of academic and scientific articles, the effect on the marketability of the composite work in which individual articles appear is not obviously related to the effect on the market for or value of the individual articles. Since (1) articles are submitted unsolicited to journals, (2) publishers do not make any payment to authors for the right to publish their articles or to acquire their copyrights, and (3) there is no evidence in the record suggesting that publishers seek to reprint particular articles in new composite works, we cannot readily conclude that evidence concerning the effect of Texaco's use on the marketability of *journals* provides an effective means to appraise the effect of Texaco's use on the market for or value of *individual journal articles.*

These considerations persuade us that evidence concerning the effect of Texaco's photocopying of individual articles within *Catalysis* on the traditional market for *Catalysis* subscriptions is of somewhat limited significance in determining and evaluating the effect of Texaco's photocopying "upon the potential market for or value of" the individual articles. We do not mean to suggest that we believe the effect on the marketability of journal subscriptions is completely irrelevant to gauging the effect on the market for and value of individual articles. Were the publishers able to demonstrate that Texaco's type of photocopying, if widespread, would impair the marketability of journals, then they might have a strong claim under the fourth factor. Likewise, were Texaco able to demonstrate that its type of photocopying, even if widespread, would have virtually no effect on the marketability of journals, then it might have a strong claim under this fourth factor.

On this record, however, the evidence is not resounding for either side. The District Court specifically found that, in the absence of photocopying, (1) "Texaco would not ordinarily fill the need now being supplied by photocopies through the purchase of back issues or back volumes . . . [or] by enormously enlarging the number of its subscriptions," but (2) Texaco still "would increase the number of subscriptions somewhat." 802 F.Supp. at 19. This moderate conclusion concerning the actual effect on the marketability of journals, combined with the uncertain relationship between the market for journals and the market for and value of individual articles, leads us to conclude that the evidence concerning sales of additional journal subscriptions, back issues, and back volumes does not strongly support either side with regard to the fourth factor. * * *

2.   *Licensing Revenues and Fees.* The District Court, however, went beyond discussing the sales of additional journal subscriptions in holding that Texaco's photocopying affected the value of the publishers' copyrights. Specifically, the Court pointed out that, if Texaco's unauthorized photocopying was not permitted as fair use, the publishers' revenues would increase significantly since Texaco would (1) obtain articles from document delivery services (which pay royalties to publishers for the right to photocopy articles), (2) negotiate photocopying licenses directly with individual publishers, and/or (3) acquire some form of photocopying license from the Copyright Clearance Center Inc. ("CCC").[16] See 802 F.Supp. at 19. Texaco claims that the District Court's reasoning is faulty because, in determining that

---

[16] The CCC is a central clearing-house established in 1977 primarily by publishers to license photocopying. The CCC offers a variety of licensing schemes; fees can be paid on a per copy basis or through blanket license arrangements. Most publishers are registered with the CCC, but the participation of for-profit institutions that engage in photocopying has been limited, largely because of uncertainty concerning the legal questions at issue in this lawsuit. The CCC is fully described in the District Court's opinion. 802 F.Supp. at 7–9. A more extended discussion of the formation, development, and effectiveness of the CCC and its licensing schemes is contained in Stanley M. Besen & Sheila Nataraj Kirby, Compensating Creators of Intellectual Property: Collectives that Collect (1989).

the value of the publishers' copyrights was affected, the Court assumed that the publishers were entitled to demand and receive licensing royalties and fees for photocopying. Yet, continues Texaco, whether the publishers can demand a fee for permission to make photocopies is the very question that the fair use trial is supposed to answer.

It is indisputable that, as a general matter, a copyright holder is entitled to demand a royalty for licensing others to use its copyrighted work, see 17 U.S.C. § 106 (copyright owner has exclusive right "to authorize" certain uses), and that the impact on potential licensing revenues is a proper subject for consideration in assessing the fourth factor, see, e.g., *Campbell*, 510 U.S. at 592–93; *Harper & Row*, 471 U.S. at 568–69; * * *.

However, not every effect on potential licensing revenues enters the analysis under the fourth factor.[17] Specifically, courts have recognized limits on the concept of "potential licensing revenues" by considering only traditional, reasonable, or likely to be developed markets when examining and assessing a secondary use's "effect upon the potential market for or value of the copyrighted work." See *Campbell*, 510 U.S. at 592 ("The market for potential derivative uses includes only those that creators of original works would in general develop or license others to develop."); *Harper & Row*, 471 U.S. at 568 (fourth factor concerned with "use that supplants any part of the *normal* market for a copyrighted work") (emphasis added) (quoting S.Rep. No. 473, 94th Cong., 1st Sess. 65 (1975)); * * *.

Though the publishers still have not established a conventional market for the direct sale and distribution of individual articles, they have created, primarily through the CCC, a workable market for institutional users to obtain licenses for the right to produce their own copies of individual articles via photocopying. The District Court found that many major corporations now subscribe to the CCC systems for photocopying licenses. 802 F.Supp. at 25. Indeed, it appears from the pleadings, especially Texaco's counterclaim, that Texaco itself has been paying royalties to the CCC. See Complaint ¶ 38; First Counterclaim ¶ 71. Since the Copyright Act explicitly provides that copyright holders have the "exclusive rights" to "reproduce" and "distribute copies" of their works, see 17 U.S.C. § 106(1) & (3), and since there currently exists a viable market for licensing these rights for individual journal articles, it is appropriate that potential licensing revenues for photocopying be considered in a fair use analysis.

Despite Texaco's claims to the contrary, it is not unsound to conclude that the right to seek payment for a particular use tends to become legally cognizable under the fourth fair use factor when the means for paying for such a use is made easier. This notion is not inherently troubling: it is sen-

---

[17] As Texaco notes and others have recognized, a copyright holder can *always* assert some degree of adverse affect on its potential licensing revenues as a consequence of the secondary use at issue simply because the copyright holder has not been paid a fee to permit that particular use. See Leval, *Toward a Fair Use Standard*, [103 Harv.L.Rev. 1105, 1124 (1990)] ("By definition every fair use involves some loss of royalty revenue because the secondary user has not paid royalties."); Fisher, *Reconstructing Fair Use*, at 1671 (noting that in almost every case "there will be *some* material adverse impact on a 'potential market'" since the secondary user has not paid for the use). Thus, were a court automatically to conclude in every case that potential licensing revenues were impermissibly impaired simply because the secondary user did not pay a fee for the right to engage in the use, the fourth fair use factor would *always* favor the copyright holder. See Leval, *Toward a Fair Use Standard*, at 1125; Fisher, *Reconstructing Fair Use*, at 1672.

For example, the Supreme Court recently explained that because of the "unlikelihood that creators of imaginative works will license critical reviews or lampoons" of their works, "the law recognizes no derivative market for critical works," *Campbell*, 510 U.S. at 592. * * *

sible that a particular unauthorized use should be considered "more fair" when there is no ready market or means to pay for the use, while such an unauthorized use should be considered "less fair" when there is a ready market or means to pay for the use. The vice of circular reasoning arises only if the availability of payment is conclusive against fair use. Whatever the situation may have been previously, before the development of a market for institutional users to obtain licenses to photocopy articles, see *Williams & Wilkins,* 487 F.2d at 1357–59, it is now appropriate to consider the loss of licensing revenues in evaluating "the effect of the use upon the potential market for or value of" journal articles. It is especially appropriate to do so with respect to copying of articles from *Catalysis,* a publication as to which a photocopying license is now available. We do not decide how the fair use balance would be resolved if a photocopying license for *Catalysis* articles were not currently available. * * *

Primarily because of lost licensing revenue, and to a minor extent because of lost subscription revenue, we agree with the District Court that "the publishers have demonstrated a substantial harm to the value of their copyrights through [Texaco's] copying," 802 F.Supp. at 21, and thus conclude that the fourth statutory factor favors the publishers.

E.   Aggregate Assessment

We conclude that three of the four statutory factors, including the important first and the fourth factors, favor the publishers. We recognize that the statutory factors provide a nonexclusive guide to analysis, see *Harper & Row,* 471 U.S. at 560, but to whatever extent more generalized equitable considerations are relevant, we are in agreement with the District Court's analysis of them. See 802 F.Supp. at 21–27. We therefore agree with the District Court's conclusion that Texaco's photocopying of eight particular articles from the *Journal of Catalysis* was not fair use. * * *

Conclusion

The order of the District Court is affirmed.[19]

■ JACOBS, CIRCUIT JUDGE, dissenting:

[Judge Jacobs took a different view of Dr. Chickering's copying, describing it as "integral to ongoing research by a scientist. In my view, all of the statutory factors organize themselves around this fact." Judge Jacobs did not think that Dr. Chickering's status as an employee of a major business corporation should alter the fair use analysis.]

The majority emphasizes *passim* that the photocopying condemned here is "systematic" and "institutional". These terms furnish a ground for distinguishing this case from the case that the majority expressly does not reach: the copying of journal articles by an individual researcher outside an institutional framework. For all the reasons adduced above, I conclude that the institutional environment in which Dr. Chickering works does not alter the character of the copying done by him or at his instance, and that the selection by an individual scientist of the articles useful to that scientist's own inquiries is not systematic copying, and does not become systematic

---

[19] Though neither the limited trial nor this appeal requires consideration of the publishers' remedy if infringement is ultimately found, we note that the context of this dispute appears to make ill-advised an injunction, which, in any event, has not been sought. If the dispute is not now settled, this appears to be an appropriate case for exploration of the possibility of a court-imposed compulsory license. See *Campbell,* 510 U.S. at 578 n. 10; 3 Nimmer on Copyright § 13.05[E][4][e], at 13–241 to 13–242.

because some number of other scientists in the same institution—four hundred or four—are doing the same thing.

[Judge Jacobs also disagreed that the development of licensing mechanisms such as the CCC should tip the balance against fair use.] I do not agree at all that a reasonable and customary use becomes unfair when the copyright holder develops a way to exact an additional price for the same product. * * *

In this case the only harm to a market is to the supposed market in photocopy licenses. The CCC scheme is neither traditional nor reasonable; and its development into a real market is subject to substantial impediments. There is a circularity to the problem: the market will not crystallize unless courts reject the fair use argument that Texaco presents; but, under the statutory test, we cannot declare a use to be an infringement unless (assuming other factors also weigh in favor of the secondary user) there is a market to be harmed. At present, only a fraction of journal publishers have sought to exact these fees. I would hold that this fourth factor decisively weighs in favor of Texaco, because there is no normal market in photocopy licenses, and no real consensus among publishers that there ought to be one.

NOTES AND QUESTIONS

(1) After its defeat in the Second Circuit, Texaco settled, agreeing to a "seven figure" payment as well as retroactive and prospective licensing fees payable through the Copyright Clearance Center. 51 Pat., Tm. & Copyr.J. (BNA) 14 (1995).

Other victories by publishers against business photocopiers include Television Digest, Inc. v. United States Telephone Ass'n, 841 F.Supp. 5 (D.D.C.1993), rejecting a fair use defense by a trade association that was making 12 to 26 extra copies of its $1250 per year subscription to plaintiff's *Communications Daily*, and Pasha Pub., Inc. v. Enmark Gas Corp., 22 U.S.P.Q.2d 1076 (N.D.Tex.1992), entering a consent judgment against a corporate subscriber that supplied its employees with copies of the plaintiff's market newsletter by photocopying and fax. A corporation's systematic posting of a plaintiff's stock market reports on the company's firm-wide intranet—it had paid for a single subscription—was held not a fair use in Lowry's Reports, Inc. v. Legg Mason, Inc., 271 F.Supp.2d 737 (D.Md.2003).[k] The photocopying practices of businesses in the wake of the *Texaco* decision are surveyed in K. Crews, Copyright at a Turning Point: Corporate Responses to the Changing Environment, 3 J.Intell.Prop.L. 277 (1996).

Is the result in *Texaco* applicable to a school or college that furnishes similar photocopying services to its faculty? (Cf. Section I of the Guidelines for Classroom Copying, p. 384 infra.)

(2) Does the court make a convincing case for including potential lost licensing fees for photocopying in its analysis of the fourth fair use factor?

---

[k] See also Washington Bureau Information v. Collier, Shannon & Scott, 42 Pat., Tm. & Copyr.J. (BNA) 619 (E.D.Va.1991), involving a settlement with a law firm for cover-to-cover photocopying of a legal newsletter. Compare Sundeman v. Seajay Soc'y, Inc., 142 F.3d 194 (4th Cir.1998), in which a defendant who sent one photocopy of a deceased author's unpublished manuscript to a literary scholar and another photocopy to a university for an authentication of authorship avoided liability with a fair use defense.

The Second Circuit revisited the relevance of lost licensing fees in Bill Graham Archives v. Dorling Kindersley Ltd., 448 F.3d 605 (2d Cir.2006). The defendant had reproduced in reduced size seven concert posters belonging to the plaintiff in a book about the Grateful Dead. The court first characterized the use as transformative, since the posters were used by the defendant as historical artifacts and not for their original artistic or promotional purposes; it then turned to the effect of the use on the potential market for the works.

"In the instant case, the parties agree that DK's use of the images did not impact BGA's primary market for the sale of the poster images. Instead, we look to whether DK's unauthorized use usurps BGA's potential to develop a derivative market. Appellant argues that DK interfered with the market for licensing its images for use in books.

" * * * [W]e do not find a harm to BGA's licensing market merely because DK did not pay a fee for BGA's copyrighted images.

"Instead, we look at the impact on potential licensing revenues for 'traditional, reasonable, or likely to be developed markets.' Texaco, 60 F.3d at 930. In order to establish a traditional license market, Appellant points to the fees paid to other copyright owners for the reproduction of their images in Illustrated Trip. Moreover, Appellant asserts that it established a market for licensing its images, and in this case expressed a willingness to license images to DK. Neither of these arguments shows impairment to a traditional, as opposed to a transformative market. * * *

"Here, unlike in Texaco, we hold that DK's use of BGA's images is transformatively different from their original expressive purpose. In a case such as this, a copyright holder cannot prevent others from entering fair use markets merely 'by developing or licensing a market for parody, news reporting, educational or other transformative uses of its own creative work.' [Castle Rock Ent., Inc. v. Carol Pub. Group, 150 F.3d 132, 146 n. 18 (2d Cir.1998).] '[C]opyright owners may not preempt exploitation of transformative markets . . . .' Id. * * * Since DK's use of BGA's images falls within a transformative market, BGA does not suffer market harm due to the loss of license fees." The court affirmed the defendant's summary judgment.

W. Gordon, Fair Use Markets: On Weighing Potential License Fees, 79 Geo.Wash.L.Rev. 1814 (2011), offers a model for determining when lost licensing revenues should be considered in the fair use calculus. S. Stadler, Relevant Markets for Copyrighted Works, 34 J.Corp.L. 1059 (2009), suggests borrowing the idea of a "relevant market" from antitrust law to help define the appropriate reach of a copyright owner's economic rights.

(3) Judge Newman in Texaco distinguished Williams & Wilkins Co. v. United States, 487 F.2d 1345 (Ct.Cl.1973)—for many years the principal precedent on photocopying. That case involved substantial copying of medical journals by two government libraries. The library at the National Institutes of Health, the Government's principal medical research organization, subscribed to about 3,000 medical journals. NIH researchers could obtain photocopies of articles from the journals in the library's collection. In a typical year it photocopied over 93,000 articles. The National Medical Library, a repository of much of the world's medical literature, cooperated with other libraries in an interlibrary loan program. Upon request, it would provide a photocopy of a journal article; in a representative year, 120,000 photocopied articles were distributed. Reversing the trial court's finding of infringement, the Court of Claims decided, 4–3, that the photocopying was fair use. "Thus, the balance of risks is definitely on defendant's side—until Congress acts more specifically, the burden on medical science of a holding that the photocopying is an infringement would appear to be much greater than the present or foreseeable burden on plaintiff and other medical publishers of a ruling that these practices fall within 'fair use.' " Has the subsequent development of licensing mechanisms such as the CCC now altered this balance? The court rejected the plaintiff's argument that its willingness to license the copying for a reasonable royalty undermined the claim of fair use. "Our difficulty with that response—in addition to the absence of proof that plaintiff has yet been hurt, and the twin doubts whether plaintiff has a viable license system and whether any satisfactory program can be created without legislation—is that the 1909 Act does not provide for compulsory licensing in this field."

The decision in the Court of Claims was affirmed without opinion by an equally-divided Supreme Court. 420 U.S. 376 (1975). Thus, of the sixteen judges who considered the case, eight thought that the use was fair and eight thought that it was infringing.

(4) The Copyright Clearance Center described in the *Texaco* case is a private, non-profit organization founded in 1978 that offers centralized licensing and collection services for photocopying and electronic dissemination. Publishers who register works with the CCC grant users such as corporations advance permission to copy registered titles. Fees are set by the individual publishers. Royalties paid to the CCC are distributed to the copyright owners; authors' shares depend on their individual publishing contracts. The CCC distributed $179 million to owners in 2012. Cooperation between the CCC and other Reproduction Rights Organizations abroad provides a degree of international enforcement.

The CCC represents thousands of publishers and licenses millions of works. Licenses from the CCC were initially available only on a transactional basis that required detailed records of copying activity. To minimize administrative costs, the CCC later inaugurated an annual blanket copying license available for a fee determined by factors such as the size of the user and the copying practices of the particular industry. More than 35,000 companies are said to have licenses from the CCC.[1]

———————

PROBLEM: Under its Google Library Project, Google made agreements to scan the contents of several major libraries, including the libraries at Harvard University, Stanford University, the University of Michigan, the New York Public Library, and the Bodleian Library at Oxford University. Google's aim is to create a comprehensive searchable text database accessible by the public over the Internet. In order to achieve that goal, Google intends to archive a digital copy of every published work. For public domain works, the entire work would be viewable by searchers. For copyrighted works, search results would be limited to fragments of text surrounding the search terms, with limits on repeated searches. The majority of copyrighted works are now out of print and thus effectively unavailable to potential users. In a concession to publishers, Google offered to allow any copyright owner to "opt out" of the database. The Authors Guild and several large

———————

[1] Information about the CCC is available on its website at www.copyright.com.

publishing companies filed suits claiming that the initiative amounted to copyright infringement on a massive scale. Google responded that its scanning, storage, and searching are in the public interest and a fair use. Would the search results displayed for copyrighted works constitute a fair use? Is the wholesale copying necessary to create the searchable database a fair use? Does it matter whether Google generates substantial advertising revenue from the search site?

The parties attempted to settle their lawsuit. Under a proposed agreement, users of the Google Library Project could preview up to 20 per cent of the pages in copyrighted books that are out of print unless the owner opted out. For books still being published, no portion of the book would be available online unless the owner opted in. Books no longer under copyright would be available for free in their entirety. Google could also sell subscriptions offering full online access. Google would retain 37 per cent of the sales and advertising revenue, with the rest going to the publishers and authors. Google also said it would finance a Book Rights Registry that would collect and distribute the funds, and it offered to pay $45 million as compensation for digitizing books for the Library Project. After considering objections from the Department of Justice, foreign governments, competitors of Google and others, Judge Chin refused to approve the 166–page proposed settlement. Authors Guild v. Google, Inc., 770 F.Supp.2d 666 (S.D.N.Y.2011). The Justice Department had argued that the opt-out structure of the settlement could effectively give Google a monopoly over the exploitation of works whose owners could not be found; foreign governments were concerned that the settlement could affect works owned by their citizens in a manner that was inconsistent with international law. Judge Chin was also concerned with the appropriate scope of judicial power: "The questions of who should be entrusted with guardianship over orphan books, under what terms, and with what safeguards are matters more appropriately decided by Congress than through an agreement among private, self-interested parties." He ended with a suggestion: "As the United States and other objectors have noted, many of the concerns raised in the objections would be ameliorated if the ASA were converted from an 'opt-out' settlement to an 'opt-in' settlement."

After seven years of litigation, the publishers finally reached a private settlement with Google that allows individual publishers to choose whether to participate in the Library Project. The settlement did not address orphan works, and apparently neither party retreated from its position on the fair use issue. 84 Pat., Tm. & Copyr.J. (BNA) 989 (2012). The class action suit brought by authors claiming that the Google Library Project infringes rights retained by authors is continuing.

In addition to their suit against Google, authors' groups filed suit in 2011 against several university libraries that are participating in the Google Library Project. Google provides each library with a digital copy of every book that it scans from the library's collection. The universities contributed those copies to the HathiTrust Digital Library. The Trust allows users to search the digital copies for particular search terms. For works under copyright, the search returns only the name and page numbers of the works on which the search term appears. No actual text is revealed. The Trust also allows full access to the works in audibly or tactilely accessible formats to users with certified print disabilities. The Trust also planned to allow full access to orphan works, that is, to works whose owners could not be found. The parties moved for summary judgment. Are any or all of these users protected by fair use? Judge Baer in Authors Guild, Inc. v. HathiTrust, 2012 WL 4808939 (S.D.N.Y.2012), first held that the associational plaintiffs lacked standing to assert the rights of their individual members. He also held that claims relating to the use of orphan works were not ripe for adjudication. As for the other uses, the court held that they were transformative. "[T]he copies serve an entirely different purpose than the original works: the purpose is superior search capabilities rather than access to copyrighted material." Use to provide access to the disabled was also transformative, since that was not an intended use of the original works. Copying of the entire works was necessary to facilitate both uses. The plaintiffs alleged harm to their emerging licensing opportunities, but Judge Baer, citing Bill Graham Archives v. Dorling Kindersley, p. 380 supra, held that harm to transformative markets does not weigh against fair use. Participation of the universities in the activities of the Trust was thus protected under the fair use doctrine. The plaintiffs have filed an appeal.

The Google litigation attracted substantial academic interest. On the merits of Google's fair use argument, see S. Hetcher, The Half–Fairness of Google's Plan to Make the World's Collection of Books Searchable, 13 Mich.Telecomm. & Tech.L.Rev. 1 (2006) (questioning the fair use defense with respect to works whose owners are identifiable); O. Bracha, Standing Copyright Law on Its Head? The Googlization of Everything and the Many Faces of Property, 85 Tex.L.Rev. 1799 (2007), argues that opt-out mechanisms like the one proposed by Google are crucial to the efficient development of a digital information society; L. Mtima and S. Jamar, Fulfilling the Copyright Social Justice Promise: Digitizing Textual Information, 55 N.Y.L.S.L.Rev. 77 (2010/11), concludes that the Google Library Project would further copyright's central purpose of advancing knowledge and culture. Some commentators urge favored treatment for digital archivers. See F. Pasquale, Copyright in an Era of Information Overload: Toward the Privileging of Categorizers, 60 Vand.L.Rev. 135 (2007), proposing to recognize the special contributions of "categorizers" as part of the first fair use factor; M. Sag, Copyright and Copy–Reliant Technology, 103 Nw.U.L.Rev. 1607 (2009), arguing against liability for technologies like search engines and archives that copy works but do not communicate them to the public.

CLASSROOM COPYING

The ease with which teachers can reproduce multiple copies of material for classroom use has created strong pressure from educators to condone such copying. Opposed to them are trade publishers and authors, especially publishers of textbooks and other teaching materials. Educators supporting extensive fair use or specific exemptions for classroom photocopying weighed in late but vigorously in the copyright revision process. The House Committee in 1976 added two phrases to § 107: in the first sentence, the phrase "(including multiple copies for classroom use)" was added to the list of examples of possible fair use; in the first of the four factors, the reference to "nonprofit educational purposes" was appended. It also added the limitation on the liability of teachers for statutory damages in § 504(c)(2). The following excerpt from the House Report deals with the issue of reproduction for classroom use.

HOUSE REPORT, PP. 66–72

Intention as to classroom reproduction

Although the works and uses to which the doctrine of fair use is applicable are as broad as the copyright law itself, most of the discussion of section 107 has centered around questions of classroom reproduction, particularly photocopying. * * *

At the Judiciary Subcommittee hearings in June 1975, Chairman Kastenmeier and other members urged the parties to meet together independently in an effort to achieve a meeting of the minds as to permissible educational uses of copyrighted material. The response to these suggestions was positive, and a number of meetings of three groups, dealing respectively with classroom reproduction of printed material, music, and audio-visual material, were held beginning in September 1975.

In a joint letter to Chairman Kastenmeier, dated March 19, 1976, the representatives of the Ad Hoc Committee of Educational Institutions and Organizations on Copyright Law Revision, and of the Authors League of America, Inc., and the Association of American Publishers, Inc., stated:

> You may remember that in our letter of March 8, 1976 we told you that the negotiating teams representing authors and publishers and the Ad Hoc Group had reached tentative agreement on guidelines to insert in the Committee Report covering educational copying from books and periodicals under Section 107 of H.R. 2223 and S. 22, and that as part of that tentative agreement each side would accept the amendments to Sections 107 and 504 which were adopted by your Subcommittee on March 3, 1976.

> We are now happy to tell you that the agreement has been approved by the principals and we enclose a copy herewith. We had originally intended to translate the agreement into language suitable for inclusion in the legislative report dealing with Section 107, but we have since been advised by committee staff that this will not be necessary.

> As stated above, the agreement refers only to copying from books and periodicals, and it is not intended to apply to musical or audiovisual works.

The full text of the agreement is as follows:

AGREEMENT ON GUIDELINES FOR CLASSROOM COPYING IN NOT–
FOR–PROFIT EDUCATIONAL INSTITUTIONS

WITH RESPECT TO BOOKS AND PERIODICALS

The purpose of the following guidelines is to state the minimum and not the maximum standards of educational fair use under Section 107 of H.R. 2223. The parties agree that the conditions determining the extent of permissible copying for educational purposes may change in the future; that certain types of copying permitted under these guidelines may not be permissible in the future; and conversely that in the future other types of copying not permitted under these guidelines may be permissible under revised guidelines.

Moreover, the following statement of guidelines is not intended to limit the types of copying permitted under the standards of fair use under judicial decision and which are stated in Section 107 of the Copyright Revision Bill. There may be instances in which copying which does not fall within the guidelines stated below may nonetheless be permitted under the criteria of fair use.

GUIDELINES

I. *Single Copying for Teachers*

A single copy may be made of any of the following by or for a teacher at his or her individual request for his or her scholarly research or use in teaching or preparation to teach a class:

    A.   A chapter from a book;

    B.   An article from a periodical or newspaper;

    C.   A short story, short essay or short poem, whether or not from a collective work;

    D.   A chart, graph, diagram, drawing, cartoon or picture from a book, periodical, or newspaper.

II. *Multiple Copies for Classroom Use*

Multiple copies (not to exceed in any event more than one copy per pupil in a course) may be made by or for the teacher giving the course for classroom use or discussion; *provided that:*

    A.   The copying meets the tests of brevity and spontaneity as defined below; *and,*

    B.   Meets the cumulative effect test as defined below; *and,*

    C.   Each copy includes a notice of copyright.

Definitions

Brevity

(*i*) Poetry: (a) A complete poem if less than 250 words and if printed on not more than two pages or (b) from a longer poem, an excerpt of not more than 250 words.

(*ii*) Prose: (a) Either a complete article, story or essay of less than 2,500 words, or (b) an excerpt from any prose work of not more than 1,000 words or 10% of the work, whichever is less, but in any event a minimum of 500 words.

[Each of the numerical limits stated in "i" and "ii" above may be expanded to permit the completion of an unfinished line of a poem or of an unfinished prose paragraph.]

(*iii*) Illustration: One chart, graph, diagram, drawing, cartoon or picture per book or per periodical issue.

(*iv*) "Special" works: Certain works in poetry, prose or in "poetic prose" which often combine language with illustrations and which are intended sometimes for children and at other times for a more general audience fall short of 2,500 words in their entirety. Paragraph "ii" above notwithstanding such "special works" may not be reproduced in their entirety; however, an excerpt comprising not more than two of the published pages of such special work and containing not more than 10% of the words found in the text thereof, may be reproduced.

Spontaneity

(*i*) The copying is at the instance and inspiration of the individual teacher, and

(*ii*) The inspiration and decision to use the work and the moment of its use for maximum teaching effectiveness are so close in time that it would be unreasonable to expect a timely reply to a request for permission.

Cumulative Effect

(*i*) The copying of the material is for only one course in the school in which the copies are made.

(*ii*) Not more than one short poem, article, story, essay or two excerpts may be copied from the same author, nor more than three from the same collective work or periodical volume during one class term.

(*iii*) There shall not be more than nine instances of such multiple copying for one course during one class term.

[The limitations stated in "ii" and "iii" above shall not apply to current news periodicals and newspapers and current news sections of other periodicals.]

III. *Prohibitions as to I and II Above*

Notwithstanding any of the above, the following shall be prohibited:

(A) Copying shall not be used to create or to replace or substitute for anthologies, compilations or collective works. Such replacement or substitution may occur whether copies of various works or excerpts therefrom are accumulated or reproduced and used separately.

(B) There shall be no copying of or from works intended to be "consumable" in the course of study or of teaching. These include workbooks, exercises, standardized tests and test booklets and answer sheets and like consumable material.

(C) Copying shall not:

(a) substitute for the purchase of books, publishers' reprints or periodicals;

(b) be directed by higher authority;

(c) be repeated with respect to the same item by the same teacher from term to term.

(D) No charge shall be made to the student beyond the actual cost of the photocopying.

Agreed March 19, 1976.

Ad Hoc Committee on Copyright Law Revision:

By Sheldon Elliott Steinbach.

Author–Publisher Group:
Authors League of America:

By IRWIN KARP, *Counsel.*

Association of American Publishers, Inc.:

By ALEXANDER C. HOFFMAN,
Chairman, Copyright Committee.

* * *

The Committee appreciates and commends the efforts and the cooperative and reasonable spirit of the parties who achieved the agreed guidelines on books and periodicals and on music. Representatives of the American Association of University Professors and of the Association of American Law Schools have written to the Committee strongly criticizing the guidelines, particularly with respect to multiple copying, as being too restrictive with respect to classroom situations at the university and graduate level. However, the Committee notes that the Ad Hoc group did include representatives of higher education, that the stated "purpose of the . . . guidelines is to state the minimum and not the maximum standards of educational fair use" and that the agreement acknowledges "there may be instances in which copying which does not fall within the guidelines . . . may nonetheless be permitted under the criteria of fair use."

The Committee believes the guidelines are a reasonable interpretation of the minimum standards of fair use. Teachers will know that copying within the guidelines is fair use. * * *

NOTES ON CLASSROOM COPYING

(1) The House Report also contains "Guidelines for Educational Uses of Music," developed by representatives of music publishers, schools, and teachers. (H.R.Rep. pp. 70–71.)

(2) In the next-to-last paragraph of the House statement, reference is made to the dissatisfaction of the American Association of University Professors and the Association of American Law Schools. Their concern that the Guidelines were too restrictive and might be misunderstood seemed warranted when after passage of the 1976 Act they were journalistically presented as "Do's and Don'ts," for example in the widely read *Chronicle of Higher Education*. This elicited the following response from representatives of educational organizations:

> The guidelines to which your article refers were signed by representatives of publishers and some education associations and were designed as an unofficial understanding of the *minimum* reach of the fair use doctrine in the context of copying for classroom teaching purposes. They are not part of the statute enacted by Congress, although they were inserted in the House and conference committee reports of the bill and referred to as a reasonable interpretation of fair use by both committees. * * *

> Perhaps some of this confusion is engendered by your apparent assumption that whatever the guidelines do not expressly permit is therefore prohibited. The guidelines themselves, the committee reports, and the floor debates all emphasize that the guidelines are a statement of the minimum scope of the fair use doctrine. They are intended as a "safe harbor,"

assuring the teacher who stays within their scope that he or she will not be liable for infringement. * * *

(Chronicle of Higher Education, Nov. 15, 1976.)

(3) Think about the copying practices at your law school. Do they comport with the statute and its legislative history? Congressman Drinan (formerly Dean of the Boston College Law School), during the House debate on the revision bill, quoted a statement from the Association of American Law Schools:

> Requiring a law school teacher to meet all three tests of brevity, spontaneity and cumulative effect stifles the use of copyrighted material for classroom purposes. The realities of classroom teaching and the economics of our students are such that they cannot purchase or pay royalties on works other than the standard text and case books that are used as the major resources in classroom teaching. Thus the teacher's choice is not between purchasing and copying; it is between copying and not using. (122 Cong.Rec. 31986 (1976))

D. Gerhardt and M. Wessel, Fair Use and Fairness on Campus, 11 N.C.J.L. & Tech. 461 (2010), emphasizes the importance of a robust fair use doctrine in higher education. Is there anything about copyright, unlike computers or photocopier supplies, that marks it for compulsory contributions at one extreme to school districts in economically depressed communities and at the other to the education of professionals whose earning prospects may exceed those of many authors?

(4) The first major precedent on classroom photocopying was Basic Books, Inc. v. Kinko's Graphics Corp., 758 F.Supp. 1522 (S.D.N.Y.1991), resulting from an ambitious attack by a coalition of publishers against the "Professor Publishing" service offered by Kinko's, a nationwide chain with hundreds of photocopying centers. The suit challenged Kinko's production and sale of photocopied course packets. (Among the examples cited was a 388–page anthology for a social science course that contained material copied from 25 books, including excerpts ranging from 14 to 53 pages taken from six books published by the plaintiffs.) The court doubted whether Kinko's, as a for-profit copier, could claim protection under the Classroom Guidelines (cf. Section III(D) of the Guidelines), but found in any event that the Guidelines had been exceeded. The court rejected Kinko's fair use defense, finding the copying to be commercial, substantial, and damaging to the copyright owners' market. Plaintiffs got a $510,000 judgment and an injunction; a later settlement added $1.6 million in legal fees.

Princeton Univ. Press v. Michigan Document Service

99 F.3d 1381 (6th Cir.1996), cert. denied, 520 U.S. 1156 (1997).

Defendant MDS is a commercial photocopying shop that produced and sold "coursepacks" at the request of professors teaching classes at the University of Michigan. MDS president James Smith, after consulting an attorney and reading what he could find on copyright law at the University of Michigan Law Library, concluded that the *Kinko's* decision was wrong; unlike most of its competitors, MDS did not seek or pay for permission to copy. The coursepacks at issue contained excerpts from the plaintiffs' copyrighted books. The excerpts ranged from 17 to 95 pages in length, the latter comprising 30 per cent of Princeton Professor Nancy Weiss' *Farewell to the*

Party of Lincoln: Black Politics in the Age of FDR. The plaintiffs got a summary judgment when the district court rejected the defendant's fair use argument.

MDS won a surprising although temporary victory when the Sixth Circuit in a 2–1 decision reversed the district court and ordered summary judgment for the defendant. 74 F.3d 1512 (6th Cir.1996) (opinion withdrawn). Judge Ryan rejected the publishers' attempt to invoke the Guidelines on Classroom Copying, holding that the four statutory fair use factors were "unambiguous," thus precluding resort to legislative history. Evaluating the "purpose and character of the use," the court refused to focus solely on the defendant's reproduction; the ultimate educational use by the students was also relevant. On the substantiality of the copying, Judge Ryan argued that even with respect to the 95–page excerpt, there was no evidence that the copying "extracted the heart of the work." [How incompetent must a professor be to extract 95 pages and fail to get the "heart" of a book?] On the fourth factor, there was no evidence of damage to the market for the original works, according to the court, since the professors had signed declarations stating that they would not have assigned the entire books. As for lost permission fees, the court rejected the Second Circuit's position in *Texaco,* concluding "[i]t is circular to argue that a use is unfair, and a fee therefore required, on the basis that the publisher is otherwise deprived a fee."

The Sixth Circuit voted for a rehearing *en banc,* vacating the panel decision in favor of MDS. After the rehearing, the court in an 8–5 decision affirmed the district court's summary judgment against the defendant (but remanded for reconsideration of damages, finding that the defendant's infringement had not been willful.) Judge Nelson, after stating the facts, began with a consideration of the fourth fair use factor.

"The burden of proof as to market effect rests with the copyright holder if the challenged use is of a 'noncommercial' nature. The alleged infringer has the burden, on the other hand, if the challenged use is 'commercial' in nature. Sony Corp. v. Universal City Studios, Inc., 464 U.S. 417, 451 (1984). In the case at bar the defendants argue that the burden of proof rests with the publishers because the use being challenged is 'noncommercial.' We disagree.

"It is true that the use to which the materials are put by the students who purchase the coursepacks is noncommercial in nature. But the use of the materials by the students is not the use that the publishers are challenging. What the publishers are challenging is the duplication of copyrighted materials for sale by a for-profit corporation that has decided to maximize its profits—and give itself a competitive edge over other copyshops—by declining to pay the royalties requested by the holders of the copyrights. * * *

"As noted above, most of the copyshops that compete with MDS in the sale of coursepacks pay permission fees for the privilege of duplicating and selling excerpts from copyrighted works. The three plaintiffs together have been collecting permission fees at a rate approaching $500,000 a year. If copyshops across the nation were to start doing what the defendants have been doing here, this revenue stream would shrivel and the potential value of the copyrighted works of scholarship published by the plaintiffs would be diminished accordingly.

"The defendants contend that it is circular to assume that a copyright holder is entitled to permission fees and then to measure market loss by reference to the lost fees. * * *

"Where * * * the copyright holder clearly does have an interest in exploiting a licensing market—and especially where the copyright holder has actually succeeded in doing so—'it is appropriate that potential licensing revenues for photocopying be considered in a fair use analysis.' American Geophysical, 60 F.3d at 930. * * *

"As to 'the purpose and character of the use, including whether such use is of a commercial nature or is for nonprofit educational purposes,' 17 U.S.C. § 107(1), we have already explained our reasons for concluding that the challenged use is of a commercial nature.

"The defendants argue that the copying at issue here would be considered 'nonprofit educational' if done by the students or professors themselves. The defendants also note that they can profitably produce multiple copies for less than it would cost the professors or the students to make the same number of copies. Most of the copyshops with which the defendants compete have been paying permission fees, however, and we assume that these shops too can perform the copying on a more cost-effective basis than the professors or students can. This strikes us as a more significant datum than the ability of a black market copyshop to beat the do-it-yourself cost.

"As to the proposition that it would be fair use for the students or professors to make their own copies, the issue is by no means free from doubt. We need not decide this question, however, for the fact is that the copying complained of here was performed on a profit-making basis by a commercial enterprise. And '[t]he courts have . . . properly rejected attempts by for-profit users to stand in the shoes of their customers making nonprofit or noncommercial uses.' Patry, Fair Use in Copyright Law, at 420 n. 34. As the House Judiciary Committee stated in its report on the 1976 legislation,

> '[I]t would not be possible for a non-profit institution, by means of contractual arrangements with a commercial copying enterprise, to authorize the enterprise to carry out copying and distribution functions that would be exempt if conducted by the non-profit institution itself.' H.R.Rep. No. 1476, 94th Cong., 2d Sess. at 74 (1976), U.S.Code Cong. & Admin.News 5659, 5687–88."

After citing J. Litman, Copyright, Compromise, and Legislative History, 72 Cornell L.Rev. 857 (1987), for its description of the private negotiations that shaped the drafting of the 1976 Act, the court concluded that it was appropriate to consider the Guidelines for Classroom Copying.

"In its systematic and premeditated character, its magnitude, its anthological content, and its commercial motivation, the copying done by MDS goes well beyond anything envisioned by the Congress that chose to incorporate the guidelines in the legislative history. Although the guidelines do not purport to be a complete and definitive statement of fair use law for educational copying, and although they do not have the force of law, they do provide us general guidance. The fact that the MDS copying is light years away from the safe harbor of the guidelines weighs against a finding of fair use.

"Although the Congress that passed the Copyright Act in 1976 would pretty clearly have thought it unfair for a commercial copyshop to appropriate as much as 30 percent of a copyrighted work without paying the license fee demanded by the copyright holder, the changes in technology and teaching practices that have occurred over the last two decades might conceivably make Congress more sympathetic to the defendants' position today. If the law on this point is to be changed, however, we think the change should be made by Congress and not by the courts. * * *

"The defendants attach considerable weight to the assertions of numerous academic authors that they do not write primarily for money and that they want their published writings to be freely copyable. The defendants suggest that unlicensed copying will 'stimulate artistic creativity for the general public good.'

"This suggestion would be more persuasive if the record did not demonstrate that licensing income is significant to the publishers. It is the publishers who hold the copyrights, of course—and the publishers obviously need economic incentives to publish scholarly works, even if the scholars do not need direct economic incentives to write such works."

There were three separate dissenting opinions. Each argued that it was wrong to take account of potential licensing fees for photocopying in judging the economic effect of the copying. Judge Martin raised another objection. "That the majority lends significance to the identity of the person operating the photocopier is a profound indication that its approach is misguided. Given the focus of the Copyright Act, the only practical difference between this case and that of a student making his or her own copies is that commercial photocopying is faster and more cost-effective." That theme was also pursued in a dissent by Judge Merritt. "There is nothing in the statute that distinguishes between copies made for students by a third person who charges a fee for their labor and copies made by students themselves who pay a fee only for use of the copy machines. Our political economy generally encourages the division and specialization of labor. There is no reason why in this instance the law should discourage high schools, colleges, students and professors from hiring the labor of others to make their copies any more than there is a reason to discourage lawyers from hiring paralegals to make copies for clients and courts. The Court's distinction in this case based on the division of labor—who does the copying—is short sighted and unsound economically." Judge Ryan dissented in an opinion that reiterated his argument in the vacated panel decision.

NOTES AND QUESTIONS

(1) In Blackwell Pub., Inc. v. Excel Research Group, LLC, 661 F.Supp.2d 786 (E.D.Mich.2009), a group of publishers won a summary judgment against a photocopy shop that kept master copies of assigned course-packs and gave them to student customers who then made a copy using the defendant's photocopy machines. "At bottom, the case is not seriously distinguishable from [Princeton Univ. Press v. Michigan Document Service]. The fact that the students push a button on a copier in the manner described is of no significance. * * * Simply put, copyright law should not turn on who presses the start button on a copier. Excel's actions violate the publishers' copyrights."

(2) Professor Jones announces in her American History 201 course that the assignment for the following week is pages 110 to 205 in *Farewell to the Party of Lincoln: Black Politics in the Age of FDR*. Professor Jones informs the students that the book is available at the University Bookstore for $16.95; she also tells them that several copies are on reserve at the library. Student A checks out a copy from the reserve desk, buys a $10 copycard for use in the library's

photocopier, and spends $9.50 making a photocopy of the required pages. Student B checks out the book, takes it across the street to a commercial copyshop, and has the pages copied for $4.75 plus tax. Is A or B liable for copyright infringement? Should the answer, as the dissenters argue, determine the liability of the commercial copyshop used by B? (Would the fair use analysis be altered if the copying consisted, not of readings assigned for class, but of research materials collected by an individual student for a term paper?)

(3) Should electronic distribution of works to students be judged by the same standards as photocopies? In Cambridge University Press v. Becker, 863 F.Supp.2d 1190 (N.D.Ga.2012), a group of publishers filed suit seeking an injunction against officials at Georgia State University in connection with excerpts of works placed on electronic reserve by faculty members. The excepts had been assigned as supplemental readings in various courses and placed on a password-protected system available only to the students in each course. A university policy required faculty members to consider the four fair use factors before submitting materials for posting. Judge Evans distinguished the *Kinko's* and *Princeton University Press* cases, saying that they involved commercial copiers; *Texaco* was also distinguished because the defendant there was a profit-making company. According to the court, the first fair use factor weighed in favor of the defendants because the use was for a non-profit educational purpose. The second factor also favored the defendants since the works were factual materials intended to inform and educate. On the third factor, although the copying exceeded the Guidelines for Classroom Copying, Judge Evans emphasized that the Guidelines were intended to state minimum and not maximum standards for copying. The court thought that copying one chapter or ten per cent of a work would generally be fair use. The excepts were sufficiently small that there was no evidence of harm to books sales under the fourth factor. Lost copying royalties were potentially relevant, but only if there was evidence that the works had been made available for licensing through the Copyright Clearance Center. Applying the analysis to the electronic excepts at issue, Judge Evans found only 5 of 75 were infringing. The publishers have appealed.

(4) In response to the *Kinko's* case, the Copyright Clearance Center established a licensing service that covers course packs, class handouts, and electronic reserves. The *Kinko's* and *Princeton Univ. Press* cases are analyzed in the course of an impassioned plea for greater educational fair use in A. Bartow, Educational Fair Use in Copyright: Reclaiming the Right to Photocopy Freely, 60 U.Pitt.L.Rev. 149 (1998).

(5) A Conference on Fair Use (CONFU) was organized to bring together copyright owners and academic users in an effort to produce guidelines for the fair use of copyrighted works in digital form. CONFU released an interim report in 1996. The report contained three sets of proposed guidelines covering the creation of digital collections of visual images, the use of copyrighted works in live interactive and recorded distance learning transmissions, and the use of copyrighted works in multimedia projects by students and teachers. The proposed guidelines are reproduced in Growing Pains: Adapting Copyright for Libraries, Education, and Society (L. Gasaway ed. 1997). However, by the time the final CONFU Report was submitted in 1998, none of the proposed guidelines had attracted sufficient support to justify formal adoption. The general utility of fair use "guidelines" is questioned in K. Crews, The Law of Fair Use and the Illusion of Fair–Use Guidelines, 62 Ohio St.L.J. 599 (2001); the use of "best practices" statements to inform fair use analysis is similarly questioned in J.

Rothman, Best Intentions: Reconsidering Best Practices Statements in the Context of Fair Use and Copyright Law, 57 J.Copyr. Soc'y 371 (2010).

LIBRARY COPYING—§ 108

According to Thomas Brennan, Chief Counsel to the Senate Subcommittee on Patents, Trademarks and Copyrights during the copyright revision process, "Next to cable television, the most interesting legislative controversy focused on the library photocopying provisions of the bill." Some Observations on the Revision of the Copyright Law From the Legislative Point of View, 24 Bull.Copyr. Soc'y 151, 156 (1977). The debate produced the intricate compromise embodied in § 108.

Initially, note that the § 108 exemptions for library copying do not extend to every entity that may style itself a "library or archives." The requirement in § 108(a) that the library must be open to the public or to researchers in a specialized field will eliminate many corporate and commercial collections; the House Report notes, however, that the prohibition against reproduction for "direct or indirect commercial advantage" refers to "the immediate commercial motivation behind the reproduction or distribution itself, rather than to the ultimate profit-making motivation behind the enterprise in which the library is located." H.R.Rep. p. 75.

Sections 108(b) and (c) govern copying for purposes such as preservation or replacement, with the exemption for copying published works subject to the requirement "that an unused replacement cannot be obtained at a fair price." A 1998 amendment allows the preservation and replacement copies to be made in digital form. A more expansive exemption applies under § 108(h) to works in the final 20 years of the copyright term, part of a compromise adopted when the duration of copyright was extended in 1998.

Copying at user request is subject to the limitations in subsections 108(d) and (e), the former for articles or small portions of copyrighted works, the latter for more extensive copying. (The warning notice required by both provisions is specified in 37 C.F.R. § 201.14.) Copying under these subsections is limited to certain materials, § 108(i), and the copies must become the property of the user. Note that the exemption from liability in subsection (d) runs to the library, not to the user. § 108(f)(2). The library is also relieved of liability for the unsupervised use of copying equipment located on its premises. § 108(f)(1). Again, the statute requires a warning notice—the Copyright Office Regulations do not specify its form. (Under what theory could such liability be imposed in the absence of a warning notice? Contributory infringement? Vicarious liability? See p. 403 infra.) Section 108(f)(4) assures us that the library exemptions do not preclude reliance on the general right of fair use. (Is copying that exceeds the limits of § 108 likely to be characterized as "fair use" under § 107?)

The heart of § 108 is subsection (g). "Isolated and unrelated" reproduction of a single copy of the same material on separate occasions is permitted, but "related or concerted" reproduction of the same material is not. The latter extends to "related" requests by members of a group. The Senate Report offers the example of students each requesting a separate copy of an article assigned by a college professor.[m] For materials described in § 108(d), chiefly articles from periodicals and journals, there is a further prohibition

---

[m] S.Rep. No. 94–473, 94th Cong., 1st Sess. 70 (1975).

against "systematic" copying. § 108(g)(2). This provision, as it came from the Senate to the House in 1976, "provoked a storm of controversy, centering around the extent to which the restrictions on 'systematic' activities would prevent the continuation and development of interlibrary networks and other arrangements involving the exchange of photocopies." H.R.Rep. pp. 77–78. When is copying "systematic"? Does the term imply some calculated plan or agreement, or will repeated copying suffice? See Nimmer on Copyright § 8.03[E][2][f].

The House softened the ban on "systematic" copying in § 108(g)(2) by adding the proviso authorizing "interlibrary arrangements" that do not "substitute for a subscription to or purchase of such work." This proviso was the subject of guidelines proposed by CONTU, with the participation and substantial agreement of representatives of libraries, publishers and authors. The guidelines appear in the House and Senate Conference Report[n] and are reproduced below. The conference committee stated that the purpose of the guidelines "is to provide guidance in the most commonly-encountered interlibrary photocopying situations, that they are not intended to be limiting or determinative in themselves or with respect to other situations, and that they deal with an evolving situation that will undoubtedly require their continuous reevaluation and adjustment." Conference Rep. p. 71.

Guidelines For the Proviso of Subsection 108(g)(2)

1.   As used in the proviso of subsection 108(g)(2), the words ". . . such aggregate quantities as to substitute for a subscription to or purchase of such work" shall mean:

(a) with respect to any given periodical (as opposed to any given issue of a periodical), filled requests of a library or archives (a "requesting entity") within any calendar year for a total of six or more copies of an article or articles published in such periodical within five years prior to the date of the request. These guidelines specifically shall not apply, directly or indirectly, to any request of a requesting entity for a copy or copies of an article or articles published in any issue of a periodical, the publication date of which is more than five years prior to the date when the request is made. These guidelines do not define the meaning, with respect to such a request, of ". . . such aggregate quantities as to substitute for a subscription to [such periodical]".

(b) With respect to any other material described in subsection 108(d), (including fiction and poetry), filled requests of a requesting entity within any calendar year for a total of six or more copies or phonorecords of or from any given work (including a collective work) during the entire period when such material shall be protected by copyright.

2.   In the event that a requesting entity—

(a) shall have in force or shall have entered an order for a subscription to a periodical, or

(b) has within its collection, or shall have entered an order for, a copy or phonorecord of any other copyrighted work,

material from either category of which it desires to obtain by copy from another library or archives (the "supplying entity"), because the material to be

---

[n]   H.R.Rep. No. 94–1733, 94th Cong., 2d Sess. 72 (1976).

copied is not reasonably available for use by the requesting entity itself, then the fulfillment of such request shall be treated as though the requesting entity made such copy from its own collection. A library or archives may request a copy or phonorecord from a supplying entity only under those circumstances where the requesting entity would have been able, under the other provisions of section 108, to supply such copy from materials in its own collection.

3.   No request for a copy or phonorecord of any material to which these guidelines apply may be fulfilled by the supplying entity unless such request is accompanied by a representation by the requesting entity that the request was made in conformity with these guidelines.

4.   The requesting entity shall maintain records of all requests made by it for copies or phonorecords of any materials to which these guidelines apply and shall maintain records of the fulfillment of such requests, which records shall be retained until the end of the third complete calendar year after the end of the calendar year in which the respective request shall have been made.

5.   As part of the review provided for in subsection 108(i), these guidelines shall be reviewed not later than five years from the effective date of this bill. (Conference Rep. pp. 72–73.)

NOTES AND QUESTIONS

(1) The guidelines are not applicable to interlibrary requests for copies of articles that are more than five years old. Should the approach to such copying be more or less generous than the guidelines? Can the interlibrary arrangements authorized under § 108(g)(2) be carried out by means of digital transmissions?

(2) The guidelines do not attempt to fix the reach of the subsection (g)(2) prohibition against "systematic reproduction" when the copying is done, not as part of an interlibrary arrangement, but rather from the library's own collection in response to requests from users. How would the claim of the Williams & Wilkins Co. against the National Institutes of Health, p. 380 supra, have fared under § 108?

Suppose that a Texaco research facility is located near a university library. After the decision in the *Texaco* case, researchers desiring copies of articles now walk across the street and request a photocopy from the library (or e-mail a request from the comfort of their desk). Can the library fill these requests under § 108(d)—or would such copying be prohibited as "related" or "systematic" under § 108(g)?

(3) In 2008 after three years of discussions, a Section 108 Study Group convened by the Copyright Office issued its recommendations for updating the library exemptions in § 108. Among other proposals, *The Section 108 Study Group Report* recommended that the rules governing interlibrary loans be replaced with standards "more appropriate" to digital materials. The workings of the Study Group are described in L. Gasaway, Amending the Copyright Act for Libraries and Society: The Section 108 Study Group, 70 Alb.L.Rev. 1331 (2007). J. Cochran, Why Can't I Watch This Video Here?: Copyright Confusion and Performances of Videocassettes and Videodiscs in Libraries, 15 Hastings Comm/Ent 837 (1993), analyzes the application of the public performance right in the library environment.

R. Tushnet, My Library: Copyright and the Role of Institutions in a Peer-to-Peer World, 53 UCLA L.Rev. 977 (2006), explores how technological and legal trends have affected the role and functioning of libraries. Conflicts between publishers and libraries arising out of the move to digital media are examined in A. Bartow, Libraries in a Digital and Aggressively Copyrighted World: Retaining Patron Access Through Changing Technologies, 62 Ohio St.L.J. 821 (2001).

2. CONTRIBUTORY AND VICARIOUS INFRINGERS

Shapiro, Bernstein & Co. v. H.L. Green Co.

United States Court of Appeals, Second Circuit, 1963.
316 F.2d 304.

■ Before WATERMAN and KAUFMAN, CIRCUIT JUDGES, and WEINFELD, DISTRICT JUDGE.

■ KAUFMAN, CIRCUIT JUDGE.

This action for copyright infringement presents us with a picture all too familiar in copyright litigation: a legal problem vexing in its difficulty, a dearth of squarely applicable precedents, a business setting so common that the dearth of precedents seems inexplicable, and an almost complete absence of guidance from the terms of the Copyright Act * * *. The plaintiffs in the court below, appellants here, are the copyright proprietors of several musical compositions, recordings of which have met with considerable popularity, especially amongst the younger set. The defendant Jalen Amusement Company, Inc. was charged in the complaint with having infringed the copyrights on these songs by manufacturing records, close copies of the "hit-type" authorized records of major record manufacturers in violation of 17 U.S.C. § 101(e): "in the absence of a license agreement" with the plaintiffs and without having served upon them a notice of intention "to use a copyrighted musical composition upon the parts of instruments serving to reproduce mechanically the musical work."

Jalen operated the phonograph record department as concessionaire in twenty-three stores of defendant H.L. Green Co., Inc., pursuant to written licenses from the Green Company. The complaint alleged that Green was liable for copyright infringement because it "sold, or contributed to and participated actively in the sale of" the so-called "bootleg" records manufactured by Jalen and sold by Jalen in the Green stores. * * *

At the time of suit, Jalen had been operating under license from Green the phonograph record department in twenty-three of its stores, in some for as long as thirteen years. The licensing agreements provided that Jalen and its employees were to "abide by, observe and obey all rules and regulations promulgated from time to time by H.L. Green Company, Inc. * * *." Green, in its "unreviewable discretion", had the authority to discharge any employee believed to be conducting himself improperly. Jalen, in turn, agreed to save Green harmless from any claims arising in connection with the conduct of the phonograph record concession. Significantly, the licenses provided that Green was to receive a percentage—in some cases 10%, in others 12%—of Jalen's gross receipts from the sale of records, as its full compensation as licensor.

In the actual day-to-day functioning of the record department, Jalen ordered and purchased all records, was billed for them, and paid for them. All sales were made by Jalen employees, who, as the District Court found, were under the effective control and supervision of Jalen. All of the daily proceeds from record sales went into Green's cash registers and were removed therefrom by the cashier of the store. At regular accounting periods, Green deducted its 10% or 12% commission and deducted the salaries of the Jalen employees, which salaries were handed over by the Green cashier to one of Jalen's employees to be distributed to the others. Social security and withholding taxes were withheld from the salaries of the employees by Green, and the withholdings then turned over to Jalen. Only then was the balance of the gross receipts of the record department given to Jalen. Customers purchasing records were given a receipt on a printed form marked "H.L. Green Company, Inc."; Jalen's name was wholly absent from the premises. The District Judge found that Green did not actively participate in the sale of the records and that it had no knowledge of the unauthorized manufacture of the records. * * *

Process

* * * It is quite clear, for example, that the normal agency rule of *respondeat superior* applies to copyright infringement by a servant within the scope of his employment. See, e.g., M. Witmark & Sons v. Calloway, 22 F.2d 412, 414 (E.D.Tenn.1927). Realistically, the courts have not drawn a rigid line between the strict cases of agency, and those of independent contract, license, and lease. See Study No. 25, Latman & Tager, "Liability of Innocent Infringers of Copyrights", prepared for the Subcommittee on Patents, Trademarks, and Copyrights of the Senate Comm. on the Judiciary, 86th Cong., 2d Sess. 146. Many of the elements which have given rise to the doctrine of *respondeat superior,* see Seavey, Studies in Agency, 145–53 (1949), may also be evident in factual settings other than that of a technical employer-employee relationship. When the right and ability to supervise coalesce with an obvious and direct financial interest in the exploitation of copyrighted materials—even in the absence of actual knowledge that the copyright monopoly is being impaired, see De Acosta v. Brown, 146 F.2d 408 (2d Cir.1944), cert. denied, Hearst Magazines v. De Acosta, 325 U.S. 862 (1945)—the purposes of copyright law may be best effectuated by the imposition of liability upon the beneficiary of that exploitation.

Respondeat Superior

The two lines of precedent most nearly relevant to the case before us are those which deal, on the one hand, with the landlord leasing his property at a fixed rental to a tenant who engages in copyright-infringing conduct on the leased premises and, on the other hand, the proprietor or manager of a dance hall or music hall leasing his premises to or hiring a dance band, which brings in customers and profits to the proprietor by performing copyrighted music but without complying with the terms of the Copyright Act. If the landlord lets his premises without knowledge of the impending infringement by his tenant, exercises no supervision over him, charges a fixed rental and receives no other benefit from the infringement, and contributes in no way to it, it has been held that the landlord is not liable for his tenant's wrongdoing. See Deutsch v. Arnold, 98 F.2d 686 (2d Cir.1938); cf. Fromont v. Aeolian Co., 254 F. 592 (S.D.N.Y.1918). But, the cases are legion which hold the dance hall proprietor liable for the infringement of copyright resulting from the performance of a musical composition by a band or orchestra whose activities provide the proprietor with a source of customers and enhanced income. He is liable whether the bandleader is considered, as a technical matter, an employee or an independent contractor,

LL leasing at fixed rate

Landlord

banquet hall

and whether or not the proprietor has knowledge of the compositions to be played or any control over their selection. * * *

We believe that the principle which can be extracted from the dance hall cases is a sound one and, under the facts of the cases before us, is here applicable. Those cases and this one lie closer on the spectrum to the employer-employee model than to the landlord-tenant model. * * * We therefore conclude, on the particular facts before us, that Green's relationship to its infringing licensee, as well as its strong concern for the financial success of the phonograph record concession, renders it liable for the unauthorized sales of the "bootleg" records. * * *

more like the hall employer-employee

Reversed and remanded.

NOTES ON VICARIOUS INFRINGEMENT

(1) Vicarious liability in copyright law, as Judge Kaufman notes, extends beyond the traditional limits of *respondeat superior*. The issue arises most frequently in connection with unauthorized performances. The House Report offers the following summation:

> The committee has considered and rejected an amendment to this section intended to exempt the proprietors of an establishment, such as a ballroom or night club, from liability for copyright infringement committed by an independent contractor, such as an orchestra leader. A well-established principle of copyright law is that a person who violates any of the exclusive rights of the copyright owner is an infringer, including persons who can be considered related or vicarious infringers. To be held a related or vicarious infringer in the case of performing rights, a defendant must either actively operate or supervise the operation of the place wherein the performances occur, or control the content of the infringing program, and expect commercial gain from the operation and either direct or indirect benefit from the infringing performance. The committee has decided that no justification exists for changing existing law, and causing a significant erosion of the public performance right. (H.R.Rep. p. 159.)

The proprietor remains liable even if the infringing performance contravenes specific instructions. See, e.g., Warner Brothers, Inc. v. O'Keefe, 468 F.Supp. 16 (S.D.Iowa 1977). When vendors at a flea market were caught selling counterfeit sound recordings, the Ninth Circuit reversed the dismissal of the copyright owners' vicarious liability claim against the operator of the flea market; the complaint alleged that the operator had the ability to control the vendors and received a financial benefit through admission fees and concession sales. (Dismissal of a claim for contributory liability, see infra, was also reversed because the complaint alleged that the operator had provided the physical site with knowledge of the infringing sales.) Fonovisa, Inc. v. Cherry Auction, Inc., 76 F.3d 259 (9th Cir.1996).

(2) In Roy Export Co. Establishment v. Trustees of Columbia Univ., 344 F.Supp. 1350 (S.D.N.Y.1972), the owner of the copyright in Charlie Chaplin's film "Modern Times" sued a student organization and its president, as well as Columbia University, for the organization's unauthorized performances. The court declined to include the university within the scope of its preliminary injunction:

"It is clear that before one may be held liable as a vicarious infringer, absent a special relationship, such as agency or partnership, he must have had the right and ability to supervise the infringing activities, as well as a direct financial interest in those activities. * * *

"We do not think, however, that the University's policy of not interfering with its student organizations is synonymous with its not having the right or ability to have supervised the present infringing activities. * * *

"However, in the present case, plaintiffs neither show benefit to the University, nor do they refute defendants Trustees' assertion that the University received no financial benefit from the two showings of the bootleg film."

(3) The vicarious liability of a sponsor of a television program was at issue in Davis v. E. I. DuPont de Nemours & Co., 240 F.Supp. 612 (S.D.N.Y.1965). After finding the writers, producers, and broadcaster liable for infringing the plaintiff's dramatization of Edith Wharton's novel "Ethan Frome," Judge Feinberg considered the vicarious liability of DuPont and its advertising agency. Relying on *Shapiro,* he concluded "that DuPont had the ultimate power to determine content of the program and exercised that power through its [advertising agency]." The program had been broadcast on the "DuPont Show of the Month." "DuPont was not merely an advertiser buying time on a program produced by a station over whom it had no control." DuPont and its advertising agency were both held liable for the infringement. For a contrary holding in the context of a "network-packaged as opposed to sponsor-packaged production," see Bevan v. CBS, Inc., 329 F.Supp. 601 (S.D.N.Y.1971) ("Hogan's Heroes").

Sony Corp. of America v. Universal City Studios, Inc.

Supreme Court of the United States, 1984.
464 U.S. 417, 104 S.Ct. 774.

[Other portions of the Court's opinion appear at pp. 3 and 341 supra.]

■ JUSTICE STEVENS * * *

III

The Copyright Act does not expressly render anyone liable for infringement committed by another. In contrast, the Patent Act expressly brands anyone who "actively induces infringement of a patent" as an infringer, 35 U.S.C. § 271(b), and further imposes liability on certain individuals labeled "contributory" infringers, § 271(c). The absence of such express language in the copyright statute does not preclude the imposition of liability for copyright infringements on certain parties who have not themselves engaged in the infringing activity.[17] For vicarious liability is imposed in

---

[17] As the District Court correctly observed, however, "the lines between direct infringement, contributory infringement, and vicarious liability are not clearly drawn . . . . " 480 F.Supp. 457–458. The lack of clarity in this area may, in part, be attributable to the fact that an infringer is not merely one who uses a work without authorization by the copyright owner, but also one who authorizes the use of a copyrighted work without actual authority from the copyright owner.

We note the parties' statements that the questions of Sony's liability under the "doctrines" of "direct infringement" and "vicarious liability" are not nominally before this Court. Compare Respondents' Brief, at 9, n. 22, 41, n. 90 with Petitioners' Reply Brief, at 1, n. 2. We also observe, however, that reasoned analysis of respondents' unprecedented contributory infringe-

virtually all areas of the law, and the concept of contributory infringement is merely a species of the broader problem of identifying the circumstances in which it is just to hold one individual accountable for the actions of another.

Such circumstances were plainly present in Kalem Co. v. Harper Brothers, 222 U.S. 55 (1911), the copyright decision of this Court on which respondents place their principal reliance. In *Kalem,* the Court held that the producer of an unauthorized film dramatization of the copyrighted book *Ben Hur* was liable for his sale of the motion picture to jobbers, who in turn arranged for the commercial exhibition of the film. Justice Holmes, writing for the Court, explained:

> "The defendant not only expected but invoked by advertisement the use of its films for dramatic reproduction of the story. That was the most conspicuous purpose for which they could be used, and the one for which especially they were made. If the defendant did not contribute to the infringement it is impossible to do so except by taking part in the final act. It is liable on principles recognized in every part of the law." 222 U.S., at 63.

* * *

Respondents argue that *Kalem* stands for the proposition that supplying the "means" to accomplish an infringing activity and encouraging that activity through advertisement are sufficient to establish liability for copyright infringement. This argument rests on a gross generalization that cannot withstand scrutiny. The producer in *Kalem* did not merely provide the "means" to accomplish an infringing activity; the producer supplied the work itself, albeit in a new medium of expression. Sony in the instant case does not supply Betamax consumers with respondents' works; respondents do. Sony supplies a piece of equipment that is generally capable of copying the entire range of programs that may be televised: those that are uncopyrighted, those that are copyrighted but may be copied without objection from the copyright holder, and those that the copyright holder would prefer not to have copied. The Betamax can be used to make authorized or unauthorized uses of copyrighted works, but the range of its potential use is much broader than the particular infringing use of the film *Ben Hur* involved in *Kalem. Kalem* does not support respondents' novel theory of liability.

Justice Holmes stated that the producer had "contributed" to the infringement of the copyright, and the label "contributory infringement" has been applied in a number of lower court copyright cases involving an ongoing relationship between the direct infringer and the contributory infringer at the time the infringing conduct occurred. In such cases, as in other situations in which the imposition of vicarious liability is manifestly just, the "contributory" infringer was in a position to control the use of copyrighted works by others and had authorized the use without permission from the copyright owner.[18] This case, however, plainly does not fall in that category.

---

ment claim necessarily entails consideration of arguments and case law which may also be forwarded under the other labels, and indeed the parties to a large extent rely upon such arguments and authority in support of their respective positions on the issue of contributory infringement.

[18]   The so-called "dance hall cases," Famous Music Corp. v. Bay State Harness Horse Racing and Breeding Ass'n, 554 F.2d 1213 (C.A.1 1977) (racetrack retained infringer to supply music to paying customers); KECA Music, Inc. v. Dingus McGee's Co., 432 F.Supp. 72 (W.D.Mo.1977) (cocktail lounge hired musicians to supply music to paying customers); Dream-

The only contact between Sony and the users of the Betamax that is dis- *only contact was at* closed by this record occurred at the moment of sale. The District Court *sale* expressly found that "no employee of Sony, Sonam or DDBI had either direct involvement with the allegedly infringing activity or direct contact with purchasers of Betamax who recorded copyrighted works off-the-air." 480 F.Supp., at 460. And it further found that "there was no evidence that any of the copies made by Griffiths or the other individual witnesses in this suit were influenced or encouraged by [Sony's] advertisements." Ibid.

If vicarious liability is to be imposed on petitioners in this case, it must rest on the fact that they have sold equipment with constructive knowledge of the fact that their customers may use that equipment to make unauthorized copies of copyrighted material. There is no precedent in the law of copyright for the imposition of vicarious liability on such a theory. The closest analogy is provided by the patent law cases to which it is appropriate to refer because of the historic kinship between patent law and copyright law.[19]

---

land Ball Room v. Shapiro, Bernstein & Co., 36 F.2d 354 (C.A.7 1929) (dance hall hired orchestra to supply music to paying customers) are often contrasted with the so-called landlord-tenant cases, in which landlords who leased premises to a direct infringer for a fixed rental and did not participate directly in any infringing activity were found not to be liable for contributory infringement. E.g., Deutsch v. Arnold, 98 F.2d 686 (C.A.2 1938).

In Shapiro, Bernstein & Co. v. H.L. Green Co., 316 F.2d 304 (C.A.2 1963), the owner of twenty-three chain stores retained the direct infringer to run its record departments. The relationship was structured as a licensing arrangement, so that the defendant bore none of the business risk of running the department. Instead, it received 10% or 12% of the direct infringer's gross receipts. The Court of Appeals concluded:

"[The dance-hall cases] and this one lie closer on the spectrum to the employer-employee model, than to the landlord-tenant model . . . . [O]n the particular facts before us, . . . Green's relationship to its infringing licensee, as well as its strong concern for the financial success of the phonograph record concession, renders it liable for the unauthorized sales of the 'bootleg' records.

". . . [T]he imposition of *vicarious* liability in the case before us cannot be deemed unduly harsh or unfair. Green has the power to police carefully the conduct of its concessionaire; our judgment will simply encourage it to do so, thus placing responsibility where it can and should be effectively exercised." Id., at 308 (emphasis in original).

In Gershwin Publishing Corp. v. Columbia Artists Management, Inc., 443 F.2d 1159 (C.A.2 1971), the direct infringers retained the contributory infringer to manage their performances. The contributory infringer would contact each direct infringer, obtain the titles of the musical compositions to be performed, print the programs, and then sell the programs to its own local organizations for distribution at the time of the direct infringement. Id., at 1161. The Court of Appeals emphasized that the contributory infringer had actual knowledge that the artists it was managing were performing copyrighted works, was in a position to police the infringing conduct of the artists, and derived substantial benefit from the actions of the primary infringers. Id., at 1163.

In Screen Gems–Columbia Music, Inc. v. Mark–Fi Records, Inc., 256 F.Supp. 399 (S.D.N.Y.1966), the direct infringer manufactured and sold bootleg records. In denying a motion for summary judgment, the District Court held that the infringer's advertising agency, the radio stations that advertised the infringer's works, and the service agency that boxed and mailed the infringing goods could all be held liable, if at trial it could be demonstrated that they knew or should have known that they were dealing in illegal goods.

[19] E.g., United States v. Paramount Pictures, 334 U.S. 131, 158 (1948); Fox Film Corp. v. Doyal, 286 U.S. 123, 131 (1932); Wheaton and Donaldson v. Peters and Grigg, 33 U.S. (8 Pet.) 591, 657–658 (1834). The two areas of the law, naturally, are not identical twins, and we exercise the caution which we have expressed in the past in applying doctrine formulated in one area to the other. See generally, Mazer v. Stein, 347 U.S. 201, 217–218 (1954); Bobbs–Merrill Co. v. Straus, 210 U.S. 339, 345 (1908).

We have consistently rejected the proposition that a similar kinship exists between copyright law and trademark law, and in the process of doing so have recognized the basic similarities between copyrights and patents. The Trade–Mark Cases, 100 U.S. 82, 91–92 (1879); see also, United Drug Co. v. Rectanus Co., 248 U.S. 90, 97 (1918) (trademark right "has little or no

Patent law & contributory infringe.

In the Patent Act both the concept of infringement and the concept of contributory infringement are expressly defined by statute. The prohibition against contributory infringement is confined to the knowing sale of a component especially made for use in connection with a particular patent. There is no suggestion in the statute that one patentee may object to the sale of a product that might be used in connection with other patents. Moreover, the Act expressly provides that the sale of a "staple article or commodity of commerce suitable for substantial noninfringing use" is not contributory infringement. * * *

We recognize there are substantial differences between the patent and copyright laws. But in both areas the contributory infringement doctrine is grounded on the recognition that adequate protection of a monopoly may require the courts to look beyond actual duplication of a device or publication to the products or activities that make such duplication possible. The staple article of commerce doctrine must strike a balance between a copyright holder's legitimate demand for effective—not merely symbolic—protection of the statutory monopoly, and the rights of others freely to engage in substantially unrelated areas of commerce. Accordingly, the sale of copying equipment, like the sale of other articles of commerce, does not constitute contributory infringement if the product is widely used for legitimate, unobjectionable purposes. Indeed, it need merely be capable of substantial noninfringing uses. * * *

Holding

In summary, the record and findings of the District Court lead us to two conclusions. First, Sony demonstrated a significant likelihood that substantial numbers of copyright holders who license their works for broadcast on free television would not object to having their broadcasts time-shifted by private viewers. And second, respondents failed to demonstrate that time-shifting would cause any likelihood of non-minimal harm to the potential market for, or the value of, their copyrighted works. The Betamax is, therefore, capable of substantial noninfringing uses. Sony's sale of such equipment to the general public does not constitute contributory infringement of respondent's copyrights. * * *

■ [JUSTICE BLACKMUN'S dissenting opinion is omitted.]

NOTES ON CONTRIBUTORY INFRINGEMENT

(1) In footnote 18 the Supreme Court makes reference to Gershwin Publishing Corp. v. Columbia Artists Management, Inc., 443 F.2d 1159 (2d Cir.1971). The defendant in *Gershwin,* in addition to managing concert artists, assisted in organizing and nurturing community associations that in turn sponsored annual concert series. It was sued in connection with an unlicensed performance that occurred during a community concert. The Second Circuit, reviewing its decision in *Shapiro,* noted that one may be a "vicarious" infringer if the person has the right and ability to supervise and a direct financial interest in the conduct. It then continued: "Similarly, one who, with knowledge of the infringing activity, induces, causes or materially contributes to the infringing conduct of another, may be held liable as a 'contributory' infringer. * * * The district court properly held [defendant] liable as a 'vicarious' and a 'contributory' infringer."

---

alogy" to copyright or patent); McLean v. Fleming, 96 U.S. 245, 254 (1877); Canal Co. v. Clark, 13 Wall. 311, 322 (1871). Given the fundamental differences between copyright law and trademark law, in this copyright case we do not look to the standard for contributory infringement set forth in Inwood Laboratories v. Ives Laboratories, 456 U.S. 844, 854–855 (1982), which was crafted for application in trademark cases. * * *

In Original Appalachian Artworks, Inc. v. Cradle Creations Inc., 223 U.S.P.Q. 80 (N.D.Ga.1983), the court, citing *Gershwin,* ordered judgment against the distributor of an instruction booklet for making "soft sculpture" dolls. "[B]ecause defendants were aware that their booklets would be used by others to make infringing copies of plaintiff's copyrighted dolls, and because defendants' booklet materially contributes to the infringing activities of others who use the instructions and patterns contained therein to produce such infringing copies, defendants' conduct constitutes contributory infringement."

(2) The House Report notes that § 106 gives to copyright owners the exclusive right "to authorize" the exercise of the specified rights. "Use of the phrase 'to authorize' is intended to avoid any questions as to the liability of contributory infringers. For example, a person who lawfully acquires an authorized copy of a motion picture would be an infringer if he or she engages in the business of renting it to others for purposes of unauthorized public performance." H.R.Rep. p. 61.

(3) In Elektra Records Co. v. Gem Electronic Distributors, Inc., 360 F.Supp. 821 (E.D.N.Y.1973), a record store installed a sophisticated self-service tape duplication system and, upon purchase of a blank cartridge, it would lend the customer a tape from its catalog of recordings. Is the store liable as a vicarious or contributory infringer? Does a library that maintains an unsupervised photocopier risk liability if it does not display a warning notice in compliance with § 108(f)(1)? The court in *Elektra Records,* justifying its preliminary injunction, distinguished the record store's library analogy, emphasizing the store's financial stake in the copying. Is there nevertheless a negative implication in the library warning requirement in § 108(f)(1)?

In a post-*Sony* case, a tape copying machine that would accept only specially-notched blank tapes was said to be a staple article of commerce, precluding contributory liability. But the manufacturer and its principal shareholder were held to be vicarious infringers when the machines were used in retail stores to copy copyrighted recordings because of their "authority to control use of the machine" (it was lent rather than sold to retailers) and their "financial interest in the copying as the source for the notched blank tapes needed to use the machine." RCA/Ariola Int'l, Inc. v. Thomas & Grayston Co., 845 F.2d 773 (8th Cir.1988); cf. A & M Records, Inc. v. General Audio Video Cassettes, Inc., 948 F.Supp. 1449 (C.D.Cal.1996), imposing contributory liability on a supplier of blank tape cut specifically to match the duration of legitimate recordings pirated by the supplier's customer.

(4) Atari, Inc. v. JS & A Group, Inc., 597 F.Supp. 5 (N.D.Ill.1983), involved a defendant that was promoting an electronic device capable of duplicating video game cartridges. A manufacturer of video games sought a preliminary injunction, alleging contributory infringement. The court saw the issue as whether the device had a "*substantial* noninfringing use." It rejected the argument that the right to use the device to copy the few games marketed by the defendant was itself a sufficient noninfringing use. It also rejected the contention that the copying was within the "archival exception" for computer programs in § 117, since the games were not subject to the risk of accidental damage for which the exemption was arguably intended. Sale of the device was enjoined. But in Vault Corp. v. Quaid Software Ltd., 847 F.2d 255 (5th Cir.1988), the court rejected the "narrow construction of the archival exception" accepted in *Atari* and found that the defendant's computer program, designed to facilitate the copying of copy-protected software, was capable of substantial noninfringing use, thus precluding contributory liability.

Sony's approach to contributory liability is defended in B. Frischmann, Peer–To–Peer Technology as Infrastructure, 52 J.Copyr. Soc'y 329 (2005); E. Lee, Freedom of the Press 2.0, 42 Ga.L.Rev. 309 (2008), argues that *Sony's* safe harbor is a first amendment safeguard, protecting speech-facilitating technologies from government control.

(5) Perfect 10 owned "tasteful copyrighted images of the world's most beautiful natural models." It alleged that numerous web sites in several countries had copied the images and were offering them for sale online. Perfect 10 brought claims of contributory and vicarious infringement against credit card companies that processed payments to the web sites selling the infringing images. The Ninth Circuit in Perfect 10, Inc. v. Visa Int'l Service Ass'n, 494 F.3d 788 (9th Cir.2007), cert. denied, 553 U.S. 1079 (2008), affirmed the dismissal of the claims. The contributory infringement count was dismissed because the defendants did not materially contribute to the infringement. Distinguishing the search engine and file-sharing cases, Judge Smith said that here, "the services provided by the credit card companies do not help locate and are not used to distribute the infringing images." There could be no vicarious infringement because "the ability to exert financial pressure does not give Defendants the right or ability to control the actual infringing activity at issue in this case." Neither argument convinced Judge Kozinski, who thought the credit cards companies should be liable for "knowingly providing a financial bridge between the buyers and sellers of pirated works, enabling them to consummate infringing transactions, while making a profit on every sale." Courts wrestling with the "material contribution" element of contributory infringement are urged to distinguish factual causation from the separate policy issue of proximate cause in M. Bartholomew and P. McArdle, Causing Infringement, 64 Vand.L.Rev. 675 (2011).

(6) M. Bartholomew and J. Tehranian, The Secret Life of Legal Doctrine: The Divergent Evolution of Secondary Liability in Trademark and Copyright Law, 21 Berk.Tech.L.J. 1363 (2006), notes the broadening of secondary liability in copyright but not trademark and blames it on the panic over digital copyright infringement; D. Lichtman and W. Landes, Indirect Liability for Copyright Infringement: An Economic Perspective, 16 Harv.J.L. & Tech. 395 (2003), offers an economic analysis of the rules governing vicarious and contributory copyright infringement.

3. COPYRIGHT IN A DIGITAL AGE

"Throughout the time I've been groping around cyberspace, an immense, unresolved conundrum has remained at the root of nearly every legal, ethical, governmental, and social vexation to be found in the Virtual World. I refer to the problem of digitized property. The enigma is this: If our property can be infinitely reproduced and instantaneously distributed all over the planet without cost, without our knowledge, without its even leaving our possession, how can we protect it? How are we going to get paid for the work we do with our minds? And, if we can't get paid, what will assure the continued creation and distribution of such work?

"Since we don't have a solution to what is a profoundly new kind of challenge, and are apparently unable to delay the galloping digitization of everything not obstinately physical, we are sailing into the future on a sinking ship.

"This vessel, the accumulated canon of copyright and patent law, was developed to convey forms and methods of expression entirely different from the vaporous cargo it is now being asked to carry. It is leaking as much from within as from without.

"Legal efforts to keep the old boat floating are taking three forms: a frenzy of deck chair rearrangement, stern warnings to the passengers that if she goes down, they will face harsh criminal penalties, and serene, glassy-eyed denial.

"Intellectual property law cannot be patched, retrofitted, or expanded to contain digitized expression any more than real property law might be revised to cover the allocation of broadcasting spectrum (which, in fact, rather resembles what is being attempted here). We need to develop an entirely new set of methods as befits this entirely new set of circumstances. * * *

"In the absence of the old containers, almost everything we think we know about intellectual property is wrong." J. Barlow, The Economy of Ideas: A Framework for Rethinking Patents and Copyrights in the Digital Age, Wired, March 1994, p. 84.⁰

"With no more than minor clarification and limited amendment, the Copyright Act will provide the necessary balance of protection of rights—and limitations on those rights—to promote the progress of science and the useful arts. Existing copyright law needs only the fine tuning that technological advances necessitate, in order to maintain the balance of the law in the face of onrushing technology." Information Infrastructure Task Force, Intellectual Property and the National Information Infrastructure 16–17 (1995) (The "White Paper").ᴾ

⁰ Reprinted with permission. The author is described as "a retired cattle rancher, a lyricist for the Grateful Dead, and co-founder and executive chair of the Electronic Frontier Foundation."

ᴾ The "White Paper" was the product of a Working Group on Intellectual Property created during the Clinton administration to recommend changes in intellectual property law and policy that would facilitate the development of digital communication. The White Paper advocated strong copyright protection for digitally-disseminated works. "Thus, the full potential of the [National Information Infrastructure] will not be realized if the education, information and entertainment products protected by intellectual property laws are not protected effectively when disseminated via the NII." It pursued this goal through broad interpretations of existing law and recommendations for congressional action. Relying on cases like MAI Systems Corp. v. Peak Computer, Inc., 991 F.2d 511 (9th Cir.1993), cert. dismissed, 510 U.S. 1033 (1994), which held that loading a computer program into the temporary RAM memory of a computer created a "copy," the White Paper concluded that digitizing, uploading, downloading, and transferring digital files all generate potentially infringing copies.

Reaction to the White Paper was varied but intense. Education and library organizations (and many academics) were strongly critical. See, e.g., J. Litman, The Exclusive Right to Read, 13 Card. A. & Ent.L.J. 29 (1994), concluding that the recommendations would amount to an exclusive right to read, view, and listen to digital works. On the other hand, film, music, and software organizations loudly applauded. For differing views on the appropriate role of intellectual property law in a digital environment, compare T. Hardy, Property (and Copyright) in Cyberspace, 1996 U.Chi.Leg. Forum 217 (1996), arguing that the practical ease of copying and low transaction costs on the Internet justify a regime of strong legal protection, and A. Ng, When Users are Authors: Authorship in the Age of Digital Media, 12 Vand.J.Ent. & Tech.L. 853 (2010), offering a strong defense of ownership rights in a digital environment, with R. Ku, The Creative Destruction of Copyright: Napster and the New Economics of Digital Technology,

———

How should the law respond to the dramatic increase in our ability to disseminate and enjoy works of authorship made possible by modern computer technology? When the 1976 Copyright Act was drafted, computers occupied entire rooms rather than laps and were fed by punch cards or reels of magnetic tape. Section 117 of the 1976 Act as originally enacted was a stand-still provision that tied a copyright owner's rights over computer use of her work to the state of the law prior to the enactment of the 1976 Act. Presumably even then, the retrieval of a work from a computer in a hard-copy form would, absent fair use, constitute infringement. As for the creation of digital copies or their input into a computer, however, the implications of White–Smith v. Apollo Co., p. 25 supra, with its emphasis on "intelligible" embodiments, left the issue in considerable doubt under the old law. The 1978 CONTU Report recommended repeal of § 117; it was replaced in 1980 by the current provision exempting certain reproductions of computer programs. As for the reproduction of other works in digital form, the CONTU Report offered this comment: "The introduction of a work into a computer memory would, consistent with the new law, be a reproduction of the work, one of the exclusive rights of the copyright proprietor. * * * Principles of fair use would be applicable in limited instances to excuse an unauthorized input of a work into computer memory." CONTU Report p. 40.

The stakes for copyright owners rose in the 1980s when personal computers began to appear in so many homes and offices. Copyright owners, particularly sellers of software, scoured copyright, patent, and trade secret law in an effort to retain control over their products and markets. The issue of intellectual property rights in an increasingly digital age was pushed to center stage by the soaring popularity of the Internet and the development of the World Wide Web. The focus on copyright law and policy grows more intense with every technological innovation. Streaming technology, which eliminated the need for users to download bulky audio and video files, made it practical to deliver live and recorded audio and video programming over the Internet. Broadband access and improvements in the compression technology that shrinks the size of digital files create ever-increasing opportunities for the digital distribution of all kinds of works, including sound recordings, software, television programs, and movies. Mobile devices like smartphones and tablets have further increased the public's appetite for digital content.

The future of the digital revolution is sometimes captured by the metaphor of a celestial jukebox—an orbiting network of satellites that can instantly deliver any requested entertainment or information product to the user's digital receiver. What role will copyright play in such a world? Is the bundle of rights in § 106 too broad, too narrow, or simply too antiquated to serve the needs of users and creators in a digital age?

———

---

69 U.Chi.L.Rev. 263 (2002), concluding that digital distribution technologies undercut the need for exclusive rights.

Religious Technology Center v. Netcom On–Line Communication Services, Inc.

United States District Court, Northern District of California, 1995.
907 F.Supp. 1361.

■ WHYTE, DISTRICT JUDGE.

This case concerns an issue of first impression regarding intellectual property rights in cyberspace. Specifically, this order addresses whether the operator of a computer bulletin board service ("BBS"), and the large Internet access provider that allows that BBS to reach the Internet, should be liable for copyright infringement committed by a subscriber of the BBS.

Plaintiffs Religious Technology Center ("RTC") and Bridge Publications, Inc. ("BPI") hold copyrights in the unpublished and published works of L. Ron Hubbard, the late founder of the Church of Scientology ("the Church"). Defendant Dennis Erlich ("Erlich")[3] is a former minister of Scientology turned vocal critic of the Church, whose pulpit is now the Usenet newsgroup[4] alt.religion.scientology ("a.r.s."), an on-line forum for discussion and criticism of Scientology. Plaintiffs maintain that Erlich infringed their copyrights when he posted portions of their works on a.r.s. Erlich gained his access to the Internet through defendant Thomas Klemesrud's ("Klemesrud's") BBS "support.com." Klemesrud is the operator of the BBS, which is run out of his home and has approximately 500 paying users. Klemesrud's BBS is not directly linked to the Internet, but gains its connection through the facilities of defendant Netcom On–Line Communications, Inc. ("Netcom"), one of the largest providers of Internet access in the United States.

After failing to convince Erlich to stop his postings, plaintiffs contacted defendants Klemesrud and Netcom. Klemesrud responded to plaintiffs' demands that Erlich be kept off his system by asking plaintiffs to prove that they owned the copyrights to the works posted by Erlich. However, plaintiffs refused Klemesrud's request as unreasonable. Netcom similarly refused plaintiffs' request that Erlich not be allowed to gain access to the Internet through its system. Netcom contended that it would be impossible to prescreen Erlich's postings and that to kick Erlich off the Internet meant

---

[3]　Issues of Erlich's liability were addressed in this court's order of September 22, 1995. That order concludes in part that a preliminary injunction against Erlich is warranted because plaintiffs have shown a likelihood of success on their copyright infringement claims against him. Plaintiffs likely own valid copyrights in Hubbard's published and unpublished works and Erlich's near-verbatim copying of substantial portions of plaintiffs' works was not likely a fair use. To the extent that Netcom and Klemesrud argue that plaintiffs' copyrights are invalid and that Netcom and Klemesrud are not liable because Erlich had a valid fair use defense, the court previously rejected these arguments and will not reconsider them here.

[4]　The Usenet has been described as

a worldwide community of electronic BBSs that is closely associated with the Internet and with the Internet community.¶ The messages in Usenet are organized into thousands of topical groups, or "Newsgroups" .... ¶ As a Usenet user, you read and contribute ("post") to your local Usenet site. Each Usenet site distributes its users' postings to other Usenet sites based on various implicit and explicit configuration settings, and in turn receives postings from other sites. Usenet traffic typically consists of as much as 30 to 50 Mbytes of messages per day. ¶ Usenet is read and contributed to on a daily basis by a total population of millions of people .... ¶ There is no specific network that is the Usenet. Usenet traffic flows over a wide range of networks, including the Internet and dial-up phone links.

Dern [The Internet Guide for New Uses (1994)] at 196–97.

kicking off the hundreds of users of Klemesrud's BBS. Consequently, plaintiffs named Klemesrud and Netcom in their suit against Erlich, although only on the copyright infringement claims. * * *

1.   Direct Infringement

Infringement consists of the unauthorized exercise of one of the exclusive rights of the copyright holder delineated in section 106. 17 U.S.C. § 501. Direct infringement does not require intent or any particular state of mind, although willfulness is relevant to the award of statutory damages. 17 U.S.C. § 504(c). * * *

a.   *Undisputed Facts*

The parties do not dispute the basic processes that occur when Erlich posts his allegedly infringing messages to a.r.s. Erlich connects to Klemesrud's BBS using a telephone and a modem. Erlich then transmits his messages to Klemesrud's computer, where they are automatically briefly stored. According to a prearranged pattern established by Netcom's software, Erlich's initial act of posting a message to the Usenet results in the automatic copying of Erlich's message from Klemesrud's computer onto Netcom's computer and onto other computers on the Usenet. In order to ease transmission and for the convenience of Usenet users, Usenet servers maintain postings from newsgroups for a short period of time—eleven days for Netcom's system and three days for Klemesrud's system. Once on Netcom's computers, messages are available to Netcom's customers and Usenet neighbors, who may then download the messages to their own computers. Netcom's local server makes available its postings to a group of Usenet servers, which do the same for other servers until all Usenet sites worldwide have obtained access to the postings, which takes a matter of hours. * * *

b.   *Creation of Fixed Copies*

The Ninth Circuit addressed the question of what constitutes infringement in the context of storage of digital information in a computer's random access memory ("RAM"). MAI Systems Corp. v. Peak Computer, Inc., 991 F.2d 511, 518 (9th Cir.1993). In *MAI,* the Ninth Circuit upheld a finding of copyright infringement where a repair person, who was not authorized to use the computer owner's licensed operating system software, turned on the computer, thus loading the operating system into RAM for long enough to check an "error log." Id. at 518–19. Copyright protection subsists in original works of authorship "*fixed* in any tangible medium of expression, now known or later developed, from which they can be perceived, reproduced, or otherwise communicated, either directly or with the aid of a machine or device." 17 U.S.C. § 102 (emphasis added). A work is "fixed" when its "embodiment in a copy . . . is sufficiently permanent or stable to permit it to be perceived, reproduced, or otherwise communicated for a period of more than transitory duration." Id. § 101. *MAI* established that the loading of data from a storage device into RAM constitutes copying because that data stays in RAM long enough for it to be perceived. *MAI Systems,* 991 F.2d at 518.

In the present case, there is no question after *MAI* that "copies" were created, as Erlich's act of sending a message to a.r.s. caused reproductions of portions of plaintiffs' works on both Klemesrud's and Netcom's storage devices. Even though the messages remained on their systems for at most eleven days, they were sufficiently "fixed" to constitute recognizable copies under the Copyright Act. See Information Infrastructure Task Force, Intellectual Property and the National Information Infrastructure: The Report of the Working Group on Intellectual Property Rights 66 (1995) ("IITF Report").

c.   *Is Netcom Directly Liable for Making the Copies?*

Accepting that copies were made, Netcom argues that Erlich, and not Netcom, is directly liable for the copying. *MAI* did not address the question raised in this case: whether possessors of computers are liable for incidental copies automatically made on their computers using their software as part of a process initiated by a third party. Netcom correctly distinguishes *MAI* on the ground that Netcom did not take any affirmative action that directly resulted in copying plaintiffs' works other than by installing and maintaining a system whereby software automatically forwards messages received from subscribers onto the Usenet, and temporarily stores copies on its system. Netcom's actions, to the extent that they created a copy of plaintiffs' works, were necessary to having a working system for transmitting Usenet postings to and from the Internet. Unlike the defendants in *MAI,* neither Netcom nor Klemesrud initiated the copying. The defendants in *MAI* turned on their customers' computers thereby creating temporary copies of the operating system, whereas Netcom's and Klemesrud's systems can operate without any human intervention. Thus, unlike *MAI,* the mere fact that Netcom's system incidentally makes temporary copies of plaintiffs' works does not mean Netcom has caused the copying. The court believes that Netcom's act of designing or implementing a system that automatically and uniformly creates temporary copies of all data sent through it is not unlike that of the owner of a copying machine who lets the public make copies with it. Although some of the people using the machine may directly infringe copyrights, courts analyze the machine owner's liability under the rubric of contributory infringement, not direct infringement. * * * It is not difficult to conclude that Erlich infringes by copying a protected work onto his computer and by posting a message to a newsgroup. However, plaintiffs' theory further implicates a Usenet server that carries Erlich's message to other servers regardless of whether that server acts without any human intervention beyond the initial setting up of the system. It would also result in liability for every single Usenet server in the worldwide link of computers transmitting Erlich's message to every other computer. These parties, who are liable under plaintiffs' theory, do no more than operate or implement a system that is essential if Usenet messages are to be widely distributed. There is no need to construe the Act to make all of these parties infringers. Although copyright is a strict liability statute, there should still be some element of volition or causation which is lacking where a defendant's system is merely used to create a copy by a third party. * * *

The court will now consider two district court opinions that have addressed the liability of BBS operators for infringing files uploaded by subscribers.

d.   *Playboy Case*

Playboy Enterprises, Inc. v. Frena involved a suit against the operator of a small BBS whose system contained files of erotic pictures. 839 F.Supp. 1552, 1554 (M.D.Fla.1993). A subscriber of the defendant's BBS had uploaded files containing digitized pictures copied from the plaintiff's copyrighted magazine, which files remained on the BBS for other subscribers to download. Id. The court did not conclude, as plaintiffs suggest in this case, that the BBS is itself liable for the unauthorized *reproduction* of plaintiffs' work; instead, the court concluded that the BBS operator was liable for violating the plaintiff's right to publicly *distribute and display* copies of its work. Id. at 1556–57.

In support of their argument that Netcom is directly liable for copying plaintiffs' works, plaintiffs cite to the court's conclusion that "[t]here is no dispute that [the BBS operator] supplied a product containing unauthorized copies of a copyrighted work. It does not matter that [the BBS operator] claims he did not make the copies [him]self." Id. at 1556. It is clear from the context of this discussion that the *Playboy* court was looking only at the exclusive right to distribute copies to the public, where liability exists regardless of whether the defendant makes copies. Here, however, plaintiffs do not argue that Netcom is liable for its public distribution of copies. Instead, they claim that Netcom is liable because its computers in fact made copies. * * *

e.   *Sega Case*

A court in this district addressed the issue of whether a BBS operator is liable for copyright infringement where it solicited subscribers to upload files containing copyrighted materials to the BBS that were available for others to download. Sega Enterprises Ltd. v. MAPHIA, 857 F.Supp. 679, 683 (N.D.Cal.1994). [The bulletin board operator in *Sega* had solicited the uploading of Sega video games by subscribers and charged a fee for downloading. The court in *Sega* said that the plaintiff had established a prima facie case of direct and contributory infringement. Judge Whyte, however, believed that the discussion of direct infringement in *Sega* was "conclusory" and "dicta"; the defendant's knowledge of the copying instead supported liability on a contributory infringement theory.] Thus, the court finds that neither *Playboy* nor *Sega* requires finding Netcom liable for direct infringement of plaintiffs' exclusive right to reproduce their works.

f.   *Public Distribution and Display?*

* * *

Playboy concluded that the defendant infringed the plaintiff's exclusive rights to publicly distribute and display copies of its works. 839 F.Supp. at 1556–57. The court is not entirely convinced that the mere possession of a digital copy on a BBS that is accessible to some members of the public constitutes direct infringement by the BBS operator. Such a holding suffers from the same problem of causation as the reproduction argument. Only the subscriber should be liable for causing the distribution of plaintiffs' work, as the contributing actions of the BBS provider are automatic and indiscriminate. * * * Where the BBS merely stores and passes along all messages sent by its subscribers and others, the BBS should not be seen as causing these works to be publicly distributed or displayed.

Even accepting the *Playboy* court's holding, the case is factually distinguishable. Unlike the BBS in that case, Netcom does not maintain an archive of files for its users. Thus, it cannot be said to be "suppl[ying] a product." In contrast to some of its larger competitors, Netcom does not create or control the content of the information available to its subscribers; it merely provides *access* to the Internet, whose content is controlled by no single entity. * * *

[margin handwritten note: Playboy ct looking only at excl. right to distribute (exists regardless of if Δ copies)]

g. *Conclusion*

The court is not persuaded by plaintiffs' argument that Netcom is directly liable for the copies that are made and stored on its computer. Where the infringing subscriber is clearly directly liable for the same act, it does not make sense to adopt a rule that could lead to the liability of countless parties whose role in the infringement is nothing more than setting up and operating a system that is necessary for the functioning of the Internet. Such a result is unnecessary as there is already a party directly liable for causing the copies to be made. Plaintiffs occasionally claim that they only seek to hold liable a party that refuses to delete infringing files after they have been warned. However, such liability cannot be based on a theory of direct infringement, where knowledge is irrelevant. The court does not find workable a theory of infringement that would hold the entire Internet liable for activities that cannot reasonably be deterred. Billions of bits of data flow through the Internet and are necessarily stored on servers throughout the network and it is thus practically impossible to screen out infringing bits from noninfringing bits. Because the court cannot see any meaningful distinction (without regard to knowledge) between what Netcom did and what every other Usenet server does, the court finds that Netcom cannot be held liable for direct infringement. Cf. IITF Report at 69 (noting uncertainty regarding whether BBS operator should be directly liable for reproduction or distribution of files uploaded by a subscriber).

2. Contributory Infringement

Netcom is not free from liability just because it did not directly infringe plaintiffs' works; it may still be liable as a contributory infringer. * * * Liability for participation in the infringement will be established where the defendant, "with knowledge of the infringing activity, induces, causes or materially contributes to the infringing conduct of another." Gershwin Publishing Corp. v. Columbia Artists Management, Inc., 443 F.2d 1159, 1162 (2d Cir.1971).

a. *Knowledge of Infringing Activity*

Plaintiffs insist that Netcom knew that Erlich was infringing their copyrights at least after receiving notice from plaintiffs' counsel indicating that Erlich had posted copies of their works onto a.r.s. through Netcom's system. Despite this knowledge, Netcom continued to allow Erlich to post messages to a.r.s. and left the allegedly infringing messages on its system so that Netcom's subscribers and other Usenet servers could access them. * * *

* * * Netcom points out that the alleged instances of infringement occurring on Netcom's system all happened prior to December 29, 1994, the date on which Netcom first received notice of plaintiffs' infringement claim against Erlich. * * * Thus, there is no question of fact as to whether Netcom knew or should have known of Erlich's infringing activities that occurred more than 11 days before receipt of the December 28, 1994 letter.

However, the evidence reveals a question of fact as to whether Netcom knew or should have known that Erlich had infringed plaintiffs' copyrights following receipt of plaintiffs' letter. Because Netcom was arguably participating in Erlich's public distribution of plaintiffs' works, there is a genuine issue as to whether Netcom knew of any infringement by Erlich before it was too late to do anything about it. If plaintiffs can prove the knowledge element, Netcom will be liable for contributory infringement since its failure to simply cancel Erlich's infringing message and thereby stop an infringing copy from being distributed worldwide constitutes substantial participation in Erlich's public distribution of the message. Cf. R.T. Nimmer, The Law of Computer Technology ¶ 15.11B, at S15–42 (2d ed. 1994) (opining the "where information service is less directly involved in the enterprise of creating unauthorized copies, a finding of contributory infringement is not likely"). * * *

b. *Substantial Participation*

Where a defendant has knowledge of the primary infringer's infringing activities, it will be liable if it "induces, causes or materially contributes to the infringing conduct of" the primary infringer. *Gershwin Publishing,* 443 F.2d at 1162. Such participation must be substantial. * * *

* * * Netcom allows Erlich's infringing messages to remain on its system and be further distributed to other Usenet servers worldwide. It does not completely relinquish control over how its system is used, unlike a landlord. Thus, it is fair, assuming Netcom is able to take simple measures to prevent further damage to plaintiffs' copyrighted works, to hold Netcom liable for contributory infringement where Netcom has knowledge of Erlich's infringing postings yet continues to aid in the accomplishment of Erlich's purpose of publicly distributing the postings. Accordingly, plaintiffs do raise a genuine issue of material fact as to their theory of contributory infringement as to the postings made after Netcom was on notice of plaintiffs' infringement claim.

3. **Vicarious Liability**

Even if plaintiffs cannot prove that Netcom is contributorily liable for its participation in the infringing activity, it may still seek to prove vicarious infringement based on Netcom's relationship to Erlich. A defendant is liable for vicarious liability for the actions of a primary infringer where the defendant (1) has the right and ability to control the infringer's acts and (2) receives a direct financial benefit from the infringement. See Shapiro, Bernstein & Co. v. H.L. Green Co., 316 F.2d 304, 306 (2d Cir.1963). Unlike contributory infringement, knowledge is not an element of vicarious liability. 3 Nimmer on Copyright § 12.04[A][1], at 12–70.

a. *Right and Ability To Control*

The first element of vicarious liability will be met if plaintiffs can show that Netcom has the right and ability to supervise the conduct of its subscribers. Netcom argues that it does not have the right to control its users' postings before they occur. Plaintiffs dispute this and argue that Netcom's terms and conditions, to which its subscribers must agree, specify that Netcom reserves the right to take remedial action against subscribers. * * * Further evidence of Netcom's right to restrict infringing activity is its prohibition of copyright infringement and its requirement that its subscribers indemnify it for any damage to third parties. Plaintiffs have thus raised a question of fact as to Netcom's right to control Erlich's use of its services.

Netcom argues that it could not possibly screen messages before they are posted given the speed and volume of the data that goes through its system. Netcom further argues that it has never exercised control over the content of its users' postings. * * * The court thus finds that plaintiffs have raised a genuine issue of fact as to whether Netcom has the right and ability to exercise control over the activities of its subscribers, and of Erlich in particular.

b. *Direct Financial Benefit*

Plaintiffs must further prove that Netcom receives a direct financial benefit from the infringing activities of its users. For example, a landlord who has the right and ability to supervise the tenant's activities is vicariously liable for the infringements of the tenant where the rental amount is proportional to the proceeds of the tenant's sales. *Shapiro, Bernstein,* 316 F.2d at 306. However, where a defendant rents space or services on a fixed rental fee that does not depend on the nature of the activity of the lessee, courts usually find no vicarious liability because there is no direct financial benefit from the infringement. * * *

* * * Plaintiffs cannot provide any evidence of a direct financial benefit received by Netcom from Erlich's infringing postings. Unlike *Shapiro, Bernstein,* * * * Netcom receives a fixed fee. There is no evidence that infringement by Erlich, or any other user of Netcom's services, in any way enhances the value of Netcom's services to subscribers or attracts new subscribers. * * * Because plaintiffs have failed to raise a question of fact on this vital element, their claim of vicarious liability fails.

[The court next concluded that Netcom was not entitled to a ruling that its use was fair as a matter of law.]

Conclusion

The court finds that plaintiffs have raised a genuine issue of fact regarding whether Netcom should have known that Erlich was infringing their copyrights after receiving a letter from plaintiffs, whether Netcom substantially participated in the infringement, and whether Netcom has a valid fair use defense. Accordingly, Netcom is not entitled to summary judgment on plaintiffs' claim of contributory copyright infringement. However, plaintiffs' claims of direct and vicarious infringement fail.

[As for Klemesrud, the bulletin board operator who dealt directly with Erlich, the court concluded that the plaintiffs' allegations of direct and vicarious infringement failed for the same reasons applicable to Netcom. As with Netcom, however, summary judgment was denied with respect to the contributory infringement claim. The court nevertheless refused a request for a preliminary injunction against both defendants since the plaintiffs had not established that they were likely to succeed in proving the knowledge and substantial participation necessary for contributory infringement.]

NOTES AND QUESTIONS

(1) The case against Netcom was ultimately settled when Netcom agreed to institute a protocol for removing material while investigating claims of infringement. It also agreed to post a warning to subscribers about copyright infringement. L.A. Times, Aug. 6, 1996, p. D2.

Netcom's approach to direct liability was adopted by the Second Circuit in Cartoon Network LP v. CSC Holdings, Inc., 536 F.3d 121 (2d Cir.2008), cert. denied, 129 S.Ct. 2890 (2009), when copyright owners sued a cable company that allowed customers to record programming on the company's remote server. The court held that the copies were "made" by the customers and the cable company's "contribution to this reproduction by providing the system does not warrant the imposition of direct liability."

(2) Fair use aside, is there any doubt that Erlich infringed when he posted substantial portions of the plaintiffs' copyrighted works on the Usenet newsgroup? The court had already issued a preliminary injunction against Erlich in an opinion at 923 F.Supp. 1231.[q] Which of the plaintiffs' § 106 rights did Erlich infringe? In its opinion on Erlich's liability, the court focused on "copying." The reproduction right was also successfully invoked by the publisher of *Playboy* against a defendant who offered photographs from the magazine on a commercial web site. Playboy Enter., Inc. v. Webbworld, Inc., 991 F.Supp. 543 (N.D.Tex.1997), aff'd, 168 F.3d 486 (5th Cir.1999).

The proposition that a reproduction of a copyrighted work in digital form is a "copy" for purposes of § 106(1) is ultimately constrained by the statutory definitions of "copies" and "fixed," which require that the embodiment be sufficiently permanent to permit the work to be perceived, reproduced, or communicated for a period of more than transitory duration. The court in *Netcom* was bound by the Ninth Circuit's holding in MAI Systems Corp. v. Peak Computer, Inc., 991 F.2d 511 (9th Cir.1993), cert. dismissed, 510 U.S. 1033 (1994), that the embodiment of a work in a computer's random access memory (which is erased when the power is turned off) is a "copy." Should the concept of a "copy" be limited to more permanent reproductions on hard drives or other storage media? Even *MAI* does not hold that all digital embodiments are "copies"—the embodiment there was sufficiently permanent to allow the user to read and use the output of the copyrighted program. The Second Circuit in the *Cartoon Network* case described in Note (1) distinguished *MAI* in holding that buffer copies made by the cable company in anticipation of customer requests for recording were not "copies" since the digital data in the buffers was continuously overwritten by new data and "no bit of data remains in any buffer for more than a fleeting 1.2 seconds."

(3) Did Erlich's posting infringe any of the other exclusive rights in § 106? The court in *Netcom* implies that Erlich caused a public distribution of the copyrighted works. Did he, under § 106(3), distribute copies to the public "by sale or other transfer of ownership, or by rental, lease, or lending"? Technically, no copies changed hands—Usenet readers each viewed a new "copy." Was there nevertheless a "distribution"?

The *DMCA Section 104 Report* issued by the Copyright Office in 2001 concluded that a digital transfer of a work, even by the owner of a lawful copy, does not fall within the protection of § 109's first sale doctrine. The first sale doctrine limits only the copyright owner's distribution right, while digital transmissions involve the creation of copies. The Report also recommended against extending the first sale doctrine to digital transmissions; since digital works can be transmitted flawlessly and almost instantaneously around the globe, digital transmissions can affect the market for a work more dramatically than the transfer of physical copies. M. Lemley, Dealing with Overlapping Copyrights on the Internet, 22 U. Dayton L.Rev. 547 (1997), points out that the

[q] A similar result was reached against another defendant who scanned and posted the same plaintiffs' texts on the Internet, see Religious Technology Center v. Lerma, 40 U.S.P.Q.2d 1569 (E.D.Va.1996), but a third defendant whose use consisted primarily of scanning the texts into a computer located in a private section of its library escaped a preliminary injunction on a fair use defense in Religious Technology Center v. F.A.C.T.NET, Inc., 901 F.Supp. 1519 (D.Colo.1995). J. Linford, A Second Look at the Right of First Publication, 58 J.Copyr. Soc'y 585 (2011), suggest a right of first online distribution that would preclude a fair use defense to an unauthorized first online dissemination.

multiple exclusive rights implicated by digital use make licensing more difficult and can frustrate statutory rules like "first sale" that were formulated with only a single right in mind; M. Van Houweling, Author Autonomy and Atomism in Copyright Law, 96 Va.L.Rev. 549 (2010), worries about the transaction costs imposed by the proliferation of works and owners in a networked environment.

(4) Are users who accessed Erlich's Usenet posting in danger of being held liable as copyright infringers? Although users might display the work on their computer screens and in other cases might perform the copyrighted work, in most instances those displays or performances are not public and hence are not infringements. Unless the user further transmits the work, she will also not violate the public distribution right. But what of the exclusive right to reproduce the work in copies? If the user downloads the work to the computer's hard drive or other storage media, or prints out a hard copy, a reproduction has clearly occurred, although it may of course be a fair use. What if a user merely "browses" the work—arguably the digital equivalent of reading a book or looking at a painting? Since a copy of the work must be created in the RAM memory of the user's computer in order to display the work on the screen, a potentially infringing reproduction has occurred. Indeed, in the process of accessing the work, the user has probably caused the creation of copies in the server on which the work resides and in numerous intermediary servers located between the host computer and the user. The situation is further complicated by the existence of caching. Caching is the temporary storage of digital information "closer" to the user in order to speed access. Caching can occur on intermediary computers in the connection between the host computer and the user as well as on the user's own computer. The user's browser software may also automatically store retrieved data on the computer's hard drive for an extended period of time. Is caching, too, a potential infringement?[r]

Suppose that, unlike the plaintiffs in *Netcom*, a copyright owner has authorized the uploading of a work onto a web site. Is there then an implied license to make the temporary copies normally associated with accessing the work? An implied license to download the work to a CD or hard drive? M. Grynberg, Property is a Two–Way Street: Personal Copyright Use and Implied Authorization, 79 Ford.L.Rev. 435 (2010), suggests an expansive view of implied license based on the reasonable expectations of the user.

Would it be wiser to abandon the structure of § 106 and wholly rethink the appropriate scope of copyright in a digital environment? There have been numerous suggestions. See, e.g., J. Litman, Revising Copyright Law for the Information Age, 75 Ore.L.Rev. 19 (1996), concluding that the touchstone for infringement should be commercial exploitation rather than reproduction; D. Tussey, From Fair Use to Filesharing: Personal Use in Cyberspace, 35 Ga.L.Rev. 1129 (2001), suggesting a legislatively defined "personal use right" to replace the de facto insulation that personal copying enjoyed in the pre-digital era; J. Lipton, Cyberspace, Exceptionalism, and Innocent Copyright Infringement, 13 Vand.J.Ent. & Tech.L. 767 (2011), believes that strict liability for copyright infringement is a poor fit with modern digital technology.

---

[r] The legal implications of caching are analyzed in T. Hardy, Computer RAM "Copies": Hit or Myth? Historical Perspectives on Caching As a Microcosm of Current Copyright Concerns, 22 U. Dayton L.Rev. 423 (1997). A. Bartow, Electrifying Copyright Norms and Making Cyberspace More Like a Book, 48 Vill.L.Rev. 13 (2003), laments the loss of analog copyright norms in the switch to digital formats.

Perfect 10, Inc. v. Amazon.com, Inc.

United States Court of Appeals, Ninth Circuit, 2007.
508 F.3d 1146.

■ Before HALL, HAWKINS, and IKUTA, CIRCUIT JUDGES.

■ IKUTA, CIRCUIT JUDGE. [Perfect 10 owned copyrights in photographs of nude models that it marketed through a password-protected web site. However, some of the photos also appeared without permission on third-party web sites. Google stored thumbnail versions of the photographs collected by its search engine web crawler from the third-party sites. Users of Google's Image Search could retrieve the thumbnails from Google's server as part of a grid of search results. If the user clicked on one of the thumbnails, Google would show the thumbnail in the upper portion of the screen along with the address of the originating web site; the lower portion of the screen showed the full-size image by means of an in-line link to the originating site. Google also operated an advertising program called AdSense that allowed Google to place advertising on participating web sites that then shared the resulting revenue with Google. Some of the third-party web sites containing infringing copies of Perfect 10's photographs were participants in Google's AdSense program. Perfect 10 claimed that Google's use of both the thumbnails and full-size images constituted direct infringement of its display and distribution rights, and that Google was also contributorily and vicariously liable for infringements by third parties.]

III

Direct Infringement

Perfect 10 claims that Google's search engine program directly infringes two exclusive rights granted to copyright holders: its display rights and its distribution rights. * * *

A.   Display Right

* * * [B]ased on the plain language of the statute, a person displays a photographic image by using a computer to fill a computer screen with a copy of the photographic image fixed in the computer's memory. There is no dispute that Google's computers store thumbnail versions of Perfect 10's copyrighted images and communicate copies of those thumbnails to Google's users.[6] Therefore, Perfect 10 has made a prima facie case that Google's communication of its stored thumbnail images directly infringes Perfect 10's display right.

Google does not, however, display a copy of full-size infringing photographic images for purposes of the Copyright Act when Google frames in-line linked images that appear on a user's computer screen. Because Google's computers do not store the photographic images, Google does not have a copy of the images for purposes of the Copyright Act. In other words, Google does not have any "material objects . . . in which a work is fixed . . . and from which the work can be perceived, reproduced, or otherwise communicated" and thus cannot communicate a copy. 17 U.S.C. § 101.

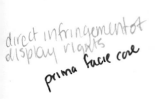

---

[6]   Because Google initiates and controls the storage and communication of these thumbnail images, we do not address whether an entity that merely passively owns and manages an Internet bulletin board or similar system violates a copyright owner's display and distribution rights when the users of the bulletin board or similar system post infringing works. Cf. CoStar Group, Inc. v. LoopNet, Inc., 373 F.3d 544 (4th Cir.2004).

Instead of communicating a copy of the image, Google provides HTML instructions that direct a user's browser to a website publisher's computer that stores the full-size photographic image. Providing these HTML instructions is not equivalent to showing a copy. First, the HTML instructions are lines of text, not a photographic image. Second, HTML instructions do not themselves cause infringing images to appear on the user's computer screen. The HTML merely gives the address of the image to the user's browser. The browser then interacts with the computer that stores the infringing image. It is this interaction that causes an infringing image to appear on the user's computer screen. Google may facilitate the user's access to infringing images. However, such assistance raises only contributory liability issues, see Metro–Goldwyn–Mayer Studios, Inc. v. Grokster, Ltd., 545 U.S. 913, 929–30 (2005), [A & M Records, Inc. v. Napster, Inc., 239 F.3d 1004, 1019 (9th Cir.2001)], and does not constitute direct infringement of the copyright owner's display rights.

Perfect 10 argues that Google displays a copy of the full-size images by framing the full-size images, which gives the impression that Google is showing the image within a single Google webpage. While in-line linking and framing may cause some computer users to believe they are viewing a single Google webpage, the Copyright Act, unlike the Trademark Act, does not protect a copyright holder against acts that cause consumer confusion. * * *

B. Distribution Right

* * * Section 106(3) provides that the copyright owner has the exclusive right "to distribute copies or phonorecords of the copyrighted work to the public by sale or other transfer of ownership, or by rental, lease, or lending." 17 U.S.C. § 106(3). As noted, "copies" means "material objects . . . in which a work is fixed." 17 U.S.C. § 101. The Supreme Court has indicated that in the electronic context, copies may be distributed electronically. See N.Y. Times Co. v. Tasini, 533 U.S. 483, 498 (2001) (a computer database program distributed copies of newspaper articles stored in its computerized database by selling copies of those articles through its database service). Google's search engine communicates HTML instructions that tell a user's browser where to find full-size images on a website publisher's computer, but Google does not itself distribute copies of the infringing photographs. It is the website publisher's computer that distributes copies of the images by transmitting the photographic image electronically to the user's computer. * * *

C. Fair Use Defense

Because Perfect 10 has succeeded in showing it would prevail in its prima facie case that Google's thumbnail images infringe Perfect 10's display rights, the burden shifts to Google to show that it will likely succeed in establishing an affirmative defense. Google contends that its use of thumbnails is a fair use of the images and therefore does not constitute an infringement of Perfect 10's copyright. See 17 U.S.C. § 107.

[In its fair use analysis, the court relied heavily on its opinion in Kelly v. Arriba Soft Corp., 336 F.3d 811 (9th Cir.2003), which found a similar use of copyrighted images to be fair use. Judge Ikuta characterized Google's use as "highly transformative." "[A] search engine provides social benefit by incorporating an original work into a new work, namely, an electronic reference tool." The district court, which held that Google's use of the thumbnails was not a fair use, had found that the transformative nature of

Google's use was undercut by the fact that the thumbnails superseded Perfect 10's ability to sell reduced-size images for use on cell phones. The lower court had also found that the commercial nature of the use was magnified by the fact that the thumbnails could lead users to AdSense web sites that contributed to Google's revenue. Judge Ikuta, however, concluded that neither the superseding use for cell phones nor the commercial advantage to Google through its AdSense program were significant. "We conclude that the significantly transformative nature of Google's search engine, particularly in light of its public benefit, outweighs Google's superseding and commercial uses of the thumbnails in this case." As in Kelly v. Arriba Soft Corp., the court held that the use of the entire copyrighted image was reasonable in light of the purpose of a search engine. As to the effect on the market for the copyrighted work, the court reasoned that since Google's thumbnails were not a substitute for the full-size images, they did not harm the market for those images. As to the market for reduced-size images for cell phone downloads, the absence of evidence of any actual downloads made that potential harm "hypothetical." "We conclude that Google is likely to succeed in proving its fair use defense and, accordingly, we vacate the preliminary injunction regarding Google's use of thumbnail images."]

IV

Secondary Liability for Copyright Infringement

We now turn to the district court's ruling that Google is unlikely to be secondarily liable for its in-line linking to infringing full-size images under the doctrines of contributory and vicarious infringement. * * *

Direct Infringement by Third Parties. As a threshold matter, before we examine Perfect 10's claims that Google is secondarily liable, Perfect 10 must establish that there has been direct infringement by third parties. See *Napster,* 239 F.3d at 1013 n.2 ("Secondary liability for copyright infringement does not exist in the absence of direct infringement by a third party.").

Perfect 10 alleges that third parties directly infringed its images in three ways. First, Perfect 10 claims that third-party websites directly infringed its copyright by reproducing, displaying, and distributing unauthorized copies of Perfect 10's images. Google does not dispute this claim on appeal.

Second, Perfect 10 claims that individual users of Google's search engine directly infringed Perfect 10's copyrights by storing full-size infringing images on their computers. We agree with the district court's conclusion that Perfect 10 failed to provide sufficient evidence to support this claim. See *Perfect 10,* 416 F.Supp.2d at 852. There is no evidence in the record directly establishing that users of Google's search engine have stored infringing images on their computers, and the district court did not err in declining to infer the existence of such evidence.

Finally, Perfect 10 contends that users who link to infringing websites automatically make "cache" copies of full size images and thereby directly infringe Perfect 10's reproduction right. The district court rejected this argument, holding that any such reproduction was likely a "fair use." Id. at 852 n.17. The district court reasoned that "[l]ocal caching by the browsers of individual users is noncommercial, transformative, and no more than necessary to achieve the objectives of decreasing network latency and minimizing unnecessary bandwidth usage (essential to the [I]nternet). It has a minimal impact on the potential market for the original work . . . . " Id. We agree; even assuming such automatic copying could constitute direct infringement, it is a fair use in this context. The copying function performed automatically by a user's computer to assist in accessing the Internet is a transformative use. Moreover, as noted by the district court, a cache copies no more than is necessary to assist the user in Internet use. It is designed to enhance an individual's computer use, not to supersede the copyright holders' exploitation of their works. Such automatic background copying has no more than a minimal effect on Perfect 10's rights, but a considerable public benefit. Because the four fair use factors weigh in favor of concluding that cache copying constitutes a fair use, Google has established a likelihood of success on this issue. Accordingly, Perfect 10 has not carried its burden of showing that users' cache copies of Perfect 10's full-size images constitute direct infringement.

> *CT: Transformative use*
>
> *no direct infringement*

Therefore, we must assess Perfect 10's arguments that Google is secondarily liable in light of the direct infringement that is undisputed by the parties: third-party websites' reproducing, displaying, and distributing unauthorized copies of Perfect 10's images on the Internet. Id. at 852.

A.   Contributory Infringement

In order for Perfect 10 to show it will likely succeed in its contributory liability claim against Google, it must establish that Google's activities meet the definition of contributory liability recently enunciated in *Grokster.* Within the general rule that "[o]ne infringes contributorily by intentionally inducing or encouraging direct infringement," *Grokster,* 545 U.S. at 930, the Court has defined two categories of contributory liability: "Liability under our jurisprudence may be predicated on actively encouraging (or inducing) infringement through specific acts (as the Court's opinion develops) or on distributing a product distributees use to infringe copyrights, if the product is not capable of 'substantial' or 'commercially significant' noninfringing uses." Id. at 942 (Ginsburg, J., concurring) (quoting *Sony,* 464 U.S. at 442); see also id. at 936–37.

> *Gen rule for contributory Liability*
>
> *Types*

Looking at the second category of liability identified by the Supreme Court (distributing products), Google relies on *Sony,* 464 U.S. at 442, to argue that it cannot be held liable for contributory infringement because liability does not arise from the mere sale of a product (even with knowledge that consumers would use the product to infringe) if the product is capable of substantial non-infringing use. Google argues that its search engine service is such a product. Assuming the principle enunciated in *Sony* is applicable to the operation of Google's search engine, then Google cannot be held liable for contributory infringement *solely* because the design of its search engine facilitates such infringement. *Grokster,* 545 U.S. at 931–32 (discussing *Sony,* 464 U.S. 417). Nor can Google be held liable solely because it did not develop technology that would enable its search engine to automatically avoid infringing images. See id. at 939 n. 12. However, Perfect 10 has not based its claim of infringement on the design of Google's search engine and the *Sony* rule does not immunize Google from other sources of contributory liability. See id. at 933–34.

> *Aargus*
>
> *G uses Sony arg.*
>
> *But Plos claim not based on the design of search engine*

We must next consider whether Google could be held liable under the first category of contributory liability identified by the Supreme Court, that is, the liability that may be imposed for intentionally encouraging infringement through specific acts.[11] * * *

---

[11] Google's activities do not meet the "inducement" test explained in *Grokster* because Google has not promoted the use of its search engine specifically to infringe copyrights. See

Our tests for contributory liability are consistent with the rule set forth in *Grokster*. We have adopted the general rule set forth in Gershwin Publishing Corp. v. Columbia Artists Management, Inc., namely: "one who, with knowledge of the infringing activity, induces, causes or materially contributes to the infringing conduct of another, may be held liable as a 'contributory' infringer," 443 F.2d 1159, 1162 (2d Cir.1971). See [Ellison v. Robertson, 357 F.3d 1072, 1076 (9th Cir.2004)]; *Napster,* 239 F.3d at 1019; Fonovisa, Inc. v. Cherry Auction, Inc., 76 F.3d 259, 264 (9th Cir.1996).

We have further refined this test in the context of cyberspace to determine when contributory liability can be imposed on a provider of Internet access or services. See *Napster,* 239 F.3d at 1019–20. In *Napster,* we considered claims that the operator of an electronic file sharing system was contributorily liable for assisting individual users to swap copyrighted music files stored on their home computers with other users of the system. *Napster,* 239 F.3d at 1011–13, 1019–22. We stated that "if a computer system operator learns of specific infringing material available on his system and fails to purge such material from the system, the operator knows of and contributes to direct infringement." Id. at 1021. Because Napster knew of the availability of infringing music files, assisted users in accessing such files, and failed to block access to such files, we concluded that Napster materially contributed to infringement. Id. at 1022.

The *Napster* test for contributory liability was modeled on the influential district court decision in Religious Technology Center v. Netcom On–Line Communication Services, Inc. (*Netcom*), 907 F.Supp. 1361, 1365–66 (N.D.Cal.1995). See *Napster,* 239 F.3d at 1021.

* * * Accordingly, we hold that a computer system operator can be held contributorily liable if it "has *actual* knowledge that *specific* infringing material is available using its system," *Napster,* 239 F.3d at 1022, and can "take simple measures to prevent further damage" to copyrighted works, *Netcom,* 907 F.Supp. at 1375, yet continues to provide access to infringing works.

* * * Applying our test, Google could be held contributorily liable if it had knowledge that infringing Perfect 10 images were available using its search engine, could take simple measures to prevent further damage to Perfect 10's copyrighted works, and failed to take such steps.

The district court did not resolve the factual disputes over the adequacy of Perfect 10's notices to Google and Google's responses to these notices. Moreover, there are factual disputes over whether there are reasonable and feasible means for Google to refrain from providing access to infringing images. Therefore, we must remand this claim to the district court for further consideration whether Perfect 10 would likely succeed in establishing that Google was contributorily liable for in-line linking to full-size infringing images under the test enunciated today.

B.   Vicarious Infringement

Perfect 10 also challenges the district court's conclusion that it is not likely to prevail on a theory of vicarious liability against Google. *Perfect 10,* 416 F.Supp.2d at 856–58. *Grokster* states that one "infringes vicariously by profiting from direct infringement while declining to exercise a right to stop or limit it." *Grokster,* 545 U.S. at 930. * * *

Grokster, 545 U.S. at 935–37. However, the Supreme Court in *Grokster* did not suggest that a court must find inducement in order to impose contributory liability under common law principles.

We evaluate Perfect 10's arguments that Google is vicariously liable in light of the direct infringement that is undisputed by the parties, namely, the third-party websites' reproduction, display, and distribution of unauthorized copies of Perfect 10's images on the Internet. *Perfect 10,* 416 F.Supp.2d at 852; see supra Section IV.A. In order to prevail at this preliminary injunction stage, Perfect 10 must demonstrate a likelihood of success in establishing that Google has the right and ability to stop or limit the infringing activities of third-party websites. In addition, Perfect 10 must establish a likelihood of proving that Google derives a direct financial benefit from such activities. Perfect 10 has not met this burden.

With respect to the "control" element set forth in *Grokster,* Perfect 10 has not demonstrated a likelihood of showing that Google has the legal right to stop or limit the direct infringement of third-party websites. See *Grokster,* 545 U.S. at 930. * * *

Because we conclude that Perfect 10 has not shown a likelihood of establishing Google's right and ability to stop or limit the directly infringing conduct of third-party websites, we agree with the district court's conclusion that Perfect 10 "has not established a likelihood of proving the [control] prong necessary for vicarious liability." *Perfect 10,* 416 F.Supp.2d at 858.

[The court also directed the district court to consider on remand whether Google would be likely to succeed in showing that it was entitled to protection under the safe harbor for providers of "information location tools" in § 512(d).]

NOTES AND QUESTIONS

(1) The court in *Perfect 10* holds that Google's links to the full-size images do not directly infringe the plaintiff's display or distribution rights. Might such "framing" links violate the exclusive right to create derivative works by presenting the copyrighted work as part of Google's own web page? In Futuredontics Inc. v. Applied Anagramics Inc., 45 U.S.P.Q.2d 2005 (C.D.Cal.), aff'd, 152 F.3d 925 (9th Cir.1998), the plaintiff argued that the defendant's framed link to the plaintiff's web site infringed the derivative right. The court denied the plaintiff's motion for a preliminary injunction, but refused to dismiss the complaint.[s]

The court concludes that the only direct infringement relevant to Google's potential contributory liability is the use of plaintiff's images by the third-party websites. Did Google materially contribute to unauthorized reproductions on those websites? To unauthorized displays or distributions by those websites?

(2) Judge Posner in Flava Works, Inc. v. Gunter, 689 F.3d 754 (7th Cir.2012), took a narrow view of contributory liability for linking when an owner of copy-

---

[s]   In a somewhat analogous situation, Judge Batts in 1–800 Contacts, Inc. v. WhenU.com, 309 F.Supp.2d 467 (S.D.N.Y.2003), rev'd on other grounds, 414 F.3d 400 (2d Cir.), cert. denied, 546 U.S. 1033 (2005), held that a defendant's "pop-up" ads that covered a portion of the plaintiff's web site did not "recast, transform or adapt" the site and thus did not create an infringing derivative work. "Moreover, if obscuring a browser window containing a copyrighted website with another computer window produces a 'derivative work,' then *any* action by a computer user that produced a computer window or visual graphic that altered the screen appearance of Plaintiff's website, however slight, would require Plaintiff's permission. A definition of 'derivative work' that sweeps within the scope of copyright law a multi-tasking Internet shopper whose word-processing program obscures the screen display of Plaintiff's website is indeed 'jarring,' and not supported by the definition set forth at 17 U.S.C. § 101."

rights in pornographic videos requested a preliminary injunction against a website that provided its users with framed links to sites containing unauthorized copies of the plaintiff's works. The court said that there was no evidence that the defendant had contributed to any infringing reproduction or distribution of the videos; as for potential contributory liability for unauthorized public performance, Judge Posner said that there was insufficient evidence in the record to establish that the defendant was "actually contributing significantly to the unauthorized performance of [plaintiff's] copyrighted works by visitors to [defendant's] website."

(3) A contributory liability claim against a defendant who linked to infringing material was successful in Intellectual Reserve, Inc. v. Utah Lighthouse Ministry, Inc., 75 F.Supp.2d 1290 (D.Utah 1999). The defendant had been required by a temporary restraining order to remove the plaintiff's *Church Handbook of Instructions* from its web site. Defendant complied but then added to its site the addresses of three other web sites that contained unauthorized copies of the work and sent e-mail messages urging people to visit those sites and download the work. The court said that even users who merely look at the copyrighted work on one of the other sites without downloading or transmitting it are infringers since browsing makes unauthorized copies in the user's RAM memory. The court held that the defendant had contributed to these infringements by encouraging the conduct and granted a preliminary injunction that prohibited the defendant from posting the addresses of other sites where the defendant had reason to know the copyrighted work was located. S. Dogan, Infringement Once Removed: The Perils of Hyperlinking to Infringing Content, 87 Iowa L.Rev. 829 (2002), concludes that existing standards for contributory and vicarious liability fail to address the different contexts in which links to infringing materials can occur; T. Folsom, Toward Non–Neutral First Principles of Private Law: Designing Secondary Liability Rules for New Technological Uses, 3 Akron Intell.Prop.J. 43 (2009), concludes more generally that the ordinary rules of secondary liability should not automatically apply in cyberspace; M. Bartholomew, Contributory Infringers and Good Samaritans, id. at 1, argues that it is generally inappropriate to impose supervisory duties on third parties who offer standardized digital functionality.

SERVICE PROVIDER "SAFE HARBORS"—§ 512

The opinion in *Netcom* notes the differing views on the appropriate scope of liability for Internet service providers like web sites that host user content or companies that provide Internet access or links to online content. Should online service providers be held strictly accountable for copyright infringement by their customers? Should knowledge be a prerequisite to liability? Online service providers pushed hard for some form of legislative protection. Their lobbying efforts ultimately produced § 512, added as part of the Digital Millennium Copyright Act in 1998. Section 512 creates a series of "safe harbors" covering many of the typical functions performed by online service providers. The section bars monetary relief and limits injunctive relief against qualifying service providers. The failure of a service provider to qualify for a safe harbor does not mean that the provider is liable for the copyright infringements of its customers. See § 512(*l*). According to the Senate Judiciary Committee Report, "Even if a service provider's activities fall outside the limitations on liability specified in the bill, the service provider is not necessarily an infringer; liability in these circumstances would be adjudicated based on the doctrines of direct, vicarious or contributory liability for infringement as they are articulated in the Copyright Act and in the court decisions interpreting and applying that statute, which are unchanged by § 512."[t]

Viacom International, Inc. v. YouTube, Inc.
United States Court of Appeals, Second Circuit, 2012.
676 F.3d 19.

■ Before CABRANES AND LIVINGSTON, CIRCUIT JUDGES.[*]

■ CABRANES, CIRCUIT JUDGE.

This appeal requires us to clarify the contours of the "safe harbor" provision of the Digital Millennium Copyright Act (DMCA) that limits the liability of online service providers for copyright infringement that occurs "by reason of the storage at the direction of a user of material that resides on a system or network controlled or operated by or for the service provider." 17 U.S.C. § 512(c).

The plaintiffs-appellants in these related actions—Viacom International, Inc. ("Viacom"), The Football Association Premier League Ltd. ("Premier League"), and various film studios, television networks, music publishers, and sports leagues (jointly, the "plaintiffs")—appeal from an August 10, 2010 judgment of the United States District Court for the Southern District of New York (Louis L. Stanton, Judge), which granted summary judgment to defendants-appellees YouTube, Inc., YouTube, LLC, and Google Inc. (jointly, "YouTube" or the "defendants"). The plaintiffs alleged direct and secondary copyright infringement based on the public performance, display, and reproduction of approximately 79,000 audiovisual "clips" that appeared on the YouTube website between 2005 and 2008. They demanded, inter alia, statutory damages pursuant to 17 U.S.C. § 504(c) or, in the alternative, actual damages from the alleged infringement, as well as declaratory and injunctive relief.

In a June 23, 2010 Opinion and Order (the "June 23 Opinion"), the District Court held that the defendants were entitled to DMCA safe harbor protection primarily because they had insufficient notice of the particular infringements in suit. Viacom Int'l, Inc. v. YouTube, Inc., 718 F.Supp.2d 514, 529 (S.D.N.Y.2010). * * *

BACKGROUND

A. The DMCA Safe Harbors

"The DMCA was enacted in 1998 to implement the World Intellectual Property Organization Copyright Treaty," Universal City Studios, Inc. v. Corley, 273 F.3d 429, 440 (2d Cir.2001), and to update domestic copyright law for the digital age, see Ellison v. Robertson, 357 F.3d 1072, 1076 (9th Cir.2004). Title II of the DMCA, separately titled the "Online Copyright Infringement Liability Limitation Act" (OCILLA), was designed to "clarif[y]

---

[t] S.Rep. No. 105-190, 105th Cong., 2d Sess. 122 (1998). See, e.g., CoStar Group, Inc. v. LoopNet, Inc., 373 F.3d 544 (4th Cir.2004), holding that § 512 does not preempt the infringement analysis in *Netcom.*

[*] The Honorable Roger J. Miner, who was originally assigned to the panel, died prior to the resolution of this case. The remaining two members of the panel, who are in agreement, have determined the matter. See 28 U.S.C. § 46(d); 2d Cir. IOP E(b); United States v. Desimone, 140 F.3d 457, 458–59 (2d Cir.1998).

the liability faced by service providers who transmit potentially infringing material over their networks." S.Rep. No. 105–190 at 2 (1998). But "[r]ather than embarking upon a wholesale clarification" of various copyright doctrines, Congress elected "to leave current law in its evolving state and, instead, to create a series of 'safe harbors[ ]' for certain common activities of service providers." Id. at 19. To that end, OCILLA established a series of four "safe harbors" that allow qualifying service providers to limit their liability for claims of copyright infringement based on (a) "transitory digital network communications," (b) "system caching," (c) "information residing on systems or networks at [the] direction of users," and (d) "information location tools." 17 U.S.C. § 512(a)–(d).

To qualify for protection under any of the safe harbors, a party must meet a set of threshold criteria. First, the party must in fact be a "service provider," defined, in pertinent part, as "a provider of online services or network access, or the operator of facilities therefor." 17 U.S.C. § 512(k)(1)(B). A party that qualifies as a service provider must also satisfy certain "conditions of eligibility," including the adoption and reasonable implementation of a "repeat infringer" policy that "provides for the termination in appropriate circumstances of subscribers and account holders of the service provider's system or network." Id. § 512(i)(1)(A). In addition, a qualifying service provider must accommodate "standard technical measures" that are "used by copyright owners to identify or protect copyrighted works." Id. § 512(i)(1)(B), (i)(2).

Beyond the threshold criteria, a service provider must satisfy the requirements of a particular safe harbor. In this case, the safe harbor at issue is § 512(c), which covers infringement claims that arise "by reason of the storage at the direction of a user of material that resides on a system or network controlled or operated by or for the service provider." Id. § 512(c)(1). The § 512(c) safe harbor will apply only if the service provider:

(A) (i) does not have actual knowledge that the material or an activity using the material on the system or network is infringing;

(ii) in the absence of such actual knowledge, is not aware of facts or circumstances from which infringing activity is apparent; or

(iii) upon obtaining such knowledge or awareness, acts expeditiously to remove, or disable access to, the material;

(B) does not receive a financial benefit directly attributable to the infringing activity, in a case in which the service provider has the right and ability to control such activity; and

(C) upon notification of claimed infringement as described in paragraph (3), responds expeditiously to remove, or disable access to, the material that is claimed to be infringing or to be the subject of infringing activity.

Id. § 512(c)(1)(A)–(C). Section 512(c) also sets forth a detailed notification scheme that requires service providers to "designate[ ] an agent to receive notifications of claimed infringement," id. § 512(c)(2), and specifies the components of a proper notification, commonly known as a "takedown notice," to that agent, see id. § 512(c)(3). Thus, actual knowledge of infringing material, awareness of facts or circumstances that make infringing activity apparent, or receipt of a takedown notice will each trigger an obligation to expeditiously remove the infringing material.

With the statutory context in mind, we now turn to the facts of this case.

B.   Factual Background

YouTube was founded in February 2005 by Chad Hurley ("Hurley"), Steve Chen ("Chen"), and Jawed Karim ("Karim"), three former employees of the internet company Paypal. When YouTube announced the "official launch" of the website in December 2005, a press release described YouTube as a "consumer media company" that "allows people to watch, upload, and share personal video clips at www.YouTube.com." Under the slogan "Broadcast yourself," YouTube achieved rapid prominence and profitability, eclipsing competitors such as Google Video and Yahoo Video by wide margins. In November 2006, Google acquired YouTube in a stock-for-stock transaction valued at $1.65 billion. By March 2010, at the time of summary judgment briefing in this litigation, site traffic on YouTube had soared to more than 1 billion daily video views, with more than 24 hours of new video uploaded to the site every minute.

The basic function of the YouTube website permits users to "upload" and view video clips free of charge. Before uploading a video to YouTube, a user must register and create an account with the website. The registration process requires the user to accept YouTube's Terms of Use agreement, which provides, *inter alia,* that the user "will not submit material that is copyrighted . . . unless [he is] the owner of such rights or ha[s] permission from their rightful owner to post the material and to grant YouTube all of the license rights granted herein." When the registration process is complete, the user can sign in to his account, select a video to upload from the user's personal computer, mobile phone, or other device, and instruct the YouTube system to upload the video by clicking on a virtual upload "button."

Uploading a video to the YouTube website triggers a series of automated software functions. During the upload process, YouTube makes one or more exact copies of the video in its original file format. YouTube also makes one or more additional copies of the video in "Flash" format, a process known as "transcoding." The transcoding process ensures that YouTube videos are available for viewing by most users at their request. The YouTube system allows users to gain access to video content by "streaming" the video to the user's computer in response to a playback request. YouTube uses a computer algorithm to identify clips that are "related" to a video the user watches and display links to the "related" clips. * * *

DISCUSSION

* * *

A.   Actual and "Red Flag" Knowledge: § 512(c)(1)(A)

The first and most important question on appeal is whether the DMCA safe harbor at issue requires "actual knowledge" or "aware[ness]" of facts or circumstances indicating "specific and identifiable infringements," *Viacom,* 718 F.Supp.2d at 523. We consider first the scope of the statutory provision and then its application to the record in this case.

Actual or red flag knows [handwritten margin note]

1.   The Specificity Requirement

"As in all statutory construction cases, we begin with the language of the statute," *Barnhart v. Sigmon Coal Co.,* 534 U.S. 438 (2002). Under § 512(c)(1)(A), safe harbor protection is available only if the service provider:

(i) does not have actual knowledge that the material or an activity using the material on the system or network is infringing;

(ii) in the absence of such actual knowledge, is not aware of facts or circumstances from which infringing activity is apparent; or

(iii) upon obtaining such knowledge or awareness, acts expeditiously to remove, or disable access to, the material . . . .

17 U.S.C. § 512(c)(1)(A). As previously noted, the District Court held that the statutory phrases "actual knowledge that the material . . . is infringing" and "facts or circumstances from which infringing activity is apparent" refer to "knowledge of specific and identifiable infringements." *Viacom,* 718 F.Supp.2d at 523. For the reasons that follow, we substantially affirm that holding.

Although the parties marshal a battery of other arguments on appeal, it is the text of the statute that compels our conclusion. In particular, we are persuaded that the basic operation of § 512(c) requires knowledge or awareness of specific infringing activity. Under § 512(c)(1)(A), knowledge or awareness alone does not disqualify the service provider; rather, the provider that gains knowledge or awareness of infringing activity retains safe-harbor protection if it "acts expeditiously to remove, or disable access to, the material." 17 U.S.C. § 512(c)(1)(A)(iii). Thus, the nature of the removal obligation itself contemplates knowledge or awareness of specific infringing material, because expeditious removal is possible only if the service provider knows with particularity which items to remove. Indeed, to require expeditious removal in the absence of specific knowledge or awareness would be to mandate an amorphous obligation to "take commercially reasonable steps" in response to a generalized awareness of infringement. Viacom Br. 33. Such a view cannot be reconciled with the language of the statute, which requires "expeditious[ ]" action to remove or disable *the material* at issue. 17 U.S.C. § 512(c)(1)(A)(iii) (emphasis added).

On appeal, the plaintiffs dispute this conclusion by drawing our attention to § 512(c)(1)(A)(ii), the so-called "red flag" knowledge provision. See id. § 512(c)(1)(A)(ii) (limiting liability where, "in the absence of such actual knowledge, [the service provider] is not aware of facts or circumstances from which infringing activity is apparent"). In their view, the use of the phrase "facts or circumstances" demonstrates that Congress did not intend to limit the red flag provision to a particular type of knowledge. The plaintiffs contend that requiring awareness of specific infringements in order to establish "aware[ness] of facts or circumstances from which infringing activity is apparent," 17 U.S.C. § 512(c)(1)(A)(ii), renders the red flag provision superfluous, because that provision would be satisfied only when the "actual knowledge" provision is also satisfied. For that reason, the plaintiffs urge the Court to hold that the red flag provision "requires less specificity" than the actual knowledge provision. Pls.' Supp. Br. 1.

* * * [C]ontrary to the plaintiffs' assertions, construing § 512(c)(1)(A) to require actual knowledge or awareness of specific instances of infringement does not render the red flag provision superfluous. The phrase "actual knowledge," which appears in § 512(c)(1)(A)(i), is frequently used to denote subjective belief. * * *

The difference between actual and red flag knowledge is thus not between specific and generalized knowledge, but instead between a subjective and an objective standard. In other words, the actual knowledge provision turns on whether the provider actually or "subjectively" knew of specific infringement, while the red flag provision turns on whether the provider was subjectively aware of facts that would have made the specific infringement "objectively" obvious to a reasonable person. The red flag provision, because it incorporates an objective standard, is not swallowed up by the actual knowledge provision under our construction of the § 512(c) safe harbor. Both provisions do independent work, and both apply only to specific instances of infringement.

The limited body of case law interpreting the knowledge provisions of the § 512(c) safe harbor comports with our view of the specificity requirement. Most recently, a panel of the Ninth Circuit addressed the scope of § 512(c) in UMG Recordings, Inc. v. Shelter Capital Partners LLC, 667 F.3d 1022 (9th Cir.2011), a copyright infringement case against Veoh Networks, a video-hosting service similar to YouTube. As in this case, various music publishers brought suit against the service provider, claiming direct and secondary copyright infringement based on the presence of unauthorized content on the website, and the website operator sought refuge in the § 512(c) safe harbor. The Court of Appeals affirmed the district court's determination on summary judgment that the website operator was entitled to safe harbor protection. With respect to the actual knowledge provision, the panel declined to "adopt[ ] a broad conception of the knowledge requirement," id. at 1038, holding instead that the safe harbor "[r]equir[es] specific knowledge of particular infringing activity," id. at 1037. The Court of Appeals "reach[ed] the same conclusion" with respect to the red flag provision, noting that "[w]e do not place the burden of determining whether [materials] are actually illegal on a service provider." Id. at 1038 (alterations in original) (quoting Perfect 10, Inc. v. CCBill LLC, 488 F.3d 1102, 1114 (9th Cir.2007)). * * *

2.   The Grant of Summary Judgment

The corollary question on appeal is whether, under the foregoing construction of § 512(c)(1)(A), the District Court erred in granting summary judgment to YouTube on the record presented. For the reasons that follow, we hold that although the District Court correctly interpreted § 512(c)(1)(A), summary judgment for the defendants was premature.

i. Specific Knowledge or Awareness

The plaintiffs argue that, even under the District Court's construction of the safe harbor, the record raises material issues of fact regarding YouTube's actual knowledge or "red flag" awareness of specific instances of infringement. To that end, the plaintiffs draw our attention to various estimates regarding the percentage of infringing content on the YouTube website. For example, Viacom cites evidence that YouTube employees conducted website surveys and estimated that 75–80% of all YouTube streams contained copyrighted material. * * * But such estimates are insufficient, standing alone, to create a triable issue of fact as to whether YouTube actually knew, or was aware of facts or circumstances that would indicate, the existence of particular instances of infringement.

Beyond the survey results, the plaintiffs rely upon internal YouTube communications that do refer to particular clips or groups of clips. The class plaintiffs argue that YouTube was aware of specific infringing material because, inter alia, YouTube attempted to search for specific Premier League videos on the site in order to gauge their "value based on video usage." * * *

The record in the *Viacom* action includes additional examples. For instance, YouTube founder Jawed Karim prepared a report in March 2006 which stated that, "[a]s of today[,] episodes and clips of the following well-known shows can still be found [on YouTube]: Family Guy, South Park, MTV Cribs, Daily Show, Reno 911, [and] Dave Chapelle [sic]." Karim further opined that, "although YouTube is not legally required to monitor content . . . and complies with DMCA takedown requests, we would benefit from *preemptively* removing content that is blatantly illegal and likely to attract criticism." He also noted that "a more thorough analysis" of the issue would be required. At least some of the TV shows to which Karim referred are owned by Viacom. A reasonable juror could conclude from the March 2006 report that Karim knew of the presence of Viacom-owned material on YouTube, since he presumably located specific clips of the shows in question before he could announce that YouTube hosted the content "[a]s of today." A reasonable juror could also conclude that Karim believed the clips he located to be infringing (since he refers to them as "blatantly illegal"), and that YouTube did not remove the content from the website until conducting "a more thorough analysis," thus exposing the company to liability in the interim.

* * * Similarly, in an August 9, 2005 e-mail exchange, Hurley urged his colleagues "to start being *diligent* about rejecting copyrighted/inappropriate content," noting that "there is a cnn clip of the shuttle clip on the site today, if the boys from Turner would come to the site, they might be pissed?" * * *

Upon a review of the record, we are persuaded that the plaintiffs may have raised a material issue of fact regarding YouTube's knowledge or awareness of specific instances of infringement. * * *

* * * Accordingly, we vacate the order granting summary judgment and instruct the District Court to determine on remand whether any specific infringements of which YouTube had knowledge or awareness correspond to the clips-in-suit in these actions.

ii. "Willful Blindness"

The plaintiffs further argue that the District Court erred in granting summary judgment to the defendants despite evidence that YouTube was "willfully blind" to specific infringing activity. On this issue of first impression, we consider the application of the common law willful blindness doctrine in the DMCA context. * * *

* * * A person is "willfully blind" or engages in "conscious avoidance" amounting to knowledge where the person " 'was aware of a high probability of the fact in dispute and consciously avoided confirming that fact.' " United States v. Aina–Marshall, 336 F.3d 167, 170 (2d Cir.2003) (quoting United States v. Rodriguez, 983 F.2d 455, 458 (2d Cir.1993)); * * *

The DMCA does not mention willful blindness. As a general matter, we interpret a statute to abrogate a common law principle only if the statute "speak[s] directly to the question addressed by the common law." Matar v. Dichter, 563 F.3d 9, 14 (2d Cir.2009) (internal quotation marks omitted). The relevant question, therefore, is whether the DMCA "speak[s] directly" to the principle of willful blindness. Id. (internal quotation marks omitted). The DMCA provision most relevant to the abrogation inquiry is § 512(m), which provides that safe harbor protection shall not be conditioned on "a service provider monitoring its service or affirmatively seeking facts indicating infringing activity, except to the extent consistent with a standard technical measure complying with the provisions of subsection (i)." 17 U.S.C. § 512(m)(1). Section 512(m) is explicit: DMCA safe harbor protection cannot be conditioned on affirmative monitoring by a service provider. For that reason, § 512(m) is incompatible with a broad common law duty to monitor or otherwise seek out infringing activity based on general awareness that infringement may be occurring. That fact does not, however, dispose of the abrogation inquiry; as previously noted, willful blindness cannot be defined as an affirmative duty to monitor. See Aina–Marshall, 336 F.3d at 170 (holding that a person is "willfully blind" where he "was aware of a high probability of the fact in dispute and consciously avoided confirming that fact"). Because the statute does not "speak[ ] directly" to the willful-blindness doctrine, § 512(m) limits—but does not abrogate—the doctrine. Accordingly, we hold that the willful blindness doctrine may be applied, in appropriate circumstances, to demonstrate knowledge or awareness of specific instances of infringement under the DMCA.

willful blindness can be applied in appropriate circumstances

The District Court cited § 512(m) for the proposition that safe harbor protection does not require affirmative monitoring, *Viacom,* 718 F.Supp.2d at 524, but did not expressly address the principle of willful blindness or its relationship to the DMCA safe harbors. As a result, whether the defendants made a "deliberate effort to avoid guilty knowledge," *In re Aimster,* [334 F.3d 643, 650 (7th Cir.2003)], remains a fact question for the District Court to consider in the first instance on remand.

B. Control and Benefit: § 512(c)(1)(B)

Apart from the foregoing knowledge provisions, the § 512(c) safe harbor provides that an eligible service provider must "not receive a financial benefit directly attributable to the infringing activity, in a case in which the service provider has the right and ability to control such activity." 17 U.S.C. § 512(c)(1)(B). The District Court addressed this issue in a single paragraph, quoting from § 512(c)(1)(B), the so-called "control and benefit" provision, and concluding that "[t]he 'right and ability to control' the activity requires knowledge of it, which must be item-specific." *Viacom,* 718 F.Supp.2d at 527. For the reasons that follow, we hold that the District Court erred by importing a specific knowledge requirement into the control and benefit provision, and we therefore remand for further fact-finding on the issue of control.

512(c)

Can't receive financial benefit directly from infringing activity

Remand
Dist. ct. wrong to import specific knowledge req.

1. "Right and Ability to Control" Infringing Activity

On appeal, the parties advocate two competing constructions of the "right and ability to control" infringing activity. 17 U.S.C. § 512(c)(1)(B). Because each is fatally flawed, we reject both proposed constructions in favor of a fact-based inquiry to be conducted in the first instance by the District Court.

The first construction, pressed by the defendants, is the one adopted by the District Court, which held that "the provider must know of the particular case before he can control it." *Viacom,* 718 F.Supp.2d at 527. The Ninth Circuit recently agreed, holding that "until [the service provider] becomes aware of specific unauthorized material, it cannot exercise its 'power or authority' over the specific infringing item. In practical terms, it does not have the kind of ability to control infringing activity the statute contemplates." UMG Recordings, Inc. v. Shelter Capital Partners LLC, 667 F.3d 1022, 1041 (9th Cir.2011). The trouble with this construction is that importing a specific knowledge requirement into § 512(c)(1)(B) renders the control provision duplicative of § 512(c)(1)(A). Any service provider that has

Δ's arg.

But this would make 512(c)(1)(A) duplicative

item-specific knowledge of infringing activity and thereby obtains financial benefit would already be excluded from the safe harbor under § 512(c)(1)(A) for having specific knowledge of infringing material and failing to effect expeditious removal. No additional service provider would be excluded by § 512(c)(1)(B) that was not already excluded by § 512(c)(1)(A). Because statutory interpretations that render language superfluous are disfavored, [Connecticut ex rel. Blumenthal v. U.S. Dept. of the Interior, 228 F.3d 82, 88 (2d Cir.2000)], we reject the District Court's interpretation of the control provision.

The second construction, urged by the plaintiffs, is that the control provision codifies the common law doctrine of vicarious copyright liability. The common law imposes liability for vicarious copyright infringement "[w]hen the right and ability to supervise coalesce with an obvious and direct financial interest in the exploitation of copyrighted materials—even in the absence of actual knowledge that the copyright mono[poly] is being impaired." Shapiro, Bernstein & Co. v. H.L. Green Co., 316 F.2d 304, 307 (2d Cir.1963); cf. Metro–Goldwyn–Mayer Studios Inc. v. Grokster, Ltd., 545 U.S. 913, 930 n. 9 (2005). * * *

* * * Under the common law vicarious liability standard, " '[t]he ability to block infringers' access to a particular environment for any reason whatsoever is evidence of the right and ability to supervise.' " Arista Records LLC v. Usenet.com, Inc., 633 F.Supp.2d 124, 157 (S.D.N.Y.2009) (alteration in original) (quoting A & M Records, Inc. v. Napster, Inc., 239 F.3d 1004, 1023 (9th Cir.2001)). To adopt that principle in the DMCA context, however, would render the statute internally inconsistent. Section 512(c) actually presumes that service providers have the ability to "block . . . access" to infringing material. Id. at 157; see Shelter Capital, 667 F.3d at 1042–43. Indeed, a service provider who has knowledge or awareness of infringing material or who receives a takedown notice from a copyright holder is required to "remove, or disable access to, the material" in order to claim the benefit of the safe harbor. 17 U.S.C. § 512(c)(1)(A)(iii) & (C). But in taking such action, the service provider would—in the plaintiffs' analysis—be admitting the "right and ability to control" the infringing material. Thus, the prerequisite to safe harbor protection under § 512(c)(1)(A)(iii) & (C) would at the same time be a disqualifier under § 512(c)(1)(B).

Moreover, if Congress had intended § 512(c)(1)(B) to be coextensive with vicarious liability, "the statute could have accomplished that result in a more direct manner." Shelter Capital, 667 F.3d at 1045. * * *

In any event, the foregoing tension—elsewhere described as a "predicament"[11] and a "catch 22"—is sufficient to establish that the control provision "dictates" a departure from the common law vicarious liability standard, [Neder v. U.S., 527 U.S. 1, 21 (1999)]. Accordingly, we conclude that the "right and ability to control" infringing activity under § 512(c)(1)(B) "requires something more than the ability to remove or block access to materials posted on a service provider's website." [Capitol Records, Inc. v. MP3Tunes, LLC, 821 F.Supp.2d 627, 645 (S.D.N.Y.2011)]; * * * The remaining—and more difficult—question is how to define the "something more" that is required.

---

[11] [Ellison v. Robertson, 189 F.Supp.2d 1051, 1061 (C.D.Cal.2002), aff'd in part and rev'd in part on different grounds, 357 F.3d 1072 (9th Cir.2004)].

To date, only one court has found that a service provider had the right and ability to control infringing activity under § 512(c)(1)(B).[13] In Perfect 10, Inc. v. Cybernet Ventures, Inc., 213 F.Supp.2d 1146 (C.D.Cal.2002), the court found control where the service provider instituted a monitoring program by which user websites received "detailed instructions regard[ing] issues of layout, appearance, and content." Id. at 1173. The service provider also forbade certain types of content and refused access to users who failed to comply with its instructions. Id. Similarly, inducement of copyright infringement under Metro–Goldwyn–Mayer Studios Inc. v. Grokster, Ltd., 545 U.S. 913 (2005), which "premises liability on purposeful, culpable expression and conduct," id. at 937, might also rise to the level of control under § 512(c)(1)(B). Both of these examples involve a service provider exerting substantial influence on the activities of users, without necessarily—or even frequently—acquiring knowledge of specific infringing activity.

In light of our holding that § 512(c)(1)(B) does not include a specific knowledge requirement, we think it prudent to remand to the District Court to consider in the first instance whether the plaintiffs have adduced sufficient evidence to allow a reasonable jury to conclude that YouTube had the right and ability to control the infringing activity and received a financial benefit directly attributable to that activity.

C. "By Reason of" Storage: § 512(c)(1)

The § 512(c) safe harbor is only available when the infringement occurs "by reason of the storage at the direction of a user of material that resides on a system or network controlled or operated by or for the service provider." 17 U.S.C. § 512(c)(1). In this case, the District Court held that YouTube's software functions fell within the safe harbor for infringements that occur "by reason of" user storage. Viacom, 718 F.Supp.2d at 526 (noting that a contrary holding would "confine[ ] the word 'storage' too narrowly to meet the statute's purpose"). For the reasons that follow, we affirm that holding with respect to three of the challenged software functions—the conversion (or "transcoding") of videos into a standard display format, the playback of videos on "watch" pages, and the "related videos" function. We remand for further fact-finding with respect to a fourth software function, involving the third-party syndication of videos uploaded to YouTube. * * *

The relevant case law makes clear that the § 512(c) safe harbor extends to software functions performed "for the purpose of facilitating access to user-stored material." Id.; see Shelter Capital, 667 F.3d at 1031–35. Two of the software functions challenged here—transcoding and playback—were expressly considered by our sister Circuit in Shelter Capital, which held that liability arising from these functions occurred "by reason of the storage at the direction of a user." 17 U.S.C. § 512(c); see Shelter Capital, 667 F.3d at 1027–28, 1031; see also UMG I [UMG Recordings, Inc. v. Veoh Networks, Inc., 620 F.Supp.2d 1081, 1089–91 (C.D.Cal.2008)]; [Io Group, Inc. v. Veoh Networks, Inc., 586 F.Supp.2d 1132, 1146–48 (N.D.Cal.2008)]. Transcoding involves "[m]aking copies of a video in a different encoding scheme" in order to render the video "viewable over the Internet to most

---

[13] Other courts have suggested that control may exist where the service provider is "actively involved in the listing, bidding, sale and delivery" of items offered for sale, Hendrickson v. eBay, Inc., 165 F.Supp.2d 1082, 1094 (C.D.Cal.2001), or otherwise controls vendor sales by previewing products prior to their listing, editing product descriptions, or suggesting prices, [Corbis Corp. v. Amazon.com, Inc., 351 F.Supp.2d 1090, 1110 (W.D.Wash.2004)]. Because these cases held that control did *not* exist, however, it is not clear that the practices cited therein are individually sufficient to support a finding of control.

[handwritten margin note: Automatic fxns preserved]

users." Supp. Joint App'x I:236. The playback process involves "deliver[ing] copies of YouTube videos to a user's browser cache" in response to a user request. Id. at 239. The District Court correctly found that to exclude these automated functions from the safe harbor would eviscerate the protection afforded to service providers by § 512(c). *Viacom*, 718 F.Supp.2d at 526–27.

[handwritten margin note: Related clips]

[handwritten margin note: C7: fully automate]

A similar analysis applies to the "related videos" function, by which a YouTube computer algorithm identifies and displays "thumbnails" of clips that are "related" to the video selected by the user. The plaintiffs claim that this practice constitutes content promotion, not "access" to stored content, and therefore falls beyond the scope of the safe harbor. * * * The record makes clear that the related videos algorithm "is fully automated and operates solely in response to user input without the active involvement of YouTube employees." Supp. Joint App'x I:237. Furthermore, the related videos function serves to help YouTube users locate and gain access to material stored at the direction of other users. Because the algorithm "is closely related to, and follows from, the storage itself," and is "narrowly directed toward providing access to material stored at the direction of users," *UMG I*, 620 F.Supp.2d at 1092, we conclude that the related videos function is also protected by the § 512(c) safe harbor.

[handwritten margin note: Safe Harbor]

[handwritten margin note: 3rd party syndic]

The final software function at issue here—third-party syndication—is the closest case. In or around March 2007, YouTube transcoded a select number of videos into a format compatible with mobile devices and "syndicated" or licensed the videos to Verizon Wireless and other companies. The plaintiffs argue—with some force—that business transactions do not occur at the "direction of a user" within the meaning of § 512(c)(1) when they involve the manual selection of copyrighted material for licensing to a third party. The parties do not dispute, however, that none of the clips-in-suit were among the approximately 2,000 videos provided to Verizon Wireless. In order to avoid rendering an advisory opinion on the outer boundaries of the storage provision, we remand for fact-finding on the question of whether any of the clips-in-suit were in fact syndicated to any other third party. * * *

[handwritten margin note: Remand]

The District Court correctly determined that a finding of safe harbor application necessarily protects a defendant from all affirmative claims for monetary relief. 17 U.S.C. § 512(c)(1); see H.R.Rep. No. 105–551(II), at 50; S.Rep. No. 105–190, at 20; cf. 17 U.S.C. § 512(j) (setting forth the scope of injunctive relief available under § 512). For the reasons previously stated, further fact-finding is required to determine whether YouTube is ultimately entitled to safe harbor protection in this case. Accordingly, we vacate the order denying summary judgment to the plaintiffs and remand the cause without expressing a view on the merits of the plaintiffs' affirmative claims. * * *

NOTES AND QUESTIONS

(1) On remand, the trial judge held that the plaintiffs had failed to establish the "something more" necessary to deprive YouTube of the safe harbor under § 512(c)(1)(B), and had also failed to establish that YouTube had actual knowledge or awareness of specific infringements or had "willfully blinded" itself to such knowledge. 2013 WL 1689071 (S.D.N.Y.2013).

Judge Cabranes' opinion for the Second Circuit disagreed with the Ninth Circuit's decision in UMG Recordings v. Shelter Capital Partners, which interpreted the § 512(c)(1)(B) financial benefit and ability to control exclusion to require knowledge of specific infringing material. After the decision in *YouTube*, the Ninth Circuit withdrew its opinion in *Shelter Capital Partners* and issued a superseding opinion at 2013 WL 1092793 (9th Cir.2013). Like *YouTube*, the new opinion does not limit the benefit and control exclusion to instances of specific knowledge. After reiterating that the exclusion requires "something more" than the vicarious liability standard of a general ability to locate and remove infringing material, the Ninth Circuit, quoting *YouTube*, said that to be excluded from the safe harbor, the service provider must "exert substantial influence on the activities of users." What does this standard require? Again tracking *YouTube*, the Ninth Circuit said that "substantial influence" may include "high levels of control over activities of users," or "purposeful conduct" such as inducement to infringement. The Ninth Circuit subsequently found "something more" than the ability to locate and remove infringing materials in Columbia Pictures Industries, Inc. v. Fung, 710 F.3d 1020 (9th Cir.2013). The court held that the defendant's BitTorrent indexing websites were excluded from safe harbor protection under § 512(c)(1)(B) because the defendant received advertising revenue from the sites, organized the files on the sites to aid potential infringers, and otherwise induced the infringing activity.

(2) As Judge Cabranes notes in *Viacom*, to be eligible for any of the safe harbors offered in § 512, service providers must adopt and reasonably implement a policy that provides for the termination of subscribers who are repeat infringers. § 512(i). According to the Ninth Circuit in Perfect 10, Inc. v. CCBill LLC, 488 F.3d 1102 (9th Cir.), cert. denied, 552 U.S. 1062 (2007), "a service provider 'implements' a policy if it has a working notification system, a procedure for dealing with DMCA-compliant notifications, and does not actively prevent copyright owners from collecting information needed to issue such notifications." "A service provider reasonably implements its repeat infringer policy if it terminates users when 'appropriate,'" but "a service provider need not affirmatively police its users for evidence of repeat infringement." In Ellison v. Robertson, 357 F.3d 1072 (9th Cir.2004), the court remanded to have a jury decide whether America Online had failed to reasonably implement a termination policy because it changed the e-mail address used by copyright owners for notices of infringements and did not close the old (now unmonitored) e-mail account or forward messages sent there to the new address.

(3) Under § 512(c)(1)(C) a service provider like Viacom must respond expeditiously to takedown notices from copyright owners by removing or disabling access to the infringing material.[u] As explained by the court in Perfect 10, Inc. v. CCBill LLC, supra, "The DMCA notification procedures place the burden of policing copyright infringement—identifying the potentially infringing material and adequately documenting infringement—squarely on the owners of the copyright." Section § 512(g) creates a procedure for users to respond to takedowns with a counter-notice in order to have the material reinstated, and § 512(f) creates liability for material misrepresentations made in a takedown notice or a counter notification.

Among other specified elements, a takedown notice must include a statement that the complaining party "has a good faith belief" that the use of the material violates the copyright law. § 512(c)(3)(A)(5). The Ninth Circuit in

---

[u]   See ALS Scan, Inc. v. RemarQ Communities, Inc., 239 F.3d 619 (4th Cir.2001), holding that a copyright owner's takedown notice complied "substantially" with the requirements of § 512(c)(3) and thus deprived a service provider of the safe harbor when the provider failed to remove the infringing material.

Rossi v. Motion Picture Ass'n of America, Inc., 391 F.3d 1000 (9th Cir.2004), cert. denied, 544 U.S. 1018 (2005), held that the "good faith belief" required for a valid takedown notice is measured by a subjective standard that does not incorporate "objective reasonableness." Originally designed to deal with the unauthorized uploading of copyrighted works, the takedown provisions are now being tested by the proliferation of user-generated derivative works on mega-sites like YouTube. When a mother uploaded to YouTube a twenty-nine second video of her children dancing in the kitchen to Prince's *Let's Go Crazy,* the copyright owner sent a takedown notice and the video was removed; the mother then send a counter notification arguing that the video was a fair use and YouTube reposted it. She also filed suit against the copyright owner under § 512(f) alleging that it had misrepresented its good faith belief that the use was infringing. The court in Lenz v. Universal Music Corp., 572 F.Supp.2d 1150 (N.D.Cal.2008), denied a motion to dismiss her claim. "An allegation that a copyright owner acted in bad faith by issuing a takedown notice without proper consideration of the fair use doctrine thus is sufficient to state a claim pursuant to Section 512(f) of the DMCA." S. Jamar, Crafting Copyright Law to Encourage and Protect User-Generated Content in the Internet Social Networking Context, 19 Widener L.J. 843 (2010), suggests revisions to the copyright law that would explicitly authorize non-commercial derivative works on social media sites like Facebook and YouTube; E. Townsend-Gard and B. Whetstone, Copyright and Social Media: A Preliminary Case Study of Pinterest, 31 Miss.Coll.L.Rev 249 (2012), uses Pinterest as a vehicle for examining copyright issues generated by large social media sites.[v]

According to one analysis, nearly one-third of the takedown notices sent to online service providers by content owners are based on claims that do not justify takedown. Examples include attempts to protect uncopyrightable material, stifle criticism, or harass competitors. 71 Pat., Tm. & Copyr.J. (BNA) 130 (2005). M. Pollack, Rebalancing Section 512 to Protect Fair Users from Herds of Mice–Trampling Elephants, 22 Santa Clara Computer & High Tech.L.J. 547 (2006), believes that the notice and takedown procedures in § 512 do not afford adequate protection to users.

(4) YouTube has instituted a new mechanism in an effort to placate content owners. When a user's video is removed due to a takedown notice, the user must now go to "Copyright School." The class consists of a five-minute video on copyright law followed by a quiz that the user must pass before being allowed to upload additional content. 81 Pat., Tm. & Copyr.J. (BNA) 828 (2011).

(5) Not all copyright owners insist on the removal of unauthorized content from YouTube. Increasingly, owners choose to permit material to remain on the site and instead allow YouTube to run ads with the material; YouTube and the copyright owner then split the revenue. Miller, YouTube Ads Turn Video Into Revenue, N.Y. Times, Sept. 3, 2010, p. B1.

(6) Section 512(d) provides a safe harbor for service providers who refer or link users to online sites containing infringing material. Again, there are requirements relating to a lack of actual or "red flag" knowledge of the infringement.

---

[v]   The difficulties of applying traditional fair use concepts to user-generated web content are considered in D. Gervais, The Tangled Web of UGC: Making Copyright Sense of User-Generated Content, 11 Vand.J.Ent. & Tech.L. 841 (2009); M. Wong, "Transformative" User-Generated Content in Copyright Law: Infringing Derivative Works or Fair Use?, id. 1075, pursues similar questions in a comparative context.

According to the Senate Report, the safe harbor for links or other location tools would not be available "if the copyright owner could prove that the location was clearly, at the time the directory provider viewed it, a 'pirate' site * * * where sound recordings, software, movies or books were available for unauthorized downloading, public performance or public display."[w] The provider must also comply with takedown notices by removing the reference or link to the infringing material. According to Google's *Transparency Report,* it now receives about *twenty million* takedown notices every month from over 3,000 copyright owners aimed at links provided by its Google Search. Record companies top the list, but other content owners like Microsoft are also prominent.[x]

(7) Service providers who offer network connections, transmission, or routing services to users are eligible for a safe harbor in § 512(a) if the provider does not determine the recipients nor select or modify the contents of the transmission. Section 512(b) creates a safe harbor for caching intermediate and temporary copies of materials transmitted by users over the provider's system. E. Lee, Decoding the DMCA Safe Harbors, 32 Colum.J.L. & Arts 233 (2009), analyzes some of the vexing interpretive issues under § 512.

FILE-SHARING

A & M Records, Inc. v. Napster, Inc.

United States Court of Appeals, Ninth Circuit, 2001.
239 F.3d 1004.

■ Before SCHROEDER, CHIEF JUDGE, BEEZER and PAEZ, CIRCUIT JUDGES.

■ BEEZER, CIRCUIT JUDGE.

[This case was the first major challenge to the unauthorized distribution of copyrighted works over peer-to-peer file-sharing networks. Napster at its height had over seventy million users. The district court issued a preliminary injunction against Napster under theories of contributory and vicarious copyright infringement. 114 F.Supp.2d 896 (N.D.Cal.2000).] *[handwritten: DCH for π prelim injunction]*

    * * *

In order to copy MP3 files through the Napster system, a user must first access Napster's Internet site and download the MusicShare software to his individual computer. See *http://www.Napster.com.* Once the software is installed, the user can access the Napster system. A first-time user is required to register with the Napster system by creating a "user name" and password.

If a registered user wants to list available files stored in his computer's hard drive on Napster for others to access, he must first create a "user li-

---

   w S.Rep. No. 105-190, 105th Cong., 2d Sess. 107 (1998).

   x When Google removes a link from its search results in response to a takedown notice, it sends a copy of the notice to a web site called chillingeffects.org, which posts the notice online. Google notifies searchers whenever a link has been deleted from their search results and provides a link to the takedown notice that prompted the deletion. The takedown notice, of course, includes the URL of the link that Google was required to delete. W. Seltzer, Free Speech Unmoored in Copyright's Safe Harbor: Chilling Effects of the DMCA on the First Amendment, 24 Harv.J.L. & Tech. 171 (2010), laments the chilling effect of the takedown regime.

brary" directory on his computer's hard drive. The user then saves his MP3 files in the library directory, using self-designated file names. He next must log into the Napster system using his user name and password. His MusicShare software then searches his user library and verifies that the available files are properly formatted. If in the correct MP3 format, the names of the MP3 files will be uploaded from the user's computer to the Napster servers. The content of the MP3 files remains stored in the user's computer. * * *

Software located on the Napster servers maintains a "search index" of Napster's collective directory. To search the files available from Napster users currently connected to the network servers, the individual user accesses a form in the MusicShare software stored in his computer and enters either the name of a song or an artist as the object of the search. The form is then transmitted to a Napster server and automatically compared to the MP3 file names listed in the server's search index. Napster's server compiles a list of all MP3 file names pulled from the search index which include the same search terms entered on the search form and transmits the list to the searching user. * * *

To transfer a copy of the contents of a requested MP3 file, the Napster server software obtains the Internet address of the requesting user and the Internet address of the "host user" (the user with the available files). * * * The Napster servers then communicate the host user's Internet address to the requesting user. The requesting user's computer uses this information to establish a connection with the host user and downloads a copy of the contents of the MP3 file from one computer to the other over the Internet, "peer-to-peer." A downloaded MP3 file can be played directly from the user's hard drive using Napster's MusicShare program or other software. The file may also be transferred back onto an audio CD if the user has access to equipment designed for that purpose.

[Judge Beezer concluded that users of the Napster system were direct infringers who were unlikely to succeed in establishing a fair use defense. See p. 350 supra. He then turned to the issues of Napster's liability for contributory and vicarious infringement.]

IV

We first address plaintiffs' claim that Napster is liable for contributory copyright infringement. Traditionally, "one who, with knowledge of the infringing activity, induces, causes or materially contributes to the infringing conduct of another, may be held liable as a 'contributory' infringer." Gershwin Publ'g Corp. v. Columbia Artists Mgmt., Inc., 443 F.2d 1159, 1162 (2d Cir.1971); see also Fonovisa, Inc. v. Cherry Auction, Inc., 76 F.3d 259, 264 (9th Cir.1996). * * *

A.   Knowledge. * * * It is apparent from the record that Napster has knowledge, both actual and constructive,[5] of direct infringement. Napster claims that it is nevertheless protected from contributory liability by the

---

[5]   The district court found actual knowledge because: (1) a document authored by Napster co-founder Sean Parker mentioned "the need to remain ignorant of users' real names and IP addresses 'since they are exchanging pirated music' "; and (2) the Recording Industry Association of America ("RIAA") informed Napster of more than 12,000 infringing files, some of which are still available. 114 F.Supp.2d at 918. The district court found constructive knowledge because: (a) Napster executives have recording industry experience; (b) they have enforced intellectual property rights in other instances; (c) Napster executives have downloaded copyrighted songs from the system; and (d) they have promoted the site with "screen shots listing infringing files." Id. at 919.

teaching of Sony Corp. v. Universal City Studios, Inc., 464 U.S. 417 (1984). We disagree. We observe that Napster's actual, specific knowledge of direct infringement renders *Sony*'s holding of limited assistance to Napster. We are compelled to make a clear distinction between the architecture of the Napster system and Napster's conduct in relation to the operational capacity of the system.

[handwritten margin note: N had knowledge but said sony protects]

The *Sony* Court refused to hold the manufacturer and retailers of video tape recorders liable for contributory infringement despite evidence that such machines could be and were used to infringe plaintiffs' copyrighted television shows. *Sony* stated that if liability "is to be imposed on petitioners in this case, it must rest on the fact that *they have sold equipment with constructive knowledge of the fact that their customers may use that equipment to make unauthorized copies* of copyrighted material." Id. at 439 (emphasis added). The *Sony* Court declined to impute the requisite level of knowledge where the defendants made and sold equipment capable of both infringing and "substantial noninfringing uses." Id. at 442 (adopting a modified "staple article of commerce" doctrine from patent law). * * *

We are bound to follow *Sony,* and will not impute the requisite level of knowledge to Napster merely because peer-to-peer file sharing technology may be used to infringe plaintiffs' copyrights. See 464 U.S. at 436 (rejecting argument that merely supplying the " 'means' to accomplish an infringing activity" leads to imposition of liability). We depart from the reasoning of the district court that Napster failed to demonstrate that its system is capable of commercially significant noninfringing uses. See *Napster,* 114 F.Supp.2d at 916, 917–18. The district court improperly confined the use analysis to current uses, ignoring the system's capabilities. See generally *Sony*, 464 U.S. at 442–43 (framing inquiry as whether the video tape recorder is "*capable* of commercially significant noninfringing uses") (emphasis added). Consequently, the district court placed undue weight on the proportion of current infringing use as compared to current and future noninfringing use. * * *

[handwritten margin note: CT: b/c of sony, can't imput knowledge to Napster just b/c tech can be used to infringe]

We agree that if a computer system operator learns of specific infringing material available on his system and fails to purge such material from the system, the operator knows of and contributes to direct infringement. See *Netcom*, 907 F.Supp. at 1374. Conversely, absent any specific information which identifies infringing activity, a computer system operator cannot be liable for contributory infringement merely because the structure of the system allows for the exchange of copyrighted material. See *Sony*, 464 U.S. at 436, 442–43. To enjoin simply because a computer network allows for infringing use would, in our opinion, violate *Sony* and potentially restrict activity unrelated to infringing use.

We nevertheless conclude that sufficient knowledge exists to impose contributory liability when linked to demonstrated infringing use of the Napster system. * * * The record supports the district court's finding that Napster has *actual* knowledge that *specific* infringing material is available using its system, that it could block access to the system by suppliers of the infringing material, and that it failed to remove the material. See *Napster*, 114 F.Supp.2d at 918, 920–21.

[handwritten margin note: CT: Here there was sufficient knowl.]

[handwritten margin note: N mat'ly cntril.]

B. Material Contribution. Under the facts as found by the district court, Napster materially contributes to the infringing activity. Relying on *Fonovisa,* the district court concluded that "[w]ithout the support services defendant provides, Napster users could not find and download the music they want with the ease of which defendant boasts." *Napster,* 114

F.Supp.2d at 919–20 ("Napster is an integrated service designed to enable users to locate and download MP3 music files."). We agree that Napster provides "the site and facilities" for direct infringement. See *Fonovisa,* 76 F.3d at 264; * * *. The district court correctly applied the reasoning in *Fonovisa,* and properly found that Napster materially contributes to direct infringement.

We affirm the district court's conclusion that plaintiffs have demonstrated a likelihood of success on the merits of the contributory infringement claim. * * *

V

We turn to the question whether Napster engages in vicarious copyright infringement. Vicarious copyright liability is an "outgrowth" of respondeat superior. *Fonovisa,* 76 F.3d at 262. In the context of copyright law, vicarious liability extends beyond an employer/employee relationship to cases in which a defendant "has the right and ability to supervise the infringing activity and also has a direct financial interest in such activities." Id. (quoting *Gershwin,* 443 F.2d at 1162); see also Polygram Int'l Publ'g, Inc. v. Nevada/TIG, Inc., 855 F.Supp. 1314, 1325–26 (D.Mass.1994) (describing vicarious liability as a form of risk allocation).

Before moving into this discussion, we note that *Sony*'s "staple article of commerce" analysis has no application to Napster's potential liability for vicarious copyright infringement. See *Sony,* 464 U.S. at 434–435; see generally 3 Melville B. Nimmer & David Nimmer, Nimmer On Copyright §§ 12.04[A][2] & [A][2][b] (2000) (confining *Sony* to contributory infringement analysis: "Contributory infringement itself is of two types—personal conduct that forms part of or furthers the infringement and contribution of machinery or goods that provide the means to infringe"). The issues of Sony's liability under the "doctrines of 'direct infringement' and 'vicarious liability'" were not before the Supreme Court, although the Court recognized that the "lines between direct infringement, contributory infringement, and vicarious liability are not clearly drawn." Id. at 435 n. 17. * * *

A. Financial Benefit. The district court determined that plaintiffs had demonstrated they would likely succeed in establishing that Napster has a direct financial interest in the infringing activity. *Napster,* 114 F.Supp.2d at 921–22. We agree. Financial benefit exists where the availability of infringing material "acts as a 'draw' for customers." *Fonovisa,* 76 F.3d at 263–64 (stating that financial benefit may be shown "where infringing performances enhance the attractiveness of a venue"). Ample evidence supports the district court's finding that Napster's future revenue is directly dependent upon "increases in userbase." More users register with the Napster system as the "quality and quantity of available music increases." 114 F.Supp.2d at 902. We conclude that the district court did not err in determining that Napster financially benefits from the availability of protected works on its system.

B. Supervision. The district court determined that Napster has the right and ability to supervise its users' conduct. *Napster,* 114 F.Supp.2d at 920–21 (finding that Napster's representations to the court regarding "its improved methods of blocking users about whom rights holders complain . . . is tantamount to an admission that defendant can, and sometimes does, police its service"). We agree in part.

The ability to block infringers' access to a particular environment for any reason whatsoever is evidence of the right and ability to supervise. See

Fonovisa, 76 F.3d at 262 ("Cherry Auction had the right to terminate vendors for any reason whatsoever and through that right had the ability to control the activities of vendors on the premises."); * * *. Here, plaintiffs have demonstrated that Napster retains the right to control access to its system. Napster has an express reservation of rights policy, stating on its website that it expressly reserves the "right to refuse service and terminate accounts in [its] discretion, including, but not limited to, if Napster believes that user conduct violates applicable law . . . or for any reason in Napster's sole discretion, with or without cause." * * *

[margin note: N has rt to ctrl acces]

The district court correctly determined that Napster had the right and ability to police its system and failed to exercise that right to prevent the exchange of copyrighted material. The district court, however, failed to recognize that the boundaries of the premises that Napster "controls and patrols" are limited. * * * Napster's reserved "right and ability" to police is cabined by the system's current architecture. As shown by the record, the Napster system does not "read" the content of indexed files, other than to check that they are in the proper MP3 format.

[margin note: Failed to ex right]

Napster, however, has the ability to locate infringing material listed on its search indices, and the right to terminate users' access to the system. The file name indices, therefore, are within the "premises" that Napster has the ability to police. We recognize that the files are user-named and may not match copyrighted material exactly (for example, the artist or song could be spelled wrong). For Napster to function effectively, however, file names must reasonably or roughly correspond to the material contained in the files, otherwise no user could ever locate any desired music. As a practical matter, Napster, its users and the record company plaintiffs have equal access to infringing material by employing Napster's "search function."

* * * Napster's failure to police the system's "premises," combined with a showing that Napster financially benefits from the continuing availability of infringing files on its system, leads to the imposition of vicarious liability. [The district court was instructed to reformulate the injunction to correspond with the boundaries of Napster's contributory and vicarious liability.]

[margin note: N = vicariously Liable]

NOTES AND QUESTIONS

(1) On remand, Judge Patel in the district court issued a preliminary injunction that required Napster to prevent the "downloading, uploading, transmitting or distributing" of a sound recording within three business days after receiving a notice from the plaintiffs that included the title of the copyrighted recording, the name of the featured artist, and the name of one or more files on Napster that contained the work. 2001 Copyr.L.Dec. ¶ 28,213 (N.D.Cal.2001). Judge Patel later ordered Napster to shut down until it could achieve 100 per cent compliance with the preliminary injunction. The modified injunction and shut-down order were affirmed by the Ninth Circuit. 284 F.3d 1091 (9th Cir.2002). Napster was eventually liquidated.

(2) Is the Ninth Circuit correct in viewing the "substantial noninfringing use" doctrine articulated by the Supreme Court in *Sony* as relevant only to whether the defendant had the requisite knowledge for contributory infringement? (If Universal City Studios had proved that Sony knew of particular owners who were using their VCRs to infringe Universal's copyrights, would the Supreme Court have imposed liability on Sony?) Are there nevertheless differences in the nature of the relationship between the two defendants and their respective customers that justify the different results? S. Dogan, Is Napster a VCR? The Implications of *Sony* for Napster and Other Internet Technologies, 52 Hastings L.J. 939 (2001), analyzes the application of *Sony* in cases like *Napster* where the defendant has some control over the direct infringers; L. Gibbons, *Napster*: The Case for the Need for a Missing Direct Infringer, 9 Vill. Sports & Ent.L.J. 57 (2002), argues that the interests of users should be considered in analyzing the contributory and vicarious liability of purveyors of new technologies.

Metro–Goldwyn–Mayer Studios Inc. v. Grokster, Ltd.

Supreme Court of the United States, 2005.
545 U.S. 913, 125 S.Ct. 2764.

■ JUSTICE SOUTER delivered the opinion of the Court.

Issue

Holding

The question is under what circumstances the distributor of a product capable of both lawful and unlawful use is liable for acts of copyright infringement by third parties using the product. We hold that one who distributes a device with the object of promoting its use to infringe copyright, as shown by clear expression or other affirmative steps taken to foster infringement, is liable for the resulting acts of infringement by third parties.

I

A

Respondents, Grokster, Ltd., and StreamCast Networks, Inc., defendants in the trial court, distribute free software products that allow computer users to share electronic files through peer-to-peer networks, so called because users' computers communicate directly with each other, not through central servers. * * * Given these benefits in security, cost, and efficiency, peer-to-peer networks are employed to store and distribute electronic files by universities, government agencies, corporations, and libraries, among others.

Other users of peer-to-peer networks include individual recipients of Grokster's and StreamCast's software, and although the networks that they enjoy through using the software can be used to share any type of digital file, they have prominently employed those networks in sharing copyrighted music and video files without authorization. A group of copyright holders (MGM for short, but including motion picture studios, recording companies, songwriters, and music publishers) sued Grokster and StreamCast for their users' copyright infringements, alleging that they knowingly and intentionally distributed their software to enable users to reproduce and distribute the copyrighted works in violation of the Copyright Act, 17 U.S.C. § 101 et seq. (2000 ed. and Supp. II). MGM sought damages and an injunction.

Discovery during the litigation revealed the way the software worked, the business aims of each defendant company, and the predilections of the users. Grokster's eponymous software employs what is known as FastTrack technology, a protocol developed by others and licensed to Grokster. StreamCast distributes a very similar product except that its software, called Morpheus, relies on what is known as Gnutella technology. A user who downloads and installs either software possesses the protocol to send requests for files directly to the computers of others using software compatible with FastTrack or Gnutella. * * *

* * * Grokster and StreamCast use no servers to intercept the content of the search requests or to mediate the file transfers conducted by users of the software, there being no central point through which the substance of the communications passes in either direction.

Although Grokster and StreamCast do not therefore know when particular files are copied, a few searches using their software would show what is available on the networks the software reaches. MGM commissioned a statistician to conduct a systematic search, and his study showed that nearly 90% of the files available for download on the FastTrack system were copyrighted works. Grokster and StreamCast dispute this figure, raising methodological problems and arguing that free copying even of copyrighted works may be authorized by the rightholders. They also argue that potential noninfringing uses of their software are significant in kind, even if infrequent in practice. Some musical performers, for example, have gained new audiences by distributing their copyrighted works for free across peer-to-peer networks, and some distributors of unprotected content have used peer-to-peer networks to disseminate files, Shakespeare being an example. * * *

Grokster and StreamCast concede the infringement in most downloads, Brief for Respondents 10, n. 6, and it is uncontested that they are aware that users employ their software primarily to download copyrighted files, even if the decentralized FastTrack and Gnutella networks fail to reveal which files are being copied, and when. From time to time, moreover, the companies have learned about their users' infringement directly, as from users who have sent e-mail to each company with questions about playing copyrighted movies they had downloaded, to whom the companies have responded with guidance. App. 559–563, 808–816, 939–954. And MGM notified the companies of 8 million copyrighted files that could be obtained using their software.

Grokster and StreamCast are not, however, merely passive recipients of information about infringing use. The record is replete with evidence that from the moment Grokster and StreamCast began to distribute their free software, each one clearly voiced the objective that recipients use it to download copyrighted works, and each took active steps to encourage infringement.

After the notorious file-sharing service, Napster, was sued by copyright holders for facilitation of copyright infringement, A & M Records, Inc. v. Napster, Inc., 114 F. Supp. 2d 896 (ND Cal. 2000), aff'd in part, rev'd in part, 239 F. 3d 1004 (CA9 2001), StreamCast gave away a software program of a kind known as OpenNap, designed as compatible with the Napster program and open to Napster users for downloading files from other Napster and OpenNap users' computers. * * *

The evidence that Grokster sought to capture the market of former Napster users is sparser but revealing, for Grokster launched its own OpenNap system called Swaptor and inserted digital codes into its Web site so that computer users using Web search engines to look for "Napster" or "[f]ree filesharing" would be directed to the Grokster Web site, where they could download the Grokster software. Id., at 992–993. And Grokster's name is an apparent derivative of Napster.

* * * Morpheus in fact allowed users to search specifically for "Top 40" songs, id., at 735, which were inevitably copyrighted. Similarly, Grokster sent users a newsletter promoting its ability to provide particular, popular copyrighted materials. Brief for Motion Picture Studio and Recording Company Petitioners 7–8.

In addition to this evidence of express promotion, marketing, and intent to promote further, the business models employed by Grokster and StreamCast confirm that their principal object was use of their software to download copyrighted works. Grokster and StreamCast receive no revenue from users, who obtain the software itself for nothing. Instead, both companies generate income by selling advertising space, and they stream the advertising to Grokster and Morpheus users while they are employing the programs. As the number of users of each program increases, advertising opportunities become worth more. Cf. App. 539, 804. While there is doubtless some demand for free Shakespeare, the evidence shows that substantive volume is a function of free access to copyrighted work. Users seeking Top 40 songs, for example, or the latest release by Modest Mouse, are certain to be far more numerous than those seeking a free Decameron, and Grokster and StreamCast translated that demand into dollars.

Finally, there is no evidence that either company made an effort to filter copyrighted material from users' downloads or otherwise impede the sharing of copyrighted files. Although Grokster appears to have sent e-mails warning users about infringing content when it received threatening notice from the copyright holders, it never blocked anyone from continuing to use its software to share copyrighted files. Id., at 75–76. StreamCast not only rejected another company's offer of help to monitor infringement, id., at 928–929, but blocked the Internet Protocol addresses of entities it believed were trying to engage in such monitoring on its networks, id., at 917–922.

B

After discovery, the parties on each side of the case cross-moved for summary judgment. The District Court limited its consideration to the asserted liability of Grokster and StreamCast for distributing the current versions of their software, leaving aside whether either was liable "for damages arising from *past* versions of their software, or from other past activities." 259 F. Supp. 2d 1029, 1033 (CD Cal. 2003). The District Court held that those who used the Grokster and Morpheus software to download copyrighted media files directly infringed MGM's copyrights, a conclusion not contested on appeal, but the court nonetheless granted summary judgment in favor of Grokster and StreamCast as to any liability arising from distribution of the then current versions of their software. * * *

The Court of Appeals affirmed. 380 F. 3d 1154 (CA9 2004). In the court's analysis, a defendant was liable as a contributory infringer when it had knowledge of direct infringement and materially contributed to the infringement. But the court read Sony Corp. of America v. Universal City Studios, Inc., 464 U.S. 417 (1984), as holding that distribution of a commercial product capable of substantial noninfringing uses could not give rise to contributory liability for infringement unless the distributor had actual knowledge of specific instances of infringement and failed to act on that knowledge. The fact that the software was capable of substantial noninfringing uses in the Ninth Circuit's view meant that Grokster and StreamCast were not liable, because they had no such actual knowledge, owing to the decentralized architecture of their software. The court also held that Grokster and StreamCast did not materially contribute to their users' infringement because it was the users themselves who searched for, retrieved, and stored the infringing files, with no involvement by the defendants beyond providing the software in the first place.

The Ninth Circuit also considered whether Grokster and StreamCast could be liable under a theory of vicarious infringement. The court held against liability because the defendants did not monitor or control the use of the software, had no agreed-upon right or current ability to supervise its use, and had no independent duty to police infringement. We granted certiorari. 543 U.S. 1032 (2004).

II

A

MGM and many of the *amici* fault the Court of Appeals's holding for upsetting a sound balance between the respective values of supporting creative pursuits through copyright protection and promoting innovation in new communication technologies by limiting the incidence of liability for copyright infringement. The more artistic protection is favored, the more technological innovation may be discouraged; the administration of copyright law is an exercise in managing the trade-off. See Sony Corp. v. Universal City Studios, supra, at 442; see generally Ginsburg, Copyright and Control Over New Technologies of Dissemination, 101 Colum. L. Rev. 1613 (2001); Lichtman & Landes, Indirect Liability for Copyright Infringement: An Economic Perspective, 16 Harv. J. L. & Tech. 395 (2003).

The tension between the two values is the subject of this case, with its claim that digital distribution of copyrighted material threatens copyright holders as never before, because every copy is identical to the original, copying is easy, and many people (especially the young) use file-sharing software to download copyrighted works. This very breadth of the software's use may well draw the public directly into the debate over copyright policy, Peters, Brace Memorial Lecture: Copyright Enters the Public Domain, 51 J. Copyright Soc. 701, 705–717 (2004) (address by Register of Copyrights), and the indications are that the ease of copying songs or movies using software like Grokster's and Napster's is fostering disdain for copyright protection, Wu, When Code Isn't Law, 89 Va. L. Rev. 679, 724–726 (2003). As the case has been presented to us, these fears are said to be offset by the different concern that imposing liability, not only on infringers but on distributors of software based on its potential for unlawful use, could limit further development of beneficial technologies. See, e.g., Lemley & Reese, Reducing Digital Copyright Infringement Without Restricting Innovation, 56 Stan. L. Rev. 1345, 1386–1390 (2004); Brief for Innovation Scholars and Economists as *Amici Curiae* 15–20; * * *

One infringes contributorily by intentionally inducing or encouraging direct infringement, see Gershwin Pub. Corp. v. Columbia Artists Management, Inc., 443 F. 2d 1159, 1162 (CA2 1971), and infringes vicariously by profiting from direct infringement while declining to exercise a right to stop or limit it, Shapiro, Bernstein & Co. v. H. L. Green Co., 316 F. 2d 304, 307 (CA2 1963).[9] * * *

---

[9] * * * In the present case MGM has argued a vicarious liability theory, which allows imposition of liability when the defendant profits directly from the infringement and has a right and ability to supervise the direct infringer, even if the defendant initially lacks knowledge of the infringement. See, e.g., Shapiro, Bernstein & Co. v. H. L. Green Co., 316 F. 2d 304, 308 (CA2 1963); Dreamland Ball Room, Inc. v. Shapiro, Bernstein & Co., 36 F.2d 354,

B

Despite the currency of these principles of secondary liability, this Court has dealt with secondary copyright infringement in only one recent case, and because MGM has tailored its principal claim to our opinion there, a look at our earlier holding is in order. In Sony Corp. v. Universal City Studios, supra, this Court addressed a claim that secondary liability for infringement can arise from the very distribution of a commercial product. There, the product, novel at the time, was what we know today as the videocassette recorder or VCR. Copyright holders sued Sony as the manufacturer, claiming it was contributorily liable for infringement that occurred when VCR owners taped copyrighted programs because it supplied the means used to infringe, and it had constructive knowledge that infringement would occur. At the trial on the merits, the evidence showed that the principal use of the VCR was for "time-shifting," or taping a program for later viewing at a more convenient time, which the Court found to be a fair, not an infringing, use. Id., at 423–424. There was no evidence that Sony had expressed an object of bringing about taping in violation of copyright or had taken active steps to increase its profits from unlawful taping. Id., at 438. Although Sony's advertisements urged consumers to buy the VCR to "record favorite shows" or "build a library" of recorded programs, id., at 459 (Blackmun, J., dissenting), neither of these uses was necessarily infringing, id., at 424, 454–455.

On those facts, with no evidence of stated or indicated intent to promote infringing uses, the only conceivable basis for imposing liability was on a theory of contributory infringement arising from its sale of VCRs to consumers with knowledge that some would use them to infringe. Id., at 439. But because the VCR was "capable of commercially significant noninfringing uses," we held the manufacturer could not be faulted solely on the basis of its distribution. Id., at 442. * * *

The parties and many of the *amici* in this case think the key to resolving it is the *Sony* rule and, in particular, what it means for a product to be "capable of commercially significant noninfringing uses." Sony Corp. v. Universal City Studios, supra, at 442. MGM advances the argument that granting summary judgment to Grokster and StreamCast as to their current activities gave too much weight to the value of innovative technology, and too little to the copyrights infringed by users of their software, given that 90% of works available on one of the networks was shown to be copyrighted. Assuming the remaining 10% to be its noninfringing use, MGM says this should not qualify as "substantial," and the Court should quantify *Sony* to the extent of holding that a product used "principally" for infringement does not qualify. See Brief for Motion Picture Studio and Recording Company Petitioners 31. As mentioned before, Grokster and StreamCast reply by citing evidence that their software can be used to reproduce public domain works, and they point to copyright holders who actually encourage copying. Even if infringement is the principal practice with their software today, they argue, the noninfringing uses are significant and will grow.

We agree with MGM that the Court of Appeals misapplied *Sony*, which it read as limiting secondary liability quite beyond the circumstances to which the case applied. *Sony* barred secondary liability based on presuming or imputing intent to cause infringement solely from the design or distribu-

---

355 (CA7 1929). Because we resolve the case based on an inducement theory, there is no need to analyze separately MGM's vicarious liability theory.

tion of a product capable of substantial lawful use, which the distributor knows is in fact used for infringement. The Ninth Circuit has read *Sony*'s limitation to mean that whenever a product is capable of substantial lawful use, the producer can never be held contributorily liable for third parties' infringing use of it; it read the rule as being this broad, even when an actual purpose to cause infringing use is shown by evidence independent of design and distribution of the product, unless the distributors had "specific knowledge of infringement at a time at which they contributed to the infringement, and failed to act upon that information." 380 F. 3d, at 1162 (internal quotation marks and alterations omitted). Because the Circuit found the StreamCast and Grokster software capable of substantial lawful use, it concluded on the basis of its reading of *Sony* that neither company could be held liable, since there was no showing that their software, being without any central server, afforded them knowledge of specific unlawful uses.

This view of *Sony*, however, was error, converting the case from one about liability resting on imputed intent to one about liability on any theory. Because *Sony* did not displace other theories of secondary liability, and because we find below that it was error to grant summary judgment to the companies on MGM's inducement claim, we do not revisit *Sony* further, as MGM requests, to add a more quantified description of the point of balance between protection and commerce when liability rests solely on distribution with knowledge that unlawful use will occur. It is enough to note that the Ninth Circuit's judgment rested on an erroneous understanding of *Sony* and to leave further consideration of the *Sony* rule for a day when that may be required.

C

Sony's rule limits imputing culpable intent as a matter of law from the characteristics or uses of a distributed product. But nothing in *Sony* requires courts to ignore evidence of intent if there is such evidence, and the case was never meant to foreclose rules of fault-based liability derived from the common law.[10] Sony Corp. v. Universal City Studios, 464 U.S., at 439 ("If vicarious liability is to be imposed on Sony in this case, it must rest on the fact that it has sold equipment with constructive knowledge" of the potential for infringement). Thus, where evidence goes beyond a product's characteristics or the knowledge that it may be put to infringing uses, and shows statements or actions directed to promoting infringement, *Sony*'s staple-article rule will not preclude liability.

The classic case of direct evidence of unlawful purpose occurs when one induces commission of infringement by another, or "entic[es] or persuad[es] another" to infringe, Black's Law Dictionary 790 (8th ed. 2004), as by advertising. Thus at common law a copyright or patent defendant who "not only expected but invoked [infringing use] by advertisement" was liable for infringement "on principles recognized in every part of the law." Kalem Co. v. Harper Brothers, 222 U.S. 55, at 62–63 (copyright infringement). * * *

The rule on inducement of infringement as developed in the early cases is no different today. Evidence of "active steps . . . taken to encourage direct infringement," Oak Industries, Inc. v. Zenith Electronics Corp., 697 F. Supp. 988, 992 (ND Ill. 1988), such as advertising an infringing use or

---

[10]   Nor does the Patent Act's exemption from liability for those who distribute a staple article of commerce, 35 U.S.C. § 271(c), extend to those who induce patent infringement, § 271(b).

instructing how to engage in an infringing use, show an affirmative intent that the product be used to infringe, and a showing that infringement was encouraged overcomes the law's reluctance to find liability when a defendant merely sells a commercial product suitable for some lawful use, see, e.g., Water Technologies Corp. v. Calco, Ltd., 850 F. 2d 660, 668 (CA Fed. 1988) (liability for inducement where one "actively and knowingly aid[s] and abet[s] another's direct infringement" (emphasis omitted)); Fromberg, Inc. v. Thornhill, 315 F. 2d 407, 412–413 (CA5 1963) (demonstrations by sales staff of infringing uses supported liability for inducement); * * *

For the same reasons that *Sony* took the staple-article doctrine of patent law as a model for its copyright safe-harbor rule, the inducement rule, too, is a sensible one for copyright. We adopt it here, holding that one who distributes a device with the object of promoting its use to infringe copyright, as shown by clear expression or other affirmative steps taken to foster infringement, is liable for the resulting acts of infringement by third parties. We are, of course, mindful of the need to keep from trenching on regular commerce or discouraging the development of technologies with lawful and unlawful potential. Accordingly, just as *Sony* did not find intentional inducement despite the knowledge of the VCR manufacturer that its device could be used to infringe, 464 U.S., at 439, n. 19, mere knowledge of infringing potential or of actual infringing uses would not be enough here to subject a distributor to liability. Nor would ordinary acts incident to product distribution, such as offering customers technical support or product updates, support liability in themselves. The inducement rule, instead, premises liability on purposeful, culpable expression and conduct, and thus does nothing to compromise legitimate commerce or discourage innovation having a lawful promise.

Inducement rule

III

A

The only apparent question about treating MGM's evidence as sufficient to withstand summary judgment under the theory of inducement goes to the need on MGM's part to adduce evidence that StreamCast and Grokster communicated an inducing message to their software users. The classic instance of inducement is by advertisement or solicitation that broadcasts a message designed to stimulate others to commit violations. MGM claims that such a message is shown here. It is undisputed that StreamCast beamed onto the computer screens of users of Napster-compatible programs ads urging the adoption of its OpenNap program, which was designed, as its name implied, to invite the custom of patrons of Napster, then under attack in the courts for facilitating massive infringement. Those who accepted StreamCast's OpenNap program were offered software to perform the same services, which a factfinder could conclude would readily have been understood in the Napster market as the ability to download copyrighted music files. Grokster distributed an electronic newsletter containing links to articles promoting its software's ability to access popular copyrighted music. And anyone whose Napster or free file-sharing searches turned up a link to Grokster would have understood Grokster to be offering the same file-sharing ability as Napster, and to the same people who probably used Napster for infringing downloads; that would also have been the understanding of anyone offered Grokster's suggestively named Swaptor software, its version of OpenNap. And both companies communicated a clear message by responding affirmatively to requests for help in locating and playing copyrighted materials. * * *

Three features of this evidence of intent are particularly notable. First, each company showed itself to be aiming to satisfy a known source of demand for copyright infringement, the market comprising former Napster users. * * *

Second, this evidence of unlawful objective is given added significance by MGM's showing that neither company attempted to develop filtering tools or other mechanisms to diminish the infringing activity using their software. While the Ninth Circuit treated the defendants' failure to develop such tools as irrelevant because they lacked an independent duty to monitor their users' activity, we think this evidence underscores Grokster's and StreamCast's intentional facilitation of their users' infringement.[12]

Third, there is a further complement to the direct evidence of unlawful objective. It is useful to recall that StreamCast and Grokster make money by selling advertising space, by directing ads to the screens of computers employing their software. As the record shows, the more the software is used, the more ads are sent out and the greater the advertising revenue becomes. Since the extent of the software's use determines the gain to the distributors, the commercial sense of their enterprise turns on high-volume use, which the record shows is infringing. This evidence alone would not justify an inference of unlawful intent, but viewed in the context of the entire record its import is clear.

The unlawful objective is unmistakable.

B

* * *

There is substantial evidence in MGM's favor on all elements of inducement, and summary judgment in favor of Grokster and StreamCast was error. On remand, reconsideration of MGM's motion for summary judgment will be in order.

The judgment of the Court of Appeals is vacated, and the case is remanded for further proceedings consistent with this opinion.

It is so ordered.

■ JUSTICE GINSBURG, with whom THE CHIEF JUSTICE and JUSTICE KENNEDY join, concurring.

I concur in the Court's decision, which vacates in full the judgment of the Court of Appeals for the Ninth Circuit, ante, at 941, and write separately to clarify why I conclude that the Court of Appeals misperceived, and hence misapplied, our holding in Sony Corp. of America v. Universal City Studios, Inc., 464 U.S. 417 (1984). There is here at least a "genuine issue as to [a] material fact," Fed. Rule Civ. Proc. 56(c), on the liability of Grokster or StreamCast, not only for actively inducing copyright infringement, but also or alternatively, based on the distribution of their software products, for contributory copyright infringement. On neither score was summary judgment for Grokster and StreamCast warranted. * * *

In sum, when the record in this case was developed, there was evidence that Grokster's and StreamCast's products were, and had been for some time, overwhelmingly used to infringe, ante, at 922–24; App. 434–

---

[12] Of course, in the absence of other evidence of intent, a court would be unable to find contributory infringement liability merely based on a failure to take affirmative steps to prevent infringement, if the device otherwise was capable of substantial noninfringing uses. Such a holding would tread too close to the Sony safe harbor.

439, 476–481, and that this infringement was the overwhelming source of revenue from the products, ante, at 925–26; 259 F. Supp. 2d, at 1043–1044. Fairly appraised, the evidence was insufficient to demonstrate, beyond genuine debate, a reasonable prospect that substantial or commercially significant noninfringing uses were likely to develop over time. On this record, the District Court should not have ruled dispositively on the contributory infringement charge by granting summary judgment to Grokster and StreamCast.

If, on remand, the case is not resolved on summary judgment in favor of MGM based on Grokster and StreamCast actively inducing infringement, the Court of Appeals, I would emphasize, should reconsider, on a fuller record, its interpretation of *Sony*'s product distribution holding.

■ JUSTICE BREYER, with whom JUSTICE STEVENS and JUSTICE O'CONNOR join, concurring.

I agree with the Court that the distributor of a dual-use technology may be liable for the infringing activities of third parties where he or she actively seeks to advance the infringement. Ante, at 919. I further agree that, in light of our holding today, we need not now "revisit" Sony Corp. of America v. Universal City Studios, Inc., 464 U.S. 417 (1984). Ante, at 934. Other Members of the Court, however, take up the *Sony* question: whether Grokster's product is "capable of 'substantial' or 'commercially significant' noninfringing uses." Ante, at 942 (GINSBURG, J., concurring) (quoting *Sony*, supra, at 442). And they answer that question by stating that the Court of Appeals was wrong when it granted summary judgment on the issue in Grokster's favor. Ante, at 944–45. I write to explain why I disagree with them on this matter. * * *

* * * The Court [in *Sony*] had before it a survey (commissioned by the District Court and then prepared by the respondents) showing that roughly 9% of all VCR recordings were of the type—namely, religious, educational, and sports programming—owned by producers and distributors testifying on Sony's behalf who did not object to time-shifting. See Brief for Respondent Universal Studios et al. O. T. 1983, No. 81–1687, pp. 52–53; see also *Sony*, supra, at 424 (7.3% of all Sony VCR use is to record sports programs; representatives of the sports leagues do not object). * * *

The Court found that the magnitude of authorized programming was "significant," and it also noted the "significant potential for future authorized copying." 464 U.S., at 444. The Court supported this conclusion by referencing the trial testimony of professional sports league officials and a religious broadcasting representative. Id., at 444, and n. 24. It also discussed (1) a Los Angeles educational station affiliated with the Public Broadcasting Service that made many of its programs available for home taping, and (2) Mr. Rogers' Neighborhood, a widely watched children's program. Id., at 445. On the basis of this testimony and other similar evidence, the Court determined that producers of this kind had authorized duplication of their copyrighted programs "in significant enough numbers to create a *substantial* market for a noninfringing use of the" VCR. Id., at 447, n. 28 (emphasis added).

The Court, in using the key word "substantial," indicated that these circumstances alone constituted a sufficient basis for rejecting the imposition of secondary liability. See id., at 456 ("Sony demonstrated a significant likelihood that *substantial* numbers of copyright holders" would not object to time-shifting (emphasis added)). Nonetheless, the Court buttressed its conclusion by finding separately that, in any event, *un*authorized time-shifting often constituted not infringement, but "fair use." Id., at 447–456.

When measured against *Sony*'s underlying evidence and analysis, the evidence now before us shows that Grokster passes *Sony*'s test—that is, whether the company's product is capable of substantial or commercially significant noninfringing uses. Id., at 442. For one thing, petitioners' (hereinafter MGM) own expert declared that 75% of current files available on Grokster are infringing and 15% are "likely infringing." See App. 436–439, ¶ ¶ 6–17 (Decl. of Dr. Ingram Olkin); cf. ante, at 922 (opinion of the Court). That leaves some number of files near 10% that apparently are noninfringing, a figure very similar to the 9% or so of authorized time-shifting uses of the VCR that the Court faced in *Sony*. * * *

Importantly, *Sony* also used the word "capable," asking whether the product is *"capable of"* substantial noninfringing uses. Its language and analysis suggest that a figure like 10%, if fixed for all time, might well prove insufficient, but that such a figure serves as an adequate foundation where there is a reasonable prospect of expanded legitimate uses over time. See ibid. (noting a "significant potential for future authorized copying"). And its language also indicates the appropriateness of looking to potential future uses of the product to determine its "capability."

Here the record reveals a significant future market for noninfringing uses of Grokster-type peer-to-peer software. Such software permits the exchange of *any* sort of digital file—whether that file does, or does not, contain copyrighted material. As more and more uncopyrighted information is stored in swappable form, it seems a likely inference that lawful peer-to-peer sharing will become increasingly prevalent. * * *

Instead, the real question is whether we should modify the *Sony* standard, as MGM requests, or interpret *Sony* more strictly, as I believe Justice Ginsburg's approach would do in practice. * * *

As I have said, *Sony* itself sought to "strike a balance between a copyright holder's legitimate demand for effective—not merely symbolic—protection of the statutory monopoly, and the rights of others freely to engage in substantially unrelated areas of commerce." Id., at 442. Thus, to determine whether modification, or a strict interpretation, of *Sony* is needed, I would ask whether MGM has shown that *Sony* incorrectly balanced copyright and new-technology interests. In particular: (1) Has *Sony* (as I interpret it) worked to protect new technology? (2) If so, would modification or strict interpretation significantly weaken that protection? (3) If so, would new or necessary copyright-related benefits outweigh any such weakening?

The first question is the easiest to answer. *Sony*'s rule, as I interpret it, has provided entrepreneurs with needed assurance that they will be shielded from copyright liability as they bring valuable new technologies to market. [Justice Breyer emphasized that *Sony* provides clear guidance to product developers and makes it appropriately difficult to impose secondary liability in connection with new technologies.]

The second, more difficult, question is whether a modified *Sony* rule (or a strict interpretation) would significantly weaken the law's ability to protect new technology. Justice Ginsburg's approach would require defendants to produce considerably more concrete evidence—more than was presented here—to earn *Sony*'s shelter. That heavier evidentiary demand, and especially the more dramatic (case-by-case balancing) modifications that

MGM and the Government seek, would, I believe, undercut the protection that *Sony* now offers. * * *

The third question—whether a positive copyright impact would outweigh any technology-related loss—I find the most difficult of the three. I do not doubt that a more intrusive *Sony* test would generally provide greater revenue security for copyright holders. But it is harder to conclude that the gains on the copyright swings would exceed the losses on the technology roundabouts. * * *

Finally, as *Sony* recognized, the legislative option remains available. Courts are less well suited than Congress to the task of "accommodat[ing] fully the varied permutations of competing interests that are inevitably implicated by such new technology." *Sony*, 464 U.S., at 431; * * *

For these reasons, I disagree with Justice Ginsburg, but I agree with the Court and join its opinion.

NOTES AND QUESTIONS ON FILE-SHARING

(1) A few months after the Supreme Court's decision, Grokster agreed to a settlement that enjoined it from further distribution of its software; it was also required to close its web site and pay $50 million in damages. 71 Pat., Tm. & Copyr.J. (BNA) 29 (2005). SteamCast fought on, but ultimately lost on a summary judgment when the trial court held on remand that "no reasonable factfinder can conclude that SteamCast provided OpenNap services and distributed Morpheus without the intent to induce infringement." Metro–Goldwyn–Mayer Studios, Inc. v. Grokster, Ltd., 454 F.Supp.2d 966 (C.D.Cal.2006).

LimeWire, a peer-to-peer software application that emerged as a successor to the networks that were shut down by the *Grokster* case, was itself held liable in Arista Records LLC v. Lime Group LLC, 784 F.Supp.2d 398 (S.D.N.Y.2011). Judge Wood found that LimeWire had induced infringement of the plaintiffs' sound recordings under the *Grokster* standard. Among other conduct, LimeWire actively targeted former customers of networks like Napster, included search functions designed to facilitate searches for copyrighted recordings, and failed to implement available technological barriers against infringing use of its system. LimeWire ultimately settled with the record companies for $105 million and ceased operations. Sisario, Music Piracy Suit to Cost LimeWire $105 Million, N.Y. Times, May 13, 2011, p. B2.

(2) *Grokster* has drawn mixed reviews. T. Wu, The Copyright Paradox, 2005 Sup.Ct.Rev. 229, questions whether the Supreme Court's focus on bad intent is a sound basis for regulating the information industries, and R. Ku, Grokking *Grokster*, 2005 Wis.L.Rev. 1217, argues that the law should not block progress by attempting to preserve existing market paradigms. N. Schaumann, Copyright Infringement and Peer-to-Peer Technology, 28 Wm. Mitchell L.Rev. 1001 (2001), urges robust application of *Sony* to peer-to-peer networks, and A. Jacob and Z. Argento, To Cache or Not To Cache—That is the Question: P2P "System Caching"—the Copyright Dilemma, 31 Whittier L.Rev. 421 (2010), analyzes the potential liability of service providers for caching content as part of peer-to-peer file sharing.

On the interaction of technological innovation and creators' rights, see B. Depoorter, Technology and Uncertainty: The Shaping Effect on Copyright Law, 157 U.Pa.L.Rev. 1831 (2009), examining how the legal uncertainties created by rapid technological change affect the evolution of copyright law, and D. Oliar, The Copyright–Innovation Tradeoff: Property Rules, Liability Rules, and Intentional Infliction of Harm, 64 Stan.L.Rev. 951 (2012), exploring how various legal entitlements can affect the respective incentives of creators and technological innovators. P. DiCola and M. Sag, An Information-Gathering Approach to Copyright Policy, 34 Cardozo L.Rev. 173 (2012), uses case studies to assess the benefits of government intervention in disputes between content owners and the makers of new technologies.

(3) The recording industry still sees peer-to-peer file-sharing as a substantial threat. Although the slide in global music sales finally ended in 2012, revenues are less than half of their 2000 level. How much of the industry's problems are due to file-sharing and how much to high prices or bad music is open to debate. The "single-bullet theory" favored by the music industry blames everything on unauthorized downloads. All of the contributors to Symposium: Piracy and File Sharing, 49 J.L. & Econ. 1 (2006), offer analyses indicating that file-sharing does indeed have a real effect on record sales.

Sales of authorized digital downloads were initially hampered by the reluctance of some record labels to license online delivery and the legal complications of clearing rights not only with record companies but also with music publishers and recording artists. W. Cardi, Über–Middleman: Reshaping the Broken Landscape of Music, 92 Iowa L.Rev. 835 (2007), blames the fractured administration of music rights for the industry's slow response to digital challenges and opportunities. In 2011, digital revenues finally exceeded revenues from physical music sales in the U.S. Although Apple's iTunes sold its 10 billionth song in 2010 (Johnny Cash's "Guess Things Happen That Way," purchased by a 71 year-old retired real estate broker, 10 Billionth Download for iTunes, N.Y. Times, Feb. 26, 2010, p. C5), the music industry complains that profit margins on 99–cent digital sales are too small. Record companies have high hopes that subscription and ad-supported music streaming services like Spotify, which are growing faster than digital purchases from sites like iTunes, will finally provide an attractive alternative to illegal downloading. Royalties paid by licensees for streaming a song, however, are much smaller than for a download. See Sisario, As Music Streaming Grows, Artists' Royalties Slow to a Trickle, N.Y. Times, Jan. 29, 2013, p. A1.

C. Sprigman, The 99¢ Question, 5 J.Telecomm. & High Tech.L. 87 (2006), examines the unusual uniformity in download prices and its implications for the structure of the music business. D. Tussey, Music at the Edge of Chaos, A Complex Systems Perspective on File Sharing, 37 Loyola U.Chi.L.J. 147 (2005), worries that legislative intervention will deprive the music market of the flexibility it needs to reach a new equilibrium, and A. Bridy, Why Pirates (Still) Won't Behave: Regulating P2P in the Decade after Napster, 40 Rutgers L.J. 565 (2009), concludes that content owners should focus on offering consumers more options and flexibility.

(4) The difficulty of pursuing decentralized file-sharing networks as well as the desire to deter illegal downloading prompted the record industry to target individual downloaders. In 2003, it began to file copyright infringement actions against file-sharers; over 35,000 suits were eventually filed. The record industry suffered a procedural setback early in its litigation campaign in Recording Industry Ass'n of America, Inc. v. Verizon Internet Services, Inc., 351 F.3d 1229 (D.C.Cir.2003), cert. denied, 543 U.S. 924 (2004). In order to trade files over a peer-to-peer network, users must disclose their Internet protocol address so that others can reach their computer. Copyright owners can trace users back to those addresses and catalog what they have downloaded. The Internet protocol address, however, is not uniquely associated with a single user or computer; at different times the address may be assigned to different users. Internet service providers typically keep records indicating to whom an address was assigned at a given time. Section 512(h) permits copyright owners to request the clerk of a U.S. District Court to issue a subpoena to a service provider demanding the identity of an alleged infringer without initiating a lawsuit. In the *Verizon* case, the RIAA served a subpoena on Verizon seeking the identity of the Verizon customer who used a specific Internet protocol address to offer 800 music files for downloading. The fast-track subpoena procedure in § 512(h) requires the copyright owner to file with the court clerk a copy of the notification of infringement described in § 512(c)(3)(A). However, that notification is part of notice and takedown provisions that only apply to service providers who store infringing material on their systems. Verizon argued that the subpoena procedure in § 512(h) did not apply to service providers like itself who merely provide transmission facilities. The D.C Circuit agreed with Verizon. The Eighth Circuit took a similar position in In re Charter Communications, Inc., 393 F.3d 771 (8th Cir.2005). As a result, the record companies were forced to use the more cumbersome and expensive procedure of filing "John Doe" lawsuits against individual defendants and then asking a judge to issue a subpoena to the service provider seeking the identity of the defendant. The procedural limitations on suits against individual file-sharers resulting from RIAA v. Verizon are criticized in L. Mtima, Whom the Gods Would Destroy: Why Congress Prioritized Copyright Protection Over Internet Privacy in Passing the DMCA, 61 Rutgers L.Rev. 627 (2009). An attempt by an alleged file-sharer to quash a court-issued subpoena based on the assertion of a right to use the Internet anonymously was rejected in Arista Records, LLC v. Doe 3, 604 F.3d 110 (2d Cir.2010).

Many of the RIAA lawsuits were settled, typically for a few thousand dollars. In the first downloading case to reach a jury, the defendant was found liable for $220,000 in statutory damages—$9,250 for each of the 24 songs involved in the litigation. However, the trial judge granted a new trial after concluding that he had wrongly instructed the jury that proof that the defendant had made the songs available for distribution was sufficient for infringement; proof of actual distribution (or downloading) should have been required. Capitol Records Inc. v. Thomas, 579 F.Supp.2d 1210 (D.Minn.2008). In the second trial, the jury awarded $1.92 million in statutory damages. Calling the damages "monstrous and shocking," the district judge said that "statutory damages must still bear *some* relation to actual damages" and granted the defendant's motion for remittitur, reducing the award to $54,000 ($2,250 per work) or granting a new trial. Capitol Records, Inc. v. Thomas–Rasset, 680 F.Supp.2d 1045 (D.Minn.2010). The record companies demanded a new trial on damages, and on the third try a the jury awarded $1.5 million in statutory damages. The defendant then filed a motion to amend the judgment on the ground that it violated due process. The court, finding the jury's award unconstitutionally severe and oppressive, again reduced it to $54,000. Capitol Records, Inc. v. Thomas–Rasset, 799 F.Supp.2d 999 (D.Minn.2011). The record companies appealed, seeking reinstatement of the first jury's verdict based on their argument that making a work available for public distribution was sufficient for infringement. The Eighth Circuit in Capitol Records, Inc. v. Thomas–Rasset, 692 F.3d 899 (8th Cir.2012), cert. denied, 133 S.Ct. 1584 (2013), found it unnecessary to decide the distribution issue and held that the $220,000 award of statutory damages did not violate the defendant's due process right.

Meanwhile, a jury in another music downloading case ordered a Boston University student to pay $675,000 in statutory damages—$22,500 per song. The defendant requested a remittitur and the court, finding that the jury award violated due process, reduce it by a factor of ten to $67,500. Sony BMG Music Entertainment v. Tenenbaum, 721 F.Supp.2d 85 (D.Mass.2010). Both parties appealed. The First Circuit held that the trial court erred when it bypassed the motion for remittitur and reached the constitutional issue. Rejecting an argument that the statutory damages provision was not applicable to "consumer copiers," the appellate court reinstated the jury award and remanded for consideration of the remittitur motion. Sony BMG Music Entertainment v. Tenenbaum, 660 F.3d 487 (1st Cir.2011), cert. denied, 132 S.Ct. 2431 (2012). On remand, the motion for remittitur was denied and the jury verdict was allowed to stand. Sony BMG Music Ent. v. Tenenbaum, 103 U.S.P.Q.2d 1902 (D. Mass.2012). Why are juries so harsh on downloaders?

The wisdom of the RIAA's litigation strategy has been hotly debated. Some academics caution against litigation as an automatic response to piracy. Public education rather than coercion is the key to maintaining the legitimacy of copyright according to J. Garon, Normative Copyright: A Conceptual Framework for Copyright Philosophy and Ethics, 88 Cornell L.Rev. 1278 (2003). Others think that the RIAA may have been right. See J. Hughes, On the Logic of Suing One's Customers and the Dilemma of Infringement–Based Business Models, 22 Cardozo Arts & Ent.L.J. 725 (2005), concluding that the "it's not good business to sue your customers" mantra may actually be wrong, and M. Sag, Piracy: Twelve Year–Olds, Grandmothers, and Other Good Targets for the Recording Industry, 4 N.W.J.Tech. & Intell.Prop. 133 (2006), arguing that the RIAA litigation is a rational response to file-sharing and that an optimal strategy would target some sympathetic, marginal file-sharers. There is also debate over the unintended consequences of the litigation spree. See N. Schaumann, Copyright Class War, 11 U.C.L.A. Ent.L.Rev. 247 (2004), hoping that the publicity will force a rebalancing of the rights of users and owners; an empirical study in B. Depoorter, A. Van Hiel, and S. Vanneste, Copyright Backlash, 84 S.Cal.L.Rev. 1251 (2011), indicates that greater copyright enforcement may actually increase infringement by eroding respect for copyrights. At the end of 2008, the RIAA announced that it had abandoned its policy of litigation against individual downloaders. It continues to insist that its litigation strategy was successful in raising public awareness that file-sharing is illegal. McBride and Smith, Music Industry to Abandon Mass Suits, Wall St.J., Dec. 19, 2008, p. B1. However, a report in 2008 estimated that 19 per cent of Internet users age thirteen and older still download music from P2P services, barely changed from the 20 per cent reported when the RIAA began its litigation campaign in 2003. Butler, Casting the Net, Billboard, June 14, 2008, p. 10. M. Schultz, Reconciling Social Norms and Copyright Law: Strategies for Persuading People to Pay for Recorded Music, 17 J.Intell.Prop.L. 59 (2009), expresses optimism that the music industry may yet succeed in reversing the social norms supporting file-sharing. That optimism may be well-founded. A 2013 study by NPD Group, a global information company, finds that P2P file-sharing was down significantly in 2012, as were the number of music files copied from CDs borrowed from friends and family and the volume of downloads from digital storage lockers. The study attributes the declines to the increasing use of legal music streaming services.

NPD Group, Music File-Sharing Declined Significantly in 2012 (Press Release, Feb 26, 2013).

(5) Spurred in part by their desire to move into content distribution, Internet service providers have finally agreed to assist content owners in the fight against piracy. In 2011 major providers AT&T, Cablevision, Comcast, Time Warner, and Verizon signed an agreement with the Recording Industry Association of America, the Motion Picture Association of America, and other representatives of content owners that establishes a systematic response to file-sharing. When notified by a content owner that a specific Internet Protocol address is suspected of illegal file-sharing, the ISPs will subject the customer to a series of up to six escalating alerts, notices, and "mitigation" measures, including reductions in connection speed and compulsory copyright education. The agreement does not require the ISP to identify the customer to the content owner and does not require a termination of service. However, recall that under § 512, the failure of a service provider to terminate the account of a repeat offender will jeopardize the service provider's safe harbor protection.[y]

A. Bridy, Graduated Response and the Turn to Private Ordering in Online Copyright Enforcement, 89 Ore.L.Rev. 81 (2010), examines the incentives for cooperation between copyright owners and ISPs, and P. Yu, The Graduated Response, 62 Fla.L.Rev. 1373 (2010), sees danger in that cooperation; M. LaFrance, Graduated Response by Industry Compact: Piercing the Black Box, 30 Cardozo Arts & Ent.L.J. 165 (2012), criticizes both the specifics of the "six strikes" agreement and the lack of consumer choice.

(6) How can performing artists best accommodate themselves to the new realities of the music marketplace? Many performers are now pursing business models based on selling tickets and merchandise rather than CDs. As one performer noted, "Thank God they can't download those." Carr, Live Music Thrives as CDs Fade, N.Y. Times, June 23, 2008, p. C1. An economic analysis of the "live performance" business model is offered in M. Schultz, Live Performance, Copyright, and the Future of the Music Business, 43 U. Richmond L.Rev. 685 (2009).

(7) The record companies and performing artists are not the only ones harmed by the unauthorized downloading of music. Songwriters, who get royalties on CD sales and authorized downloads, are also suffering. According to the National Music Publishers' Association, royalties to songwriters and music publishers from record sales have fallen substantially since Napster emerged in 1999. Bernstein, Songwriters Say Piracy Eats Into Their Pay, N.Y. Times, Jan. 5, 2004, p. C6. Sheet music too is now available online, although the threat of unauthorized downloading may be no worse than the risk of photocopying for sheet music in the traditional print format. Both songwriters and the record companies got some relief from a new market—tunes sold as cellphone ring tones, but that market too may have peaked. Shannon, Global Market for Cellphone Ring Tones is Shrinking, N.Y. Times, Dec. 31, 2007, p. C2.

(8) Although music has attracted the most attention, the ability to transfer large files over the Internet creates similar risks and opportunities for other media. Rising storage capacities, faster connections, improved compression technology, and more efficient file-sharing networks combined to erode the

---

[y] Information on the "Copyright Alert System" can be found at www.copyrightinformation.org, the website of the Center for Copyright Information, formed to administer the policy.

technical limitations that once gave the movie industry a degree of practical protection against file-sharing never enjoyed by the record companies. Like the music industry, movie studios now keep a close eye on the Internet. The hit movie *Avatar,* for example, was illegally downloaded on the BitTorrent network almost a million times in the week following its release. Itzkoff, "Avatar" Commandeers Film Piracy Record, N.Y. Times, Jan. 6, 2010, p. C2. (Morality apparently plays no role—at one point in 2004, Mel Gibson's *The Passion of the Christ* was the most pirated movie on the Internet. L.A. Times, May 13, 2004, p. E5.) Following the trail blazed but ultimately abandoned by the music industry, some independent movie producers have authorized law firms to file barrages of suits against downloaders, relying on the leverage of statutory damages to extract settlements of a few thousand dollars each. By some counts more than 135,000 defendants alleged to have used the BitTorrent transfer protocol to share movie files have been targeted. Hanners, Grandma's a Movie Pirate? Are You Sure?, St. Paul Pioneer Press, Apr. 9, 2011, p. A7. BitTorrent users obtain a file associated with the desired movie from an indexing website. The file is then used to contact an intermediary server that connects the user with other BitTorrent users who have the desired movie. The user can then download the movie file in pieces from multiple sources. Numerous John Doe lawsuits have been filed against large groups of BitTorrent users alleged to have been part of a "swarm" related to a particular movie; the plaintiffs then subpoena the Internet service providers to learn the identities of the individual users. The courts are split over whether participation in a "swarm" satisfies the "same transaction" requirement for joining all of the defendants in a single lawsuit. Compare Third Degree Films v. Does 1-47, 286 F.R.D. 188 (D.Mass.2012) (finding joinder technically proper but nevertheless exercising its discretion to sever), with Hard Drive Prods., Inc., v. Does 1-188, 809 F.Supp.2d 1150 (N.D.Cal.2011) (holding that joinder was improper). An operator of BitTorrent indexing websites was held contributorily liable for inducing copyright infringement under the *Grokster* standard in Columbia Pictures Industries, Inc. v. Fung, 710 F.3d 1020 (9th Cir.2013).

In a sign of the dwindling market for DVDs, 2009 was the first year since 2002 that movie box office receipts exceeded DVD and Blu-ray sales. Wall St.J., Jan. 4, 2010, p. B3. With less need to worry about preserving a DVD market, the studios are putting greater emphasis on video-on-demand services through the early availability of major releases. The Federal Communications Commission offered a boost to video-on-demand by approving a request from the studios to allow cable and satellite companies to turn off the output connections on their set-top boxes for limited times to prevent copying of newly-released video-on-demand movies. Verrier, First–Run Movies Can Open at Home, L.A. Times, May 8, 2010, p. 1. Following the lead of the record industry, the movie studios are also increasingly turning to the Internet to supplement their revenue, offering digital streaming through companies like Netflix and Amazon. (Netflix is apparently the largest source of U.S. Internet traffic during peak hours. Arango and Carr, Netflix Move Onto the Web Stirs Rivalries, N.Y. Times, Nov. 25, 2010, p. A1.)

Television networks have also embraced the Internet, but authorized access remains somewhat chaotic with a mix of free and pay streaming that varies from network to network. Some of the problems may be traceable to production contracts drafted when producers still associated the Internet only with piracy. Boutin, Surfing Required, and Maybe a Fee, for TV on the Web, N.Y.

Times, July 8, 2010, p. B9. All the major networks offer free streaming of some popular shows, and ad-free downloads and streaming episodes are also available on sites like iTunes, Amazon, and Hulu. However, a larger selection of programming is available on unauthorized sites and file-sharing networks. An episode of HBO's *Game of Thrones* was apparently the most pirated program of 2012, with 4.28 million illegal downloads, mostly outside the U.S. Itzkoff, "Game of Thrones" Popular with Pirates, N.Y. Times, Dec. 25, 2012, p. C2.

(9) Books too are sold—and pirated—online. Publishers and online booksellers have competed for the electronic rights to popular books, which some authors retain under their original publishing contracts. See p. 512 infra.[z] The market for electronic books has benefitted from the arrival of a new generation of e-book readers like the Kindle that allow users to wirelessly download books—typically at less cost than a hard copy. Amazon now sells more e-books than print books. N.Y. Times, May 20, 2011, p. B2. Stieg Larson's *The Girl with the Dragon Tattoo* became the first book to sell a million digital copies. N.Y. Times, Apr. 8, 2011, p. C2. E-books create unique issues for libraries. Although the major publishers sell e-books to libraries under agreements that permit the books to be lent to one reader at a time, some require annual licensing payments or restrict the number of times an e-book can be lent. Marx, E-Books and Democracy, N.Y. Times, May 1, 2013, p. A25. As predicted, the growing popularity of e-books and e-book readers has lead to an increase in the availability of pirated copies on the Internet. Rich, Print Books are Target of Pirates on the Web, N.Y. Times, May 12, 2009, p. B1.

In an attempt to boost a different format, major book publishers are following the lead of the record companies and abandoning anti-piracy software on audio book downloads. Stone, Publishers Phase Out Piracy Protection on Audio Books, N.Y. Times, March 3, 2008, p. C2.

(10) File-sharing networks also present challenges for the software industry. Like movies, popular software is often available on peer-to-peer networks before its official release. Even high-end technical programs can be found on the Internet. Some software producers try to limit piracy through mandatory program activation procedures, but the schemes are often cracked by hackers. A study released by the Business Software Alliance estimated that worldwide software piracy rates increased to 42 per cent in 2011, due in part to increased computer sales in high-piracy countries such as China and India, resulting in losses said to exceed $63 billion; the U.S. piracy rate was the lowest at 19 per cent, but represented the largest dollar loss at $9.7 billion. However, a report by the U.S. Government Accountability Office in 2010 was highly skeptical of software industry loss estimates. It pointed out, for example, that the Business Software Alliance estimate of software losses was based on a one-to-one substitution rate that assumes every user of a pirated copy would otherwise purchase the real thing. 79 Pat., Tm. & Copyr.J. (BNA) 749 (2010.)

(11) Although file-sharing systems like BitTorrent continue to elude control, attention is shifting toward another online threat to copyright owners. Huge Internet storage lockers, supported by subscription fees and advertising, allow and sometimes encourage users to store copyrighted works that can then be streamed or downloaded by other users. The U.S. Government has begun a crackdown, using its authority to seize property involved in the commission of a

---

[z]   Thousands of public domain works are available online through Project Gutenberg at www.gutenberg.org., and through the Google Book Search project at www.books.google.com.

crime to take control of domain names used by pirate websites, although the sites often quickly reappear under a new name. See, e.g., Sisario, U.S. Shuts Web Sites in its Battle to Stop Online Piracy, N.Y. Times, Nov. 27, 2010, p. B2. The most well-known case involves Megaupload, a storage locker website whose domain name was seized by the Department of Justice in 2012. A federal indictment against the operators of the site alleged that it was the 13th most popular website on the entire Internet with fifty million visitors every day, generating $175 million since 2005. The indictment included charges of criminal copyright infringement, wire fraud, and racketeering. 83 Pat., Tm. & Copyr.J. (BNA) 573 (2012). Although a number of the foreign defendants have been arrested, extradition for copyright infringement is problematic. Exactly one year after his New Zealand mansion was raided by police, Kim Dotcom, the principal figure behind Megaupload, unveiled a new storage site called Mega that automatically encrypts a users' files prior to uploading, thus preventing the both the company and copyright owners from identifying the contents of stored files. Users can share files with others by sending their encryption key. Hutchison, A Year After the Closing of Megaupload, a File-Sharing Tycoon Opens a New Site, N.Y. Times, Jan. 21, 2013, p. B5. Will encryption insulate the new Mega site from liability?

(12) Copyright and trademark owners launched a major effort in 2011 to strengthen enforcement of intellectual property rights against pirates and counterfeiters. The Protect IP Act (PIPA), S. 968, and the Stop Online Piracy Act (SOPA), H.R. 3261, were directed at websites "dedicated" to infringing activities. Both bills authorized the U.S. Attorney General to institute actions against foreign websites that could result in court orders requiring ISPs to block access to the site, requiring financial transaction service providers to withdraw their support from the site, ordering Internet advertising services to cease doing business with the site, and requiring search engines to remove links to the site. Both bills also established private rights of action against foreign and domestic websites dedicated to infringing activities, and SOPA permitted content owners to file notifications without judicial involvement on financial transaction and internet advertising service providers requiring them to suspend services to the website. Opponents objected that the broad definitions of illegal sites contained in the bills invited censorship and effectively removed the safe harbor protection of § 512 by requiring sites to monitor their content. The bills were stopped in their tracks when major online providers like Google, Wikipedia, Craigslist, and others either blacked out their sites for a day in protest or encouraged their users to contact Congress. 83 Pat., Tm. & Copyr.J. (BNA) 360 (2012). The volume of opposition was so unexpectedly intense that future bills may be handicapped by lawmakers' fears of being "SOPAed."

(13) The ultimate outcome of the contest between content owners and digital innovators remains uncertain. It may still be true, as a t-shirt advised, that "Copyright Infringement Is Your Best Entertainment Value." Some argue that it's time for a completely different approach. See, e.g., N. Netanel, Impose a Noncommercial Use Levy to Allow Free Peer-to-Peer File Sharing, 17 Harv.J.L. & Tech. 1 (2003), advocating unrestricted noncommercial file-sharing in exchange for a levy on goods and services such as Internet access, CD and DVD burners, and blank media, to be divided among copyright holders based on the popularity of their works; R. Chused, Rewrite Copyright: Protecting Creativity and Social Utility in the Digital Age, 38 Israel L.Rev. 80 (2005), proposes a bar code levy system that would guarantee both access and remuneration. J. Grimmelmann, The Ethical Visions of Copyright Law, 77 Fordham L.Rev. 2005 (2009), examines the ethics behind competing rhetoric like "respect copyrights" and "sharing." Defenders of activities like file-sharing, however, face an uphill battle. At a hearing on peer-to-peer networks, Senator Orrin Hatch, former Chair of the Senate Judiciary Committee's Subcommittee on Intellectual Property and composer of songs such as "The Answer's Not in Washington," casually endorsed technology that would, after two warnings, destroy a file-sharer's computer. Healey, Deep–Six Computers to Sink Net Pirates?, L.A. Times, June 18, 2003, p. C1.

THE WIPO COPYRIGHT TREATY

A diplomatic conference in Geneva sponsored by the World Intellectual Property Organization in 1996 adopted two treaties designed to insure copyright protection in the emerging digital environment—the Copyright Treaty and the Performances and Phonograms Treaty.[aa] (On the latter, see p. 272 supra).

The WIPO Copyright Treaty requires contracting nations to treat computer programs as "literary works" within the meaning of the Berne Convention and requires protection for compilations of data that display creativity in selection or arrangement. The treaty also recognizes an exclusive distribution right for tangible copies and requires protection against the commercial rental of computer programs, phonograms, and cinematographic works (with an exception that protection for the latter works is not required absent widespread copying attributable to rentals).

The most significant provision in the treaty is Article 8, which declares that "authors of literary and artistic works shall enjoy the exclusive right of authorizing any communication to the public of their works, by wire or wireless means, including the making available to the public of their works in such a way that members of the public may access these works from a place and at a time individually chosen by them." In a concession to online service providers, an agreed statement interpreting Article 8 specifies that "the mere provision of physical facilities for enabling or making a communication does not in itself amount to communication." There is also an agreed statement that "the storage of a protected work in digital form in an electronic medium constitutes a reproduction within the meaning of Article 9 of the Berne Convention."

The Copyright Treaty imposes two other significant obligations. Article 11 requires contracting nations to provide adequate protection and remedies "against the circumvention of effective technological measures" employed by authors to restrict unauthorized uses not permitted by law. Article 12 requires remedies against persons who remove or alter "electronic rights management information" or who knowingly distribute works with removed or altered information if the person has reason to know that the conduct will facilitate or conceal an infringement. The protected information includes the identity of the work, author, and copyright owner, as

---

[aa] The WIPO treaties are reprinted in the Statutory Supplement. See also the WIPO website at www.wipo.org. P. Yu, Anticircumvention and Anti–Anticircumvention, 84 Denver U.L.Rev. 13 (2006), urges developing nations to be very cautious about implementing the treaties.

well as information on the terms and conditions of use. About ninety nations have ratified the treaty, including the United States.

ANTI–CIRCUMVENTION

The WIPO Copyright Treaty and the Performances and Phonograms Treaty were implemented in 1998 by Title I of the Digital Millennium Copyright Act, Pub.L. 105–304, 112 Stat. 2860 (1998), which added Chapter 12 to the Copyright Act. Section 1201(a)(1) prohibits "circumventing a technological measure that effectively controls access to a work." Technological measures that control access include, for example, password protection and encryption designed to prevent unauthorized access. According to the House Judiciary Committee, gaining access to a work by circumventing a technological protection measure "is the electronic equivalent of breaking into a locked room in order to obtain a copy of a book."[bb]

Although the WIPO treaties require only protection against the *act* of circumventing technological control measures, § 1201(a)(2) also prohibits the manufacture or sale of "any technology, product, service, device, component, or part thereof" that is primarily designed for the purpose of circumventing access control measures. Additionally, § 1201(b) prohibits the manufacture or sale of devices or services primarily designed to circumvent "a technological measure that effectively protects a right of a copyright owner under this title"—for example, technological measures intended to prevent unauthorized copying of the work. (The absence of a corresponding prohibition against the *act* of circumventing a technological measure that protects a right of the copyright owner is explained in the Senate Report: "The copyright law has long forbidden copyright infringements, so no new prohibition was necessary. The device limitation in 1201(b) enforces the longstanding prohibitions on infringements.")[cc] Since not all copying that occurs after the circumvention of a protective measure will constitute copyright infringement, critics argue that the ban on providing circumvention devices can effectively prevent users from making fair use of the protected works.[dd]

[bb] H.R. Rep. No. 105–551I, 105th Cong., 2d Sess. 47 (1998). Sections 1201(d)–(j) allow circumvention for a series of narrowly-defined purposes such as library acquisition decisions, analysis of computer programs, and encryption research.

Section 1201(a)(1)(C) authorizes the Librarian of Congress to exempt particular classes of works from the prohibition on circumventing access controls. There are currently five classes of works that have been exempted: circumvention to access the read-aloud functions of e-books to assist the blind; to achieve interoperability of mobile phones with legally obtained software; to unlock mobile phones purchased prior to February, 2013 to enable use with a different service provider; circumvention of protection on DVDs or online movies for the purpose of criticism, or making noncommercial videos or documentaries, or e-books offering film analysis, or for use in film studies classes; and circumvention of protection on DVDs for the purpose of developing captioning. 77 Fed.Reg. 65,266 (2012). Note that the exemptions apply only to the prohibition against circumvention in § 1201(a)(1); they do not cover parties who provide products or services that assist in such circumventions in violation of the prohibition in § 1201(a)(2).

[cc] S.Rep. 105–190, 105th Cong., 2d Sess. 12 (1998).

[dd] The inconsistencies and overbreadth of the anti-circumvention provisions are described in P. Samuelson, Intellectual Property and the Digital Economy: Why the Anti–Circumvention Regulations Need to Be Revised, 14 Berk.Tech.L.J. 519 (1999); L. Gasaway, The New Access Right and Its Impact on Libraries and Library Users, 10 J.Intell.Prop.L. 269 (2003), sees the anti-circumvention provisions as unwisely adding an exclusive right of access to the existing rights of copyright owners, a view only partly shared in M. Landau, Has the

Section 1201(c)(1) states that nothing in § 1201 "shall affect defenses to copyright infringement, including fair use." Note however that violations of the device and circumvention prohibitions in § 1201 are not "copyright infringement"; they are independent violations separately actionable under § 1203, which contains its own remedial provisions, including statutory damages up to $2,500 for each violation of the anti-circumvention provisions.[ee] Criminal penalties may be imposed under § 1204.

In addition to the anti-circumvention provisions, the Digital Millennium Copyright Act also added protection for "copyright management information" in § 1202. Removal or alteration of identifying information or information on the terms and conditions of use, or the distribution of works after removal or alteration of the information, is prohibited under § 1202(b) if there are reasonable grounds to know that it will facilitate or conceal an infringement.[ff] Violations are actionable under § 1203.[gg]

Universal City Studios, Inc. v. Corley

United States Court of Appeals, Second Circuit, 2001.
273 F.3d 429.

■ Before NEWMAN and CABRANES, CIRCUIT JUDGES, and THOMPSON, DISTRICT JUDGE.

■ NEWMAN, CIRCUIT JUDGE:

When the Framers of the First Amendment prohibited Congress from making any law "abridging the freedom of speech," they were not thinking about computers, computer programs, or the Internet. But neither were they thinking about radio, television, or movies. Just as the inventions at the beginning and middle of the 20th century presented new First Amend-

---

DMCA Really Created a New Exclusive Right of Access? Attempting to Reach a Balance Between Users' and Content Providers' Rights, 49 J.Copyr.Soc'y 277 (2001).

[ee] The statutory damages provision in § 1203(c)(3) was applied in EchoStar Satellite LLC v. ViewTech, Inc., 98 U.S.P.Q.2d 1757 (S.D.Cal.2011). The court awarded the minimum $200 damages for each of the 1,074,493 unauthorized satellite receivers sold by the defendant, putting total damages at $214,898,600.

[ff] Judge Greenaway in IQ Group, Ltd. v. Wiesner Pub., LLC, 409 F.Supp.2d 587 (D.N.J.2006), granted summary judgment against an advertising company claiming that a competitor who removed the plaintiff's logo and link from email advertisements had violated § 1202 by removing "copyright management information." The court held that the definition of that term in § 1202(c) included only information that "function[s] as a component of an automated copyright protection or management system." Judge Abrams in Textile Secrets Int'l, Inc. v. Ya–Ya Brand Inc., 524 F.Supp.2d 1184 (C.D.Cal.2007), agreed with *IQ Group* and held that § 1202 only applies to copyright information that is related to technological measures or processes contemplated by the DMCA. However, when a photographer complained about the removal of a credit line identifying him as the author of a photograph posted online by the defendant, the Third Circuit in Murphy v. Millennium Radio Group LLC, 650 F.3d 295 (3d Cir.2011), disagreed with both decisions, holding that under the "plain language" of § 1202(c), the prohibition against removal is not limited to information used by automated protection or management systems and the credit line qualified as "copyright management information" protected by the statute.

[gg] G. Lunney, The Death of Copyright: Digital Technology, Private Copying, and the Digital Millennium Copyright Act, 87 Va.L.Rev. 813 (2001), questions whether § 1201 is really necessary to prevent market failures, but J. Garon, What If DRM Fails?, 2008 Mich.St.L.Rev. 103, believes that digital rights management is needed to preserve incentives; T. Bell, Fair Use vs. Fared Use: The Impact of Automated Rights Management on Copyright's Fair Use Doctrine, 76 N.C.L.Rev. 557 (1998), offers efficiency arguments in support of rights management systems; D. Post, His Napster's Voice, 20 Temp.Envt'l L. & Tech.J. 35 (2001), thinks that helping owners control their works in cyberspace might at least help constrain legal restrictions on file-sharing.

ment issues, so does the cyber revolution at the end of that century. This appeal raises significant First Amendment issues concerning one aspect of computer technology—encryption to protect materials in digital form from unauthorized access. The appeal challenges the constitutionality of the Digital Millennium Copyright Act ("DMCA"), 17 U.S.C. § 1201 et seq. (Supp. V 1999) and the validity of an injunction entered to enforce the DMCA.

Defendant–Appellant Eric C. Corley and his company, 2600 Enterprises, Inc., (collectively "Corley," "the Defendants," or "the Appellants") appeal from the amended final judgment of the United States District Court for the Southern District of New York (Lewis A. Kaplan, District Judge), entered August 23, 2000, enjoining them from various actions concerning a decryption program known as "DeCSS." *Universal City Studios, Inc. v. Reimerdes*, 111 F. Supp. 2d 346 (S.D.N.Y. 2000) (*"Universal II"*). The injunction primarily bars the Appellants from posting DeCSS on their web site and from knowingly linking their web site to any other web site on which DeCSS is posted. Id. at 346–47. We affirm.

Introduction

* * *

This appeal concerns the anti-trafficking provisions of the DMCA, which Congress enacted in 1998 to strengthen copyright protection in the digital age. Fearful that the ease with which pirates could copy and distribute a copyrightable work in digital form was overwhelming the capacity of conventional copyright enforcement to find and enjoin unlawfully copied material, Congress sought to combat copyright piracy in its earlier stages, before the work was even copied. The DMCA therefore backed with legal sanctions the efforts of copyright owners to protect their works from piracy behind digital walls such as encryption codes or password protections. In so doing, Congress targeted not only those pirates who would *circumvent* these digital walls (the "anti-circumvention provisions," contained in 17 U.S.C. § 1201(a)(1)), but also anyone who would *traffic* in a technology primarily designed to circumvent a digital wall (the "anti-trafficking provisions," contained in 17 U.S.C. § 1201 (a)(2), (b)(1)).

Corley publishes a print magazine and maintains an affiliated web site geared towards "hackers," a digital-era term often applied to those interested in techniques for circumventing protections of computers and computer data from unauthorized access. * * *

In November 1999, Corley posted a copy of the decryption computer program "DeCSS" on his web site, http://www.2600.com ("2600.com"). DeCSS is designed to circumvent "CSS," the encryption technology that motion picture studios place on DVDs to prevent the unauthorized viewing and copying of motion pictures. Corley also posted on his web site links to other web sites where DeCSS could be found.

Plaintiffs–Appellees are eight motion picture studios that brought an action in the Southern District of New York seeking injunctive relief against Corley under the DMCA. Following a full non-jury trial, the District Court entered a permanent injunction barring Corley from posting DeCSS on his web site or from knowingly linking via a hyperlink to any other web site containing DeCSS. *Universal II*, 111 F. Supp. 2d at 346–47. The District Court rejected Corley's constitutional attacks on the statute and the injunction. *Universal I* [Universal City Studios, Inc. v. Reimerdes, 111 F.Supp.2d 294, 325–45 (S.D.N.Y. 2000)].

A challenges

Corley renews his constitutional challenges on appeal. Specifically, he argues primarily that: (1) the DMCA oversteps limits in the Copyright Clause on the duration of copyright protection; (2) the DMCA as applied to his dissemination of DeCSS violates the First Amendment because computer code is "speech" entitled to full First Amendment protection and the DMCA fails to survive the exacting scrutiny accorded statutes that regulate "speech"; and (3) the DMCA violates the First Amendment and the Copyright Clause by unduly obstructing the "fair use" of copyrighted materials. Corley also argues that the statute is susceptible to, and should therefore be given, a narrow interpretation that avoids alleged constitutional objections.

Background

For decades, motion picture studios have made movies available for viewing at home in what is called "analog" format. Movies in this format are placed on videotapes, which can be played on a video cassette recorder ("VCR"). In the early 1990s, the studios began to consider the possibility of distributing movies in digital form as well. Movies in digital form are placed on disks, known as DVDs, which can be played on a DVD player (either a stand-alone device or a component of a computer). DVDs offer advantages over analog tapes, such as improved visual and audio quality, larger data capacity, and greater durability. However, the improved quality of a movie in a digital format brings with it the risk that a virtually perfect copy, i.e., one that will not lose perceptible quality in the copying process, can be readily made at the click of a computer control and instantly distributed to countless recipients throughout the world over the Internet. This case arises out of the movie industry's efforts to respond to this risk by invoking the anti-trafficking provisions of the DMCA.

I.   CSS

The movie studios were reluctant to release movies in digital form until they were confident they had in place adequate safeguards against piracy of their copyrighted movies. The studios took several steps to minimize the piracy threat. First, they settled on the DVD as the standard digital medium for home distribution of movies. The studios then sought an encryption scheme to protect movies on DVDs. They enlisted the help of members of the consumer electronics and computer industries, who in mid–1996 developed the Content Scramble System ("CSS"). CSS is an encryption scheme that employs an algorithm configured by a set of "keys" to encrypt a DVD's contents. The algorithm is a type of mathematical formula for transforming the contents of the movie file into gibberish; the "keys" are in actuality strings of 0's and 1's that serve as values for the mathematical formula. Decryption in the case of CSS requires a set of "player keys" contained in compliant DVD players, as well as an understanding of the CSS encryption algorithm. Without the player keys and the algorithm, a DVD player cannot access the contents of a DVD. With the player keys and the algorithm, a DVD player can display the movie on a television or a computer screen, but does not give a viewer the ability to use the copy function of the computer to copy the movie or to manipulate the digital content of the DVD.

* * *

II.   DeCSS

In September 1999, Jon Johansen, a Norwegian teenager, collaborating with two unidentified individuals he met on the Internet, reverse-engineered a licensed DVD player designed to operate on the Microsoft operating system, and culled from it the player keys and other information necessary to decrypt CSS. The record suggests that Johansen was trying to develop a DVD player operable on Linux, an alternative operating system that did not support any licensed DVD players at that time. In order to accomplish this task, Johansen wrote a decryption program executable on Microsoft's operating system. That program was called, appropriately enough, "DeCSS."

If a user runs the DeCSS program (for example, by clicking on the DeCSS icon on a Microsoft operating system platform) with a DVD in the computer's disk drive, DeCSS will decrypt the DVD's CSS protection, allowing the user to copy the DVD's files and place the copy on the user's hard drive. The result is a very large computer file that can be played on a non-CSS-compliant player and copied, manipulated, and transferred just like any other computer file. DeCSS comes complete with a fairly user-friendly interface that helps the user select from among the DVD's files and assign the decrypted file a location on the user's hard drive. The quality of the resulting decrypted movie is "virtually identical" to that of the encrypted movie on the DVD. *Universal I*, 111 F. Supp. 2d at 308, 313. And the file produced by DeCSS, while large, can be compressed to a manageable size by a compression software called "DivX," available at no cost on the Internet. This compressed file can be copied onto a DVD, or transferred over the Internet (with some patience).

Johansen posted the executable object code, but not the source code, for DeCSS on his web site. * * * Within months of its appearance in executable form on Johansen's web site, DeCSS was widely available on the Internet, in both object code and various forms of source code. * * *

In November 1999, Corley wrote and placed on his web site, 2600.com, an article about the DeCSS phenomenon. His web site is an auxiliary to the print magazine, *2600: The Hacker Quarterly*, which Corley has been publishing since 1984. * * *

Corley's article about DeCSS detailed how CSS was cracked, and described the movie industry's efforts to shut down web sites posting DeCSS. It also explained that DeCSS could be used to copy DVDs. At the end of the article, the Defendants posted copies of the object and source code of DeCSS. In Corley's words, he added the code to the story because "in a journalistic world, . . . you have to show your evidence . . . and particularly in the magazine that I work for, people want to see specifically what it is that we are referring to," including "what evidence . . . we have" that there is in fact technology that circumvents CSS. Trial Tr. at 823. Writing about DeCSS without including the DeCSS code would have been, to Corley, "analogous to printing a story about a picture and not printing the picture." Id. at 825. Corley also added to the article links that he explained would take the reader to other web sites where DeCSS could be found. Id. at 791, 826, 827, 848.

2600.com was only one of hundreds of web sites that began posting DeCSS near the end of 1999. The movie industry tried to stem the tide by sending cease-and-desist letters to many of these sites. These efforts met with only partial success; a number of sites refused to remove DeCSS. In January 2000, the studios filed this lawsuit.

III. The DMCA

[Judge Newman identified the prohibition against trafficking in devices designed to circumvent access controls in § 1201(a)(2) as the applicable provision.]

* * *

IV. Procedural History

Invoking subsection 1203(b)(1), the Plaintiffs sought an injunction against the Defendants, alleging that the Defendants violated the anti-trafficking provisions of the statute. On January 20, 2000, after a hearing, the District Court issued a preliminary injunction barring the Defendants from posting DeCSS. *Universal City Studios, Inc. v. Reimerdes*, 82 F. Supp. 2d 211 (S.D.N.Y. 2000).

The Defendants complied with the preliminary injunction, but continued to post links to other web sites carrying DeCSS, an action they termed "electronic civil disobedience." *Universal I*, 111 F. Supp. 2d at 303, 312. Under the heading "Stop the MPAA [(Motion Picture Association of America)]," Corley urged other web sites to post DeCSS lest "we . . . be forced into submission." Id. at 313.

The Plaintiffs then sought a permanent injunction barring the Defendants from both posting DeCSS and linking to sites containing DeCSS. After a trial on the merits, the Court issued a comprehensive opinion, *Universal I*, and granted a permanent injunction, *Universal II*. * * *

Discussion

I.   Narrow Construction to Avoid Constitutional Doubt

The Appellants first argue that, because their constitutional arguments are at least substantial, we should interpret the statute narrowly so as to avoid constitutional problems. They identify three different instances of alleged ambiguity in the statute that they claim provide an opportunity for such a narrow interpretation.

First, they contend that subsection 1201(c)(1), which provides that "nothing in this section shall affect rights, remedies, limitations or defenses to copyright infringement, including fair use, under this title," can be read to allow the circumvention of encryption technology protecting copyrighted material when the material will be put to "fair uses" exempt from copyright liability. We disagree that subsection 1201(c)(1) permits such a reading. Instead, it clearly and simply clarifies that the DMCA targets the *circumvention* of digital walls guarding copyrighted material (and trafficking in circumvention tools), but does not concern itself with the use of those materials after circumvention has occurred. Subsection 1201(c)(1) ensures that the DMCA is not read to prohibit the "fair use" of information just because that information was obtained in a manner made illegal by the DMCA. The Appellants' much more expansive interpretation of subsection 1201(c)(1) is not only outside the range of plausible readings of the provision, but is also clearly refuted by the statute's legislative history.[13] See Commodity Fu-

---

[13] The legislative history of the enacted bill makes quite clear that Congress intended to adopt a "balanced" approach to accommodating both piracy and fair use concerns, eschewing the quick fix of simply exempting from the statute all circumventions for fair use. H.R. Rep. No. 105–551, pt. 2, at 25 (1998). It sought to achieve this goal principally through the use of what it called a "fail-safe" provision in the statute, authorizing the Librarian of Congress to exempt certain users from the anti-circumvention provision when it becomes evident that in practice, the statute is adversely affecting certain kinds of fair use. See 17 U.S.C.

tures Trading Commission v. Schor, 478 U.S. 833, 841 (1986) (constitutional doubt canon "does not give a court the prerogative to ignore the legislative will").

Second, the Appellants urge a narrow construction of the DMCA because of subsection 1201(c)(4), which provides that "nothing in this section shall enlarge or diminish any rights of free speech or the press for activities using consumer electronics, telecommunications, or computing products." This language is clearly precatory: Congress could not "diminish" constitutional rights of free speech even if it wished to, and the fact that Congress also expressed a reluctance to "enlarge" those rights cuts against the Appellants' effort to infer a narrowing construction of the Act from this provision.

Third, the Appellants argue that an individual who buys a DVD has the "authority of the copyright owner" to view the DVD, and therefore is exempted from the DMCA pursuant to subsection 1201(a)(3)(A) when the buyer circumvents an encryption technology in order to view the DVD on a competing platform (such as Linux). The basic flaw in this argument is that it misreads subsection 1201(a)(3)(A). That provision exempts from liability those who would "decrypt" an encrypted DVD with the authority of a copyright owner, not those who would "view" a DVD with the authority of a copyright owner. In any event, the Defendants offered no evidence that the Plaintiffs have either explicitly or implicitly authorized DVD buyers to circumvent encryption technology to support use on multiple platforms. * * *

II.   Constitutional Challenge Based on the Copyright Clause

In a footnote to their brief, the Appellants appear to contend that the DMCA, as construed by the District Court, exceeds the constitutional authority of Congress to grant authors copyrights for a "limited time," U.S. Const. art. I, § 8, cl. 8, because it "empowers copyright owners to effectively secure perpetual protection by mixing public domain works with copyrighted materials, then locking both up with technological protection measures." Brief for Appellants at 42 n.30. * * *

[T]o whatever extent the argument might have merit at some future time in a case with a properly developed record, the argument is entirely premature and speculative at this time on this record. There is not even a claim, much less evidence, that any Plaintiff has sought to prevent copying of public domain works, or that the injunction prevents the Defendants from copying such works. As Judge Kaplan noted, the possibility that encryption would preclude access to public domain works "does not yet appear to be a problem, although it may emerge as one in the future." *Universal I*, 111 F. Supp. 2d at 338 n.245.

---

§ 1201(a)(1)(C); H.R. Rep. No. 105–551, pt. 2, at 36 ("Given the threat of a diminution of otherwise lawful access to works and information, the Committee on Commerce believes that a 'fail-safe' mechanism is required. This mechanism would . . . allow the . . . [waiver of the anticircumvention provisions], for limited time periods, if necessary to prevent a diminution in the availability to individual users of a particular category of copyrighted materials.").

Congress also sought to implement a balanced approach through statutory provisions that leave limited areas of breathing space for fair use. A good example is subsection 1201(d), which allows a library or educational institution to circumvent a digital wall in order to determine whether it wishes legitimately to obtain the material behind the wall. See H.R. Rep. No. 105–551, pt. 2, at 41. It would be strange for Congress to open small, carefully limited windows for circumvention to permit fair use in subsection 1201(d) if it then meant to exempt in subsection 1201(c)(1) any circumvention necessary for fair use.

III. Constitutional Challenges Based on the First Amendment

A.   Applicable Principles

* * *

1.   Code as Speech

Communication does not lose constitutional protection as "speech" simply because it is expressed in the language of computer code. * * * The undisputed evidence reveals that even pure object code can be, and often is, read and understood by experienced programmers. And source code (in any of its various levels of complexity) can be read by many more. See *Universal I*, 111 F. Supp. 2d at 326. Ultimately, however, the ease with which a work is comprehended is irrelevant to the constitutional inquiry. If computer code is distinguishable from conventional speech for First Amendment purposes, it is not because it is written in an obscure language. See Junger v. Daley, 209 F.3d 481, 484 (6th Cir. 2000).

2.   Computer Programs as Speech

* * * Arguably distinguishing computer programs from conventional language instructions is the fact that programs are executable on a computer. But the fact that a program has the capacity to direct the functioning of a computer does not mean that it lacks the additional capacity to convey information, and it is the conveying of information that renders instructions "speech" for purposes of the First Amendment. The information conveyed by most "instructions" is how to perform a task.

Instructions such as computer code, which are intended to be executable by a computer, will often convey information capable of comprehension and assessment by a human being. A programmer reading a program learns information about instructing a computer, and might use this information to improve personal programming skills and perhaps the craft of programming. Moreover, programmers communicating ideas to one another almost inevitably communicate in code, much as musicians use notes. * * *

[W]e join the other courts that have concluded that computer code, and computer programs constructed from code can merit First Amendment protection * * *

computer code is protected by 1st amend as speech

3.   The Scope of First Amendment Protection for Computer Code

Having concluded that computer code conveying information is "speech" within the meaning of the First Amendment, we next consider, to a limited extent, the scope of the protection that code enjoys. As the District Court recognized, *Universal I*, 111 F. Supp. 2d at 327, the scope of protection for speech generally depends on whether the restriction is imposed because of the content of the speech. *content based* Content-based restrictions are permissible only if they serve compelling state interests and do so by the least restrictive means available. See Sable Communications of California, Inc. v. FCC, 492 U.S. 115 (1989). A *content-neutral* content-neutral restriction is permissible if it serves a substantial governmental interest, the interest is unrelated to the suppression of free expression, and the regulation is narrowly tailored, which "in this context requires . . . that the means chosen do not 'burden substantially more speech than is necessary to further the government's legitimate interests.'" Turner Broadcasting System, Inc. v. FCC, 512 U.S. 622, 662 (1994) (quoting Ward v. Rock Against Racism, 491 U.S. 781, 799 (1989)). * * *

4.   The Scope of First Amendment Protection for Decryption Code

In considering the scope of First Amendment protection for a decryption program like DeCSS, we must recognize that the essential purpose of encryption code is to prevent unauthorized access. Owners of all property rights are entitled to prohibit access to their property by unauthorized persons. Homeowners can install locks on the doors of their houses. Custodians of valuables can place them in safes. Stores can attach to products security devices that will activate alarms if the products are taken away without purchase. These and similar security devices can be circumvented. Burglars can use skeleton keys to open door locks. Thieves can obtain the combinations to safes. Product security devices can be neutralized. * * *

At first glance, one might think that Congress has as much authority to regulate the distribution of computer code to decrypt DVD movies as it has to regulate distribution of skeleton keys, combinations to safes, or devices to neutralize store product security devices. However, despite the evident legitimacy of protection against unauthorized access to DVD movies, just like any other property, regulation of decryption code like DeCSS is challenged in this case because DeCSS differs from a skeleton key in one important respect: it not only is capable of performing the function of unlocking the encrypted DVD movie, it also is a form of communication, albeit written in a language not understood by the general public. As a communication, the DeCSS code has a claim to being "speech," and as "speech," it has a claim to being protected by the First Amendment. But just as the realities of what any computer code can accomplish must inform the scope of its constitutional protection, so the capacity of a decryption program like DeCSS to accomplish unauthorized—indeed, unlawful—access to materials in which the Plaintiffs have intellectual property rights must inform and limit the scope of its First Amendment protection. Cf. [Red Lion Broadcasting Co. v. FCC, 395 U.S. 367, 386 (1969)] ("Differences in the characteristics of new media justify differences in the First Amendment standards applied to them.").

With all of the foregoing considerations in mind, we next consider the Appellants' First Amendment challenge to the DMCA as applied in the specific prohibitions that have been imposed by the District Court's injunction.

B.   First Amendment Challenge

* * *

1.   Posting

The initial issue is whether the posting prohibition is content-neutral, since, as we have explained, this classification determines the applicable constitutional standard. The Appellants contend that the anti-trafficking provisions of the DMCA and their application by means of the posting prohibition of the injunction are content-based. They argue that the provisions "specifically target ... scientific expression based on the particular topic addressed by that expression—namely, techniques for circumventing CSS." Supplemental Brief for Appellants at 1. We disagree. The Appellants' argument fails to recognize that the target of the posting provisions of the injunction—DeCSS—has both a nonspeech and a speech component, and that the DMCA, as applied to the Appellants, and the posting prohibition of the injunction target only the nonspeech component. Neither the DMCA nor the posting prohibition is concerned with whatever capacity DeCSS might have for conveying information to a human being, and that capacity, as previously explained, is what arguably creates a speech component of the decryption code. The DMCA and the posting prohibition are applied to DeCSS solely because of its capacity to instruct a computer to decrypt CSS. That functional capability is not speech within the meaning of the First Amendment. The Government seeks to "justify," [Hill v. Colorado, 530 U.S. 703, 720 (2000)], both the application of the DMCA and the posting prohibition to the Appellants solely on the basis of the functional capability of DeCSS to instruct a computer to decrypt CSS, i.e., "without reference to the content of the regulated speech," id. This type of regulation is therefore content-neutral, just as would be a restriction on trafficking in skeleton keys identified because of their capacity to unlock jail cells, even though some of the keys happened to bear a slogan or other legend that qualified as a speech component.

As a content-neutral regulation with an incidental effect on a speech component, the regulation must serve a substantial governmental interest, the interest must be unrelated to the suppression of free expression, and the incidental restriction on speech must not burden substantially more speech than is necessary to further that interest. *Turner Broadcasting*, 512 U.S. at 662. The Government's interest in preventing unauthorized access to encrypted copyrighted material is unquestionably substantial, and the regulation of DeCSS by the posting prohibition plainly serves that interest. Moreover, that interest is unrelated to the suppression of free expression. The injunction regulates the posting of DeCSS, regardless of whether DeCSS code contains any information comprehensible by human beings that would qualify as speech. Whether the incidental regulation on speech burdens substantially more speech than is necessary to further the interest in preventing unauthorized access to copyrighted materials requires some elaboration.

Posting DeCSS on the Appellants' web site makes it instantly available at the click of a mouse to any person in the world with access to the Internet, and such person can then instantly transmit DeCSS to anyone else with Internet access. Although the prohibition on posting prevents the Appellants from conveying to others the speech component of DeCSS, the Appellants have not suggested, much less shown, any technique for barring them from making this instantaneous worldwide distribution of a decryption code that makes a lesser restriction on the code's speech component. It is true that the Government has alternative means of prohibiting unauthorized access to copyrighted materials. For example, it can create criminal and civil liability for those who gain unauthorized access, and thus it can be argued that the restriction on posting DeCSS is not absolutely necessary to preventing unauthorized access to copyrighted materials. But a content-neutral regulation need not employ the least restrictive means of accomplishing the governmental objective. Id. It need only avoid burdening "substantially more speech than is necessary to further the government's legitimate interests." Id. (internal quotation marks and citation omitted). The prohibition on the Defendants' posting of DeCSS satisfies that standard.

2.   Linking

* * *

In applying the DMCA to linking (via hyperlinks), Judge Kaplan recognized, as he had with DeCSS code, that a hyperlink has both a speech and a nonspeech component. It conveys information, the Internet address of the linked web page, and has the functional capacity to bring the content of the linked web page to the user's computer screen (or, as Judge Kaplan put it, to "take one almost instantaneously to the desired destination." Id.). As he had ruled with respect to DeCSS code, he ruled that application of the DMCA to the Defendants' linking to web sites containing DeCSS is content-neutral because it is justified without regard to the speech component of the hyperlink. Id. The linking prohibition applies whether or not the hyperlink contains any information, comprehensible to a human being, as to the Internet address of the web page being accessed. The linking prohibition is justified solely by the functional capability of the hyperlink. * * *

To avoid applying the DMCA in a manner that would "burden substantially more speech than is necessary to further the government's legitimate interests," *Turner Broadcasting*, 512 U.S. at 662 (internal quotation marks and citation omitted), Judge Kaplan adapted the standards of New York Times Co. v. Sullivan, 376 U.S. 254 (1964), to fashion a limited prohibition against linking to web sites containing DeCSS. He required clear and convincing evidence

> that those responsible for the link (a) know at the relevant time that the offending material is on the linked-to site, (b) know that it is circumvention technology that may not lawfully be offered, and (c) create or maintain the link for the purpose of disseminating that technology.

Universal I, 111 F. Supp. 2d at 341. He then found that the evidence satisfied his three-part test by his required standard of proof. Id.

* * *

Mindful of the cautious approach to First Amendment claims involving computer technology expressed in [Name.Space, Inc. v. Network Solutions, Inc., 202 F.3d 573, 584 n. 11 (2d Cir.2000)], we see no need on this appeal to determine whether a test as rigorous as Judge Kaplan's is required to respond to First Amendment objections to the linking provision of the injunction that he issued. * * * Under the circumstances amply shown by the record, the injunction's linking prohibition validly regulates the Appellants' opportunity instantly to enable anyone anywhere to gain unauthorized access to copyrighted movies on DVDs.[32]

* * *

IV. Constitutional Challenge Based on Claimed Restriction of Fair Use

Asserting that fair use "is rooted in and required by both the Copyright Clause and the First Amendment," Brief for Appellants at 42, the Appellants contend that the DMCA, as applied by the District Court, unconstitutionally *"eliminates* fair use" of copyrighted materials, id. at 41 (emphasis added). We reject this extravagant claim.

Preliminarily, we note that the Supreme Court has never held that fair use is constitutionally required, although some isolated statements in its opinions might arguably be enlisted for such a requirement. In Stewart v. Abend, 495 U.S. 207 (1990), cited by the Appellants, the Court merely noted that fair use " 'permits courts to avoid rigid application of the copyright statute when, on occasion, it would stifle the very creativity which that law is designed to foster,' " id. (quoting Iowa State University Research

---

[32] We acknowledge that the prohibition on linking restricts more than Corley's ability to facilitate instant access to DeCSS on linked web sites; it also restricts his ability to facilitate access to whatever protected speech is available on those sites. However, those who maintain the linked sites can instantly make their protected material available for linking by Corley by the simple expedient of deleting DeCSS from their web sites.

Foundation, Inc. v. American Broadcasting Cos., 621 F.2d 57, 60 (2d Cir. 1980)); see also Harper & Row, Publishers, Inc. v. Nation Enterprises, 471 U.S. 539, 560 (1985) (noting "the First Amendment protections already embodied in the Copyright Act's distinction between copyrightable expression and uncopyrightable facts and ideas, and the latitude for scholarship and comment traditionally afforded by fair use"). In Campbell v. Acuff–Rose Music, Inc., 510 U.S. 569 (1994), the Court observed, "From the infancy of copyright protection, some opportunity for fair use of copyrighted materials has been thought necessary to fulfill copyright's very purpose, 'to promote the Progress of Science and useful Arts . . . . ' "[33] Id. at 575 (citation omitted); see generally William F. Patry, The Fair Use Privilege in Copyright Law 573–82 (2d ed. 1995) (questioning First Amendment protection for fair use).

We need not explore the extent to which fair use might have constitutional protection, grounded on either the First Amendment or the Copyright Clause, because whatever validity a constitutional claim might have as to an application of the DMCA that impairs fair use of copyrighted materials, such matters are far beyond the scope of this lawsuit for several reasons. In the first place, the Appellants do not claim to be making fair use of any copyrighted materials, and nothing in the injunction prohibits them from making such fair use. They are barred from trafficking in a decryption code that enables unauthorized access to copyrighted materials.

Second, as the District Court properly noted, to whatever extent the anti-trafficking provisions of the DMCA might prevent others from copying portions of DVD movies in order to make fair use of them, "the evidence as to the impact of the anti-trafficking provisions of the DMCA on prospective fair users is scanty and fails adequately to address the issues." *Universal I*, 111 F. Supp. 2d at 338 n.246.

Third, the Appellants have provided no support for their premise that fair use of DVD movies is constitutionally required to be made by copying the original work in its original format. Their examples of the fair uses that they believe others will be prevented from making all involve copying in a digital format those portions of a DVD movie amenable to fair use, a copying that would enable the fair user to manipulate the digitally copied portions. One example is that of a school child who wishes to copy images from a DVD movie to insert into the student's documentary film. We know of no authority for the proposition that fair use, as protected by the Copyright Act, much less the Constitution, guarantees copying by the optimum method or in the identical format of the original. Although the Appellants insisted at oral argument that they should not be relegated to a "horse and buggy" technique in making fair use of DVD movies, the DMCA does not impose even an arguable limitation on the opportunity to make a variety of traditional fair uses of DVD movies, such as commenting on their content, quoting excerpts from their screenplays, and even recording portions of the video images and sounds on film or tape by pointing a camera, a camcorder, or a microphone at a monitor as it displays the DVD movie. The fact that the resulting copy will not be as perfect or as manipulable as a digital copy obtained by having direct access to the DVD movie in its digital form, pro-

---

[33] Although we have recognized that the First Amendment provides no entitlement to use copyrighted materials beyond that accorded by the privilege of fair use, except in "an extraordinary case," Twin Peaks Productions, Inc. v. Publications International, Ltd., 996 F.2d 1366, 1378 (2d Cir. 1993), we have not ruled that the Constitution guarantees any particular formulation or minimum availability of the fair use defense.

vides no basis for a claim of unconstitutional limitation of fair use. A film critic making fair use of a movie by quoting selected lines of dialogue has no constitutionally valid claim that the review (in print or on television) would be technologically superior if the reviewer had not been prevented from using a movie camera in the theater, nor has an art student a valid constitutional claim to fair use of a painting by photographing it in a museum. Fair use has never been held to be a guarantee of access to copyrighted material in order to copy it by the fair user's preferred technique or in the format of the original.

Conclusion

We have considered all the other arguments of the Appellants and conclude that they provide no basis for disturbing the District Court's judgment. Accordingly, the judgment is affirmed.

NOTES AND QUESTIONS ON ANTI–CIRCUMVENTION

(1) Is it clear that CSS is a technological measure that "controls access to a work," rather than a measure that "protects a right of a copyright owner"? Would that make a difference in the outcome of the case? In what kind of a case *would* it make a difference? See R. Denicola, Access Controls, Rights Protection, and Circumvention: Interpreting the Digital Millennium Copyright Act to Preserve Noninfringing Use, 31 Colum.J.L. and Arts 209 (2008).

(2) The plaintiffs in *Corley* sought relief against the dissemination of the DeCSS computer code. Would the anti-trafficking provisions in § 1201 also reach the dissemination of a verbal description of the ideas embodied in the computer program if it would enable another programmer to create similar software? A dispute under § 1201 arose from a challenge issued by a group of record and electronics companies to anyone who could overcome a new encryption system for CDs. The encryption was defeated by a research team led by Princeton Professor Edward Felten, but when the team prepared to present its results at an academic conference, the Recording Industry Association of America threatened suit under § 1201. The presentation was postponed, but the researchers then filed a lawsuit arguing that the use of § 1201 to restrain the publication of their research would violate the first amendment. The research was eventually presented at a subsequent conference. Lee, Delayed Report on Encryption Flaws to be Presented, N.Y. Times, Aug. 15, 2001, p. C6. The researchers' lawsuit was dismissed when the RIAA promised not to sue.

(3) "DVD Jon," the Norwegian teenager who wrote the DeCSS decryption program, was indicted under the computer hacking provisions of the Norwegian criminal code. He was acquitted by a three-member panel of the Oslo City Court, which apparently believed that he could not be convicted of breaking into his own DVDs. A seven-judge appellate panel unanimously upheld the acquittal. Hollywood Rep., Dec. 23, 2003, p. 3.

(4) Record companies have experimented for years with digital locks on CDs. Sony Music, for example, came up with an early technology designed to prevent users from playing (and copying) CDs on personal computers. The CDs contained an initial track of bogus data, which CD players ignored but PCs continuously tried to read, preventing them from accessing the subsequent music tracks. Music fans soon figured out that if they marked over the edge of the CD with a felt-tipped pen, PCs would ignore the bogus data track and go straight to the music. They quickly spread the word over the Internet. Richtel, Digital

Lock? Try a Hairpin, N.Y. Times, May 26, 2002, Sec. 4, p. 12. Would a purchaser who used that technique be liable under § 1201(a)(1)(A) for circumventing "a technological measure that *effectively* controls access to a work"? Would the pen company be liable under § 1201(a)(2) for trafficking in a circumvention device?

Another experiment with copy-protected CDs in 2003 was also a disaster. BMG Music sold CDs that contained anti-copying technology developed by SunnComm that was designed to limit the number of times the CD could be copied on a PC. Alex Halderman, a Princeton University graduate student, discovered that the protection could be defeated by holding down the shift key when the CD was inserted into the computer—a standard Windows technique used to block a program from running. He posted his findings on the Internet and SunnComm's stock dropped 25 per cent in two days. SunnComm's president threatened to sue Halderman for violating § 1201, but backed down under pressure from BMG Music following a web and e-mail campaign mounted by Halderman's supporters. Maney, Debate Heats Up as Student Spots Hole in CD Protection, USA Today, Oct. 27, 2003, p. A1.

A later attempt to resurrect copy-protection for CDs produced yet another debacle for Sony BMG when it included aggressive copy-protection software on millions of CDs. When the CDs were played on a computer, the anti-copying software surreptitiously downloaded and hid itself in the computer's hard drive. The software also proved capable of hiding other programs, and Internet-borne worms were soon discovered trying to take advantage of the software. The Texas Attorney General brought suit against Sony BMG for violating that state's Consumer Protection Against Computer Spyware Act; numerous class action suits were also filed. Zeller, Sony BMG Stirs a Debate Over Software Used to Guard Content, N.Y. Times, Nov. 14, 2005, p. C1. Sony BMG was ultimately forced to settle the suits with promises of cash, free CDs and music downloads for consumers, and restrictions on further use of copy-protection. N.Y. Times, Dec. 30, 2005, p. C4. No major record labels currently employ copy-protection on their CDs, and privately they admit that they do not foresee it returning until improvements in technology can prevent unfavorable consumer experiences. Thompson and Ferguson, Copy Protection Curtailed, Billboard, Dec. 16, 2006, p. 27. Apple's iTunes dropped its digital rights management system on music downloads in 2009. However, technological protection persists on movie DVDs and is a staple on e-books. Do differences in the works or markets explain this disparity? J. Rothchild, Economic Analysis of Technological Protection Measures, 84 Ore.L.Rev. 489 (2005), concludes that the competitiveness of particular markets will drive decisions about the use of protective technologies.

(5) The absence of a fair use exception to the circumvention and trafficking prohibitions in § 1201 was at the heart of a suit between seven Hollywood studios and a software company called 321 Studios whose product, DVD X Copy, allowed users to make copies of encrypted DVDs. The movie studios sought to ban the product as a circumvention device, fearing that users would sell or trade the DVD copies, or worse, distribute the temporary copy that the software created on the user's hard drive over the Internet. 321 Studios countered that the product allowed users to exercise their fair use right to make back-up copies of purchased DVDs. The movie studios won an injunction in 321 Studios v. Metro Goldwyn Mayer Studios, Inc., 307 F.Supp.2d 1085 (N.D.Cal.2004). Judge Illston ruled that the possibility of fair use by customers was not a defense to 321 Studios' violation of the anti-trafficking provisions. The company quickly went out of business. A similar result was reached when RealNetworks began distributing software called RealDVD that allowed users to copy CSS-protected DVDs onto their hard drive or portable media. The studios worried that the copying would undermine the market for movie streaming and downloads and that DVD sales would suffer when consumers copied rented or borrowed DVDs. Judge Patel in RealNetworks, Inc. v. DVD Copy Control Ass'n, 641 F.Supp.2d 913 (N.D.Cal.2009), held that the RealNetworks product circumvented access and copy controls on the plaintiffs' DVDs and its sale was a violation of §§ 1201(a) and (b). Citing cases like *321 Studios* and *Corley*, the court rejected RealNetworks' fair use defense, stating, "the fair use of the copyrighted material by end users is not a defense to, and plays no role in determining, liability under the DMCA." RealNetworks was preliminarily enjoined from offering its software to the public; it later agreed to a permanent injunction.

(6) There have been legislative proposals to amend § 1201 to create fair use exceptions to the circumvention and trafficking prohibitions. Could a circumvention device be designed to allow only fair uses? The bills have not made any headway against the opposition of content owners. There have also been numerous scholarly suggestions. T. Armstrong, Digital Rights Management and the Process of Fair Use, 20 Harv.J.L. & Tech. 49 (2006), explores technical solutions to the fair use problem that could permit and monitor asserted fair uses; J. Gibson, Once and Future Copyright, 81 Notre Dame L.Rev. 167 (2005), argues that owners should at least be required to deposit an unencumbered copy of the work with the Copyright Office to protect the public interest in access.

Will market forces constrain the deployment of technological protection measures? To facilitate that process, R. Denicola, Fair's Fair: An Argument for Mandatory Disclosure of Technological Protection Measures, 11 Mich.Telecomm. & Tech.L.Rev. 1 (2004), suggests that disclosure of technological protection measures to consumers should be a prerequisite to an owner's protection against circumvention; H. Melendez–Juarbe, DRM Interoperability, 15 B.U.J.Sci. & Tech.L. 181 (2009), wonders why the market has made little progress toward standardized digital rights management systems.

(7) The criminal penalties in § 1204 were invoked against a Russian graduate student named Dmitri Sklyarov and his employer when they created a program to defeat the electronic protection for e-books developed by Adobe Systems. Sklyarov was arrested at the instigation of Adobe Systems at a convention of computer hackers in Las Vegas where he made a presentation on e-book security. Adobe Systems quickly backed away when the case became a cause célèbre, with supporters sporting "Free Sklyarov" t-shirts and bumper stickers. The charges against Sklyarov were eventually dropped in exchange for his testimony at the trial of his employer. The employer's motion to dismiss the charges was denied in United States v. Elcom Ltd., 203 F.Supp.2d 1111 (N.D.Cal.2002). The court held that the anti-trafficking provisions were not unconstitutionally vague nor invalid under the first amendment. In the subsequent trial, a jury acquitted the company, apparently because of doubt about whether it had "willfully" violated § 1201 as required for conviction under § 1204. Richtel, Russian Company Cleared of Illegal Software Sales, N.Y. Times, Dec. 18, 2002, p. C4.

(8) How do the first amendment issues raised by the anti-circumvention provisions in § 1201 differ from those arising from traditional copyright protection for works of authorship as discussed at p. 367 supra? S. McJohn, *Eldred*'s Aftermath: Tradition, the Copyright Clause, and the Constitutionalization of Fair Use, 10 Mich.Telcomm. & Tech.L.Rev. 95 (2003), thinks that nontraditional protections like the anti-circumvention rules remain open to constitutional challenge; however, C. Bohannan, Reclaiming Copyright, 23 Cardozo Arts & Ent.L.J. 567 (2006), concludes that statutory construction rather than constitutional attack is the best tool for reasserting the public interest under the DMCA and elsewhere in copyright law.

Chamberlain Group, Inc. v. Skylink Technologies, Inc.

381 F.3d 1178 (Fed.Cir.2004), cert. denied, 544 U.S. 923 (2005).

Plaintiff Chamberlain sold garage door openers; defendant Skylink sold remote controllers that could operate Chamberlain's system. Chamberlain claimed that Skylink's controllers circumvented a technological security code in its door openers in order to gain access to the copyrighted computer program that operated the openers. Chamberlain sued, alleging that sales of Skylink's controllers violated the anti-trafficking provision in § 1201(a)(2). Skylink countered that under § 1201(a)(3), circumvention of access controls is actionable only when done "without the authority of the copyright owner." Since Chamberlain had not placed any restrictions on the type of controller that a purchaser of its system could use, Skylink argued that homeowners had Chamberlain's implicit authorization to access the opener's computer program by means of any controller. The trial court granted defendant Skylink's motion for summary judgment. 292 F.Supp.2d 1040 (N.D.Ill.2003). The Federal Circuit, with appellate jurisdiction because of a patent infringement count, affirmed the summary judgment on broader grounds.

" * * * Statutory structure and legislative history both make it clear that § 1201 applies only to circumventions reasonably related to protected rights. Defendants who traffic in devices that circumvent access controls in ways that facilitate infringement may be subject to liability under § 1201(a)(2). Defendants who use such devices may be subject to liability under § 1201(a)(1) whether they infringe or not. * * * And finally, defendants whose circumvention devices do not facilitate infringement are not subject to § 1201 liability. * * *

"Chamberlain urges us to read the DMCA as if Congress simply created a new protection for copyrighted works without any reference at all either to the protections that copyright owners already possess or to the rights that the Copyright Act grants to the public. Chamberlain has not alleged that Skylink's Model 39 infringes its copyrights, nor has it alleged that the Model 39 contributes to third-party infringement of its copyrights. Chamberlain's allegation is considerably more straightforward: The only way for the Model 39 to interoperate with a Security+ GDO is by 'accessing' copyrighted software. Skylink has therefore committed a per se violation of the DMCA. Chamberlain urges us to conclude that no necessary connection exists between access and *copyrights*. Congress could not have intended such a broad reading of the DMCA." (In a footnote, Judge Gajarsa added, "We do not reach the relationship between § 107 fair use and violations of § 1201. The District Court in *Reimerdes* rejected the DeCSS defendants' argument that fair use was a *necessary* defense to § 1201(a), *Reimerdes*, 111 F.Supp.2d at 317; because *any* access enables some fair uses, any act of circumvention would embody its own defense. We leave open the question as to when § 107 might serve as an affirmative defense to a prima facie violation of § 1201. For the moment, we note only that though the traditional fair use doctrine of § 107 remains unchanged as a defense to copyright infringement under § 1201(c)(1), circumvention is not infringement.")

" * * * Chamberlain's proposed construction would allow any manufacturer of any product to add a single copyrighted sentence or software fragment to its product, wrap the copyrighted material in a trivial 'encryption' scheme, and thereby gain the right to restrict consumers' rights to use its products in conjunction with competing products. In other words, Chamberlain's construction of the DMCA would allow virtually any company to attempt to leverage its sales into aftermarket monopolies—a practice that both the antitrust laws, see *Eastman Kodak Co. v. Image Tech. Servs.*, 504 U.S. 451, 455 (1992), and the doctrine of copyright misuse, *Assessment Techs. of WI, LLC v. WIREdata, Inc.*, 350 F.3d 640, 647 (7th Cir.2003), normally prohibit. * * *

"Finally, the requisite 'authorization,' on which the District Court granted Skylink summary judgment, points to yet another inconsistency in Chamberlain's proposed construction. * * * Underlying Chamberlain's argument on appeal that it has not granted such authorization lies the necessary assumption that Chamberlain is entitled to prohibit legitimate purchasers of its embedded software from 'accessing' the software by using it. Such an entitlement, however, would go far beyond the idea that the DMCA allows copyright owner to prohibit 'fair uses . . . as well as foul.' *Reimerdes*, 111 F.Supp.2d at 304. Chamberlain's proposed construction would allow copyright owners to prohibit *exclusively fair* uses even in the absence of any feared foul use. It would therefore allow any copyright owner, through a combination of contractual terms and technological measures, to repeal the fair use doctrine with respect to an individual copyrighted work—or even selected copies of that copyrighted work. Again, this implication contradicts § 1201(c)(1) directly. Copyright law itself authorizes the public to make certain uses of copyrighted materials. Consumers who purchase a product containing a copy of embedded software have the inherent legal right to use that copy of the software. What the law authorizes, Chamberlain cannot revoke. * * * We conclude that 17 U.S.C. § 1201 prohibits only forms of access that bear a reasonable relationship to the protections that the Copyright Act otherwise affords copyright owners."

Lexmark International, Inc. v. Static Control Components, Inc.

387 F.3d 522 (6th Cir.2004).

Lexmark is a major manufacturer of printers. "[T]he 'Printer Engine Program,' controls various printer functions on Lexmark printers. * * * Lexmark began selling discount toner cartridges for its printers that only Lexmark could re-fill and that contained a microchip designed to prevent Lexmark printers from functioning with toner cartridges that Lexmark had not re-filled. In an effort to support the market for competing toner cartridges, Static Control Components (SCC) mimicked Lexmark's computer chip and sold it to companies interested in selling remanufactured toner cartridges. * * * [Lexmark] claimed that SCC's chip violated the DMCA by circumventing a technological measure designed to control access to the Printer Engine Program." The district court had granted a preliminary injunction. Judge Sutton reversed.

" * * * Because Congress did not explain what it means to 'gain access to the work,' the district court relied on the 'ordinary, customary meaning' of 'access': 'the ability to enter, to obtain, or to make use of,' D. Ct. Op. at 41 (quoting *Merriam-Webster's Collegiate Dictionary* 6 (10th ed. 1999)). Based on this definition, the court concluded that 'Lexmark's authentication sequence effectively "controls access" to the Printer Engine Program because it controls the consumer's ability to *make use of* these programs.' D. Ct. Op. at 41 (emphasis added).

"We disagree. It is not Lexmark's authentication sequence that 'controls access' to the Printer Engine Program. See 17 U.S.C. § 1201(a)(2). It is the purchase of a Lexmark printer that allows 'access' to the program. Anyone who buys a Lexmark printer may read the literal code of the Printer Engine Program directly from the printer memory, with or without the benefit of the authentication sequence, and the data from the program may be translated into readable source code after which copies may be freely distributed. Maggs Hr'g Test., JA 928. No security device, in other words, protects access to the Printer Engine Program Code and no security device accordingly must be circumvented to obtain access to that program code.

"The authentication sequence, it is true, may well block one form of 'access'—the 'ability to . . . make use of' the Printer Engine Program by preventing the printer from functioning. But it does not block another relevant form of 'access'—the 'ability to [ ] obtain' a copy of the work or to 'make use of' the literal elements of the program (its code). Because the statute refers to 'control[ling] access to a work protected under this title,' it does not naturally apply when the 'work protected under this title' is otherwise accessible.

" * * * Because Lexmark has not directed any of its security efforts, through its authentication sequence or otherwise, to ensuring that its copyrighted work (the Printer Engine Program) cannot be read and copied, it cannot lay claim to having put in place a 'technological measure that effectively controls access to a work protected under [the copyright statute]. § 17 U.S.C. § 1201(a)(2)(B)."

Judge Sutton then moved to higher ground. "Nowhere in its deliberations over the DMCA did Congress express an interest in creating liability for the circumvention of technological measures designed to prevent consumers from using consumer goods while leaving the copyrightable content of a work unprotected."

Judge Merritt concurred, stressing the underlying policy argument. "We should make clear that in the future companies like Lexmark cannot use the DMCA in conjunction with copyright law to create monopolies of manufactured goods for themselves just by tweaking the facts of this case: by, for example * * * cutting off other access to the Printer Engine Program. The crucial point is that the DMCA forbids anyone from trafficking in any technology that 'is primarily designed or produced for the purpose of circumventing a technological measure that effectively controls access to a [protected] work. § 17 U.S.C. § 1201(2)(A) (emphasis added). The key question is the 'purpose' of the circumvention technology. The microchip in SCC's toner cartridges is intended * * * only for the purpose of making SCC's competing toner cartridges work with printers manufactured by Lexmark. * * * If we were to adopt Lexmark's reading of the statute, manufacturers could potentially create monopolies for replacement parts simply by using similar, but more creative, lock-out codes. * * * Congress did not intend to allow the DMCA to be used offensively in this manner, but rather only sought to reach those who circumvented protective measures 'for the purpose' of pirating works protected by the copyright statute."

NOTES AND QUESTIONS

(1) In Storage Tech. Corp. v. Custom Hardware Eng'g & Consulting, Inc., 421 F.3d 1307 (Fed.Cir.2005), a software owner complained about a defendant who by-passed the plaintiff's password protection scheme in order to reconfigure the program in the course of diagnosing and repairing problems with the software. The Federal Circuit, applying First Circuit law, vacated a preliminary injunction. The court held first that loading the plaintiff's program likely fell within the computer "maintenance or repair" exception in § 117(c) and thus was not copyright infringement. The plaintiff also claimed a violation of the anti-circumvention rule in § 1201(a)(1), but the court held that the claim was unlikely to succeed.

"We held above that it is unlikely StorageTek will succeed on the merits of its copyright claim. To the extent that CHE's activities do not constitute copyright infringement or facilitate copyright infringement, StorageTek is foreclosed from maintaining an action under the DMCA. See [Chamberlain Group, Inc. v. Skylink Technologies, Inc., 381 F.3d 1178, 1202 (Fed.Cir.2004)]. That result follows because the DMCA must be read in the context of the Copyright Act, which balances the rights of the copyright owner against the public's interest in having appropriate access to the work. See id. at 1199 * * *. Therefore, courts generally have found a violation of the DMCA only when the alleged access was intertwined with a right protected by the Copyright Act. See, e.g., Lexmark Int'l, Inc. v. Static Control Components, Inc., 253 F.Supp.2d 943, 987 (E.D.Ky.2003), vacated and remanded on other grounds, 387 F.3d 522 (6th Cir.2004) * * *. To the extent that StorageTek's rights under copyright law are not at risk, the DMCA does not create a new source of liability."

Would circumvention in order to make fair use of a work be immune from liability under the rationale in *Storage Tech*?

(2) The Ninth Circuit took a different view of § 1201(a) in MDY Industries, LLC v. Blizzard Entertainment, Inc., 629 F.3d 928 (9th Cir.2010). Blizzard Entertainment, producer of the popular World of Warcraft online game, claimed that MDY Industries was violating § 1201(a)(2) by marketing a software "bot" that allowed users to automate play of the early levels of WoW. Blizzard had deployed technology designed to prevent players who were using bots from connecting to the WoW servers; MDY had responded by adding an anti-detection feature to its bot. According to Judge Callahan, "One of the issues raised by this appeal is whether certain provisions of § 1201 prohibit circumvention of access controls when access does not constitute copyright infringement."

" * * * First, § 1201(a)(2) prohibits the circumvention of a measure that 'effectively controls access to *a work protected under this title*,' whereas § 1201(b)(1) concerns a measure that 'effectively protects *a right of a copyright owner under this title in a work or portion thereof*.' (emphasis added). We read § 1201(b)(1)'s language—'right of a copyright owner under this title'—to reinforce copyright owners' traditional exclusive rights under § 106 by granting them an additional cause of action against those who traffic in circumventing devices that facilitate infringement. Sections 1201(a)(1) and (a)(2), however, use the term 'work protected under this title.' Neither of these two subsections explicitly refers to traditional copyright infringement under § 106. Accordingly,

we read this term as extending a new form of protection, i.e., the right to prevent circumvention of access controls, broadly to works protected under Title
17, i.e., copyrighted works." Specifically rejecting the Federal Circuit's decisions
in Chamberlain Group v. Skylink Techs. and Storage Tech. Corp. v. Custom
Hardware Eng'g, the court concluded, "Our review of the legislative history
supports our reading of § 1201: that section (a) creates a new anticircumvention
right distinct from copyright infringement, while section (b) strengthens the
traditional prohibition against copyright infringement. * * * "

"While we appreciate the policy considerations expressed by the Federal
Circuit in *Chamberlain*, we are unable to follow its approach because it is contrary to the plain language of the statute. * * *

"Were we to follow *Chamberlain* in imposing an infringement nexus requirement, we would have to disregard the plain language of the statute. Moreover, there is significant textual evidence showing Congress's intent to create a
new anticircumvention right in § 1201(a) distinct from infringement. As set
forth supra, this evidence includes: (1) Congress's choice to link only
§ 1201(b)(1) explicitly to infringement; (2) Congress's provision in
§ 1201(a)(3)(A) that descrambling and decrypting devices can lead to § 1201(a)
liability, even though descrambling and decrypting devices may only enable
non-infringing access to a copyrighted work; and (3) Congress's creation of a
mechanism in § 1201(a)(1)(B)–(D) to exempt certain non-infringing behavior
from § 1201(a)(1) liability, a mechanism that would be unnecessary if an infringement nexus requirement existed. * * *

"In sum, we conclude that a fair reading of the statute (supported by legislative history) indicates that Congress created a distinct anti-circumvention
right under § 1201(a) without an infringement nexus requirement."

(3) J. Lipton, The Law of Unintended Consequences: The DMCA and Interoperability, 62 Wash & Lee L.Rev. 487 (2005), argues for a presumption against
liability under the DMCA for a competitor's sale of interoperable goods when
the protected software is merely incidental to the product; T. Armstrong, Fair
Circumvention, 74 Brooklyn L.Rev. 1 (2008), analogizes the judicial limits on
circumvention liability to the common law development of fair use; D. Burk,
Anticircumvention Misuse, 50 UCLA L.Rev. 1095 (2003), suggests that abuses
of the anti-circumvention rules could be controlled by judicial recognition of a
misuse doctrine analogous to patent and copyright misuse.

(4) Does the digital world demand a reassessment of the nature or scope of
copyright? D. Zimmerman, Living Without Copyright in a Digital World, 70
Alb.L.Rev. 1375 (2007), thinks copyright is simply not up to the job in
cyberspace; instead of tinkering with fair use, G. Parchomovsky and P. Weiser,
Beyond Fair Use, 96 Cornell L.Rev. 91 (2010), proposes creation of a system of
user privileges to insure an appropriate level of digital access and use; R.
Denicola, Mostly Dead? Copyright Law in the New Millennium, 47 J.Copyr.
Soc'y 193 (2000), wonders whether public pressure might eventually force
Congress to reassert the public's interest. Taking a different perspective, D.
Long, First "Let's Kill All the Intellectual Property Lawyers!": Musings on the
Decline and Fall of the Intellectual Property Empire, 34 J. Marshall L.Rev. 851
(2001), laments domestic and international hostility to intellectual property
protection.

A 2004 report by the Congressional Budget Office entitled *Copyright Issues in Digital Media* hazards no legislative recommendations but does offer this advice to Congress: "Property rights and other elements of a regulatory regime for creative works should be regarded as instruments for allocating creative resources. Hence, existing copyright law should not be viewed as an absolute, inviolable set of rights to which either creators or consumers are entitled." At a conference celebrating the 300th anniversary of modern copyright law and the 1710 Statute of Anne, the then-Register of Copyrights admitted that modern copyright law "is out of balance" and has lost the respect of the public. She was not optimistic about a remedy. "Work on the copyright law right now is nonexistent. Nothing in copyright is going to happen." 79 Pat., Tm. & Copyr.J. (BNA) 765 (2010). Another assessment by a copyright attorney was similarly bleak. "The major players in the debate—big copyright owners, artists, distributors, technology companies, libraries and groups purporting to represent 'the public,' among others—simply have profound, deeply felt and entirely legitimate disagreements over what kind of 'reform' the system needs. Different players live on different planets: Some look around today and see a world with too much infringement. Others see too much enforcement. And that isn't a gap easily bridged through compromise." Sheffner, Legal Matters: Copyright Reform? Don't Hold Your Breath, Billboard, Apr. 3, 2010, p. 11. Nevertheless, in April, 2013, the Chair of the House Judiciary Committee, with the support of the Register of Copyrights, announced that the Committee would begin a comprehensive review of U.S. copyright law.

CHAPTER 5

THE CALCULUS OF RIGHTS

1. DURATION AND TERMINATION OF TRANSFERS

Eldred v. Ashcroft

Supreme Court of the United States, 2003.
537 U.S. 186, 123 S.Ct. 769.

■ JUSTICE GINSBURG delivered the opinion of the Court.

This case concerns the authority the Constitution assigns to Congress to prescribe the duration of copyrights. The Copyright and Patent Clause of the Constitution, Art. I, § 8, cl. 8, provides as to copyrights: "Congress shall have Power . . . [t]o promote the Progress of Science . . . by securing [to Authors] for limited Times . . . the exclusive Right to their . . . Writings." In 1998, in the measure here under inspection, Congress enlarged the duration of copyrights by 20 years. Copyright Term Extension Act (CTEA), Pub.L. 105–298, § 102(b) and (d), 112 Stat. 2827–2828 (amending 17 U.S.C. §§ 302, 304). As in the case of prior extensions, principally in 1831, 1909, and 1976, Congress provided for application of the enlarged terms to existing and future copyrights alike.

Petitioners are individuals and businesses whose products or services build on copyrighted works that have gone into the public domain. They seek a determination that the CTEA fails constitutional review under both the Copyright Clause's "limited Times" prescription and the First Amendment's free speech guarantee. Under the 1976 Copyright Act, copyright protection generally lasted from the work's creation until 50 years after the author's death. Pub.L. 94–553, § 302(a), 90 Stat. 2572 (1976 Act). Under the CTEA, most copyrights now run from creation until 70 years after the author's death. 17 U.S.C. § 302(a). Petitioners do not challenge the "life-plus–70–years" time span itself. "Whether 50 years is enough, or 70 years too much," they acknowledge, "is not a judgment meet for this Court." Brief for Petitioners 14. Congress went awry, petitioners maintain, not with respect to newly created works, but in enlarging the term for published works with existing copyrights. The "limited Tim[e]" in effect when a copyright is secured, petitioners urge, becomes the constitutional boundary, a clear line beyond the power of Congress to extend. See ibid. As to the First Amendment, petitioners contend that the CTEA is a content-neutral regulation of speech that fails inspection under the heightened judicial scrutiny appropriate for such regulations.

In accord with the District Court and the Court of Appeals, we reject petitioners' challenges to the CTEA. In that 1998 legislation, as in all previous copyright term extensions, Congress placed existing and future copyrights in parity. In prescribing that alignment, we hold, Congress acted within its authority and did not transgress constitutional limitations.

I

A

We evaluate petitioners' challenge to the constitutionality of the CTEA against the backdrop of Congress' previous exercises of its authority under the Copyright Clause. The Nation's first copyright statute, enacted in 1790, provided a federal copyright term of 14 years from the date of publication, renewable for an additional 14 years if the author survived the first term. Act of May 31, 1790, ch. 15, § 1, 1 Stat. 124 (1790 Act). The 1790 Act's renewable 14–year term applied to existing works (i.e., works already published and works created but not yet published) and future works alike. Ibid. Congress expanded the federal copyright term to 42 years in 1831 (28 years from publication, renewable for an additional 14 years), and to 56 years in 1909 (28 years from publication, renewable for an additional 28 years). Act of Feb. 3, 1831, ch. 16, §§ 1, 16, 4 Stat. 436, 439 (1831 Act); Act of Mar. 4, 1909, ch. 320, §§ 23–24, 35 Stat. 1080–1081 (1909 Act). Both times, Congress applied the new copyright term to existing and future works, 1831 Act §§ 1, 16; 1909 Act §§ 23–24; to qualify for the 1831 extension, an existing work had to be in its initial copyright term at the time the Act became effective, 1831 Act §§ 1, 16.

In 1976, Congress altered the method for computing federal copyright terms. 1976 Act §§ 302–304. For works created by identified natural persons, the 1976 Act provided that federal copyright protection would run from the work's creation, not—as in the 1790, 1831, and 1909 Acts—its publication; protection would last until 50 years after the author's death. § 302(a). In these respects, the 1976 Act aligned United States copyright terms with the then-dominant international standard adopted under the Berne Convention for the Protection of Literary and Artistic Works. See H.R.Rep. No. 94–1476, p. 135 (1976), U.S.Code Cong. & Admin.News 1976, p. 5659. For anonymous works, pseudonymous works, and works made for hire, the 1976 Act provided a term of 75 years from publication or 100 years from creation, whichever expired first. § 302(c).

These new copyright terms, the 1976 Act instructed, governed all works not published by its effective date of January 1, 1978, regardless of when the works were created. §§ 302–303. For published works with existing copyrights as of that date, the 1976 Act granted a copyright term of 75 years from the date of publication, § 304(a) and (b), a 19–year increase over the 56–year term applicable under the 1909 Act.

The measure at issue here, the CTEA, installed the fourth major duration extension of federal copyrights. Retaining the general structure of the 1976 Act, the CTEA enlarges the terms of all existing and future copyrights by 20 years. For works created by identified natural persons, the term now lasts from creation until 70 years after the author's death. 17 U.S.C. § 302(a). This standard harmonizes the baseline United States copyright term with the term adopted by the European Union in 1993. See Council Directive 93/98/EEC of 29 October 1993 Harmonizing the Term of Protection of Copyright and Certain Related Rights, 1993 Official J. Eur. Cmty. 290 (EU Council Directive 93/98). For anonymous works, pseudonymous works, and works made for hire, the term is 95 years from publication or 120 years from creation, whichever expires first. 17 U.S.C. § 302(c).

Paralleling the 1976 Act, the CTEA applies these new terms to all works not published by January 1, 1978. §§ 302(a), 303(a). For works published before 1978 with existing copyrights as of the CTEA's effective date, the CTEA extends the term to 95 years from publication. § 304(a) and (b). Thus, in common with the 1831, 1909, and 1976 Acts, the CTEA's new terms apply to both future and existing copyrights.

B

* * *

We granted certiorari to address two questions: whether the CTEA's extension of existing copyrights exceeds Congress' power under the Copyright Clause; and whether the CTEA's extension of existing and future copyrights violates the First Amendment. 534 U.S. 1126 and 1160 (2002). We now answer those two questions in the negative and affirm.

II

A

We address first the determination of the courts below that Congress has authority under the Copyright Clause to extend the terms of existing copyrights. Text, history, and precedent, we conclude, confirm that the Copyright Clause empowers Congress to prescribe "limited Times" for copyright protection and to secure the same level and duration of protection for all copyright holders, present and future.

The CTEA's baseline term of life plus 70 years, petitioners concede, qualifies as a "limited Tim[e]" as applied to future copyrights.[4] Petitioners contend, however, that existing copyrights extended to endure for that same term are not "limited." Petitioners' argument essentially reads into the text of the Copyright Clause the command that a time prescription, once set, becomes forever "fixed" or "inalterable." The word "limited," however, does not convey a meaning so constricted. * * *

To comprehend the scope of Congress' power under the Copyright Clause, "a page of history is worth a volume of logic." New York Trust Co. v. Eisner, 256 U.S. 345, 349 (1921) (Holmes, J.). History reveals an unbroken congressional practice of granting to authors of works with existing copyrights the benefit of term extensions so that all under copyright protection will be governed evenhandedly under the same regime. * * *

Congress' consistent historical practice of applying newly enacted copyright terms to future and existing copyrights reflects a judgment stated concisely by Representative Huntington at the time of the 1831 Act: "[J]ustice, policy, and equity alike forb[id]" that an "author who had sold his [work] a week ago, be placed in a worse situation than the author who should sell his work the day after the passing of [the] act." 7 Cong. Deb. 424 (1831); accord Symposium, The Constitutionality of Copyright Term Extension, 18 Cardozo Arts & Ent. L.J. 651, 694 (2000) (Prof. Miller) ("[S]ince 1790, it has indeed been Congress's policy that the author of yesterday's work should not get a lesser reward than the author of tomorrow's work just because Congress passed a statute lengthening the term today."). The CTEA follows this historical practice by keeping the duration provisions of the 1976 Act largely in place and simply adding 20 years to each of them. Guided by text, history, and precedent, we cannot agree with petitioners' submission that extending the duration of existing

---

[4] We note again that Justice Breyer makes no such concession. * * * He does not train his fire, as petitioners do, on Congress' choice to place existing and future copyrights in parity. Moving beyond the bounds of the parties' presentations, and with abundant policy arguments but precious little support from precedent, he would condemn Congress' entire product as irrational.

copyrights is categorically beyond Congress' authority under the Copyright Clause.

Satisfied that the CTEA complies with the "limited Times" prescription, we turn now to whether it is a rational exercise of the legislative authority conferred by the Copyright Clause. On that point, we defer substantially to Congress. *Sony,* 464 U.S., at 429 ("[I]t is Congress that has been assigned the task of defining the scope of the limited monopoly that should be granted to authors . . . in order to give the public appropriate access to their work product.").[10]

The CTEA reflects judgments of a kind Congress typically makes, judgments we cannot dismiss as outside the Legislature's domain. As respondent describes, see Brief for Respondent 37–38, a key factor in the CTEA's passage was a 1993 European Union (EU) directive instructing EU members to establish a copyright term of life plus 70 years. EU Council Directive 93/98, p. 4; see 144 Cong. Rec. S12377–S12378 (daily ed. Oct. 12, 1998) (statement of Sen. Hatch). Consistent with the Berne Convention, the EU directed its members to deny this longer term to the works of any non-EU country whose laws did not secure the same extended term. See Berne Conv. Art. 7(8); P. Goldstein, International Copyright § 5.3, p. 239 (2001). By extending the baseline United States copyright term to life plus 70 years, Congress sought to ensure that American authors would receive the same copyright protection in Europe as their European counterparts. The CTEA may also provide greater incentive for American and other authors to create and disseminate their work in the United States. * * *

In addition to international concerns, Congress passed the CTEA in light of demographic, economic, and technological changes, Brief for Respondent 25–26, 33, and nn. 23 and 24,[14] and rationally credited projections that longer terms would encourage copyright holders to invest in the restoration and public distribution of their works, id., at 34–37; see H.R.Rep. No. 105–452, p. 4 (1998) (term extension "provide[s] copyright owners generally with the incentive to restore older works and further disseminate them to the public").[15]

---

[10] Justice Breyer would adopt a heightened, three-part test for the constitutionality of copyright enactments. Post, at 245. He would invalidate the CTEA as irrational in part because, in his view, harmonizing the United States and European Union baseline copyright terms "apparent[ly]" fails to achieve "significant" uniformity. Post, at 264. But see infra, at 206. The novelty of the "rational basis" approach he presents is plain. Cf. Board of Trustees of Univ. of Ala. v. Garrett, 531 U.S. 356, 383 (2001) (Breyer, J., dissenting) ("Rational-basis review—with its presumptions favoring constitutionality—is 'a paradigm of *judicial* restraint.' ") (quoting FCC v. Beach Communications, Inc., 508 U.S. 307, 314 (1993)). Rather than subjecting Congress' legislative choices in the copyright area to heightened judicial scrutiny, we have stressed that "it is not our role to alter the delicate balance Congress has labored to achieve." Stewart v. Abend, 495 U.S., at 230; see Sony Corp. of America v. Universal City Studios, Inc., 464 U.S. 417, 429 (1984). Congress' exercise of its Copyright Clause authority must be rational, but Justice Breyer's stringent version of rationality is unknown to our literary property jurisprudence.

[14] Members of Congress expressed the view that, as a result of increases in human longevity and in parents' average age when their children are born, the pre-CTEA term did not adequately secure "the right to profit from licensing one's work during one's lifetime and to take pride and comfort in knowing that one's children—and perhaps their children—might also benefit from one's posthumous popularity." 141 Cong. Rec. 6553 (1995) (statement of Sen. Feinstein); * * *

[15] Justice Breyer urges that the economic incentives accompanying copyright term extension are too insignificant to "mov[e]" any author with a "rational economic perspective." Post, at 255; see post, at 254–257. Calibrating rational economic incentives, however, like "fashion[ing] . . . new rules [in light of] new technology," *Sony,* 464 U.S., at 431, is a task pri-

In sum, we find that the CTEA is a rational enactment; we are not at liberty to second-guess congressional determinations and policy judgments of this order, however debatable or arguably unwise they may be. Accordingly, we cannot conclude that the CTEA—which continues the unbroken congressional practice of treating future and existing copyrights in parity for term extension purposes—is an impermissible exercise of Congress' power under the Copyright Clause.

B

Petitioners' Copyright Clause arguments rely on several novel readings of the Clause. We next address these arguments and explain why we find them unpersuasive.

1

Petitioners contend that even if the CTEA's 20–year term extension is literally a "limited Tim[e]," permitting Congress to extend existing copyrights allows it to evade the "limited Times" constraint by creating effectively perpetual copyrights through repeated extensions. We disagree.

As the Court of Appeals observed, a regime of perpetual copyrights "clearly is not the situation before us." 239 F.3d, at 379. Nothing before this Court warrants construction of the CTEA's 20–year term extension as a congressional attempt to evade or override the "limited Times" constraint. * * *

2

Petitioners dominantly advance a series of arguments all premised on the proposition that Congress may not extend an existing copyright absent new consideration from the author. They pursue this main theme under three headings. Petitioners contend that the CTEA's extension of existing copyrights (1) overlooks the requirement of "originality," (2) fails to "promote the Progress of Science," and (3) ignores copyright's *quid pro quo.*

Petitioners' "originality" argument draws on Feist Publications, Inc. v. Rural Telephone Service Co., 499 U.S. 340 (1991). In *Feist,* we observed that "[t]he *sine qua non* of copyright is originality," id., at 345, and held that copyright protection is unavailable to "a narrow category of works in which the creative spark is utterly lacking or so trivial as to be virtually nonexistent," id., at 359. Relying on *Feist,* petitioners urge that even if a work is sufficiently "original" to qualify for copyright protection in the first instance, any extension of the copyright's duration is impermissible because, once published, a work is no longer original.

Feist, however, did not touch on the duration of copyright protection. Rather, the decision addressed the core question of copyrightability, i.e., the "creative spark" a work must have to be eligible for copyright protection at all. Explaining the originality requirement, *Feist* trained on the Copyright Clause words "Authors" and "Writings." Id., at 346–347. The decision did not construe the "limited Times" for which a work may be protected, and the originality requirement has no bearing on that prescription.

---

marily for Congress, not the courts. Congress heard testimony from a number of prominent artists; each expressed the belief that the copyright system's assurance of fair compensation for themselves and their heirs was an incentive to create. See, e.g., House Hearings 233–239 (statement of Quincy Jones); Copyright Term Extension Act of 1995: Hearings before the Senate Committee on the Judiciary, 104th Cong., 1st Sess., 55–56 (1995) (statement of Bob Dylan); id., at 56–57 (statement of Don Henley); id., at 57 (statement of Carlos Santana). * * *

More forcibly, petitioners contend that the CTEA's extension of existing copyrights does not "promote the Progress of Science" as contemplated by the preambular language of the Copyright Clause. Art. I, § 8, cl. 8. To sustain this objection, petitioners do not argue that the Clause's preamble is an independently enforceable limit on Congress' power. See 239 F.3d, at 378 (Petitioners acknowledge that "the preamble of the Copyright Clause is not a substantive limit on Congress' legislative power." (internal quotation marks omitted)). Rather, they maintain that the preambular language identifies the sole end to which Congress may legislate; accordingly, they conclude, the meaning of "limited Times" must be "determined in light of that specified end." Brief for Petitioners 19. The CTEA's extension of existing copyrights categorically fails to "promote the Progress of Science," petitioners argue, because it does not stimulate the creation of new works but merely adds value to works already created.

As petitioners point out, we have described the Copyright Clause as "both a grant of power and a limitation," Graham v. John Deere Co. of Kansas City, 383 U.S. 1, 5 (1966), and have said that "[t]he primary objective of copyright" is "[t]o promote the Progress of Science," Feist, 499 U.S., at 349. The "constitutional command," we have recognized, is that Congress, to the extent it enacts copyright laws at all, create a "system" that "promote[s] the Progress of Science." Graham, 383 U.S., at 6.[18]

We have also stressed, however, that it is generally for Congress, not the courts, to decide how best to pursue the Copyright Clause's objectives. * * * The justifications we earlier set out for Congress' enactment of the CTEA, supra, at 205–207, provide a rational basis for the conclusion that the CTEA "promote[s] the Progress of Science." * * *

Closely related to petitioners' preambular argument, or a variant of it, is their assertion that the Copyright Clause "imbeds a quid pro quo." Brief for Petitioners 23. They contend, in this regard, that Congress may grant to an "Autho[r]" an "exclusive Right" for a "limited Tim[e]," but only in exchange for a "Writin[g]." Congress' power to confer copyright protection, petitioners argue, is thus contingent upon an exchange: The author of an original work receives an "exclusive Right" for a "limited Tim[e]" in exchange for a dedication to the public thereafter. Extending an existing copyright without demanding additional consideration, petitioners maintain, bestows an unpaid-for benefit on copyright holders and their heirs, in violation of the *quid pro quo* requirement.

We can demur to petitioners' description of the Copyright Clause as a grant of legislative authority empowering Congress "to secure a bargain—

---

[18] Justice Stevens' characterization of reward to the author as "a secondary consideration" of copyright law, post, at 227, n. 4 (internal quotation marks omitted), understates the relationship between such rewards and the "Progress of Science." As we have explained, "[t]he economic philosophy behind the [Copyright] [C]lause . . . is the conviction that encouragement of individual effort by personal gain is the best way to advance public welfare through the talents of authors and inventors." Mazer v. Stein, 347 U.S. 201, 219 (1954). Accordingly, "copyright law *celebrates* the profit motive, recognizing that the incentive to profit from the exploitation of copyrights will redound to the public benefit by resulting in the proliferation of knowledge . . . . The profit motive is the engine that ensures the progress of science." American Geophysical Union v. Texaco Inc., 802 F.Supp. 1, 27 (S.D.N.Y.1992), aff'd, 60 F.3d 913 (C.A.2 1994). Rewarding authors for their creative labor and "promot[ing] . . . Progress" are thus complementary; as James Madison observed, in copyright "[t]he public good fully coincides . . . with the claims of individuals." The Federalist No. 43, p. 272 (C. Rossiter ed.1961). Justice Breyer's assertion that "copyright statutes must serve public, not private, ends" post, at 247, similarly misses the mark. The two ends are not mutually exclusive; copyright law serves public ends by providing individuals with an incentive to pursue private ones.

this for that." Brief for Petitioners 16; see Mazer v. Stein, 347 U.S. 201, 219 (1954) ("The economic philosophy behind the clause empowering Congress to grant patents and copyrights is the conviction that encouragement of individual effort by personal gain is the best way to advance public welfare through the talents of authors and inventors in 'Science and useful Arts.' "). But the legislative evolution earlier recalled demonstrates what the bargain entails. Given the consistent placement of existing copyright holders in parity with future holders, the author of a work created in the last 170 years would reasonably comprehend, as the "this" offered her, a copyright not only for the time in place when protection is gained, but also for any renewal or extension legislated during that time.[21] Congress could rationally seek to "promote . . . Progress" by including in every copyright statute an express guarantee that authors would receive the benefit of any later legislative extension of the copyright term. Nothing in the Copyright Clause bars Congress from creating the same incentive by adopting the same position as a matter of unbroken practice. See Brief for Respondent 31–32. * * *

* * * Accordingly, we reject the proposition that a *quid pro quo* requirement stops Congress from expanding copyright's term in a manner that puts existing and future copyrights in parity. * * *

III

Petitioners separately argue that the CTEA is a content-neutral regulation of speech that fails heightened judicial review under the First Amendment. We reject petitioners' plea for imposition of uncommonly strict scrutiny on a copyright scheme that incorporates its own speech-protective purposes and safeguards. The Copyright Clause and First Amendment were adopted close in time. This proximity indicates that, in the Framers' view, copyright's limited monopolies are compatible with free speech principles. Indeed, copyright's purpose is to *promote* the creation and publication of free expression. As *Harper & Row* observed: "[T]he Framers intended copyright itself to be the engine of free expression. By establishing a marketable right to the use of one's expression, copyright supplies the economic incentive to create and disseminate ideas." 471 U.S., at 558.

In addition to spurring the creation and publication of new expression, copyright law contains built-in First Amendment accommodations. See id., at 560. First, it distinguishes between ideas and expression and makes only the latter eligible for copyright protection. Specifically, 17 U.S.C. § 102(b) provides: "In no case does copyright protection for an original work of authorship extend to any idea, procedure, process, system, method of operation, concept, principle, or discovery, regardless of the form in which it is described, explained, illustrated, or embodied in such work." As we said in *Harper & Row,* this "idea/expression dichotomy strike[s] a definitional balance between the First Amendment and the Copyright Act by permitting free communication of facts while still protecting an author's expression." 471 U.S., at 556 (internal quotation marks omitted). Due to this distinction, every idea, theory, and fact in a copyrighted work becomes instantly available for public exploitation at the moment of publication. See *Feist,* 499 U.S., at 349–350.

---

[21] Standard copyright assignment agreements reflect this expectation. See, e.g., A. Kohn & B. Kohn, Music Licensing 471 (3d ed.1992–2002) (short form copyright assignment for musical composition, under which assignor conveys all rights to the work, "including the copyrights and proprietary rights therein and in any and all versions of said musical composition(s), and any renewals and extensions thereof (whether presently available *or subsequently available as a result of intervening legislation)*" (emphasis added)); * * *

Second, the "fair use" defense allows the public to use not only facts and ideas contained in a copyrighted work, but also expression itself in certain circumstances. Codified at 17 U.S.C. § 107, the defense provides: "[T]he fair use of a copyrighted work, including such use by reproduction in copies . . . , for purposes such as criticism, comment, news reporting, teaching (including multiple copies for classroom use), scholarship, or research, is not an infringement of copyright." The fair use defense affords considerable "latitude for scholarship and comment," *Harper & Row,* 471 U.S., at 560, and even for parody, see Campbell v. Acuff–Rose Music, Inc., 510 U.S. 569 (1994) (rap group's musical parody of Roy Orbison's "Oh, Pretty Woman" may be fair use). * * *

[The CTEA] protects authors' original expression from unrestricted exploitation. Protection of that order does not raise the free speech concerns present when the government compels or burdens the communication of particular facts or ideas. The First Amendment securely protects the freedom to make—or decline to make—one's own speech; it bears less heavily when speakers assert the right to make other people's speeches. To the extent such assertions raise First Amendment concerns, copyright's built-in free speech safeguards are generally adequate to address them. We recognize that the D.C. Circuit spoke too broadly when it declared copyrights "categorically immune from challenges under the First Amendment." 239 F.3d, at 375. But when, as in this case, Congress has not altered the traditional contours of copyright protection, further First Amendment scrutiny is unnecessary. See *Harper & Row,* 471 U.S., at 560; cf. San Francisco Arts & Athletics, Inc. v. United States Olympic Comm., 483 U.S. 522 (1987).

IV

If petitioners' vision of the Copyright Clause held sway, it would do more than render the CTEA's duration extensions unconstitutional as to existing works. Indeed, petitioners' assertion that the provisions of the CTEA are not severable would make the CTEA's enlarged terms invalid even as to tomorrow's work. The 1976 Act's time extensions, which set the pattern that the CTEA followed, would be vulnerable as well.

As we read the Framers' instruction, the Copyright Clause empowers Congress to determine the intellectual property regimes that, overall, in that body's judgment, will serve the ends of the Clause. See *Graham,* 383 U.S., at 6 (Congress may "implement the stated purpose of the Framers by selecting the policy which *in its judgment* best effectuates the constitutional aim." (emphasis added)). Beneath the facade of their inventive constitutional interpretation, petitioners forcefully urge that Congress pursued very bad policy in prescribing the CTEA's long terms. The wisdom of Congress' action, however, is not within our province to second guess. Satisfied that the legislation before us remains inside the domain the Constitution assigns to the First Branch, we affirm the judgment of the Court of Appeals.

It is so ordered.

■ JUSTICE STEVENS, dissenting.

* * * *Ex post facto* extensions of copyrights result in a gratuitous transfer of wealth from the public to authors, publishers, and their successors in interest. Such retroactive extensions do not even arguably serve either of the purposes of the Copyright/Patent Clause. The reasons why such extensions of the patent monopoly are unconstitutional apply to copyrights as well. * * *

* * * The federal Copyright Act was first amended in 1831. That amendment, like later amendments, not only authorized a longer term for new works, but also extended the terms of unexpired copyrights. Respondent argues that that historical practice effectively establishes the constitutionality of retroactive extensions of unexpired copyrights. Of course, the practice buttresses the presumption of validity that attaches to every Act of Congress. But, as our decision in INS v. Chadha, 462 U.S. 919 (1983), demonstrates, the fact that Congress has repeatedly acted on a mistaken interpretation of the Constitution does not qualify our duty to invalidate an unconstitutional practice when it is finally challenged in an appropriate case. As Justice White pointed out in his dissent in *Chadha,* that case sounded the "death knell for nearly 200 other statutory provisions" in which Congress had exercised a "legislative veto." Id., at 967. * * *

Respondent also argues that the Act promotes the useful arts by providing incentives to restore old movies. For at least three reasons, the interest in preserving perishable copies of old copyrighted films does not justify a wholesale extension of existing copyrights. First, such restoration and preservation will not even arguably promote any new works by authors or inventors. And, of course, any original expression in the restoration and preservation of movies will receive new copyright protection. Second, however strong the justification for preserving such works may be, that justification applies equally to works whose copyrights have already expired. Yet no one seriously contends that the Copyright/Patent Clause would authorize the grant of monopoly privileges for works already in the public domain solely to encourage their restoration. Finally, even if this concern with aging movies would permit congressional protection, the remedy offered—a blanket extension of all copyrights—simply bears no relationship to the alleged harm.

Finally, respondent relies on concerns of equity to justify the retroactive extension. If Congress concludes that a longer period of exclusivity is necessary in order to provide an adequate incentive to authors to produce new works, respondent seems to believe that simple fairness requires that the same lengthened period be provided to authors whose works have already been completed and copyrighted. This is a classic non sequitur. The reason for increasing the inducement to create something new simply does not apply to an already-created work. To the contrary, the equity argument actually provides strong support for petitioners. Members of the public were entitled to rely on a promised access to copyrighted or patented works at the expiration of the terms specified when the exclusive privileges were granted. On the other hand, authors will receive the full benefit of the exclusive terms that were promised as an inducement to their creativity, and have no equitable claim to increased compensation for doing nothing more. * * *

■ JUSTICE BREYER, dissenting.

* * * The economic effect of this 20–year extension—the longest blanket extension since the Nation's founding—is to make the copyright term not limited, but virtually perpetual. Its primary legal effect is to grant the extended term not to authors, but to their heirs, estates, or corporate successors. And most importantly, its practical effect is not to promote, but to inhibit, the progress of "Science"—by which word the Framers meant learning or knowledge, E. Walterscheid, The Nature of the Intellectual Property Clause: A Study in Historical Perspective 125–126 (2002). * * *

The Copyright Clause and the First Amendment seek related objectives—the creation and dissemination of information. When working in tandem, these provisions mutually reinforce each other, the first serving as an "engine of free expression," Harper & Row, Publishers, Inc. v. Nation Enterprises, 471 U.S. 539 (1985), the second assuring that government throws up no obstacle to its dissemination. At the same time, a particular statute that exceeds proper Copyright Clause bounds may set Clause and Amendment at cross-purposes, thereby depriving the public of the speech-related benefits that the Founders, through both, have promised.

Consequently, I would review plausible claims that a copyright statute seriously, and unjustifiably, restricts the dissemination of speech somewhat more carefully than reference to this Court's traditional Commerce Clause jurisprudence might suggest, cf. ante, at 204–205, and n. 10. * * * Rather, it is necessary only to recognize that this statute involves not pure economic regulation, but regulation of expression, and what may count as rational where economic regulation is at issue is not necessarily rational where we focus on expression—in a Nation constitutionally dedicated to the free dissemination of speech, information, learning, and culture. * * *

First, the present statute primarily benefits the holders of existing copyrights, i.e., copyrights on works already created. And a Congressional Research Service (CRS) study prepared for Congress indicates that the added royalty-related sum that the law will transfer to existing copyright holders is large. E. Rappaport, CRS Report for Congress, Copyright Term Extension: Estimating the Economic Values (1998) (hereinafter CRS Report). In conjunction with official figures on copyright renewals, the CRS Report indicates that only about 2% of copyrights between 55 and 75 years old retain commercial value—i.e., still generate royalties after that time. Brief for Petitioners 7 (estimate, uncontested by respondent, based on data from the CRS, Census Bureau, and Library of Congress). But books, songs, and movies of that vintage still earn about $400 million per year in royalties. CRS Report 8, 12, 15. Hence, (despite declining consumer interest in any given work over time) one might conservatively estimate that 20 extra years of copyright protection will mean the transfer of several billion extra royalty dollars to holders of existing copyrights—copyrights that, together, already will have earned many billions of dollars in royalty "reward." See id., at 16. * * *

A second, equally important, cause for concern arises out of the fact that copyright extension imposes a "permissions" requirement—not only upon potential users of "classic" works that still retain commercial value, but also upon potential users of *any other work* still in copyright. Again using CRS estimates, one can estimate that, by 2018, the number of such works 75 years of age or older will be about 350,000. * * *

What copyright-related benefits might justify the statute's extension of copyright protection? First, no one could reasonably conclude that copyright's traditional economic rationale applies here. The extension will not act as an economic spur encouraging authors to create new works. * * * No potential author can reasonably believe that he has more than a tiny chance of writing a classic that will survive commercially long enough for the copyright extension to matter. After all, if, after 55 to 75 years, only 2% of all copyrights retain commercial value, the percentage surviving after 75 years or more (a typical pre-extension copyright term)—must be far smaller. See supra, at 804; CRS Report 7 (estimating that, even after copyright renewal, about 3.8% of copyrighted books go out of print each year). And any remaining monetary incentive is diminished dramatically by the fact that the relevant royalties will not arrive until 75 years or more into the future, when, not the author, but distant heirs, or shareholders in a successor corporation, will receive them. Using assumptions about the time value of money provided us by a group of economists (including five Nobel prize winners), Brief for George A. Akerlof et al. as *Amici Curiae* 5–7, it seems fair to say that, for example, a 1% likelihood of earning $100 annually for 20 years, starting *75 years into the future,* is worth less than seven cents today. See id., at 3a; see also CRS Report 5. See generally Appendix, Part A, infra.

What potential Shakespeare, Wharton, or Hemingway would be moved by such a sum? What monetarily motivated Melville would not realize that he could do better for his grandchildren by putting a few dollars into an interest-bearing bank account? * * *

* * * The present extension will produce a copyright period of protection that, even under conservative assumptions, is worth more than *99.8%* of protection *in perpetuity* (more than *99.99%* for a songwriter like Irving Berlin and a song like Alexander's Ragtime Band). See Appendix, Part A, infra. The lack of a practically meaningful distinction from an author's *ex ante* perspective between (a) the statute's extended terms and (b) an infinite term makes this latest extension difficult to square with the Constitution's insistence on "limited Times." * * *

In any event, the incentive-related numbers are far too small for Congress to have concluded rationally, even with respect to new works, that the extension's economic-incentive effect could justify the serious expression-related harms earlier described. See Part II–B, supra. And, of course, in respect to works already created—the source of many of the harms previously described—*the statute creates no economic incentive at all.* See ante, at 226–227 (Stevens, J., dissenting).

Second, the Court relies heavily for justification upon international uniformity of terms. * * *

Despite appearances, the statute does *not* create a uniform American–European term with respect to the lion's share of the economically significant works that it affects—*all* works made "for hire" and *all* existing works created prior to 1978. See Appendix, Part B, infra. With respect to those works the American statute produces an extended term of 95 years while comparable European rights in "for hire" works last for periods that vary from 50 years to 70 years to life plus 70 years. * * *

[T]he statute's legislative history suggests another possible justification. That history refers frequently to the financial assistance the statute will bring the entertainment industry, particularly through the promotion of exports. See, e.g., S.Rep. No. 104–315, p. 3 (1996) ("The purpose of this bill is to ensure adequate copyright protection for American works in foreign nations and the continued economic benefits of a healthy surplus balance of trade"); * * * I can find nothing in the Copyright Clause that would authorize Congress to enhance the copyright grant's monopoly power, likely leading to higher prices both at home and abroad, *solely* in order to produce higher foreign earnings. That objective is not a *copyright* objective. Nor, standing alone, is it related to any other objective more closely tied to the Clause itself. Neither can higher corporate profits alone justify the grant's enhancement. The Clause seeks public, not private, benefits. * * *

I respectfully dissent.

[The Appendix to Justice Breyer's dissent is omitted.]

DURATION OF COPYRIGHT FOR WORKS CREATED AFTER 1977

The revision process leading to the 1976 Act raised basic questions about the appropriate duration of copyright: Should copyright protection run for a single term or for an original and a renewal term as under the 1909 Act? Should the period of protection be a stated number of years (running from publication, creation, or registration), or should the period (excluding works by corporations, etc.) be the author's life plus a stated number of years after death? Should there be different periods for different classes of works?

How would you go about deciding the optimum duration for copyright? What values and expectations should be maximized? The limits range from zero to as close to perpetuity as the "limited times" constraint in the Constitution will allow.[a]

In framing the 1976 Act, strong support emerged for a single term measured by the life of the author plus 50 years. That term was originally adopted in § 302(a), with § 302(c) providing for anonymous and pseudonymous works and for works made for hire a term of 75 years from publication or 100 years from creation, whichever expired first. The House Report, supporting the life-plus–50 year term, noted that "a very large majority of the world's countries have adopted" this term, which is the minimum required by the Berne Convention. (H.R.Rep. p. 135.)

As Justice Ginsburg explains in *Eldred,* the 1993 European Union Directive extending the term of copyright to life-plus-seventy years prompted calls for a similar extension here. Proponents of an extension argued that because of the Berne Convention's "rule of the shorter term" in art. 7(8), U.S. copyright owners were unable to take advantage of the longer protection abroad; extension of our own copyright term would thus allow domestic owners to receive foreign royalties for an additional twenty years.[b] The music and movies industries were big supporters of extension. Opponents ar-

---

[a]   Although he apparently favored perpetual copyright, Samuel Clemens testified before Congress in 1906 in support of an unsuccessful proposal to extend the duration of copyright to life plus fifty years. "I think that will satisfy any reasonable author, because it will take care of his children," he said. "Let the grandchildren take care of themselves." Fox, Rights of Writers as a Mark Twain Obsession, N.Y. Times, Feb. 16, 1998, p. E1. American poet Ezra Pound's intricate proposal for perpetual copyright is examined in R. Spoo, Ezra Pound's Copyright Statute: Perpetual Rights and the Problem of Heirs, 56 U.C.L.A. L.Rev. 1775 (2009). D. Desai, The Life and Death of Copyright, 2011 Wis.L.Rev. 219 (2011), concludes that there is no convincing historical, philosophical, or economic justification for continuing copyright protection after death.

The constitutional emanations from the "limited times" constraint are explored in M. Pollack, Unconstitutional Incontestability? The Intersection of the Intellectual Property and Commerce Clauses of the Constitution, 18 Seattle U.L.Rev. 259 (1995); D. Shipley, Congressional Authority Over Intellectual Property Policy After Eldred v. Ashcroft: Deference, Empty Limitations, and Risks to the Public Domain, 70 Alb.L.Rev. 1255 (2007), concludes that the limitations in the copyright clause have become largely irrelevant.

[b]   The ratcheting up of duration can work both ways. European countries typically provided fifty years of protection to sound recordings. Citing the longer protection for sound recordings in the U.S., the European Union has extended the term of copyright on sound recordings to 70 years, thus avoiding the imminent entry into the public domain of early recordings by groups like the Beatles and the Rolling Stones.

gued that the public got nothing in return for an extension of existing copyrights. As for future works, as Justice Breyer points out in his dissent, it seems unlikely that additional creative output will be called forth by the prospect of an extra twenty years of protection that commences fifty years after the author's death. The proponents of extension prevailed in 1998 with the Copyright Term Extension Act that added twenty years to the duration of copyright. Section 302(a) now provides a basic term of life plus 70 years; for anonymous and pseudonymous works and works made for hire, § 302(c) now gives a term of 95 years from publication or 120 years from creation.

NOTES AND QUESTIONS

(1) A patent for an invention lasts for 20 years from the date of the patent application. 35 U.S.C. § 154(a)(2). There seems to be tacit acceptance of the large gap between the duration of patent and copyright. Is it justified?

(2) Have difficulties of administration and classification obscured the possibility of varying the length of copyright with the nature of the work? There are some instances of this in foreign systems, such as shorter terms for photographs and sound recordings.

(3) How long will a copyright in fact last under a life-plus–70 year regime? Studies by the Copyright Office on the life-plus–50 year term suggested an average span of around 75 years, so the current term should average about 95 years; this explains the extension of subsisting copyrights to 95 years, which more than triples the term available under the first Copyright Act of 1790: 14 years, renewable for 14 more by the author only.[c]

DURATION OF COPYRIGHT FOR WORKS CREATED BEFORE 1978

Works created after the effective date of the 1976 Act are entitled to the single term of copyright provided in § 302. The 1976 Act also makes elaborate arrangements for works that were already under copyright when the 1976 Act took effect on Jan. 1, 1978. Under the 1909 Copyright Act, copyright protection lasted for an initial term of 28 years, with a renewal term available for an additional 28 years. For existing copyrights already in their twenty-eight year renewal term when the 1976 Act took effect, § 304(b) as originally enacted provided that the copyright would endure for 75 years rather than the 56 years granted under the old statute. In the expectation that the slowly emerging copyright revision bill would extend the terms of existing copyrights, Congress had already begun extending the terms of renewed copyrights in 1962 and continued this process until the

---

[c]   A few old copyrights produce handsome returns all the way to expiration. *Happy Birthday to You*, written by the Hill sisters in 1935—and still under copyright—pulls in about $2 million a year in royalties. Cato, City May Owe Royalty If It Sings "Happy Birthday," Pittsburgh Tribune Rev., Aug. 31, 2008. (What kinds of uses would you imagine are the primary contributors to this royalty stream?) The complicated history of *Happy Birthday to You* and its dubious copyright is recounted R. Brauneis, Copyright and the World's Most Popular Song, 56 J.Copyr.Soc'y 335 (2009). R. Spoo, Three Myths for Aging Copyrights: Tithonus, Dorian Gray, and Ulysses, 31 Cardozo Arts & Ent.L.J. 77 (2012), counts the cultural costs of the vigorous assertions of copyright by the estate of James Joyce in the author's almost century-old works.

1976 Act was passed. Accordingly, all renewal copyrights that would otherwise have expired after 1962 were still subsisting on Jan. 1, 1978, and eligible for the extension to 75 years.[d] In 1998, the Copyright Term Extension Act upheld in *Eldred* amended § 304(b) to add twenty additional years to the duration of copyright for works that were still in their extended renewal term at the time of the Extension Act, thus providing those works with a total term of 95 years.

For existing copyrights that were in their first twenty-eight year term when the 1976 Act took effect in 1978, § 304(a) as initially enacted required the owner to file a renewal application in order to obtain an additional term of 47 years, for a total duration of 75 years. Effective on June 26, 1992, § 304(a) was amended to grant the renewal term automatically to copyrights still then in their first term, thus doing away with the need for a renewal application. However, there was still an incentive to file a renewal application. Failure to file an application for renewal registration in the year preceding expiration of the original term deprived the renewal owner of the right to prevent continued exploitation of authorized derivative works prepared by others during the original term. (See § 304(a)(4)(A) and Stewart v. Abend, p. 526 infra.). Despite the incentive, reports from the Copyright Office indicate that renewal registrations went down dramatically after the advent of automatic renewal.[e] In 1998, as part of the Copyright Term Extension Act, the renewal term in § 304(a) was extended from 47 to 67 years, thus providing a total copyright term of 95 years.

NOTES AND QUESTIONS

(1) It was the lengthening of existing copyrights that made the 1998 Copyright Term Extension Act particularly controversial. The extension postponed the imminent entry into the public domain of works that include novels by Ernest Hemingway and F. Scott Fitzgerald, movies like as *Casablanca*, *The Wizard of Oz*, and *Gone With the Wind*, music such as George Gershwin's *Rhapsody in Blue*, and Disney characters Mickey Mouse, Donald Duck, Goofy, and Pluto. Critics see a certain irony in Disney's successful push for the extension, noting that many of Disney's most popular works, including *Snow White*, *The Jungle Book*, *Pinocchio*, and *Treasure Island*, were based on public domain stories. See Streitfeld, The Cultural Anarchist vs. The Hollywood Police State, L.A. Times, Sept. 22, 2002, p. I10. A statistical analysis of copyrighted and public domain works of fiction offered in P. Heald, Property Rights and the Efficient Exploitation of Copyrighted Works, 92 Minn.L.Rev. 1031 (2008), challenges the asser-

---

[d]   An extraordinary special-interest extension of copyright was enacted in 1971 when the copyright in all editions of Mary Baker Eddy's *Science and Health with Key to the Scriptures* was extended for an *additional* period of 75 years. Priv.Law 92–60, 92d Cong. (1971). First published in 1875 and last revised by the author in 1906, copyright in the 1906 edition was subsisting as a result of the interim extensions described above. The 75–year extension was struck down under the establishment clause of the first amendment in United Christian Scientists v. Christian Science Board of Directors, First Church of Christ, Scientist, 829 F.2d 1152 (D.C.Cir.1987).

[e]   Since the first twenty-eight year term of copyright for all works published prior to the 1978 effective date of the 1976 Copyright Act has now expired, it is too late to gain the control over existing derivative works that was available if a timely renewal application had been filed. To assist users in determining the copyright status of works whose initial copyright term expired prior to the advent of automatic renewal in 1992, Stanford University Libraries and Academic Information Resources have created an on-line database of renewal records for works published between 1923 and 1963. See http://collections.stanford.edu/copyrightrenewals.

tion that the lack of continuing copyright protection results in inefficient exploitation of a work; R. Bard and L. Kurlantzick, Copyright Duration at the Millennium, 47 J.Copyr. Soc'y 13 (2000), use the term extension to demonstrate the costs imposed when producers' interests dominate over economic analysis and social interests in the formulation of copyright policy.

(2) Debate over the wisdom and legitimacy of the copyright term extension has been extensive. See T. Nachbar, Constructing Copyright's Mythology, 6 Green Bag 2d 37 (2002), expressing skepticism about the extension opponents' appeals to a romanticized vision of copyright, and C. Dallon, Original Intent and the Copyright Clause: *Eldred v. Ashcroft* Gets It Right, 50 St. Louis L.J. 307 (2006), concluding that *Eldred* is correct as a matter of constitutional law; S. Fischer, Threatening the Founding Ideal of a Republic of Letters, 5 Akron Intell.Prop.J. 205 (2011), worries that decisions like *Eldred* will undermine public confidence in copyright law. R. Ku, J. Sun, and Y. Fan, Does Copyright Law Promote Creativity? An Empirical Analysis of Copyright's Bounty, 62 Vand.L.Rev. 1669 (2009), uses a statistical analysis of copyright registrations to conclude that there is no predictable relationship between changes in copyright law and the number of new works produced.

Will there be another Copyright Term Extension Act when the extra years added in 1998 are about to expire? T. Lee, *Eldred v. Ashcroft* and the (Hypothetical) Copyright Term Extension Act of 2020, 12 Tex.Intell.Prop.L.J. 1 (2003), examines the implications of *Eldred* for future extension legislation.

(3) Two recent articles take a different perspective on copyright duration, arguing that as a work moves further into its copyright term, the scope of permissible fair use should increase. See J. Liu, Copyright and Time: A Proposal, 101 Mich.L.Rev. 409 (2002), and J. Hughes, Fair Use Across Time, 50 UCLA L.Rev. 775 (2003).

(4) In response to a Senate request, the Copyright Office undertook a study of so-called "orphan works"—works whose copyright owner cannot be identified or located by persons wishing to make use of the work. With the elimination of formalities as a prerequisite to copyright and the increasing duration of protection, more and more works are likely to become orphaned. In its 2006 Report on Orphan Works, the Copyright Office recommended legislation to facilitate the use of orphan works. Bills introduced in Congress would have limited liability for the use of a work if the user was unable to locate the owner despite a qualifying, good faith search; if the owner later resurfaced, remedies would be limited to "reasonable compensation" for the use. 77 Pat., Tm. & Copyr.J. (BNA) 75 (2008). Professional photographers have been the most vocal opponents of orphan works legislation. 75 id. 526. Why are *they* particularly concerned? In 2012 the Copyright Office announced a new inquiry into the orphan works issue, with special emphasis on the problems that orphan works create in the context of mass digitization efforts like Google's Library Project.

(5) While examining a box of manuscripts at the Mark Twain Papers, a major research collection at the University of California at Berkeley, a graduate student uncovers an unpublished manuscript on copyright law written by Samuel Clemens in 1898. (Clemens died in 1910.) The student would like to publish the manuscript in a book of Clemens' writings on law. Is it in the public domain? See § 303 on the duration of copyright in works that were unpublished when the 1976 Act took effect.

(6) Peter Hirtle of the Cornell University Library tells the story of a letter written in 1755 by John Adams. All rights in the letter were transferred to the Massachusetts Historical Society, which first published the letter and registered the copyright in 1956 and filed a renewal in 1984. When will John Adams' letter be in the public domain? P. Hirtle, When is 1923 Going to Arrive and Other Complications of the U.S. Public Domain, 20 Searcher 7 (Sept. 2012).

SUMMARY OF COPYRIGHT TERMS

Works published before 1923	Public domain. (Even if renewed, the 47–year extended renewal term that followed the 28–year first term would have expired prior to the 20–year term extension in 1998.)
Works published with copyright notice between 1923 and 1963	28 years, with an additional 67–year renewal term if the copyright was renewed, for a maximum duration of 95 years.
Works published with copyright notice between 1964 and 1977	95 years. (Renewal for a 67–year renewal term following the 28–year first term became automatic in 1992.)
Works created before 1978 but not published when the 1976 Act took effect on Jan. 1, 1978	Life of the author plus 70 years or until the end of 2002, whichever is longer. If the work was published before 2003 (and if the copyright notice or cure provisions were satisfied for any pre–1989 publications), life of the author plus 70 years or until the end of 2047, whichever is longer.
Works created after the 1976 Act took effect on Jan. 1, 1978 (if the copyright notice or cure provisions were satisfied for any pre–1989 publications)	Life of the author plus 70 years; for anonymous, pseudonymous, or works made for hire, 95 years from publication or 120 years from creation, whichever expires first.

NOTES AND QUESTIONS ON RENEWAL—§ 304(A)

(1) Under the 1909 Act, the right to the renewal term of a copyright belonged to the author if living, otherwise to the author's spouse, children, executor, or next of kin. This scheme is continued in § 304(a) of the 1976 Act for works that were still in their first term of copyright when the 1976 Act took effect in 1978. This reversion of the renewal term to the author or her statutory successors reflected a paternalistic attempt to protect authors from an improvident assignment of rights during the initial copyright term. In Fred Fisher Music Co. v. M. Witmark & Sons, 318 U.S. 643 (1943), the Supreme Court faced this issue: "Concededly, the author can assign the original copyright and, after he has secured it, the renewal copyright as well. The question is—does the Act prevent the author from assigning his interest in the renewal copyright before he has secured it?" Justice Frankfurter, arguing that a rule against advance transfers of the renewal term would prevent authors from selling an asset when they might be most in need, concluded that authors were not precluded from assigning their renewal rights during the initial term. Assignees thus often demanded that authors assign rights in both the initial and renewal terms. An assignee's right to the renewal term, however, was precarious, since it was also accepted that an author's advance assignment was effective only if the author was still living when the time came for renewal; unless the author's statutory successors had joined in the assignment, they took the renewal term despite a prior assignment by the deceased author.

Assignees rights are still contingent

(2) Suppose that an author during the original term of a pre–1978 copyright assigned the copyright and the renewal term to his friend A. The author then died prior to the end of the original term. He had no widow or children. Under his will, the author's residual estate, including any copyrights, passed to his nephew B. Who owns the renewal term under § 304(a)(1)(C)? See Miller Music Corp. v. Charles N. Daniels, Inc., 362 U.S. 373 (1960), holding that the executor's statutory succession is free of any obligations arising from the deceased author's prior assignment.

(3) Must the author, in order for an assignment of the renewal right to be effective, survive until the first day of the twenty-eighth year, the date on which the renewal application is filed, or through the end of the twenty-eighth year? As a result of the amendments made by Pub.L. 102–307 (1992), § 304(a)(2)(B) provides that if a renewal application had been filed in the year preceding expiration of the original term, the renewal term vests in the person who was entitled to claim the renewal at the time the application was filed; in the absence of a renewal application, the renewal term vests in whomever was entitled to claim it as of the end of the original term. The rule was applied in Roger Miller Music, Inc. v. Sony/ATV Publishing, LLC, 672 F.3d 434 (6th Cir.2012), to confirm ownership in the songwriter's assignee since the writer was living when the assignee filed an application to register the renewal copyright, even though he died before the start of the renewal term.

1st day or last day or date of renewal

• If in year preceding → vests in person entitled

(4) How is the renewal term shared among a surviving widow and two children under § 304(a)(1)(C)? Cf. § 304(c)(2) and § 203(a)(2), which specify half to the surviving spouse and half to the children following the termination of an assignment and which influenced the court in Broadcast Music, Inc. v. Roger Miller Music, Inc., 396 F.3d 762 (6th Cir.), cert. denied, 546 U.S. 871 (2005), to adopt the same rule for renewal interests. The First Circuit agreed in Venegas–Hernandez v. Asociacion De Compositores, 424 F.3d 50 (1st Cir.2005).

(5) The creators of Superman, Siegel and Shuster, were bound by a contract with National Comics. In a state court action in 1948, facing a likely judgment that they had in 1938 conveyed "all rights" in Superman to National, they agreed to a settlement including a consent judgment that recited that they had validly transferred "all of their rights in and to the comic strip Superman." Later, they claimed rights in the renewal term. The Second Circuit held that the consent judgment was res judicata and that it included the renewal rights even

Consented to valid transfer

though those words had not been used. Siegel v. National Periodical Pub., 508 F.2d 909 (2d Cir.1974). Absent the consent judgment, would that be the proper interpretation of an assignment of "all rights"? Cf. Corcovado Music Corp. v. Hollis Music, Inc., 981 F.2d 679 (2d Cir.1993), invoking a presumption against inclusion of the renewal term if the contract did not expressly refer to future rights. A grant of rights "in perpetuity," however, was found sufficient to include the renewal term in P.C. Films Corp. v. MGM/UA Home Video Inc., 138 F.3d 453 (2d Cir.), cert. denied, 525 U.S. 1017 (1998).

On the various workings of the renewal scheme, see F. Nevins, The Magic Kingdom of Will Bumping: Where Estates Law and Copyright Law Collide, 35 J.Copyr. Soc'y 77 (1988).

————————

TERMINATION OF TRANSFERS

(1) One advantage of a renewal term is that it gave give authors a second bite at the apple. With the single term of copyright for post–1977 works, a new mechanism was needed to maintain this benefit for authors. Section 203 provides for an inalienable power, exercisable by the author, or the author's surviving spouse and issue, to terminate any assignment or license granted by the author after Jan. 1, 1978 otherwise than by will. This power can be exercised during a five-year period that begins 35 years after the execution of the grant. (If the grant covers the right to publish the work, the termination period begins at the earlier of 35 years from the publication under the grant or 40 years from execution.) With the experience under the renewal procedures of the 1909 Act to guide them, the drafters produced an intricate scheme that avoids most of the infelicities of those rules, while doubtless creating others. Compare the problems that have arisen in the interpretation of the renewal rules in § 304(a) and see if you can find reactions to them in § 203. See H.R.Rep. pp. 124–28.

The right in § 203 to terminate post–1977 transfers and licenses of copyrights after 35 years finally came into play in 2013. In one early dispute over the validity of a § 203 termination notice, Victor Willis, lead singer of the Village People, won dismissal of a challenge to his notice seeking to reclaim his copyright interests in thirty-three musical compositions including *YMCA* and *In the Navy*. Scorpio Music S.A. v. Willis, 102 U.S.P.Q.2d 1606 (S.D.Cal.2012). A suggestion to amend the termination of transfer rules in § 203 to provide a mechanism to protect authors who are minors at the time of a transfer is offered in J. Young, From the Mouths of Babes: Protecting Child Authors from Themselves, 112 W.Va.L.Rev. 431 (2010).

(2) Consider also the operation of § 304(c), which creates a right parallel but not quite identical to § 203 applicable to the termination of pre–1978 assignments and licenses; it can be invoked within five years after the 56th year of copyright to recapture for the author or the author's statutory successors the 39 years that have been added to subsisting copyrights. For example, popular songwriters including Paul McCartney, Bob Dylan, and Willie Nelson have filed § 304(c) termination notices to reclaim songs assigned to music publishers in the 1950s and 1960s. Christman, Going for a Song, Billboard, March 30, 2013, p. 28.

One case that arose under this termination provision stemmed from an attempt by the heirs of Edgar Rice Burroughs to terminate under § 304(c) a

1931 grant to MGM that authorized it to use the character Tarzan in an original screenplay and remakes of that screenplay. The action was aimed at stopping a 1981 remake starring Bo Derek as Jane. The Second Circuit held that the notice of termination was ineffective because it failed to list five Tarzan books encompassed by the original grant. The bulk of the opinion is an engaging exploration of copying: had MGM, in view of changing times and mores (it maintained that the 1981 version appropriately subordinated violence in favor of nudity) stuck to its 1931 screenplay as required by the license or had it infringed the original Tarzan story? The court found no breach of MGM's contractual obligation to follow the original screenplay. Burroughs v. Metro–Goldwyn–Mayer, Inc., 683 F.2d 610 (2d Cir.1982).

(3) In 1998 the Copyright Term Extension Act added a new termination right in § 304(d). For works in their renewal term at the time of the Extension Act, it creates a new right to terminate pre–1978 transfers and licenses if the § 304(c) 56th-year termination right had already expired unexercised. The § 304(d) termination right (available for five years beginning at the end of the 75th year of copyright) thus provides an opportunity in such circumstances for the author or the author's successors to regain the copyright for the twenty years added by the 1998 Copyright Term Extension Act.[f]

(4) With Fred Fisher Music v. Witmark, p. 497 supra, surely in mind, the drafters attempted to make certain that termination rights could not be lost before they became exercisable by allowing termination "notwithstanding any agreement to the contrary." See § 203(a)(5) and § 304(c)(5). "These limitations," Professor Nimmer once observed, "are subject to all of the challenges that the ingenuity of the bar representing so-called user groups can muster." Does your ingenuity suggest any?

Alan Alexander Milne, author of the "Winnie the Pooh" children's books, licensed rights to Slesinger in 1930, who later assigned the rights to Walt Disney. Faced with the possibility that Milne's son, Christopher, might terminate the original grant to Slesinger under § 304(c), Disney and Christopher renegotiated the rights in 1983. In 2002, Christopher's daughter, Clare, filed a notice to terminate the 1930 license under § 304(d). The court in Milne v. Stephen Slesinger, Inc., 430 F.3d 1036 (9th Cir.2005), cert. denied, 548 U.S. 904 (2006), held that the 1930 grant had been terminated by the new agreement in 1983, and hence there was no grant "executed before January 1, 1978" to be terminated under § 304(d). Clare argued that the 1983 agreement was an invalid "agreement to the contrary" under § 304(c)(5) that could not prevent termination of the original grant. Judge Callahan concluded that the renegotiated agreement "exemplifies the increased bargaining power that Congress intended to bestow on authors" through the statutory termination right and said that the legislative history indicated that Congress explicitly endorsed the right of the parties to terminate an existing grant and negotiate a new one. An analogous result was reached by the Second Circuit in Penguin Group (USA) Inc. v. Steinbeck, 537 F.3d 193 (2d Cir.2008), cert. denied, 129 S.Ct.. 2383 (2009). John Steinbeck had executed a publishing agreement in 1938 covering some of his most famous works. On his death in 1968, he bequeathed his interests in the copyrights to his widow, Elaine. In 1994 she entered into a new agreement with the holder of the publishing rights. A year after Elaine's death in 2003, Steinbeck's surviving son, together with the surviv-

---

[f]   A software tool to help authors navigate the thicket of termination windows and deadlines under §§ 203 and 304 is available at http://labs.creativecommons.org/termination.

ing child of Steinbeck's deceased son, filed a notice to terminate the 1938 publishing grant under § 304(d). The publisher sought a declaratory judgment that the termination notice was invalid. The court agreed, holding that the 1994 agreement had terminated the original grant. The court also held that the 1994 agreement was not an invalid "agreement to the contrary" under § 304(c)(5). "There is no indication in the statutory text or the legislative history of the Copyright Act that elimination of a termination right through termination of a pre–1978 contractual grant was to be precluded or was undesirable."

In Classic Media, Inc. v. Mewborn, 532 F.3d 978 (9th Cir.2008), the Ninth Circuit distinguished its decision in Milne v. Slesinger when the daughter of Eric Knight, author of *Lassie Come Home*, sought to terminate a grant of television and movie rights in the story under § 304(c). The current owner, citing *Milne*, argued that a subsequent grant had replaced the original grant, which was thus no longer available for statutory termination. The court held that here the later grant had not revoked the initial one, but instead simply assigned additional rights. But the court also emphasized that *Milne* was different because there the second grant was made at a time when the first grant could have been terminated under the statute, thus providing the grantor with the bargaining leverage that the termination provisions were meant to create. Here, the new grant was made well before the original grant could have been terminated. "Thus, unlike Milne, Mewborn had nothing in hand with which to bargain," and the subsequent notice terminating the original grant was effective.

(5) The widow and daughter of Superman co-creator Jerome Siegel won a summary judgment that they had successfully exercised their right under § 304(c) to terminate Siegel's 1938 assignment of the Superman copyright to Detective Comics for $130. Siegel v. Warner Bros. Ent. Inc., 542 F.Supp.2d 1098 (C.D.Cal.2008).[g] Judge Larson pointed out that under § 304(c)(6)(E), Warner Brothers and DC Comics still retained unfettered rights to the Superman character in foreign countries. In the U.S., they were now co-owners of the copyright with the plaintiffs and must account for profits from U.S. exploitation. That co-ownership interest arose from the fact that no termination notice had been filed with respect to the 1938 assignment by Siegel's co-creator, Joseph Shuster. Section 304(d) gave Shuster's heirs another opportunity to terminate the assignment at the end of 75 years, and his estate filed the required termination notice. In DC Comics v. Pacific Pictures Corp., 104 U.S.P.Q.2d 1596 (C.D.Cal.2012), the court found that a 1992 agreement between DC Comics and Shuster's brother and sister had superseded the prior transfer and regranted the rights to DC for $25,000 per year. Citing the *Milne* and *Steinbeck* cases, the court held that there was thus no longer any pre-1978 grant to terminate under § 304(d).

(6) In Mills Music, Inc. v. Snyder, 469 U.S. 153 (1985), the Supreme Court decided a § 304(c) case arising out of an important exception to the termination right:

---

[g]   In a later decision the district court found that almost all of the subsequent work done by Jerome Siegel on Superman was work for hire under the 1909 Act and thus not subject to termination. Siegel v. Warner Bros. Ent. Inc., 658 F.Supp.2d 1036 (C.D.Cal.2009). The Ninth Circuit subsequently concluded that Siegel's heirs were bound by a post-termination agreement with Warner Bros. that settled the terms for future use. Larson v. Warner Bros. Ent., Inc., 2013 WL 1113259 (9th Cir.2013) (unpublished). Absent the agreement, what kinds of uses of the character could Warner Bros. make without infringing the terminated rights?

A derivative work prepared under authority of the grant before its termination may continue to be utilized under the terms of the grant after its termination, but this privilege does not extend to the preparation after the termination of other derivative works based on the copyrighted work covered by the terminated grant. § 304(c)(6)(A); see also § 203(b)(1).

This was overtly intended to respond to the complaints of moviemakers that, in view of their mammoth investment in making a film, the author of a story from which the film derived should not be in a position to block exhibition of the film by terminating the grant.

In the music industry, composers routinely assign their copyrights to music publishers who license a variety of uses, usually keeping half of the proceeds. *Mills Music* dealt with recording rights to a 1923 standard, "Who's Sorry Now." Snyder, one of the authors of the song, had transferred the renewal copyright to a music publisher, Mills Music, in exchange for an advance payment and 50% of the recording royalties. Mills Music, through the Harry Fox Agency, had issued more than 400 recording licenses for the song, including renditions by Judy Garland, Liza Minelli, and Nat King Cole. The recording rights were still pumping out $15,000 a year to the Harry Fox Agency, which brought this interpleader action to ascertain whether it should continue to pay 50% of the royalties to Mills Music now that Snyder had exercised his § 304(c) right to terminate his grant of the renewal term to Mills Music.

Mills Music maintained that the right to continue to utilize a derivative work under § 304(c)(6)(A), a right which the record-makers clearly enjoyed, also protected its own right to royalties. Surprisingly, the drafters had not expressly addressed the status of an intermediate grantee (from the author) who is the grantor (to the record companies) of the protected derivative right.

The Supreme Court, in a 5–4 decision, held in favor of Mills Music. Justice Stevens found the "key" to the dispute in the statutory right to continue use of a derivative work "under the terms of the grant"—a phrase that he read "to encompass the original grant from Snyder to Mills."

" * * * If the Exception is narrowly read to exclude Mills from its coverage, thus protecting only the class of 'utilizers' as the Snyders wish, the crucial link between the record companies and the Snyders will be missing, and the record companies will have no contractual obligation to pay royalties to the Snyders. If the statute is read to preserve the total contractual relationship, which entitled Mills to make duly authorized derivative works, the record companies continue to be bound by the terms of their licenses, including any terms requiring them to continue to pay royalties to Mills."

Four dissenters, led by Justice White, remained unconvinced:

"The majority places great emphasis on indications that Congress was aware of multi-party arrangements in the movie and music-publishing industries, positing from this awareness an intention to extend the benefits of the Exception to middlemen such as Mills. But the majority cites not one word to indicate that Congress did in fact contemplate such a result when it enacted the Exception. * * * That middlemen such as music publishers were to be excluded from the benefits conferred by the Exception is strongly supported by statements to that effect by music publishers themselves, made in the discussions that took place before the Copyright Office. When a version of the Exception first appeared in the 1964 preliminary draft bill, representatives of the music publishing industry protested. A representative of the Music Publishers Association of the United States stated that under the proposed exception, 'the royalties resulting from the license presumably rever[t] entirely to the author.'[5] A spokesman for the Music Publishers Protective Association construed the exception as being 'for the benefit of everyone acquiring rights under a copyright other than the publisher.'[6]"

Mills Music is thoroughly analyzed in H. Abrams, Who's Sorry Now? Termination Rights and the Derivative Works Exception, 62 U.Det.L.Rev. 181 (1985). Abrams cautiously concludes that the intention, at least of the Copyright Office drafters, was to give all of the reversion to the author. At a 1985 hearing on an unsuccessful bill to change the outcome in Mills Music, former Register of Copyrights Barbara Ringer declared, "It was my pen that drafted the section." Mills Music, she said, is "just dead wrong." 32 Pat., Tm. & Copyr.J. (BNA) 82 (1985).

(7) The scope of the § 304(c)(6)(A) right to continued use of pre-termination derivative works came before the Second Circuit in Fred Ahlert Music Corp. v. Warner/Chappell Music, Inc., 155 F.3d 17 (2d Cir.1998). Prior to termination, the defendant music publisher had authorized the use of the copyrighted song "Bye Bye Blackbird" in a sound recording by Joe Cocker. After termination, with the permission of the successor-in-interest to the composer's heirs, an edited version of that sound recording was used on the soundtrack of the motion picture Sleepless in Seattle. When the movie soundtrack album was released, the defendant publisher claimed a right to royalties from the album as a post-termination use of a pre-termination derivative work. Judge Walker said that the issue was whether the use of the pre-termination recording on the movie soundtrack was a use covered by the terms of the terminated grant. That in turn depended on the terms of both the original grant from the composer to the defendant publisher and the terms of the publisher's subsequent grant authorizing the production of the Joe Cocker derivative work. Since the latter grant was limited to use of the song on a record, use on the movie soundtrack did not fall within the exception for continued use of derivative works produced under authority of the terminated grant. (The opinion also illustrates an important limitation on the ability to terminate transfers and licenses. Only domestic rights are affected by a termination. See § 304(c)(6)(E).)

(8) Note that termination rights do not exist in works made for hire. §§ 203(a), 304(c),(d). What is the purpose of this exception? To protect employers from terminations by employees? (Does an employer own a work for hire by virtue of a "transfer or license" that could otherwise be terminated under § 203 or § 304? See § 201(b).) To exclude grants made by employers, who are presumptively less in need of protection against unremunerative transfers?

The Second Circuit in Marvel Characters, Inc. v. Simon, 310 F.3d 280 (2d Cir.2002), rationalized the exclusion of works for hire from the termination provisions this way: "Because an employer-publisher does not face the

⁵ Preliminary Draft for Revised U.S. Copyright Law and Discussions and Comments on the Draft, 88th Cong., 2d Sess., Copyright Law Revision, Part 3, pp. 284–285 (H. Judiciary Comm. Print 1964) (statement of Phillip Wattenberg). See also id., at 296–297 (termination clause, including exception, would give author 100% of royalties) (statement of Mr. Kaminstein).

⁶ Id., at 318–319 (written submission of Julian Abeles). * * *

same potential unequal bargaining position as an individual author, it follows that an employer-publisher does not need the same protections as an individual author." The court also held that the rule in § 304(c)(5) permitting termination "notwithstanding any agreement to the contrary" allowed a party who had conceded in an earlier settlement agreement that the work was made for hire to argue that in fact the work was not for hire and thus subject to the termination provisions. Otherwise, Judge McLaughlin said, "litigation-savvy publishers would be able to utilize their superior bargaining position to compel authors to agree that a work was created for hire," thus nullifying the termination right.[h]

(9) Suppose Author created a work in 1969. In 1975 she assigned the copyright, including the renewal term, to Publisher, and the work was first published with a notice of copyright in that year. Author died in 2005, leaving a spouse, daughter, and two grandchildren of a deceased son. When can the assignment to Publisher be terminated, and who must sign the notice of termination? See § 304(c)(1)–(4).

(10) Suppose Author created a work in 1969 and first published the work with a notice of copyright in 1975. In 1985 she assigned the copyright, including the renewal term, to Publisher. Author dies in 2005, leaving a spouse, daughter, and two grandchildren of a deceased son. When can the assignment to Publisher be terminated, and who must sign the notice of termination? See § 203(a)(1)–(4).

2. TRANSFERS OF INTERESTS: ASSIGNMENTS AND LICENSES

The chief economic value of a work often lies, not in its exploitation in the form originally created by the author, but rather in the exploitation of forms derived from it, such as a motion picture based on a novel or play. The author is often incapable of transforming the work into other artistic media and is usually incapable of managing the commercial exploitation of the work either in its original form or in any of its derivative forms. Hence the multitudinous transfers of interests, large and small, in copyrights.

We can assume that in early days transfers of interests in copyrights tended to be transfers of all rights. Even when the rights had obviously been divided, there was still a certain convenience in locating "the copyright" in one person so that in the event of infringement there would be a single person having the right to sue—a means of avoiding multiple suits and recoveries. The owner of a copyright by transfer was denominated an assignee, and subtle disputes abound in the older cases about whether particular transfers were an assignment or a license. In early cases it was said that only a transfer of all the rights comprised in the copyright could make the transferee an assignee; a transfer of less than all rights made the transferee a mere licensee who did not have standing to sue for infringement. This was an example of the concept of "indivisibility" of copyright.

---

[h]   A battle over superheroes is taking shape as a result of termination notices filed by the heirs of Jack Kirby, who created many of the Marvel Comics characters now owned by Walt Disney. Kirby's wife and children filed termination notices under § 304(c) in connection with Kirby's work on Marvel characters such as the Fantastic Four, Incredible Hulk, X–Men, Spiderman, Thor, and Iron Man. In a declaratory judgment action brought by Marvel, Judge McMahon held that Kirby's contributions were works for hire and thus not subject to termination. Marvel Worldwide, Inc. v. Kirby, 777 F.Supp.2d 720 (S.D.N.Y.2011).

The 1976 Act in § 201(d)(2) and in the definition of "copyright owner" in § 101 goes pretty much all out in eliminating "indivisibility" and authorizing separate transfer and ownership of the rights that comprise a copyright. The concept of a "transfer of copyright ownership" as defined in § 101 now turns on whether the recipient obtains an exclusive or nonexclusive right.[i]

Section 204(a) says that a "transfer of copyright ownership" is not valid "unless an instrument of conveyance, or a note or memorandum of the transfer, is in writing and signed by the owner." The writing requirement has been interpreted to apply also to *agreements* to transfer copyright ownership. See Valente–Kritzer Video v. Pinckney, 881 F.2d 772 (9th Cir.1989), cert denied, 493 U.S. 1062 (1990). What functions does the writing requirement serve? Do the rationales for the requirement exclude writings that are not contemporaneous with the purported transfer? Judge Kozinski was emphatic in Konigsberg Int'l Inc. v. Rice, 16 F.3d 355 (9th Cir.1994), that to comply with § 204(a), "the writing in question must, at the very least, be executed more or less contemporaneously with the agreement and must be a product of the parties' negotiations." But the Ninth Circuit later distinguished *Konigsberg* and held that an oral assignment can be confirmed by a subsequent writing, at least when it is a third party who complains about the delay. Magnuson v. Video Yesteryear, 85 F.3d 1424 (9th Cir.1996). The Seventh Circuit in Billy–Bob Teeth, Inc. v. Novelty, Inc., 329 F.3d 586 (7th Cir.2003), went further, stating flatly that the statute of frauds in § 204(a) is intended to resolve disputes between the copyright owner and the transferee, and hence third parties do not have standing to object to the absence of a writing memorializing an assignment. In Schiller & Schmidt, Inc. v. Nordisco Corp., 969 F.2d 410 (7th Cir.1992), Judge Posner held that the writing required under § 204(a) need not mention the word "copyright"; an agreement for the sale of a photography business, including negatives, carried with it the copyrights in the photographs.[j]

Judge Kozinski had previously invoked § 204(a) to defeat a claimed assignment in Effects Associates, Inc. v. Cohen, 908 F.2d 555 (9th Cir.1990), cert. denied, 498 U.S. 1103 (1991) ("It doesn't have to be the Magna Charta; a one-line pro forma statement will do," rejecting defendant's "Moviemakers do lunch, not contracts" defense); however, he concluded on the facts that an implied, nonexclusive license (which does not require a writing since it is not a "transfer of copyright ownership" under the § 101 definition) arose from the transfer to a movie studio of film footage showing the destruction of "an alien life form that looks (and tastes) like frozen yogurt" for use in a motion picture. The Ninth Circuit in Foad Consulting Group, Inc. v. Azzalino, 270 F.3d 821 (9th Cir.2001), emphasizing that state law determines whether an implied, non-exclusive license has arisen, found that a contract for the creation of a plot plan for a shopping center made

---

[i]   Although an exclusive license is a "transfer of copyright ownership" under the definition in § 101, an exclusive licensee's ownership does not carry with it the right to further assign or sublicense its rights according to Gardner v. Nike, Inc., 279 F.3d 774 (9th Cir.2002).

[j]   See Playboy Enter., Inc. v. Dumas, 53 F.3d 549 (2d Cir.), cert. denied, 516 U.S. 1010 (1995), deferring to the district court's determination that a legend on a check stating that endorsement acknowledges assignment "of all right, title and interest" in the described works was insufficient to evidence an intent to assign the copyright as opposed to one-time publication rights. A university's policy statement that copyright in works resulting from the performance of university duties belonged to the employee was found insufficient under § 204(a) to transfer copyright ownership in a work made for hire when a university employee claimed copyright in photographs taken at the direction of the university. Foraste v. Brown University, 290 F.Supp.2d 234 (D.R.I.2003).

between an engineering firm and a developer gave rise to an implied license for the developer to reproduce and adapt the plan and distribute it to prospective tenants.[k]

These materials furnish only a brief introduction to the question of how transferees of interests in published and unpublished works can assure themselves that they are getting what they think they have bargained for and that they will not be cut off by interests of whose existence they may be quite justifiably ignorant. The recordation of transfers provisions in § 205 give some assurances, but surely do not eliminate the problem. It is hard to imagine a recording system for this species of property that could approach the efficiency of modern land recording systems.[l]

3. CONTRACT INTERPRETATION WITH RESPECT TO NEW USES

Boosey & Hawkes Music Publishers, Ltd. v. Walt Disney Co.

United States Court of Appeals, Second Circuit, 1998.
145 F.3d 481.

■ Before LEVAL AND PARKER, CIRCUIT JUDGES, and BAER, DISTRICT JUDGE.

■ LEVAL, CIRCUIT JUDGE:

Boosey & Hawkes Music Publishers Ltd., an English corporation and the assignee of Igor Stravinsky's copyrights for "The Rite of Spring," brought this action alleging that the Walt Disney Company's foreign distribution in video cassette and laser disc format ("video format") of the film "Fantasia," featuring Stravinsky's work, infringed Boosey's rights. In 1939 Stravinsky licensed Disney's distribution of The Rite of Spring in the motion picture. Boosey, which acquired Stravinsky's copyright in 1947, contends that the license does not authorize distribution in video format.

The district court (Duffy, J.) granted partial summary judgment to Boosey, declaring that Disney's video format release was not authorized by the license agreement. Disney appeals from that ruling. * * *

---

[k] An organization called the Creative Commons at www.creativecommons.org assists authors who are willing to license their work to the public on generous terms such as unrestricted noncommercial use or any use with attribution to the author. Software is sometimes distributed under a variety of "open source" licenses that may allow free use and modification of the software and sometimes require that distributions of new versions created by users be on the same terms as the original license. In Jacobsen v. Katzer, 535 F.3d 1373 (Fed.Cir.2008), the court held that use of a work in violation of the terms of an "open source" license was actionable as copyright infringement. T. Armstrong, Shrinking the Commons: Termination of Copyright Licenses and Transfers for the Benefit of the Public, 47 Harv.J.Leg. 359 (2010), worries about the effect of the termination provisions on Creative Commons and other "open content" licenses.

[l] Where should security interests in copyrights be filed? According to the Ninth Circuit, "[W]hen a copyright has been registered, a security interest can be perfected only by recording the transfer in the Copyright Office. * * * [B]ecause unregistered copyrights don't have a registered name and number, under the Copyright Act there isn't any place to file anything regarding unregistered copyrights that makes any legal difference. So, as a matter of state law, the U.C.C. doesn't step back in deference to federal law, but governs perfection and priority of security interests in unregistered copyrights itself." In re World Auxiliary Power Co., 303 F.3d 1120 (9th Cir.2002).

During 1938, Disney sought Stravinsky's authorization to use The Rite of Spring (sometimes referred to as the "work" or the "composition") throughout the world in a motion picture. Because under United States law the work was in the public domain, Disney needed no authorization to record or distribute it in this country, but permission was required for distribution in countries where Stravinsky enjoyed copyright protection. In January 1939 the parties executed an agreement (the "1939 Agreement") giving Disney rights to use the work in a motion picture in consideration of a fee to Stravinsky of $6000.

The 1939 Agreement provided that

> In consideration of the sum of Six Thousand ($6,000) Dollars, receipt of which is hereby acknowledged, [Stravinsky] does hereby give and grant unto Walt Disney Enterprises, a California corporation ... the nonexclusive, irrevocable right, license, privilege and authority to record in any manner, medium or form, and to license the performance of, the musical composition hereinbelow set out ...

Under "type of use" in ¶ 3, the Agreement specified that

> The music of said musical composition may be used in one motion picture throughout the length thereof or through such portion or portions thereof as the Purchaser shall desire. The said music may be used in whole or in part and may be adapted, changed, added to or subtracted from, all as shall appear desirable to the Purchaser in its uncontrolled discretion .... The title "Rites of Spring" or "Le Sacre de Printemps", or any other title, may be used as the title of said motion picture and the name of [Stravinsky] may be announced in or in connection with said motion picture.

The Agreement went on to specify in ¶ 4 that Disney's license to the work "is limited to the use of the musical composition in synchronism or timed-relation with the motion picture."

Paragraph Five of the Agreement provided that

> The right to record the musical composition as covered by this agreement is conditioned upon the performance of the musical work in theatres having valid licenses from the American Society of Composers, Authors and Publishers, or any other performing rights society having jurisdiction in the territory in which the said musical composition is performed.

We refer to this clause, which is of importance to the litigation, as "the ASCAP Condition."

Finally, ¶ 7 of the Agreement provided that "the licensor reserves to himself all rights and uses in and to the said musical composition not herein specifically granted" (the "reservation clause").

Disney released Fantasia, starring Mickey Mouse, in 1940. The film contains no dialogue. It matches a pantomime of animated beasts and fantastic creatures to passages of great classical music, creating what critics celebrated as a "partnership between fine music and animated film." The soundtrack uses compositions of Bach, Beethoven, Dukas, Schubert, Tchaikovsky, and Stravinsky, all performed by the Philadelphia Orchestra under the direction of Leopold Stokowski. As it appears in the film soundtrack, The Rite of Spring was shortened from its original 34 minutes to about

22.5; sections of the score were cut, while other sections were reordered. For more than five decades Disney exhibited The Rite of Spring in Fantasia under the 1939 license. The film has been re-released for theatrical distribution at least seven times since 1940, and although Fantasia has never appeared on television in its entirety, excerpts including portions of The Rite of Spring have been televised occasionally over the years. Neither Stravinsky nor Boosey has ever previously objected to any of the distributions.

In 1991 Disney first released Fantasia in video format. The video has been sold in foreign countries, as well as in the United States. To date, the Fantasia video release has generated more than $360 million in gross revenue for Disney. * * *

* * * In determining that the license did not cover the distribution of a video format, the district court found that while the broad language of the license gave Disney "the right to record [the work] on video tape and laser disc," the ASCAP Condition "prevents Disney from distributing video tapes or laser discs directly to consumers." Boosey & Hawkes Music Publishers Ltd. v. Walt Disney Co., 934 F.Supp. 119, 123 (S.D.N.Y.1996). The court therefore concluded that Disney's video format sales exceeded the scope of the license. * * *

Boosey's request for declaratory judgment raises two issues of contract interpretation: whether the general grant of permission under the 1939 Agreement licensed Disney to use The Rite of Spring in the video format version of Fantasia (on which the district court found in Disney's favor); and, if so, whether the ASCAP Condition barred Disney from exploiting the work through video format (on which the district court found for Boosey).

1. *Whether the "motion picture" license covers video format.* Boosey contends that the license to use Stravinsky's work in a "motion picture" did not authorize distribution of the motion picture in video format, especially in view of the absence of an express provision for "future technologies" and Stravinsky's reservation of all rights not granted in the Agreement. Disputes about whether licensees may exploit licensed works through new marketing channels made possible by technologies developed after the licensing contract—often called "new-use" problems—have vexed courts since at least the advent of the motion picture. See 3 Melville B. Nimmer and David Nimmer, Nimmer on Copyright, § 10.10[A] at 10–86 (hereinafter "Nimmer"); Kirke La Shelle Co. v. Paul Armstrong Co., 263 N.Y. 79, 188 N.E. 163 (1933) (deciding whether a license for a stage production also conveyed rights in sound motion pictures).

In *Bartsch v. Metro–Goldwyn–Mayer, Inc.* we held that "licensee[s] may properly pursue any uses which may reasonably be said to fall within the medium as described in the license." 391 F.2d 150, 155 (2d Cir.1968) (Friendly, J.)(quoting Nimmer). We held in *Bartsch* that a license of motion picture rights to a play included the right to telecast the motion picture. We observed that "[i]f the words are broad enough to cover the new use, it seems fairer that the burden of framing and negotiating an exception should fall on the grantor," at least when the new medium is not completely unknown at the time of contracting. Id. at 154, 155.

The 1939 Agreement conveys the right "to record [the composition] in any manner, medium or form" for use "in [a] motion picture." We believe this language is broad enough to include distribution of the motion picture in video format. At a minimum, *Bartsch* holds that when a license includes a grant of rights that is reasonably read to cover a new use (at least where the new use was foreseeable at the time of contracting), the burden of excluding the right to the new use will rest on the grantor. 391 F.2d at 155; see also Bloom v. Hearst Entertainment Inc., 33 F.3d 518, 524–25 (5th Cir.1994) (applying *Bartsch* to hold that a grant of movie and television rights to a book encompassed video rights as well). The license "to record in any manner, medium or form" doubtless extends to videocassette recording and we can see no reason why the grant of "motion picture" reproduction rights should not include the video format, absent any indication in the Agreement to the contrary. See Bourne v. Walt Disney Co., 68 F.3d 621, 630 (2d Cir.1995); *Bloom*, 33 F.3d at 525. If a new-use license hinges on the foreseeability of the new channels of distribution at the time of contracting—a question left open in *Bartsch*—Disney has proffered unrefuted evidence that a nascent market for home viewing of feature films existed by 1939. The *Bartsch* analysis thus compels the conclusion that the license for motion picture rights extends to video format distribution.

We recognize that courts and scholars are not in complete accord on the capacity of a broad license to cover future developed markets resulting from new technologies. The Nimmer treatise describes two principal approaches to the problem. According to the first view, advocated here by Boosey, "a license of rights in a given medium (e.g., 'motion picture rights') includes only such uses as fall within the unambiguous core meaning of the term (e.g., exhibition of motion picture film in motion picture theaters) and exclude any uses that lie within the ambiguous penumbra (e.g., exhibition of motion picture on television)." Nimmer, § 10.10[B] at 10–90; see also Cohen v. Paramount Pictures Corp., 845 F.2d 851, 853–54 (9th Cir.1988) (holding that license to use musical score in television production does not extend to use in videocassette release); Rey v. Lafferty, 990 F.2d 1379, 1390–91 (1st Cir.1993) (holding that license to portray Curious George in animations for "television viewing" does not extend to videocassette release). Under this approach, a license given in 1939 to "motion picture" rights would include only the core uses of "motion picture" as understood in 1939—presumably theatrical distribution—and would not include subsequently developed methods of distribution of a motion picture such as television videocassettes or laser discs. See Nimmer § 10.10[b] at 10–90.

The second position described by Nimmer is "that the licensee may properly pursue any uses that may reasonably be said to fall within the medium as described in the license." Id. at 10–91. Nimmer expresses clear preferences for the latter approach on the ground that it is "less likely to prove unjust." Id. As Judge Friendly noted in *Bartsch*, "[S]o do we." 391 F.2d at 155.

We acknowledge that a result which deprives the author-licensor of participation in the profits of new unforeseen channels of distribution is not an altogether happy solution. Nonetheless, we think it more fair and sensible than a result that would deprive a contracting party of the rights reasonably found in the terms of the contract it negotiates. This issue is too often, and improperly, framed as one of favoritism as between licensors and licensees. Because licensors are often authors—whose creativity the copyright laws intend to nurture—and are often impecunious, while licensees are often large business organizations, there is sometimes a tendency in copyright scholarship and adjudication to seek solutions that favor licensors over licensees. Thus in *Cohen*, 845 F.2d at 854, the Ninth Circuit wrote that a "license must be construed in accordance with the purpose underlying federal copyright law," which the court construed as the granting of valuable, enforceable rights to authors and the encouragement of the production of literary works. Asserting that copyright law "is enacted for the benefit of the composer," (quoting Jondora Music Publish. Co. v. Melody Recordings, Inc., 506 F.2d 392, 395 (3rd Cir.1974) (as amended)), the court concluded that it would "frustrate the purposes of the [copyright] Act" to construe the license as encompassing video technology, which did not exist when the license was granted. Id.; see also Warner Bros. Pictures v. Columbia Broadcasting System, 216 F.2d 945, 949 (9th Cir.1954) ("Such doubt as there is should be resolved in favor of the composer. The clearest language is necessary to divest the author from the fruit of his labor."); William F. Patry, 1 Copyright Law and Practice 392 (1994) (arguing that "agreements should, wherever possible, be construed in favor of the copyright transferor," to reflect Congress's "policy judgment that copyright owners should retain all rights unless specifically transferred").

In our view, new-use analysis should rely on neutral principles of contract interpretation rather than solicitude for either party. Although *Bartsch* speaks of placing the "burden of framing and negotiating an exception ... on the grantor," 391 F.2d at 155, it should not be understood to adopt a default rule in favor of copyright licensees or any default rule whatsoever.[3] What governs under *Bartsch* is the language of the contract. If the contract is more reasonably read to convey one meaning, the party benefitted by that reading should be able to rely on it; the party seeking exception or deviation from the meaning reasonably conveyed by the words of the contract should bear the burden of negotiating for language that would express the limitation or deviation. This principle favors neither licensors nor licensees. It follows simply from the words of the contract.

The words of Disney's license are more reasonably read to include than to exclude a motion picture distributed in video format. Thus, we conclude that the burden fell on Stravinsky, if he wished to exclude new markets arising from subsequently developed motion picture technology, to insert such language of limitation in the license, rather than on Disney to add language that reiterated what the license already stated.

Other significant jurisprudential and policy considerations confirm our approach to new-use problems. We think that our view is more consistent with the law of contract than the view that would exclude new technologies even when they reasonably fall within the description of what is licensed. Although contract interpretation normally requires inquiry into the intent of the contracting parties, intent is not likely to be helpful when the subject of the inquiry is something the parties were not thinking about. See Nimmer, § 10.10[B] at 10–90 (noting that usually "there simply was no intent at all at the time of execution with respect to ... whether the grant includes a new use developed at a later time"). Nor is extrinsic evidence such as past dealings or industry custom likely to illuminate the intent of the parties, because the use in question was, by hypothesis, new, and could

---

[3]   We note that commentators and courts have misinterpreted *Bartsch* in just this way. See, e.g., Filmvideo Releasing Corp. v. Hastings, 426 F.Supp. 690, 695 (S.D.N.Y.1976) (interpreting *Bartsch* to mean that "the words of the grant are to be construed against the grantor"); James W. Dabney, Licenses and New Technology: Apportioning and Benefits, C674 ALI–ABA 85, 89, 96 (characterizing *Bartsch* as a "pro-licensee" decision that articulates a rule of contract construction favoring licensees in new-use cases). We emphasize that *Bartsch* favors neither party and announces no special rule of contract interpretation for the new-use context. Rather, it instructs courts to rely on the language of the license contract and basic principles of interpretation.

not have been the subject of prior negotiations or established practice. * * * Moreover, many years after formation of the contract, it may well be impossible to consult the principals or retrieve documentary evidence to ascertain the parties' intent, if any, with respect to new uses. On the other hand, the parties or assignees of the contract should be entitled to rely on the words of the contract. Especially where, as here, evidence probative of intent is likely to be both scant and unreliable, the burden of justifying a departure from the most reasonable reading of the contract should fall on the party advocating the departure.[4]

Neither the absence of a future technologies clause in the Agreement nor the presence of the reservation clause alters that analysis. The reservation clause stands for no more than the truism that Stravinsky retained whatever he had not granted. It contributes nothing to the definition of the boundaries of the license. See *Bartsch*, 391 F.2d at 154 n. 1. And irrespective of the presence or absence of a clause expressly confirming a license over future technologies, the burden still falls on the party advancing a deviation from the most reasonable reading of the license to insure that the desired deviation is reflected in the final terms of the contract. As we have already stated, if the broad terms of the license are more reasonably read to include the particular future technology in question, then the licensee may rely on that language.

Bartsch therefore continues to articulate our "preferred" approach to new-use questions, Nimmer, § 10.10[B] at 10–91, and we hold that the district court properly applied it to find that the basic terms of Disney's license included the right to record and distribute Fantasia in video format.

2.   *The ASCAP Condition.* Boosey further contends that distribution of Fantasia in video format violated the ASCAP Condition. The district court agreed. It granted summary judgment to Boosey declaring that the ASCAP Condition "prevents Disney from distributing video tapes and laser discs directly to consumers." Boosey & Hawkes, 934 F.Supp. at 123. We disagree with the district court's analysis.

[The court found that the ASCAP Condition, which it characterized as "industry boilerplate" appearing in "countless synchronization licenses," did "not unambiguously prohibit Disney from exhibiting the composition in non-ASCAP theaters, or from distributing the film directly to consumers." It therefore vacated Boosey's summary judgment and remanded for a trial to determine whether Disney's video release violated the ASCAP Condition.]

---

[4]   We note also that an approach to new-use problems that tilts against licensees gives rise to antiprogressive incentives. Motion picture producers would be reluctant to explore and utilize innovative technologies for the exhibition of movies if the consequence would be that they would lose the right to exhibit pictures containing licensed works. See *Bartsch*, 391 F.2d at 155.

Nor do we believe that our approach disadvantages licensors. By holding contracting parties accountable to the reasonable interpretation of their agreements, we encourage licensors and licensees to anticipate and bargain for the full value of potential future uses. Licensors reluctant to anticipate future developments remain free to negotiate language that clearly reserves the rights to future uses. But the creation of exceptional principles of contract construction that places doubt on the capacity of a license to transfer new technologies is likely to harm licensors together with licensees, by placing a significant percentage of the profits they might have shared in the hands of lawyers instead.

NOTES AND QUESTIONS

(1) Is the court correct in concluding that "[t]he words of Disney's license are more reasonably read to include than to exclude a motion picture distributed in video format"?

(2) As *Boosey & Hawkes* indicates, the burgeoning popularity of videocassettes beginning in the 1980s raised the "new use" question with respect to movies made before that use was fully anticipated. An early case was Platinum Record Co. v. Lucasfilm, Ltd., 566 F.Supp. 226 (D.N.J.1983). Plaintiff's predecessor in interest had granted Lucasfilm a "synchronization" right to use four songs on the soundtrack of the motion picture "American Graffiti." The grantee had the right "to exhibit, distribute, exploit, market and perform said motion picture * * * perpetually throughout the world by any means or methods now or hereafter known." Plaintiff made no objection to broadcasts of the film on over-the-air and cable television, but complained when the movie was released for sale and rental on videocassette. Citing the Second Circuit's analysis in *Bartsch v. Metro–Goldwyn–Mayer* that was reaffirmed in *Boosey & Hawkes*, the court granted the defendants' motion for summary judgment. "A motion picture is exhibited when it is presented for viewing by an audience on a theater or television screen; the video cassette and video disc operate as a means of exhibition, not as something of an altogether different nature from exhibition." The court thought it "immaterial whether plaintiff anticipated all potential future developments in the manner of exhibiting motion pictures."

As noted by Judge Leval in *Boosey & Hawkes*, a different result emerged in Cohen v. Paramount Pictures Corp., 845 F.2d 851 (9th Cir.1988). Although the transaction involved another synchronization license to use a song in a movie, the contract was different. It granted "authority * * * to record in any manner, medium, form or language" (but it did not include "now or hereafter known"). It did include exhibition "by means of television * * * including 'pay television', 'subscription television' and 'closed circuit into homes' television." All rights except those granted were retained. "Perhaps the primary reason why the words 'exhibition by means of television' in the license cannot be construed as including videocassette reproduction is that, although in use by the networks, VCRs for home use were not invented or known in 1969, when the license was executed." According to the court in *Cohen*, to deprive the author of a reward for the "virtually unlimited access" that the public would now have to his song through videocassettes would "frustrate the purposes of the [Copyright] Act to reward authorship." *Platinum Record* was distinguished because here the grant did not refer to methods yet to be invented and reserved all rights not expressly granted.[m] T. Hardy, Copyright and "New–Use" Technologies, 23 Nova L.Rev. 659 (1999), argues that since we aren't very good at predicting the impact of new technologies, uncertainties over new uses should be resolved in favor of the author to preserve incentive.; J. Harrison, A Positive

---

[m] Citing its analysis in Cohen v. Paramount, the Ninth Circuit in Welles v. Turner Ent. Co., 503 F.3d 728 (9th Cir.2007), vacated a summary judgment against the daughter of Orson Welles, who sought a declaratory judgment that she owned the home video rights to *Citizen Kane*. The 1939 grant of rights in the screenplay covered "motion picture and television rights," but retained "publication, radio, dramatic and other rights." "[I]n light of the narrow scope of rights granted to RKO and the broad reservation of rights by [the grantor], we cannot conclude with certainty that the parties would have given RKO home video rights had they contemplated the issue." Finding a genuine issue of fact regarding the parties' intentions, the court remanded the case to the district court.

Externalities Approach to Copyright Law: Theory and Application, 13 J.Intell.Prop.L. 1 (2005), offers an economic perspective on when an author's rights should extend to new uses; S. Balganesh, Foreseeability and Copyright Incentives, 122 Harv.L.Rev. 1569 (2009), pursues a similar theme, concluding that to align the scope of protection with the incentive to create, the author's protection should be limited to uses that were foreseeable when the work was created.

Platinum Record was again distinguished when the First Circuit interpreted a contract granting rights in the *Curious George* children's books "for television viewing"; unlike *Platinum Records*, this contract "contained no general grant of rights in technologies yet to be developed, and no explicit reference to 'future methods' of exhibition." The court held that videocassette rights were not covered by the agreement. The contract had been drafted "by a professional investment firm accustomed to licensing agreements," while the copyright owner was "an elderly woman" not represented by counsel for much of the transaction; the ambiguities were construed against the drafter. Rey v. Lafferty, 990 F.2d 1379 (1st Cir.), cert. denied, 510 U.S. 828 (1993).

Was the Second Circuit in *Boosey & Hawkes* correct in giving little weight to the absence of a "future technologies" clause?[n]

(3) The "new use" issue arose again with the sale of television programs on DVDs. Music owners argue that standard television licenses that predate the DVD market do not encompass that use and have demanded substantial sums to license their music for a complete season's DVD release. Some producers are simply replacing the show's original music with cheaper alternatives on the DVD version. Kipnis, Licensing an Issue for TV DVDs, Billboard, Nov. 8, 2003, p. 8. For new programs, the producers now demand an all-encompassing rights package that will allow them to market the television series in any format. Yet another dispute over "new use" rights in the television industry involved arguments between content owners like Viacom and cable television providers like Time Warner and Cablevision over whether their existing distribution contracts cover the delivery of programming to portable devices like iPads. Stelter, Viacom Sues Cablevision; Time Warner Case is Delayed, N.Y. Times, June 24, 2011, p. B3. The parties eventually resolved their dispute.

(4) Book publishers too must sort out the ownership of rights to new uses. Random House sued Internet publisher Rosetta Books for offering e-book versions of works by Random House authors such as Kurt Vonnegut and William Styron. The authors had publishing contracts that granted Random House the right to "print, publish and sell the work in book form," but they subsequently granted electronic rights to the defendant. Random House requested a prelimi-

---

[n]   Rapper Eminem's production company sued a subsidiary of UMG Recordings over the interpretation of contractual royalty provisions applicable to online record distributions in F.B.T. Productions, LLC v. Aftermath Records, 621 F.3d 958 (9th Cir.2010), cert. denied, 131 S.Ct. 1677 (2011). The 1998 agreement called for one royalty rate for "records sold," and a higher rate for "masters licensed" to others. The record company later entered into agreements with businesses like Apple's iTunes that duplicate and sell sound recordings in digital formats. The plaintiffs claimed that the latter deals were licenses of the master recordings entitled to the higher royalty rate. The defendants argued that digital downloads did not exist when the contract was made and the provision for master licensing royalties had previously been applied only to compilation records, television shows, movies, and commercials. The court responded that the contract allowed the record company to exploit the master recordings "in any and all forms of media now known and hereinafter developed" and thus the "masters licensed" provision applied to licensed downloads.

nary injunction on a copyright infringement theory, alleging a violation of its rights as an exclusive licensee. Judge Stein in Random House, Inc. v. Rosetta Books LLC, 150 F.Supp.2d 613 (S.D.N.Y.2001), aff'd, 283 F.3d 490 (2d Cir.2002), denied the plaintiff's motion, holding that the grants to Random House did not extend to publication in electronic form. *Boosey & Hawkes* was distinguished because there the language conveying the rights was broader. The court also argued that *Boosey & Hawkes* involved a "new use" in the "same medium as the original grant"—display of a motion picture in theaters and on videocassette—while here the "new use"—electronic signals sent over the Internet—was a "separate medium" from the original printed words on paper. Despite Random House's unsuccessful assertion of electronic publication rights against Rosetta Stone, it continues to claim that it has the exclusive right to publish e-book versions of titles covered by contracts that predate the explicit grant of e-book rights that it added to its publishing agreements in 1994. Agents representing authors, however, have forced Random House and other publishers to renegotiate for e-book rights to older works. Bosman, Random House Wins Battle for E–Book Rights, N.Y. Times, Aug. 25, 2010, p. B3. L. Mtima, *Tasini* and Its Progeny: The New Exclusive Right or Fair Use on the Electronic Publishing Frontier?, 14 Fordham Intell.Prop., Media & Ent.L.J. 369 (2004), examines *Random House* and other digital republication issues.

New York Times Company, Inc. v. Tasini

Supreme Court of the United States, 2001.
533 U.S. 483, 121 S.Ct. 2381.

■ JUSTICE GINSBURG delivered the opinion of the Court.

This copyright case concerns the rights of freelance authors and a presumptive privilege of their publishers. The litigation was initiated by six freelance authors and relates to articles they contributed to three print periodicals (two newspapers and one magazine). Under agreements with the periodicals' publishers, but without the freelancers' consent, two computer database companies placed copies of the freelancers' articles—along with all other articles from the periodicals in which the freelancers' work appeared—into three databases. Whether written by a freelancer or staff member, each article is presented to, and retrievable by, the user in isolation, clear of the context the original print publication presented.

The freelance authors' complaint alleged that their copyrights had been infringed by the inclusion of their articles in the databases. The publishers, in response, relied on the privilege of reproduction and distribution accorded them by § 201(c) of the Copyright Act, which provides:

> "Copyright in each separate contribution to a collective work is distinct from copyright in the collective work as a whole, and vests initially in the author of the contribution. In the absence of an express transfer of the copyright or of any rights under it, the owner of copyright in the collective work is presumed to have acquired only the privilege of reproducing and distributing the contribution as part of that particular collective work, any revision of that collective work, and any later collective work in the same series." 17 U.S.C. § 201(c).

Specifically, the publishers maintained that, as copyright owners of collective works, i.e., the original print publications, they had merely exercised "the privilege" § 201(c) accords them to "reproduc[e] and distribut[e]" the author's discretely copyrighted contribution.

In agreement with the Second Circuit, we hold that § 201(c) does not authorize the copying at issue here. The publishers are not sheltered by § 201(c), we conclude, because the databases reproduce and distribute articles standing alone and not in context, not "as part of that particular collective work" to which the author contributed, "as part of . . . any revision" thereof, or "as part of . . . any later collective work in the same series." Both the print publishers and the electronic publishers, we rule, have infringed the copyrights of the freelance authors.

I

A

Respondents Jonathan Tasini, Mary Kay Blakely, Barbara Garson, Margot Mifflin, Sonia Jaffe Robbins, and David S. Whitford are authors (Authors). Between 1990 and 1993, they wrote the 21 articles (Articles) on which this dispute centers. Tasini, Mifflin, and Blakely contributed 12 Articles to The New York Times, the daily newspaper published by petitioner The New York Times Company (Times). Tasini, Garson, Robbins, and Whitford wrote eight Articles for Newsday, another New York daily paper, published by petitioner Newsday, Inc. (Newsday). Whitford also contributed one Article to Sports Illustrated, a weekly magazine published by petitioner Time, Inc. (Time). The Authors registered copyrights in each of the Articles. The Times, Newsday, and Time (Print Publishers) registered collective work copyrights in each periodical edition in which an Article originally appeared. The Print Publishers engaged the Authors as independent contractors (freelancers) under contracts that in no instance secured consent from an Author to placement of an Article in an electronic database.

At the time the Articles were published, all three Print Publishers had agreements with petitioner LEXIS/NEXIS (formerly Mead Data Central Corp.), owner and operator of NEXIS, a computerized database that stores information in a text-only format. NEXIS contains articles from hundreds of journals (newspapers and periodicals) spanning many years. The Print Publishers have licensed to LEXIS/NEXIS the text of articles appearing in the three periodicals. The licenses authorize LEXIS/NEXIS to copy and sell any portion of those texts.

Pursuant to the licensing agreements, the Print Publishers regularly provide LEXIS/NEXIS with a batch of all the articles published in each periodical edition. The Print Publisher codes each article to facilitate computerized retrieval, then transmits it in a separate file. After further coding, LEXIS/NEXIS places the article in the central discs of its database.

Subscribers to NEXIS, accessing the system through a computer, may search for articles by author, subject, date, publication, headline, key term, words in text, or other criteria. Responding to a search command, NEXIS scans the database and informs the user of the number of articles meeting the user's search criteria. The user then may view, print, or download each of the articles yielded by the search. The display of each article includes the print publication (e.g., The New York Times), date (September 23, 1990), section (Magazine), initial page number (26), headline or title ("Remembering Jane"), and author (Mary Kay Blakely). Each article appears as a separate, isolated "story"—without any visible link to the other stories originally published in the same newspaper or magazine edition. NEXIS does not contain pictures or advertisements, and it does not reproduce the original print publication's formatting features such as headline size, page placement (e.g., above or below the fold for newspapers), or location of continuation pages.

The Times (but not Newsday or Time) also has licensing agreements with petitioner University Microfilms International (UMI). The agreements authorize reproduction of Times materials on two CD–ROM products, the New York Times OnDisc (NYTO) and General Periodicals OnDisc (GPO).

Like NEXIS, NYTO is a text-only system. Unlike NEXIS, NYTO, as its name suggests, contains only the Times. Pursuant to a three-way agreement, LEXIS/NEXIS provides UMI with computer files containing each article as transmitted by the Times to LEXIS/NEXIS. Like LEXIS/NEXIS, UMI marks each article with special codes. UMI also provides an index of all the articles in NYTO. Articles appear in NYTO in essentially the same way they appear in NEXIS, i.e., with identifying information (author, title, etc.), but without original formatting or accompanying images.

GPO contains articles from approximately 200 publications or sections of publications. Unlike NEXIS and NYTO, GPO is an image-based, rather than a text-based, system. The Times has licensed GPO to provide a facsimile of the Times' Sunday Book Review and Magazine. UMI "burns" images of each page of these sections onto CD–ROMs. The CD–ROMs show each article exactly as it appeared on printed pages, complete with photographs, captions, advertisements, and other surrounding materials. UMI provides an index and abstracts of all the articles in GPO.

Articles are accessed through NYTO and GPO much as they are accessed through NEXIS. The user enters a search query using similar criteria (e.g., author, headline, date). The computer program searches available indexes and abstracts, and retrieves a list of results matching the query. The user then may view each article within the search result, and may print the article or download it to a disc. The display of each article provides no links to articles appearing on other pages of the original print publications.

B

* * *

The District Court granted summary judgment for the Publishers, holding that § 201(c) shielded the Database reproductions. 972 F.Supp. 804, 806 (S.D.N.Y.1997). * * *

The Authors appealed, and the Second Circuit reversed. 206 F.3d 161 (C.A.2 1999). The Court of Appeals granted summary judgment for the Authors on the ground that the Databases were not among the collective works covered by § 201(c), and specifically, were not "revisions" of the periodicals in which the Articles first appeared. Id., at 167–170. * * *

II

* * *

Section 201(c) both describes and circumscribes the "privilege" a publisher acquires regarding an author's contribution to a collective work:

> "In the absence of an express transfer of the copyright or of any rights under it, the owner of copyright in the collective work is presumed to have acquired *only* the privilege of reproducing and distributing the contribution as part of that particular collective work, any revision of that collective work, and any later collective work in the same series." (Emphasis added.)

A newspaper or magazine publisher is thus privileged to reproduce or distribute an article contributed by a freelance author, absent a contract otherwise providing, only "as part of" any (or all) of three categories of collective works: (a) "that collective work" to which the author contributed her work, (b) "any revision of that collective work," or (c) "any later collective work in the same series." In accord with Congress' prescription, a "publishing company could reprint a contribution from one issue in a later issue of its magazine, and could reprint an article from a 1980 edition of an encyclopedia in a 1990 revision of it; the publisher could not revise the contribution itself or include it in a new anthology or an entirely different magazine or other collective work." H.R. Rep. 122–123, U.S.Code Cong. & Admin.News 1976, pp. 5659, 5738.

Essentially, § 201(c) adjusts a publisher's copyright in its collective work to accommodate a freelancer's copyright in her contribution. If there is demand for a freelance article standing alone or in a new collection, the Copyright Act allows the freelancer to benefit from that demand; after authorizing initial publication, the freelancer may also sell the article to others. * * * It would scarcely "preserve the author's copyright in a contribution" as contemplated by Congress, H.R. Rep. 122, U.S.Code Cong. & Admin.News 1976, pp. 5659, 5738, if a newspaper or magazine publisher were permitted to reproduce or distribute copies of the author's contribution in isolation or within new collective works. See Gordon, Fine–Tuning *Tasini*: Privileges of Electronic Distribution and Reproduction, 66 Brooklyn L.Rev. 473, 484 (2000).

III

In the instant case, the Authors wrote several Articles and gave the Print Publishers permission to publish the Articles in certain newspapers and magazines. It is undisputed that the Authors hold copyrights and, therefore, exclusive rights in the Articles.[7] It is clear, moreover, that the Print and Electronic Publishers have exercised at least some rights that § 106 initially assigns exclusively to the Authors: LEXIS/NEXIS' central discs and UMI's CD–ROMs "reproduce . . . copies" of the Articles, § 106(1); UMI, by selling those CD–ROMs, and LEXIS/NEXIS, by selling copies of the Articles through the NEXIS Database, "distribute copies" of the Articles "to the public by sale," § 106(3); and the Print Publishers, through contracts licensing the production of copies in the Databases, "authorize" reproduction and distribution of the Articles, § 106.[8] * * *

In determining whether the Articles have been reproduced and distributed "as part of" a "revision" of the collective works in issue, we focus on the Articles as presented to, and perceptible by, the user of the Databases. See § 102 (copyright protection subsists in original works fixed in any medium "from which they can be perceived, reproduced, or otherwise communicated"); see also § 101 (definitions of "copies" and "fixed"); Haemmerli,

---

[7] The Publishers do not claim that the Articles are "work[s] made for hire." 17 U.S.C. § 201(b). As to such works, the employer or person for whom a work was prepared is treated as the author. Ibid. The Print Publishers, however, neither engaged the Authors to write the Articles as "employee[s]" nor "commissioned" the Articles through "a written instrument signed by [both parties]" indicating that the Articles shall be considered "work[s] made for hire." § 101 (1994 ed., Supp. V) (defining "work made for hire").

[8] Satisfied that the Publishers exercised rights § 106 initially assigns exclusively to the Author, we need resolve no more on that score. Thus, we do not reach an issue the Register of Copyrights has argued vigorously. The Register maintains that the Databases publicly "display" the Articles, § 106(5); because § 201(c) does not privilege "display," the Register urges, the § 201(c) privilege does not shield the Databases. See Peters Letter E182–E183.

Commentary: *Tasini v. New York Times Co.*, 22 Colum.-VLA. J.L. & Arts 129, 142–143 (1998). In this case, the three Databases present articles to users clear of the context provided either by the original periodical editions or by any revision of those editions. The Databases first prompt users to search the universe of their contents: thousands or millions of files containing individual articles from thousands of collective works (i.e., editions), either in one series (the Times, in NYTO) or in scores of series (the sundry titles in NEXIS and GPO). When the user conducts a search, each article appears as a separate item within the search result. In NEXIS and NYTO, an article appears to a user without the graphics, formatting, or other articles with which the article was initially published. In GPO, the article appears with the other materials published on the same page or pages, but without any material published on other pages of the original periodical. In either circumstance, we cannot see how the Database perceptibly reproduces and distributes the article "as part of" either the original edition or a "revision" of that edition.

One might view the articles as parts of a new compendium—namely, the entirety of works in the Database. In that compendium, each edition of each periodical represents only a minuscule fraction of the ever-expanding Database. The Database no more constitutes a "revision" of each constituent edition than a 400–page novel quoting a sonnet in passing would represent a "revision" of that poem. "Revision" denotes a new "version," and a version is, in this setting, a "distinct form of something regarded by its creators or others as one work." Webster's Third New International Dictionary 1944, 2545 (1976). The massive whole of the Database is not recognizable as a new version of its every small part.

Alternatively, one could view the Articles in the Databases "as part of" no larger work at all, but simply as individual articles presented individually. That each article bears marks of its origin in a particular periodical (less vivid marks in NEXIS and NYTO, more vivid marks in GPO) suggests the article was *previously* part of that periodical. But the markings do not mean the article is *currently* reproduced or distributed as part of the periodical. The Databases' reproduction and distribution of individual Articles—simply *as individual Articles*—would invade the core of the Authors' exclusive rights under § 106.[9]

The Publishers press an analogy between the Databases, on the one hand, and microfilm and microfiche, on the other. We find the analogy wanting. Microforms typically contain continuous photographic reproductions of a periodical in the medium of miniaturized film. Accordingly, articles appear on the microforms, writ very small, in precisely the position in which the articles appeared in the newspaper. * * * In short, unlike microforms, the Databases do not perceptibly reproduce articles as part of the collective work to which the author contributed or as part of any "revision" thereof. * * *

---

[9] The dissenting opinion takes as its starting point "what is sent from the New York Times to the Electronic Databases." See post, at 512–516. This case, however, is not ultimately about what is sent between Publishers in an intermediate step of Database production; it is about what is presented to the general public in the Databases. See supra, at 499–500. Those Databases simply cannot bear characterization as a "revision" of any one periodical edition. We would reach the same conclusion if the Times sent intact newspapers to the Electronic Publishers.

IV

The Publishers warn that a ruling for the Authors will have "devastating" consequences. Brief for Petitioners 49. The Databases, the Publishers note, provide easy access to complete newspaper texts going back decades. A ruling for the Authors, the Publishers suggest, will punch gaping holes in the electronic record of history. The Publishers' concerns are echoed by several historians, see Brief for Ken Burns et al. as *Amici Curiae*, but discounted by several other historians, see Brief for Ellen Schrecker et al. as *Amici Curiae*; Brief for Authors' Guild, Jacques Barzun et al. as *Amici Curiae*.

Notwithstanding the dire predictions from some quarters, see also post, at 520 (STEVENS, J., dissenting), it hardly follows from today's decision that an injunction against the inclusion of these Articles in the Databases (much less all freelance articles in any databases) must issue. See 17 U.S.C. § 502(a) (court "may" enjoin infringement); Campbell v. Acuff–Rose Music, Inc., 510 U.S. 569, 578, n. 10 (1994) (goals of copyright law are "not always best served by automatically granting injunctive relief"). The parties (Authors and Publishers) may enter into an agreement allowing continued electronic reproduction of the Authors' works; they, and if necessary the courts and Congress, may draw on numerous models for distributing copyrighted works and remunerating authors for their distribution. See, e.g., 17 U.S.C. § 118(b); Broadcast Music, Inc. v. Columbia Broadcasting System, Inc., 441 U.S. 1, 4–6, 10–12 (1979) (recounting history of blanket music licensing regimes and consent decrees governing their operation).[13] In any event, speculation about future harms is no basis for this Court to shrink authorial rights Congress established in § 201(c). Agreeing with the Court of Appeals that the Publishers are liable for infringement, we leave remedial issues open for initial airing and decision in the District Court.

* * *

We conclude that the Electronic Publishers infringed the Authors' copyrights by reproducing and distributing the Articles in a manner not authorized by the Authors and not privileged by § 201(c). We further conclude that the Print Publishers infringed the Authors' copyrights by authorizing the Electronic Publishers to place the Articles in the Databases and by aiding the Electronic Publishers in that endeavor. We therefore affirm the judgment of the Court of Appeals.

It is so ordered.

■ JUSTICE STEVENS, with whom JUSTICE BREYER joins, dissenting.

* * *

---

[13] Courts in other nations, applying their domestic copyright laws, have also concluded that Internet or CD–ROM reproduction and distribution of freelancers' works violate the copyrights of freelancers. See, e.g., Union Syndicale des Journalistes Franais v. SDV Plurimdia (T.G.I., Strasbourg, Fr., Feb. 3, 1998), in Lodging of International Federation of Journalists (IFJ) as *Amicus Curiae*; S.C.R.L. Central Station v. Association Generale des Journalistes Professionnels de Belgique (CA, Brussels, Belg., 9e ch., Oct. 28, 1997), transl. and ed. in 22 Colum.-VLA J.L. & Arts 195 (1998); Heg v. De Volskrant B.V. (Dist.Ct., Amsterdam, Neth., Sept. 24, 1997), transl. and ed. in 22 Colum.-VLA J.L. & Arts, at 181. After the French *Plurimdia* decision, the journalists' union and the newspaper-defendant entered into an agreement compensating authors for the continued electronic reproduction of their works. See FR3 v. Syndicats de Journalistes (CA, Colmar, Sept. 15, 1998), in Lodging of IFJ as *Amicus Curiae*. In Norway, it has been reported, a similar agreement was reached. See Brief for IFJ as *Amicus Curiae* 18.

In contrast, I think that a proper respect for media neutrality suggests that the New York Times, reproduced as a collection of individual ASCII files, should be treated as a "revision" of the original edition, as long as each article explicitly refers to the original collective work and as long as substantially the rest of the collective work is, at the same time, readily accessible to the reader of the individual file. * * *

To see why an electronic version of the New York Times made up of a group of individual ASCII article-files, standing alone, may be considered a § 201(c) revision, suppose that, instead of transmitting to NEXIS the articles making up a particular day's edition, the New York Times saves all of the individual files on a single floppy disk, labels that disk "New York Times, October 31, 2000," and sells copies of the disk to users as the electronic version of that day's New York Times. The disk reproduces the creative, editorial selection of that edition of the New York Times. The reader, after all, has at his finger tips substantially all of the relevant content of the October 31 edition of the collective work. Moreover, each individual article makes explicit reference to that selection by including tags that remind the reader that it is a part of the New York Times for October 31, 2000. Such a disk might well constitute "that particular collective work"; it would surely qualify as a "revision" of the original collective work. Yet all the features identified as essential by the majority and by the respondents would still be lacking. An individual looking at one of the articles contained on the disk would still see none of the original formatting context and would still be unable to flip the page. * * *

If my hypothetical October 31, 2000, floppy disk can be a revision, I do not see why the inclusion of other editions and other periodicals is any more significant than the placement of a single edition of the New York Times in a large public library or in a book store. Each individual file still reminds the reader that he is viewing "part of" a particular collective work. And the *entire* editorial content of that work still exists at the reader's fingertips.

It is true that, once the revision of the October 31, 2000, New York Times is surrounded by the additional content, it can be conceptualized as existing as part of an even larger collective work (e.g., the entire NEXIS database). See ante, at 500. The question then becomes whether this ability to conceive of a revision of a collective work as existing within a larger "collective work" changes the status of the original revision. Section 201(c)'s requirement that the article be published only as "part of . . . any revision of *that collective work*" does not compel any particular answer to that question. A microfilm of the New York Times for October 31, 2000, does not cease to be a revision of that individual collective work simply because it is stored on the same roll of film as other editions of the Times or on a library shelf containing hundreds of other microfilm periodicals. Nor does § 201(c) compel the counterintuitive conclusion that the microfilm version of the Times would cease to be a revision simply because its publishers might choose to sell it on rolls of film that contained a year's editions of both the New York Times *and* the Herald–Tribune. Similarly, the placement of our hypothetical electronic revision of the October 31, 2000, New York Times within a larger electronic database does nothing to alter either the nature of our original electronic revision or the relationship between that revision and the individual articles that exist as "part of" it. * * *

The majority discounts the effect its decision will have on the availability of comprehensive digital databases, ante, at 504–505, but I am not as confident. As petitioners' *amici* have persuasively argued, the difficulties of locating individual freelance authors and the potential of exposure to statutory damages may well have the effect of forcing electronic archives to purge freelance pieces from their databases. "The omission of these materials from electronic collections, for any reason on a large scale or even an occasional basis, undermines the principal benefits that electronic archives offer historians—efficiency, accuracy and comprehensiveness." Brief for Ken Burns et al. as *Amici Curiae* 13. * * *

NOTES AND QUESTIONS

(1) Immediately after the Supreme Court's decision, the New York Times said that it would begin removing freelance articles from databases such as LEXIS/NEXIS, estimating that 115,000 stories by 27,000 freelance authors were involved. N.Y. Times, July 6, 2001, p. C4. The suit was later settled. Under the Supreme Court's reasoning, could *any* electronic version of the *New York Times* fall within the § 201(c) privilege? W. Gordon, Fine–Tuning *Tasini*: Privileges of Electronic Distribution and Reproduction, 60 Brooklyn L.Rev. 473 (2000), argues that since individual articles can be downloaded, the freelancers' contributions were not being distributed "as part of" the collective work as required under § 201(c).

(2) While the *Tasini* case was before the Supreme Court, several writers' organizations filed a class action suit raising similar claims against a number of newspapers and electronic archives, including the New York Times and the owners of Westlaw and Lexis/Nexis. Included among the classes of plaintiffs were authors who had not registered the copyrights in their works. A settlement intended to ensure that digital archives remain intact in exchange for payments to authors was approved by the trial court, but the Second Circuit in In re Literary Works in Electronic Databases Copyright Litigation, 509 F.3d 116 (2d Cir.2007), held that the registration requirement in § 411(a) deprived the district court of subject-matter jurisdiction to approve a settlement that included unregistered copyrights. That ruling was overturned by the Supreme Court in Reed Elsevier, Inc. v. Muchnick, 130 S.Ct. 1237 (2010). The Court held that the registration requirement in § 411 "is a precondition to filing a claim that does not restrict a federal court's subject-matter jurisdiction." Thus, the district court had jurisdiction to approve a settlement of the class action even though the settlement included claims relating to unregistered works. However, the Second Circuit on remand again rejected the settlement, which had established damage formulas for registered and unregistered works and included a release of liability for future uses by publishers, holding that the authors of unregistered works had not been adequately represented. In re Literary Works in Electronic Databases Copyright Litigation, 654 F.3d 242 (2d Cir.2011).

(3) In Faulkner v. National Geographic Enter., 409 F.3d 26 (2d Cir.), cert. denied, 546 U.S. 1076 (2005), freelance writers and photographers who had contributed material to issues of *National Geographic* complained when the publisher offered a collection of thirty CD–ROMs with every issue of the magazine beginning in 1888. The CDs contained an exact reproduction of every page so that users saw precise copies of the magazine pages except in size and resolution. The CDs also contained an introductory sequence of covers from the magazine as well as navigation software. The Second Circuit held that the exact reproduction of the magazine pages in the CDs was privileged under *Tasini*'s reading of § 201(c). The Eleventh Circuit in an en banc opinion reached a similar conclusion with respect to the same product in Greenberg v. National Geographic Society, 533 F.3d 1244 (11th Cir.), cert. denied, 555 U.S. 1070 (2008). The addition of the introductory montage and the software's search and zoom capabilities did not remove the product from the scope of the "revision" privilege in § 201(c).

(4) If disparity in bargaining power between contributors and publishers is the real problem, will interpreting the default rule in § 201(c) to favor contributors afford them any genuine relief? Justice Stevens in his dissent in *Tasini* noted that since 1995 the New York Times has required freelance authors to grant electronic rights, with no apparent increase in compensation.

4. DERIVATIVE WORKS AND UNDERLYING WORKS

G. Ricordi & Co. v. Paramount Pictures, Inc.

United States Court of Appeals, Second Circuit, 1951.
189 F.2d 469.
Certiorari denied, 342 U.S. 849.

■ Before L. HAND, CHIEF JUDGE, and SWAN and FRANK, CIRCUIT JUDGES.

■ SWAN, CIRCUIT JUDGE. This is a suit for a declaratory judgment with respect to motion picture rights in the copyrighted opera "Madame Butterfly," the renewal copyright of which is owned solely by the plaintiff. Federal jurisdiction is claimed on diversity of citizenship, the plaintiff being a partnership composed of Italian citizens and the defendant a New York corporation. After answer, both parties moved for summary judgment upon the pleadings, affidavits and exhibits. The district court granted the plaintiff's motion and awarded a judgment declaring the plaintiff to be the exclusive owner of motion picture rights in the renewal copyright of the opera and enjoining the defendant from interfering with the plaintiff's exercise of such rights. The defendant has appealed.

There is no dispute as to the facts. In 1897 John Luther Long wrote a novel entitled "Madame Butterfly," which was published in the Century Magazine and copyrighted by the Century Company. In 1900 David Belasco, with the consent of the copyright owner, wrote a play based upon the novel and having the same title. The play was not copyrighted until 1917. In 1901 Long and Belasco made a contract with the plaintiff by which they gave it "the exclusive rights * * * to make a libretto for an Opera of his [Belasco's] dramatic version of Madame Butterfly, founded on the original theme, written by Mr. John Luther Long * * * the said Libretto and all rights therein, dramatic or otherwise, to be the exclusive property of Messrs. G. Ricordi & Company for all countries of the world." It is upon this agreement that the plaintiff grounds its claim to motion picture rights in the world-famous opera, with music and lyrics by Puccini in collaboration with Giacosa and Illica, which was copyrighted by the plaintiff in 1904, and of which the renewal copyright was acquired by the plaintiff from the son of Puccini.

The defendant does not deny that the plaintiff is the sole owner of the renewal copyright of the opera but it asserts that it owns the motion picture rights in the John Luther Long basic story and in the Belasco dramatic version thereof, and, consequently, if the plaintiff wishes to make a motion

Δ:
π needs Δ's
consent

Δ: '01 K btw
L, B & π ≠ grant
movie rights

②© expired for
novel & play ∴
ended excl. Licenses
of opera

Dist. Ct.

• CT: JLL's right
to make movies
did not extend beyond
term of ©

• Assign. ≠ include
right of renewal

π not entitled
to make gen'l use
of novel for movie

picture version of the opera, the defendant's consent must be obtained for the use of the Long novel and the Belasco play. Its primary contentions are two: (1) that the 1901 agreement of Long and Belasco with the plaintiff did not grant any motion picture rights; and (2) that in any event the expiration in 1925 of the copyright of Long's novel and the expiration in 1945 of the copyright of Belasco's play put an end to any exclusive license of the plaintiff to use the novel and the play for a motion picture version of the opera. Long had obtained in 1925 a renewal of the copyright on his novel and in 1932 his administrator granted to the defendant the motion picture rights therein. In the same year, 1932, the defendant obtained from the trustee under Belasco's will an assignment of the motion picture rights in Belasco's play. So far as appears there was no renewal of copyright in the play.

The district court was of opinion that the primary question for decision was whether the 1901 agreement granted to the plaintiff motion picture rights in the operatic version of the novel and of Belasco's dramatization of it. After an extensive review of the authorities, the court concluded that it did. The appellant argues strenuously that the court erred in so construing the agreement, but we do not find it necessary to decide this question. The right which Long had to make motion pictures of the story of his copyrighted novel did not extend beyond the term of the copyright; hence, if it be assumed that he assigned to the plaintiff any moving picture rights, they were necessarily similarly limited to the term of the copyright, unless the assignment included the right of renewal. It did not; the 1901 agreement made no allusion to renewal of copyright. In Fred Fisher Music Co. v. M. Witmark & Sons, 318 U.S. 643, which held that an author has power to assign his right of renewal during the term of the original copyright, no one suggested that rights assigned under the original copyright did not end with it, if nothing was said of renewal. We think they do. A copyright renewal creates a new estate, and the few cases which have dealt with the subject assert that the new estate is clear of all rights, interests or licenses granted under the original copyright.[1] It is true that the expiration of Long's copyright of the novel did not affect the plaintiff's copyright of so much of the opera as was a "new work" and entitled to be independently copyrighted as such. But the plaintiff has acquired no rights under Long's renewal of the copyright on his novel and the plaintiff's renewal copyright of the opera gives it rights only in the new matter which it added to the novel and the play. It follows that the plaintiff is not entitled to make general use of the novel for a motion picture version of Long's copyrighted story; it must be restricted to what was copyrightable as new matter in its operatic version.

The next question is whether the plaintiff's right to make use of Belasco's play for a motion picture version thereof is similarly restricted to what was copyrightable as new matter in its operatic version. After Long's novel was copyrighted, Belasco was given permission—a license—to make use of the story for a play. Apparently the license was oral and its precise terms are not disclosed by the record. If it be assumed that the license gave Belasco any motion picture rights, they were necessarily limited to the term of the copyright of the novel. However, Belasco as author of the play

---

[1] See Fitch v. Shubert, D.C.N.Y., 20 F.Supp. 314, 315; Fox Film Corp. v. Knowles, D.C.N.Y., 274 F. 731, 732, reversed on other grounds, 261 U.S. 326; Ball, Law of Copyright and Literary Property, p. 535. Cf. In re Paper Bag Cases, 105 U.S. 766; Silverman v. Sunrise Pictures Corp., 2 Cir., 273 F. 909; White–Smith Music Pub. Co. v. Goff, 1 Cir., 187 F. 247.

had the common law rights of an author, which include the right to copyright it. This was done in 1917. By so doing the play was dedicated to the public except for the rights reserved by the copyright, for that is the condition upon the grant of any copyright. When the copyright expired, the play was property in the public demesne, since the record discloses no renewal of the copyright. Consequently, the exclusive motion picture rights in the play, which the trustee under Belasco's will assigned to the defendant by the 1932 agreement, expired in 1945 with the expiration of the copyright of the play. Thereafter the plaintiff was as free to use the play as was the defendant in making a motion picture version of the play.

However, the defendant still has the motion picture rights in the renewal copyright of Long's novel. Therefore it may assert, as it did, that the plaintiff cannot make general use of the story of the novel for a motion picture version of its opera; and, as already stated, the plaintiff is restricted to using what was copyrightable as new matter in its operatic version of the novel but is not so restricted in using the play which is now in public demesne. It scarcely need be added that the defendant, while free to use the novel and the play in making a motion picture, may not make use of the plaintiff's opera without its consent.

The remaining contentions of the parties have been examined and found without merit. Discussion of them is deemed unnecessary.

So much of the judgment as declares that the plaintiff is "the rightful owner and sole proprietor of the valid renewal copyright in the Opera entitled Madame Butterfly and of all rights and interest therein including the sole and exclusive motion picture rights" is affirmed. The injunction granted the plaintiff is too broad unless it be construed to forbid only such assertions of claims by the defendant as exceed those which the defendant is entitled to make as shown by the foregoing opinion. Accordingly the injunction is modified to conform to our opinion. Each party shall bear its own appellate costs and no attorney's fees are awarded to either party.

On Petition for Clarification

Paramount Pictures, Inc., asks for a clarification of that part of our opinion relating to the expiration and dedication of Belasco's copyright. We there said: "When the copyright expired, the play was property in the public demesne, since the record discloses no renewal of the copyright." What the petitioner desires is an express statement that only the new matter which Belasco's play added to Long's novel came into the public demesne upon the expiration of Belasco's copyright. It is implicit in the opinion as a whole that what is dedicated to the public as a condition of obtaining a copyright is only such matter as is copyrightable, but to avoid any possible cavil we will amend the above quoted sentence to read as follows: "When the copyright expired, the copyrightable new matter in the play was property in the public demesne, since the record discloses no renewal of the copyright".

NOTES AND QUESTIONS

(1) Under the decision of the court, what is the nature of the motion picture, if any, that Ricordi would be entitled to make without obtaining Paramount's consent?

(2) Does the decision have any bearing on Ricordi's right to publish the opera, if sued by the owner of the renewal term in Long's novel?

Russell v. Price

612 F.2d 1123 (9th Cir.1979), cert. denied, 446 U.S. 952 (1980).

George Bernard Shaw copyrighted his play "Pygmalion" in 1913. The 1941 renewal, as extended, was good until 1988. A licensed motion picture was made in 1938; its copyright was allowed to expire in 1966. This action was brought under the 1909 Act by the owner of the renewal copyright in the play to enjoin the unlicensed rental of the film following the expiration of its copyright.

" * * * [W]e reaffirm, without finding it necessary to repeat the rationale, the well-established doctrine that a derivative copyright protects only the new material contained in the derivative work, not the matter derived from the underlying work. 1 Nimmer on Copyright § 3.04 (1979). Thus, although the derivative work may enter the public domain, the matter contained therein which derives from a work still covered by statutory copyright is not dedicated to the public. * * * The established doctrine prevents unauthorized copying or other infringing use of the underlying work or any part of that work contained in the derivative product so long as the underlying work itself remains copyrighted. Therefore, since exhibition of the film 'Pygmalion' necessarily involves exhibition of parts of Shaw's play, which is still copyrighted, plaintiffs here may prevent defendants from renting the film for exhibition without their authorization."

The court distinguished Classic Film Museum, Inc. v. Warner Bros., Inc., 597 F.2d 13 (1st Cir.1979), which gave a declaratory judgment that a plaintiff could exhibit the 1937 motion picture "A Star is Born", on which copyright had expired, despite the defendant's claim that the exhibition would infringe its common law copyright in the underlying story and screenplay. According to *Classic Film*, "Defendant's reliance upon the *Ricordi* line of cases is misplaced. Those cases solely concerned underlying works which were statutorily copyrighted; thus, any protection offered by the *Ricordi* doctrine was limited to the fixed life of the underlying copyright * * *. The *Ricordi* doctrine is not equally applicable where there is an underlying common-law copyright which might extend indefinitely." (Can this be explained by saying that publication of the derivative work also published the portions of the underlying work that it incorporated, thus ending common law protection?)°

Filmvideo Releasing Corp. v. Hastings

668 F.2d 91 (2d Cir.1981).

On the basis of a 1935 agreement with Clarence Mulford, author of the Hopalong Cassidy cowboy books, Paramount had made 23 movies exploiting the character. Mulford or his estate had renewed the copyrights on all the novels; Paramount had let all the movie copyrights expire. Plaintiff, in a declaratory judgment action, maintained that it could license the films for television although Mulford in the 1935 agreement had reserved television and radio rights. Mulford's successors counterclaimed for infringement and

---

° See Batjac Prod. Inc. v. GoodTimes Home Video Corp., 160 F.3d 1223 (9th Cir.1998), cert. denied, 526 U.S. 1158 (1999), holding that common law copyright in an underlying screenplay had been lost as a result of its publication in a motion picture that had fallen into the public domain. The Second Circuit reached an analogous result in Shoptalk, Ltd. v. Concorde–New Horizons Corp., 168 F.3d 586 (2d Cir.), cert. denied, 527 U.S. 1038 (1999).

prevailed. After three reported opinions in the district court, the Court of Appeals was terse.

"The principal question on this appeal is whether a licensed, derivative, copyrighted work and the underlying copyrighted matter which it incorporates both fall into the public domain where the underlying copyright has been renewed but the derivative copyright has not. We agree with the Ninth Circuit, Russell v. Price * * * that the answer is 'No'."

"Since 1909," Judge Van Graafeiland wrote, "the courts of this circuit have held almost without exception that a derivative copyright is a good copyright only with regard to the original embellishments and additions it has made to the underlying work. * * * Since the proprietor of a derivative copyright cannot convey away that which he does not own * * * it follows that he cannot release that which he does not own into the public domain."

NOTES AND QUESTIONS

(1) *Russell* and *Filmvideo* were followed in CBS Operations Inc. v. Reel Funds Int'l, Inc., 2007 WL 2325218 (N.D.Tex.2007), when the defendant distributed 16 episodes of *The Andy Griffith Show* to televisions stations. Copyrights in the 16 episodes had not been renewed, but CBS claimed that the use infringed the copyrights owned by CBS in 79 prior episodes. Finding that the 16 episodes were derivative works that contained preexisting copyrighted material from the earlier episodes (including film footage and protectable characters such as Sheriff Andy, Deputy Barney Fife, Aunt Bee, and Opie), the court held that the defendant's use infringed CBS's copyrights in the earlier works.

(2) The preceding cases hold that derivative works on which copyright has expired cannot be exhibited if they embody material from underlying works that are still under copyright. But consider this alternative solution: the derivative works are in the public domain and thus open to use as a necessary consequence of the expiration of copyright, but this does not divest copyright in the underlying work or in any other derivations; thus, the derivative works can be exhibited, but no other use of the underlying work is permissible. Is that a better resolution?

(3) G. Ricordi v. Paramount and its sequels spawned a formidable body of commentary. See, e.g., R. Brown, The Widening Gyre: Are Derivative Works Getting Out of Hand?, 3 Cardozo Arts & Ent.L.J. 1 (1984); P. Goldstein, Derivative Rights and Derivative Works in Copyright, 30 J.Copyr. Soc'y 209 (1983); F. Nevins, The Doctrine of Copyright Ambush: Limitations on the Free Use of Public Domain Derivative Works, 25 St. Louis U.L.J. 58 (1981).

Why so much about so little? Obstructed access to old movies stirs feelings, even passions. Several writers had propounded a "new property" theory in support of the film-maker. The film-maker, they argued, is not simply an embellisher of the underlying work, but a creator who transforms a simple story into a larger art form. Such works should not be at the mercy of an underlying copyright owner, any more than Puccini's genius should be hobbled by John Luther Long, the Philadelphia lawyer in *Ricordi* with a flair for Japanese fantasies. That is the policy argument, oversimplified. It suffered a major setback in Stewart v. Abend.

Stewart v. Abend

Supreme Court of the United States, 1990.
495 U.S. 207, 110 S.Ct. 1750.

■ JUSTICE O'CONNOR delivered the opinion of the Court.

The author of a pre-existing work may assign to another the right to use it in a derivative work. In this case the author of a pre-existing work agreed to assign the rights in his renewal copyright term to the owner of a derivative work, but died before the commencement of the renewal period. The question presented is whether the owner of the derivative work infringed the rights of the successor owner of the pre-existing work by continued distribution and publication of the derivative work during the renewal term of the pre-existing work.

Cornell Woolrich authored the story "It Had to Be Murder," which was first published in February 1942 in Dime Detective Magazine. The magazine's publisher, Popular Publications, Inc., obtained the rights to magazine publication of the story and Woolrich retained all other rights. Popular Publications obtained a blanket copyright for the issue of Dime Detective Magazine in which "It Had to Be Murder" was published.

The Copyright Act of 1909, 17 U.S.C. § 1 et seq. (1976 ed.) (1909 Act), provided authors a 28–year initial term of copyright protection plus a 28–year renewal term. See 17 U.S.C. § 24 (1976 ed.). In 1945, Woolrich agreed to assign the rights to make motion picture versions of six of his stories, including "It Had to Be Murder," to B.G. De Sylva Productions for $9,250. He also agreed to renew the copyrights in the stories at the appropriate time and to assign the same motion picture rights to De Sylva Productions for the 28–year renewal term. In 1953, actor Jimmy Stewart and director Alfred Hitchcock formed a production company, Patron, Inc., which obtained the motion picture rights in "It Had to Be Murder" from De Sylva's successors in interest for $10,000.

In 1954, Patron, Inc., along with Paramount Pictures, produced and distributed, "Rear Window," the motion picture version of Woolrich's story "It Had to Be Murder." Woolrich died in 1968 before he could obtain the rights in the renewal term for petitioners as promised and without a surviving spouse or child. He left his property to a trust administered by his executor, Chase Manhattan Bank, for the benefit of Columbia University. On December 29, 1969, Chase Manhattan Bank renewed the copyright in the "It Had to Be Murder" story pursuant to 17 U.S.C. § 24 (1976 ed.). Chase Manhattan assigned the renewal rights to respondent Abend for $650 plus 10% of all proceeds from exploitation of the story.

"Rear Window" was broadcast on the ABC television network in 1971. Respondent then notified petitioners Hitchcock (now represented by co-trustees of his will), Stewart, and MCA Inc., the owners of the "Rear Window" motion picture and renewal rights in the motion picture, that he owned the renewal rights in the copyright and that their distribution of the motion picture without his permission infringed his copyright in the story. Hitchcock, Stewart, and MCA nonetheless entered into a second license with ABC to rebroadcast the motion picture. In 1974, respondent filed suit against these same petitioners, and others, in the United States District Court for the Southern District of New York, alleging copyright infringement. Respondent dismissed his complaint in return for $25,000.

Three years later, the United States Court of Appeals for the Second Circuit decided Rohauer v. Killiam Shows, Inc., 551 F.2d 484, cert. denied, 431 U.S. 949 (1977), in which it held that the owner of the copyright in a derivative work may continue to use the existing derivative work according to the original grant from the author of the pre-existing work even if the grant of rights in the pre-existing work lapsed. 551 F.2d, at 494. Several years later, apparently in reliance on *Rohauer,* petitioners re-released the motion picture in a variety of media, including new 35 and 16 millimeter prints for theatrical exhibition in the United States, videocassettes, and videodiscs. They also publicly exhibited the motion picture in theaters, over cable television, and through videodisc and videocassette rentals and sales.

Respondent then brought the instant suit in the United States District Court for the Central District of California against Hitchcock, Stewart, MCA, and Universal Film Exchanges, a subsidiary of MCA and the distributor of the motion picture. Respondent's complaint alleges that the re-release of the motion picture infringes his copyright in the story because petitioners' right to use the story during the renewal term lapsed when Woolrich died before he could register for the renewal term and transfer his renewal rights to them. * * *

* * * The District Court granted petitioners' motions for summary judgment based on *Rohauer* and the fair use defense and denied respondent's motion for summary judgment, as well as petitioners' motion for summary judgment alleging defects in the story's copyright. Respondent appealed to the United States Court of Appeals for the Ninth Circuit and petitioners cross-appealed.

The Court of Appeals reversed, holding that respondent's copyright in the renewal term of the story was not defective. 863 F.2d 1465, 1472 (1988). The issue before the court, therefore, was whether petitioners were entitled to distribute and exhibit the motion picture without respondent's permission despite respondent's valid copyright in the pre-existing story. * * *

Petitioners also relied, as did the District Court, on the decision in Rohauer v. Killiam Shows, Inc., supra. In *Rohauer,* the Court of Appeals for the Second Circuit held that statutory successors to the renewal copyright in a pre-existing work under § 24 could not "depriv[e] the proprietor of the derivative copyright of a right . . . to use so much of the underlying copyrighted work as already has been embodied in the copyrighted derivative work, as a matter of copyright law." Id., at 492. The Court of Appeals in the instant case rejected this reasoning, concluding that even if the pre-existing work had been incorporated into a derivative work, use of the pre-existing work was infringing unless the owner of the derivative work held a valid grant of rights in the renewal term.

The court relied on Miller Music Corp. v. Charles N. Daniels, Inc., 362 U.S. 373 (1960), in which we held that assignment of renewal rights by an author before the time for renewal arrives cannot defeat the right of the author's statutory successor to the renewal rights if the author dies before the right to renewal accrues. * * *

In its debates leading up to the Copyright Act of 1909, Congress elaborated upon the policy underlying a system comprised of an original term and a completely separate renewal term. See G. Ricordi & Co. v. Paramount Pictures, Inc., 189 F.2d 469, 471 (CA2) (the renewal right "creates a new estate, and the . . . cases which have dealt with the subject assert that the new estate is clear of all rights, interests or licenses granted under the original copyright"), cert. denied, 342 U.S. 849 (1951). "It not infrequently happens that the author sells his copyright outright to a publisher for a comparatively small sum." H.R.Rep. No. 2222, 60th Cong., 2d Sess., 14 (1909). The renewal term permits the author, originally in a poor bargaining position, to renegotiate the terms of the grant once the value of the work has been tested. * * *

* * * If the assignee of all of the renewal rights holds nothing upon the death of the assignor before arrival of the renewal period, then, *a fortiori,* the assignee of a portion of the renewal rights, e.g., the right to produce a derivative work, must also hold nothing. See also Brief for Register of Copyrights as *Amicus Curiae* 22 ("[A]ny assignment of renewal rights made during the original term is void if the author dies before the renewal period"). Therefore, if the author dies before the renewal period, then the assignee may continue to use the original work only if the author's successor transfers the renewal rights to the assignee. This is the rule adopted by the Court of Appeals below and advocated by the Register of Copyrights. See 863 F.2d, at 1478; Brief for Register of Copyrights as *Amicus Curiae* 22. Application of this rule to this case should end the inquiry. Woolrich died before the commencement of the renewal period in the story, and, therefore, petitioners hold only an unfulfilled expectancy. Petitioners have been "deprived of nothing. Like all purchasers of contingent interests, [they took] subject to the possibility that the contingency may not occur." *Miller Music,* supra, 362 U.S., at 378.

The reason that our inquiry does not end here, and that we granted certiorari, is that the Court of Appeals for the Second Circuit reached a contrary result in Rohauer v. Killiam Shows, Inc., 551 F.2d 484 (1977). Petitioners' theory is drawn largely from *Rohauer.* The Court of Appeals in *Rohauer* attempted to craft a "proper reconciliation" between the owner of the pre-existing work, who held the right to the work pursuant to *Miller Music,* and the owner of the derivative work, who had a great deal to lose if the work could not be published or distributed. 551 F.2d, at 490. Addressing a case factually similar to this case, the court concluded that even if the death of the author caused the renewal rights in the pre-existing work to revert to the statutory successor, the owner of the derivative work could continue to exploit that work. * * *

Properly conceding there is no explicit support for their theory in the 1909 Act, its legislative history, or the case law, petitioners contend, as did the court in *Rohauer,* that the termination provisions of the 1976 Act, while not controlling, support their theory of the case. For works existing in their original or renewal terms as of January 1, 1978, the 1976 Act added 19 years to the 1909 Act's provision of 28 years of initial copyright protection and 28 years of renewal protection. See 17 U.S.C. §§ 304(a) and (b) (1988 ed.). For those works, the author has the power to terminate the grant of rights at the end of the renewal term and, therefore, to gain the benefit of that additional 19 years of protection. See 17 U.S.C. § 304(c). In effect, the 1976 Act provides a third opportunity for the author to benefit from a work in its original or renewal term as of January 1, 1978. Congress, however, created one exception to the author's right to terminate: the author may not, at the end of the renewal term, terminate the right to use a derivative work for which the owner of the derivative work has held valid rights in the original and renewal terms. See § 304(c)(6)(A). The author, however, may terminate the right to create new derivative works. Ibid. For example, if the petitioners held a valid copyright in the story throughout the original and renewal terms, and the renewal term in "Rear Window" were about to expire, petitioners could continue to distribute the motion picture even if respondent terminated the grant of rights, but could not create a new motion picture version of the story. Both the court in *Rohauer* and petitioners infer from this exception to the right to terminate an intent by Congress to prevent authors of pre-existing works from blocking distribution of derivative works. In other words, because Congress decided not to permit authors to exercise a third opportunity to benefit from a work incorporated into a derivative work, the Act expresses a general policy of undermining the author's second opportunity. We disagree. * * *

Reject Rohauer

    * * * Congress would not have stated explicitly in § 304(c)(6)(A) that, at the end of the renewal term, the owner of the rights in the pre-existing work may not terminate use rights in existing derivative works unless Congress had assumed that the owner continued to hold the right to sue for infringement even after incorporation of the pre-existing work into the derivative work. * * *

    Accordingly, we conclude that neither the 1909 Act nor the 1976 Act provides support for the theory set forth in *Rohauer*. * * *

    Finally, petitioners urge us to consider the policies underlying the Copyright Act. They argue that the rule announced by the Court of Appeals will undermine one of the policies of the Act—the dissemination of creative works—by leading to many fewer works reaching the public. *Amicus* Columbia Pictures asserts that "[s]ome owners of underlying work renewal copyrights may refuse to negotiate, preferring instead to retire their copyrighted works, and all derivative works based thereon, from public use. Others may make demands—like respondent's demand for 50% of petitioners' future gross proceeds in excess of advertising expenses . . . —which are so exorbitant that a negotiated economic accommodation will be impossible." Brief for Columbia Pictures et al. as *Amicus Curiae* 21. These arguments are better addressed by Congress than the courts. * * *

    [The Court also rejected petitioners' fair use defense.]

    For the foregoing reasons, the judgment of the Court of Appeals is affirmed and the case is remanded for further proceedings consistent with this opinion.

    It is so ordered.

■ JUSTICE WHITE, concurring in the judgment.

    Although I am not convinced, as the Court seems to be, that the decision in Miller Music Corp. v. Charles N. Daniels, Inc., 362 U.S. 373 (1960), was required by the Copyright Act, neither am I convinced that it was an impermissible construction of the statute. And because *Miller Music,* in my view, requires the result reached by the Court in this case, I concur in the judgment of affirmance.

■ JUSTICE STEVENS, with whom THE CHIEF JUSTICE and JUSTICE SCALIA join, dissenting.

    * * *

    [Section 7 of the 1909 Act] deals with derivative works—works that include both old material and new material. The plain language of § 7 confers on the entire derivative work—not just the new material contained therein—the status of all other works of authorship, that of "new works subject to copyright under the provisions of this title." * * * Section 7, read together with § 3, plainly indicates that the copyright on a derivative work extends to both the new material and that "in which copyright is already subsisting." § 3. The author or proprietor of the derivative work therefore has the statutory right to publish and distribute the entire work. * * *

* * * In my opinion, § 7 was intended to do something more: to give the original author the power to sell the right to make a derivative work that upon creation and copyright would be completely independent of the original work. * * *

* * * By designating derivative works as "new works" that are subject to copyright and accorded the two terms applicable to original works, Congress evinced its intention that the derivative copyright not lapse upon termination of the original author's interest in the underlying copyright. The continued publication of the derivative work, after the expiration of the original term of the prior work, does not infringe any of the statutory successor's rights in the renewal copyright of the original work. The author's right to sell his derivative rights is exercised when consent is conveyed and completed when the derivative work is copyrighted. At that point, prior to the end of the first term, the right to prevent publication of the derivative work is no longer one of the bundle of rights attaching to the copyright. The further agreement to permit use of the underlying material during the renewal term does not violate § 24 because at the moment consent is given and the derivative work is created and copyrighted, a new right of property comes into existence independent of the original author's copyright estate.

* * * Ironically, by restricting the author's ability to consent to creation of a derivative work with independent existence, the Court may make it practically impossible for the original author to sell his derivative rights late in the original term and to reap the financial and artistic advantage that comes with the creation of a derivative work.[18]

NOTES AND QUESTIONS

(1) The Supreme Court's decision generated critical commentary and inventive titles. See D. Hughes, Jurisprudential Vertigo: The Supreme Court's View of "Rear Window" is for The Birds, 60 Miss.L.J. 239 (1990); for guarded support of the decision, see D. Nimmer, Refracting the Window's Light: *Stewart v. Abend* in Myth and Fact, 39 J.Copyr. Soc'y 18 (1991).[p]

(2) One consequence of Stewart v. Abend is that Christmas must now be celebrated without the continuous airing of Frank Capra's *It's A Wonderful Life,* in

---

[18] The creation of a derivative work often is in the best interests of both the original author and his statutory successors. As one commentator has noted: "The movie Rear Window became a selling point for anthologies containing the Woolrich story. The musical play Cats no ⸱⸱ sent many people who dimly remembered the Love Song of J. Alfred Prufrock as the ⸱⸱ only oeuvre of T. S. Eliot to the bookstore for Old Possum's Book of Practical ⸱⸱⸱ air's Fair: A Comment on the Fair Use Doctrine, 103 Harv. L. Rev. 1137,

⸱⸱ r of rights in Cornell Woolrich's *It Had to Be Murder* had less success against ⸱⸱ g's film *Disturbia* in Sheldon Abend Revocable Trust v. Spielberg, 748 ⸱⸱ S.D.N.Y.2010). "It cannot be disputed that both works tell the story of a male ⸱⸱fined to his home, who spies on neighbors to stave off boredom and, in so do-⸱⸱hat one of his neighbors is a murderer. The voyeur is himself discovered by the ⸱derer, is attacked by the murderer, and is ultimately vindicated." Nevertheless, ⸱udge Swain, "This broad plot idea, or premise, is not a protectible element." The ⸱hat "[t]here is no substantial similarity between the total concept and feel of the ⸱and that of *Disturbia*."

which despondent banker George Bailey (Jimmy Stewart again) is saved with the help of a whimsical angel named Clarence. Copyright in the 1946 film had expired in 1974 when Republic Pictures failed to renew. Everyone, including the film's owner, assumed that it was in the public domain and thus available for unlicensed broadcast. But inspired by Stewart v. Abend, Republic looked more closely and found that it still owned the copyright in *The Greatest Gift,* an obscure short story on which the film was loosely based. (Republic also quietly bought up rights in the music used in the movie.) It now asserts that further unauthorized broadcasts of the movie are an infringement of its rights in the underlying works. One programming executive said sadly, "I used to work in an independent station and everyone was so happy when *It's A Wonderful Life* went into the public domain. It was like a gift, and now we hate to return it." Koseluk, Not a Wonderful Year, Chicago Tribune, Dec. 19, 1993, Arts, p. 22.

(3) The 1976 Act's termination of transfers provisions, with their exemption for continued use of derivative works, p. 500 supra, lighten for movie-makers the consequences of terminations.

For movies made after 1978 as works for hire, i.e., made by the corporate employer of the many contributors, the copyright term is 95 years from publication. § 302(c). Is it possible that there could still be underlying rights that might prevent the free exploitation of such works even after 95 years? Consider this example:

> An author born in 1965 publishes a novel in 2000. A movie based on the novel appears in 2008. The copyright in the movie will expire in 2103. But if the author dies in 2050, the copyright in the novel will last until 2120.

What will you advise a would-be distributor or exhibitor of the movie in 2104?

5. WORK MADE FOR HIRE AND JOINT WORK

COPYRIGHT IN "WORK MADE FOR HIRE"

The 1909 Act in its skimpy definition section (§ 26) declared that "the word 'author' shall include an employer in the case of works made for hire." As the statute came to be interpreted, persons who in other contexts would be considered "independent contractors," in that they created works on commission without having any continuing employment relationship with the commissioning party, were brought within the reach of the "work made for hire" doctrine. "Direction" and "supervision" by the "employer" became the touchstone for finding a work to be for hire.

In the 1976 Act, § 201(b) continues the rule that "[i]n the case of a work made for hire, the employer or other person for whom the work was prepared is considered the author." The definition of "work made for hire" in § 101 is crucial. In addition to "a work prepared by an employee within the scope of his or her employment" under part (1) of the definition, nine kinds of commissioned works can also be work for hire under part (2) of the definition, but only "if the parties expressly agree in a written instrument signed by them that the work shall be considered a work made for hire." Note that photographs are not listed, nor architectural drawings, nor computer programs.

For a time, the leading case under the 1976 Act was Aldon Accessories Ltd. v. Spiegel, Inc., 738 F.2d 548 (2d Cir.), cert. denied, 469 U.S. 982 (1984). It relied almost entirely on cases decided under the 1909 Act and failed to find in the legislative history any intention to depart from the "supervision" test.

The Fifth Circuit in Easter Seal Society for Crippled Children and Adults, Inc. v. Playboy Enterprises, 815 F.2d 323 (5th Cir.1987), cert. denied, 485 U.S. 981 (1988), departed significantly from *Aldon* in rejecting the "supervision" test: "Today we adopt a bright-line rule for determining whether a work was made 'for hire' under the 1976 Act. Only works by actual employees and independent contractors who fulfill the requirements of § 101(2) can be 'for hire' under the new statute. Copyright 'employees' are those persons called 'employees' or 'servants' for purposes of agency law."

The Ninth Circuit in Dumas v. Gommerman, 865 F.2d 1093 (9th Cir.1989), went beyond *Easter Seal* to a strict reading of the statutory reference to "employee." The court said that "only works produced by formal, salaried employees are covered by 17 U.S.C. § 101(1). Works by independent contractors are works for hire only when the requirements of 17 U.S.C. § 101(2) are satisfied." The invocation of "agency law principles" to find employee status, Judge Fletcher wrote, would reintroduce "the rejected 'supervision and control' test."

Each of these interpretations of "work made for hire" was urged upon the Supreme Court in the following case.

Community for Creative Non–Violence v. Reid

Supreme Court of the United States, 1989.
490 U.S. 730, 109 S.Ct. 2166.

■ JUSTICE MARSHALL delivered the opinion of the Court.

In this case, an artist and the organization that hired him to produce a sculpture contest the ownership of the copyright in that work. To resolve this dispute, we must construe the "work made for hire" provisions of the Copyright Act of 1976 (Act or 1976 Act), 17 U.S.C. §§ 101 and 201(b), and in particular, the provision in § 101, which defines as a "work made for hire" a "work prepared by an employee within the scope of his or her employment" (hereinafter § 101(1)).

I

Petitioners are the Community for Creative Non–Violence (CCNV), a nonprofit unincorporated association dedicated to eliminating homelessness in America, and Mitch Snyder, a member and trustee of CCNV. In the fall of 1985, CCNV decided to participate in the annual Christmas-time Pageant of Peace in Washington, D.C., by sponsoring a display to dramatize the plight of the homeless. As the District Court recounted:

"Snyder and fellow CCNV members conceived the idea for the nature of the display: a sculpture of a modern Nativity scene in which, in lieu of the traditional Holy Family, the two adult figures and the infant would appear as contemporary homeless people huddled on a streetside steam grate. The family was to be black (most of the homeless in Washington being black); the figures were to be life-sized, and the steam grate would be positioned atop a platform 'pedestal,' or base, within which special-effects equipment would be enclosed to emit stimulated 'steam' through the grid to swirl about the figures. They also settled upon a title for the work—'Third World America'—and a legend for the pedestal: 'and still there is no room at the inn.'" 652 F.Supp. 1453, 1454 (DC 1987).

Snyder made inquiries to locate an artist to produce the sculpture. He was referred to respondent James Earl Reid, a Baltimore, Maryland, sculptor. In the course of two telephone calls, Reid agreed to sculpt the three human figures. CCNV agreed to make the steam grate and pedestal for the statue. Reid proposed that the work be cast in bronze, at a total cost of approximately $100,000 and taking six to eight months to complete. Snyder rejected that proposal because CCNV did not have sufficient funds, and because the statute had to be completed by December 12 to be included in the pageant. Reid then suggested, and Snyder agreed, that the sculpture would be made of a material known as "Design Cast 62," a synthetic substance that could meet CCNV's monetary and time constraints, could be tinted to resemble bronze, and could withstand the elements. The parties agreed that the project would cost no more than $15,000, not including Reid's services, which he offered to donate. The parties did not sign a written agreement. Neither party mentioned copyright.

After Reid received an advance of $3,000, he made several sketches of figures in various poses. At Snyder's request, Reid sent CCNV a sketch of a proposed sculpture showing the family in a creche-like setting: the mother seated, cradling a baby in her lap; the father standing behind her, bending over her shoulder to touch the baby's foot. Reid testified that Snyder asked for the sketch to use in raising funds for the sculpture. Snyder testified that it was also for his approval. Reid sought a black family to serve as a model for the sculpture. Upon Snyder's suggestion, Reid visited a family living at CCNV's Washington shelter but decided that only their newly born child was a suitable model. While Reid was in Washington, Snyder took him to see homeless people living on the streets. Snyder pointed out that they tended to recline on steam grates, rather than sit or stand, in order to warm their bodies. From that time on, Reid's sketches contained only reclining figures.

Throughout November and the first two weeks of December 1985, Reid worked exclusively on the statue, assisted at various times by a dozen different people who were paid with funds provided in installments by CCNV. On a number of occasions, CCNV members visited Reid to check on his progress and to coordinate CCNV's construction of the base. CCNV rejected Reid's proposal to use suitcases or shopping bags to hold the family's personal belongings, insisting instead on a shopping cart. Reid and CCNV members did not discuss copyright ownership on any of these visits.

On December 24, 1985, 12 days after the agreed upon date, Reid delivered the completed statue to Washington. There it was joined to the steam grate and pedestal prepared by CCNV and placed on display near the site of the pageant. Snyder paid Reid the final installment of the $15,000. The statue remained on display for a month. In late January 1986, CCNV members returned it to Reid's studio in Baltimore for minor repairs. Several weeks later, Snyder began making plans to take the statue on a tour of several cities to raise money for the homeless. Reid objected, contending that the Design Cast 62 material was not strong enough to withstand the ambitious itinerary. He urged CCNV to cast the statue in bronze at a cost of $35,000, or to create a master mold at a cost of $5,000. Snyder declined to spend more of CCNV's money on the project.

In March 1986, Snyder asked Reid to return the sculpture. Reid refused. He then filed a certificate of copyright registration for "Third World
America" in his name and announced plans to take the sculpture on a more
modest tour than the one CCNV had proposed. Snyder, acting in his capacity as CCNV's trustee, immediately filed a competing certificate of copyright
registration.

[The District Court held that the sculpture was a work made for hire,
reasoning that CCNV was the "motivating force" in its production and "directed enough of [Reid's] effort to assure that, in the end, he had produced
what they, not he, wanted."]

The Court of Appeals for the District of Columbia reversed and remanded, holding that Reid owned the copyright because "Third World
America" was not a work for hire. 846 F.2d 1485, 1494 (1988). Adopting
what it termed the "literal interpretation" of the Act as articulated by the
Fifth Circuit in Easter Seal Society for Crippled Children and Adults of
Louisiana, Inc. v. Playboy Enterprises, 815 F.2d 323, 329 (1987), cert. denied, 485 U.S. 981 (1988), the court read § 101 as creating "a simple dichotomy in fact between employees and independent contractors." 846 F.2d, at
1492. Because, under agency law, Reid was an independent contractor, the
court concluded that the work was not "prepared by an employee" under
§ 101(1). Id., 846 F.2d, at 1494. Nor was the sculpture a "work made for
hire" under the second subsection of § 101 (hereinafter § 101(2)): sculpture
is not one of the nine categories of works enumerated in that subsection,
and the parties had not agreed in writing that the sculpture would be a
work for hire. Ibid. The court suggested that the sculpture nevertheless
may have been jointly authored by CCNV and Reid, id., 846 F.2d, at 1495,
and remanded for a determination whether the sculpture is indeed a joint
work under the Act. Id., 846 F.2d, at 1498–1499.

We granted certiorari to resolve a conflict among the Courts of Appeals
over the proper construction of the "work made for hire" provisions of the
Act. 488 U.S. 940 (1988). We now affirm.

II

A

The Copyright Act of 1976 provides that copyright ownership "vests initially in the author or authors of the work." 17 U.S.C. § 201(a). As a general rule, the author is the party who actually creates the work, that is, the
person who translates an idea into a fixed, tangible expression entitled to
copyright protection. § 102. The Act carves out an important exception,
however, for "works made for hire."[3] If the work is for hire, "the employer or
other person for whom the work was prepared is considered the author"
and owns the copyright, unless there is a written agreement to the contrary. § 201(b). Classifying a work as "made for hire" determines not only the
initial ownership of its copyright, but also the copyright's duration, § 302(c),
and the owners' renewal rights, § 304(a), termination rights, § 203(a), and
right to import certain goods bearing the copyright, § 601(b)(1). See 1 M.
Nimmer & D. Nimmer, Nimmer on Copyright § 5.03[A], pp. 5–10 (1988).
The contours of the work for hire doctrine therefore carry profound significance for freelance creators—including artists, writers, photographers, de-

---

[3]   We use the phrase "work for hire" interchangeably with the more cumbersome statutory phrase "works made for hire."

signers, composers, and computer programmers—and for the publishing, advertising, music, and other industries which commission their works.[4]

* * * The petitioners do not claim that the statue satisfies the terms of § 101(2). Quite clearly, it does not. Sculpture does not fit within any of the nine categories of "specially ordered or commissioned" works enumerated in that subsection, and no written agreement between the parties establishes "Third World America" as a work for hire.

The dispositive inquiry in this case therefore is whether "Third World America" is "a work prepared by an employee within the scope of his or her employment" under § 101(1). The Act does not define these terms. In the absence of such guidance, four interpretations have emerged. The first holds that a work is prepared by an employee whenever the hiring party[6] retains the right to control the product. See Peregrine v. Lauren Corp., 601 F.Supp. 828, 829 (Colo.1985); Clarkstown v. Reeder, 566 F.Supp. 137, 142 (S.D.N.Y.1983). Petitioners take this view. Brief for Petitioners 15; Tr. of Oral Arg. 12. A second, and closely related, view is that a work is prepared by an employee under § 101(1) when the hiring party has actually wielded control with respect to the creation of a particular work. This approach was formulated by the Court of Appeals for the Second Circuit, Aldon Accessories Ltd. v. Spiegel, Inc., 738 F.2d 548, cert. denied, 469 U.S. 982 (1984), and adopted by the Fourth Circuit, Brunswick Beacon, Inc. v. Schock–Hopchas Publishing Co., 810 F.2d 410 (1987), the Seventh Circuit, Evans Newton, Inc. v. Chicago Systems Software, 793 F.2d 889, cert. denied, 479 U.S. 949 (1986), and, at times, by petitioners, Brief for Petitioners 17. A third view is that the term "employee" within § 101(1) carries its common law agency meaning. This view was endorsed by the Fifth Circuit in Easter Seal Society for Crippled Children and Adults of Louisiana, Inc. v. Playboy Enterprises, 815 F.2d 323 (1987), and by the Court of Appeals below. Finally, respondent and numerous *amici curiae* contend that the term "employee" only refers to "formal, salaried" employees. See, e.g., Brief for Respondents 23–24; Brief for Register of Copyrights as *Amicus Curiae* 7. The Court of Appeals for the Ninth Circuit recently adopted this view. See Dumas v. Gommerman, 865 F.2d 1093 (1989).

The starting point for our interpretation of a statute is always its language. Consumer Product Safety Comm'n v. GTE Sylvania, Inc., 447 U.S. 102, 108 (1980). The Act nowhere defines the terms "employee" or "scope of employment." It is, however, well established that "[w]here Congress uses terms that have accumulated settled meaning under . . . the common law, a court must infer, unless the statute otherwise dictates, that Congress means to incorporate the established meaning of these terms." NLRB v. Amax Coal Co., 453 U.S. 322, 329 (1981); see also Perrin v. United States, 444 U.S. 37, 42 (1979). In the past, when Congress has used the term "employee" without defining it, we have concluded that Congress intended to describe the conventional master-servant relationship as understood by common-law agency doctrine. See, e.g., Kelley v. Southern Pacific Co., 419 U.S. 318, 322–323 (1974); Baker v. Texas & Pacific R. Co., 359 U.S. 227,

---

[4]   As of 1955, approximately 40 percent of all copyright registrations were for works for hire, according to a Copyright Office study. See Varmer, Works Made for Hire and On Commission, in Studies Prepared for the Subcommittee on Patents, Trademarks, and Copyrights of the Senate Committee on the Judiciary, Study No. 13, 86th Cong., 2d Sess. 139, n. 49 (Comm.Print, 1960) (hereinafter Varmer, Works Made for Hire). The Copyright Office does not keep more recent statistics on the number of work for hire registrations.

[6]   By "hiring party," we mean to refer to the party who claims ownership of the copyright by virtue of the work for hire doctrine.

228 (1959) (*per curiam*); Robinson v. Baltimore & Ohio R. Co., 237 U.S. 84, 94 (1915). Nothing in the text of the work for hire provisions indicates that Congress used the words "employee" and "employment" to describe anything other than " 'the conventional relation of employer and employee.' " *Kelley,* supra, at 323, quoting *Robinson,* supra, at 94; compare NLRB v. Hearst Publications, Inc., 322 U.S. 111, 124–132 (1944) (rejecting agency law conception of employee for purposes of the National Labor Relations Act where structure and context of statute indicated broader definition). On the contrary, Congress' intent to incorporate the agency law definition is suggested by § 101(1)'s use of the term, "scope of employment," a widely used term of art in agency law. See Restatement (Second) of Agency § 228 (1958) (hereinafter Restatement).

In past cases of statutory interpretation, when we have concluded that Congress intended terms such as "employee," "employer," and "scope of employment" to be understood in light of agency law, we have relied on the general common law of agency, rather than on the law of any particular State, to give meaning to these terms. See, e.g., *Kelley,* 419 U.S., at 323–324, and n. 5; id., at 332 (Stewart, J., concurring in judgment); Ward v. Atlantic Coast Line R. Co., 362 U.S. 396, 400 (1960); *Baker,* supra, at 228. This practice reflects the fact that "federal statutes are generally intended to have uniform nationwide application." Mississippi Choctaw Indian Band v. Holyfield, 490 U.S. 30, 43 (1989). Establishment of a federal rule of agency, rather than reliance on state agency law, is particularly appropriate here given the Act's express objective of creating national, uniform copyright law by broadly pre-empting state statutory and common-law copyright regulation. See 17 U.S.C. § 301(a). We thus agree with the Court of Appeals that the term "employee" should be understood in light of the general common law of agency.

In contrast, neither test proposed by petitioners is consistent with the text of the Act. The exclusive focus of the right to control the product test on the relationship between the hiring party and the product clashes with the language of § 101(1), which focuses on the relationship between the hired and hiring parties. The right to control the product test also would distort the meaning of the ensuing subsection, § 101(2). Section 101 plainly creates two distinct ways in which a work can be deemed for hire: one for works prepared by employees, the other for those specially ordered or commissioned works which fall within one of the nine enumerated categories and are the subject of a written agreement. The right to control the product test ignores this dichotomy by transforming into a work for hire under § 101(1) any "specially ordered or commissioned" work that is subject to the supervision and control of the hiring party. Because a party who hires a "specially ordered or commissioned" work by definition has a right to specify the characteristics of the product desired, at the time the commission is accepted, and frequently until it is completed, the right to control the product test would mean that many works that could satisfy § 101(2) would already have been deemed works for hire under § 101(1). Petitioners' interpretation is particularly hard to square with § 101(2)'s enumeration of the nine specific categories of specially ordered or commissioned works eligible to be works for hire, e.g., "a contribution to a collective work," "a part of a motion picture," and "answer material for a test." The unifying feature of these works is that they are usually prepared at the instance, direction, and risk of a publisher or producer.[7] By their very nature, therefore, these types of works would be works by an employee under petitioners' right to control the product test.

The actual control test, articulated by the Second Circuit in *Aldon Accessories,* fares only marginally better when measured against the language and structure of § 101. Under this test, independent contractors who are so controlled and supervised in the creation of a particular work are deemed "employees" under § 101(1). Thus work for hire status under § 101(1) depends on a hiring party's *actual* control, rather than *right to* control, the product. *Aldon Accessories,* 738 F.2d, at 552. Under the actual control test, a work for hire could arise under § 101(2), but not under § 101(1), where a party commissions, but does not actually control, a product which falls into one of the nine enumerated categories. Nonetheless, we agree with the Fifth Circuit Court of Appeals that "[t]here is simply no way to milk the 'actual control' test of *Aldon Accessories* from the language of the statute." *Easter Seal Society,* 815 F.2d, at 334. Section 101 clearly delineates between works prepared by an employee and commissioned works. Sound though other distinctions might be as a matter of copyright policy, there is no statutory support for an additional dichotomy between commissioned works that are actually controlled and supervised by the hiring party and those that are not.

We therefore conclude that the language and structure of § 101 of the Act do not support either the right to control the product or the actual control approaches.[8] The structure of § 101 indicates that a work for hire can arise through one of two mutually exclusive means, one for employees and one for independent contractors, and ordinary canons of statutory interpretation indicate that the classification of a particular hired party should be made with reference to agency law.

[The Court reviewed the legislative history and found an intention to preclude hiring parties from imposing work for hire status on commissioned works that did not fall within the specifically enumerated categories.]

* * *

Finally, petitioners' construction of the work for hire provisions would impede Congress' paramount goal in revising the 1976 Act of enhancing predictability and certainty of copyright ownership. See H.R.Rep. No. 94–1476, supra, at 129. In a "copyright marketplace," the parties negotiate

---

[7] See Supplementary Report of the Register of Copyrights on the General Revision of the US Copyright Law: 1965 Revision Bill, 89th Cong., 1st Sess., Copyright Law Revision, pt. 6, pp. 66–67 (H. R. Judiciary Comm. Print 1965) (hereinafter Supplementary Report); Hardy, Copyright Law's Concept of Employment—What Congress Really Intended, 35 J. Copr. Soc. USA 210, 244–245 (1988).

[8] We also reject the suggestion of respondent and *amici* that the § 101(1) term "employee" refers only to formal, salaried employees. While there is some support for such a definition in the legislative history, see Varmer, Works Made for Hire 130; n. 11, infra, the language of § 101(1) cannot support it. The Act does not say "formal" or "salaried" employee, but simply "employee." Moreover, the respondent and those *amici* who endorse a formal, salaried employee test do not agree upon the content of this test. Compare, e.g., Brief for Respondent 37 (hired party who is on payroll is an employee within § 101(1)) with Tr. of Oral Arg. 31 (hired party who receives a salary or commissions regularly is an employee within § 101(1)); and Brief for Volunteer Lawyers for the Arts Inc. et al. as *Amici Curiae* 4 (hired party who receives a salary *and* is treated as an employee for Social Security and tax purposes is an employee within § 101(1)). Even the one Court of Appeals to adopt what it termed a formal, salaried employee test in fact embraced an approach incorporating numerous factors drawn from the agency law definition of employee which we endorse. See *Dumas,* 865 F.2d, at 1104.

with an expectation that one of them will own the copyright in the completed work. *Dumas,* 865 F.2d, at 1104–1105, n. 18. With that expectation, the parties at the outset can settle on relevant contractual terms, such as the price for the work and the ownership of reproduction rights.

To the extent that petitioners endorse an actual control test, CCNV's construction of the work for hire provisions prevents such planning. Because that test turns on whether the hiring party has closely monitored the production process, the parties would not know until late in the process, if not until the work is completed, whether a work will ultimately fall within § 101(1). Under petitioners' approach, therefore, parties would have to predict in advance whether the hiring party will sufficiently control a given work to make it the author. "If they guess incorrectly, their reliance on 'work for hire' or on assignment may give them a copyright interest that they did not bargain for." *Easter Seal Society,* 815 F.2d, at 333; accord *Dumas,* 865 F.2d, at 1103. This understanding of the work for hire provisions clearly thwarts Congress' goal of ensuring predictability through advance planning. Moreover, petitioners' interpretation "leaves the door open for hiring parties, who have failed to get a full assignment of copyright rights from independent contractors falling outside the subdivision (2) guidelines, to unilaterally obtain work-made-for-hire rights years after the work has been completed as long as they directed or supervised the work, a standard that is hard not to meet when one is a hiring party." Hamilton, Commissioned Works as Works Made for Hire Under the 1976 Copyright Act: Misinterpretation and Injustice, 135 U.Pa.L.Rev. 1281, 1304 (1987).

In sum, we must reject petitioners' argument. Transforming a commissioned work into a work by an employee on the basis of the hiring party's right to control, or actual control of, the work is inconsistent with the language, structure, and legislative history of the work for hire provisions. To determine whether a work is for hire under the Act, a court first should ascertain, using principles of general common law of agency, whether the work was prepared by an employee or an independent contractor. After making this determination, the court can apply the appropriate subsection of § 101.

B

We turn, finally, to an application of § 101 to Reid's production of "Third World America." In determining whether a hired party is an employee under the general common law of agency, we consider the hiring party's right to control the manner and means by which the product is accomplished. Among the other factors relevant to this inquiry are the skill required; the source of the instrumentalities and tools; location of the work; the duration of the relationship between the parties; whether the hiring party has the right to assign additional projects to the hired party; the extent of the hired party's discretion over when and how long to work; the method of payment; the hired party's role in hiring and paying assistants; whether the work is part of the regular business of the hiring party; whether the hiring party is in business; the provision of employee benefits; and the tax treatment of the hired party. See Restatement § 220(2) (setting forth a nonexhaustive list of factors relevant to determining whether a hired party is an employee). No one of these factors is determinative. See *Ward,* 362 U.S., at 400; Hilton Int'l Co. v. NLRB, 690 F.2d 318, 321 (CA2 1982).

Examining the circumstances of this case in light of these factors, we agree with the Court of Appeals that Reid was not an employee of CCNV but an independent contractor. 846 F.2d, at 1494, n. 11. True, CCNV members directed enough of Reid's work to ensure that he produced a sculpture that met their specifications. 652 F.Supp., at 1456. But the extent of control the hiring party exercises over the details of the product is not dispositive. Indeed, all the other circumstances weigh heavily against finding an employment relationship. Reid is a sculptor, a skilled occupation. Reid supplied his own tools. He worked in his own studio in Baltimore, making daily supervision of his activities from Washington practicably impossible. Reid was retained for less than two months, a relatively short period of time. During and after this time, CCNV had no right to assign additional projects to Reid. Apart from the deadline for completing the sculpture, Reid had absolute freedom to decide when and how long to work. CCNV paid Reid $15,000, a sum dependent on "completion of a specific job, a method by which independent contractors are often compensated." Holt v. Winpisinger, 811 F.2d 1532, 1540 (1987). Reid had total discretion in hiring and paying assistants. "Creating sculptures was hardly 'regular business' for CCNV." 846 F.2d, at 1494, n. 11. Indeed, CCNV is not a business at all. Finally, CCNV did not pay payroll or social security taxes, provide any employee benefits, or contribute to unemployment insurance or workers' compensation funds.

Because Reid was an independent contractor, whether "Third World America" is a work for hire depends on whether it satisfies the terms of § 101(2). This petitioners concede it cannot do. Thus, CCNV is not the author of "Third World America" by virtue of the work for hire provisions of the Act. However, as the Court of Appeals made clear, CCNV nevertheless may be a joint author of the sculpture if, on remand, the District Court so determines that CCNV and Reid prepared the work "with the intention that their contributions be merged into inseparable or interdependent parts of a unitary whole." 17 U.S.C. § 101.[32] In that case, CCNV and Reid would be co-owners of the copyright in the work. See § 201(a).

For the aforestated reasons, we affirm the judgment of the Court of Appeals for the District of Columbia.

It is so ordered.

NOTES AND QUESTIONS

(1) The Second Circuit in Aymes v. Bonelli, 980 F.2d 857 (2d Cir.1992), concluding that software written for the plaintiff's business was not a work for hire, held that the weight accorded to the individual agency factors should vary with their significance in the particular case.[q] D. Tussey, What If Employees

---

[32] Neither CCNV nor Reid sought review of the Court of Appeals' remand order. We therefore have no occasion to pass judgment on applicability of the Act's joint authorship provisions to this case.

[q] For another application of the *CCNV* test for "employee" see Kirk v. Harter, 188 F.3d 1005 (8th Cir.1999), focusing mostly on pay and benefits in concluding that a software developer was an independent contractor rather than an employee and thus retained rights in the computer program. Connoisseurs of modern dance will enjoy Martha Graham School v. Martha Graham Center of Contemporary Dance, Inc., 380 F.3d 624 (2d Cir.2004), cert. denied, 544 U.S. 1060 (2005), sorting out the work for hire status of seventy dances created by the renowned choreographer under both the 1909 and 1976 Acts.

N. Schaumann, Small Business and Copyright Ownership, 22 Wm. Mitchell L.Rev. 1469 (1996), emphasizes that even for an employee, a work is for hire only when created within the scope of the employment. See Avtec Systems, Inc. v. Peiffer, 21 F.3d 568 (4th Cir.1994), remanding for reconsideration of whether an employee's work on a computer program was within the scope of employment. In another computer software case, the development of litigation

Owned Their Copyrights, 2008 Mich.St.U.L.Rev. 233, points out that the work-for-hire doctrine facilitates access by creating a single owner for collaborative works like motion pictures.

In JustMed, Inc. v. Byce, 600 F.3d 1118 (9th Cir.2010), the court placed special emphasis on the way technology start-up companies operate in deciding that a software developer who worked at home without benefits and who was paid mostly in stock was nevertheless an employee and the resulting source code was thus a work made for hire. J. Garon and E. Ziff, The Work Made for Hire Doctrine Revisited: Startup and Technology Employees and the Use of Contracts in a Hiring Relationship, 12 Minn.J.L.Sci. & Tech. 489 (2011), offers advice to technology startups navigating the work for hire rules; J. Silbey, Harvesting Intellectual Property: Inspired Beginnings and "Work–Makes–Work," Two Stages in the Creative Processes of Artists and Innovators, 86 Notre Dame L.Rev. 2091 (2011), uses interviews with creators and lawyers to explore the role of intellectual property in the early stages of the creative process.

Should the 1976 Act as interpreted in *CCNV* be applied to settle ownership issues relating to works created when the 1909 Act was in effect? Roth v. Pritikin, 710 F.2d 934 (2d Cir.), cert. denied, 464 U.S. 961 (1983), held that for pre–1978 works, the old rules on work for hire still apply.

(2) T. Hardy, An Economic Understanding of Copyright Law's Work–Made–for–Hire Doctrine, 12 Colum.J.L. & Arts 181 (1988), argues that what the courts have been trying to do (and as a policy matter should do?) is to allocate copyright in a commissioned work to the participant in the deal who can most effectively exploit the work. How would one identify the most efficient exploiter? Will the determination of copyright ownership indeed influence the efficiency of exploitation? Recall that copyrights are transferable. In an efficient market, the rights granted by copyright will move to the best exploiter regardless of initial ownership. Are there reasons why the market in copyrights might not operate efficiently?

(3) There is said to be acute dissatisfaction among freelancers who create the types of commissioned works that can be considered "work made for hire" under the second part of the definition in § 101 and who deal with buyers who know how to draft contracts that satisfy the statute.[r] There have been proposals to remove major categories of commissioned works from the § 101 definition. What arguments can be made either for retaining or eliminating any of the principal categories? An argument for eliminating all of them is made in M. Landau, "Works Made For Hire" After *Community for Creative Non–Violence v. Reid:* The Need for Statutory Reform and the Importance of Contract, 9 Cardozo Arts & Ent.L.J. 107 (1990).

In 1999, without any congressional hearings or debate, "a sound recording" was added to the list of commissioned works that can be a work for hire.

---

management software by a city attorney after hours with his own resources was found to fall outside the scope of his employment. Quinn v. City of Detroit, 988 F.Supp. 1044 (E.D.Mich.1997). *Quinn* was distinguished in a later case holding that software created at home during off-duty hours by an employee involved in research project was within the scope of employment and hence a work for hire. Genzmer v. Public Health Trust of Miami–Dade County, 219 F.Supp.2d 1275 (S.D.Fla.2002).

[r] In Playboy Enter., Inc. v. Dumas, 53 F.3d 549 (2d Cir.), cert. denied, 516 U.S. 1010 (1995), Judge Oakes said that although the agreement necessary to turn a listed commissioned work into a work for hire must come before the work is created, the writing memorializing the agreement can come later.

Pub.L. No. 106–113 (1999). Recording artists argued that sound recordings had not previously been works for hire since the performers are not "employees"; they complained that the new work for hire status would deprive them of the opportunity under § 203 to terminate their transfers of rights to the record companies. Apparently embarrassed that the change had been passed off as "clarifying and technical" by a House committee counsel who later went to work for the Recording Industry Association of America,[8] Congress quickly retreated and removed sound recordings from the work for hire definition in 2000. Pub.L. No. 106–379 (2000). The record companies apparently believe that most sound recordings still qualify for work for hire status as a commissioned "contribution to a collective work" under § 101(2). M. LaFrance, Authorship and Termination Rights in Sound Recordings, 75 S.Cal.L.Rev. 375 (2002), concludes that there is a strong argument that many sound recordings are indeed works for hire. The dispute between the record companies and performers over the work for hire status of sound recordings will soon reach a climax as performers begin to assert termination rights under § 203 beginning in 2013. Rohter, Record Industry Braces for Artists' Battles Over Song Rights, N.Y. Times, Aug. 16, 2011, p. C1.

(4) Even without any copyright interest, writers and performers involved in the production of television programs and motion pictures normally share in the revenues from subsequent uses such as television reruns, DVD sales, and uses in foreign markets through collective bargaining agreements that require "residual" payments. See Thomas Selz, Melvin Simensky, Patricia Acton, and Robert Lind, Entertainment Law (3d ed. Thomson West) § 8:16. Guilds representing actors and writers are constantly fighting for a larger share of DVD and Internet revenues.

In 2012 after more than a dozen years of negotiations, delegates from over fifty countries including the United States adopted the World Intellectual Property Organization's Beijing Treaty on Audiovisual Performances (reprinted in the Statutory Supplement). The treaty recognizes audiovisual performers' rights in their performances that are similar to those provided to musical performers under the WIPO Performances and Phonograms Treaty, p. 272 infra. However, art. 12 of the treaty specifically allows countries to permit the transfer of the performers' economic rights to the producer of the audiovisual work. The treaty will take effect after formal ratification by thirty countries.

(5) If a work is clearly produced "within the scope of * * * employment," a creator who wishes to retain the copyright must get an express written agreement. § 201(b). What does this do to the academic practice that lets professors keep the copyrights in their scholarly work? See S. Burr, A Critical Assessment of *Reid's* Work for Hire Framework and Its Potential Impact on the Marketplace for Scholarly Works, 24 J. Marshall L.Rev. 119 (1990), illustrating the difficulty of applying the *CCNV* criteria in an academic environment. R. Dreyfuss, The Creative Employee and the Copyright Act of 1976, 54 U.Chi.L.Rev. 590 (1987), musters a battery of arguments to preserve copyrights in faculty. See also Weinstein v. University of Illinois, 811 F.2d 1091 (7th Cir.1987) ("This has been the academic tradition since copyright law began * * *") (dictum by Judge Easterbrook, formerly of the University of Chicago law faculty). In Hays v. Sony Corp., 847 F.2d 412 (7th Cir.1988), Judge Posner (of identical background) discussed at some length the case for a "teacher exception" to the work for hire rules and opined that, despite the seemingly literal grip of § 201(b), "we

---

[8] See 60 Pat., Tm. & Copyr.J. (BNA) 391 (2000).

might, if forced to decide the issue, conclude that the exception had survived the enactment of the 1976 Act." R. VerSteeg, Copyright and the Educational Process: The Right of Teacher Inception, 75 Iowa L.Rev. 381 (1990), finds a "teacher exception" desirable but ultimately recommends reliance on contractual arrangements; university copyright policies are reviewed in L. Lape, Ownership of Copyrightable Works of University Professors: The Interplay Between the Copyright Act and University Copyright Policies, 37 Vill.L.Rev. 223 (1992). University policies have traditionally allowed faculty to retain copyright in their writings and teaching materials, but that is being reconsidered in light of the potential economic value of digital works such as computer programs and online courses now being developed by faculty at many colleges.

Faculty ownership of copyright in their research articles has financial repercussions for universities and libraries. Much of the research that was formerly published by non-profit organizations now appears in for-profit journals owned by a few large publishing companies. The commercial publishers typically demand a transfer of copyright from the faculty author. Faced with dramatically escalating subscription costs, universities complain that the commercial publishers get articles for free from university faculty and then demand exorbitant prices to sell the articles back to the universities that paid for the research in the first place. A suggestion that universities should assert their right in works for hire and deposit copies of faculty research publications in open-access electronic repositories is made in R. Denicola, Copyright and Open Access: Reconsidering University Ownership of Faculty Research, 85 Neb.L.Rev. 351 (2006). University faculties are now experimenting with mechanisms to increase open access to their research. See, e.g., 84 Pat., Tm. & Copyr.J. (BNA) 181 (2012) (University of California at San Francisco faculty grant the university a nonexclusive, irrevocable, worldwide license to distribute their scholarly articles). In 2013 the Obama administration announced a new policy that requires all federal agencies with more than $100 million in annual research expenditures to implement procedures that insure free public access to publications arising from their federally-funded research within twelve months of publication. 85 Pat., Tm. & Copyr.J. (BNA) 565 (2013).

(6) You have photographs taken at your wedding. For an agreed fee, the photographer delivers an agreed number of prints. There is no written contract. Who owns the copyright? Can you make extra copies of the prints? Can you post the photos on Facebook[t] or e-mail copies to friends? See Marco v. Accent Pub. Co., 969 F.2d 1547 (3d Cir.1992), holding that photographs of jewelry were not works for hire despite some exercise of control by the commissioning party. To avoid the risk of liability for infringement, many photo labs will not print copies of photographs that look like they were taken by a professional photographer, such as school photos or posed pictures of children with stylish backgrounds or photos that simply look too good to have been taken by the customer. Bergstein, Digital Photography Hampered by Old Laws, Philadelphia Inquirer, June 19, 2005, p. E12.

(7) At this late date, is it still arguable that there are constitutional limitations on declaring employers to be "authors"? See Judge Friendly's dissent in Scherr v. Universal Match Corp., 417 F.2d 497 (2d Cir.1969), cert. denied, 397 U.S. 936 (1970). A. Ng, Authors and Readers: Conceptualizing Authorship in Copy-

---

[t]   In a 2012 filing with the Securities and Exchange Commission, Facebook estimated that 250 million photos are uploaded by Facebook users every day.

right Law, 30 Hastings Comm. & Ent. L.J. 377 (2008), believes the law should recognize greater rights in the actual author; T. Wu, On Copyright's Authorship Policy, 2008 U.Chi.Leg. Forum 335 (2008), argues that giving copyright to authors rather than distributors promotes innovation.

(8) No matter how the law defines works for hire, is there any way that commissioning parties with sufficient economic power can be prevented from exacting "all rights" assignments from writers and artists? In what ways will a copyright owner's rights differ if instead of taking under the work for hire rules, it relies on an assignment of copyright from the commissioned party? See, e.g., §§ 203, 302(c), 304(c). When, if ever, are the differences likely to be important?

S. Burnham, The Interstices of Copyright Law and Contract Law: Finding the Terms of an Implied Nonexclusive License in a Failed Work for Hire Agreement, 46 J.Copyr.Soc'y 333 (1999), sorts out the scope of use available under an implied license theory to a commissioning party who does not own the copyright through either assignment or work for hire. In Attig v. DRG, Inc., 74 U.S.P.Q.2d 1614 (E.D.Pa.2005), the defendant hired a computer consultant to create a web site for its business. The defendant did not get an assignment of copyright in the web site, but the court held that even absent ownership rights under the work for hire doctrine, the defendant had the right to reproduce and display the web site under an implied nonexclusive license arising from the plaintiff's delivery of the work with the intent that the defendant use it as planned. See also Asset Marketing Systems, Inc. v. Gagnon, 542 F.3d 748 (9th Cir.2008), cert. denied, 129 S.Ct. 2442 (2009) (finding that the commissioning party had an implied, nonexclusive license "to retain, use, and modify" the commissioned computer programs).

JOINT WORK

"The authors of a joint work are coowners of copyright in the work." § 201(a). The House Report summarizes the consequences of co-ownership: "Under the bill, as under the present law, coowners of a copyright would be treated generally as tenants in common, with each coowner having an independent right to use or license the use of a work, subject to a duty of accounting to the other coowners for any profits." H.R. Rep. p. 121.

What is a "joint work"? It is defined in § 101 as "a work prepared by two or more authors with the intention that their contributions be merged into inseparable or interdependent parts of a unitary whole." This is amplified in the House Report: "The touchstone here is the intention, at the time the writing is done, that the parts be absorbed or combined into an integrated unit, although the parts themselves may be either 'inseparable' (as in the case of a novel or painting) or 'interdependent' (as in the case of a motion picture, opera, or the words and music of a song.)" H.Rep. p. 120. See also § 302(b) on the duration of copyright in joint works.

The definition of joint work is tailored to correct the odd consequences of a series of older cases mostly concerning the interests of lyricists and composers of popular music. The Second Circuit consistently found a "joint" relationship between words and music created at different times without overt collaboration. The high-water mark was the *Twelfth Street Rag* case, Shapiro Bernstein & Co. v. Jerry Vogel Music Co., 115 F.Supp. 754 (S.D.N.Y.1953), rev'd, 221 F.2d 569 (2d Cir.), modified, 223 F.2d 252 (2d

Cir.1955). There the music was written and published without words. The composer assigned all rights to a publisher, who had words written and published with the music without the composer's knowledge. The Court of Appeals held that the relevant intent was that of the assignee "to merge the two contributions into a single work." As interpreted in the House Report, the 1976 Act requires an intention by the authors at the time of creation to merge their contributions into a unitary whole.

Recognition of joint ownership has been used as a solution in disputed work for hire cases. We return to the homeless Holy Family case, this time to the decision below in the Court of Appeals.

Community for Creative Non–Violence v. Reid

United States Court of Appeals, District of Columbia Circuit, 1988.
846 F.2d 1485.
Aff'd, 490 U.S. 730, 109 S.Ct. 2166 (1989).

■ Before MIKVA, RUTH BADER GINSBURG, and SILVERMAN, CIRCUIT JUDGES.

■ RUTH BADER GINSBURG, CIRCUIT JUDGE:

* * *

III.

CCNV sought a declaration of copyright ownership. We have held that CCNV is not author of a work made for hire and see no other basis for a claim that CCNV is sole owner of copyright in "Third World America." But neither does the existing record bear out Reid's assertion that he is the exclusive owner of copyright in the work. The facts thus far found by the district court, however, indicate that "Third World America" may indeed qualify as a joint work. [The court set forth the relevant statutory provisions.]

Most prominently undercutting Reid's claim of sole ownership, the district court found that CCNV "was the motivating factor in the procreation of 'Third World America,'" "conceived the idea in starkly specific detail," and "directed enough of [Reid's] effort to assure that, in the end, he had produced what [CCNV] not he, wanted . . . . " 652 F.Supp. at 1456. In making this point, we do not overlook the "idea/expression dichotomy"; as stated in the 1976 Act, "[i]n no case does copyright protection for an original work of authorship extend to any idea . . . regardless of the form in which it is . . . embodied in such work." 17 U.S.C. § 102(b). * * * "Third World America," however, was more than CCNV's abstract idea. Following CCNV's original conception of the sculpture, Snyder and other CCNV members, the district court found, monitored the progress of the work, not simply to approve Reid's embodiment of their idea, but to guide his expression and coordinate with his effort CCNV's construction of the steam grate pedestal. See 652 F.Supp. at 1455–56.[17]

In sum, were it not for the prevailing confusion over the work for hire doctrine, this case—once more taking the record in its current state—might qualify as a textbook example of a jointly-authored work in which the joint

---

[17] Case law concerning joint authorship in relation to the idea/expression dichotomy is sparse largely because the broad scope of the work for hire doctrine under the 1909 Act tended to draw disputes in which one party claimed to be the creative motivating force in the production of a copyrightable work into the ambit of that doctrine. With the substantial cutback of the work for hire doctrine under the 1976 Act, more cases of this genre can be expected to appear under the joint authorship rubric.

authors co-own the copyright. We note in this regard Reid's original and creative contribution to the figures; CCNV's contribution to the steam grate pedestal added to its initial conceptualization and ongoing direction of the realization of "Third World America"; and the various indicia of the parties' intent, from the outset, to merge their contributions into a unitary whole, and not to construct and separately preserve discrete parts as independent works. * * *

[The court took note of suggestions that other participants in the undertaking might also be joint authors and not simply employees of CCNV or Reid.] We therefore refer the matter to the district court with instructions to determine if there are any other parties who might qualify as "Third World America" authors and, on that account, should be joined in this action. * * *

We address, finally, a peculiar feature of this case * * * on which the parties' presentations are cloudy. There is only one "copy" of the copyrighted work at issue, and that only existing copy is exclusively owned by CCNV. Joint authors co-owning copyright in a work "are deemed to be tenants in common," with "each having an independent right to use or license the copyright, subject only to a duty to account to the other co-owner for any profits earned thereby." W. Patry, [Latman's The Copyright Law (6th ed.1986)] at 116 (footnotes omitted). In the absence of an agreement specifying otherwise, any profits earned are to be divided equally, "even where it is clear that [the] respective contributions to the joint work are not equal." 1 M. Nimmer & D. Nimmer, supra note 8, § 6.08, at 6–20 (footnote omitted). But singular works of art, we recognize, do not fit comfortably into a scheme centrally concerned with reproduction of the underlying work. See Brenner, A Two–Phase Approach to Copyrighting the Fine Arts, 24 Bull. Copyright Soc'y 85, 85 (1976–77).

Reid, as we mentioned earlier, objected to CCNV's travel plans for "Third World America," and planned a more modest exhibition tour of his own. See 652 F.Supp. at 1456. Co-ownership (or even sole ownership) of the copyright does not appear to carry with it a right to stop or limit CCNV's tour or to gain possession of the unique work of art. * * *

If CCNV reproduces "Third World America" in any medium and profits thereby, however, an accounting would be due to Reid as a copyright owner. Independent of Reid's ownership of the copyright, CCNV might be obliged to credit Reid as an author of the sculpture. * * * Furthermore, Reid, as an author, may have rights against CCNV should it publish an excessively mutilated or altered version of "Third World America." See Gilliam v. American Broadcasting Co., 538 F.2d 14 (2d Cir.1976); Kwall, Copyright and the Moral Right: Is an American Marriage Possible?, 38 Vand. L. Rev. 1, 17–34 (1985) (discussing various common law and statutory doctrines available to protect a creator against publication of excessively mutilated versions of his work but not against destruction); * * *

* * * [We] remand the case for further proceedings consistent with this opinion, particularly, for comprehensive consideration whether the sculpture called "Third World America" is a joint work and, if it is, for determination of the owners of copyright in the work.

NOTES AND QUESTIONS

(1) The Court of Appeals decided, with no apparent difficulty, that the sole copy of the sculpture belonged to CCNV. Can you imagine a case where a unique

copy would also be jointly owned? The question of joint ownership was ultimately settled by the parties. Reid was recognized as the sole author of the work, with control over three–dimensional reproductions. The original copy belonged to CCNV, and the parties agreed to co-ownership of rights in two–dimensional reproductions. Community for Creative Non–Violence v. Reid, 1991-92 Copyright Law Dec. (CCH) ¶ 26,753 (D.D.C.1991). Reid's access to the sculpture in exercise of his 3–dimensional reproduction rights, however, required further judicial intervention. See id. ¶ 26,860 (D.D.C.1991), recognizing an "implied easement of necessity" in favor of Reid.

(2) In Ashton–Tate Corp. v. Ross, 916 F.2d 516 (9th Cir.1990), the Ninth Circuit concluded that joint authorship requires each author to make a copyrightable contribution to the joint work. Cases in other circuits have reached similar conclusions. See, e.g., Forward v. Thorogood, 985 F.2d 604 (1st Cir.1993) (logistical support is insufficient for joint authorship); Erickson v. Trinity Theatre, Inc., 13 F.3d 1061 (7th Cir.1994) (noting that other contributors can protect their interests by contract). See also Andrien v. Southern Ocean County Chamber of Commerce, 927 F.2d 132 (3d Cir.1991) (one who acts as a mere amanuensis in fixing another's expression is not a joint author). R. VerSteeg, Defining "Author" for Purposes of Copyright, 45 Am.U.L.Rev. 1323 (1996), supports the case law requiring a contribution of copyrightable expression for joint authorship.[u]

(3) The Second Circuit in Childress v. Taylor, 945 F.2d 500 (1991), agreed that a joint author must make a copyrightable contribution and must intend, according to the statutory definition, that the contributions be merged into a unitary whole; but the court held that this was not sufficient for joint authorship. "[A]n inquiry so limited would extend joint author status to many persons who are not likely to have been within the contemplation of Congress. For example, a writer frequently works with an editor who makes revisions to the first draft, some of which will consist of additions of copyrightable expression. Both intend their contributions to be merged into inseparable parts of a unitary whole, yet very few editors and even fewer writers would expect the editor to be accorded the status of a joint author, enjoying an undivided half interest in the copyright in the published work. * * * What distinguishes the writer-editor relationship * * * from the true joint author relationship is the lack of intent of both parties in the venture to regard themselves as joint authors. * * * Joint authorship entitles the co-authors to equal undivided interests in the work, see 17 U.S.C. § 201(a); Community for Creative Non–Violence v. Reid, 846 F.2d 1485, 1498 (D.C.Cir.1988), aff'd without consideration of this point, 490 U.S. 730 (1989). That equal sharing of rights should be reserved for relationships in which all participants fully intend to be joint authors." The court held that a defendant who contributed research, incidental suggestions, and minor bits of expression was not a joint author. Is this an appropriate gloss on the statutory definition? R. Kwall, "Author-Stories": Narrative's Implications for Moral Rights and Copyright's Joint

---

[u]		The U.S. Government's claim to joint authorship of the Korean War Veterans Memorial was rejected in Gaylord v. United States, 595 F.3d 1364 (Fed.Cir.2010), when the sculptor objected to the U.S. Postal Service's use of a photograph of the Memorial on a stamp. Holding that one who "merely describes to an author what the commissioned work should do or look like is not a joint author," the court found that suggestions by government agents about the ethnicities, age, and equipment of the soldiers depicted in the Memorial were uncopyrightable ideas. J. Young, Copyright in Memoriam, 13 Vand.J.Ent. & Tech.L. 507 (2011), searches for theories that would limit copyright protection for public monuments.

Authorship Doctrine, 75 S.Cal.L.Rev. 1 (2001), expresses sympathy for the non-dominant collaborator and suggests that the ownership interests recognized in joint authors could in some cases be unequal.[v]

The *Childress* formulation proved decisive when a "dramaturg"—a "combination script doctor, editor, researcher, advice-giver and hand-holder"—claimed joint authorship of the Broadway smash hit *Rent*, which was taking in over $500,000 per week. The Second Circuit in Thomson v. Larson, 147 F.3d 195 (2d Cir.1998), held that the fact that author Jonathan Larson retained sole decision-making authority over the final work, was billed as the sole author, and entered into agreements as the sole author all indicated his lack of intent to make the plaintiff a co-author. The plaintiff argued that if she was not a co-author, she must instead have exclusive rights in her own contributions to the play. Since the plaintiff had not raised a claim of infringement in the trial court, Judge Calabresi said that issue was not properly before the court on appeal. Soon after the Second Circuit's decision, the plaintiff did bring an infringement action based on the inclusion of her copyrightable contributions in the play. The litigation was settled for an undisclosed sum and credit to the plaintiff as dramaturg on the title page of the *Rent* playbill. McKinley, Family of "Rent" Creator Settles Suit Over Authorship, N.Y. Times, Sept. 10, 1998, p. B3.[w]

The Ninth Circuit in Aalmuhammed v. Lee, 202 F.3d 1227 (9th Cir.2000), noted a further level of complexity in the joint work issue. The plaintiff made copyrightable contributions to the Spike Lee movie *Malcolm X* in the form of specific dialogue and scenes. The court agreed with the *Childress* position that a copyrightable contribution was not sufficient in itself to establish joint authorship. It is true, the court said, that a creator of expression is the "author" of that contribution for purposes of its independent copyrightability; the contributor, however, is not necessarily an "author" of the joint work. The latter turns on several factors, including who superintends the work by controlling its creation and whether there is an objective manifestation of intent to be co-authors. Here, the creation of the film was controlled by Warner Brothers and Spike Lee, and plaintiff's contributions were subject to Lee's approval. Warner Brothers had refused to recognize even Lee as a co-author, requiring him to sign a work-for-hire agreement, and it would be illogical to assume that Warner Brothers intended to share ownership with people who worked under Lee. The special problems of authorship and ownership in the motion picture industry are analyzed in J. Dougherty, Not a Spike Lee Joint? Issues in the Authorship of Motion Pictures Under U.S. Copyright Law, 49 UCLA L.Rev. 225 (2001).

(4) Joint ownership of the copyright, although a seemingly Solomonic solution in difficult situations, creates its own problems of discordant use by co-owners

---

[v]   For criticism of the judicial restrictions on joint work status, see L. Lape, A Narrow View of Creative Cooperation: The Current State of Joint Work Doctrine, 61 Alb.L.Rev. 43 (1997). M. LaFrance, Authorship, Dominance, and the Captive Collaborator: Preserving the Rights of Joint Authors, 50 Emory L.J. 193 (2001), questions any "relationship test" for joint authorship, urging instead a focus on the nature of the contribution made by the less-dominant contributor.

[w]   The issues raised by attempts to gain recognition of a "director's copyright" in the "staging" directions for a play—vigorously opposed by playwrights—are debated in Green, Exit, Pursued by a Lawyer, N.Y. Times, Jan. 29, 2006, Sec. 2, p. 1. M. Livingston, Inspiration or Imitation: Copyright Protection for Stage Directions, 50 B.C.L.Rev. 427 (2009), examines the scope of copyright protection that might be available to theater directors for their stage directions.

who may be at odds, mitigated only somewhat by the obligation of each to account to the other. M. Chon, New Wine Bursting From Old Bottles: Collaborative Internet Art, Joint Works, and Entrepreneurship, 75 Ore.L.Rev. 257 (1996), uses the joint work doctrine to illustrate the misalignment of traditional ownership principles with the fluidity of the networked computer environment; E. Lee, Warming Up to User–Generated Content, 2008 U.Ill.L.Rev. 1459, points to user-generated web content as an example of the informal practices that fill in the gaps of copyright law. See also S. Hetcher, Using Social Norms to Regulate Fan Fiction and Remix Culture, 157 U.Pa.L.Rev. 1869 (2009), crediting social norms with facilitating the explosion of "remix" works created by combining pieces of existing works.

The confusing relationship between state community property law and the federal rules on intellectual property ownership is analyzed in J. Cochran, It Takes Two to Tango!: Problems with Community Property Ownership of Copyrights and Patents in Texas, 58 Baylor L.Rev. 407 (2006).

(5) Authors of joint works, unlike creators of works for hire, do have the power to terminate grants. This has its problems too. Consider this situation:

> In 1985, *A* and *B* collaborated on a novel; the work was registered as a joint work. *A* and *B* immediately granted exclusive movie rights to Studio. In 2020, *A* is dead, survived by her husband and one child. *B* is living, and wishes to terminate the grant to Studio. Who must join *B* in exercising the termination right? See § 203(a).

6. INDUSTRIES AFFECTED BY COMPULSORY COPYRIGHT LICENSING

We now turn to situations where Congress has decided, for reasons that vary with each setting, that copyrights must be made available on terms that are outlined in the statute and administratively regulated. We have already encountered the compulsory license in § 114 for the digital performance of sound recordings, p. 284 supra. The others cover noncommercial broadcasting, § 118; the production of phonorecords, § 115; "coin-operated phonorecord players"—jukeboxes, now superseded by § 116; and cable and satellite transmissions of television programs, §§ 111, 119, and 122.

COPYRIGHT ROYALTY JUDGES

One creation of the 1976 Act was an administrative body called the Copyright Royalty Tribunal. The Tribunal was charged with "periodically reviewing and adjusting statutory royalty rates for use of copyrighted materials pursuant to compulsory licenses provided in sections 111 (secondary transmissions by cable systems), 115 (mechanical royalties)[x] and 116 (jukebox) of the bill. In addition, the Commission will make determinations as to reasonable terms and rates of royalty payments as provided in section 118 (public broadcasting), and to resolve disputes over the distribution of royal-

----

[x]　This label persists, although it profoundly misdescribes modern music recording technology, as a remnant of § 1(e) of the 1909 Act, which spoke of "copyright controlling the parts of instruments serving to reproduce mechanically the musical work."

ties paid pursuant to the statutory licenses in sections 111 and 116." H.R.Rep. p. 173.

The Tribunal had a turbulent career. One chair of the Tribunal in 1981 proposed its abolition and resigned. In 1990, the number of commissioners was reduced from five to three. In 1993, the chair charged her two colleagues, both of whom favored dissolution of the Tribunal, with professional misconduct. The Copyright Royalty Tribunal was finally abolished in 1993 amid complaints that its proceedings were costly and inefficient. The rate-setting and royalty distributing duties of the Tribunal were transferred to ad hoc Copyright Arbitration Royalty Panels convened by the Librarian of Congress. But after a decade of experience with CARPs, the content providers who are regular participants in the rate-setting and royalty distribution proceedings complained that the CARP system too was inefficient and relied on inappropriate standards in setting rates. In 2004, Congress changed the system again, creating the Copyright Royalty Board consisting of three Copyright Royalty Judges serving six-year terms and eligible for reappointment. At least one of the Judges "shall have significant knowledge of copyright law"; another "shall have significant knowledge of economics." § 802 (a). The Register of Copyrights has the authority to "review for legal error the resolution by the Copyright Royalty Judges of a material question of substantive law under this title," § 802(f)(1)(D); an appeal from a determination of the Copyright Royalty Judges can be taken to the Court of Appeals for the District of Columbia Circuit. § 803(d).[y]

PUBLIC BROADCASTING AND § 118

Both ASCAP and BMI at one time gave free licenses to educational broadcasters, with certain restrictions on popular songs. The public broadcasters, worried that they might someday have to start paying, pushed for protection during the drafting of the 1976 Act. The outcome is § 118. See B. Korman, Performance Rights in Music under Sections 110 and 118 of the 1976 Copyright Act, 22 N.Y.L.S.L.Rev. 521 (1977).

Section 118 covers the performance and display of published nondramatic musical works and published pictorial, graphic, and sculptural works by public broadcasting entities. It explicitly encourages voluntary agreement. The rates for musical works are generally negotiated. Rates for works not covered by a voluntary agreement are set by the Copyright Royalty Judges.

---

[y] The constitutionality of the Copyright Royalty Board was called into question in Intercollegiate Broadcasting Sys., Inc. v. Copyright Royalty Bd., 684 F.3d 1332 (D.C.Cir.2012), when a group of noncommercial webcasters appealed a rate-setting decision. The webcasters argued that the Copyright Royalty Judges, who are appointed by the Librarian of Congress, are "principal" officers who must be appointed by the President with Senate confirmation. The court agreed, but as a remedy it invalidated the restrictions in § 802(i) on the Librarian's ability to remove a Copyright Royalty Judge. Without the restrictions on removal, the court said that the Judges were now "inferior" officers who did not require Presidential appointment. However, the court vacated and remanded the rate decision because "the Board's structure was unconstitutional at the time it issued its determination." It is unclear whether other prior determinations of the Board are now open to a similar challenge.

THE RECORD INDUSTRY AND § 115

When recording rights were added to copyright in the 1909 Act, fears were expressed that the granting of exclusive recording licenses by the owners of popular music would consolidate the monopoly of a "music trust" in the then-dominant form of recorded music—player-piano rolls; hence the compulsory license that first appeared in § 1(e) of the 1909 Act. Although concern over the piano roll monopoly had subsided considerably by 1976, similar fears with respect to competition in the record industry prompted the continuation of the compulsory license in § 115. The compulsory license to record a musical work is available only after "phonorecords of a nondramatic musical work have been distributed to the public in the United States under the authority of the copyright owner." § 115(a)(1). The compulsory license can be invoked only if the licensee's "primary purpose in making phonorecords is to distribute them to the public for private use"; it cannot be used, for example, to record music for movies or television programs, often referred to as "synchronous" use.[z] Recognizing that sound recordings can be delivered online, Congress in 1995 expanded the compulsory license to cover the digital distribution of sound recordings. Section 115(c)(3) endeavors to distinguish between a digital performance and the digital distribution of a sound recording through the definition of a "digital phonorecord delivery" in § 115(d); a defining characteristic of a "digital phonorecord delivery" is the creation of "a specifically identifiable reproduction" of the recording by or for the recipient.

Does the structure of the modern music industry support the earlier rationale for a compulsory license? Less than two decades ago there were still six major record companies, but today there are only three, although there are also a number of smaller independent labels.[aa] What effect does the availability of a compulsory license to record musical works have on the competitiveness of the record industry? The license makes possible the release of "cover" records. If a song becomes a hit, other performers can and will record it, and there is thus no way to maintain a monopoly in the recording of a popular song. And what does the songwriter get? Her contract with the music publisher will usually divide evenly the recording right royalties as well as other payments from third parties. If the music and lyrics have separate authors, another split occurs. The initial recording contract is not legally constrained by the compulsory license rate, but that rate is

---

[z]   What exactly does the compulsory license permit? When a defendant invoked the license to record a karaoke CD–ROM that included a video track that scrolled the lyrics across the screen, the court held that the use was beyond the scope of § 115. "[W]hile a compulsory license permits the recording of a 'cover' version of a song, it does not permit the inclusion of a copy of the lyrics. That requires the separate permission of the copyright holder." ABKCO Music, Inc. v. Stellar Records, Inc., 96 F.3d 60 (2d Cir.1996).

Section 115(a)(2) allows a compulsory licensee to arrange the music "to the extent necessary to conform it to the style or manner of interpretation of the performance," but does not allow changes in "the basic melody or fundamental character of the work" and precludes compulsory licensees from claiming copyright in their derivative versions. Could 2 Live Crew have invoked the compulsory license to insulate its parody recording of *Oh, Pretty Woman*? See footnote 4 of the *Campbell* opinion, p. 354 supra. Musician Jonathan Coulton publicly complained that the television show *Glee* used a version of his folksy, banjo-infused cover of the 1992 hip-hop hit *Baby Got Back* by Sir Mix-A-Lot. Would Coulton have a claim for infringement of his arrangement? Might he himself be liable to Sir Mix-A-Lot for exceeding the scope of the compulsory license? Zakarin, Musician Claims "Glee" Stole His Version of "Baby Got Back," Hollywood Reporter, Jan. 25, 2013.

[aa]   For extensive information on the recording industry, consult M. Krasilovsky, S. Shemel, J. Gross, and J. Feinstein, This Business of Music (2007).

often used; "cover" records of course need pay no more than the statutory royalty.

The 1976 Act originally set the compulsory license rate at 2.75 cents per track. As soon as the law allowed, copyright owners resorted to the Copyright Royalty Tribunal, which after extensive hearings set a rate of 4 cents. Both sides appealed. In Recording Industry Ass'n of America v. Copyright Royalty Tribunal, 662 F.2d 1 (D.C.Cir.1981), the court found that the Tribunal had adequately justified the four–cent rate.[bb] The Tribunal had also proposed annual proceedings "to calculate appropriate interim adjustment figures." The court remanded this arrangement, finding it unauthorized in view of the precise and widely-separated adjustment intervals prescribed in the statute. But the court helpfully observed that "we see nothing in the statute precluding the Tribunal from adopting a reasonable mechanism for automatic rate changes in interim years." The Tribunal did just that. Succeeding increases brought the rate to 9.1 cents in 2006. In a subsequent rate proceeding, the Copyright Royalty Board decided to keep the rate at 9.1 cents through 2012 for both physical recordings and permanent digital downloads. In 2012 the Board adopted an agreement negotiated by the Recording Industry Association of America, the National Music Publishers' Association, and the Digital Media Association that continues the 9.1 cent rate for physical records and permanent downloads and the 24 cent rate for ringtones. The agreement also includes rates for services such as on-demand streaming and digital lockers. 77 Fed.Reg. 29259 (May 17, 2012).

NOTES AND QUESTIONS

(1) Can you think of any reason, aside from habit, why the basic statutory rate remains a flat amount, rather than a percentage of record prices or revenues, as is the case in some other countries?

(2) For the composer-performer, the mechanical royalty is merely part of a package that also includes performers' royalties; the latter are limited only by bargaining strength, and for superstars can reach superfigures like 15 per cent or more of retail prices.[cc] But on "cover" records made by other performers, the composer gets only the mechanical royalties. The desire to share in those royalties is one incentive for record companies to have music publishing affiliates.

(3) Music owners have sometimes been accused of "double-dipping," claiming that the downloading of a digital music file also constitutes a public performance for which separate royalties are due, or that streamed performances result in temporary RAM or "buffer" copies that necessitate a mechanical license royalty under § 115. In a 2001 DMCA Report mandated by Congress, the Copyright Office recommended amending § 115 to preclude liability for temporary buffer copies that are incidental to a licensed digital performance of a musical work. The Report also concluded that no liability should result from any technical performance of a musical work that may occur in the course of licensed digital downloads of sound recordings.

[bb]   Among the Tribunal's findings: "[F]rom 1955 to 1979 composers' royalties had declined from being slightly greater than performers' royalties to barely a quarter of the performers' share, * * * and that from 1964 to 1974 copyright owners' royalty payments declined from 11.2% of wholesale record price to 7.2%." 662 F.2d 11 n. 25.

[cc]   The arcane accounting practices of the record companies sometimes leave performers with less than they expect. Gundersen, Bye, Bye, A Piece of the Pie; Music Veterans Sue for Record Royalties, But the Accounting Can Be Confounding, USA Today, May 17, 2004, p. D1.

The conclusion that digital downloads do not generally constitute a performance was confirmed by the Second Circuit in United States v. ASCAP, 627 F.3d 64 (2d Cir.2010), cert. denied, 132 S.Ct. 366 (2011). "In answering the question of whether a download is a public performance, we turn to Section 101 of the Copyright Act, which states that '[t]o "perform" a work means to recite, render, play, dance, or act it, either directly or by means of any device or process.' 17 U.S.C. § 101. A download plainly is neither a 'dance' nor an 'act.' Thus, we must determine whether a download of a musical work falls within the meaning of the terms 'recite,' 'render,' or 'play.' * * * The ordinary sense of the words 'recite,' 'render,' and 'play' refer to actions that can be perceived contemporaneously." The court concluded, "The downloads at issue in this appeal are not musical performances that are contemporaneously perceived by the listener. They are simply transfers of electronic files containing digital copies from an on-line server to a local hard drive. The downloaded songs are not performed in any perceptible manner during the transfers; the user must take some further action to play the songs after they are downloaded. Because the electronic download itself involves no recitation, rendering, or playing of the musical work encoded in the digital transmission, we hold that such a download is not a performance of that work, as defined by § 101." In a footnote the court added a caution: "Our opinion does not foreclose the possibility, under certain circumstances not presented in this case, that a transmission could constitute both a stream and a download, each of which implicates a different right of the copyright holder."

(4) The opposite issue—do streamed performances also result in a "digital phonorecord delivery" that requires a license under § 115—remains unsettled. See P. Goldstein, Goldstein on Copyright § 7.2.1. Section 115(c)(3)(C) does include "digital phonorecord deliveries where the reproduction or distribution of a phonorecord is incidental to the transmission which constitutes the digital phonorecord delivery," although it specifies that the terms and rates for such deliveries should be distinguished from digital phonorecord deliveries in general. However, the argument that "buffering" used to effectuate a digital performance does not constitute a digital reproduction that triggers § 115 got a boost from the Second Circuit's decision in Cartoon Network LP v. CSC Holdings, Inc., 536 F.3d 121 (2d Cir.2008), cert. denied 129 S.Ct. 2890 (2009). The court concluded that Cablevision's buffering of television programming streams in connection with its Remote Storage DVR system did not infringe the copyright owners' reproduction right. Judge Walker noted that the definition of "fixed" in § 101 requires that the embodiment of the work persist "for a period of more than transitory duration." Here the buffered data was replaced every 1.2 seconds. The court held that the programming had not been "fixed" and hence the buffering did not create potentially infringing copies.[dd]

(5) Noting that other countries have eliminated the compulsory license to distribute phonorecords, the Register of Copyrights suggested in 2005 that § 115 be repealed so that the market could develop one-stop licensing mechanisms for all uses of musical works. 70 Pat., Tm. & Copyr.J. (BNA) 232 (2005). By 2007 however, the Register had given up hope that § 115 would be scrapped anytime soon, proposing instead more modest amendments. 73 id. 652 (2007). M. Einhorn and L. Kurlantzick, Traffic Jam on the Music Highway: Is It a Repro-

---

[dd] A. Perzanowski, Fixing RAM Copies, 104 Nw.U.L.Rev. 1067 (2010), uses the *Cartoon Network* case as the starting point to analyze the "more than transitory duration" requirement for fixation in a copy.

duction or a Performance?, 49 J.Copyr. Soc'y 417 (2001), argue for a compulsory licensing regime for downloading and streaming that will not distort choices among alternative delivery systems by burdening digital deliveries with costs not assessed on physical phonorecord deliveries; H. Abrams, Copyright's First Compulsory License, 26 Santa Clara Computer & High Tech.L.J. 215 (2010), argues against continuation of the compulsory license for phonorecords.

(6) An important entity in the world of music is the Harry Fox Agency. It represents over 45,000 music publishers in licensing recording rights through contracts that bypass some of the compulsory licensing formalities in § 115.[ee] "Synchronization" of music on works such as motion pictures, television programs, and commercials must be licensed directly from the individual music publishers.

JUKEBOXES AND § 116

Performance of copyrighted music on "coin-operated machines" was exempted from the public performance for profit right in the 1909 Act because the penny-arcade machines of that era were believed to be unprofitable. Then came the once ubiquitous jukebox, which in its heyday may have swallowed half a billion dollars a year in nickels, dimes, and quarters. Attempts to repeal the exemption were frequent but unsuccessful. The operators who supply the machines and the taverns and other establishments who by custom get half the take constituted a broad political base, in contrast to the concentration of the popular music industry in a few urban centers. Their only contention of any weight against paying was that they bought a lot of records. (See H.R.Rep. pp. 112–13 for a summary of the arguments for and against the exemption.)

The 1976 Act in § 116 initially replaced the jukebox exemption with a compulsory license. However, art. 11 of the Berne Convention has been interpreted to prohibit compulsory licensing of public performance rights in musical works. (Article 13(1) permits compulsory licensing of recording rights as in § 115.) In 1993, the compulsory license in § 116 was eliminated, replaced with procedures for voluntary negotiations backed by administrative rate-setting proceedings.

CABLE AND SATELLITE TELEVISION

1. *Introduction*

The last compulsory licenses to be considered are by all odds the most intricate. They can be understood, moreover, only in the context of an industry that has been on a roller coaster ride for almost fifty years. Cable television has been alternately advanced and retarded by the Federal Communications Commission, the Congress, the courts, and the Copyright Office. Meanwhile, technological advances, notably satellite transmission, have created both new opportunities and new forms of competition.

During the 1960s the Federal Communications Commission was urged to move against cable television by the broadcasters, who saw cable as a

------

[ee] Information on the Harry Fox Agency is available at www.harryfox.com. A press release lists Irving Berlin's *White Christmas* as the most licensed song in the Harry Fox catalog.

threat to "free" television. At first, cable merely provided wider and better reception of local stations. But then cable began to import signals from distant stations and to carry its own programming. (Recall the very different settings of the *Fortnightly* and *Teleprompter* cases, pp. 273 and 275 supra.)

The FCC in 1972 promulgated regulations based on a "consensus agreement," a compromise between broadcasters, program producers, and cable operators.[ff] The regulations severely restricted the ability of cable operators to import the most attractive distant signals. Another part of the consensus agreement insured protection for territorial exclusivity of syndicated programs. Both for the makers of programs and for the networks and other broadcasters, syndicated exclusivity was thought to be the key to maximizing revenues. But as long as cable was free of copyright liability under *Fortnightly* and *Teleprompter,* FCC action was necessary to protect the separation of first runs and reruns and control their timing and marketing. The rules required imported cable signals to be blacked out whenever they carried programs covered under exclusive contracts in the local market.

Meanwhile, copyright revision was at a standstill, in part because of the lack of agreement over the obligation of cable operators to pay copyright owners. A compromise was finally reached.

2.   *Section 111*

The compromise, § 111, is one of the most indigestible segments of the 1976 Act. The House Report attempted this summary:

"In general, the Committee believes that cable systems are commercial enterprises whose basic retransmission operations are based on the carriage of copyrighted program material and that copyright royalties should be paid by cable operators to the creators of such programs. The Committee recognizes, however, that it would be impractical and unduly burdensome to require every cable system to negotiate with every copyright owner whose work was retransmitted by a cable system. Accordingly, the Committee has determined to maintain the basic principle of the Senate bill to establish a compulsory copyright license for the retransmission of those over-the-air broadcast signals that a cable system is authorized to carry pursuant to the rules and regulations of the FCC.

"The compulsory license is conditioned, however, on certain requirements and limitations. These include compliance with reporting requirements, payment of the royalty fees established in the bill, a ban on the substitution or deletion of commercial advertising, and geographic limits on the compulsory license for copyrighted programs broadcast by Canadian or Mexican stations. Failure to comply with these requirements and limitations subjects a cable system to a suit for copyright infringement and the remedies provided under the bill for such actions.

" * * * The Committee determined, however, that there was no evidence that the retransmission of 'local' broadcast signals by a cable operator threatens the existing market for copyright program owners. Similarly, the retransmission of network programing, including network programing which is broadcast in 'distant' markets, does not injure the copyright owner. The copyright owner contracts with the network on the basis of his programing reaching all markets served by the network and is compensated accordingly.

[ff]   See 37 Fed.Reg. 3341 (Feb. 12, 1972).

"By contrast, their transmission of distant non-network programing by cable systems causes damage to the copyright owner by distributing the program in an area beyond which it has been licensed. Such retransmission adversely affects the ability of the copyright owner to exploit the work in the distant market. It is also of direct benefit to the cable system by enhancing its ability to attract subscribers and increase revenues. For these reasons, the Committee has concluded that the copyright liability of cable television systems under the compulsory license should be limited to the retransmission of distant non-network programing."[gg]

Section 111 has survived, with repeated tinkering, for over three decades despite dramatic changes in technology. Among the major developments were these:

3.   *An Interlude of Deregulation*

Heralded by two massive economic reports in 1979[hh] and encouraged by political pressure toward deregulation, the FCC in 1980 abolished both distant signal restrictions and the safeguards for syndicated exclusivity. In 1981, the Second Circuit upheld everything that the FCC had done, or rather undone. Malrite T.V. v. FCC, 652 F.2d 1140 (2d Cir.1981), cert. denied, 454 U.S. 1143 (1982). The Copyright Royalty Tribunal responded to this unshackling of cable by setting higher royalty rates under § 111. The Tribunal's action was upheld in National Cable Television Ass'n v. Copyright Royalty Tribunal, 724 F.2d 176 (D.C.Cir.1983).

4.   *Satellite Retransmission*

Satellites that can receive broadcast transmissions and redirect them to receiving dishes were initially used by cable systems for bringing in programs beyond those of the local broadcasters. Satellite transmissions, however, can also be distributed to individual home viewers. The obligations of satellite disseminators to copyright owners remained unresolved until Congress in the Satellite Home Viewer Act, Pub.L. No. 100–667, added § 119 to the Copyright Act in 1988. It creates a compulsory license covering satellite retransmission for private home viewing, but network stations can be delivered only to "unserved households" that cannot receive an over-the-air signal of specified quality from a network affiliate.[ii]

In an effort to make satellite transmission more competitive with cable, Congress in 1999 added § 122 to the Copyright Act, which provides a royalty-free compulsory license for the satellite retransmission of local television broadcasts into the broadcaster's local market. Pub.L. No. 106–113.[jj]

[gg] H.R.Rep. pp. 89–90.

[hh] 71 F.C.C.2d 632 and 951 (1979).

[ii] When EchoStar, operator of the DISH satellite television network, was found to have engaged in a "pattern or practice" of violating the restriction against delivery of distant network stations to homes that were not "unserved" by local network stations, the Eleventh Circuit ordered a nationwide injunction under § 119(a)(7)(B) barring EchoStar from delivering any distant network programming under the compulsory license in § 119. CBS Broadcasting, Inc. v. EchoStar Communications Corp., 450 F.3d 505 (11th Cir. 2006), cert. denied, 549 U.S. 1113 (2007). Congress effectively overturned the injunction in 2010. See § 119(g).

[jj] Satellite transmissions (as opposed to the programs being transmitted) are the subject of the Brussels Convention Relating to the Distribution of Programme—Carrying Signals Transmitted by Satellite (1974). The purpose of the Brussels Convention is to combat commercial piracy of satellite signals; it does not encompass reception for private use. The United States, viewing its existing copyright and communications laws as sufficient to satisfy the Convention, ratified it in 1984.

5. *The Roller Coaster Rolls On*

Meanwhile, FCC and Congressional momentum favoring cable continued. The Cable Communications Policy Act of 1984, Pub.L. No. 98–549, 47 U.S.C.A. § 521 et seq., gave cable a boost when it drastically curtailed state and local authority over franchises and customer rates. The courts also contributed to cable's emancipation. A substantial element in the 1976 compromise behind § 111 was cable's "must carry" obligation imposed by the FCC with respect to local channels. In 1985, the Court of Appeals for the District of Columbia surprised many observers by holding that the "must carry" rules violated the hitherto quiescent first amendment rights of cable operators. Quincy Cable TV, Inc. v. FCC, 768 F.2d 1434 (D.C.Cir.1985), cert. denied, 476 U.S. 1169 (1986). This alarmed independent broadcast stations of all types. The FCC was quickly persuaded to restore "must carry" for five years. These interim regulations also fell before the first amendment in Century Communications Corp. v. FCC, 835 F.2d 292 (D.C.Cir.1987), cert. denied, 486 U.S. 1032 (1988).

About the only thing the FCC did in the 1980s that in any way curbed cable was to reinstate exclusive programming contracts for broadcasters—the syndicated exclusivity that it had abolished in 1980. This meant that cable had to black out programs (typically reruns) if either local or superstations had exclusive rights in them. A challenge by the cable companies to the reinstatement of syndicated exclusivity was rejected in United Video, Inc. v. FCC, 890 F.2d 1173 (D.C.Cir.1989).

6. *Putting the Brakes on Cable: The 1992 Cable Act*

The Cable Television Consumer Protection and Competition Act of 1992, Pub.L. No. 102–385, refashioned the regulation of cable on several fronts. In an effort to insure access to program material, cable operators with an interest in a programmer or vendor were generally prohibited from restricting access to the programming by competitors. The Act also imposed a complicated system of rate regulation that yielded only limited results.

In yet another attempt to give broadcasters the power to insist that cable systems carry their signals, the 1992 Act revived "must carry" obligations for cable operators (but also offered broadcasters the option to forgo their "must carry" rights and instead negotiate with cable operators for consent to retransmit their signal under the threat of withholding permission). The "must carry" requirement, which had twice before been struck down as a burden on first amendment rights, was quickly challenged. When the issue reached the Supreme Court in Turner Broadcasting System v. FCC, 520 U.S. 180 (1997), the "must carry" obligation survived in a 5–4 decision.[kk]

7. *The Forces of Competition?*

After years of struggle, Congress rewrote the nation's communications laws in the Telecommunications Act of 1996, Pub.L. No. 104–104. Among other changes, the law encouraged cable and telephone companies to enter each others' markets with a full range of services such as telephone, video, and broadband. In particular, the Telecommunications Act created an "open video system" that allowed telephone companies to retransmit broad-

---

[kk] The version of the "must carry" rules applicable to satellite transmitters who take advantage of the compulsory license in § 122 to retransmit a broadcast into the broadcaster's local market was upheld against first amendment challenge in Satellite Broadcasting and Communications Ass'n v. FCC, 275 F.3d 337 (4th Cir.2001), cert. denied, 536 U.S. 922 (2002).

cast television signals, subject to "must carry" obligations. This attempt to unleash the forces of competition in the television industry initially flopped as telephone companies shelved their once ambitious plans to enter the television market. Recently however, companies such as AT&T and Verizon have emerged as competitors of cable and satellite providers by offering video services over their networks.[ll] FCC rules designed to expedite the local approval process for the new video services were upheld against a challenge by cable operators and local government organizations in Alliance for Community Media v. FCC, 529 F.3d 763 (6th Cir.2008), cert. denied, 129 S.Ct. 2821 (2009).

8.   *The Future of the Compulsory Licenses*

Amidst all this change, the compulsory licenses in § 111, § 119, and § 122 occupy an inconspicuous but not insignificant corner. Although the royalties generated by the licenses are relatively small,[mm] the guaranteed access to programming that they provide is crucial, at least according to cable and satellite operators.

In the Satellite Home Viewer Extension and Reauthorization Act § 109 Report (2008) on the statutory licensing regimes in §§ 111, 119, and 122, the Copyright Office was unambiguous: "The principal recommendation in the Report is that Congress move toward abolishing Section 111 and Section 119 of the Act. The cable and satellite industries are no longer nascent entities in need of government subsidies through a statutory licensing system. They have substantial market power and are able to negotiate private agreements with copyright owners for programming carried on distant broadcast signals." The Report specifically recommended against extending a compulsory license for Internet transmission of broadcast programming.[nn]

After preserving the satellite retransmission licenses in §§ 119 and 122 through a series of temporary extensions, Congress eventually enacted a five-year renewal in the Satellite Television Extension and Localism Act of 2010, P.L. 111–175 (2010). Passage of the renewal followed a year of hearings at which satellite operators argued for looser rules on the retransmission of signals and broadcasters and program owners urged an end to the compulsory license. Despite increased support for ending the licenses, the status quo largely prevailed, with satellite operators gaining an expansion of the compulsory license to cover digital transmissions and a loosening of the rules on transmitting local stations into local markets. The Register of Copyrights was directed to submit a report to Congress containing recommendations on how to implement a phase-out of the statutory licenses in §§ 111, 119, and 122. The Satellite Television Extension and Localism Act § 302 Report (2011) concluded that copyright owners should be

---

[ll]   According to the FCC's 2012 Annual Assessment of the Status of Competition in the Market for the Delivery of Video Programming, telephone video services account for 7 percent of the television subscriber market. Cable still leads with 60 percent, followed by satellite providers at 33 percent.

[mm]   Cable companies paid about $200 million in royalties under § 111 in 2010; total satellite royalties under § 119 are considerably less. See U.S. Copyright Office, Satellite Television Extension and Localism Act § 302 Report (2011).

[nn]   In WPIX, Inc. v. ivi, Inc., 691 F.3d 275 (2d Cir.2012), cert. denied, 133 S.Ct. 1585 (2013), copyright owners sued a company that captured over-the-air television broadcasts and simultaneously streamed the broadcasts over the Internet to subscribers. The defendant claimed that it was entitled to a compulsory license under § 111 as a "cable system." The court rejected the defendant's contention, agreeing with the Copyright Office that despite the lack of clarity in the statutory language, Congress never intended § 111 to apply to an Internet distributor.

allowed to develop marketplace licensing options to replace the compulsory licenses. Possible mechanisms might include sublicensing cable and satellite retransmission rights through the broadcast stations, collective licensing organizations that could issue blanket licenses, and direct licensing between copyright owners and cable and satellite systems. Bills to dismantle the compulsory licenses faced immediate opposition. 83 Pat., Tm. & Copyr.J. (BNA) 481 (2012).

The only certainty in all of this is that things will not remain as they are.

CHAPTER 6

JURISDICTION AND REMEDIES

1. JURISDICTION OF FEDERAL AND STATE COURTS

28 U.S.C. § 1338

(a) The district courts shall have original jurisdiction of any civil action arising under any Act of Congress relating to patents, plant variety protection, copyrights and trademarks. No State court shall have jurisdiction over any claim for relief arising under any Act of Congress relating to patents, plant variety protection, or copyrights. For purposes of this subsection, the term "State" includes any State of the United States, the District of Columbia, the Commonwealth of Puerto Rico, the United States Virgin Islands, American Samoa, Guam, and the Northern Mariana Islands.

(b) The district courts shall have original jurisdiction of any civil action asserting a claim of unfair competition when joined with a substantial and related claim under the copyright, patent, plant variety protection or trademark laws.

(c) Subsections (a) and (b) apply to exclusive rights in mask works under chapter 9 of title 17, and to exclusive rights in designs under chapter 13 of title 17, to the same extent as such subsections apply to copyrights.

NOTES AND QUESTIONS

(1) It is plain enough under 28 U.S.C. § 1338 that if a copyright owner brings an infringement action against a stranger who has reproduced the copyrighted work, the federal courts have exclusive subject matter jurisdiction. What is it about copyright (and patent) that justifies the denial of concurrent jurisdiction in state courts?

(2) Not every cause of action that invokes the word "copyright" will be treated as "arising under" the Copyright Act. An action to enforce a contract to pay royalties for use of a copyrighted work, for example, must be brought in state court, absent some other basis for federal jurisdiction. See, e.g., Danks v. Gordon, 272 Fed. 821 (2d Cir.1921); Golden West Melodies, Inc. v. Capitol Records, Inc., 274 Cal.App.2d 713, 79 Cal.Rptr. 442 (1969). Similarly, an action to foreclose a security interest in a copyright remains within the jurisdiction of the state courts. Republic Pictures Corp. v. Security–First National Bank of Los Angeles, 197 F.2d 767 (9th Cir.1952).

(3) Allocating jurisdiction in disputes over the ownership of a copyright has proved particularly troublesome. When the primary objective of the litigation is to determine the enforceability or effect of an assignment, federal jurisdiction is usually denied. See, e.g., T.B. Harms Co. v. Eliscu, 339 F.2d 823 (2d Cir.1964), cert. denied, 381 U.S. 915 (1965); Scholastic Ent., Inc. v. Fox Ent. Group, Inc., 336 F.3d 982 (9th Cir.2003). Yet, if the complaint also raises a genuine issue of infringement, federal jurisdiction may be upheld. See Topolos v. Caldewey, 698 F.2d 991 (9th Cir.1983). As the latter case notes, "Courts have directed inquiry to what they have variously described as the 'primary and controlling purpose'

of the suit, the 'principal issue,' the 'fundamental controversy,' and the 'gist' or 'essence' of the plaintiff's claim." If subsequently, "affidavits or other materials reveal the infringement claim to be spurious," the federal action should be dismissed. Vestron, Inc. v. Home Box Office, 839 F.2d 1380 (9th Cir.1988).

How strong is the claim for exclusive federal jurisdiction in suits to establish joint authorship? See Goodman v. Lee, 815 F.2d 1030 (5th Cir.1987) (federal jurisdiction accepted); Merchant v. Levy, 92 F.3d 51 (2d Cir.1996), cert. denied, 519 U.S. 1108 (1997) ("Unlike a case where a dispute as to copyright ownership arises under an agreement between the parties, resolution of which depends on state contract law * * * copyright ownership by reason of one's status as a co-author of a joint work arises directly from the terms of the Copyright Act itself.").[a]

In *T.B. Harms,* supra, Judge Friendly offered this oft-quoted summary:

"Mindful of the hazards of formulation in this treacherous area, we think that an action 'arises under' the Copyright Act if and only if the complaint is for a remedy expressly granted by the Act, e.g., a suit for infringement or for the statutory royalties for record reproduction, * * * or asserts a claim requiring construction of the Act, * * * or, at the very least and perhaps more doubtfully, presents a case where a distinctive policy of the Act requires that federal principles control the disposition of the claim."

(4) Suppose a licensee, in making use of a copyrighted work, exceeds the scope of its license. It is often advantageous, particularly with respect to remedies, for the copyright owner to pursue a claim for infringement in lieu of, or in addition to, one for breach of contract. Jurisdiction over such a claim will generally lie in federal court, see, e.g., Frankel v. Stein and Day, Inc., 470 F.Supp. 209 (S.D.N.Y.1979), aff'd, 646 F.2d 560 (2d Cir.1980); Greenfield v. Twin Vision Graphics, Inc., 268 F.Supp.2d 358 (D.N.J.2003), even when the case requires interpretation of the agreement.

In Bassett v. Mashantucket Pequot Tribe, 204 F.3d 343 (2d Cir.2000), the court upheld federal jurisdiction over a claim that the defendant had infringed the copyright in a motion picture script after it terminated a movie production agreement with the author. Judge Leval held that as to claims of infringement arising in the context of a breach of contract, Judge Friendly's criteria in *T.B. Harms Co. v. Eliscu* remained the proper standard. Since the plaintiff alleged copyright infringement and sought a remedy under the Copyright Act, the claim arose under the Act for purposes of federal jurisdiction. The jurisdictional issue is analyzed in A. Cohen, "Arising Under" Jurisdiction and the Copyright Laws, 44 Hastings L.J. 337 (1993).

(5) May a plaintiff who successfully invokes federal jurisdiction by alleging copyright infringement join a claim for breach of contract? The Ninth Circuit, noting § 1338(b)'s explicit reference to "unfair competition," said, "We do not read it to limit pendent jurisdiction in appropriate cases over other types of claims." Lone Ranger Television, Inc. v. Program Radio Corp., 740 F.2d 718, 724 (9th Cir.1984) (state law conversion claim). See Frederick Fell Pub. v.

---

[a]   Although the plaintiff in JustMed, Inc. v. Byce, 600 F.3d 1118 (9th Cir.2010), raised only state law claims, removal to federal court was proper since resolution of the state claims required application of the work for hire rules: "The instant case, therefore, arises under the federal law governing copyrights."

Lorayne, 422 F.Supp. 808 (S.D.N.Y.1976) (pendent jurisdiction over contract claim accepted).

(6) There is also a special provision on venue in copyright actions—28 U.S.C.A. § 1400 (actions "may be instituted in the district in which the defendant or his agent resides or may be found"). See Milwaukee Concrete Studios, Ltd. v. Fjeld Mfg. Co., 8 F.3d 441 (7th Cir.1993) (venue is determined by contacts with the particular judicial district, not contacts with the state in which the district is located).

(7) Acts of infringement occurring wholly outside the territory of the United States are not actionable under the Copyright Act. See, e.g., Subafilms, Ltd. v. MGM–Pathe Communications Co., 24 F.3d 1088 (9th Cir.) (en banc), cert. denied, 513 U.S. 1001 (1994). *Subafilms* held that this principle applies even if a defendant has authorized the foreign conduct from within this country, interpreting the copyright owner's right under § 106 "to authorize" the exercise of its exclusive rights as establishing a kind of contributory liability, violated only if the acts authorized by the defendant are themselves cognizable under U.S. law. But see Curb v. MCA Records, Inc., 898 F.Supp. 586 (M.D.Tenn.1995), rejecting *Subafilms* and holding that unlawful authorization can itself amount to a domestic infringement cognizable under the Copyright Act even if the infringing acts occur abroad. A similar conclusion was reached in Expediters Int'l, Inc. v. Direct Line Cargo Management Services, 995 F.Supp. 468 (D.N.J.1998). However, Armstrong v. Virgin Records, Ltd., 91 F.Supp.2d 628 (S.D.N.Y.2000), adhered to *Subafilms* in holding that domestic authorization of foreign infringement is not actionable.

Several courts have endorsed a "predicate act" doctrine that permits a plaintiff to recover damages for foreign infringements if those infringements were made possible by a predicate act of infringement committed within the United States. For example, the plaintiff in Tire Eng'g and Distrib., LLC v. Shandong Linglong Rubber Co., 682 F.3d 292 (4th Cir.2012), cert. denied, 133 S.Ct. 846 (2013), was allowed to recover for infringing uses of its blueprints in a foreign country since those uses were made possible by an initial unauthorized reproduction in the United States. See also, e.g., Los Angeles News Serv. v. Reuters Television Int'l Ltd., 340 F.3d 926 (9th Cir.2003), cert. denied, 541 U.S. 1041 (2004).

The court in Blue Ribbon Pet Products, Inc. v. Rolf C. Hagen (USA) Corp., 66 F.Supp.2d 454 (E.D.N.Y.1999), held that acts committed in a foreign country can be the basis for contributory liability when committed with knowledge that they will induce or contribute to infringement within the United States. A U.S. subsidiary that sold infringing copies of the plaintiff's aquarium ornaments was liable for importing the infringing items in violation of the plaintiff's distribution right; the Canadian parent company that arranged for the production and delivery of the infringing items to the U.S. subsidiary was held liable for contributory infringement.

NOTE ON STATE LIABILITY FOR COPYRIGHT INFRINGEMENT

The 11th Amendment to the Constitution reads as follows: "The Judicial power of the United States shall not be construed to extend to any suit in law or equity, commenced or prosecuted against one of the United States by Citizens of another State, or by Citizens or Subjects of any Foreign State."

The 11th Amendment, as it has come to be understood, prohibits suit in federal court by an individual against a state without its consent. See, e.g., Hans v. Louisiana, 134 U.S. 1 (1890). Given the exclusive federal jurisdiction over copyright claims, this interpretation seems to preclude the imposition of liability against a state for copyright infringement. However, in Pennsylvania v. Union Gas Co., 491 U.S. 1 (1989), the Supreme Court indicated that Congress had the authority to abrogate a state's 11th Amendment immunity in the exercise of its powers under Article I of the Constitution, in that case the power over interstate commerce. In 1990, Congress attempted to do precisely that through the addition to the Copyright Act of § 511. See B. Jones, Copyrights and State Liability, 76 Iowa L.Rev. 701 (1991). However, a subsequent decision by the Supreme Court soon raised doubts about § 511. Seminole Tribe v. Florida, 517 U.S. 44 (1996), involved a challenge to a federal statute granting Indian tribes the right to sue states in federal court on issues relating to the operation of gambling casinos on tribal land. Overruling Pennsylvania v. Union Gas, the Supreme Court in a 5–4 decision held that Congress could not abrogate a state's 11th Amendment immunity by invoking federal power under Article I's Indian commerce clause, or by implication, any other of its Article I powers, including the patent and copyright clause. Seminole Tribe did not affect, and indeed reaffirmed, congressional power over the states exercised pursuant to the 14th Amendment's prohibition against deprivations of "property" without due process.[b]

The issue of state liability for copyright infringement under § 511 was clarified by the Supreme Court's subsequent decision in Florida Prepaid Postsecondary Ed. Expense Bd. v. College Savings Bank, 527 U.S. 627 (1999). Plaintiff sued the state of Florida for patent infringement and for false advertising under § 43(a) of the Lanham Act. The district court refused to dismiss the patent claim, holding that the Patent Act's abrogation of state sovereign immunity was a valid exercise of congressional power under the 14th Amendment; the court did dismiss the Lanham Act claim, holding that no 14th Amendment property interest was implicated by a false advertising claim. The Third Circuit affirmed the dismissal of the Lanham Act claim. 131 F.3d 353 (3d Cir.1997). The Federal Circuit, with jurisdiction over the patent appeal, affirmed the refusal to dismiss the patent infringement claim, holding that patents are "property" and thus within Congress' power under the enforcement provision of the 14th Amendment. 148 F.3d 1343 (Fed.Cir.1998). The Supreme Court held, 5–4, that the attempt to abrogate state sovereign immunity in the Patent Act was not a valid exercise of congressional power. Chief Justice Rehnquist said that it was clear after Seminole Tribe that Congress could not rely on its Article I powers under the commerce clause or the patent and copyright clause. The Supreme Court then concluded that the statute was not a valid exercise of congressional power to enforce the 14th Amendment's guarantee against deprivations of property without due process. Although patents were "property," the Court said that the legislative history of the patent act amendment that purported to abrogate state immunity did not suggest that Congress was responding to constitutional violations of due process. There was

---

[b]   Seminole Tribe and the overruling of Pennsylvania v. Union Gas Co. is dissected in L. Bloom, Interpretive Issues in Seminole and Alden, 55 SMU L.Rev. 377 (2002).

little congressional consideration of the availability of state law remedies in tort or restitution for state patent infringements that might satisfy due process requirements, and there was no evidence of a consistent pattern of constitutional violations that would justify congressional action under the 14th Amendment. However, state officials with a sufficient connection to the infringement still remain subject to suit for injunctive relief to stop a continuing violation of federal law under the rule in Ex Parte Young, 209 U.S. 123 (1908). (In a separate opinion, 527 U.S. 666 (1999), the Supreme Court held that protection against false advertising under § 43(a) of the Lanham Act did not implicate any property rights that could serve as the basis for an abrogation of state sovereign immunity under the 14th Amendment.)

Justice Stevens in dissent pointed out that the legislative history of § 511 of the Copyright Act is more extensive in its investigation of the extent and ramifications of copyright infringement by the states and hence might present a stronger case for validity under the majority's 14th Amendment analysis than did the patent provision. The Fifth Circuit, however, subsequently held that the majority's analysis of congressional power under the 14th Amendment with respect to patent infringement also applied to the attempt to impose liability on the states for copyright infringement under § 511. In Chavez v. Arte Publico Press, 204 F.3d 601 (5th Cir.2000), it ordered dismissal of the plaintiff's claim against the University of Houston for reproducing her book without permission.

Relying on the Fifth Circuit's opinion in *Chavez*, Judge Donald in Jacobs v. Memphis Convention and Visitors Bureau, 710 F.Supp.2d 663 (W.D.Tenn.2010), held that sovereign immunity precluded suit against a state entity that allegedly infringed the copyright in the plaintiff's photograph. Holding that *Florida Prepaid* applied to copyright claims, the court said, "Congress did not create a record sufficient to justify prophylactic legislation abrogating state sovereign immunity under § 5 of the Fourteenth Amendment." Taking a more individualistic approach, the Eleventh Circuit affirmed the dismissal of a copyright infringement claim brought by an association of pharmacy boards alleging that the University of Georgia had copied questions from the association's licensing tests. The court held that the plaintiff had not alleged an actual due process violation that would support the abrogation of state immunity; the state through its Tort Claims Act and its legislative review procedure provided sufficient post-deprivation remedies to avoid any due process violation. National Ass'n of Bds. of Pharmacy v. Board of Regents of Univ. of Georgia, 633 F.3d 1297 (11th Cir.2011).

The Supreme Court's decision in *Florida Prepaid* is attacked as inconsistent with its own "takings" jurisprudence in S. Ghosh, Toward a Theory of Regulatory Takings for Intellectual Property: The Path Left Open After *College Savings v. Florida Prepaid*, 37 San Diego L.Rev. 637 (2000); the decision gets a lukewarm endorsement in E. Volokh, Sovereign Immunity and Intellectual Property, 73 S.Cal.L.Rev. 1161 (2000).

Meanwhile, Congress has considered possible ways to overcome the constitutional barriers to state liability for infringement of intellectual property rights. Some bills would condition a state's ability to enforce its own intellectual property rights on a waiver of sovereign immunity from suit in federal court for infringement. See 66 Pat., Tm., & Copyr.J. (BNA) 230 (2003). The proposal raised concern among public universities, who often make millions from patented research, copyrighted sports broadcasts, and merchandising of logos and mascots (and who also sometimes raise sovereign immunity as a defense to their own infringements). They worried that their state governments will refuse to waive immunity under such proposals, leaving their federal intellectual property rights at risk. Foster, Piracy Without Penalty?, Chronicle of Higher Ed., July 25, 2003, p. A25. The limits on congressional power to alter the current situation are considered in C. Bohannan and T. Cotter, When the State Steals Ideas: Is the Abrogation of State Sovereign Immunity From Federal Infringement Claims Constitutional in Light of *Seminole Tribe*?, 67 Fordham L.Rev. 1435 (1999); M. Landau, State Sovereign Immunity and Intellectual Property Revisited, 22 Fordham Intell.Prop., Media & Ent.L.J. 513 (2012), examines the "twisted" history of 11th Amendment jurisprudence and offers hope for a legislative solution.

Finally, note that the *federal* government has waived its own immunity for patent and copyright infringement in 28 U.S.C.A. § 1498. The remedy for copyright infringement, however, is limited to an action by the copyright owner "for the recovery of his reasonable and entire compensation as damages for such infringement, including the minimum statutory damages as set forth in section 504(c) of title 17"ᶜ; thus, a plaintiff cannot enjoin an infringement by the federal government.

2. STANDING TO SUE

(1) Under the 1909 Act, the various rights comprising copyright were considered an indivisible whole. A transfer of anything less than this whole was characterized as a mere license. Licensees did not have standing to sue for infringement, although an exclusive licensee could maintain an action by joining the copyright owner. The 1976 Act in § 201(d) expressly abandons indivisibility. Exclusive rights, and subdivisions of exclusive rights, may be separately owned. Further, the definition of "transfer of copyright ownership" in § 101 includes not only an assignment of a copyright or an exclusive right, but also an exclusive license. Thus, as the "owner" of an exclusive right, both an assignee and an exclusive licensee of any of the rights under copyright may, according to § 501(b), "institute an action for any infringement of that particular right committed while he or she is the owner of it." The exclusive right upon which the owner relies can be quite limited. The House Report states, "It is thus clear, for example, that a local broadcasting station holding an exclusive license to transmit a particular work within a particular geographic area and for a particular period of time, could sue, in its own name as copyright owner, someone who infringed that particular exclusive right." H.R.Rep. p. 123. See Eden Toys, Inc. v. Florelee Undergarment Co., Inc., 697 F.2d 27 (2d Cir.1982) (exclusive licensee for use of drawings of "Paddington Bear" on clothing has standing to sue for infringement); Gamma Audio & Video, Inc. v. Ean–Chea, 11 F.3d 1106 (1st Cir.1993) (exclusive licensee of distribution rights in particular states has standing). On the other hand, the holder of a non-exclusive license does not have standing to sue for infringement. See, e.g., Sybersound Records, Inc. v. UAV Corp., 517 F.3d 1137 (9th Cir.2008). R. Blair and T. Cotter, The

---

ᶜ   The reference to "the minimum statutory damages" was interpreted by the Court of Federal Claims in Wechsberg v. United States, 54 Fed.Cl. 158 (2002), as setting a floor but not a ceiling on recovery when a copyright owner seeks statutory damages under § 504(c) against the federal government; contra Cohen v. U.S., 105 Fed.Cl. 733 (Fed.Cl.2012) ("Following the cross-reference in § 1498(b) to the 1976 Copyright Act, it is apparent that the phrase 'the minimum statutory damages' means $750.00.")

Elusive Logic of Standing Doctrine in Intellectual Property Law, 74 Tulane L.Rev. 1323 (2000), attributes the liberal standing rules for copyright to the independent value of the exclusive rights and the low risk that a copyright will be declared invalid.

(2) An action for infringement of an exclusive right may be instituted by the "legal or beneficial owner." § 501(b). The most significant example of the latter is "an author who had parted with legal title to the copyright in exchange for percentage royalties based on sales or license fees." H.R.Rep. p. 159. See, e.g., Cortner v. Israel, 732 F.2d 267 (2d Cir.1984) (brought by the composers of the theme music for ABC's Monday Night Football). A work-for-hire employee, however, has no beneficial interest even if the compensation takes the form of a royalty agreement according to Warren v. Fox Family Worldwide, Inc., 328 F.3d 1136 (9th Cir.2003).

(3) Section 501(b) encourages a flexible response to the procedural problems inherent in divisibility. The court may order notice of the action served on all persons having an interest in the copyright; when the interest is "likely to be affected," notice is mandatory. Third parties claiming an interest in the copyright have a right to intervene, and the court, in its discretion, may order their joinder.

(4) Section 507(b) bars a civil action for infringement "unless it is commenced within three years after the claim accrued." In William A. Graham Co. v. Haughey, 568 F.3d 425 (3d Cir.), cert. denied, 130 S.Ct. 503 (2009), the court debated whether a claim for infringement accrues when the injury occurs or when the plaintiff discovered or with reasonable diligence should have discovered the injury. Finding that eight other circuits had previously applied the discovery rule to civil actions for copyright infringement, the Third Circuit agreed, concluding that "use of the discovery rule comports with the text, structure, legislative history and underlying policies of the Copyright Act."

Although Taylor v. Meirick, 712 F.2d 1112 (7th Cir.1983), suggests that if some portion of the infringing acts occurred within the limitations period, the copyright owner may recover for the whole of the infringement, most cases hold that recovery is limited to infringing acts that occurred within the limitations period. See, e.g., Stone v. Williams, 970 F.2d 1043 (2d Cir.1992), cert. denied, 508 U.S. 906 (1993); Roley v. New World Pictures, Ltd., 19 F.3d 479 (9th Cir.1994). Which approach best advances the rationale for a statute of limitation?[d]

---

[d] Application of the statute of limitations to claims of joint authorship has proven particularly troublesome. The limitations period proved fatal to a claim of joint authorship of the song *Why Do Fools Fall in Love* brought 32 years after the song was written, Merchant v. Levy, 92 F.3d 51 (2d Cir.1996), cert. denied, 519 U.S. 1108 (1997). The Ninth Circuit in Aalmuhammed v. Lee, 202 F.3d 1227 (9th Cir.2000), said, "A claim of authorship of a joint work must be brought within three years of when it accrues. Because creation rather than infringement is the gravamen of an authorship claim, the claim accrues on account of creation, not subsequent infringement, and is barred three years from 'plain and express repudiation' of authorship." However, when the plaintiff in Goodman v. Lee, 78 F.3d 1007 (5th Cir.), cert. denied, 519 U.S. 861 (1996), claimed joint authorship and an accounting in 1985 for the 1956 hit *Let the Good Times Roll*, the court said that the state ten-year limitations period for an accounting by a co-owner, running from when demand is made, was controlling. Judge Posner's analysis in Gaiman v. McFarlane, 360 F.3d 644 (7th Cir.2004), concludes that the state statute of limitations applies if co-ownership is conceded and only accounting matters are at issue, but copyright's three-year statute applies if joint authorship is contested.

Laches can also serve as a defense in a copyright infringement action. In Petrella v. Metro-Goldwyn-Mayer, Inc., 695 F.3d 946 (9th Cir.2012), a claim raised against the continuing infringement of a screenplay that was used to produce the movie *Raging Bull* was barred by the plaintiff's eighteen-year delay in filing suit. Even a delay of less than the three-year limitations period can raise a laches issue. In Chirco v. Crosswinds Communities, Inc., 474 F.3d 227 (6th Cir.), cert. denied, 551 U.S. 1131 (2007), the Sixth Circuit held that the plaintiffs' eighteen-month delay in bringing suit for infringement of architectural works and plans made a request for destruction of the infringing buildings unduly prejudicial to the defendants.

(5) "Misuse" of the copyright monopoly may preclude relief for infringement. See Lasercomb America, Inc. v. Reynolds, 911 F.2d 970 (4th Cir.1990) (restrictions in the plaintiff's licensing agreements against the creation of competing works constituted misuse of the copyright that barred recovery for infringement, even against a defendant who was not a party to the offending license). In Alcatel USA, Inc. v. DGI Tech., Inc., 166 F.3d 772 (5th Cir.1999), the Fifth Circuit, citing *Lasercomb*, held that by requiring licensees to use the copyrighted software only with the plaintiff's own microprocessor cards, the plaintiff had misused the copyright in an attempt to secure commercial control over an unprotected product. That misuse precluded an injunction against a defendant who downloaded the software in the course of creating a competing card. *Lasercomb* was also invoked by the Ninth Circuit in holding that the American Medical Association had committed copyright misuse when it licensed a government agency to use its medical procedure code on the condition that the agency not use any competing system. Practice Management Information Corp. v. American Medical Ass'n, 121 F.3d 516 (9th Cir.), cert. denied, 522 U.S. 933 (1997).[e]

The Third Circuit in Video Pipeline, Inc. v. Buena Vista Home Ent., Inc., 342 F.3d 191 (3d Cir.2003), cert. denied, 540 U.S. 1178 (2004), rejected a misuse defense raised by a party who had been enjoined from using film clips from Walt Disney movies on its web site. Although Disney's licenses prohibited licensed web sites from including material that was derogatory or critical of Disney or its films, the court concluded that the restriction did not interfere with public access to criticism of Disney and a copyright owner should not be required to license its works without regard to the other content displayed on the web site. D. Olson, First Amendment Based Copyright Misuse, 52 Wm. & Mary L.Rev. 537 (2010), suggests that the misuse doctrine should reach owners who use their copyright to chill or control speech.

J. Cross and P. Yu, Competition Law and Copyright Misuse, 56 Drake L.Rev. 427 (2008), explores various mechanisms, including the misuse doctrine, for dealing with anticompetitive assertions of copyright; C. Bohannan, IP Misuse as Foreclosure, 96 Iowa L.Rev. 475 (2011), argues that the copyright

---

[e]   After the Supreme Court affirmed the Ninth Circuit's rejection of defendant Costco's first sale defense in Omega's suit against the unauthorized importation of watches bearing a small copyrighted design on the back, Omega S.A. v. Costco Wholesale Corp., 541 F.3d 982 (9th Cir.2008), aff'd by equally divided Court, 131 S.Ct. 565 (2010), Costco won a summary judgment on a theory of copyright misuse. Omega conceded that it had added the design in order to take advantage of copyright law's importation restrictions. Citing the Ninth Circuit's analysis of copyright misuse in *Practice Management Information*, the court held that Omega had misused its copyright by attempting to leverage its monopoly over the design to control the importation of its watches. Omega S.A. v. Costco Wholesale Corp., 2011 WL 8492716 (C.D.Cal.2011).

misuse doctrine should focus on conduct that forecloses competition, innovation, or access to the public domain. Writing about a different form of "misuse," J. Tehranian, Curbing Copyblight, 14 Vand.J.Ent. & Tech.L. 993 (2012), advocates creation of a private right of action against false claims of copyright ownership or unreasonable claims about the extent of the owner's rights.

3. THE BATTERY OF REMEDIES

ACTUAL DAMAGES AND PROFITS

Section 504(b) authorizes the copyright owner to recover "the actual damages suffered by him or her as a result of the infringement." Lost profits on lost sales are a common measure of damage. As in other contexts, however, it may be difficult to establish lost profits with the requisite certainty. When should the court assume that every sale made by the infringer is a sale lost by the plaintiff? When are comparisons with the sales of other works relevant? Should expert projections suffice? See Stevens Linen Associates v. Mastercraft Corp., 656 F.2d 11 (2d Cir.1981). And lost sales are not the same as lost profits. If you sell less, you will ordinarily save some production costs, and these should be taken into account in computing damages. Taylor v. Meirick, 712 F.2d 1112 (7th Cir.1983). In some instances, damages may instead be measured by the decrease in the market value of the copyrighted work. See Universal Pictures Co. v. Harold Lloyd Corp., 162 F.2d 354 (9th Cir.1947). In others, it may be appropriate to measure the plaintiff's damages by the fair market value of a license that would cover the defendant's infringing use. On Davis v. The Gap, Inc., 246 F.3d 152 (2d Cir.2001).[f] Are there losses in addition to the economic injury occasioned by lost sales or diminished market value that might be recovered by the victim of an infringement?

The copyright owner is not limited to an award of damages. Section 504(b) authorizes recovery of both actual damages "and any profits of the infringer that are attributable to the infringement and are not taken into account in computing the actual damages." Section 504(b) clearly authorizes an award of both the plaintiff's damages and the defendant's profits, but the right to a cumulative recovery is not unlimited. The copyright owner may recover only defendant's profits that "are not taken into account in computing the actual damages." What is the effect of this limitation? The House Report offers this explanation:

> In allowing the plaintiff to recover "the actual damages suffered by him or her as a result of the infringement," plus any of the infringer's profits "that are attributable to the infringement and are not taken into account in computing the actual damages," section 504(b) recognizes the different purposes served by awards of damages and profits. Damages are awarded to compensate the copyright owner for losses from the infringement, and profits are awarded to prevent the infringer from unfairly benefiting from a wrongful act. Where the de-

---

[f]   Software company Oracle won what was probably the largest damage award ever made in a copyright infringement case when a jury set actual damages at $1.3 billion in a suit against competitor SAP America for copying Oracle's business management software. The award was based on the fair market value of a license for the use. However, the trial judge subsequently found the jury's award contrary to the weight of the evidence and grossly excessive since the evidence was insufficient to establish an objective, non-speculative license price. Oracle USA, Inc. v. SAP AG, 100 U.S.P.Q.2d 1450 (N.D.Cal.2011).

fendant's profits are nothing more than a measure of the damages suffered by the copyright owner, it would be inappropriate to award damages and profits cumulatively, since in effect they amount to the same thing. However, in cases where the copyright owner has suffered damages not reflected in the infringer's profits, or where there have been profits attributable to the copyrighted work but not used as a measure of damages, subsection (b) authorizes the award of both. H.R.Rep. p. 161.

When are the defendant's profits "nothing more than a measure of the damages"? When instead are damages "not reflected in the infringer's profits"? Suppose that a construction company, having contracted to use a set of architectural plans for one apartment building, copies them without permission for a second. Should the architect who owns the copyright in the plans be permitted to recover, in addition to damages for the re-use measured by the fair market value of the plans, the defendant's net profit on the second construction contract? Compare Aitken, Hazen, Hoffman, Miller, P.C. v. Empire Construction Co., 542 F.Supp. 252 (D.Neb.1982), with Robert Jones Associates, Inc. v. Nino Homes, p. 153 supra. Taylor v. Meirick, supra, held that the owner of copyrighted maps that were reproduced and sold by an infringer could not recover both its lost profits resulting from the diverted trade and the defendant's profits on the infringing sales; the plaintiff would be entitled to the defendant's profits only to the extent that they exceeded the plaintiff's own lost profits recovered as damages. The Second Circuit in Abeshouse v. Ultragraphics, Inc., 754 F.2d 467 (2d Cir.1985), acknowledged that "[d]ouble-counting may occur when an infringing seller has to disgorge profits on sales that a copyright holder might have made and for which he may therefore claim damages in the form of lost profits." But on the facts before it the court concluded that there was no double-counting in permitting the owner of a copyrighted poster to recover from a faithless exclusive distributor both its lost profits resulting from the defendant's purchases of infringing posters and the defendant's profits on subsequent sales of the infringing items to wholesalers. Plaintiffs "could not have sold their posters domestically to anyone but their exclusive distributor," and thus "could not properly have made the latter sales and therefore cannot claim any lost profits on them. Thus, requiring [defendant] to disgorge to appellees its profits on those sales contains no element of double-counting * * *." R. Blair and T. Cotter, An Economic Analysis of Damages Rules in Intellectual Property Law, 39 Wm. & Mary L.Rev. 1585 (1998), concludes that the baseline recovery should be the greater of the plaintiff's loss or the defendant's gain from the infringement.

Determining the "profits of the infringer that are attributable to the infringement" is itself a complex task. The Ninth Circuit, distinguishing "direct profits"—those made by selling an infringing product—and "indirect profits"—revenue with a more attenuated nexus to the infringement—said that to recover "indirect profits," the plaintiff "must proffer sufficient non-speculative evidence to support a causal relationship between the infringement and the profits generated indirectly from such an infringement." The court affirmed a summary judgment against an artist whose work had been photographed and used without permission in a promotional brochure for the Seattle Symphony; there was insufficient evidence of a link between the infringement and the Symphony's revenues. Mackie v. Rieser, 296 F.3d 909 (9th Cir.2002), cert. denied, 537 U.S. 1189 (2003). In Andreas v. Volkswagen of America, Inc., 336 F.3d 789 (8th Cir.2003), the court reinstated a jury's award of profits against a defendant auto maker who ran a television commercial that infringed the plaintiff's copyrighted text. The court held that there was sufficient circumstantial evidence to establish a nexus between the infringing text and the defendant's car sales. The jury awarded ten per cent of the profits earned on sales of the advertised car while the commercial aired.

In many instances, even a defendant's "direct" profits will reflect in part the value of the defendant's own contributions. According to the House Report, "where some of the defendant's profits result from the infringement and other profits are caused by different factors, it will be necessary for the court to make an apportionment." H.R.Rep. p. 161.

Sheldon v. Metro–Goldwyn Pictures Corp.
309 U.S. 390, 60 S.Ct. 681 (1940).

After the Second Circuit found the defendant's motion picture "Letty Lynton" to be an infringement of the copyrighted play "Dishonored Lady" (p. 176 supra), the district court awarded to the plaintiffs the defendant's total profit from the movie, amounting to $587,604. 26 F.Supp. 134. The Second Circuit, on appeal, apportioned the profits, awarding 20%. 106 F.2d 45. The plaintiffs sought reinstatement of the district court's award in the Supreme Court. Chief Justice Hughes, after deciding that apportionment was proper, turned to the method of apportionment:

"Third. The controlling fact in the determination of the apportionment was that the profits had been derived, not from the mere performance of a copyrighted play, but from the exhibition of a motion picture which had its distinctive profit-making features, apart from the use of any infringing material, by reason of the expert and creative operations involved in its production and direction. In that aspect the case has a certain resemblance to that of a patent infringement, where the infringer has created profits by the addition of non-infringing and valuable improvements. And, in this instance, it plainly appeared that what respondents had contributed accounted for by far the larger part of their gains. * * *

"The testimony showed quite clearly that in the creation of profits from the exhibition of a motion picture, the talent and popularity of the 'motion picture stars' generally constitutes the main drawing power of the picture, and that this is especially true where the title of the picture is not identified with any well-known play or novel. Here, it appeared that the picture did not bear the title of the copyrighted play and that it was not presented or advertised as having any connection whatever with the play. It was also shown that the picture had been 'sold,' that is, licensed to almost all the exhibitors as identified simply with the name of a popular motion picture actress before even the title 'Letty Lynton' was used. In addition to the drawing power of the 'motion picture stars,' other factors in creating the profits were found in the artistic conceptions and in the expert supervision and direction of the various processes which made possible the composite result with its attractiveness to the public.

"Upon these various considerations, with elaboration of detail, respondents' expert witnesses gave their views as to the extent to which the use of the copyrighted material had contributed to the profits in question. The underlying facts as to the factors in successful production and exhibition of motion pictures were abundantly proved, but, as the court below recognized, the ultimate estimates of the expert witnesses were only the expression 'of their very decided opinions.' These witnesses were in complete agreement that the portion of the profits attributable to the use of the copyrighted play in the circumstances here disclosed was very small. Their estimates given in percentages of receipts ran from five to twelve per cent; the estimate apparently most favored was ten per cent as the limit. One finally expressed the view that the play contributed nothing. There was no rebuttal. But the court below was not willing to accept the experts' testimony 'at its face value.' The court felt that it must make an award 'which by no possibility shall be too small.' Desiring to give petitioners the benefit of every doubt, the court allowed for the contribution of the play twenty per cent of the net profits.

"Petitioners are not in a position to complain that the amount thus allowed by the court was greater than the expert evidence warranted. Nor is there any basis for attack, and we do not understand that any attack is made, upon the qualifications of the experts. By virtue of an extensive experience, they had an intimate knowledge of all pertinent facts relating to the production and exhibition of motion pictures. Nor can we say that the testimony afforded no basis for a finding. What we said in [Dowagiac Mfg. Co. v. Minnesota Moline Plow Co., 235 U.S. 641 (1915)] is equally true here,—that what is required is not mathematical exactness but only a reasonable approximation. That, after all, is a matter of judgment; and the testimony of those who are informed by observation and experience may be not only helpful but, as we have said, may be indispensable. Equity is concerned with making a fair apportionment so that neither party will have what justly belongs to the other. Confronted with the manifest injustice of giving to petitioners all the profits made by the motion picture, the court in making an apportionment was entitled to avail itself of the experience of those best qualified to form a judgment in the particular field of inquiry and come to its conclusion aided by their testimony. We see no greater difficulty in the admission and use of expert testimony in such a case than in the countless cases involving values of property rights in which such testimony often forms the sole basis for decision.

"Petitioners also complain of deductions allowed in the computation of the net profits. These contentions involve questions of fact which have been determined below upon the evidence and we find no ground for disturbing the court's conclusions.

"The judgment of the Circuit Court of Appeals is Affirmed."

NOTES ON RECOVERY OF DEFENDANT'S PROFITS

(1) In Sheldon v. Moredall Realty Corp., 29 F.Supp. 729 (S.D.N.Y.1939), the defendant was the operator of the Capitol Theatre in New York City, which showed "Letty Lynton" for two weeks. Although "unquestionably an innocent infringer," it was required to give up 20% of its profits. Presumably the plaintiffs could have made a similar demand on other theaters.

"Innocent" infringement may take several forms. The copying may be subconscious. (See Judge Hand's charitable concession in *Sheldon* that the defendants may have "forgot" what they took from the copyrighted play.) Or the defendant may in good faith believe that the use does not infringe the plaintiff's copyright. Or, as here, it may be unaware of the infringing activities of a related party. Such "innocence," however, is not itself a defense to liability for the plaintiff's actual damages or the defendant's profits.

(2) Problems of apportioning a defendant's profits become particularly intricate when the infringing work is sold as part of a larger unit—a song on an album, for example. After George Harrison's "My Sweet Lord" was found to infringe the Chiffons' 1963 hit, "He's So Fine," the court was forced to apportion profits both with respect to the relative contributions to the infringing work, as in *Sheldon* (75% due to the plagiarized tune), and the percentage of profits from the album (50%) and "single" (70%)—there was a "flip side"—that were attributable to the presence of the infringing song. ABKCO Music, Inc. v. Harrisongs Music, Ltd., 508 F.Supp. 798 (S.D.N.Y.1981), modified, 722 F.2d 988 (2d Cir.1983). In Lottie Joplin Thomas Trust v. Crown Pub., Inc., 592 F.2d 651 (2d Cir.1978), an award of 50% of the defendant's profits was upheld despite the fact that the infringing work occupied only 10% of defendant's five-record set of Scott Joplin music. The inclusion of the infringing work had made the defendant's collection the only "complete set."

How much did the unauthorized use of a photograph of actress Raquel Welch (unclad) on the cover of "Celebrity Skin" contribute to its profits? In Sygma Photo News, Inc. v. High Society Magazine, Inc., 778 F.2d 89 (2d Cir.1985), the magistrate said 20%, but the district court said 75%. The Court of Appeals settled for 50%. For a more prosaic illustration, see Orgel v. Clark Boardman Co., 301 F.2d 119 (2d Cir.1962), where the court awarded 50% of the profits from the defendant's legal treatise, although only 35% of the work made use of material from the plaintiff's copyrighted text.

(3) The plaintiff can recover the defendant's profit, not the defendant's gross revenue. Thus, aside from problems of apportionment, there are the inevitable disputes about the deduction of expenses. The most obvious deductions are those directly related to the labor and materials expended by the defendant in the production of the infringing work. See, e.g., Taylor v. Meirick, 712 F.2d 1112 (7th Cir.1983). Beyond that, questions quickly multiply. Should a defendant be allowed a credit for income taxes paid on its profits? Should any deduction be permitted for "overhead"? If so, how should it be allocated? Judge Hand, in *Sheldon,* said that the "correct rule" as to overhead permits an allocated deduction for overhead that would "assist in the production of the infringement." 106 F.2d at 54. Judge Oakes in Hamil America Inc. v. GFI, 193 F.3d 92 (2d Cir.1999), cert. denied, 528 U.S. 1160 (2000), adhered to Judge Hand's formulation: "The first step is to determine what overhead expense categories (such as rent, business, entertainment, personnel and public relations) are actually implicated by the production of the infringing product. * * * The second step is to arrive at a fair, accurate, and practical method of allocating the implicated overhead to the infringement." Judge Posner, no stranger to economic analysis, said in *Taylor,* "Costs that would be incurred anyway should not be subtracted, because by definition they cannot be avoided by curtailing the profit-making activity"—deductions are limited to "variable costs." Are these approaches consistent? If not, which one is more in keeping with the principle stated in the House Report, that "profits are awarded to prevent the infringer from unfairly benefiting from a wrongful act"? H.R.Rep. p. 161. The difficulties of apportionment and deductions are lessened for the copyright owner by the burden of proof in § 504(b).

STATUTORY DAMAGES

(1) Section 504(c) offers the copyright owner an election. In lieu of a recovery measured by the plaintiff's actual damages and the defendant's profits, the copyright owner may elect to recover "statutory damages * * * in a sum of not less than $750 or more than $30,000 as the court considers just."

What is the purpose of such an award? As the preceding materials illustrate, proof of actual damages and profits is often difficult, sometimes impossible. The availability of statutory damages insures a remedy. It also insures a measure of deterrence. This may be particularly significant with respect to infringements such as unauthorized performances or downloads, where actual damages in individual cases may be trivial, yet aggregate effects substantial. Statutory damages can also provide the copyright owner with significant bargaining leverage, sometimes perhaps too much. See R. Brown, The Operation of the Damage Provisions of the Copyright Law: An Exploratory Study, Copyr.L. Revision Study No. 23 (1958), in 2 Studies on Copyr. 1067 (1963).

The House Report emphasizes that the recovery of actual damages and profits under § 504(b) and the award of statutory damages under § 504(c) are mutually exclusive and the election is left to the copyright owner. An owner who delays registration of the copyright, however, may forfeit the right to claim statutory damages as a result of the limitation in § 412.

(2) What factors should influence the determination, within the statutory limits, of a "just" sum? Although a plaintiff who has elected to recover statutory damages is not obliged to submit proof of actual damages or the defendant's profits, the House Report notes that nothing in § 504 prevents a court from taking into account evidence of actual damages and profits in fixing a statutory award. The nature of the defendant's conduct will also be weighed. The statute alters the minimum and maximum awards when the infringement is committed either innocently or willfully. § 504(c)(2). How should the latter term be interpreted? In Fitzgerald Pub. Co. v. Baylor Pub. Co., Inc., 807 F.2d 1110 (2d Cir.1986), where a defendant printing company dealt with a scoundrel who it knew or should have known lacked authority, the "knowledge that its actions constitute an infringement establishes that the defendant acted willfully." See also Video Views, Inc. v. Studio 21, Ltd., 925 F.2d 1010 (7th Cir.), cert. denied, 502 U.S. 861 (1991) ("An infringement is 'willful' if the infringer knows that its conduct is an infringement or if the infringer has acted in reckless disregard of the copyright owner's right.") Innocent infringement, also specially treated in § 504(c)(2), justified an award of reduced statutory damages against small, unsophisticated retailers of infringing Batman merchandise in D.C. Comics Inc. v. Mini Gift Shop, 912 F.2d 29 (2d Cir.1990).

The opportunity to preclude a defendant from seeking refuge in "innocent" infringement to mitigate statutory or actual damages is the sole surviving statutory incentive to the use of a copyright notice. See §§ 401(d) and 402(d).[g] Note also, in § 504(c)(2), the small victory achieved by educators. In light of the ability to increase statutory damages in instances of willful in-

---

[g]   A claim of "innocent" infringement in mitigation of statutory damages raised by a music downloader was rejected in Maverick Recording Co. v. Harper, 598 F.3d 193 (5th Cir.), cert. denied, 131 S.Ct. 590 (2010), because the defense was precluded under § 402(d) by the presence of copyright notices on the phonorecords from which the songs were taken. (Does that satisfy the requirement in § 402(d) that the notice "appears on the published phonorecord or phonorecords to which a defendant in a copyright infringement suit has access."?)

fringement, separate punitive damages are not available in copyright infringement actions. See On Davis v. The Gap, Inc., 246 F.3d 152 (2d Cir.2001).

(3) A recovery of statutory damages within the prescribed limits is to be awarded for all infringements "with respect to any one work." The House Report explains that the statutory minimum and maximum are to be applied individually in the case of multiple works—if the defendant has publicly performed or downloaded three of the plaintiff's songs, statutory damages of at least $2,250 must be awarded.[h]

Statutory damages can multiply quickly. A total of $9.1 million representing $100,000 per work for the willful duplication and sale of ninety-one sound recordings was awarded in Sony Music Ent. v. Cassette Prod., Inc., 41 U.S.P.Q.2d 1198 (D.N.J.1996). A licensor of syndicated television programs got $9 million in statutory damages when a licensee continued to broadcast the programs after the license was terminated. The court said it was awarding $10,000 for each of 900 unauthorized broadcasts; the defendant's failure to produce supporting evidence precluded its argument that many of the infringements involved multiple broadcasts of the same episode and thus the number of infringed works was substantially less than 900. MCA Television Ltd. v. Feltner, 89 F.3d 766 (11th Cir.1996), cert. denied, 520 U.S. 1117 (1997). In Capitol Records, Inc. v. Thomas-Rasset, p. 452 supra, the Eighth Circuit held that an award of $220,000 in statutory damages representing $9,250 for each of twenty-four downloaded songs, did not violate the defendant's due process rights.

P. Samuelson and T. Wheatland, Statutory Damages in Copyright Law: A Remedy in Need of Reform, 51 Will. & Mary L.Rev. 439 (2009), offers principles to guide application of the statutory damages remedy; A. Garfield, Calibrating Copyright Statutory Damages to Promote Speech, 38 Fla.St.U.L.Rev. 1 (2010), advocates a nuanced approach to statutory damages to avoid chilling beneficial uses. J. Tehranian, Infringement Nation: Copyright Reform and the Law/Norm Gap, 2007 Utah L.Rev. 537, illustrates how a hypothetical professor can easily rack up $4.5 billion in statutory damages, even without downloading any music.

(4) What is the effect of multiple acts of infringement? Under the 1909 Act, courts sometimes treated a series of infringements as separate transactions, each supporting an award of at least minimum statutory damages. See, e.g., Robert Stigwood Group Ltd. v. O'Reilly, 530 F.2d 1096 (2d Cir.), cert. denied, 429 U.S. 848 (1976), in which separate statutory damages were awarded for each of forty-eight unauthorized performances of "Jesus Christ Superstar." Section 504(c), however, provides for an award within the statutory limits "for all infringements involved in the action, with respect to any one work." The House Report is emphatic: "A single infringer of a single work is liable for a single amount [between the statutory minimum and maximum], no matter how many acts of infringement are in-

---

[h] When a distributor sold unauthorized digital copies of two music albums through Internet retailers like iTunes, an appellate court affirmed the trial court's decision to limit statutory damages to one award per album rather than one award for each of the twenty individual songs on the albums. Judge Wood in Bryant v. Media Right Productions, Inc., 603 F.3d 135 (2d Cir.), cert. denied, 131 S.Ct. 656 (2010), relying on the language in § 504(c)(1) stating that for purposes of statutory damages, "all the parts of a compilation or derivative work constitute one work," specifically rejected an "independent economic value" test for determining the number of works.

volved in the action and regardless of whether the acts were separate, isolated, or occurred in a related series." H.R.Rep. p. 162.

(5) Because copyright is divisible, a single infringing act can violate the exclusive rights of numerous "owners." The defendant, however, remains liable for only a single award of statutory damages. The House Report explains that "although the minimum and maximum amounts are to be multiplied where multiple 'works' are involved in the suit, the same is not true with respect to multiple copyrights, multiple owners, multiple exclusive rights, or multiple registrations." H.R.Rep. p. 162.

INJUNCTIVE RELIEF

(1) Injunctive relief for copyright infringement, both preliminary and permanent, is authorized in § 502. The Supreme Court's decision in eBay Inc. v. MercExchange, 547 U.S. 388 (2006), emphasizing in a patent case that injunctions are discretionary and subject to traditional principles of equity, may have dramatic consequences for copyright litigation. The trial court in Salinger v. Colting, 641 F.Supp.2d 250 (S.D.N.Y.2009), for example, had granted a preliminary injunction barring publication of a novel based on the Holden Caulfield character from J.D. Salinger's *Catcher in the Rye.* Finding infringement of the Caulfield character and rejecting a fair use defense, the district court stated that the defendants' work "contains no reasonably perceived parodic character." Although the work was unlikely to affect the market for *Catcher in the Rye,* Judge Batts held that it was appropriate to consider the market for a sequel or other derivative works in the fair use analysis, even though Salinger had not demonstrated any interest in publishing such works. Concluding that the plaintiff was likely to succeed on the merits of his infringement claim, the court invoked the traditional rule that irreparable harm from copyright infringement is presumed and granted a preliminary injunction. On appeal, the Second Circuit in Salinger v. Colting, 607 F.3d 68 (2d Cir.2010), while finding no fault with the trial court's conclusion as to plaintiff's likelihood of success on the merits, held that the traditional presumption of irreparable harm in copyright cases is inconsistent with the Supreme Court's decision in *eBay* and vacated the lower court's preliminary injunction. Although *eBay* involved a permanent injunction in a patent case, Judge Calabresi held that the case applied with equal force to preliminary injunctions and copyright cases. Thus, in addition to likelihood of success, "plaintiffs must show that, on the facts of their case, the failure to issue an injunction would actually cause irreparable harm." Instead of a presumption, "the court must actually consider the injury the plaintiff will suffer if he or she loses on the preliminary injunction but ultimately prevails on the merits," paying particular attention to whether remedies such as damages are inadequate. The court conceded, however, that "[h]arm might be irremediable, or irreparable, for many reasons, including that a loss is difficult to replace or difficult to measure, or that it is a loss that one should not be expected to suffer." In addition, trial courts considering preliminary injunctions in copyright infringement cases must consider the balance of hardships between the parties and whether the public interest would be disserved by an injunction.[i] The Ninth Circuit reached a similar conclusion in Flexible Lifeline Systems, Inc. v. Precision

---

[i]   After the appellate court decision in *Salinger*, the parties agreed to a settlement that bars publication of the defendant's sequel in the United States. L.A. Times, Jan. 14, 2011, p. 2.

Lift, Inc., 654 F.3d 989 (9th Cir.2011), remanding for further consideration of a motion for a preliminary injunction after the district court erroneously relied on a presumption of irreparable harm.

The plaintiff in Suntrust Bank v. Houghton Mifflin Co., 268 F.3d 1257 (11th Cir.2001), controlled the copyright in *Gone With the Wind* (said to be second in sales only to the Bible since its 1936 publication). It won a preliminary injunction against the publication of *The Wind Done Gone*, a novel that appropriated the characters, plot, and major scenes from the copyrighted work to criticize its depiction of slavery. The Court of Appeals vacated the injunction, finding that the plaintiff had not established a likelihood of success on the merits in light of the defendant's fair use defense. But the court also said that damages would be an adequate remedy and the injunction was at odds with the first amendment as a prior restraint on the author's speech.[j]

M. Lemley and E. Volokh, Freedom of Speech and Injunctions in Intellectual Property Cases, 48 Duke L.J. 147 (1998), argue that the traditional rule against prior restraints applied in libel, obscenity, and other speech cases should temper preliminary relief in copyright cases; J. Tehranian, Wither Copyright? Transformative Use, Free Speech, and an Intermediate Liability Proposal, 2005 B.Y.U.L.Rev. 1201, concludes that free speech interests may justify limiting the remedy for infringing but transformative uses to an accounting of profits. However, the Ninth Circuit, upholding a preliminary injunction against a sixteen-hour documentary on Elvis Presley that made substantial unauthorized use of copyrighted materials, said flatly, "[I]f the use of the alleged infringer is not a fair use, there are no First Amendment prohibitions against granting a preliminary injunction." Elvis Presley Enters., Inc. v. Passport Video, 349 F.3d 622 (9th Cir.2003), amended, 357 F.3d 896 (9th Cir.), cert. denied, 542 U.S. 921 (2004).

(2) Despite the frequent reliance on injunctions, a permanent injunction does not always follow a decision for the plaintiff. See, e.g., Love v. Kwitny, 772 F.Supp. 1367 (S.D.N.Y.1991), aff'd, 963 F.2d 1521 (2d Cir.), cert. denied, 506 U.S. 862 (1992) (non-willful infringement comprised 2.6% of the defendant's book; the court withheld an injunction and awarded the plaintiff 2.6% of the profits). In Abend v. MCA, Inc., 863 F.2d 1465 (9th Cir.1988), aff'd sub nom. Stewart v. Abend, 495 U.S. 207 (1990), p. 526 supra, the speculator who had bought the renewal term in the story on which *Rear Window* was based got only monetary relief. This resolution was later endorsed by the Supreme Court in footnote 10 of its opinion in Campbell v. Acuff–Rose Music, Inc., p. 354 supra. In eBay Inc. v. MercExchange, the Supreme Court drew support from footnote 10 in *Campbell*. In a concurrence, Chief Justice Roberts noted that the tradition of injunctions in patent cases wasn't surprising, "given the difficulty of protecting a right to *exclude* through monetary remedies that allow an infringer to *use* an invention * * *." However, in a separate concurrence, Justice Kennedy argued that when the threat of an injunction is used by the owner simply as leverage in negotiating licensing fees, damages may well be sufficient. The *eBay* case was cited by the Fourth Circuit in Christopher Phelps & Associates, LLC v. Galloway, 492 F.3d 532 (4th Cir.2007), when it denied an injunction against the sale or lease of a house built with infringing plans. (What right

---

[j] The suit was eventually settled. At the plaintiff's request, the defendant made a contribution to Morehouse College, and the book, which could remain on sale, would be labeled "an unauthorized parody." Kirkpatrick, Mitchell Estate Settles "Gone With the Wind" Suit, N.Y. Times, May 10, 2002, p. C6.

would such a sale or lease infringe?) The influence of *eBay* on permanent injunctions in copyright cases is examined in C. Bohannan, Copyright Harm and Injunctions, 30 Cardozo Arts & Ent.L.J. 11 (2012). A. Ng, Rights, Privileges, and Access to Information, 42 Loy.U.Chi.L.J. 89 (2010), uses property law principles to distinguish a right to compensation from a right to exclude, but H. Gomez–Arostegui, Prospective Compensation in Lieu of a Final Injunction in Patent and Copyright Cases, 78 Fordham L.Rev. 1661 (2010), argues that courts do not have the authority to order continuing royalties or other compensation for post-judgment infringements.

THE RIGHT TO A JURY TRIAL

When the plaintiff in an infringement action seeks to recover actual damages and profits, either party is entitled, upon demand, to a jury. Conversely, if the plaintiff seeks only an injunction, the action is "equitable," and there is no right to a jury trial. But plaintiffs often demand both an injunction and damages. As a consequence of Beacon Theatres, Inc. v. Westover, 359 U.S. 500 (1959), and Dairy Queen, Inc. v. Wood, 369 U.S. 469 (1962), all damage claims in such actions are triable by a jury.

When a plaintiff elects to forego actual damages and profits and seeks instead only statutory damages, the right to a jury trial had been unsettled. Some courts, viewing the remedy of statutory damages as "legal," found a seventh amendment right to trial by jury. E.g., Cass County Music Co. v. C.H.L.R., Inc., 88 F.3d 635 (8th Cir.1996) (surveying the split among the circuits); cf. Video Views, Inc. v. Studio 21, Ltd., 925 F.2d 1010 (7th Cir.), cert. denied, 502 U.S. 861 (1991) (recognizing a right to a jury trial on issues of infringement and willfulness, but with the judge determining the amount of statutory damages). Others cases considered the remedy "equitable," raising no constitutional or statutory right to a jury. E.g., Twentieth Century Music Corp. v. Frith, 645 F.2d 6 (5th Cir.1981). (The plaintiffs in several of these cases were music publishers complaining of unauthorized public performances. Why might they want to avoid a jury?)

In Feltner v. Columbia Pictures Television, Inc., 523 U.S. 340 (1998), the Supreme Court held that there is a right to a jury in statutory damage cases. The trial judge had awarded $8.8 million in statutory damages for a broadcaster's "willful" infringement, denying the defendant's request for a jury trial. The Ninth Circuit affirmed, 106 F.3d 284 (9th Cir.1997), but the Supreme Court reversed. Attempting to avoid the constitutional issue, the Supreme Court first considered whether the Copyright Act itself granted a jury trial in statutory damages cases, but concluded that "[t]he language of § 504(c) does not grant a right to have a jury assess statutory damages." Referring to § 504(c)'s requirement that damages be assessed in an amount that "the court considers just," Justice Thomas said that "[t]he word 'court' in this context appears to mean judge, not jury." Although the statute did not require a jury trial, the Court concluded that the constitution did. "Before the adoption of the Seventh Amendment, the common law and statutes in England and this country granted copyright owners causes of action for infringement. More importantly, copyright suits for monetary damages were tried in courts of law, and thus before juries. * * * [W]e hold that the Seventh Amendment provides a right to a jury trial on all issues pertinent to an award of statutory damages under § 504(c) of the Copyright Act, including the amount itself."[k]

IMPOUNDMENT AND DISPOSITION

The court in an infringement action has discretion to order the impoundment of allegedly infringing copies and related articles. § 503(a). Impoundments are governed by the safeguards in Federal Rule of Civil Procedure 65. See Fed.R.Civ.P. 65(f). Upon final judgment, destruction or other disposition of infringing copies may be ordered. § 503(b).

COSTS AND ATTORNEY'S FEES

The court in its discretion may award costs and "a reasonable attorney's fee." § 505. Although the former may be assessed against either side, the latter is reserved for the "prevailing party." (It is not always easy to decide who has in fact prevailed. See Shapiro, Bernstein & Co. v. 4636 S. Vermont Ave., Inc., 367 F.2d 236 (9th Cir.1966).) The opportunity for attorney's fees, like statutory damages, may be lost if the copyright owner delays registration. § 412.

Fee awards have been the subject of considerable judicial discussion, perhaps reflecting the mounting encroachments on the entrenched "American rule" that parties must pay their own legal expenses. Prevailing plaintiffs frequently received attorney's fees. The criteria for awards to prevailing defendants, however, varied among the circuits. The variations were surveyed in Lieb v. Topstone Indus., Inc., 788 F.2d 151 (3d Cir.1986), but were wiped out by the Supreme Court in Fogerty v. Fantasy, Inc., 510 U.S. 517 (1994), endorsing the "even-handed" approach exemplified by the Third Circuit in *Lieb*. "Prevailing plaintiffs and prevailing defendants," Chief Justice Rehnquist wrote, "are to be treated alike, but attorney's fees are to be awarded to prevailing parties only as a matter of the court's discretion." The Third Circuit's description in *Lieb* of the factors that may guide the exercise of that discretion was endorsed by the Supreme Court: "These factors include 'frivolousness, motivation, objective unreasonableness (both in the factual and in the legal components of the case) and the need in particular circumstances to advance considerations of compensation and deterrence.'"[l]

---

[k]   On remand, the defendant in *Feltner* got his jury trial, but the jury set statutory damages at $31.68 million—$23 million more than the original judgment by the trial judge. The award was upheld on appeal at 259 F.3d 1186 (9th Cir.2001), cert. denied, 534 U.S. 1127 (2002).

[l]   Judge Posner suggested a "refinement" of the standard for awarding attorney's fees announced in *Fogerty*: "[T]he prevailing party in a copyright case in which the monetary stakes are small should have a presumptive entitlement to an award of attorneys' fees." Otherwise, Judge Posner worried, the effect "would be to allow minor infringements, though willful, to be committed with impunity, to be in effect privileged, immune from legal address." Gonzales v. Transfer Technologies, Inc., 301 F.3d 608 (7th Cir.2002). Judge Posner continued his "simplification" of the relevant factors for attorney's fees in Assessment Tech., LLC v. WIREdata, Inc., 361 F.3d 434 (7th Cir.2004), arguing that the "two most important considerations" are the strength of the prevailing party's case and the amount of the recovery. "When the prevailing party is the defendant, who by definition receives not a small award but no award, the presumption in favor of awarding fees is very strong."

The Third Circuit in *Lieb* had also discussed factors relevant to the amount of the award. As for "what amount is reasonable under the circumstances * * * the relative complexity of the litigation is relevant. Also, a sum greater than what the client has been charged may not be assessed, but the award need not be that large. * * * The relative financial strength of the parties is a valid consideration * * * as are the damages * * *. Where bad faith is present that, too, may affect the size of the award. * * * We emphasize that the aims of the statute are compensation and deterrence where appropriate, but not ruination." The Second Circuit, however, took a somewhat different view of "a reasonable attorney's fee" in Crescent Pub. Group, Inc. v. Playboy Enter., Inc., 246 F.3d 142 (2d Cir.2001). Adopting the "lodestar method" that looks to the rates of lawyers of similar skill and experience in the community, the court declined to adopt a rule that the actual billing arrangement placed a ceiling on the fee award, although it acknowledged that the actual billing remained a significant factor in determining a "reasonable" fee.[m]

CRIMINAL INFRINGEMENT

Willful copyright infringement done for purposes of commercial advantage or private financial gain is a criminal offense. § 506(a)(1)(A). Responding to United States v. LaMacchia, 871 F.Supp. 535 (D.Mass.1994), where a defendant who had provided free access to copyrighted software through a computer bulletin board escaped criminal sanctions due to the absence of financial gain, Congress in 1997 expanded criminal liability to encompass the reproduction or distribution, including by electronic means, of infringing copies with a total retail value of more than $1,000 during any 180-day period. § 506(a)(1)(B). It also added the liberal definition of "financial gain" in § 101. In 2005, Congress expanded criminal liability again to include unauthorized distribution of works that have not yet been commercially distributed. § 506(a)(1)(C). Record and movie piracy account for most of the criminal prosecutions, although other infringers (including, alas, the Marx Brothers) are not immune. See Marx v. United States, 96 F.2d 204 (9th Cir.1938). The criminal penalties for infringement are specified in 18 U.S.C.A. § 2319 (reproduced in the Statutory Supplement). They can be severe.[n] E. Goldman, A Road to No Warez: The No Electronic Theft Act and Criminal Copyright Infringement, 82 Ore.L.Rev. 369 (2003), critically reviews the expansion of criminal copyright liability.

On the relationship between civil and criminal infringement actions, see United States v. Cohen, 946 F.2d 430 (6th Cir.1991), allowing the in-

---

[m] The American Intellectual Property Law Association says that the median cost of litigating a copyright infringement case with a value of less than $1 million is $350,000. AIPLA, Report of the Economic Survey 35 (2011).

[n] The Department of Justice has increased its enforcement of the criminal provisions of the Copyright Act. Particular targets include so-called "warez" groups that compete to provide the fastest and highest quality pirated works over the Internet, as well as traditional organized crime groups specializing in hard copies like CDs and DVDs. In what may be the largest seizure of pirated CDs, 500,000 counterfeit music and software CDs were seized from a piracy ring that allegedly brought in $100 million a year; the chief defendant was sentenced to 37 months in prison. 74 Pat., Tm. & Copyr.J. (BNA) 461 (2007). The tools and resources available to the federal government for enforcement of intellectual property rights were enhanced by passage of the Enforcement of Intellectual Property Rights Act of 2008, P.L. 110–403 (2008). E. Goldman, Warez Trading and Criminal Copyright Infringement, 51 J.Copyr.Soc'y 395 (2004), analyzes enforcement of the criminal copyright provisions.

troduction of evidence from a civil infringement case in a criminal prosecution for duplicating video cassettes. In Columbia Pictures Indus., Inc. v. T & F Enter., 68 F.Supp.2d 833 (E.D.Mich.1999), the court permitted the plaintiff movie studios to invoke the doctrine of collateral estoppel in their civil action against movie pirates in order to prevent the defendants from denying facts admitted in their guilty pleas to criminal copyright infringement.

It is a violation of federal law, punishable by fine and ten years imprisonment, to transport "in interstate or foreign commerce any goods, wares, merchandise, securities or money, of the value of $5,000 or more, knowing the same to have been stolen, converted or taken by fraud." 18 U.S.C.A. § 2314. Does the interstate transportation of unauthorized copies of copyrighted works fall within the scope of this prohibition? The Supreme Court held that it does not in Dowling v. United States, 473 U.S. 207 (1985).

Can the states apply their own criminal statutes to conduct that infringes a federal copyright? See § 301; Crow v. Wainwright, 720 F.2d 1224 (11th Cir.1983), cert. denied, 469 U.S. 819 (1984) (criminal conviction under a state record piracy statute overturned as preempted by federal copyright law). A state criminal prosecution under Ohio law for unauthorized use of another's property brought against a defendant who used his computer bulletin board to distribute copies of copyrighted software was held preempted under § 301 in State v. Perry, 83 Ohio St.3d 41, 697 N.E.2d 624 (1998). But see State v. Smith, 115 Wash.2d 434, 798 P.2d 1146 (1990) (defendant would buy a computer program, make copies for sale, and then return it; a state prosecution for theft was not preempted). Can the latter two cases be distinguished?

PART 2

UNFAIR COMPETITION AND OTHER DOCTRINES BEYOND COPYRIGHT

CHAPTER 7

THE ROOTS OF UNFAIR COMPETITION

1. PASSING OFF

Boston Professional Hockey Association, Inc. v. Dallas Cap & Emblem Manufacturing, Inc.

United States Court of Appeals, Fifth Circuit, 1975.
510 F.2d 1004.
Certiorari denied, 423 U.S. 868.

■ Before BROWN, CHIEF JUDGE, and GODBOLD and RONEY, CIRCUIT JUDGES.

■ RONEY, CIRCUIT JUDGE:

Nearly everyone is familiar with the artistic symbols which designate the individual teams in various professional sports. The question in this case of first impression is whether the unauthorized, intentional duplication of a professional hockey team's symbol on an embroidered emblem, to be sold to the public as a patch for attachment to clothing, violates any legal right of the team to the exclusive use of that symbol. Contrary to the decision of the district court, we hold that the team has an interest in its own individualized symbol entitled to legal protection against such unauthorized duplication.

The National Hockey League (NHL) and thirteen of its member hockey teams brought this action to enjoin Dallas Cap & Emblem Manufacturing, Inc., from manufacturing and selling embroidered emblems depicting their trademarks. All plaintiffs assert a cause of action for common law unfair competition. The NHL and twelve of the plaintiff teams have secured federal registration of their team symbols as service marks for ice hockey entertainment services and seek relief under both provisions of the Lanham Act, 15 U.S.C.A. §§ 1114, 1125, which give statutory protection to such marks. The Toronto team has not secured federal registration of its symbol and, thus, has not alleged a cause of action against defendant for infringement of a registered mark under 15 U.S.C.A. § 1114, but is restricted to § 1125 which can encompass unregistered marks. The Vancouver team did not secure registration until after the alleged infringing act and has sued only for injunctive relief under § 1114, not for damages. None of the symbols of the various teams have been copyrighted.

The district court denied Lanham Act relief and granted only limited relief for unfair competition, requiring solely that defendant place on the emblems or the package a notice that the emblems are not authorized by or have not emanated from the plaintiffs. The claim for damages was denied.

d.c.

The Facts

The controlling facts of the case at bar are relatively uncomplicated and uncontested. Plaintiffs play ice hockey professionally. In producing and promoting the sport of ice hockey, plaintiffs have each adopted and widely publicized individual team symbols. * * *

Plaintiffs have authorized National Hockey League Services, Inc. (NHLS) to act as their exclusive licensing agent. NHLS has licensed various manufacturers to use the team symbols on merchandise and has granted to one manufacturer, Lion Brothers Company, Inc., the exclusive license to manufacture embroidered emblems depicting the marks in question. In the spring of 1972, NHLS authorized the sale of NHL team emblems in connection with the sale of Kraft candies. That promotion alone was advertised on more than five million bags of candy.

Defendant Dallas Cap & Emblem Manufacturing, Inc., is in the business of making and selling embroidered cloth emblems. In August of 1968 and June of 1971, defendant sought to obtain from NHLS an exclusive license to make embroidered emblems representing the team motifs. Although these negotiations were unsuccessful, defendant went ahead and manufactured and sold without authorization emblems which were substantial duplications of the marks. During the month of April 1972, defendant sold approximately 24,603 of these emblems to sporting goods stores in various states. Defendant deliberately reproduced plaintiffs' marks on embroidered emblems and intended the consuming public to recognize the emblems as the symbols of the various hockey teams and to purchase them as such.

The Law

The complaint alleged that defendant's manufacture and sale of the team symbols constitutes (1) an infringement of the plaintiffs' registered marks in violation of 15 U.S.C.A. § 1114;[2] (2) false designation of origin in violation of 15 U.S.C.A. § 1125;[3] and (3) common law unfair competition.

The statutory cause of action emanates from what is commonly called the Lanham Act. 15 U.S.C.A. § 1051 et seq. The Lanham Act defines a service mark as "a mark used in the sale or advertising of services to identify the services of one person and distinguish them from the services of others" and a trademark as "any word, name, symbol, or device or any combination thereof adopted and used by a manufacturer or merchant to identify his goods and distinguish them from those manufactured or sold by others." 15 U.S.C.A. § 1127. Service mark infringement and trademark infringement are governed by identical standards. The terms can be used interchangea-

---

[2]   15 U.S.C.A. § 1114 reads in pertinent part:

(1) Any person who shall, without the consent of the registrant—

(a) use in commerce any reproduction, counterfeit, copy, or colorable imitation of a registered mark in connection with the sale, offering for sale, distribution, or advertising of any goods or services on or in connection with which such use is likely to cause confusion, or to cause mistake, or to deceive;

* * *

shall be liable in a civil action by the registrant for the remedies hereinafter provided.

[3]   15 U.S.C.A. § 1125 reads in pertinent part:

(a) Any person who shall affix, apply, or annex, or use in connection with any goods or services, or any container or containers for goods, a false designation of origin, or any false description or representation, including words or other symbols tending falsely to describe or represent the same, and shall cause such goods or services to enter into commerce, . . . shall be liable to a civil action by any person doing business in the locality falsely indicated as that of origin or in the region in which said locality is situated, or by any person who believes that he is or is likely to be damaged by the use of any such false description or representation.

[The text of § 1125(a) as subsequently amended in 1988 appears at p. 593 infra.]

bly when the marks are both service marks and trademarks. For convenience we use the word trademark in this opinion to designate both service mark and trademark use of the symbols involved.

A cause of action for the infringement of a registered mark in violation of 15 U.S.C.A. § 1114 exists where a person uses (1) any reproduction, counterfeit, copy or colorable imitation of a mark; (2) without the registrant's consent; (3) in commerce; (4) in connection with the sale, offering for sale, distribution or advertising of any goods; (5) where such use is likely to cause confusion, or to cause mistake or to deceive. A broadening of the protection afforded by the statute occurred by amendment in 1962 which deleted the previously existing requirement that the confusion or deception must relate to the "source of origin of such goods or service." Pub.L. 87–772, § 17, 76 Stat. 773 (1962). Continental Motors Corp. v. Continental Aviation Corp., 375 F.2d 857, 860 at n. 8 (5th Cir.1967).

* * * The use of an unregistered trademark can constitute a violation of § 1125 where

> . . . the alleged unregistered trademarks used by the plaintiff are so associated with its goods that the use of the same or similar marks by another company constitutes a representation that its goods come from the same source.

Joshua Meier Co. v. Albany Novelty Mfg. Co., 236 F.2d 144, 147 (2d Cir.1956). * * * Under § 1125, the registration of a mark is not a prerequisite of recovery as it is under § 1114.

Unfair competition is a broader area of the law than statutory trademark infringement. B.H. Bunn Co. v. AAA Replacement Parts Co., 451 F.2d 1254 (5th Cir.1971). Unfair competition is almost universally regarded as a question of whether the defendant is passing off his goods or services as those of the plaintiff by virtue of substantial similarity between the two, leading to confusion on the part of potential customers. * * * As a general rule, therefore, the same facts which would support an action for trademark infringement would also support an action for unfair competition.

The Case

The difficulty with this case stems from the fact that a reproduction of the trademark itself is being sold, unattached to any other goods or services. The statutory and case law of trademarks is oriented toward the use of such marks to sell something other than the mark itself. The district court thought that to give plaintiffs protection in this case would be tantamount to the creation of a copyright monopoly for designs that were not copyrighted. The copyright laws are based on an entirely different concept than the trademark laws, and contemplate that the copyrighted material, like patented ideas, will eventually pass into the public domain. The trademark laws are based on the needed protection of the public and business interests and there is no reason why trademarks should ever pass into the public domain by the mere passage of time.

Although our decision here may slightly tilt the trademark laws from the purpose of protecting the public to the protection of the business interests of plaintiffs, we think that the two become so intermeshed when viewed against the backdrop of the common law of unfair competition that both the public and plaintiffs are better served by granting the relief sought by plaintiffs. * * *

As to 15 U.S.C.A. § 1114.

Plaintiffs indisputably have established the first three elements of a § 1114 cause of action. Plaintiffs' marks are validly registered and defendant manufactured and sold emblems which were (1) substantial duplications of the marks, (2) without plaintiffs' consent, and (3) in interstate commerce. The issue is whether plaintiffs have proven elements four and five of an action for mark infringement under the Lanham Act, i.e., whether the symbols are used in connection with the sale of goods and whether such use is likely to cause confusion, mistake or deception.

The fourth requisite of a § 1114 cause of action is that the infringing use of the registered mark must be in connection with the sale, offering for sale, distribution or advertising of any goods. Although the district court did not expressly find that plaintiffs had failed to establish element four, such a finding was implicit in the court's statement that "in the instant case, the registered trade mark is, in effect, the product itself."

Defendant is in the business of manufacturing and marketing emblems for wearing apparel. These emblems are the products, or goods, which defendant sells. When defendant causes plaintiffs' marks to be embroidered upon emblems which it later markets, defendant uses those marks in connection with the sale of goods as surely as if defendant had embroidered the marks upon knit caps. * * *

The fifth element of a cause of action for mark infringement under 15 U.S.C.A. § 1114 is that the infringing use is likely to cause confusion, or to cause mistake or to deceive. The district court decided that there was no likelihood of confusion because the usual purchaser, a sports fan in his local sporting goods store, would not be likely to think that defendant's emblems were manufactured by or had some connection with plaintiffs. Cf. Sun–Maid Raisin Growers of California v. Sunaid Food Products, Inc., 356 F.2d 467 (5th Cir.1966). This court has held that the findings of a district court as to likelihood of confusion are factual and not to be overturned unless clearly erroneous. Hang Ten International v. Sherry Manufacturing Co., 498 F.2d 326 (5th Cir.1974); American Foods, Inc. v. Golden Flake, Inc., 312 F.2d 619 (5th Cir.1963). In this case, however, the district court overlooked the fact that the act was amended to eliminate the source of origin as being the only focal point of confusion. The confusion question here is conceptually difficult. It can be said that the public buyer *knew* that the emblems portrayed the teams' symbols. Thus, it can be argued, the buyer is not confused or deceived. This argument misplaces the purpose of the confusion requirement. The confusion or deceit requirement is met by the fact that the defendant duplicated the protected trademarks and sold them to the public knowing that the public would identify them as being the teams' trademarks. The certain knowledge of the buyer that the source and origin of the trademark symbols were in plaintiffs satisfies the requirement of the act. The argument that confusion must be as to the source of the manufacture of the emblem itself is unpersuasive, where the trademark, originated by the team, is the triggering mechanism for the sale of the emblem.

The plaintiffs, with the exception of Toronto, have satisfied all elements of a cause of action for mark infringement in violation of 15 U.S.C.A. § 1114. Plaintiffs are entitled to an injunction permanently enjoining defendant from the manufacture and sale, in interstate commerce, of emblems embroidered with substantial duplications of plaintiffs' marks without plaintiffs' consent, and such other relief as might flow from the facts.

As to 15 U.S.C.A. § 1125.

The district court held that plaintiffs failed to prove a cause of action under 15 U.S.C.A. § 1125 for false designation of origin of the goods in question or for false description by means of symbols. Because all plaintiffs, with the exception of Toronto, have established a cause of action for registered mark infringement, the district court's decision in regard to a § 1125 cause of action only affects plaintiff Toronto. The district court based its denial of a § 1125 cause of action on two findings of fact: (1) there was no likelihood of confusion as to the source of the emblems and (2) defendant did not make any false representations concerning the origin of the emblems. Our decision that confusion is self-evident from the nature of defendant's use of plaintiffs' marks applies with equal force in plaintiff Toronto's case. We reverse. * * *

* * * In the language of § 1125, defendant used a symbol, Toronto's mark, which tended falsely to represent goods, the embroidered emblems, in commerce. Where the consuming public had the certain knowledge that the source and origin of the trademark symbol was in the Toronto team, the reproduction of that symbol by defendant constituted a violation of § 1125.

To warrant injunctive relief under § 1125, a plaintiff must demonstrate that the false representations have a tendency to deceive the consumer. Geisel v. Poynter Products, Inc., 283 F.Supp. 261 (S.D.N.Y.1968). Our decision that defendant's use of plaintiffs' marks entails a likelihood of confusion under § 1114 establishes that defendant's identical use of Toronto's mark constitutes a false representation under § 1125. See Girl Scouts v. Personality Posters Mfg. Co., 304 F.Supp. 1228 (S.D.N.Y.1969). Accordingly, we reverse the decision of the district court and hold that Toronto has established a cause of action under 15 U.S.C.A. § 1125.

As to Unfair Competition.

Although the district court denied plaintiffs relief under the applicable provisions of the Lanham Act, the court found that the actions of defendant constituted unfair competition. The court stated that defendant's use of plaintiffs' marks had "... the prospect of trading on the competitive advantage the mark originator has to the public which desires the 'official' product." Unfair competition is a question of fact, Volkswagenwerk Aktiengesellschaft v. Rickard, 492 F.2d 474 (5th Cir.1974). Our review is narrowly circumscribed by F.R.Civ.P. 52(a). We find that there is substantial evidence which reflects that defendant competed unfairly with plaintiffs and, accordingly, we affirm the decision of the district court in this regard.

The unfair competition cannot, however, be rendered fair by the disclaimer ordered by the district court. The exact duplication of the symbol and the sale as the team's emblem satisfying the confusion requirement of the law, words which indicate it was not authorized by the trademark owner are insufficient to remedy the illegal confusion. Only a prohibition of the unauthorized use will sufficiently remedy the wrong.

Additional Defenses to Relief

Defendant makes two arguments against an extension of Lanham Act protection to plaintiffs which need consideration. Adopting the district court's rationale, defendant asserts first, that plaintiffs' marks when embroidered on emblems for wearing apparel are functional and, thus, serve no trademark purpose and, second, that there is some overriding concept of free competition which, under the instant facts, would remove plaintiffs from the protective ambits of the Lanham Act.

The short answer to defendant's arguments is that the emblems sold because they bore the identifiable trademarks of plaintiffs. This fact clearly distinguishes the case from Pagliero v. Wallace China Co., 198 F.2d 339 (9th Cir.1952), relied upon by the district court. *Pagliero* involved designs on chinaware which were neither trademarked, patented nor copyrighted. The court found no unfair competition on the ground that the designs were functional, that is, they connoted other than a trademark purpose. "The attractiveness and eye-appeal of the design sells the china," 198 F.2d at pp. 343–344, not the trademark character of the designs. In the case at bar, the embroidered symbols are sold not because of any such aesthetic characteristic but because they are the trademarks of the hockey teams. * * *

The argument that the symbols could be protected only if copyrighted likewise misses the thrust of trademark protection. A trademark is a property right which is acquired by use. Trade–Mark Cases, 100 U.S. 82 (1879). It differs substantially from a copyright, in both its legal genesis and its scope of federal protection. The legal cornerstone for the protection of copyrights is Article I, section 8, clause 8 of the Constitution. In the case of a copyright, an individual creates a unique design and, because the Constitutional fathers saw fit to encourage creativity, he can secure a copyright for his creation for a period of 28 years, renewable once. After the expiration of the copyright, his creation becomes part of the public domain. In the case of a trademark, however, the process is reversed. An individual selects a word or design that might otherwise be in the public domain to represent his business or product. If that word or design comes to symbolize his product or business in the public mind, the individual acquires a property right in the mark. The acquisition of such a right through use represents the passage of a word or design out of the public domain into the protective ambits of trademark law. Under the provisions of the Lanham Act, the owner of a mark acquires a protectable property interest in his mark through registration and use. * * *

Reversed and remanded.

NOTES AND QUESTIONS

(1) Would copyright be a serviceable alternative to the trademark and unfair competition claims raised by the plaintiffs to protect what Judge Roney describes as their "artistic symbols"?

(2) Consider the various theories discussed in *Boston Hockey*. Each appears to require a finding that confusion is likely. The typical trademark case involves allegations that a defendant has used a trademark similar to one associated with the plaintiff in a manner that is likely to cause confusion as to the source or sponsorship of the defendant's goods. About what, exactly, were purchasers of the defendant's patches confused? Should the teams have a right to prevent even non-confusing exploitation of their symbols? Later decisions have criticized *Boston Hockey* for its loose interpretation of the confusion requirement. The issue is considered further at p. 694 infra.

(3) The 1909 Copyright Act included "prints or labels used for articles of merchandise" among its classification of copyrightable works. See Kitchens of Sara Lee, Inc. v. Nifty Foods Corp., 266 F.2d 541 (2d Cir.1959) (copyright in illustrations of bakery products held valid and infringed). In the 1976 Act, prints and labels are absorbed into the category of "pictorial, graphic, and sculptural works," with no intention, it is said, to narrow the scope of copyright. H.R.Rep. p. 54. But copyright in labels and packaging is sharply limited by the requirement of authorship. The cases, echoing Copyright Office policy, demand "an appreciable amount of original text or pictorial material." *Kitchens of Sara Lee,* supra; Alberto–Culver Co. v. Andrea Dumon, Inc., 466 F.2d 705 (7th Cir.1972). Lists of ingredients or contents, serving directions, and brief descriptive texts are thus excluded from copyright, as are short phrases such as slogans, names, and titles. See 37 C.F.R. § 202.1(a).

A NOTE ON THE LAW OF TRADEMARKS AND UNFAIR COMPETITION

The preceding case brings into consideration a number of important elements of the law of trademarks and unfair competition. It accepts as axiomatic that attempts to pass off one's goods as those of another are actionable. This is the foundation of the expanding law of unfair competition. Unfair competition is a vigorous and sometimes unconfined companion of copyright. Application of its doctrines to literary and artistic works has become commonplace; the next two chapters offer numerous illustrations. An understanding of the scope of contemporary unfair competition law calls for some knowledge of both common law trademark protection and the federal statutory regime that supplements (but does not supplant) it.

(1) *Common Law Protection.* The law of trademarks and unfair competition has its roots in the common law action of deceit. The gravamen of the original tort was the fraudulent marketing of goods through the imitation of another's trademark. Injury to the aggrieved trademark owner was direct— customers who wished to patronize the plaintiff were diverted instead to an imposter. Consumer confusion was thus the touchstone.

The common law of trademarks soon became entangled in an etymological thicket that sometimes obscured the dominant role of the confusion rationale. Marks that consist of a coined word, such as EXXON on petroleum products or KODAK on cameras, or an arbitrary word whose primary meaning is not related to the goods on which it appears, such as APPLE on computers or SHELL on gasoline, are protectable as trademarks immediately upon adoption. However, words whose primary meanings are descriptive of the goods to which they are affixed, such as CHAP STICK on a lip balm or FOOD FAIR on a supermarket, are not immediately accorded the status of a trademark. This distinction reflects a reluctance to permit the exclusive appropriation of terms in which competitors can claim some legitimate interest. Yet even the use of a "descriptive" term can cause confusion if the public has come to associate that term with a particular producer. This source significance for descriptive terms is what, in a triumph of obfuscation, came to be called "secondary meaning"—this despite the fact that in the relevant market the primary significance of the term is now one of identification rather than description. The word WHEATIES on a box of cereal, for example, is understood as more than a description of the physical ingredients; use on a cereal sold by a competitor of General Mills is likely to cause confusion about the source of the product. The common law thus also offers redress for appropriations of descriptive terms that have acquired "secondary meaning." But the owner's rights extend only to the secondary meaning—a "fair use" of the term in its original, descriptive sense will not infringe. The existence of "source significance," whether inherent or acquired, and the likelihood of consumer confusion, are the dominant issues.

Protection against unfair competition can reach beyond words and symbols used on goods or services. The themes of source significance and confusion extended easily to business and corporate names, and these too are protected at common law. The general appearance of labels and packaging, if duplicated by a competitor, also can create confusion, and the common law stood ready, upon a showing of source significance, to prohibit the infringement of a seller's "trade dress." Indeed, the appearance and design of the goods themselves can sometimes serve as an indication of their origin; thus, product copying that causes confusion of source can be actionable as "unfair competition."

The common law proscription against trademark infringement was eventually supplemented at the state level by statutory trademark protection. Much of the modern state legislation derives from the Model State Trademark Bill. With the exception of the anti-dilution provisions noted below, however, these state statutes largely reaffirm basic common law principles.

(2) *Registration Under the Lanham Act.* The federal trademark statute, known as the Lanham Act, 15 U.S.C.A. § 1051 et seq., establishes a trademark registration system administered by the Patent and Trademark Office. (Selected provisions of the Lanham Act are reproduced in the Statutory Supplement.) The system follows the general contours of the common law. Protection extends chiefly to "trademarks" and "service marks" that have been registered on the Principal Register. Business and corporate names, which the Lanham Act calls "trade names," are not registrable as such, but if the name is also used as a trademark or service mark, it is in that capacity eligible for registration. Before the 1988 revision of the Lanham Act, actual use of the mark in interstate commerce was a prerequisite to registration. Section 1(b), 15 U.S.C.A. § 1051(b), now permits an application based on a bona fide intention to use the mark, thus providing a measure of security for pre-marketing expenditures. But intent must be followed in due course (generally six months) by actual use.

There are several important restrictions on the kinds of marks that can be registered on the Principal Register. Section 2(d) of the Lanham Act, 15 U.S.C.A. § 1052(d), prohibits the registration of a mark which so resembles a mark or trade name used by another "as to be likely, when used on or in connection with the goods of the applicant, to cause confusion, or to cause mistake, or to deceive"; section 2(e) excludes "a mark which, (1) when used on or in connection with the goods of the applicant is merely descriptive or deceptively misdescriptive of them, (2) when used on or in connection with the goods of the applicant is primarily geographically descriptive of them * * * [or] (4) is primarily merely a surname." These subsection (e) exclusions can be overcome, however, by meeting the requirements of § 2(f), which authorizes "the registration of a mark used by the applicant which has become distinctive of the applicant's goods in commerce"—that is, which has acquired secondary meaning. (A "Supplemental Register" is maintained for marks that are merely "capable of distinguishing" source, in aid of registration abroad where a domestic registration is often a prerequisite to foreign registration. §§ 23–28, 15 U.S.C.A. §§ 1091–96.)

A distinction is drawn both at common law and under the Lanham Act between marks that are *descriptive* (and thus require proof of secondary meaning) and those that are instead merely *suggestive* of the virtues or characteristics of the goods (and thus entitled to immediate registration and protection as inherently distinctive). TENDER VITTLES is descriptive of a moist cat food, Ralston Purina Co. v. Thomas J. Lipton, Inc., 341 F.Supp. 129 (S.D.N.Y.1972), but TAIL WAGGER is merely suggestive of a dog food, Allied Mills, Inc. v. Kal Kan Foods, Inc., 203 U.S.P.Q. 390 (Tm.Tr.App.Bd.1979). HOLIDAY INN is descriptive of a hotel, Zimmerman v. Holiday Inns, Inc., 438 Pa. 528, 266 A.2d 87 (1970), cert. denied, 400 U.S. 992 (1971), but ROACH MOTEL is merely suggestive of an insect trap. American Home Prod. Corp. v. Johnson Chemical Co., 589 F.2d 103 (2d Cir.1978). The distinction is obviously fragile.

When a designation is said to be "generic," it means that it is used by consumers as the name of the product itself, regardless of source, and cannot be monopolized by a single producer. Thus, the Supreme Court held that "Shredded Wheat" was the generic name for the pillow-shaped breakfast cereal; the original producer could not prevent competitors from using that name, at least if they took reasonable steps to minimize the likelihood of confusion. Kellogg Co. v. National Biscuit Co., 305 U.S. 111 (1938). Even a coined word that initially qualifies as a trademark can become generic. Famous examples include "aspirin" and "cellophane." Bayer Co., Inc. v. United Drug Co., 272 Fed. 505 (S.D.N.Y.1921); DuPont Cellophane Co. v. Waxed Products Co., 85 F.2d 75 (2d Cir.1936). Under § 14(3) of the Lanham Act, a registration may be canceled if the mark becomes the generic name for the goods or services. 15 U.S.C.A. § 1064(3). Such determinations can be delicate; a single word may function both as a product name and an indication of source. (For a case that stirred considerable controversy as a result of its unusual formulation of the applicable standard, see Anti–Monopoly, Inc. v. General Mills Fun Group, Inc., 684 F.2d 1316 (9th Cir.1982), cert. denied, 459 U.S. 1227 (1983), holding generic the registered trademark MONOPOLY as used on the well-known board game. It prompted an amendment to § 14 emphasizing that a mark is not generic merely because it is also used as the name of a "unique" product.)

Early decisions read the Lanham Act's definition of "trademark" to preclude registration on the Principal Register of product and packaging configurations; a more liberal view took root in 1958 with the registration by Haig & Haig of its "Pinch" bottle for scotch whisky. Ex parte Haig & Haig, Ltd., 118 U.S.P.Q. 229 (Comm'r Pat.1958). Although a packaging feature is occasionally considered to be inherently distinctive and thus entitled to immediate registration, applicants are usually required to demonstrate that the packaging has achieved secondary meaning as an indication of source. The Supreme Court in Wal–Mart Stores, Inc. v. Samara Brothers, Inc., 529 U.S. 205 (2000), p. 649 infra, held that product (as opposed to packaging) features always require a showing of secondary meaning as a prerequisite to protection under the Lanham Act.

Even if the appearance of a product is distinctive of its source, neither the Lanham Act nor the common law will forbid others to imitate it if the design is "functional." See §§ 2(e)(5), 33(b)(8), 43(a)(3), 15 U.S.C.A. §§ 1052(e)(5), 1115(b)(8), 1125(a)(3). Functional in this context means that the feature contributes to the efficient manufacture or performance of the product or otherwise yields a competitive advantage. The Supreme Court in the "Shredded Wheat" case, for example, found the shape of the wheat biscuit to be functional and thus not susceptible of exclusive appropriation as a trademark. Plaintiffs proving source significance for functional features must be content with relief mandating labeling or other measures intended to minimize confusion. See, e.g., American Greetings Corp. v. Dan–Dee Imports, Inc., 807 F.2d 1136 (3d Cir.1986); Keene Corp. v. Paraflex Industries, Inc., 653 F.2d 822 (3d Cir.1981).

When goods are purchased in part for their aesthetic qualities, ornamental features unrelated to the physical operation of the product may be considered "functional" if a prohibition on imitation would substantially hinder competition. Thus, "aesthetic functionality" is not unknown in the case law. See, e.g., Wallace Int'l Silversmiths, Inc. v. Godinger Silver Art Co., 916 F.2d 76 (2d Cir.1990). It was to these cases that the defendant in *Boston Hockey* unsuccessfully appealed.

(3) *The Test for Infringement.* Although registration under the Lanham Act provides a variety of procedural and substantive advantages, the standard of infringement remains, as at common law, a likelihood of confusion. Section 32(1), quoted by the court in *Boston Hockey,* bears repeating:

> Any person who shall, without the consent of the registrant—
>
> (a) use in commerce any reproduction, counterfeit, copy, or colorable imitation of a registered mark in connection with the sale, offering for sale, distribution, or advertising of any goods or services on or in connection with which such use is likely to cause confusion, or to cause mistake, or to deceive * * * shall be liable in a civil action by the registrant for the remedies hereinafter provided. * * * (15 U.S.C.A. § 1114(1))

One court set the stage for a determination of infringement by declaring:

> We begin with the oft-repeated observation that the essential question in any case of alleged trademark infringement brought under the Lanham Act or under the law of unfair competition is "whether a substantial number of ordinarily prudent purchasers are likely to be misled or confused as to the source of different products."[a]

Establishing a likelihood of confusion can be difficult. The plaintiff's burden is sometimes lightened by the willingness of judges and juries to project a likelihood of confusion on the basis of their own evaluation of the marks, the goods, and any other aspects of the marketing context that may affect the likelihood of confusion. Consumer surveys, properly conducted, can be decisive.

For a time the law of trademarks seemed concerned only with the use of confusingly similar marks on directly competing goods. Yet a trademark owner's reputation and goodwill may be endangered even when its mark is applied to products that the trademark owner does not sell. During the first half of the last century the concept of unfair competition grew to include the unauthorized use of marks on non-competing goods, provided that the goods were sufficiently related to the plaintiff's to cause a likelihood of confusion. As usual, the classic formulation is Judge Hand's:

> There is indeed a limit; the goods on which the supposed infringer puts the mark may be too remote from any that the owner would be likely to make or sell. It would be hard, for example, for the seller of a steam shovel to find ground for complaint in the use of his trade-mark on a lipstick.

---

[a] Information Clearing House, Inc. v. Find Magazine, 492 F.Supp. 147, 154 (S.D.N.Y.1980) (quoting Mushroom Makers, Inc. v. R.G. Barry Corp., 441 F.Supp. 1220, 1225 (S.D.N.Y.1977), aff'd, 580 F.2d 44 (2d Cir.1978), cert. denied, 439 U.S. 1116 (1979)).

L.E. Waterman Co. v. Gordon, 72 F.2d 272, 273 (2d Cir.1934).

The likelihood of confusion can turn on a number of variables. Among the most important is the distinctiveness of the plaintiff's mark, often described in terms of "strong" versus "weak" marks. The archetype of a strong mark is KODAK—fanciful, non-descriptive, prestigious, yet devoid of generic overtones. Probably no one else can use that word as a trademark on anything. Weak marks are typically descriptive or common—"National" or "Acme." Their scope of protection is accordingly narrow.

In an extension of the non-competing goods cases, confusion of sponsorship has come to be an accepted basis for a finding of infringement. Unauthorized use of the name of a teenage fashion magazine in connection with the sale of girls clothing led to an early articulation of the principle. See Triangle Pub. v. Rohrlich, 167 F.2d 969 (2d Cir.1948). Confusion of sponsorship claims appear frequently in cases challenging the unauthorized use of symbols derived from the worlds of sports and entertainment. See, e.g., Dallas Cowboys Cheerleaders, Inc. v. Pussycat Cinema, Ltd., 604 F.2d 200 (2d Cir.1979); National Football League Properties, Inc. v. Wichita Falls Sportswear, Inc., 532 F.Supp. 651 (W.D.Wash.1982).

Neither the Lanham Act nor the common law, however, prohibits the non-deceptive use of another's trademark to communicate truthful information about a product, for example, in comparative advertising. See, e.g., Prestonettes, Inc. v. Coty, 264 U.S. 359 (1924); Smith v. Chanel, Inc., 402 F.2d 562 (9th Cir.1968).

(4) *Section 43(a) of the Lanham Act.* This section is an oddity among the provisions of the Lanham Act; unlike most of the remainder of the Act, § 43(a), 15 U.S.C.A. § 1125, is not about registered trademarks:

> (1) Any person who, on or in connection with any goods or services, or any container for goods, uses in commerce any word, term, name, symbol, or device, or any combination thereof, or any false designation of origin, false or misleading description of fact, or false or misleading representation of fact, which—

> (A) is likely to cause confusion, or to cause mistake, or to deceive as to the affiliation, connection, or association of such person with another person, or as to the origin, sponsorship, or approval of his or her goods, services, or commercial activities by another person, or

> (B) in commercial advertising or promotion, misrepresents the nature, characteristics, qualities, or geographic origin of his or her or another person's goods, services, or commercial activities,

> shall be liable in a civil action by any person who believes that he or she is or is likely to be damaged by such act.

Section § 43(a) was intended to overcome a much-criticized common law rule that false statements by a seller about itself or its products were not actionable by a competitor unless the plaintiff could prove that the falsehoods necessarily resulted in a direct diversion of trade from the plaintiff to the defendant. This was the rule of American Washboard Co. v. Saginaw Mfg. Co., 103 Fed. 281 (6th Cir.1900), as reinforced by Mosler Safe Co. v. Ely–Norris Safe Co., 273 U.S. 132 (1927). Although § 43(a) may have been envisioned initially as a federal false advertising statute, it has evolved into something of a federal law of unfair competition, encompassing the infringement of unregistered trademarks, trade names, and trade dress. It was for this purpose that the section was invoked by the plaintiffs in *Boston Hockey*. Section 43(a) is an important adjunct to copyright; it will be encountered often in the succeeding materials.

(5) *Dilution.* The prevention of confusion is the primary aim of conventional trademark doctrine. But there is also a persistent view that emphasizes the undoubted advertising and commercial values that inhere in successful marks. These symbols, it is argued, should be protected against dilution, that is, against any use that may drain away the potency of the mark, regardless of the likelihood of confusion. This view was first propounded in this country in F. Schechter, The Rational Basis of Trademark Protection, 40 Harv.L.Rev. 813 (1927), although the wisdom of shielding marks against a dilution of their advertising value has also been questioned. See, e.g., R. Brown, Advertising and the Public Interest: Legal Protection of Trade Symbols, 57 Yale L.J. 1165 (1948), arguing that protection should be confined to the informational value of trademarks. Protection against dilution first achieved statutory recognition in many states through the formulation in the Model State Trademark Bill (1964):

> Likelihood of injury to business reputation or of dilution of the distinctive quality of a mark registered under this Act, or a mark valid at common law, or a trade name valid at common law, shall be a ground for injunctive relief notwithstanding the absence of competition between the parties or the absence of confusion as to the source of goods or services.

Most states have now replaced this formulation with the revised versions in the Model State Trademark Bill that parallel § 43(c) of the Lanham Act.

State dilution statutes have been invoked in two distinct situations. The distinctiveness of a mark as the identifying symbol of a particular company can be vitiated, even in the absence of confusion, if others use the same mark to identify themselves or their own products. This was the theory relied upon by the owner of the LEXIS legal research service in its unsuccessful attempt to stop the use by Toyota of LEXUS on luxury cars. Mead Data Central, Inc. v. Toyota Motor Sales, U.S.A., Inc., 875 F.2d 1026 (2d Cir.1989). (Did the defendant's use in *Boston Hockey* pose any threat to the distinctiveness of the plaintiffs' marks?) In addition to this "blurring" of distinctiveness, courts have sometimes been induced to enjoin the "tarnishment" of trademarks. Confusion aside, the image of a prestigious mark can be damaged by its appearance on inferior products or on goods incompatible with those of the trademark owner, or by its use in other unflattering or unwholesome settings. Such injury has frequently been forestalled through manipulation of the confusion rationale;[b] the dilution statutes offer more direct protection. However, if the defendant's use can be characterized as noncommercial speech, plaintiff's objection to the unwelcome reference may be met by an assertion of first amendment rights. Film-maker George Lucas, for example, was unsuccessful in his attempt to stop the media from using his STAR WARS trademark to characterize President Reagan's Strategic Defense Initiative, Lucasfilm Ltd. v. High Frontier, 622 F.Supp. 931 (D.D.C.1985), and L.L. Bean failed in an attempt

---

[b]   See, e.g., Mutual of Omaha Ins. Co. v. Novak, 836 F.2d 397 (8th Cir.1987) (likelihood of confusion found in the use of a distorted version of an insurance company's Indian Head logo on T-shirts with the words "Mutant of Omaha" and "Nuclear Holocaust Insurance"); General Electric v. Alumpa Coal Co., 205 U.S.P.Q. 1036 (D.Mass.1979) ("Genital Electric" on T-shirts and briefs enjoined based on a likelihood of confusion); Coca–Cola Co. v. Gemini Rising, Inc., 346 F.Supp. 1183 (E.D.N.Y.1972) ("Enjoy Coca-Cola" design altered on posters to advocate "Enjoy Cocaine"; injunction granted on a likelihood of confusion rationale).

to enjoin a prurient parody of its famous catalog. L.L. Bean, Inc. v. Drake Publishers, Inc., 811 F.2d 26 (1st Cir.), cert. denied, 483 U.S. 1013 (1987). Some of these issues are discussed in R. Denicola, Trademarks as Speech: Constitutional Implications of the Emerging Rationales for the Protection of Trade Symbols, 1982 Wis.L.Rev. 158. G. Myers, Trademark Parody: Lessons from the Copyright Decision in *Campbell v. Acuff–Rose Music, Inc.*, 59 L. & Contemp.Prob. (No. 2) 181 (1996), applies learning from the copyright parody cases to trademark parodies.

In 1995, protection against the "dilution" of "famous" marks (both registered and unregistered) became available under the Lanham Act with the addition of § 43(c); the provision was amended in 2006 to emphasize that uses *likely* to cause dilution are sufficient for liability, and that "dilution" includes both "blurring" and "tarnishment." "[D]ilution by blurring" is defined as "association arising from the similarity between a mark or trade name and a famous mark that impairs the distinctiveness of the famous mark"; "dilution by tarnishment" is "association arising from the similarity between a mark or trade name and a famous mark that harms the reputation of the famous mark." There are exclusions for the "fair use" of a mark, including use in comparative advertising or to parody, criticize, or comment on the mark owner or its goods, as well as for use in "news reporting" and "noncommercial use of a mark."[c]

(6) *Domain Names.* Internet domain names that identify the location of web sites have become a fertile ground for trademark disputes. A defendant who offers goods or services on a web site with a domain name that creates a likelihood of confusion because of its similarity to another's trademark is liable for infringement. See, e.g., Brookfield Communications, Inc. v. West Coast Ent. Corp., 174 F.3d 1036 (9th Cir.1999) (plaintiff's MovieBuff trademark for an entertainment database was infringed by a defendant who offered a similar product at its moviebuff.com web site). Domain names can also result in liability for trademark dilution. See, e.g., Hasbro, Inc. v. Internet Ent. Group, 40 U.S.P.Q.2d 1479 (W.D.Wash.1996) (plaintiff's CANDY LAND game mark was diluted by tarnishment caused by the defendant's candyland.com adult web site). The most common complaint about domain names, however, involves "cyberpiracy," in which a person registers a domain name containing another's trademark with the intention of selling it at a profit to the trademark owner. The possible variations on a mark, combined with the numerous "top level" domains (.com, .org, .net, .info, etc., with more on the way),[d] create headaches for trademark owners. Congress responded in 1999 with the addition to the Lanham Act of § 43(d), 15 U.S.C.A. § 1125(d). Owners of registered and unregistered marks are protected against the registration of a domain name that is identical or confusingly similar to the mark (or "dilutive" of a famous mark), but only if there is "a bad faith intent to profit" from the mark. The statute lists nine non-exclusive factors relevant to "bad faith" that attempt to balance the interests of trademark owners and domain name registrants.

---

[c] The exclusion for "noncommercial use of a mark" was interpreted by Judge Kozinski in Mattel, Inc. v. MCA Records, Inc., 296 F.3d 894 (9th Cir.2002), cert. denied, 537 U.S. 1171 (2003), to preclude liability when the defendant's use consists entirely of noncommercial speech. Use of the BARBIE trademark in a song poking fun at the Barbie doll and the values she represents was thus outside the reach of § 43(c).

[d] Applicants can now register their own "top level" domains, whether trademarks like .google or terms like .music or .sucks. See Perlroth, Imagining Dot Magic in a Name, N.Y. Times, June 14, 2012, p. B1.

(7) *References.* A number of substantial areas of trademark law have not even been mentioned in this brief introduction, including matters such as registration procedures, the geographic limits of protection, assignment and licensing of marks, remedies, and international protection. The most helpful treatise on trademark law is J. McCarthy, Trademarks and Unfair Competition (Thomson West). See also Restatement (Third) of Unfair Competition (1995). On registration under the Lanham Act, see A. Lalonde, Gilson on Trademarks (LexisNexis).

2. MISAPPROPRIATION

International News Service v. Associated Press

Supreme Court of the United States, 1918.
248 U.S. 215, 39 S.Ct. 68.

■ MR. JUSTICE PITNEY delivered the opinion of the Court.

The parties are competitors in the gathering and distribution of news and its publication for profit in newspapers throughout the United States. The Associated Press, which was complainant in the District Court, is a cooperative organization, incorporated under the Membership Corporations Law of the State of New York, its members being individuals who are either proprietors or representatives of about 950 daily newspapers published in all parts of the United States. * * * Complainant gathers in all parts of the world, by means of various instrumentalities of its own, by exchange with its members, and by other appropriate means, news and intelligence of current and recent events of interest to newspaper readers and distributes it daily to its members for publication in their newspapers. The cost of the service, amounting approximately to $3,500,000 per annum, is assessed upon the members and becomes a part of their costs of operation, to be recouped, presumably with profit, through the publication of their several newspapers. Under complainant's by-laws each member agrees upon assuming membership that news received through complainant's service is received exclusively for publication in a particular newspaper, language, and place specified in the certificate of membership, that no other use of it shall be permitted, and that no member shall furnish or permit anyone in his employ or connected with his newspaper to furnish any of complainant's news in advance of publication to any person not a member. And each member is required to gather the local news of his district and supply it to the Associated Press and to no one else.

Defendant is a corporation organized under the laws of the State of New Jersey, whose business is the gathering and selling of news to its customers and clients, consisting of newspapers published throughout the United States, under contracts by which they pay certain amounts at stated times for defendant's service. It has wide-spread news-gathering agencies; the cost of its operations amounts, it is said, to more than $2,000,000 per annum; and it serves about 400 newspapers located in the various cities of the United States and abroad, a few of which are represented, also, in the membership of the Associated Press.

The parties are in the keenest competition between themselves in the distribution of news throughout the United States; and so, as a rule, are the newspapers that they serve, in their several districts. * * *

The bill was filed to restrain the pirating of complainant's news by defendant in three ways: First, by bribing employees of newspapers published by complainant's members to furnish Associated Press news to defendant before publication, for transmission by telegraph and telephone to defendant's clients for publication by them; Second, by inducing Associated Press members to violate its by-laws and permit defendant to obtain news before publication; and, Third, by copying news from bulletin boards and from early editions of complainant's newspapers and selling this, either bodily or after rewriting it, to defendant's customers.

The District Court, upon consideration of the bill and answer, with voluminous affidavits on both sides, granted a preliminary injunction under the first and second heads; but refused at that stage to restrain the systematic practice admittedly pursued by defendant, of taking news bodily from the bulletin boards and early editions of complainant's newspapers and selling it as its own. The court expressed itself as satisfied that this practice amounted to unfair trade, but as the legal question was one of first impression it considered that the allowance of an injunction should await the outcome of an appeal. 240 Fed. 983, 996. Both parties having appealed, the Circuit Court of Appeals sustained the injunction order so far as it went, and upon complainant's appeal modified it and remanded the cause with directions to issue an injunction also against any bodily taking of the words or substance of complainant's news until its commercial value as news had passed away. 245 Fed. 244, 253. The present writ of certiorari was then allowed. 245 U.S. 644.

The only matter that has been argued before us is whether defendant may lawfully be restrained from appropriating news taken from bulletins issued by complainant or any of its members, or from newspapers published by them, for the purpose of selling it to defendant's clients. Complainant asserts that defendant's admitted course of conduct in this regard both violates complainant's property rights in the news and constitutes unfair competition in business. And notwithstanding the case has proceeded only to the stage of a preliminary injunction, we have deemed it proper to consider the underlying questions, since they go to the very merits of the action and are presented upon facts that are not in dispute. As presented in argument, these questions are: (1) Whether there is any property in news; (2) Whether, if there be property in news collected for the purpose of being published, it survives the instant of its publication in the first newspaper to which it is communicated by the news-gatherer; and (3) Whether defendant's admitted course of conduct in appropriating for commercial use matter taken from bulletins or early editions of Associated Press publications constitutes unfair competition in trade.

The federal jurisdiction was invoked because of diversity of citizenship, not upon the ground that the suit arose under the copyright or other laws of the United States. Complainant's news matter is not copyrighted. It is said that it could not, in practice, be copyrighted, because of the large number of dispatches that are sent daily; and, according to complainant's contention, news is not within the operation of the copyright act. * * *

In considering the general question of property in news matter, it is necessary to recognize its dual character, distinguishing between the substance of the information and the particular form or collocation of words in which the writer has communicated it.

No doubt news articles often possess a literary quality, and are the subject of literary property at the common law; nor do we question that such an article, as a literary production, is the subject of copyright by the terms of the act as it now stands. * * *

But the news element—the information respecting current events contained in the literary production—is not the creation of the writer, but is a report of matters that ordinarily are *publici juris;* it is the history of the day. It is not to be supposed that the framers of the Constitution, when they empowered Congress "to promote the progress of science and useful arts, by securing for limited times to authors and inventors the exclusive right to their respective writings and discoveries" (Const. art. 1, § 8, par. 8), intended to confer upon one who might happen to be the first to report a historic event the exclusive right for any period to spread the knowledge of it.

We need spend no time, however, upon the general question of property in news matter at common law, or the application of the copyright act, since it seems to us the case must turn upon the question of unfair competition in business. And, in our opinion, this does not depend upon any general right of property analogous to the common-law right of the proprietor of an unpublished work to prevent its publication without his consent; nor is it foreclosed by showing that the benefits of the copyright act have been waived. We are dealing here not with restrictions upon publication but with the very facilities and processes of publication. The peculiar value of news is in the spreading of it while it is fresh; and it is evident that a valuable property interest in the news, as news, cannot be maintained by keeping it secret. Besides, except for matters improperly disclosed, or published in breach of trust or confidence, or in violation of law, none of which is involved in this branch of the case, the news of current events may be regarded as common property. What we are concerned with is the business of making it known to the world, in which both parties to the present suit are engaged. * * * The parties are competitors in this field; and, on fundamental principles, applicable here as elsewhere, when the rights or privileges of the one are liable to conflict with those of the other, each party is under a duty so to conduct its own business as not unnecessarily or unfairly to injure that of the other. * * *

* * * The question here is not so much the rights of either party as against the public but their rights as between themselves. See Morison v. Moat, 9 Hare, 241, 258. And, although we may and do assume that neither party has any remaining property interest as against the public in uncopyrighted news matter after the moment of its first publication, it by no means follows that there is no remaining property interest in it as between themselves. For, to both of them alike, news matter, however little susceptible of ownership or dominion in the absolute sense, is stock in trade, to be gathered at the cost of enterprise, organization, skill, labor, and money, and to be distributed and sold to those who will pay money for it, as for any other merchandise. Regarding the news, therefore, as but the material out of which both parties are seeking to make profits at the same time and in the same field, we hardly can fail to recognize that for this purpose, and as between them, it must be regarded as *quasi* property, irrespective of the rights of either as against the public. * * *

Not only do the acquisition and transmission of news require elaborate organization and a large expenditure of money, skill, and effort; not only has it an exchange value to the gatherer, dependent chiefly upon its novelty and freshness, the regularity of the service, its reputed reliability and thoroughness, and its adaptability to the public needs; but also, as is evident, the news has an exchange value to one who can misappropriate it.

The peculiar features of the case arise from the fact that, while novelty and freshness form so important an element in the success of the business, the very processes of distribution and publication necessarily occupy a good deal of time. Complainant's service, as well as defendant's, is a daily service to daily newspapers; most of the foreign news reaches this country at the Atlantic seaboard, principally at the city of New York, and because of this, and of time differentials due to the earth's rotation, the distribution of news matter throughout the country is principally from east to west; and, since in speed the telegraph and telephone easily outstrip the rotation of the earth, it is a simple matter for defendant to take complainant's news from bulletins or early editions of complainant's members in the eastern cities and at the mere cost of telegraphic transmission cause it to be published in western papers issued at least as early as those served by complainant. Besides this, and irrespective of time differentials, irregularities in telegraphic transmission on different lines, and the normal consumption of time in printing and distributing the newspaper, result in permitting pirated news to be placed in the hands of defendant's readers sometimes simultaneously with the service of competing Associated Press papers, occasionally even earlier. * * *

* * * The right of the purchaser of a single newspaper to spread knowledge of its contents gratuitously, for any legitimate purpose not unreasonably interfering with complainant's right to make merchandise of it, may be admitted; but to transmit that news for commercial use, in competition with complainant—which is what defendant has done and seeks to justify—is a very different matter. In doing this defendant, by its very act, admits that it is taking material that has been acquired by complainant as the result of organization and the expenditure of labor, skill, and money, and which is salable by complainant for money, and that defendant in appropriating it and selling it as its own is endeavoring to reap where it has not sown, and by disposing of it to newspapers that are competitors of complainant's members is appropriating to itself the harvest of those who have sown. Stripped of all disguises, the process amounts to an unauthorized interference with the normal operation of complainant's legitimate business precisely at the point where the profit is to be reaped, in order to divert a material portion of the profit from those who have earned it to those who have not; with special advantage to defendant in the competition because of the fact that it is not burdened with any part of the expense of gathering the news. The transaction speaks for itself and a court of equity ought not to hesitate long in characterizing it as unfair competition in business. * * *

The contention that the news is abandoned to the public for all purposes when published in the first newspaper is untenable. Abandonment is a question of intent, and the entire organization of the Associated Press negatives such a purpose. The cost of the service would be prohibitive if the reward were to be so limited. No single newspaper, no small group of newspapers, could sustain the expenditure. Indeed, it is one of the most obvious results of defendant's theory that, by permitting indiscriminate publication by anybody and everybody for purposes of profit in competition with the news-gatherer, it would render publication profitless, or so little profitable as in effect to cut off the service by rendering the cost prohibitive in comparison with the return. The practical needs and requirements of the business are reflected in complainant's by-laws which have been referred to.

Their effect is that publication by each member must be deemed not by any means an abandonment of the news to the world for any and all purposes, but a publication for limited purposes; for the benefit of the readers of the bulletin or the newspaper as such; not for the purpose of making merchandise of it as news, with the result of depriving complainant's other members of their reasonable opportunity to obtain just returns for their expenditures. * * *

It is said that the elements of unfair competition are lacking because there is no attempt by defendant to palm off its goods as those of the complainant, characteristic of the most familiar, if not the most typical, cases of unfair competition. Howe Scale Co. v. Wyckoff, Seamans, etc., 198 U.S. 118, 140. But we cannot concede that the right to equitable relief is confined to that class of cases. In the present case the fraud upon complainant's rights is more direct and obvious. Regarding news matter as the mere material from which these two competing parties are endeavoring to make money, and treating it, therefore, as *quasi* property for the purposes of their business because they are both selling it as such, defendant's conduct differs from the ordinary case of unfair competition in trade principally in this that, instead of selling its own goods as those of complainant, it substitutes misappropriation in the place of misrepresentation, and sells complainant's goods as its own.

Besides the misappropriation, there are elements of imitation, of false pretense, in defendant's practices. The device of rewriting complainant's news articles, frequently resorted to, carries its own comment. The habitual failure to give credit to complainant for that which is taken is significant. Indeed, the entire system of appropriating complainant's news and transmitting it as a commercial product to defendant's clients and patrons amounts to a false representation to them and to their newspaper readers that the news transmitted is the result of defendant's own investigation in the field. But these elements, although accentuating the wrong, are not the essence of it. It is something more than the advantage of celebrity of which complainant is being deprived. * * *

As to securing "tips" from a competing news agency, the District Court (240 Fed. 991, 995), while not sanctioning the practice, found that both parties had adopted it in accordance with common business usage, in the belief that their conduct was technically lawful, and hence did not find in it any sufficient ground for attributing unclean hands to complainant. The Circuit Court of Appeals (245 F. 247) found that the tip habit, though discouraged by complainant, was "incurably journalistic," and that there was "no difficulty in discriminating between the utilization of tips and the bodily appropriation of another's labor in accumulating and stating information."

We are inclined to think a distinction may be drawn between the utilization of tips and the bodily appropriation of news matter, either in its original form or after rewriting and without independent investigation and verification; whatever may appear at the final hearing, the proofs as they now stand recognize such a distinction; both parties avowedly recognize the practice of taking tips, and neither party alleges it to be unlawful or to amount to unfair competition in business. * * *

There is some criticism of the injunction that was directed by the District Court upon the going down of the mandate from the Circuit Court of Appeals. In brief, it restrains any taking or gainfully using of the complainant's news, either bodily or in substance, from bulletins issued by the complainant or any of its members, or from editions of their newspapers, "*until its commercial value as news to the complainant and all of its members has passed away.*" The part complained of is the clause we have italicized; but if this be indefinite, it is no more so than the criticism. Perhaps it would be better that the terms of the injunction be made specific, and so framed as to confine the restraint to an extent consistent with the reasonable protection of complainant's newspapers, each in its own area and for a specified time after its publication, against the competitive use of pirated news by defendant's customers. But the case presents practical difficulties; and we have not the materials, either in the way of a definite suggestion of amendment, or in the way of proofs, upon which to frame a specific injunction; hence, while not expressing approval of the form adopted by the District Court, we decline to modify it at this preliminary stage of the case, and will leave that court to deal with the matter upon appropriate application made to it for the purpose.

The decree of the Circuit Court of Appeals will be

Affirmed.[e]

■ MR. JUSTICE CLARKE took no part in the consideration or decision of this case.

■ MR. JUSTICE HOLMES dissenting.

When an uncopyrighted combination of words is published there is no general right to forbid other people repeating them—in other words there is no property in the combination or in the thoughts or facts that the words express. Property, a creation of law, does not arise from value, although exchangeable—a matter of fact. Many exchangeable values may be destroyed intentionally without compensation. Property depends upon exclusion by law from interference, and a person is not excluded from using any combination of words merely because some one has used it before, even if it took labor and genius to make it. If a given person is to be prohibited from making the use of words that his neighbors are free to make some other ground must be found. One such ground is vaguely expressed in the phrase unfair trade. This means that the words are repeated by a competitor in business in such a way as to convey a misrepresentation that materially injures the person who first used them, by appropriating credit of some kind which the first user has earned. The ordinary case is a representation by device, appearance, or other indirection that the defendant's goods come from the plaintiff. But the only reason why it is actionable to make such a representation is that it tends to give the defendant an advantage in his competition with the plaintiff and that it is thought undesirable that an advantage should be gained in that way. Apart from that the defendant may use such unpatented devices and uncopyrighted combinations of words as he likes. The ordinary case, I say, is palming off the defendant's product as the plaintiff's but the same evil may follow from the opposite falsehood— from saying whether in words or by implication, that the plaintiff's product is the defendant's, and that, it seems to me, is what has happened here.

Fresh news is got only by enterprise and expense. To produce such news as it is produced by the defendant represents by implication that it has been acquired by the defendant's enterprise and at its expense. When it comes from one of the great news collecting agencies like the Associated

---

[e]   The decree ultimately entered by consent of the defendant on May 19, 1919, simply enjoined it from "gainfully using * * * complainant's news, either bodily or in substance, * * * until its commercial value as news to the complainant and all of its members has passed away."

Press, the source generally is indicated, plainly importing that credit; and that such a representation is implied may be inferred with some confidence from the unwillingness of the defendant to give the credit and tell the truth. If the plaintiff produces the news at the same time that the defendant does, the defendant's presentation impliedly denies to the plaintiff the credit of collecting the facts and assumes that credit to the defendant. If the plaintiff is later in western cities it naturally will be supposed to have obtained its information from the defendant. The falsehood is a little more subtle, the injury a little more indirect, than in ordinary cases of unfair trade, but I think that the principle that condemns the one condemns the other. It is a question of how strong an infusion of fraud is necessary to turn a flavor into a poison. The dose seems to me strong enough here to need a remedy from the law. But as, in my view, the only ground of complaint that can be recognized without legislation is the implied misstatement, it can be corrected by stating the truth; and a suitable acknowledgment of the source is all that the plaintiff can require. I think that within the limits recognized by the decision of the Court the defendant should be enjoined from publishing news obtained from the Associated Press for ___ hours after publication by the plaintiff unless it gives express credit to the Associated Press; the number of hours and the form of acknowledgment to be settled by the District Court.

▪ MR. JUSTICE MCKENNA concurs in this opinion.

▪ MR. JUSTICE BRANDEIS dissenting. * * *

No question of statutory copyright is involved. The sole question for our consideration is this: Was the International News Service properly enjoined from using, or causing to be used gainfully, news of which it acquired knowledge by lawful means (namely, by reading publicly posted bulletins or papers purchased by it in the open market) merely because the news had been originally gathered by the Associated Press and continued to be of value to some of its members, or because it did not reveal the source from which it was acquired? * * *

News is a report of recent occurrences. The business of the news agency is to gather systematically knowledge of such occurrences of interest and to distribute reports thereof. The Associated Press contended that knowledge so acquired is property, because it costs money and labor to produce and because it has value for which those who have it not are ready to pay; that it remains property and is entitled to protection as long as it has commercial value as news; and that to protect it effectively the defendant must be enjoined from making, or causing to be made, any gainful use of it while it retains such value. An essential element of individual property is the legal right to exclude others from enjoying it. If the property is private, the right of exclusion may be absolute; if the property is affected with a public interest, the right of exclusion is qualified. But the fact that a product of the mind has cost its producer money and labor, and has a value for which others are willing to pay, is not sufficient to ensure to it this legal attribute of property. The general rule of law is, that the noblest of human productions—knowledge, truths ascertained, conceptions, and ideas—become, after voluntary communication to others, free as the air to common use. Upon these incorporeal productions the attribute of property is continued after such communication only in certain classes of cases where public policy has seemed to demand it. These exceptions are confined to productions which, in some degree, involve creation, invention, or discovery. But by no means all such are endowed with this attribute of property. The creations which are recognized as property by the common law are literary, dramatic, musical, and other artistic creations; and these have also protection under the copyright statutes. The inventions and discoveries upon which this attribute of property is conferred only by statute, are the few comprised within the patent law. There are also many other cases in which courts interfere to prevent curtailment of plaintiff's enjoyment of incorporeal productions; and in which the right to relief is often called a property right, but is such only in a special sense. In those cases, the plaintiff has no absolute right to the protection of his production; he has merely the qualified right to be protected as against the defendant's acts, because of the special relation in which the latter stands or the wrongful method or means employed in acquiring the knowledge or the manner in which it is used. Protection of this character is afforded where the suit is based upon breach of contract or of trust or upon unfair competition.

The knowledge for which protection is sought in the case at bar is not of a kind upon which the law has heretofore conferred the attributes of property; nor is the manner of its acquisition or use nor the purpose to which it is applied, such as has heretofore been recognized as entitling a plaintiff to relief.

First: Plaintiff's principal reliance was upon the "ticker" cases; but they do not support its contention. The leading cases on this subject rest the grant of relief, not upon the existence of a general property right in news, but upon the breach of a contract or trust concerning the use of news communicated; and that element is lacking here. * * *

Second: Plaintiff also relied upon the cases which hold that the common law right of the producer to prohibit copying is not lost by the private circulation of a literary composition, the delivery of a lecture, the exhibition of a painting, or the performance of a dramatic or musical composition. These cases rest upon the ground that the common law recognizes such productions as property which, despite restricted communication, continues until there is a dedication to the public under the copyright statutes or otherwise. But they are inapplicable for two reasons: (1) At common law, as under the copyright acts, intellectual productions are entitled to such protection only if there is underneath something evincing the mind of a creator or originator, however modest the requirement. The mere record of isolated happenings, whether in words or by photographs not involving artistic skill, are denied such protection. (2) At common law, as under the copyright acts, the element in intellectual productions which secures such protection is not the knowledge, truths, ideas, or emotions which the composition expresses, but the form or sequence in which they are expressed; that is "some new collocation of visible, or audible points—of lines, colors, sounds, or words." See White–Smith Music Co. v. Apollo Co., 209 U.S. 1, 19; Kalem Co. v. Harper Bros., 222 U.S. 55, 63. An author's theories, suggestions, and speculations, or the systems, plans, methods, and arrangements of an originator, derive no such protection from the statutory copyright of the book in which they are set forth; and they are likewise denied such protection at common law. * * *

Third: If news be treated as possessing the characteristics not of a trade secret, but of literary property, then the earliest issue of a paper of general circulation or the earliest public posting of a bulletin which embodies such news would, under the established rules governing literary property, operate as a publication, and all property in the news would then cease. * * *

Fourth: Plaintiff further contended that defendant's practice constitutes unfair competition, because there is "appropriation without cost to itself of values created by" the plaintiff; and it is upon this ground that the decision of this court appears to be based. To appropriate and use for profit, knowledge and ideas produced by other men, without making compensation or even acknowledgment, may be inconsistent with a finer sense of propriety; but, with the exceptions indicated above, the law has heretofore sanctioned the practice. Thus it was held that one may ordinarily make and sell anything in any form, may copy with exactness that which another has produced, or may otherwise use his ideas without his consent and without the payment of compensation, and yet not inflict a legal injury; and that ordinarily one is at perfect liberty to find out, if he can by lawful means, trade secrets of another, however valuable, and then use the knowledge so acquired gainfully, although it cost the original owner much in effort and in money to collect or produce.

Such taking and gainful use of a product of another which, for reasons of public policy, the law has refused to endow with the attributes of property, does not become unlawful because the product happens to have been taken from a rival and is used in competition with him. The unfairness in competition which hitherto has been recognized by the law as a basis for relief, lay in the manner or means of conducting the business; and the manner or means held legally unfair involves either fraud or force or the doing of acts otherwise prohibited by law. * * *

Fifth: The great development of agencies now furnishing countrywide distribution of news, the vastness of our territory, and improvements in the means of transmitting intelligence, have made it possible for a news agency or newspapers to obtain, without paying compensation, the fruit of another's efforts and to use news so obtained gainfully in competition with the original collector. The injustice of such action is obvious. But to give relief against it would involve more than the application of existing rules of law to new facts. It would require the making of a new rule in analogy to existing ones. The unwritten law possesses capacity for growth; and has often satisfied new demands for justice by invoking analogies or by expanding a rule or principle. This process has been in the main wisely applied and should not be discontinued. Where the problem is relatively simple, as it is apt to be when private interests only are involved, it generally proves adequate. But with the increasing complexity of society, the public interest tends to become omnipresent; and the problems presented by new demands for justice cease to be simple. Then the creation or recognition by courts of a new private right may work serious injury to the general public, unless the boundaries of the right are definitely established and wisely guarded. In order to reconcile the new private right with the public interest, it may be necessary to prescribe limitations and rules for its enjoyment; and also to provide administrative machinery for enforcing the rules. It is largely for this reason that, in the effort to meet the many new demands for justice incident to a rapidly changing civilization, resort to legislation has latterly been had with increasing frequency.

The rule for which the plaintiff contends would effect an important extension of property rights and a corresponding curtailment of the free use of knowledge and of ideas; and the facts of this case admonish us of the danger involved in recognizing such a property right in news, without imposing upon news-gatherers corresponding obligations. A large majority of the newspapers and perhaps half the newspaper readers of the United

States are dependent for their news of general interest upon agencies other than the Associated Press. The channel through which about 400 of these papers received, as the plaintiff alleges, "a large amount of news relating to the European war of the greatest importance and of intense interest to the newspaper reading public" was suddenly closed. The closing to the International News Service of these channels for foreign news (if they were closed) was due not to unwillingness on its part to pay the cost of collecting the news, but to the prohibitions imposed by foreign governments upon its securing news from their respective countries and from using cable or telegraph lines running therefrom.[f] [Brandeis speculates on the possibility that newspapers subscribing to the INS service might have been glad to become members of AP if they could have done so. A legislature urged to enact a law to protect news from appropriation would have to consider what evils it might bring, whether an injunction in addition to damages should be provided, whether a public utility concept should be adopted, etc.]

Courts are ill-equipped to make the investigations which should precede a determination of the limitations which should be set upon any property right in news or of the circumstances under which news gathered by a private agency should be deemed affected with a public interest. Courts would be powerless to prescribe the detailed regulations essential to full enjoyment of the rights conferred or to introduce the machinery required for enforcement of such regulations. Considerations such as these should lead us to decline to establish a new rule of law in the effort to redress a newly disclosed wrong, although the propriety of some remedy appears to be clear.

RECEPTION OF THE MISAPPROPRIATION RATIONALE

Despite the broad implications of the Supreme Court's decision, it had for many years only sporadic influence. Judge Learned Hand, repeating the objections of Justice Brandeis, thought the decision a threat to the balance struck by Congress in the federal copyright and patent laws. In a series of opinions for the Second Circuit, he tried to read *INS* out of existence.[g] Although his views eventually lost sway,[h] similar concerns would later reappear within the Supreme Court itself. The next section reviews the subsequent upheaval.

Typical of the cases rejecting a misappropriation claim is Germanow v. Standard Unbreakable Watch Crystals, 283 N.Y. 1, 27 N.E.2d 212 (1940). The plaintiff, with about 50% of the business in replacement watch crystals, supplied a special cabinet, together with a numbering system for locating the right crystal. The defendant offered, at a lower price, a line of crystals specifically adapted for the plaintiff's cabinet and system. The plaintiff had no patent or other statutory protection, and the dealers who were customers of both parties were not deceived. A decree for the plaintiff was reversed.

---

[f]   INS had been denied the use of cables controlled by the Allied powers in November 1916, for alleged violations of censorship and distortion of the news. See O. Gramling, AP: The Story of News 285 (1940).

[g]   See, e.g., Cheney Brothers v. Doris Silk Corp., p. 647 infra; RCA Mfg. Co. v. Whiteman, 114 F.2d 86 (2d Cir.), cert. denied, 311 U.S. 712 (1940); G. Ricordi & Co. v. Haendler, 194 F.2d 914 (2d Cir.1952).

[h]   See Capitol Records v. Mercury Records Corp., 221 F.2d 657 (2d Cir.1955).

A misappropriation claim raised by the National Football League against the use of its football scores in a state lottery was rejected in National Football League v. Governor of Delaware, 435 F.Supp. 1372 (D.Del.1977). "It is true that Delaware is thus making profits it would not make but for the existence of the NFL, but I find this difficult to distinguish from the multitude of charter bus companies who generate profit from servicing those of plaintiffs' fans who want to go to the stadium or, indeed, the sidewalk popcorn salesman who services the crowd as it surges towards the gate." Attempts to invoke the doctrine to prohibit the imitation of successful products have also been consistently rejected. See, e.g., Cheney Brothers v. Doris Silk Corp., p. 647 infra. Nevertheless, in a few areas, the doctrine flourished.

On the specific issue decided in *INS*—appropriation of news by a competitor—plaintiffs continued to prevail. Radio stations that relied on newspaper subscriptions rather than news reporters, and trade journals guilty of appropriating information from competitors, were unable to escape the reach of *INS*.[i]

Another line of cases in which misappropriation arguments have sometimes succeeded involves the unauthorized broadcasting of sporting events. A leading case is Pittsburgh Athletic Co. v. KQV Broadcasting Co., 24 F.Supp. 490 (W.D.Pa.1938). The plaintiff granted a third party exclusive broadcasting rights to its baseball games; the defendant was enjoined from broadcasting the games from vantage points outside the park. (But cf. WCVB–TV v. Boston Athletic Ass'n, 926 F.2d 42 (1st Cir.1991), refusing to enjoin an unauthorized telecast of the Boston Marathon, run on the public streets of Boston and neighboring towns.)

The *INS* rationale has occasionally triumphed in other contexts. It became an important tool in the early battles against record piracy.[j] It has also been invoked to prevent the unauthorized sale of items as varied as photographs of a World's Fair,[k] recorded performances of the Metropolitan Opera,[l] answers to problems in a college textbook,[m] and a photographic reproduction of another's typeset edition of a public domain book.[n] The misappropriation doctrine was also employed to restrict the unauthorized use of well-known stock indices such as the Dow Jones Industrial Average in connection with the sale of stock market index contracts.[o] Another decision,

---

[i]   See, e.g., Associated Press v. KVOS, 80 F.2d 575 (9th Cir.1935), reversed for want of jurisdiction, 299 U.S. 269 (1936); Pottstown Daily News Pub. Co. v. Pottstown Broadcasting Co., 411 Pa. 383, 192 A.2d 657 (1963); McCord Co. v. Plotnick, 108 Cal.App.2d 392, 239 P.2d 32 (1951)

[j]   See, e.g., A & M Records, Inc. v. M.V.C. Distrib. Corp., 574 F.2d 312 (6th Cir.1978); Mercury Record Prod., Inc. v. Economic Consultants, Inc., 64 Wis.2d 163, 218 N.W.2d 705 (1974), appeal dismissed, 420 U.S. 914 (1975). See p. 669 infra.

[k]   New York World's Fair 1964–1965 Corp. v. Colourpicture Pub., Inc., 141 U.S.P.Q. 939 (N.Y.Sup.Ct.), aff'd, 21 A.D.2d 896, 251 N.Y.S.2d 885 (1964).

[l]   Metropolitan Opera Ass'n v. Wagner–Nichols Recorder Corp., 199 Misc. 786, 101 N.Y.S.2d 483 (Sup.Ct.1950), aff'd, 279 A.D. 632, 107 N.Y.S.2d 795 (1951).

[m]   Addison–Wesley Pub. Co. v. Brown, 207 F.Supp. 678 (E.D.N.Y.1962) (see also 223 F.Supp. 219 (E.D.N.Y.1963)).

[n]   Grove Press, Inc. v. Collectors Pub., Inc., 264 F.Supp. 603 (C.D.Cal.1967).

[o]   Standard & Poor's Corp. v. Commodity Exchange, Inc., 683 F.2d 704 (2d Cir.1982) (but also finding a likelihood of confusion); Board of Trade of Chicago v. Dow Jones & Co., 98 Ill.2d 109, 456 N.E.2d 84 (1983). The stock market index cases were distinguished in Dow Jones & Co. v. International Securities Exchange, Inc., 451 F.3d 295 (2d Cir.2006). The plaintiff stock index owners had licensed the creation of stock funds based on their indices. The defendants offered options trading on the shares of those index funds. Judge Leval affirmed the dismissal

however, drew back from the stock indices cases in a suit involving use of the U.S. Golf Association's handicapping formula by a computerized handicapping service. After tracing the development of the misappropriation doctrine, the Third Circuit in United States Golf Ass'n v. St. Andrews Systems, Data–Max, Inc., 749 F.2d 1028 (3d Cir.1984), distinguished *INS* in that here the defendant's use was only indirectly competitive with the plaintiff and thus "falls outside the misappropriation doctrine, since the public interest in free access outweighs the public interest in providing an additional incentive to the creator or gatherer of information." The court affirmed the defendant's summary judgment. "Where such a monopoly is unnecessary to protect the basic incentive for the production of the idea or information involved, we do not believe that the creator's interest in its ideas or information justifies such an extensive restraint on competition."

NOTES AND QUESTIONS

(1) The opinion of the Supreme Court in *INS* invites analysis. Is the case best understood as an assertion of natural law property rights? Why did the Court so intently examine the economics of news-gathering? What is the cost of prohibiting the defendant's appropriation and from whom is it extracted?

Is it of any relevance that three decades after the *INS* decision the Associated Press was found to have violated the antitrust laws by unduly restricting both its membership and the disposition of news by its members? See Associated Press v. United States, 326 U.S. 1 (1945).

(2) Does a cause of action for the misappropriation of facts raise first amendment concerns, or is the traditional insulation of copyright from free speech limitations equally applicable here?

(3) The attempt to curtail the misappropriation doctrine in § 38 of the Restatement (Third) of Unfair Competition is applauded in G. Myers, The Restatement's Rejection of the Misappropriation Tort: A Victory for the Public Domain, 47 S.Car.L.Rev. 673 (1996). See also W. Gordon, On Owning Information: Intellectual Property and the Restitutionary Impulse, 78 Va.L.Rev. 149 (1992), worrying that the impulse to grant relief results in overprotection at the expense of the community interest in access.

In defining the formal precedential scope of *INS,* note that it was a diversity case, presumably at that time declaring federal common law. But may a state adopt the rationale as part of its own law of unfair competition? Only to the extent that the misappropriation doctrine survives federal preemption, the topic of the following section.

---

of complaints alleging misappropriation. "Because plaintiffs have permitted the buying and selling of the [stock index] shares, plaintiffs may not prevent exchanges from offering marketplaces for buyers and sellers to come together to effectuate their transactions." The court distinguished *Standard & Poor's* and *Board of Trade* because there the defendants had created their own stock index funds based on the plaintiffs' indices.

3. PREEMPTION

Sears, Roebuck & Co. v. Stiffel Co.

Supreme Court of the United States, 1964.
376 U.S. 225, 84 S.Ct. 784.

■ MR. JUSTICE BLACK delivered the opinion of the Court.

The question in this case is whether a State's unfair competition law can, consistently with the federal patent laws, impose liability for or prohibit the copying of an article which is protected by neither a federal patent nor a copyright. The respondent, Stiffel Company, secured design and mechanical patents on a "pole lamp"—a vertical tube having lamp fixtures along the outside, the tube being made so that it will stand upright between the floor and ceiling of a room. Pole lamps proved a decided commercial success, and soon after Stiffel brought them on the market Sears, Roebuck & Company put on the market a substantially identical lamp, which it sold more cheaply, Sears' retail price being about the same as Stiffel's wholesale price. Stiffel then brought this action against Sears in the United States District Court for the Northern District of Illinois, claiming in its first count that by copying its design Sears had infringed Stiffel's patents and in its second count that by selling copies of Stiffel's lamp Sears had caused confusion in the trade as to the source of the lamps and had thereby engaged in unfair competition under Illinois law. There was evidence that identifying tags were not attached to the Sears lamps although labels appeared on the cartons in which they were delivered to customers, that customers had asked Stiffel whether its lamps differed from Sears', and that in two cases customers who had bought Stiffel lamps had complained to Stiffel on learning that Sears was selling substantially identical lamps at a much lower price.

The District Court, after holding the patents invalid for want of invention, went on to find as a fact that Sears' lamp was "a substantially exact copy" of Stiffel's and that the two lamps were so much alike, both in appearance and in functional details, "that confusion between them is likely, and some confusion has already occurred." On these findings the court held Sears guilty of unfair competition, enjoined Sears "from unfairly competing with [Stiffel] by selling or attempting to sell pole lamps identical to or confusingly similar to" Stiffel's lamp, and ordered an accounting to fix profits and damages resulting from Sears' "unfair competition."

The Court of Appeals affirmed.[1] 313 F.2d 115. That court held that, to make out a case of unfair competition under Illinois law, there was no need to show that Sears had been "palming off" its lamps as Stiffel lamps; Stiffel had only to prove that there was a "likelihood of confusion as to the source of the products"—that the two articles were sufficiently identical that customers could not tell who had made a particular one. Impressed by the "remarkable sameness of appearance" of the lamps, the Court of Appeals upheld the trial court's findings of likelihood of confusion and some actual confusion, findings which the appellate court construed to mean confusion "as to the source of the lamps." The Court of Appeals thought this enough under Illinois law to sustain the trial court's holding of unfair competition, and thus held Sears liable under Illinois law for doing no more than copy-

---

[1] No review is sought here of the ruling affirming the District Court's holding that the patent is invalid.

ing and marketing an unpatented article. We granted certiorari to consider whether this use of a State's law of unfair competition is compatible with the federal patent law. 374 U.S. 826.

Before the Constitution was adopted, some States had granted patents either by special act or by general statute, but when the Constitution was adopted provision for a federal patent law was made one of the enumerated powers of Congress because, as Madison put it in The Federalist No. 43, the States "cannot separately make effectual provision" for either patents or copyrights.[4] That constitutional provision is Art. I, § 8, cl. 8, which empowers Congress "To promote the Progress of Science and useful Arts, by securing for limited Times to Authors and Inventors the exclusive Right to their respective Writings and Discoveries." Pursuant to this constitutional authority, Congress in 1790 enacted the first federal patent and copyright law, 1 Stat. 109, and ever since that time has fixed the conditions upon which patents and copyrights shall be granted, see 17 U.S.C.A. §§ 1–216; 35 U.S.C.A. §§ 1–293. These laws, like other laws of the United States enacted pursuant to constitutional authority, are the supreme law of the land. See Sperry v. Florida, 373 U.S. 379 (1963). When state law touches upon the area of these federal statutes, it is "familiar doctrine" that the federal policy "may not be set at naught, or its benefits denied" by the state law. Sola Elec. Co. v. Jefferson Elec. Co., 317 U.S. 173, 176 (1942). This is true, of course, even if the state law is enacted in the exercise of otherwise undoubted state power.

The grant of a patent is the grant of a statutory monopoly; indeed, the grant of patents in England was an explicit exception to the statute of James I prohibiting monopolies. Patents are not given as favors, as was the case of monopolies given by the Tudor monarchs, see The Case of Monopolies (Darcy v. Allein), 11 Co.Rep. 84 b., 77 Eng.Rep. 1260 (K.B.1602), but are meant to encourage invention by rewarding the inventor with the right, limited to a term of years fixed by the patent, to exclude others from the use of his invention. During that period of time no one may make, use, or sell the patented product without the patentee's authority. 35 U.S.C.A. § 271. But in rewarding useful invention, the "rights and welfare of the community must be fairly dealt with and effectually guarded." Kendall v. Winsor, 21 How. 322, 329 (1859). To that end the prerequisites to obtaining a patent are strictly observed, and when the patent has issued the limitations on its exercise are equally strictly enforced. To begin with, a genuine "invention" or "discovery" must be demonstrated "lest in the constant demand for new appliances the heavy hand of tribute be laid on each slight technological advance in an art." Cuno Engineering Corp. v. Automatic Devices Corp., 314 U.S. 84, 92 (1941); see Great Atlantic & Pacific Tea Co. v. Supermarket Equipment Corp., 340 U.S. 147, 152–153 (1950); Atlantic Works v. Brady, 107 U.S. 192, 199–200 (1883). Once the patent issues, it is strictly construed, United States v. Masonite Corp., 316 U.S. 265, 280 (1942), it cannot be used to secure any monopoly beyond that contained in the patent, Morton Salt Co. v. G.S. Suppiger Co., 314 U.S. 488, 492 (1942), the patentee's control over the product when it leaves his hands is sharply limited, see United States v. Univis Lens Co., 316 U.S. 241, 250–252 (1942), and the patent monopoly may not be used in disregard of the antitrust laws, see International Business Machines Corp. v. United States, 298 U.S. 131 (1936); United Shoe Machinery Corp. v. United States, 258 U.S. 451, 463–464 (1922). Finally, and especially relevant here, when the

---

[4] The Federalist (Cooke ed. 1961) 288.

patent expires the monopoly created by it expires, too, and the right to make the article—including the right to make it in precisely the shape it carried when patented—passes to the public. Kellogg Co. v. National Biscuit Co., 305 U.S. 111, 120–122 (1938); Singer Mfg. Co. v. June Mfg. Co., 163 U.S. 169, 185 (1896).

Thus the patent system is one in which uniform federal standards are carefully used to promote invention while at the same time preserving free competition.[7] Obviously a State could not, consistently with the Supremacy Clause of the Constitution,[8] extend the life of a patent beyond its expiration date or give a patent on an article which lacked the level of invention required for federal patents. To do either would run counter to the policy of Congress of granting patents only to true inventions, and then only for a limited time. Just as a State cannot encroach upon the federal patent laws directly, it cannot, under some other law, such as that forbidding unfair competition, give protection of a kind that clashes with the objectives of the federal patent laws.

In the present case the "pole lamp" sold by Stiffel has been held not to be entitled to the protection of either a mechanical or a design patent. An unpatentable article, like an article on which the patent has expired, is in the public domain and may be made and sold by whoever chooses to do so. What Sears did was to copy Stiffel's design and to sell lamps almost identical to those sold by Stiffel. This it had every right to do under the federal patent laws. That Stiffel originated the pole lamp and made it popular is immaterial. "Sharing in the goodwill of an article unprotected by patent or trade-mark is the exercise of a right possessed by all—and in the free exercise of which the consuming public is deeply interested." Kellogg Co. v. National Biscuit Co., supra, 305 U.S. at 122. To allow a State by use of its law of unfair competition to prevent the copying of an article which represents too slight an advance to be patented would be to permit the State to block off from the public something which federal law has said belongs to the public. The result would be that while federal law grants only 14 or 17 years' protection to genuine inventions, see 35 U.S.C.A. §§ 154, 173, States could allow perpetual protection to articles too lacking in novelty to merit any patent at all under federal constitutional standards. This would be too great an encroachment on the federal patent system to be tolerated.

Sears has been held liable here for unfair competition because of a finding of likelihood of confusion based only on the fact that Sears' lamp was copied from Stiffel's unpatented lamp and that consequently the two looked exactly alike. Of course there could be "confusion" as to who had manufactured these nearly identical articles. But mere inability of the public to tell two identical articles apart is not enough to support an injunction against copying or an award of damages for copying that which the federal patent laws permit to be copied. Doubtless a State may, in appropriate circumstances, require that goods, whether patented or unpatented, be labeled or that other precautionary steps be taken to prevent customers from being misled as to the source, just as it may protect businesses in the use of their trademarks, labels, or distinctive dress in the packaging of goods so as

---

[7]   The purpose of Congress to have national uniformity in patent and copyright laws can be inferred from such statutes as that which vests exclusive jurisdiction to hear patent and copyright cases in federal courts, 28 U.S.C.A. § 1338(a), and that section of the Copyright Act which expressly saves state protection of unpublished writings but does not include published writings, 17 U.S.C.A. § 2.

[8]   U.S. Const., Art. VI.

to prevent others, by imitating such markings, from misleading purchasers as to the source of the goods. But because of the federal patent laws a State may not, when the article is unpatented and uncopyrighted, prohibit the copying of the article itself or award damages for such copying. Cf. G. Ricordi & Co. v. Haendler, 194 F.2d 914, 916 (C.A.2d Cir.1952). The judgment below did both and in so doing gave Stiffel the equivalent of a patent monopoly on its unpatented lamp. That was error, and Sears is entitled to a judgment in its favor.

Reversed.

Compco Corp. v. Day–Brite Lighting, Inc.

Supreme Court of the United States, 1964.
376 U.S. 234, 84 S.Ct. 779.

■ MR. JUSTICE BLACK delivered the opinion of the Court.

As in Sears, Roebuck & Co. v. Stiffel Co., 376 U.S. 225, the question here is whether the use of a state unfair competition law to give relief against the copying of an unpatented industrial design conflicts with the federal patent laws. Both Compco and Day–Brite are manufacturers of fluorescent lighting fixtures of a kind widely used in offices and stores. Day–Brite in 1955 secured from the Patent Office a design patent on a reflector having cross-ribs claimed to give both strength and attractiveness to the fixture. Day–Brite also sought, but was refused, a mechanical patent on the same device. After Day–Brite had begun selling its fixture, Compco's predecessor began making and selling fixtures very similar to Day–Brite's. This action was then brought by Day–Brite. One count alleged that Compco had infringed Day–Brite's design patent; a second count charged that the public and the trade had come to associate this particular design with Day–Brite, that Compco had copied Day–Brite's distinctive design so as to confuse and deceive purchasers into thinking Compco's fixtures were actually Day–Brite's, and that by doing this Compco had unfairly competed with Day–Brite. The complaint prayed for both an accounting and an injunction.

The District Court held the design patent invalid; but as to the second count, while the court did not find that Compco had engaged in any deceptive or fraudulent practices, it did hold that Compco had been guilty of unfair competition under Illinois law. The court found that the overall appearance of Compco's fixture was "the same, to the eye of the ordinary observer, as the overall appearance" of Day–Brite's reflector, which embodied the design of the invalidated patent; that the appearance of Day–Brite's design had "the capacity to identify [Day–Brite] in the trade and does in fact so identify [it] to the trade"; that the concurrent sale of the two products was "likely to cause confusion in the trade"; and that "[a]ctual confusion has occurred." On these findings the court adjudged Compco guilty of unfair competition in the sale of its fixtures, ordered Compco to account to Day–Brite for damages, and enjoined Compco "from unfairly competing with plaintiff by the sale or attempted sale of reflectors identical to, or confusingly similar to" those made by Day–Brite. The Court of Appeals held there was substantial evidence in the record to support the District Court's finding of likely confusion and that this finding was sufficient to support a holding of unfair competition under Illinois law.[2] 311 F.2d 26. Although the

---

2   The Court of Appeals also affirmed the holding that the design patent was invalid. No review of this ruling is sought here.

District Court had not made such a finding, the appellate court observed that "several choices of ribbing were apparently available to meet the functional needs of the product," yet Compco "chose precisely the same design used by the plaintiff and followed it so closely as to make confusion likely." 311 F.2d, at 30. A design which identifies its maker to the trade, the Court of Appeals held, is a "protectable" right under Illinois law, even though the design is unpatentable. We granted certiorari. 374 U.S. 825.

To support its findings of likelihood of confusion and actual confusion, the trial court was able to refer to only one circumstance in the record. A plant manager who had installed some of Compco's fixtures later asked Day–Brite to service the fixtures, thinking they had been made by Day–Brite. There was no testimony given by a purchaser or by anyone else that any customer had ever been misled, deceived, or "confused," that is, that anyone had ever bought a Compco fixture thinking it was a Day–Brite fixture. All the record shows, as to the one instance cited by the trial court, is that both Compco and Day–Brite fixtures had been installed in the same plant, that three years later some repairs were needed, and that the manager viewing the Compco fixtures—hung at least 15 feet above the floor and arranged end to end in a continuous line so that identifying marks were hidden—thought they were Day–Brite fixtures and asked Day–Brite to service them. Not only is this incident suggestive only of confusion *after* a purchase had been made, but also there is considerable evidence of the care taken by Compco to prevent customer confusion, including clearly labeling both the fixtures and the containers in which they were shipped and not selling through manufacturers' representatives who handled competing lines.

Notwithstanding the thinness of the evidence to support findings of likely and actual confusion among purchasers, we do not find it necessary in this case to determine whether there is "clear error" in these findings. They, like those in Sears, Roebuck & Co. v. Stiffel Co., 376 U.S. 225, were based wholly on the fact that selling an article which is an exact copy of another unpatented article is likely to produce and did in this case produce confusion as to the source of the article. Even accepting the findings, we hold that the order for an accounting for damages and the injunction are in conflict with the federal patent laws. Today we have held in Sears, Roebuck & Co. v. Stiffel Co., 376 U.S. 225, that when an article is unprotected by a patent or a copyright, state law may not forbid others to copy that article. To forbid copying would interfere with the federal policy, found in Art. I, § 8, cl. 8, of the Constitution and in the implementing federal statutes, of allowing free access to copy whatever the federal patent and copyright laws leave in the public domain. Here Day–Brite's fixture has been held not to be entitled to a design or mechanical patent. Under the federal patent laws it is, therefore, in the public domain and can be copied in every detail by whoever pleases. It is true that the trial court found that the configuration of Day–Brite's fixture identified Day–Brite to the trade because the arrangement of the ribbing had, like a trademark, acquired a "secondary meaning" by which that particular design was associated with Day–Brite. But if the design is not entitled to a design patent or other federal statutory protection, then it can be copied at will.

As we have said in *Sears*, while the federal patent laws prevent a State from prohibiting the copying and selling of unpatented articles, they do not stand in the way of state law, statutory or decisional, which requires those who make and sell copies to take precautions to identify their products as their own. A State of course has power to impose liability upon those who, knowing that the public is relying upon an original manufacturer's reputation for quality and integrity, deceive the public by palming off their copies as the original. That an article copied from an unpatented article could be made in some other way, that the design is "nonfunctional" and not essential to the use of either article, that the configuration of the article copied may have a "secondary meaning" which identifies the maker to the trade, or that there may be "confusion" among purchasers as to which article is which or as to who is the maker, may be relevant evidence in applying a State's law requiring such precautions as labeling; however, and regardless of the copier's motives, neither these facts nor any others can furnish a basis for imposing liability for or prohibiting the actual acts of copying and selling. Cf. Kellogg Co. v. National Biscuit Co., 305 U.S. 111, 120 (1938). And of course a State cannot hold a copier accountable in damages for failure to label or otherwise to identify his goods unless his failure is in violation of valid state statutory or decisional law requiring the copier to label or take other precautions to prevent confusion of customers as to the source of the goods.

Since the judgment below forbids the sale of a copy of an unpatented article and orders an accounting for damages for such copying, it cannot stand.

Reversed.

■ MR. JUSTICE HARLAN, concurring in the result.*

In one respect I would give the States more leeway in unfair competition "copying" cases than the Court's opinions would allow. If copying is found, other than by an inference arising from the mere act of copying, to have been undertaken with the dominant purpose and effect of palming off one's goods as those of another or of confusing customers as to the source of such goods, I see no reason why the State may not impose reasonable restrictions on the future "copying" itself. Vindication of the paramount federal interest at stake does not require a State to tolerate such specifically oriented predatory business practices. Apart from this, I am in accord with the opinions of the Court, and concur in both judgments since neither case presents the point on which I find myself in disagreement.

NOTE

The reaction to *Sears* and *Compco* was mixed, due in part to disagreement about what they meant. Do the cases hold that the patent and copyright clause of the Constitution itself precludes state interference with the right to copy objects within its scope? Or are the cases instead applications of the supremacy clause, holding that the state doctrines interfered with the policies implemented by Congress in the federal patent statute? The distinction is significant. It had implications, for example, in connection with attempts by the states to rein in the burgeoning trade in pirated records and tapes. If the patent and copyright clause is read to exclude all state regulation of "writings" and "discoveries," state protection of sound recordings would be void on its face. If the issue is instead the supremacy of federal law, the question becomes whether state protection interferes with the congressional policies embodied in copyright law, which did not extend protection to sound recordings until 1972. That issue and others were decided in the following case.

---

* [This opinion applies also to Sears, Roebuck & Co. v. Stiffel Co., 376 U.S. 225.]

Goldstein v. California

Supreme Court of the United States, 1973.
412 U.S. 546, 93 S.Ct. 2303.

■ MR. CHIEF JUSTICE BURGER delivered the opinion of the Court.

We granted certiorari to review petitioners' conviction under a California statute making it a criminal offense to "pirate" recordings produced by others.

In 1971, an information was filed by the State of California, charging petitioners in 140 counts with violating § 653h of the California Penal Code. The information charged that, between April 1970 and March 1971, petitioners had copied several musical performances from commercially sold recordings without the permission of the owner of the master record or tape.[1] Petitioners moved to dismiss the complaint on the grounds that § 653h was in conflict with Art. I, § 8, cl. 8, of the Constitution, the "Copyright Clause," and the federal statutes enacted thereunder. Upon denial of their motion, petitioners entered pleas of *nolo contendere* to 10 of the 140 counts; the remaining counts were dismissed. On appeal, the Appellate Department of the Superior Court sustained the validity of the statute. After exhausting other state appellate remedies, petitioners sought review in this Court.

I

Petitioners were engaged in what has commonly been called "record piracy" or "tape piracy"—the unauthorized duplication of recordings of performances by major musical artists. Petitioners would purchase from a retail distributor a single tape or phonograph recording of the popular performances they wished to duplicate. The original recordings were produced and marketed by recording companies with whom petitioners had no contractual relationship. At petitioners' plant, the recording was reproduced on blank tapes, which could in turn be used to replay the music on a tape player. The tape was then wound on a cartridge. A label was attached, stating the title of the recorded performance—the same title as had appeared on the original recording, and the name of the performing artists.[4] After final packaging, the tapes were distributed to retail outlets for sale to the public, in competition with those petitioners had copied.

Petitioners made no payments to the artists whose performances they reproduced and sold, nor to the various trust funds established for their benefit; no payments were made to the producers, technicians, or other

---

[1] In pertinent part, the California statute provides:

"(a) Every person is guilty of a misdemeanor who:

"(1) Knowingly and willfully transfers or causes to be transferred any sounds recorded on a phonograph record, . . . tape, . . . or other article on which sounds are recorded, with intent to sell or cause to be sold, . . . such article on which such sounds are so transferred, without the consent of the owner.

"(2) . . .

"(b) As used in this section, 'person' means any individual, partnership, corporation or association; and 'owner' means the person who owns the master phonograph record, . . . master tape, . . . or other device used for reproducing recorded sounds on phonograph records, . . . tapes, . . . or other articles on which sound is recorded, and from which the transferred recorded sounds are directly or indirectly derived." * * *

[4] An additional label was attached to each cartridge by petitioners, stating that no relationship existed between petitioners and the producer of the original recording or the individuals whose performances had been recorded. Consequently, no claim is made that petitioners misrepresented the source of the original recordings or the manufacturer of the tapes.

staff personnel responsible for producing the original recording and paying the large expenses incurred in production. No payments were made for the use of the artists' names or the album title. * * *

Petitioners' attack on the constitutionality of § 653h has many facets. First, they contend that the statute establishes a state copyright of unlimited duration, and thus conflicts with Art. I, § 8, cl. 8, of the Constitution. Second, petitioners claim that the state statute interferes with the implementation of federal policies inherent in the federal copyright statutes. 17 U.S.C.A. § 1 et seq. According to petitioners, it was the intention of Congress, as interpreted by this Court in Sears, Roebuck and Co. v. Stiffel Co., 376 U.S. 225 (1964), and Compco Corp. v. Day–Brite Lighting, 376 U.S. 234 (1964), to establish a uniform law throughout the United States to protect original writings. As part of the federal scheme, it is urged that Congress intended to allow individuals to copy any work which was not protected by a federal copyright. Since § 653h effectively prohibits the copying of works which are not entitled to federal protection, petitioners contend that it conflicts directly with congressional policy and must fall under the Supremacy Clause of the Constitution. Finally, petitioners argue that 17 U.S.C.A. § 2, which allows States to protect unpublished writings, does not authorize the challenged state provision; since the records which petitioners copied had previously been released to the public, petitioners contend that they had, under federal law, been published.

We note at the outset that the federal copyright statutes to which petitioners refer were amended by Congress while their case was pending in the state courts. In 1971, Pub.L. 92–140, 85 Stat. 391, was passed to allow federal copyright protection of recordings. However, § 3 of the amendment specifically provides that such protection is to be available only to sound recordings "fixed, published, and copyrighted" on and after February 15, 1972, and before January 1, 1975, and that nothing in Title 17, as amended is to "be applied retroactively or [to] be construed as affecting in any way any rights with respect to sound recordings fixed before" February 15, 1972. The recordings which petitioners copied were all "fixed" prior to February 15, 1972. Since, according to the language of § 3 of the amendment, Congress did not intend to alter the legal relationships which govern these recordings, the amendments have no application in petitioners' case.[7]

II

Petitioners' first argument rests on the premise that the state statute under which they were convicted lies beyond the powers which the States reserved in our federal system. If this is correct, petitioners must prevail, since the States cannot exercise a sovereign power which, under the Constitution, they have relinquished to the Federal Government for its exclusive exercise.

A

The principles which the Court has followed in construing state power were stated by Alexander Hamilton in Number 32 of The Federalist:

"An entire consolidation of the States into one complete national sovereignty would imply an entire subordination of the parts; and whatever powers might remain in them, would be altogether dependent on the general will. But as the plan of the [Constitutional] convention

---

[7] No question is raised in the present case as to the power of the States to protect recordings fixed after February 15, 1972.

aims only at a partial union or consolidation, the State governments would clearly retain all the rights of sovereignty which they before had, and which were not, by that act, *exclusively* delegated to the United States. This exclusive delegation, or rather this alienation, of State sovereignty, would only exist in three cases: where the Constitution in express terms granted an exclusive authority to the Union; where it granted in one instance an authority to the Union, and in another prohibited the States from exercising the like authority; and where it granted an authority to the Union, to which a similar authority in the States would be absolutely and totally *contradictory and repugnant*."[8]

The first two instances mentioned present no barrier to a State's enactment of copyright statutes. The clause of the Constitution granting to Congress the power to issue copyrights does not provide that such power shall vest exclusively in the Federal Government. Nor does the Constitution expressly provide that such power shall not be exercised by the States.

In applying the third phase of the test, we must examine the manner in which the power to grant copyrights may operate in our federal system. The objectives of our inquiry were recognized in Cooley v. Board of Wardens, 12 How. (53 U.S.) 299 (1851), when, in determining whether the power granted to Congress to regulate commerce was "compatible with the existence of a similar power in the States," the Court noted:

"Whatever subjects of this power are in their nature national, or admit of only one uniform system, or plan of regulation, may justly be said to be of such a nature as to require exclusive legislation by Congress." Id., at 319.

* * * We must also be careful to distinguish those situations in which the concurrent exercise of a power by the Federal Government and the States or by the States alone *may possibly* lead to conflicts and those situations where conflicts *will necessarily* arise. "It is not . . . a mere possibility of inconvenience in the exercise of powers, but an immediate constitutional repugnancy that can by implication alienate and extinguish a pre-existing right of [state] sovereignty." The Federalist, No. 32, at 243. * * *

The objective of the Copyright Clause was clearly to facilitate the granting of rights national in scope. While the debates on the clause at the Constitutional Convention were extremely limited, its purpose was described by James Madison in No. 43 of the Federalist Papers:

"The utility of this power will scarcely be questioned. The copyright of authors has been solemnly adjudged, in Great Britain, to be a right of common law. The right to useful inventions seems with equal reason to belong to the inventors. The public good fully coincides in both cases with the claims of individuals. The States cannot separately make effectual provision for either of the cases, and most of them have anticipated the decision of this point, by laws passed at the instance of Congress."[11]

The difficulty noted by Madison relates to the burden placed on an author or inventor who wishes to achieve protection in all States when no federal system of protection is available. To do so, a separate application is re-

---

[8]   The Federalist No. 32, p. 241 (B. Wright ed. 1961); see Cooley v. Board of Wardens, 12 How. 299, 318–319 (1851).

[11]   The Federalist, at 309.

quired to each state government; the right which in turn may be granted has effect only within the granting State's borders.[12] The national system which Madison supported eliminates the need for multiple applications and the expense and difficulty involved. In effect, it allows Congress to provide a reward greater in scope than any particular State may grant to promote progress in those fields which Congress determines are worthy of national action.

Although the Copyright Clause thus recognizes the potential benefits of a national system, it does not indicate that all writings are of national interest or that state legislation is, in all cases, unnecessary or precluded. The patents granted by the States in the 18th century show, to the contrary, a willingness on the part of the States to promote those portions of science and the arts which were of local importance. Whatever the diversity of people's backgrounds, origins, and interests, and whatever the variety of business and industry in the 13 colonies, the range of diversity is obviously far greater today in a country of 210 million people in 50 states. In view of that enormous diversity, it is unlikely that all citizens in all parts of the country place the same importance on works relating to all subjects. Since the subject matter to which the Copyright Clause is addressed may thus be of purely local importance and not worthy of national attention or protection, we cannot discern such an unyielding national interest as to require an inference that state power to grant copyrights has been relinquished to *exclusive* federal control.

The question to which we next turn is whether, in actual operation, the exercise of the power to grant copyrights by some States will prejudice the interests of other States. As we have noted, a copyright granted by a particular State has effect only within its boundaries. If one State grants such protection, the interests of States which do not are not prejudiced since their citizens remain free to copy within their borders those works which may be protected elsewhere. The interests of a State which grants copyright protection may, however, be adversely affected by other States that do not; individuals who wish to purchase a copy of a work protected in their own State will be able to buy unauthorized copies in other States where no protection exists. However, this conflict is neither so inevitable nor so severe as to compel the conclusion, that state power has been relinquished to the exclusive jurisdiction of the Congress. * * *

Similarly, it is difficult to see how the concurrent exercise of the power to grant copyrights by Congress and the States will necessarily and inevitably lead to difficulty. At any time Congress determines that a particular category of "writing" is worthy of national protection and the incidental expenses of federal administration, federal copyright protection may be authorized. Where the need for free and unrestricted distribution of a writing is thought to be required by the national interest, the Copyright Clause and the Commerce Clause would allow Congress to eschew all protection. In such cases, a conflict would develop if a State attempted to protect that

---

[12] Numerous examples may be found in our early history of the difficulties which the creators of items of national import had in securing protection of their creations in all States. For example, Noah Webster, in his effort to obtain protection for his book, A Grammatical Institute of the English Language, brought his claim before the legislatures of at least six States, and perhaps as many as 12. See B. Bugbee, The Genesis of American Patent and Copyright Law 108–110, 120–124 (Wash., D.C., 1967); H.R.Rep. No. 2222, 60th Cong., 2d Sess., at 2 (1909). Similar difficulties were experienced by John Fitch and other inventors who desired to protect their efforts to perfect a steamboat. See Federico, State Patents, 13 J.Pat.Off.Soc. 166, 170–176 (1931).

which Congress intended to be free from restraint or to free that which Congress had protected. However, where Congress determines that neither federal protection nor freedom from restraint is required by the national interest, it is at liberty to stay its hand entirely. Since state protection would not then conflict with federal action, total relinquishment of the States' power to grant copyright protection cannot be inferred.

As we have seen, the language of the Constitution neither explicitly precludes the State from granting copyrights nor grants such authority exclusively to the Federal Government. The subject matter to which the Copyright Clause is addressed may at times be of purely local concern. No conflict will necessarily arise from a lack of uniform state regulation, nor will the interest of one State be significantly prejudiced by the actions of another. No reason exists why Congress must take affirmative action either to authorize protection of all categories of writings or to free them from all restraint. We therefore conclude that, under the Constitution, the States have not relinquished all power to grant to authors "the exclusive Right to their respective Writings."

B

Petitioners base an additional argument on the language of the Constitution. The California statute forbids individuals from appropriating recordings at any time after release. From this, petitioners argue that the State has created a copyright of *unlimited* duration, in violation of that portion of Art. I, § 8, cl. 8, which provides that copyrights may only be granted "for limited Times." Read literally, the text of Art. I does not support petitioners' position. Section 8 enumerates those powers which have been granted *to Congress;* whatever limitations have been appended to such powers can only be understood as a limit on congressional, and not state, action. Moreover, it is not clear that the dangers to which this limitation was addressed apply with equal force to both the Federal Government and the States. When Congress grants an exclusive right or monopoly, its effects are pervasive; no citizen or State may escape its reach. As we have noted, however, the exclusive right granted by a State is confined to its borders. Consequently, even when the right is unlimited in duration, any tendency to inhibit further progress in science or the arts is narrowly circumscribed. The challenged statute cannot be voided for lack of a durational limitation.

III

Our conclusion that California did not surrender its power to issue copyrights does not end the inquiry. We must proceed to determine whether the challenged state statute is void under the Supremacy Clause. No simple formula can capture the complexities of this determination; the conflicts which may develop between state and federal action are as varied as the fields to which congressional action may apply. "Our primary function is to determine whether, under the circumstances of this particular case, [the state] law stands as an obstacle to the accomplishment and execution of the full purposes and objectives of Congress." Hines v. Davidowitz, 312 U.S. 52, 67 (1941). We turn then to federal copyright law to determine what objectives Congress intended to fulfill.

By Art. I, § 8, cl. 8, of the Constitution, the States granted to Congress the power to protect the "Writings" of "Authors." These terms have not been construed in their narrow literal sense but, rather, with the reach necessary to reflect the broad scope of constitutional principles. While an "author" may be viewed as an individual who writes an original composition, the term, in its constitutional sense, has been construed to mean an "originator," "he to whom anything owes its origin." Burrow–Giles Lithographic Co. v. Sarony, 111 U.S. 53, 58 (1884). Similarly, although the word "writings" might be limited to script or printed material, it may be interpreted to include any physical rendering of the fruits of creative intellectual or aesthetic labor. Id.; Trade Mark Cases, 100 U.S. 82, 94 (1879). Thus, recordings of artistic performances may be within the reach of Clause 8.

While the area in which Congress *may* act is broad, the enabling provision of Clause 8 does not require that Congress act in regard to all categories of materials which meet the constitutional definitions. Rather, whether any specific category of "Writings" is to be brought within the purview of the federal statutory scheme is left to the discretion of the Congress. The history of federal copyright statutes indicates that the congressional determination to consider specific classes of writings is dependent not only on the character of the writing, but also on the commercial importance of the product to the national economy. As our technology has expanded the means available for creative activity and has provided economical means for reproducing manifestations of such activity, new areas of federal protection have been initiated.

Petitioners contend that the actions taken by Congress in establishing federal copyright protection preclude the States from granting similar protection to recordings of musical performances. According to petitioners, Congress addressed the question of whether recordings of performances should be granted protection in 1909; Congress determined that any individual who was entitled to a copyright on an original musical composition should have the right to control to a limited extent the use of that composition on recordings, but that the record itself, and the performance which it was capable of reproducing were not worthy of such protection. In support of their claim, petitioners cite the House Report on the 1909 Act, which states:

> "It is not the intention of the committee to extend the right of copyright to the mechanical reproductions themselves, but only to give the composer or copyright proprietor the control, in accordance with the provisions of the bill, of the manufacture and use of such devices." H.R.Rep. No. 2222, 60th Cong., 2d Sess., 9 (1909).

* * * The section of the House Report cited by petitioners was intended only to establish the limits of *the composer's* right; composers were to have no control over the recordings themselves. Nowhere does the report indicate that Congress considered records as anything but a component part of a machine, capable of reproducing an original composition or that Congress intended records, as *renderings of original artistic performance,* to be free from state control.

Petitioners' argument does not rest entirely on the belief that Congress intended specifically to exempt recordings of performances from state control. Assuming that no such intention may be found, they argue that Congress so occupied the field of copyright protection as to pre-empt all comparable state action. Rice v. Santa Fe Elevator Corporation, 331 U.S. 218 (1947). This assertion is based on the language of 17 U.S.C.A. §§ 4 and 5, and on this Court's opinions in Sears, Roebuck and Co. v. Stiffel Co., 376 U.S. 225 (1964), and Compco Corp. v. Day–Brite Lighting, 376 U.S. 234 (1964).

Section 4 of the federal copyright laws provides:

"The works for which copyright may be secured under this title shall include all the writings of an author."

Section 5, which lists specific categories of protected works, adds:

"The above specifications shall not be held to limit the subject-matter of copyright as defined in section 4 of this title . . . ."

Since § 4 employs the constitutional term "writings," it may be argued that Congress intended to exercise its authority over all works to which the constitutional provision might apply. However, in the more than 60 years which have transpired since enactment of this provision, neither the Copyright Office, the courts, nor the Congress has so interpreted it. The Register of Copyrights, who is charged with administration of the statute, has consistently ruled that "claims to exclusive rights in mechanical recordings . . . or in the performances they reproduce" are not entitled to protection under § 4. 37 CFR § 202.8(b) (1972). With one early exception,[26] American courts have agreed with this interpretation;[27] and in 1971, prior to passage of the statute which extended federal protection to recordings fixed on or after Feb. 15, 1972, Congress acknowledged the validity of that interpretation. Both the House and Senate Reports on the proposed legislation recognized that recordings qualified as "writings" within the meaning of the Constitution, but had not previously been protected under the federal copyright statute. H.R.Rep. No. 92–487, 92d Cong., 1st Sess. (1971), at 2, 5; S.Rep. No. 92–72, 92d Cong., 1st Sess. (1971), at 4. In light of this consistent interpretation by the courts, the agency empowered to administer the copyright statutes, and Congress itself, we cannot agree that §§ 4 and 5 have the broad scope petitioners claim.

Sears and *Compco*, on which petitioners rely, do not support their position. In those cases, the question was whether a State could, under principles of state unfair competition law, preclude the copying of mechanical configurations which did not possess the qualities required for the granting of a federal design or mechanical patent. * * *

In regard to mechanical configurations, Congress had balanced the need to encourage innovation and originality of invention against the need to insure competition in the sale of identical or substantially identical products. The standards established for granting federal patent protection to machines thus indicated not only which articles in this particular category Congress wished to protect, but which configurations it wished to remain free. The application of state law in these cases to prevent the copying of articles which did not meet the requirements for federal protection disturbed the careful balance which Congress had drawn and thereby necessarily gave way under the Supremacy Clause of the Constitution. No comparable conflict between state law and federal law arises in the case of recordings of musical performances. In regard to this category of "Writings," Congress has drawn no balance; rather, it has left the area unattended, and no reason exists why the State should not be free to act.[28]

---

[26] Fonotipia Limited v. Bradley, 171 F. 951, 963 (EDNY 1909).

[27] Aeolian Co. v. Royal Music Roll Co., 196 F. 926, 927 (W.D.N.Y.1912); Waring v. WDAS Broadcasting Station, 327 Pa. 433, 437–438, 194 A. 631 (1937); Capitol Records v. Mercury Records Corp., 221 F.2d 657, 661–662 (C.A.2 1955); Jerome v. Twentieth Century Fox–Film Corp., 67 F.Supp. 736, 742 (S.D.N.Y.1946).

[28] Petitioners place great stress on their belief that the records or tapes which they copied had been "published." We have no need to determine whether, *under state law*, these recordings had been published or what legal consequences such publication might have. *For*

IV

* * *

In sum, we have shown that § 653h does not conflict with the federal copyright statute enacted by Congress in 1909. Similarly, no conflict exists between the federal copyright statute passed in 1971 and the present application of § 653h, since California charged petitioners only with copying recordings fixed prior to February 15, 1972. Finally, we have concluded that our decisions in *Sears* and *Compco,* which we reaffirm today, have no application in the present case, since Congress has indicated neither that it wishes to protect, nor to free from protection, recordings of musical performances fixed prior to February 15, 1972.

We conclude that the State of California has exercised a power which it retained under the Constitution, and that the challenged statute, as applied in this case, does not intrude into an area which Congress has, up to now, pre-empted. Until and unless Congress takes further action with respect to recordings fixed prior to February 15, 1972, the California statute may be enforced against acts of piracy such as those which occurred in the present case.

Affirmed.

■ MR. JUSTICE DOUGLAS, with whom MR. JUSTICE BRENNAN and MR. JUSTICE BLACKMUN concur, dissenting. * * *

Prior to February 25, 1972, copyright protection was not extended to sound recordings. *Sears* and *Compco* make clear that the federal policy expressed in Art. I, § 8, cl. 8, is to have "national uniformity in patent and copyright laws," 376 U.S., at 231 n. 7, a policy bolstered by Acts of Congress which vest "exclusive jurisdiction to hear patent and copyright cases in federal courts . . . and that section of the Copyright Act which expressly saves state protection of unpublished writings but does not include published writings." Ibid. * * *

California's law promotes monopoly; the federal policy promotes monopoly only when a copyright is issued, and it fosters competition in all other instances. Moreover, federal law limits its monopoly to 28 years plus a like renewal period, while California extends her monopoly into perpetuity.

Cases like *Sears* were surcharged with "unfair competition" and the present one with "pirated recordings." But free access to products on the market is the consumer interest protected by the failure of Congress to extend patents or copyrights into various areas. * * *

I would reverse the judgment below.

■ MR. JUSTICE MARSHALL, with whom MR. JUSTICE BRENNAN and MR. JUSTICE BLACKMUN join, dissenting.

* * * In my view, Congress has demonstrated its desire to exercise the full grant of constitutional power. Title 17, U.S.C.A. § 4, states: "The works for which copyright may be secured under this title shall include *all the writings of an author*" (emphasis added). The use of the constitutional terms "writings" and "author" rather strongly suggests that Congress in-

---

purposes of federal law, "publication" serves only as a term of the art which defines the legal relationships which Congress has adopted under the federal copyright statutes. As to categories of writings which Congress has not brought within the scope of the federal statute, the term has no application.

tended to follow the constitutional grant. It could exercise the power given it by the Constitution in two ways: either by protecting all writings, or by protecting all writings within designated classes and leaving open to competition all writings in other classes. Section 5 shows that the latter course was chosen, for it enumerates various classes of works that may be registered. * * *

* * * [W]e should not let our distaste for "pirates" interfere with our interpretation of the copyright laws. I would therefore hold that, as to sound recordings fixed before February 15, 1972, the States may not enforce laws limiting reproduction.

Kewanee Oil Co. v. Bicron Corp.
416 U.S. 470, 94 S.Ct. 1879 (1974).

Plaintiff Kewanee had a secret process for producing synthetic crystals. Defendants, former employees of Kewanee, formed a competitor called Bicron. The district court enjoined the defendants from using the plaintiff's trade secrets, but the court of appeals held that Ohio trade secret law was in conflict with federal patent law in that the plaintiff's techniques might have been patentable, but having been in commercial use for more than a year, they were no longer eligible for federal protection due to the one-year restriction in 35 U.S.C.A. § 102. The Supreme Court, in an opinion by Chief Justice Burger, reinstated the judgment of the district court:

"The first issue we deal with is whether the States are forbidden to act at all in the area of protection of the kinds of intellectual property which may make up the subject matter of trade secrets. * * *

"Just as the States may exercise regulatory power over writings so may the States regulate with respect to discoveries. States may hold diverse viewpoints in protecting intellectual property relating to invention as they do in protecting the intellectual property relating to the subject matter of copyright. The only limitation on the States is that in regulating the area of patents and copyrights they do not conflict with the operation of the laws in this area passed by Congress, and it is to that more difficult question we now turn.

"The question of whether the trade secret law of Ohio is void under the Supremacy Clause involves a consideration of whether that law 'stands as an obstacle to the accomplishment and execution of the full purposes and objectives of Congress.' Hines v. Davidowitz, 312 U.S. 52, 67 (1941). * * *

"The laws which the Court of Appeals in this case held to be in conflict with the Ohio law of trade secrets were the patent laws passed by the Congress in the unchallenged exercise of its clear power under Art. I, § 8, cl. 8, of the Constitution. The patent law does not explicitly endorse or forbid the operation of trade secret law. However, as we have noted, if the scheme of protection developed by Ohio respecting trade secrets 'clashes with the objectives of the federal patent laws,' Sears, Roebuck & Co. v. Stiffel Co., supra, 376 U.S. at 231, then the state law must fall. To determine whether the Ohio law 'clashes' with the federal law it is helpful to examine the objectives of both the patent and trade secret laws.

"The stated objective of the Constitution in granting the power to Congress to legislate in the area of intellectual property is to 'promote the Progress of Science and useful Arts.' The patent laws promote this progress by offering a right of exclusion for a limited period as an incentive for inventors to risk the often enormous costs in terms of time, research, and development. The productive effort thereby fostered will have a positive effect on society through the introduction of new products and processes of manufacture into the economy, and the emanations by way of increased employment and better lives for our citizens. In return for the right of exclusion—this 'reward for inventions,' Universal Oil Co. v. Globe Co., 322 U.S. 471, 484 (1944)—the patent laws impose upon the inventor a requirement of disclosure. To insure adequate and full disclosure so that upon the expiration of the 17–year period 'the knowledge of the invention enures to the people, who are thus enabled without restriction to practice it and profit by its use,' United States v. Dubilier Condenser Corp., 289 U.S. 178, 187 (1933), the patent laws require that the patent application shall include a full and clear description of the invention and 'of the manner and process of making and using it' so that any person skilled in the art may make and use the invention. 35 U.S.C.A. § 112. When a patent is granted and the information contained in it is circulated to the general public and those especially skilled in the trade, such additions to the general store of knowledge are of such importance to the public weal that the Federal Government is willing to pay the high price of 17 years of exclusive use for its disclosure, which disclosure, it is assumed, will stimulate ideas and the eventual development of further significant advances in the art. The Court has also articulated another policy of the patent law: that which is in the public domain cannot be removed therefrom by action of the States.

> '[F]ederal laws requires that all ideas in general circulation be dedicated to the common good unless they are protected by a valid patent.' Lear, Inc. v. Adkins, 395 U.S., at 668.

See also Goldstein v. California, 412 U.S., at 570–571; Sears, Roebuck & Co. v. Stiffel Co., supra; Compco Corp. v. Day–Brite Lighting, Inc., 376 U.S. 234, 237–238 (1964); International News Service v. Associated Press, 248 U.S. 215, 250 (1918) (Brandeis, J., dissenting.)"

Chief Justice Burger next examined the policies that underlie state trade secret law, and then turned to the question of whether state trade secret protection constituted "too great an encroachment on the federal patent system to be tolerated."

"As we noted earlier, trade secret law protects items which would not be proper subjects for consideration for patent protection under 35 U.S.C. § 101. As in the case of the recordings in Goldstein v. California, Congress, with respect to nonpatentable subject matter, 'has drawn no balance; rather, it has left the area unattended, and no reason exists why the State should not be free to act.' Goldstein v. California, supra, at 570. * * *

"Congress has spoken in the area of those discoveries which fall within one of the categories of patentable subject matter of 35 U.S.C. § 101 and which are, therefore, of a nature that would be subject to consideration for a patent. Processes, machines, manufactures, compositions of matter, and improvements thereof, which meet the tests of utility, novelty, and nonobviousness are entitled to be patented, but those which do not, are not. The question remains whether those items which are proper subjects for consideration for a patent may also have available the alternative protection accorded by trade secret law.

"Certainly the patent policy of encouraging invention is not disturbed by the existence of another form of incentive to invention. In this respect the two systems are not and never would be in conflict. Similarly, the policy that matter once in the public domain must remain in the public domain is not incompatible with the existence of trade secret protection. By definition a trade secret has not been placed in the public domain.

"The more difficult objective of the patent law to reconcile with trade secret law is that of disclosure, the *quid pro quo* of the right to exclude."

The Court concluded that "there is no real possibility that trade secret law will conflict with the federal policy favoring disclosure," chiefly because the scope of trade secret protection is limited; anyone not bound by confidence or contract may independently discover and exploit the secret. "The possibility that an inventor who believes his invention meets the standards of patentability will sit back, rely on trade secret law, and after one year of use forfeit any right to patent protection, 35 U.S.C. § 102(b), is remote indeed."

The Chief Justice also noted that "[t]rade secret law and patent law have co-existed in this country for over one hundred years," and concluded that "Congress, by its silence over these many years, has seen the wisdom of allowing the States to enforce trade secret protection. Until Congress takes affirmative action to the contrary, States should be free to grant protection to trade secrets."

Justice Marshall concurred in the result, accepting the co-existence argument. Justices Douglas and Brennan dissented, invoking *Sears* and *Compco* and the federal policy favoring disclosure in return for the patent monopoly.

Bonito Boats, Inc. v. Thunder Craft Boats, Inc.
489 U.S. 141, 109 S.Ct. 971 (1989).

Justice O'Connor wrote the opinion for a unanimous Court sustaining the defendant's challenge to a Florida statute that declared it "unlawful for any person to use the direct molding process to duplicate for the purpose of sale any manufactured vessel hull or component part of a vessel made by another without the written permission of that other person."

"We must decide today what limits the operation of the federal patent system places on the States' ability to offer substantial protection to utilitarian and design ideas which the patent laws leave otherwise unprotected. * * *

" * * * The federal patent system thus embodies a carefully crafted bargain for encouraging the creation and disclosure of new, useful, and nonobvious advances in technology and design in return for the exclusive right to practice the invention for a period of years. * * *

"The attractiveness of such a bargain, and its effectiveness in inducing creative effort and disclosure of the results of that effort, depend almost entirely on a backdrop of free competition in the exploitation of unpatented designs and innovations. The novelty and nonobviousness requirements of patentability embody a congressional understanding, implicit in the Patent Clause itself, that free exploitation of ideas will be the rule, to which the protection of a federal patent is the exception. Moreover, the ultimate goal of the patent system is to bring new designs and technologies into the public domain through disclosure. State law protection for techniques and designs whose disclosure has already been induced by market rewards may conflict with the very purpose of the patent laws by decreasing the range of ideas available as the building blocks of further innovation. The offer of federal protection from competitive exploitation of intellectual property would be rendered meaningless in a world where substantially similar state law protections were readily available. To a limited extent, the federal patent laws must determine not only what is protected, but also what is free for all to use. * * *

"The pre-emptive sweep of our decisions in *Sears* and *Compco* has been the subject of heated scholarly and judicial debate. See, e.g., Symposium, Product Simulation: A Right or a Wrong?, 64 Colum.L.Rev. 1178 (1964); Lear, Inc. v. Adkins, 395 U.S. 653, 676 (1969) (Black, J., concurring in part and dissenting in part). Read at their highest level of generality, the two decisions could be taken to stand for the proposition that the States are completely disabled from offering any form of protection to articles or processes which fall within the broad scope of patentable subject matter. See id., at 677. Since the potentially patentable includes 'anything under the sun that is made by man,' Diamond v. Chakrabarty, 447 U.S. 303, 309 (1980) (citation omitted), the broadest reading of *Sears* would prohibit the States from regulating the deceptive simulation of trade dress or the tortious appropriation of private information.

"That the extrapolation of such a broad pre-emptive principle from *Sears* is inappropriate is clear from the balance struck in *Sears* itself. The *Sears* Court made it plain that the States 'may protect businesses in the use of their trademarks, labels, or distinctive dress in the packaging of goods so as to prevent others, by imitating such markings, from misleading purchasers as to the source of the goods.' *Sears,* supra, 376 U.S., at 232 (footnote omitted). Trade dress is, of course, potentially the subject matter of design patents. See W.T. Rogers Co. v. Keene, 778 F.2d 334, 337 (C.A.7 1985). Yet our decision in *Sears* clearly indicates that the States may place limited regulations on the circumstances in which such designs are used in order to prevent consumer confusion as to source. Thus, while *Sears* speaks in absolutist terms, its conclusion that the States may place some conditions on the use of trade dress indicates an implicit recognition that all state regulation of potentially patentable but unpatented subject matter is not *ipso facto* pre-empted by the federal patent laws. * * *

"We believe that the Florida statute at issue in this case so substantially impedes the public use of the otherwise unprotected design and utilitarian ideas embodied in unpatented boat hulls as to run afoul of the teaching of our decisions in *Sears* and *Compco*. It is readily apparent that the Florida statute does not operate to prohibit 'unfair competition' in the usual sense that the term is understood. The law of unfair competition has its roots in the common-law tort of deceit: its general concern is with protecting *consumers* from confusion as to source. While that concern may result in the creation of 'quasi-property rights' in communicative symbols, the focus is on the protection of consumers, not the protection of producers as an incentive to product innovation. Judge Hand captured the distinction well in Crescent Tool Co. v. Kilborn & Bishop Co., 247 F. 299, 301 (C.A.2 1917), where he wrote:

'[T]he plaintiff has the right not to lose his customers through false representations that those are his wares which in fact are not, but he may not monopolize any design or pattern, however trifling. The defendant, on the other hand, may copy plaintiff's goods slavishly down to the minutest detail: but he may not represent himself as the plaintiff in their sale.'

"With some notable exceptions, including the interpretation of the Illinois law of unfair competition at issue in *Sears* and *Compco,* see *Sears,* supra, 376 U.S., at 227–228, n. 2, the common-law tort of unfair competition has been limited to protection against copying of nonfunctional aspects of consumer products which have acquired secondary meaning such that they operate as a designation of source. See generally P. Kaufmann, Passing Off and Misappropriation, in 9 IIC Studies in Industrial Property and Copyright Law 100–109 (1986). The 'protection' granted a particular design under the law of unfair competition is thus limited to one context where consumer confusion is likely to result; the design 'idea' itself may be freely exploited in all other contexts.

"In contrast to the operation of unfair competition law, the Florida statute is aimed directly at preventing the exploitation of the design and utilitarian conceptions embodied in the product itself. The sparse legislative history surrounding its enactment indicates that it was intended to create an inducement for the improvement of boat hull designs. * * *

"Our decisions since *Sears* and *Compco* have made it clear that the Patent and Copyright Clauses do not, by their own force or by negative implication, deprive the States of the power to adopt rules for the promotion of intellectual creation within their own jurisdictions. * * *

"Nor does the fact that a particular item lies within the subject matter of the federal patent laws necessarily preclude the States from offering limited protection which does not impermissibly interfere with the federal patent scheme. As *Sears* itself makes clear, States may place limited regulations on the use of unpatented designs in order to prevent consumer confusion as to source. In *Kewanee,* we found that state protection of trade secrets, as applied to both patentable and unpatentable subject matter, did not conflict with the federal patent laws. In both situations, state protection was not aimed exclusively at the promotion of invention itself, and the state restrictions on the use of unpatented ideas were limited to those necessary to promote goals outside the contemplation of the federal patent scheme. Both the law of unfair competition and state trade secret law have coexisted harmoniously with federal patent protection for almost 200 years, and Congress has given no indication that their operation is inconsistent with the operation of the federal patent laws. See Florida Lime & Avocado Growers, Inc. v. Paul, 373 U.S. 132, 144 (1963); United States v. Bass, 404 U.S. 336, 349 (1971).

"Indeed, there are affirmative indications from Congress that both the law of unfair competition and trade secret protection are consistent with the balance struck by the patent laws. Section 43(a) of the Lanham Act, 60 Stat. 441, 15 U.S.C. § 1125(a), creates a federal remedy for making 'a false designation of origin, or any false description or representation, including words or other symbols tending falsely to describe or represent the same . . . . ' Congress has thus given federal recognition to many of the concerns which underlie the state tort of unfair competition, and the application of *Sears* and *Compco* to nonfunctional aspects of a product which have been shown to identify source must take account of competing federal policies in this regard. * * *

"The Florida statute is aimed directly at the promotion of intellectual creation by substantially restricting the public's ability to exploit ideas which the patent system mandates shall be free for all to use. Like the interpretation of Illinois unfair competition law in *Sears* and *Compco,* the Florida statute represents a break with the tradition of peaceful coexistence between state market regulation and federal patent policy. * * *

" * * * By offering patent-like protection for ideas deemed unprotected under the present federal scheme, the Florida statute conflicts with the 'strong federal policy favoring free competition in ideas which do not merit patent protection.' *Lear, Inc.,* 395 U.S., at 656. We therefore agree with the majority of the Florida Supreme Court that the Florida statute is preempted by the Supremacy Clause, and the judgment of that court is hereby affirmed."

NOTES AND QUESTIONS ON THE PREEMPTION CASES

(1) In distinguishing *Sears* and *Compco,* the majority opinion in *Goldstein* concludes that in regard to mechanical configurations, Congress, through the patent laws, has determined not only what is to be protected, but also what is to be left in the public domain. In regard to writings, the Supreme Court concludes that, as to some, Congress "has left the area unattended." Is the distinction justified? Congressional intent on the issue of pre–1972 sound recordings is considerably less ambiguous under the 1976 Copyright Act. See § 301(c).

(2) The Supreme Court considered the preemptive effect of federal patent law again in Aronson v. Quick Point Pencil Co., 440 U.S. 257 (1979), and upheld a state contract law claim for royalties due on sales of an article embodying an innovation that was denied a patent subsequent to the contract.

(3) Does Justice O'Connor's opinion in *Bonito Boats*—by its interpretation of the Illinois law at issue in *Sears* and *Compco* and its caution that "application of *Sears* and *Compco* to nonfunctional aspects of a product which have been shown to identify source must take account of the competing federal policies" reflected in patent law and § 43(a) of the Lanham Act—rehabilitate state trademark protection for nonfunctional product features with secondary meaning? If so, the case represents a significant retreat from the sweeping language in *Compco.* See the analysis of *Bonito Boats* in D. Shipley, Refusing to Rock the Boat: The *Sears–Compco* Preemption Doctrine Applied to *Bonito Boats v. Thunder Craft,* 25 Wake Forest L.Rev. 385 (1990). See also P. Heald, Federal Intellectual Property Law and the Economics of Preemption, 76 Iowa L.Rev. 959 (1991), applying the *Bonito Boats* rationale to other state doctrines including publicity rights, resale royalty rights, and trademark dilution.

STATUTORY PREEMPTION—§ 301

HOUSE REPORT

Preemption of State law

The intention of section 301 is to preempt and abolish any rights under the common law or statutes of a State that are equivalent to copyright and that extend to works coming within the scope of the Federal copyright law. The declaration of this principle in section 301 is intended to be stated in the clearest and most unequivocal language possible, so as to foreclose any conceivable misinterpretation of its unqualified intention that Congress shall act preemptively, and to avoid the development of any vague border-line areas between State and Federal protection.

Under section 301(a) all "legal or equitable rights that are equivalent to any of the exclusive rights within the general scope of copyright as specified by section 106" are governed exclusively by the Federal copyright statute if the works involved are "works of authorship that are fixed in a tangible medium of expression and come within the subject matter of copyright as specified by sections 102 and 103." All corresponding State laws, whether common law or statutory, are preempted and abrogated. Regardless of when the work was created and whether it is published or unpublished, disseminated or undisseminated, in the public domain or copyrighted under the Federal statute, the States cannot offer it protection equivalent to copyright. H.R.Rep. pp. 130–31.

———————

At the time the House Report was prepared, § 301(b) of the revision bill read as follows:

> (b) Nothing in this title annuls or limits any rights or remedies under the common law or statutes of any State with respect to * * *

> (3) activities violating legal or equitable rights that are not equivalent to any of the exclusive rights within the general scope of copyright as specified by section 106, including rights against misappropriation not equivalent to any of such exclusive rights, breaches of contract, breaches of trust, trespass, conversion, invasion of privacy, defamation, and deceptive trade practices such as passing off and false representation. H.R.Rep. p. 24.

The inclusion of "rights against misappropriation not equivalent to" copyright on the list of non-preempted rights was a complete turnabout. An earlier House Report, commenting on a version of § 301(b) that did not include misappropriation in its list of preserved rights, had said:

> In accordance with the Supreme Court's decision in Sears, Roebuck & Co. v. Stiffel Co., section 301 is not intended to preempt common law protection in cases involving activities such as false labeling, fraudulent representation, and passing off, even where the subject matter involved comes within the scope of the copyright statute. However, where the cause of action involves the form of unfair competition commonly referred to as "misappropriation," which is nothing more than copyright protection under another name, section 301 is intended to have preemptive effect.[p]

The Antitrust Division of the Department of Justice opposed the addition of misappropriation to the § 301(b)(3) list of preserved state rights and pressed for its deletion when the bill was about to pass the Senate. See 122 Cong.Rec. 3836 (Feb. 19, 1976) (letter to Senator Scott). When this move was unsuccessful, a letter was written to the House committee stressing the Department's position that remedies against misappropriation were anti-competitive and expressing concern that the list of allowable state rights might be misused "to nullify preemption." See H. Fetter, Copyright Revision and the Preemption of State "Misappropriation" Law, 25 Bull.Copyr. Soc'y 367, 418–24 (1978). Nothing happened. But at the very last moment before passage of the bill in the House, Congressman

———————

[p]   H.R.Rep. No. 2237, 89th Cong., 2d Sess. 129 (1966).

Seiberling offered an amendment to strike the entire list of examples from subsection (b)(3). It evoked the following dialogue:

> Mr. SEIBERLING. Mr. Chairman, my amendment is intended to save the "Federal preemption" of State law section, which is section 301 of the bill, from being inadvertently nullified because of the inclusion of certain examples in the exemptions from preemption.
>
> This amendment would simply strike the examples listed in section 301(b)(3).
>
> The amendment is strongly supported by the Justice Department, which believes that it would be a serious mistake to cite as an exemption from preemption the doctrine of "misappropriation." The doctrine was created by the Supreme Court in 1922 [sic], and it has generally been ignored by the Supreme Court itself and by the lower courts ever since.
>
> Inclusion of a reference to the misappropriation doctrine in this bill, however, could easily be construed by the courts as authorizing the States to pass misappropriation laws. We should not approve such enabling legislation, because a misappropriation law could be so broad as to render the preemption section meaningless.
>
> Mr. RAILSBACK. Mr. Chairman, will the gentleman yield?
>
> Mr. SEIBERLING. I yield to the gentleman from Illinois.
>
> Mr. RAILSBACK. Mr. Chairman, may I ask the gentleman from Ohio, for the purpose of clarifying the amendment that by striking the word "misappropriation," the gentleman in no way is attempting to change the existing state of the law, that is as it may exist in certain States that have recognized the right of recovery relating to "misappropriation"; is that correct?
>
> Mr. SEIBERLING. That is correct. All I am trying to do is prevent the citing of them as examples in a statute. We are, in effect, adopting a rather amorphous body of State law and codifying it, in effect. Rather I am trying to have this bill leave the State law alone and make it clear we are merely dealing with copyright laws, laws applicable to copyrights.
>
> Mr. RAILSBACK. Mr. Chairman, I personally have no objection to the gentleman's amendment in view of that clarification and I know of no objections from this side.
>
> Mr. SEIBERLING. I thank the gentleman.
>
> 122 Cong.Rec. 32015 (Sept. 22, 1976).

The amendment was adopted and the revision bill passed.

NOTES AND QUESTIONS ON § 301

(1) Only state-created rights in works "within the subject matter of copyright as specified by sections 102 and 103" are subject to preemption under § 301. How should this criterion be interpreted? The House Report offers a partial explanation: "As long as a work fits within one of the general subject matter categories of sections 102 and 103, the bill prevents the State from protecting it even if it fails to achieve Federal statutory copyright because it is too minimal or lacking in originality to qualify, or because it has fallen into the public domain." H.R.Rep. p. 131. But what of works specifically excluded from copyright, such as the designs of useful articles that fail to satisfy the separability test in § 101? May state law, for instance, prohibit the copying of dress designs? They are not, literally, within the "subject matter of copyright." And what of ideas and facts, excluded from copyright by § 102(b)? Are these, by virtue of that exclusion, eligible for state protection?[q]

A few cases, equating "subject matter" with protected matter, have concluded that material excluded from copyright under the 1976 Act remains open to state protection. Thus, in Bromhall v. Rorvik, 478 F.Supp. 361 (E.D.Pa.1979), a state-law claim based on the appropriation of ideas from the plaintiff's doctoral dissertation escaped preemption on the reasoning that "[c]opyright protection extends only to *expression* of an idea, not the idea itself." Similarly, in Vermont Castings, Inc. v. Evans Prod. Co., 215 U.S.P.Q. 758 (D.Vt.1981), the court concluded that because the inseparable design features of a stove could not command copyright protection, "there can be no preemption under § 301 of the Copyright Act of common law remedies for protection." See also H$_2$O Swimwear, Ltd. v. Lomas, 164 A.D.2d 804, 560 N.Y.S.2d 19 (1990) (because clothing designs are excluded from copyright, state protection is not preempted).

Should the subject-matter test in § 301 be seen instead as a codification of *Goldstein*, intended to distinguish "attended" from "unattended" matter? In Hoehling v. Universal City Studios, p. 235 supra, the Second Circuit, operating under the 1909 Act, refused to permit a state unfair competition claim premised on the appropriation of the plaintiff's facts and research: "Where, as here, historical facts, themes, and research have been deliberately exempted from the scope of copyright protection to vindicate the overriding goal of encouraging contributions to recorded knowledge, the states are pre-empted from removing such material from the public domain." The Second Circuit took the same position under the 1976 Act in National Basketball Ass'n v. Motorola, Inc., 105 F.3d 841 (2d Cir.1997) ("Section 301 preemption bars state law misappropriation claims with respect to uncopyrightable as well as copyrightable elements."). Several other circuits have agreed. See, e.g., ProCD, Inc. v. Zeidenberg, 86 F.3d 1447 (7th Cir.1996), holding that data in an uncopyrightable compilation falls within the subject matter of the Copyright Act: "One function of § 301 is to prevent states from giving special protection to works of authorship that Congress has decided should be in the public domain, which it can accomplish only if 'subject matter of copyright' includes all works of a type covered by sections 102 and 103, even if federal law does not afford protection to them."; United States ex rel. Berge v. Board of Trustees of Univ. of Alabama, 104 F.3d 1453 (4th Cir.), cert. denied, 522 U.S. 916 (1997), concluding that although the ideas in the plaintiff's dissertation were excluded from copyright, they were still within the subject matter of the statute. However, that conclusion was questioned by the Eleventh Circuit in Dunlap v. G & L Holding Group, Inc., 381 F.3d 1285 (11th Cir.2004), holding that a state law claim for conversion of an idea is not preempted because the subject matter of copyright requirement in § 301 includes only elements that are substantively qualified for copyright protection.

(2) Section 301 preempts only state rights that are "equivalent" to the rights specified in § 106. How is equivalency to be determined? The House Report,

---

[q]   Compare R. Brown, Unification: A Cheerful Requiem for Common–Law Copyright, 24 UCLA. L.Rev. 1070 (1977), with P. Goldstein, Preempted State Doctrines, Involuntary Transfers and Compulsory Licenses, id. at 1107.

commenting on the penultimate version of § 301 (with its illustrative examples of non-equivalent rights), offers this analysis:

> The examples in clause (3), while not exhaustive, are intended to illustrate rights and remedies that are different in nature from the rights comprised in a copyright and that may continue to be protected under State common law or statute. The evolving common law rights of "privacy," "publicity," and trade secrets, and the general laws of defamation and fraud, would remain unaffected as long as the causes of action contain elements, such as an invasion of personal rights or a breach of trust or confidentiality, that are different in kind from copyright infringement. Nothing in the bill derogates from the rights of parties to contract with each other and to sue for breaches of contract; however, to the extent that the unfair competition concept known as "interference with contract relations" is merely the equivalent of copyright protection, it would be preempted.

> The last example listed in clause (3)—"deceptive trade practices such as passing off and false representation"—represents an effort to distinguish between those causes of action known as "unfair competition" that the copyright statute is not intended to preempt and those that it is. Section 301 is not intended to preempt common law protection in cases involving activities such as false labeling, fraudulent representation, and passing off even where the subject matter involved comes within the scope of the copyright statute. (H.R.Rep. p. 132.)

When does a state cause of action "contain elements * * * that are different in kind from copyright infringement"? Suppose the state doctrine demands a showing of wrongful intent? In Crow v. Wainwright, 720 F.2d 1224 (11th Cir.1983), cert. denied, 469 U.S. 819 (1984), a state criminal conviction for record piracy was overturned on the basis of federal preemption. "The additional element of scienter traditionally necessary to establish a criminal case merely narrows the applicability of the statute. The prohibited act—wrongfully distributing a copyrighted work—remains the same."[r] The Second Circuit in Harper & Row Pub., Inc. v. Nation Enterprises, 723 F.2d 195 (2d Cir.1983), rev'd on other grounds, 471 U.S. 539 (1985), determining equivalency by whether the "right defined by state law may be abridged by an act which, in and of itself, would infringe one of the exclusive rights," held that the plaintiffs' claims for conversion and interference with contractual relations were preempted; the additional element of "intentional interference, not part of a copyright infringement claim, goes merely to the scope of the right; it does not establish qualitatively different conduct on the part of the infringing party, nor a fundamental nonequivalence between the state and federal rights implicated."[s] In

---

[r] The Supreme Court of Illinois in People v. Williams, 235 Ill.2d 178, 920 N.E.2d 446 (2009), drew a distinction between a state criminal statute prohibiting the piracy of sound recordings and a statute requiring labeling that discloses the manufacturer and performers; only the former is preempted by federal copyright law since a labeling requirement is not equivalent to any of the exclusive rights of copyright. California has a statute, Cal. Penal C. § 653aa, that imposes criminal liability on a person who "knowingly electronically disseminates" a commercial recording or audiovisual work to more than ten people without disclosing his or her e-mail address and the title of the work. Can the statute survive preemption?

[s] A claim for intentional interference with contractual relations did escape preemption in Sturdza v. United Arab Emirates, 281 F.3d 1287 (D.C.Cir.2002). The court said that a claim for interference with a plaintiff's contract would be preempted if the interference involved nothing more than the reproduction of a copyrighted work. Here however, the alleged interference included not only the copying of the plaintiff's architectural design by the defendant, but

Rosciszewski v. Arete Associates, Inc., 1 F.3d 225 (4th Cir.1993), a plaintiff brought a civil action under the Virginia Computer Crimes Act (Va.Code Ann. §§ 18.2–152.1 et seq.) against a former employee who made an unauthorized copy of the plaintiff's software. The state statute required proof that the defendant "use[d] a computer," "without authority," "with the intent to * * * [c]onvert the property of another." As applied to the facts, the statutory cause of action was preempted; the court said that the elements of the claim were not qualitatively different from copyright infringement.

The case law on "equivalent" state rights continues to accumulate. Claims involving allegations of passing off or trademark infringement, with their required element of consumer confusion, generally escape preemption, even when the confusion results from the use of a copyrighted work. See, e.g., Donald Frederick Evans & Associates, Inc. v. Continental Homes, Inc., 785 F.2d 897 (11th Cir.1986); John H. Harland Co. v. Clarke Checks, Inc., 207 U.S.P.Q. 664 (N.D.Ga.1980), aff'd, 711 F.2d 966 (11th Cir.1983); Warner Brothers v. ABC, Inc., p. 701 infra. Similarly, protection under state trade secret law is not preempted, at least if there are allegations of a breach of confidence. Compare Gates Rubber Co. v. Bando Chemical Industries, Ltd., 9 F.3d 823 (10th Cir.1993) and Computer Associates Int'l, Inc. v. Altai, Inc., 982 F.2d 693 (2d Cir.1992), with Avco Corp. v. Precision Air Parts, Inc., 210 U.S.P.Q. 894 (M.D.Ala.1980), aff'd, 676 F.2d 494 (11th Cir.), cert. denied, 459 U.S. 1037 (1982). For conversion claims, courts have drawn a distinction between actions seeking redress for deprivations of physical property and those relating to exploitation through reproduction; the latter are preempted. See, e.g., Carson v. Dynegy, Inc., 344 F.3d 446 (5th Cir.2003); Ehat v. Tanner, 780 F.2d 876 (10th Cir.1985), cert. denied, 479 U.S. 820 (1986).

What of claims for unjust enrichment? When the "enrichment" consists of the use of material within the subject matter of copyright, the state cause of action has generally failed. See, e.g., Briarpatch Ltd., L.P. v. Phoenix Pictures, Inc., 373 F.3d 296 (2d Cir.2004), cert. denied, 544 U.S. 949 (2005); Del Madera Properties v. Rhodes and Gardner, Inc., 820 F.2d 973 (9th Cir.1987).

Is the Supreme Court's preemption analysis in *Kewanee* useful in determining when rights are equivalent under § 301?

(3) Unwilling to rely solely on the protection afforded by intellectual property law, creators often seek to impose contractual limitations on the use of their creations. Do claims for breach of contract survive analysis under § 301? For the most part, the courts have said that they do. See, e.g., Acorn Structures, Inc. v. Swantz, 846 F.2d 923 (4th Cir.1988). In ProCD, Inc. v. Zeidenberg, 86 F.3d 1447 (7th Cir.1996), Judge Easterbrook broadly stated that since contracts affect only the parties, they do not create "exclusive rights" and hence are not equivalent to copyright. Equivalency aside, is there anything to the district court's argument in *ProCD* that a contractual restriction on the reproduction of uncopyrightable data contained in a publicly distributed work should be preempted because it "erects a barrier on access to information that under copyright law should be accessible"? 908 F.Supp. 640, 658 (W.D.Wis.1996).

In National Car Rental Sys., Inc. v. Computer Associates Int'l, Inc., 991 F.2d 426 (8th Cir.), cert. denied, 510 U.S. 861 (1993), the Eighth Circuit held

---

also the formation of a competing contract between the defendant and the other contracting party.

that a claim for breach of contract was not preempted under § 301, at least
when the contract created rights that are not equivalent to any of the exclusive
rights of copyright (in that case a restriction on certain uses of the work). Is
this caveat appropriate? The Sixth Circuit too added a caveat to *ProCD*'s blanket preservation of contract rights in Wrench LLC v. Taco Bell Corp., 256 F.3d
446 (6th Cir.2001), cert. denied, 534 U.S. 1114 (2002). Plaintiff sought recovery
on an implied-in-fact contract claiming that the chihuahua used in a Taco Bell
advertising campaign had been based on a cartoon chihuahua that the plaintiff
had pitched to the defendant's executives. The court held that the defendant's
implied promise to pay for the use of the work made the plaintiff's claim qualitatively different from copyright infringement. According to the court, only a
promise "to refrain from reproducing, performing, distributing or displaying the
work" would be preempted; here the promise to pay was a sufficient "extra element" that made the contract claim not equivalent to copyright. However, the
Eleventh Circuit in Lipscher v. LRP Publications Inc., 266 F.3d 1305 (11th
Cir.2001), adopted *ProCD*'s unrestricted preservation of private contract rights.
The same result was reached by the Federal Circuit applying First Circuit law
in Bowers v. Baystate Technologies, Inc., 320 F.3d 1317 (Fed.Cir.), cert. denied,
539 U.S. 928 (2003), holding that the mutual assent necessary for a contract
claim renders it qualitatively different from copyright. D. Wanat, Copyright
Law, Contract Law, and Preemption under § 301(a) of the Copyright Act of
1976, 31 Vt.L.Rev. 707 (2007), argues for an end to the "extra element" approach to contract preemption, replaced by a direct emphasis on preemption
policy.

(4) As the Wrench v. Taco Bell case indicates, claims based on implied-in-
fact contracts have generally escaped preemption. In Montz v. Pilgrim Films &
Television, Inc., 649 F.3d 975 (9th Cir.) (en banc), cert. denied, 132 S.Ct. 550
(2011), p. 788 infra, a plaintiff who had pitched an idea for a television show
alleged breach of an implied-in-fact contract based on an understanding of
payment if the concept was used. The district court held that the claim was
preempted by federal copyright law and a panel of the Ninth Circuit affirmed.
606 F.3d 1153 (9th Cir. 2010). The preemption holding was reversed after a
rehearing en banc. The court began by noting that "the scope of copyright subject matter does not extend to ideas that are not within a fixed medium. * * *
Ideas that are still purely airborne are thus not even within the subject matter
of copyright." However, "ideas and concepts that are fixed in a tangible medium
fall within the scope of copyright * * * and thus satisfy the first prong of the
statutory preemption test, despite the exclusion of fixed ideas from the scope of
actual federal copyright protection." The court then focused on the equivalent
right portion of the preemption test. "To survive preemption, a state cause of
action must assert rights that are qualitatively different from the rights protected by copyright. * * * Contract claims generally survive preemption because
they require proof of such an extra element. * * * The extra element, the implied agreement of payment for use of a concept, is a personal one, between the
parties." (The plaintiff's claim for breach of confidence also survived preemption.) The Second Circuit agreed that implied-in-fact contracts claims are not
preempted in Forest Park Pictures v. Universal Television Network, Inc., 683
F.3d 424 (2d Cir.2012), when several writers claimed that the USA Network
show *Royal Pains* was based on a treatment that they had pitched to the network. They alleged there was an implied promise to pay if the network used
their idea. "In this case, we need not address whether preemption is precluded

whenever there is a contract claim, or only when the contract claim includes a promise to pay."

(5) The drafting history of § 301 attests to the uncertain status of state rights against misappropriation. Is a cause of action for "misappropriation" equivalent to the exclusive rights of reproduction, distribution, or performance? Misappropriation claims seeking redress for the reproduction of works within the subject matter of copyright have generally failed to survive analysis under § 301. See, e.g., Stromback v. New Line Cinema, 384 F.3d 283 (6th Cir.2004) (screenplay); Alcatel USA, Inc. v. DGI Technologies, Inc., 166 F.3d 772 (5th Cir.1999) (computer software); Warner Brothers, Inc. v. ABC (p. 701 infra) (character). Misappropriation claims directed at unauthorized performances have also been unsuccessful. See Orth–O–Vision, Inc. v. Home Box Office, 474 F.Supp. 672 (S.D.N.Y.1979). However, when the claim relates to an appropriation of facts as in INS v. AP, the preemption analysis has proved more difficult.

Barclays Capital Inc. v. Theflyonthewall.com, Inc.

United States Court of Appeals, Second Circuit, 2011.
650 F.3d 876.

■ Before POOLER, SACK, and RAGGI, CIRCUIT JUDGES.

■ SACK, CIRCUIT JUDGE.

The parties, the district court, and amici have raised a wide variety of interesting legal and policy issues during the course of this litigation. We need not address most of them. We conclude that under principles that are well established in this Circuit, the plaintiffs' claim against the defendant for "hot news" misappropriation of the plaintiff financial firms' recommendations to clients and prospective clients as to trading in corporate securities is preempted by federal copyright law. Based upon principles explained and applied in National Basketball Association v. Motorola, Inc., 105 F.3d 841 (2d Cir.1997) (sometimes hereinafter "*NBA*"), we conclude that because the plaintiffs' claim falls within the "general scope" of copyright, 17 U.S.C. § 106, and involves the type of works protected by the Copyright Act, 17 U.S.C. §§ 102 and 103, and because the defendant's acts at issue do not meet the exceptions for a "hot news" misappropriation claim as recognized by *NBA*, the claim is preempted. We therefore reverse the judgment of the district court with respect to that claim.

The plaintiffs-appellees—Barclays Capital Inc. ("Barclays"); Merrill Lynch, Pierce, Fenner & Smith Inc. ("Merrill Lynch"); and Morgan Stanley & Co. Inc. ("Morgan Stanley") (collectively, the "Firms")—are major financial institutions that, among many other things, provide securities brokerage services to members of the public. Largely in that connection, they engage in extensive research about the business and prospects of publicly traded companies, the securities of those companies, and the industries in which those companies are engaged. The results of the research are summarized by the Firms in reports, which customarily contain recommendations as to the wisdom of purchasing, holding, or selling securities of the subject companies. Although the recommendations and the research underlying them in the reports are inextricably related, it is the alleged misappropriation of the recommendations, each typically contained in a single sentence, that is at the heart of the district court's decision and the appeal here. * * *

The defendant-appellant is the proprietor of a news service distributed electronically, for a price, to subscribers. In recent years and by various means, the defendant has obtained information about the Firms' recommendations before the Firms have purposely made them available to the general public and before exchanges for trading in those shares open for the day. Doing so tends to remove the informational and attendant trading advantage of the Firms' clients and prospective clients who are authorized recipients of the reports and recommendations. The recipients of the information are, in turn, less likely to buy or sell the securities using the brokerage services of the reporting and recommending Firms, thereby reducing the incentive for the Firms to create such reports and recommendations in the first place. This, the Firms assert, will destroy their business models and have a severely deleterious impact on their ability to engage in further research and to create further reports and recommendations. * * *

The cornerstone of Fly's offerings is its online newsfeed, which it continually updates between 5:00 a.m. and 7:00 p.m. during days on which the New York Stock Exchange is open. The newsfeed typically streams more than 600 headlines a day in ten different categories, including "hot stocks," "rumors," "technical analysis," and "earnings." One such category is "recommendations." There, Fly posts the recommendations (but not the underlying research reports or supporting analysis) produced by sixty-five investment firms' analysts, including those at the plaintiff Firms. A typical Recommendation headline from 2009, for example, reads "EQIX: Equinox initiated with a Buy at BofA/Merrill. Target $110." [Barclays Capital Inc. v. Theflyonthewall.com., 700 F.Supp.2d. 310, 323.] * * *

According to Fly, over time it has changed the way in which it obtains information about recommendations. Some investment firms, such as Wells Fargo's investment services, will send Fly research reports directly as soon as they are released. Others, including the plaintiff Firms, do not. Until 2005, for recommendations of firms that do not, including the plaintiff Firms, Fly relied on employees at the investment firms (without the firms' authorization) to e-mail the research reports to Fly as they were released. * * *

Fly maintains that because of threats of litigation in 2005, it no longer obtains recommendations directly from such investment firms. Instead, it gathers them using a combination of other news outlets, chat rooms, "blast IMs" sent by people in the investment community to hundreds of recipients, and conversations with traders, money managers, and its other contacts involved in the securities markets. Fly also represents that it no longer publishes excerpts from the research reports themselves, and now disseminates only the Recommendations, typically summarizing only the rating and price target for a particular stock. * * *

In 2004, the Firms identified Fly as one of several entities systematically publishing the Recommendations without the Firms' permission. Others doing the same included larger and better-known news outlets with far broader audiences, such as Bloomberg, Dow Jones, and Thomson Reuters. All of them regularly post short headlines reporting Recommendations soon after they become available. The Firms nonetheless focused their legal actions in this regard on Fly. * * *

Having concluded that the Firms had established the tort of "hot news" misappropriation, the district court entered a permanent injunction barring Fly from reporting a Recommendation until either (a) half an hour after the market opens, if the report containing the recommendation was released before 9:30 a.m., or (b) two hours after release, if the report was released after 9:30 a.m. * * *

We need not address the viability *vel non* of a "hot news" misappropriation tort under New York law. Were we to do so, though, plainly we would be bound by the conclusion of the previous Second Circuit panel in *NBA* that the tort survives. See, e.g., United States v. Jass, 569 F.3d 47, 58 (2d Cir.2009) (explaining the binding nature of one panel opinion on a subsequent panel of the same circuit); Meacham v. Knolls Atomic Power Lab., 461 F.3d 134, 141 (2d Cir.2006) (similar), rev'd on other grounds, 554 U.S. 84 (2008). We are therefore without the authority to "repudiate" that view. * * *

National Basketball Association v. Motorola, Inc., 105 F.3d 841 (2d Cir.1997), appears to be the only judicial decision—surely the only decision binding upon us—that addresses directly the preemption issue raised in this appeal.

There, defendant Motorola, Inc. produced and sold (or otherwise provided) to members of the public a telephonic pager called SportsTrax. Motorola's co-defendant, STATS, Inc., supplied statistical information about National Basketball Association ("NBA") professional basketball games. The information was transmitted to SportsTrax pagers owned or leased by Motorola and STATS customers roughly simultaneously with the playing of the games. *NBA,* 105 F.3d at 843. The information included "(i) the teams playing; (ii) score changes; (iii) the team in possession of the ball; (iv) whether the team is in the free-throw bonus; (v) the quarter of the game; and (vi) time remaining in the quarter." Id. at 844. * * *

SportsTrax gathered the information for the service by employing persons who would watch the games on television or listen to accounts of them on the radio and supply the information to STATS's host computer. The computer compiled, analyzed, and formatted the data for retransmission. The information was then sent to FM radio stations which retransmitted them to the subscribers' individual SportsTrax pagers. Id. * * *

The *NBA* panel observed that "[t]he subject matter requirement"—the second factor in a preemption analysis—"is met when the work of authorship being copied or misappropriated 'falls within the ambit of copyright protection.'" Id. at 849 (quoting Harper & Row, Inc. v. Nation Enters., 723 F.2d 195, 200 (2nd Cir.1983) (brackets omitted), rev'd on other grounds, 471 U.S. 539 (1985)). In deciding whether a state-law claim is preempted by the Copyright Act, then, it is not determinative that the plaintiff seeks redress with respect to a defendant's alleged misappropriation of uncopyrightable material—e.g., facts—contained in a copyrightable work. "Copyrightable material often contains uncopyrightable elements within it, but Section 301 preemption bars state law misappropriation claims with respect to uncopyrightable as well as copyrightable elements," if the work as a whole satisfies the subject matter requirement. *NBA,* 105 F.3d at 849; see also id. at 850 (quoting ProCD, Inc. v. Zeidenberg, 86 F.3d 1447, 1453 (7th Cir.1996)).

* * * The claim of tortious behavior in *NBA* was indeed for the acts of reproduction, distribution, and display of facts by the defendants of material taken from the copyrighted broadcasts. The *NBA* panel therefore concluded that the plaintiff's tort claim was within the general scope of copyright.

The court was thus satisfied that both preemption factors were met. * * *

Having decided that the two preliminary factors counseled in favor of preemption, the *NBA* panel observed:

> [C]ertain forms of commercial misappropriation otherwise within the general scope requirement will survive preemption if an "extra-element" test is met. As stated in *Altai:*
>
>> But if an "extra element" is "required instead of or in addition to the acts of reproduction, performance, distribution or display, in order to constitute a state-created cause of action, then the right does not lie 'within the general scope of copyright,' and there is no preemption."
>
> [Computer Assocs. Int'l, Inc. v. Altai, Inc., 982 F.2d 693, 716 (2d Cir. 1992)] (quoting 1 Melville B. Nimmer & David Nimmer, *Nimmer on Copyright* § 1.01[B] at 1–14–15 (1991)).

NBA, 105 F.3d at 850; * * *. It is with respect to the "extra elements" that the *NBA* Court proffered a three-factor analysis: "We . . . find the extra elements—those in addition to the elements of copyright infringement—that allow a 'hot news' claim to survive preemption are: (i) the time-sensitive value of factual information, (ii) the free-riding by a defendant, *and* (iii) the threat to the very existence of the product or service provided by the plaintiff." Id. at 853 (emphasis added). * * *

The House of Representatives Report with respect to the preemption provisions of the 1976 Copyright Act amendments commented in this regard:

> "Misappropriation" is not necessarily synonymous with copyright infringement, and thus a cause of action labeled as "misappropriation" is not preempted if it is in fact based neither on a right within the general scope of copyright as specified by [17 U.S.C. §] 106 [specifying the general scope of copyright] nor on a right equivalent thereto. For example, state law should have the flexibility to afford a remedy (under traditional principles of equity) against a consistent pattern of unauthorized appropriation by a competitor of the facts (i.e., not the literary expression) constituting "hot" news, whether in the traditional mold of [International News Service v. Associated Press, 248 U.S. 215 (1918)], or in the newer form of data updates from scientific, business, or financial data bases.

H.R. No. 94–1476 at 132, reprinted in 1976 U.S.C.C.A.N. at 5748 (footnote omitted), quoted in *NBA,* 105 F.3d at 850. The House Report thus anticipated that *INS*-like state-law torts would survive preemption. It did not itself create such a cause of action or recognize the existence of one under federal law. It allowed instead for the survival of such a state-law claim.

The *NBA* Court thus used *INS* as a description of the type of claims—"*INS*-like"—that, Congress has said, are not necessarily preempted by federal copyright law. * * *

Before concluding that the NBA's claim was preempted, the *NBA* panel set forth in its opinion—twice—a five-part "test" for identifying a non-preempted "hot news" misappropriation claim. * * *. [T]he panel restated the five-part inquiry later in its opinion:

> In our view, the elements central to an *INS* claim are: (i) the plaintiff generates or collects information at some cost or expense, see

> [Financial Information, Inc. v. Moody's Investors Serv., 808 F.2d 204, 206 (2d Cir.1986) ("*FII*")]; *INS*, 248 U.S. at 240; (ii) the value of the information is highly time-sensitive, see *FII*, 808 F.2d at 209; *INS*, 248 U.S. at 231; Restatement (Third) Unfair Competition, § 38 cmt. c.; (iii) the defendant's use of the information constitutes free-riding on the plaintiff's costly efforts to generate or collect it, see *FII*, 808 F.2d at 207; *INS*, 248 U.S. at 239–40; Restatement § 38 at cmt. c.; *McCarthy*, § 10:73 at 10–139; (iv) the defendant's use of the information is in direct competition with a product or service offered by the plaintiff, *FII*, 808 F.2d at 209, *INS*, 248 U.S. at 240; (v) the ability of other parties to free-ride on the efforts of the plaintiff would so reduce the incentive to produce the product or service that its existence or quality would be substantially threatened, *FII*, 808 F.2d at 209; Restatement, § 38 at cmt. c.; *INS*, 248 U.S. at 241 ("[INS's conduct] would render [AP's] publication profitless, or so little profitable as in effect to cut off the service by rendering the cost prohibitive in comparison with the return.").

NBA, 105 F.3d at 852. * * *

It is axiomatic that appellate judges cannot make law except insofar as they reach a conclusion based on the specific facts and circumstances presented to the court in a particular appeal. Subordinate courts and subsequent appellate panels are required to follow only these previous appellate legal "holdings." The *NBA* panel decided the case before it, and we think that the law it thus made regarding "hot news" preemption is, as we have tried to explain, determinative here. But the Court's various explanations of its five-part approach are not.[32] * * *

Applying the principles of preemption it had identified, the *NBA* Court concluded that the tort claim that the NBA sought to assert against Motorola and STATS was preempted by the Copyright Act because, the "general scope requirement" and the "subject matter requirement" having been satisfied, the "extra elements" necessary for such a claim nonetheless to survive preemption were absent. This was so despite the fact that Motorola and STATS were indeed disseminating, on a timely basis, information about NBA games that the NBA was also circulating. The Court concluded that:

> An indispensable element of an *INS* "hot news" claim is free-riding by a defendant on a plaintiff's product, enabling the defendant to produce a directly competitive product for less money because it has lower costs .... Appellants are in no way free-riding on [the NBA service that provided game statistics to the public]. Motorola and STATS expend their own resources to collect purely factual information generated in NBA games to transmit to [Motorola] pagers. They have their own network and assemble and transmit data themselves.

> To be sure, if appellants in the future were to collect facts from an enhanced [NBA] pager to retransmit them to [Motorola's] pagers, that would constitute free-riding and might well cause [the NBA service] to be unprofitable because it had to bear costs to collect facts that

---

[32] Indeed, rather than identifying a set of required and specific "extra elements" essential to a non-preempted *INS*-like "hot news" claim, the Court in *NBA* was opining about the hypothetical set of circumstances—not present in that case—that might give rise to such a claim. Because the *NBA* Court concluded that no such claim could be established on the facts of that case because of the absence of free-riding, its conjecture was descriptive and a helpful window into its reasoning, but could not bind subsequent courts. * * *

[Motorola] did not. If the appropriation of facts from one pager to another pager service were allowed, transmission of current information on NBA games to pagers or similar devices would be substantially deterred because any potential transmitter would know that the first entrant would quickly encounter a lower cost competitor free-riding on the originator's transmissions.

However, that is not the case in the instant matter. [Motorola] and [the NBA] are each bearing [its] own costs of collecting factual information on NBA games, and, if one produces a product that is cheaper or otherwise superior to the other, that producer will prevail in the marketplace. This is obviously not the situation against which *INS* was intended to prevent: the potential lack of any such product or service because of the anticipation of free-riding.

NBA, 105 F.3d at 854 (footnote omitted). * * *

We conclude that applying *NBA* and copyright preemption principles to the facts of this case, the Firms' claim for "hot news" misappropriation fails because it is preempted by the Copyright Act. First, the Firms' reports culminating with the Recommendations satisfy the "subject matter" requirement because they are all works "of a type covered by section[ ] 102," i.e., "original works of authorship fixed in a[ ] tangible medium of expression." 17 U.S.C. § 102. As discussed above, it is not determinative for the Copyright Act preemption analysis that the facts of the Recommendations themselves are not copyrightable. See *NBA,* 105 F.3d at 850. Second, the reports together with the Recommendations fulfill the "general scope" requirement because the rights "may be abridged by an act which, in and of itself, would infringe one of the exclusive rights provided by federal copyright law," *Altai, Inc.,* 982 F.2d at 716 (citing *Harper & Row,* 723 F.2d at 200), i.e., "acts of reproduction, performance, distribution or display," id. (internal quotation marks omitted).

Third and finally, the Firms' claim is not a so-called *INS*-type non-preempted claim because Fly is not, under *NBA*'s analysis, "free-riding." It is collecting, collating and disseminating factual information—the *facts* that Firms and others in the securities business have made recommendations with respect to the value of and the wisdom of purchasing or selling securities—and attributing the information to its source. The Firms are making the news; Fly, despite the Firms' understandable desire to protect their business model, is breaking it * * *

The practice of what *NBA* referred to as "free-riding" was further described by *INS*. The *INS* Court defined the "hot news" tort in part as "taking material that has been acquired by complainant as the result of organization and the expenditure of labor, skill, and money, and which is salable by complainant for money, and . . . appropriating it and selling it as [the defendant's] own . . . . " *INS,* 248 U.S. at 239. That definition fits the facts of *INS:* The defendant was taking news gathered and in the process of dissemination by the Associated Press and selling that news as though the defendant itself had gathered it. But it does not describe the practices of Fly. The Firms here may be "acquiring material" in the course of preparing their reports, but that is not the focus of this lawsuit. In pressing a "hot news" claim against Fly, the Firms seek only to protect their Recommendations, something they *create* using their expertise and experience rather than *acquire* through efforts akin to reporting. * * *

We do not perceive a meaningful difference between (a) Fly's taking material that a Firm has *created* (not "acquired") as the result of organization and the expenditure of labor, skill, and money, and which is (presumably) salable by a Firm for money, and selling it *by ascribing the material to its creator Firm* and author (not selling it as Fly's own), and (b) what appears to be unexceptional and easily recognized behavior by members of the traditional news media—to report on, say, winners of Tony Awards or, indeed, scores of NBA games with proper attribution of the material to its creator. *INS* did not purport to address either.

It is also noteworthy, if not determinative, that *INS* referred to INS's tortious behavior as "amount[ing] to an unauthorized interference with the normal operation of complainant's legitimate business *precisely at the point where the profit is to be reaped,* in order to *divert a material portion of the profit* from those who have earned it to those who have not . . . ." Id. at 240 (emphases added). As we have seen, the point at which the Firms principally reap their profit is upon the execution of sales or purchases of securities. It is at least arguable that Fly's interference with the "normal operation" of the Firms' business is indeed at a "point" where the Firms' profits are reaped. But it is not at all clear that *that* profit is being in any substantial sense "diverted" to Fly by its publication of Recommendations news. The lost commissions are, we would think, diverted to whatever broker happens to execute a trade placed by the recipient of news of the Recommendation from Fly. * * *

By way of comparison, we might, as the *NBA* Court did, see id., 105 F.3d at 854, speculate about a product a Firm *might* produce which *might* indeed give rise to an non-preempted "hot-news" misappropriation claim. If a Firm were to collect and disseminate to some portion of the public facts about securities recommendations in the brokerage industry (including, perhaps, such facts it generated itself—its own Recommendations), and were Fly to copy the facts contained in the Firm's hypothetical service, it might be liable to the Firm on a "hot-news" misappropriation theory. That would appear to be an *INS*-type claim and might survive preemption. * * *

We conclude that in this case, a Firm's ability to make news—by issuing a Recommendation that is likely to affect the market price of a security—does not give rise to a right for it to control who breaks that news and how. We therefore reverse the judgment of the district court to that extent and remand with instructions to dismiss the Firms' misappropriation claim.

■ RAGGI, CIRCUIT JUDGE, concurring:

I join the court in reversing the judgment in favor of the Firms on their state law claims of "hot news" misappropriation on the ground that such claims are preempted by federal copyright law. See 17 U.S.C. § 301. Unlike my colleagues in the majority, I do not reject the five-part test enunciated in National Basketball Association v. Motorola, Inc., 105 F.3d 841 (2d Cir.1997) ("*NBA*"), to reach this result. Whatever reservations I may have about that test as a means for identifying non-preempted "hot news" claims, I do not think it can be dismissed as *dictum.* Accordingly, I write separately to explain why I conclude that the Firms failed to satisfy the "direct competition" requirement of *NBA*'s test. * * *

In *NBA,* this court applied the "extra element" test to determine "the extent to which a 'hot news' misappropriation claim," originally identified by the Supreme Court in *INS* prior to the Copyright Act of 1976, avoided

§ 301 preemption. See 105 F.3d at 850–51. In concluding that "some form" of "hot news" claim was not preempted, *NBA* relied first on a House Report to the 1976 Act stating that " 'state law should have the flexibility to afford a remedy . . . against a consistent pattern of unauthorized appropriation by a competitor of the facts (i.e., not the literary expression) constituting "hot" news, whether in the traditional mold' " of *INS* " 'or in the newer form of data updates from scientific, business, or financial data bases.' " Id. at 850 (quoting H.R.Rep. No. 94–1476, at 132, 1976 U.S.C.C.A.N. 5659, 5748 (1976)); see id. (citing Financial Info., Inc. v. Moody's Investors Serv., Inc., 808 F.2d at 209 (relying on House Report in noting that "hot news" claims not preempted)).

Although this legislative history is some evidence that Congress did not intend federal copyright law to preempt all "hot news" claims, the scope of that intent is not easily discerned. The House Report references an *earlier* version of the 1976 Act containing examples of non-preempted actions, including "rights against misappropriation not equivalent to" the exclusive § 106 rights, "breaches of contract, breaches of trust . . . and deceptive trade practices such as passing off and false representation." H.R.Rep. No. 94– 1476, at 24, 1976 U.S.C.C.A.N. 5659, 5748; see also [5 William F. Patry, *Patry on Copyright*] § 18:8, at 18–21 to 18–27. After the Justice Department raised concerns about the identification of misappropriation as a non-preempted action, Congress chose to omit the entire list from the final bill. See 5 Patry, supra, § 18:8, at 18–27 to 18–31 (discussing confusing colloquy between House Judiciary Committee members regarding deletion of list). Thus, it is not clear what weight the Report excerpt quoted in *NBA* can bear in any assessment of whether a particular "hot news" claim survives federal copyright preemption. See generally Architectronics, Inc. v. Control Sys., Inc., 935 F.Supp. 425, 440–41 (S.D.N.Y.1996) (declining to rely on § 301's "puzzling and unreliable" legislative history); * * *

NBA next identified five factors central to a non-preempted "*INS*-like" claim: (1) the plaintiff incurred costs to generate or gather information (2) that is time-sensitive and (3) used by the defendant in a manner constituting free-riding (4) in direct competition with plaintiff's product when (5) the ability of parties to free-ride so reduces the incentive to produce the product that its existence or quality is substantially threatened. 105 F.3d at 852. I share the concern expressed by some courts and commentators as to whether these "extra elements" *qualitatively* differentiate a "hot news" tort from a claim of unauthorized copying or distribution, activities violating rights equivalent to those within the general scope of § 106. See 5 Patry, supra, § 18:40, at 18–139 to 18–141 (questioning whether *NBA*'s factors are sufficient to avoid preemption). "Free riding" in this context appears synonymous with proscribed copying. See id. § 18:40, at 18–140 ("[C]opying information someone else generated . . . can always be characterized as free riding . . . . "); Lowry's Reports, Inc. v. Legg Mason, Inc., 271 F.Supp.2d 737, 756 (D.Md.2003) (noting that free riding "may be a pejorative description of copying, but it is still copying" (internal quotation marks omitted)). Although the other four *NBA* factors may narrow the tort's scope to egregious instances of "free riding" factually similar to *INS*, they do not appear to alter the nature of the claim. See Lowry's Reports, Inc. v. Legg Mason, Inc., 271 F.Supp.2d at 756 (noting that "cost," "time sensitivity," and "direct competition . . . merely define pre-existing conditions" while "threat" to plaintiff's business "merely identifies a consequence of" free riding). Accordingly, I share some of the majority's doubt regarding the viability of *NBA*'s test, but for a different reason. I question whether the test adequately identifies tort claims with "extra elements" qualitatively different from the rights protected by copyright. * * *

In concluding that the Firms failed to establish a non-preempted "hot news" claim under the test identified in *NBA,* I rely on facts emphasized by the majority, namely, that Fly produces an aggregate product reporting many Firms' Recommendations among other financial news, and attributing each Recommendation to its source, while the Firms each disseminate only their own Recommendations to clients who engage in a particular level of trading with the Firms. See ante at 901–06. The majority, however, uses these facts to draw a bright line distinguishing between the Firms, who generate news, and Fly and other news aggregators, who "break" the news, with the former falling outside of hot-news protection. See ante at 902. I am not convinced that this distinction is determinative here because the Firms appear to play both roles. Not only do they generate their Recommendations, they then disseminate them, recouping the cost of generation through trading revenue. I am not prepared to foreclose the possibility of a "hot news" claim by a party who disseminates news it happens to create. I conclude simply that the facts emphasized by the majority preclude the Firms from stating a non-preempted "hot news" claim for a different reason derived from *NBA*: the Firms' product and Fly's newsfeed do not *directly* compete. * * *

NOTES AND QUESTIONS

(1) Is Judge Raggi's concurrence correct in cautioning against reliance on comments in the House Report preserving the *INS* tort that were written before Congress deleted the language preserving rights against misappropriation from § 301 of the copyright revision bill? *Barclays* and the preemption of state misappropriation law are analyzed in R. Denicola, News on the Internet, 23 Fordham Intell.Prop., Media & Ent.L.J. 68 (2012).

(2) The preemption issue is analyzed in H. Abrams, Copyright, Misappropriation, and Preemption: Constitutional and Statutory Limits of State Law Protection, 1983 Sup.Ct.Rev. 509 (1984). After a comprehensive survey of the case law, J. Bauer, Addressing the Incoherency of the Preemption Provisions of the Copyright Act of 1976, 10 Vand.J.Ent. & Tech.L. 1 (2007), advocates a broad interpretation of § 301.

PREEMPTION BEYOND § 301

(1) Does the preemptive effect of the 1976 Copyright Act extend beyond § 301? What of state laws that may undermine rights granted by the Act to owners or users; if any such law "stands as an obstacle to the accomplishment and execution of the full purposes and objectives of Congress," Hines v. Davidowitz, 312 U.S. 52, 67 (1941), would it not be preempted under the supremacy clause? For example, some states have tried to regulate the manner in which motion picture distributors license their films to theaters. Is this an impermissible interference with federal copyright policy? In Orson, Inc. v. Miramax Film Corp., 189 F.3d 377 (3d Cir.1999), cert. denied, 529 U.S. 1012 (2000), the Third Circuit *en banc* ruled that a Pennsylvania statute that prohibited movie distributors from granting exclusive first-run licenses lasting more than forty-two days was preempted by federal copyright law. "[W]e hold that because section 203–7 of the Pennsylvania Feature Motion Picture Fair Business Practices Law 'stands as an obstacle' to

the federally created exclusive rights given to a copyright holder, namely, the exclusive right to distribute the copyrighted work, it is preempted by the federal Copyright Act." Enforcement of a New York statute requiring performing rights organizations like ASCAP to notify proprietors within 72 hours after commencing an investigation of unauthorized performances was enjoined in ASCAP v. Pataki, 930 F.Supp. 873 (S.D.N.Y.1996); the court said the statute was preempted under the supremacy clause as "an obstacle to the enforcement of the federal copyright statute."

In Rano v. Sipa Press, Inc., 987 F.2d 580 (9th Cir.1993), the Ninth Circuit reached the surprising conclusion that a California rule permitting at will termination of contracts that do not specify a particular duration was preempted when applied to copyright licenses; the court thought that the rule was in conflict with § 203 of the Copyright Act, which permits termination of copyright licenses after 35 years. Is it? The Seventh Circuit in Walthal v. Rusk, 172 F.3d 481 (7th Cir.1999), specifically rejected *Rano* and held that § 203's 35–year time period set a maximum but not a minimum duration for licenses, and thus an Illinois rule allowing at will termination of contracts without a specific duration did not conflict with federal copyright policy. The Eleventh Circuit agreed with *Walthal* in Korman v. HBC Florida, Inc., 182 F.3d 1291 (11th Cir.1999).

When New York passed a statute requiring the public filing of questions and answers used on standardized tests within 30 days after the release of the tests results, the law was challenged by the owner of the copyright in the MCAT test used in medical school admissions. The plaintiff argued that the statute was in conflict with its exclusive rights under § 106 to publish, copy, and distribute the test; it also argued that the statute facilitated infringement of its copyright. The district court granted summary judgment against New York. On appeal, the Second Circuit in Association of American Medical Colleges v. Cuomo, 928 F.2d 519 (2d Cir.), cert. denied, 502 U.S. 862 (1991), said that if the statute facilitated infringement, it would be preempted, but the court remanded the case for further consideration of New York's argument that the statute merely facilitated "fair uses."

(2) If contract rights generally survive § 301 as not equivalent to copyright, might some contracts nevertheless interfere with federal copyright policy and thus fail under the supremacy clause? Does enforcement of the buyer's promise in *ProCD* not to make commercial use of the uncopyrightable data in the plaintiff's directory interfere with the balance drawn by Congress in the Copyright Act? Would the court in *ProCD* uphold a shrink-wrap license accompanying a biography that required purchasers to promise that they would not use any of the facts in a competing book?[t]

In Bowers v. Baystate Technologies, 320 F.3d 1317 (Fed.Cir.), cert. denied, 539 U.S. 928 (2003), the Federal Circuit was faced with a contractual provision forbidding the reverse engineering of software. Although the court had earlier ruled in Atari Games Corp. v. Nintendo (p. 257 supra) that such reverse engineering could be a fair use, it applied First Circuit law to uphold a claim for breach of contract. "[C]ase law

---

[t] The Maryland Bar Association apparently included a shrink-wrap contract within the plastic covering of its annual directory of lawyers. The contract prohibited loaning or reselling the book. Business Week, Dec. 9, 2002, p. 8. Assuming that shrink-wrap contracts are otherwise enforceable under Maryland contract law, would a claim for breach against a member of the bar who gave the book to a compiler of mailing lists be preempted in light of copyright's first sale doctrine?

indicates the First Circuit would find that private parties are free to contractually forego the limited ability to reverse engineer a software product under the exemptions of the Copyright Act." The court also held that the contract claim did not conflict with the exemption from the anti-circumvention rules for the reverse engineering of software in § 1201(f).[u] Judge Dyk in dissent argued that the majority's approach "permits state law to eviscerate an important federal copyright policy reflected in the fair use defense." "If state law provided that a copyright holder could bar fair use of the copyrighted material by placing a black dot on each copy of the work offered for sale, there would be no question but that the state law would be preempted," citing Bonito Boats v. Thunder Craft, p. 624 supra. Although agreeing with the majority that state law could permit parties to contract away a fair use defense in a "freely negotiated" agreement, Judge Dyk thought that shrink-wrap contracts were different. "However, state law giving effect to shrinkwrap licenses is no different in substance from a hypothetical black dot law. Like any other contract of adhesion, the only choice offered to the purchaser is to avoid making the purchase in the first place. * * * State law thus gives the copyright holder the ability to eliminate the fair use defense in each and every instance at its option." In Vault Corp. v. Quaid Software Ltd., 847 F.2d 255 (5th Cir.1988), the court said that a Louisiana statute permitting software manufacturers to restrict copying and modification by buyers through "shrink wrap" licenses was in conflict with the rights granted users under § 117 and hence preempted.

(3) The move to online dissemination of copyrighted works (backed by the anti-circumvention rules in § 1201) increases the opportunities for owners to impose contractual restrictions on users through click-on licenses and similar mechanisms. That has worried a number of scholars. M. Madison, Legal–Ware: Contract and Copyright in the Digital Age, 67 Fordham L.Rev. 1025 (1998), is concerned that cases validating contractual restrictions on use will marginalize public policy; W. Fisher, Property and Contract on the Internet, 73 Chi.-Kent L.Rev. 1203 (1998), tries to define the appropriate boundaries of private authority to alter copyright doctrine through contract; worried that routine validation of standard form licenses will threaten the balance between incentive and competition, J. Reichman and J. Franklin, Privately Legislated Intellectual Property Rights: Reconciling Freedom of Contract with the Public Good Uses of Information, 147 U.Penn.L.Rev. 875 (1999), proposes new doctrinal tools to limit the adverse effects of mass-market licensing.

Preserving fair use is a particular concern. C. McManis, The Privatization (or "Shrink–Wrapping") of American Copyright Law, 87 Calif.L.Rev. 173 (1999), urges limits on mass-market licenses that circumvent privileges such as fair use; V. Moffat, Super–Copyright: Contracts, Preemption, and the Structure of Copyright Policymaking, 41 U.C. Davis L.Rev. 45 (2007), forcefully argues that enforcement of adhesion contracts restricting fair use should be preempted; T. Bell, Codifying Copyright's Misuse Defense, 2007 Utah L.Rev. 573, proposes a statutory bar to copyright infringement actions by parties who contractually limit fair use; and C. Bohannan, Copyright Preemption of Contracts, 67 Md.L.Rev. 616 (2008), suggests a preemption analysis based on the principles governing waivers of statutory rights, dis-

---

[u]   The Eighth Circuit in Davidson & Associates v. Jung, 422 F.3d 630 (8th Cir.2005), agreed with *Bowers* and held that enforcement of an end-user license restricting reverse engineering was not preempted by § 1201(f).

tinguishing waivable rights that protect individual users from non-waivable rights like fair use that protect the public interest.

CHAPTER 8

APPLICATIONS OF UNFAIR COMPETITION

1. IMITATION OF DESIGN AND APPEARANCE

To what extent can the state and federal law of unfair competition be enlisted as a complement to copyright in the protection of artistic and literary works? The Second Circuit some 35 years before *Sears* and *Compco*, in a notable opinion by Judge Learned Hand, had declared a broad privilege to copy matter left unprotected by federal copyright.

Cheney Brothers v. Doris Silk Corp.

35 F.2d 279 (2d Cir.1929), cert. denied, 281 U.S. 728 (1930).

The plaintiff manufactured silks; most of the designs had a short seasonal life. Design patents were not practically obtainable on the many patterns put out each year, and copyright was not then available for textile designs. A bill in equity was brought against a copier.

"The plaintiff asks for protection only during the season, and needs no more, for the designs are all ephemeral. It seeks in this way to disguise the extent of the proposed innovation, and to persuade us that, if we interfere only a little, the solecism, if there be one, may be pardonable. But the reasoning which would justify any interposition at all demands that it cover the whole extent of the injury. A man whose designs come to harvest in two years, or in five, has prima facie as good right to protection as one who deals only in annuals. Nor could we consistently stop at designs; processes, machines, and secrets have an equal claim. The upshot must be that, whenever any one has contrived any of these, others may be forbidden to copy it. This is not the law. In the absence of some recognized right at common law, or under the statutes—and the plaintiff claims neither—a man's property is limited to the chattels which embody his invention. * * *

"Of the cases on which the plaintiff relies, the chief is International News Service v. Associated Press, 248 U.S. 215. Although that concerned another subject-matter—printed news dispatches—we agree that, if it meant to lay down a general doctrine, it would cover this case; at least, the language of the majority opinion goes so far. We do not believe that it did. While it is of course true that law ordinarily speaks in general terms, there are cases where the occasion is at once the justification for, and the limit of, what is decided. This appears to us such an instance; we think that no more was covered than situations substantially similar to those then at bar. The difficulties of understanding it otherwise are insuperable. We are to suppose that the court meant to create a sort of common-law patent or copyright for reasons of justice. Either would flagrantly conflict with the scheme which Congress has for more than a century devised to cover the subject-matter.

"Qua patent, we should at least have to decide, as tabula rasa, whether the design or machine was new and required invention; further, we must ignore the Patent Office whose action has always been a condition upon the creation of this kind of property. Qua copyright, although it would be simpler to decide upon the merits, we should equally be obliged to dispense with the conditions imposed upon the creation of the right. Nor, if we went so far, should we know whether the property so recognized should be limited to the periods prescribed in the statutes, or should extend as long as the author's grievance. It appears to us incredible that the Supreme Court should have had in mind any such consequences. To exclude others from the enjoyment of a chattel is one thing; to prevent any imitation of it, to set up a monopoly in the plan of its structure, gives the author a power over his fellows vastly greater, a power which the Constitution allows only Congress to create. * * *

"True, it would seem as though the plaintiff had suffered a grievance for which there should be a remedy, perhaps by an amendment of the Copyright Law, assuming that this does not already cover the case, which is not urged here. It seems a lame answer in such a case to turn the injured party out of court, but there are larger issues at stake than his redress. Judges have only a limited power to amend the law; when the subject has been confided to a Legislature, they must stand aside, even though there be an hiatus in completed justice. An omission in such cases must be taken to have been as deliberate as though it were express, certainly after long-standing action on the subject-matter. Indeed, we are not in any position to pass upon the questions involved, as Brandeis, J., observed in International News Service v. Associated Press. We must judge upon records prepared by litigants, which do not contain all that may be relevant to the issues, for they cannot disclose the conditions of this industry, or of the others which may be involved. Congress might see its way to create some sort of temporary right, or it might not. Its decision would certainly be preceded by some examination of the result upon the other interests affected. Whether these would prove paramount we have no means of saying; it is not for us to decide. Our vision is inevitably contracted, and the whole horizon may contain much which will compose a very different picture.

"The order is affirmed, and, as the bill cannot in any event succeed, it may be dismissed, if the defendant so desires."

NOTES

(1) Copyright in textile designs became secure after Mazer v. Stein, p. 124 supra, but Judge Hand's views on the freedom to copy absent a copyright or patent still resonate in the wake of the Supreme Court's decision in *Bonito Boats,* p. 624 supra. On the issues raised in this section, see generally R. Brown, Design Protection: An Overview, 34 UCLA L.Rev. 1341 (1987).

(2) As we have seen, a state unfair competition claim based solely on the copying of a work within the subject matter of copyright is preempted by § 301. For works outside the scope of copyright, the supremacy clause analysis in *Sears* and *Compco*, as interpreted in *Bonito Boats*, still controls. However, both constrain only state law; § 43(a) of the federal Lanham Act has now become a substantial adjunct to copyright.

Wal–Mart Stores, Inc. v. Samara Brothers, Inc.

Supreme Court of the United States, 2000.
529 U.S. 205, 120 S.Ct. 1339.

■ JUSTICE SCALIA delivered the opinion of the Court.

In this case, we decide under what circumstances a product's design is distinctive, and therefore protectible, in an action for infringement of unregistered trade dress under § 43(a) of the Trademark Act of 1946 (Lanham Act), 60 Stat. 441, as amended, 15 U.S.C. § 1125(a).

I

Respondent Samara Brothers, Inc., designs and manufactures children's clothing. Its primary product is a line of spring/summer one-piece seersucker outfits decorated with appliques of hearts, flowers, fruits, and the like. A number of chain stores, including JCPenney, sell this line of clothing under contract with Samara.

Petitioner Wal–Mart Stores, Inc., is one of the nation's best known retailers, selling among other things children's clothing. In 1995, Wal–Mart contracted with one of its suppliers, Judy–Philippine, Inc., to manufacture a line of children's outfits for sale in the 1996 spring/summer season. Wal–Mart sent Judy–Philippine photographs of a number of garments from Samara's line, on which Judy–Philippine's garments were to be based; Judy–Philippine duly copied, with only minor modifications, 16 of Samara's garments, many of which contained copyrighted elements. In 1996, Wal–Mart briskly sold the so-called knockoffs, generating more than $1.15 million in gross profits.

In June 1996, a buyer for JCPenney called a representative at Samara to complain that she had seen Samara garments on sale at Wal–Mart for a lower price than JCPenney was allowed to charge under its contract with Samara. The Samara representative told the buyer that Samara did not supply its clothing to Wal–Mart. Their suspicions aroused, however, Samara officials launched an investigation, which disclosed that Wal–Mart and several other major retailers—Kmart, Caldor, Hills, and Goody's—were selling the knockoffs of Samara's outfits produced by Judy–Philippine.

After sending cease-and-desist letters, Samara brought this action in the United States District Court for the Southern District of New York against Wal–Mart, Judy–Philippine, Kmart, Caldor, Hills, and Goody's for copyright infringement under federal law, consumer fraud and unfair competition under New York law, and—most relevant for our purposes—infringement of unregistered trade dress under § 43(a) of the Lanham Act, 15 U.S.C. § 1125(a). All of the defendants except Wal–Mart settled before trial.

After a weeklong trial, the jury found in favor of Samara on all of its claims. Wal–Mart then renewed a motion for judgment as a matter of law, claiming, *inter alia*, that there was insufficient evidence to support a conclusion that Samara's clothing designs could be legally protected as distinctive trade dress for purposes of § 43(a). The District Court denied the motion, 969 F.Supp. 895 (S.D.N.Y.1997), and awarded Samara damages, interest, costs, and fees totaling almost $1.6 million, together with injunctive relief, see App. to Pet. for Cert. 56–58. The Second Circuit affirmed the denial of the motion for judgment as a matter of law, 165 F.3d 120 (1998), and we granted certiorari, 528 U.S. 808 (1999).

II

* * * In addition to protecting registered marks, the Lanham Act, in § 43(a), gives a producer a cause of action for the use by any person of "any word, term, name, symbol, or device, or any combination thereof . . . which . . . is likely to cause confusion . . . as to the origin, sponsorship, or approval of his or her goods . . . ." 15 U.S.C. § 1125(a). It is the latter provision that is at issue in this case.

The breadth of the definition of marks registrable under § 2, and of the confusion-producing elements recited as actionable by § 43(a), has been held to embrace not just word marks, such as "Nike," and symbol marks, such as Nike's "swoosh" symbol, but also "trade dress"—a category that originally included only the packaging, or "dressing," of a product, but in recent years has been expanded by many courts of appeals to encompass the design of a product. * * *

The text of § 43(a) provides little guidance as to the circumstances under which unregistered trade dress may be protected. It does require that a producer show that the allegedly infringing feature is not "functional," see § 43(a)(3), and is likely to cause confusion with the product for which protection is sought, see § 43(a)(1)(A), 15 U.S.C. § 1125(a)(1)(A). Nothing in § 43(a) explicitly requires a producer to show that its trade dress is distinctive, but courts have universally imposed that requirement, since without distinctiveness the trade dress would not "cause confusion . . . as to the origin, sponsorship, or approval of [the] goods," as the section requires. Distinctiveness is, moreover, an explicit prerequisite for registration of trade dress under § 2, and "the general principles qualifying a mark for registration under § 2 of the Lanham Act are for the most part applicable in determining whether an unregistered mark is entitled to protection under § 43(a)." Two Pesos, Inc. v. Taco Cabana, Inc., 505 U.S. 763, 768 (1992) (citations omitted).

In evaluating the distinctiveness of a mark under § 2 (and therefore, by analogy, under § 43(a)), courts have held that a mark can be distinctive in one of two ways. First, a mark is inherently distinctive if "[its] intrinsic nature serves to identify a particular source." Ibid. In the context of word marks, courts have applied the now-classic test originally formulated by Judge Friendly, in which word marks that are "arbitrary" ("Camel" cigarettes), "fanciful" ("Kodak" film), or "suggestive" ("Tide" laundry detergent) are held to be inherently distinctive. See Abercrombie & Fitch Co. v. Hunting World, Inc., 537 F.2d 4, 10–11 (C.A.2 1976). Second, a mark has acquired distinctiveness, even if it is not inherently distinctive, if it has developed secondary meaning, which occurs when, "in the minds of the public, the primary significance of a [mark] is to identify the source of the product rather than the product itself." Inwood Laboratories, Inc. v. Ives Laboratories, Inc., 456 U.S. 844, 851, n. 11 (1982).

The judicial differentiation between marks that are inherently distinctive and those that have developed secondary meaning has solid foundation in the statute itself. Section 2 requires that registration be granted to any trademark "by which the goods of the applicant may be distinguished from the goods of others"—subject to various limited exceptions. 15 U.S.C. § 1052. It also provides, again with limited exceptions, that "nothing in this chapter shall prevent the registration of a mark used by the applicant which has become distinctive of the applicant's goods in commerce"—that is, which is not inherently distinctive but has become so only through secondary meaning. § 2(f), 15 U.S.C. § 1052(f). Nothing in § 2, however, demands the conclusion that *every* category of mark necessarily includes some marks "by which the goods of the applicant may be distinguished from the goods of others" *without* secondary meaning—that in every category some marks are inherently distinctive.

Indeed, with respect to at least one category of mark—colors—we have held that no mark can ever be inherently distinctive. See [Qualitex Co. v. Jacobson Products Co., 514 U.S. 159, 162–163 (1995)]. In *Qualitex*, petitioner manufactured and sold green-gold dry-cleaning press pads. After respondent began selling pads of a similar color, petitioner brought suit under § 43(a), then added a claim under § 32 after obtaining registration for the color of its pads. We held that a color could be protected as a trademark, but only upon a showing of secondary meaning. * * *

It seems to us that design, like color, is not inherently distinctive. The attribution of inherent distinctiveness to certain categories of word marks and product packaging derives from the fact that the very purpose of attaching a particular word to a product, or encasing it in a distinctive packaging, is most often to identify the source of the product. Although the words and packaging can serve subsidiary functions—a suggestive word mark (such as "Tide" for laundry detergent), for instance, may invoke positive connotations in the consumer's mind, and a garish form of packaging (such as Tide's squat, brightly decorated plastic bottles for its liquid laundry detergent) may attract an otherwise indifferent consumer's attention on a crowded store shelf—their predominant function remains source identification. Consumers are therefore predisposed to regard those symbols as indication of the producer, which is why such symbols "almost *automatically* tell a customer that they refer to a brand," id., at 162–163, and "immediately . . . signal a brand or a product 'source,'" id., at 163. And where it is not reasonable to assume consumer predisposition to take an affixed word or packaging as indication of source—where, for example, the affixed word is descriptive of the product ("Tasty" bread) or of a geographic origin ("Georgia" peaches)—inherent distinctiveness will not be found. That is why the statute generally excludes, from those word marks that can be registered as inherently distinctive, words that are "merely descriptive" of the goods, § 2(e)(1), 15 U.S.C. § 1052(e)(1), or "primarily geographically descriptive of them," see § 2(e)(2), 15 U.S.C. § 1052(e)(2). In the case of product design, as in the case of color, we think consumer predisposition to equate the feature with the source does not exist. Consumers are aware of the reality that, almost invariably, even the most unusual of product designs—such as a cocktail shaker shaped like a penguin—is intended not to identify the source, but to render the product itself more useful or more appealing.

The fact that product design almost invariably serves purposes other than source identification not only renders inherent distinctiveness problematic; it also renders application of an inherent-distinctiveness principle more harmful to other consumer interests. Consumers should not be deprived of the benefits of competition with regard to the utilitarian and esthetic purposes that product design ordinarily serves by a rule of law that facilitates plausible threats of suit against new entrants based upon alleged inherent distinctiveness. How easy it is to mount a plausible suit depends, of course, upon the clarity of the test for inherent distinctiveness, and where product design is concerned we have little confidence that a reasonably clear test can be devised. Respondent and the United States as *amicus curiae* urge us to adopt for product design relevant portions of the test formulated by the Court of Customs and Patent Appeals for product packaging in Seabrook Foods, Inc. v. Bar–Well Foods, Ltd., 568 F.2d 1342 (1977). That opinion, in determining the inherent distinctiveness of a product's packaging, considered, among other things, "whether it was a 'common' basic shape or design, whether it was unique or unusual in a particular field, [and] whether it was a mere refinement of a commonly-adopted and well-known form of ornamentation for a particular class of goods viewed by the public as a dress or ornamentation for the goods." Id., at 1344 (footnotes omitted). Such a test would rarely provide the basis for summary disposition of an anticompetitive strike suit. Indeed, at oral argument, counsel for the United States quite understandably would not give a definitive answer as to whether the test was met in this very case, saying only that "[t]his is a very difficult case for that purpose." Tr. of Oral Arg. 19.

It is true, of course, that the person seeking to exclude new entrants would have to establish the nonfunctionality of the design feature, see § 43(a)(3), 15 U.S.C.A. § 1125(a)(3) (Oct.1999 Supp.)—a showing that may involve consideration of its esthetic appeal, see *Qualitex*, 514 U.S., at 170. Competition is deterred, however, not merely by successful suit but by the plausible threat of successful suit, and given the unlikelihood of inherently source-identifying design, the game of allowing suit based upon alleged inherent distinctiveness seems to us not worth the candle. That is especially so since the producer can ordinarily obtain protection for a design that is inherently source identifying (if any such exists), but that does not yet have secondary meaning, by securing a design patent or a copyright for the design—as, indeed, respondent did for certain elements of the designs in this case. The availability of these other protections greatly reduces any harm to the producer that might ensue from our conclusion that a product design cannot be protected under § 43(a) without a showing of secondary meaning.

Respondent contends that our decision in *Two Pesos* forecloses a conclusion that product-design trade dress can never be inherently distinctive. In that case, we held that the trade dress of a chain of Mexican restaurants, which the plaintiff described as "a festive eating atmosphere having interior dining and patio areas decorated with artifacts, bright colors, paintings and murals," 505 U.S., at 765 (internal quotation marks and citation omitted), could be protected under § 43(a) without a showing of secondary meaning, see id., at 776. *Two Pesos* unquestionably establishes the legal principle that trade dress can be inherently distinctive, see, e.g., id., at 773, but it does not establish that *product-design* trade dress can be. *Two Pesos* is inapposite to our holding here because the trade dress at issue, the decor of a restaurant, seems to us not to constitute product *design*. It was either product packaging—which, as we have discussed, normally *is* taken by the consumer to indicate origin—or else some *tertium quid* that is akin to product packaging and has no bearing on the present case.

Respondent replies that this manner of distinguishing *Two Pesos* will force courts to draw difficult lines between product-design and product-packaging trade dress. There will indeed be some hard cases at the margin: a classic glass Coca–Cola bottle, for instance, may constitute packaging for those consumers who drink the Coke and then discard the bottle, but may constitute the product itself for those consumers who are bottle collectors, or part of the product itself for those consumers who buy Coke in the classic glass bottle, rather than a can, because they think it more stylish to drink from the former. We believe, however, that the frequency and the difficulty of having to distinguish between product design and product packaging will be much less than the frequency and the difficulty of having to decide when a product design is inherently distinctive. To the extent there are close cases, we believe that courts should err on the side of caution and classify ambiguous trade dress as product design, thereby requiring secondary meaning. The very closeness will suggest the existence of relatively small utility in adopting an inherent-distinctiveness principle, and relatively great consumer benefit in requiring a demonstration of secondary meaning.

Classify ambiguous trade dress as product design

* * *

We hold that, in an action for infringement of unregistered trade dress under § 43(a) of the Lanham Act, a product's design is distinctive, and therefore protectible, only upon a showing of secondary meaning. The judgment of the Second Circuit is reversed, and the case is remanded for further proceedings consistent with this opinion.

It is so ordered.

NOTES AND QUESTIONS

(1) Plaintiff Roulo designed a line of greeting cards. Roulo's cards were "beige, single-face (no fold) cards containing sentimental verses and frequently using ellipses written in Roulo's handwriting with brown ink. * * * Flanking the message on the left and right borders are a series of four stripes, two silver foil stripes enveloping one brown and one colored stripe in the middle." Defendant Berrie, a former distributor of Roulo's cards, produced a line of cards designed for similar occasions "employing like, although not identical verses." "The [defendant's] cards are identically sized and priced, single-face cards on cream paper with cursive written messages in brown ink. The cards combine two stripes of color on the left side and one colored stripe on the right side, none of which are in foil. A colored butterfly is superimposed on the left stripes." How could the plaintiff go about proving that the design of her cards has acquired "secondary meaning" and is thus protectable as a trademark in an action under § 43(a)? How could she prove that the defendant's cards are "likely to cause confusion"? See Roulo v. Russ Berrie & Co., 886 F.2d 931 (7th Cir.1989), cert. denied, 493 U.S. 1075 (1990), holding that the plaintiff's cards were inherently distinctive (a theory now presumably barred by *Wal–Mart*) and that the evidence was sufficient to support a jury verdict that confusion of source was likely. The court also upheld a verdict of copyright infringement. See also Hartford House, Ltd. v. Hallmark Cards, Inc., 846 F.2d 1268 (10th Cir.), cert. denied, 488 U.S. 908 (1988).

Greetings card

Δ produced line of cards that were similar

Distinguishing the "concrete expression" protected as trade dress in cases such as *Roulo*, Judge Newman in Jeffrey Milstein, Inc. v. Greger, Lawlor, Roth, Inc., 58 F.3d 27 (2d Cir.1995), held that a trade dress claim cannot be used to protect "an idea, a concept, or a generalized type of appearance." The court rejected the plaintiff's attempt to protect vertically-folded greeting cards cut to the outline of the object depicted in the color photograph on the front panel of the card; the plaintiff "is effectively seeking protection for an idea or concept—die-cut photographic greeting cards."

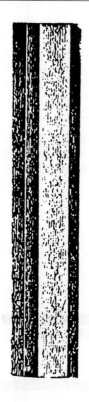

I want to shout
and tell the
world how much
I love you...
but instead
I'll just...
whisper.

(Roulo card)

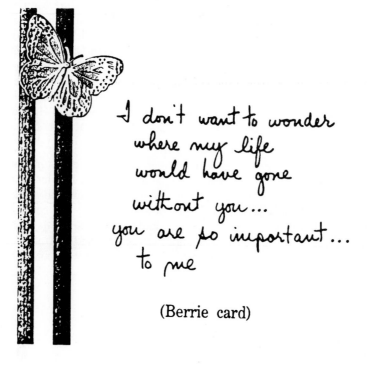

I don't want to wonder
where my life
would have gone
without you...
you are so important...
to me

(Berrie card)

(2) Is the protection afforded to product designs under the law of trademarks a workable substitute for a general design protection law? D. Welkowitz, Trade Dress and Patent—The Dilemma of Confusion, 30 Rutgers L.J. 289 (1999), concludes that it is not. See also A. Oddi, Product Simulation: From Tort to Intellectual Property, 88 Trademark Rep. 101 (1998), arguing that injunctions against copying should be a last resort in product design trademark cases. What other remedies might be available to avert consumer confusion?

(3) Trademark law was enlisted to prevent the imitation of an artistic style in Romm Art Creations Ltd. v. Simcha Int'l, Inc., 786 F.Supp. 1126 (E.D.N.Y.1992). The plaintiff was the exclusive distributor of limited edition prints and posters by Israeli artist Itzchak Tarkay. The litigation concerned a series of Tarkay's works known as "Women and Cafes"; the plaintiff complained that the defendant was selling reproductions of similar paintings by another artist. The court, describing the case as involving "the application of trade dress protection to works of art," found that the defendant's sales created a likelihood of confusion. A preliminary injunction was granted against the sale of a number of specifically identified works. Is this an appropriate application of "trade dress" protection? Does it cross the line propounded by Judge Newman in *Jeffrey Milstein*, supra? Cf. Galerie Furstenberg v. Coffaro, 697 F.Supp. 1282 (S.D.N.Y.1988), refusing to recognize trademark rights in images by Salvador Dali.

Under pressure from the estate of artist Alexander Calder, who died in 1976, several museums that display Calder mobiles removed mobiles created by other artists from their gift shops. The estate argued that some customers would assume that the mobiles were reproductions of Calder works or had been endorsed by the estate. Acknowledging that Calder is famous as an innovator of mobiles as an art form, the head of an organization of artists argued that it was like saying, "Don't use acrylic paint because I'm the first artist to use it." Hu, Store Wars: When a Mobile is Not a Calder, N.Y. Times, Aug. 6, 1998, p. E1.

(4) An attempt to use trademark law to stop a motion picture company from using a clip taken from a Three Stooges movie in a new film was rebuffed in Comedy III Productions, Inc. v. New Line Cinema, 200 F.3d 593 (9th Cir.2000). Although the film clip was in the public domain due to the expiration of copyright, the plaintiff argued that the use infringed its trademark rights in the "name, the characters, the likeness, and the overall 'act' of The Three Stooges." The argument did not move the Ninth Circuit: "Essentially, Comedy III is arguing that the clip at issue falls under the protection of the Lanham Act because it contains elements that in other contexts might serve as trademarks. Had New Line used the likeness of The Three Stooges on t-shirts which it was selling, Comedy III might have an arguable claim for trademark violation. But we will not entertain this expedition of trademark protection squarely into the domain of copyright law, to allow for Lanham Act coverage of a piece of footage taken directly from a film by The Three Stooges." M. McKenna, *Dastar*'s Next Stand, 19 J.Intell.Prop.L. 357 (2012), argues generally that trademark law should never impose liability for the use of material as part of the content of a work.

The Second Circuit reached an analogous result when it rejected a song owner's attempt to stop the use of a similar song on a commercial by claiming, in effect, that the song was a trademark for the song itself. Such a conclusion would "give trademark law a role in protecting the very essence of the song, an unwarranted extension into an area already protected by copyright." EMI Catalogue Partnership v. Hill, Holliday, Connors, Cosmopulos Inc., 228 F.3d 56 (2d Cir.2000). A trade dress claim under § 43(a) of the Lanham Act seeking to protect the "total image and appearance of 'Wife Swap US' as shaped by the selection, compilation, arrangement, sequence, and combination of the expressive elements of the program" was dismissed in RDF Media Ltd. v. Fox Broadcasting Co., 372 F.Supp.2d 556 (C.D.Cal.2005). The plaintiff had alleged that the television show's "trade dress" was infringed by a similar show called "Trading Spouses." Judge Otero said that the plaintiff was asking the court "to recognize the reality show itself as the trade dress," but the program was protectable, if at all, only under copyright law.

(5) The plaintiff in *Wal–Mart* invoked the concept of "trade dress" in an attempt to prohibit the imitation of its product. More typically, as in the following case, trade dress claims relate to packaging or labeling elements that contribute to the appearance of the product as presented to prospective purchasers. On the protection of packaging and product designs as trademarks, see generally J. McCarthy, Trademarks and Unfair Competition §§ 7:53–62 and §§ 8:1–21; Restatement, Third, Unfair Competition § 16 (1995).

Harlequin Enterprises Ltd. v. Gulf & Western Corp.
United States Court of Appeals, Second Circuit, 1981.
644 F.2d 946.

■ Before LUMBARD, MANSFIELD and MESKILL, CIRCUIT JUDGES.

■ LUMBARD, CIRCUIT JUDGE:

Defendant appeals from a preliminary injunction order entered by Judge Owen of the Southern District of New York. The order directs Simon & Schuster, a division of the defendant, to cease using the cover format it had adopted for a new series of romance novels titled "Silhouette Romance." Judge Owen granted this relief on the ground that the "Silhouette Romance" cover design infringes upon that of the "Harlequin Presents" romance novel series sold by plaintiff Harlequin Enterprises Limited ("Harlequin") in violation of § 43(a) of the Lanham Act, 15 U.S.C. § 1125(a). He also decided that Harlequin's delay in seeking an injunction did not bar relief. We agree and, accordingly, affirm the order of the district court. * * *

For many years, Simon & Schuster was the exclusive United States distributor of the Harlequin Presents series and other books published by Harlequin. In early 1979, however, Harlequin notified Simon & Schuster that it planned to let the distributorship agreement expire by its terms and, beginning January 1, 1980, to conduct its own distribution in the United States.

Shortly thereafter, Simon & Schuster decided to launch its own line of romance fiction under the rubric "Silhouette Romance." In March, 1980, approximately one month before the Silhouette Romance series appeared on the market, Harlequin filed a trade dress infringement suit alleging that the Silhouette Romance cover design is virtually identical to that of the Harlequin Presents series. On July 3, 1980, Harlequin moved for preliminary relief against the use of the Silhouette Romance cover. * * *

On the undisputed facts in the record before us, we hold that the district court did not abuse its discretion in enjoining Simon & Schuster from further use of the Silhouette Romance cover.

The district court's conclusion that the Silhouette Romance cover is "substantially similar" to the Harlequin Presents cover is clearly supported by the evidence. Both books are bound with glossy white covers and are of identical dimensions in height, width and thickness. The series' number is set in black type in the upper left hand corner and the price is printed on the upper right hand corner of each book. Both books retail for $1.50. A collage of gold filigree, the publisher's colophon and the series' title appears in the top center of each cover. Harlequin's colophon, a black and white harlequin, is framed by a gold diamond; Simon & Schuster's colophon, black silhouettes of a man and woman, is cast in a gold oval. The series' titles are printed in similar black script with one word of the series' title appearing on each side of the colophon. Beneath the collage on each book, the author's name is printed in bold, colored capital letters. The book's title is printed below the author's name on both books in black lettering. The bottom half of each cover is devoted to an illustration of a man and a woman in a romantic setting suggesting the book's story line.

While there are also some differences, such as the series' names and the publishers' colophons, it is the "combination of features as a whole rather than a difference in some of the details which must determine whether the competing product is likely to cause confusion in the mind of the public." Perfect Fit Industries, Inc. v. Acme Quilting Co., 618 F.2d 950, 955 (2d Cir.1980). We, like the district court, are convinced that an ordinary buyer of romance fiction would not recognize the disparities without setting out to find them. A buyer who did notice the difference between the names and the colophons would be reasonably justified in believing both products come from the same publisher.

In addition to the startling similarities between the covers, the district judge determined that there was actual confusion between the two covers among romance readers and members of the trade. These findings are substantiated by the inquiries directed to Harlequin about the Silhouette Romance series and the extraordinary number of Silhouette Romance book returns sent to Harlequin by retailers. Finally, the district court received and credited substantial evidence that Simon & Schuster deliberately imitated the Harlequin Presents cover. Evidence of conscious imitation is pertinent because the law presumes that an intended similarity is likely to cause confusion. Perfect Fit Industries, Inc. v. Acme Quilting Co., 618 F.2d at 954; RJR Foods, Inc. v. White Rock Corp., 603 F.2d 1058, 1060 (2d Cir.1979); Harold Ritchie, Inc. v. Chesebrough–Pond's, Inc., 281 F.2d 755, 758–60 (2d Cir.1960).

Harlequin has also adduced sufficient evidence to support the district court's preliminary finding that the Harlequin Presents cover has a "secondary meaning" for romance readers. By secondary meaning, we mean that romance readers associate the Harlequin Presents cover with a particular series and publisher. See RJR Foods, Inc. v. White Rock Corp., 603 F.2d at 1059. Harlequin's extensive national advertising, its phenomenal sales success and the results of a consumer survey[2] indicate that romance readers correlate the Harlequin Presents cover with Harlequin and the

---

[2] Spencer Bruno Research Associates interviewed 500 romance readers in three cities. The readers were shown copies of unpublished Harlequin Presents titles with the Harlequin name and colophon deleted and asked to name the publisher. Fifty percent of the readers correctly identified Harlequin as the publisher. While these results are not conclusive evidence of secondary meaning, particularly in light of Harlequin's market dominance, the district court properly found the results probative of secondary meaning. RJR Foods, Inc. v. White Rock Corp., 603 F.2d 1058, 1060 (2d Cir.1979).

Harlequin Presents series. See id. at 1060. The fact that the enthusiasm and loyalty of Harlequin's readers have been the subject of extensive, unsolicited media coverage further supports the district court's finding of secondary meaning. Scarves By Vera, Inc. v. Todo Imports, Ltd., 544 F.2d 1167, 1174 (2d Cir.1976). Perhaps the most significant evidence of secondary meaning in this case, however, was the attempt by Simon & Schuster to capitalize on the Harlequin Presents cover when it introduced its own romance series. RJR Foods, Inc. v. White Rock Corp., 603 F.2d at 1060.

Although secondary meaning usually is a prerequisite to trademark protection, New York law shields trade dress from deliberate copying even if it has not acquired a secondary meaning. Perfect Fit Industries, Inc. v. Acme Quilting Co., 618 F.2d 950 (2d Cir.1980). Thus, even if romance readers did not associate the Harlequin Presents cover with a specific series and publisher, Harlequin would be entitled to an injunction against Simon & Schuster's deliberate imitation of its cover. * * *

The findings of the district court and terms of its preliminary injunction are amply supported by the record.

Affirmed.

NOTES AND QUESTIONS

(1) Why would New York law prohibit the imitation of trade dress "even if it has not acquired a secondary meaning"? Is this merely a recognition of "inherent distinctiveness" for product packaging? If "readers did not associate the Harlequin Presents cover with a specific series and publisher," how could a similar cover be "likely to cause confusion"? The "New York rule" is criticized in J. McCarthy, Trademarks and Unfair Competition §§ 15:12–20.

(2) The publisher of *Reader's Digest* successfully invoked § 43(a) when the *Conservative Digest* adopted a cover format similar in size and graphic design to the cover used by the plaintiff. The similarities, according to the court, were likely to cause consumers to think that the two magazines came from the same publisher. As in *Harlequin Enterprises*, the court said that its finding of secondary meaning was bolstered by proof of intentional copying. Why is that relevant to secondary meaning? There was also a finding of copyright infringement. Reader's Digest Ass'n v. Conservative Digest, 821 F.2d 800 (D.C.Cir.1987).

Another publisher was less successful in fending off imitation by a competitor in Publications Int'l, Ltd. v. Landoll, Inc., 164 F.3d 337 (7th Cir.1998), cert. denied, 526 U.S. 1088 (1999); the oilcloth covers, large pages, and gilded edges of its cookbooks were functional and also not distinctive of books coming from the plaintiff.

(3) Beatrix Potter brought to life Peter Rabbit and other endearing characters in a series of books published by Frederick Warne & Co. beginning in 1902. In 1977 another publisher collected in a single volume seven of Miss Potter's stories that had entered the public domain. Included within the book were redrawings of the cover illustrations from the original Warne editions. Warne, claiming trademark rights in the illustrations, brought suit under § 43(a) and § 32 of the Lanham Act—three of the covers had been registered as trademarks for books. The defendant claimed a right to unrestricted use, insisting that the cover illustrations were now in the public domain. Summary judgment motions by both parties were denied: "[T]he proper factual inquiry in this case is not

whether the cover illustrations were once copyrightable and have fallen into the public domain, but whether they have acquired secondary meaning, identifying Warne as the publisher or sponsor of goods bearing those illustrations, and if so, whether defendant's use of these illustrations in 'packaging' or 'dressing' its editions is likely to cause confusion." But plaintiff's burden was formidable—"it would not be enough that the illustrations in question have come to signify Beatrix Potter as author of the books; plaintiff must show that they have come to represent its goodwill and reputation as *publisher* of those books." Frederick Warne & Co. v. Book Sales Inc., 481 F.Supp. 1191 (S.D.N.Y.1979).

(4) The plaintiff in Original Appalachian Artworks, Inc. v. Toy Loft, Inc., 684 F.2d 821 (11th Cir.1982), hit upon a novel technique for marketing dolls; the dolls were "adopted" rather than sold—a birth certificate and adoption papers accompanied the transaction, and a birthday card was sent to the buyer on the anniversary of the happy event. (These were the enormously successful "Cabbage Patch" dolls. They merited a cover story in *Newsweek,* What a Doll!: The Cabbage Patch Craze, Dec. 12, 1983, p. 78.) Defendant embarked on a similar marketing campaign. (He also copied the plaintiff's dolls, prompting a finding of copyright infringement.) The trial court thought confusion likely. Declaring the adoption procedures to be protectable trade dress, the Eleventh Circuit affirmed an injunction under § 43(a). Should all this pandering to sentimentalism be protectable as trade dress?

Brandir International, Inc. v. Cascade Pacific Lumber Co.

United States Court of Appeals, Second Circuit, 1987.
834 F.2d 1142.

■ Before OAKES and WINTER, CIRCUIT JUDGES, and ZAMPANO, DISTRICT JUDGE.

■ OAKES, CIRCUIT JUDGE:

[The portion of the court's opinion dealing with the plaintiff's copyright infringement claim appears at p. 142 supra.]

As to whether the configuration of Brandir's bicycle rack can be protected under either section 43(a) of the Lanham Act, 15 U.S.C. § 1125(a), or New York State unfair competition law, we are reminded that the design of a product itself may function as its packaging or protectable trade dress. See LeSportsac, Inc. v. K mart Corp., 754 F.2d 71, 75 (2d Cir.1985). The district court dismissed Brandir's claims, saying that its analysis of the copyright issue was sufficient to dispose of the Lanham Act and common law claims. The court stated "the design feature of the Ribbon Racks is clearly dictated by the function to be performed, namely, holding up bicycles. If the steam pipes were not bent into the design, but instead remained flat, the bicycles would not stand up, they would fall down." But as Judge Newman noted in his dissent in *Carol Barnhart,* 773 F.2d at 420 n. 1, the principle of conceptual separability of functional design elements in copyright law is different from the somewhat similar principle of functionality as developed in trademark law. For trademark purposes, he pointed out, a design feature "has been said to be functional if it is 'essential to the use or purpose of the article' or 'affects the cost or quality of the article.'" Id. (quoting Inwood Laboratories, Inc. v. Ives Laboratories, Inc., 456 U.S. 844, 850 n. 10 (1982)); see LeSportsac, Inc. v. K mart Corp., 754 F.2d at 75–76 (trade dress of a product is eligible for protection if it has acquired a secondary meaning and is nonfunctional).[4]

Here, the district court limited its inquiry to determining whether portions of the RIBBON Rack performed the function of a bicycle rack. But the fact that a design feature performs a function does not make it essential to the performance of that function; it is instead the absence of alternative constructions performing the same function that renders the feature functional. Thus, the true test of functionality is not whether the feature in question performs a function, but whether the feature "is dictated by the functions to be performed," Warner Bros. Inc. v. Gay Toys, Inc., 724 F.2d 327, 331 (2d Cir.1983) (quoted in LeSportsac, Inc. v. K mart Corp., 754 F.2d at 76), as evidenced by available alternative constructions. See Metro Kane Imports, Ltd. v. Rowoco, Inc., 618 F.Supp. 273, 275–76 (S.D.N.Y.1985), aff'd mem., 800 F.2d 1128 (2d Cir.1986) (finding high-tech design of orange juice squeezer not dictated by function to be performed as there was no evidence that design permitted juicer to be manufactured at lower price or with altered performance). There are numerous alternative bicycle rack constructions. The nature, price, and utility of these constructions are material issues of fact not suitable for determination by summary judgment.[5] For example, while it is true that the materials used by Brandir are standard-size pipes, we have no way of knowing whether the particular size and weight of the pipes used is the best, the most economical, or the only available size and weight pipe in the marketplace. We would rather think the opposite might be the case. So, too, with the dimension of the bends being dictated by a standard formula corresponding to the pipe size; it could be that there are many standard radii and that the particular radius of Brandir's RIBBON Rack actually required new tooling. This issue of functionality on remand should be viewed in terms of bicycle racks generally and not one-piece undulating bicycle racks specifically. See id. at 330–32; see also In re DC Comics, Inc., 689 F.2d 1042, 1045 (C.C.P.A.1982) (dolls generally and not Superman dolls are the class by which functionality is determined). We reverse and remand as to the trademark and unfair competition claims.

Wallace International Silversmiths, Inc. v. Godinger Silver Art Co.

United States Court of Appeals, Second Circuit, 1990.
916 F.2d 76.
Certiorari denied, 499 U.S. 976 (1991).

■ Before WINTER, MAHONEY and WALKER, CIRCUIT JUDGES.

■ WINTER, CIRCUIT JUDGE:

Wallace International Silversmiths ("Wallace") appeals from Judge Haight's denial of its motion for a preliminary injunction under Section 43(a) of the Lanham Act, 15 U.S.C. § 1125(a) (1988), prohibiting Godinger Silver Art Co., Inc. ("Godinger") from marketing a line of silverware with ornamentation that is substantially similar to Wallace's GRANDE BAROQUE line. Judge Haight held that the GRANDE BAROQUE design is "a

---

[4] Because the district court viewed the rack as entirely functional, it therefore did not reach the next step of determining whether Brandir's RIBBON Rack had acquired secondary meaning by the time Cascade started to manufacture its bicycle rack.

[5] Indeed, in addition to the numerous bicycle racks on the market, one may observe trees, awning supports, parking meters, signs, fire plugs, and many other objects used as bicycle racks.

functional feature of 'Baroque' style silverware" and thus not subject to protection as a trademark. We affirm.

Wallace, a Delaware corporation, has sold sterling silver products for over one hundred years. Its GRANDE BAROQUE pattern was introduced in 1941 and is still one of the best-selling silverware lines in America. Made of fine sterling silver, a complete place setting costs several thousand dollars. Total sales of GRANDE BAROQUE silverware have exceeded fifty million dollars. The GRANDE BAROQUE pattern is fairly described as "ornate, massive and flowery [with] indented, flowery roots and scrolls and curls along the side of the shaft, and flower arrangements along the front of the shaft." Wallace owns a trademark registration for the GRANDE BAROQUE name as applied to sterling silver flatware and hollowware. The GRANDE BAROQUE design is not patented, but on December 11, 1989, Wallace filed an application for trademark registration for the GRANDE BAROQUE pattern. This application is still pending.

Godinger, a New York corporation, is a manufacturer of silver-plated products. The company has recently begun to market a line of baroque-style silver-plated serving pieces. The suggested retail price of the set of four serving pieces is approximately twenty dollars. Godinger advertised its new line under the name 20TH CENTURY BAROQUE and planned to introduce it at the Annual New York Tabletop and Accessories Show, the principal industry trade show at which orders for the coming year are taken. Like Wallace's silverware, Godinger's pattern contains typical baroque elements including an indented root, scrolls, curls, and flowers. The arrangement of these elements approximates Wallace's design in many ways, although their dimensions are noticeably different. The most obvious difference between the two designs is that the Godinger pattern extends further down the handle than the Wallace pattern does. The Wallace pattern also tapers from the top of the handle to the stem while the Godinger pattern appears bulkier overall and maintains its bulk throughout the decorated portion of the handle. Although the record does not disclose the exact circumstances under which Godinger's serving pieces were created, Godinger admits that its designers were "certainly inspired by and aware of [the Wallace] design when [they] created [the 20TH CENTURY BAROQUE] design." * * *

The core purpose of trademark law is to prevent competitors from copying those aspects of a product or its trade dress that identify the source of the product to prospective consumers. See Inwood Laboratories v. Ives Laboratories, 456 U.S. 844, 854 n. 14 (1982); Bose Corp. v. Linear Design Labs, Inc., 467 F.2d 304, 309–10 (2d Cir.1972). By giving the first user of a trademark exclusive rights in that mark, the law protects trademark owners' investments in creating goodwill and affords consumers a low-cost means of identifying the source of goods. See *Inwood Laboratories,* supra; W.T. Rogers Co. Inc. v. Keene, 778 F.2d 334 (7th Cir.1985). Although the paradigmatic trademark is a distinctive name, the "trade dress" of a product may also serve as a trademark. A product's trade dress ordinarily consists of its packaging. However, the design given a product by its manufacturer also may serve to distinguish it from the products of other manufacturers and hence be protectible trade dress. See, e.g., Stormy Clime Ltd. v. Progroup, Inc., 809 F.2d 971, 974 (2d Cir.1987) ("The trade dress of a product 'involves the total image of a product and may include features such as size, shape, color or color combinations, texture, [or] graphics.'") (quoting John H. Harland Co. v. Clarke Checks, Inc., 711 F.2d 966, 980 (11th Cir.1983)); [Warner Bros. v. Gay Toys, Inc., 658 F.2d 76 (2d Cir.1981)] (color and symbols on toy car); Harlequin Enterprises Ltd. v. Gulf & Western Corp., 644 F.2d 946 (2d Cir.1981) (paperback book covers).

In order to maintain an action for trade dress infringement under Section 43(a) of the Lanham Act, the plaintiff must show that its trade dress has acquired secondary meaning—that is, the trade dress identifies the source of the product—and that there is a likelihood of confusion between the original trade dress and the trade dress of the allegedly infringing product. LeSportsac, Inc. v. K Mart Corp., 754 F.2d 71, 75 (2d Cir.1985). Even if the plaintiff establishes these elements, the defendant may still avoid liability on a variety of grounds, including the so-called functionality doctrine. Our present view of that doctrine is derived from the Supreme Court's dictum in *Inwood Laboratories,* stating that "[i]n general terms, a product feature is functional if it is essential to the use or purpose of the article or if it affects the cost or quality of the article." 456 U.S. at 850 n. 10. Our most recent elaboration of the doctrine was in *Stormy Clime,* where Judge Newman stated:

> the functionality inquiry . . . should [focus] on whether bestowing trade dress protection upon [a particular] arrangement of features " 'will hinder competition or impinge upon the rights of others to compete effectively in the sale of goods.' " Sicilia di R. Biebow & Co. v. Cox, 732 F.2d 417, 429 (5th Cir.1984) (quoting In re Morton–Norwich Products, Inc., 671 F.2d 1332, 1342 (Cust. & Pat.App.1982)).

Id. at 976–77. * * *

Turning to the instant case, Judge Haight found that the similarities between the Godinger and Wallace designs involved elements common to all baroque-style designs used in the silverware market. He noted that many manufacturers compete in that market with such designs and found that "[t]he 'Baroque' curls, roots and flowers are not 'mere indicia of source.' Instead, they are requirements to compete in the silverware market." Judge Haight concluded that "the 'Grande Baroque' design is a functional feature of 'Baroque' style silverware," relying on Pagliero v. Wallace China Co., 198 F.2d 339 (9th Cir.1952).

Although we agree with Judge Haight's decision, we do not endorse his reliance upon *Pagliero.* That decision allowed a competitor to sell exact copies of china bearing a particular pattern without finding that comparably attractive patterns were not available to the competitor. It based its holding solely on the ground that the particular pattern was an important ingredient in the commercial success of the china. Id. at 343–44. We rejected *Pagliero* in *LeSportsac,* supra at 77, and reiterate that rejection here. Under *Pagliero,* the commercial success of an aesthetic feature automatically destroys all of the originator's trademark interest in it, notwithstanding the feature's secondary meaning and the lack of any evidence that competitors cannot develop non-infringing, attractive patterns. By allowing the copying of an exact design without any evidence of market foreclosure, the *Pagliero* test discourages both originators and later competitors from developing pleasing designs. See Keene Corp. v. Paraflex Industries, Inc., 653 F.2d 822, 824–25 (3d Cir.1981).

Our rejection of *Pagliero,* however, does not call for reversal. Quite unlike *Pagliero,* Judge Haight found in the instant matter that there is a substantial market for baroque silverware and that effective competition in that market requires "use [of] essentially the same scrolls and flowers" as are found on Wallace's silverware. Based on the record at the hearing, that finding is not clearly erroneous and satisfies the requirement of *Stormy Clime* that a design feature not be given trade dress protection where use of that feature is necessary for effective competition. 809 F.2d at 976–77.

Stormy Clime is arguably distinguishable, however, because it involved a design that had both aesthetic and utilitarian features. If read narrowly, *Stormy Clime* might be limited to cases in which trademark protection of a design would foreclose competitors from incorporating utilitarian features necessary to compete in the market for the particular product. In the instant case, the features at issue are strictly ornamental because they neither affect the use of the silverware nor contribute to its efficient manufacture. The question, therefore, is whether the doctrine of functionality applies to features of a product that are purely ornamental but that are essential to effective competition.

Our only hesitation in holding that the functionality doctrine applies is based on nomenclature. "Functionality" seems to us to imply only utilitarian considerations and, as a legal doctrine, to be intended only to prevent competitors from obtaining trademark protection for design features that are necessary to the use or efficient production of the product. * * *

We put aside our quibble over doctrinal nomenclature, however, because we are confident that whatever secondary meaning Wallace's baroque silverware pattern may have acquired, Wallace may not exclude competitors from using those baroque design elements necessary to compete in the market for baroque silverware. It is a first principle of trademark law that an owner may not use the mark as a means of excluding competitors from a substantial market. * * *

In the instant matter, Wallace seeks trademark protection, not for a precise expression of a decorative style, but for basic elements of a style that is part of the public domain. As found by the district court, these elements are important to competition in the silverware market. We perceive no distinction between a claim to exclude all others from use on silverware of basic elements of a decorative style and claims to generic names, basic colors or designs important to a product's utility. In each case, trademark protection is sought, not just to protect an owner of a mark in informing the public of the source of its products, but also to exclude competitors from producing similar products. We therefore abandon our quibble with the aesthetic functionality doctrine's nomenclature and adopt the Draft Restatement's view that, where an ornamental feature is claimed as a trademark and trademark protection would significantly hinder competition by limiting the range of adequate alternative designs, the aesthetic functionality doctrine denies such protection. See Third Restatement of the Law, Unfair Competition (Preliminary Draft No. 3), Ch. 3, § 17(c) at 213–14. This rule avoids the overbreadth of *Pagliero* by requiring a finding of foreclosure of alternatives while still ensuring that trademark protection does not exclude competitors from substantial markets.

Of course, if Wallace were able to show secondary meaning in a precise expression of baroque style, competitors might be excluded from using an identical or virtually identical design. In such a case, numerous alternative baroque designs would still be available to competitors. Although the Godinger design at issue here was found by Judge Haight to be "substantially similar," it is not identical or virtually identical, and the similarity involves design elements necessary to compete in the market for baroque silverware. Because according trademark protection to those elements would significantly hinder competitors by limiting the range of adequate alternative designs, we agree with Judge Haight's denial of a preliminary injunction.

Affirmed.

NOTES AND QUESTIONS

(1) Which party should have the burden of proof on the functionality issue? Responding to a split in the circuits, Congress in 1999 added § 43(a)(3), which places the burden in a § 43(a) case on the party claiming trademark rights.

(2) Does the functionality limitation on trademark protection for product designs fully harmonize the respective spheres of patent and trademark law? In TrafFix Devices, Inc. v. Marketing Displays, Inc., 532 U.S. 23 (2001), the plaintiff manufactured outdoor signs with a spring mechanism to hold them upright against the wind. The mechanism had been covered by a utility patent, now expired. It claimed that its signs were recognizable to buyers because of the spring mechanism and filed suit against a competitor who sold signs with a spring mechanism that looked liked the plaintiff's. Justice Kennedy wrote for a unanimous Court:

> The principal question in this case is the effect of an expired patent on a claim of trade dress infringement. A prior patent, we conclude, has vital significance in resolving the trade dress claim. A utility patent is strong evidence that the features therein claimed are functional. If trade dress protection is sought for those features the strong evidence of functionality based on the previous patent adds great weight to the statutory presumption that features are deemed functional until proved otherwise by the party seeking trade dress protection. Where the expired patent claimed the features in question, one who seeks to establish trade dress protection must carry the heavy burden of showing that the feature is not functional, for instance by showing that it is merely an ornamental, incidental, or arbitrary aspect of the device.[a]

(3) Should the aesthetic functionality doctrine as interpreted in *Wallace International* operate to limit protection for the greeting cards in Roulo v. Russ Berrie, p. 653 supra? For the artwork in Romm Art Creations v. Simcha Int'l, p. 655 supra? And what of the "adoption" procedure protected as "trade dress" in Original Appalachian Artworks v. Toy Loft, p. 659 supra? See generally Restatement, Third, Unfair Competition § 17 (1995).

---

[a] The Supreme Court's decision in *TrafFix* also called into question the relevance of alternative designs in analyzing utilitarian functionality. "There is no need, furthermore, to engage, as did the Court of Appeals, in speculation about other design possibilities * * *. Here, the functionality of the spring design means that competitors need not explore whether other spring juxtapositions might be used." Some courts have understood *TrafFix* to mean that if the feature is necessary to the operation of the product, the existence of alternative designs that would work just as well is irrelevant to functionality. See Eppendorf–Netheler–Hinz GMBH v. Ritter GMBH, 289 F.3d 351 (5th Cir.), cert. denied, 537 U.S. 1071 (2002); other courts believe that alternative designs remain relevant in determining whether a design is functional in the first place. See Valu Engineering, Inc. v. Rexnord Corp., 278 F.3d 1268 (Fed.Cir.2002). A. Cohen, Following the Direction of *TrafFix*: Trade Dress Law and Functionality Revisited, 50 Idea 593 (2010), reviews the varying interpretations of the *TrafFix* case and ultimately urges an end to registration and protection of product configurations.

LANHAM ACT REGISTRATION OF PRODUCT CONFIGURATIONS

Kohler Co. v. Moen Inc.

United States Court of Appeals, Seventh Circuit, 1993.
12 F.3d 632.

■ Before CUDAHY and COFFEY, CIRCUIT JUDGES, and ESCHBACH, SENIOR CIRCUIT JUDGE.

■ COFFEY, CIRCUIT JUDGE.

This action began in 1987 when Moen, Incorporated ("Moen") filed two applications in the United States Patent and Trademark Office ("PTO") to register a faucet design and a faucet handle design as trademarks. Kohler Company ("Kohler") opposed the applications before the PTO's Trademark Trial and Appeal Board ("TTAB") on the ground that product shapes were not registrable as trademarks. The TTAB dismissed Kohler's oppositions. Kohler sought review of the TTAB's decision under 15 U.S.C. § 1071(b) in the district court. The parties filed cross summary judgment motions and stipulated first that they would rely on the record before the TTAB and further that no new evidence would be submitted. The district court entered summary judgment in favor of Moen and against Kohler. Kohler filed a timely appeal from the district court's judgment. We affirm.

Kohler and Moen are competitors in the business of manufacturing and selling plumbing products, including faucets and faucet handles. Moen sought and obtained trademark registration of its "LEGEND" kitchen faucet and the appearance of the handle used on the "LEGEND" and other Moen faucets. In support of registration of its product configurations as trademarks, Moen introduced voluminous evidence of sales and promotional expenses with respect to each design, and also submitted substantial evidence that purchasers of its products recognized the source of the faucets by their distinctive shapes. The record included hundreds of declarations from persons in the plumbing business and from individual purchasers attesting to the distinctiveness of the shape of Moen's faucet and handle without reference to any markings. One of Moen's vice-presidents submitted a declaration stating that Moen's faucet design is not based upon utility or function, is not inexpensive to manufacture, and is only one of many competitive designs in the industry performing the same function. Moen also submitted a declaration from the chairman of one of its chief competitors, Price Pfister, that stated that Moen's faucet is distinctive, its design indicates a single point of origin, the design is neither functional nor utilitarian, and that trademark protection for the configuration would not hinder competition in the plumbing trade. Finally, a market research survey of 273 licensed plumbers in six cities revealed that eighty-two percent of those surveyed identified the faucet as a Moen product, and eighty-three percent identified the handle as a Moen product. * * *

In dismissing Kohler's oppositions, the TTAB necessarily concluded that § 45 of the Act provides trademark protection for product configurations. Section 45 of the Act defines trademark to "*include*[ ] any word, name, symbol, or device or any combination thereof adopted and used by a manufacturer or merchant to identify his goods and distinguish them from those manufactured or sold by others." 15 U.S.C. § 1127 (1988). As Kohler notes, § 45 does not list "product configuration" among its examples of trademarks. Early decisions under the Act strictly construed the language of § 45 and held that a product or container shape was not entitled to trademark protection. See 1 McCarthy, McCarthy on Trademarks and Unfair Competition, § 7.31 (3d ed. 1992) [hereinafter McCarthy on Trademarks]; Ex Parte Minnesota Mining & Mfg. Co., 92 U.S.P.Q. 74 (1952). Subsequent TTAB decisions and the courts reviewing TTAB rulings, however, have interpreted § 45 to allow trademark protection for product configurations.

In Application of Kotzin, 276 F.2d 411, 414–15 (C.C.P.A.1960), the Court of Customs and Patent Appeals ("C.C.P.A.") held that the § 45 list ("word, name, symbol or device") did not restrict other items from receiving trademark protection if they satisfied the requirements for registration on the Principal Register. The court in *Kotzin* supported its interpretation of the statute by noting that the provision stated that trademarks *"include"* words, names, symbols or devices, not that "trademark" *"means"* words, names, symbols or devices. * * *

In Application of Mogen David, 328 F.2d 925 (C.C.P.A.1964), the C.C.P.A. held that the configuration of a container could be registered as a trademark for the product it contains. Id. at 929–30. The C.C.P.A. thereafter held that a product configuration itself could be registered as a trademark in Application of Honeywell, Inc., 497 F.2d 1344 (C.C.P.A.), cert. denied, 419 U.S. 1080 (1974). The C.C.P.A., the Federal Circuit, and the TTAB have since interpreted § 45 to allow trademark protection for qualifying product configurations. * * *

* * * The persuasiveness of the TTAB and the Federal Circuit's interpretation of § 45 is reinforced by the legislative history accompanying the 1988 Lanham Act amendments. See Trademark Law Revision Act of 1988, Pub.L. 100–667, § 38, S.Rep. 515, 100th Cong., 2d Sess. 44 (1988), reprinted in, 1988 U.S.C.C.A.N. 5577, 5607. Although these amendments did not take effect until November 1989, approximately two years after the TTAB's decision in this case, as a codification of prior case law they validate the uniform preamendment interpretation of § 45 on the Act. The Senate Report accompanying the 1988 amendments specifically states "the words 'symbol or device,'" were retained in the Trademark Revision Act's revised definition of trademark "so as not to preclude the registration of colors, shapes, sounds *or configurations* where they function as trademarks." S.Rep. 100–515, 100th Cong., 2d Sess. at 44, reprinted in, 1988 U.S.C.C.A.N. at 5607 (emphasis added). Congress thus specifically approved the broad judicial interpretation of § 45's definition of "trademark" to include product configurations. * * *

Kohler asserts that granting trademark protection and allowing trademark registration for a product configuration directly conflicts with the rationale of the Constitution's Patent Clause and the Patent Act, 35 U.S.C. §§ 1–376 (1988). Kohler alleges that the Supreme Court's interpretation of the Patent Clause in Bonito Boats, Inc. v. Thunder Craft Boats, Inc., 489 U.S. 141, 146 (1989); Sears Roebuck & Co. v. Stiffel Co., 376 U.S. 225 (1964), and Compco Corp. v. Day–Brite Lighting, Inc., 376 U.S. 234 (1964), indicates that the TTAB and lower courts' interpretation of the Act to allow trademark protection for product configurations contravenes the Patent Clause's requirement that the exclusive right to "Writings and Discoveries" be for a "limited Time[]." To analyze the soundness of Kohler's claim that courts' interpretation of the Act runs afoul of the Patent Clause and implementing patent law, a brief discussion of the purpose of each is necessary.

To obtain patent protection, an applicant has to show that an invention or design is both novel and "not obvious at the time the invention was made to a person having ordinary skill in the art to which said art pertains." 35 U.S.C. § 103 (1988). Patent protection is limited in duration * * *. The innovation passes into the public domain after the patent expires.

Compared to patent protection, trademark protection is relatively weak because it precludes competitors only from using marks that are likely to confuse or deceive the public. Trademark protection is dependent only on public reaction to the trademark in the marketplace rather than solely on the similarity of the configurations. * * * Significantly, while a patent creates a type of monopoly pricing power by giving the patentee the exclusive right to make and sell the innovation, a trademark gives the owner only the right to preclude others from using the mark when such use is likely to cause confusion or to deceive. See 1 McCarthy on Trademarks § 2.05[1]. * * *

In the *Sears/Compco* decisions, the Supreme Court reviewed two decisions from this court which held that Illinois unfair competition law prohibited unauthorized copying of unpatentable lighting fixture designs. The Supreme Court held in both cases that federal copyright and patent law preempted the state unfair competition law which prohibited the copying of a nonpatented product. *Sears*, 376 U.S. at 231–32; *Compco*, 376 U.S. at 237–38. Kohler argues that because state unfair competition and federal trademark law serve the same purpose, federal patent law also conflicts with federal trademark law. Kohler is mistaken. First, no Lanham Act issue was raised in either *Sears* or *Compco;* the decision in each case was based on the Supremacy Clause. Second, the Court in *Compco* noted that a defendant may copy at will if the design is "not entitled to a design patent *or other federal statutory protection* . . . . " *Compco*, 376 U.S. at 238. Of course, the Lanham Act falls under the rubric of "other federal statutory protection," and courts have expressly held that *Sears* and *Compco* do not preclude federal trademark protection of designs. * * *

As in *Sears,* however, the *Bonito Boats* Court recognized that states have the power to give unfair competition and trademark protection to trade dress. * * * The Court's holding in *Bonito Boats* is also inapplicable to federal trademark law because the Florida statute granted boat manufacturers patent-like rights far exceeding any right available under the Lanham Act. * * * As described earlier in this opinion, the underlying policies of federal trademark law, and the nature of the protection afforded, do not approximate the sweeping, perpetual patent-like state statutes that the Supreme Court found impermissible in *Sears, Compco,* and *Bonito Boats.* * * *

Kohler has conceded that under the facts of this case, Moen satisfied all of the requirements for trademark protection for product configurations. The Supreme Court's holdings and dicta in *Sears, Compco, Bonito Boats,* and *Two Pesos* offer no reason for this court to hold that every court that has allowed federal trademark protection for product configurations was mistaken. * * *

The district court's judgment is affirmed.

■ CUDAHY, CIRCUIT JUDGE, dissenting.

[Judge Cudahy, after extensive analysis, concluded that in view of the statutory provision for design patents, trademark registration for product configurations was fundamentally inconsistent with the Supreme Court's preemption cases.]

In my view, whatever new law has been developed in the lower courts to authorize the use of product configuration trademarks as a substitute for design patents is without sanction from the Supreme Court. The Court has spoken repeatedly to disfavor the use of unfair competition law to avoid the "limited times" provision of the Patent Clause. The Court has emphasized the importance of the right to copy as an aspect of the Patent Clause. The right to copy is constitutionally protected and is absolutely essential to the successful long-term operation of a free and competitive economy. I therefore respectfully dissent.

NOTES AND QUESTIONS

(1) Section 45 of the Lanham Act states, "The term 'trademark' includes any word, name, symbol, or device, or any combination thereof * * *." "Device" was the gateway for registration of the path-breaking PINCH scotch bottle, Ex parte Haig & Haig Ltd., 118 U.S.P.Q. 229 (Comm'r Pat.1958). The shape and packaging of a candy bar was approved for registration in In re World's Finest Chocolate, Inc., 474 F.2d 1012 (C.C.P.A.1973); In re Ovation Instruments, Inc., 201 U.S.P.Q. 116 (Tm.Tr. & App.Bd.1978), accepted the shape of a guitar for registration. Even building designs appear on the Principal Register. See, e.g., Fotomat Corp. v. Ace Corp., 208 U.S.P.Q. 92 (S.D.Cal.1980). If a *packaging* configuration is sufficiently unique ("inherently distinctive"), may it be registered without a demonstration of secondary meaning on the theory that it will presumptively serve to identify the goods of the applicant to consumers? See, e.g., In re Days–Ease Home Products Corp., 197 U.S.P.Q. 566 (Tm.Tr. & App.Bd.1977) (container for a liquid drain opener shaped to resemble a pipe trap registered as inherently distinctive). *Wal–Mart* now bars this attempt to avoid the necessity of proving secondary meaning for the registration of a *product* design.

G. Lunney, The Trade Dress Emperor's New Clothes: Why Trade Dress Does Not Belong on the Principal Register, 51 Hastings L.J. 1131 (2000), maintains, contrary to *Kohler*, that Congress never intended the federal registration system to encompass product configurations.

(2) The Lanham Act in § 2(e), 15 U.S.C. § 1052(e), precludes trademark registration of functional matter. See, e.g., Valu Engineering, Inc. v. Rexnord Corp., 278 F.3d 1268 (Fed.Cir.2002).

2. SOUND RECORDINGS

STATE PROTECTION AGAINST DUPLICATION

State record piracy statutes such as the one applied in Goldstein v. California, p. 614 supra, undertake to penalize the duplication of sound recordings. *Goldstein* considered the duplication of records that were made before sound recordings were given federal copyright protection in 1972; the Supreme Court said Congress had left these recordings subject to state control. There was some fumbling in the revision bill about these old recordings; the outcome was § 301(c). State anti-piracy protection remains effective until the year 2067 with respect to recordings fixed before Feb. 15, 1972, but those recordings continue to be excluded from federal copyright.[b] (Why 2067? Because it is 95 years from 1972, the same duration given to pre-1978 copyrights in § 304(a),(b).) For sound recordings made after the extension of federal copyright in 1972, state protection against duplication is preempted.[c]

Goldstein validated a state criminal statute against record piracy. Many state statutes also offer civil remedies. Note that § 301(c) also preserves state common law protection for pre–1972 recordings. Relief against unauthorized duplication of sound recordings has sometimes been achieved under a common law misappropriation theory. In Capitol Records v. Mercury Records Corp., 221 F.2d 657 (2d Cir.1955), the Second Circuit, over a strong dissent by Learned Hand, held that New York law would recognize in the originator an exclusive right to reproduce and sell its recordings.[d] A misappropriation claim against a record pirate was enthusiastically upheld in Mercury Record Prod., Inc. v. Economic Consultants, Inc., 64 Wis.2d 163, 218 N.W.2d 705 (1974). After reviewing the attacks on *INS,* which it associated chiefly with Learned Hand, the Wisconsin Supreme Court concluded that "*Goldstein* completely repudiates Judge Hand's rationale criticizing *I.N.S.* * * * *I.N.S.* stands." This view has been influential in subsequent record piracy cases. See, e.g., A & M Records, Inc. v. M.V.C. Distrib. Corp., 574 F.2d 312 (6th Cir.1978); GAI Audio of New York, Inc. v. Columbia Broadcasting System, Inc., 27 Md.App. 172, 340 A.2d 736 (1975).

IMITATION OF SOUND RECORDINGS

Waits v. Frito–Lay, Inc.

United States Court of Appeals, Ninth Circuit, 1992.
978 F.2d 1093.
Certiorari denied, 506 U.S. 1080 (1993).

■ Before BROWNING, BOOCHEVER, and REINHARDT, CIRCUIT JUDGES.

■ BOOCHEVER, CIRCUIT JUDGE:

Defendants Frito–Lay, Inc., and Tracy–Locke, Inc., appeal a jury verdict and award of $2.6 million in compensatory damages, punitive damages, and attorney's fees, in favor of singer Tom Waits. Waits sued the snack food manufacturer and its advertising agency for voice misappropriation and false endorsement following the broadcast of a radio commercial for

---

[b] A 2011 Copyright Office report recommends extending federal copyright protection to pre–1972 sound recordings, primarily to provide greater certainty for preservation efforts by libraries and archives. See 83 Pat., Tm. & Copyr.J. (BNA) 291 (2012).

[c] Even post–1971 recordings are not entirely beyond the reach of the states. See Anderson v. Nidorf, 26 F.3d 100 (9th Cir.1994), upholding a California criminal statute prohibiting sales of recordings and audiovisual works that do not conspicuously disclose the identity of the manufacturer. The Supreme Court of Georgia reached an analogous conclusion in Briggs v. Georgia, 281 Ga. 329, 638 S.E.2d 292 (2006).

[d] In response to a certified question from the Second Circuit, the New York Court of Appeals relied on a detailed history of British and American copyright law in reaching the conclusion that pre–1972 sound recordings made in England were protected under the common law of New York even if the recordings had entered the public domain in their country of origin. Capitol Records, Inc. v. Naxos, Inc., 4 N.Y.3d 540, 797 N.Y.S.2d 352, 830 N.E.2d 250 (2005).

SalsaRio Doritos which featured a vocal performance imitating Waits' raspy singing voice. On appeal, the defendants mount attacks on nearly all aspects of the judgment. * * *

BACKGROUND

Tom Waits is a professional singer, songwriter, and actor of some renown. Waits has a raspy, gravelly singing voice, described by one fan as "like how you'd sound if you drank a quart of bourbon, smoked a pack of cigarettes and swallowed a pack of razor blades . . . . Late at night. After not sleeping for three days." Since the early 1970s, when his professional singing career began, Waits has recorded more than seventeen albums and has toured extensively, playing to sold-out audiences throughout the United States, Canada, Europe, Japan, and Australia. * * * Tom Waits does not, however, do commercials. He has maintained this policy consistently during the past ten years, rejecting numerous lucrative offers to endorse major products. Moreover, Waits' policy is a public one: in magazine, radio, and newspaper interviews he has expressed his philosophy that musical artists should not do commercials because it detracts from their artistic integrity.

Frito–Lay, Inc. is in the business of manufacturing, distributing, and selling prepared and packaged food products, including Doritos brand corn chips. Tracy–Locke, Inc. is an advertising agency which counts Frito–Lay among its clients. In developing an advertising campaign to introduce a new Frito–Lay product, SalsaRio Doritos, Tracy–Locke found inspiration in a 1976 Waits song, "Step Right Up." Ironically, this song is a jazzy parody of commercial hucksterism, and consists of a succession of humorous advertising pitches. The commercial the ad agency wrote echoed the rhyming word play of the Waits song. * * *

The story of Tracy–Locke's search for a lead singer for the commercial suggests that no one would do but a singer who could not only capture the feeling of "Step Right Up" but also imitate Tom Waits' voice. The initial efforts of the ad agency's creative team, using a respected professional singer with a deep bluesy voice, met with disapproval from executives at both Tracy–Locke and Frito–Lay. Tracy–Locke then auditioned a number of other singers who could sing in a gravelly style.

Stephen Carter was among those who auditioned. A recording engineer who was acquainted with Carter's work had recommended him to Tracy–Locke as someone who did a good Tom Waits imitation. Carter was a professional musician from Dallas and a Tom Waits fan. Over ten years of performing Waits songs as part of his band's repertoire, he had consciously perfected an imitation of Waits' voice. When Carter auditioned, members of the Tracy–Locke creative team "did a double take" over Carter's near-perfect imitation of Waits, and remarked to him how much he sounded like Waits. In fact, the commercial's musical director warned Carter that he probably wouldn't get the job because he sounded too much like Waits, which could pose legal problems. Carter, however, did get the job. * * *

The commercial was broadcast in September and October 1988 on over 250 radio stations located in 61 markets nationwide, including Los Angeles, San Francisco, and Chicago. Waits heard it during his appearance on a Los Angeles radio program, and was shocked. He realized "immediately that whoever was going to hear this and obviously identify the voice would also identify that [Tom Waits] in fact had agreed to do a commercial for Doritos."

In November 1988, Waits sued Tracy–Locke and Frito–Lay, alleging claims of misappropriation under California law and false endorsement under the Lanham Act. The case was tried before a jury in April and May 1990. The jury found in Waits' favor, awarding him $375,000 compensatory damages and $2 million punitive damages for voice misappropriation, and $100,000 damages for violation of the Lanham Act. The court awarded Waits attorneys' fees under the Lanham Act. This timely appeal followed.

DISCUSSION

I.   *Voice Misappropriation*

In Midler v. Ford Motor Co., 849 F.2d 460, 463 (9th Cir.1988), cert. denied, 503 U.S. 951 (1992), we held that "when a distinctive voice of a professional singer is widely known and is deliberately imitated in order to sell a product, the sellers have appropriated what is not theirs and have committed a tort in California." The *Midler* tort is a species of violation of the "right of publicity," the right of a person whose identity has commercial value—most often a celebrity—to control the commercial use of that identity. See Motschenbacher v. R.J. Reynolds Tobacco Co., 498 F.2d 821, 824–25 (9th Cir.1974). See generally J.T. McCarthy, The Rights of Publicity and Privacy (1987) (hereafter Publicity and Privacy). We recognized in *Midler* that when voice is a sufficient indicia of a celebrity's identity, the right of publicity protects against its imitation for commercial purposes without the celebrity's consent. See Midler, 849 F.2d at 463. * * *

A.   *Continuing Viability of Midler*

As a threshold matter, the defendants ask us to rethink *Midler,* and to reject it as an inaccurate statement of California law. *Midler,* according to the defendants, has been "impliedly overruled" by the Supreme Court's decision in Bonito Boats, Inc. v. Thunder Craft Boats, Inc., 489 U.S. 141 (1989). Additionally, they argue that the *Midler* tort is preempted by the federal Copyright Act. We review these questions of law de novo. See Kruso v. International Tel. & Tel. Corp., 872 F.2d 1416, 1421 (9th Cir.1989), cert. denied, 496 U.S. 937 (1990).

Bonito Boats involved a Florida statute giving perpetual patent-like protection to boat hull designs already on the market, a class of manufactured articles expressly excluded from federal patent protection. The Court ruled that the Florida statute was preempted by federal patent law because it directly conflicted with the comprehensive federal patent scheme. In reaching this conclusion, the Court cited its earlier decisions in Sears Roebuck & Co. v. Stiffel Co., 376 U.S. 225 (1964), and Compco Corp. v. Day–Brite Lighting, 376 U.S. 234 (1964), for the proposition that "publicly known design and utilitarian ideas which were unprotected by patent occupied much the same position as the subject matter of an expired patent," i.e., they are expressly unprotected. *Bonito Boats,* 489 U.S. at 152.

The defendants seize upon this citation to *Sears* and *Compco* as a reaffirmation of the sweeping preemption principles for which these cases were once read to stand. They argue that *Midler* was wrongly decided because it ignores these two decisions, an omission that the defendants say indicates an erroneous assumption that *Sears* and *Compco* have been "relegated to the constitutional junkyard." Thus, the defendants go on to reason, earlier cases that rejected entertainers' challenges to imitations of their performances based on federal copyright preemption, were correctly decided because they relied on *Sears* and *Compco.* See Sinatra v. Goodyear Tire & Rubber Co., 435 F.2d 711, 716–18 (9th Cir.1970), cert. denied, 402 U.S. 906

(1971); Booth v. Colgate–Palmolive Co., 362 F.Supp. 343, 348 (S.D.N.Y.1973); Davis v. Trans World Airlines, 297 F.Supp. 1145, 1147 (C.D.Cal.1969). This reasoning suffers from a number of flaws.

Bonito Boats itself cautions against reading *Sears* and *Compco* for a "broad pre-emptive principle" and cites subsequent Supreme Court decisions retreating from such a sweeping interpretation. "[T]he Patent and Copyright Clauses do not, by their own force or by negative implication, deprive the States of the power to adopt rules for the promotion of intellectual creation." *Bonito Boats*, 489 U.S. at 165 (citing, *inter alia,* Goldstein v. California, 412 U.S. 546, 552–61, (1973) and Kewanee Oil Co. v. Bicron Corp., 416 U.S. 470, 478–79 (1974)). Instead, the Court reaffirmed the right of states to "place limited regulations on the use of unpatented designs in order to prevent consumer confusion as to source." Id. *Bonito Boats* thus cannot be read as endorsing or resurrecting the broad reading of *Compco* and *Sears* urged by the defendants, under which Waits' state tort claim arguably would be preempted. * * *

The defendants ask that we rethink *Midler* anyway, arguing as the defendants did there that voice misappropriation is preempted by section 114 [301?] of the Copyright Act. Under this provision, a state cause of action escapes Copyright Act preemption if its subject matter "does not come within the subject matter of copyright . . . including works or authorship not fixed in any tangible medium of expression." 17 U.S.C. § 301(b)(1). We rejected copyright preemption in *Midler* because voice is not a subject matter of copyright: "A voice is not copyrightable. The sounds are not 'fixed.'" *Midler,* 849 F.2d at 462. As a three-judge panel, we are not at liberty to reconsider this conclusion, and even if we were, we would decline to disturb it.

Waits' claim, like Bette Midler's, is for infringement of voice, not for infringement of a copyrightable subject such as sound recording or musical composition. Moreover, the legislative history of section 114 [301?] indicates the express intent of Congress that "[t]he evolving common law rights of 'privacy,' 'publicity,' and trade secrets . . . remain unaffected [by the preemption provision] as long as the causes of action contain elements, such as an invasion of personal rights . . . that are different in kind from copyright infringement." H.R.Rep. No. 1476, 94th Cong., 2d Sess. 132, reprinted in 1976 U.S.C.C.A.N. 5659, 5748. Waits' voice misappropriation claim is one for invasion of a personal property right: his right of publicity to control the use of his identity as embodied in his voice. See *Midler,* 849 F.2d at 462–63 ("What is put forward as protectable here is more personal than any work of authorship . . . . A voice is as distinctive and personal as a face.") The trial's focus was on the elements of voice misappropriation, as formulated in *Midler:* whether the defendants had deliberately imitated Waits' voice rather than simply his style and whether Waits' voice was sufficiently distinctive and widely known to give him a protectable right in its use. These elements are "different in kind" from those in a copyright infringement case challenging the unauthorized use of a song or recording. Waits' voice misappropriation claim, therefore, is not preempted by federal copyright law.

B.   *Jury Instructions*

The defendants next contend that the district court committed prejudicial error by rejecting their proposed jury instructions on three elements of the *Midler* tort: the deliberate misappropriation for commercial purposes of (1) a voice, that is (2) distinctive and (3) widely known. * * *

(1) *"Voice" vs. "Style"*

The defendants argued at trial that although they had consciously copied Tom Waits' style in creating the Doritos commercial, they had not deliberately imitated his voice. * * *

* * * The court's voice misappropriation instructions limited the jury's consideration to voice, and in no way implied that it could consider style. Indeed, in addressing the jury in closing argument, Waits' attorney agreed with the defendants that style was not protected. Moreover, the court included an additional instruction that effectively narrowed the jury's focus to Waits' voice and indicated that style imitation alone was insufficient for tort liability. For the defendants to be liable for voice misappropriation, the court stated, the imitation had to be so good that "people who were familiar with plaintiff's voice who heard the commercial *believed plaintiff performed it*. In this connection it is not enough that they were reminded of plaintiff or thought the singer sounded like plaintiff . . . . "[3] (Emphasis added.) Even if the jury were initially confused about whether the defendants could be liable simply for imitating Waits' style, this instruction would have disabused them of this notion.

(2) *Definition of "Distinctive"*

The defendants next argue that the court's instruction concerning the meaning of "distinctive" was an unfair and inaccurate statement of the law because it confuses the "distinctiveness" of a voice with its identifiability or recognizability. * * *

The defendants' technical argument that distinctiveness is a separate concept from identifiability, while supported by their experts' testimony, has no basis in law. Identifiability is properly considered in evaluating distinctiveness, for it is a central element of a right of publicity claim. See Publicity and Privacy § 3.4[A] & n. 1 (citing cases). Our *Midler* holding is premised on the fact that a person is as identifiable by voice as by any other indicia of identity previously recognized as protectable. Although we did not define "distinctiveness" in *Midler,* we stated: "A voice is as *distinctive* and personal as a face. The human voice is one of the most palpable ways *identity is manifested.* We are all aware that a friend is at once known by a few words on the phone . . . . [T]hese observations hold true of singing . . . . " Midler v. Ford, 849 F.2d at 463 (emphasis added). See also *Motschenbacher,* 498 F.2d at 826–27 (rejecting trial court's ruling that because plaintiff's face was not recognizable in advertisement photograph, his identity had not been misappropriated, and finding that plaintiff was identifiable from distinctive decorations on race car).

The court's "distinctiveness" instruction informed the jury that it could consider the recordings of Waits' voice introduced into evidence and the testimony of expert and other witnesses. The court thus invited members of the jury to use their common sense in determining whether Waits has a distinctive enough voice to warrant protection, and to consider as well what the experts had to say. This was entirely appropriate. * * *

(3) *Definition of "Widely Known"*

The defendants next object to the district court's instruction concerning the element of "widely known" on the ground that it was too vague to

---

[3] This instruction effectively added an additional element to *Midler's* formulation of voice misappropriation: actual confusion. The validity of this instruction is not before us in this appeal and we express no opinion on this issue.

guide the jury in making a factual determination of the issue. The court instructed the jury: "A professional singer's voice is widely known if it is known to a *large number* of people throughout a *relatively large* geographic area." (Emphasis added.) The court rejected an instruction proposed by the defendants, which reflected their contention at trial that Tom Waits is a singer known only to music insiders and to a small but loyal group of fans: "A singer is not widely known if he is only recognized by his own fans, or fans of a particular sort of music, or a small segment of the population."

The legal underpinnings of this proposed instruction are questionable. The defendants assert that because Waits has not achieved the level of celebrity Bette Midler has, he is not well known under the *Midler* standard. We reject this crabbed interpretation of *Midler*. The defendants' proposed instruction would have excluded from legal protection the voices of many popular singers who fall short of superstardom. "Well known" is a relative term, and differences in the extent of celebrity are adequately reflected in the amount of damages recoverable. * * *

C.   *Compensatory Damage Award*

The jury awarded Waits the following compensatory damages for voice misappropriation: $100,000 for the fair market value of his services; $200,000 for injury to his peace, happiness and feelings; and $75,000 for injury to his goodwill, professional standing and future publicity value. The defendants contest the latter two awards, disputing both the availability of such damages in a voice misappropriation action and the sufficiency of the evidence supporting the awards. * * *

[The court upheld the award of damages for mental distress, relying in part on testimony from Waits that the commercial embarrassed him. "I had to call all my friends, that if they hear this thing, please be informed this is not me. I was on the phone for days. I also had people calling me saying, Gee Tom, I heard the new Doritos ad." The court also upheld the award for damage to Waits' goodwill and reputation.]

D.   *Punitive Damage Award*

The jury awarded Waits a total of $2 million in punitive damages for voice misappropriation: $1.5 million against Tracy–Locke and $500,000 against Frito–Lay. The defendants ask that we vacate this award, arguing that punitive damages are unavailable as a matter of law, and alternatively, that the evidence was insufficient to support their award.

In California, exemplary or punitive damages are available "where it is proven by clear and convincing evidence that the defendant has been guilty of oppression, fraud, or malice." Cal.Civ.Code § 3294(a) (West Supp.1992). * * *

The defendants argue, however, that although they may have been aware that legal risks were involved, they had a good faith belief that Waits' rights would not be infringed because they read the legal precedents differently. This argument leaves us unpersuaded. Good faith cannot be manufactured by looking to the law of other jurisdictions to define the rights of California residents. *Midler* could not be more clear that, in California at least, a well-known singer with a distinctive voice has a property right in that voice. * * *

II.   *Lanham Act Claim*

Section 43(a) of the Lanham Act, 15 U.S.C. § 1125(a), prohibits the use of false designations of origin, false descriptions, and false representations in the advertising and sale of goods and services. Smith v. Montoro, 648 F.2d 602, 603 (9th Cir.1981). Waits' claim under section 43(a) is premised on the theory that by using an imitation of his distinctive voice in an admitted parody of a Tom Waits song, the defendants misrepresented his association with and endorsement of SalsaRio Doritos. The jury found in Waits' favor and awarded him $100,000 in damages. The district court also awarded him attorneys' fees under section 35 of the Lanham Act. On appeal, the defendants argue that Waits lacks standing to bring a Lanham Act claim, that Waits' false endorsement claim fails on its merits, that the damage award is duplicative, and that attorneys' fees are improper. Before we address these contentions, however, we turn to the threshold issue of whether false endorsement claims are properly cognizable under section 43(a) of the Lanham Act, a question of first impression in this circuit.

A. *False Endorsement*

* * * Courts in other jurisdictions have interpreted [§ 43(a)] as authorizing claims for false endorsement. E.g., Better Business Bureau v. Medical Directors, Inc., 681 F.2d 397 (5th Cir.1982); Jackson v. MPI Home Video, 694 F.Supp. 483 (N.D.Ill.1988); Wildlife Internationale, Inc. v. Clements, 591 F.Supp. 1542 (S.D.Oh.1984); Geisel v. Poynter Prods., Inc., 283 F.Supp. 261, 267 (S.D.N.Y.1968). Moreover, courts have recognized false endorsement claims brought by plaintiffs, including celebrities, for the unauthorized imitation of their distinctive attributes, where those attributes amount to an unregistered commercial "trademark." See Dallas Cowboys Cheerleaders, Inc. v. Pussycat Cinema, Ltd., 604 F.2d 200, 205 (2d Cir.1979) (recognizing claim under § 43(a) because uniform worn by star of X-rated movie was confusingly similar to plaintiffs' trademark uniforms, falsely creating impression that plaintiffs "sponsored or otherwise approved the use" of the uniform); Allen v. Men's World Outlet, Inc., 679 F.Supp. 360, 368 (S.D.N.Y.1988) (celebrity states a claim under § 43(a) by showing that advertisement featuring photograph of a look-alike falsely represented that advertised products were associated with him); Allen v. National Video, Inc., 610 F.Supp. 612, 625–26 (S.D.N.Y.1985) (recognizing celebrity's false endorsement claim under § 43(a) because celebrity has commercial investment in name and face tantamount to interests of a trademark holder in distinctive mark); see also Lahr v. Adell Chemical Co., 300 F.2d 256, 258 (1st Cir.1962) (imitation of unique voice actionable as common law unfair competition); cf. Sinatra v. Goodyear Tire & Rubber Co., 435 F.2d 711, 716 (9th Cir.1970) (rejecting common law unfair competition claim because plaintiff's voice not sufficiently unique to be protectable), cert. denied, 402 U.S. 906 (1971).

The persuasiveness of this case law as to the cognizability of Waits' Lanham Act claim is reinforced by the 1988 Lanham Act amendments. * * * Specifically, we read the amended language to codify case law interpreting section 43(a) to encompass false endorsement claims. In light of persuasive judicial authority and the subsequent congressional approval of that authority, we conclude that false endorsement claims, including those premised on the unauthorized imitation of an entertainer's distinctive voice, are cognizable under section 43(a).

B. *Standing*

According to the defendants, however, Waits lacks standing to sue for false endorsement. They assert that because he is not in competition with the defendants, he cannot sue under the Lanham Act. Common sense contradicts this argument, for the purported endorser who is commercially damaged by the false endorsement will rarely if ever be a competitor, and yet is the party best situated to enforce the Lanham Act's prohibition on such conduct. * * *

[Holding that the "dispositive question" on standing is whether plaintiff "has a reasonable interest to be protected against false advertising," the court concluded that § 43(a) "does not require 'actual competition' in the traditional sense; it extends to a purported endorser who has an economic interest akin to that of a trademark holder in controlling the commercial exploitation of his or her identity."]

C. *Merits*

The defendants next argue that Waits' false endorsement claim must fail on its merits because the Doritos commercial "did not represent that . . . [Waits] sponsored or endorsed their product." We disagree. The court correctly instructed the jury that in considering Waits' Lanham Act claim, it must determine whether "ordinary consumers . . . would be confused as to whether Tom Waits sang on the commercial . . . and whether he sponsors or endorses SalsaRio Doritos." The jury was told that in making this determination, it should consider the totality of the evidence, including the distinctiveness of Waits' voice and style, the evidence of actual confusion as to whether Waits actually sang on the commercial, and the defendants' intent to imitate Waits' voice. * * *

At trial, the jury listened to numerous Tom Waits recordings, and to a recording of the Doritos commercial in which the Tom Waits impersonator delivered this "hip" endorsement of SalsaRio Doritos: "It's buffo, boffo, bravo, gung-ho, tally-ho, but never mellow . . . try 'em, buy 'em, get 'em, got 'em." The jury also heard evidence, relevant to the likelihood of consumer confusion, that the Doritos commercial was targeted to an audience which overlapped with Waits' audience, males between the ages of 18 to 35 who listened to the radio. Finally, there was evidence of actual consumer confusion: the testimony of numerous witnesses that they actually believed it was Tom Waits singing the words of endorsement.

This evidence was sufficient to support the jury's finding that consumers were likely to be misled by the commercial into believing that Waits endorsed SalsaRio Doritos.

[The jury award of $100,000 on the Lanham Act claim, representing the fair market value of Waits' services, was vacated as duplicative of the damages awarded on the voice misappropriation claim. The court did, however, uphold an award of attorney's fees under the Lanham Act.]

Affirmed in part and vacated in part.

NOTES AND QUESTIONS

(1) In the Midler v. Ford Motor Co. case on which Judge Boochever so heavily relies, the Young and Rubicam advertising agency had prepared a series of television commercials for Ford designed to build an emotional connection with "yuppies" by stirring memories of their college days. The commercials used popular songs from the seventies, in many instances sung by the original artist. When Bette Midler refused to participate, Young and Rubicam used one of Midler's former backup singers to imitate Midler's rendition of her 1973 hit *Do You Want to Dance.* In the opinion cited in *Waits,* the Ninth Circuit overturned a summary judgment for the defendants on Midler's appropriation of identity claim. She eventually won a $400,000 jury award, which was affirmed by the

Ninth Circuit. See 22 U.S.P.Q.2d 1478 (9th Cir.1991), cert. denied, 503 U.S. 951 (1992).

(2) The opinion in *Midler* distinguished the Ninth Circuit's earlier decision in Sinatra v. Goodyear Tire & Rubber Co., 435 F.2d 711 (9th Cir.1970), cert. denied, 402 U.S. 906 (1971), which at the time was the leading case on voice imitation. In *Sinatra,* an advertising agency (once again Young and Rubicam) created a campaign for Goodyear to promote its "wide boots" tires. The commercials centered around the music and revised lyrics from *These Boots are Made for Walkin',* a song made popular by plaintiff Nancy Sinatra. According to the court, Sinatra's "complaint is not that her sound is uniquely personal; it is that the sound in connection with the music, lyrics and arrangement, which made her the subject of popular identification, ought to be protected." The Ninth Circuit affirmed a summary judgment in favor of the defendants. The court in *Midler* distinguished the *Sinatra* case with the following comments:

> The basis of Nancy Sinatra's complaint was unfair competition; she claimed that the song and the arrangement had acquired "a secondary meaning" which, under California law, was protectible. This court noted that the defendants "had paid a very substantial sum to the copyright proprietor to obtain the license for the use of the song and all of its arrangements." To give Sinatra damages for their use of the song would clash with federal copyright law. Summary judgment for the defendants was affirmed. * * * If Midler were claiming a secondary meaning to "Do You Want To Dance" or seeking to prevent the defendants from using that song, she would fail like Sinatra. But that is not this case. Midler does not seek damages for Ford's use of "Do You Want To Dance," and thus her count is not preempted by federal copyright law. Copyright protects "original works of authorship fixed in any tangible medium of expression." 17 U.S.C. § 102(a). A voice is not copyrightable. The sounds are not "fixed."

The Ninth Circuit offered an extensive analysis of its voice appropriation case law in Laws v. Sony Music Ent., Inc., 448 F.3d 1134 (9th Cir.2006), cert. denied, 549 U.S. 1252 (2007). Plaintiff Laws raised common law and statutory right of publicity claims against Sony, who had used samples from Laws's recording of "Very Special" in producing the Jennifer Lopez recording of "All I Have." Sony, however, had a license from Elektra Records, owner of the copyright in Laws's sound recording. Judge Bybee thought that Laws's claim was different from the voice appropriation claims upheld in Waits v. Frito–Lay and Midler v. Ford. "In contrast to *Midler* and *Waits,* where the licensing party obtained only a license to the song, and then imitated the artist's voice, here Sony obtained a license to use Laws's recording itself." The court agreed with Sony that the claims were preempted under § 301. "Her state tort action challenges control of the artistic work itself and could hardly be more closely related to the subject matter of the Copyright Act."

(3) Is the decision in *Midler* imposing liability for an imitation of Bette Midler's recorded performance of *Do You Want to Dance* inconsistent with § 114 of the Copyright Act, which protects sound recordings against duplication, but not against imitation? Is the distinction in *Waits* between the imitation of "voice" and "style" sufficient to avoid potential conflict?

(4) On the imitation of a performing "style," see Shaw v. Time–Life Records, 38 N.Y.2d 201, 379 N.Y.S.2d 390, 341 N.E.2d 817 (1975), in which bandleader Artie Shaw objected to a re-creation of his "sound" in a newly-recorded collection of

"Swing Era" classics. The New York Court of Appeals affirmed that Shaw had no property interest in his "sound," but said that he was entitled to explore at trial whether the advertising and labeling of the records might cause purchasers to believe that the recordings were actual Artie Shaw performances.

On the possibility of protecting elements of a performer's "style" as an aspect of the right of publicity (p. 743 infra), see Estate of Presley v. Russen, 513 F.Supp. 1339 (D.N.J.1981), in which the court, although declining to issue a preliminary injunction, found a likelihood of success on a right of publicity claim directed against a live stage production imitating an Elvis Presley performance.

3. TITLES

Centaur Communications, Ltd. v. A/S/M Communications, Inc.

United States Court of Appeals, Second Circuit, 1987.
830 F.2d 1217.

■ Before CARDAMONE and MINER, CIRCUIT JUDGES, and SPRIZZO, DISTRICT JUDGE.

■ CARDAMONE, CIRCUIT JUDGE:

* * *

In a judgment of the United States District Court for the Southern District of New York (Pollack, J.) entered on January 20, 1987, the district court judge found that the plaintiff-appellee Centaur Communications, Ltd. (Centaur or appellee) had established that the phrase, "Marketing Week," the title of a Centaur publication, was a protectible trademark under both federal and state law. The trial judge also ruled that the defendant-appellant A/S/M Communications, Inc. (A/S/M or appellant) had infringed upon the mark because the title of its publication, "ADWEEK's Marketing Week," would be likely to create confusion among consumers as to the source or origin of A/S/M's magazine. Based on these findings, it granted injunctive relief. We subsequently stayed a portion of the injunction pending appeal. We now affirm.

This appeal involves two weekly publications with similar titles, both of which focus on marketing news. For purposes of clarity, we will refer to Centaur's publication as *Marketing Week* and A/S/M's as *ADWEEK's Marketing Week*. Although both magazines are concerned with marketing, the emphasis of each is different. *Marketing Week* concentrates on the British market, though it does have a page devoted to marketing news in the United States, and *ADWEEK's Marketing Week* is geared towards the American market. * * *

The main issue raised is the correctness of the district court's determination that by its use of the term "Marketing Week" A/S/M violated § 43(a) of the Lanham Act.

I. *The Lanham Act Claim*

Section 43(a) of the Lanham Act proscribes "false designation of origin" in relation to goods or services. 15 U.S.C. § 1125(a) (1982). This section is the only provision in the Lanham Act that protects an unregistered mark like Centaur's. Its purpose is to prevent consumer confusion regarding a product's source, see Lois Sportswear, U.S.A., Inc. v. Levi Strauss & Co., 799 F.2d 867, 871 (2d Cir.1986), and to enable those that fashion a product to differentiate it from others on the market. International Order of Job's Daughters v. Lindeburg & Co., 633 F.2d 912, 918 (9th Cir.1980), cert. denied, 452 U.S. 941 (1981). In that way producers create goodwill with consumers. The device used to protect both groups is a trademark. * * *

Because the title, "Marketing Week," is not registered, Centaur may only succeed in this infringement suit if it proves that (1) the mark has acquired secondary meaning and (2) there is a likelihood of confusion as to the source of the publication. See Thompson Medical Co. v. Pfizer Inc., 753 F.2d 208, 213, 216 (2d Cir.1985); [20th Century Wear, Inc. v. Sanmark–Stardust Inc., 747 F.2d 81, 90 (2d Cir.1984), cert. denied, 470 U.S. 1052 (1985)]. This two-step analysis reflects two different questions. The inquiry into the existence of secondary meaning examines whether the proponent of the mark has acquired a protectible interest in it. See American Television & Communications Corp. v. American Communications & Television, Inc., 810 F.2d 1546, 1548 (11th Cir.1987); Security Center, Ltd. v. First Nat'l Sec. Centers, 750 F.2d 1295, 1298 (5th Cir.1985). An examination into the likelihood of confusion considers whether that interest has been infringed. See *Lois Sportswear*, 799 F.2d at 871. We discuss each of these questions.

A.   *Secondary Meaning*

A mark acquires secondary meaning when "it [is] shown that the *primary* significance of the term in the minds of the consuming public is not the product but the producer." 20th Century Wear, Inc. v. Sanmark–Stardust Inc., 815 F.2d 8, 10 (2d Cir.1987) (quoting Ralston Purina Co. v. Thomas J. Lipton, Inc., 341 F.Supp. 129, 133 (S.D.N.Y.1972) (emphasis in original)). Thus, the crux of the doctrine of secondary meaning "is that the mark comes to identify not only the goods but the source of those goods," even though the relevant consuming public might not know the name of the producer. Id. ("[C]onsumers often buy goods without knowing the personal identity or actual name of the [producer]."). Nonetheless, someone seeking to establish secondary meaning must show that the purchasing public associates goods designated by a particular mark with but a single—although anonymous—source. Id. * * *

Moreover, it is only necessary to show that a substantial segment of the relevant group of consumers made the requisite association between the product and the producer. * * * The district court here found that the relevant consuming public (i.e., market) of the magazines was "executives in the international marketing and advertising community in the United States." 652 F.Supp. at 1110. Because neither party challenges this definition of the group, it is the starting point for analysis.

In *Thompson Medical* we collected the various precedents that discussed the question of secondary meaning, 753 F.2d at 271, and drew from them the elements utilized in determining whether secondary meaning had been created, noting that "no 'single factor [was] determinative,' and [that] every element need not be proved." Id. (quoting American Footwear Corp. v. General Footwear Co., 609 F.2d 655, 663 (2d Cir.1979)). The elements are (1) advertising expenditures, (2) consumer studies linking the mark to a source, (3) unsolicited media coverage of the product, (4) sales success, (5) attempts to plagiarize the mark, and, (6) length and exclusivity of the mark's use. Id. After applying these criteria to its definition of the relevant market the district court found that the mark "Marketing Week" had acquired a secondary meaning. * * *

(1) *Advertising Expenditures*

The characteristics of the relevant market are important in considering advertising expenditures. Compared to other advertising campaigns, Centaur's efforts were relatively modest. * * * It expended $10,000 in a direct mail solicitation campaign targeted at 26,000 subscribers of *Advertising Age.*

Nonetheless, the record discloses that Centaur publicized *Marketing Week* by other means. For the past three years it has mailed brochures to the top 100 American advertising agencies. Its senior director has traveled to the United States twice a year for the last eight years to make sales presentations to advertising agencies and the media. * * * Moreover, Centaur produces a video guide to advertising agencies in England, many of which are overseas offices of American agencies. Centaur has also sponsored various conferences featuring speakers from American advertising agencies and companies under the "Marketing Week" title. And, it has generated in recent years up to $250,000 in revenues from U.S. advertisers buying space in *Marketing Week.*

Thus, these activities support the conclusion that Centaur's efforts were effective in causing the relevant group of consumers to associate *Marketing Week* with it. * * *

(2) *Consumer Studies Linking Mark to Source*

The most vigorously disputed aspect of this case is the evidence of consumer associations linking the mark to appellee. The dispute encompasses the district court's reliance on "anecdotal" testimony by Centaur's witnesses and its treatment of A/S/M's survey. The trial court credited testimony of the head of another trade magazine, *Advertising Age,* Mr. Rance Crain, and of the chief executive officer of a large advertising agency, Mr. Edward Ney, that *Marketing Week* had substantial recognition and acceptance in the relevant market.

Appellant mounts several challenges to the use of this evidence. First, it attacks reliance on anecdotal testimony by consumers instead of use of a consumer survey. This attack is misplaced. We have never rejected use of direct testimony by consumers. Cf. *20th Century,* 815 F.2d at 10 (in passing on the question of secondary meaning, the court noted the absence of testimony from consumers or a consumer survey). And, though surveys have become the usual way of demonstrating secondary meaning, see Mattel, Inc. v. Azrak–Hamway Int'l, Inc., 724 F.2d 357, 361 (2d. Cir.1983) (per curiam), they are not the only way. * * *

A/S/M conducted two surveys designed to test consumer association of the mark "Marketing Week" to Centaur. No consumer in either survey made the association. These surveys were admitted into evidence, but their significance was discounted by the district court, which stated that they were "of dubious value in the totality of the evidence." 652 F.Supp. at 1110. * * *

The surveys here, according to the testimony of Dr. Hans Zeisel, were designed to test the reactions of "people in executive positions in marketing in American business enterprises and institutions." These people did not correspond to the relevant group—"executives in the international marketing and advertising community in the United States"—defined by the district court. Thus, the value of the surveys was correctly discounted, leaving direct evidence of consumer association of "Marketing Week" with Centaur as inconclusive.

(3) *Sales Success*

As previously mentioned, American subscriptions to *Marketing Week* are limited. In another context, such a small base might be fatal. But the paucity of subscribers in the instant case must be considered in light of two factors. First, some of the subscriptions are held by large advertising agencies and companies where the magazine is read by more than one person. Second, Centaur sold advertising to *Business Week,* the *New York Times,* Hilton International, and McGraw Hill. Because these advertising decisions typically involve advertising agencies and client companies, they suggest a recognition among the relevant group of consumers. In sum, the limited success of Centaur in attracting subscribers tends to undercut a finding of secondary meaning, but in light of the discussed considerations, it is not dispositive.

(4) *Unsolicited Media Coverage*

With respect to unsolicited media coverage, *Marketing Week* has been cited in such publications as *Business Week* and the Associated Press. Not much significance may be ascribed to such citations because it is not clear what they indicate about the relevant group of consumers. * * *

(5) *Attempts to Plagiarize*

The most persuasive *Thompson Medical* factor is the finding that A/S/M had intentionally copied Centaur's mark. See *20th Century*, 815 F.2d at 10 (finding of intentional copying was persuasive, if not conclusive, evidence of consumer recognition and goodwill). Appellant was aware of appellee's publication. Its executive vice-president and principal stockholder had copies of *Marketing Week* in his office. Additionally, the parties previously had discussed a joint video venture, as well as Centaur's possible acquisition of some shares in A/S/M. * * *

(6) *Length and Exclusivity*

Another *Thompson Medical* factor that supports the finding of secondary meaning is the length and exclusivity of Centaur's use of the mark. From 1978 Centaur had continuously and exclusively used "Marketing Week" as its mark until A/S/M changed the title of *ADWEEK's National Marketing Edition* in September 1986. * * *

To summarize: given the findings of intentional copying of the mark, its duration and exclusive use, and the relative significance of advertising expenditures, considered in the context of the relevant consumer group, we are unable to say that the district court was clearly erroneous in concluding that "Marketing Week" had achieved secondary meaning. Accordingly, we turn to the second part of the Lanham Act analysis to explore whether the use of "Marketing Week" by A/S/M was likely to confuse consumers as to the source of the product.

B. *Likelihood of Confusion*

Having determined that Centaur has a protectible property interest in its mark, we take up the question of whether A/S/M has infringed upon that right. In order to succeed on this sort of Lanham Act claim, a plaintiff must show a "likelihood that an appreciable number of ordinarily prudent purchasers are likely to be misled, or indeed simply confused, as to the source of the goods in question." Mushroom Makers, Inc. v. R.G. Barry

Corp., 580 F.2d 44, 47 (2d Cir.1978) (per curiam), cert. denied, 439 U.S. 1116 (1979). * * *

In Polaroid Corp. v. Polarad Elecs. Corp., 287 F.2d 492 (2d Cir), cert. denied, 368 U.S. 820 (1961), Judge Friendly set out a multifactor balancing test. The factors are: (1) the strength of the mark, (2) the degree of similarity between the two marks, (3) the proximity of the products, (4) the likelihood that the senior user of the mark will bridge the gap, (5) evidence of actual confusion, (6) the junior user's bad faith *vel non* in adopting the mark, (7) the quality of the junior user's product, and, finally, (8) the sophistication of the relevant consumer group. Id. at 495. * * * We turn then to the various *Polaroid* findings.

(1) *Strength of the Mark*

Addressing the first *Polaroid* factor, the district court found that "Marketing Week" had achieved a position of relative strength. 652 F.Supp. at 1112. The strength of a mark is its tendency to identify the goods sold as emanating from a particular source, even when the source is unknown to the consumer. [McGregor–Doniger Inc. v. Drizzle Inc., 599 F.2d 1126, 1131 (2d Cir.1979)]. As discussed above, the degree of the mark's distinctiveness depends in part upon its type. * * * Thus, "Marketing Week," as a descriptive mark is, by definition, somewhat weak. Yet, a mark's category is not alone controlling. * * *

Marketing Week has been in circulation a comparatively short time with modest sales. But, it circulates in a small market that does not require a large circulation base in order to acquire consumer identification. We think that when this is considered together with Centaur's various promotional activities, consumers in that small market would associate the mark with its source. Thus, the trial court correctly concluded that "Marketing Week" has achieved relative—if not great—strength in its market context.

(2) *Degree of Similarity*

The second factor is the similarity of the two marks. * * *

A/S/M contends that the presence of "Adweek" in its title makes the two titles dissimilar. The argument proves too little. The titles are not identical; yet given the size and logotype of "Adweek", it does not occupy a significant place in the title. Thus, appellant has not shown that the titles are distinct. Hence, this *Polaroid* factor supports the conclusion that the two titles presented a potential for consumer confusion.

(3) *Proximity*

The third factor is the proximity of the products, perhaps more accurately described as "competitive proximity." The concern is whether "it is likely that customers mistakenly will assume either that [the junior user's goods] somehow are associated with [the senior user] or are made by [the senior user]." *Lois Sportswear*, 799 F.2d at 874. * * *

A/S/M correctly points out that the different editorial emphasis—one publication is primarily concerned with marketing news in America and the other with marketing news in Britain—militates against a finding of proximity. * * * This does not end the inquiry however. Both magazines are high quality weekly publications concerned with marketing news. Thus, consumers in the market interested in American marketing news well might assume that Centaur had decided to launch a different magazine primarily concerned with that topic. See *Lois Sportswear*, 799 F.2d at 874 (consumers of non-designer jeans might assume that maker of designer jeans had entered a different market because of similarity of mark on non-designer jeans). Consequently, there is competitive proximity because consumers could have mistakenly assumed that *ADWEEK's Marketing Week* was another Centaur publication, particularly in light of the publications' similarity.

(4) *Bridging the Gap*

The fourth factor looks to whether the senior user of the mark is likely to enter the market in which the junior user is operating, that is, bridge the gap. If the senior user can show such an intention, it "helps to establish a future likelihood of confusion as to source." *Lois Sportswear*, 799 F.2d at 874. One interest that the trademark law protects is "the senior user's interest in being able to enter a related field at some future time." Scarves by Vera, Inc. v. Todo Imports Ltd., 544 F.2d 1167, 1172 (2d Cir.1976). The district court found that Centaur had shown a "clear intention to publish an edition of the magazine with an American focus." 652 F.Supp. at 1113. * * *

(5) *Actual Confusion*

The fifth factor looks to whether any consumers had actually been confused by the products bearing the allegedly confusing marks. The district court found actual confusion in this instance based upon misattributions in *The Wall Street Journal* and *New York Times* as well as certain responses given by interviewees in the survey conducted at appellant's instigation. A/S/M's surveyor found that the interviewers referred to *ADWEEK's Marketing Week* as *Marketing Week*.

* * * The newspaper misattributions found in the present case are isolated incidents that are not probative on the issue of actual confusion. * * * Nor do the responses of those surveyed demonstrate instances of actual confusion. Because the surveyors used an improper frame of reference, it is impossible to determine whether the interviewees were aware of Centaur's publication; therefore, their answers cannot be interpreted as mistakenly referring to one publication when they meant the other.

Evidence of *actual* confusion is not required to prove the likelihood of confusion between the two marks. Ideal Industries, Inc. v. Gardner Bender, Inc., 612 F.2d 1018, 1024 (7th Cir.1979). The absence of such proof is not especially significant in the present case, particularly given the short time before trial—four months—in which the marks were "competing." * * *

(6) *Junior User's Good Faith*

The sixth *Polaroid* factor examines the good faith of the junior user in selecting the mark. * * * As we have previously noted: "We have recognized that evidence of intentional copying raises a presumption that a second comer intended to create a confusing similarity of appearance and succeeded . . . . But if comparison of the [marks] reveals no fair jury issue concerning likelihood of confusion, then intent to copy, even if found from the proffered evidence, would not establish a Lanham Act violation." Warner Bros. v. American Broadcasting Co., 720 F.2d 231, 246–47 (2d Cir.1983).

Here, appellant was well aware of Centaur's use of "Marketing Week" as its mark. This awareness can give rise to an inference of bad faith. * * *

(7) *Quality of Junior User's Product*

The seventh factor looks to the quality of the junior user's product. The district court's finding that *ADWEEK's Marketing Week* is a product of high quality is not disputed and it supports a finding of a likelihood of confusion.

The lack of marked difference in quality between goods supports the inference that they emanate from the same source. * * *

(8) *Sophistication of Consumers*

The final *Polaroid* factor examines the sophistication of the consumers in the relevant market. The parties concede that these consumers are sophisticated. Sophistication of consumers usually militates against a finding of a likelihood of confusion * * *. Here it decreased the likelihood of confusion since neither the products nor the marks are identical. * * *

Upon review of the district court's findings on the various *Polaroid* factors, we agree with its legal conclusion that there existed a likelihood of confusion as to source as a result of A/S/M's use of "Marketing Week" in the title of its magazine. Although there have been no instances of actual confusion of the products among the sophisticated consumers, the findings concerning the relative strength of "Marketing Week", the degree of similarity of the marks, the competitive proximity of the products as well as their quality, Centaur's intention to bridge the gap, and A/S/M's intentional copying of Centaur's mark in bad faith all present a potential for confusion.

In summary, given the correctness of the findings of secondary meaning and a likelihood of confusion, we affirm the district court's conclusion that A/S/M infringed Centaur's trademark and, hence, need not address Centaur's state law claims. * * *

Jackson v. Universal International Pictures

36 Cal.2d 116, 222 P.2d 433 (1950).

The plaintiff Jackson, a writer of long experience, wrote a play that he entitled "Slightly Scandalous." It rehearsed in Los Angeles, opened in Philadelphia, and flopped in New York, closing after seven performances in 1944. About two years later, Universal, aware of Jackson's play, released a movie to which it gave the same name. There was no claim of any similarity in content. Jackson's action was based on the use of his title, for which he claimed secondary meaning. A jury awarded him $17,500. Judge Edmunds, writing for a unanimous court, affirmed:

"There is substantial evidence in the record to support the implied finding of the jury that 'Slightly Scandalous' had acquired a secondary meaning. Jackson's play was publicized in three of the largest cities in this country. The rehearsal and production of the play were announced in dramatic and motion picture journals in Hollywood and New York. Although only about 3,750 persons attended performances of the play, there is no basis for a holding, as a matter of law, that they and the undetermined number who saw the advertising are not sufficient in number to provide a basis for secondary meaning. * * *

"Universal claims that, in order to gain secondary meaning, the title must be associated specifically with the author of the play rather than with the play. The contention is unrealistic and contrary to authority. * * *

"In all probability only a very small percentage of persons who know something about plays can remember or identify the names of the authors. Usually, advertising and publicity are concentrated upon the title and the actors rather than the name of the playwright. There is no logical basis for holding that a public well acquainted with the title and the play could not confer secondary meaning upon that title merely because of unfamiliarity with the author's name."

NOTES ON THE PROTECTION OF LITERARY TITLES

(1) According to the regulations of the Copyright Office, "The following are examples of works not subject to copyright * * *: (a) Words and short phrases such as names, titles, and slogans * * *." 37 C.F.R. § 202.1. The protection of literary titles rests instead on the common law of unfair competition, supplemented by the federal codification in § 43(a) of the Lanham Act. Judge Learned Hand put it this way: "The plaintiff succeeds as soon as he shows an audience educated to understand that the title means his play * * *." International Film Service Co. v. Associated Producers, Inc., 273 Fed. 585 (S.D.N.Y.1921). But of course, the plaintiff must also show that the defendant's use creates a likelihood of confusion.

Priority of use, absent secondary meaning, will not secure exclusive rights. To illustrate, in 1936 the defendants published two issues of a magazine entitled "Information Please," printing a total of 18,000 copies. No further issues were published. A year and a half later, the plaintiff initiated a stump-the-experts radio program also called "Information Please." (The court said that the plaintiff adopted the name "in good faith," but it does not appear whether it was aware of the prior use.) Within a year, after the plaintiff's program had achieved wide popularity, the defendants made arrangements to resume publication under their old title. The plaintiff successfully enjoined the defendants' use. Golenpaul v. Rosett, 174 Misc. 114, 18 N.Y.S.2d 889 (Sup.Ct.1940). See also Gordon v. Warner Bros. Pictures, Inc., 269 Cal.App.2d 31, 74 Cal.Rptr. 499 (1969) (prior use of "FBI Story" for a novel was not sufficient in itself to establish liability for the defendant's later use of "The FBI Story" for a motion picture starring Jimmy Stewart).

Is it possible to acquire rights in a title prior to the release of the work? That was the issue in Metro–Goldwyn Mayer, Inc. v. Lee, 212 Cal.App.2d 23, 27 Cal.Rptr. 833 (1963). MGM was in the process of producing a motion picture based on the fairy tales of the Grimm brothers, all in the public domain; the film was to be released under the title "The Wonderful World of The Brothers Grimm." The defendant, distributing a German film entitled "Grimms Fairy Tales," adopted in its advertising the phrase "A wonderful world of the Grimm Brothers." The court held that the pre-release publicity surrounding the MGM movie (which had been mentioned in gossip columns, trade journals, newspapers, and magazines) was sufficient to support a finding of secondary meaning; the defendant's ads were found to be confusing. In Orion Pictures Co. v. Dell Pub. Co., 471 F.Supp. 392 (S.D.N.Y.1979), the court found that pre-release advertising had created secondary meaning in the movie title "A Little Romance"; a paperback publisher who had changed the name of the book on which the movie was based to exploit the popularity of the film was enjoined.

Secondary meaning, once established, can eventually be lost. The plaintiff in Kirkland v. NBC, Inc., 425 F.Supp. 1111 (E.D.Pa.1976), aff'd, 565 F.2d 152 (3d Cir.1977), had in 1933 written a story entitled "Land of the Lost," which later became a radio program broadcast from 1943 to 1948. In 1974, NBC adopted the same name for a Saturday morning children's television program. In response to the plaintiff's claim of unfair competition, the court found that the public had ceased to associate the title with the plaintiff or her work.

(2) Titles of periodicals and other literary series can sometimes receive protection without a demonstration of secondary meaning if the title is arbitrary or suggestive rather than descriptive of the periodical's content and hence is considered "inherently distinctive." See C.L.A.S.S. Promotions, Inc. v. D.S. Magazines, Inc., 753 F.2d 14 (2d Cir.1985). However, titles of individual works have been subject to a different rule both in actions at common law and under § 43(a) of the Lanham Act. "Ordinarily a suggestive mark is entitled to protection without any showing of secondary meaning because it is inherently distinctive. However, we have applied a more stringent rule to literary titles in requiring the trademark proprietor to demonstrate secondary meaning notwithstanding the suggestive nature of the title." Twin Peaks Prod., Inc. v. Publications Int'l, Ltd., 996 F.2d 1366 (2d Cir.1993). On the protection of titles, see generally J. McCarthy, Trademarks and Unfair Competition §§ 10:1–40.

(3) As *Centaur Communications* shows, the likelihood of confusion may depend on more than the similarity of the titles. Comparisons of content, marketing techniques, and visual appearance often influence the result. In Playboy Enterprises, Inc. v. Chuckleberry Pub., Inc., 687 F.2d 563 (2d Cir.1982), the plaintiff was granted an injunction against the use of "Playmen" as the title for a magazine adopting a cover and format similar to "Playboy." The court found it likely that some consumers would confuse the magazines themselves, while others might assume that the defendant's publication was sponsored by the plaintiff.[e]

Visual comparison proved fatal to a claim of unfair competition in Brown v. Lyle Stuart, Inc., 42 Misc.2d 909, 249 N.Y.S.2d 370 (Sup.Ct.1964). "Sex and the Single Girl" was a collection of advice by a magazine editor. She, her publisher, and Warner Brothers, which had bought the movie rights, sued the author and publisher of "Sex and the Single Man," a more explicit work by "an expert sexologist." Examination of the books and jackets revealed differences that made confusion unlikely. The court also made this observation: "Where titles of books are involved, as distinguished from those of plays, motion pictures and the like, the court will be much more reluctant to find unfair competition because book buyers generally place more importance upon the author than upon the title of a literary work." But the court was more sympathetic to Warner Brothers' concern that the defendants might sell their own movie rights and prejudice Warner's almost completed film. Because the defendants disclaimed any such intention, arguing that their work "is scarcely the kind of book that lends itself to motion picture treatment," the court saw no harm in granting the request for a limited injunction.

Some cases raise the bar for likelihood of confusion when the challenged title has significant "artistic relevance" to the underlying work. In Rogers v. Grimaldi, 875 F.2d 994 (2d Cir.1989), a case brought under § 43(a) of the Lanham Act against a movie title that included the first names of dancers Fred Astaire and Ginger Rogers, Judge Newman said, "The title of a movie may be both an integral element of the film-maker's expression as well as a significant means of marketing the film to the public. * * * [T]he expressive element of titles requires more protection than the labeling of ordinary commercial products." To accommodate the interest in free expression, the court held that un-

---

[e] So-called "reverse confusion," wherein the infringer's use of the title causes confusion as to the source of the *plaintiff's* work, can also support a finding of unfair competition. See Capital Films Corp. v. Charles Fries Prod., Inc., 628 F.2d 387 (5th Cir.1980) ("The Trial of Lee Harvey Oswald" used first as the title of the plaintiff's film and later for an ABC television movie).

less the title was confusingly similar to another title, the author should not be liable "unless the title has no artistic relevance to the underlying work whatsoever, or, if it has some artistic relevance, unless the title explicitly misleads as to the source or the content of the work." See, e.g., Twin Peaks Prod., Inc. v. Publications Int'l, Ltd., 996 F.2d 1366 (2d Cir.1993) (remanding on the issue of likely confusion between the plaintiff's *Twin Peaks* television series and the defendant's book entitled *Welcome to Twin Peaks: A Complete Guide to Who's Who and What's What*). The Ninth Circuit in Mattel, Inc. v. MCA Records, Inc., 296 F.3d 894 (9th Cir.2002), cert. denied, 537 U.S. 1171 (2003), adopting the *Rogers* standard, held that the defendants' song *Barbie Girl* did not infringe the plaintiff's rights in its BARBIE doll trademark.

(4) Returning to "Sex and the Single Girl," it appears that Warner Brothers had paid a substantial sum for the movie rights, essentially for the title, for that book too scarcely lent itself to movie treatment. But if secondary meaning is the touchstone, what exactly did Warner Brothers buy? Or take the more extreme case where a seller has merely thought up an attractive title, but has not used it in connection with any work. If sales of titles are assimilated to sales of trademarks, they may be embarrassed by the orthodox rule that trademark rights cannot be transferred in gross (i.e., without a transfer of the business or goodwill associated with the mark). Restatement, Third, Unfair Competition § 34 (1995); see also § 10 of the Lanham Act, 15 U.S.C.A. § 1060. Should titles be assimilated for this purpose to other commercial marks?

There is apparently a lively market in movie titles, supported by an unofficial title registry run by the Motion Picture Association of America. The MPAA issues registration reports, giving studios time to file a protest if they believe a new title is too similar to a registered title of their own. Among the hundreds of protests filed each year, only a few go to formal arbitration; most are settled through buy-outs or trades. See Goldstein, Hey, Let's Play the Movie Title Game!, L.A. Times, Aug. 20, 1997, p. F1. The workings of the title registry are described in E. McCarthy, How Important is a Title? An Examination of the Private Law Created by the Motion Picture Association of America, 56 U. Miami L.Rev. 1071 (2002).

(5) Attempts to obtain federal trademark registration for titles of literary works have generally been unsuccessful. Application of Cooper, 254 F.2d 611 (C.C.P.A.1958), remains influential. Cooper, author of a children's book entitled "Teeny–Big," the story of "a little elf with magic powers of self-expansion," applied for registration of the title as a trademark for books. Registration was refused, the court likening the title to "a descriptive name like 'canned beans,' rather than a trademark like 'Sunkist.'" It concluded that since "Teeny–Big is no more than the name of a book, its only name, it is not a trademark under the statute, Section 2." (Is this exclusion consistent with § 14(3) of the Lanham Act, 15 U.S.C.A. § 1064(3), which says that a "mark shall not be deemed to be the generic name of goods or services solely because such mark is also used as a name of or to identify a unique product or service"?) The court conceded that the title of a series of works and the names of periodicals such as magazines and newspapers can be registered as trademarks. Is there a sound distinction? The Federal Circuit reiterated the rule that the title of a single work cannot be registered as a trademark under the Lanham Act in Herbko Int'l, Inc. v. Kappa Books, Inc., 308 F.3d 1156 (Fed.Cir.2002). The court said that the rule insures that after the copyright expires, others will be free to publish the work under the original title. The court also emphasized in a footnote that titles of single works remain protectable under § 43(a) upon proof of secondary meaning.

(6) Is state law free to offer protection against the confusing use of a title? Is a right to prevent the use of a confusing title "equivalent to any of the exclusive rights" of copyright under the test for preemption in § 301?

The preemption issue is moot when § 43(a) of the Lanham Act is invoked to protect a title. (See § 301(d).) In National Lampoon, Inc. v. American Broadcasting Co., 376 F.Supp. 733 (S.D.N.Y.), aff'd, 497 F.2d 1343 (2d Cir.1974), the plaintiff was the publisher of the magazine "National Lampoon" (having obtained a license for the name from the publishers of the "Harvard Lampoon," a century-old college humor magazine). It successfully invoked § 43(a) to enjoin the use of "Lampoon" as the title for a television show. Similarly, Simon & Schuster, publisher of *The Book of Virtues,* offered sufficient proof of secondary meaning and likelihood of confusion under § 43(a) to enjoin *The Children's Audiobook of Virtues.* Simon & Schuster, Inc. v. Dove Audio, Inc., 970 F.Supp. 279 (S.D.N.Y.1997). The owners of the 1956 movie *Bridge on the River Kwai* used § 43(a) to prevent the release of a film entitled *Return from the River Kwai*; the plaintiffs had established secondary meaning for the title and there was evidence that some reviewers thought that the defendants' movie was a sequel. Tri–Star Pictures, Inc. v. Unger, 14 F.Supp.2d 339 (S.D.N.Y.1998). But a plaintiff cannot succeed under § 43(a) absent proof of secondary meaning and a likelihood of confusion. The heirs of the author of a famous short story entitled *First Contact*, published in 1945, sued Paramount Pictures over its use of the title *Star Trek: First Contact* for a 1996 motion picture. The court granted Paramount a summary judgment, holding that the title had become generic for a class of stories about a first encounter with extraterrestrial life, and in any event there was insufficient proof of secondary meaning. Estate of Jenkins v. Paramount Pictures Corp., 90 F.Supp.2d 706 (E.D.Va.2000), aff'd, 7 Fed.Appx. 270 (4th Cir.2001). See also Davis v. United Artists, Inc., 547 F.Supp. 722 (S.D.N.Y.1982) (denying relief under § 43(a) against the use of "Coming Home" as a movie title, despite the plaintiff's prior use on a novel).

(7) Can the use of names or titles be challenged under the misappropriation doctrine? In Universal City Studios, Inc. v. Montgomery Ward & Co., 207 U.S.P.Q. 852 (N.D.Ill.1980), the owner of the movies *Jaws* and *Jaws 2* obtained a preliminary injunction against the use of those terms in connection with a line of food waste disposers marketed by the defendant: "Likelihood of confusion is not required. Under the laws of Illinois, one may not use the mark of another to obtain a 'free ride' on his efforts to promote that mark." The court cited *INS,* but it also found a likelihood of confusion as to approval, association, or sponsorship. For a similar result, see Universal City Studios, Inc. v. Kamar Industries, Inc., 217 U.S.P.Q. 1162 (S.D.Tex.1982) ("I Love E.T." on drinking mugs enjoined). Can these results survive analysis under § 301? Is a right to prevent the misappropriation of a title "equivalent" to an exclusive right of reproduction? Is it a right in "the subject matter of copyright as specified by sections 102 and 103"?

———————

TITLES OF WORKS OUT OF COPYRIGHT

Gotham Music Service v. Denton & Haskins Music Publishing Co.

Court of Appeals of New York, 1932.
259 N.Y. 86, 181 N.E. 57.

Appeal from Supreme Court, Appellate Division, First Department.

Action by the Gotham Music Service, Inc., and another, against the Denton & Haskins Music Publishing Company, Inc. From a final judgment of the Appellate Division granting a permanent injunction and awarding damages, and an order of the Appellate Division reversing an order of the Special Term on reargument and directing resettlement of an interlocutory judgment (233 App.Div. 839, 250 N.Y.S. 929), defendant appeals.

Judgment reversed, and complaint dismissed.

■ POUND, C.J. Some years ago, as far back as 1925, a song called "Gambler's Blues" was sung and played throughout the country. It was a melancholy ballad purporting to have been sung by a gambler in a barroom after he had seen his sweetheart lying dead in the infirmary. It was not a copyrighted publication. Both song and melody became publici juris or of public right. Any one was free to produce them.

In March, 1929, the plaintiffs revived the old song under the title "St. James' Infirmary." The infirmary heretofore unidentified was given a name. They put forward an advertising and publicity campaign to sell the old composition under the new name. They made the song popular. On or about March, 1930, the defendant, a rival music publishing house, put on the market the same song and melody under the title "St. James' Infirmary or Gambler's Blues." Its nominal purpose was to link both titles under one name so that a customer who called for either might be supplied. The defendant has been restrained from using the title "St. James' Infirmary" or any simulation or imitation thereof as the title of a (i.e., any) musical composition, and judgment for damages has been entered against it.

Infringement of copyright is not involved. Respondents' brief so states, and the complaint contains no claim that copyright property has been misappropriated. If such were the grievance, the remedy would be in the federal courts. Underhill v. Schenck, 238 N.Y. 7, 143 N.E. 773. Plaintiffs have no property in the name "St. James' Infirmary." The name describes the song and, generally speaking, any one may use it to describe the same song. Black v. Ehrich (C.C.) 44 F. 793; Atlas Mfg. Co. v. Street & Smith (C.C.A.) 204 F. 398, 404; Merriam Co. v. Syndicate Pub. Co., 237 U.S. 618. The plaintiffs must establish that defendant's acts amount to an unlawful abuse of competition by creating a reasonable likelihood of deception; that persons who desire the song and melody because plaintiffs have made them popular may be misled by defendant into thinking that they are purchasing the plaintiffs' version of the song. This they have wholly failed to accomplish.

Defendant is not deceiving the public. The song is popular, not because plaintiffs publish it, but because they have advertised it and thus made it known to the public. Their names are not identified with the new name. The demand is for the song, and not for the publisher. * * *

* * * A name which is descriptive of one song may not be attached by a competitor to another when the duplication will mislead the public into the

belief that the two songs are alike; but the name, so far as it is a symbol descriptive of the old song, is not protected unless it is identified with the source or origin of production. Underhill v. Schenck, supra. Here it is sought to protect the title because plaintiffs invented it, but no question of imitation or deception or mistake arises. No unlawful competition in trade is shown, nor breach of contract or trust. In the absence of the use of the name in such a way as to create a likelihood that people will be misled, the name is publici juris, and may be used by all.

The judgment of the Appellate Division should be reversed and the complaint dismissed, with costs in all courts.

■ CRANE, J. (dissenting). I view this case somewhat differently from the Chief Judge. True, the song, called "Gambler's Blues," became publici juris, and any one was free to use it, print copies of it, and sell it on the market. No one had or could have a restricted right to sell the song. Also, the name, the original name, "Gambler's Blues," followed the song, and any one could use this name in reproducing it. The plaintiffs, however, did more than this to make the song valuable. No one wanted it; it had passed out of use, had ceased to be popular; there was no demand for it. The plaintiffs made changes in tempo of the music, added a few verses, and gave it a new name, "St. James' Infirmary," and then started an advertising campaign, spending thousands of dollars in making the name, "St. James' Infirmary," known to the public. Under this name the plaintiffs advertised extensively throughout the country their rearrangement of this old song.

Now comes the defendant and seeks to reap the harvest of this advertising. It publishes the old song and gives it the name which the plaintiffs have made popular; namely, "St. James' Infirmary." If they had called it by its original name, "Gambler's Blues," no one could complain, and no rights would have been violated. This would not do; the defendant must reap the profits which legitimately should go to the plaintiffs as the result of their expenditures for advertising, and so the defendant takes "St. James' Infirmary" for no other reason than to gain the reward of others' work. * * *

"If a copyright does not exist, or, once existing, has been lost, the name is lost, too, in so far as it is merely a symbol descriptive of the copyrighted thing." Underhill v. Schenck, 238 N.Y. 7, 20, 143 N.E. 773, 778. Thus, the old name, "Gambler's Blues," is as free for use in connection with the old song as the song itself. This does not mean, however, that an established trade may not be built up for an arrangement under a new name which will prevent unfair competition by use of the same name and arrangement, even though no copyrights exist. * * *

Here the copyright on the song had expired; but this did not prevent the plaintiffs from having a right to their rearrangement and the new name which they had given it, especially when through much expenditure of money they had built up a demand for the song under that name.

The full and complete answer to the plea of the defendant is to go out and sell the original song under its old name and see how far it gets with it. When the defendant refuses to do this, it is evident that it wants the benefits coming from the plaintiffs' new arrangement and new name, which they have given the song. This is not fair.

The judgment should be affirmed.

G. & C. Merriam Co. v. Ogilvie

United States Circuit Court of Appeals, First Circuit, 1908.
159 Fed. 638.
Certiorari denied 209 U.S. 551.

Appeal from the Circuit Court of the United States for the District of Massachusetts.

■ Before PUTNAM and LOWELL, CIRCUIT JUDGES, and ALDRICH, DISTRICT JUDGE.

■ ALDRICH, DISTRICT JUDGE. This case involves a bill and a crossbill, each party claiming injunction relief against the other. There was an injunction below against each party. The Merriam Company appeal upon the ground that it should not be restrained, and also upon the ground that the injunction against Ogilvie was not broad enough. Ogilvie did not appeal. * * *

The name "Webster" having been copyrighted by the Merriams, they were protected in its use under a statutory right during an expressed term of years. The protection, therefore, in that respect, came by virtue of the copyright rather than by virtue of its use in publication and trade.[f]

The statutory monopoly having expired under statutory limitation, the word "Webster," used in connection with a dictionary, became public property, and any relief granted upon the idea of title or proprietorship in the trade-name of "Webster" would necessarily involve an unwarrantable continuance of the statutory monopoly secured by the copyright.

The authorities and the discussion of this phase of the case by the learned judge in the Circuit Court (Ogilvie v. Merriam Co. [C.C.] 149 Fed. 858, where the facts sufficiently appear)[g] satisfy us in respect to the soundness of the proposition that upon the expiration of the copyright the name "Webster" passed into the field of public right.

* * * [T]hough the name "Webster" as applied to the Merriam Company's dictionary had acquired a secondary meaning, indicating a particular book published and sold by them, it became public property when the copyright expired.

---

[f]   Is this correct?

[g]   The lower court took the facts to be as follows: Having previously acquired all rights in Noah Webster's Dictionary from Webster's heirs, Merriam Company published a number of editions under the title "Webster's." It published Webster's Unabridged Dictionary in 1847; the copyright on this edition expired in 1889. Until 1889, Merriam Company was the sole publisher of dictionaries under the title "Webster's." After 1889, various editions of Webster's Dictionary were published by other publishers, "but, notwithstanding this circumstance, it is shown by a preponderance of evidence that the name 'Webster' still indicates to the public the dictionaries published and sold by the Merriam Company."

The last edition published by Merriam Company prior to the suit was Webster's International Dictionary. Plaintiff Ogilvie proceeded to put out a dictionary called Webster's Imperial Dictionary, "an enlarged and revised edition of Webster's Dictionary, based upon Webster's Unabridged Dictionary." On the cover of the Ogilvie book appeared the name "George W. Ogilvie," and on the title page, "George W. Ogilvie, Publisher." Ogilvie's circulars and advertisements conveyed the impression "that the Ogilvie book is a new edition of Webster's Dictionary published by the Merriam Company, and that it is the successor of Webster's International Dictionary"; Ogilvie had inserted in his circulars and advertisements material taken from Merriam's promotional literature for the International.

Ogilvie in his bill sought to restrain Merriam Company from sending letters to the trade stating that it had the exclusive right to the use of "Webster's" on dictionaries. By cross-bill Merriam Company sought to stop Ogilvie from using "Webster's" on his dictionary and from sending out misleading literature.

The right to use a copyrighted name, however, upon the expiration of the copyright, goes out to the public subject to a certain and well-understood limitation or condition, namely, that the public right to use shall be so exercised as not to deceive members of the public and lead them into the belief that they are buying the particular or identical thing which was produced under the copyright. That the right of public user of the name "Webster" was subject to such a condition was fully recognized by the learned judge who decided this case in the Circuit Court, and, indeed, the principle was forcibly stated by Mr. Justice White in the Singer case.

We think the conclusion reached by the Circuit Court, that the Merriam Company should be enjoined from sending out circulars to the effect that it has the exclusive right to use the name "Webster" in connection with dictionaries, was justified by the evidence and the authorities, and we are content to leave that branch of the case upon the reasoning contained in the opinion of the learned judge of the Circuit Court.

That court also points out, and we think the situation justifies it, that the Ogilvie circulars and advertisements are misleading and deceptive, and show an intention on the part of Ogilvie to trespass upon the reputation of the Merriam Company and to deceive purchasers into buying his dictionary for one of the series of Webster's dictionaries published by the Merriam Company, and it was held that Ogilvie should be enjoined from sending out circulars and advertisements in their present form. We agree that this should be so upon equitable principles, because it presents a situation in which a member of the public seeks to appropriate more than fairly and equitably belongs to him.

It is also our conclusion that the same purpose and the same reasoning hold good with respect to the title page of the Ogilvie publication.

It seems pretty evident from consideration of all the circumstances surrounding these publications, including the correspondence, the circulars, the advertisements, and the character of the litigation, that the purpose of Ogilvie was to put out such a publication and such circulars and advertisements as would lead the public into the supposition that they were buying the Webster Dictionary as improved and added to by the Merriam Publishing Company, and we think that the reasoning of the Circuit Court with respect to the circulars and advertisements applies with equal force to the title page of the Ogilvie publication.

We also think, in view of the ingenious arrangement of the prominent features of the Ogilvie title page, that its weight in the public eye is not fully and unmistakably overcome by printing the name "George W. Ogilvie" upon the back of the cover, or by printing the words "George W. Ogilvie, Publisher," as a part of the title page. * * *

If the title page of the Ogilvie dictionaries had contained, for instance, the words "Webster's Dictionary, published by George W. Ogilvie," with other expressions correctly indicating the identity of the publication, the Merriam Company would have no just cause for complaint. But such is not this case. * * * [Judge Aldrich then describes a number of ways that Ogilvie subordinated his own name and suggested a connection with the Merriam dictionaries.]

It seems to us that Ogilvie was not content with using the word "Webster," which was at large as a word entitled to be used in connection with a dictionary, but purposely used words of description calculated to lead the ordinary purchaser to suppose that he was getting the publication which had been built up by the Merriams. This, we think, was an appropriation of something which he was not entitled to appropriate, and under the circumstances amounts to unfair competition. * * *

The decree of the Circuit Court with respect to the injunction against the Merriam Company is affirmed.

The decree of the Circuit Court for an injunction against Ogilvie in respect to circulars and advertisements is affirmed, and the case is remanded to that court with directions that the injunction against George W. Ogilvie, his agents, attorneys and servants, be so enlarged as to include the title pages and the backs of the dictionaries in the present form, or in any form calculated to deceive members of the public into purchasing his dictionary under the belief that it is a Merriam Webster's Dictionary, and for further proceedings not inconsistent with the opinion passed down this day. All questions of accounting, including the question whether or not the Merriam Company is entitled to an accounting, are open to the Circuit Court. Neither party recovers costs in this court.

NOTES AND QUESTIONS

(1) Upon remand, the lower court entered a decree unsatisfactory to Merriam Company, who again appealed. The Court of Appeals ordered the decree modified so as to require Ogilvie to print on the title page of his book: "This dictionary is not published by the original publishers of Webster's Dictionary, or by their successors." G. & C. Merriam Co. v. Ogilvie, 170 Fed. 167 (1st Cir.1909).

Merriam Company, still seeking to prevent competitors from using the word "Webster's," advanced a different theory in litigation against Syndicate Publishing Co., namely, that the competitor's dictionaries had departed so far from the old Webster's that it would deceive the public if they were allowed to use that name on their altered versions. District Judge Learned Hand pointed out that Merriam had itself in its more recent editions come a long way from the original Webster's. Even its 1847 edition was markedly different from Noah Webster's 1828 original; it had not been edited by Noah, who died in 1843. "Webster's," Hand decided, must accordingly be taken to mean any work which could claim "literary descent" from the original Webster's, and the defendant's dictionary had almost as much claim to this distinction as the plaintiff's current works. G. & C. Merriam Co. v. Syndicate Pub. Co., 207 Fed. 515 (2d Cir.1913) (per curiam affirmance reproducing Judge Hand's opinion in the lower court), appeal dism'd, 237 U.S. 618 (1915). Suppose that the defendant's dictionary could not claim such "literary descent." Would use of the "Webster's" name by the defendant then be actionable as deceptive advertising under § 43(a)(1)(B)?

"Webster's" litigation rolls on. See Merriam–Webster, Inc. v. Random House, Inc., 35 F.3d 65 (2d Cir.1994), cert. denied, 513 U.S. 1190 (1995) (trade dress for the plaintiff's "Webster's Ninth New Collegiate Dictionary" was not infringed by the trade dress used for Random House's "Webster's College Dictionary").

(2) In Walt Disney Prod. v. Souvaine Selective Pictures, 98 F.Supp. 774 (S.D.N.Y.), aff'd, 192 F.2d 856 (2d Cir.1951), the plaintiff had at great expense produced an animated cartoon film based on Lewis Carroll's "Alice in Wonderland," carrying the same title. Advance ballyhoo was considerable and costly. Meanwhile, a competitor also produced an "Alice in Wonderland" movie based on Carroll, using puppets with a live Alice; the production was less expensive and had been given little advance publicity. The pictures were scheduled to open in New York at about the same time. The plaintiff sought an injunction, but its application was denied: "Anyone has a legal right to make a picture based on Louis [sic] Carroll's book and entitled 'Alice in Wonderland.'" What additional facts might justify some measure of relief?

(3) On all these matters, consult L. Kurtz, Protection of Titles of Literary Works in the Public Domain, 37 Rutgers L.Rev. 53 (1984), advocating freedom to use public domain titles, even on derivative works, but with adequate protection against confusion, chiefly through explanatory disclaimers.

A NOTE ON MERCHANDISING RIGHTS

Several of the cases in this section find a likelihood of confusion even when the defendant's use of the name or title occurs in a different medium—a play and a film, a magazine and a radio program. But suppose a title is used in connection with an article of merchandise? If the secondary meaning of the title is sufficiently strong, even this may cause confusion, if not of origin, at least of sponsorship. The PLAYBOY mark, for example, has been protected against unauthorized use on theaters and automobile parts in addition to competing publications,[h] and other magazine, television, and motion picture titles have received similar protection under the confusion rationale.[i] But does the unauthorized use of well-known names and titles inevitably cause a likelihood of confusion? The National Football League has produced surveys indicating that a majority of consumers who encounter clothing bearing its team names and insignia believe that the product is officially sponsored.[j] The decision in Boston Professional Hockey Ass'n v. Dallas Cap & Emblem Mfg., p. 583 supra, goes further, apparently equating mere recognition with confusion of sponsorship. But other cases decline to indulge in any presumption of confusion. When a fraternal organization sought an injunction against the sale of jewelry bearing its insignia, the Ninth Circuit in International Order of Job's Daughters v. Lindeburg & Co., 633 F.2d 912 (9th Cir.1980), cert. denied, 452 U.S. 941 (1981), ordered judgment for the defendant, specifically rejecting *Boston Hockey*:

> It is not uncommon for a name or emblem that serves in one context as a collective mark or trademark also to be merchandised for its

---

[h] See HMH Pub. Co. v. Turbyfill, 330 F.Supp. 830 (M.D.Fla.1971); HMH Pub. Co. v. Brincat, 504 F.2d 713 (9th Cir.1974); Playboy Enterprises, Inc. v. Chuckleberry Pub., Inc., 687 F.2d 563 (2d Cir.1982). See also Turner v. HMH Pub. Co., 380 F.2d 224 (5th Cir.), cert. denied, 389 U.S. 1006 (1967) (restaurant).

[i] See, e.g., Triangle Publications, Inc. v. Rohrlich, 167 F.2d 969 (2d Cir.1948) ("Seventeen" magazine title used on girl's clothing); Paramount Pictures Corp. v. Dorney Park Coaster Co., 698 F.Supp. 1274 (E.D.Pa.1988) ("Top Gun" used on an amusement park ride); Penthouse Int'l Ltd. v. Penthouse Party & Travel Club, Ltd., 184 U.S.P.Q. 479 (E.D.Mich.1974) ("Penthouse" on a travel agency); Esquire, Inc. v. Maira, 101 F.Supp. 398 (M.D.Pa.1951) ("Esquire" on men's clothing); Aurora Products Corp. v. Schisgall Enterprises Inc., 176 U.S.P.Q. 184 (S.D.N.Y.1972) ("Monday Night Football" used on a football game); Wyatt Earp Enterprises, Inc. v. Sackman, Inc., 157 F.Supp. 621 (S.D.N.Y.1958) ("Wyatt Earp" on children's clothing).

[j] See National Football League Properties, Inc. v. Wichita Falls Sportswear, Inc., 532 F.Supp. 651 (W.D.Wash.1982); National Football League Properties, Inc. v. Dallas Cap & Emblem Mfg. Inc., 26 Ill.App.3d 820, 327 N.E.2d 247 (1975). Cf. Processed Plastic Co. v. Warner Communications, Inc., 675 F.2d 852 (7th Cir.1982) (survey indicating that children believed a toy car was sponsored by a television show). The NFL sells over $3 billion in licensed products each year. Major League Baseball does at least equally well.

own intrinsic utility to consumers. We commonly identify ourselves by displaying emblems expressing allegiances. Our jewelry, clothing, and cars are emblazoned with inscriptions showing the organizations we belong to, the schools we attend, the landmarks we have visited, the sports teams we support, the beverages we imbibe. Although these inscriptions frequently include names and emblems that are also used as collective marks or trademarks, it would be naive to conclude that the name or emblem is desired because consumers believe that the product somehow originated with or was sponsored by the organization the name or emblem signifies. * * *

Our holding does not mean that a name or emblem could not serve simultaneously as a functional component of a product and a trademark. * * * Accordingly, a court must closely examine the articles themselves, the defendant's merchandising practices, and any evidence that consumers have actually inferred a connection between the defendant's product and the trademark owner.

In a case similar on its facts to *Job's Daughters,* the Fifth Circuit, narrowly construing its prior decision in *Boston Hockey,* also denied relief:

> * * * Acknowledging, in reference to the *Boston Hockey* decision, that "[i]t is not unreasonable to conclude, given the degree to which sports emblems are used to advertise teams and endorse products, that a consumer seeing the emblem or name of a team on or associated with a good or service would assume some sort of sponsorship or association between the product's seller and the team," the district court in this case found that "[t]he practice with respect to fraternal emblems, and, in particular, fraternal jewelry is markedly different." That finding is supported by the evidence. In Kentucky Fried Chicken Corp. v. Diversified Packaging Corp., 549 F.2d 368 (5th Cir.1977), we explained that *Boston Hockey* does not always equate knowledge of a symbol's source with confusion sufficient to establish trademark infringement and we treated as a fact question the question whether in a given case knowledge of the source of the *symbol* supports the inference that many of the product's typical purchasers would believe that the *product itself* originated with or was somehow endorsed by the owner of the mark. 549 F.2d at 389.

Supreme Assembly, Order of Rainbow for Girls v. J.H. Ray Jewelry Co., 676 F.2d 1079 (5th Cir.1982).

Reliance on *Boston Hockey* also proved futile when the University of Pittsburgh complained about the unauthorized use of its "Pitt" insignia on shirts, jackets, and other apparel made by Champion, the leading producer of "imprinted soft goods." "The notion that a university's name and insignia are its own property, to do with as it chooses, has a certain common-sense appeal. An examination of the law and the facts in this case has convinced us, however, that neither Congress, nor the Pennsylvania Legislature, nor the common law has created the property right that Pitt asserts here." The court found "as a matter of fact, that there is no likelihood of confusion, whether of source, origin, sponsorship, endorsement, or any other nature * * *." University of Pittsburgh v. Champion Products, Inc., 566 F.Supp. 711 (W.D.Pa.1983). However, the tide has clearly turned in favor of the colleges. For example, in Board of Supervisors for Louisiana State Univ. v. Smack Apparel Co., 550 F.3d 465 (5th Cir.2008), cert. denied, 129 S.Ct. 2759 (2009), the court held that even the color scheme of a university can be protected as a trademark, at least when used together with other references to the school; citing *Boston Hockey*, it said that "the overwhelming similarity between the defendant's t-shirts and the Universities' licensed products, and the defendant's admitted intent to create an association with the plaintiffs and to influence consumers in calling the plaintiffs to mind," resulted in the inescapable conclusion "that many consumers would likely be confused and believe that Smack's t-shirts were sponsored or endorsed by the Universities."[k] *Boston Hockey* was also endorsed, and *Job's Daughters* disapproved, in Univ. of Georgia Athletic Ass'n v. Laite, 756 F.2d 1535 (11th Cir.1985) (defendant imitated Georgia's Bulldog mascot on beer cans, although with a disclaimer). See also Boston Athletic Ass'n v. Sullivan, 867 F.2d 22 (1st Cir.1989) (rebuttable presumption of confusion arose from the defendant's references to the plaintiff's Boston Marathon mark on T-shirts, also citing the *INS* case). But the Eleventh Circuit in Univ. of Alabama Bd. of Trustees v. New Life Art, Inc., 683 F.3d 1266 (11th Cir.2012), rejected the contention that a painter who depicted football scenes that included the University of Alabama's uniforms and colors in paintings, prints, and calendars infringed the university's trademarks. The court held that the public interest in free expression outweighed the interest in avoiding confusion from the artistically expressive use since the works had not been marketed as sponsored products.

Should a trademark owner be permitted to enjoin even a non-confusing appropriation of its mark? Could state misappropriation law prohibit the non-deceptive reproduction of the Boston Bruins insignia on caps or shirts? A few cases, citing the Supreme Court's decision in *INS,* have indeed enjoined the "misappropriation of merchandising properties." See Universal City Studios, Inc. v. Montgomery Ward & Co., 207 U.S.P.Q. 852 (N.D.Ill.1980); Universal City Studios, Inc. v. Kamar Industries, Inc., 217 U.S.P.Q. 1162 (S.D.Tex.1982). But others have reached a different conclusion. One court offered this analysis: "Although industry and investment are encouraged by protecting distinctive marks, they are also encouraged by a system that allows entrepreneurs to copy and exploit such marks in nonconfusing ways. Indeed, a system that permits nonconfusing copying may achieve greater social utility and wealth than a system that protects marks without a showing of confusion. The originator of a mark may in some circumstances lose far less in economic value because of copying by others than is gained by the copiers and the public." Bi–Rite Enterprises, Inc. v. Button Master, 555 F.Supp. 1188, 1194–95 (S.D.N.Y.1983) (but granting relief on right of publicity grounds). See also WCVB–TV v. Boston Athletic Ass'n, 926 F.2d 42 (1st Cir.1991) (interpreting its earlier reference to the *INS* case in Boston Athletic Ass'n v. Sullivan, supra, as not indicating a departure from the traditional requirement of a likelihood of confusion.)

Who would be the primary beneficiaries of an exclusive merchandising right? At whose expense? Some tentative conclusions are offered in R. Denicola, Institutional Publicity Rights: An Analysis of the Merchandising of Famous Trade Symbols, 62 N.C.L.Rev. 603 (1984); S. Dogan and M. Lemley, The Merchandising Right: Fragile Theory or *Fait Accompli?*, 54 Emory L.J. 461 (2005), argue that pre-sale or post-sale confusion should

---

[k] The Collegiate Licensing Company serves as the licensing agent for almost 200 universities and athletic conferences in the $4 billion college merchandise market. Its top moneymakers are said to include Florida, Michigan, North Carolina, Notre Dame, and Alabama. Texas is apparently the top earner, bringing in over $10 million a year in licensing royalties. Eight per cent seems to be the customary royalty rate, (with higher rates for bowl game and national championship merchandise).

remain a necessary prerequisite of liability for an unauthorized merchandising use of another's trademark.

4. CHARACTERS

Chaplin v. Amador

93 Cal.App. 358, 269 P. 544 (1928).

Commencing in 1913, Charlie Chaplin adopted a characteristic garb and behavior in motion pictures—he "has generally worn a kind of attire peculiar and individual to himself, consisting of a particular kind or type of mustache, old and threadbare hat, clothes, and shoes, a decrepit derby, ill-fitting vest, tight-fitting coat, and trousers and shoes much too large for him, and with this attire, a flexible cane usually carried, swung, and bent as he performs his part. This character, and the manner of dress, has been used and portrayed by Charles Chaplin for so long and with such artistry, that he has become well known all over the world in this character to such an extent that a display of his picture with the word 'Charlie,' or even with no name at all, has come to mean the plaintiff."

In the 1920s one Charles Amador and others produced a motion picture, "The Race Track," in which Amador appeared under the stage name "Charlie Aplin." Aplin's dress and antics were similar to Chaplin's. In advertising "The Race Track" as the first of a series of twelve comedies, the producers spoke of "record breaking comedies featuring 'Charlie Aplin' in the well-known character, famous the world over." "Our comedian is a world beater in this famous character." Along with views of Charlie Aplin in stage dress, the producers included a quotation from a newspaper stating, "Aplin, whose name is like that of Charlie Chaplin, who looks like him and acts like him, and who is a regular fellow with it all * * *."

Chaplin sought injunctive relief in a California court against Amador. At the opening of the trial, the defendants stated their willingness to abandon the use of any name similar to Charlie Chaplin and to settle on those terms. This was evidently unsatisfactory to the plaintiff and the trial proceeded. The decree entered against the defendants after trial was summarized by the appellate court: "perpetually enjoining and restraining them, their servants, agents, and employees, and all persons acting in privity with them from, (a) disposing of, advertising, or dealing in a motion picture called 'The Race Track'; (b) from using the name 'Charles Aplin' or 'Charlie Aplin,' or any other name similar to that of plaintiff in connection with said motion picture, or any motion picture, in imitation of the motion pictures of plaintiff, which will be likely to deceive the public into believing that plaintiff is acting the role therein hereafter referred to; (c) from advertising, selling, or dealing in any motion pictures which are an imitation of the motion pictures of plaintiff, or style of dress, costume, or mannerisms constituting an imitation of the plaintiff in his name or in his playing or acting the part or character or role of Charlie Chaplin, and which are so like the motion pictures acted in and produced by the plaintiff, and in which the plaintiff plays the principal or leading or any part in such role, as to be likely to deceive the public in believing that said motion pictures are the motion pictures produced and acted by plaintiff, or which would have the likely effect of so deceiving." The injunction was affirmed.

NOTES AND QUESTIONS

(1) Should it make any difference whether Charlie Chaplin originated his garb and behavior or instead copied portions of his characterization from others?

(2) Is it relevant whether the Chaplin films were under copyright? Would the defendants' activities infringe the motion picture copyrights?

Lone Ranger, Inc. v. Cox

United States Circuit Court of Appeals, Fourth Circuit, 1942.
124 F.2d 650.

■ Before PARKER and DOBIE, CIRCUIT JUDGES, and CHESTNUT, DISTRICT JUDGE.

■ PARKER, CIRCUIT JUDGE. This is an action for damages and for injunction based upon alleged infringement of copyright and unfair competition. The plaintiff is the Lone Ranger, Inc., a Michigan corporation, which since the year 1933 has been broadcasting over the radio copyrighted dramatic serial stories featuring the heroic exploits of a mythical western cowboy, "The Lone Ranger", who rides about masked and on a white horse, called "Silver", championing the cause of the oppressed and redressing the wrongs of the community. Plaintiff has licensed a comic strip, entitled "The Lone Ranger", appearing in a number of newspapers and has licensed the use of the name, "The Lone Ranger", as a trademark to vendors of various articles. The radio programs of plaintiff are broadcast from one hundred or more radio stations, are very popular and appeal particularly to children. A "Lone Ranger" safety club, promoted in connection with the programs, has attained a membership of between three and four million young people.

The defendant Powell is a motion picture actor, who in 1937 played the part of Allan King as the "Lone Ranger" in a motion picture produced under license from plaintiff. He has been appearing, under contract with the defendant Cox, in a small circus in which he takes the part of the "Lone Ranger", riding masked on a white horse and giving the cry "Hi, yo Silver" or "Hi, yo, Silver, away!", which is the distinctive call of the "Lone Ranger" to his horse in each of plaintiff's radio programs. He is advertised by the circus as the original "Lone Ranger" or the "Lone Ranger" in person. The words "talking picture" or "of talking picture fame" are prefixed or added to the words "Lone Ranger" in the advertisements, but these qualifying words are in smaller lettering than "Lone Ranger", which is given great prominence. In some, the call to the horse, "Hi, yo, Silver" is prominently displayed. Newspaper advertisements are addressed particularly to children and stress that the "Lone Ranger" is appearing in person. In all, the effect of the advertisements is to create the impression that the original "Lone Ranger", made famous by the radio programs, is appearing with the circus—a result more easily achieved because the public interested is composed very largely of children.

The plaintiff did not produce its copyrights in evidence, relying upon the principles of unfair competition. Its contention is that the advertising and appearances of Powell are unfair in that they are an attempt on his part to appropriate to himself a portion of the good will which plaintiff has built up in connection with its radio programs, and in that the inevitable effect of this infringement upon its rights is to destroy the element of mystery surrounding the character of the "Lone Ranger" as presented by its programs and show him to be a very commonplace person in whom the young people have no further interest, once he has been seen. Plaintiff relies, also, upon a consent decree entered by the United States District Court for the Middle District of Pennsylvania, in which the same defendants were enjoined at the suit of plaintiff from using the name "Lone Ranger" except with reference to the fact that Powell had played the part of Allan King in the motion picture serial of that name, from using the phrases "Hi, yo, Silver" and "Hi, yo, Silver, away!", and from representing in any way, or doing anything that would lead the public to believe, that Powell was identified with the radio programs of plaintiff. * * *

Quite apart from any rights under the Pennsylvania decree or the copyrights relied on, we think that plaintiff, under the principles of unfair competition, was entitled to relief. Under the name or title of "The Lone Ranger", plaintiff had built up a radio feature of great value. The exploits of this mythical character, as portrayed in the radio programs, had become of great interest to countless young people throughout the country and were a source of large revenue to plaintiff. Defendants were attempting to avail themselves of the good will created by the broadcasting of the radio programs and the advertising connected therewith, including the "Lone Ranger" safety clubs. Their conduct in advertising Powell as the "Original Lone Ranger" was manifestly calculated and intended to lead the public to believe that he was the "Lone Ranger" of the radio programs and to attract to the circus those who were interested in the programs and particularly the young people who were members of the safety clubs. The fact that the advertisements contained a reference to the talking picture did little, if anything, to minimize the deception of the children to whom they were primarily addressed, and this deception was accentuated by use of the call "Hi, yo, Silver" in some of the advertisements and in Powell's act in the circus. The defendants were in the business of furnishing entertainment, just as was plaintiff, and there can be no doubt but that they were attempting to pass off their show as being identified with the radio programs of plaintiff, or at least as being connected in some manner therewith, and thus to benefit from the good will which had been built up by plaintiff through its broadcasts and advertising.

We entertain no doubts as to the power and duty of a court of equity to afford relief under such circumstances. While the case presented is not precisely similar to that kind of unfair competition involving the use of a corporate or business name or to the ordinary case involving the unfair use of trademarks and trade names, the principle involved is the same as that recognized in these cases, viz., that a court of equity should enjoin any form of "passing off" which involves fraudulent appropriation, through devices calculated to deceive or mislead the public, of the business or good will which another has built up. * * * We see no reason why the same principles are not applicable in the case of one who perpetrates a fraud both upon the public and upon the producer of radio programs by representing that his performance is connected in some way with such programs. * * *

"Obviously, the question of what is unfair competition in business must be determined with particular reference to the character and circumstances of the business." International News Service v. Associated Press, 248 U.S. 215, 236. * * * Here it is the use of the term "Lone Ranger" and his distinctive call to his horse in such way as to lead to the belief on the part of children interested in the programs of the radio broadcast that the entertainment of defendants is connected in some way with these programs. In all, there is involved the element of fraudulent attempt of some one to "reap where he has not sown" and to appropriate himself "the harvest of those who have sown". Cf. Chafee, Unfair Competition, 53 Harvard Law Review 1289, 1311. Even if relief under the principles of unfair competition were confined to cases of palming off of goods or services, we think that the case at bar would be one calling for relief; but we do not understand that relief in this class of cases is so limited. As said by the Supreme Court in International News Service v. Associated Press, supra: "It is said that the elements of unfair competition are lacking because there is no attempt by defendant to palm off its goods as those of the complainant, characteristic of the most familiar, if not the most typical, cases of unfair competition. Howe Scale Co. v. Wyckoff, Seamans [& Benedict], 198 U.S. 118. But we cannot concede that the right to equitable relief is confined to that class of cases." * * *

And we are not impressed by the argument that defendants are protected in what they have done because of Powell's connection with the motion pictures licensed by plaintiff. The contention that the advertisement is true is not correct. Powell is not the "Lone Ranger" at all.[1] He is merely a moving picture actor who took the part of the "Lone Ranger" in a motion picture play of that name produced long after the "Lone Ranger" of radio had become widely known. The only reason that defendant's desire to call him the "talking picture Lone Ranger" or the "Lone Ranger of talking picture fame", with "Lone Ranger" emphasized and the qualifying words in smaller lettering, is to attract the patronage of those who will confuse him in some way with the "Lone Ranger" of the radio programs; and the principle is applicable that, not only must one tell the truth, but he must tell it in a truthful way, i.e., so as not to deceive the public. 38 Cyc. 847. Thus, one may not use even his own name or the name of the town in which he does business as descriptive of his goods, if the effect will be to mislead the public to the prejudice of a competitor. See opinion of Holmes, J., in American Waltham Watch Co. v. United States Watch Co., 173 Mass. 85, 53 N.E. 141, and cases there cited; Nims, Unfair Competition, 3rd Ed. sec. 72; Chafee, Unfair Competition, 53 Harvard Law Review 1289, 1296. The use of the words "talking picture" or "of talking picture fame" in the advertisements was insufficient to protect defendants because the use of these words as they were used in the advertisements would not obviate the tendency of the use of "Lone Ranger" as emphasized therein to deceive and mislead the public. If it is desired to advertise Powell as the man who played the part of Allan King as the "Lone Ranger" in the motion picture of that name, this should be allowed; but any advertisement that he is the "Lone Ranger" must be avoided, as must any other language tending to imply connection with the "Lone Ranger" of plaintiff's radio programs or any form of advertising which will lead the public to believe that there is such connection. * * *

For the reasons stated, the judgment appealed from will be reversed and the cause will be remanded for further proceedings in accordance with this opinion.

Reversed.

---

[1] Who *was* the Lone Ranger? The New York Times, March 2, 1965, in an obituary of Brace Beemer, who played the part on radio from 1941 until the last live radio program in 1954, said that Beemer had two predecessors on the program.

NOTES AND QUESTIONS

(1) On Judge Parker's reasoning, how should the injunction be formulated? Does he recognize in the plaintiff any interest beyond the prevention of confusion?

What relief could the plaintiff have secured on the basis of its copyrights in the radio programs? Would the defendant's conduct infringe any of the plaintiff's exclusive rights in § 106?

(2) The New York Times, Sept. 7, 1979, p. 12, reports on the unmasking of another Lone Ranger. Clayton Moore had portrayed the character in more than 200 half-hour television programs from 1949 to 1956. Since then he had made his living through personal appearances wearing a mask, white hat, and six-shooters. Lone Ranger Television, Inc., which had arranged for the production of a new motion picture based on the character, argued that at age sixty-four Moore was "no longer an appropriate physical representative of the trim 19th-century Western hero." "It's our mask. By wearing the mask, Moore is appearing as the Lone Ranger. But in spite of what Mr. Moore feels in his heart, he is not the Lone Ranger. We own the Lone Ranger." A judge ordered Moore to remove his mask. He replaced it with dark sunglasses. "They tried to shoot me down, but I stood up to them. I've lived by the Lone Ranger creed for 30 years and I'm fighting now for fair play, justice, law and order." These virtues triumphed. In 1985 the Wrather Corp., parent of Lone Ranger Television, lifted the restraint. (The 1981 movie it had sought to protect lost $11 million.) Moore claimed that one million signatures had been collected in support of his appearances as the Lone Ranger. Time, Feb. 4, 1985, p. 69.

(3) Bud Fisher created the comic strip character "Mutt" in 1907 and his sidekick "Jeff" in 1908. The strips were published in the *New York American* newspaper, but apparently were not copyrighted. In 1915, Fisher made an exclusive contract with a syndicator. However, the *American* continued to publish "Mutt and Jeff" strips, drawn now by its own employees. Fisher sought an injunction, alleging unfair competition. Judge Chase found that the characters had acquired secondary meaning indicating a product originating from Fisher and that the defendant was passing off its strips as Fisher's work. According to the court, "The only purpose that another than [Fisher] can have in using the figures or names of 'Mutt' and 'Jeff' is to appropriate the financial value that such figures and names have acquired by reason of the skill of [Fisher]." Fisher v. Star Co., 231 N.Y. 414, 132 N.E. 133, cert. denied, 257 U.S. 654 (1921). Does Judge Chase recognize rights beyond the prevention of confusion? Would a claim for misappropriation of "the financial value that such figures and names have acquired by reason of the skill" of the plaintiff survive analysis under § 301? Judge Newman in Warner Brothers, Inc. v. ABC, the "Greatest American Hero" case, p. 229 supra, thought that a state law claim against ABC that relied "on the misappropriation branch of unfair competition" would be preempted under § 301. When the plaintiff in Kodadek v. MTV Networks, Inc., 152 F.3d 1209 (9th Cir.1998), brought suit under California unfair competition law complaining that MTV's *Beavis and Butthead* animated television series had been based on his earlier drawings, the court affirmed a summary judgment for the defendant, holding that the claim was preempted.

In Ideal Toy Corp. v. Kenner Products, Inc., 443 F.Supp. 291 (S.D.N.Y.1977), the producer of the movie *Star Wars* and one of its licensees failed to enjoin the sale of three toys "similar to the characters in the movie in that a tall, black-robed evil figure in a black helmet is an adversary to a medium-sized metallic humanoid robot and a smaller computer-type, round, metallic robot." The toys did not use the characters' names from the film. The court thought confusion unlikely: "A finding of general 'association'—that the toys 'look like' the movie or remind someone of the movie—does not mean that the prospective purchaser thinks that the toys are derived from the movie or 'sponsored' by the movie." A copyright infringement claim was also rejected.

Toho Co. v. William Morrow and Co.

United States District Court, Central District of California, 1998.
33 F.Supp.2d 1206.

■ TEVRIZIAN, DISTRICT JUDGE.

Plaintiff Toho Co., Ltd. ("Toho" or "Plaintiff") brings this action against Defendant William Morrow and Company, Inc. ("Morrow" or "Defendant") alleging various causes of action for alleged infringement of Toho's intellectual property rights in the fictional character "Godzilla," and subsequent derivative works based thereon. * * *

In or about 1954, Toho alleges that it created the fictional character "Godzilla", a giant prehistoric monster brought to life in the modern world. [Complaint], ¶ 5. At the same time, Toho produced and distributed a feature-length motion picture entitled *Godzilla,* based upon the reawakening of Godzilla by the detonation of an atomic bomb. The film was allegedly released in the United States in or about 1956 under the title *Godzilla, King of the Monsters.* Id. Toho alleges that it has subsequently produced and distributed throughout the world a series of motion pictures based upon the further adventures of Godzilla, including such purported "classics" as *Godzilla vs. Mothra,* and *Son of Godzilla.* Id. Toho contends that it is the owner of the exclusive rights and privileges in and to the copyright in its original motion picture *Godzilla* and in the subsequent Godzilla motion pictures. Id., ¶ 6.

Toho alleges that as a result of its success and popularity, it has continuously engaged in the business of merchandising the Godzilla character. Id., ¶ 8. Toho alleges that it licenses others to use the name and likeness of Godzilla on and in the connection with toys, clothing, books, games, records, posters and various other types of merchandise. Id.

Beginning in about 1981, Toho alleges that it duly registered the name "Godzilla" as a service mark and trademark under the Lanham Act, 15 U.S.C. § 1051, and that Toho remains to this date the owner of said trademark and service mark. Id., ¶ 9.

On May 20, 1998, Toho contends that Tri–Star pictures plans to release a big-budget style motion picture featuring the Godzilla character. The motion picture is entitled *Godzilla* and is being produced with Toho's permission. Toho avers that in connection with the impending release of the Godzilla motion picture, Toho and its authorized merchandising agent are engaged in an extensive licensing and merchandising campaign. Id., 12. Among the licensees are Random House, Inc. ("Random House"), who was allegedly granted the exclusive right to publish a wide variety of books concerning Godzilla, including compendium books. Id., ¶ 13. Pursuant to this license, Toho alleges that Random House is publishing a compendium book of Toho's Godzilla films entitled "The Official Godzilla Compendium" (hereinafter the "Random House Book"). Id., ¶ 14.

Toho alleges that Morrow is currently advertising and publishing, and plans to make available to the public beginning on April 1, 1998, a 227–page Godzilla compendium book entitled "Godzilla!" (hereinafter the "Morrow Book"). Id., ¶ 15. Toho contends that the cover of the Morrow Book features an illustration of Toho's copyrighted Godzilla character, and the title is written in the distinctive lettering style used by Toho and its licensees in their merchandising activities. Id. Toho asserts that the Morrow Book will contain more than ninety (90) photographs from or concerning Toho's copyrighted films, and that several of these photographs will comprise full pages in said Book. Id. Toho alleges that Morrow's unauthorized Book is substantially similar to the Toho authorized Random House Book. Id., ¶ 16
* * *

1. *Toho Has Demonstrated a Likelihood of Success on the Merits of Its Trademark Claim.*

Toho has brought trademark and unfair competition claims against Morrow under 15 U.S.C. § 1114(a) and 1125(a). When trademark and unfair competition claims are based on the same infringing conduct, courts apply the same analysis to both claims. E. & J. Gallo Winery v. Gallo Cattle Co., 967 F.2d 1280, 1288 n. 2 (9th Cir.1992). To succeed on a claim for trademark infringement or unfair competition, the moving party must establish:

> (1) ownership of the trademark at issue;

> (2) use by defendant, without authorization, of a copy, reproduction, counterfeit or colorable imitation of the moving party's mark in connection with the sale, distribution or advertising of goods or services; and

> (3) that defendant's use of the mark is likely to cause confusion, or to cause mistake or to deceive.

15 U.S.C. § 1114(a); *Gallo,* 967 F.2d at 1288 n. 2. The Court notes also that for preliminary injunctive relief, the Court need only find a probability that necessary facts will be established, not that such facts actually exist. Sierra On–Line, Inc. v. Phoenix Software, 739 F.2d 1415, 1423 (9th Cir.1984).

a. *Nominative Fair Use by Defendant.*

Defendant asserts that its use of the Godzilla trademark is protected by the nominative fair use defense. * * * [T]o be entitled to the non-statutory nominative fair use defense, Defendant must satisfy the three part test:

> First, the product or service in question must be one not readily identifiable without use of the trademark; second, only so much of the mark or marks may be used as is reasonably necessary to identify the product or service; and third, the user must do nothing that would, in conjunction with the mark, suggest sponsorship or endorsement by the trademark holder. New Kids on the Block v. News America Publishing Inc., 971 F.2d 302 (9th Cir.1992). * * *

Turning to the requirements of the three part test, this Court finds that the first prong of the test is satisfied. The product (the Godzilla character) is one not readily identifiable without the use of the trademark. A "giant sized pre-historic dragon-like monsters" may be an adequate description of Plaintiff's product, but use of the "Godzilla" mark is required to readily identify Plaintiff's product. The second prong, "only so much of the mark or marks may be used as is reasonably necessary to identify the product or service," appears to derive from a concern that confusion as to affiliation may result if the defendant's use of the plaintiff's mark exceeds its legitimate referential purpose. The cover of the Morrow Book contains Toho's trademark in bold orange lettering prominently displayed. This prong of the test does not appear to be satisfied because Morrow's use exceeds its legitimate referential purpose.

The third prong of test, "the user must do nothing that would, in conjunction with the mark, suggest sponsorship or endorsement by the trademark holder," essentially goes to consumer confusion as to the source of Toho's mark, as well as the actions and intent of Morrow in utilizing the mark. The issue thus becomes whether "a reasonable consumer of average intelligence and experience would be confused as to the source" of the product. New West Corp. v. NYM Co., 595 F.2d 1194 (9th Cir.1979). The Ninth Circuit has established a multi-factored test to make this determination, including a commonly-used eight-factor set forth in AMF, Inc. v. Sleekcraft Boats, 599 F.2d 341 (9th Cir.1979). This Court notes that this test is merely "a non-exclusive series of factors," not "hoops that a district court need jump through to make the determination." Eclipse Assoc. Ltd. v. Data General Corp., 894 F.2d 1114, 1118 (9th Cir.1990). However, before this Court undertakes an analysis of the *Sleekcraft* factors, Morrow's First Amendment and Disclaimers defenses must be addressed.

i.   Morrow's First Amendment Defense is Unavailing.

Morrow contends that there is a significant First Amendment interest associated with choosing an appropriate title for a book or other work. E.g. Rogers v. Grimaldi, 875 F.2d 994, 998–99 (2d Cir.1989). Morrow contends that the Lanham Act does not apply "unless [1] the title has no artistic relevance to the underlying work whatsoever, or, [2] if it has some artistic relevance, unless the title explicitly misleads as to the source or the content of the work." Id. at 999. The Second Circuit added however that, "this limiting construction would not apply to misleading titles that are confusingly similar to other titles. The public interest in sparing consumers this type of confusion outweighs the *slight* public interest in permitting authors to use such titles." Id. at 999, n. 5 (emphasis added). Furthermore the court noted that the Lanham Act should be construed to apply to "artistic works only where the public interest in avoiding consumer confusion outweighs the public interest in free expression." Id. In this case, because the Morrow Book's title does indeed have some artistic relevance to the underlying work, the Lanham Act will only apply if the title unreasonably creates confusion as to the source of the work. With regards to the second test, "the finding of likelihood of confusion must be particularly compelling to outweigh the First Amendment interest" of the defendant. [Twin Peaks Prods. v. Publications Intern., 996 F.2d 1366, 1379 (2d Cir.1993).] For the reasons stated infra, the likelihood of confusion in this action is strong, and therefore Morrow's First Amendment defense is unavailing.

ii.   Morrow's Disclaimers Are Ineffective.

Prior to an analysis of the *Sleekcraft* factors, this Court must also decide the issue of the effectiveness of Morrow's disclaimers. If a court determines that a disclaimer is adequate to alleviate potential confusion, that ends the inquiry; there is no need to proceed through the multi-factor *Sleekcraft* test. Sardi's Restaurant Corp. v. Sardie, 755 F.2d 719, 723–26 (9th Cir.1985). With regards to the disclaimer, Morrow argues that it has included prominent disclaimers on both the front and back covers of the

Morrow Book. On the front cover, the word "UNAUTHORIZED" appears at the very top of the page, in relatively small lettering, surrounded by an orange bordering. Morrow Exhibit 1. On the *back* cover the following disclaimer appears, highlighted by its appearance against a blue background: "THIS BOOK WAS NOT PREPARED, APPROVED, LICENSED OR ENDORSED BY ANY ENTITY INVOLVED IN CREATING OR PRODUCING ANY GODZILLA MOVIE, INCLUDING COLUMBIA/TRISTAR AND TOHO CO. LTD." Id. * * *

This Court finds that the disclaimers do not alleviate the potential for consumer confusion. The word "UNAUTHORIZED" on the front cover only conveys a limited amount of information. It is not necessarily clear that alerting the average consumer to the word "UNAUTHORIZED" would negate consumer confusion as to Toho's sponsorship or endorsement of the Morrow Book. As the court in Twin Peaks Productions v. Publications Intern., 996 F.2d 1366, 1379 (2nd Cir. 1993) stated, the disclaimer would have been far more effective had it simply stated "that the publication has not been prepared, approved, or licensed by any entity that created or produced the" original Toho Godzilla films. That this information is conveyed on the back cover does not suffice. This Court is of the belief that most consumers look primarily at the front cover of a book prior to purchase. Moreover, the color of the disclaimer on the front cover does not effectively draw the attention of the average consumer as its bordering is in the same shade as the title. Further, the word is placed at the top of the page where most consumers' eyes are not likely to dwell. Perhaps if the information contained on the back cover were placed on the front cover, consumer confusion could be negated. The disclaimer is also not placed on the spine of the Morrow Book, a place where many consumers are likely to view before seeing the cover. Toho also asserts that the advertisement for the Morrow Book placed on the Internet at sites such as "Amazon.com" does not even contain the disclaimer. In summary, this Court finds that the disclaimers are ineffective.

iii. The Sleekcraft Factors Favor Toho.

[After examining various factors relevant to the likelihood of confusion, Judge Tevrizian concluded that confusion as to the sponsorship of Morrow's book was indeed likely.] [T]his Court finds that the likelihood of confusion is strong. The products are identical, the disclaimers are ineffective, the Godzilla trademark is strong, the similarity of the marks is strong, and the marketing channels are identical. The aforementioned reasons compel this Court to find that consumer confusion is likely. Therefore, it appears that Morrow is not entitled to rely on the non-statutory nominative fair use defense.

[Finding that Toho was likely to prevail on the merits of its trademark and unfair competition claims, the court granted a preliminary injunction. Judge Tevrizian also found that Toho was likely to prevail on its copyright infringement claim. Toho had demonstrated prima facie ownership of both the Godzilla movies and "the Godzilla character apart from any film." Although Morrow's book included commentary on the films, it also included photographs and detailed plot summaries "that cannot be considered necessary for a critical commentary." "Due to the strong similarity between the two books, the conclusion is inescapable that the Morrow book will affect the potential market for Toho's book." Since Morrow was thus unlikely to prevail on a fair use defense, a preliminary injunction was appropriate.]

NOTES ON CHARACTERS AND UNFAIR COMPETITION

(1) Section 43(a) of the Lanham Act has become a popular vehicle for asserting trademark rights in characters. Judge Urbom in Midway Mfg. Co. v. Dirkschneider, 543 F.Supp. 466 (D.Neb.1981), held that the shapes and colors of the characters in the plaintiff's *Pac–Man* video game were "non-functional design features" protectable under § 43(a) upon a showing of secondary meaning and likelihood of confusion. In DC Comics, Inc. v. Filmation Associates, 486 F.Supp. 1273 (S.D.N.Y.1980), the court, on defendant's motion to overturn a jury verdict, broadly construed the scope of trademark protection for characters. The plaintiff had produced comic books and television shows featuring an extraordinary array of characters including Aquaman and Plastic Man; the defendant, who once produced a television series under contract with the plaintiff, began distributing its own animated television series with similar characters, including Manta and Superstretch. The court said that "where the product sold by plaintiff is 'entertainment' in one form or another * * * an ingredient of the product itself can amount to a trademark protectable under § 43(a) because the ingredient can come to symbolize the plaintiff or its product in the public mind." These "ingredients" include "names and nicknames of entertainment characters, as well as their physical appearances and costumes" (but not, the court thought, their personality traits or abilities, since these could not attain the "consistency of representation" necessary to constitute a symbol recognized by the public).[m]

A claim under § 43(a) was rejected in the "Greatest American Hero" case. The lack of substantial similarity between Superman and the television character that had proved fatal to the plaintiff's copyright infringement claim also precluded, as a matter of law, any likelihood of confusion. The court acknowledged that "the image of a cartoon character and some indicia of that character can function as a trademark to identify the source of a work," and conceded that "there may be some viewers among the television audience who think that the *Hero* series was produced or authorized by those responsible for the Superman movies," but Judge Newman concluded that the issue of likelihood of confusion must be judged within an "outer limit" of reasonableness. A state law "passing off" count was also rejected on similar reasoning after Judge Newman held that the state claim was not preempted under § 301.

The owner of the children's dinosaur character "Barney" unsuccessfully invoked trademark law in an attempt to stop a parody of the character during appearances by "The Famous Chicken," a popular performer at sporting events. Although the character appearing with the Chicken closely resembled Barney,

---

[m] The value of merchandising rights in famous characters is increasingly apparent. According to an article in *The Sunday Times* on the *Harry Potter* books and movies, "Children can spend an entire 24–hour day wrapped up in the Potter fantasy. They can wake up on Harry Potter sheets, brush their teeth with his toothpaste, wash their hair with his shampoo, take their Harry Potter rucksack to school, use their Hedwig, Bertie Botts and Gryffindor notebooks in class, drink their Harry Potter Colas, eat from themed lunch boxes, check the end of the school day on their Harry Potter watches and go home to play on electronic games starring the boy hero before doing their homework on Harry Potter desk sets and curling up again in bed in pyjamas emblazoned with his image to reread the novels using a Harry Potter bookmark." Harlow and Chittenden, Movie Pirates Cash in on Harry Potter Mania, The Sunday Times, Nov. 4, 2001, p. 24. When the Batman movie *The Dark Knight* was released in 2008, it was accompanied by 950 toys and another 4,000 merchandising items, plus the hundreds of Batman toys and clothing items that had been available since the movie franchise began in 1989. A popular movie can bring in over $100 million in merchandising royalties. Bowles, Summer Movies Drive Toys Full–Speed to Shelves, USA Today, Apr. 29, 2008, p. 9B.

there was little likelihood of confusion. Despite tales of young children crying "Chicken step on Barney!," the court affirmed a summary judgment against the plaintiff; since the largely adult audience would understand the use as a parody, confusion was unlikely. Lyons Partnership v. Giannoulas, 179 F.3d 384 (5th Cir.1999).

(2) A character can be used to identify the source of goods or services and thus qualify for registration as a trademark under the Lanham Act. The Pillsbury character "Poppin' Fresh," for example, is registered as a trademark, but the registration was of no help when *Screw* magazine published a picture depicting the character engaged in sexual intercourse with "Poppie Fresh," another Pillsbury trade character; the court found no likelihood of confusion as to sponsorship. Pillsbury Co. v. Milky Way Productions, Inc., 215 U.S.P.Q. 124 (N.D.Ga.1981) (but relief was granted under the Georgia anti-dilution statute). In re DC Comics, Inc., 689 F.2d 1042 (C.C.P.A.1982), declared that a drawing of Superman (and also of Batman and Joker) could be registered as a trademark for toy versions of the characters.

(3) The *Los Angeles Times* reported on a suit filed by the Academy of Motion Picture Arts and Sciences to protect its "Oscar" statuette from a defendant who was selling an anatomically correct (indeed enhanced) version of the statuette on the Internet. The Academy claimed copyright infringement, trademark infringement, and dilution by tarnishment. O'Neill, California Academy Sues Over "Obscene" Replicas of Oscar, L.A. Times, Feb. 7, 2002, p. C2. Would the copyright claim survive a fair use defense? Is there a likelihood of confusion for trademark infringement? As for "tarnishment" under § 43(c), would the use fall under the exception in § 43(c)(3)(A)(ii) for "identifying and parodying, criticizing, or commenting upon the famous mark owner or the goods or services of the famous mark owner"? Cf. Lucasfilm Ltd. v. Media Market Group, Ltd., 182 F.Supp.2d 897 (N.D.Cal.2002), denying a preliminary injunction on copyright, trademark infringement, and dilution grounds sought by the plaintiff to protect its STAR WARS mark against a pornographic movie entitled "Starballz."

(4) If the name or appearance of a cartoon character becomes protectable as a trademark, will the protection be affected by the expiration of copyright in some or all of the cartoons? In Harvey Cartoons v. Columbia Pictures Indus., 645 F.Supp. 1564 (S.D.N.Y.1986), the question was whether the defendant's "Ghostbusters" movie logo infringed the plaintiff's creation, "The Ghostly Trio," companions of "Casper, The Friendly Ghost." Copyrights on early representations of the "Trio" had not been renewed, but the plaintiff had a registered trademark. The court, concluding that there was no confusing similarity, apparently assumed that the trademark remained enforceable despite the expiration of the copyrights.

The question of trademark life after copyright death was avoided in Silverman v. CBS Inc., 870 F.2d 40 (2d Cir.), cert. denied, 492 U.S. 907 (1989), p. 228 supra, involving Amos 'n Andy and related characters. Copyrights on the radio programs had expired because of non-renewal and the characters were therefore in the public domain. The court accepted that CBS once had trademark rights in the characters, but found that the rights had been abandoned by more than 20 years of nonuse.[n]

---

[n]   Cf. Siegel v. Warner Bros. Ent. Inc., 542 F.Supp.2d 1098 (C.D.Cal.2008). After declaring that the heirs of Jerry Siegel had successfully terminated the assignment of copyright in the Superman character, Judge Larson noted that under § 304(c)(6)(E), the termination did

On trademark protection for characters no longer under copyright, see L. Kurtz, The Methuselah Factor: When Characters Outlive Their Copyrights, 11 U. Miami Ent. & Sports L.Rev. 437 (1994) (advocating disclaimers to avoid any likelihood of confusion).

Columbia Broadcasting System, Inc. v. DeCosta

United States Court of Appeals, First Circuit, 1967.
377 F.2d 315.
Certiorari denied 389 U.S. 1007.

■ Before ALDRICH, CHIEF JUDGE, MCENTEE and COFFIN, CIRCUIT JUDGES.

■ COFFIN, CIRCUIT JUDGE.

This is an appeal by defendants from jury verdicts in the total amount of $150,000 awarded plaintiff on his claim that he created, and the defendants misappropriated, the character of Paladin, the protagonist of the CBS television series entitled "Have Gun Will Travel".

The story of this case—more bizarre than most television serial installments—is one of "coincidence" run riot. The plaintiff, of Portuguese parents, is a Rhode Island mechanic whose formal education ceased after the fourth grade. During the Depression, having tired of factory work, he hopped a freight for the West, lived in hobo jungles, and eventually became a range hand on a Texas ranch. After two years of riding and roping he returned to Rhode Island to work as a mechanic and later received training as a motor machinist in the Coast Guard. But he retained his passion for all things western. In 1947 he began to participate in rodeos, horse shows, horse auctions, and parades.

From the beginning plaintiff indulged a penchant for costume. He was already equipped with a moustache. He soon settled on a black shirt, black pants, and a flat-crowned black hat. He had acquired a St. Mary's medal at a parade and affixed this to his hat. He adopted the name Paladin after an onlooker of Italian descent had hurled an epithet at him containing the word "Paladino". On looking up the word Paladin in a dictionary he found it meant "champion of Knights" and was content that people began so to call him. One day when he had donned his costume in preparation for a horse show, and was about to mount his horse, one of a group waiting for him shouted "Have Gun Will Travel", a cry immediately picked up by the children present.

The finishing touches were a chess knight, bought for fifteen cents at an auction, which plaintiff thought was a good symbol, and which he used on a business card along with the words "Have", "Gun", "Will", "Travel", and "Wire Paladin, N. Court St., Cranston, R.I.", hand-printed with separate rubber stamps; a silver copy of the chess piece on his holster; and an antique derringer strapped under his arm. So accoutered, he would appear in parades, the openings and finales of rodeos, auctions, horse shows, and a pony ring he once operated. From time to time at rodeos he would stage a western gunfight, featuring his quick draw and the timely use of his hidden derringer. He would pass out photographs of himself and cards—printed versions soon replacing the rubber-stamped ones. Hospitals, drug stores, barber shops, sports shops, diners—all were the repositories of his cards,

---

not affect rights under other law. Thus, the plaintiffs were not entitled to an accounting of profits "purely attributable to [Superman] trademark rights," which were still owned by the defendants.

some 250,000 of them. Children clamored for the cards, and clustered about him to the extent that he was likened to the Pied Piper and Gene Autry. This was perhaps one of the purest promotions ever staged, for plaintiff did not seek anything but the entertainment of others. He sold no product, services, or institution, charged no fees, and exploited only himself.

Ten years after he had begun to live his avocational role of Paladin, he and his friends saw the first CBS television production of "Have Gun Will Travel", starring moustachioed Richard Boone, who played the part of an elegant knight errant of the Old West, always on the side of Good—for a fee. The television Paladin also wore a black costume, a flat-crowned black hat bearing an oval silver decoration, and a silver chess knight on his holster, and announced himself with a card featuring a chess piece virtually— if not absolutely—identical with the plaintiff's and the words "HAVE GUN WILL TRAVEL. WIRE PALADIN, SAN FRANCISCO". The series was notably successful; it appeared in 225 first-run episodes in the United States, was licensed in foreign countries, and by the time of trial had grossed in excess of fourteen million dollars.

The writers and network executives responsible for the series testified in detail that the television Paladin was a spontaneous creation, developed in total ignorance of the attributes of his Rhode Island predecessor. The writers, Herb Meadow and Sam Rolfe, testified that the germ of the idea was the title, "Have Gun Will Travel", which Meadow had evolved from mulling over a familiar theatrical advertising phrase, "Have tux, will travel". The character was originally conceived as a denizen of contemporary New York, but was changed to a western hero because the network hoped to cast Randolph Scott in the role. The name "Paladin" resulted from a thesaurus search for words meaning "knight" or "hero" or "champion". The chess piece symbol was inspired by Meadow's observation, while teaching his son the game, that the knight's movements were uniquely erratic and unpredictable. In the pilot script for the series, Paladin used a hidden derringer because it was a convenient way to extricate him from the obligatory dangerous situation.

The show's original producer, Julian Claman, testified that after Randolph Scott and other "fairly well known" actors were found to be unavailable he selected Richard Boone to be tested for the role of Paladin. Boone appeared for the test with a moustache, for reasons unknown, and was outfitted in a black suit because it was the only available costume that fitted. The hat, bearing a silver "conche", was selected by Claman because it looked appropriate. The card, which had been described in Meadow and Rolfe's original prospectus, was realized by the CBS art department from a rough sketch by Claman. The "shocking similarity" to DeCosta's cards was pure coincidence. Boone's test was successful, and Claman, reluctant to change any element of a winning combination, decided to keep card, costume, and moustache intact for the pilot film. He also decided to add the silver chess knight to Paladin's holster because it produced a distinct article that would be marketable if the series succeeded.

DeCOSTA AS PALADIN (1975)

Meadow, Rolfe, Claman, and the other witnesses for the defendants all testified that they had never seen DeCosta or any of his cards. The jury obviously disbelieved at least this much of their testimony, and we think it clear that they were amply justified. Thus, the plaintiff has had the satisfaction of proving the defendants pirates. But we are drawn to conclude that that proof alone is not enough to entitle him to a share of the plunder. Our Paladin is not the first creator to see the fruits of his creation harvested by another, without effective remedy; and although his case is undeniably hard, to affirm the judgments below would, we think, allow a hard case to make some intolerably bad law.

In the first place, it is by no means clear that such state law of intellectual property as we have found supports relief on these facts. Several cases have been cited around the general proposition that it is an actionable wrong to appropriate and exploit the product of another's creative effort; but all seem to involve distinguishable wrongs of at least equal or even superior significance. Most rest on the tort of "passing off": appropriation not of the creation but of the value attached to it by public association (the so-called "secondary meaning"), by misleading the public into thinking that the defendant's offering is the product of the plaintiff's established skill. E.g., Lone Ranger, Inc. v. Cox, 4 Cir., 1942, 124 F.2d 650; Chaplin v. Amador, 1928, 93 Cal.App. 358, 269 P. 544.[4] Others add an element of injury to reputation caused by a poor imitation. E.g., Lahr v. Adell Chem. Co., 1 Cir., 1962, 300 F.2d 256. * * *

Plaintiff argues that he has established "secondary meaning" through testimony of some witnesses that they thought he was the Paladin on television and evidence that most people knew him only as Paladin, not as Victor DeCosta. Whether or not this assertion is true, it is here irrelevant, for the issue was not submitted to the jury. The complaint alleged three causes of action: misappropriation, trade and/or service mark infringement, and unfair competition by "passing off" the television Paladin as the plaintiff. Only the first was tried, the court reserving judgment on defendant's motions to dismiss the other two. The jury was instructed that the plaintiff would be entitled to the verdict if he established:

> "First. That he conceived and created said idea and character of 'Paladin, Have Gun Will Travel'; and that said idea and character was novel, original, and unique; and that he did not at any time abandon said idea and character by a publication thereof.

> "Second. That the defendants * * * did copy said idea and character without the permission of the plaintiff and used them in the television series, 'Have Gun Will Travel.'

> And

> "Third. That the plaintiff sustained damages as a result of such copying and use of said idea and character. * * * "

Thus, the judgment can only be supported on a rule of law that would allow recovery upon proof of creation by the plaintiff and copying by the defendants, and nothing else. We do not find such a rule in the cases cited above.

Moreover, the leading case affording a remedy for mere copying, International News Serv. v. Associated Press, 1918, 248 U.S. 215, is no longer authoritative for at least two reasons: it was decided as a matter of general federal law before the decision in Erie R.R. v. Tompkins, 1938, 304 U.S. 64; and, as it prohibited the copying of published written matter that had not been copyrighted (indeed, as news it could not be copyrighted, 248 U.S. at 234), it has clearly been overruled by the Supreme Court's recent decisions in Sears, Roebuck & Co. v. Stiffel Co., 1964, 376 U.S. 225, and Compco Corp. v. Day–Brite Lighting, Inc., 1964, 376 U.S. 234. While this normally would not prevent the state court from adopting the reasoning of *INS* in fashioning a rule of state law, we think it important to consider the scope of state power in this area in view of *Sears* and *Compco*. * * *

Does the language in *Compco*, "whatever the federal patent and copyright laws leave in the public domain", refer to creations that Congress has

---

[4]   The plaintiff quotes the *Lone Ranger* case as involving "the element of fraudulent attempt of someone to 'reap where he has not sown' and to appropriate to himself 'the harvest of those who have sown' ". 124 F.2d at 653. But the opinion makes it clear that the "harvest" is the goodwill generated by long establishment of the Lone Ranger in the public eye, and the element of fraud is quite as important as the element of appropriation.

deliberately chosen not to protect or more broadly to those it has simply not protected, whether by choice or by chance? In the case of patents the two questions are coterminous, for Congress has deliberately chosen not to protect inventions lacking the element of originality, and an invention is thus either patentable or unprotectible. In the case of "writings" there is no such universal test of qualification. But Congress has established a procedural scheme of protection by notice and registration. The necessary implication of this approach, we conclude, is that, absent compliance with the scheme, the federal policy favoring free dissemination of intellectual creations prevails. Thus, if a "writing" is within the scope of the constitutional clause, and Congress has not protected it, whether deliberately or by unexplained omission, it can be freely copied. See Cheney Bros. v. Doris Silk Corp., 2 Cir., 1929, 35 F.2d 279. * * *

* * * [Plaintiff] argues that a character is not copyrightable—by which we must understand that it is not within the scope of Congress's power under the copyright clause * * *.

A more substantial argument for this first proposition is that the plaintiff's creation is not a "writing" in the sense used in the copyright clause (or, what is the same thing, that it is not an "article" in the sense used in *Sears* and *Compco*). There is no question that the term is to be interpreted more broadly than its common meaning would indicate. See, e.g., Mazer v. Stein, 1954, 347 U.S. 201 (statuette used as a lamp base). But it has been argued that it should be limited to mean some identifiable, durable, material form. Nimmer, Copyright Publication, 56 Colum.L.Rev. 185, 196 n. 98 (1956). And it is argued here that the plaintiff's creation, being a personal characterization, was not reduced and could not be reduced to such a form.

To this argument there are several answers. First, while more precise limitations on "writings" might be convenient in connection with a statutory scheme of registration and notice, we see no reason why Congress's power is so limited. Second, we cannot say that it would be impracticable to incorporate into the copyright system a procedure for registering "characters" by filing pictorial and narrative description in an identifiable, durable, and material form. Finally, however, there comes a point where what is created is so slight a thing as not to warrant protection by any law. All human beings—and a good part of the animal kingdom—create characters every day of their lives. Individuals often go beyond the realm of unconscious creation and devise characterizations for their own and others' amusement. Many a starred performer has so begun, and continued to grow on the borrowings from others. At some point his innate talent and eclectic poaching may enable him to attract a following, and ultimately to secure the law's protection against imitators. At what point short of this there should be additional protection we do not say. But in view of the federal policy of encouraging intellectual creation by granting a limited monopoly at best, we think it sensible to say that the constitutional clause extends to any concrete, describable manifestation of intellectual creation; and to the extent that a creation may be ineffable, we think it ineligible for protection against copying *simpliciter* under either state or federal law.

* * * We accordingly reverse.

NOTES AND QUESTIONS

(1) When DeCosta's case returned to the district court, he won an accounting of profits on his service mark infringement and unfair competition counts based on findings that the "Paladin" name and card had acquired secondary meaning and the television series created a likelihood of confusion. CBS appealed again. In DeCosta v. Columbia Broadcasting System, Inc., 520 F.2d 499 (1st Cir.1975), cert. denied, 423 U.S. 1073 (1976) (*DeCosta II*), the same panel of judges who had reversed DeCosta's misappropriation verdict eight years earlier reversed again. The court began with an acknowledgement that its earlier analysis of the misappropriation count had been in error. "We now know, after Goldstein v. California, 412 U.S. 546, 560 (1973), that 'under the Constitution, the States have not relinquished all power to grant to authors "the exclusive Right to their respective Writings".' * * * We face a dilemma. *Goldstein* tells us that we were, in our interpretation of the preemptive reach of the Copyright Clause, over-inclusive. And yet, what we decided in *DeCosta I* has settled, for this case, the issue of misappropriation." The court then turned to the service mark infringement and unfair competition counts. "We shall assume, therefore, [despite the non-commercial nature of DeCosta's activities] that plaintiff's marks meet the requirements of common law service marks. We also shall assume that they are distinctive enough so that proof of secondary meaning is not essential. In the alternative, we shall accept the finding of the magistrate, adopted by the district court, that, at least among some people, plaintiff's name and card had come to be associated with him." On the issue of likelihood of confusion, however, the court was less charitable. "[T]he testimony of six witnesses that they thought, on first viewing the program, that the television character Paladin was plaintiff, seems to us either no evidence at all or such minimal evidence as not to support a finding of likelihood of confusion requiring an accounting of defendants' profits from a highly successful, 225 episode series grossing over fourteen million dollars."

DeCosta did not give up. In 1976, he succeeded in obtaining a federal service mark registration for *Have Gun Will Travel. Wire Paladin*. See Columbia Broadcasting System, Inc. v. DeCosta, 192 U.S.P.Q. 453 (Tm.Tr.App.Bd.1976). Years later, when Viacom began broadcasting re-runs of "Have Gun Will Travel," DeCosta sued again. This time, DeCosta based his claim on "reverse confusion," arguing that the television series caused confusion as to the source or sponsorship of DeCosta's own activities. A jury found in DeCosta's favor. Viacom appealed, asserting that under the doctrine of collateral estoppel, DeCosta was precluded from relitigating issues that had already been decided against him. DeCosta countered that "reverse confusion" was a new legal principle not available to him in his initial case. Judge Breyer in DeCosta v. Viacom Int'l, Inc., 981 F.2d 602 (1st Cir.1992), cert. denied, 509 U.S. 923 (1993) (*DeCosta III*), disagreed, holding that the principle of reverse confusion was "nothing particularly new." The only change in the law since *DeCosta II* was dicta in a few cases suggesting "that a plaintiff, claiming reverse confusion, can recover for harm suffered, not because the buying public may wrongly believe that the defendant makes or sponsors the plaintiff's product, but simply because the public wrongly believes that the plaintiff copied the defendant's name. * * * The fatal problem for DeCosta in respect to this 'change in the law,' however, lies in our view that this change is not sound law. * * * For these reasons, insofar as the doctrine of 'reverse confusion' may be thought significantly 'new' (reverse confusion about 'piracy'), we do not accept it. Insofar as we accept it (reverse confusion involving source or sponsorship), we do not believe it is significantly new. Hence, we do not believe that there are changes in the law here that can overcome the effects of 'collateral estoppel.'" DeCosta's judgment was reversed yet again.

(2) Was DeCosta's creation, in the words of *DeCosta I,* too "slight a thing" to merit protection on one theory or another?

(3) Would the misappropriation claim pressed in *DeCosta I* survive § 301? Was DeCosta's creation "within the subject matter of copyright"? (Was it "fixed in a tangible medium of expression"?) Is the case, in this regard, distinguishable from those involving cartoon or audiovisual characters?

(4) The court's decision in *DeCosta III* wiped out a $3.5 million judgment and an injunction that had effectively prohibited further broadcast of the television series, leaving DeCosta with nothing to show for thirty years of litigation except a jury verdict that CBS had stolen his creation. DeCosta died at age 84 a month after the First Circuit's final decision. His obituary by United Press International described him as the "former cowboy, rodeo star and construction worker who created the 'Have Gun, Will Travel' TV Western character known as Paladin."

CHAPTER 9

MORAL RIGHTS AND PUBLICITY RIGHTS

1. PROTECTION OF "MORAL RIGHTS"

Article 6*bis* of the Berne Convention for the Protection of Literary and Artistic Works (Paris Revision, 1971), reprinted in the Statutory Supplement, provides as follows:

> (1) Independently of the author's economic rights, and even after the transfer of the said rights, the author shall have the right to claim authorship of the work and to object to any distortion, mutilation or other modification of, or other derogatory action in relation to, the said work, which would be prejudicial to his honour or reputation.

> (2) The rights granted to the author in accordance with the preceding paragraph shall, after his death, be maintained, at least until the expiry of the economic rights, and shall be exercisable by the persons or institutions authorized by the legislation of the country where protection is claimed. However, those countries whose legislation, at the moment of their ratification of or accession to this Act, does not provide for the protection after the death of the author of all the rights set out in the preceding paragraph may provide that some of these rights may, after his death, cease to be maintained.

> (3) The means of redress for safeguarding the rights granted by this Article shall be governed by the legislation of the country where protection is claimed.

These rights are sometimes called "moral rights." They include the author's right to claim "paternity" of a work and to protect the "integrity" of a work. One of the copyright studies done in preparation for the drafting of the copyright revision bill describes the former as "the author's right to be made known to the public as the creator of his work, to prevent others from usurping his work by naming another person as the author, and to prevent others from wrongfully attributing to him a work he has not written." W. Strauss, The Moral Right of the Author, Copyr. Law Revision Study No. 4, 116 (1959), in 2 Studies on Copyr. 963, 966 (1963). The latter, the right to protect the integrity of a work, entitles the author to prevent harmful alterations. Moral rights are sometimes said to extend beyond paternity and integrity to encompass the right to publish or not to publish a work, to withdraw a work from sale, and to prevent other injuries to the author's personality as embodied in the work. The doctrine of moral rights finds its most complete expression in French law—hence the frequent reference, even in America, to *droit moral*.[a]

---

[a] See generally R. Kwall, Copyright and the Moral Right: Is an American Marriage Possible?, 38 Vand.L.Rev. 1 (1985). J. Fromer, Expressive Incentives in Intellectual Property, 98 Va.L.Rev. 1745 (2012), points out that protecting the non-pecuniary and personal interests of authors in their creations furthers copyright's goal by strengthening incentives to create.

In the debates preceding our accession to the Berne Convention, the issue of moral rights provoked sharp disagreement. One group, composed mostly of magazine publishers and broadcasters, opposed our adherence to Berne out of fears that writers and other contributors would cripple the editing process by threatening to assert integrity rights. The motion picture studios, although anxious for Berne's increased copyright protection abroad, expressed similar concerns. These fears were nourished by the supposed position under French law that moral rights cannot be waived or transferred. At the other extreme were authors and film directors who argued that we could not join Berne in good faith without federal legislation that would recognize and strengthen moral rights. In the middle were "minimalists" who asserted that existing elements of federal and state law adequately recognized paternity and integrity rights, so that we could and should adhere to Berne.

The minimalist position triumphed,[b] and except for the Visual Artists Rights Act of 1990 described later in this section, it continues to reflect the American response to the protection of moral rights as required under Berne. The Berne Convention Implementation Act of 1988 (Pub.L. 100–568) emphasized in § 2 that the Berne Convention was "not self-executing under the Constitution and laws of the United States" and that the obligations under Berne "may be performed only pursuant to appropriate domestic law." Section 3 of the Act reiterated that the provisions of the Convention "shall be given effect under title 17, as amended by this Act, and any other relevant provision of Federal or State law, including the common law," but "shall not be enforceable in any action brought pursuant to the provisions of the Berne Convention itself." See also § 104(c) of the Copyright Act.

What is this body of existing law so solicitously enshrined?

Smith v. Montoro

United States Court of Appeals, Ninth Circuit, 1981.
648 F.2d 602.

■ Before PECK, ANDERSON, and PREGERSON, CIRCUIT JUDGES.

■ PREGERSON, CIRCUIT JUDGE:

This is an appeal from a judgment granting defendant's motion to dismiss under Fed.R.Civ.P. 12(b)(6) for failure to state a federal claim. The district court held that the complaint did not allege facts sufficient to constitute a violation of section 43(a) of the Lanham Act, 15 U.S.C. § 1125(a). Appellant argues that the district court erred since the acts alleged in the complaint are the economic equivalent of "palming off," or misuse of a trade name, thus meeting the district court's standard for stating a claim under section 43(a). For the reasons stated below, we reverse.

Paul Smith contracted to star in a film to be produced by Producioni Atlas Cinematografica ("PAC"), an Italian film company. The contract allegedly provided that Smith would receive star billing in the screen credits and advertising for the film and that PAC would so provide in any subsequent contracts with distributors of the film. PAC then licensed defendants

---

[b]   On this controversy as it appeared on the eve of adherence, see R. Brown, Adherence to the Berne Copyright Convention: The Moral Rights Issue, 35 J.Copyr.Soc'y 196 (1988).

Edward Montoro and Film Venture International, Inc. ("FVI") to distribute the film in this country under the name "Convoy Buddies." Plaintiff complains, however, that Montoro and FVI removed Smith's name and substituted the name of another actor, "Bob Spencer," in place of Smith's name in both the film credits and advertising material. Plaintiff alleges that, as a result of defendants' substitution, plaintiff has been damaged in his reputation as an actor, and has lost specific employment opportunities. * * *

[handwritten margin note: Starred in film but they said it was a diff. guy]

Appellant argues that defendants violated section 43(a) by affixing or using "a false designation or representation," i.e., another actor's name in place of appellant's, in connection with the movie's advertising and credits. Appellant claims standing under section 43(a) as a person "who believes that he is or is likely to be damaged" by the use of another actor's name in place of his. Thus, appellant's claim, although one of first impression, appears to fall within the express language of section 43(a).

[handwritten margin note: Appant :]

The district court appears to have rejected appellant's argument on the ground that, to state a claim under section 43(a), a complaint must allege merchandising practices "in the nature of, or economically equivalent to, palming off . . . and/or misuse of trademarks and trade names." * * *

To the extent that the district court's standard for section 43(a) claims could be read as limiting such claims to cases of palming off, such a narrow rule would be contrary to established case law. * * *

The district court's ruling was entirely consistent with the vast majority of section 43(a) cases, however, to the extent that it indicated that a section 43(a) claim may be based on economic practices or conduct "economically equivalent" to palming off. Such practices would include "reverse passing off," which occurs when a person removes or obliterates the original trademark, without authorization, before reselling goods produced by someone else. See Borchard, Reverse Passing Off—Commercial Robbery or Permissible Competition?, 67 Trademark Rep. 1 (1977). Reverse passing off is accomplished "expressly" when the wrongdoer removes the name or trademark on another party's product and sells that product under a name chosen by the wrongdoer. "Implied" reverse passing off occurs when the wrongdoer simply removes or otherwise obliterates the name of the manufacturer or source and sells the product in an unbranded state.

In the instant case, appellant argues that the defendants' alleged conduct constitutes *reverse* passing off and that appellant's complaint therefore stated a section 43(a) claim even under the district court's own standard. Appellees argue, however, that the protection afforded by the Lanham Act is limited to "sales of goods" and does not extend to claims that a motion picture shown to the public might contain false information as to origin.

The short answer to appellees' argument is that the Lanham Act explicitly condemns false designations or representations in connection with "*any* goods or *services*." The prohibitions of this section have been applied to motion picture representations. See, e.g., Dallas Cowboys Cheerleaders, Inc. v. Pussycat Cinema Ltd., 467 F.Supp. 366 (S.D.N.Y.), aff'd, 604 F.2d 200 (2d Cir.1979). * * *

According to appellant's complaint, defendants not only removed appellant's name from all credits and advertising, they also substituted a name of their own choosing. Appellees' alleged conduct therefore amounts to *express* reverse passing off. As a matter of policy, such conduct, like traditional palming off, is wrongful because it involves an attempt to misappropriate or profit from another's talents and workmanship. Moreover, in reverse palming off cases, the originator of the misidentified product is involuntarily deprived of the advertising value of its name and of the goodwill that otherwise would stem from public knowledge of the true source of the satisfactory product. * * * The ultimate purchaser (or viewer) is also deprived of knowing the true source of the product and may even be deceived into believing that it comes from a different source. Borchard, supra, at 4–5.

In the film industry, a particular actor's performance, which may have received an award or other critical acclaim, may be the primary attraction for movie-goers. Some actors are said to have such drawing power at the box office that the appearance of their names on the theater marquee can almost guarantee financial success. Such big box office names are built, in part, through being prominently featured in popular films and by receiving appropriate recognition in film credits and advertising. Since actors' fees for pictures, and indeed, their ability to get any work at all, is often based on the drawing power their name may be expected to have at the box office, being accurately credited for films in which they have played would seem to be of critical importance in enabling actors to sell their "services," i.e., their performances. We therefore find that appellant has stated a valid claim for relief under section 43(a) of the Lanham Act. * * *

As the district court stated, a section 43(a) claim may be based on practices or conduct "economically equivalent" to palming off. We find that appellant did state such a claim by alleging that defendants engaged in conduct amounting to "express reverse palming off." Since appellant also has standing to sue under section 43(a), the district court's dismissal of the complaint for failure to state a federal claim is reversed. The dismissal of the pendent state law claims is also reversed.

Reversed and remanded.

Dastar Corp. v. Twentieth Century Fox Film Corp.

Supreme Court of the United States, 2003.
539 U.S. 23, 123 S.Ct. 2041.

■ JUSTICE SCALIA delivered the opinion of the Court.

In this case, we are asked to decide whether § 43(a) of the Lanham Act, 15 U.S.C. § 1125(a), prevents the unaccredited copying of a work, and if so, whether a court may double a profit award under § 1117(a), in order to deter future infringing conduct.

I

In 1948, three and a half years after the German surrender at Reims, General Dwight D. Eisenhower completed Crusade in Europe, his written account of the allied campaign in Europe during World War II. Doubleday published the book, registered it with the Copyright Office in 1948, and granted exclusive television rights to an affiliate of respondent Twentieth Century Fox Film Corporation (Fox). Fox, in turn, arranged for Time, Inc., to produce a television series, also called Crusade in Europe, based on the book, and Time assigned its copyright in the series to Fox. The television series, consisting of 26 episodes, was first broadcast in 1949. It combined a soundtrack based on a narration of the book with film footage from the United States Army, Navy, and Coast Guard, the British Ministry of Information and War Office, the National Film Board of Canada, and unidentified "Newsreel Pool Cameramen." In 1975, Doubleday renewed the copyright on the book as the " 'proprietor of copyright in a work made for hire.' " App. to Pet for Cert. 9a. Fox, however, did not renew the copyright on the Crusade television series, which expired in 1977, leaving the television series in the public domain.

In 1988, Fox reacquired the television rights in General Eisenhower's book, including the exclusive right to distribute the Crusade television series on video and to sub-license others to do so. Respondents SFM Entertainment and New Line Home Video, Inc., in turn, acquired from Fox the exclusive rights to distribute Crusade on video. SFM obtained the negatives of the original television series, restored them, and repackaged the series on videotape; New Line distributed the videotapes.

Enter petitioner Dastar. In 1995, Dastar decided to expand its product line from music compact discs to videos. Anticipating renewed interest in World War II on the 50th anniversary of the war's end, Dastar released a video set entitled World War II Campaigns in Europe. To make Campaigns, Dastar purchased eight beta cam tapes of the *original* version of the Crusade television series, which is in the public domain, copied them, and then edited the series. Dastar's Campaigns series is slightly more than half as long as the original Crusade television series. Dastar substituted a new opening sequence, credit page, and final closing for those of the Crusade television series; inserted new chapter-title sequences and narrated chapter introductions; moved the "recap" in the Crusade television series to the beginning and retitled it as a "preview"; and removed references to and images of the book. Dastar created new packaging for its Campaigns series and (as already noted) a new title.

Dastar manufactured and sold the Campaigns video set as its own product. The advertising states: "Produced and Distributed by: *Entertainment Distributing*" (which is owned by Dastar), and makes no reference to the Crusade television series. Similarly, the screen credits state "DASTAR CORP presents" and "an ENTERTAINMENT DISTRIBUTING Production," and list as executive producer, producer, and associate producer, employees of Dastar. Supp.App. 2–3, 30. The Campaigns videos themselves also make no reference to the Crusade television series, New Line's Crusade videotapes, or the book. Dastar sells its Campaigns videos to Sam's Club, Costco, Best Buy, and other retailers and mail-order companies for $25 per set, substantially less than New Line's video set.

In 1998, respondents Fox, SFM, and New Line brought this action alleging that Dastar's sale of its Campaigns video set infringes Doubleday's copyright in General Eisenhower's book and, thus, their exclusive television rights in the book. Respondents later amended their complaint to add claims that Dastar's sale of Campaigns "without proper credit" to the Crusade television series constitutes "reverse passing off" in violation of § 43(a) of the Lanham Act, 15 U.S.C. § 1125(a), and in violation of state unfair-competition law. App. to Pet. for Cert. 31a. On cross-motions for summary judgment, the District Court found for respondents on all three counts, id., at 54a–55a, treating its resolution of the Lanham Act claim as controlling on the state-law unfair-competition claim because "the ultimate test under both is whether the public is likely to be deceived or confused," id., at 54a. The court awarded Dastar's profits to respondents and doubled them pursuant to § 35 of the Lanham Act, 15 U.S.C. § 1117(a), to deter future infringing conduct by petitioner.

The Court of Appeals for the Ninth Circuit affirmed the judgment for respondents on the Lanham Act claim, but reversed as to the copyright claim and remanded. 34 Fed.Appx. 312, 316 (2002). (It said nothing with regard to the state-law claim.) With respect to the Lanham Act claim, the Court of Appeals reasoned that "Dastar copied substantially the entire *Crusade in Europe* series created by Twentieth Century Fox, labeled the resulting product with a different name and marketed it without attribution to Fox [, and] therefore committed a 'bodily appropriation' of Fox's series." Id., at 314. It concluded that "Dastar's 'bodily appropriation' of Fox's original [television] series is sufficient to establish the reverse passing off." Ibid.[2] The court also affirmed the District Court's award under the Lanham Act of twice Dastar's profits. We granted certiorari. 537 U.S. 1099 (2003).

II

* * * [E]very Circuit to consider the issue found [the original version of] § 43(a) broad enough to encompass reverse passing off. See, e.g., Williams v. Curtiss–Wright Corp., 691 F.2d 168, 172 (C.A.3 1982); Arrow United Indus., Inc. v. Hugh Richards, Inc., 678 F.2d 410, 415 (C.A.2 1982); F.E.L. Publications, Ltd. v. Catholic Bishop of Chicago, 214 USPQ 409, 416, (C.A.7 1982); Smith v. Montoro, 648 F.2d 602, 603 (C.A.9 1981); Bangor Punta Operations, Inc. v. Universal Marine Co., 543 F.2d 1107, 1109 (C.A.5 1976). The Trademark Law Revision Act of 1988 made clear that § 43(a) covers origin of production as well as geographic origin. Its language is amply inclusive, moreover, of reverse passing off—if indeed it does not implicitly adopt the unanimous court-of-appeals jurisprudence on that subject. See, e.g., ALPO Petfoods, Inc. v. Ralston Purina Co., 913 F.2d 958, 963–964, n.6 (C.A.D.C.1990) (Thomas, J.).

Thus, as it comes to us, the gravamen of respondents' claim is that, in marketing and selling Campaigns as its own product without acknowledging its nearly wholesale reliance on the Crusade television series, Dastar has made a "false designation of origin, false or misleading description of fact, or false or misleading representation of fact, which . . . is likely to cause confusion . . . as to the origin . . . of his or her goods." See, e.g., Brief for Respondents 8, 11. That claim would undoubtedly be sustained if Dastar had bought some of New Line's Crusade videotapes and merely repackaged them as its own. Dastar's alleged wrongdoing, however, is vastly different: it took a creative work in the public domain—the Crusade television series—copied it, made modifications (arguably minor), and produced its very own series of videotapes. If "origin" refers only to the manufacturer or producer of the physical "goods" that are made available to the public (in this case the videotapes), Dastar was the origin. If, however, "origin" includes the creator of the underlying work that Dastar copied, then someone else (perhaps Fox) was the origin of Dastar's product. At bottom, we must decide what § 43(a)(1)(A) of the Lanham Act means by the "origin" of "goods."

III

The dictionary definition of "origin" is "[t]he fact or process of coming into being from a source," and "[t]hat from which anything primarily proceeds; source." Webster's New International Dictionary 1720–1721 (2d ed.1949). And the dictionary definition of "goods" (as relevant here) is

---

[2] As for the copyright claim, the Ninth Circuit held that the tax treatment General Eisenhower sought for his manuscript of the book created a triable issue as to whether he intended the book to be a work for hire, and thus as to whether Doubleday properly renewed the copyright in 1976. See 34 Fed.Appx., at 314. The copyright issue is still the subject of litigation, but is not before us. We express no opinion as to whether petitioner's product would infringe a valid copyright in General Eisenhower's book.

"[w]ares; merchandise." Id., at 1079. We think the most natural understanding of the "origin" of "goods"—the source of wares—is the producer of
the tangible product sold in the marketplace, in this case the physical
Campaigns videotape sold by Dastar. The concept might be stretched (as it
was under the original version of § 43(a)) to include not only the actual
producer, but also the trademark owner who commissioned or assumed responsibility for ("stood behind") production of the physical product. But as
used in the Lanham Act, the phrase "origin of goods" is in our view incapable of connoting the person or entity that originated the ideas or communications that "goods" embody or contain. Such an extension would not only
stretch the text, but it would be out of accord with the history and purpose
of the Lanham Act and inconsistent with precedent.

Section 43(a) of the Lanham Act prohibits actions like trademark infringement that deceive consumers and impair a producer's goodwill. It forbids, for example, the Coca–Cola Company's passing off its product as
Pepsi–Cola or reverse passing off Pepsi–Cola as its product. But the brand-
loyal consumer who prefers the drink that the Coca–Cola Company or Pep-
siCo sells, while he believes that that company produced (or at least stands
behind the production of) that product, surely does not necessarily believe
that that company was the "origin" of the drink in the sense that it was the
very first to devise the formula. The consumer who buys a branded product
does not automatically assume that the brand-name company is the same
entity that came up with the idea for the product, or designed the product—
and typically does not care whether it is. The words of the Lanham Act
should not be stretched to cover matters that are typically of no consequence to purchasers.

It could be argued, perhaps, that the reality of purchaser concern is
different for what might be called a communicative product—one that is
valued not primarily for its physical qualities, such as a hammer, but for
the intellectual content that it conveys, such as a book or, as here, a video.
The purchaser of a novel is interested not merely, if at all, in the identity of
the producer of the physical tome (the publisher), but also, and indeed primarily, in the identity of the creator of the story it conveys (the author).
And the author, of course, has at least as much interest in avoiding passing-off (or reverse passing-off) of his creation as does the publisher. For
such a communicative product (the argument goes) "origin of goods" in
§ 43(a) must be deemed to include not merely the producer of the physical
item (the publishing house Farrar, Straus and Giroux, or the video producer Dastar) but also the creator of the content that the physical item conveys
(the author Tom Wolfe, or—assertedly—respondents).

The problem with this argument according special treatment to communicative products is that it causes the Lanham Act to conflict with the
law of copyright, which addresses that subject specifically. The right to
copy, and to copy without attribution, once a copyright has expired, like
"the right to make [an article whose patent has expired]—including the
right to make it in precisely the shape it carried when patented—passes to
the public." Sears, Roebuck & Co. v. Stiffel Co., 376 U.S. 225, 230 (1964);
see also Kellogg Co. v. National Biscuit Co., 305 U.S. 111, 121–122 (1938).
"In general, unless an intellectual property right such as a patent or copyright protects an item, it will be subject to copying." TrafFix Devices, Inc. v.
Marketing Displays, Inc., 532 U.S. 23, 29 (2001). The rights of a patentee or
copyright holder are part of a "carefully crafted bargain," Bonito Boats, Inc.
v. Thunder Craft Boats, Inc., 489 U.S. 141, 150–151 (1989), under which,

once the patent or copyright monopoly has expired, the public may use the invention or work at will and without attribution. * * * Assuming for the sake of argument that Dastar's representation of itself as the "Producer" of its videos amounted to a representation that it originated the creative work conveyed by the videos, allowing a cause of action under § 43(a) for that representation would create a species of mutant copyright law that limits the public's "federal right to 'copy and to use,'" expired copyrights, *Bonito Boats*, supra, at 165.

When Congress has wished to create such an addition to the law of copyright, it has done so with much more specificity then the Lanham Act's ambiguous use of "origin." The Visual Artists Rights Act of 1990, § 603(a), 104 Stat. 5128, provides that the author of an artistic work "shall have the right . . . to claim authorship of that work." 17 U.S.C. § 106(A)(a)(1)(A). That express right of attribution is carefully limited and focused. It attaches only to specified "work[s] of visual art," § 101, is personal to the artist, §§ 106A(b) and (e), and endures only for "the life of the author," at § 106(A)(d)(1). Recognizing in § 43(a) a cause of action for misrepresentation of authorship on noncopyrighted works (visual or otherwise) would render these limitations superfluous. A statutory interpretation that renders another statute superfluous is of course to be avoided. E.g., Mackey v. Lanier Collection Agency & Service, Inc., 486 U.S. 825 (1988).

Reading "origin" in § 43(a) to require attribution of uncopyrighted materials would pose serious practical problems. Without a copyrighted work as the basepoint, the word "origin" has no discernable limits. A video of the MGM film Carmen Jones, after its copyright has expired, would presumably require attribution not just to MGM, but to Oscar Hammerstein II (who wrote the musical on which the film was based), to Georges Bizet (who wrote the opera on which the musical was based), and to Prosper Merimee (who wrote the novel on which the opera was based). In many cases, figuring out who is in the line of "origin" would be no simple task. Indeed, in the present case it is far from clear that respondents have that status. Neither SFM nor New Line had anything to do with the production of the Crusade television series—they merely were licensed to distribute the video version. While Fox might have a claim to being in the line of origin, its involvement with the creation of the television series was limited at best. Time, Inc., was the principal if not the exclusive creator, albeit under arrangement with Fox. And of course it was neither Fox nor Time, Inc., that shot the film used in the Crusade television series. Rather, that footage came from the United States Army, Navy, and Coast Guard, the British Ministry of Information and War Office, the National Film Board of Canada, and unidentified "Newsreel Pool Cameramen." If anyone has a claim to being the *original* creator of the material used in both the Crusade television series and the Campaigns videotapes, it would be those groups, rather than Fox. We do not think the Lanham Act requires this search for the source of the Nile and all its tributaries.

Another practical difficulty of adopting a special definition of "origin" for communicative products is that it places the manufacturers of those products in a difficult position. On the one hand, they would face Lanham Act liability for *failing* to credit the creator of a work on which their lawful copies are based; and on the other hand they could face Lanham Act liability for *crediting* the creator if that should be regarded as implying the creator's "sponsorship or approval" of the copy, 15 U.S.C. § 1125(a)(1)(A). In this case, for example, if Dastar had simply "copied [the television series] as

Crusade in Europe and sold it as Crusade in Europe," without changing the title or packaging (including the original credits to Fox), it is hard to have confidence in respondents' assurance that they "would not be here on a Lanham Act cause of action," Tr. of Oral Arg. 35. * * *

In sum, reading the phrase "origin of goods" in the Lanham Act in accordance with the Act's common-law foundations (which were *not* designed to protect originality or creativity), and in light of the copyright and patent laws (which *were*), we conclude that the phrase refers to the producer of the tangible goods that are offered for sale, and not to the author of any idea, concept, or communication embodied in those goods. Cf. 17 U.S.C. § 202 (distinguishing between a copyrighted work and "any material object in which the work is embodied"). To hold otherwise would be akin to finding that § 43(a) created a species of perpetual patent and copyright, which Congress may not do. See Eldred v. Ashcroft, 537 U.S. 186, 208 (2003).

* * * If, moreover, the producer of a video that substantially copied the Crusade series were, in advertising or promotion, to give purchasers the impression that the video was quite different from that series, then one or more of the respondents might have a cause of action—not for reverse passing off under the "confusion . . . as to the origin" provision of § 43(a)(1)(A), but for misrepresentation under the "misrepresents the nature, characteristics [or] qualities" provision of § 43(a)(1)(B). For merely saying it is the producer of the video, however, no Lanham Act liability attaches to Dastar. * * *

Because we conclude that Dastar was the "origin" of the products it sold as its own, respondents cannot prevail on their Lanham Act claim. We thus have no occasion to consider whether the Lanham Act permitted an award of double petitioner's profits. The judgment of the Court of Appeals for the Ninth Circuit is reversed, and the case is remanded for further proceedings consistent with this opinion.

It is so ordered.

■ JUSTICE BREYER took no part in the consideration or decision of this case.

NOTES AND QUESTIONS ON "PATERNITY"

(1) The Ninth Circuit eventual held that Dastar's video infringed the copyright in Eisenhower's underlying book, which it found to be a work for hire under the 1909 Act and hence validly renewed for a second term by its publisher. Twentieth Century Fox Film Corp. v. Entertainment Distrib., 429 F.3d 869 (9th Cir.2005), cert. denied, 548 U.S. 919 (2006).

(2) Is the rule in *Dastar* applicable to the unattributed copying of a *copyrighted* work? In Williams v. UMG Recordings, Inc., 281 F.Supp.2d 1177 (C.D.Cal.2003), the court dismissed a claim under § 43(a) alleging a failure to credit the plaintiff for his work on the defendant's movie, holding that *Dastar* "is in no way limited to uncopyrighted material." The First Circuit in Zyla v. Wadsworth, 360 F.3d 243 (1st Cir.2004), affirmed a summary judgment against a co-author who claimed that an acknowledgment understating her contribution to a copyrighted textbook was a false designation of origin; the court said "*Dastar* controls."

(3) Does *Dastar* overrule Smith v. Montoro? (Note the Supreme Court's citation to *Smith* as an illustration of "reverse passing off" under § 43(a).) Even if "origin" under § 43(a)(1)(A) means the producer of the tangible product rather than the "author," isn't there still a misrepresentation in *Smith?* Does the substitution of names misrepresent "the nature, characteristics [or] qualities" of the movie, actionable under § 43(a)(1)(B)? *Dastar* leaves open the possibility of a false advertising claim under that subsection by any person "likely to be damaged" by misrepresentations made in advertising or promoting a work.[c] J. Ginsburg, The Right to Claim Authorship in U.S. Copyright and Trademark Law, 41 Houston L.Rev. 263, 274–75 (2004), thinks that Smith might still have a claim after *Dastar.* Professor Goldstein, however, believes that reliance on § 43(a) to redress the false attribution of an author's work to another may well be barred by *Dastar.* P. Goldstein, Copyright § 17.24.2.2.[d]

(4) Would *Dastar* require a different outcome in any of the following pre-*Dastar* decisions?

(a) Two plaintiffs alleged that they had coauthored two songs with a third person named Crosby. When Crosby's band released the songs on an album, authorship of one song was attributed solely to Crosby and the second song was attributed to Crosby and another person. Plaintiffs sued Crosby and the record company. The Ninth Circuit reversed a summary judgment against the plaintiffs, holding that they had stated a cause of action for false designation of origin under § 43(a). Lamothe v. Atlantic Recording Corp., 847 F.2d 1403 (9th Cir.1988).

(b) Plaintiff published a series of abbreviated adaptations of famous public domain works like *Robin Hood* and *Black Beauty*, with simplified language and illustrations for small children. Defendant substantially copied the works and attributed them to its own authors and illustrators. Plaintiff had not registered the copyrights in its works; it claimed instead that the attributions by the defendant were false designations of origin under § 43(a). The Second Circuit agreed in Waldman Publishing Corp. v. Landoll, Inc., 43 F.3d 775 (2d Cir.1994).

(c) Plaintiff architect produced drawings and plans for an elaborate home but stopped work following a contract dispute with the owner. Another architect then removed the plaintiff's name and seal from the designs, replaced them with his own name and seal, and submitted the designs to the city inspector. The Sixth Circuit found a false designation of origin under § 43(a). Johnson v. Jones, 149 F.3d 494 (6th Cir.1998). (After *Dastar,* would it matter if instead of simply re-labeling the plaintiff's originals, the defendant architect first copied the plans and then switched names on the copies and hence was the "origin" of the tangible product? *Should* it matter?)

---

[c] Romero v. Buhimschi, 396 Fed.Appx. 224 (6th Cir.2010) (unpublished), cert. denied, 131 S.Ct. 1695 (2011), involved a claim by a medical researcher that he had been improperly denied credit on a research paper. The court held that *Dastar* precluded a claim for false designation of origin under § 43(a)(1)(A) of the Lanham Act; as for a false advertising claim under $43(a)(1)(B), the court said that advertising attributing the research to another "related to authorship, rather than the nature, characteristics, or qualities of the research" as required under the statutory text.

[d] L. McLain, Thoughts on *Dastar* From a Copyright Perspective: A Welcome Step Toward Respite for the Pubic Domain, 11 U.Balt.Intell.Prop.L.J. 71 (2003), applauds *Dastar's* holding that public domain works can be used without attribution, but distinguishes cases involving a false representation; M. LaFrance, When You Wish Upon *Dastar*: Creative Provenance and the Lanham Act, 23 Cardozo Arts & Ent.L.J. 197 (2005), argues that *Dastar* should be limited to omitted attributions and should not apply to false attributions that constitute passing off or reverse passing off; G. Lastowka, Digital Attribution: Copyright and the Right to Credit, 87 B.U.L.Rev. 41 (2007), would further an author's attribution right by making attribution an explicit factor in the § 107 fair use analysis.

(5) Can a plaintiff successfully invoke *state* law to remedy a misattribution? An Ohio court, declaring that "[i]t makes no difference whether we label this claim for relief plagiarism, invasion of privacy, or *prima facie* tort," reversed a summary judgment against a medical researcher who alleged that the laboratory's director had presented a discovery made by the plaintiff as his own at a national scientific society. "[I]s there a right in plaintiff to be recognized for his work product which was violated by defendant's claiming that the work product was his own? We conclude that there is such a right. Although such right may not be invaded by a failure to give recognition to another upon an authorized publication, it is invaded when one claims the other's work product as his own." Bajpayee v. Rothermich, 53 Ohio App.2d 117, 372 N.E.2d 817 (1977). In light of *Datsar*'s argument that a cause of action under § 43(a) for misrepresenting the creative origin of a work "limits the public's 'federal right to "copy and to use" ' expired copyrights," would relief for such a misrepresentation under state law be preempted? The court in Aagard v. Palomar Builders, Inc., 344 F.Supp.2d 1211 (E.D.Cal.2004), held that under *Dastar*, a state unfair competition claim alleging reverse-passing off of a communicative product was preempted by federal copyright law. T. Bell, Misunderestimating *Dastar*: How the Supreme Court Unwittingly Revolutionized Copyright Preemption, 65 Md.L.Rev. 206 (2006), emphasizes *Dastar*'s broad implications for the preemption of state claims that fall outside the scope of § 301.

(6) A creator can impose a duty of attribution through a contract with her assignees and licensees, but absent an express obligation, the assignee or licensee is under no duty to credit the creator. Vargas v. Esquire, Inc., 164 F.2d 522 (7th Cir.1947), is a frequently-cited example. For several years plaintiff Vargas had furnished drawings for publication in the defendant's *Esquire* magazine under the title "Varga Girls," with plaintiff acknowledged as the artist. When the relationship terminated amid charges of fraud on the part of the defendant, it began publishing the remaining drawings under the title "Esquire Girls" with no attribution to the plaintiff. The assignments did not mention attribution, but Vargas argued that a duty to credit authorship should nevertheless be implied. The Seventh Circuit refused. "Such a reservation will not be presumed; it must be expressed and clearly imposed." See also Harris v. Twentieth Century Fox Film Corp., 43 F.Supp. 119 (S.D.N.Y.1942).

(7) American law has consistently afforded redress when someone else's work is falsely attributed to the plaintiff. (*Dastar* does not affect such claims, does it? J. Hughes, American Moral Rights and Fixing the *Dastar* "Gap," 2007 Utah L.Rev. 659, concludes that *Dastar* does not preclude a claim for the misattribution of another's work to the plaintiff.) False or misleading attributions have been successfully contested under a variety of theories, most often unfair competition. When Time–Life Records began promoting "Artie Shaw versions" of "Swing Era" classics, for example, bandleader Shaw was held entitled under a claim of common law unfair competition to explore whether consumers realized that the versions were not in fact Artie Shaw performances. Shaw v. Time–Life Records, 38 N.Y.2d 201, 379 N.Y.S.2d 390, 341 N.E.2d 817 (1975).

Novelist Ken Follett invoked § 43(a) of the Lanham Act to enjoin the publication of a nonfiction work attributed to him as principal author; he had in fact only edited the work. The court ordered an accurate credit line. Follett v. New American Library, Inc., 497 F.Supp. 304 (S.D.N.Y.1980). Stephen King, prolific author of horror stories, successfully invoked § 43(a) against a motion picture advertised as "Stephen King's Lawnmower Man." Although King had assigned the movie rights to his short story of that name, the court found that the attribution used with the movie (which only loosely tracked the story) misrepresented King's involvement; he had no role in producing or approving the script or film. However, the defendant was permitted to describe the film as "based on" King's story. King v. Innovation Books, 976 F.2d 824 (2d Cir.1992). Jazz musician George Benson was also successful in a claim alleging a misleading attribution. Distribution of a record album entitled "George Benson, Erotic Moods" was enjoined under § 43(a); the title was likely to mislead the public because the recordings, all several years old, involved a then unknown Benson playing merely as a group member. Benson v. Paul Winley Record Sales Corp., 452 F.Supp. 516 (S.D.N.Y.1978). See also PPX Enterprises, Inc. v. Audiofidelity Enterprises, Inc., 818 F.2d 266 (2d Cir.1987) (Jimi Hendrix absent from some recordings and only a sideman on others). Another record case, in which the defendant had overdubbed words and music onto the unfinished performance of the named artists, was won on a passing off theory under the Uniform Deceptive Trade Practices Act. Bonner v. Westbound Records, Inc., 49 Ill.App.3d 543, 364 N.E.2d 570 (1977).

A defamation claim involving an inaccurate attribution survived in Clevenger v. Baker Voorhis & Co., 8 N.Y.2d 187, 203 N.Y.S.2d 812 (1960). The plaintiff, author of "Clevenger's Annual Practice of New York," complained of a revised edition published under his name without permission. He alleged that the more than two hundred errors in the revision irreparably injured his reputation as a lawyer and legal writer; a jury award of $50,000 in compensatory and punitive damages was reduced on appeal to $10,000. 14 N.Y.2d 536, 248 N.Y.S.2d 396 (1964). In another unauthorized revision case, continued use of the original author's name was held an invasion of privacy. Zim v. Western Publishing Co., 573 F.2d 1318 (5th Cir.1978).

Shostakovich v. Twentieth Century–Fox Film Corp.

196 Misc. 67, 80 N.Y.S.2d 575 (Sup.Ct.1948).

"Plaintiffs are composers of international renown. They are citizens and residents of the Union of Soviet Socialist Republics. Defendant, a domestic corporation, has produced a picture known as 'The Iron Curtain' which is now being exhibited in theatres throughout this country. In the public mind, this title has come to indicate the boundary between that part of Europe which is under the sovereignty of, occupied by or under the influence of the U.S.S.R., as distinguished from the rest of the continent. The picture depicts recent disclosures of espionage in Canada attributed to representatives of the U.S.S.R. There is shown, preliminarily, but not as part of the picture proper, as is customary in the showing of motion pictures, the names of the players, the producer, the cameramen, and similar informative data. Included is this statement: 'Music—From The Selected Works of the Soviet Composers—Dmitry Shostakovich, Serge Prokofieff, Aram Khachaturian, Nicholai Miaskovsky—Conducted by Alfred Newman'. Such practice in the theatrical, advertising and kindred businesses is known as giving a 'credit line'. During the picture, music of the several plaintiffs is reproduced, from time to time, for a total period of approximately 45 minutes. The entire running time of the film is 87 minutes. The use of the music can best be described as incidental, background matter. Aside from the use of their music neither the plot nor the theme of the play, in any manner, concerns plaintiffs. In addition to the use of their names on the 'credit lines' the name of one plaintiff is used when one of the characters in the play is shown placing a recording of this particular plaintiff's music on a phonograph. Again this is incidental, the name is mentioned in an appreciative, familiar fashion, the impression given being that the character has come upon a record of a composition which he recognizes and appreciates hearing. All the music, it is conceded, for the purposes of this motion, is in the public domain and enjoys no copyright protection whatever.

"Plaintiffs seek to enjoin pendente lite and permanently the use of their names and music in the picture and in any advertising or publicity matter relating to it. * * *

" * * * The lack of copyright protection has long been held to permit others to use the names of authors in copying, publishing or compiling their works. Clemens v. Belford, Clark & Co., C.C., 14 F. 728. * * *

" * * * The wrong which is alleged here is the use of plaintiffs' music in a moving picture whose theme is objectionable to them in that it is unsympathetic to their political ideology. The logical development of this theory leads inescapably to the Doctrine of Moral Right (53 Harvard Law Rev. 554). There is no charge of distortion of the compositions nor any claim that they have not been faithfully reproduced. Conceivably, under the doctrine of Moral Right the court could in a proper case, prevent the use of a composition or work, in the public domain, in such a manner as would be violative of the author's rights. The application of the doctrine presents much difficulty however. With reference to that which is in the public domain there arises a conflict between the moral right and the well established rights of others to use such works. Clemens v. Belford Clark & Co., supra. So, too, there arises the question of the norm by which the use of such work is to be tested to determine whether or not the author's moral right as an author has been violated. Is the standard to be good taste, artistic worth, political beliefs, moral concepts or what is it to be? In the present state of our law the very existence of the right is not clear, the relative position of the rights thereunder with reference to the rights of others is not defined nor has the nature of the proper remedy been determined. * * * The motion is accordingly denied in all respects."

NOTE

The Appellate Division affirmed with the following memorandum: "We assume that the film in question is not a news film. We do not pass upon the sufficiency of the alleged cause of action, but think that, under the circumstances of this case, the motion for a temporary injunction was properly denied." 275 A.D. 692, 87 N.Y.S.2d 430 (1949). Would a judgment for the plaintiffs be inconsistent with the concept of a public domain?

The *Shostakovich* case was later relitigated in France when an assignee of the Russian composers protested the use of their music in the film "Le Rideau de Fer." An appellate court, finding the composers entitled to copyright in France, justified seizure of the film on a copyright infringement theory, but also found that there was "undoubtedly a moral damage."[e]

---

[e]   See W. Strauss, The Moral Right of the Author, Copyr. Law Revision Study No. 4, 139 n. 133 (1959), in 2 Studies on Copyr. 963, 989 n. 133 (1963). The great-great-grandson of Victor Hugo fought a seven-year legal battle in France against the publisher of two modern sequels to Hugo's 1862 classic *Les Miserables*, claiming that the works violated the integrity of the original novel. (The plaintiff seemed particularly upset that the works resurrected Inspec-

Gilliam v. American Broadcasting Companies

United States Court of Appeals, Second Circuit, 1976.
538 F.2d 14.

■ Before LUMBARD, HAYS and GURFEIN, CIRCUIT JUDGES.

■ LUMBARD, CIRCUIT JUDGE. Plaintiffs, a group of British writers and performers known as "Monty Python," appeal from a denial by Judge Lasker in the Southern District of a preliminary injunction to restrain the American Broadcasting Company (ABC) from broadcasting edited versions of three separate programs originally written and performed by Monty Python for broadcast by the British Broadcasting Corporation (BBC). We agree with Judge Lasker that the appellants have demonstrated that the excising done for ABC impairs the integrity of the original work. We further find that the countervailing injuries that Judge Lasker found might have accrued to ABC as a result of an injunction at a prior date no longer exist. We therefore direct the issuance of a preliminary injunction by the district court.

Since its formation in 1969, the Monty Python group has gained popularity primarily through its thirty-minute television programs created for BBC as part of a comedy series entitled "Monty Python's Flying Circus." In accordance with an agreement between Monty Python and BBC, the group writes and delivers to BBC scripts for use in the television series. This scriptwriters' agreement recites in great detail the procedure to be followed when any alterations are to be made in the script prior to recording of the program. The essence of this section of the agreement is that, while BBC retains final authority to make changes, appellants or their representatives exercise optimum control over the scripts consistent with BBC's authority and only minor changes may be made without prior consultation with the writers. Nothing in the scriptwriters' agreement entitles BBC to alter a program once it has been recorded. The agreement further provides that, subject to the terms therein, the group retains all rights in the script. * * *

In October 1973, Time–Life Films acquired the right to distribute in the United States certain BBC television programs, including the Monty Python series. Time–Life was permitted to edit the programs only "for insertion of commercials, applicable censorship or governmental . . . rules and regulations, and National Association of Broadcasters and time segment requirements." No similar clause was included in the scriptwriters' agreement between appellants and BBC. Prior to this time, ABC had sought to acquire the right to broadcast excerpts from various Monty Python programs in the spring of 1975, but the group rejected the proposal for such a disjoined format. Thereafter, in July 1975, ABC agreed with Time–Life to broadcast two ninety-minute specials each comprising three thirty-minute Monty Python programs that had not previously been shown in this country. * * *

ABC broadcast the first of the specials on October 3, 1975. Appellants did not see a tape of the program until late November and were allegedly "appalled" at the discontinuity and "mutilation" that had resulted from the editing done by Time–Life for ABC. Twenty-four minutes of the original 90 minutes of recording had been omitted. Some of the editing had been done in order to make time for commercials; other material had been edited, ac-

---

tor Javert, who drowns in the Seine at the conclusion of the original.) The Paris High Court refused to stop publication, holding that the works did not threaten the integrity of Hugo's novel. Samuel, *Les Mis*, The Sequels, Daily Telegraph (UK), Dec. 20, 2008, p. 14.

cording to ABC, because the original programs contained offensive or obscene matter.

In early December, Monty Python learned that ABC planned to broadcast the second special on December 26, 1975. The parties began negotiations concerning editing of that program and a delay of the broadcast until Monty Python could view it. These negotiations were futile, however, and on December 15 the group filed this action to enjoin the broadcast and for damages. Following an evidentiary hearing, Judge Lasker found that "the plaintiffs have established an impairment of the integrity of their work" which "caused the film or program . . . to lose its iconoclastic verve." According to Judge Lasker, "the damage that has been caused to the plaintiffs is irreparable by its nature." Nevertheless, the judge denied the motion for the preliminary injunction on the grounds that it was unclear who owned the copyright in the programs produced by BBC from the scripts written by Monty Python; that there was a question of whether Time–Life and BBC were indispensable parties to the litigation; that ABC would suffer significant financial loss if it were enjoined a week before the scheduled broadcast; and that Monty Python had displayed a "somewhat disturbing casualness" in their pursuance of the matter.

Judge Lasker granted Monty Python's request for more limited relief by requiring ABC to broadcast a disclaimer during the December 26 special to the effect that the group dissociated itself from the program because of the editing. A panel of this court, however, granted a stay of that order until this appeal could be heard and permitted ABC to broadcast, at the beginning of the special, only the legend that the program had been edited by ABC. We heard argument on April 13 and, at that time, enjoined ABC from any further broadcast of edited Monty Python programs pending the decision of the court.

I

* * *

Judge Lasker denied the preliminary injunction in part because he was unsure of the ownership of the copyright in the recorded program. Appellants first contend that the question of ownership is irrelevant because the recorded program was merely a derivative work taken from the script in which they hold the uncontested copyright. Thus, even if BBC owned the copyright in the recorded program, its use of that work would be limited by the license granted to BBC by Monty Python for use of the underlying script. We agree. * * *

Since the copyright in the underlying script survives intact despite the incorporation of that work into a derivative work, one who uses the script, even with the permission of the proprietor of the derivative work, may infringe the underlying copyright. See Davis v. E.I. DuPont deNemours & Co., 240 F.Supp. 612 (S.D.N.Y.1965) (defendants held to have infringed when they obtained permission to use a screenplay in preparing a television script but did not obtain permission of the author of the play upon which the screenplay was based).

If the proprietor of the derivative work is licensed by the proprietor of the copyright in the underlying work to vend or distribute the derivative work to third parties, those parties will, of course, suffer no liability for their use of the underlying work consistent with the license to the proprietor of the derivative work. Obviously, it was just this type of arrangement that was contemplated in this instance. The scriptwriters' agreement between Monty Python and BBC specifically permitted the latter to license the transmission of the recordings made by BBC to distributors such as Time–Life for broadcast in overseas territories.

One who obtains permission to use a copyrighted script in the production of a derivative work, however, may not exceed the specific purpose for which permission was granted. Most of the decisions that have reached this conclusion have dealt with the improper extension of the underlying work into media or time, i.e., duration of the license, not covered by the grant of permission to the derivative work proprietor. See Bartsch v. Metro–Goldwyn–Mayer, Inc., 391 F.2d 150 (2d Cir.), cert. denied, 393 U.S. 826 (1968); G. Ricordi & Co. v. Paramount Pictures Inc., 189 F.2d 469 (2d Cir.), cert. denied, 342 U.S. 849 (1951). Cf. Rice v. American Program Bureau, 446 F.2d 685 (2d Cir.1971). Appellants herein do not claim that the broadcast by ABC violated media or time restrictions contained in the license of the script to BBC. Rather, they claim that revisions in the script, and ultimately in the program, could be made only after consultation with Monty Python, and that ABC's broadcast of a program edited after recording and without consultation with Monty Python exceeded the scope of any license that BBC was entitled to grant.

The rationale for finding infringement when a licensee exceeds time or media restrictions on his license—the need to allow the proprietor of the underlying copyright to control the method in which his work is presented to the public—applies equally to the situation in which a licensee makes an unauthorized use of the underlying work by publishing it in a truncated version. Whether intended to allow greater economic exploitation of the work, as in the media and time cases, or to ensure that the copyright proprietor retains a veto power over revisions desired for the derivative work, the ability of the copyright holder to control his work remains paramount in our copyright law. We find, therefore, that unauthorized editing of the underlying work, if proven, would constitute an infringement of the copyright in that work similar to any other use of a work that exceeded the license granted by the proprietor of the copyright. * * *

Finally, ABC contends that appellants must have expected that deletions would be made in the recordings to conform them for use on commercial television in the United States. ABC argues that licensing in the United States implicitly grants a license to insert commercials in a program and to remove offensive or obscene material prior to broadcast. According to the network, appellants should have anticipated that most of the excised material contained scatological references inappropriate for American television and that these scenes would be replaced with commercials, which presumably are more palatable to the American public.

The proof adduced up to this point, however, provides no basis for finding any implied consent to edit. Prior to the ABC broadcasts, Monty Python programs had been broadcast on a regular basis by both commercial and public television stations in this country without interruption or deletion. Indeed, there is no evidence of any prior broadcast of edited Monty Python material in the United States. These facts, combined with the persistent requests for assurances by the group and its representatives that the programs would be shown intact belie the argument that the group knew or should have known that deletions and commercial interruptions were inevitable.

Several of the deletions made for ABC, such as elimination of the words "hell" and "damn," seem inexplicable given today's standard television fare. If, however, ABC honestly determined that the programs were obscene in substantial part, it could have decided not to broadcast the specials at all, or it could have attempted to reconcile its differences with appellants. The network could not, however, free from a claim of infringement, broadcast in a substantially altered form a program incorporating the script over which the group had retained control.

Our resolution of these technical arguments serves to reinforce our initial inclination that the copyright law should be used to recognize the important role of the artist in our society and the need to encourage production and dissemination of artistic works by providing adequate legal protection for one who submits his work to the public. See Mazer v. Stein, 347 U.S. 201 (1954). We therefore conclude that there is a substantial likelihood that, after a full trial, appellants will succeed in proving infringement of their copyright by ABC's broadcast of edited versions of Monty Python programs. In reaching this conclusion, however, we need not accept appellants' assertion that any editing whatsoever would constitute infringement. Courts have recognized that licensees are entitled to some small degree of latitude in arranging the licensed work for presentation to the public in a manner consistent with the licensee's style or standards. See Stratchborneo v. Arc. Music Corp., 357 F.Supp. 1393, 1405 (S.D.N.Y.1973); Preminger v. Columbia Pictures Corp., 49 Misc.2d 363, 267 N.Y.S.2d 594 (Sup.Ct.), aff'd 25 A.D.2d 830, 269 N.Y.S.2d 913 (1st Dept.), aff'd 18 N.Y.2d 659, 273 N.Y.S.2d 80, 219 N.E.2d 431 (1966). That privilege, however, does not extend to the degree of editing that occurred here especially in light of contractual provisions that limited the right to edit Monty Python material.

II

It also seems likely that appellants will succeed on the theory that, regardless of the right ABC had to broadcast an edited program, the cuts made constituted an actionable mutilation of Monty Python's work. This cause of action, which seeks redress for deformation of an artist's work, finds its roots in the continental concept of droit moral, or moral right, which may generally be summarized as including the right of the artist to have his work attributed to him in the form in which he created it. See 1 M. Nimmer, supra, at § 110.1.

American copyright law, as presently written, does not recognize moral rights or provide a cause of action for their violation, since the law seeks to vindicate the economic, rather than the personal, rights of authors. Nevertheless, the economic incentive for artistic and intellectual creation that serves as the foundation for American copyright law, Goldstein v. California, 412 U.S. 546 (1973); Mazer v. Stein, 347 U.S. 201 (1954), cannot be reconciled with the inability of artists to obtain relief for mutilation or misrepresentation of their work to the public on which the artists are financially dependent. Thus courts have long granted relief for misrepresentation of an artist's work by relying on theories outside the statutory law of copyright, such as contract law, Granz v. Harris, 198 F.2d 585 (2d Cir.1952) (substantial cutting of original work constitutes misrepresentation), or the tort of unfair competition, Prouty v. National Broadcasting Co., 26 F.Supp. 265 (D.Mass.1939). See Strauss, The Moral Right of the Author 128–138, in Studies on Copyright (1963). Although such decisions are clothed in terms of proprietary right in one's creation, they also properly vindicate the author's personal right to prevent the presentation of his work to the public in a distorted form. See Gardella v. Log Cabin Products Co., 89 F.2d 891, 895–

96 (2d Cir.1937); Roeder, The Doctrine of Moral Right, 53 Harv.L.Rev. 554, 568 (1940).

Here, the appellants claim that the editing done for ABC mutilated the original work and that consequently the broadcast of those programs as the creation of Monty Python violated the Lanham Act § 43(a), 15 U.S.C.A. § 1125(a). This statute, the federal counterpart to state unfair competition laws, has been invoked to prevent misrepresentations that may injure plaintiff's business or personal reputation, even where no registered trademark is concerned. See Mortellito v. Nina of California, 335 F.Supp. 1288, 1294 (S.D.N.Y.1972). It is sufficient to violate the Act that a representation of a product, although technically true, creates a false impression of the product's origin. See Rich v. RCA Corp., 390 F.Supp. 530 (S.D.N.Y.1975) (recent picture of plaintiff on cover of album containing songs recorded in distant past held to be a false representation that the songs were new); Geisel v. Poynter Products, Inc., 283 F.Supp. 261, 267 (S.D.N.Y.1968).

These cases cannot be distinguished from the situation in which a television network broadcasts a program properly designated as having been written and performed by a group, but which has been edited, without the writer's consent, into a form that departs substantially from the original work. "To deform his work is to present him to the public as the creator of a work not his own, and thus makes him subject to criticism for work he has not done." Roeder, supra, at 569. In such a case, it is the writer or performer, rather than the network, who suffers the consequences of the mutilation, for the public will have only the final product by which to evaluate the work. Thus, an allegation that a defendant has presented to the public a "garbled," Granz v. Harris, supra (Frank, J., concurring), distorted version of plaintiff's work seeks to redress the very rights sought to be protected by the Lanham Act, 15 U.S.C.A. § 1125(a), and should be recognized as stating a cause of action under that statute. See Autry v. Republic Productions, Inc., 213 F.2d 667 (9th Cir.1954); Jaeger v. American Intn'l Pictures, Inc., 330 F.Supp. 274 (S.D.N.Y.1971), which suggest the violation of such a right if mutilation could be proven.

During the hearing on the preliminary injunction, Judge Lasker viewed the edited version of the Monty Python program broadcast on December 26 and the original, unedited version. After hearing argument of this appeal, this panel also viewed and compared the two versions. We find that the truncated version at times omitted the climax of the skits to which appellants' rare brand of humor was leading and at other times deleted essential elements in the schematic development of a story line.[12] We therefore agree with Judge Lasker's conclusion that the edited version broadcast by ABC impaired the integrity of appellants' work and represented to the public as the product of appellants what was actually a mere caricature of their talents. We believe that a valid cause of action for such distortion ex-

---

[12] A single example will illustrate the extent of distortion engendered by the editing. In one skit, an upper class English family is engaged in a discussion of the tonal quality of certain words as "woody" or "tinny." The father soon begins to suggest certain words with sexual connotations as either "woody" or "tinny," whereupon the mother fetches a bucket of water and pours it over his head. The skit continues from this point. The ABC edit eliminates this middle sequence so that the father is comfortably dressed at one moment and, in the next moment, is shown in a soaked condition without any explanation for the change in his appearance.

ists and that therefore a preliminary injunction may issue to prevent repetition of the broadcast prior to final determination of the issues.[13] * * *

For these reasons we direct that the district court issue the preliminary injunction sought by the appellants.

■ GURFEIN, CIRCUIT JUDGE (concurring):

I concur in my brother Lumbard's scholarly opinion, but I wish to comment on the application of Section 43(a) of the Lanham Act, 15 U.S.C.A. § 1125(a). * * *

So far as the Lanham Act is concerned, it is not a substitute for *droit moral* which authors in Europe enjoy. If the licensee may, by contract, distort the recorded work, the Lanham Act does not come into play. If the licensee has no such right by contract, there will be a violation in breach of contract. The Lanham Act can hardly apply literally when the credit line correctly states the work to be that of the plaintiffs which, indeed it is, so far as it goes. The vice complained of is that the truncated version is not what the plaintiffs wrote. But the Lanham Act does not deal with artistic integrity. It only goes to misdescription of origin and the like. See Societe Comptoir De L'Industrie Cotonniere Etablissements Boussac v. Alexander's Dept. Stores, Inc., 299 F.2d 33, 36 (2 Cir.1962).

The misdescription of origin can be dealt with, as Judge Lasker did below, by devising an appropriate legend to indicate that the plaintiffs had not approved the editing of the ABC version. With such a legend, there is no conceivable violation of the Lanham Act. If plaintiffs complain that their artistic integrity is still compromised by the distorted version, their claim does not lie under the Lanham Act, which does not protect the copyrighted work itself but protects only against the misdescription or mislabelling.

So long as it is made clear that the ABC version is not approved by the Monty Python group, there is no misdescription of origin. So far as the content of the broadcast itself is concerned, that is not within the proscription of the Lanham Act when there is no misdescription of the authorship.

I add this brief explanation because I do not believe that the Lanham Act claim necessarily requires the drastic remedy of permanent injunction. That form of ultimate relief must be found in some other fountainhead of equity jurisprudence.

NOTES AND QUESTIONS ON "INTEGRITY"

(1) The theory adopted in *Gilliam* had been presaged in Jaeger v. American Int'l Pictures, Inc., 330 F.Supp. 274 (S.D.N.Y.1971). The plaintiff, a film director, complained of alterations made by the American distributor of his film. The court, denying a motion to dismiss, found it "at least arguable" that the use of the plaintiff's name on the altered work was actionable under § 43(a), but it declined to issue a preliminary injunction, noting that the scope of the defend-

---

[13] Judge Gurfein's concurring opinion suggests that since the gravamen of a complaint under the Lanham Act is that the origin of goods has been falsely described, a legend disclaiming Monty Python's approval of the edited version would preclude violation of that Act. We are doubtful that a few words could erase the indelible impression that is made by a television broadcast, especially since the viewer has no means of comparing the truncated version with the complete work in order to determine for himself the talents of plaintiffs. Furthermore, a disclaimer such as the one originally suggested by Judge Lasker in the exigencies of an impending broadcast last December would go unnoticed by viewers who tuned in to the broadcast a few minutes after it began. * * *

ant's rights under the distribution contract would be determinative. (Does *Dastar* curtail the use of § 43(a) to remedy the attribution of an altered work to the original author? Professor Goldstein thinks it does not. P. Goldstein, Copyright § 17.24.1.) A similar claim prevailed under a contract theory in Granz v. Harris, 198 F.2d 585 (2d Cir.1952). The defendant had purchased master tapes of musical performances produced by the plaintiff and later sold records containing abbreviated versions. The harm, the court said, was not in the alterations themselves, but rather in the use of the plaintiff's name on the altered versions; since the contract required attribution to the plaintiff, it carried "by implication" a "duty not to sell records which make the required legend a false representation."

Gilliam was cited with approval in National Bank of Commerce v. Shaklee Corp., 503 F.Supp. 533 (W.D.Tex.1980). The case was brought by Heloise Bowles, who wrote newspaper columns and books offering household hints. The defendant, a direct sales organization operating through independent distributors, purchased 100,000 copies of her book "All Around the House" as part of a promotional scheme. Prior to distribution, Shaklee placed advertisements for its products on the cover of the book and at the conclusion of each chapter. Despite copyright in the name of her publisher, the court said that Heloise had standing as "equitable owner" to claim infringement since her publishing contract provided for royalties and for reassignment of the copyright at the conclusion of the agreement. The court held that the addition of the advertising material infringed the copyright. (On what theory?) It also found Shaklee guilty of unfair competition in causing consumers to believe that Heloise had endorsed its products.[f]

(2) Under the 1976 Act, statutory copyright could subsist in a work such as the Monty Python script. Which of the § 106 rights would be infringed by the ABC broadcasts? The performance right, despite the licenses? The right "to prepare derivative works"?[g] An author's rights as the copyright owner, however, ultimately depend on the terms of the author's licenses. How likely is it that an author or artist will have sufficient bargaining power to reserve or restrict the right to modify or alter the work? And of course rights under copyright are of no use to an author who has assigned the copyright in the work.

---

[f]   A law student complaining of the alleged mutilation of his Comment by the editors of a law review failed in an attempt to invoke the rationale of *Gilliam*. The court concluded that the student had not been presented as the author of a work not his own. (The student did not help his case when he submitted an affidavit criticizing typographical errors that appeared in the article; the affidavit said that the typos were as much the "copy's [*sic*] editors' " fault as his own, "if not moreso [*sic*].") Choe v. Fordham Univ. School of Law, 920 F.Supp. 44 (S.D.N.Y.1995), aff'd, 81 F.3d 319 (2d Cir.1996).

[g]   Copyright ownership remains the most effective vehicle for protecting an author's artistic vision. When the licensor of the play *Steel Magnolias* learned that a Memphis theater intended to use a man in the role of Truvy (played by Dolly Parton in the movie version), it ordered the producer to recast the role or lose the right to stage the play: "Robert Harling, the author of the play, does not want that. And considering it is his property, he has every right to disapprove and say no." Yellen, Man Seeks Female Role, But Playwright Says No, N.Y. Times, Sept. 22, 1996, p. 20. M. Caroll, Copyright's Creative Hierarchy in the Performing Arts, 14 Vand.J.Ent. & Tech.L. 797 (2012), laments the degree of control that copyright gives playwrights over the nature and content of performances of their works.

The National Cathedral in Washington and the sculptor who created its renowned entryway bas-relief *Ex Nihilo* depicting the Biblical creation scene invoked copyright to force Warner Brothers to alter a scene in the video version of its film *Devil's Advocate*, in which figures in a substantially similar sculptural work come alive and engage in erotic groping. Clines, Creator of Religious Art Prevails on "Devil" Film, N.Y. Times, Feb. 14, 1998, p. A5.

R. Kwall, Inspiration and Innovation: The Intrinsic Dimension of the Artistic Soul, 81 Notre Dame L.Rev. 1945 (2006), uses an examination of the motivations for creativity to justify a proposal for general legislative recognition of moral rights.

(3) Suppose an artist sells a painting, assigning the copyright to the buyer. Does the artist have any right to prevent destruction of the work by the owner? Crimi v. Rutgers Presbyterian Church, 194 Misc. 570, 89 N.Y.S.2d 813 (Sup.Ct.1949), concluded that the artist did not. The work was a twenty-six by thirty-five foot fresco on the rear chancel wall of a church. The church had paid $6,800 for the work and taken an assignment of the copyright. Eight years later, without notice to the artist, the work was painted over. (There were indications that some parishioners objected that its portrayal of a bare-chested Christ emphasized physical at the expense of spiritual qualities.) The artist sought restoration of the work, removal from the church at the defendant's expense, or damages. Judgment was entered for the defendant. "The time for the artist to have reserved any rights was when he and his attorney participated in the drawing of the contract with the church." Would the outcome be different if the artist had retained the copyright?[h]

Would the artist now prevail under the Visual Artists Rights Act of 1990, infra, which added § 106A? See § 106A(a)(3)(B). What is the purpose of the statutory requirement that the work be "of recognized stature"? To protect elementary school teachers who throw away student artwork? How can "stature" be appraised? See also the special rules in § 113(d) for visual art that has been incorporated into a building.

(4) Some years ago a furniture manufacturer reproduced in an advertisement Rembrandt's *Aristotle Contemplating the Bust of Homer*—it is of course in the public domain. The painting was altered in that the bust was shown resting on a mirrored dining table and the caption read, "Contemplating a Table." More recently, an insurance company reproduced Vincent van Gogh's *The Starry Night,* put Snoopy and his doghouse in the foreground, and said, "We're the Old Masters of Financial Security." Would Rembrandt or van Gogh, if living, have any claim for relief?

THE VISUAL ARTISTS RIGHTS ACT

In 1990, moral rights received their first express recognition under federal law when the 1976 Copyright Act was amended by the Visual Artists Rights Act, Pub.L. 101–650. The rights created by the addition of § 106A extend only to a "work of visual art" as defined in § 101. What prin-

---

[h] An article by G. Schwartz, Ars Moriendi: The Mortality of Art, Art in America, Nov. 1996, p. 72, includes a curious account of the funeral plans made by Japanese industrialist Ryoei Saito, who in 1990 purchased Vincent van Gogh's *Portrait of Dr. Gachet* and Renoir's *Au Moulin de la Galette* for some $160 million. Saito later announced that he intended to have the two paintings incinerated with him on his funeral pyre. (He retracted the announcement in response to public outcries, and the two paintings survived his death in 1996.) Kernan, The Great Debate Over Artists' Rights, Wash. Post, May 22, 1988, p. F1, recounts famous instances of art mutilation, including an incident in which two Australians purchased a Picasso lino-cut for $10,000 and cut it into 500 one-inch squares which they offered for $135 apiece. The problem is as old as art. The article reminds readers of the 17th century monks who cut a door through Leonardo da Vinci's *The Last Supper* and the owner of Rembrandt's *Polish Rider* who cut off the horse's legs to fit the painting into a frame.

ciples might explain the particular selection of subject matter encompassed by that definition? (Note the exclusion of work made for hire.) Authors of works of visual art have the right under § 106A(a) to "claim authorship" of their work. (Does this include a right to have their name appear on the work?) They can prevent the use of their name on works that they did not create or on a distorted, mutilated, or modified version of their work that would be prejudicial to their honor or reputation. They also have the right to prevent any such distortion, mutilation, or modification of their work, as well as the right to prevent destruction of a work "of recognized stature."

A substantial limitation on the artist's paternity and integrity rights is imposed in § 106A(c)(3)—use of the work by another in connection with any of the items excluded from the § 101 definition of a "work of visual art," including posters, motion pictures, books, magazines, newspapers, periodicals, and advertising material, is exempt from liability. This point is emphasized in the legislative history. "For example, a newspaper, book, or magazine may include a photograph of a painting or a piece of sculpture. A motion picture may include a scene in an art gallery. The exclusion from the definition of a work of visual art would be of little or no value if these industries could be held liable under section 106A for the manner in which they depict, portray, reproduce, or otherwise make use of such a work. Moreover, because such actions do not affect the single or limited edition copy, imposing liability in these situations would not further the paramount goal of the legislation: to preserve and protect certain categories of original works of art." H.R.Rep. No. 101–514, 101st Cong., 2d Sess. 17–18 (1990).[i] Section 106A would thus be of no help to the artists in Note (4) supra, or to Alberto Vargas in his dispute over the unattributed reproduction of his drawings in *Esquire* magazine, p. 725 supra.

In an early test of the Visual Artists Rights Act, three artists convinced a district judge to issue a permanent injunction against the removal of a large "walk-through sculpture" located in the lobby of a building; the new owner wanted to get rid of it. The Second Circuit reversed, holding that the sculpture was a work for hire and thus beyond the protection of § 106A. Carter v. Helmsley–Spear, Inc., 71 F.3d 77 (2d Cir.1995), cert. denied, 517 U.S. 1208 (1996). Another artist who created a ten-by-thirty foot mural on heavy paper for use as a backdrop at an advocacy group's information table was also excluded from the protection of § 106A when she complained that the work had been damaged during its removal; the banner was not a "work of visual art" since it was "advertising" or "promotional" material excluded under the § 101 definition. Pollara v. Seymour, 344 F.3d 265 (2d Cir.2003).

The creator of a sculptural work entitled *Symphony #1* was successful with a claim under § 106A(a)(3)(B) against the city of Indianapolis when it destroyed the work after acquiring the property on which it was located. The court found the work to be "of recognized stature"—the model for it had

---

[i] In Silberman v. Innovation Luggage, Inc., 67 U.S.P.Q.2d 1489 (S.D.N.Y.2003), the plaintiff was a photographer who created 200 numbered and signed prints of a photograph of New York; he gave a license to a company to use the work for a poster. The defendant scanned the work from a poster catalog, changed the tint, and used a portion of the new image as a poster in its retail stores. The defendant claimed a violation of his attribution and integrity rights under § 106A. Although the numbered prints were protected as a "work of visual art," the court dismissed the claim because the defendant had copied the mass-produced poster, which is expressly excluded from protection in the § 101 definition. (Would it matter, in light of § 106A(c)(3), if the defendant had instead scanned one of the numbered prints to create its advertising poster?) The plaintiff did succeed on a copyright infringement count.

won best of show at the 55th Annual Hoosier Salon Art Show and there were articles and letters praising the work from academics and art critics. The Seventh Circuit affirmed an award of maximum statutory damages under § 504(c)(1) (which applies, along with the other remedial provisions of the 1976 Act, to violations of § 106A as a result of § 501(a)). However, the court concluded that the plaintiff was not entitled to increased damages under § 504(c)(2) for a willful violation in the absence of evidence that the city had been aware of the plaintiff's statutory rights in the work. Martin v. City of Indianapolis, 192 F.3d 608 (7th Cir.1999). According to the artist, although nothing can compensate for the loss of the work, "[T]he ironic thing is that there's a really nice picture of the sculpture in the court's ruling, so it lives on in the law books." ABA Journal, Dec. 1999, p. 38. Another court refused to dismiss an artist's claim under § 106A(a)(3)(A) for intentional mutilation of a sculptural work when the owner hired an alleged incompetent to repair the face of the figure; the owner raised § 106A(c)(2) as a defense since the "modification" was the result of "conservation," but the court held that the artist's allegations might bring the case within that subsection's exception for "gross negligence." Flack v. Friends of Queen Catherine Inc., 139 F.Supp.2d 526 (S.D.N.Y.2001).

A failed endeavor involving a museum and artist aimed at the creation of a huge art installation led to a detailed analysis of § 106A by the First Circuit in Massachusetts Museum of Contemporary Art Fd., Inc. v. Buchel, 593 F.3d 38 (1st Cir.2010). A Swiss artist had agreed to create a football field-size installation at the museum, but the project was abandoned prior to completion. The incomplete work, partially covered by tarpaulins, was visible to visitors at the museum. The artist claimed that exhibition of the work violated his attribution and integrity rights under § 106A. The court examined the language protecting the integrity right in § 106A(a)(3), noting that it not only creates rights to prevent certain conduct, but also states that the occurrence of that conduct is "a violation of that right." The attribution rights in § 106A(a)(1)–(2), however, create only rights "to claim authorship" or "to prevent" use of the artist's name, with no language making any conduct a "violation." This, the court concluded, indicated a congressional intent to limit attribution remedies to injunctions; monetary recoveries are available only for violations of the integrity rights. On the latter claim, the court held that by continuing to work on the installation without authorization from the artist, the museum could be liable under § 106A(a)(3) for intentional distortion, mutilation, or other modification of the work. However, merely showing the work in an unfinished state or covered with tarpaulins did not itself constitute a distortion, mutilation, or modification actionable under the statute.

The rights under § 106A are exercisable only by the author, whether or not the author still owns the copyright in the work. § 106A(b). For works created after the effective date of the Act (June 1, 1991), the rights endure for the life of the author. Preexisting works also qualify for protection if the author had not transferred title to the work prior to the Act, but for these works the § 106A rights terminate on the expiration of the copyright. § 106A(d).

Although the rights provided by § 106A cannot be transferred, they can be waived by the author in a signed writing that identifies the work and the uses to which the waiver applies. § 106A(e)(1). Concerned that artists might be forced to waive their rights without fair compensation, Congress directed the Copyright Office to undertake a study on the use and effect of the waiver provision. Although artists urged its repeal, a 1996 Copyright Office report entitled Waiver of Moral Rights in Visual Artworks cautioned that it was premature to assess the effect of the provision and concluded that no legislative action was warranted (except perhaps, in light of some broadly-worded waivers, for clarification of the requirement that the waiver must specifically identify the covered uses). The report is analyzed in R. Kwall, How Fine Art Fares Post VARA, 1 Marq.Intell.Prop.L.Rev. 1 (1997), also reviewing the slowly accumulating case law under § 106A. See also T. Cotter, Pragmatism, Economics, and the *Droit Moral*, 76 N.C.L.Rev. 1 (1997), cautiously favoring a waivable right.

The effect of the Visual Artists Rights Act on bargaining between producers and buyers of art is discussed in R. VerSteeg, Federal Moral Rights for Visual Artists: Contract Theory and Analysis, 67 Wash.L.Rev. 827 (1992); L. Gibbons, Visual Artists Rights Act (VARA) and the Protection of Digital Works of "Photographic" Art, 11 N.C.J.L. & Tech. 531 (2010), examines the uncertain application of VARA to digital works; M. Carpenter, Drawing a Line in the Sand: Copyright Law and New Museums, 13 Vand.J.Ent. & Tech.L. 463 (2011), wonders how VARA and the copyright owner's derivative right may limit attempts by museums to create interactive experiences for visitors.

MORAL RIGHTS AND THE COLORIZATION OF FILMS

The motion picture studios have long been vocal opponents of moral rights. The studios worry that broad recognition of moral rights will disrupt the production of films and hamper their ability to adapt movies for the home video and broadcast markets. Producers, directors, writers, and cinematographers all at various times urged Congress to legislate in favor of creators' rights in motion pictures, but the unanimity dissipated on the issue of who in the creative process should be entitled to such rights. See 39 Pat., Tm. & Copyr.J. (BNA) 206 (1990). Although artistic objections have been aimed at editing techniques such as "panning and scanning" that select portions of the original image to fit onto television screens, and "time compression" that speeds up movies to fit broadcast time constraints, the lightening rod for the debate was the colorization of black and white films. The campaign to block colorization was waged on two fronts. The first attacked the acceptance of colorized films as copyrightable derivative works. The colorizers won.

The second and more flamboyant front tried to advance the moral rights of film creators who did not want their classic works defaced (as they viewed it) by color. Film greats such as Woody Allen, Frank Capra, Walter Huston, and Jimmy Stewart were passionately engaged. There were years of bills, hearings, and panels, but in the end moral rights were not extended to motion pictures. The last word may be Ted Turner's, who paid $1.3 billion for MGM's collection of pre–1948 films: "The last time I checked I owned those films." See D. Kohs, Paint Your Wagon—Please! Colorization, Copyright, and the Search for Moral Rights, 40 Fed.Comm.L.J. 1, 2 (1988). But in a few cases, contract rights prevailed. Woody Allen, for example, apparently retained the right to prevent "panning and scanning" of his films. See 38 Pat., Tm. & Copyr.J. (BNA) 680 (1989). And we were spared a colorized version of *Citizen Kane* because of the nearly total artistic control written into Orson Welles' 1939 contract with RKO Pictures. Masters, Turner Won't Colorize "Kane," Wash. Post, Feb. 15, 1989, p. C1.

Meanwhile in France, director John Huston and later his children sought an injunction against the showing on French television of a color-ized version of his 1950 film *The Asphalt Jungle.* In 1991 the Huston heirs prevailed in the highest court in France, winning an injunction against broadcast of the colorized version on the ground that it would violate Hus-ton's moral rights. 42 Pat., Tm. & Copyr.J. (BNA) 236 (1991).

STATE MORAL RIGHTS STATUTES

(1) The California Art Preservation Act, Cal.Civil Code § 987, took ef-fect on Jan. 1, 1980. It begins with the following declaration:

> The Legislature hereby finds and declares that the physical alter-ation or destruction of fine art, which is an expression of the artist's personality, is detrimental to the artist's reputation, and artists there-fore have an interest in protecting their works of fine art against any alteration or destruction; and that there is also a public interest in preserving the integrity of cultural and artistic creations.

The substance of the Act is contained in subsections (c) and (d):

> (c)(1) No person, except an artist who owns and possesses a work of fine art which the artist has created, shall intentionally commit, or authorize the intentional commission of, any physical defacement, mu-tilation, alteration, or destruction of a work of fine art.

> (2) In addition to the prohibitions contained in paragraph (1), no person who frames, conserves, or restores a work of fine art shall commit, or authorize the commission of, any physical defacement, mu-tilation, alteration, or destruction of a work of fine art by any act con-stituting gross negligence. For purposes of this section, the term "gross negligence" shall mean the exercise of so slight a degree of care as to justify the belief that there was an indifference to the particular work of fine art.

> (d) The artist shall retain at all times the right to claim author-ship, or, for a just and valid reason, to disclaim authorship of his or her work of fine art.

The California Art Preservation Act protects only "fine art," defined in subsection (b) as "an original painting, sculpture, or drawing, or an original work of art in glass, of recognized quality, but shall not include work pre-pared under contract for commercial use by its purchaser." "Commercial use" is defined as "fine art created under a work-for-hire arrangement for use in advertising, magazines, newspapers, or other print and electronic media." What is the justification for this exclusion? And what of the re-quirement that the work be "of recognized quality"—does it raise difficul-ties of artistic judgment akin to those foreseen by Justice Holmes in *Bleistein,* p. 50 supra? The Act in subsection (f) states that "the trier of fact shall rely on the opinions of artists, art dealers, collectors of fine art, cura-tors of art museums" and others in determining "recognized quality."

What is the effect of subsection (d)? Can the artist insist that her name appear on the work? And what "just and valid" reasons might justify a dis-claimer of authorship—would anything other than alteration suffice?

The Act offers injunctive relief, actual and punitive damages, and at-torney's fees. The statutory rights subsist in the artist or "his or her heir, beneficiary, devisee, or personal representative" until fifty years after the artist's death. The rights and duties created by the Act may be waived by an instrument in writing signed by the artist.[j]

Can the California Art Preservation Act survive a challenge under § 301? Is a right to claim or disclaim authorship, or a right to prevent mutilation or destruction, "equivalent" to copyright? What of a right to prevent "alteration"? And when invoked by a living artist to protect a "work of visual art," can any applications of the statute escape preemption under § 301(f) as not "equivalent" to the rights conferred by § 106A?

Massachusetts has a statute, Mass.Gen.Laws Ann. c. 231, § 85S, that is similar to California's but of wider reach. It encompasses "any original work of visual or graphic art of any media which shall include, but not limited to, any painting, print, drawing, sculpture, craft object, photograph, audio or video tape, film, hologram, or any combination thereof, of recognized quality."[k] Other statutes on the California model include Connecticut, Gen.Stat.Ann. §§ 42–116s and 116t; New Mexico, Stat.Ann. §§ 13–4B–1 et seq.; and Pennsylvania, Stat.Ann. tit. 73, §§ 2101–2110.

(2) New York has also enacted a "moral rights" statute. Its Artists' Authorship Rights Act, N.Y.Arts & Cult.Aff.L. § 14.03, took effect in 1984. Like the California Act, it grants to the artist "the right to claim authorship, or, for just and valid reason, to disclaim authorship," and it expressly provides that this "shall include the right of the artist to have his or her name appear on or in connection with such work as the artist." § 14.03(2).

"Integrity" rights are protected only indirectly under the New York statute. Section 14.03(1) provides that no person "shall knowingly display in a place accessible to the public or publish a work of fine art * * * or a reproduction thereof in an altered, defaced, mutilated or modified form if the work is displayed, published or reproduced as being the work of the artist, or under circumstances under which it would reasonably be regarded as being the work of the artist, and damage to the artist's reputation is reasonably likely to result therefrom." Can liability be avoided simply by removing the artist's name from the altered work? But what of the statutory right to claim authorship? Would a disclaimer suffice? The Act excludes works "prepared under contract for advertising or trade use unless the contract so provides," and the right to seek redress in an action for "legal and injunctive relief" runs only to the artist.

---

[j]   A *Los Angeles Times* article reports on some of the litigation under the California statute. The article was prompted by a suit initiated by an artist against a framer and others in connection with a dark and blotchy varnish that had been applied to his still lifes of fruits and vegetables done for a San Diego hotel. "The subtle color nuances were totally destroyed," according to artist Brian Ura. "I'm embarrassed to have people see my name on them." The article also reports on a small judgment won by an artist after his ex-girlfriend ripped up a painting he had given her and scribbled profanities on the pieces before mailing them back to him. In another case an artist won a settlement from a collector who removed $50 bills that were part of the artist's avant-garde work and apparently spent them. Lerner, Painter Going to the Mat Over Changes in Artwork for Hotel, L.A. Times, Mar. 5, 1990, p. B3.

[k]   An artist who had created a series of sculptural works for a public park attempted to prevent the works from being moved to a new location by arguing that the work was so site-specific that moving it would amount to destruction or modification in violation of § 106A. The First Circuit in Phillips v. Pembroke Real Estate, Inc., 459 F.3d 128 (1st Cir.2006), held that § 106A does not cover site-specific art, at least in the sense of prohibiting its removal from the original location. The lower court had certified the question whether the Massachusetts Art Preservation Act protects the placement of site-specific art to the Supreme Judicial Court of Massachusetts. That court responded that the state act did not protect against "the conceptual destruction or decontextualization" that may result from removing the art from its intended physical environment; only physical alteration or destruction was prohibited. Phillips v. Pembroke Real Estate, Inc., 443 Mass. 110, 819 N.E.2d 579 (2004).

Statutes on the New York model include Louisiana, Rev.Stat.Ann. § 51:2151 et seq.; Maine, Rev.Stat.Ann. tit. 27, § 303; New Jersey, Stat.Ann. 2A:24A–1 et seq.; and Rhode Island, Gen.L. § 5–62–2 et seq.

(3) The New York statute was successfully invoked in Wojnarowicz v. American Family Ass'n, 745 F.Supp. 130 (S.D.N.Y.1990), by an artist whose works had been presented at an exhibition supported by the National Endowment for the Arts. The defendant, objecting to the sexually explicit images in the plaintiff's works, published a pamphlet attacking the use of public funds for such an exhibition; the pamphlet included fragmentary images of fourteen of the plaintiff's works. After concluding that attribution of the modified images to the plaintiff was a violation of the New York statute, the court enjoined further distribution of the pamphlet. In a footnote the court noted that Congress was then considering the Visual Artists Rights Act. Would § 106A afford any relief to the plaintiff? Would the Act, through § 301(f), now preempt the plaintiff's claim for relief under the New York statute? J. Cross, Reconciling the "Moral Rights" of Authors with the First Amendment Right of Free Speech, 1 Akron Intell.Prop.J. 185 (2007), examines the first amendment implications of federal and state moral rights regimes.

DROIT DE SUITE

Article 14*ter* of the Berne Convention (Paris Revision, 1971) provides:

1. The author, or, after his death, the persons or institutions authorized by national legislation shall, with respect to original works of art and original manuscripts of writers and composers, enjoy the inalienable right to an interest in any sale of the work subsequent to the first transfer by the author of the work.

2. The protection provided by the preceding paragraph may be claimed in a country of the Union only if legislation in the country to which the author belongs so permits, and to the extent permitted by the country where this protection is claimed.

3. The procedure for collection and the amounts shall be matters for determination by national legislation.

This article acknowledges the *droit de suite*—the right of an artist to share in the proceeds of subsequent resales of the work. The *droit de suite* in one form or another is recognized in a number of foreign countries.[1]

In 1976 California adopted the *droit de suite*. Cal.Civil Code § 986. Subsection (a) of the California Resale Royalties Act provides in part:

(a) Whenever a work of fine art is sold and the seller resides in California or the sale takes place in California, the seller or the seller's agent shall pay to the artist of such work of fine art or to such artist's agent 5 percent of the amount of such sale. The right of the artist to receive an amount equal to 5 percent of the amount of such sale may

---

[1] The European Union in 2001 adopted a directive that requires its member states to provide resale royalty rights to artists and their heirs for seventy years after the artist's death. The directive requires resale royalties only for works sold for more than 3,000 euros and caps the maximum royalty on a single sale at 12,500 euros. China has now overtaken Britain as the second largest art market, trailing only the United States. Some British art sellers blame their decline on the EU's resale royalty mandate. Daily Telegraph (UK), Mar. 15, 2011.

be waived only by a contract in writing providing for an amount in excess of 5 percent of the amount of such sale. An artist may assign the right to collect the royalty payment provided by this section to another individual or entity. However, the assignment shall not have the effect of creating a waiver prohibited by this subdivision.

The obligation to pay resale royalties does not apply if the resale price is less than $1,000, or less than the original price paid by the seller. § 986(b). Upon the death of the artist, the royalty right "shall inure to his or her heirs, legatees, or personal representative, until the 20th anniversary of the death of the artist." § 986(a)(7).

NOTES AND QUESTIONS

(1) What is the justification for the *droit de suite*? Do the creators of "fine art" deserve economic rights beyond those furnished by copyright?

(2) Consider the various factors that affect the resale price of art. Which support a claim by the artist to share in any appreciation?

(3) Who are the chief beneficiaries of the *droit de suite*? Is there any reason to expect that resales will yield royalties that correlate with private equities or public policy? A study by T. Camp, Art Resale Rights and the Art Resale Market, 28 Bull.Copyr. Soc'y 146 (1980), concluded on the basis of an analysis of auctions at Sotheby's that most of the benefits would go to a few important artists. This is confirmed in J. Wu, Art Resale Rights and the Art Resale Market: A Follow–Up Study, 46 J.Copyr.Soc'y 531 (1999), finding that only a tiny fraction of contemporary artists have a significant resale market.

Perhaps due to the fear of alienating art collectors and galleries, or because the amount of the royalty is typically small, artists have not been aggressive in enforcing the California statute. According to the California Arts Council, in the 34 years that the law has been in effect, only about 400 artists received royalties, and total payments amounted to only $328,000. Cohen, Artists File Lawsuits, Seeking Royalties, N.Y. Times, Nov. 2, 2011, p. C1.

(4) Is the California Resale Royalties Act preempted by federal copyright law? An art dealer challenged the constitutionality of the statute soon after it took effect. In Morseburg v. Balyon, 621 F.2d 972 (9th Cir.), cert. denied, 449 U.S. 983 (1980), the Ninth Circuit, in an opinion treating only the 1909 Act, found the Supreme Court's decision in Goldstein v. California controlling: "This is an additional right similar to the additional protection afforded by California's anti-pirating statute upheld in *Goldstein*." (*Goldstein* is in fact clearly inapposite, is it not?) The court rejected the dealer's contention that the Act contravened the first sale doctrine. "The work can be transferred without restriction. The fact that a resale may create a liability to the creator artist or a state instrumentality and, at the same time, constitute an exercise of a right guaranteed by the Copyright Act does not make the former a legal restraint on the latter."

Can the California statute survive § 301 of the 1976 Act? Is the *droit de suite* "equivalent" to the distribution right? The legislative history of the Visual Artists Rights Act says that state resale royalty rights are not preempted under § 301(f). H.R.Rep. No. 101–514, 101st Cong., 2d Sess. 21 (1990).

The California Resale Royalties Act eventually fell before a different constitutional limitation when several California artists sued New York auction houses Sotheby's and Christie's for failing to comply with the California law in connection with sales by California residents. In Estate of Graham v. Sotheby's Inc., 860 F.Supp.2d 1117 (C.D.Cal.2012), the court held that the California statute violated the Commerce Clause because it regulated sales occurring outside the state. Finding that the California legislature would not have enacted the law without its extraterritorial reach, Judge Nguyen stuck down the entire Act.

(5) As part of the Visual Artists Rights Act, the Copyright Office was directed to report on the feasibility of implementing a federal resale royalty system. In a report issued in 1992, the Copyright Office concluded that there was insufficient justification for establishing a federal resale royalty right. The report noted that most artists do not have a resale market for their work, and a right to resale royalties might depress prices for initial sales in anticipation of future royalty obligations. Bills to establish a federal resale royalty right applicable to art resales of $10,000 or more at major auction houses have been introduced, but with no indication that passage is likely. See 83 Pat., Tm., & Copyr.J. (BNA) 265 (2011). In response to a request from members of Congress, the Copyright Office is preparing a new report on a federal resale royalty right.

2. PUBLICITY AND PRIVACY

Haelan Laboratories, Inc. v. Topps Chewing Gum, Inc.

United States Court of Appeals, Second Circuit, 1953.
202 F.2d 866.
Certiorari denied, 346 U.S. 816.

■ Before SWAN, CHIEF JUDGE, and CLARK and FRANK, CIRCUIT JUDGES.

■ FRANK, CIRCUIT JUDGE. After a trial without a jury, the trial judge dismissed the complaint on the merits. The plaintiff maintains that defendant invaded plaintiff's exclusive right to use the photographs of leading baseball-players. Probably because the trial judge ruled against plaintiff's legal contentions, some of the facts were not too clearly found.

    1.   So far as we can now tell, there were instances of the following kind:

    (a). The plaintiff, engaged in selling chewing-gum, made a contract with a ball-player providing that plaintiff for a stated term should have the exclusive right to use the ball-player's photograph in connection with the sales of plaintiff's gum; the ball-player agreed not to grant any other gum manufacturer a similar right during such term; the contract gave plaintiff an option to extend the term for a designated period.

    (b). Defendant, a rival chewing-gum manufacturer, knowing of plaintiff's contract, deliberately induced the ball-player to authorize defendant, by a contract with defendant, to use the player's photograph in connection with the sales of defendant's gum either during the original or extended term of plaintiff's contract, and defendant did so use the photograph.

Defendant argues that, even if such facts are proved, they show no actionable wrong, for this reason: The contract with plaintiff was no more than a release by the ball-player to plaintiff of the liability which, absent the release, plaintiff would have incurred in using the ball-player's photograph, because such a use, without his consent, would be an invasion of his right of privacy under Section 50 and Section 51 of the New York Civil Rights Law; this statutory right of privacy is personal, not assignable; therefore, plaintiff's contract vested in plaintiff no "property" right or other legal interest which defendant's conduct invaded.

Both parties agree, and so do we, that, on the facts here, New York "law" governs. And we shall assume, for the moment, that, under the New York decisions, defendant correctly asserts that any such contract between plaintiff and a ball-player, in so far as it merely authorized plaintiff to use the player's photograph, created nothing but a release of liability. On that basis, were there no more to the contract, plaintiff would have no actionable claim against defendant. But defendant's argument neglects the fact that, in the contract, the ball-player also promised not to give similar releases to others. If defendant, knowing of the contract, deliberately induced the ball-player to break that promise, defendant behaved tortiously. See, e.g., Hornstein v. Podwitz, 254 N.Y. 443, 173 N.E. 674; 6 Corbin, Contracts (1951) Sec. 1470.

Some of defendant's contracts were obtained by it through its agent, Players Enterprise, Inc.; others were obtained by Russell Publishing Co., acting independently, and were then assigned by Russell to defendant. Since Players acted as defendant's agent, defendant is liable for any breach of plaintiff's contracts thus induced by Players. However, as Russell did not act as defendant's agent when Russell, having knowledge of plaintiff's contract with a player, by subsequently contracting with that player, induced a breach of plaintiff's contract, defendant is not liable for any breach so induced; nor did there arise such a liability against defendant for such an induced breach when defendant became the assignee of one of those Russell contracts.

2.   The foregoing covers the situations where defendant, by itself or through its agent, induced breaches. But in those instances where Russell induced the breach, we have a different problem; and that problem also confronts us in instances—alleged in one paragraph of the complaint and to which the trial judge in his opinion also (although not altogether clearly) refers—where defendant, "with knowledge of plaintiff's exclusive rights," used a photograph of a ball-player without his consent during the term of his contract with plaintiff.

With regard to such situations, we must consider defendant's contention that none of plaintiff's contracts created more than a release of liability, because a man has no legal interest in the publication of his picture other than his right of privacy, i.e., a personal and non-assignable right not to have his feelings hurt by such a publication.

A majority of this court rejects this contention. We think that, in addition to and independent of that right of privacy (which in New York derives from statute), a man has a right in the publicity value of his photograph, i.e., the right to grant the exclusive privilege of publishing his picture, and that such a grant may validly be made "in gross," i.e., without an accompanying transfer of a business or of anything else. Whether it be labelled a "property" right is immaterial; for here, as often elsewhere, the tag "property" simply symbolizes the fact that courts enforce a claim which has pecuniary worth.

This right might be called a "right of publicity." For it is common knowledge that many prominent persons (especially actors and ballplayers), far from having their feelings bruised through public exposure of their likenesses, would feel sorely deprived if they no longer received money for authorizing advertisements, popularizing their countenances, displayed in newspapers, magazines, busses, trains and subways. This right of publicity would usually yield them no money unless it could be made the subject of an exclusive grant which barred any other advertiser from using their pictures. * * *

* * * [P]laintiff, in its capacity as exclusive grantee of a player's "right of publicity," has a valid claim against defendant if defendant used that player's photograph during the term of plaintiff's grant and with knowledge of it. It is no defense to such a claim that defendant is the assignee of a subsequent contract between that player and Russell, purporting to make a grant to Russell or its assignees. For the prior grant to plaintiff renders that subsequent grant invalid during the period of the grant (including an exercised option) to plaintiff, but not thereafter. * * *

Reversed and remanded.

■ SWAN, CHIEF JUDGE (concurring in part). I agree that the cause should be reversed and remanded, and I concur in so much of the opinion as deals with the defendant's liability for intentionally inducing a ball-player to breach a contract which gave plaintiff the exclusive privilege of using his picture. * * *

NOTES AND QUESTIONS ON PRIVACY AND PUBLICITY RIGHTS

(1) In *Haelan,* Judge Frank gave a name to an emerging right and launched it on a lively course. Why was it necessary for the opinion to move beyond the New York privacy statute, which authorizes a suit for monetary and injunctive relief by "[a]ny person whose name, portrait, picture or voice is used within this state for advertising purposes or for the purposes of trade * * *."? N.Y. Civ. Rights Law § 51.[m]

Our interest in privacy here is confined to the fourth of Dean Prosser's famous four-fold classification of the privacy tort—the right against the commercial appropriation of one's identity, usually through the use of a name or likeness. The other three are (1) the right against intrusion; (2) the right against unwarranted disclosure of private facts; and (3) the right against disclosure of information that puts one in a "false light."[n]

The right of privacy is usually thought of as protecting ordinary people who have hurt feelings to be salved. For celebrities however, publicity is something they seek, yet at the same time wish to control. This is the essence of the "right of publicity," which protects not hurt feelings but rather the commercial value of a person's identity. About twenty states, including the entertainment

---

[m] Background on the *Haelan* case is provided in G. Hylton, Baseball Cards and the Birth of the Right of Publicity: The Curious Case of Haelan Laboratories v. Topps Chewing Gum, 12 Marq. Sports L.Rev. 273 (2001).

[n] The right against intrusion refers largely to physical intrusions or surveillance or harassment. The protection against the harmful disclosure of truthful private facts (e.g., a long-past criminal record) is readily overcome by a showing of newsworthiness. The classic case is Sidis v. F–R Pub. Corp., 113 F.2d 806 (2d Cir.), cert. denied, 311 U.S. 711 (1940). The "false light" branch of privacy is so close to defamation that the Supreme Court in Time, Inc. v. Hill, 385 U.S. 374 (1967), held that it is subject to the constitutional standards of New York Times Co. v. Sullivan, 376 U.S. 254 (1964). Another related tort is the intentional infliction of emotional distress. Its invocation by public figures was severely curtailed by the Supreme Court in Hustler Magazine v. Falwell, 485 U.S. 46 (1988).

centers of New York and California, offer such protection by statute; in a number of other states it has been recognized as part of the common law. In some jurisdictions, protection for the commercial value of a person's identity is accomplished through interpretations of the privacy tort; in others, a distinct "right of publicity" affords an independent basis for relief. In still others, the existence of the right remains unsettled. See generally Restatement, Third, Unfair Competition §§ 46–49 (1995).

(2) The New York Court of Appeals subsequently held (contrary to cases such as *Haelan*) that the New York privacy statute preempts recognition of any separate common law rights against the commercial exploitation of identity, notably in Arrington v. New York Times Co., 55 N.Y.2d 433, 449 N.Y.S.2d 941 (1982), and Stephano v. News Group Pubs. Inc., 64 N.Y.2d 174, 485 N.Y.S.2d 220 (1984). As for an assignee's standing under the New York statute, the cases have treated the statutory right as personal and non-assignable. J. Rothman, The Inalienable Right of Publicity, 101 Geo.L.J. 185 (2012), questions the common assumption that publicity rights should be fully alienable.

(3) Typical of "routine" right of publicity cases are the many decisions enjoining the unauthorized use of a celebrity's name or likeness on merchandise such as posters, t-shirts, and buttons. See, e.g., Factors Etc., Inc. v. Pro Arts, Inc., 579 F.2d 215 (2d Cir.1978), cert. denied, 440 U.S. 908 (1979) (Elvis Presley poster); Bi–Rite Enterprises, Inc. v. Button Master, 555 F.Supp. 1188 (S.D.N.Y.1983) (likeness of rock musicians on buttons); Winterland Concessions Co. v. Sileo, 528 F.Supp. 1201 (N.D.Ill.1981), aff'd, 735 F.2d 257 (7th Cir.1984) (t-shirts). But cf. Allison v. Vintage Sports Plaques, 136 F.3d 1443 (11th Cir.1998), applying a "first sale" limitation on the common law right of publicity to protect a defendant who mounted and sold trading cards purchased from licensed distributors.

The other "routine" type of publicity case involves the unauthorized use of a celebrity's identity in advertising. See, e.g., Waits v. Frito–Lay, p. 669 supra; Downing v. Abercrombie & Fitch, 265 F.3d 994 (9th Cir.2001) (use of a photo of the plaintiff in a clothing catalog); Negri v. Schering Corp., 333 F.Supp. 101 (S.D.N.Y.1971) (photograph of an actress used in an advertisement).[o]

(4) What policies support the recognition of a right of publicity? An incentive rationale similar to that underlying copyright? Prevention of unjust enrichment? A regard for personal integrity and autonomy?[p] Consider whether these

---

[o] The advertising value of a famous identity can be very substantial. Appliance maker Salton, for example, paid former heavyweight boxing champion George Foreman $137 million for the right to use his name and image to sell its cooking grills. N.Y. Times, Dec. 10, 1999, p. C2. Even non-celebrities can have publicity rights. Facebook encountered a class action lawsuit when it automatically generated paid advertisements based on users who clicked the "Like" button for particular commercial products. The user's Facebook name and photograph were sent to the user's Facebook "friends" as part of a "sponsored story" indicating that the user liked the product. The plaintiffs, alleging economic injury rather than metal anguish, claimed that the use violated the California right of publicity statute. In Fraley v. Facebook, Inc., 830 F.Supp.2d 785 (N.D.Cal.2011), the court held that the statutory right applied to celebrities and non-celebrities alike. "Plaintiffs' allegations suggest that advertisers' abilities to conduct targeted marketing has now made friend endorsements 'a valuable marketing tool,' just as celebrity endorsements have always been so considered." See also Bullard v. MRA Holding, LLC, 2013 WL 1247976 (Ga.2013) (plaintiff can recover the value of the advertising use without proof that her identity had inherent commercial value).

[p] K. Greene, Intellectual Property Expansion: The Good, The Bad, and the Right of Publicity, 11 Chap.L.Rev. 521 (2008), finds at least limited justification for the publicity right in its protection of dignitary interests; M. Bartholomew, A Right Is Born: Celebrity, Property,

or other interests justify protection in the following situations, some of which are discussed in the cases that follow:

(a) Johnny Carson, then host of "The Tonight Show," complains that the phrase "Here's Johnny" (which he employed nightly as an introduction) is being used by a defendant engaged in renting and selling "Here's Johnny" portable toilets. See Carson v. Here's Johnny Portable Toilets, Inc., 698 F.2d 831 (6th Cir.1983). Elroy Hirsch, an All–American football player at the University of Wisconsin and later a star with the Los Angeles Rams who earned the nickname "Crazylegs" complains of the use of that name on a women's shaving gel. Hirsch v. S.C. Johnson & Son, Inc., 90 Wis.2d 379, 280 N.W.2d 129 (1979). Should the right of publicity extend to phrases and nicknames?

(b) The plaintiff, a well-known race car driver, has come to be associated with a distinctively decorated car. The R.J. Reynolds Tobacco Company used a photograph of the car in a television commercial, but the plaintiff's face was not visible. After altering the photo by placing the word "Winston" on the car, it added a series of comic strip style "balloons"; one emanating from the plaintiff's car read, "Did you know that Winston tastes good, like a cigarette should?" See Motschenbacher v. R.J. Reynolds Tobacco Co., 498 F.2d 821 (9th Cir.1974). Brooklyn Dodger pitching great Don Newcombe complains about a beer advertisement that contains a drawing of an old-time baseball scene based on a newspaper photograph of Newcombe pitching in the 1949 World Series. The players' uniforms have been altered so they do not depict an actual team and Newcombe's uniform number has been changed from 36 to 39. Newcombe v. Adolf Coors Co., 157 F.3d 686 (9th Cir.1998). Have the plaintiffs' identities been appropriated?

(c) A group of professional athletes seek to enjoin the distribution of games that, while making no use of their names or likenesses in promotions, include the names as part of the contents of the game, together with accurate data on the players' careers. See Uhlaender v. Henricksen, 316 F.Supp. 1277 (D.Minn.1970); Palmer v. Schonhorn Enterprises, Inc., 96 N.J.Super. 72, 232 A.2d 458 (1967). *Life* magazine in 1945 published a photograph of a sailor kissing a nurse in Times Square in celebration of the end of World War II. The picture became famous. Forty years later (having learned the identity of the sailor) *Life* offers a limited-edition print at $1600. See Mendonsa v. Time Inc., 678 F.Supp. 967 (D.R.I.1988). Should these uses fall within the scope of the publicity right?

(d) In Apple Corps Ltd. v. Leber, 229 U.S.P.Q. 1015 (Cal.Super.1986), Leber had created a production that featured Beatles imitators performing Beatles songs. (The imitators had a license to perform the songs.) It was a great success, grossing $45 million. Apple, as assignee of the Beatles' publicity rights, alleged invasion of those rights as well as unfair competition. The plaintiff won on both right of publicity and unfair competition grounds. As to unfair competition, the judge said that viewers might be confused into thinking that the Beatles had authorized or approved the production. See also Estate of Presley v. Russen, 513 F.Supp. 1339 (D.N.J.1981), p. 678 supra.

(e) What about the use of deceptive look-alikes in advertisements? A look-alike of Jackie Onassis was included with some consenting celebrities in an

and Postmodern Lawmaking, 44 Conn.L.Rev. 301 (2011), offers an explanation of the right that emphasizes social rather than commercial forces.

advertisement depicting a group of guests at a fictitious wedding of the "Dior family." The resemblance was held close enough to constitute a "portrait" or "picture" under the New York privacy statute. Onassis v. Christian Dior–New York, Inc., 122 Misc.2d 603, 472 N.Y.S.2d 254 (Sup.Ct.1984), aff'd, 110 A.D.2d 1095, 488 N.Y.S.2d 943 (1985). When Woody Allen had a similar grievance, Judge Motley had doubts about the applicability of the New York statute, but found enough likelihood of confusion as to Allen's endorsement to invoke § 43(a) of the Lanham Act. Allen v. National Video, Inc., 610 F.Supp. 612 (S.D.N.Y.1985). Another Woody Allen case was decided the same way by the same judge. A disclaimer was considered inadequate. Allen v. Men's World Outlet, Inc., 679 F.Supp. 360 (S.D.N.Y.1988). Is Judge Motley correct in hesitating to apply the language of the New York privacy statute to look-alikes?

(5) For more on the scope and rationale of the publicity right, see R. Kwall, Fame, 73 Ind.L.Rev. 1 (1997), a broad-based defense of the right from a cultural and historical perspective; an attempt to define the scope of the right in terms of the purpose of the appropriation is made in H. Hetherington, Direct Commercial Exploitation of Identity: A New Age for the Right of Publicity, 17 Colum.J.L. & Arts 1 (1992); M. McKenna, The Right of Publicity and Autonomous Self–Definition, 67 U.Pitt.L.Rev. 225 (2005), concludes that the right of publicity should redress only injuries to personal rather than economic interests. The leading treatise on the right of publicity is J. McCarthy, The Rights of Publicity and Privacy (Thomson West).

Martin Luther King, Jr., Center for Social Change, Inc. v. American Heritage Products, Inc.

United States Court of Appeals, Eleventh Circuit, 1983.
694 F.2d 674.

■ Before HENDERSON and CLARK, CIRCUIT JUDGES, and TUTTLE, SENIOR CIRCUIT JUDGE.

PER CURIAM:

In our previous consideration of this case, The Martin Luther King, Jr., Center for Social Change, Inc. v. American Heritage Products, Inc., No. 81–7264 (11th Cir., Apr.1, 1982), we certified the following questions to the Supreme Court of Georgia pursuant to Georgia Code Annotated § 24–3902 permitting such procedure:

(1) Is the "right to publicity" recognized in Georgia as a right distinct from the right to privacy?

(2) If the answer to question (1) is affirmative, does the "right to publicity" survive the death of its owner? Specifically, is the right inheritable and devisable?

(3) If the answer to question (2) is also affirmative, must the owner have commercially exploited the right before it can survive his death?

(4) Assuming affirmative answers to questions (1), (2) and (3), what is the guideline to be followed in defining commercial exploitation and what are the evidentiary prerequisites to a showing of commercial exploitation?

The Supreme Court of Georgia, The Martin Luther King, Jr., Center for Social Change, Inc. v. American Heritage Products, Inc., 250 Ga. 135, 296 S.E.2d 697 (1982), has answered questions (1) and (2) affirmatively and question (3) in the negative in an opinion attached hereto as Exhibit A.

Pursuant to this opinion, the opinion of the Supreme Court of Georgia, and that court's answers to the first three certified questions, we reverse the judgment of the district court and remand for further proceedings.

Reversed and Remanded.

Exhibit A

In the Supreme Court of Georgia

Decided: Oct. 28, 1982

38748.   THE MARTIN LUTHER KING, JR., CENTER FOR SOCIAL CHANGE, INC., ET AL. v. AMERICAN HERITAGE PRODUCTS, INC., ET AL.

■ HILL, PRESIDING JUSTICE.

These are certified questions regarding the "right of publicity". The certification comes from the United States Court of Appeals for the Eleventh Circuit. Code Ann. § 24–3902; see Miree v. United States of America, 242 Ga. 126, 131–133, 249 S.E.2d 573 (1978). The facts upon which the questions arise are as follows:

The plaintiffs are the Martin Luther King, Jr. Center for Social Change (the Center), Coretta Scott King, as administratrix of Dr. King's estate, and Motown Record Corporation, the assignee of the rights to several of Dr. King's copyrighted speeches. Defendant James F. Bolen is the sole proprietor of a business known as B & S Sales, which manufactures and sells various plastic products as funeral accessories. Defendant James E. Bolen, the son of James F. Bolen, developed the concept of marketing a plastic bust of Dr. Martin Luther King, Jr., and formed a company, B & S Enterprises, to sell the busts, which would be manufactured by B & S Sales. B & S Enterprises was later incorporated under the name of American Heritage Products, Inc.

Although Bolen sought the endorsement and participation of the Martin Luther King, Jr. Center for Social Change, Inc., in the marketing of the bust, the Center refused Bolen's offer. Bolen pursued the idea, nevertheless, hiring an artist to prepare a mold and an agent to handle the promotion of the product. Defendant took out two half-page advertisements in the November and December 1980 issues of Ebony magazine, which purported to offer the bust as "an exclusive memorial" and "an opportunity to support the Martin Luther King, Jr., Center for Social Change." The advertisement stated that "a contribution from your order goes to the King Center for Social Change." Out of the $29.95 purchase price, defendant Bolen testified he set aside 3% or $.90, as a contribution to the Center. The advertisement also offered "free" with the purchase of the bust a booklet about the life of Dr. King entitled "A Tribute to Dr. Martin Luther King, Jr."

In addition to the two advertisements in Ebony, defendant published a brochure or pamphlet which was inserted in 80,000 copies of newspapers across the country. The brochure reiterated what was stated in the magazine advertisements, and also contained photographs of Dr. King and excerpts from his copyrighted speeches. * * *

* * * Testimony in the district court disclosed that money had been tendered to the Center, but was not accepted by its governing board. * * *

On November 21, 1980, and December 19, 1980, the plaintiffs demanded that the Bolens cease and desist from further advertisements and sales of the bust, and on December 31, 1980, the plaintiffs filed a complaint in the United States District Court for the Northern District of Georgia. The district court held a hearing on the plaintiffs' motion for a preliminary injunction and the defendants' motion to dismiss the complaint. The motion to dismiss was denied and the motion for a preliminary injunction was granted in part and denied in part. The motion for an injunction sought (1) an end to the use of the Center's name in advertising and marketing the busts, (2) restraint of any further copyright infringement and (3) an end to the manufacture and sale of the plastic busts. The defendants agreed to discontinue the use of the Center's name in further promotion. Therefore, the court granted this part of the injunction. The district court found that the defendants had infringed the King copyrights and enjoined all further use of the copyrighted material.

In ruling on the third request for injunction, the court confronted the plaintiffs' claim that the manufacture and sale of the busts violated Dr. King's right of publicity which had passed to his heirs upon Dr. King's death. The defendants contended that no such right existed, and hence, an injunction should not issue. The district court concluded that it was not necessary to determine whether the "right of publicity" was devisable in Georgia because Dr. King did not commercially exploit this right during his lifetime. As found by the district court, the evidence of exploitation by Dr. King came from his sister's affidavit which stated that he had received "thousands of dollars in the form of honorariums from the use of his name, likeness, literary compositions, and speeches." The district court further found that "Dr. King apparently sold his copyrights in several speeches to Motown Records Corporation." Martin Luther King, Jr. Center for Social Change, Inc. v. American Heritage Products, Inc., 508 F.Supp. 854 (N.D.Ga.1981).

On plaintiffs' appeal of the partial denial of the preliminary injunction, the Eleventh Circuit Court of Appeals has certified the following questions: * * *

1. Is the "right of publicity" recognized in Georgia as a right distinct from the right of privacy?

Georgia has long recognized the right of privacy. Following denial of the existence of the right of privacy in a controversial decision by the New York Court of Appeals in Roberson v. Rochester Folding–Box Co., 171 N.Y. 538, 64 N.E. 442 (1902), the Georgia Supreme Court became the first such court to recognize the right of privacy in Pavesich v. New England Life Ins. Co., 122 Ga. 190, 50 S.E. 68 (1905). See Prosser, Law of Torts, pp. 802–804 (1971).

In Pavesich v. New England Life Ins. Co., supra, the picture of an artist was used without his consent in a newspaper advertisement of the insurance company. Analyzing the right of privacy, this court held: "The publication of a picture of a person, without his consent, as a part of an advertisement, for the purpose of exploiting the publisher's business, is a violation of the right of privacy of the person whose picture is reproduced, and entitles him to recover without proof of special damage." 122 Ga. at 191(11), 50 S.E. at 68(11). * * *

Recognizing the possibility of a conflict between the right of privacy and the freedoms of speech and press, this court said: "There is in the publication of one's picture for advertising purposes not the slightest semblance of an expression of an idea, a thought, or an opinion, within the meaning of the constitutional provision which guarantees to a person the right to publish his sentiments on any subject." 122 Ga. at 219, 50 S.E. at 80. The defendants in the case now before us make no claim under these freedoms and we find no violation thereof. * * *

The "right of publicity" was first recognized in Haelan Laboratories, Inc. v. Topps Chewing Gum, Inc., 202 F.2d 866 (2d Cir.1953). * * *

The right to publicity is not absolute. In Hicks v. Casablanca Records, 464 F.Supp. 426 (S.D.N.Y.1978), the court held that a fictional novel and movie concerning an unexplained eleven day disappearance by Agatha Christie, author of numerous mystery novels, were permissible under the first amendment. * * *

The right of publicity was first recognized in Georgia by the Court of Appeals in Cabaniss v. Hipsley, 114 Ga.App. 367, 151 S.E.2d 496 (1966). There the court held that the plaintiff, an exotic dancer, could recover from the owner of the Atlanta Playboy Club for the unauthorized use of the dancer's misnamed photograph in an entertainment magazine advertising the Playboy Club. Although plaintiff had had her picture taken to promote her performances, she was not performing at the Playboy Club. * * *

Thus, the courts in Georgia have recognized the rights of private citizens, *Pavesich,* supra, as well as entertainers, *Cabaniss* * * *, supra, not to have their names and photographs used for the financial gain of the user without their consent, where such use is not authorized as an exercise of freedom of the press. We know of no reason why a public figure prominent in religion and civil rights should be entitled to less protection than an exotic dancer or a movie actress. Therefore, we hold that the appropriation of another's name and likeness, whether such likeness be a photograph or sculpture, without consent and for the financial gain of the appropriator is a tort in Georgia, whether the person whose name and likeness is used is a private citizen, entertainer, or as here a public figure who is not a public official.

In *Pavesich,* supra, 122 Ga. 190, 50 S.E. 68, this right not to have another appropriate one's photograph was denominated the right of privacy; in Cabaniss v. Hipsley, supra, 114 Ga.App. 367, 151 S.E.2d 496, it was the right of publicity. Mr. Pavesich was not a public figure; Ms. Hipsley was. We conclude that while private citizens have the right of privacy, public figures have a similar right of publicity, and that the measure of damages to a public figure for violation of his or her right of publicity is the value of the appropriation to the user. Cabaniss v. Hipsley, supra; see also Uhlaender v. Henricksen, 316 F.Supp. 1277, 1279–1280 (Minn.1970). As thus understood the first certified question is answered in the affirmative.

    2.   Does the "right of publicity" survive the death of its owner (i.e., is the right inheritable and devisable)? * * *

The right of publicity is assignable during the life of the celebrity, for without this characteristic, full commercial exploitation of one's name and likeness is practically impossible. Haelan Laboratories v. Topps Chewing Gum, supra, 202 F.2d at 868. That is, without assignability the right of publicity could hardly be called a "right". Recognizing its assignability, most commentators have urged that the right of publicity must also be inheritable. Felcher and Rubin, The Descendibility of the Right of Publicity: Is there Commercial Life After Death?, 89 Yale L.J. 1125 (1980); Gordon, Right of Property in Name, Likeness, Personality and History, 55 Nw.U.L.Rev. 553 (1960); * * *

In Factors Etc., Inc. v. Pro Arts, Inc., 579 F.2d 215 (2d Cir.1978), Elvis Presley had assigned his right of publicity to Boxcar Enterprises, which assigned that right to Factors after Presley's death. Defendant Pro Arts published a poster of Presley entitled "In Memory". In affirming the grant of injunction against Pro Arts, the Second Circuit Court of Appeals said (579 F.2d at 221): "The identification of this exclusive right belonging to Boxcar as a transferable property right compels the conclusion that the right survives Presley's death. The death of Presley, who was merely the beneficiary of an income interest in Boxcar's exclusive right, should not in itself extinguish Boxcar's property right. Instead, the income interest, continually produced from Boxcar's exclusive right of commercial exploitation, should inure to Presley's estate at death like any other intangible property right. To hold that the right did not survive Presley's death, would be to grant competitors of Factors, such as Pro Arts, a windfall in the form of profits from the use of Presley's name and likeness. At the same time, the exclusive right purchased by Factors and the financial benefits accruing to the celebrity's heirs would be rendered virtually worthless."

In Lugosi v. Universal Pictures, 25 Cal.3d 813, 160 Cal.Rptr. 323, 603 P.2d 425 (1979), the Supreme Court of California, in a 4 to 3 decision, declared that the right of publicity expires upon the death of the celebrity and is not descendible. See Guglielmi v. Spelling–Goldberg Productions, 25 Cal.3d 860, 160 Cal.Rptr. 352, 603 P.2d 454 (1979), decided two days after *Lugosi,* supra. Bela Lugosi appeared as Dracula in Universal Picture's movie by that name. Universal had acquired the movie rights to the novel by Bram Stoker. Lugosi's contract with Universal gave it the right to exploit Lugosi's name and likeness in connection with the movie. The majority of the court held that Lugosi's heirs could not prevent Universal's continued exploitation of Lugosi's portrayal of Count Dracula after his death. The court did not decide whether Universal could prevent unauthorized third parties from exploitation of Lugosi's appearance as Dracula after Lugosi's death.

In Memphis Development Foundation v. Factors Etc., Inc., 616 F.2d 956 (6th Cir.1980), Factors, which had won its case against Pro Arts in New York (see above), lost against the Memphis Development Foundation under the Court of Appeals for the Sixth Circuit's interpretation of Tennessee law. There, the Foundation, a non-profit corporation, planned to erect a statue of Elvis Presley in Memphis and solicited contributions to do so. Donors of $25 or more received a small replica of the proposed statue. The Sixth Circuit reversed the grant of an injunction favoring Factors, holding that a celebrity's right of publicity was not inheritable even where that right had been exploited during the celebrity's life.[4] The court reasoned that although recognition of the right of publicity during life serves to encourage effort and inspire creative endeavors, making the right inheritable would not. The court also was concerned with unanswered legal questions which recognizing inheritability would create. We note, however, that the court was dealing with a non-profit foundation attempting to promote Presley's adopted homeplace, the City of Memphis. The court was not dealing, as we do here, with a profit making endeavor. * * *

For the reasons which follow we hold that the right of publicity survives the death of its owner and is inheritable and devisable. Recognition of the right of publicity rewards and thereby encourages effort and creativity.

---

[4] The Second Circuit has now accepted the Sixth Circuit's interpretation of Tennessee law. Factors Etc., Inc. v. Pro Arts, Inc., 652 F.2d 278 (2d Cir.1981).

If the right of publicity dies with the celebrity, the economic value of the right of publicity during life would be diminished because the celebrity's untimely death would seriously impair, if not destroy, the value of the right of continued commercial use. Conversely, those who would profit from the fame of a celebrity after his or her death for their own benefit and without authorization have failed to establish their claim that they should be the beneficiaries of the celebrity's death. Finally, the trend since the early common law has been to recognize survivability, notwithstanding the legal problems which may thereby arise. We therefore answer question 2 in the affirmative.

3.   Must the owner of the right of publicity have commercially exploited that right before it can survive?

Exploitation is understood to mean commercial use by the celebrity other than the activity which made him or her famous, e.g., an inter vivos transfer of the right to the use of one's name and likeness.

The requirement that the right of publicity be exploited by the celebrity during his or her lifetime in order to render the right inheritable arises from the case involving Agatha Christie, Hicks v. Casablanca Records, supra, 464 F.Supp. at 429. * * * [T]he *Hicks* court held that the fictional account of Agatha Christie's 11 day disappearance was protected by the first amendment. Thus, the finding that exploitation during life was necessary to inheritability was actually unnecessary to that decision.

Nevertheless, the *Hicks* dicta has been relied upon. See Groucho Marx Productions, Inc. v. Day and Night Co., 523 F.Supp. 485, 490 (S.D.N.Y.1981).[5] However, in this case, involving the Marx brothers, it was found that, although Leo and Adolpho Marx ("Chico" and "Harpo") had not made inter vivos or specific testamentary dispositions of their rights, they had earned their livelihoods by exploiting the unique characters they created and thus had exploited their rights to publicity so as to make such rights descendible. Thus, even in the Southern District of New York where the requirement arose, exploitation beyond the "activity which made him or her famous" is not now required.

The cases which have considered this issue, see above, involved entertainers. The net result of following them would be to say that celebrities and public figures have the right of publicity during their lifetimes (as others have the right of privacy), but only those who contract for bubble gum cards, posters and tee shirts have a descendible right of publicity upon their deaths. See Groucho Marx Productions, Inc. v. Day and Night Co., supra, 523 F.Supp. at 490, 491–492. That we should single out for protection after death those entertainers and athletes who exploit their personae during life, and deny protection after death to those who enjoy public acclamation but did not exploit themselves during life, puts a premium on exploitation. Having found that there are valid reasons for recognizing the right of publicity during life, we find no reason to protect after death only those who took commercial advantage of their fame.

Perhaps this case more than others brings the point into focus. A well known minister may avoid exploiting his prominence during life because to do otherwise would impair his ministry. Should his election not to take commercial advantage of his position during life ipso facto result in permit-

---

[5]   On appeal of this case, the Second Circuit reversed, finding the law of California applicable, where, as noted above, the right of publicity is not inheritable. Groucho Marx Productions, Inc. v. Day & Night Co., 689 F.2d 317 (2d Cir.1982).

ting others to exploit his name and likeness after his death? In our view, a person who avoids exploitation during life is entitled to have his image protected against exploitation after death just as much if not more than a person who exploited his image during life.

Without doubt, Dr. King could have exploited his name and likeness during his lifetime. That this opportunity was not appealing to him does not mean that others have the right to use his name and likeness in ways he himself chose not to do. Nor does it strip his family and estate of the right to control, preserve and extend his status and memory and to prevent unauthorized exploitation thereof by others. Here, they seek to prevent the exploitation of his likeness in a manner they consider unflattering and unfitting. We cannot deny them this right merely because Dr. King chose not to exploit or commercialize himself during his lifetime.

Question 3 is answered in the negative, and therefore we need not answer question 4.

Certified questions 1 and 2 answered in the affirmative, question 3 answered in the negative, and question 4 not answered.

All the Justices concur, except Weltner, J., who concurs specially.

■ WELTNER, JUSTICE, concurring specially.

I concur specially because, although this matter is one of certified questions, I believe that the complaint states a claim upon which relief can be granted. I disagree most decidedly with the substantive portion of the majority opinion, for reason that it generates more unsettling questions than it resolves. * * *

[T]he majority says that the fabrication and commercial distribution of a likeness of Dr. King is not "speech," thereby removing the inquiry from the ambit of First Amendment or Free Speech inquiries. * * *

Do not the statues of the Confederate soldiers which inhabit so many of our courthouse squares express the sentiments of those who raised them?

Are not the busts of former chief justices, stationed within the rotunda of this very courthouse, expressions of sentiments of gratitude and approval?

Is not the portrait of Dr. King which hangs in our Capitol an expression of sentiment?

Manifestly so.

If, then, a two-dimensional likeness in oil and canvas is an expression of sentiment, how can it be said that a three-dimensional likeness in plastic is *not*?

But, says the majority, our new right to publicity is violated only in cases involving financial gain. * * *

Did the sculptors of our Confederate soldiers, and of our chief justices, labor without gain? Was Dr. King's portraitist unpaid for his work?

If "financial gain" is to be the watershed of violation *vel non* of this new-found right, it cannot withstand scrutiny. It is rare, indeed, that any expression of sentiment beyond casual conversation is not somehow connected, directly or indirectly, to "financial gain." For example, a school child wins a $25 prize for the best essay on Dr. King's life. Is this "financial gain?" Must the child then account for the winnings?

The essay, because of its worth, is reprinted in a commercial publication. Must the publisher account?

The publication is sold on the newsstand. Must the vendor account?

The majority will say "free speech." Very well. The same child wins a $25 prize in the school art fair. His creation—a bust of Dr. King.

Must he account?

The local newspaper prints a photograph of the child and of his creation. Must it account?

The school commissions replicas of the bust to raise money for its library. Must it account?

UNICEF reproduces the bust on its Christmas cards. Must it account?

Finally, a purely commercial venture undertakes to market replicas of the bust under circumstances similar to those of this case. Must it account?

Obviously, the answers to the above questions will vary, and properly so, because the circumstances posited are vastly different. The dividing line, however, cannot be fixed upon the presence or absence of "financial gain." Rather, it must be grounded in the community's judgment of what, *ex aequo et bono,* is unconscionable. * * *

NOTES ON THE DESCENDIBILITY OF PUBLICITY RIGHTS

(1) Consider again the interests underlying the right of publicity. Which, if any, support a post-mortem right? Other cases finding a descendible right of publicity at common law include Nature's Way Products, Inc. v. Nature–Pharma, Inc., 736 F.Supp. 245 (D.Utah 1990) (Utah law); and Estate of Presley v. Russen, 513 F.Supp. 1339 (D.N.J.1981) (New Jersey law).

Did the majority indeed neglect significant free speech interests as argued in Justice Weltner's concurrence? The first amendment issue is pursued later in this section.

(2) In the *Memphis Development Foundation* case summarized by Justice Hill, the Sixth Circuit, after concluding "that making the right of publicity inheritable would not significantly inspire the creative endeavors of individuals," posed the following "practical problems" raised by a descendible publicity right: "How long would the 'property' interest last? In perpetuity? For a term of years? Is the right of publicity taxable? At what point does the right collide with the right of free expression guaranteed by the first amendment? Does the right apply to elected officials and military heroes whose fame was gained on the public payroll, as well as to movie stars, singers and athletes? Does the right cover posters or engraved likenesses of, for example, Farah Fawcett Majors or Mahatma Gandhi, kitchen utensils ('Revere Ware'), insurance ('John Hancock'), electric utilities ('Edison'), a football stadium ('RFK'), a pastry ('Napoleon'), or the innumerable urban subdivisions and apartment complexes named after famous people? Our legal system normally does not pass on to heirs other similar personal attributes even though the attributes may be shared during life by others or have some commercial value. Titles, offices and reputation are not inheritable. Neither are trust or distrust and friendship or enmity descendible. An employment contract during life does not create the right for heirs to take over the job. Fame falls in the same category as reputation; it is an attribute from which others may benefit but may not own." 616 F.2d at 959.

The Tennessee legislature responded to the *Memphis Development* decision with the Personal Rights Protection Act of 1984, which declares that publicity rights survive for a period of ten years after death and continue thereafter absent proof of non-use by the heirs or devisees for any two-year period subsequent to the initial ten-year term. Tenn.Code Ann. § 47–25–1101 et seq.[q]

(3) Hicks v. Casablanca Records, cited by Justice Hill for its holding that the right must be "exploited" during life in order to render it inheritable, involved an attempt by the heirs and assignees of Dame Agatha Christie to enjoin distribution of the motion picture "Agatha," which presented a fictionalized account of an incident in the author's life. On the question of inheritability the court said, "it would appear that a party claiming the right must establish that the decedent acted in such a way as to evidence his or her own recognition of the extrinsic commercial value of his or her name or likeness, and manifested that recognition in some overt manner, e.g., making an *inter vivos* transfer of the rights in the name (*Factors*), or posing for bubble gum cards (see *Haelan Laboratories, Inc.* * * *)." The court found sufficient exploitation in assignments by Agatha Christie of rights to her literary works, including contracts for the use of her name in connection with movies and plays based on her books. A motion for preliminary relief was nevertheless denied; citing first amendment interests, the court held that the right of publicity could not be invoked to stop a motion picture.

What function, if any, is served by making "exploitation" a prerequisite to descendibility? The limitation has not been widely adopted.

(4) The reluctance of the California Supreme Court to recognize a descendible right is discussed by the Second Circuit in Groucho Marx Productions, Inc. v. Day and Night Co., 689 F.2d 317 (2d Cir.1982), which also makes the point that if a name or likeness that is used in connection with a product or service acquires secondary meaning as an indication of source, post-mortem rights can be sustained on a trademark theory.

In 1984 the California legislature established the descendibility of publicity rights in elaborate legislation that includes registration procedures and a scheme of statutory succession. The right lasts for 70 years after death. Among the exemptions are uses in books, magazines, newspapers, music, audiovisual works, television programs, and single and original works of art. Cal.Civ.C. § 3344.1. In addition to California and Tennessee, statutes in at least a half-dozen other states recognize descendible publicity rights ranging in duration from 20 years (Va.C.Ann. § 8.01–40) to 100 years! (Ind.C. § 32-36-1-8 and

---

[q]   The Tennessee legislation, attributable to the lobbying efforts of the Elvis Presley estate, has nurtured a remarkable empire. A media entrepreneur paid $100 million in 2006 for a 90–year lease on Elvis Presley's Graceland home and an 85 per cent interest in the Presley estate that controls the use of his name and likeness (but not his music, which belongs to Presley's record label). Bosman, $50 Million Puts Ali in the Ring with Elvis and "American Idol", N.Y. Times, April 12, 2006, p. C1. According to *Forbes* magazine, Michael Jackson has at least temporarily surpassed Elvis as the top earning deceased celebrity, taking in $170 million in 2011, followed by Elvis at $55 million, and Marilyn Monroe at $27 million. The Marilyn Monroe estate, however, suffered a major defeat in 2012 when the Ninth Circuit in Milton H. Greene Archives, Inc. v. Marilyn Monroe LLC, 692 F.3d 983 (9th Cir.2012), held that the estate did not own a posthumous right of publicity. Having consistently maintained for tax purposes that Monroe had been domiciled in New York at the time of her death, the estate was estopped from claiming that she was instead domiciled in California. New York and not California law thus governed, and since New York does not recognize a descendible right of publicity, no right passed to her estate.

Okla.Stat. tit. 12, § 1448(G)). Several other states, following New York, limit publicity rights to living persons.

(5) A different durational issue arose in Abdul–Jabbar v. General Motors Corp., 85 F.3d 407 (9th Cir.1996). The defendant, charged with making a false claim of endorsement under § 43(a) and infringement of the right of publicity, defended by arguing that basketball star Kareem Abdul–Jabbar had "abandoned" his former name, Lew Alcindor, which the defendant had used in its advertising. The court rejected the defendant's analogy to trademark abandonment and reversed a summary judgment against the plaintiff.

(6) A *New York Times* story (inspired by a law review article—J. Beard, Casting Call at Forest Lawn: The Digital Resurrection of Deceased Entertainers—A 21st Century Challenge for Intellectual Property Law, 8 High Tech.L.J. 101 (1993)) speculates on the legal implications of emerging computer technology that enables the digital reanimation of deceased film stars. Computers can extract digital images of performers from earlier works and manipulate them to create new performances—a western with Kevin Costner and John Wayne, for instance, or *Schindler's List* starring Clark Gable.[r] Would such works violate anyone's legal rights? Recall the exclusion in California's descendible right of publicity for use in audiovisual works and television programs. See Restatement, Third, Unfair Competition § 47, Comments *c–d* (1995). Would extraction of the digital data necessary to recreate the performer infringe the copyright in the original film?

White v. Samsung Electronics America, Inc.

United States Court of Appeals, Ninth Circuit, 1992.
971 F.2d 1395.
Petition for rehearing en banc denied, 989 F.2d 1512 (1993).
Certiorari denied, 508 U.S. 951.

■ Before GOODWIN, PREGERSON, and ALARCON, CIRCUIT JUDGES.

■ GOODWIN, SENIOR CIRCUIT JUDGE:

This case involves a promotional "fame and fortune" dispute. In running a particular advertisement without Vanna White's permission, defendants Samsung Electronics America, Inc. (Samsung) and David Deutsch Associates, Inc. (Deutsch) attempted to capitalize on White's fame to enhance their fortune. White sued, alleging infringement of various intellectual property rights, but the district court granted summary judgment in favor of the defendants. We affirm in part, reverse in part, and remand.

Plaintiff Vanna White is the hostess of "Wheel of Fortune," one of the most popular game shows in television history. An estimated forty million people watch the program daily. Capitalizing on the fame which her participation in the show has bestowed on her, White markets her identity to various advertisers.

The dispute in this case arose out of a series of advertisements prepared for Samsung by Deutsch. The series ran in at least half a dozen pub-

---

[r] Weber, Why Marilyn and Bogie Still Need a Lawyer, N.Y. Times, March 11, 1994, p. B18. With the permission of his family, the Coors beer company digitally extracted the image of John Wayne playing a general in the 1965 film *To Cast a Giant Shadow* and used it in a commercial in which a drill sergeant grilling his platoon about beer in the barracks is interrupted by Wayne as the general looking for his Coors Light. Coors made a "seven-figure" donation to the John Wayne Cancer Institute. USA Today, May, 21 1996, p. 4B.

lications with widespread, and in some cases national, circulation. Each of the advertisements in the series followed the same theme. Each depicted a current item from popular culture and a Samsung electronic product. Each was set in the twenty-first century and conveyed the message that the Samsung product would still be in use by that time. By hypothesizing outrageous future outcomes for the cultural items, the ads created humorous effects. For example, one lampooned current popular notions of an unhealthy diet by depicting a raw steak with the caption: "Revealed to be health food. 2010 A.D." Another depicted irreverent "news"-show host Morton Downey Jr. in front of an American flag with the caption: "Presidential candidate. 2008 A.D."

The advertisement which prompted the current dispute was for Samsung video-cassette recorders (VCRs). The ad depicted a robot, dressed in a wig, gown, and jewelry which Deutsch consciously selected to resemble White's hair and dress. The robot was posed next to a game board which is instantly recognizable as the Wheel of Fortune game show set, in a stance for which White is famous. The caption of the ad read: "Longest-running game show. 2012 A.D." Defendants referred to the ad as the "Vanna White" ad. Unlike the other celebrities used in the campaign, White neither consented to the ads nor was she paid.

Following the circulation of the robot ad, White sued Samsung and Deutsch in federal district court under: (1) California Civil Code § 3344; (2) the California common law right of publicity; and (3) § 43(a) of the Lanham Act, 15 U.S.C. § 1125(a). The district court granted summary judgment against White on each of her claims. White now appeals.

I.   Section 3344

White first argues that the district court erred in rejecting her claim under section 3344. Section 3344(a) provides, in pertinent part, that "[a]ny person who knowingly uses another's name, voice, signature, photograph, or likeness, in any manner, . . . for purposes of advertising or selling, . . . without such person's prior consent . . . shall be liable for any damages sustained by the person or persons injured as a result thereof."

White argues that the Samsung advertisement used her "likeness" in contravention of section 3344. * * *

In this case, Samsung and Deutsch used a robot with mechanical features, and not, for example, a manikin molded to White's precise features. Without deciding for all purposes when a caricature or impressionistic resemblance might become a "likeness," we agree with the district court that the robot at issue here was not White's "likeness" within the meaning of section 3344. Accordingly, we affirm the court's dismissal of White's section 3344 claim.

II.   Right of Publicity

White next argues that the district court erred in granting summary judgment to defendants on White's common law right of publicity claim. In Eastwood v. Superior Court, 149 Cal.App.3d 409, 198 Cal.Rptr. 342 (1983), the California court of appeal stated that the common law right of publicity cause of action "may be pleaded by alleging (1) the defendant's use of the plaintiff's identity; (2) the appropriation of plaintiff's name or likeness to defendant's advantage, commercially or otherwise; (3) lack of consent; and (4) resulting injury." Id. at 417, 198 Cal.Rptr. 342 (citing Prosser, Law of Torts (4th ed. 1971) § 117, pp. 804–807). The district court dismissed White's claim for failure to satisfy Eastwood's second prong, reasoning that

defendants had not appropriated White's "name or likeness" with their robot ad. We agree that the robot ad did not make use of White's name or
likeness. However, the common law right of publicity is not so confined.
* * *

The "name or likeness" formulation referred to in *Eastwood* originated
not as an element of the right of publicity cause of action, but as a description of the types of cases in which the cause of action had been recognized.
The source of this formulation is Prosser, Privacy, 48 Cal.L.Rev. 383, 401–
07 (1960), one of the earliest and most enduring articulations of the common law right of publicity cause of action. In looking at the case law to that
point, Prosser recognized that right of publicity cases involved one of two
basic factual scenarios: name appropriation, and picture or other likeness
appropriation. Id. at 401–02, nn. 156–57.

Even though Prosser focused on appropriations of name or likeness in
discussing the right of publicity, he noted that "[i]t is not impossible that
there might be appropriation of the plaintiff's identity, as by impersona-
tion, without the use of either his name or his likeness, and that this would
be an invasion of his right of privacy." Id. at 401, n. 155. At the time
Prosser wrote, he noted however, that "[n]o such case appears to have aris-
en." Id.

Since Prosser's early formulation, the case law has borne out his insight that the right of publicity is not limited to the appropriation of name
or likeness. In Motschenbacher v. R.J. Reynolds Tobacco Co., 498 F.2d 821
(9th Cir.1974), the defendant had used a photograph of the plaintiff's race
car in a television commercial. Although the plaintiff appeared driving the
car in the photograph, his features were not visible. Even though the defendant had not appropriated the plaintiff's name or likeness, this court
held that plaintiff's California right of publicity claim should reach the jury.

In [Midler v. Ford Motor Company, 849 F.2d 460 (9th Cir.1988)], this
court held that, even though the defendants had not used Midler's name or
likeness, Midler had stated a claim for violation of her California common
law right of publicity because "the defendants . . . for their own profit in
selling their product did appropriate part of her identity" by using a Midler
sound-alike. Id. at 463–64.

In Carson v. Here's Johnny Portable Toilets, Inc., 698 F.2d 831 (6th
Cir.1983), the defendant had marketed portable toilets under the brand
name "Here's Johnny"—Johnny Carson's signature "Tonight Show" introduction—without Carson's permission. The district court had dismissed
Carson's Michigan common law right of publicity claim because the defendants had not used Carson's "name or likeness." Id. at 835. In reversing the
district court, the sixth circuit found "the district court's conception of the
right of publicity . . . too narrow" and held that the right was implicated
because the defendant had appropriated Carson's identity by using, inter
alia, the phrase "Here's Johnny." Id. at 835–37.

These cases teach not only that the common law right of publicity
reaches means of appropriation other than name or likeness, but that the
specific means of appropriation are relevant only for determining whether
the defendant has in fact appropriated the plaintiff's identity. The right of
publicity does not require that appropriations of identity be accomplished
through particular means to be actionable. It is noteworthy that the *Midler*
and *Carson* defendants not only avoided using the plaintiff's name or like-

ness, but they also avoided appropriating the celebrity's voice, signature, and photograph. The photograph in *Motschenbacher* did include the plaintiff, but because the plaintiff was not visible the driver could have been an actor or dummy and the analysis in the case would have been the same.

Although the defendants in these cases avoided the most obvious means of appropriating the plaintiffs' identities, each of their actions directly implicated the commercial interests which the right of publicity is designed to protect. As the *Carson* court explained:

> [t]he right of publicity has developed to protect the commercial interest of celebrities in their identities. The theory of the right is that a celebrity's identity can be valuable in the promotion of products, and the celebrity has an interest that may be protected from the unauthorized commercial exploitation of that identity . . . . If the celebrity's identity is commercially exploited, there has been an invasion of his right whether or not his "name or likeness" is used.

Carson, 698 F.2d at 835. It is not important *how* the defendant has appropriated the plaintiff's identity, but *whether* the defendant has done so. *Motschenbacher, Midler,* and *Carson* teach the impossibility of treating the right of publicity as guarding only against a laundry list of specific means of appropriating identity. A rule which says that the right of publicity can be infringed only through the use of nine different methods of appropriating identity merely challenges the clever advertising strategist to come up with the tenth. * * *

Viewed separately, the individual aspects of the advertisement in the present case say little. Viewed together, they leave little doubt about the celebrity the ad is meant to depict. The female-shaped robot is wearing a long gown, blond wig, and large jewelry. Vanna White dresses exactly like this at times, but so do many other women. The robot is in the process of turning a block letter on a game-board. Vanna White dresses like this while turning letters on a game-board but perhaps similarly attired Scrabble-playing women do this as well. The robot is standing on what looks to be the Wheel of Fortune game show set. Vanna White dresses like this, turns letters, and does this on the Wheel of Fortune game show. She is the only one. Indeed, defendants themselves referred to their ad as the "Vanna White" ad. We are not surprised.

Television and other media create marketable celebrity identity value. Considerable energy and ingenuity are expended by those who have achieved celebrity value to exploit it for profit. The law protects the celebrity's sole right to exploit this value whether the celebrity has achieved her fame out of rare ability, dumb luck, or a combination thereof. We decline Samsung and Deutch's invitation to permit the evisceration of the common law right of publicity through means as facile as those in this case. Because White has alleged facts showing that Samsung and Deutsch had appropriated her identity, the district court erred by rejecting, on summary judgment, White's common law right of publicity claim.

III. The Lanham Act

[The court also reversed defendants' summary judgment on White's claim under § 43(a) of the Lanham Act. Judge Goodwin said that there was a genuine issue of material fact as to whether the advertisement created a likelihood of confusion concerning White's endorsement of the product.]

IV. The Parody Defense

In defense, defendants cite a number of cases for the proposition that their robot ad constituted protected speech. The only cases they cite which are even remotely relevant to this case are Hustler Magazine v. Falwell, 485 U.S. 46 (1988) and L.L. Bean, Inc. v. Drake Publishers, Inc., 811 F.2d 26 (1st Cir.1987). Those cases involved parodies of advertisements run for the purpose of poking fun at Jerry Falwell and L.L. Bean, respectively. This case involves a true advertisement run for the purpose of selling Samsung VCRs. The ad's spoof of Vanna White and Wheel of Fortune is subservient and only tangentially related to the ad's primary message: "buy Samsung VCRs." Defendants' parody arguments are better addressed to non-commercial parodies.[3] The difference between a "parody" and a "knock-off" is the difference between fun and profit.

V. Conclusion

In remanding this case, we hold only that White has pleaded claims which can go to the jury for its decision.

Affirmed in Part, Reversed in Part, and Remanded.

■ ALARCON, CIRCUIT JUDGE, concurring in part, dissenting in part:

* * *

I must dissent from the majority's holding on Vanna White's right to publicity claim. The district court found that, since the commercial advertisement did not show a "likeness" of Vanna White, Samsung did not improperly use the plaintiff's identity. The majority asserts that the use of a likeness is not required under California common law. According to the majority, recovery is authorized if there is an appropriation of one's "identity." I cannot find any holding of a California court that supports this conclusion. Furthermore, the record does not support the majority's finding that Vanna White's "identity" was appropriated. * * *

The majority contends that "the individual aspects of the advertisement . . . [v]iewed together leave little doubt about the celebrity the ad is meant to depict." Majority Opinion at p. 1399. It derives this conclusion from the fact that Vanna White is "the only one" who "dresses like this, turns letters, and does this on the Wheel of Fortune game show." Id. In reaching this conclusion, the majority confuses Vanna White, the person, with the role she has assumed as the current hostess on the "Wheel of For-

---

[3] In warning of a first amendment chill to expressive conduct, the dissent reads this decision too broadly. See Dissent at 1407. This case concerns only the market which exists in our society for the exploitation of celebrity to sell products, and an attempt to take a free ride on a celebrity's celebrity value. Commercial advertising which relies on celebrity fame is different from other forms of expressive activity in two crucial ways. First, for celebrity exploitation advertising to be effective, the advertisement must evoke the celebrity's identity. The more effective the evocation, the better the advertisement. If, as Samsung claims, its ad was based on a "generic" game-show hostess and not on Vanna White, the ad would not have violated anyone's right of publicity, but it would also not have been as humorous or as effective. Second, even if some forms of expressive activity, such as parody, do rely on identity evocation, the first amendment hurdle will bar most right of publicity actions against those activities. Cf. *Falwell,* 485 U.S. at 46. In the case of commercial advertising, however, the first amendment hurdle is not so high. Central Hudson Gas & Electric Corp. v. Public Service Comm'n of New York, 447 U.S. 557, 566 (1980). Realizing this, Samsung attempts to elevate its ad above the status of garden-variety commercial speech by pointing to the ad's parody of Vanna White. Samsung's argument is unavailing. See Board of Trustees, State Univ. of N.Y. v. Fox, 492 U.S. 469, 474–75 (1988); Bolger v. Youngs Drug Products Corp., 463 U.S. 60, 67–68 (1983). Unless the first amendment bars all right of publicity actions—and it does not, see Zacchini v. Scripps–Howard Broadcasting Co., 433 U.S. 562 (1977)—then it does not bar this case.

tune" television game show. A recognition of the distinction between a performer and the part he or she plays is essential for a proper analysis of the facts of this case. As is discussed below, those things which Vanna White claims identify her are not unique to her. They are, instead, attributes of the *role* she plays. The representation of those attributes, therefore, does not constitute a representation of Vanna White. See Nurmi v. Peterson, 10 U.S.P.Q.2d 1775 (C.D.Cal.1989) (distinguishing between performer and role). * * *

The only characteristic in the commercial advertisement that is not common to many female performers or celebrities is the imitation of the "Wheel of Fortune" set. This set is the only thing which might possibly lead a viewer to think of Vanna White. The Wheel of Fortune set, however, is not an attribute of Vanna White's identity. It is an identifying characteristic of a television game show, a prop with which Vanna White interacts in her role as the current hostess. To say that Vanna White may bring an action when another blond female performer or robot appears on such a set as a hostess will, I am sure, be a surprise to the owners of the show. Cf. Baltimore Orioles, Inc. v. Major League Baseball Players Ass'n, 805 F.2d 663 (7th Cir.1986) (right to publicity in videotaped performances preempted by copyright of owner of telecast).

* * * The advertisement was intended to depict a robot, playing the role Vanna White currently plays on the Wheel of Fortune. I quite agree that anyone seeing the commercial advertisement would be reminded of Vanna White. *Any* performance by another female celebrity as a game-show hostess, however, will also remind the viewer of Vanna White because Vanna White's celebrity is so closely associated with the role. But the fact that an actor or actress became famous for playing a particular role has, until now, never been sufficient to give the performer a proprietary interest in it. I cannot agree with the majority that the California courts, which have consistently taken a narrow view of the right to publicity, would extend law to these unique facts.

[Judge Alarcon also disagreed with the majority's reversal of the summary judgment on White's § 43(a) claim, concluding that the evidence did not permit a finding that confusion was likely. He also thought that the majority gave "short shrift" to the defendant's first amendment argument merely because the parody took the form of an advertisement. The latter issue was taken up by Judge Kozinski in a dissent from the denial of the defendant's request for rehearing en banc at 989 F.2d 1512.]

■ KOZINSKI, CIRCUIT JUDGE, with whom CIRCUIT JUDGES O'SCANNLAIN and KLEINFELD join, dissenting from the order rejecting the suggestion for rehearing en banc.

Vanna White

Ms. C3PO?

Saddam Hussein wants to keep advertisers from using his picture in unflattering contexts.[1] Clint Eastwood doesn't want tabloids to write about him.[2] Rudolf Valentino's heirs want to control his film biography.[3] The Girl

---

[1]   See Eben Shapiro, Rising Caution on Using Celebrity Images, N.Y. Times, Nov. 4, 1992, at D20 (Iraqi diplomat objects on right of publicity grounds to ad containing Hussein's picture and caption "History has shown what happens when one source controls all the information").

[2]   Eastwood v. Superior Court, 149 Cal.App.3d 409, 198 Cal.Rptr. 342 (1983).

[3]   Guglielmi v. Spelling–Goldberg Prods., 25 Cal.3d 860, 160 Cal.Rptr. 352, 603 P.2d 454 (1979) (Rudolph Valentino); see also Maheu v. CBS, Inc., 201 Cal.App.3d 662, 668, 247 Cal.Rptr. 304 (1988) (aide to Howard Hughes). * * *

Scouts don't want their image soiled by association with certain activities.[4] George Lucas wants to keep Strategic Defense Initiative fans from calling it "Star Wars."[5] * * *

Something very dangerous is going on here. Private property, including intellectual property, is essential to our way of life. It provides an incentive for investment and innovation; it stimulates the flourishing of our culture; it protects the moral entitlements of people to the fruits of their labors. But reducing too much to private property can be bad medicine. Private land, for instance, is far more useful if separated from other private land by public streets, roads and highways. Public parks, utility rights-of-way and sewers reduce the amount of land in private hands, but vastly enhance the value of the property that remains.

So too it is with intellectual property. Overprotecting intellectual property is as harmful as underprotecting it. Creativity is impossible without a rich public domain. Nothing today, likely nothing since we tamed fire, is genuinely new: Culture, like science and technology, grows by accretion, each new creator building on the works of those who came before. Overprotection stifles the very creative forces it's supposed to nurture.[11]

The panel's opinion is a classic case of overprotection. Concerned about what it sees as a wrong done to Vanna White, the panel majority erects a property right of remarkable and dangerous breadth: Under the majority's opinion, it's now a tort for advertisers to *remind* the public of a celebrity. Not to use a celebrity's name, voice, signature or likeness; not to imply the celebrity endorses a product; but simply to evoke the celebrity's image in the public's mind. This Orwellian notion withdraws far more from the public domain than prudence and common sense allow. It conflicts with the Copyright Act and the Copyright Clause. It raises serious First Amendment problems. It's bad law, and it deserves a long, hard second look. * * *

Consider how sweeping this new right is. What is it about the ad that makes people think of White? It's not the robot's wig, clothes or jewelry; there must be ten million blond women (many of them quasi-famous) who wear dresses and jewelry like White's. It's that the robot is posed near the "Wheel of Fortune" game board. Remove the game board from the ad, and no one would think of Vanna White. See Appendix. But once you include the game board, anybody standing beside it—a brunette woman, a man wearing women's clothes, a monkey in a wig and gown—would evoke White's image, precisely the way the robot did. It's the "Wheel of Fortune" set, not the robot's face or dress or jewelry that evokes White's image. The panel is giving White an exclusive right not in what she looks like or who she is, but in what she does for a living.[18]

---

[4] Girl Scouts v. Personality Posters Mfg., 304 F.Supp. 1228 (S.D.N.Y.1969) (poster of a pregnant girl in a Girl Scout uniform with the caption "Be Prepared").

[5] Lucasfilm Ltd. v. High Frontier, 622 F.Supp. 931 (D.D.C.1985).

[11] See Wendy J. Gordon, A Property Right in Self Expression: Equality and Individualism in the Natural Law of Intellectual Property, 102 Yale L.J. 1533, 1556–57 (1993).

[18] Once the right of publicity is extended beyond specific physical characteristics, this will become a recurring problem: Outside name, likeness and voice, the things that most reliably remind the public of celebrities are the actions or roles they're famous for. A commercial with an astronaut setting foot on the moon would evoke the image of Neil Armstrong. Any masked man on horseback would remind people (over a certain age) of Clayton Moore. And any number of songs—"My Way," "Yellow Submarine," "Like a Virgin," "Beat It," "Michael, Row the Boat Ashore," to name only a few—instantly evoke an image of the person or group who made them famous, regardless of who is singing. * * *

This is entirely the wrong place to strike the balance. Intellectual property rights aren't free: They're imposed at the expense of future creators and of the public at large. Where would we be if Charles Lindbergh had an exclusive right in the concept of a heroic solo aviator? If Arthur Conan Doyle had gotten a copyright in the idea of the detective story, or Albert Einstein had patented the theory of relativity? If every author and celebrity had been given the right to keep people from mocking them or their work? Surely this would have made the world poorer, not richer, culturally as well as economically.[19] * * *

The panel, however, does more than misinterpret California law: By refusing to recognize a parody exception to the right of publicity, the panel directly contradicts the federal Copyright Act. Samsung didn't merely parody Vanna White. It parodied Vanna White appearing in "Wheel of Fortune," a copyrighted television show, and parodies of copyrighted works are governed by federal copyright law. * * *

The majority's decision decimates this federal scheme. It's impossible to parody a movie or a TV show without at the same time "evok[ing]" the "identit[ies]" of the actors. You can't have a mock *Star Wars* without a mock Luke Skywalker, Han Solo and Princess Leia, which in turn means a mock Mark Hamill, Harrison Ford and Carrie Fisher. You can't have a mock *Batman* commercial without a mock Batman, which means someone emulating the mannerisms of Adam West or Michael Keaton. See Carlos V. Lozano, West Loses Lawsuit over Batman TV Commercial, L.A. Times, Jan. 18, 1990, at B3 (describing Adam West's right of publicity lawsuit over a commercial produced under license from DC Comics, owner of the *Batman* copyright). The public's right to make a fair use parody and the copyright owner's right to license a derivative work are useless if the parodist is held hostage by every actor whose "identity" he might need to "appropriate." * * *

Finally, I can't see how giving White the power to keep others from evoking her image in the public's mind can be squared with the First Amendment. * * *

The majority dismisses the First Amendment issue out of hand because Samsung's ad was commercial speech. Id. at 1401 & n. 3. So what? Commercial speech may be less protected by the First Amendment than noncommercial speech, but less protected means protected nonetheless. Central Hudson Gas & Elec. Corp. v. Public Serv. Comm'n, 447 U.S. 557 (1980). * * *

Commercial speech is a significant, valuable part of our national discourse. The Supreme Court has recognized as much, and has insisted that lower courts carefully scrutinize commercial speech restrictions, but the panel totally fails to do this. The panel majority doesn't even purport to apply the *Central Hudson* test, which the Supreme Court devised specifically for determining whether a commercial speech restriction is valid. The majority doesn't ask, as *Central Hudson* requires, whether the speech restriction is justified by a substantial state interest. It doesn't ask whether the restriction directly advances the interest. It doesn't ask whether the restriction is narrowly tailored to the interest. See id. at 566. These are all

---

[19] See generally Gordon, supra note 11; see also Michael Madow, Private Ownership of Public Image: Popular Culture and Publicity Rights, 81 Cal.L.Rev. 125, 201–03 (1993) (an excellent discussion).

things the Supreme Court told us—in no uncertain terms—we must consider; the majority opinion doesn't even mention them. * * *

For better or worse, we are the Court of Appeals for the Hollywood Circuit. Millions of people toil in the shadow of the law we make, and much of their livelihood is made possible by the existence of intellectual property rights. But much of their livelihood—and much of the vibrancy of our culture—also depends on the existence of other intangible rights: The right to draw ideas from a rich and varied public domain, and the right to mock, for profit as well as fun, the cultural icons of our time.

In the name of avoiding the "evisceration" of a celebrity's rights in her image, the majority diminishes the rights of copyright holders and the public at large. In the name of fostering creativity, the majority suppresses it. Vanna White and those like her have been given something they never had before, and they've been given it at our expense. I cannot agree.

NOTES AND QUESTIONS

(1) The dissenting opinions in *White* bring forward two points: first, that the use should not be considered an appropriation of White's "identity," and second, that the imposition of liability may contravene the first amendment. Are these issues related? On the former, do you agree with the dissenters that the majority failed to distinguish the performer from the role she performed?[s] The distinction between the performer and the role performed was before the Ninth Circuit again in Wendt v. Host Int'l, Inc., 125 F.3d 806 (9th Cir.1997), cert. denied, 531 U.S. 811 (2000), when actors George Wendt and John Ratzenberger objected to the use of "animatronic robotic figures" based on their characters Norm and Cliff from the television series *Cheers*. A licensee of copyright owner Paramount had placed the figures in airport bars that were modeled after the set used on the show. The defendants argued that the use appropriated only the identities of the television characters and won a summary judgment in the district court. Judge Fletcher, finding issues of fact concerning the degree to which the figures resembled the plaintiffs, reinstated their right of publicity claims. Is it possible for a copyright owner to exploit television characters in a commercially viable manner *without* appropriating the identity of the actors who portrayed them? The Ninth Circuit denied the defendants' request for a rehearing en banc; Judge Kozinski dissented, arguing that the plaintiffs' right of publicity should not trump Paramount's right to exploit its copyrighted characters. 197 F.3d 1284 (9th Cir.1999).

The Sixth Circuit, expressing support for Judge Kozinski's concern about overextending the publicity right, affirmed a summary judgment against an actor who played a minor role in the Arnold Schwarzenegger movie *Predator*; the plaintiff was complaining about a line of action figures that included his character. The court agreed that the use of a fictional character could be actionable as an exploitation of the actor's identity when "the two personalities are inseparable in the public's mind," but "the focus of any right of publicity analysis must always be on the actor's own persona and not on the character's." Here the toy (only an inch and a half tall with no eyes or mouth) did not invoke

---

[s] D. Welkowitz, Catching Smoke, Nailing JELL–O to a Wall: The *Vanna White* Case and the Limits of Celebrity Rights, 3 J.Intell.Prop.L. 67 (1995), argues that the defendant's "metaphoric" use was not an appropriation of identity; S. Dogan, An Exclusive Right to Evoke, 44 B.C.L.Rev. 291 (2003), is also critical of liability for merely "evoking" a celebrity.

the actor's persona. Landham v. Lewis Galoob Toys, Inc., 227 F.3d 619 (6th Cir.2000).

(2) On the first amendment issue, pursuing Judge Kozinski's view, how would Vanna White's claim fare under an explicit application of the *Central Hudson* standard for regulating commercial speech?[t]

Comedy III Productions, Inc. v. Saderup

Supreme Court of California, 2001.
25 Cal.4th 387, 106 Cal.Rptr.2d 126, 21 P.3d 797.
Certiorari denied, 534 U.S. 1078 (2002).

■ MOSK, J.

A California statute grants the *right of publicity* to specified successors in interest of deceased celebrities, prohibiting any other person from using a celebrity's name, voice, signature, photograph, or likeness for commercial purposes without the consent of such successors. (Former Civ.Code, § 990 [now § 3344.1].) The United States Constitution prohibits the states from abridging, among other fundamental rights, freedom of speech. (U.S. Const., 1st and 14th Amends.) In the case at bar we resolve a conflict between these two provisions. The Court of Appeal concluded that the lithographs and silkscreened T-shirts in question here received no First Amendment protection simply because they were reproductions rather than original works of art. As will appear, this was error: reproductions are equally entitled to First Amendment protection. We formulate instead what is essentially a balancing test between the First Amendment and the right of publicity based on whether the work in question adds significant creative elements so as to be transformed into something more than a mere celebrity likeness or imitation. Applying this test to the present case, we conclude that there are no such creative elements here and that the right of publicity prevails. On this basis, we will affirm the judgment of the Court of Appeal.
* * *

Comedy III is the registered owner of all rights to the former comedy act known as The Three Stooges, who are deceased personalities within the meaning of the statute.

Saderup is an artist with over 25 years' experience in making charcoal drawings of celebrities. These drawings are used to create lithographic and silkscreen masters, which in turn are used to produce multiple reproductions in the form, respectively, of lithographic prints and silkscreened images on T-shirts. Saderup creates the original drawings and is actively involved in the ensuing lithographic and silkscreening processes.

Without securing Comedy III's consent, Saderup sold lithographs and T-shirts bearing a likeness of The Three Stooges reproduced from a charcoal drawing he had made. These lithographs and T-shirts did not constitute an advertisement, endorsement, or sponsorship of any product. * * *

---

[t]   For more on Judge Kozinski's views, see his Trademarks Unplugged, 68 N.Y.U.L.Rev. 960 (1993), vividly describing the variety of roles, some protected and some not, played by trademarks in modern society; S. Dogan and M. Lemley, What the Right of Publicity Can Learn from Trademark Law, 58 Stan.L.Rev. 1161 (2006), uses trademark law analogies in an effort to restrain expansion of the right of publicity.

[The court concluded that by selling the lithographs and T-shirts, Saderup had used the likenesses of the Three Stooges "on . . . products, merchandise, or goods" within the meaning of the California statute.]

Saderup next contends that enforcement of the judgment against him violates his right of free speech and expression under the First Amendment. He raises a difficult issue, which we address below.

The right of publicity is often invoked in the context of commercial speech when the appropriation of a celebrity likeness creates a false and misleading impression that the celebrity is endorsing a product. (See Waits v. Frito–Lay, Inc. (9th Cir.1992) 978 F.2d 1093; Midler v. Ford Motor Co. (9th Cir.1988) 849 F.2d 460.) Because the First Amendment does not protect false and misleading commercial speech (Central Hudson Gas & Elec. Corp. v. Public Serv. Com'n (1980) 447 U.S. 557, 563–564), and because even nonmisleading commercial speech is generally subject to somewhat lesser First Amendment protection (*Central Hudson,* at p. 566), the right of publicity may often trump the right of advertisers to make use of celebrity figures.

But the present case does not concern commercial speech. As the trial court found, Saderup's portraits of The Three Stooges are expressive works and not an advertisement for or endorsement of a product. * * *

The right of publicity has a potential for frustrating the fulfillment of [the purposes of the First Amendment]. Because celebrities take on public meaning, the appropriation of their likenesses may have important uses in uninhibited debate on public issues, particularly debates about culture and values. And because celebrities take on personal meanings to many individuals in the society, the creative appropriation of celebrity images can be an important avenue of individual expression. As one commentator has stated: "Entertainment and sports celebrities are the leading players in our Public Drama. We tell tales, both tall and cautionary, about them. We monitor their comings and goings, their missteps and heartbreaks. We copy their mannerisms, their styles, their modes of conversation and of consumption. Whether or not celebrities are 'the chief agents of moral change in the United States,' they certainly are widely used—far more than are institutionally anchored elites—to symbolize individual aspirations, group identities, and cultural values. Their images are thus important expressive and communicative resources: the peculiar, yet familiar idiom in which we conduct a fair portion of our cultural business and everyday conversation." (Madow, Private Ownership of Public Image: Popular Culture and Publicity Rights (1993) 81 Cal. L.Rev. 125, 128 (Madow), italics and fns. omitted.) * * *

Although surprisingly few courts have considered in any depth the means of reconciling the right of publicity and the First Amendment, we follow those that have in concluding that depictions of celebrities amounting to little more than the appropriation of the celebrity's economic value are not protected expression under the First Amendment. We begin with Zacchini v. Scripps–Howard Broadcasting Co. (1977) 433 U.S. 562, 576 (*Zacchini*), the only United States Supreme Court case to directly address the right of publicity. Zacchini, the performer of a human cannonball act, sued a television station that had videotaped and broadcast his entire performance without his consent. The court held the First Amendment did not protect the television station against a right of publicity claim under Ohio common law. In explaining why the enforcement of the right of publicity in this case would not violate the First Amendment, the court stated: " '[T]he rationale for [protecting the right of publicity] is the straightforward one of preventing unjust enrichment by the theft of good will. No social purpose is served by having the defendant get free some aspect of the plaintiff that would have market value and for which he would normally pay.'" (Id. at p. 576.) The court also rejected the notion that federal copyright or patent law preempted this type of state law protection of intellectual property: "[Copyright and patent] laws perhaps regard the 'reward to the owner [as] a secondary consideration,' [citation], but they were 'intended definitely to grant valuable, enforceable rights' in order to afford greater encouragement to the production of works of benefit to the public. [Citation.] The Constitution does not prevent Ohio from making a similar choice here in deciding to protect the entertainer's incentive in order to encourage the production of this type of work." (Id. at p. 577.)

To be sure, *Zacchini* was not an ordinary right of publicity case: the defendant television station had appropriated the plaintiff's entire act, a species of common law copyright violation. Nonetheless, two principles enunciated in *Zacchini* apply to this case: (1) state law may validly safeguard forms of intellectual property not covered under federal copyright and patent law as a means of protecting the fruits of a performing artist's labor; and (2) the state's interest in preventing the outright misappropriation of such intellectual property by others is not automatically trumped by the interest in free expression or dissemination of information; rather, as in the case of defamation, the state law interest and the interest in free expression must be balanced, according to the relative importance of the interests at stake. * * *

It is admittedly not a simple matter to develop a test that will unerringly distinguish between forms of artistic expression protected by the First Amendment and those that must give way to the right of publicity. Certainly, any such test must incorporate the principle that the right of publicity cannot, consistent with the First Amendment, be a right to control the celebrity's image by censoring disagreeable portrayals. Once the celebrity thrusts himself or herself forward into the limelight, the First Amendment dictates that the right to comment on, parody, lampoon, and make other expressive uses of the celebrity image must be given broad scope. The necessary implication of this observation is that the right of publicity is essentially an economic right. What the right of publicity holder possesses is not a right of censorship, but a right to prevent others from misappropriating the economic value generated by the celebrity's fame through the merchandising of the "name, voice, signature, photograph, or likeness" of the celebrity. (§ 990.)

Beyond this precept, how may courts distinguish between protected and unprotected expression? Some commentators have proposed importing the fair use defense from copyright law (17 U.S.C. § 107), which has the advantage of employing an established doctrine developed from a related area of the law. (See Barnett, First Amendment Limits on the Right of Publicity (1995) 30 Tort & Ins. L.J. 635, 650–657; Coyne, Toward a Modified Fair Use Defense in Right of Publicity Cases (1988) 29 Wm. & Mary L.Rev. 781, 812–820.) Others disagree, pointing to the murkiness of the fair use doctrine and arguing that the idea/expression dichotomy, rather than fair use, is the principal means of reconciling copyright protection and First Amendment rights. (2 McCarthy, [The Rights of Publicity and Privacy] § 8.38, pp. 8–358 to 8–360; see also Kwall, The Right of Publicity vs. The

First Amendment: A Property and Liability Rule Analysis (1994) 70 Ind. L.J. 47, 58, fn. 54.)

We conclude that a wholesale importation of the fair use doctrine into right of publicity law would not be advisable. * * *

Nonetheless, the first fair use factor—"the purpose and character of the use" (17 U.S.C. § 107(1))—does seem particularly pertinent to the task of reconciling the rights of free expression and publicity. * * *

This inquiry into whether a work is "transformative" appears to us to be necessarily at the heart of any judicial attempt to square the right of publicity with the First Amendment. * * * When artistic expression takes the form of a literal depiction or imitation of a celebrity for commercial gain, directly trespassing on the right of publicity without adding significant expression beyond that trespass, the state law interest in protecting the fruits of artistic labor outweighs the expressive interests of the imitative artist. (See *Zacchini*, supra, 433 U.S. at pp. 575–576.)

On the other hand, when a work contains significant transformative elements, it is not only especially worthy of First Amendment protection, but it is also less likely to interfere with the economic interest protected by the right of publicity. As has been observed, works of parody or other distortions of the celebrity figure are not, from the celebrity fan's viewpoint, good substitutes for conventional depictions of the celebrity and therefore do not generally threaten markets for celebrity memorabilia that the right of publicity is designed to protect. (See Cardtoons, L.C. v. Major League Baseball Players Association (10th Cir.1996) 95 F.3d 959, 974 (*Cardtoons*).) Accordingly, First Amendment protection of such works outweighs whatever interest the state may have in enforcing the right of publicity. The right-of-publicity holder continues to enforce the right to monopolize the production of conventional, more or less fungible, images of the celebrity.

Cardtoons, supra, 95 F.3d 959, cited by Saderup, is consistent with this "transformative" test. There, the court held that the First Amendment protected a company that produced trading cards caricaturing and parodying well-known major league baseball players against a claim brought under the Oklahoma right of publicity statute. The court concluded that "[t]he cards provide social commentary on public figures, major league baseball players, who are involved in a significant commercial enterprise, major league baseball," and that "[t]he cards are no less protected because they provide humorous rather than serious commentary." (*Cardtoons*, at p. 969.) The *Cardtoons* court weighed these First Amendment rights against what it concluded was the less-than-compelling interests advanced by the right of publicity outside the advertising context—especially in light of the reality that parody would not likely substantially impact the economic interests of celebrities—and found the cards to be a form of protected expression. (*Cardtoons*, at pp. 973–976.) While *Cardtoons* contained dicta calling into question the social value of the right of publicity, its conclusion that works parodying and caricaturing celebrities are protected by the First Amendment appears unassailable in light of the test articulated above.

We emphasize that the transformative elements or creative contributions that require First Amendment protection are not confined to parody and can take many forms, from factual reporting (see, e.g., Rosemont Enterprises, Inc. v. Random House, Inc. (N.Y.Sup.Ct.1968) 58 Misc.2d 1, 294 N.Y.S.2d 122, 129, affd. mem. (1969) 32 A.D.2d 892, 301 N.Y.S.2d 948) to fictionalized portrayal ([Guglielmi v. Spelling–Goldberg Productions (1979)

25 Cal.3d 860, 871–872, 160 Cal.Rptr. 352, 603 P.2d 454]; see also Parks v. LaFace Records (E.D.Mich.1999) 76 F.Supp.2d 775, 779–782 [use of civil rights figure Rosa Parks in song title is protected expression]), from heavy-handed lampooning (see Hustler Magazine v. Falwell (1988) 485 U.S. 46) to subtle social criticism (see Coplans et al., Andy Warhol (1970) pp. 50–52 [explaining Warhol's celebrity portraits as a critique of the celebrity phenomenon]). * * *

We further emphasize that in determining whether the work is transformative, courts are not to be concerned with the quality of the artistic contribution—vulgar forms of expression fully qualify for First Amendment protection. (See, e.g., Hustler Magazine v. Falwell, supra, 485 U.S. 46; see also Campbell v. Acuff—Rose Music, Inc., supra [510 U.S. 569, 582].) On the other hand, a literal depiction of a celebrity, even if accomplished with great skill, may still be subject to a right of publicity challenge. The inquiry is in a sense more quantitative than qualitative, asking whether the literal and imitative or the creative elements predominate in the work.

Furthermore, in determining whether a work is sufficiently transformative, courts may find useful a subsidiary inquiry, particularly in close cases: does the marketability and economic value of the challenged work derive primarily from the fame of the celebrity depicted? If this question is answered in the negative, then there would generally be no actionable right of publicity. When the value of the work comes principally from some source other than the fame of the celebrity—from the creativity, skill, and reputation of the artist—it may be presumed that sufficient transformative elements are present to warrant First Amendment protection. If the question is answered in the affirmative, however, it does not necessarily follow that the work is without First Amendment protection—it may still be a transformative work.

In sum, when an artist is faced with a right of publicity challenge to his or her work, he or she may raise as affirmative defense that the work is protected by the First Amendment inasmuch as it contains significant transformative elements or that the value of the work does not derive primarily from the celebrity's fame. * * *

* * * [T]he inquiry is into whether Saderup's work is sufficiently transformative. Correctly anticipating this inquiry, he argues that all portraiture involves creative decisions, that therefore no portrait portrays a mere literal likeness, and that accordingly all portraiture, including reproductions, is protected by the First Amendment. We reject any such categorical position. Without denying that all portraiture involves the making of artistic choices, we find it equally undeniable, under the test formulated above, that when an artist's skill and talent is manifestly subordinated to the overall goal of creating a conventional portrait of a celebrity so as to commercially exploit his or her fame, then the artist's right of free expression is outweighed by the right of publicity. As is the case with fair use in the area of copyright law, an artist depicting a celebrity must contribute something more than a " 'merely trivial' variation, [but must create] something recognizably 'his own' " (L. Batlin & Son, Inc. v. Snyder (2d Cir.1976) 536 F.2d 486, 490), in order to qualify for legal protection.

On the other hand, we do not hold that all reproductions of celebrity portraits are unprotected by the First Amendment. The silkscreens of Andy Warhol, for example, have as their subjects the images of such celebrities as Marilyn Monroe, Elizabeth Taylor, and Elvis Presley. Through distortion and the careful manipulation of context, Warhol was able to convey a message that went beyond the commercial exploitation of celebrity images and became a form of ironic social comment on the dehumanization of celebrity itself. (See Coplans et al., supra, at p. 52.) Such expression may well be entitled to First Amendment protection. * * *

Turning to Saderup's work, we can discern no significant transformative or creative contribution. His undeniable skill is manifestly subordinated to the overall goal of creating literal, conventional depictions of The Three Stooges so as to exploit their fame. Indeed, were we to decide that Saderup's depictions were protected by the First Amendment, we cannot perceive how the right of publicity would remain a viable right other than in cases of falsified celebrity endorsements.

Moreover, the marketability and economic value of Saderup's work derives primarily from the fame of the celebrities depicted. While that fact alone does not necessarily mean the work receives no First Amendment protection, we can perceive no transformative elements in Saderup's works that would require such protection. * * *

The judgment of the Court of Appeal is affirmed.

■ GEORGE, C.J., KENNARD, J., BAXTER, J., WERDEGAR, J., CHIN, J., BROWN, J., concur.

APPENDIX

NOTES ON PUBLICITY RIGHTS AND FREE SPEECH

(1) When, as in *Comedy III*, the appropriation of identity involves little more than the merchandising of a famous name or likeness on goods such as clothing or posters, first amendment defenses have usually been rejected. See, e.g., Factors Etc., Inc. v. Pro Arts, Inc., 579 F.2d 215 (2d Cir.1978), cert. denied, 440 U.S. 908 (1979) (posters). Cases involving games have also rejected first amendment defenses. See, e.g., Rosemont Enterprises, Inc. v. Urban Systems, Inc., 42 A.D.2d 544, 345 N.Y.S.2d 17 (1973). Are the game cases such as those described on p. 747 supra truly devoid of free speech interests?

In C.B.C. Distrib. and Marketing, Inc. v. Major League Baseball Advanced Media, L.P., 505 F.3d 818 (8th Cir.2007), cert. denied, 553 U.S. 1090 (2008), the plaintiff operated a web site that offered fantasy baseball games for a fee. The success of a customer's fantasy team depends on the actual performances of major league baseball players. The CBC web site contained up-to-date information on player performances, including, for example, batting averages, home runs, etc. Although CBC at one time had a license from the Major League Players Association, the license had expired. CBC sought declaratory and injunctive relief against Advanced Media, the Internet arm of Major League Baseball, which had been granted exclusive rights by the Players Association for all interactive media. The Players Association and Advanced Media counterclaimed, asserting that CBC was violating the players' rights of publicity. Affirming a summary judgment in favor of CBC, the Eighth Circuit conceded that the Players Association had stated a cause of action for violation of the right of publicity under Missouri law—the players' identities had been used without consent to obtain a commercial advantage. However, the interests protected by the publicity right, including economic incentive and the avoidance of emotional distress and consumer confusion, were not threatened by the use. On the other hand, "the information used in CBC's fantasy baseball games is all readily available in the public domain, and it would be strange law that a person would not have a first amendment right to use information that is available to everyone." The court held that CBC's first amendment right superseded the players' rights of publicity.

Former college athletes have raised claims against the N.C.A.A. and its licensed merchandisers, particular electronic game makers, for use of their likenesses in sports video games. In one case, the court denied a game manufacturer's motion to dismiss a California right of publicity claim raised by a former college quarterback whose likeness appeared in a video game. Keller v. Electronics Arts, Inc., 94 U.S.P.Q.2d 1130 (N.D.Cal.2010). The depiction of the plaintiff was not sufficiently transformative to escape liability under the rule in *Comedy III*, and a "public interest" defense of the kind that succeeded in CBC v. Major League Baseball was not available since the use did not involve the dissemination of real-life information. Another federal court reached a different conclusion on the first amendment implications of the video games. In a class action suit by former college football players alleging violations of the right of publicity under New Jersey law, the court in Hart v. Electronic Arts, Inc., 808 F.Supp.2d 757 (D.N.J.2011), granted summary to the defendant video game maker on first amendment grounds. Judge Wolfson cited the Supreme Court's decision in Brown v. Entertainment Merchants Association, 131 S.Ct. 2729 (2011), invalidating a California law prohibiting the sale of violent video games to minors. Justice Scalia wrote, "Like the protected books, plays, and movies that preceded them video games communicate ideas—and even social messages—through many familiar literary devices (such as characters, dialogue, plot, and music) and through features distinctive to the medium (such as the player's interaction with the virtual world). That suffices to confer First Amendment protection." The trial judge in *Hart* held that the expressive content added by the defendant in the form of a virtual world of stadiums, coaches, fans, sound effects, and commentary, together with the interactive nature of the game, made the use transformative under the test in *Comedy III*. However, the Third Circuit reversed in Hart v. Electronic Arts, Inc., 2013 WL 2161317 (3d Cir.2013), holding that the game's realistic depiction of the plaintiffs was not sufficiently transformative under *Comedy III* to earn immunity under the first amendment. The case was remanded to the district court. (If, as the Supreme Court said, video games are like books and movies, should they be entitled to the apparently wholesale immunity from publicity claims traditionally enjoyed by those works?)

(2) Applying the test that it had developed in the *Comedy III* case, the California Supreme Court held that a defendant's use of comic book characters based on musician brothers Johnny and Edgar Winter involved significant creative elements that transformed the use into something more than a mere celebrity likeness; the use was thus entitled to first amendment protection. Winter v. DC Comics, 30 Cal.4th 881, 134 Cal.Rptr.2d 634 (2003). However, the Supreme Court of Missouri reached a different conclusion in "a case with a remarkably similar fact situation." The plaintiff was a former hockey player known for his rough play; the defendant used his name for a "Mafia don" character in a comic book, although there was no physical resemblance or other similarities. There was some evidence that the defendant had marketed the comics to hockey fans. The defendant argued that the plaintiff's right of publicity claim was barred by the first amendment. The court rejected the "transformative" test because it could preclude a cause of action whenever the use was expressive regardless of the extent of the commercial exploitation. Instead, the court said it would balance the expressive and commercial aspects and found that the defendant's use of the name was predominantly a ploy to sell comic books. Doe v. TCI Cablevision, 110 S.W.3d 363 (Mo.2003), cert. denied, 540 U.S. 1106 (2004).

The *Comedy III* test was adopted by the Sixth Circuit in ETW Corp. v. Jireh Publishing, Inc., 332 F.3d 915 (6th Cir.2003). Artist Rick Rush created a painting entitled *The Masters of Augusta* commemorating Tiger Woods' record-breaking win at the 1997 Masters golf tournament in Augusta, Georgia. The painting featured three different views of Tiger Woods in the foreground and the Augusta National Clubhouse and the Masters Leaderboard in the background; beyond the Clubhouse were likenesses of famous past winners of the Masters looking down on the scene. The defendant Jireh Publishing marketed prints of the painting, including two hundred and fifty 22 by 30 inch reproductions for $700 and five thousand 9 by 11 inch copies for $100. The plaintiff ETW was the assignee of Tiger Woods' publicity rights. The Sixth Circuit held that Ohio would adopt the limitations on the publicity right suggested in Restatement (Third) of Unfair Competition § 47 and *Comedy III*. Judge Graham said the painting embodied "substantial informational and creative content which outweighs any adverse effect on ETW's market," and "[u]nlike the unadorned, nearly photographic reproduction of the faces of The Three Stooges in *Comedy III*," Rush's work contained "significant transformative elements" that entitled it to full first amendment protection. Judge Clay dissented, concluding that the right of publicity was not outweighed by free speech interests since "the prints gain their commercial value by exploiting the fame and celebrity status that Woods has worked to achieve."

T. Cotter and I. Dmitrieva, Integrating the Right of Publicity with First Amendment and Copyright Preemption Analysis, 33 Colum.J.L. & Arts 165 (2010), argues that while publicity claims involving commercial speech should survive first amendment challenge, non-commercial speech cases require a careful analysis of the state interests advanced by the asserted right; J. Dougherty, All the World's Not a Stooge: The "Transformativeness" Test for Analyzing a First Amendment Defense to a Right of Publicity Claim Against Distribution of a Work of Art, 27 Colum.J.L. & Arts 1 (2003), concludes that the transformation test in *Comedy III* inadequately protects free speech interests and urges more categorical protection for works that are not incorporated into merchandise; E. Volokh, Freedom of Speech and the Right of Publicity, 40 Houston L.Rev. 903 (2003), is also skeptical of the *Comedy III* approach and argues that publicity rights should yield to all non-commercial speech.

(3) Are the identities of political figures fair game for use on merchandise? The image of Barack Obama, for example, has appeared on everything from plates to soap. S. Ghosh, On Bobbling Heads, Paparazzi, and Justice Hugo Black, 45 Santa Clara L.Rev. 617 (2005), proposes absolute immunity for use of the name or likeness of public officials, responding to the settlement of a suit brought by Governor Arnold Schwarzenegger against sales of a bobble-head doll showing him in a suit and tie brandishing an assault rifle. Is use in advertising different? A clothing company displayed a billboard in New York's Times Square featuring President Obama walking on the Great Wall of China wearing one of the company's coats. The ad said, "A Leader in Style." The photo had been purchased from the Associated Press. It was reported that the White House contacted the company to express its displeasure, and the company announced that it would no longer use the image in its advertising. 79 Pat., Tm. & Copyr.J. (BNA) 268 (2010).

(4) The use of a celebrity's name and photograph in newspaper or magazine articles is normally shielded by the first amendment. See Cher v. Forum Int'l, Ltd., 692 F.2d 634 (9th Cir.1982), cert. denied, 462 U.S. 1120 (1983); Ann–Margret v. High Society Magazine, Inc., 498 F.Supp. 401 (S.D.N.Y.1980). The former case also holds that a magazine may use a celebrity's name and likeness in advertising for the limited purpose of indicating its content; see also Namath v. Sports Illustrated, 48 A.D.2d 487, 371 N.Y.S.2d 10 (1975), aff'd, 39 N.Y.2d 897, 386 N.Y.S.2d 397 (1976). The *Ann–Margret* case emphasizes that good taste is not a prerequisite to first amendment protection. See also Hoffman v. Capital Cities/ABC, Inc., 255 F.3d 1180 (9th Cir.2001) (a photograph of Dustin Hoffman dressed as a woman from the movie *Tootsie* used in a magazine article about Hollywood fashions was not actionable); New Kids on the Block v. News America Pub., Inc., 971 F.2d 302 (9th Cir.1992) (use of entertainers' names in a newspaper survey was "in connection with" a news account and not actionable under the California statute or the common law). Cf. Titan Sports, Inc. v. Comics World Corp., 870 F.2d 85 (2d Cir.1989), reversing a defendant publisher's summary judgment because of uncertainty as to whether posters stapled inside the defendant's wrestling magazine were entitled to first amendment protection. In Toffoloni v. LFP Pub. Group, LLC, 572 F.3d 1201 (11th Cir.2009), cert. denied, 130 S.Ct. 1689 (2010), the court reversed the dismissal of a right of publicity claim brought under Georgia law by the estate of a murder victim over publication in *Hustler* magazine of nude photographs of the victim taken twenty years earlier. The court held that the use did not fall within the "newsworthiness" exception to the publicity right. "These private, nude photographs were not incident to a newsworthy article; rather, the brief biography was incident to the photographs. Additionally, these photographs were neither related in time nor concept to the current incident of public interest."

Books too are generally beyond the reach of the publicity right. Although reclusive billionaire Howard Hughes through Rosemont Enterprises successfully suppressed Howard Hughes games and t-shirts, he could not enjoin publication of an unauthorized biography. "The publication of a biography is clearly outside the ambit of the 'commercial use' contemplated by the 'right of publicity' * * *." Rosemont Enterprises, Inc. v. Random House, Inc., 58 Misc.2d 1, 294 N.Y.S.2d 122 (Sup.Ct.1968), aff'd, 32 A.D.2d 892, 301 N.Y.S.2d 948 (1969). The estate of Marilyn Monroe met a similar response when it objected to Norman Mailer's *Marilyn*: "We think it does not matter whether the book is properly described as a biography, a fictional biography, or any other kind of literary work. * * * It is enough that the book is a literary work and not simply a disguised commercial advertisement for the sale of goods or services." Frosch v. Grosset & Dunlap, Inc., 75 A.D.2d 768, 427 N.Y.S.2d 828 (1980). Hicks v. Casablanca Records, the Agatha Christie case, p. 756 supra, reached the same conclusion with respect to a fictional account in a motion picture. Responding to a certified question from the Eleventh Circuit, the Supreme Court of Florida answered that the phrase "for purposes of trade or for any commercial or advertising purpose" in the Florida right of publicity statute did not extend to the use of a person's identity in a motion picture; the plaintiffs were children of the fishermen whose loss at sea is depicted in the film *The Perfect Storm*. Tyne v. Time Warner Ent. Co., 901 So.2d 802 (Fla.2005). The Supreme Court of Kentucky held that country music star John Michael Montgomery's use of audio clips and pictures of his father in a music video was protected by the first amendment and affirmed a summary judgment against the father's second wife who had raised a publicity claim as executrix of his estate. Montgomery v. Montgomery, 60 S.W.3d 524 (Ky.2001).

(5) As noted by Judge Mosk in *Comedy III*, the United States Supreme Court considered the right of publicity in Zacchini v. Scripps–Howard Broadcasting Co., 433 U.S. 562 (1977). The defendant, without permission, filmed the plaintiff's "human cannonball" act at a county fair and showed the fifteen-second film on the eleven o'clock news, with commentary urging viewers to go see it. The Ohio Supreme Court held that the defendant's use was privileged under the first amendment. The U.S. Supreme Court reversed, 5–4. Drawing an analogy to the goals of patent and copyright law, the Supreme Court said that "Ohio's decision to protect petitioner's right of publicity here rests on more than a desire to compensate the performer for the time and effort invested in his act; the protection provides an economic incentive for him to make the investment required to produce a performance of interest to the public." As for the first amendment, the Court held: "It is evident, and there is no claim here to the contrary, that petitioner's state-law right of publicity would not serve to prevent respondent from reporting the newsworthy facts about petitioner's act. Wherever the line in particular situations is to be drawn between media reports that are protected and those that are not, we are quite sure that the First and Fourteenth Amendments do not immunize the media when they broadcast a performer's entire act without his consent."

The Supreme Court also noted that Zacchini's claim involved "not the appropriation of an entertainer's reputation to enhance the attractiveness of a commercial product, but the appropriation of the very activity by which the entertainer acquired his reputation in the first place." Is *INS* the more relevant precedent?

(6) When Ginger Rogers, dancing partner of Fred Astaire, objected to a Fellini film entitled "Ginger and Fred," about a pair of "tattered, retired hoofers" who had adopted that stage name, Judge Newman for the Second Circuit concluded that the interest in free expression in the choice of a title would defeat her right of publicity claim, holding that Oregon law would not permit "the right of publicity to bar the use of a celebrity's name in a movie title unless the title was 'wholly unrelated' to the movie or was 'simply a disguised commercial advertisement for the sale of goods or services.'" Rogers v. Grimaldi, 875 F.2d 994

(2d Cir.1989). The Rogers v. Grimaldi standard was adopted by the Sixth Circuit in Parks v. LaFace Records, 329 F.3d 437 (6th Cir.), cert. denied, 540 U.S. 1074 (2003), when Rosa Parks, who became a symbol of the civil rights movement in 1955 when she refused to give up her seat and move to the back of a Montgomery, Alabama bus, brought a common law right of publicity claim against defendants who put out a record by the musical group Outkast entitled *Rosa Parks*. Although the song was not about Rosa Parks or the civil rights movement, the chorus included the words, "Ah, ha hush that fuss. Everyone move to the back of the bus." Holding that a right of publicity claim against the title of an expressive work could succeed only if the title was "wholly unrelated" to the work, the court decided that here that question presented a genuine issue of fact that precluded a summary judgment.

(7) Are any of the manifestations of the right of publicity preempted under § 301? In Midler v. Ford, p. 676 supra, the Ninth Circuit rejected Ford's argument that Bette Midler's right of publicity claim was preempted, holding that the claim did not concern the subject matter of copyright: "A voice is not copyrightable." The Ninth Circuit later reached an analogous result with respect to a person's name and likeness in Downing v. Abercrombie & Fitch, 265 F.3d 994 (9th Cir.2001). "A person's name or likeness is not a work of authorship within the meaning of 17 U.S.C. § 102. This is true notwithstanding the fact that Appellants' names and likenesses are embodied in a copyrightable photograph." The Seventh Circuit came to a similar conclusion in Toney v. L'Oreal USA, Inc., 406 F.3d 905 (7th Cir.2005), holding that a person's likeness and persona are not within the subject matter of copyright and hence a right of publicity claim against the use of a copyrighted photograph in advertising was not preempted under § 301.

Even if publicity claims generally survive analysis under § 301, might they sometimes be preempted under the supremacy clause as obstructing congressional objectives under copyright law? The Fifth Circuit considered the preemptive effect of copyright law on the right of publicity in Brown v. Ames, 201 F.3d 654 (5th Cir.), cert. denied, 531 U.S. 925 (2000). The plaintiffs complained about the use of their names and likenesses in connection with unauthorized sales of their musical recordings. After rejecting a preemption argument under § 301 since an individual's "persona" is not within the subject matter of copyright, the court considered a supremacy clause argument. Judge Jones said that preemption might occur if the right of publicity was used against authorized publishers of copyrighted or public domain works, but since the right of publicity would not prevent authorized publishers from identifying the author or creator of a work, it does not threaten the objectives of copyright. A similar distinction surfaced in KNB Enter. v. Matthews, 78 Cal.App.4th 362, 92 Cal.Rptr.2d 713 (2000). The plaintiff owned the copyrights in 417 erotic photographs depicting 452 models that defendant had displayed without permission on a commercial web site. Instead of suing for copyright infringement, the plaintiff got an assignment of publicity rights from the models and brought suit under California's right of publicity statute. The court rejected the defendant's argument that the claim was preempted. The court distinguished Fleet v. CBS, Inc., 50 Cal.App.4th 1911, 58 Cal.Rptr.2d 645 (1996), where motion picture actors involved in a pay dispute sought to use a right of publicity claim to stop distribution of a film. That case held that their claims were preempted, concluding that performers in a copyrighted work could not use their publicity rights to prevent the copyright owner from distributing the work. In *KNB*, the court said, "we distinguish this case from *Fleet* because this is not a situation where the models are asserting a right of publicity claim against the exclusive copyright holder in an effort to halt the authorized distribution of their photographs." An analogous approach was adopted by the Third Circuit in Facenda v. N.F.L. Films, Inc., 542 F.3d 1007 (3d Cir.2008), when the defendant used a narrator's voice-overs from NFL game films on a promotional feature for the Madden NFL video game. The narrator's estate claimed the use violated Pennsylvania's right of publicity statute; NFL Films argued preemption. The court said there was no preemption under § 301 since a voice is outside the subject matter of copyright. Distinguishing *Fleet,* the court also held that the claim was not preempted under the supremacy clause because the defendant had used the work for a commercial purpose to which the decedent had never agreed.

The question of federal preemption of the right of publicity was muddied, however, when the Ninth Circuit reviewed a claim by an adult movie actor complaining about the defendants' unauthorized reproduction and sale of thirteen DVDs. Jules Jordan Video, Inc. v. 144942 Canada Inc., 617 F.3d 1146 (9th Cir. 2010), cert. denied, 133 S.Ct. 133 (2012). In addition to a (successful) copyright claim, the plaintiff also alleged a violation of his right of publicity under California law. The district court had ruled that the publicity claim was not preempted, relying on KNB Enters. v. Matthews and its distinction between publicity claims asserted against an authorized distributor, which are preempted, and claims against an unauthorized distributor as here. The Ninth Circuit rejected that distinction and stated that preemption did not depend on the rights held by the defendant. "In the instant case, we conclude that [plaintiff's] right of publicity claim falls within the subject matter of copyright, and that the rights he asserts are equivalent to the rights within the scope of § 106 of the Copyright Act. The essence of [plaintiff's] claim is that the Kaytel defendants reproduced and distributed the DVDs without authorization. His claim is under the Copyright Act." Plaintiff's judgment on the right of publicity claim was vacated.

CHAPTER 10

COMPENSATION FOR "IDEAS"

This Chapter concerns rights in ideas, especially ideas of potential value in the entertainment business. The cases are drawn from New York and California, the two centers of the entertainment business. The law in other jurisdictions, although generally less developed, favors one or another variation on these basic themes.

NEW YORK LAW

Murray v. National Broadcasting Co.

United States Court of Appeals, Second Circuit, 1988.
844 F.2d 988.
Certiorari denied, 488 U.S. 955.

■ Before WINTER, PRATT and ALTIMARI, CIRCUIT JUDGES.

■ ALTIMARI, CIRCUIT JUDGE:

It was almost a generation ago that a young comedian named Bill Cosby became the first black entertainer to star in a dramatic network television series. That program, *I Spy,* earned Cosby national recognition as an actor, including three Emmy Awards (1966, 1967 and 1968) for best performance in a dramatic series, and critical acclaim for the portrayal of a character without regard to the actor's race. Although keenly aware of the significance of his achievement in breaking the color line on network television, Cosby set his sights then on "accomplish[ing] something more significant for the Negro on TV."[1] In an interview in 1965, he envisioned a different approach to the situation comedy genre made popular by *The Dick Van Dyke Show.* The *Daily News* described Cosby's "dream" series as not

> unlike other situation comedies. There'll be the usual humorous exchanges between husband and wife . . . . Warmth and domestic cheerfulness will pervade the entire program.
>
> Everything on the screen will be familiar to TV viewers. But this series will be radically different. Everyone in it will be a Negro.
>
> * * *
>
> . . . "I'm interested in proving there's no difference between people," [explained Cosby]. "My series would take place in a middle-income Negro neighborhood. People who really don't know Negroes would find on this show that they're just like everyone else."[2]

Nearly twenty years later, on September 20, 1984, Cosby's dream for a "color-blind" family series materialized with the premier of *The Cosby Show*—a situation comedy about a family known as the Huxtables. Bill

---

[1] Lardine, Looking to the Future: Bill Cosby Has Dreams of an All–Negro TV Series, New York Daily News, Sept. 19, 1965, Sunday Magazine, at 6.

[2] Id.

Cosby stars in the leading role as Heathcliff ("Cliff") Huxtable together with his TV wife Clair and their five children.

Plaintiff-appellant Hwesu Murray, an employee of defendant-appellee ("NBC"), claims in the instant case that in 1980, four years prior to the premier of *The Cosby Show* on NBC's television network, he proposed to NBC a "new" idea for a half-hour situation comedy starring Bill Cosby. * * *

* * * Because we agree with the district court's conclusion that, under New York law, lack of novelty in an idea precludes plaintiff from maintaining a cause of action to prevent its unauthorized use, we affirm the district court's order granting summary judgment and dismissing the complaint.

Plaintiff Hwesu S. Murray has been employed in the television industry for the past ten years. Murray holds a Bachelor of Arts degree in English and graduate degrees in broadcast journalism and law. In 1979, defendant-appellee NBC hired Murray as a Unit Manager and financial analyst in its sports division. A year later, plaintiff contacted an NBC official outside of NBC Sports about some "extracurricular" ideas he had for future television programs, and the official apparently instructed him to submit his proposals in writing. Soon thereafter, in June 1980, plaintiff submitted five written proposals, one of which was entitled "Father's Day." Murray allegedly informed NBC that if it were interested in any of the proposals, he expected to be named executive producer and to receive appropriate credit and compensation as the creator of the eventual program. Plaintiff also allegedly told NBC that his ideas were being submitted in confidence.

Murray's proposal for "Father's Day" is the subject matter of this action. The NBC official who originally had requested it encouraged Murray to "flesh out" his proposal and submit it to Josh Kane, then an NBC vice-president and a top official with NBC Entertainment, the division of NBC responsible for network television programming. Plaintiff thereupon submitted to Kane an expanded proposal for "Father's Day." In a two-page memorandum dated November 1, 1980, Murray first suggested that Bill Cosby play the part of the father. At that time, plaintiff also made several other casting suggestions, including roles for a working spouse and five children, and again indicated that the proposed series would "combine humor with serious situations in a manner similar to that of the old *Dick Van Dyke Show*" but "with a Black perspective." Murray's expanded proposal concluded with the observation that, "[l]ike *Roots,* the show will attempt to depict life in a [closely-knit] Black family, with the addition of a contemporary, urban setting."

NBC apparently decided not to pursue Murray's proposal. On November 21, 1980, Kane returned the "Father's Day" submission to plaintiff and informed him that "we are not interested in pursuing [its] development at this time."

Four years later, in the fall of 1984, *The Cosby Show* premiered on NBC. * * *

Less than a month after viewing the premier, plaintiff wrote to NBC to advise it that *The Cosby Show* had been derived from his idea for "Father's Day." In January 1985, NBC responded through its Law Department, stating its position that " 'Father's Day' played absolutely no role in the development of 'The Cosby Show' . . . [since m]uch of the substance and style of 'The Cosby Show' is an outgrowth of the humor and style developed by Bill Cosby throughout his career." NBC further maintained that *The Cosby Show* was developed and produced by The Carsey–Werner Company

("Carsey–Werner"), an independent production company and the executive producers of the series.

In his complaint, plaintiff claimed that *The Cosby Show's* portrayal of a strong black family in a nonstereotypical manner is the essence of "Father's Day," and "[i]t is that portrayal of Black middle-class life that originated with plaintiff." Murray also alleged that Josh Kane showed plaintiff's "Father's Day" proposal to his superiors at NBC, including defendant-appellee Brandon Tartikoff, President of NBC Entertainment. Tartikoff, together with Cosby and Carsey–Werner, have been credited with the creation and development of *The Cosby Show.* Plaintiff maintains that NBC and Tartikoff deliberately deceived plaintiff into believing that NBC had no interest in "Father's Day" and then proceeded to develop and eventually produce plaintiff's idea as *The Cosby Show.*

Plaintiff's complaint stated a number of causes of action arising out of defendants' alleged appropriation of his idea. Among those relevant to this appeal are plaintiff's claims of race discrimination under 42 U.S.C. §§ 1981 and 1982, false designation of origin under the Lanham Act, 15 U.S.C. § 1125, and various state law claims, including misappropriation, conversion, breach of implied contract, unjust enrichment and fraud. Plaintiff sought, *inter alia,* damages and declaratory and injunctive relief as the "sole owner of all rights in and to the idea, proposal and property [known as] 'Father's Day.' "

In a decision dated July 15, 1987, 671 F.Supp. 236 (S.D.N.Y.), the district court considered whether plaintiff's idea was "property" that could be subject to legal protection. Since the parties agreed that New York law applied to plaintiff's claims, the district court proceeded to analyze defendants' motion for summary judgment in light of the New York Court of Appeals decision in Downey v. General Foods Corp., 31 N.Y.2d 56, 334 N.Y.S.2d 874, 286 N.E.2d 257 (1972). In *Downey,* the New York court established the general proposition that "[l]ack of novelty in an idea is fatal to *any* cause of action for its unlawful use." 334 N.Y.S.2d at 877, 286 N.E.2d at 259 (quoting Bram v. Dannon Milk Prods., Inc., 33 A.D.2d 1010, 307 N.Y.S.2d 571, 571 (1st Dep't 1970)) (emphasis added). The district court, therefore, determined that the "sole issue" before it was the novelty of plaintiff's "Father's Day" proposal, and accordingly assumed, for purposes of defendants' motion, that defendants in fact used plaintiff's idea in the development of *The Cosby Show.* See Ed Graham Productions, Inc. v. National Broadcasting Co., 75 Misc.2d 334, 347 N.Y.S.2d 766, 769 (Sup.Ct.N.Y.Cty.1973) (even assuming defendant used plaintiff's idea, plaintiff may not recover if idea is "wholly lacking in novelty"). * * *

As the district court recognized, the dispositive issue in this case is whether plaintiff's idea is entitled to legal protection. Plaintiff points to "unique"—"even revolutionary"—aspects of his "Father's Day" proposal that he claims demonstrate "genuine novelty and invention," see Educational Sales Programs, Inc. v. Dreyfus Corp., 65 Misc.2d 412, 317 N.Y.S.2d 840, 844 (Sup.Ct.N.Y.Cty.1970), which preclude the entry of summary judgment against him. Specifically, plaintiff contends that his idea suggesting the nonstereotypical portrayal of black Americans on television is legally protectible because it represents a real breakthrough. * * *

We certainly do not dispute the fact that the portrayal of a nonstereotypical black family on television was indeed a breakthrough. Nevertheless, that breakthrough represents the achievement of what many black Americans, including Bill Cosby and plaintiff himself, have recognized for many years—namely, the need for a more positive, fair and realistic portrayal of blacks on television. While NBC's decision to broadcast *The Cosby Show* unquestionably was innovative in the sense that an intact, nonstereotypical black family had never been portrayed on television before, the mere fact that such a decision had not been made before does not necessarily mean that the idea for the program is itself novel. See *Educational Sales Programs,* 317 N.Y.S.2d at 843 ("[n]ot every 'good idea' is a legally protectible idea"). * * *

Appellant would have us believe that by interpreting New York law as we do, we are in effect condoning the theft of ideas. On the contrary, ideas that reflect "genuine novelty and invention" are fully protected against unauthorized use. *Educational Sales Programs,* 317 N.Y.S.2d at 844. But those ideas that are not novel "are in the public domain and may freely be used by anyone with impunity." *Ed Graham Productions,* 347 N.Y.S.2d at 769. Since such non-novel ideas are not protectible as property, they cannot be stolen. * * *

Finally, as an alternative attack on the propriety of the district court's order granting summary judgment, plaintiff posits that even if his idea was not novel as a matter of law, summary judgment still was inappropriate because his proposal was solicited by defendants and submitted to them in confidence. In this regard, Murray relies on Cole v. Phillips H. Lord, Inc., 262 A.D. 116, 28 N.Y.S.2d 404 (1st Dep't 1941). Murray contends that *Cole* stands for the proposition that when an idea is protected by an agreement or a confidential relationship, a cause of action arises for unauthorized use of that idea irrespective of the novelty of the subject matter of the contract. Plaintiff's reliance on *Cole* is misplaced in light of subsequent cases, particularly the New York Court of Appeals decision in Downey v. General Foods Corp., 31 N.Y.2d 56, 334 N.Y.S.2d 874, 286 N.E.2d 257 (1972). See also Ferber v. Sterndent Corp., 51 N.Y.2d 782, 433 N.Y.S.2d 85, 86, 412 N.E.2d 1311 (1980) ("[a]bsent a showing of novelty, plaintiff's action to recover damages for illegal use of 'confidentially disclosed ideas' must fail as a matter of law"); *Educational Sales Programs,* 317 N.Y.S.2d at 844 ("[o]ne cannot be forever barred from using a worthwhile but unoriginal idea merely because it was once asked to be treated in confidence").

Consequently, we find that New York law requires that an idea be original or novel in order for it to be protected as property. See *Downey,* 334 N.Y.S.2d at 877, 286 N.E.2d at 259. Since, as has already been shown, plaintiff's proposal for "Father's Day" was lacking in novelty and originality, we conclude that the district court correctly granted defendants' motion for summary judgment.

Having determined that plaintiff's idea is not property under New York law, we turn now to a consideration of the district court's dismissal of the various claims in the complaint.

A.   *State law claims*

"[W]hen one submits an idea to another, no promise to pay for its use may be implied, and no asserted agreement enforced, if the elements of novelty and originality are absent . . . . " *Downey,* 334 N.Y.S.2d at 877, 286 N.E.2d at 259. As the district court recognized, non-novel ideas do not constitute property. As a result, there can be no cause of action for unauthorized use of Murray's proposal since it was not unlawful for defendants to use a non-novel idea. We conclude therefore that the district court properly dismissed plaintiff's state law claims for breach of implied contract, misappropriation, conversion, and unjust enrichment. * * *

Similarly, plaintiff's fraud claim also fails since, as the district court recognized, plaintiff "cannot be defrauded of property that he does not own." Essential to a cause of action for fraud is a showing of injury as the proximate result of the alleged fraudulent conduct. See Dress Shirt Sales, Inc. v. Hotel Martinique Assocs., 12 N.Y.2d 339, 239 N.Y.S.2d 660, 663, 190 N.E.2d 10 (1963). Because plaintiff's idea for "Father's Day" was in the public domain when NBC allegedly used it in the creation of *The Cosby Show,* Murray suffered no injury. His cause of action for fraud thus was properly dismissed.

B.   *Civil Rights claims*

[The court held that the plaintiff's civil rights claims were also properly dismissed.]

C.   *Lanham Act claim*

Lastly, we find that Judge Cedarbaum correctly determined that plaintiff's claim for false designation of origin, see Lanham Act § 43(a), 15 U.S.C. § 1125(a), regarding the credits to *The Cosby Show,* cannot survive in light of the court's granting of summary judgment against plaintiff on the issue of novelty. Even assuming defendants used plaintiff's idea, NBC's failure to designate Murray as the creator of *The Cosby Show* does not mean that the credits to the program are false since ideas in the public domain may be used with impunity and thus do not require attribution. * * *

Affirmed.

■ GEORGE C. PRATT, CIRCUIT JUDGE, dissenting:

Today this court holds that the idea underlying what may well be the most successful situation comedy in television history was, in 1980, so unoriginal and so entrenched in the public domain that, as a matter of law, it did not constitute intellectual property protected under New York law. Because I am convinced that the novelty issue in this case presents a factual question subject to further discovery and ultimate scrutiny by a trier of fact, I respectfully dissent. * * *

I agree with the majority that there is some evidence that Murray's idea was not novel. But clearly, there is also evidence indicating novelty. Initially, there is the admission by NBC, in its agreement with Carsey–Werner, that the television series is "unique, intellectual property." * * *

Novelty, by its very definition, is highly subjective. As fashion, advertising, and television and radio production can attest, what is novel today may not have been novel 15 years ago, and what is commonplace today may well be novel 15 years hence. In this instance, where Cosby expressed the concept almost a decade and a half before Murray submitted his proposal, where it was Murray's idea that NBC actually used, where there is no evidence indicating NBC knew anything of the program idea until Murray submitted it, compare Downey v. General Foods Corp., 31 N.Y.2d 56, 60, 334 N.Y.S.2d 874, 877–78, 286 N.E.2d 257 (1972) (no novelty because defendant had "envisaged" *and* "utilized" plaintiff's idea for "years before the plaintiff submitted it") with Werlin v. Readers Digest Ass'n Inc., 528 F.Supp. 451, 466 (S.D.N.Y.1981) (even though plaintiff's idea was in public domain, no evidence that defendant knew about or would have discovered the idea except through plaintiff's proposal; hence, the "idea was novel" as far as defendant was concerned), and where substantial conflicting evidence exists as to the "novelty" of the idea under New York law, there seems to be at least a triable issue.

The majority's decision prematurely denies Murray a fair opportunity to establish his right to participate in the enormous wealth generated by *The Cosby Show*. Accordingly, I would reverse the district court judgment and remand the case for further consideration.

NOTES AND QUESTIONS

(1) Did the Second Circuit intend to suggest that in the absence of novelty, even an *express* contract for the sale of an idea is unenforceable? See, in addition to the *Downey* case discussed in *Murray,* Granoff v. Merrill Lynch & Co., 775 F.Supp. 621 (S.D.N.Y.1991), aff'd, 962 F.2d 2 (2d Cir.1992), holding that under New York law, "to meet the requirement of minimal consideration, even actions on express contracts must involve the use of an idea which is novel."

The New York rule on express contracts was refined by the New York Court of Appeals in Apfel v. Prudential–Bache Securities Inc., 81 N.Y.2d 470, 600 N.Y.S.2d 433, 616 N.E.2d 1095 (1993). The court explained that the novelty requirement serves "to establish both the attributes of ownership necessary for a property-based claim and the value of the consideration—the disclosure— necessary for contract-based claims." But here, the contract to pay for use of the idea was made subsequent to the plaintiff's disclosure. "In such a case, buyer knows what he or she is buying and has agreed that the idea has value, and the Court will not ordinarily go behind that determination. The lack of novelty, in and of itself, does not demonstrate a lack of value * * *."

(2) Mrs. Galanis wrote an unsolicited letter to Procter & Gamble stating that she had an idea for a new kind of soap, which she called "Blue." It was a soap with bluing added, to be used for washing laundry. The company replied, thanking Mrs. Galanis for her interest and saying that it had considered such a soap many times in the past but had decided against it; it would be excellent for regular laundry, but was likely to be unpopular for colored fabrics and lingerie. The company later put out a soap called "Blue Cheer" that according to the plaintiff combined soap with bluing as she had suggested. She sued the company for $1 million. On the defendant's motion for summary judgment, Judge Dawson said, "The general rule of law is that a mere idea is not property and that any right to its exclusive use is lost by its voluntary disclosure." Yet "courts have in certain cases recognized that even if plaintiff has no property right in an idea, and even though no contract for the sale or use of such idea has been established, nevertheless the defendant may be held liable in *quantum meruit* on the theory of unjust enrichment, where defendant utilized a concrete and novel idea submitted by plaintiff." For the plaintiff to recover, she would have to establish that her idea was novel and concrete and that it had been appropriated by the defendant in developing its product. The court doubted that the plaintiff could succeed in proving these propositions at trial, but felt constrained to deny summary judgment. Galanis v. Procter & Gamble Corp., 153 F.Supp. 34 (S.D.N.Y.1957).

See also Werlin v. Reader's Digest Ass'n, Inc., 528 F.Supp. 451 (S.D.N.Y.1981), reiterating the elements of novelty, concreteness, and appropriation. The court awarded damages on a quasi-contract theory to an author who, encouraged by Reader's Digest, submitted an article that inspired the magazine to prepare its own story based on the plaintiff's idea. The court also held that the cause of action was not preempted by federal copyright law. Is that correct?

(3) How can a plaintiff prove "appropriation" or "use" of an idea by a defendant? Is it enough to avoid liability for the defendant to demonstrate access to the idea from a different source? Suppose the defendant utilizes the idea in the sense of experimenting with it, but finishes with a product deviating materially from the idea as submitted?

Switching to the West Coast for a moment, consider, on the question of appropriation, the express contract claim brought by columnist Art Buchwald against Paramount Pictures, which had purchased an option on his "treatment" for a movie tailored for Eddie Murphy. It was about an African ruler who is deposed while visiting the United States. Buchwald claimed that Paramount, after allowing the option to lapse, derived *Coming to America* (starring Eddie Murphy) from his synopsis. The contract required payment if Paramount made a movie "based upon Author's work." Should the test be "substantial similarity" in the copyright sense? The court in Buchwald v. Paramount Pictures Corp., 13 U.S.P.Q.2d 1497 (Cal.Super.1990), said that Paramount was liable if *Coming to America* was "based upon a material element of or was inspired by Buchwald's treatment"; the court held that it was.[a] In Benay v. Warner Bros. Ent., Inc., 607 F.3d 620 (9th Cir.2010), plaintiffs pitched a screenplay entitled *The Last Samurai* to the defendants, who "passed" on the offer but later produced a movie with the same title. The appellate court upheld a summary judgment for the defendants on a copyright infringement claim, finding insufficient similarity of protected elements to satisfy the Ninth Circuit's "extrinsic test" of substantial similarity. However, the court reversed the defendants' summary judgment on a breach of implied-in-fact contract claim, rejecting the defendants' contention that the plaintiffs could not prove "use" of their screenplay. "In breach of contract claims, the level of similarity that permits an inference of actionable use depends on the nature of the agreement between the parties. See 4 Nimmer § 19D.08. In cases of explicit contracts where the terms of the agreement are spelled out, the level of similarity required depends on those terms. * * * *Where the contract is implied-in-fact rather than explicit*, the parties have not specified any standard. In such cases, 'the weight of California authority is that there must be "substantial similarity" between plaintiff's idea and defendant's production to render defendant liable.'" However, "because the claim is based in contract, unauthorized use can be shown by substantially similar elements that are not protected under copyright law. * * * Therefore, our holding (above) that the Screenplay and the Film are not substantially similar for purposes of copyright infringement does not preclude a finding of substantial similarity for purposes of an implied-in-fact contract under California law."

(4) The Second Circuit made a further attempt to summarize New York law on idea submissions in Nadel v. Play–By–Play Toys & Novelties, Inc., 208 F.3d 368 (2d Cir.2000). Plaintiff, "a toy idea man," disclosed to the defendant toy

---

[a]   Buchwald's contract called for a share of the net profits, but Paramount rejoined that the film, which grossed over $300 million at the box office, produced no net profit to Paramount under the formula contained in the contract. The court later held that the contract formula was unconscionable. Buchwald got a judgment for $900,000; first Paramount appealed, but then it settled for more than $1 million. It may have been worried that an appeal might set a legal precedent that would later haunt it; in another dispute it was claiming that *Forrest Gump*, which grossed $650 million, had yet to turn a profit. Abelson, The Shell Game of Hollywood "Net Profits," N.Y. Times, Mar. 4, 1996, p. D1.

company his idea for a plush toy figure that spun around when placed on a flat surface. Industry custom called for the company to treat the disclosure as confidential and to compensate the inventor for subsequent use unless the idea was already known to the company. The plaintiff, claiming that the defendant used the idea without paying him, brought claims for breach of contract, quasi-contract, and unfair competition (which the Second Circuit treated as a claim for misappropriation of the idea). Relying primarily on *Apfel*, Note (1) supra, Judge Sotomayor described New York law as follows:

> In sum, we find that New York law in submission-of-idea cases is governed by the following principles: Contract-based claims require only a showing that the disclosed idea was novel to the buyer in order to find consideration. Such claims involve a fact-specific inquiry that focuses on the perspective of the particular buyer. By contrast, misappropriation claims require that the idea at issue be original and novel in absolute terms. This is so because unoriginal, known ideas have no value as property and the law does not protect against the use of that which is free and available to all. Finally, an idea may be so unoriginal or lacking in novelty generally that, as a matter of law, the buyer is deemed to have knowledge of the idea. In such cases, neither a property-based nor a contract-based claim for uncompensated use of the idea may lie.

CALIFORNIA LAW

Montz v. Pilgrim Films & Television, Inc.

United States Court of Appeals, Ninth Circuit (en banc), 2011.
649 F.3d 975.
Certiorari denied, 132 S.Ct. 550.

■ Before KOZINSKI, CHIEF JUDGE, AND SCHROEDER, REINHARDT, O'SCANNLAIN, THOMAS, WARDLAW, GOULD, PAEZ, TALLMAN, BEA, and SMITH, JR., CIRCUIT JUDGES.

■ SCHROEDER, CIRCUIT JUDGE.

In Hollywood, writers commonly submit copyrighted scripts to producers with the understanding that if the script is used, the producer must compensate the writer for the use of the copyrighted material. But what happens when the producer uses the idea or concept embodied in the script, but doesn't pay? The Supreme Court of California, in 1956, answered this question by recognizing an implied contractual right to compensation when a writer submits material to a producer with the understanding that the writer will be paid if the producer uses the concept. Desny v. Wilder, 46 Cal.2d 715, 299 P.2d 257 (1956).

A so-called "*Desny* claim" has remained viable under California law for over fifty years. See Gunther–Wahl Productions, Inc. v. Mattel, Inc., 104 Cal.App.4th 27, 128 Cal.Rptr.2d 50 (2002). This court applied that California law in Grosso v. Miramax Film Corp., 383 F.3d 965 (9th Cir.2004), amended 400 F.3d 658 (9th Cir.2005), cert. denied 546 U.S. 824 (2005), where we held that such an implied contractual claim is not preempted by federal copyright law. We explained that the contractual claim requires that there be an expectation on both sides that use of the idea requires

compensation, and that such bilateral understanding of payment constitutes an additional element that transforms a claim from one asserting a
right exclusively protected by federal copyright law, to a contractual claim
that is not preempted by copyright law. *Grosso* has firm roots in our federal
law as well as in the California law. Earlier, we recognized that a claim for
unjust enrichment is essentially equivalent to a claim of copyright infringement and is therefore preempted. See Del Madera Props. v. Rhodes &
Gardner, Inc., 820 F.2d 973, 977 (9th Cir.1987), overruled on other grounds
by Fogerty v. Fantasy, Inc., 510 U.S. 517 (1994). * * *

We again hold that copyright law does not preempt a contract claim
where plaintiff alleges a bilateral expectation that he would be compensated for use of the idea, the essential element of a *Desny* claim that separates it from preempted claims for the use of copyrighted material. We see
no meaningful difference between the conditioning of use on payment in
Grosso and conditioning use in this case on the granting of a partnership
interest in the proceeds of the production. Montz, as did the plaintiffs in
Desny and *Grosso,* has alleged he revealed his concept to defendants reasonably expecting to be compensated, if his concept was used. We conclude
that the district court's judgment dismissing the contractual claim as
preempted must be reversed. * * *

I. Factual Background

In 1981, Plaintiff Larry Montz, a parapsychologist, conceived of an
idea for a television show that would follow a team of paranormal investigators conducting field investigations. As envisioned, each episode would
follow the team to different real-world locations, where they would use
magnetometers, infrared cameras, and other devices to investigate reports
of paranormal activity. According to the complaint, from 1996 to 2003,
Montz and Plaintiff Daena Smoller, a publicist and a producer, pitched
Montz's idea to television studios, producers, and their representatives, including representatives of NBC and the Sci–Fi channel. A number of meetings and discussions took place, and Montz and Smoller presented screenplays, videos, and other materials relating to their proposed show. Ultimately, the studios indicated that they were not interested.

Three years later, in November 2006, Montz and Smoller filed a complaint against Pilgrim Films & Television, Inc., NBC Universal Inc., Craig
Piligian, Jason Conrad Hawes, and ten unknown defendants in federal district court, alleging copyright infringement, breach of implied contract,
breach of confidence, and several other causes of action. According to the
complaint, after the meetings with Montz and Smoller, NBC partnered
with Piligian and Pilgrim to produce a series on the Sci–Fi Channel based
on the plaintiffs' materials. The show, called *Ghost Hunters,* starred Hawes
as the leader of a team of investigators who travel across the country to
study paranormal activity.

Plaintiffs' complaint specifically alleged that defendants breached an
implied-in-fact contract. The complaint described the terms of the agreement:

> Plaintiffs communicated their ideas and creative concepts for the
> "Ghost Hunters" Concept to the Defendants, pursuant to the standard
> custom and practice in the industry with respect to the exchange of
> creative ideas, under the following terms:
>
>> a. that Plaintiffs' disclosure of their ideas and concepts was strict-
>> ly confidential;

b. that the Defendants would not disclose, divulge or exploit the Plaintiffs' ideas and concepts without compensation and without obtaining the Plaintiffs' consent; and

c. that, by accepting the Plaintiffs' disclosure of its concept, the Defendants accepted and agreed to abide by the foregoing terms.

Compl. at ¶ 46. The complaint further alleged that plaintiffs presented the concept on the express condition that they made the presentation as an offer to partner with the defendants and that plaintiffs justifiably expected to receive a share of the profits derived from any use of the idea:

The Plaintiffs presented their ideas for the "Ghost Hunter" Concept to the Defendants' [sic] in confidence, pursuant to the custom and practice of the entertainment industry, for the express purpose of offering to partner with the Defendants in the production, broadcast and distribution of the Concept. Accordingly, the Plaintiffs justifiably expected to receive a share of any profits and credit that might be derived from the exploitation of its ideas and concepts for the Concept.

Id. at ¶ 47. The dissent appears to overlook these clear allegations that compensation was expected in accord with industry practice.

Plaintiffs also alleged that defendants breached their confidential relationship "by taking Plaintiffs' novel ideas and concepts, exploiting those ideas and concepts, and profiting therefrom to the Plaintiffs' exclusion. . . ." Id. at ¶ 59. The complaint therefore alleged a claim under California law of breach of confidence.

II. Procedural Background

Defendants moved to dismiss the complaint under Federal Rule of Civil Procedure 12(b)(6) for failure to state a claim upon which relief can be granted. The district court granted in part and denied in part the defendants' motion. The court concluded that the complaint alleged facts sufficient to state a federal copyright claim, but that federal copyright law preempted the plaintiffs' state-law claims. The court dismissed the state-law claims with prejudice and without leave to amend.

Plaintiffs amended their copyright claim and added Universal Television Networks as a defendant. Subsequently, the parties stipulated to the voluntary dismissal of the amended copyright claim with prejudice. With no remaining claims to be adjudicated, the district court entered final judgment in favor of the defendants. The plaintiffs timely appealed the dismissal of their breach of implied contract and breach of confidence claims.

On June 3, 2010, the three-judge panel affirmed, holding both claims preempted by federal copyright law. Montz v. Pilgrim Films & Television, Inc., 606 F.3d 1153, 1158 (9th Cir.2010). We ordered a rehearing of this case en banc pursuant to a vote of the majority of active judges. See 28 U.S.C. § 46(c) and Fed. R.App. P. 35.

III. California Implied–in–Fact Contract Law

Writers in the Hollywood film industry often submit scripts to producers, or set up meetings with them, in the hope of selling them scripts and concepts for movies. The practice has carried over into television. Since the writer is looking for someone to turn the written work into an entertainment production, writers often pitch scripts or concepts to producers with the understanding that the writer will be paid if the material is used. Since an idea cannot be copyrighted, a concept for a film or television show cannot be protected by a copyright. 17 U.S.C. § 102. But the concept can still be stolen if the studio violates an implied contract to pay the writer for using it.

In *Desny,* the California Supreme Court recognized that a writer and producer form an implied contract under circumstances where both understand that the writer is disclosing his idea on the condition that he will be compensated if it is used. 299 P.2d at 270. There, defendant Billy Wilder, famed director of *Sunset Boulevard* and *Witness for the Prosecution,* allegedly entered into an implied contractual arrangement that was initiated when the plaintiff telephoned Wilder's office and pitched a movie idea to Wilder's secretary who, along with Wilder, understood Wilder was to pay if he used the story. Id. at 273–74. Wilder produced a film, *Ace in the Hole,* allegedly based on the idea plaintiff had pitched for a movie inspired by the "life story of Floyd Collins who was trapped [in a cave] and made sensational news for two weeks." Id. at 262. Wilder allegedly failed to compensate the plaintiff, and the California Supreme Court held that, given the entertainment industry norms, the plaintiff had sufficiently pled the breach of an implied contract to pay for use of his idea. The issue here is whether copyright law now preempts such claims.

IV. Copyright Preemption

[The court held that the implied-in-fact contract claim was not preempted under § 301. See supra p. 633.]

Plaintiffs' claim for breach of confidence also survives copyright preemption. The claim protects the duty of trust or confidential relationship between the parties, an extra element that makes it qualitatively different from a copyright claim. See Computer Assocs. Int'l, Inc. v. Altai, Inc., 982 F.2d 693, 717 (2d Cir.1992); Fischer v. Viacom Int'l, Inc., 115 F.Supp.2d 535, 542 (D.Md.2000); Berkla v. Corel Corp., 66 F.Supp.2d 1129, 1150–51 (E.D.Cal.1999); Nimmer at § 19D.03[C][1].

V. Sufficiency of the Complaint as to the Breach of Implied Contract and Breach of Confidence Claims

Defendants argue that the complaint fails to allege sufficient facts to make out a claim for breach of implied contract. They assert that it lacks any allegation (1) that Montz and Smoller disclosed their idea for sale, (2) that they expected to be reasonably compensated for the idea, and (3) that defendants knew the conditions on which it was offered. Yet the complaint makes all three allegations and closely tracks the complaint we found sufficient in *Grosso.*

Defendants similarly argue that Montz and Smoller failed to allege sufficient facts to make out their claim for breach of confidence. They argue that there is no allegation (1) that plaintiffs disclosed "confidential and novel information," and (2) that defendants knew it was supposed to be kept confidential. See Entm't Research Grp., Inc. v. Genesis Creative Grp., Inc., 122 F.3d 1211, 1227 (9th Cir.1997). But the complaint clearly contains these allegations as well.

VI. Conclusion

The judgment of the district court is REVERSED and the matter REMANDED for further proceedings on plaintiffs' remaining claims.

■ O'SCANNLAIN, CIRCUIT JUDGE, Joined by GOULD, TALLMAN, and BEA, CIRCUIT JUDGES, dissenting:

Montz does not claim to have sold his rights as a copyright owner. To the contrary, he alleges that he retained those rights, and that Pilgrim implicitly promised *not* to use or to disclose his ideas *without his consent*. As the district court properly held, an action to enforce a promise not to use or to disclose ideas embodied in copyrighted material without authorization asserts rights equivalent to those protected by the Copyright Act. Accordingly, the district court's determination that the Copyright Act preempts Montz's claims should be affirmed. I respectfully dissent from the Court's opinion to the contrary. * * *

Under section 106, a copyright owner has the exclusive rights to reproduce, to distribute, and to display the copyrighted work, as well as to prepare derivative works based on the copyrighted work. 17 U.S.C. § 106. Section 106 also provides a copyright owner with the exclusive rights to authorize such reproduction, distribution, display, and preparation. Id. Montz alleges that "by producing and broadcasting" *Ghost Hunters,* "[t]he Defendants breached their implied agreement not to disclose, divulge or exploit the Plaintiffs' ideas and concepts without the[ir] express consent." In other words, Montz asserts that Pilgrim produced and broadcast a television program derived from Montz's screenplays, video, and other materials *without authorization*. These rights are equivalent to the rights of copyright owners under section 106—namely, the exclusive rights to authorize reproduction, distribution, and display of original works, and to authorize preparation of derivative works. See Del Madera Props. v. Rhodes & Gardner, Inc., 820 F.2d 973, 977 (9th Cir.1987), overruled on other grounds by Fogerty v. Fantasy, Inc., 510 U.S. 517 (1994) ("[A]n implied promise not to use or copy materials within the subject matter of copyright is equivalent to the protection provided by section 106 of the Copyright Act.").

* * * [A]ccording to the complaint, Pilgrim did not promise to pay for the use of Montz's ideas. Rather, it promised (implicitly) to respect Montz's rights to the production, distribution, and broadcast of his work. Put differently, it promised to respect the rights afforded to Montz by the Copyright Act.

The majority asserts that there is "no meaningful difference between the conditioning of use on payment in *Grosso* and conditioning use in this case on the granting of a partnership interest in the proceeds of the production." Maj. Op. at 977. This was never the issue. The *Montz* panel did not rely on the difference between seeking compensation in the form of a lump sum versus a percentage of profits. Rather, it relied on the difference between authorizing the use of one's work in exchange for money, and not authorizing the use of one's work at all. See Montz v. Pilgrim Films & Television, Inc., 606 F.3d 1153, 1158 (9th Cir.2010) ("Whereas the breach of the alleged agreement in *Grosso* violated the plaintiff's right to payment on a sale, the breach of the alleged agreement in this case violated the plaintiffs' exclusive rights to use and to authorize use of their work. . . ."). * * * There is thus nothing in the complaint that "qualitatively distinguish[es]" the breach-of-implied-contract claim from a copyright claim. * * *

NOTES AND QUESTIONS ON CONTRACTS IMPLIED–IN–FACT

(1) It is easy enough to remit "idea" cases to the general canons of contract law, but it is apparent on reflection that interpretation of the varying situations in which ideas are submitted presents serious difficulties. The person with the idea is reluctant to disclose it without some promise of compensation, but the

potential buyer is reluctant to make any promises without more than an ink-
ling of what the idea merchant has to sell. The transactions are therefore likely
to be fuzzy ones in which express words of agreement may not be found. When
it comes to "implications," the trier of fact can make no headway without asking what, specifically, are the terms that the plaintiff seeks to imply, and what,
specifically, are the features of the transaction from which these terms may
fairly arise. In such an analysis it may be hard to choose between conflicting
interpretations of the facts.[b]

Counsel for plaintiffs have urged in effect, without a nice regard for contract theory, that a recipient is liable if after submission of an idea it comes out
with a product embodying the idea or something reasonably close to it—unless
perhaps it can show that it already had the idea in mind. Cf. Teich v. General
Mills, Inc., 170 Cal.App.2d 791, 339 P.2d 627 (1959). On the other side, defendants' counsel have urged that recovery should be barred unless the idea is submitted in response to a definite invitation. Meanwhile, corporations seek to invent routines for handling submissions that will avoid lawsuits and the perils
of jury verdicts. These range from extreme measures such as routing letters
from outsiders to independent readers so that the submitted idea never reaches
decision-makers, to form contracts that seek to regulate the relationship expressly (in the recipient's favor of course) and thereby avoid claims based on
inchoate and conflicting versions of the facts.

(2) Is it significant that *Montz*'s description of the California rules on implied-
in-fact contracts makes no mention of "novelty" or "concreteness"? Under the
California cases, neither is a prerequisite to recovery on a contract claim. California courts have almost routinely upheld the triability of contract claims derived from idea and format submissions for movies and television programs.
Examples include Grosso v. Miramax Film Corp., 383 F.3d 965 (9th Cir.2004),
amended, 400 F.3d 658, cert. denied, 546 U.S. 658 (2005); Minniear v. Tors, 266
Cal.App.2d 495, 72 Cal.Rptr. 287 (1968); Blaustein v. Burton, 9 Cal.App.3d 161,
88 Cal.Rptr. 319 (1970), an account of a producer's promotion and demotion in
the Richard Burton–Elizabeth Taylor version of "The Taming of the Shrew";
Fink v. Goodson–Todman Enterprises, Ltd., 9 Cal.App.3d 996, 88 Cal.Rptr. 679
(1970). But see Faris v. Enberg, 97 Cal.App.3d 309, 158 Cal.Rptr. 704 (1979),
affirming a summary judgment for the defendant on the plaintiff's implied-in-
fact contract count in a suit involving the disclosure to sportscaster Dick
Enberg of an idea for a sports quiz show; there was no evidence that the plaintiff had communicated an expectation of payment. M. LaFrance, Something
Borrowed, Something New: The Changing Role of Novelty in Idea Protection
Law, 34 Seton Hall L.Rev. 485 (2004), argues in favor of the California position
that does not require novelty for the contractual protection of ideas; A. Miller,
Common Law Protection for Products of the Mind: An "Idea" Whose Time Has
Come, 119 Harv.L.Rev. 703 (2006), goes further, questioning the utility of both
the "concreteness" and "novelty" requirements under any theory of idea protec-
tion.

---

[b] See B. Kaplan, Implied Contract and the Law of Literary Property, 42 Calif.L.Rev. 28
(1954); B. Kaplan, Further Remarks on Compensation for Ideas in California, 46 id. 699
(1958). Idea submitters in the entertainment business sometimes attempt to protect their
creations by registering them with the Writers Guild of America, which receives over 30,000
submissions a year. See Craft, Hollywood's Storehouse of Scripts, Ideas, Movies, L.A. Times,
Mar. 18, 1992, p. F3. The online registration system is described in Calvo, WGA Puts Writers
One Click Closer, L.A. Times, Dec. 3, 2002, p. E1.

(3) Landsberg v. Scrabble Crossword Game Players, Inc., 802 F.2d 1193 (9th Cir.1986), invoked the implied-in-fact contract theory outside the television and film settings of the previous cases. The defendant plagiarized Landsberg's manuscript on Scrabble strategy, although not enough to constitute copyright infringement. See 736 F.2d 485 (9th Cir.1984), p. 243 supra. In this second appeal, the court upheld a substantial recovery for breach of an implied-in-fact contract stemming from the plaintiff's submission of the manuscript at the defendant's request.

A jury verdict against an idea submitter was overturned in Gunther–Wahl Productions, Inc. v. Mattel, Inc., 104 Cal.App.4th 27, 128 Cal.Rptr.2d 50 (2002). The plaintiffs, at Mattel's request, pitched an idea for "Flutter Faeries"—dolls that were half-human and half-butterfly. They claimed that the company later used some of their concepts without compensation and sued on an implied-in-fact contract theory. The trial court had instructed the jury that the plaintiffs had to prove that "they clearly conditioned their disclosure on Mattel's agreement to pay." The appellate court said the instruction was incorrect, since no express representation about payment is necessary for the creation of an implied-in-fact contract.

(4) In Reeves v. Alyeska Pipeline Serv. Co., 926 P.2d 1130 (Alaska 1996), the Supreme Court of Alaska examined the various theories available to an idea submitter, including contract implied-in-fact. After allegedly receiving assurances that his disclosure would be "between us," plaintiff Reeves revealed to a manager of the defendant (operator of the Trans–Alaska Pipeline) his idea for a visitor's center at a highway turnoff on the defendant's property. Unknown at the time to either the manager or Reeves, the company had rejected a suggestion for a visitor's center at that location four years earlier. This time it went ahead with the center. Reeves brought suit on a variety of theories, but the trial court granted summary judgment against him on all counts because his idea lacked novelty.

Considering first Reeves' express contract claim, the appellate court said that since Reeves alleged other consideration, it need not decide whether a non-novel idea could serve as consideration for an express contract. It turned next to the circumstances that might justify recognition of a contract implied-in-fact.

"There are three primary factual scenarios under which ideas may be submitted to another. See Nimmer, supra § 16.05. The first involves an unsolicited submission that is involuntarily received. Id. at 16–33. The idea is submitted without warning; it is transmitted before the recipient has taken any action which would indicate a promise to pay for the submission. Id. at 16–33 to 16–34. Under this scenario, a contract will not be implied. [Desny v. Wilder, 46 Cal.2d 715, 299 P.2d 257, 270 (1956)], Nimmer, supra, § 16.05[B], at 16–34.

"The second involves an unsolicited submission that is voluntarily received. Nimmer, supra, § 16.05[C], at 16–36. In this situation, the idea person typically gives the recipient advance warning that an idea is to be disclosed; the recipient has an opportunity to stop the disclosure, but through inaction allows the idea to be disclosed. Id. at 16–36 to 16–37. Under California law, if the recipient at the time of disclosure understands that the idea person expects to be paid for the disclosure of the idea, and does not attempt to stop the disclosure, inaction may be seen as consent to a contract. *Desny*, 299 P.2d at 267; Donahue v. Ziv Television Programs, Inc., 245 Cal.App.2d 593, 54 Cal.Rptr. 130, 139 (1966).

"This view has been criticized as unfairly placing a duty on the recipient to take active measures to stop the submission. Nimmer, supra § 16.05[C], at 16–38. The critics argue that inaction generally should not be considered an expression of consent to a contract. Id.

"We believe that a contract should not be implied under this scenario. An implied-in-fact contract is based on circumstances that demonstrate that the parties intended to form a contract but failed to articulate their promises. * * * Only under exceptional circumstances would inaction demonstrate an intent to enter a contract.

"The third scenario involves a solicited submission. Nimmer, supra § 16.05[D], at 16–40. Here, a request by the recipient for disclosure of the idea usually implies a promise to pay for the idea if the recipient uses it. *Desny*, 299 P.2d at 267; Nimmer, supra § 16.05[D] at 16–40."

Since the plaintiff alleged that the defendant had requested the disclosure, summary judgment against him was improper. The court did agree, however, with the California rule that novelty is not a prerequisite for an implied-in-fact contract claim, rejecting the contrary rule in New York. "An idea may be valuable to the recipient merely because of its timing or the manner in which it is presented. * * * If the parties voluntarily choose to bargain for an individual's services in disclosing or developing a non-novel or unoriginal idea, they have the power to do so."

As for plaintiff's quasi-contact claim for unjust enrichment, that, the court said, was a property-based claim, sustainable only if the idea was novel. Summary judgment on that count was affirmed.

BREACH OF CONFIDENCE

If there is a legally recognized confidential relationship between the parties, it is clear that they will be held to high standards in dealing with each other. See Carpenter Foundation v. Oakes, 26 Cal.App.3d 784, 103 Cal.Rptr. 368 (1972). But existing fiduciary-like relationships aside, courts sometimes speak of a "confidential relationship" merely to describe what happens when one person discloses information to another "in confidence." Is a "breach of confidence" in this sense actionable as such by the disclosing party? In Davies v. Krasna, 14 Cal.3d 502, 121 Cal.Rptr. 705 (1975), a confused and protracted idea-submission case, the plaintiff had lost with a jury on her contract claims. She had also pleaded a "breach of confidence" count. (The precise question was what statute of limitations should apply to such a count. The California Supreme Court held that it was a tort or quasi-contract, barred after two years, not constructive fraud with a three-year limit, which would be applicable to the breach of a true fiduciary relationship.) Justice Tobriner said "this court has never ruled that a cause of action for breach of confidence can rest upon a basis other than a contract that protects that confidence." Here it was settled that there was no contract. But the court felt obliged to accept as the law of the case that, "When defendant received Valentine Davies' idea, with the understanding that this idea was confidential, defendant incurred an obligation not to use or disclose that idea without the creator's consent." It proceeded to decide the limitations issue on that assumption, but it refused "to create a new genre of liability without full argumentation."

In Faris v. Enberg, Note (2) supra, where the plaintiff had disclosed his idea for a sports quiz show, a California Court of Appeal did assert a willingness to recognize a cause of action for "breach of confidence." "An actionable breach of confidence will arise when an idea, whether or not protectable, is offered to another in confidence, and is voluntarily received by the offeree in confidence with the understanding that it is not to be disclosed to others, and is not to be used by the offeree for purposes beyond the limits of the confidence without the offeror's permission." But the court rejected the claim on the facts, finding no evidence that the disclosure was made in confidence. "[A] confidential relationship will not be created from the mere submission of an idea to another. There must exist evidence of the communication of the confidentiality of the submission or evidence from which a confidential relationship can be inferred." 158 Cal.Rptr. at 712. Faris v. Enberg was dissected in Tele–Count Engineers, Inc. v. Pacific Tel. & Tel. Co., 168 Cal.App.3d 455, 214 Cal.Rptr. 276 (1985), a business system case concluding that the plaintiff had failed to achieve the necessary understanding that the defendant was to treat the submitted forms in confidence. After noting that *Faris* had established that information need not be copyrightable to be the subject of a breach of confidence action, the court said, "Nevertheless, appellate decisions have uniformly required that an idea must be confidential and novel to warrant protection."

The Ninth Circuit attempted a summary of the California rules on "breach of confidence" in a case involving a manufacturer's disclosure to a distributor of design information on inflatable promotional costumes:

> To prevail on a claim for breach of confidence under California law, a plaintiff must demonstrate that: (1) the plaintiff conveyed "confidential and novel information" to the defendant; (2) the defendant had knowledge that the information was being disclosed in confidence; (3) there was an understanding between the defendant and the plaintiff that the confidence would be maintained; and (4) there was a disclosure or use in violation of the understanding.

The court upheld the defendant's summary judgment since the plaintiff's information was not confidential; the costumes had been placed on the market prior to the disclosure. Entertainment Research Group, Inc. v. Genesis Creative Group, Inc., 122 F.3d 1211 (9th Cir.1997), cert. denied, 523 U.S. 1021 (1998).[c]

The California decisions seem to present a doctrinal bias that is different from the New York cases. Judge Friendly, in Lehman v. Dow Jones & Co., 783 F.2d 285 (2d Cir.1986), remarked that "California law has gone

----

[c]   The Uniform Trade Secrets Act has been successfully invoked by idea providers complaining that a recipient has used the idea in breach of confidence. See, e.g., Learning Curve Toys, Inc. v. Playwood Toys, Inc., 342 F.3d 714 (7th Cir.2003). The court reinstated a jury verdict in favor of a plaintiff who disclosed an idea for a realistic looking and sounding toy railroad track in confidence to a manufacturer who used it without permission. The court held that the idea qualified for protection as the plaintiff's "trade secret." "It is irrelevant under Illinois law that [plaintiff] did not actually use the concept in its business." The Act's preemption section, displacing conflicting state law pertaining to the misappropriation of trade secrets, was invoked in HDNet, LLC v. North American Boxing Council, 972 N.E.2d 920 (Ind.App. 2012), to defeat a claim for "idea misappropriation" brought by a martial arts fight sanctioning body that had pitched an idea for a television fight series to a cable network channel. The court held that the Act abolished all alternative non-contractual causes of action for the misappropriation of confidential information, even if the information fails to qualify for protection under the Act as a trade secret.

quite far in finding implied-in-fact contracts" and also noted the absence of any novelty prerequisite to the enforcement of implied-in-fact idea submission contracts. Perhaps California law simply reflects more emphatically the values of the entertainment business, where ideas and other intangibles that the law recognizes only dimly, if at all, can be worth large sums of money. See L. Sobel, The Law of Ideas, Revisited, 1 UCLA Ent.L.Rev. 9 (1994).

PART 3

INTERNATIONAL COPYRIGHT

CHAPTER 11

U.S. INTERNATIONAL COPYRIGHT RELATIONS

1. THE POSITION BEFORE 1891

The Copyright Act of 1790 (1 Stat. 124) gave protection to "the author and authors * * * being a citizen or citizens [of the United States], or resident within the same," § 1, and emphasized in § 5 that "nothing in this act shall be construed to extend to prohibit the importation or vending, reprinting or publishing within the United States, of any map, chart, book or books, written, printed, or published by any person not a citizen of the United States, in foreign parts or places without the jurisdiction of the United States." It is perhaps not surprising that a newly-founded country would permit and even encourage poaching on foreign works, but the same policy continued even as the nation grew. The Act of 1831 (4 Stat. 436) accorded protection to "any person or persons, being a citizen or citizens of the United States, or resident therein, who shall be the author or authors," § 1, but stated in § 8 that "nothing in this act shall be construed to extend to prohibit the importation or vending, printing, or publishing, of any map, chart, book, musical composition, print or engraving, written, composed, or made, by any person not being a citizen of the United States, nor resident within the jurisdiction thereof." Again, the Revised Statutes of 1873 granted rights to "Any citizen of the United States or resident therein, who shall be the author," § 4952, and reaffirmed in § 4971: "Nothing in this chapter shall be construed to prohibit the printing, publishing, importation, or sale of any book, map, chart, dramatic or musical composition, print, cut, engraving, or photograph, written, composed or made by any person not a citizen of the United States nor resident therein."

BRITISH–AMERICAN COPYRIGHT RELATIONS

ADDRESS OF BRITISH AUTHORS

(Presented to the Senate by Henry Clay, February 2, 1837)[a]

The humble address and petition of certain authors of Great Britain, to the Senate and House of Representatives of the United States, in Congress assembled, respectfully showeth—

1. That your petitioners have long been exposed to injury in their reputation and property, from the want of a law by which the exclusive right to their respective writings may be secured to them in the United States of America.

2. That, for want of such law, deep and extensive injuries have, of late, been inflicted on the reputation and property of certain of your petitioners; and on the interests of literature and science, which ought to con-

---

[a]   S.Rep. No. 134, 24th Cong., 2d Sess. (1837), reproduced in R. Bowker, Copyright, Its History and Its Law 341 (1912).

stitute a bond of union and friendship between the United States and Great Britain.

3.   That, from the circumstance of the English language being common to both nations, the works of British authors are extensively read throughout the United States of America, while the profits arising from the sale of their works may be wholly appropriated by American booksellers, not only without the consent of the authors, but even contrary to their express desire—a grievance under which your petitioners have, at present, no redress.

4.   That the works thus appropriated by American booksellers are liable to be mutilated and altered, at the pleasure of the said booksellers, or of any other persons who may have an interest in reducing the price of the works, or in conciliating the supposed principles or prejudice of purchasers in the respective sections of your union: and that, the names of the authors being retained, they may be made responsible for works which they no longer recognize as their own. * * *

8.   That American authors are injured by the non-existence of the desired law. While American publishers can provide themselves with works for publication by unjust appropriation, instead of by equitable purchase, they are under no inducement to afford to American authors a fair remuneration for their labours: under which grievance American authors have no redress but in sending over their works to England to be published, an expedient which has become an established practice with some of whom their country has most reason to be proud.

9.   That the American public is injured by the non-existence of the desired law. The American public suffers, not only from the discouragement afforded to native authors, as above stated, but from the uncertainty now existing as to whether the books presented to them as the works of British authors, are the actual and complete productions of the writers whose names they bear. * * *

11.   That your petitioners, deeply impressed with the conviction that the only firm ground of friendship between nations, is a strict regard to simple justice, earnestly pray that your Honours, the representatives of the United States in Congress assembled, will speedily use, in behalf of the authors of Great Britain, your power "of securing to the authors the exclusive right to their respective writings."

NOTES AND QUESTIONS

(1) The Address of British Authors assumes that British writers could obtain no protection in the United States for their published books. But the American statutes allowed copyright not only to citizens but to residents of the United States, and the question naturally arose whether a temporary sojourn by an alien author could be recognized as residence. Eaton Drone, writing in 1879, was of the opinion that resident "refers to a person who is residing in the United States with the intention of making this country his permanent place of abode." E. Drone on Copyright 233 (1879). Further, although the American statutes did not expressly provide where publication must be made in order to entitle the author to copyright, Drone thought that "an author forfeits his claim to copyright in this country by a first, but not by a contemporaneous, publication of his work abroad." Id. at 296.

Could American authors obtain protection for their works in Great Britain? British law at that date appears to have given no copyright to an alien author who first published a book outside Great Britain. Legislation commencing in 1838 (the so-called International Copyright Acts), together with Orders in Council and a network of treaties, did have the effect of extending copyright to such works, but on the condition (among others) that the alien's country granted reciprocal rights to British authors. The United States of course did not qualify. It appears to have been accepted, however, that an alien who first published a book in Great Britain could claim the benefit of the general British copyright statutes even though he had no other connection with that country. In the case of Jefferys v. Boosey, 4 H.L.Cas. 815, 10 Eng.Rep. 681 (1854), the House of Lords took the position that (apart from the International Copyright Acts) an alien author could obtain British copyright by a first publication in Great Britain only if he was physically present within the British dominions at the time of the publication. By 1868 there was some opinion in the House of Lords that the visit to the British dominions at the time of first publication could be dispensed with. See Low v. Routledge, 3 H.L. 100 (1868) (judgments of Lords Cairns and Westbury). But for better assurance American authors still made the trip. The effect of these and other requirements was that a very cautious American author seeking British as well as American copyright would, while physically present somewhere in the British dominions, publish simultaneously in Great Britain and the United States.

(2) The piracy of British books by American publishers through most of the 19th century has been celebrated in song and story.[b] What is not so well known is the very considerable piracy of American works by British publishers during the same period—for it was a rare American author who could thread his way through the British law, which was in fact more complex and less certain than this short sketch suggests, and who could indulge in the luxury of complying with all its requirements.[c]

B. Matthews, American Authors and British Pirates, 4 New Princeton Rev. 201 (1887), 5 id. 47 (1888), recounts an amusing exchange between lawyer-critic Brander Matthews and Samuel Clemens. Matthews deplores the British piracies. With his customary gusto and ironic reflections on Matthews' lawyerly abilities, Clemens answers that he has been enjoying British copyright by following the British law; Matthews replies that the expedients Clemens has been using are not in practice available to less affluent authors.[d]

(3) Copyright relations among important European countries including Great Britain were simplified and improved with the coming into effect of the Berne Convention in 1887, but there was no essential change in British–American copyright relations. In practice, however, piracy of British books in America had been brought under some unofficial restraint. According to a "trade understanding" of American publishers, when an American publisher bought sheets of a British work and republished the work in the United States, respectable

---

[b]   For Anthony Trollope's measured condemnation of American piracies, see *An Autobiography*, ch. XVII (1883).

[c]   See C. Gohdes, American Literature in 19th Century England (1944); C. Gohdes, Longfellow and His Authorized British Publishers, 55 Pub.Mod.Lang. Ass'n 1165 (1940).

[d]   Samuel Clemens was no admirer of copyright statutes. "Only one thing is impossible for God: to find any sense in any copyright law on the planet. Whenever a copyright law is to be made or altered, then the idiots assemble." Mark Twain's Notebook 381–82 (Harper & Bros. 1935).

competitors would ordinarily refrain from piracy. There was in fact a lively market for early sheets of important British books, and British publishers and authors did in many cases profit from American publication.

2. FROM THE CHACE ACT TO THE UNIVERSAL COPYRIGHT CONVENTION

THE CHACE ACT OF 1891

On September 9, 1886, ten nations signed the Berne Convention, Additional Article and Final Protocol for the creation of an International Union for the Protection of Literary and Artistic Works—one of the great steps forward in securing international copyright protection.[e] Although the United States sent a delegation to the Berne meeting, it did not adhere to the Convention. Within a short time, however, the United States adopted legislation granting a measure of copyright protection to nationals of foreign countries. This was the Chace Act. (Act of March 3, 1891, 26 Stat. 1106.) Section 13 of the Act provided:

> That this act shall apply to a citizen or subject of a foreign state or nation when such foreign state or nation permits to citizens of the United States of America the benefit of copyright on substantially the same basis as [to] its own citizens [so-called "national treatment"]; or when such foreign state or nation is a party to an international agreement which provides for reciprocity in the granting of copyright, by the terms of which agreement the United States of America may, at its pleasure, become a party to such agreement. The existence of either of the conditions aforesaid shall be determined by the President of the United States by proclamation made from time to time as the purposes of this act may require.[f]

Fears that the American printing and publishing trades would be overwhelmed by foreign competition, however, were reflected in § 3 of the Act. This provided that "in the case of a book, photograph, chromo or lithograph, the two copies" required to be deposited with the Library of Congress "shall be printed from type set within the limits of the United States, or from plates made therefrom, or from negatives, or drawings on stone made within the limits of the United States, or from transfers made therefrom"; and it further provided that during the existence of copyright, the importation of books not complying with these requirements was prohibited. This was the first appearance of the so-called "manufacturing clause."

THE 1909 COPYRIGHT ACT

The situation of foreign authors seeking copyright protection in the United States was somewhat improved by the 1909 Copyright Act.

Section 8 of the original 1909 Act (later codified in § 9 of the Act) went beyond the Chace Act in allowing an alien author or proprietor domiciled in the United States at the time of first publication of the work to obtain a

---

[e]   Texts of the international treaties on copyright and related subjects, together with information on adherences, are available at the World Intellectual Property Organization's web site, www.wipo.org.

[f]   It appears that no Presidential proclamation ever issued on the latter basis of the existence of an "open" international agreement.

copyright even if his country had not been "proclaimed." A non-domiciled alien, however, could obtain American copyright only if his country had been proclaimed, and the 1909 Act added to the two Chace Act bases for proclamation a third alternative, namely: "When the foreign state * * * grants * * * to citizens of the United States * * * copyright protection, substantially equal to the protection secured to such foreign author under this title or by treaty"—so-called "reciprocal treatment." But foreigners qualifying by American domicile or by reason of proclamations covering their countries also had to comply with the requirements for obtaining and preserving copyright in the United States, of which the most onerous was the manufacturing requirement. Under § 16 of the 1909 Act, copyright could be secured in books and periodicals only on condition of domestic manufacture—i.e., the type must be set, plates made, lithographic or photoengraving process performed, and printing and binding accomplished in the United States. Excepted was "the original text of a book or periodical of foreign origin in a language or languages other than English." Importation of copies of copyrighted works not complying with the manufacturing requirement was prohibited, subject to some exceptions. § 107. The 1909 Act introduced special "ad interim" protection for books published abroad in English before publication in this country; deposit of a copy of the foreign edition could secure a short-term copyright while the owner decided whether to publish an American edition in compliance with the manufacturing requirements. §§ 22–23.

The manufacturing clause, despite the ad interim arrangements, continued to hinder our international copyright relations. Its impact was lessened, however, by our adherence to the Universal Copyright Convention, infra, and the addition of § 9(c) to the 1909 Act that eliminated the manufacturing requirement for foreign authors claiming protection through the UCC.

The manufacturing clause in attenuated form survived temporarily in § 601 of the 1976 Copyright Act. It was limited essentially to nondramatic literary works in English by American authors domiciled in the United States—that is, its effect was to prevent domestic authors from taking advantage of cheap foreign printing.

As enacted, the manufacturing requirements of § 601 were to expire on July 1, 1982. But when the time came, the usual protectionist arguments prevailed. (The arguments pro and con are rehashed in the House Report, pp. 165–66.) Congress voted a four-year extension, and the manufacturing requirement eventually expired on July 1, 1986.[g]

FOREIGN AUTHORS AND THE 1976 ACT

(1) In the 1976 Act, the status of foreign works is governed by § 104. Note first that under § 104(a) any unpublished work satisfying the standards of copyrightability is protected "without regard to the nationality or domicile of the author."

For foreign authors seeking protection for published works under the 1976 Act, § 104(b) offers six overlapping points of attachment that make a work eligible for copyright. Authors who at the time of first publication are nationals or domiciliaries of a treaty party (including nations adhering to

---

[g]   Just before its expiration, an attempt to declare the manufacturing clause unconstitutional was rebuffed in *Authors League of America v. Oman*, 790 F.2d 220 (2d Cir.1986).

Berne or the UCC) can claim protection pursuant to § 104(b)(1). Works first published in the United States or in a treaty party (or published in such a country within thirty days after publication elsewhere) are protected under (b)(2). Can you describe a work that would *not* fall within either of the preceding categories?

Proclamations (see § 104(b)(6)) and bilateral treaties are now of diminished importance in view of the combined reach of the UCC and Berne. Two other multinational conventions, Mexico City of 1908 and Buenos Aires of 1911, are also now essentially obsolete; all of their participants are members of Berne or the UCC. Article 3 of the Buenos Aires Convention had a notice requirement: "[A] statement that indicates the reservation of the property right" had to appear on copies of the work. From this came the familiar legend, "All Rights Reserved."[h]

(2) Whose law applies when foreign authors seek copyright protection in the United States? In Bridgeman Art Library, p. 68 supra, Judge Kaplan decided that under § 104 the copyrightability of foreign works is determined by United States copyright law. In Itar–Tass Russian News Agency v. Russian Kurier, Inc., 153 F.3d 82 (2d Cir.1998), Judge Newman faced a claim of copyright infringement brought by Russian newspaper publishers against a New York Russian-language newspaper that had copied individual articles from the plaintiffs' newspapers. On the issue of whether the newspapers or their reporters owned the copyrights in the individual articles, the court held that Russian law controlled. Once the nature of the plaintiffs' copyright ownership had been established, the court said that the question of infringement was determined by United States law. See the comprehensive analysis of the choice of law issue in W. Patry, Choice of Law and International Copyright, 48 Am.J.Comp.L. 383 (2000).

3. THE UNIVERSAL COPYRIGHT CONVENTION

THE ORIGIN OF THE UCC

For a long time some Americans felt uneasy about our failure to enter wholeheartedly into international arrangements for copyright protection. Bills introduced in Congress from 1924 to 1940[i] sought—vainly, as it turned out—to create a pattern of law that would qualify the U.S. for entrance into the Berne Union. These bills were not merely altruistic efforts to improve the position of foreign authors in this country. In the absence of an international modus vivendi comparable to Berne, American authors and producers seeking foreign markets were often obliged to inquire into and comply with the varying requirements of the laws of foreign countries in an attempt to secure protection for their works, and the measure of protection actually secured was frequently in doubt.

It is true that Americans found a "back door" to Berne by which they could gain the benefit of the Convention even though the United States was not a member. Article 3(1) of the Berne Convention extends the protection of Berne to "authors who are not nationals of one of the countries of the Union, for their works first published in one of those countries, or simultaneously in a country outside the Union and in a country of the Union." Thus

---

[h]   See A. Rinaldo, The Scope of Copyright Protection in the United States Under Existing Inter–American Relations, 22 Bull.Copyr. Soc'y 417 (1975).

[i]   See A. Goldman, The History of U.S.A. Copyright Law Revision From 1901–1954, Copyr. Law Revision Study No. 1 (1955), in 2 Studies on Copyr. 1101 (1963).

the practice sprang up of American authors making token publications of their works in Berne countries like Canada or Great Britain simultaneously with publication in the United States. This tactic could not fail to arouse resentment abroad. As early as 1914 a section was added to art. 6 of Berne that created the possibility of retaliation: "Where any country outside the Union fails to protect in an adequate manner the works of authors who are nationals of one of the countries of the Union, the latter country may restrict the protection given to the works of authors who are, at the date of the first publication thereof, nationals of the other country and are not habitually resident in one of the countries of the Union." Although this provision was not in fact used against American authors, it stood as a threat.

As the adherents to Berne were not disposed to alter the Convention to accommodate American law, and as efforts to change American law to accommodate to Berne had not succeeded, some new approach was needed. A solution satisfactory to the United States was found by creating a new convention that could co-exist with Berne. A large intergovernmental project to formulate the new convention was launched shortly after World War II. The effort culminated on September 6, 1952, with the signing of the Universal Copyright Convention at Geneva. The UCC text with 1971 revisions is set out in the Statutory Supplement. Domestic legislation needed to prepare this country for adherence to the UCC was approved in 1954. On September 16, 1955, the Convention came into force.

The essentials of the Universal Copyright Convention are summarized by former Register of Copyrights Barbara Ringer as follows:

"1. *Adequate and effective protection.* Under article I, the contracting states are obliged to 'provide for the adequate and effective protection of the rights of authors and other copyright proprietors * * *.'

"2. *National treatment.* Article II provides that the 'published works of nationals of any Contracting State and works first published in that State shall enjoy in each other Contracting State the same protection as that other State accords to works of its nationals first published in its own territory.' There is a similar provision for unpublished works.

"3. *Formalities.* Article III, which represents the great compromise of the U.C.C., provides that the formal requirements, such as notice, registration, and manufacture, of a contracting state's copyright law are satisfied with respect to foreign U.C.C. works 'if from the time of first publication all of the copies of the work * * * bear the symbol © accompanied by the name of the copyright proprietor and the year of first publication placed in such manner and location as to give reasonable notice of claim of copyright.'

"4. *Duration of protection.* Another major compromise is embodied in article IV of the U.C.C. The minimum term, subject to various detailed qualifications and exceptions, is to be either 25 years from the death of the author or from the date of first publication.

"5. *Translation rights.* The U.C.C., in article V, requires contracting states to give exclusive translation rights to foreign U.C.C. authors for at least seven years; thereafter a rather cumbersome compulsory licensing system can be established. [This translation right was liberalized with respect to 'developing countries' in article V*ter* of the 1971 Paris revision.]

"6. *Nonretroactivity*. Under article VII a contracting state is not obliged to protect works that are permanently in its public domain on the date the Convention becomes effective in that state.

"7. *Berne safeguard clause*. An enormously important provision of the U.C.C. is found in article XVII and the 'Appendix Declaration' attached to it. These provide, in effect, that no Berne country can denounce the Berne Convention and rely on the U.C.C. in its copyright relations with Berne Union members. [This was relaxed with respect to developing countries in the 1971 Paris revision.]

"Thus, at least in comparison with the 1948 Brussels revision of the Berne Convention, the Universal Copyright Convention represents a rather low-level copyright arrangement, resembling in many ways the original 1886 Berne text."[j]

STOCKHOLM (1967) TO PARIS (1971)

As the time approached for a conference at Stockholm in 1967 to consider revisions to the Berne Convention, hopes for the general revision of the United States copyright statute were high, and it was possible to give serious consideration to closing the gaps that still remained between Berne and American law. But at the same time, developing nations, many of them newly created, were organizing resistance to the trend of the multinational conventions toward ever-increasing protection of authors.

The Stockholm Conference produced a "Protocol Regarding Developing Countries" allowing such nations to make certain reservations with respect to the provisions of Berne. These included a shorter term of protection and broadened translation privileges and reproduction rights in connection with educational and instructional uses in developing nations.[k] The victory of the developing countries, however, was an empty one. The developed countries could not be compelled to accede to the Protocol, and they did not.

Ringer, writing while the next steps were still in doubt, concluded, "The irony of the present American position in international copyright needs no elaboration. After a century as a virtual outlaw, a half century as an outsider, and 15 years as a stranger at the feast, the United States suddenly finds itself cast as a leading champion of literary property. Having refused to join the Berne Union because its standards were too high, the United States is now faced with the prospect of being unable to join it because the standards have become too low."[l]

The Register of Copyrights, Abraham Kaminstein, took the lead in fashioning compromises that facilitated a concurrent revision of both the UCC and Berne Conventions. This feat was successfully performed in 1971 at parallel conferences in Paris. The UCC was extended to secure to authors the rights of reproduction, public performance and broadcasting as minimum rights. In both Conventions, concessions were made to the developing countries, including limitations on the rights of translation and reproduction for certain privileged purposes. Another change was the modifi-

---

[j]   B. Ringer, The Role of the United States in International Copyright—Past, Present, and Future, 56 Geo.L.J. 1050, 1061–62 (1968). The author was then Assistant Register of Copyrights. Reprinted by permission of the Georgetown Law Journal.

[k]   See id. at 1070-74.

[l]   Id. at 1078.

cation of the "Berne safeguard" in the UCC. As explained by Kaminstein, "Article XVII and its Appendix Declaration constitute the 'Berne Safeguard Clause', one of the major compromises of the Geneva Conference establishing the UCC in 1952. The provision as it now exists makes the Berne Convention predominant over the UCC as between two countries, both of which belong to the two Conventions; and, equally important, it would preclude a Berne country from leaving the Berne Union and relying on the Universal Convention for protection of its works in Berne Union–UCC countries. The [Paris] text would remove the latter condition with respect to developing countries, leaving them free, without fear of retaliation or loss of protection, to be party to either or both Conventions."[m]

The United States ratified the 1971 Paris revision of the UCC in 1972. It came into force on July 10, 1974. Approximately one hundred countries are parties to the UCC. About two-thirds have ratified the 1971 Paris text; the 1952 Geneva text remains in force for those countries who have not ratified the Paris revision.

NOTES AND QUESTIONS ON THE UCC

(1) Even after the UCC, works of foreign authors could fall into the public domain in the United States if the author failed to obtain relief from our copyright formalities by using the UCC notice specified in art. III of the Convention. (Recall that until March 1, 1989, the 1976 Act required a copyright notice on works "published in the United States or elsewhere.") Many of these lost copyrights have now been restored under § 104A. See p. 40 supra.

(2) In 1973 the former Soviet Union unexpectedly joined the UCC. It had not been a party to any multinational copyright arrangement, nor was there any bilateral treaty with the United States. But gratification at the Soviet action soon curdled. Senator McClellan explained:

> Unfortunately, it now appears that the Soviet Government may contemplate using its adherence [to] the Universal Copyright Convention as a tool to tighten its control over the circulation of literature which does not meet with Communist approval. On February 21, the Supreme Soviet adopted a decree amending the Soviet copyright law in connection with that country's adherence to the Copyright Convention. According to an Associated Press dispatch from Moscow the law "could sharply restrict publication in the West of works by Russian authors considered anti-Soviet." The news reports indicate that the new Soviet law apparently is designed to permit that country to prevent publication abroad of anti-Soviet works by bringing suits for infringement of United States or other copyrights, against publishers in foreign countries who issue these works. Presumably the Soviet Union under its domestic statute would claim proprietary rights in the United States or other foreign copyrights in the works of these authors. 119 Cong.Rec. 9387 (March 26, 1973).

A proposed anti-Soviet amendment metamorphosed into § 201(e) of the 1976 Act, which denies effect to involuntary transfers of copyright. It was a misguided attempt to generalize from a suspicion.

---

[m]　A. Kaminstein, Report of the General Rapporteur of the Conference for Revision of the Universal Copyright Convention, 19 Bull.Copyr. Soc'y 211, 259 (1972), a valuable guide to the revisions.

In 1995, Russia joined the UCC and the Berne Convention. Concern over Russian enforcement of intellectual property rights was one of the primary issues that impeded its entry into the World Trade Organization. An eighteen-year effort finally culminated in WTO membership for Russia in 2012.

4. THE BERNE CONVENTION, TRIPS, AND BEYOND

At several points in these materials we have addressed the changes in American law that flowed from the United States accession to the Berne Convention for the Protection of Literary and Artistic Works in 1988. (The 1971 Paris text of the Convention appears in the Statutory Supplement.) What follows is an overview of Berne, extracted from the House Judiciary Committee Report of May 6, 1988,[n] advocating adherence.

A. THE BERNE CONVENTION IN INTERNATIONAL COPYRIGHT

In order to appreciate the importance of U.S. adherence to the Berne Convention, it is useful to start with the Convention's history and successive revisions, its role in international copyright, administration of the Convention by the World Intellectual Property Organization, the relationship of Berne to the Universal Copyright Convention, and Berne and developing countries.

The Berne Convention is the oldest and most respected international copyright treaty.

In 1886, the Convention was concluded at Berne, Switzerland and the Berne Union came into being. Since then, the Convention has been successively completed and revised seven times: at Paris (1896), Berlin (1908), Berne (1914), Rome (1928), Brussels (1948), Stockholm (1967), and most recently, at Paris (1971). * * *

1. History of the Convention

The Berne Convention of 1886 culminated over 25 years of study and conferences which were undertaken by representatives of authors and artists, journalists, publishers, academics and governments, acting to replace the growing patchwork of European bilateral copyright arrangements with a simple, multilateral treaty respecting authors rights. These bilateral agreements often imposed a variety of conditions and restrictions upon rights as well as a variety of formalities which had to be complied with as conditions of protection. * * *

The original Convention was intended to promote five objectives: (1) the development of copyright laws in favor of authors in all civilized countries; (2) the elimination over time of basing rights upon reciprocity; (3) the end of discrimination in rights between domestic and foreign authors in all countries; (4) the abolition of formalities for the recognition and protection of copyright in foreign works; and, (5) ultimately, the promotion of uniform international legislation for the protection of literary and artistic works.

The first Berne Convention was a simple document in which two cardinal principles were established, both of continuing vitality today:

---

[n]   H.R.Rep. No. 100–609, 100th Cong., 2d Sess. 11–19 (1988).

a. *The Union:* the states adhering to the Convention organized themselves into a Union for the protection of the rights of authors in their literary and artistic works. In forming the Union, the original members contemplated an essentially political as well as legal undertaking: that adherents to the Convention would function as a cooperative unit which would continue in existence regardless of future accessions or withdrawals from the Convention itself.

b. *The Rule of National Treatment:* one of the cornerstones of international copyright is the rule, first recognized for copyright in the Berne Convention, that authors should enjoy in other countries the same protection for their works as those countries accord their own authors.

During the century of its existence, the Convention has been revised five times to meet changed conditions and technological development affecting authors' rights. Successive texts have generally improved and extended rights accorded authors and copyright proprietors; and, in 1967, the Berne Union confronted the special challenges to copyright policy posed by the emergence of numerous developing countries on the world scene.

2. *Successive Revisions of the Berne Convention*

a. *1908 Berlin Act.* The principal achievement of the Berlin Revision Conference was the prohibition of formalities as a condition of the enjoyment and exercise of rights under the Convention. The minimum duration of protection was set at the life of the author and fifty years post mortem, but made subject to exceptions for each country so as to make it less than a mandatory rule. The Convention further expanded the minimum subject matter of copyright under the Convention, including photographs. Moreover, the Berlin Revision recognized the exclusive rights of composers of musical works to authorize the adaptation of these works and gave explicit protection to the authors of cinematographic works.

b. *1928 Rome Act.* This revision was the first to recognize expressly the "moral rights" of authors: the right to claim authorship of a work and the right to object to modifications of the work which prejudiced the honor or reputation of the author. The Rome revision specifically recognized the right to authorize broadcasting of works, leaving details to be elaborated by national legislation.

c. *1948 Brussels Act.* This revision established the term of protection of life of the author and fifty years post mortem as mandatory. It added improvements in copyright protection including recognition of the right of public recitation; rules governing mutual recognition of optional "resale royalty" laws (so-called "droit de suite"); extension of the broadcasting article to secondary transmissions, including by wire; and, express recognition of cinematographic works and works produced by processes analogous to cinematography as distinct subjects of copyright protection.

d. *1967 Stockholm Act.* For the first time, the implicit right of reproduction was expressly established in the Convention and special rules governing exceptions to that right were also included. Significant new rules relating to reconciling different national rules of authorship and ownership of motion pictures, defining the "nationality" of films for Convention purposes, were added at this revision. Protection was extended to include authors having habitual residence in a Union country, regardless of their citizenship. Finally, this revision established a "Protocol Regarding Developing Countries," which would have allowed developing countries broadly to limit rights of translation and reproduction. The 1967 Stockholm Act has not and will not come into force. It has effectively been superseded by the 1971 Paris Act.

   e.   *1971 Paris Act.* The 1971 Paris Act of Berne—the only Act now open to accession—is essentially the 1967 Stockholm Act with significant revisions made to the Protocol Regarding Developing Countries. The thrust of these revisions will be discussed in the context of relations with developing countries.

3.   *The Administration of the Convention*

   The Berne Convention is administered by the World Intellectual Property Organization (W.I.P.O.), an intergovernmental organization with headquarters located in Geneva, Switzerland. The W.I.P.O. is a specialized agency within the United Nations system of organizations. It is responsible for the administration of various Unions, each rooted in a multilateral treaty and dealing with aspects of intellectual property. The twin objectives of the W.I.P.O. are to promote the protection of intellectual property throughout the world and to ensure administrative cooperation among Union states. * * *

   Within this framework, the Berne Union through the W.I.P.O. conducts an ambitious program examining the relevance of the Convention to new media of creation, exploitation and consumption of copyrighted works. During the past decade, the W.I.P.O. has facilitated examination within the Union of the copyright aspects of cable television, satellite transmissions, including direct broadcast satellites, the rental of copies of protected works, private copying, and access to protected works by developing countries. * * *

5.   *The Berne Convention and Developing Countries*

   [The Report here describes the Stockholm episode, p. 808 supra.]

   In 1970, largely under the leadership of the United States through the Universal Copyright Convention, a compromise program was developed under which both Berne and the UCC would be revised to include less drastic concessions to developing countries, centered largely upon limited compulsory licensing options for translation and reprint rights in support of educational and developmental objectives. This program succeeded and in 1971 Berne and the UCC were jointly revised at Paris.

   Since that time, relative stability in the Berne Convention has prevailed. Only two members of the Berne Convention and four members of the UCC have declared their intention, in accordance with the requirements of the two Conventions, to avail themselves of the compulsory licensing privileges of the Conventions. * * *

B.   THE BERNE CONVENTION AND INTERNATIONAL TRADE

   Recently, protection of intellectual property, including copyrights, has become an international trade issue. Improved technology and communications greatly facilitate the global dissemination of ideas, cultural views, and creative activity. Technological changes also facilitate the unauthorized copying of the creative work-product.

   The United States, as a leader in the creation and global exploitation of copyrighted works, has a great interest in a strong and viable international copyright system. Under the U.S. Constitution, the primary objective of copyright law is not to reward the author, but rather to secure for the public the benefits derived from the authors' labors. By giving authors an incentive to create, the public benefits in two ways: when the original expression is created and second when the limited term of protection expires and the creation is added to the public domain.

If framed properly, copyright protection fosters creative activity and innovation and encourages investment in commercialization of new ideas and technology. Trade in goods protected by American copyright law and the licensing of the rights to copyrighted works have expanded rapidly in the recent past. Domestic industries relying upon copyright protection to stimulate creative efforts represent a broad range of interests including all types of publishing, motion pictures, music and sound recordings and computer software. Goods and services produced by these industries consistently results in a trade surplus for the United States. A positive trade balance also sustains American jobs thereby stimulating the domestic economy. * * *

The United States successfully placed the topic of trade-related aspects of intellectual property on the agenda of the Uruguay Round Negotiations under the auspices of the General Agreement of Tariffs and Trade (GATT). The GATT meeting of Trade Ministers in Punte del Este recognized the relationship between trade and the protection and enforcement of intellectual property rights. Implicit in this recognition is the presumption that inadequate and ineffective protection of intellectual property rights can result in trade distortions. * * *

The Berne Convention represents an international consensus on copyright protection. The United States should be in a position to take advantage of that consensus, to encourage other countries to join the common ground, and to use it to encourage expansion of legitimate trade. As to the latter, the relationship of Berne adherence to promotion of U.S. trade is clear. American popular culture and information products have become precious export commodities of immense economic value. That value is badly eroded by low international copyright standards. Berne standards are both high, reasonable and widely accepted internationally. * * *

NOTES ON THE BERNE CONVENTION AND THE TRIPS AGREEMENT

(1) Approximately 165 nations have adhered to the Berne Convention. Recall, however, that the Berne Convention is not self-executing under United States law; the rights recognized under the Convention must be pursued through our domestic law. Among other changes, the Berne Convention Implementation Act of 1988, Pub.L. No. 100–568, abolished the requirement of copyright notice, eliminated the necessity of recording transfers of copyright (and for foreign works, of registering the copyright) prior to commencing suit, and weakened the jukebox compulsory license (later wholly repealed). Our treaty obligations under Berne also played a significant role in bringing architectural works within the subject matter of copyright and extending moral rights to works of visual art.°

°   The pressure to harmonize U.S. and foreign copyright laws is critically analyzed in K. Crews, Harmonization and the Goals of Copyright: Property Rights or Cultural Progress, 6 Ind.J. Global Leg.Stud. 117 (1998); P. Yu, Currents and Crosscurrents in the International Intellectual Property Regime, 38 Loy.L.A.L.Rev. 323 (2004), provides an historical perspective

For information on the Berne Convention, see S. Ricketson and J. Ginsburg, International Copyright and Neighbouring Rights Agreements from 1886 to the Present: The Berne Convention and Beyond (2006); Papers Presented at a Conference to Celebrate the Centenary of the Berne Convention, 1886–1986, 11 Colum.J.L. & Arts 1 (1986).

(2) In the 1980s the United States won inclusion of intellectual property rights as a component in international trade negotiations. The aim was to insure a high level of intellectual property protection throughout the world, backed by effective enforcement mechanisms that were lacking in the international conventions. The result was the Agreement on Trade–Related Aspects of Intellectual Property Rights (TRIPS), overseen by the World Trade Organization. (The TRIPS Agreement is reproduced in the Statutory Supplement.)

With respect to copyright, TRIPS takes what has been described as a "Berne plus" approach. The Agreement incorporates by reference the minimum substantive standards contained in articles 1–21 of Berne (with the exception, at U.S. insistence, of article 6*bis* on moral rights).[p] TRIPS goes beyond Berne, however, in requiring protection for computer programs and creative compilations. Member countries must also provide rights against the commercial rental of computer programs, phonorecords, and cinematographic works, although protection for the latter is not required "unless such rental has led to widespread copying of such works which is materially impairing the exclusive right of reproduction."

The chief contribution of TRIPS, however, is in its provisions on enforcement. Member countries are required to implement adequate procedures and remedies for enforcement of the intellectual property rights guaranteed by TRIPS, and unlike Berne or the UCC, the World Trade Organization has substantial means available, including trade sanctions, to spur compliance with the national obligations imposed by the Agreement.[q]

(3) In 1990, the People's Republic of China enacted its first copyright law, which recognized both economic and moral rights. See 41 Pat., Tm. & Copyr.J. (BNA) 37 (1990). In 1992, prompted by a trade agreement with the United States, China also joined both the UCC and Berne. However, Chinese compliance with its international obligations to protect intellectual property remains an issue. Tension between the United States and China over the protection of intellectual property escalated in 2007 when the U.S. filed two complaints against China with the World Trade Organization. One focused on China's lax enforcement of copyright and trademark rights. A WTO dispute panel ruled that some of the Chinese practices violated its obligations under TRIPS. 77 Pat., Tm. & Copyr.J. (BNA) 307 (2009). China later announced that amendments to its copyright law and customs regulations dealing with the disposal of infringing products brought it into full compliance with the WTO ruling. The

---

on the clash between the forces of harmonization and multilateralism versus national autonomy and access.

   [p] The renewed pressure under TRIPS to comply with art. 18 of Berne relating to the protection of works that have not yet fallen into the public domain in their country of origin led to the enactment of § 104A restoring copyright in certain foreign works. See p. 40 supra. The requirement under TRIPS to provide protection against the unauthorized recording of unfixed performances prompted the anti-bootlegging provision in § 1101. See p. 21 supra.

   [q] Some of the technical shortcomings of TRIPS, especially in high technology areas, are examined in C. McManis, Taking TRIPS on the Information Superhighway: Int'l Intellectual Property Protection and Emerging Computer Technology, 41 Vill.L.Rev. 207 (1996).

United States and China have reached a procedural agreement that preserves the U.S. right to challenge China's implementation of the ruling. 79 Pat., Tm. & Copyr.J. (BNA) 767 (2010). P. Yu, The TRIPS Enforcement Dispute, 89 Neb.L.Rev. 1046 (2011), critiques the WTO case challenging China's enforcement of intellectual property rights. The second WTO complaint challenged barriers to the sale of U.S. works in China. A WTO dispute panel largely upheld the U.S. claims that China improperly restricted the importation and distribution of goods such as theatrical films, DVDs, music, and books. That determination was sustained by the WTO's Appellate Body following China's appeal of the dispute panel ruling. 79 Pat., Tm. & Copyr.J. (BNA) 226 (2010). In May, 2012, China claimed that it had moved to full compliance with the ruling, but the United States did not agree that there had been a final resolution of all issues.

(4) Although generally supported by copyright owners, not everyone is enthusiastic about TRIPS. Some economists argue that TRIPS was a triumph for American industry at the expense of developing nations who are denied cheap access to intellectual property—an ironic twist given that the rapid development of the U.S. in the 19th century and Japan in the 20th century may have been due in part to the absence of strong international protection for intellectual property.[r]

D. Long, The Impact of Foreign Investment on Indigenous Culture: An Intellectual Property Perspective, 23 N.C.J. Int'l L. & Comm.Reg. 229 (1998), suggests strategies for developing nations to use the intellectual property norms imposed by TRIPS to protect their own cultural heritage, including folklore, rituals, and costumes; M. Chon, Intellectual Property "From Below": Copyright and Capability for Education, 40 U.C. Davis L.Rev. 803 (2007), reimagines the international regime as a means of insuring access to educational resources in developing countries; M. Wong, Toward an Alternative Normative Framework for Copyright: From Private Property to Human Rights, 26 Cardozo A. & Ent.L.J. 775 (2009), urges a move to a human rights orientation on international intellectual property protection.

(5) In addition to multinational agreements such as Berne and TRIPS, the United States is actively pursuing an agenda for increased copyright protection abroad through bilateral and multilateral trade agreements, focusing particularly on the duration of copyright and on technological protection similar to that in our Digital Millennium Copyright Act. See Congressional Research Service, Intellectual Property Rights and International Trade 28–34 (2007). For example, as part of a free trade agreement with the U.S., Australia agreed to a package of amendments to its copyright act, including a life-plus-seventy year term of copyright and new liability measures directed at persons who circumvent technological protection measures; the opposition party said the government "has surrendered to American interests, rather than Australian consumers." 73 Pat., Tm. & Copyr.J. (BNA) 159 (2006).

(6) The monetary stakes in international copyright protection are huge. According to the International Intellectual Property Alliance, the core copyright industries (primarily music, movies, television, print, and software) contributed $932 billion to the U.S. economy in 2010, or about 6.4 percent of the total gross domestic product. Foreign sales accounted for $134 billion, far more than any

---

[r]   See Lohr, The Intellectual Property Debate Takes a Page from 19th–Century America, N.Y. Times, Oct. 14, 2002, p. C4.

other export sector. Copyright Industries in the U.S. Economy: The 2011 Report.

(7) Helpful works on foreign and international copyright include P. Geller, International Copyright Law and Practice (Matthew Bender); P. Goldstein and P. Hugenholtz, International Copyright—Principles, Law and Practice (Oxford Univ. Press 2012).

———————

INDEX